Jeremiah R. Donovan

DOCUMENTARY BACKGROUND
OF WORLD WAR II

1931 to 1941

DOCUMENTARY BACKGROUND OF WORLD WAR II

1931 to 1941

Compiled and Edited by
JAMES W. GANTENBEIN

New York
COLUMBIA UNIVERSITY PRESS
1948

COPYRIGHT 1948 COLUMBIA UNIVERSITY PRESS, NEW YORK

PUBLISHED IN GREAT BRITAIN AND INDIA BY GEOFFREY CUMBERLEGE
OXFORD UNIVERSITY PRESS, LONDON AND BOMBAY

MANUFACTURED IN THE UNITED STATES OF AMERICA

There can be no peace if the reign of law is to be replaced by a recurrent sanctification of sheer force.

There can be no peace if national policy adopts as a deliberate instrument the threat of war.

There can be no peace if national policy adopts as a deliberate instrument the dispersion all over the world of millions of helpless and persecuted wanderers with no place to lay their heads.

There can be no peace if humble men and women are not free to think their own thoughts, to express their own feelings, to worship God.

—PRESIDENT FRANKLIN D. ROOSEVELT
Address, October 26, 1938

There can be no peace if the reign of law is to be replaced by a recurrent sanctification of sheer force.

There can be no peace if national policy adopts as a deliberate instrument the threat of war.

There can be no peace if national policy adopts as a deliberate instrument the dispersion all over the world of millions of helpless and persecuted wanderers with no place to lay their heads.

There can be no peace if humble men and women are not free to think their own thoughts, to express their own feelings, to worship God.

—President Franklin D. Roosevelt
Address, October 26, 1938

PREFACE

On september 18–19, 1931, the world was shocked by the news that a member of the family of nations had invaded Manchuria. It was by no means the first disillusion experienced since the World War of 1914–18 by those millions of men and women in all parts of the world who had assumed that international relations had been placed on a firmer basis of law and fair dealing, such as had long characterized the relations among most civilized individuals. Nevertheless, the Japanese invasion of Manchuria marked the end of the hopeful and fairly happy postwar period and the beginning of a new pre-war period that was to come to an end with the Japanese attack upon Pearl Harbor a decade later. During those intervening years, there was witnessed one of the great dramas of history, in which it seemed that the forces of peace were contending with the forces of war in a heroic but losing struggle that had many of the qualities of an ancient Greek tragedy.

The collection of papers that follows represents an effort to trace, through speeches of statesmen, diplomatic correspondence, and other documents, the story of the foreign policies that various of the leading countries of the world were following during that fateful decade. The idea of the compilation occurred to me in March, 1939. Mussolini had just said in a speech at Rome that "no matter how things go we wish to hear no more about brotherhood, sisterhood, cousins and such other bastard relationships because relationships between States are relations of force and these relations of force are the determining elements of their policy"; that "we must arm"; and that "the watchword is this: more cannon, more ships, more airplanes, at whatever cost, with whatever means, even if it should mean wiping out all that is called civil life." Two days before, Mr. Cordell Hull had said in a public statement that "we in this country have striven, particularly during recent years, and we shall continue to strive, to strengthen the threatened structure of world peace by fostering in every possible way the rule of law and the building of sound economic relationships upon which alone peace can rest." It seemed that it might aid in an appreciation of the issues, including the political philosophies, at stake if there could be brought together in parallel form and as objectively as possible the pronouncements of those who were playing the leading roles in this world drama.

The compilation makes no pretenses with respect to completeness. A great many important documents in the international relations of the period will not be found here. I have attempted simply to bring together in a single volume a group of documents that, by either their intrinsic importance or their representative character, might be useful in tracing the main lines of foreign policy of a number of countries during the years mentioned. In many cases, limitations of space have not permitted including the entire documents, but I have endeavored to avoid removing passages from contexts which are necessary for purposes of conveying accurate impressions. As it is contemplated that the compilation will be used chiefly in the United States, I have included more papers relating to United States foreign policy than documents from other countries.

The collection is not to be construed as being in any way official or as having the endorsement or approval of the United States Government. Responsibility for the choice, arrangement and editing of the material rests solely with me personally.

As to sources, the majority of the documents have been taken directly from official publications of the United States, British, and French Governments, and of the League of Nations. A number of papers, however, have been reprinted from *The New York Times* and the annual compilations of the Royal Institute of International Affairs, *Documents on International Affairs;* and documents have been taken also from the semi-monthly publication, *Vital Speeches of the Day* (New York), *International Conciliation* (published monthly by the Carnegie Endowment for International Peace), the two volumes of *Documents on American Foreign Relations* covering the period from the beginning of 1938 to the middle of 1940, compiled by S. Shepard Jones and Denys P. Myers and published by the World Peace Foundation, and *My New Order,* a collection of speeches by Hitler compiled by Raoul de Roussey de Sales and published by Reynal and Hitchcock. For permission to reprint, I am very grateful to the compilers and publishers of these works and publications, as well as to His Majesty's Stationery Office in London, the Associated Press, the United Press, Reynal and Hitchcock, as publishers of the *French Yellow Book* (the collection of official French documents relating to the outbreak of the war), and Farrar and Rinehart, publishers in the United States of *The British War Blue Book.*

I wish to acknowledge a particular debt to my wife, Mary Gantenbein, for her generous and painstaking assistance in the assembling of the documents, which formed a large part of the work involved. I am also grateful to Miss Matilda L. Berg of Columbia University Press for her valuable aid in the preparation of the manuscript for publication.

J.W.G.

Berlin
March 22, 1948

CONTENTS

PART ONE: THE UNITED STATES
GENERAL STATEMENTS OF POLICY

Address by Henry L. Stimson, Secretary of State, at Pittsburgh, October 26, 1932 — 3
Inaugural Address by President Franklin D. Roosevelt, March 4, 1933 — 10
Address by President Franklin D. Roosevelt at Washington, December 28, 1933 — 11
Address by Cordell Hull, Secretary of State, "Eight Pillars of Enduring Peace," at Buenos Aires, December 5, 1936 — 14
Statement by Cordell Hull, Secretary of State, July 16, 1937 — 24
Address by President Franklin D. Roosevelt at the Dedication of the Outerlink Bridge, Chicago, October 5, 1937 — 25
Radio Address by President Franklin D. Roosevelt, October 26, 1938 — 30
Address by Cordell Hull, Secretary of State, "Our Foreign Policy," at Washington, October 26, 1940 — 32

DISARMAMENT

Address by Hugh S. Gibson, Acting Chairman of the American Delegation at the First General Disarmament Conference at Geneva, February 9, 1932 — 42
Statement Issued by the White House, June 22, 1932 — 47
Message of President Franklin D. Roosevelt to the Heads of Other Nations Participating in the Disarmament Conference and the World Monetary and Economic Conference, May 16, 1933 — 49
Statement by Norman H. Davis, Chairman of the United States Delegation to the General Disarmament Conference, at Geneva, May 29, 1934 — 51
Statement by Norman H. Davis, Chairman of the United States Delegation to the Conference for the Limitation of Naval Armament at London, before the Senate Committee on Foreign Relations, May 13, 1936 — 56
Statement Issued by the Department of State, February 5, 1938 — 60
Statement Issued by the Department of State, June 30, 1938 — 62

RELATIONS WITH JAPAN

Memorandum Handed by Henry L. Stimson, Secretary of State, to the Japanese Ambassador to the United States (Katsuji Debuchi), September 22, 1931 — 65
Telegram from Henry L. Stimson, Secretary of State, to the American Consul at Geneva (Prentiss B. Gilbert), October 9, 1931 — 66

x   CONTENTS

Telegram from Henry L. Stimson, Secretary of State, to the American Ambassador to Great Britain (Charles G. Dawes), November 10, 1931   67

Telegram from Henry L. Stimson, Secretary of State, to the American Ambassador to Japan (William Cameron Forbes), January 7, 1932   71

Telegram from Henry L. Stimson, Secretary of State, to the American Minister to Switzerland (Hugh R. Wilson), February 12, 1932   71

Communication from Henry L. Stimson, Secretary of State, to the Secretary-General of the League of Nations (Joseph Avenol), February 25, 1933   75

Communication from Joseph C. Grew, American Ambassador to Japan, to the Secretary of State of the United States (Cordell Hull), December 27, 1934   76

Telegram from Cordell Hull, Secretary of State, to the American Ambassador to Japan (Joseph C. Grew), September 2, 1937   81

Note from Joseph C. Grew, United States Ambassador to Japan, by Instruction of the Department of State, to the Japanese Minister for Foreign Affairs (Koki Hirota), December 14, 1937   84

Announcement Issued by the Department of State, April 22, 1938   85

Note from Joseph C. Grew, American Ambassador to Japan, to the Japanese Minister for Foreign Affairs (Hachiro Arita), December 30, 1938   85

Telegram from Joseph C. Grew, American Ambassador to Japan, to the Secretary of State of the United States (Cordell Hull), May 18, 1939   91

Note from Cordell Hull, Secretary of State, to the Japanese Ambassador to the United States (Kensuke Horinouchi), July 26, 1939   94

Memorandum of Cordell Hull, Secretary of State, Regarding a Conversation with the Japanese Ambassador to the United States (Kensuke Horinouchi), August 26, 1939   95

Statement by Cordell Hull, Secretary of State, March 30, 1940   97

Address by Sumner Welles, Under Secretary of State, "Our Foreign Policy and National Defense," at Cleveland, September 28, 1940   98

Memorandum of Cordell Hull, Secretary of State, Regarding a Conversation with the Japanese Ambassador to the United States (Kensuke Horinouchi), October 8, 1940   100

Statement Issued by the White House, December 10, 1940   102

Statement by Cordell Hull, Secretary of State, before the Foreign Affairs Committee of the House of Representatives, January 15, 1941   102

Telegram from Joseph C. Grew, American Ambassador to Japan, to the Secretary of State of the United States (Cordell Hull), January 27, 1941   104

Statement by Sumner Welles, Acting Secretary of State, July 24, 1941   105

Statement Issued by the White House, July 25, 1941   106

Communication Presented by Cordell Hull, Secretary of State, to the Japanese Ambassador to the United States (Admiral Kichisaburo Nomura), November 26, 1941   107

Statement by President Franklin D. Roosevelt, Handed by Sumner Welles, Under Secretary of State, to the Japanese Ambassador (Ad-

CONTENTS

miral Kichisaburo Nomura) and the Japanese Special Representative (Saburo Kurusu), December 2, 1941 ... 111

Memorandum of a Conversation between Cordell Hull, Secretary of State, the Japanese Ambassador (Admiral Kichisaburo Nomura), and the Japanese Special Representative (Saburo Kurusu), December 5, 1941 ... 112

Message from President Franklin D. Roosevelt to Emperor Hirohito of Japan, the Afternoon of December 6, 1941 ... 115

Message of President Franklin D. Roosevelt to Congress, December 15, 1941, Containing a Summary of United States Past Policy in the Pacific ... 117

GERMAN AND ITALIAN AGGRESSIONS

GENERAL

Annual Message of President Franklin D. Roosevelt to Congress, January 3, 1936 ... 129
Statement by President Franklin D. Roosevelt, November 15, 1938 ... 132
Statement by Cordell Hull, Secretary of State, at a Press Conference, August 4, 1941 ... 132

AGAINST EUROPEAN AND AFRICAN COUNTRIES

Ethiopia

Statement by Cordell Hull, Secretary of State, September 13, 1935 ... 133
Statement by President Franklin D. Roosevelt, October 30, 1935 ... 136

Czechoslovakia

Note from Sumner Welles, Acting Secretary of State, to the German Chargé d'Affaires at Washington (Hans Thomsen), March 20, 1939 ... 137

Albania

Statement by Cordell Hull, Secretary of State, April 8, 1939 ... 138

Entry of Italy into the European War

Address by President Franklin D. Roosevelt, Delivered at the Commencement Exercises of the University of Virginia, at Charlottesville, Virginia, June 10, 1940 ... 138

German Execution of Hostages

Statement by President Franklin D. Roosevelt, October 25, 1941 ... 141

AGAINST THE UNITED STATES

American Citizens in Germany

Note from Prentiss B. Gilbert, American Chargé d'Affaires at Berlin, to the German Minister for Foreign Affairs (Joachim von Ribbentrop), December 14, 1938 ... 142

Note from Prentiss B. Gilbert, American Chargé d'Affaires at Berlin, to the German Minister for Foreign Affairs (Joachim von Ribbentrop), January 11, 1939 ... 143

Sinking of the "Robin Moor"

Message of President Franklin D. Roosevelt to Congress, June 20, 1941 — 144
Note from Cordell Hull, Secretary of State, to the German Chargé d'Affaires at Washington (Hans Thomsen), September 19, 1941 — 147

APPEALS FOR PEACE

Message from President Franklin D. Roosevelt Direct to the President of Czechoslovakia and the Chancellor of Germany, and through the Secretary of State to the Prime Minister of Great Britain and the Premier of France, the Morning of September 26, 1938 — 148
Telegram from Cordell Hull, Secretary of State, to All American Diplomatic Missions Accredited to Governments from Which the United States Government Had Not Already Received Messages or Which Had Not Already Taken Action, on the Afternoon of September 27, 1938 — 149
Message from President Franklin D. Roosevelt to the Chancellor of Germany (Adolf Hitler), the Night of September 27, 1938 — 150
Message from President Franklin D. Roosevelt to the Chancellor of Germany (Adolf Hitler) and *mutatis mutandis* to the Premier of Italy (Benito Mussolini), April 14, 1939 — 152
Message from President Franklin D. Roosevelt to King Victor Emmanuel of Italy, August 23, 1939 — 155
Message from President Franklin D. Roosevelt to the President of Poland (Ignace Moscicki), August 24, 1939 — 156
Message from President Franklin D. Roosevelt to the Chancellor of Germany (Adolf Hitler), August 24, 1939 — 157
Message from President Franklin D. Roosevelt to the Chancellor of Germany (Adolf Hitler), August 25, 1939 — 158
Message from President Franklin D. Roosevelt to the Premier of Italy (Benito Mussolini), April 29, 1940 — 159
Message from President Franklin D. Roosevelt to the Premier of Italy (Benito Mussolini), May 14, 1940 — 161
Telegram from William Phillips, American Ambassador to Italy, to the Secretary of State of the United States (Cordell Hull), May 27, 1940 — 161
Telegram from Cordell Hull, Secretary of State, to the American Ambassador to Italy (William Phillips), May 30, 1940 — 163
Telegram from William Phillips, American Ambassador to Italy, to the Secretary of State of the United States (Cordell Hull), June 1, 1940 — 164

NATIONAL AND CONTINENTAL DEFENSE, AND AID TO THE DEMOCRACIES

GENERAL

Message of President Franklin D. Roosevelt to Congress, January 28, 1938 — 166

CONTENTS xiii

Message of President Franklin D. Roosevelt to Congress, January 12, 1939   168
Statement by Cordell Hull, Secretary of State, August 25, 1940   172
Radio Address by President Franklin D. Roosevelt, Delivered from the White House over a Nation-wide Network and Broadcast to Foreign Countries, December 29, 1940   172
Annual Message of President Franklin D. Roosevelt to Congress, January 6, 1941   181
Radio Address by President Franklin D. Roosevelt, May 27, 1941   189

DECLARATIONS OF NATIONAL EMERGENCY

Proclamation of National Emergency by President Franklin D. Roosevelt, September 8, 1939   199
Proclamation of Unlimited National Emergency by President Franklin D. Roosevelt, May 27, 1941   200

AID TO FRANCE

Message from President Franklin D. Roosevelt to the Premier of France (Paul Reynaud), June 13, 1940   201
Message from President Franklin D. Roosevelt to the Premier of France (Paul Reynaud), June 15, 1940   202

EUROPEAN POSSESSIONS IN THE WESTERN HEMISPHERE

Statement Issued by the Department of State, June 19, 1940   203
Statement by Cordell Hull, July 5, 1940, Regarding the German Reply to the United States Note Dated June 18, 1940   203

LEASE OF BRITISH NAVAL AND AIR BASES

Message of President Franklin D. Roosevelt to Congress, September 3, 1940   205

LEND-LEASE ACT OF MARCH 11, 1941

An Act to Promote the Defense of the United States   206

DEFENSE OF GREENLAND

Announcement by the Department of State, April 10, 1941, of an Agreement between Denmark and the United States   210

FREEZING OF GERMAN AND ITALIAN ASSETS IN THE UNITED STATES

Statement Issued by the White House, June 14, 1941   212

CLOSING OF GERMAN AND ITALIAN CONSULAR OFFICES AND OTHER AGENCIES IN THE UNITED STATES

Note from Sumner Welles, Under Secretary of State, to the German Chargé d'Affaires at Washington (Hans Thomsen), June 16, 1941   213
Note from Sumner Welles, Under Secretary of State, to the Italian

Ambassador to the United States (Don Ascanio dei Principi Colonna), June 20, 1941 ... 214

DEFENSE OF ICELAND

Message of President Franklin D. Roosevelt to Congress, July 7, 1941 ... 215

THE "BLACK LIST"

Statement on the Proclaimed List of Certain Blocked Nationals, Issued by the Department of State, July 17, 1941 ... 216

ANNOUNCEMENT OF THE "ATLANTIC CHARTER"

Message from President Roosevelt to Congress Concerning His Conferences at Sea with the Prime Minister of Great Britain (Winston Churchill) in August, 1941 ... 220

PROTECTION OF AMERICAN VESSELS

Radio Address by President Franklin D. Roosevelt, September 11, 1941 ... 221
Address by President Franklin D. Roosevelt at Washington, D.C., October 27, 1941, Delivered at a Dinner on "Navy and Total Defense Day" ... 228

NEUTRALITY AND NEUTRALITY LEGISLATION

Radio Address by Cordell Hull, Secretary of State, "Our Foreign Policy with Respect to Neutrality," November 6, 1935 ... 232
Letter from Cordell Hull, Secretary of State, to the Chairman of the Committee on Foreign Relations of the Senate (Key Pittman), May 12, 1938 ... 235
Radio Address by President Franklin D. Roosevelt, September 3, 1939 ... 236
Message of President Franklin D. Roosevelt to Congress, September 21, 1939 ... 239
Message of President Franklin D. Roosevelt to Congress, October 9, 1941 ... 247

ENTRY OF THE UNITED STATES INTO THE WAR, DECEMBER 7–11, 1941

Statement by Cordell Hull, Secretary of State, December 7, 1941 ... 251
Message of President Franklin D. Roosevelt to Congress, December 8, 1941, Requesting a Declaration of War against Japan ... 252
Declaration by Congress of a State of War with Japan, December 8, 1941 ... 253
Radio Address by President Franklin D. Roosevelt to the Nation, December 9, 1941 ... 254
Message of President Franklin D. Roosevelt to Congress, December 11, 1941, Requesting Declarations of War against Germany and Italy ... 260
Declarations by Congress of a State of War with Germany and Italy, December 11, 1941 ... 261

CONTENTS xv

ECONOMIC AND FINANCIAL POLICY

Address by Cordell Hull, Secretary of State, before the World Monetary and Economic Conference at London, July 27, 1933 262
Message of President Franklin D. Roosevelt to Congress, June 1, 1934 267
Trade Agreements Act of June 12, 1934 273
Address by Cordell Hull, Secretary of State, "The Foreign Policy of the United States," at Washington, D.C., May 2, 1935 276
Statement by Henry Morgenthau, Jr., Secretary of the Treasury, September 25, 1936, Issued Simultaneously with Similar Statements by the Governments of Great Britain and France 282
Memorandum Left by Sumner Welles, Under Secretary of State, with Paul Reynaud, French Minister of Finance, in Paris, March 9, 1940 283

PART TWO: GREAT BRITAIN

GENERAL STATEMENTS OF POLICY

Address by Viscount Cecil, Chief of the British Delegation to the Assembly of the League of Nations, before the Assembly, September 10, 1931 287
Address by J. Ramsay MacDonald, Prime Minister, Delivered at the Guildhall Banquet, London, November 9, 1934 290
Statement by J. Ramsay MacDonald, Prime Minister, March 1, 1935 293
Address by Anthony Eden, Secretary of State for Foreign Affairs, before the Assembly of the League of Nations, September 20, 1937 298
Address by Anthony Eden, Secretary of State for Foreign Affairs, in the House of Commons, November 1, 1937 301
Address by Viscount Halifax, Secretary of State for Foreign Affairs, at Chatham House, London, June 29, 1939 302

DISARMAMENT AND SECURITY

Address by J. Ramsay MacDonald, Prime Minister, in the House of Commons, June 29, 1931 311
Draft Disarmament Convention, Submitted by J. Ramsay MacDonald, Prime Minister, to the General Commission of the Conference for the Reduction and Limitation of Armaments, at Geneva, March 16, 1933 319
Memorandum of the British Government, January 29, 1934 330
Statement by Viscount Monsell, British Delegate to the Conference for the Limitation of Naval Armament at London, January 15, 1936 342
Address by Anthony Eden, Secretary of State for Foreign Affairs, in the House of Commons, March 2, 1937 346

RELATIONS WITH GERMANY AND OUTBREAK OF THE WAR 1934–1937

Address by Stanley Baldwin, Lord President of the Council, in the House of Commons, November 28, 1934 348

Communication from Anthony Eden, Secretary of State for Foreign Affairs, to the British Ambassador to Germany (Sir Eric Phipps), March 26, 1936   350

Address by Anthony Eden, Secretary of State for Foreign Affairs, in the House of Commons, January 19, 1937   360

THE CZECHOSLOVAKIAN CRISIS, 1938

Letter from Neville Chamberlain, Prime Minister, to the Chancellor of Germany (Adolf Hitler), September 23, 1938   362

Second Letter from Neville Chamberlain, Prime Minister, to the Chancellor of Germany (Adolf Hitler), September 23, 1938   363

Letter from Neville Chamberlain, Prime Minister, to the Chancellor of Germany (Adolf Hitler), September 26, 1938   364

Message from Neville Chamberlain, Prime Minister, to the Secretary of State of the United States (Cordell Hull), September 26, 1938, in Reply to the Appeal for Peace by President Franklin D. Roosevelt on the Same Day   366

Address of Neville Chamberlain, Prime Minister, in the House of Commons, September 28, 1938   367

Address by Neville Chamberlain, Prime Minister, in the House of Commons, October 3, 1938   381

Address by Lord Halifax, Secretary of State for Foreign Affairs, in the House of Lords, October 3, 1938   383

1939

Address by Neville Chamberlain, Prime Minister, at Birmingham, March 17, 1939   385

Letter from Neville Chamberlain, Prime Minister, to the Chancellor of Germany (Adolf Hitler), August 22, 1939   391

Address by Neville Chamberlain, Prime Minister, in the House of Commons, August 24, 1939   392

Communication from the British Government to the German Government, August 28, 1939, Replying to the Communication of the German Chancellor (Adolf Hitler) of August 25, 1939   399

Communication from the British Government to the German Government, August 30, 1939, Replying to the Communication of the German Chancellor (Adolf Hitler) Dated August 29, 1939   401

Address by Neville Chamberlain, Prime Minister, in the House of Commons, September 1, 1939   403

Address by Neville Chamberlain, Prime Minister, in the House of Commons, September 3, 1939   408

Radio Address by Neville Chamberlain, Prime Minister, September 3, 1939   409

Final Report by Sir Nevile Henderson, British Ambassador to Germany, to the Foreign Office, September 20, 1939, on the Circumstances Leading to the Termination of His Mission   410

CONTENTS xvii

RELATIONS WITH ITALY

Statement by Anthony Eden, Minister for League of Nations Affairs, in the House of Commons, July 1, 1935   417
Statement by Anthony Eden, Minister for League of Nations Affairs, in the Committee of Eighteen of the League of Nations, October 12, 1935   418
Address by Anthony Eden, Secretary of State for Foreign Affairs, in the House of Commons, November 1, 1937   420
Address by Neville Chamberlain, Prime Minister, in the House of Commons, November 2, 1938   421
Radio Address by Winston Churchill, Prime Minister, to the Italian People, December 23, 1940   425

RELATIONS WITH JAPAN

Note from the British Government to the Japanese Government, August 29, 1937, Regarding the Wounding of the British Ambassador to China   430
Note from Sir Robert Leslie Craigie, British Ambassador to Japan, to the Japanese Minister for Foreign Affairs (Koki Hirota), December 16, 1937, Regarding the Bombing of British Vessels   432
Note from Sir Robert Leslie Craigie, British Ambassador to Japan, to the Japanese Minister for Foreign Affairs (Hachiro Arita), January 14, 1939   433
Radio Address by Winston Churchill, Prime Minister, August 24, 1941   436
Address by Winston Churchill, Prime Minister, in the House of Commons, December 8, 1941   436

PART THREE: FRANCE

GENERAL STATEMENTS OF POLICY

Address by Aristide Briand, Minister for Foreign Affairs, before the Assembly of the League of Nations, September 11, 1931   443
Address by Edouard Daladier, Premier, before the Congress of the Radical-Socialist Party at Vichy, October 8, 1933   450
Address by Pierre Laval, Premier, before the Assembly of the League of Nations, September 13, 1935   452
Statement by Léon Blum, Premier, in the French Senate, June 23, 1936   455
Address by Yvon Delbos, Minister for Foreign Affairs, in the Chamber of Deputies, November 19, 1937   462
Statement by Georges Bonnet, Minister for Foreign Affairs, in the Council of the League of Nations, May 23, 1939   470

Disarmament and Security

Communication from the French Government to the German Government, September 11, 1932 — 472
Memorandum Communicated by Louis Barthou, Minister for Foreign Affairs, to the British Embassy at Paris, April 17, 1934 — 477
Draft of an Eastern Pact Submitted by the French Government to the British Government in a Memorandum of the French Ambassador at London, June 27, 1934 — 480
Statement by Pierre Laval, Minister for Foreign Affairs, January 7, 1935, Regarding Rapprochement with Italy — 481

Relations with Germany and Outbreak of the War

Letter from Pierre Laval, Minister for Foreign Affairs, to the Secretary-General of the League of Nations (Joseph Avenol), April 9, 1935, Transmitting Memorandum Regarding Decisions of the German Government Relating to Armaments — 483
Statement by Pierre-Etienne Flandin, Minister for Foreign Affairs, in the Council of the League of Nations, March 14, 1936 — 487
Message from Edouard Daladier, Premier, to the President of the United States (Franklin D. Roosevelt), September 26, 1938, in Reply to the Latter's Appeal for Peace the Same Day — 491
Address by Edouard Daladier, Premier, in the Chamber of Deputies, October 4, 1938 — 491
Communication from André François—Poncet, French Ambassador to Germany, to the French Minister for Foreign Affairs (Georges Bonnet), October 20, 1938 — 500
Instruction from Georges Bonnet, Minister for Foreign Affairs, to the French Ambassadors at London, Berlin, Brussels, Rome, and Barcelona, and the French Minister at Prague, December 14, 1938 — 507
Communication from Robert Coulondre, French Ambassador to Germany, to the French Minister for Foreign Affairs (Georges Bonnet), March 16, 1939, Regarding the Dismemberment of Czechoslovakia — 509
Instruction from Georges Bonnet, Minister for Foreign Affairs, to the French Ambassador to Germany (Robert Coulondre), March 17, 1939, Regarding the Annexation of Bohemia and Moravia — 516
Communication Handed by Georges Bonnet, Minister for Foreign Affairs, to the German Ambassador to France (Count Johannes von Welczeck), July 1, 1939 — 517
Personal Letter from Georges Bonnet, Minister for Foreign Affairs, to the German Minister for Foreign Affairs (Joachim von Ribbentrop), July 21, 1939 — 518
Instruction from Georges Bonnet, Minister for Foreign Affairs, to the French Ambassador to Poland, August 24, 1939 — 521
Telephone Communication from Robert Coulondre, French Ambassador to Germany, to the French Minister for Foreign Affairs (Georges Bonnet), August 25, 1939, Transmitting Message from the

CONTENTS xix

   Chancellor of Germany (Adolf Hitler) to the French Premier (Edouard Daladier)   522
Message from Edouard Daladier, Premier, to the Chancellor of Germany (Adolf Hitler), August 26, 1939, Communicated through the French Foreign Office and the French Ambassador to Germany (Robert Coulondre)   524
Communication from Robert Coulondre, French Ambassador to Germany, to the French Minister for Foreign Affairs (Georges Bonnet), August 27, 1939   526
Address by Edouard Daladier, Premier, in the Chamber of Deputies, September 2, 1939   527
Telephone Communication from Robert Coulondre, French Ambassador to Germany, to the French Minister for Foreign Affairs (Georges Bonnet), September 3, 1939   534
Statement by Edouard Daladier, Premier, to the Nation, September 3, 1939   535

PART FOUR: THE UNION OF SOVIET SOCIALIST REPUBLICS

GENERAL STATEMENTS OF POLICY

Address by Maxim Litvinov, People's Commissar for Foreign Affairs, before the Central Executive Committee of the U.S.S.R., December 29, 1933   540
Letter from Maxim Litvinov, People's Commissar for Foreign Affairs, to the President of the Assembly of the League of Nations (R. J. Sandler), Regarding Membership in the League, September 15, 1934   550
Report by Vyacheslav M. Molotov, President of the Soviet of People's Commissars, to the Seventh All-Union Soviet Congress at Moscow, January 28, 1935   551
Address by Vyacheslav M. Molotov, President of the Soviet of People's Commissars, before the Central Executive Committee of the U.S.S.R., January 11, 1936   557
Address by Maxim Litvinov, People's Commissar for Foreign Affairs, before the Assembly of the League of Nations, September 21, 1938   560
Address by Vyacheslav M. Molotov, President of the Council of People's Commissars and People's Commissar for Foreign Affairs, before the Supreme Soviet, May 31, 1939   564
Address by Vyacheslav M. Molotov, President of the Council of People's Commissars and People's Commissar for Foreign Affairs, before the Supreme Soviet, October 31, 1939   570

DISARMAMENT AND SECURITY

Minutes of a Meeting of the General Commission of the Conference for the Reduction and Limitation of Armaments, February 25, 1932 — 582

Minutes of a Meeting of the General Commission of the Conference for the Reduction and Limitation of Armaments, May 29, 1934 — 587

Statement by Maxim Litvinov, People's Commissar for Foreign Affairs, Regarding the German Denunciation of the Treaty of Locarno, in the Council of the League of Nations, March 17, 1936 — 594

OTHER SUBJECTS BEFORE 1941

RESPONSIBILITY FOR ACTS OF THE COMMUNIST INTERNATIONAL

Note from N. Krestinski, Acting People's Commissar for Foreign Affairs, to the American Ambassador to the Union of Soviet Socialist Republics (William C. Bullitt), August 27, 1935 — 600

CZECHOSLOVAKIAN CRISIS, 1938

Address by Maxim Litvinov, People's Commissar for Foreign Affairs, before the Assembly of the League of Nations, September 21, 1938 — 601

WAR WITH FINLAND, 1939–1940

Radio Address by Vyacheslav M. Molotov, President of the Council of People's Commissars and People's Commissar for Foreign Affairs, November 29, 1939 — 602

Telegram from Vyacheslav M. Molotov, President of the Council of People's Commissars and People's Commissar for Foreign Affairs, to the Secretary-General of the League of Nations (Joseph Avenol), December 5, 1939 — 605

PART FIVE: GERMANY

GENERAL STATEMENTS OF POLICY

Address by Julius Curtius, Minister for Foreign Affairs, before the Assembly of the League of Nations, September 12, 1931 — 609

Radio Address by Adolf Hitler, Chancellor of the Reich, October 14, 1933 — 614

Address by Baron Konstantin von Neurath, Minister for Foreign Affairs, before the Seventh International Road Congress at Berlin, October 12, 1934 — 619

Address by Adolf Hitler, Chancellor of the Reich, at the Party Congress at Nuremberg, September 13, 1937 — 624

Address by Adolf Hitler, Chancellor of the Reich, before the Reichstag, February 20, 1938 — 628

CONTENTS

DISARMAMENT AND SECURITY

Address by Julius Curtius, Minister for Foreign Affairs, in the Council of the League of Nations, January 20, 1931 — 636

Communication from Baron Konstantin von Neurath, Minister for Foreign Affairs, to the President of the Conference for the Reduction and Limitation of Armaments (Arthur Henderson), September 14, 1932 — 637

Communication Telegraphed by Baron Konstantin von Neurath, Minister for Foreign Affairs, to the President of the Conference for the Reduction and Limitation of Armaments (Arthur Henderson), October 14, 1933 — 638

Proclamation by Adolf Hitler, Chancellor of the Reich, to the German Nation, October 14, 1933, Regarding the Withdrawal of Germany from the Disarmament Conference and the League of Nations — 639

Statement Issued by the German Government, April 16, 1934, Regarding the British Memorandum on Disarmament of January 29, 1934 — 640

Proclamation by Adolf Hitler, Chancellor of the Reich, Denouncing Part V of the Treaty of Versailles, March 16, 1935 — 641

Address by Adolf Hitler, Chancellor of the Reich, before the Reichstag, May 21, 1935 — 647

Memorandum Presented by Leopold von Hoesch, German Ambassador to Great Britain, to the British Secretary of State for Foreign Affairs (Anthony Eden), March 7, 1936, Regarding the Franco-Soviet Treaty, the Treaty of Locarno, and the Demilitarized Zone in the Rhineland — 651

Memorandum Presented by Joachim von Ribbentrop, German Ambassador-at-Large, to the British Secretary of State for Foreign Affairs (Anthony Eden), April 1, 1936 — 655

Address by Adolf Hitler, Chancellor of the Reich, at the Party Congress at Nuremberg, September 9, 1936 — 659

Memorandum Communicated by the German Government to the British Government on April 27, 1939, Denouncing the Anglo-German Naval Agreement of 1935, the Supplementary Declaration of 1937, and Part III of the Anglo-German Naval Agreement of 1937 — 662

ACQUISITION OF AUSTRIA

Manifesto Broadcast by Theo Habicht, "Inspector for Austria," July 5, 1933 — 664

Communiqué of the German Government Broadcast by Joseph Goebbels, Minister of Propaganda, July 11, 1936 — 665

Address by Adolf Hitler, Chancellor of the Reich, at Linz, Austria, March 12, 1938, Delivered Following the Entry of German Military Forces into Austria on March 11 and 12 — 666

Acquisition of Czechoslovakia

Memorandum by the Foreign Office, Regarding a Conversation between Field Marshal Hermann Goering and the Hungarian Minister (Döme Sztójay), September 16, 1938   668

Memorandum by the Foreign Office, Regarding a Conversation between Adolf Hitler, Chancellor of the Reich, the Premier of Hungary (Béla Imredy), and the Hungarian Minister for Foreign Affairs (Kálmán de Kánya), September 20, 1938   670

Letter from Adolf Hitler, Chancellor of the Reich, to the British Prime Minister (Neville Chamberlain), September 23, 1938   671

Memorandum Presented by Adolf Hitler, Chancellor of the Reich, to the British Prime Minister (Neville Chamberlain), September 23, 1938   674

Radio Address by Adolf Hitler, Chancellor of the Reich, September 26, 1938   676

Message from Adolf Hitler, Chancellor of the Reich, to the President of the United States (Franklin D. Roosevelt), September 26, 1938, in Reply to the Latter's Appeal for Peace of the Same Date   685

Letter from Adolf Hitler, Chancellor of the Reich, to the British Prime Minister (Neville Chamberlain), September 27, 1938   688

Note from Hans Thomsen, German Chargé d'Affaires at Washington, to the Secretary of State of the United States (Cordell Hull), March 17, 1939   690

Relations with France, Great Britain, and Poland: Outbreak of the War

Statement by Joachim von Ribbentrop, Minister for Foreign Affairs, December 6, 1938, Regarding the Franco-German Declaration of the Same Date   693

Address by Adolf Hitler, Chancellor of the Reich, before the Reichstag, January 30, 1939   694

Personal Letter from Joachim von Ribbentrop, Minister for Foreign Affairs, to the French Minister for Foreign Affairs (Georges Bonnet), July 13, 1939   694

Communication from Adolf Hitler, Chancellor of the Reich, to the Prime Minister of Great Britain (Neville Chamberlain), August 23, 1939   696

Verbal Communication Made by Adolf Hitler, Chancellor of the German Reich, to the British Ambassador to Germany (Sir Nevile Henderson) at an Interview, August 25, 1939   699

Personal Letter from Adolf Hitler, Chancellor of the Reich, to the French Premier (Edouard Daladier), August 27, 1939   701

Communication from Adolf Hitler, Chancellor of the Reich, to the British Government, Handed to the British Ambassador to Germany (Sir Nevile Henderson) during the Evening of August 29,

CONTENTS

1939, in Reply to the British Government's Communication of August 28, 1939 — 705
Communication from the German Government to the British Government, Handed by the German State Secretary (Baron Ernst von Weizsäcker) to the British Ambassador (Sir Nevile Henderson) at 9:15 P.M. on August 31, 1939 — 707
Communication from Hans Thomsen, German Chargé d'Affaires at Washington, to the Secretary of State of the United States (Cordell Hull), August 31, 1939, Replying to President Roosevelt's Appeals for Peace on August 25 and 26, 1939 — 712
Proclamation by Adolf Hitler, Chancellor of the Reich, to the German Army, September 1, 1939 — 712
Address by Adolf Hitler, Chancellor of the Reich, before the Reichstag, September 1, 1939 — 713
Communication from the German Government to the British Government, Handed by Joachim von Ribbentrop, Minister for Foreign Affairs, to the British Ambassador (Sir Nevile Henderson) at 11:20 A.M., September 3, 1939 — 718
Proclamation by Adolf Hitler, Chancellor of the Reich, to the German People, September 3, 1939 — 721

RELATIONS WITH CERTAIN OTHER COUNTRIES

ITALY

Official Communiqué Issued after the Visit to Germany of Count Galeazzo Ciano, Italian Minister for Foreign Affairs, October 25, 1936 — 723
Address by Adolf Hitler, Chancellor of the Reich, at Berlin, September 28, 1937, Delivered during the Visit to Berlin of Premier Benito Mussolini — 723

THE UNITED STATES

Note from the German Foreign Office to the American Chargé d'Affaires at Berlin (Prentiss B. Gilbert), December 30, 1938 — 725
Memorandum of a Conversation between Adolf Hitler, Chancellor of the Reich, and the Chief of the Spanish State (General Francisco Franco) at Hendaye, October 23, 1940 — 727
Communiqué Issued by the Official German News Agency, September 6, 1941, Regarding the Attack on the U.S.S. *Greer* — 729
Note from Hans Thomsen, German Chargé d'Affaires at Washington, to the Secretary of State of the United States (Cordell Hull), September 26, 1941, Regarding the Sinking of the *Robin Moor* — 730
Communiqué Issued by the German Government from the Military Headquarters of Adolf Hitler, Chancellor of the Reich, November 1, 1941, Referring to the Address of President Franklin D. Roosevelt on October 28, 1941 — 730
Second Communiqué Issued by the German Government from the Military Headquarters of Adolf Hitler, Chancellor of the Reich,

xxiv   CONTENTS

   November 1, 1941, Referring to the Address of President Franklin
      D. Roosevelt on October 28, 1941   732
Note from Joachim von Ribbentrop, Minister for Foreign Affairs, to
   the American Chargé d'Affaires at Berlin (Leland B. Morris), Delivered the Morning of December 11, 1941   733
Address by Adolf Hitler, Chancellor of the Reich, before the Reichstag, December 11, 1941   734

JAPAN

Memorandum of a Conversation between Baron Ernst von Weiz-
   säcker, State Secretary, and the Japanese Ambassador (Hiroshi
   Oshima), September 18, 1939   739
Telegram from Eugen Ott, German Ambassador to Japan, to the Ger-
   man Foreign Office, June 19, 1940, with Foreign Office Notation   740
Memorandum of a Conversation between Joachim von Ribbentrop,
   Minister for Foreign Affairs, the Premier of Italy (Benito Musso-
   lini), and the Italian Minister for Foreign Affairs (Count Galeazzo
   Ciano), at the Palazzo Venezia, Rome, May 13, 1941   743
Telegram from Joachim von Ribbentrop, Minister for Foreign Af-
   fairs, to the German Ambassador to Japan (Eugen Ott), July 1, 1941   744

THE UNION OF SOVIET SOCIALIST REPUBLICS

Address by Adolf Hitler, Chancellor of the Reich, before the Reichstag, October 6, 1939   747
Proclamation by Adolf Hitler, Chancellor of the Reich, June 22, 1941   749

INVASIONS OF VARIOUS COUNTRIES

DENMARK AND NORWAY

Memorandum of the German Government Presented to the Norwegian Government and *mutatis mutandis* to the Danish Government, April 9, 1940   758

BELGIUM AND THE NETHERLANDS

Memorandum of the German Government Presented to the Governments of Belgium and the Netherlands, May 10, 1940   759

YUGOSLAVIA

Order of the Day Issued by Adolf Hitler, Chancellor of the Reich, to
   the Soldiers of the Southeast Front, April 6, 1941   760

ECONOMIC AND FINANCIAL POLICY

Address by Hjalmar Schacht, President of the Reichsbank, at Bad
   Eilsen, August 30, 1934, Given before the International Conference
   of Agricultural Science   763
Announcement of the "New Plan" by Hjalmar Schacht, President of
   the Reichsbank, in September, 1934   765

CONTENTS xxv

Address by Adolf Hitler, Chancellor of the Reich, at the Party Congress at Nuremberg, September 9, 1936 766
Address by Adolf Hitler, Chancellor of the Reich, before the Reichstag, January 30, 1939 767

PART SIX: ITALY

GENERAL STATEMENTS OF POLICY

Address by Dino Grandi, Minister for Foreign Affairs, before the Assembly of the League of Nations, September 8, 1931 775
Address by Benito Mussolini, Premier, before the General Staff of the Italian Army, August 24, 1934 779
Address by Benito Mussolini, Premier, at Milan, October 6, 1934 781
Address by Benito Mussolini, Premier, in the Chamber of Deputies, May 25, 1935 782
Address by Benito Mussolini, Premier, at Avellino, Italy, August 30, 1936 785
Statement by Count Galeazzo Ciano, Minister for Foreign Affairs, at the End of His Visit to Germany, October 25, 1936 787
Address by Benito Mussolini, Premier, at Milan, November 1, 1936 789
Address by Count Galeazzo Ciano, Minister for Foreign Affairs, before the Fascist Chamber, May 13, 1937 793
Address by Benito Mussolini, Premier, at Berlin, September 28, 1937 804
Statement by Count Galeazzo Ciano, Minister for Foreign Affairs, November 6, 1937, Referring to Italy's Accession of the Same Date to the German-Japanese Agreement of November 25, 1936 806
Address by Benito Mussolini, Premier, at Rome, December 11, 1937 806
Address by Benito Mussolini, Premier, at Rome, March 26, 1939, in Commemoration of the 20th Anniversary of the Founding of the First Fascist Squad 808

DISARMAMENT AND SECURITY

Memorandum of the Italian Government, Published in Rome, January 31, 1934 812
Statement by Dino Grandi, Italian Delegate to the Conference for the Limitation of Naval Armament at London, March 25, 1936 818

WAR WITH ETHIOPIA

Radio Address by Benito Mussolini, Premier, October 2, 1935 819
Statement by Baron Pompeo Aloisi, Representative of Italy in the Council of the League of Nations, October 5, 1935 820

FROM THE OUTBREAK OF THE WAR IN EUROPE

Communication from King Victor Emmanuel to the President of the United States (Franklin D. Roosevelt), August 30, 1939, in Reply to the Latter's Appeal for Peace of August 23, 1939 825

Address by Benito Mussolini, Premier, before Leaders of the Fascist
 Party at Rome, September 23, 1939 825
Communication from Benito Mussolini, Premier, to the President of
 the United States (Franklin D. Roosevelt), May 2, 1940 827
Communication from Benito Mussolini, Premier, to the President of
 the United States (Franklin D. Roosevelt), May 18, 1940 827
Radio Address by Benito Mussolini, June 10, 1940 828
Communication from Emmanuele Grazzi, Italian Minister at Athens,
 to the Greek Government, October 28, 1940, Regarding the Occupation of Strategic Points in Greek Territory by Italian Armed
 Forces 830
Address by Benito Mussolini, Premier, at the Palazzo Venezia, Rome,
 December 11, 1941 832

PART SEVEN: JAPAN

GENERAL STATEMENTS OF POLICY

Address by Kenkichi Yoshizawa, Japanese Ambassador to France and
 Chief of the Japanese Delegation to the Assembly of the League of
 Nations, before the Assembly, September 9, 1931 835
Address by Koki Hirota, Minister for Foreign Affairs, in the Imperial
 Diet, January 23, 1934 838
Address by Koki Hirota, Minister for Foreign Affairs, in the Imperial
 Diet, January 21, 1936 842
Address by Koki Hirota, Minister for Foreign Affairs, in the Imperial
 Diet, January 22, 1938 848
Address by Hachiro Arita, Minister for Foreign Affairs, in the Imperial
 Diet, February 1, 1940 852
Address by Shigenori Togo, Minister for Foreign Affairs, in the Imperial Diet, November 17, 1941 857

DISARMAMENT

Note *verbale* from Hirosi Saito, Japanese Ambassador to the United
 States, to the Secretary of State of the United States (Cordell Hull),
 December 29, 1934 861
Statement by Admiral Osami Nagano, Chairman of the Japanese Delegation to the Conference for the Limitation of Naval Armament at
 London, in the First Committee of the Conference, January 15, 1936 862
Letter from Admiral Osami Nagano, Chairman of the Japanese Delegation to the Conference for the Limitation of Naval Armament at
 London, to the Chairman of the Conference (Lord Monsell), January 15, 1936 864
Note from Koki Hirota, Minister for Foreign Affairs, to the American
 Ambassador to Japan (Joseph C. Grew), February 12, 1938 . . . 865

CONTENTS

INVASIONS OF CHINA AND RELATIONS WITH THE UNITED STATES

Statement Issued by the Japanese Government after an Extraordinary Cabinet Meeting, September 24, 1931	867
Note from Kenkichi Yoshizawa, Minister for Foreign Affairs, to the American Ambassador to Japan (W. Cameron Forbes), January 16, 1932	869
Statement Issued by the Japanese Government, September 15, 1932	870
Statement by Yosuke Matsuoka, Chief of the Japanese Delegation to the Special Session of the Assembly of the League of Nations Convened at the Request of the Chinese Government, February 24, 1933	873
Statement Issued by the Japanese Government in Virtue of Paragraph 5 of Article 15 of the Covenant of the League of Nations, February 25, 1933	874
Telegram from Count Yasuya Uchida, Minister for Foreign Affairs, to the Secretary-General of the League of Nations (Sir Eric Drummond), March 27, 1933, Regarding the Japanese Withdrawal from the League	888
Reply of the Japanese Government, October 27, 1937, to the Invitation of the Belgian Government to Hold a Conference at Brussels	890
Statement Issued by the Japanese Foreign Office, October 28, 1937, Regarding the Convoking of the Conference of Brussels	892
Note from Koki Hirota, Minister for Foreign Affairs, to the American Ambassador to Japan (Joseph C. Grew), December 14, 1937	897
Statement by Prince Konoe, Prime Minister, January 18, 1938	898
Note from Hachiro Arita, Minister for Foreign Affairs, to the American Ambassador to Japan (Joseph C. Grew), November 18, 1938	899
Statement by Prince Konoe, Prime Minister, December 22, 1938	903
Statement by Admiral Kichisaburo Nomura, Minister for Foreign Affairs, at a Meeting of the Japanese Cabinet, October 27, 1939, as Published in the Japanese Press	904
Pro-Memoria from Admiral Kichisaburo Nomura, Minister for Foreign Affairs, to the American Ambassador (Joseph C. Grew), December 18, 1939	905
Draft Proposal Handed by Admiral Kichisaburo Nomura, Japanese Ambassador to the United States, to the Secretary of State of the United States (Cordell Hull), September 6, 1941	908
Draft Proposal Handed by Admiral Kichisaburo Nomura, Japanese Ambassador to the United States, to the Secretary of State of the United States (Cordell Hull), November 20, 1941	909
Memorandum Presented by Admiral Kichisaburo Nomura, Japanese Ambassador to the United States, to the Secretary of State of the United States (Cordell Hull), December 7, 1941	910

PART EIGHT: INTERNATIONAL AGREEMENTS AND RESOLUTIONS, JOINT COMMUNIQUÉS

ACTION BY THE LEAGUE OF NATIONS IN CERTAIN CASES

JAPANESE INVASION OF MANCHURIA IN 1931

Resolution Adopted by the Council of the League of Nations, September 30, 1931	919
Resolution Adopted by the Council of the League of Nations, October 24, 1931	920
Resolution Adopted by the Council of the League of Nations, December 10, 1931	922
Report Adopted by the Assembly of the League of Nations, February 24, 1933	923
Resolution Adopted by the Assembly of the League of Nations, February 24, 1933	934

RETURN OF THE SAAR TO GERMANY

Resolution Adopted by the Council of the League of Nations, January 17, 1935	936

GERMAN DENUNCIATION OF PART V OF THE TREATY OF VERSAILLES

Resolution Submitted by the Governments of France, Great Britain, and Italy, and Adopted by the Council of the League of Nations, April 17, 1935	937

ITALIAN-ETHIOPIAN WAR

Minutes of Meeting of the Council of the League of Nations, October 7, 1935	938
Minutes of Meeting of the Assembly of the League of Nations, October 11, 1935	940
Resolutions Recommended by the Committee of Seventeen (later the Committee of Eighteen) and Adopted by the Coordination Committee of the League of Nations, October 11–19, 1935	941
Resolutions Recommended by the Committee of Eighteen and Adopted by the Coordination Committee of the League of Nations, November 2, 1935	947
Resolution Adopted by the Assembly of the League of Nations, July 4, 1936	949
Minutes of the Final Meeting of the Coordination Committee, July 6, 1936	949

GERMAN VIOLATION OF ARTICLE 43 OF THE TREATY OF VERSAILLES

Resolution Adopted by the Council of the League of Nations, March 19, 1936	953

CONTENTS   xxix

GERMAN DENUNCIATION OF THE LOCARNO TREATY

Resolution Adopted by the Council of the League of Nations, March 24, 1936 953

JAPANESE AGGRESSIONS AGAINST CHINA, 1937–1939

First Report of the Sub-Committee of the Far-East Advisory Committee of the League of Nations, Adopted by the Committee, October 5, 1937, and by the Assembly of the League, October 6, 1937 ... 954

Second Report of the Sub-Committee of the Far-East Advisory Committee of the League of Nations, Adopted by the Committee, October 5, 1937, and by the Assembly of the League, October 6, 1937 ... 955

Resolution Adopted by the Assembly of the League of Nations, October 6, 1937 957

Resolution Adopted by the Council of the League of Nations, February 2, 1938 957

Resolution Adopted by the Council of the League of Nations, May 14, 1938 958

Resolutions Adopted by the Council of the League of Nations, May 22, 1939 959

WITHDRAWAL OF NON-SPANISH COMBATANTS FROM SPAIN

Resolution Adopted by the Council of the League of Nations, September 30, 1938 960

EXPULSION OF THE U.S.S.R. FROM THE LEAGUE

Resolutions Adopted by the Assembly of the League of Nations, December 14, 1939 961

Resolution Adopted by the Council of the League of Nations, December 14, 1939 962

REDUCTION AND LIMITATION OF ARMAMENTS

Resolution Adopted by the Assembly of the League of Nations, September 29, 1931 964

Resolution Adopted by the General Commission of the Conference for the Reduction and Limitation of Armaments, July 23, 1932 ... 965

Communication from Arthur Henderson, President of the Conference for the Reduction and Limitation of Armaments, to the German Minister for Foreign Affairs (Baron Konstantin von Neurath), September 18, 1932 969

Declarations by the Governments of the United States, Great Britain, France, Germany, and Italy (Sometimes Known as the "Five-Power Agreement"), Regarding the Work of the Disarmament Conference, Communicated to the President of the Conference (Arthur Henderson), December 11, 1932 971

Communication Telegraphed by Arthur Henderson, President of the Conference for the Reduction and Limitation of Armaments,

to the German Minister for Foreign Affairs (Baron Konstantin von Neurath), October 16, 1933, Regarding the German Withdrawal from the Conference ... 972
Resolution Adopted by the General Commission of the Conference for the Reduction and Limitation of Armaments, June 8, 1934 ... 973
Anglo-German Naval Agreement, June 18, 1935 ... 975
Note from Sir Samuel Hoare, Secretary of State for Foreign Affairs, to Joachim von Ribbentrop, German Ambassador-at-Large, June 18, 1935 ... 975
Note from Joachim von Ribbentrop, German Ambassador-at-Large, to the British Secretary of State for Foreign Affairs (Sir Samuel Hoare), June 18, 1935 ... 977
Treaty for the Limitation of Naval Armament between the United States, France, Great Britain, Canada, Australia, New Zealand, and India, Signed at London, March 25, 1936 ... 978
Procès-verbal Relating to the Rules of Submarine Warfare as Set Forth in Part IV of the Treaty of London of April 22, 1930, Signed by Representatives of the United States, Australia, Canada, France, Great Britain, India, the Irish Free State, Italy, Japan, New Zealand, and the Union of South Africa, at London, November 6, 1936 ... 985
Protocol of June 30, 1938, Modifying the Treaty for the Limitation of Naval Armament, Signed March 25, 1936 ... 986

Rome-Berlin-Tokyo Axis Agreements

German-Japanese Agreement and Supplementary Protocol, Signed at Berlin, November 25, 1936 ... 988
Protocol Concluded by Italy, Germany, and Japan, at Rome, November 6, 1937 ... 990
Summary of the Three-Power Pact between Germany, Italy, and Japan, Signed at Berlin, September 27, 1940 ... 991

American Solidarity

Declaration of the Principles of the Solidarity of America (the "Declaration of Lima"), Adopted at the Eighth International Conference of American States, at Lima, December 24, 1938 ... 993
The "Declaration of Panama," Adopted at the Meeting of the Ministers for Foreign Affairs of the American Republics at Panama, October 3, 1939 ... 994
Joint Declaration by the American Republics, May 19, 1940 ... 996
Declaration XV, "Reciprocal Assistance and Cooperation for the Defense of the Nations of the Americas," Adopted at the Meeting of the Ministers for Foreign Affairs of the American Republics at Habana, July 30, 1940 ... 997
Declaration I, "Breaking of Diplomatic Relations," Adopted at the

CONTENTS xxxi

Meeting of the Ministers for Foreign Affairs of the American Republics at Rio de Janeiro, January 28, 1942 998

OTHER AGREEMENTS AND JOINT COMMUNIQUÉS

German-Polish Agreement of January 26, 1934 999
Joint Communiqué Issued by the French, British, and Italian Governments, Regarding the Independence of Austria, February 17, 1934 1000
Communiqué Issued by the Premier of Italy and the Minister for Foreign Affairs of France at Rome, January 7, 1935 1001
Joint Resolution of Representatives of the Governments of France, Great Britain, and Italy at the Conference of Stresa, Including the Anglo-Italian Declaration and the Final Declaration, April 14, 1935 1001
Treaty of Mutual Assistance between France and the Union of Soviet Socialist Republics, Signed at Paris, May 2, 1935 1004
Declaration by the British and Italian Governments Regarding the Mediterranean, January 2, 1937 1008
The Nyon Arrangement between Great Britain, Bulgaria, Egypt, France, Greece, Rumania, Turkey, the Union of Soviet Socialist Republics, and Yugoslavia, Signed at Nyon, September 14, 1937 1008
Agreement Supplementary to the Nyon Arrangement, between Great Britain, Bulgaria, Egypt, France, Greece, Rumania, Turkey, the Union of Soviet Socialist Republics, and Yugoslavia, Signed at Geneva, September 17, 1937 1011
Report Adopted by the Conference of Brussels, November 24, 1937, and Declaration of the Conference of the Same Date 1012
Agreement between Great Britain and Italy, Signed at Rome, April 16, 1938 1017
Proposals Presented by the French and British Governments to the Czechoslovakian Government, September 19, 1938 1019
Agreements between Germany, Great Britain, France, and Italy, Signed at Munich, September 29, 1938 1021
Joint Communiqué Issued by Adolf Hitler, Chancellor of Germany, and Neville Chamberlain, Prime Minister of Great Britain, at Munich, September 30, 1938 1023
Declaration by the French and German Governments, Signed at Paris, December 6, 1938 1024
Communiqué Issued by the British and Polish Governments, April 6, 1939 1025
Treaty of Non-Aggression between Germany and the Union of Soviet Socialist Republics, Signed at Moscow, August 23, 1939 1025
Agreement of Mutual Assistance between Great Britain and Poland, August 25, 1939 1027
Agreements between Germany and the Union of Soviet Socialist Republics, Signed at Moscow, September 28, 1939 1029

Agreements between the Union of Soviet Socialist Republics and Japan, Signed at Moscow, April 13, 1941 ... 1031
Joint Declaration of President Franklin D. Roosevelt, of the United States, and Winston Churchill, Prime Minister of Great Britain, at Sea, August 14, 1941 (the "Atlantic Charter") ... 1033
Joint Declaration by Twenty-six United Nations, January 1, 1942, Regarding Cooperative War Efforts against the Axis Countries ... 1035

APPENDICES

I: SELECTED DOCUMENTS FROM "NAZI-SOVIET RELATIONS," 1939–1941, PUBLISHED BY THE DEPARTMENT OF STATE IN 1948

Secret Additional Protocol to the Treaty of Non-Aggression between Germany and the Union of Soviet Socialist Republics, Signed at Moscow, August 23, 1939 ... 1037
Telegram from Joachim von Ribbentrop, German Minister for Foreign Affairs, to the German Ambassador to the Union of Soviet Socialist Republics (Count Friedrich Werner von der Schulenburg), September 15, 1939 ... 1038
Telegram from Count Friedrich Werner von der Schulenburg, German Ambassador to the Union of Soviet Socialist Republics, to the German Foreign Office, September 20, 1939 ... 1040
Telegram from Joachim von Ribbentrop, German Minister for Foreign Affairs, to the German Ambassador to the Union of Soviet Socialist Republics (Count Friedrich Werner von der Schulenburg), September 23, 1939 ... 1040
Confidential and Secret Protocols to the Boundary and Friendship Treaty between Germany and the Union of Soviet Socialist Republics, Signed at Moscow, September 28, 1939 ... 1041
Memorandum of a Conversation between Adolf Hitler and Vyacheslav M. Molotov, at Berlin, November 12, 1940 ... 1043
Memorandum of a Conversation between Adolf Hitler and Vyacheslav M. Molotov, at Berlin, November 13, 1940, in the Presence of Joachim von Ribbentrop ... 1051
Memorandum of a Conversation between Joachim von Ribbentrop and Vyacheslav M. Molotov, at Berlin, Novemer 13, 1940 ... 1063
Circular Telegram from Baron Ernst von Weizsäcker to All German Diplomatic Missions and the Offices in Paris and Brussels, November 15, 1940 ... 1070
Telegram from Count Friedrich Werner von der Schulenburg to the German Foreign Office, November 26, 1940 ... 1071
Military Directive for "Operation Barbarossa" of Adolf Hitler, December 18, 1940 ... 1073
Telegram from Count Friedrich Werner von der Schulenburg to the German Foreign Office, January 17, 1941 ... 1077

CONTENTS   xxxiii

Telegram from Joachim von Ribbentrop to Baron Ernst von Weizsäcker, January 21, 1941   1078
Telegram from Joachim von Ribbentrop to Count Friedrich Werner von der Schulenburg, February 27, 1941   1080
Telegram from Count Friedrich Werner von der Schulenburg to the German Foreign Office, March 1, 1941   1081
Telegram from Count Friedrich Werner von der Schulenburg to the German Foreign Office, March 1, 1941   1082
Memorandum of a Conversation between Adolf Hitler and Yosuke Matsuoka, at Berlin, March 27, 1941, in the Presence of Joachim von Ribbentrop and Other Officials   1083
Memorandum of a Conversation between Joachim von Ribbentrop and Yosuke Matsuoka, at Berlin, March 29, 1941   1086
Memorandum of a Conversation between Adolf Hitler and Yosuke Matsuoka, at Berlin, April 4, 1941, in the Presence of Joachim von Ribbentrop and Other Officials   1090
Letter from Adolf Hitler to Benito Mussolini, June 21, 1941   1093

APPENDIX II: CHRONOLOGY OF INTERNATIONAL EVENTS, MARCH, 1938, TO DECEMBER, 1941, ISSUED BY THE DEPARTMENT OF STATE, DECEMBER 18, 1941   1098

INDEX   1113

PART ONE
THE UNITED STATES

GENERAL STATEMENTS OF POLICY

ADDRESS by Henry L. Stimson, Secretary of State, "The Work of the United States Government in the Promotion of Peace during the Past Three Years," at Pittsburgh, October 26, 1932

Delivered before the Council of the Methodist Episcopal Church for the Pittsburgh area. Department of State, Publication No. 398; excerpts

I AM GLAD to have this opportunity of laying before you the work which the American Government has been doing during the past three years in the cause of peace. That, of course, is only one of the objectives towards which the work of the Department of State is directed, but it is the fundamental objective and the one on which our main efforts are constantly spent. All of the social, commercial, and other relations of the members of the family of nations are dependent upon the existence among them of conditions of amity and good will; and, therefore, the efforts of the foreign ministries of each of those nations are fundamentally and constantly concerned with promoting such relations. . . .

Ever since I assumed the duties of my present office, three years and a half ago, I have been working by the side of a President whose chief preoccupation in the conduct of foreign relations has been to promote this great cause of peace. He believes, and I believe, that peace is for the best interests of the United States not only on moral grounds but on material grounds. We feel that no nation in the world has been provided by Providence with such a secure position from which to promote the cause of good relations among the nations of the world, or is so deeply interested, from the aspect of both its moral and material welfare, in the existence of peace. From our secure position in the New Hemisphere, surrounded only by friendly nations whose proximity has never given us cause for real anxiety, we have an assured base from which the influence of America may be exerted, without fear throughout the world, towards the establishment of better world relations.

From this base of secured position, Mr. Hoover's administration has been working along various lines, each of which has been intended to reach the same ultimate goal. I shall try to give you this evening a hasty sketch of those various paths and something of what we have accomplished in our progress along them. In the time which I have, it necessarily must be cursory and imperfect.

I. In the first place, the maintenance of peace is fundamentally dependent upon the cultivation of a common understanding among the various nations. Hostility and enmity arise more commonly out of a failure to understand each other's aims or position than from almost any other cause. The stranger has traditionally been considered an enemy ever since the Romans used the same word for each. But the modern world, by its development of easy travel and systems of communication, is daily making it more possible to cultivate this common understanding. Two foreign ministers, or secretaries of state, have a much better chance of reaching an agreement when they can pick up the telephone or make a personal visit and talk directly with each other than when their communication is limited to written messages sent through envoys.

Mr. Hoover appreciated this fully and signalized his understanding of it by making a trip which was a unique precedent in American history. You will remember that in 1928, immediately after his election and before his inauguration, he visited most of the countries of South America. In that way he established personal contact with those peoples and their rulers; he gained a face-to-face knowledge of their problems and conditions; and he was able to appraise the work being done by our ministers and ambassadors, and to form his own estimates for future development. The effect of his trip has been shown again and again by both his own better understanding of the problems of that continent and the many evidences of appreciation which have come to us.

The same method of direct contact has been carried out so far as possible during the subsequent years of his administration. The Presidents of Mexico, Colombia, and Panama, the Prime Ministers of Great Britain and Canada, the President of the Council of Ministers of France, and the Minister of Foreign Affairs of Italy have all made personal visits to Washington and talked over their problems face to face with us here. Three times I myself, at the President's direction, have visited Europe and have formed contacts with my colleagues in corresponding positions in European countries which have been of inestimable value to me in understanding their problems. I stress this direct method of international intercourse not only because I believe it to be vitally important, but because it marks a virtually new chapter in the methods of American foreign relations.

II. Closely akin to these steps have been those which we have taken to remove historic sources of friction between us and some of our neighbors, notably our Latin American neighbors. We are withdrawing our Marines from Nicaragua and Haiti as rapidly as possible and are winding up, I am glad to say successfully, the problems which caused those Marines to be landed there many years ago. Very early in 1929, during an insurrection in Mexico, we showed our friendship to that country by giving to the Mexican Government all the help which, under international law, was possible. And I am glad to say that, largely owing to that step and the cordial relations with the Mexican Government which were established by Ambassador Morrow, the newspapers of Mexico now currently state that their national relations with us have never been on a sounder or more friendly basis.

These acts are merely typical of a continuous and consistent policy of our Government towards our southern neighbors; and the favorable effect of this policy has been widespread and fundamental, and evidence of it has come from every quarter and in many ways. It is shown, for example, by the way in which they do not hesitate to turn to us for help in soothing sore spots which exist among themselves. For instance, the conference held in Washington in 1930 to deal with the disputed boundary between Guatemala and Honduras, resulted in the appointment of a special tribunal presided over by our own Chief Justice, Mr. Hughes. This tribunal has been at work all summer. Another example is the long and patient efforts of our Government, in connection with four other countries, Mexico, Cuba, Colombia, and Uruguay, to settle the difficult and persistent controversy between Paraguay and Bolivia in the Chaco. In all these matters our chief concern is for the preservation of sound and friendly international relations and the eradication of friction which may lead to the use of force and to war.

III. There is also being gradually built up in the world a great system of machinery intended to promote peace in more formal ways by direct agreements between the different nations. Under this head come particularly the treaties and agreements which directly provide for the settlement of international quarrels and disputes by peaceful and judicial methods, and the treaties which are intended to prevent the provocation of war which may come through excessive and competitive armaments.

We have taken a vigorous course in promoting all of these forms of treaties. In the first place, we have signed and ratified, within the past three years and a half, 28 treaties of arbitration and conciliation. We have signed the treaty for the World Court and have urged its ratification before the United States Senate. We believe that by joining that Court we would not only facilitate the quick and easy settlement of many irritating and troublesome controversies, but that we would also give a great assurance to the other nations of the world of our devotion to the cause of peace, which has been somewhat shaken by the length of time it has taken to get us into the Court, an institution for the original suggestion of which our country was more responsible than any other country of the world.

But I want to refer especially to two particular classes of treaties in which we have made distinct progress.

IV. The first of these classes consists of treaties limiting and reducing the size of armaments, the so-called treaties of disarmament. They form a very important class of the peace machinery of the world, because the suspicion and rivalry which comes out of competition between the different nations in building up armaments is one of the most fertile sources out of which war may arise. If you have ever had the misfortune to visit a community where everybody was carrying arms, as I have, you will know what I mean. Casualties are constantly happening. One man pulls and shoots because he thinks the other man is going to. The first step towards law and order is always to get rid of those pistols.

Now that is just the object intended to be accomplished between nations by an agreement reducing and limiting arms. It moreover stops the rivalry, which in turn breeds suspicion and ill will, and which in turn leads to an outbreak of hostilities. Except for our Navy the United States is not really an armed nation. While our Army is a most excellent nucleus of defense and a means for training our citizen soldiery in case any great emergency should arise, it is far too small to excite any apprehension on the part of our neighbors. Now in 1930 by the London Naval Treaty we reached an agreement with the two other large naval powers, Great Britain and Japan, by which a limitation was placed upon every class of vessels in our respective fleets. The first step had been taken eight years before in the Washington treaty, where an agreement was reached as to capital ships. But that proved only partially effective because competition afterwards grew up in cruisers and other vessels which led to suspicion and ill will. At London in 1930, after long efforts, we finally succeeded in getting an agreement which settled and restricted the size of the entire fleets of the three great naval powers of the world. That marked an event in disarmament which was unprecedented. For instance, it wiped out all of the petty irritation, suspicion, and rivalry which had for several years been growing up between us and Great Britain, and it inaugurated an era of good will and confidence between those two countries which has made all of our relations easy ever since. When that treaty was ratified by the United States Senate by a vote of 58 to 9, after all the fight which some of our militaristic news-

GENERAL STATEMENTS OF POLICY

papers and citizens could put up against it, more was done for the cause of peaceful settlements in this country than anything which had been done for a long time. For it showed that the moral standards of this country call for fair and just dealings with other nations and not for an aggressive show of force.

The success of the three great naval powers in reaching an agreement in the London treaty has furthermore led to hope and encouragement for the success of the great General Disarmament Conference which was afterwards called in Geneva and which is now under way. This is a much more gigantic problem because it includes all of the nations of the world with all of their different problems and relations and rivalries and suspicions, as well as all of the classes of weapons with which they may fight. That Conference met last February and for the first five months of its debates made slight progress beyond uncovering the concrete difficulties and obstacles which must be overcome to reach a successful conclusion. Inasmuch as we had already limited our Navy and as our Army, as I have already said, was not a menace or a cause of anxiety to any one, the chief problems of the Conference and the responsibility for their solution necessarily rested upon the shoulders of the other nations. We have, however, made important suggestions designed to help towards ultimate success.

To begin with, we have pointed out the importance of putting a limit on the power of offense by limiting or abolishing weapons which belong purely to the offensive class. If that idea can be carried out, it would tend to make it impossible for any nation to surprise another nation with a knockout blow at the beginning of hostilities. It would tend to discourage sudden aggressive action in the world. It would promote security and peace by strengthening defense among nations at the cost of offense.

Secondly, when the deliberations of the other nations seemed to be getting into a stalemate, our Government came forward last June with the Hoover proposal. This cut through all the maze of technicalities which had been raised and proposed that all nations should agree upon a cut of substantially one third in existing armaments. Mr. Hoover's offer came like a breath of fresh air to the atmosphere of the Conference and revived the hopes which had been waning. To-day the various delegations are engaged in working over the details of his proposal, and there has been manifested a growing spirit of hope that along this line a great beneficent result may finally be accomplished by the Conference.

V. The other class of treaties to which I wish especially to refer are the great multilateral treaties which have been adopted since the

World War in the hope of minimizing and preventing all war in the future. There have been two of these treaties. One of them is the Covenant of the League of Nations, which has been adopted by most of the other nations of the world but to which we are not a party; and the other is the Pact of Paris, the so-called Kellogg-Briand Pact. To this last we are not only a party, but it was originated by my predecessor as Secretary of State, Mr. Kellogg, in conjunction with Mr. Briand, the then Foreign Minister of France. It has also been executed by practically all of the nations of the world. The nations which signed the treaty renounce war as an instrument of national policy and agree that the settlement of all disputes and conflicts of whatever nature among them shall never be sought except by pacific means. It is a great treaty, a great simple concept, carrying with it the chief hopes of the world for a new and better era. And I regard the work which this administration has been privileged to do in the interpretation and carrying forward of this treaty as perhaps the chief work which we have accomplished in the cause of peace.

When we came into office the treaty had not yet come into force. The ceremony of proclamation took place at Washington on the 24th day of July, 1929. The treaty at that time was, of course, entirely untested, and there were many critics in the world, as there always are, who were ready to believe the worst. In the first place, some of them said that it was not a covenant at all, but simply a group of voluntary declarations made by the various nations which had signed it, expressing their pious intentions for the future for which nobody could call them to account or hold them responsible. It was said that each signatory was to be the sole judge of its own behavior. There was, however, nothing in the treaty to warrant such a destructive interpretation, but everything to the contrary. And we went to work from the very beginning to show what the treaty meant to us and what we should contend that it necessarily meant to every one else.

When Mr. MacDonald, the Prime Minister of Great Britain, came over here and visited Mr. Hoover at the Rapidan on October 9, 1929, those two gentlemen made public an historic statement as to their views of the Kellogg-Briand Treaty. They said, speaking for the United States and Great Britain:

. . . Both our Governments resolve to accept the Peace Pact not only as a declaration of good intentions but as a positive obligation to direct national policy in accordance with its pledge.

From that time onward, on every proper occasion, our Government has made it clear what our views were and what we should expect; and I think I can say that those views are now becoming the

GENERAL STATEMENTS OF POLICY

views of the entire world. We have made it clear that in our opinion the declaration in the treaty carries with it the duty of performance. We have made it clear that it necessarily alters the whole attitude of the world towards war; that, whereas during the centuries hitherto war has been one of the natural functions of government, hereafter, among the signers of this treaty, war will be an illegal thing—a disease instead of a normal state function; that, whereas hitherto a breach between two nations has been nobody's business but their own, now, under the treaty, it has become the rightful concern of the whole world, because practically the whole world has signed the treaty; and that this being so, whenever a breach of the treaty is threatened by approaching hostilities, it implies a duty of consultation among the other parties in order that public opinion may be mobilized against the impending disaster of war.

These views have been expressed by our Government in step after step relating to the recent troubles in the Far East; and the policy of this Government, announced in its note of January 7 last, not to recognize the fruits of aggression obtained by a violation of the treaty, has been formally approved in a resolution of the Assembly of the League of Nations as the proper policy for all the nations which are members of that League. It has also more recently been adopted by all of the 19 neutral nations of this hemisphere in respect to the quarrel between Bolivia and Paraguay as the proper policy for the nations of these continents. And, so far as formal and general adoption can thus make it, it has become a recognized principle of international law and practice.

The attitude which your Government has taken towards the Kellogg Pact in these proceedings has had at least two other results. In the first place, it has tended to strengthen the sanctity of treaties. If, when the trouble broke out in Manchuria, we had turned away our heads, irreparable damage would have been done not only to the standing of the Kellogg Pact but also to every other peace treaty of the world. But when the United States showed that the sanctity of the Kellogg Treaty was of keen interest and importance to us, and when our view was followed by the rest of the world, a new breath of vigor and of life was infused into the vitality of all such treaties and their obligations.

In the second place, the action which has taken place among the nations of the world in respect to the troubles in Manchuria has marked a new milestone in the development of actual international cooperation when war threatens the world. In the new international world created by these treaties, the basic idea is that war anywhere is of concern everywhere. The necessary resulting process of this has been shown by the events of the past year to be a consultation between the nations of the world and a call to public opinion to exert itself. The nations of the world have consulted together as to the threat to peace even in far-off Manchuria. They have consulted as to the means to avoid the breach or to moderate and appease it. As a part of this effort to ascertain the true facts involved in the fog of mutual recrimination and intelligently to inform public opinion, a neutral investigating commission has, with the consent of both the disputant nations, been sent to the seat of the quarrel and is about to present the result of its findings to the nations members of the League of Nations assembled in Geneva.

These are all new and important landmarks in the realm of international controversy. They evidence a new orientation of the world attitude towards war. They make it clear that after centuries of effort based upon other and more backward theories, the world is now moving forward upon these new lines.

We have a right to take courage in the light of such events. For ourselves, we believe that eventually the reign of peace will come. There will be among nations in respect to public war, war between nations, the same development that has been seen in individual communities in respect to private combat between individual men. We do not delude ourselves as to the difficulty of the road that lies before us nor as to the obstacles and trials which stand in our way. We are well aware that it will require the utmost patience and faith. We know that all such developments in human organization are extremely slow. We realize that it took centuries to eliminate ordeal by battle in the settlement of the individual quarrels of individual men. But we are unshakably confident that the same process is on its way among the nations and will eventually arrive. And during the brief term in which we have been invested with the heavy responsibility of guiding the foreign policy of this country, we have tried to act in that faith.

INAUGURAL ADDRESS by President Franklin D. Roosevelt, March 4, 1933

Congressional Record, 77.1, 73d Congress, Special Session, p. 5; excerpt

IN THE FIELD of world policy I would dedicate this Nation to the policy of the good neighbor—the neighbor who resolutely respects himself and, because he does so, respects the rights of others—the neighbor who respects his obligations and respects the sanctity of his agreements in and with a world of neighbors. We now realize as we have never realized before our interdependence on each other; that we cannot merely take, but must give as well.

ADDRESS by President Franklin D. Roosevelt, Delivered at Washington, D.C., before the Woodrow Wilson Foundation, December 28, 1933

Department of State, *Press Releases,* December 30, 1933, p. 380; excerpts

"COMPREHENSION must be the soil in which shall grow all the fruits of friendship." Those words, used by President Wilson in the Mobile speech in 1913, can well serve as a statement of policy by the Government of the United States. That policy applies equally to a comprehension of our internal problems and our international relations. . . .

In that speech in Mobile, President Wilson first enunciated the definite statement "that the United States will never again seek one additional foot of territory by conquest." The United States accepted that declaration of policy. President Wilson went further pointing out with special reference to our Latin American neighbors that material interests must never be made superior to human liberty.

Nevertheless, and largely as a result of the convulsion of the World War and its after effects, the complete fruition of that policy of unselfishness has not in every case been obtained. And in this we, all of us, have to share the responsibility.

I do not hesitate to say that if I had been engaged in a political campaign as a citizen of some other American republic, I might have been strongly tempted to play upon the fears of my compatriots of that republic by charging the United States of North America with some form of imperialistic desire for selfish aggrandizement. As a citizen of some other republic I might have found it difficult to believe fully in the altruism of the richest American republic. In particular, as a citizen of some other republic, I might have found it hard to approve of the occupation of the territory of other republics, even as a temporary measure.

It therefore has seemed clear to me as President that the time has come to supplement and to implement the declaration of President Wilson by the further declaration that the definite policy of the United States from now on is one opposed to armed intervention.

The maintenance of constitutional government in other nations is not a sacred obligation devolving upon the United States alone. The maintenance of law and the orderly processes of government in this hemisphere is the concern of each individual nation within its own borders first of all. It is only if and when the failure of orderly processes affects the other nations of the continent that it becomes their concern; and the point to stress is that in such an event it becomes the joint concern of a whole continent in which we are all neighbors.

It is the comprehension of that doctrine—a comprehension not by the leaders alone but by the peoples of all the American republics, that has made the conference now concluding its labors in Montevideo such a fine success. A better state of feeling among the neighbor nations of North and Central and South America exists today than at any time within a generation. For participation in the bringing about of that result we can feel proud that so much credit belongs to the Secretary of State of the United States, Cordell Hull.

In the wider world field a chain of events has led, of late, away from rather than towards the ultimate objectives of Woodrow Wilson.

The superficial observer charges this failure to the growth of the spirit of nationalism. But in so doing he suggests a nationalism in its narrower, restrictive sense, and a nationalism of that kind supported by the overwhelming masses of the people themselves in each nation.

I challenge that description of the world population today.

The blame for the danger to world peace lies not in the world population but in the political leaders of that population.

The imagination of the masses of world population was stirred, as never before, by President Wilson's gallant appeal to them—to those masses—to banish future war. His appeal meant little to the imagination or the hearts of a large number of the so-called statesmen who gathered in Paris to assemble a treaty of so-called peace in 1919. I saw that with my own eyes and heard that with my own ears. Political profit, personal prestige, national aggrandizement attended the birth of the League of Nations, and handicapped it from its infancy by seeking their own profit and their own safety first.

Nevertheless, through the League directly, or through its guiding motives indirectly, the states of the world have groped forward to find something better than the old way of composing their differences.

The League has provided a common meeting place; it has provided machinery which serves for international discussion; and in very many practical instances it has helped labor and health and commerce and education, and, last but not least, the actual settlement of many disputes great and small among nations great and small.

Today the United States is cooperating openly in the fuller utilization of the League of Nations machinery than ever before.

I believe that I express the views of my countrymen when I state that the old policies, alliances, combinations, and balances of power have proved themselves inadequate for the preservation of world peace. The League of Nations, encouraging as it does the extension of nonaggression pacts, of reduction of armament agreements, is a prop in the world peace structure.

We are not members and we do not contemplate membership. We are giving cooperation to the League in every matter which is not primarily political and in every matter which obviously represents the views and the good of the peoples of the world as distinguished from the views and the good of political leaders, of privileged classes, or of imperialistic aims.

If you figure the world's population at approximately one billion and a half people, you will find it safe to guess that a least 90 percent of all of them are today content with the territorial limits of their respective nations and are willing further to reduce their armed forces tomorrow if every other nation in the world will agree to do the same thing. Back of the threat to world peace lies the fear and perhaps even the possibility that the other 10 percent of the people of the world may go along with a leadership which seeks territorial expansion at the expense of neighbors and which under various pleas in avoidance are unwilling to reduce armament or stop rearmament even if everybody else agrees to nonaggression and to arms reduction.

If this 10 percent can be persuaded by the other 90 percent to do their own thinking and not to be led, we will have practical peace, permanent peace, real peace throughout the world. Our own country has reduced the immediate steps to this greatest of objectives to practical and reasonable terms.

I have said to every nation in the world something to this effect:

1. Let every nation agree to eliminate over a short period of years, and by progressive steps, every weapon of offense in its possession and to create no additional weapons of offense. This does not guarantee a nation against invasion unless you implement it with the right to fortify its own border with permanent and nonmobile defenses; and also with the right to assure itself through international continuing inspection that its neighbors are not creating nor maintaining offensive weapons of war.

2. A simple declaration that no nation will permit any of its armed forces to cross its own borders into the territory of another nation. Such an act would be regarded by humanity as an act of aggression and as an act, therefore, that would call for condemnation by humanity.

3. It is clear, of course, that no such general agreement for the elimination of aggression and of the weapons of offensive warfare would be of

any value to the world unless every nation, without exception, entered into the agreement by solemn obligation. If, then, such an agreement were signed by a great majority of the nations on the definite condition that it would go into effect only when signed by all the nations, it would be a comparatively easy matter to determine which nations in this enlightened time are willing to go on record as belonging to the small minority of mankind which still believes in the use of the sword for invasion of and attack upon their neighbors.

I did not make this suggestion until I felt assured, after a hardheaded practical survey, that the temper of the overwhelming majority of all men and women in my own country, as well as those who make up the world's population, subscribes to the fundamental objective I have set forth and to the practical road to that objective. The political leaders of many of these peoples interpose and will interpose argument, excuse, befogging amendment—yes, and even ridicule. But I tell them that the men and women they serve are so far in advance of that type of leadership that we could get a world accord on world peace immediately if the people of the world spoke for themselves.

Through all the centuries and down to the world conflict of 1914 to 1918, wars were made by governments. Woodrow Wilson challenged that necessity. That challenge made the people who create and who change governments think. They wondered with Woodrow Wilson whether the people themselves could not some day prevent governments from making war.

It is but an extension of the challenge of Woodrow Wilson for us to propose in this newer generation that from now on war by governments shall be changed to peace by peoples.

ADDRESS by Cordell Hull, Secretary of State, "Eight Pillars of Enduring Peace," at Buenos Aires, December 5, 1936

Delivered at the Inter-American Conference for the Maintenance of Peace, the Secretary being the Chairman of the United States Delegation. Department of State, *Press Releases*, December 5, 1936, p. 432

THE PRIMARY purpose of this Conference is to banish war from the Western Hemisphere. In its earnest pursuit of this great undertaking, it is necessary at the outset to visualize numerous dangerous conditions and practices in general international affairs to the extent that they bear upon and affect the work of this Conference. It is manifest that every country today is faced with a supreme alternative.

GENERAL STATEMENTS OF POLICY

Each must play its part in determining whether the world will slip backward toward war and savagery, or whether it can maintain and will advance the level of civilization and peace. None can escape its responsibility.

The 21 American republics cannot remain unconcerned by the grave and threatening conditions in many parts of the world. Our convocation here in Buenos Aires utters this hemisphere's common voice of its interest, nay, its intense concern, over the determination of this momentous question. The repercussions of wars and preparations for wars have been so universally disastrous that it is now as plain as mathematical truth that each nation in any part of the world is concerned in peace in every part of the world. The nations of all the Americas, through their chosen delegates, have assembled to make careful survey and analysis of all aspects of their responsibilities; to take account of their common duties; and to plan accordingly for the safety and welfare of their peoples.

The Western Hemisphere must now face squarely certain hard realities. For the purpose of our undertaking, we must frankly recognize that for some time the forces of militarism have been in the ascendant in a large part of the world; those of peace have been correspondingly on the decline. We should be lacking in common sense if we ignored the plain fact that the effects of these forces will unavoidably have direct impact upon all of us. We should be lacking in ordinary caution if we fail to counsel together for our common safety and welfare.

It is bad enough when many statesmen and peoples close their minds and memories to the awful lesson taught by the millions of soldiers sacrificed in the World War; the shattered cities, the desolated fields, and all the other material, moral, and spiritual ravages of that conflict. Still worse, that war has brought in its train wounds to man's heart and spirit, national hatreds and fears, the dislocation or destruction of indispensable political and governmental structures, and the collapse or cool abandonment of former high standards of national conduct. The supreme tragedy is completed by the breakdown of the commerce of mind and culture, the attempt to isolate the nations of the earth into sealed compartments, all of which have made war a burden not to be endured by mankind.

The delegates of the American nations, meeting here in the face of these grave and threatening world conditions, must realize that mere words will not suffice. From every wise and practical viewpoint, concrete peace planning, peace views, and peace objectives are imperative. We must quicken our words and our hopes into a specific, embracing program to maintain peace. Such a program, adequately implemented, should constitute an armory of peace. It should comprise a structure affording all practical means for safeguarding peace. At a time when many other governments or peoples fail or fear to proclaim and embrace a broad or definite peace plan or movement, while their statesmen are shouting threats of war, it is all the more necessary that we of the Americas must cry out for peace, keep alive the spirit of peace, live by the rules of peace, and forthwith perfect the machinery for its maintenance. Should we fail to make this outstanding contribution, it would be a practical desertion of the cause of peace and a tragic blow to the hopes of humanity.

In meeting this problem, the American republics are in a peculiarly advantageous situation. There are among us no radical differences, no profound mistrusts or deep hatreds. On the contrary we are inspired by the impulse to be constant friends and the determination to be peaceful neighbors.

We recognize the right of all nations to handle their affairs in any way they choose, and this quite irrespective of the fact that their way may be different from our way or even repugnant to our ideas. But we cannot fail to take cognizance of the international aspect of their policies when and to the extent that they may react upon us. I, myself, am unalterably of the view that a policy leading to war may react upon us. In the face of any situation directly leading to war, can we therefore be other than apprehensive?

In sustaining the firm determination that peace must be maintained and that any country whose policies make war likely is threatening injury to all, I believe that the nations of this hemisphere would find themselves in accord with governments elsewhere. I strongly entertain the hope that a united group of American nations may take common action at this Conference further to assure peace among themselves and define their attitude toward war; and that this action may not only demonstrate the happy position of the New World, but, though designed primarily for our own benefit, embody policies of world application and correspond to the views and interests of nations outside this hemisphere.

There is no need for war. There is a practical alternative policy at hand, complete and adequate. It is no exclusive policy aimed at the safety or supremacy of a few, leaving others to struggle with distressful situations. It demands no sacrifices comparable to the advantages which will result to each nation and to each individual.

In these circumstances the representatives of the 21 American republics should frankly call the attention of the people of this hemisphere to the possibilities of danger to their future peace and progress and at the same time set forth the numerous steps that can well be undertaken as the most effective means of improving and safeguarding the conditions of permanent peace.

While carefully avoiding any political entanglements, my Government strives at all times to cooperate with other nations to every practical extent in support of peace objectives, including reduction or limitation of armaments, the control of traffic in arms, taking the profits out of war, and the restoration of fair and friendly economic relationships. We reject war as a method of settling international disputes and favor such methods as conference, conciliation, and arbitration.

Peace can be partially safeguarded through international agreements. Such agreements, however, must reflect the utmost good faith; this alone can be the guaranty of their significance and usefulness. Contemporary events clearly show that, where mutual trust, good will, and sincerity of purpose are lacking, pacts or agreements fail; and the world is seized by fear and left to the mercy of the wreckers.

The Conference has the duty of considering all peace proposals of merit. Let me enumerate and briefly discuss eight separate and vitally important principles and proposals for a comprehensive peace program and peace structure. They are not designed to be all-inclusive. In considering them, we should be guided by the knowledge that other forces and agencies of peace exist besides those made and to be made on our continents; what we do contemplates no conflict with sincere efforts the world over.

First. I would emphasize the local and unilateral responsibility of each nation carefully to educate and organize its people in opposition to war and its underlying causes. Support must be given to peace, to the most effective policies for its preservation; and, finally, each nation must maintain conditions within its own borders which will permit it to adopt national policies that can be peacefully pursued. More than any other factor, a thoroughly informed and alert public opinion in each country as to the suitable and desirable relationships with other nations and the principles underlying them, enables a government in time of crisis to act promptly and effectively for peace.

The forces of peace everywhere are entitled to function both through governments and through public opinion. The peoples of the world would be far wiser if they expended more of their hard-earned money in organizing the forces of peace and fewer of the present 5 billion dollars in educating and training their military forces.

Since the time when Thomas Jefferson insisted upon a "decent respect to the opinions of mankind," public opinion has controlled foreign policy in all democracies. It is, therefore, all important that every platform, every pulpit, and every forum should become constant and active agencies in the great work of education and organization. The limited extent of such highly organized and intelligent public opinion in support of peace is by far the largest drawback to any plan to prevent war. Truly the first step is that each nation must thus make itself safe for peace. This, too, develops a common will for freedom, the soil from which peace springs.

People everywhere should be made to know of the peace mechanisms. Even more, there should be brought home to them the knowledge that trade, commerce, finance, debts, communications, have a bearing on peace. The workman at his bench, the farmer on his land, the shopkeeper by his shelves, the clerk at his books, the laborer in factory, plantation, mine, or construction camp, must realize that his work is the work of peace; that to interrupt it for ends of national or personal rapacity is to drive him toward quick death by bayonets, or to slower, but not less grievous suffering, through economic distress.

In all our countries we have scholars who can demonstrate these facts; let them not be silent. Our churches have direct contact with all groups; may they remember that the peacemakers are the children of God. We have artists and poets who can distill their needed knowledge into trenchant phrase and line; they have work to do. Our great journals on both continents cover the world. Our women are awake; our youth sentient; our clubs and organizations make opinion everywhere. There is a strength here available greater than that of armies. We have but to ask its aid; it will be swift to answer, not only here, but in continents beyond the seas.

Second. Indispensable in their influence for peace and well-being are frequent conferences between representatives of the nations and intercourse between their peoples. Collaboration and the exchange of views, ideas, and information are the most effective means of establishing understanding, friendship, and trust. I would again emphasize that any written pacts or agreements not based upon such relationships as these too often exist on paper only. Development of the atmosphere of peace, understanding, and good will during our sessions here will alone constitute a vast accomplishment.

Third. Any complete program would include safeguarding the nations of this hemisphere from using force, one against the other, through the consummation of all the five well-known peace agreements, produced in chief part by previous conferences, as well as through the Draft Convention Coordinating the Existing Treaties between the American States and Extending Them in Certain Re-

GENERAL STATEMENTS OF POLICY

spects, which the Delegation of the United States is presenting for the consideration of this Conference.

In these, virtually all of the essentials of adequate machinery are present. If their operation is somewhat implemented by provisions in the draft proposal I have just mentioned to be considered by this Conference, such machinery would be complete.

The first of these is the Treaty to Avoid and Prevent Conflicts between the American States, which was signed in Santiago in 1923.

The second is the Treaty for the Renunciation of War, known as the Kellogg-Briand Pact, or the Pact of Paris, signed at Paris in 1928.

The third is the General Convention of Inter-American Conciliation, signed at Washington in 1929.

The fourth is the General Treaty of Inter-American Arbitration, signed at Washington in 1929.

The fifth is the Anti-War Treaty of Nonaggression and Conciliation, signed at Rio de Janeiro in 1933.

While the Montevideo Conference in 1933 went on record in favor of the valid execution of these five agreements by each of the 21 governments represented, several have not yet completed this ratification. These agreements provide a many-sided and flexible functioning machinery for the adjustment of difficulties that may arise in this hemisphere. A government could not give more tangible proof of its readiness to translate into practicable form its desire to promote and to maintain peace. Swift action by all of us to ratify these agreements should be the natural assertion of our intentions.

Fourth. If war should occur, any peace program must provide for the problem then presented. For the belligerent, there is the ruin and suffering of war. For the neutrals, there is the task of remaining neutral, of not being too disturbed in their own affairs, of not having their own peace imperiled, of working in common to restrict the war and bring it to an end. Can we in this Conference work out for ourselves a common line of policy that might be pursued during a period of neutrality? Some first broad approaches toward that end are, I think, possible. If these are to be sound they must be inspired by the determination to stay at peace. When interests are challenged, when minds are stirred, when entry into war in some particular juncture may appear to offer to some country the chance of national advantage, then determination is needed to retain neutrality. The maintenance of neutrality is an achievement to be attained more readily if undertaken jointly. Such agreement would be a tremendous safeguard for each of us. It might be a powerful means of ending war.

When we have done all that seems to be possible in extending and perfecting an integrated and permanent mechanism for preserving peaceful relations among ourselves, and when we have placed in operation these various instruments, the 21 republics of this hemisphere will have given overt expression to the most determined will for peace to be found in the world today. In the face of a weakening elsewhere in the world of reliance on and observance of international agreements, we shall have proclaimed our firm intention that these peaceful instruments shall be the foundation of relations between nations throughout this whole region.

If we can endow peace with certainty, if we can make it glow in our part of the world, then we may indulge the hope that our example will not be in vain.

Fifth. The peoples of this region have a further opportunity. They must make headway with a liberal policy of commerce, which would lower excessive barriers to trade and lessen injurious discriminations as between the trade of different countries. This means the substitution of a policy of economic benefit, good will, and fair dealing for one stimulated by greedy and short-sighted calculations of momentary advantage in an impractical isolation. It would have most beneficial effects, both direct and indirect, upon political difficulties and antagonisms.

A thriving international commerce, well adjusted to the resources and talents of each country, brings benefit to all. It keeps men employed, active and usefully supplying the wants of others. It leads each country to look upon others as helpful counterparts to itself rather than as antagonists. It opens up to each country, to the extent mutually profitable and desirable, the resources and the organized productive power of other countries; by its benefits small nations with limited territory or resources can have a varied, secure, and prosperous life; it can bring improvement to those who feel their toil too hard and their reward too meager.

Prosperity and peace are not separate entities. To promote one is to promote the other. The economic well-being of peoples is the greatest single protection against civil strife, large armaments, war. Economic isolation and military force go hand in hand; when nations cannot get what they need by the normal processes of trade, they will continue to resort to the use of force. A people employed and in a state of reasonable comfort is not a people among whom class struggles, militarism, and war can thrive. But a people driven to desperation by want and misery is at all times a threat to peace, their conditions an invitation to disorder and chaos, both internal and external.

The intervening years have given added significance to the eco-

GENERAL STATEMENTS OF POLICY

nomic program adopted at the Conference at Montevideo 3 years ago. That program is today the greatest potential force both for peace and prosperity. Our present Conference should reaffirm and secure action upon this program of economic intelligence.

One feature of the resolutions adopted at Montevideo was the support for the principle of equality of treatment as the basis of acceptable commercial policy. This rule has been followed in a number of commercial agreements that have already been concluded between American nations. Their benefits are already becoming manifest and will continue to grow. We cannot blind ourselves to the fact, however, that at the same time there has taken place even among the American nations a growth in the restrictions upon trade and an extension of discriminatory practices; these have tended to counteract the advantages resulting from the liberalizing terms embodied in other agreements.

I would urge again the wisdom of avoiding discrimination in our commercial policy. The practice of discrimination prevents trade from following the lines which would produce the greatest economic benefits—it inevitably in the long run must provoke retaliation from those who suffer from discrimination; makes it more difficult for countries eager to pursue a liberal trade policy to secure the fair gains from this policy, and thereby checks the lowering of restrictions. It will not serve our broad and deep aims; on the contrary, if steadily extended will lead us into new controversies and difficulties. The Montevideo program offers the only alternative to the present short-sighted, war-breeding bilateral bargaining method of trade, to the exclusion of triangular and multilateral trade, which is being employed in many parts of the world with sterile results.

The ends we seek can best be achieved by the concurrent or concerted action of many countries. Each can exert itself steadfastly amidst the particular circumstances of its economic situation to make its contribution toward the rebuilding of trade. Each can grant new opportunities to others as it receives new opportunities for itself. All are called upon to share in the concurrent or concerted action which is required. Any country which seeks the benefits of the program while avoiding its responsibilities, will in time shut itself off from the benefits. Any country which is tempted or forced by some special calculation to depart from these lines of action and which conveys and seeks special advantage jeopardizes the progress, and perhaps the very existence, of the program. Faithful dealing, without favor, between equal partners will be required to readjust trade along the lines of growth, which is our goal.

Sixth. The Conference must recognize the all-important principle of practical international cooperation to restore many indispensable relationships between nations; for international relationships, in many vital respects, are at a low ebb. The entire international order is severely dislocated. Chaotic conditions in the relations between nations have appeared. Human progress already has slowed down.

Nations in recent years have sought to live a hermit existence by isolating themselves from each other in suspicion and fear. The inevitable result is not unlike that experienced by a community where individuals undertake to live a hermit existence, with the resultant decline and decay of the spiritual, the moral, the educational, and the material benefits and blessings which spring from community organization and effort. The difference, when nations live apart, is that the entire human race in countless instances suffers irreparable injury—political, moral, material, spiritual, and social. Today, for illustration, through lack of comprehension, understanding, and confidence, we see many nations exhausting their material substance and the vitality of their people by piling up huge armaments. We behold others, in their attempted isolation, becoming more indifferent and less considerate toward the rights, privileges, and honest opinions of others. National character and conduct are threatened with utter demoralization. At no distant time we shall see a state of moral and spiritual isolation, bringing with it the condemnation of the world, covering great parts of the earth, unless peoples halt and turn toward a sane course.

Seventh. International law has been in large measure flouted. It should be reestablished, revitalized, and strengthened by general demand. International law protects the peace and security of nations and so safeguards them against maintaining great armaments and wasting their substance in continual readiness for war. Founded upon justice and humanity, the great principles of international law are the source and fountain of the equality, the security, and the very existence of nations. Armies and navies are no permanent substitute. Abandonment of the rule of law would not only leave small or unarmed states at the mercy of the reckless and powerful but would hopelessly undermine all international order. It is inconceivable that the civilized nations would long delay a supreme effort to reestablish that rule of law.

Eighth. Observance of understandings, agreements, and treaties between nations constitutes the foundation of international order. May I say here that this is not a time for crimination or recrimination, nor is such in my mind during this discussion. There must be the fullest patience and forbearance, one country with another, as the nations endeavor to climb back to that high ground of wholesome and elevating relationship of loyalty to the given word and faithful fair dealing.

International agreements have lost their force and reliability as a basis of relations between nations. This extremely ominous and fateful development constitutes the most dangerous single phenomenon in the world of today; not international law merely, but that which is higher—moral law—and the whole integrity and honor of governments are in danger of being ruthlessly trampled upon. There has been a failure of the spirit. There is no task more urgent than that of remaking the basis of trusted agreement between nations. They must ardently seek the terms of new agreements and stand behind them with unfailing will. The vitality of international agreements must be restored.

If the solemn rights and obligations between nations are to be treated lightly or brushed aside, the nations of the world will head straight toward international anarchy and chaos. And soon, too, the citizen begins to lower his individual standards of personal, moral, and business conduct to those of his government. Trust in each nation's honor and faith in its given word must be restored by the concerted resolve of all governments.

It is to the interest of everyone that there be an end of treaties broken by arbitrary unilateral action. Peaceful procedure, agreements between the signatories, and mutual understanding must be restored as the means of modifying or ending international agreements.

In the accomplishment of the high aims and purposes of this eightfold program, the people of every nation have an equal interest. We of this hemisphere have reason to hope that these great objectives may receive the support of all peoples. If peace and progress are to be either maintained or advanced, the time is overripe for renewed effort on each nation's part. There can be no delay. Through past centuries, the human race fought its way up from the low level of barbarism and war to that of civilization and peace. This accomplishment has only been partial, and it may well be but temporary.

It would be a frightful commentary on the human race if, with the awful lesson of its disastrous experience, responsible and civilized governments should now fail.

The nations of this continent should omit no word or act in their attempt to meet the dangerous conditions which endanger peace. Let our actions here at Buenos Aires constitute the most potent possible appeal to peacemakers and warmakers throughout the world.

So only does civilization become real. So only can we rightly ask that universal support which entitles governments to speak for their peoples to the world not with the voice of propaganda but with that of truth. Having affirmed our faith, we should be remiss if we were to leave anything undone which will tend to assure our peace here and make us powerful for peace elsewhere. In a very real sense, let this continent set the high example of championing the forces of peace, democracy, and civilization.

Digest of the Address

1. Peoples must be educated for peace. Each nation must make itself safe for peace.
2. Frequent conferences between representatives of nations and intercourse between their peoples are essential.
3. The consummation of the five well-known peace agreements will provide adequate peace machinery.
4. In the event of war in this hemisphere there should be a common policy of neutrality.
5. The nations should adopt commercial policies to bring each that prosperity upon which enduring peace is founded.
6. Practical international cooperation is essential to restore many indispensable relationships between nations and prevent the demoralization with which national character and conduct are threatened.
7. International law should be reestablished, revitalized, and strengthened. Armies and navies are no permanent substitute for its great principles.
8. Faithful observance of undertakings between nations is the foundation of international order, and rests upon moral law, the highest of all law.

STATEMENT by Cordell Hull, Secretary of State, July 16, 1937

Department of State, *Press Releases,* July 17, 1937, p. 41

I HAVE BEEN receiving from many sources inquiries and suggestions arising out of disturbed situations in various parts of the world.

Unquestionably there are in a number of regions tensions and strains which on their face involve only countries that are near neighbors but which in ultimate analysis are of inevitable concern to the whole world. Any situation in which armed hostilities are in progress or are threatened is a situation wherein rights and interests of all nations either are or may be seriously affected. There can be no serious hostilities anywhere in the world which will not one way or another affect interests or rights or obligations of this country. I therefore feel warranted in making—in fact, I feel it a duty to make—a statement of this Government's position in regard to international problems and situations with respect to which this country feels deep concern.

This country constantly and consistently advocates maintenance of peace. We advocate national and international self-restraint. We advocate abstinence by all nations from use of force in pursuit of policy and from interference in the internal affairs of other nations. We advocate adjustment of problems in international relations by processes of peaceful negotiation and agreement. We advocate faithful observance of international agreements. Upholding the principle of the sanctity of treaties, we believe in modification of provisions of treaties, when need therefor arises, by orderly processes carried out in a spirit of mutual helpfulness and accommodation. We believe in respect by all nations for the rights of others and performance by all nations of established obligations. We stand for revitalizing and strengthening of international law. We advocate steps toward promotion of economic security and stability the world over. We advocate lowering or removing of excessive barriers in international trade. We seek effective equality of commercial opportunity and we urge upon all nations application of the principle of equality of treatment. We believe in limitation and reduction of armament. Realizing the necessity for maintaining armed forces adequate for national security, we are prepared to reduce or to increase our own armed forces in proportion to reductions or increases made by other countries. We avoid entering into alliances or entangling commitments but we believe in cooperative effort by peaceful and practicable means in support of the principles hereinbefore stated.

ADDRESS by President Franklin D. Roosevelt at the Dedication of the Outerlink Bridge, Chicago, October 5, 1937

Department of State, *Press Releases*, October 9, 1937, p. 275

I AM GLAD to come once again to Chicago and especially to have the opportunity of taking part in the dedication of this important project of civic betterment.

On my trip across the continent and back I have been shown many evidences of the result of common-sense cooperation between municipalities and the Federal Government, and I have been greeted by tens of thousands of Americans who have told me in every look and word that their material and spiritual well-being has made great strides forward in the past few years.

And yet, as I have seen with my own eyes, the prosperous farms, the thriving factories, and the busy railroads—as I have seen the happiness and security and peace which covers our wide land—almost inevitably I have been compelled to contrast our peace with very different scenes being enacted in other parts of the world.

It is because the people of the United States under modern conditions must, for the sake of their own future, give thought to the rest of the world, that I, as the responsible executive head of the Nation, have chosen this great inland city and this gala occasion to speak to you on a subject of definite national importance.

The political situation in the world, which of late has been growing progressively worse, is such as to cause grave concern and anxiety to all the peoples and nations who wish to live in peace and amity with their neighbors.

Some 15 years ago the hopes of mankind for a continuing era of international peace were raised to great heights when more than 60 nations solemnly pledged themselves not to resort to arms in furtherance of their national aims and policies. The high aspirations expressed in the Briand-Kellogg Peace Pact and the hopes for peace thus raised have of late given way to a haunting fear of calamity. The present reign of terror and international lawlessness began a few years ago.

It began through unjustified interference in the internal affairs of other nations or the invasion of alien territory in violation of treaties and has now reached a stage where the very foundations of civilization are seriously threatened. The landmarks and traditions which have marked the progress of civilization toward a condition of law, order, and justice are being wiped away.

Without a declaration of war and without warning or justification of any kind, civilians, including women and children, are being ruthlessly murdered with bombs from the air. In times of so-called peace ships are being attacked and sunk by submarines without cause or notice. Nations are fomenting and taking sides in civil warfare in nations that have never done them any harm. Nations claiming freedom for themselves deny it to others.

Innocent peoples and nations are being cruelly sacrificed to a greed for power and supremacy which is devoid of all sense of justice and humane consideration.

To paraphrase a recent author, "perhaps we foresee a time when men, exultant in the technique of homicide, will rage so hotly over

GENERAL STATEMENTS OF POLICY

the world that every precious thing will be in danger, every book and picture and harmony, every treasure garnered through two millenniums, the small, the delicate, the defenseless—all will be lost or wrecked or utterly destroyed."

If those things come to pass in other parts of the world let no one imagine that America will escape, that it may expect mercy, that this Western Hemisphere will not be attacked, and that it will continue tranquilly and peacefully to carry on the ethics and the arts of civilization.

If those days come "there will be no safety by arms, no help from authority, no answer in science. The storm will rage till every flower of culture is trampled and all human beings are leveled in a vast chaos."

If those days are not to come to pass—if we are to have a world in which we can breathe freely and live in amity without fear—the peace-loving nations must make a concerted effort to uphold laws and principles on which alone peace can rest secure.

The peace-loving nations must make a concerted effort in opposition to those violations of treaties and those ignorings of humane instincts which today are creating a state of international anarchy and instability from which there is no escape through mere isolation or neutrality.

Those who cherish their freedom and recognize and respect the equal right of their neighbors to be free and live in peace, must work together for the triumph of law and moral principles in order that peace, justice, and confidence may prevail in the world. There must be a return to a belief in the pledged word, in the value of a signed treaty. There must be recognition of the fact that national morality is as vital as private morality.

A bishop wrote me the other day:

It seems to me that something greatly needs to be said in behalf of ordinary humanity against the present practice of carrying the horrors of war to helpless civilians, especially women and children. It may be that such a protest might be regarded by many, who claim to be realists, as futile, but may it not be that the heart of mankind is so filled with horror at the present needless suffering that that force could be mobilized in sufficient volume to lessen such cruelty in the days ahead. Even though it may take twenty years, which God forbid, for civilization to make effective its corporate protest against this barbarism, surely strong voices may hasten the day.

There is a solidarity and interdependence about the modern world, both technically and morally, which makes it impossible for any nation completely to isolate itself from economic and political upheavals in the rest of the world, especially when such upheavals appear to be spreading and not declining. There can be no stability or peace either within nations or between nations except under laws and moral standards adhered to by all. International anarchy destroys every foundation for peace. It jeopardizes either the immediate or the future security of every nation, large or small. It is, therefore, a matter of vital interest and concern to the people of the United States that the sanctity of international treaties and the maintenance of international morality be restored.

The overwhelming majority of the peoples and nations of the world today want to live in peace. They seek the removal of barriers against trade. They want to exert themselves in industry, in agriculture, and in business, that they may increase their wealth through the production of wealth-producing goods rather than striving to produce military planes and bombs and machine guns and cannon for the destruction of human lives and useful property.

In those nations of the world which seem to be piling armament on armament for purposes of aggression, and those other nations which fear acts of aggression against them and their security, a very high proportion of their national income is being spent directly for armaments. It runs from 30 to as high as 50 percent.

The proportion that we in the United States spend is far less—11 or 12 percent.

How happy we are that the circumstances of the moment permit us to put our money into bridges and boulevards, dams and reforestation, the conservation of our soil, and many other kinds of useful works rather than into huge standing armies and vast supplies of implements of war.

I am compelled and you are compelled, nevertheless, to look ahead. The peace, the freedom, and the security of 90 percent of the population of the world is being jeopardized by the remaining 10 percent, who are threatening a breakdown of all international order and law. Surely the 90 percent who want to live in peace under law and in accordance with moral standards that have received almost universal acceptance through the centuries, can and must find some way to make their will prevail.

The situation is definitely of universal concern. The questions involved relate not merely to violations of specific provisions of particular treaties; they are questions of war and of peace, of international law, and especially of principles of humanity. It is true that they involve definite violations of agreements, and especially of the Covenant of the League of Nations, the Briand-Kellogg Pact, and

GENERAL STATEMENTS OF POLICY

the Nine Power Treaty. But they also involve problems of world economy, world security, and world humanity.

It is true that the moral consciousness of the world must recognize the importance of removing injustices and well-founded grievances; but at the same time it must be aroused to the cardinal necessity of honoring sanctity of treaties, of respecting the rights and liberties of others, and of putting an end to acts of international aggression.

It seems to be unfortunately true that the epidemic of world lawlessness is spreading.

When an epidemic of physical disease starts to spread, the community approves and joins in a quarantine of the patients in order to protect the health of the community against the spread of the disease.

It is my determination to pursue a policy of peace and to adopt every practicable measure to avoid involvement in war. It ought to be inconceivable that in this modern era, and in the face of experience, any nation could be so foolish and ruthless as to run the risk of plunging the whole world into war by invading and violating in contravention of solemn treaties the territory of other nations that have done them no real harm and which are too weak to protect themselves adequately. Yet the peace of the world and the welfare and security of every nation is today being threatened by that very thing.

No nation which refuses to exercise forbearance and to respect the freedom and rights of others can long remain strong and retain the confidence and respect of other nations. No nation ever loses its dignity or good standing by conciliating its differences and by exercising great patience with and consideration for the rights of other nations.

War is a contagion, whether it be declared or undeclared. It can engulf states and peoples remote from the original scene of hostilities. We are determined to keep out of war, yet we cannot insure ourselves against the disastrous effects of war and the dangers of involvement. We are adopting such measures as will minimize our risk of involvement, but we cannot have complete protection in a world of disorder in which confidence and security have broken down.

If civilization is to survive the principles of the Prince of Peace must be restored. Shattered trust between nations must be revived.

Most important of all, the will for peace on the part of peace-loving nations must express itself to the end that nations that may be tempted to violate their agreements and the rights of others will desist from such a cause. There must be positive endeavors to preserve peace.

America hates war. America hopes for peace. Therefore, America actively engages in the search for peace.

RADIO ADDRESS by President Franklin D. Roosevelt, October 26, 1938. Delivered in Connection with the Eighth Annual *New York Herald Tribune* Forum on Current Problems

Broadcast from the White House. Department of State, *Press Releases,* October 29, 1938, p. 281

No one who lived through the grave hours of last month can doubt the longing of most of the peoples of the world for an enduring peace. Our business now is to utilize the desire for peace to build principles which are the only basis of permanent peace.

It is becoming increasingly clear that peace by fear has no higher or more enduring quality than peace by the sword.

There can be no peace if the reign of law is to be replaced by a recurrent sanctification of sheer force.

There can be no peace if national policy adopts as a deliberate instrument the threat of war.

There can be no peace if national policy adopts as a deliberate instrument the dispersion all over the world of millions of helpless and persecuted wanderers with no place to lay their heads.

There can be no peace if humble men and women are not free to think their own thoughts, to express their own feelings, to worship God.

There can be no peace if economic resources that ought to be devoted to social and economic reconstruction are to be diverted to an intensified competition in armaments which will merely heighten the suspicions and fears and threaten the economic prosperity of each and every nation.

At no time in modern history has the responsibility which rests upon governments been more obvious or more profound.

I speak for a United States which has no interest in war. We covet nothing save good relations with our neighbors; and we recognize that the world today has become our neighbor.

But in the principle of the good neighbor certain fundamental reciprocal obligations are involved. There must be a deliberate and conscious will that such political changes as changing needs require shall be made peacefully.

That means a due regard for the sanctity of treaties. It means deliberate avoidance of policies which arouse fear and distress. It means the self-restraint to refuse strident ambitions which are sure to breed insecurity and intolerance and thereby weaken the prospect of that economic and moral recovery the world so sadly needs.

You cannot organize civilization around the core of militarism and at the same time expect reason to control human destinies.

For more than 12 years, the United States has been steadily seeking disarmament.

Yet we have consistently pointed out that neither we, nor any nation, will accept disarmament while neighbor nations arm to the teeth. If there is not general disarmament, we ourselves must continue to arm. It is a step we do not like to take, and do not wish to take. But, until there is general abandonment of weapons capable of aggression, ordinary rules of national prudence and common sense require that we be prepared.

We still insist that an armament race among nations is absurd unless new territories or new controls are coveted. We are entitled, I think, to greater reassurance than can be given by words: The kind of proof which can be given, for example, by actual discussions, leading to actual disarmament. Not otherwise can we be relieved of the necessity of increasing our own military and naval establishments. For while we refuse to accept as a permanent necessity the idea of force, and reject it as an ideal of life, we must be prepared to meet with success any application of force against us.

We in the United States do not seek to impose on any other people either our way of life or our internal form of government. But we are determined to maintain and protect that way of life and that form of government for ourselves. And we are determined to use every endeavor in order that the Western Hemisphere may work out its own interrelated salvation in the light of its own interrelated experience.

And we affirm our faith that, whatever choice of way of life a people makes, that choice must not threaten the world with the disaster of war. The impact of such a disaster cannot be confined. It releases a floodtide of evil emotions fatal to civilized living. That statement applies not to the Western Hemisphere alone but to the whole of Europe and Asia and Africa and the islands of the seas.

In all that I have said to you I have reaffirmed the faith of the American people in democracy. The way of democracy is free discussion—as exemplified by the objectives of the Forum to which I am speaking. Free discussion is most greatly useful when it is restrained and relates to facts. It is not useful to suggest either to the American people or to the peoples of other nations that the American Government, its policies, its practices, and its servants are actuated by motives of dishonor or corruption. To do so is, of necessity, an attack on the American system of constitutional representative government itself.

Let us work with greater unity for peace among the nations of the world, for restraint, for negotiation, and for community of effort. Let us work for the same ideals within our own borders in our relations with each other, so that we may, if the test ever comes, have that unity of will with which alone a democracy can successfully meet its enemies.

ADDRESS by Cordell Hull, Secretary of State, "Our Foreign Policy," at Washington, D.C., October 26, 1940

Delivered at the National Press Club Dinner. Department of State, *Bulletin,* October 26, 1940, p. 331

IT IS WITH no light heart that I address you and any others who may be listening tonight on the subject of our international relations. I should be lacking in candor if I did not emphasize the gravity of the present situation.

Only once before in our national existence has as grave a danger from without threatened this Nation as the danger which looms today on the international horizon. That was in the stirring days when the founders of this Republic staked everything on their unshakable conviction that a nation of free men could be established and would endure on the soil of America. Theirs was a struggle and a victory the fruits of which have been the proud inheritance of succeeding generations of Americans for more than a century and a half. These generations, including our own, have enjoyed this inheritance in a world where human freedom, national independence, and order under law were steadily becoming more and more firmly established as a system of civilized relations among nations and among individuals.

Today that system and all peaceful nations, including our own, are gravely menaced. The danger arises out of the plans and acts of a small group of national rulers who have succeeded in transforming their peoples into forceful instruments for widespread domination by conquest.

To understand the significance of this danger and to prepare to meet it successfully we must see clearly the tragic lessons taught by what has occurred since the protagonists of conquest began their march across the earth. I ask you to review with me the whirlwind

GENERAL STATEMENTS OF POLICY

developments of one of the saddest and most crucial decades in the history of mankind—that of the nineteen-thirties.

I

The opening years of the decade were filled with ominous rumblings of impending disaster. Profound economic dislocation had spread rapidly to every part of the world. It had disrupted international economic relations and was causing untold distress everywhere. The structure of international peace was still intact, but a dangerous breach was opened in it by the Japanese occupation of Manchuria in 1931. That act, universally condemned at the time, proved to be only the beginning of an epidemic of callous disregard of international commitments—probably unparalleled in the annals of history. International discussions for the reduction and limitation of armaments, begun much earlier, were dragging along. Their failure to result in effective agreements was adding to the general feeling of apprehension and insecurity.

These developments were bound to create grave difficulties and grave dangers for our country, as well as for the rest of the world. The problems which they presented imperatively demanded on our part vigorous initiative and leadership in the promotion and defense of the national interest.

Accordingly, in the conduct of foreign policy, this Government directed its efforts to the following objectives: (1) Peace and security for the United States with advocacy of peace and limitation of armament as universal international objectives; (2) support for law, order, justice, and morality and the principle of nonintervention; (3) restoration and cultivation of sound economic methods and relations; (4) development of the maximum measure of international cooperation; (5) promotion of the security, solidarity, and general welfare of the Western Hemisphere. These basic objectives of a good-neighbor policy represented a sound and practical middle course between the extremes of internationalism and isolation. They have been consistently pursued throughout. The sweep of events has, of course, required the focusing of our attention at different periods upon different problems and different geographic areas.

II

In the early thirties, the relations among the American republics left much to be desired. Elements of mistrust, apprehension, and disunion had to be eliminated if a good-neighbor policy was really to prevail on the American Continent and provide a foundation upon which 21 free and independent American republics could establish peaceful and mutually beneficial relations among themselves and with the rest of the world.

The Seventh International Conference of American States, meeting at Montevideo in December 1933, offered an opportunity for a far-reaching move in this direction. There, a solid foundation was laid for a new structure of inter-American relations built on lines so broad that the entire program of principles was of universal application. At that meeting, the American republics took effective action for the maintenance of inter-American peace, ageed upon nonintervention, and adopted an economic program of common benefit based on the rule of equal treatment. During the years which immediately followed, the United States gave tangible proofs of its determination to act in accordance with the newly created system of inter-American relations.

At the same time we inaugurated a new policy in the sphere of economic relations. In the summer of 1934, this country adopted the reciprocal-trade-agreements program, designed to restore and expand international commerce through the reduction of unreasonable trade barriers and the general reestablishment of the rule of equality of commercial treatment. This program proved to be the greatest constructive effort in a world racing toward economic destruction.

In the meantime, other phases of international relations were undergoing further and rapid deterioration. Efforts to achieve international security through the reduction and limitation of armaments were unsuccessful. The long and weary conferences at Geneva during which plan after plan failed of adoption showed that the world was not ready to grasp an opportunity for action which, had it been taken, might have prevented subsequent disasters. This and the notice given by Japan in December 1934 of her intention to terminate the Washington Treaty for the Limitation of Naval Armaments opened the way for a new armament race.

At this juncture, Italy announced her intention to secure control over Ethiopia—by force of arms, if necessary. While there was still a possibility for an amicable settlement of the difficulties between Italy and Ethiopia, the attitude of the Government of the United States was made clear on September 13, 1935, in a statement which read in part as follows:

"Under the conditions which prevail in the world today, a threat of hostilities anywhere cannot but be a threat to the interests—political, economic, legal and social—of all nations. Armed conflict in any part of the world cannot but have undesirable and adverse effects in every part of the world. All nations have the right to ask that any and all issues between whatsoever nations be resolved by pacific means. Every nation has the right to ask that no nations subject it and other nations to the hazards and uncertainties that must inevitably accrue to all from resort to arms by any two."

During the summer of 1935 under the influence of these rapidly unfolding developments threatening the peace of the world the Congress enacted a statute known as the Neutrality Act of 1935. The purpose of this act was to reduce the risks of our becoming involved in war. Unfortunately, it contained as its principal feature the provision for a rigid embargo on export of arms to belligerents. This provision was adopted under the influence of a fallacious concept temporarily accepted by a large number of our people that this country's entrance into the World War had been brought about by the sale of arms to belligerents and the machinations of so-called "international bankers."

It was clear then, and has become even clearer since, that a rigid embargo on export of arms might have an effect the opposite of that which was intended. On the occasion of the signing of the act, the President pointed out that "history is filled with unforeseeable situations" and that conditions might arise in which the wholly inflexible provision for an arms embargo "might drag us into war instead of keeping us out." I myself repeatedly pointed out that in addition to the unforeseeable consequences of the provision itself reliance upon that concept might mean the closing of our eyes to manifold dangers in other directions and from other sources.

By 1938, there was no longer any doubt that the existence of the arms embargo provision was definitely having the effect of making widespread war more likely. Accordingly, early in 1939, the executive branch of the Government urgently recommended to Congress the repeal of that provision. That was finally accomplished, after the outbreak of war in Europe, at a special session of Congress called by the President for that specific purpose.

III

The Italo-Ethiopian war and its attendant circumstances left, in an already shaken Europe, a new condition of intense bitterness and unsettlement. Into that situation, Germany, after three years of intensive military preparation, flung, early in 1936, her first serious challenge to world order under law. The German Government tore up the Treaty of Locarno, into which Germany had freely and voluntarily entered, and proceeded to fortify the Rhineland in violation of the express provisions of that treaty. In the summer of that year, a violent civil conflict flared up in Spain, and that unfortunate country became a battleground of newly emerging power politics.

During this period, the President and I on numerous occasions emphasized the gathering dangers in the world situation. In June 1935, I made the following statement:

"We witness all about us a reckless, competitive building up of armaments, a recurrence of the mad race which prior to 1914 led the nations of the world headlong to destruction. If persisted in, this course will again plunge the world into disaster."

Tragic indeed is the fact that, from the end of 1935, the voice of reason became increasingly drowned by the rising clangor of the furious rearmament by nations preparing for conquest.

We continued our efforts for peace. We continued to carry forward our program of economic restoration through the trade-agreements policy. We intensified the process of strengthening our naval armaments and of improving in other ways our means of defense. Speaking for the Government, I pointed out that we would not serve the cause of peace by not having adequate powers of self-defense; that we must be sure that in our desire for peace we would not appear to any other country unable to protect our just rights.

In view of the imminence of an impending world crisis, we proposed to our sister republics of the Americas, in January, 1936, an extraordinary conference to consider the best means of safeguarding the peace of this hemisphere. At this Inter-American Conference for the Maintenance of Peace, convoked at Buenos Aires, the 21 American republics, building on the foundations laid down at Montevideo, adopted for the first time the great principle that a threat from without the continent to the peace of any of them should be regarded by the American republics as a threat to each and every one of them. They established in contractual form the obligation to consult together whenever the peace of the Americas is menaced, either from within or from without.

During the year 1937, while the cauldron of European politics seethed dangerously, the focus of world events again shifted to the Far East. In the summer of that year, Japan struck a further and more extensive blow at China. This new threat to the peace of the world rendered appropriate a restatement of the fundamental aims and principles of the foreign policy of the United States. In a statement issued on July 16, 1937, I set forth those principles. We urged upon all nations the acceptance and observance of those principles. We repeatedly offered to be of assistance toward composing the Chinese-Japanese conflict in accordance with those principles. We participated —and Japan refused to participate—in the Brussels conference of the signatories to the Nine Power Pact, convoked for the purpose of bringing about a peaceful solution of that conflict.

IV

During the year 1938, the focus of events returned to Europe. In March of that year, the armed forces of Germany passed beyond that country's borders, and the annexation of Austria marked the first forcible alteration of the frontiers established in Europe by the treaties of peace. This was followed, within a few months, by an intense crisis, culminating in the Munich conference and the first dismemberment of Czechoslovakia. The darkening shadows of an approaching war deepened over the fields and homes of the European Continent.

It is not necessary for me to dwell in detail on the kaleidoscopic events of the anguished year that preceded the outbreak of the European war, nor of the 14 months we have since lived through. All of us recall the feverish activity in Europe which became a prelude to war and our repeated attempts to influence the contending nations to adjust their differences by pacific means on the basis of justice, equality, and fair-dealing, without recourse to force or threat of force. The tragic and the heroic developments of the war months and the brutal invasion and ruthless extinguishment of the independence and freedom of many countries are too vivid in the minds of all of us to need recapitulation.

The appalling tragedy of the present world situation lies in the fact that peacefully disposed nations failed to recognize in time the true nature of the aims and ambitions which have actuated the rulers of the heavily arming nations. Recoiling from the mere contemplation of the possibility of another widespread war, the peoples of the peaceful nations permitted themselves to be lulled into a false sense of security by the assurances made by these rulers that their aims were limited. This continued even as succeeding events left less and less room for doubt that, behind the screen of these assurances, preparations were being made for new attempts at widespread conquest. To mask still further this monstrous deception, these rulers and their satellites attempted to brand as "war mongers" and "imperialists" all who warned against the clearly emerging dangers, and poured upon them vituperation and abuse.

The United States, together with most other nations, has stood firmly for the basic principles underlying civilized international relations—peace, law, justice, treaty observance, non-intervention, peaceful settlement of differences, and fair-dealing, supported by the fullest practicable measure of international cooperation. The advocacy of these principles has won for us the friendship of all nations, except those which, vaguely describing themselves as the "have-nots" and claiming a superior right to rule over other peoples, are today on the march with great armies, air fleets, and navies to take by force what they say they need or want.

The rulers of these nations have repudiated and violated in every essential respect the long-accepted principles of peaceful and orderly international relations. Merciless armed attack; unrestrained terrorization through slaughter of non-combatant men, women, and children; deceit, fraud, and guile; forced labor; confiscation of property; imposed starvation and deprivations of every sort—all these are weapons constantly used by the conquerors for the invasion and subjugation of other nations.

They adhere to no geographic lines and they fix no time limit on their programs of invasion and destruction. They cynically disregard every right of neutral nations, and, having occupied several such countries, they then proceed to warn all peaceful nations that they must remain strictly neutral until an invading force is actually crossing their borders. They have as a fixed objective the securing of control of the high seas. They threaten peaceful nations with the direst consequences if those nations do not remain acquiescent, while the conquerors are seizing the other continents and most of the seven seas of the earth.

Let no one comfort himself with the delusion that these are mere excesses or exigencies of war, to be voluntarily abandoned when fighting ceases. By deed and by utterance, the would-be conquerors have made it abundantly clear that they are engaged upon a relentless attempt to transform the civilized world as we have known it into a world in which mankind will be reduced again to the degradation of a master-and-slave relationship among nations and among individuals, maintained by brute force.

The hand of crushing assault has struck again and again at peaceful nations, complacent and unprepared in their belief that mere intention on their part to keep peace was an ample shield of security.

There can be nothing more dangerous for our Nation than for us to assume that the avalanche of conquest could under no circumstances reach any vital portion of this hemisphere. Oceans give the nations of this hemisphere no guaranty against the possibility of economic, political, or military attack from abroad. Oceans are barriers but they are also highways. Barriers of distance are merely barriers of time. Should the would-be conquerors gain control of other continents, they would next concentrate on perfecting their control of the seas, of the air over the seas, and of the world's economy; they might then be able with ships and with planes to strike at the communication lines, the commerce, and the life of this hemisphere; and ultimately we might find ourselves compelled to fight on our own soil, under our own skies, in defense of our independence and our very lives.

These are some of the governing facts and conditions of the present-day international situation. These are the dangers which must be recognized. Against these dangers, our policies and measures must provide defense.

V

We are in the presence not of local or regional wars, but of an organized and determined movement for steadily expanding conquest. Against this drive for power no nation and no region is secure save as its inhabitants create for themselves means of defense so formidable that even the would-be conquerors will not dare to raise against them the hand of attack.

The first need for all nations still masters of their own destiny is to create for themselves, as speedily and as completely as possible, impregnable means of defense. This is the staggering lesson of mankind's recent experience.

To meet that need, we are bringing our military, naval, and air establishments to maximum practicable strength. Production of military supplies is being brought to a greater and greater pitch of speed and effectiveness. Wherever necessary for the carrying out of the defense program, export of essential materials is being stringently regulated. Arrangements are being carried forward to provide military and technical training for the youth of this country. We intend to continue and intensify our effort in all these directions.

We are taking measures toward dealing with subversive activities in this country directed from abroad. The experience of many other countries has brought us the shocking realization of the manner in which, and the extent to which, such activities are employed to undermine social and political institutions and to bring about internal disintegration and decay in the countries which they plan to make their victims. We intend to act in this field with unremitting vigor.

We are seeking to advance by every appropriate means the spirit of inter-American solidarity and the system of continental defense. In conformity with the procedure set up at Buenos Aires and Lima, the Panama Consultative Meeting of the Ministers of Foreign Affairs of the American Republics adopted important measures to safeguard the national and collective interests of the American nations, their peace, and their economic security. Last summer they met again, at Habana, to consult with regard to several threats to the peace and security of the Americas, the danger of which, they unanimously agreed, existed. To ward off these threats, they took positive steps to prevent any transfer of sovereignty in the Western Hemisphere from one non-American nation to another, embodied in an international convention and in the Act of Habana. They also agreed upon procedures for combating subversive activities in the American nations and they adopted measures of economic defense and collaboration.

We have concluded an arrangement with Great Britain under which we have acquired long-time leases of eight strategically located naval and air bases which will enable us to create a protective girdle of steel along the Atlantic seaboard of the American Continent—bases which will be available for use by all of the American republics. We are engaged in defense consultations with our neighbors to the south, and we have created facilities for such consultations with Canada. In all these fields, we intend to continue vigorous effort.

We have sought in every appropriate way to discourage conquest and to limit the area of war. We have followed consistently the policy of refusing recognition of territorial changes effected by force or threat of force. We have taken every opportunity to express our concern over threatened changes by force in the existing political status of colonial possessions, disturbance of which would extend the area of hostilities. We have placed under license the funds of invaded countries. In these respects, too, we intend to continue our activities.

We believe that the safety and the primary interests of the United States must be upheld with firmness and resolution—supported by the speediest and fullest possible armament for all defensive purposes. In view of the unprecedented character of menacing developments abroad, we have frankly recognized the danger involved and the increasing need for defense against it. As an important means of strengthening our own defense and of preventing attack on any part of the Western Hemisphere, this country is affording all feasible facilities for the obtaining of supplies by nations which, while defending themselves against barbaric attack, are checking the spread of violence and are thus reducing the danger to us. We intend to continue doing this to the greatest practicable extent. Any contention, no matter from what source, that this country should not take such action is equivalent, in the present circumstances, to a denying of the inalienable right of self-defense.

VI

In our democracy the basic determination of foreign policy rests with the people. As I sense the will of our people today, this Nation is determined that its security and rightful interests shall be safeguarded.

GENERAL STATEMENTS OF POLICY

The dangers with which we are confronted are not of our making. We cannot know at what point, or when, we may possibly be attacked. We can, however, be prepared, first, to discourage any thought of assault upon our security and, if any such assault should be attempted, to repel it.

The people of this country want peace. To have peace, we must have security. To have security, we must be strong. These are times that test the fiber of men and of nations.

Our system of defense must, of necessity, be many-sided, because the dangers against which safeguards are imperatively required are manifold. Essential to effective national defense are constant and skilful use of political and economic measures, possession of military weapons, and continuous exercise of wisdom and of high moral qualities. We must have planes and tanks and ships and guns. We must have trained men. We must hold to the ideal of a world in which the rights of all nations are respected and each respects the rights of all; in which principles of law and order and justice and fair-dealing prevail. Above all, we must be a united people—united in purpose and in effort to create impregnable defense.

Thus can we maintain our inheritance. Thus will we continue to make this country's high contribution toward the progress of mankind on the roadway of civilized effort.

DISARMAMENT

ADDRESS by Hugh S. Gibson, Acting Chairman of the American Delegation at the First General Disarmament Conference, Geneva, February 9, 1932

Department of State, *Press Releases*, February 13, 1932, p. 147

The United States enters the first world conference on the limitation and reduction of armaments with the determination to leave nothing undone to achieve substantial progress. It assumes that the same will predominates among all the nations represented in this conference. Nothing is contributed to our deliberations, indeed our efforts are only clouded with insincerity and pretense, if we fail to acknowledge the difficulties which just now surround the project before us. The part of statecraft is, however, neither to gloss over difficulties and thereby contribute to defeat, nor to invite despair by overemphasis on the difficulties in the foreground. The situation demands calm consideration of the facts as they exist and courageous efforts to obtain a substantial solution. The impediments are familiar to the most elementary observer of international affairs of this kind. We meet with the necessity of coordinating motives and maturing agreement in a congress of nations larger than has ever before been assembled. We meet under the strain of economic distresses, international uncertainties, and popular emotions which might easily engulf anything smaller in stature than the cause presented here. Our conference must not be diverted from achieving success on the vital questions by minor differences of a technical nature. The task before the nations of the world is not to minimize these problems but, fully mindful of them, to gather strength and determination from the conviction that the demand for a régime of international confidence, cooperation, and peace will in the end have its way; that the men and nations of our own day who contribute to it will be counted in the end as enrolled in a victorious cause, and that in the long perspective of history those who are to-day reluctant and preoccupied with smaller interests will stand only as temporary impediments to a world-wide and inevitable movement.

The people of the United States have during the past generation played a useful and leading part in the movement for the limitation and reduction of arms. The Washington Conference of 1922 made the first concrete contribution in voluntary limitation. It met the then existing problem of armament at its most acute, its most threatening, and its most conspicuous point, and by a restriction of naval armament among the powers who found themselves setting an unhappy example, made a long and decisive stride in the direction demanded by world opinion. Our people at that conference sacrificed, if not a real predominance, at least a potential predominance in weight and strength for warfare. The American people have been proud of the contribution which they made to that pact of temperate conduct and common sense. In the London Naval Conference of 1930 the principle of limitation established for capital ships at the Washington meeting was enlarged to cover the whole field of equipment for warfare at sea by the three most heavily armed of the nations, and some progress was made toward including the two other powers most concerned. We enter the Conference to-day with the practicability of the limitation upon arms established, with the demand for it augmented by general pride and satisfaction in the achievement already made, and with the United States again willing to play its appropriate part in further progress. The American Delegation is prepared to consider any form of military limitation and reduction which promises real progress toward the feeling of international security, protection against surprise, and restraint on the use of arms for purposes of aggression.

The burden and dangers of the gigantic machinery of warfare which are now being maintained in times of peace have reached a point where they threaten civilization itself. For two years past the people of every race have been confronted with an economic crisis from which no nation has been free. All the governments of the world have faced reduction of income, unsettled budgets, and dangers to the very stability of government itself. The United States, while seriously affected by these difficulties, has suffered somewhat less severely than many of the other nations. It is to-day able to maintain the burden of armaments as readily as any of the nations, but it views that burden as unnecessary and inexcusable. No one will doubt the political instability of the world, of which these arms are not alone the effect but also the cause. No one will doubt that they not only contribute to the economic debacle but that they threaten the peace of the world. Our American people look upon the statesmanship which permits the continuance of existing conditions as nothing less than failure. The time has gone by when the peoples of the world will long permit the continuance of this failure.

There is a feeling sometimes expressed that the convictions of the United States in this field, the faith of our people in an orderly and stable régime among the nations, and our conviction that the very existence of armaments unbalances the equilibrium, are a product of our geographical isolation and of our lack of experience of and exposure to the rivalries and strains of the European Continent. In answer, the American people point to the fact that the system of competitive armament, of alliances and cross alliances which has existed for centuries in Europe has failed to maintain peace and seems indeed to have been provocative of war, the results of which are such that victors and vanquished are victims alike. Furthermore, the altered conditions of international relationships, the development of communication and transport within the last generation to a point where the whole world is knit together by strands of commerce, finance, and intimate contact, have to-day produced new international relationships which are utterly inconsistent with the older methods and formulas. America is convinced that the world should not go on to new movements and new tasks hampered by the garments of an older régime, and that the problem is only how promptly and smoothly mankind will cast aside the weapons and traditions of the old.

In the past every nation has justified its level of armament, however high, by the claim such levels were necessary for its national defense. Let us not forget, however, that new international commitments of binding force have introduced a new conception of what is needed by a nation for the purpose of defense. Such treaties and commitments bear upon practically all the nations here represented. In view of this new situation calling for new methods and new formulas, the lessons of the old strategy must be unlearned in order that we may advance. The new conception of national armaments has never been put into words in any of our commitments, but it is so implicit in their terms that it can be reduced almost to a formula. Every nation has not only the right but the obligation to its own people to maintain internal order. This obviously calls for an adequate military force for internal police work. Beyond and above this there is the obligation of each government to its people to maintain a sufficient increment of military strength to defend the national territory against aggression and invasion. We therefore have this formula dividing our military forces into two parts. Beyond this reasonable supplement to the police force we have taken an implicit obligation to restrict ourselves. Our problem is therefore to establish by honest scrutiny and agreement the margin that now exists beyond what is essential for the maintenance of internal order and defense of our territories. Controlled by prudence but not by fear, let us then proceed in a practical way to reduce armaments to the level to which we are all committed.

DISARMAMENT

The American Delegation has listened with interest to the speeches of Sir John Simon and M. Tardieu and has been interested to note that each of them has begun this general discussion by concrete proposals, setting forth at the very beginning of the Conference the contributions which their Governments can make to the cause for which we are assembled. These proposals and any others which may be put before the Conference will be examined with an open mind by my Government; and we feel that the best road to success lies in a similar statement from every delegation that has something positive to lay before us, so that we may set out upon our labors with the benefit of all the practical proposals which it is possible to bring forward at the outset.

The American Delegation has not attempted to formulate and submit any comprehensive plan for overcoming all of the obstacles that exist in the way of achieving a general limitation and reduction in armaments. In the first place, we do not desire to raise new questions which increase the points of difference and thus delay taking the forward steps which could otherwise be taken. In the second place, we do not believe the human mind is capable of so projecting itself into the future as to devise a plan which will adequately provide for all future developments and contingencies.

Since practically all the nations of the world have now pledged themselves not to wage aggressive war, we believe this Conference should and can successfully devote itself to the abolition of weapons which are devoted primarily to aggressive war, and we are prepared to give earnest and sympathetic consideration to any plans or proposals which seem to furnish a practicable and sound basis upon which we may effect a general limitation and reduction of armaments and establish a more healthy and peaceful state of affairs. It is my purpose to-day to lay before you certain points which the American Delegation advocates. Let me say that this list is not exclusive and contains merely some of the thoughts which we feel will carry on some of the purposes of the Conference.

1. The American Government advocates consideration of the draft convention as containing the outlines for a convenient basis for discussion, while expressing its entire willingness to give full consideration to any supplementary proposals calculated to advance the end we all seek.

2. We suggest the possibility of prolonging the existing naval agreements concluded at Washington and London, and we advocate completing the latter as soon as possible by the adherence of France and Italy.

3. We advocate proportional reduction from the figures laid down in the Washington and London agreements on naval tonnage as soon as all parties to the Washington agreement have entered this framework.

4. We advocate, as we long have done, the total abolition of submarines.

5. We will join in formulating the most effective measures to protect civilian population against aerial bombing.

6. We advocate the total abolition of lethal gases and bacteriological warfare.

7. We advocate, as I have already stated, the computation of the number of armed forces on the basis of the effectives necessary for the maintenance of internal order plus some suitable contingent for defense. The former are obviously impossible of reduction; the latter is a question of relativity.

8. We agree in advocating special restrictions for tanks and heavy mobile guns; in other words, for those arms of a peculiarly offensive character.

9. We are prepared to consider a limitation of expenditure on material as a complementary method to direct limitation, feeling that it may prove useful to prevent a qualitative race, if and when quantitative limitation has been effected.

I have already said these nine points are in no sense exclusive, but I mention them merely in order to focus attention upon the methods in which we have the greatest hope of early practical realization.

The nations of the Western Hemisphere have long since prepared themselves for an international life in which the solution of difficulties will be sought by pacific means only. The problem of armaments is not of the Western Hemisphere. Of the five principal navies of the world only one belongs to an American nation, and to this navy the principle of proportionate limitation and reduction has been comprehensively applied. Not a single American nation possesses an army which brings fear to its neighbors. For half a century no international war has occurred between the nations of our hemisphere. There is no surer evidence that self-restraint from over-armament safeguards peace. There is more security to be had in friendly cooperation between nations than in reliance on force. The best defense a nation can have is the good will of its neighbors. Nevertheless, and in spite of the fact that we ourselves have reduced the personnel of our land forces to a figure below the proportion reached by any great European power, we are here to cooperate to the utmost of our ability. We are prepared to discuss and to extend to other fields the principles of limitation and reduction of armaments already established and to examine and accept new principles if they contribute genuinely to the end defined. We join our sister nations with the deep conviction that the cause at issue must not be diverted by lack of frank discussion, by preoccupation with the difficulties in the foreground, or by a weak surrender to the obvious impediments to progress. The Delegation of the United States is representing not only a government but a people; and the mandate from both is in the same

DISARMAMENT 47

unmistakable terms, that decrease in arms is an essential not alone to economic recovery of the world but also to the preservation of the whole fabric of peace.

STATEMENT Issued by the White House, June 22, 1932

Department of State, *Press Releases,* June 25, 1932, p. 593

THE DELEGATIONS at the World Conference on Disarmament at Geneva are engaged in discussions as to methods by which a more comprehensive effort can be made toward disarmament.

The following is the substance of instructions which have been given by the President to the American Delegation for guidance in the discussions which are now occupying them.

The time has come when we should cut through the brush and adopt some broad and definite method of reducing the overwhelming burden of armament which now lies upon the toilers of the world. This would be the most important world step that could be taken to expedite economic recovery. We must make headway against the mutual fear and friction arising out of war armament which kill human confidence throughout the world. We can still remain practical in maintaining an adequate self-defense among all nations; we can add to the assurances of peace and yet save the people of the world from 10 to 15 billions of wasted dollars during the next 10 years.

I propose that the following principles should be our guide:

First: The Kellogg-Briand Pact, to which we are all signatories, can only mean that the nations of the world have agreed that they will use their arms solely for defense.

Second: This reduction should be carried out not only by broad general cuts in armaments but by increasing the comparative power of defense through decreases in the power of the attack.

Third: The armaments of the world have grown up in general mutual relation to each other. And, speaking generally, such relativity should be preserved in making reductions.

Fourth: The reductions must be real and positive. They must effect economic relief.

Fifth: There are three problems to deal with—land forces, air forces and naval forces. They are all interconnected. No part of the proposals which I make can be disassociated one from the other.

Based on these principles, I propose that the arms of the world should be reduced by nearly one-third.

Land forces. In order to reduce the offensive character of all land forces as distinguished from their defensive character, I propose the adoption of the presentation already made at the Geneva conference for the abolition of all tanks, all chemical warfare and all large mobile guns. This would not prevent the establishment or increase of fixed fortifications of any character for the defense of frontiers and seacoasts. It would give an increased relative strength to such defenses as compared with the attack.

I propose furthermore that there should be a reduction of one-third in strength of all land armies over and above the so-called police component.

The land armaments of many nations are considered to have two functions. One is the maintenance of internal order in connection with the regular peace forces of the country. The strength required for this purpose has been called the "police component." The other function is defense against foreign attack. The additional strength required for this purpose has been called the "defense component." While it is not suggested that these different components should be separated, it is necessary to consider this contention as to functions in proposing a practical plan of reduction in land forces. Under the Treaty of Versailles and the other peace treaties, the Armies of Germany, Austria, Hungary and Bulgaria were reduced to a size deemed appropriate for the maintenance of internal order, Germany being assigned 100,000 troops for a population of approximately 65,000,000 people. I propose that we should accept for all nations a basis police component of soldiers proportionate to the average which was thus allowed Germany and these other states. This formula, with necessary corrections for powers having colonial possessions, should be sufficient to provide for the maintenance of internal order by the nations of the world. Having analyzed these two components in this fashion, I propose as stated above that there should be a reduction of one-third in the strength of all land armies over and above the police component.

Air forces. All bombing planes to be abolished. This will do away with the military possessions of types of planes capable of attacks upon civil populations and should be coupled with the total prohibition of all bombardment from the air.

Naval forces. I propose that the treaty number and tonnage of battleships shall be reduced by one-third; that the treaty tonnage of aircraft carriers, cruisers and destroyers shall be reduced by one-fourth; that the treaty tonnage of submarines shall be reduced by one-third, and that no nation shall retain a submarine tonnage greater than 35,000.

The relative strength of naval arms in battleships and aircraft carriers, as between the five leading naval powers, was fixed by the Treaty of Washington. The relative strength in cruisers, destroyers and submarines was fixed, as between the United States, Great Britain and Japan, by the Treaty of London. For the purposes of this proposal, it is suggested that the French and Italian strength in cruisers and destroyers be calculated as though they had joined in the Treaty of London on a basis approximating the so-called accord of March 1, 1931. There are various technical considerations connected with these naval discussions which will be presented by the Delegation.

DISARMAMENT

General. The effect of this plan would be to effect an enormous saving in cost of new construction and replacements of naval vessels. It would also save large amounts in the operating expense in all nations of land, sea and air forces. It would greatly reduce offensive strength compared to defensive strength in all nations.

These proposals are simple and direct. They call upon all nations to contribute something. The contribution here proposed will be relative and mutual. I know of nothing that would give more hope for humanity to-day than the acceptance of such a program with such minor changes as might be necessary. It is folly for the world to go on breaking its back over military expenditure and the United States is willing to take its share of responsibility by making definite proposals that will relieve the world.

MESSAGE of President Franklin D. Roosevelt Telegraphed to the Heads of the Other Nations Participating in the Disarmament Conference and the World Monetary and Economic Conference, May 16, 1933

Department of State, *Press Releases,* May 20, 1933, p. 349

A PROFOUND HOPE of the people of my country impels me, as the head of their government, to address you and, through you, the people of your nation. This hope is that peace may be assured through practical measures of disarmament and that all of us may carry to victory our common struggle against economic chaos.

To these ends the nations have called two great world conferences. The happiness, the prosperity, and the very lives of the men, women and children who inhabit the world are bound up in the decisions which their governments will make in the near future. The improvement of social conditions, the preservation of individual human rights, and the furtherance of social justice are dependent upon these decisions.

The World Economic Conference will meet soon and must come to its conclusions quickly. The world can not await deliberations long drawn out. The Conference must establish order in place of the present chaos by a stabilization of currencies, by freeing the flow of world trade, and by international action to raise price levels. It must, in short, supplement individual domestic programs for economic recovery, by wise and considered international action.

The Disarmament Conference has labored for more than a year and, as yet, has been unable to reach satisfactory conclusions. Confused purposes still clash dangerously. Our duty lies in the direction of bringing practical results through concerted action based upon the greatest good to the greatest number. Before the imperative call of this great duty, petty obstacles must be swept away and petty aims forgotten. A selfish victory is always destined to be an ultimate defeat. The furtherance of durable peace for our generation in every part of the world is the only goal worthy of our best efforts.

If we ask what are the reasons for armaments, which, in spite of the lessons and tragedies of the World War, are today a greater burden on the peoples of the earth than ever before, it becomes clear that they are two-fold: First, the desire, disclosed or hidden, on the part of Governments to enlarge their territories at the expense of a sister nation. I believe that only a small minority of Governments or of peoples harbor such a purpose. Second, the fear of nations that they will be invaded. I believe that the overwhelming majority of peoples feel obliged to retain excessive armaments because they fear some act of aggression against them and not because they themselves seek to be aggressors.

There is justification for this fear. Modern weapons of offense are vastly stronger than modern weapons of defense. Frontier forts, trenches, wire entanglements, coast defense—in a word, fixed fortifications—are no longer impregnable to the attack of war planes, heavy mobile artillery, land battleships called tanks, and poison gas.

If all nations will agree wholly to eliminate from possession and use the weapons which make possible a successful attack, defenses automatically will become impregnable, and the frontiers and independence of every nation will become secure.

The ultimate objective of the Disarmament Conference must be the complete elimination of all offensive weapons. The immediate objective is a substantial reduction of some of these weapons and the elimination of many others.

This Government believes that the program for immediate reduction of aggressive weapons, now under discussion at Geneva, is but a first step toward our ultimate goal. We do not believe that the proposed immediate steps go far enough. Nevertheless, this Government welcomes the measures now proposed and will exert its influence toward the attainment of further successive steps of disarmament.

Stated in the clearest way, there are three steps to be agreed upon in the present discussions:

First, to take, at once, the first definite step toward this objective, as broadly outlined in the MacDonald Plan.

Second, to agree upon time and procedure for taking the following steps.

Third, to agree that while the first and the following steps are being taken, no nation shall increase its existing armaments over and above the limitations of treaty obligations.

But the peace of the world must be assured during the whole period of disarmament and I, therefore, propose a fourth step concurrent with and wholly dependent on the faithful fulfillment of these three proposals and subject to existing treaty rights:

That all the nations of the world should enter into a solemn and definite pact of non-aggression: That they should solemnly reaffirm the obligations they have assumed to limit and reduce their armaments, and, provided these obligations are faithfully executed by all signatory powers, individually agree that they will send no armed force of whatsoever nature across their frontiers.

Common sense points out that if any strong nation refuses to join with genuine sincerity in these concerted efforts for political and economic peace, the one at Geneva and the other at London, progress can be obstructed and ultimately blocked. In such event the civilized world, seeking both forms of peace, will know where the responsibility for failure lies. I urge that no nation assume the responsibility, and that all the nations joined in these great conferences translate their professed policies into action. This is the way to political and economic peace.

I trust that your government will join in the fulfillment of these hopes.

STATEMENT by Norman H. Davis, Chairman of the United States Delegation to the General Disarmament Conference, at Geneva, May 29, 1934

Department of State, *Press Releases,* June 2, 1934, p. 330

(1) Twenty-seven months and more have passed since we met, in high hopes, to frame a general disarmament convention. No one foresaw a short or easy negotiation; the difficulties were more apparent than the solution; but the goal was so clear and the need for agreement so vital and so pressing that we confidently expected success. Now we meet once again but with hopes dimmed. One great power has chosen to withdraw from the Conference; parallel and private conversations have not smoothed out the principal difficulties nor given the results we hoped for; certain powers are talking not in terms

of reduction of armaments but in terms of mere limitation, and others of actual increase. In this confused situation, we can well ask ourselves: "Whither are we going?"

(2) Notwithstanding the inherent difficulties it is, I believe, the consensus of opinion of the delegates to this Conference that disarmament is a problem susceptible of a practical solution if the nations most vitally concerned will only cooperate in the proper spirit to that end.

(3) As a result of thorough studies and discussions here, a remarkable and considerable measure of accord has actually been reached with respect to the technical aspects of armaments and the kind of a disarmament convention that would be effective. Nevertheless, other questions and considerations have intervened which have not only prevented a general agreement but which now actually threaten the failure of the Conference.

(4) Every nation here has the same basic thought, how to remove the menace and lighten the burden of competitive armaments without reducing its security. It is somewhat difficult for anxious public opinions of countries which have armed primarily because of fear, to realize that the apparent sacrifice of national defense involved in reduction of armaments may be fully compensated for by an increase of security along other lines. It is nevertheless the view of the American Government that such a compensatory advantage would be in fact obtainable through a mutual reduction and limitation of armaments in accordance with the revised draft convention that was accepted a year ago as the basis of our negotiations.

(5) Reduced to its simplest terms, there are two ways and only two conceivable ways to achieve security. The first is by overwhelming superiority in armament, coupled perhaps with reinsurance in the form of alliances; but this system has led first to a race in armaments and then to a war, from which we have not yet recovered and from a repetition of which we might never recover. Arms certainly did not prevent the World War, nor did they save either victor or vanquished from the terrible consequences of that war. The other way is to increase the power of defense and decrease the power of attack—in other words, to reduce the chances of a successful campaign of aggression—by a progressive abolition of those types of weapons peculiarly suitable for invasion, namely, heavy mobile artillery, tanks, and bombing planes. This method of disarmament, besides avoiding the complexities incident to limitation and reduction, which is solely numerical, constitutes a realistic aid to peace not only through reducing the sum total of means of war but more particularly by doing away with the very instruments which are indispensable for

successful aggression and by giving supremacy to fortifications and other means of defense. In fact, this method was accepted by the Conference in the resolution of July 23, 1932.

(6) Such is the choice. For its part, the American Government earnestly and sincerely believes that only by following the second path—that of disarmament—can the peace and progress of the world and the national security of each country be truly promoted. Unfortunately there is at present a distinct tendency in Europe toward the old policy of political alignments accompanied by an uncontrolled race in armaments which, if persisted in, will recreate the conditions which preceded the World War. Those who are today pursuing that policy, rather than one which promotes good will and increases security through a reduction of armaments, are inviting a terrible risk for the future.

(7) The United States has repeatedly stated in unequivocal terms its belief in the value and efficacy of a drastic reduction of armaments and its willingness to join with other powers in bringing armaments down to a level to be determined by the needs of actual self-defense. On May 22, 1933, in support of the draft convention which had been submitted to the Conference by the British Delegation, I outlined, with the approval of the President, the views of the United States Government on disarmament, its willingness to join in a decisive and progressive reduction of armaments through international agreement, and the extent to which it was prepared to cooperate to that end. It was with a view of helping indirectly to meet a given situation (in the event that the European powers should find it necessary or desirable to supplement a general convention by special regional agreements applicable to Europe) that I made on behalf of the United States Government this very considered statement of what its policy in certain circumstances would be. At that time it was our understanding that if the United States would be willing to adopt, subject to the conditions indicated, a policy that would not hamper the possible organization of European peace, it would be possible to conclude an agreement for a reduction and limitation of armaments along the lines of the draft convention then under consideration.

(8) In fact, President Roosevelt has authorized me to summarize the attitude and policy of the United States as follows: We are prepared to cooperate in every practicable way in efforts to secure a general disarmament agreement and thus to help promote the general peace and progress of the world. We are furthermore willing in connection with a general disarmament convention, to negotiate a universal pact of nonaggression and to join with other nations in conferring on international problems growing out of any treaties to which

we are a party. The United States will not, however, participate in European political negotiations and settlements and will not make any commitment whatever to use its armed forces for the settlement of any dispute anywhere. In effect, the policy of the United States is to keep out of war, but to help in every possible way to discourage war.

(9) We have no new cures to offer. We suggested in the proposals of President Hoover in June 1932 a percentage cut covering all types of armaments. We suggested at that time a method of computing effectives to reach a basis of internal police requirements which was regarded by nearly all the powers as the only proposal which promised a fair and reasonable solution of this difficult question. A year later President Roosevelt, in his message to the chiefs of state, suggested the abolition of weapons of invasion and, to make this more effective, a pact of nonaggression, and then the establishment of an effective system of supervision and control. We are willing to go further and work out by international agreement an effective system for the regulation of the manufacture of and traffic in arms and munitions of war. Let me quote one paragraph from a recent message to Congress by President Roosevelt on this subject:

It is my earnest hope that the representatives of the nations who will reassemble at Geneva on May 29 will be able to agree upon a convention containing provisions for the supervision and control of the traffic in arms even more far-reaching than those which were embodied in the convention of 1925. Some suitable international organization must and will take such action. The peoples of many countries are being taxed to the point of poverty and starvation in order to enable governments to engage in a mad race in armament which, if permitted to continue, may well result in war. This grave menace to the peace of the world is due in no small measure to the uncontrolled activities of the manufacturers and merchants of engines of destruction, and it must be met by the concerted action of the peoples of all nations.

The people of the United States are aroused at the evils which are being revealed in the production and traffic of munitions of war. The American people and Government are convinced that by some means the production and traffic in engines of death, and the profits resulting therefrom, must be controlled or eliminated. Those who have a sordid financial interest in fomenting international suspicion and discord, which in turn increases the demand for what they have to sell, must be put in a position in which they do not have the power or the incentive to do so much evil. If we are to foment international good will and stability we must take effective steps to control or suppress the forces which have a material interest in fomenting mistrust and

DISARMAMENT

discord. My Government is ready to join in measures for suppressing this evil, and is prepared to negotiate in connection with disarmament a treaty that would deal drastically with this problem.

(10) We still stand ready to advance along any constructive lines. Even where our arms are already limited, we are prepared to agree upon further reductions. Thus, in the matter of naval armaments, although we have felt it necessary to build up approximately to the treaty limits, largely in replacement ships, we are none the less willing to join the other interested powers in a substantial proportionate reduction of naval tonnage. In fact, our efforts remain directed toward disarmament in all branches and not toward either truce or rearmament.

(11) The Disarmament Conference recessed on the 16th of October last in order that there might be given an opportunity to carry on diplomatic negotiations with the view of reconciling the divergent views which stood in the way of agreement. Unfortunately these negotiations did not result in agreement, and they have now been terminated. On the other hand, they have served a necessary and useful purpose in clarifying the fundamental differences and issues. I feel, therefore, that in taking the initiative in these negotiations the British Government has rendered a real service. Nevertheless the termination of these parallel efforts brings us face to face with an emergency situation demanding a grave decision. We must determine whether our efforts shall result in a controlled disarmament, or in a mere limitation of armaments at a level so high as to be of doubtful value and effect, or in an uncontrolled race in armaments which would be disastrous. Surely no nation represented here wishes to take the responsibility for a failure of the Conference or to face the consequences of a failure. Let us therefore go back to the last stage in our negotiations where a general agreement was in sight, namely, to June 8 last year, when the British draft convention was accepted by all nations, including Germany, as the basis of the future convention. In doing so we may of course have due regard for subsequent contributions that may have been made toward agreement. If Germany desires a disarmament convention, which surely must be the case, then I cannot easily believe that she would not be willing to resume negotiations on the basis to which she previously agreed.

The negotiations of the past 6 months were terminated by the demand that bilateral discussions be discontinued and that the work be brought back to Geneva. Very good. We are back in Geneva. I for one am glad to be here. I have stated the views of my Government, and I think every one here would consider it timely if all would explain their positions. The issue cannot be avoided. I am unshaken in my belief that with a real spirit of cooperation we can still achieve success.

STATEMENT by Norman H. Davis, Chairman of the United States Delegation to the Conference for the Limitation of Naval Armament at London, before the Senate Committee on Foreign Relations, May 13, 1936

Department of State, *Press Releases*, May 16, 1936, p. 486

A FULL REPORT of the recent Naval Conference in London and of the treaty which was signed on March 25 last has been made to the President, who in turn has transmitted this to the Senate. I should like, however, to make certain additional observations with regard to the treaty that is now before you for ratification.

At the outset, I must state that there are two regrettable but unavoidable omissions in this treaty. One is that two of the Washingon Treaty powers, Japan and Italy, have not yet signed it; the other is that this treaty does not provide for any reduction in total tonnage or for a continuance of the principle of quantitative limitation established by the two previous treaties. The facts are, however, that it was not possible to secure agreement to that effect because all of the naval powers represented at the Conference, with exception of Great Britain and the United States, refused to enter into a new treaty which continued the limitations and the ratios established by the present treaties. In fact, Japan left the Conference a few weeks after it began because the other powers were unable to accept as a basis for negotiation the Japanese proposal for a so-called common upper limit which, in effect, was to scrap the present system of naval limitation and, without regard to relative needs and security, to change the present ratio of 5–5–3 to 3–3–3 or 5–5–5. While recognizing Japan's right to equal security, which we believe was achieved under the Washington and London Treaties, it was obviously impossible to accept the Japanese proposal because, owing to the difference in relative needs and vulnerability, naval parity would give to Japan naval superiority.

As it was impossible to agree to continue existing treaties beyond the end of this year, it was necessary, after the Japanese withdrawal from the Conference, for the remaining powers to decide whether to throw up their hands and quit or whether to proceed to the negotiation of such a treaty as might be possible, in order to prevent if possible the chaotic situation that would develop upon the termination of the existing treaties in case there should be nothing to take their place.

Notwithstanding the difficulties that were inherent in this situation, it was decided to continue in conference, with the result that after considerable time and patient effort we succeeded in negotiating a treaty which, while preserving in a modified but practical way the principle of naval limitation, contains new and important provisions which largely offset the omissions.

Although some things which we wanted are not in this treaty, there is nothing in it to which we object. There is, in fact, no single provision of the treaty which is objectionable or unfair to any participating state or to any of the other naval powers, but there is much that should prove to be mutually beneficial. It can thus be hoped that those states who have not yet signed the treaty will readily adhere to its provisions.

The main objectives of this treaty are twofold: First, to preserve the foundation of general naval limitation; and, second, to prevent a naval race. To accomplish this it standardizes and limits the size of ships and the caliber of their guns, and provides for a full exchange of information between the contracting powers as to all projected and actual construction.

In substance, this treaty differs from its predecessors in that there are no provisions for the direct quantitative limitation of naval armaments. As a result of the elimination of this principle, more prominence is given to restrictions upon the size and gun caliber of the different classes of naval vessels. Although the absence of quantitative limits is a matter of regret, it is believed that qualitative limitation will serve effectively to eliminate competitive construction in naval armaments and thus to avoid dangerous rivalry in the construction of new types. Governments know today what the existing sizes are both as to type and number, and their respective naval strength is accordingly adjusted to this. If, however, countries are permitted to build new types of ships, such building might overnight render obsolete existing classes of ships and necessitate replacement of one or more categories, thereby creating heavy additional costs. Such competition may easily become even more expensive than competition in numbers.

The maximum size of battleships is left at 35,000 tons, but the treaty provides for a reduction in the caliber of guns on future battleships from 16 to 14 inches provided all of the Washington Treaty powers enter into an agreement to that effect before the new treaty comes into force. The age limit for battleships has been increased by 6 years, thus prolonging their life and effecting substantial savings in their replacement. To insure that no hybrid vessel between battleships and cruisers will be built which would create a new type and upset existing classes, a zone of nonconstruction between these two categories has been created.

Aircraft carriers are to be reduced from 27,000 to 23,000 tons, and the maximum size of submarines is placed at 2,000 tons.

In respect to cruisers we in effect agreed, upon certain conditions, not to increase our present number of 10,000-ton cruisers during the next 6 years. In so doing, however, we did not sacrifice any American principle or agree to anything that is detrimental to our own national security. The United States now has, either built or building, all of the 10,000-ton cruisers which we were permitted to have under the London Treaty. This, in fact, gives us all of the cruisers of this type which we expect to need for the next few years unless the construction of cruisers by some other power or powers upsets the balance of this type, in which case we have the right under the treaty to terminate the so-called cruiser holiday and to construct such 10,000-ton cruisers as we may deem necessary in the circumstances.

While the new treaty has not been signed by Japan and Italy, it has been left open for their future adherence. It may be pointed out, however, that Italy collaborated in the formation of the treaty, which it is expected she will sign at a later date. Also, Japanese observers remained throughout the Conference, and it is hoped that Japan will see fit later on to adhere to the treaty. It is, furthermore, expected that Germany and Russia, two other principal powers who were not parties to the present treaties, will come into the new treaty system through bilateral treaties with Great Britain.

There has been some comment on the so-called safeguarding clauses of this treaty, to the effect that the treaty is so full of holes as to have no substance whatever. No one will question, I am sure, the necessity for providing that, in case the construction of powers outside the scope of the treaty should menace the national security of any of the contracting parties, such contracting party shall have the right to depart from the limits established by the treaty. These clauses, however, are so drafted that, although they give each power ample assurance that it will be able to meet an emergency, they do not contemplate that the whole structure of the treaty will be destroyed by a simple noncompliance with the letter or spirit of its provisions. Only if a country considers that the requirements of its national defense are seriously threatened by the action of a non-contracting party will it undertake to put into operation the machinery to release it from its treaty obligations. Experience has shown that such action is not apt to be taken lightly. It is further provided that each power wishing to avail itself of this right must set forth in detail the reason for so doing and justify its action to the other powers.

The new treaty provides for much more elaborate and detailed exchange of information than has heretofore existed. Under the provisions for exchange of information, no program of construction is to be put into effect and no keel is to be laid without 4 months' advance notice and full information to all the parties to the treaty. This is a considerable improvement over the present naval treaties. To the layman it may seem unimportant, but to all naval experts and to you who are conversant with the problem, this feature of the treaty is of considerable importance. It removes an element of uncertainty and guards against any sudden development of naval building as to type or quantity which would seriously disturb confidence or the relative security. In effect, it reduces suspicion and the danger of the most harmful and costly kind of naval competition.

Although no limits have been placed on total naval tonnages, and each power is therefore free to build as many or as few of the permitted types of craft as it sees fit, England and America are in agreement that there shall be no competitive building between them. The exchange of letters which took place between the British Foreign Secretary and myself as chairman of the American delegation, recognized this point of fundamental importance. These letters reaffirmed the understanding between England and America that the principle of parity between the fleets of the United States and of the British Commonwealth of Nations is an established principle which shall continue to govern their naval policies. The reaffirmation of this basic principle of the preceding treaties should go far, in these days of uncertainty, to show that at least as between the two greatest naval powers, the United States of America and Great Britain, there is no thought of naval competition.

When one considers the difficulties which stood in the way of negotiating any treaty whatsoever, and what the situation would be without any treaty at all, it is indeed a source of real satisfaction that we were able to achieve as much as we did. We were indeed fortunate in being able to negotiate a treaty which not only preserves a structure of naval limitation but which establishes a basis for further progress toward naval reduction under more favorable conditions than now exist.

While the new naval treaty is less rigid and less far-reaching than the previous treaties, it has many advantages, and its lack of rigidity may well be one of them. The fact is that the Washington Treaty has been denounced because of its rigidity, and for the same reason the London Treaty could not be renewed, whereas the new treaty, which is more flexible, may be more enduring and prove in the long run to be more practical. At any rate, we have nothing to lose in trying it out, and possibly much to gain.

STATEMENT Issued by the Department of State, February 5, 1938

Department of State, *Press Releases*, February 5, 1938, p. 223

Since December 31, 1936, when the Washington Naval Treaty of 1922 and the London Naval Treaty of 1930 expired, as a result of denunciation by Japan, there has been no quantitative naval limitation, that is, a limit on the number of ships which a nation may build.

There has been qualitative limitation, that is, a limit on the types of ships which a nation may build. This limitation has been in effect between the signatories of the London Naval Treaty of 1936—the United States, Great Britain, and France—and between Great Britain on the one hand, and Germany and the Soviet Union on the other.

Japan took part in the early stages of the London Naval Conference of 1935–1936 but withdrew when the other participants were unable to accept the Japanese demand for a common upper limit, which meant that Japan would have naval equality in principle with the United States and Great Britain.

Subsequently, in 1936, Japan was approached by the British Government and asked if it would not give assurances that the treaty limits on types of ships would in practice be adhered to by it even though it could not see its way to subscribing to the London Naval Treaty.

The Japanese Government declined to give these assurances.

This Government took up with Japan the limit of the size of guns on capital ships. Under article 4 of the London Naval Treaty, 1936, it is provided that 14 inches should be the limit of the caliber of guns on capital ships; however, if any of the parties to the Washington Naval Treaty of February 6, 1922, should fail to accept this limit by April 1, 1937, 16 inches would become the treaty limit of guns carried on capital ships.

Despite the efforts of this Government, Japan declined to accept the limit of 14 inches, and, as a consequence of the Japanese refusal, the limit of the guns on capital ships rose to 16 inches.

Recently, reports have been recurrent that Japan not only is ex-

DISARMAMENT

ceeding the limits provided in the London Naval Treaty, 1936, on the size of guns of cruisers and capital ships but is building, or is planning to build, above the limit of types of ships as well.

The question arises, therefore, whether these reports are correct and if so whether it will be necessary for the parties to the London Naval Treaty, 1936, to escalate, in accordance with the provision of the naval treaty which gives a signatory the right of escalation in the event of building not in conformity with treaty limits by a power not a party thereto. Before the parties to the Treaty can escalate, under its provisions they must consult. A preliminary consultation has taken place and the British, French and American Governments have decided to approach the Japanese Government with a request for information.

In the following note to be delivered to the Japanese Government by the American Ambassador at Tokyo, Mr. Joseph C. Grew, on February 5, it is suggested that the United States, as a party to the London Naval Treaty, will be glad to receive a reply to the inquiry with regard to the size and armament of Japanese capital ships and cruisers not later than February 20 next. The reason for fixing February 20 is that it is incumbent upon this Government, under the London Naval Treaty, to furnish information with regard to its naval program to the treaty powers within the first 4 months of the calendar year and that in order to prepare its estimates and have them ready for communication to the other naval powers parties to the London Naval Treaty, it is essential that the facts upon which the estimates are based be wholly assembled at the latest by the end of February. The hope is therefore expressed that a reply will be received from the Japanese Government by February 20, in order that the exchange of information may be completed by the final date referred to in the note, that is, May 1.

The text of the American note follows:

1. The Japanese Government will be aware that under the London Naval Treaty 1936 the American Government is precluded from constructing capital ships (i. e. vessels of more than ten thousand standard displacement or with a gun of more than eight inches) which exceed thirty five thousand tons or carry a gun of more than sixteen inches, or which are of less than seventeen thousand five hundred tons or carry a gun of less than ten inches. As regards cruisers (i. e. vessels of not more than ten thousand tons with gun of not more than eight inches) the American Government is limited to a maximum of eight thousand tons with six inch guns.

2. The Japanese Government has unfortunately not seen its way to subscribing to the London Naval Treaty nor has it hitherto felt able to give any assurances that treaty limits would in practice be adhered to by it.

3. As the Japanese Government will be aware, the naval treaty gives the

American Government a right of escalation in the event of building not in conformity with treaty limits by a power not a party thereto. There have for some time been persistent and cumulative reports, which in the absence of explicit assurances from the Japanese Government that they are ill-founded, must be deemed to be authentic, that Japan has undertaken or intends to undertake construction of capital ships and cruisers not in conformity with the above-mentioned limits. The American Government has therefore decided that it will be necessary for it to exercise its right of escalation unless the Japanese Government can furnish the aforesaid assurances and can satisfy the American Government that it will not, prior to January 1, 1943, lay down, complete or acquire any vessel which does not conform to the limits in question, without previously informing the American Government of its intention to do so and of tonnage and caliber of the largest gun of the vessel or vessels concerned.

4. In view of the forthcoming publication of naval estimates and necessity for giving other treaty powers information as to intended American construction, the American Government will be glad to receive a reply not later than February 20 next. Should no reply be received by that date or should the reply be lacking in the desired information and assurances, it will be compelled to assume that the Japanese Government either is constructing or acquiring or has authorized the construction or acquisition of vessels not in conformity with the limits referred to. The American Government would thereupon be obliged in consultation with the other naval powers with which it is in treaty relations to resume full liberty of action. If, however, the Japanese Government though engaged in, or intending to engage in, construction not in conformity with treaty limits, were willing to indicate forthwith the tonnages and calibers of guns of the vessels which it was constructing, or was intending to construct, the American Government for its part would be ready to discuss with the Japanese Government the question of the tonnages and gun calibers to be adhered to in future if Japan were now prepared to agree to some limitation. It would however be necessary that such consultation should be completed by May 1.

STATEMENT Issued by the Department of State, June 30, 1938

Department of State, *Press Releases,* July 2, 1938, p. 10

FOLLOWING the refusal of Japan to furnish information with regard to its naval construction, or its plans for future construction, the powers parties to the London Naval Treaty of 1936—that is, the United States, Great Britain, and France—mutually reached the decision to depart from the limits of the treaty in the battleship category and, on April 1, exchanged notes announcing their intention to escalate.

DISARMAMENT

Under the terms of the treaty, the next step following the formal announcement of intention to escalate is consultation over a period of 3 months to determine whether new limits can be fixed and if so what these new limits will be. Accordingly, the representatives of the three powers met at London on April 12 and at intervals thereafter in order to explore the possibilities of limitation.

All three powers, in this consultation, took the ground that, in view of all the circumstances, there must be a departure from the limits of the treaty. The United States, wishing to maintain in effect naval limitation insofar as possible, informed the other signatory powers of its willingness to accept a new limitation of 45,000 tons on the size and 16 inches in the armament of capital ships. When it is decided to build larger capital ships, these limits are, from a technical point of view, believed most nearly to correspond with the naval defense needs of the United States.

The protocol signed today at London by the signatories to the London treaty of 1936 gives formal approval to the fixing of the new limitation to the tonnage of capital ships.

The protocol was signed on behalf of the United States by Mr. Herschel V. Johnson, the American Chargé d'Affaires. The text is as follows:

Whereas by Article Four (1) of the Treaty for the Limitation of Naval Armaments signed in London on the 25th March, 1936, it is provided that no capital ship shall exceed 35,000 tons (35,560 metric tons) standard displacement;

And whereas by reason of Article Four (2) of the said Treaty the maximum calibre of gun carried by capital ships is 16 inches (406 mm.);

And whereas on the 31st March, 1938, His Majesty's Government in the United Kingdom of Great Britain and Northern Ireland and the Government of the United States of America gave notice under paragraph (2) of Article 25 of the said Treaty of their decision to exercise the right provided for in paragraph (1) of the said Article to depart from the limitations and restrictions of the Treaty in regard to the upper limits of capital ships of subcategory (a);

And whereas consultations have taken place as provided in paragraph (3) of Article 25, with a view to reaching agreement in order to reduce to a minimum the extent of the departures from the limitations and restrictions of the Treaty;

The undersigned, duly authorized by their respective governments, have agreed as follows:

One. As from this day's date the figure of 35,000 tons (35,560 metric tons) in Article Four (1) of the said Treaty shall be replaced by the figure of 45,000 tons (45,720 metric tons).

Two. The figure of 16 inches (406 mm.) in Article Four (2) remains unaltered.

Three. The present protocol, of which the French and English texts shall both be equally authentic, shall come into force on this day's date.

In faith whereof the undersigned have signed the present protocol.

Done in London the 30th day of June 1938.

The British Government has today addressed a note to the Government of the United States stating that the two capital ships provided for in the current year's estimates will not exceed 40,000 tons (40,640 metric tons). The note also states that should it at any time be found necessary to construct capital ships of a higher tonnage than 40,000 tons (40,640 metric tons) notification of such intention would be made in the ordinary way to the other interested powers in accordance with the provisions of the London Naval Treaty of 1936.

RELATIONS WITH JAPAN

MEMORANDUM Handed by Henry L. Stimson, Secretary of State, to the Japanese Ambassador to the United States (Katsuji Debuchi), September 22, 1931

Department of State, *Peace and War,* p. 156

WITHOUT GOING into the background, either as to the immediate provocation or remote causes or motivation, it appears that there has developed within the past four days a situation in Manchuria which I find surprising and view with concern. Japanese military forces, with some opposition at some points by Chinese military forces, have occupied the principal strategic points in South Manchuria, including the principal administrative center, together with some at least of the public utilities. It appears that the highest Chinese authority ordered the Chinese military not to resist, and that, when news of the situation reached Tokyo, but after most of the acts of occupation had been consummated, the Japanese Government ordered cessation of military activities on the part of the Japanese forces. Nevertheless, it appears some military movements have been continuously and are even now in process. The actual situation is that an arm of the Japanese Government is in complete control of South Manchuria.

The League of Nations has given evidence of its concern. The Chinese Government has in various ways invoked action on the part of foreign governments, citing its reliance upon treaty obligations and inviting special reference to the Kellogg Pact.

This situation is of concern, morally, legally and politically to a considerable number of nations. It is not exclusively a matter of concern to Japan and China. It brings into question at once the meaning of certain provisions of agreements, such as the Nine-Powers Treaty of February 6, 1922, and the Kellogg-Briand Pact.

The American Government is confident that it has not been the intention of the Japanese Government to create or to be a party to the creation of a situation which brings the applicability of treaty provisions into consideration. The American Government does not wish to be hasty in formulating its conclusions or in taking a position. However, the American Government feels that a very unfortunate situation exists, which no doubt is embarrassing to the Japanese Government. It would seem that the responsibility for determining the course of events with regard to the liquidating of this situation rests largely upon Japan, for the simple reason that Japanese armed forces have seized and are exercising *de facto* control in South Manchuria.

It is alleged by the Chinese, and the allegation has the support of circumstantial evidence, that lines of communication outward from Manchuria have been cut or interfered with. If this is true, it is unfortunate.

It is the hope of the American Government that the orders which it understands have been given both by the Japanese and the Chinese Governments to their military forces to refrain from hostilities and further movements will be respected and that there will be no further application of force. It is also the hope of the American Government that the Japanese and the Chinese Governments will find it possible speedily to demonstrate to the world that neither has any intention to take advantage, in furtherance of its own peculiar interests, of the situation which has been brought about in connection with and in consequence of this use of force.

What has occurred has already shaken the confidence of the public with regard to the stability of conditions in Manchuria, and it is believed that the crystallizing of a situation suggesting the necessity for an indefinite continuance of military occupation would further undermine that confidence.

TELEGRAM from Henry L. Stimson, Secretary of State, to the American Consul at Geneva (Prentiss B. Gilbert), October 9, 1931

Department of State, *Foreign Relations of the United States: Japan, 1931–1941*, I, 17; paraphrase

73. Consulate's 162, October 8[7], 5 p. m. A memorandum in writing containing the following message from me dated as of October 5, 1931, may be handed by you to Sir Eric Drummond. This he may feel free to communicate confidentially to the Council members.

I believe that our cooperation in the future handling of this difficult matter should proceed along the course which has been followed ever since the first outbreak of the trouble fortunately found the Assembly and Council of the League of Nations in session. The Council has deliberated long and earnestly on this matter and the Covenant of the League of Nations provides permanent and already tested machinery for handling such issues as between States members of the League. Both the Chinese and

Japanese have presented and argued their cases before the Council and the world has been informed through published accounts with regard to the proceedings there. The Council has formulated conclusions and outlined a course of action to be followed by the disputants; and as the said disputants have made commitments to the Council, it is most desirable that the League in no way relax its vigilance and in no way fail to assert all the pressure and authority within its competence towards regulating the action of China and Japan in the premises.

On its part the American Government acting independently through its diplomatic representatives will endeavor to reinforce what the League does and will make clear that it has a keen interest in the matter and is not oblivious to the obligations which the disputants have assumed to their fellow signatories in the Pact of Paris as well as in the Nine Power Pact should a time arise when it would seem advisable to bring forward those obligations. By this course we avoid any danger of embarrassing the League in the course to which it is now committed.

TELEGRAM from Henry L. Stimson, Secretary of State, to the American Ambassador to Great Britain (Charles G. Dawes), November 10, 1931

Department of State, *Foreign Relations of the United States: Japan, 1931–1941*, I, 41; paraphrase, in part

326. [Paraphrase.] With regard to our conversation this morning over the telephone, it is my desire that during the next few days you should be in Paris so that you may be available for conference with Monsieur Briand and possibly with the representatives of the other nations who are assembling on November 16 for the adjourned meeting of the League of Nations Council concerning the problem which has arisen out of the developments in, and in connection with, Manchuria. That you will find it necessary to attend the Council meetings is not anticipated. It is desired, however, that you be available for conference on matters which affect treaty rights and general interest of the United States, in view of the fact that the developments in Manchuria and the discussions which will take place in Paris will presumably involve matters pertinent thereto.

It is assumed that you know generally of the events in Manchuria and of the discussion which has occurred at Geneva and the action taken by the Council and by the American Government.

Your Government sees it as follows: The armed forces of Japan for practical purposes have in South Manchuria taken control of all important cities, the railway lines, the telephone, telegraph, radio systems, and some other public utilities, and have destroyed or seriously disrupted there the administrative machinery of the Chinese.

It is the contention of the Japanese Government that all measures taken have been necessary in order to protect the lives and property of Japanese subjects and to protect the South Manchuria Railway. [End paraphrase.]

The Council of the League was in session when this trouble began and China immediately appealed to it. Both China and Japan are represented on the Council. On September 30, the Council unanimously adopted a resolution in which it was affirmed that Japan had no territorial designs on Manchuria; that Japan would withdraw its troops as rapidly as possible into the Railway Zone, in proportion as the safety of the lives and property of Japanese nationals was effectively assured; and that the Chinese Government would assume responsibility for the safety of Japanese lives and property as the withdrawal continued. The Council then adjourned, to meet on October 14.

When the Council met again on October 14 [*13*], no progress had been made in the matter of withdrawal. The Japanese military had somewhat extended its activities. It appeared that the question of invoking the Kellogg Pact must be dealt with. We authorized Gilbert to accept an invitation of the Council to sit with the Council as an observer, to take part in the discussions in so far as they might relate to the Kellogg Pact, but to participate in no discussions which did not relate to the Pact. He of course had no vote. The first result was a request by several governments represented on the Council to signatories of the Kellogg Pact to call attention to that treaty. The governments thus acting immediately sent notes to Japan and to China invoking that treaty, and several other governments, including the American, soon did likewise.

The Council continued in session and Briand, Reading, Grandi and others endeavored to persuade Japan and China to agree to a new resolution intended to hasten the resolving of the military situation and a solution by peaceful means. It became apparent, however, that, among other matters, Japan was now insisting as a condition precedent to withdrawal that China expressly confirm certain old treaties and treaty obligations which had been in dispute over a number of years. When it finally appeared that Japan insisted absolutely on that point, the Council drew up a resolution, which was voted upon affirmatively by all the representatives except the Japanese on October 24. This resolution, in view of the fact that the vote was not unanimous, lacks legal force. Its essential features were as follows: The points made in the September 30 resolution were reiterated. Japan was called upon to withdraw its forces before the next meeting of the Council on November 16. China was called upon to make arrangements for taking over the territory evacuated and to associate with her authorities designated for that purpose representatives of other powers to follow execution of these arrangements. It was recommended that China and Japan appoint representatives to meet and arrange details of evacuation and taking over. It was recommended that as soon as the evacuation was complete China and Japan should begin direct negotiations and, if necessary, set up a committee of conciliation. The Council was to adjourn until November 16.

At the last meeting, the Japanese made a counter-proposal, which was not accepted. Examination of this and of subsequent statements of the Japanese Government indicate that the real issue is as follows: The Japanese insist that before releasing the military grip which they have gained, matters of long-standing dispute between them and the Chinese shall be settled. These matters appear to include questions of validity of treaties which China disputes and details of interpretation of treaties which China does not dispute. The Chinese have stated in a formal note to the League that they regard themselves as bound by the League Covenant to a scrupulous respect for all treaty obligations and they have offered to submit to arbitration or judicial settlement. They have not denied that they dispute the validity of certain treaties. It appears that at one point the Japanese stated that they would give the Council a list of the treaties for which they demand respect; but we are not informed that they have submitted such a list.

[Paraphrase.] Japan has not appeared to us to be justified in insisting that all these matters should be settled as a prerequisite to withdrawal; in fact, it has seemed to us that to insist thus would amount to exerting military pressure in order to bring about a settlement. In addition, we have taken the position from the outset that, while acting independently, we should endeavor, insofar as might be proper, to reinforce the League's action. Therefore, we stated to Shidehara in a memorandum left with him by Forbes, November 5, that the use of military force in order to influence negotiations would be deprecated by us, and that our attitude was the same as that expressed by the Council in its resolutions; that is, withdrawal of Japan's forces should not be conditioned upon the settling of long-standing questions. Since we did not wish to give an opinion one way or the other concerning the wisdom of the Council's strategy in setting a date for the evacuation, we did not mention the date specified in the resolution.

Although, technically speaking, war has been avoided so far, these efforts seem as yet to have produced no very effective results. Realizing from the beginning that conflict in regard to policy existed within Japan, our purpose has been to avoid any measure which might help in the gaining of uncontested control by the military element. China has also had her conflicts within, and it has been our hope that the Chinese would themselves view the situation and its requirements more realistically than they seem to have done so far.

We still feel that it should be possible for a method to be found for the peaceful settlement of this issue. Careful consideration should be given to the respecting by both China and Japan of the treaty rights between those two countries and those of other powers.

The disputants must be made to realize that we have no intention of taking sides as between them, nor do we intend to allow a line of cleavage to be created between us and the Council, since we feel that our objectives are the same: namely, to effect a peaceful settlement and prevent war. We can associate ourselves with the Council's efforts on behalf of peace although we cannot ally ourselves with it. The obvious fact that the whole world desires peace must be impressed on both the Japanese and Chinese.

In view of the above, it is my desire to send you to Paris and place you in close touch with the Council's leading members in order to add force to my efforts here along these lines. Leaving the lead to Briand, you should, in your discretion, contribute by your counsel to the search for a way of obtaining the agreement of China and Japan to some method of peaceful solution. I do not want us to push or lead in this matter; neither do I want the American Government to be placed in the position of initiating or instigating League action. I do desire that we confer with the principal Council members on this difficult problem of common concern and that our efforts shall be added to theirs.

My suggestion is that you feel your way cautiously. Notify me fully in regard to such possibilities as you may envisage, as well as in regard to actual developments.

I have in mind other possibilities which I shall indicate to you in a later telegram. [End paraphrase.]

TELEGRAM from Henry L. Stimson, Secretary of State, to the American Ambassador to Japan (William Cameron Forbes), January 7, 1932

Department of State, *Foreign Relations of the United States: Japan, 1931–1941*, I, 76

7. Please deliver to the Foreign Office on behalf of your Government as soon as possible the following note:

With the recent military operations about Chinchow, the last remaining administrative authority of the Government of the Chinese Republic in South Manchuria, as it existed prior to September 18th, 1931, has been destroyed. The American Government continues confident that the work of the neutral commission recently authorized by the Council of the League of Nations will facilitate an ultimate solution of the difficulties now existing between China and Japan. But in view of the present situation and of its own rights and obligations therein, the American Government deems it to be its duty to notify both the Imperial Japanese Government and the Government of the Chinese Republic that it cannot admit the legality of any situation *de facto* nor does it intend to recognize any treaty or agreement entered into between those Governments, or agents thereof, which may impair the treaty rights of the United States or its citizens in China, including those which relate to the sovereignty, the independence, or the territorial and administrative integrity of the Republic of China, or to the international policy relative to China, commonly known as the open door policy; and that it does not intend to recognize any situation, treaty or agreement which may be brought about by means contrary to the covenants and obligations of the Pact of Paris of August 27, 1928, to which Treaty both China and Japan, as well as the United States, are parties.

State that an identical note is being sent to the Chinese government.

TELEGRAM from Henry L. Stimson, Secretary of State, to the American Minister to Switzerland (Hugh R. Wilson), February 12, 1932

Department of State, *Foreign Relations of the United States: Japan, 1931–1941*, I, 80–82

11. Reference Department's 9, February 12, noon. There follows the text of a draft concerning which I have just talked with Sir John Simon. Please deliver a copy to Sir John before he leaves Geneva, ex-

plaining that this is merely a rough draft; that I shall be working further on it; that I shall welcome his comments and suggestions.

To the nations who are either signatories or adherents of the so-called Nine Power Treaty regarding principles and policies to be followed in matters concerning China:

The (blank) Governments, signatories of the Nine-Power Treaty, pursuant to Article seventh thereof, desire to communicate to their fellow signatories and adherents to this Treaty their views as to certain matters which have recently occurred within the territory of the Republic of China.

I. This Treaty was concluded in 1922 in the city of Washington at a conference, participated in by many powers, at which the policy of these powers towards the Republic of China was fully discussed and the attitude which they should hereafter adopt towards the Republic of China was set forth in this treaty. The treaty represented the culmination of a policy towards China which had been developed between these powers for many years, known as the Open Door policy. In the first article of that Treaty the Contracting Powers, other than China, agreed:

"1. To respect the sovereignty, the independence, and the territorial and administrative integrity of China.

"2. To provide the fullest and most unembarrassed opportunity to China to develop and maintain for herself and [an] effective and stable government."

The Treaty thus represents a carefully developed and matured international policy intended to afford to the people of China the fullest possible opportunity of developing, without molestation, their sovereignty and independence among the nations of the world, according to the modern and enlightened standards believed now to maintain among the peoples of this earth. It was known that China was in the process of developing the free institutions of a self-governing Republic after her recent revolution from an autocratic form of government; that she would require many years of both economic and political effort to that end, and that the process would necessarily be a very long one. The Treaty was thus a deliberate covenant of self-denial among the signatory powers of all acts of aggression which were calculated to interfere with that development. But it was believed, and a study of the Treaty reveals that faith, that only by such a process of development could the fullest interests, not only of China but of all nations having intercourse with her, best be served.

II. Six years later the general policy upon which the Nine-Power Treaty was based received a powerful reinforcement in the execution, by substantially all the nations of the world, of the Pact of Paris. These two treaties represent successive steps taken for the purpose of aligning the conscience and public opinion of the world in favor of a system of orderly development by the law of nations, including the settlement of all controversies by the methods of justice and peace instead of by arbitrary force. The program for the protection of China from outside aggression is an essential part of any such development. The signatories and the adherents of the Nine-Power Treaty rightly felt that the orderly and peaceful development of the four hundred millions of people inhabiting China was necessary to the peaceful welfare of the people of the entire world and that no program for the welfare of the world as a whole could afford to neglect the protection of the development of China.

III. Although they have withheld adverse judgment pending the investigation which is to be made by the commission appointed by the League of Nations under the resolution of December 9, the nations of the world have watched with apprehension the events in Manchuria which have taken place during recent months. This apprehension was based upon the tragic experience of the last two decades which have made manifest the fact that in case of war no nation is immune from the danger of becoming involved in the conflict, however remote in its inception. The recent spread of these disturbances in Manchuria to the area of Shanghai, involving as it does the direct threat of danger to the interests of many nations, is further powerful evidence of this fact.

IV. The rapid development of events in Shanghai seems to the (blank) Governments to give full cause for the deepest apprehension of all nations who have been interested in the policy of the two treaties to which we have referred. It is unnecessary to attempt to analyze the origin of the controversy or to apportion the blame between the two nations which unhappily are involved. For it is clear beyond peradventure that a situation has now developed which can not under any circumstances be reconciled with the covenants and the obligations of these two treaties and which is wholly abhorrent to the enlightened purpose for which they were conceived. There is now assembled in the port of Shanghai a Japanese force including over forty vessels of war and reenforced by a large expeditionary force of land troops. The very size of such an expedition is not only disproportionate to its avowed objective of protecting life and property in the city of Shanghai but is in itself provocative of counter-violence. Military airplanes have been bombing areas densely populated by helpless civilians of a nation with whom their operators are not ostensibly at war. Many miles away from the city where the alleged violence against Japanese nationals occurred, the Japanese Government is now engaged in military operations on a large scale. It is inconceivable that if the leaders of these two nations had been fully and equally inbued with the purpose underlying these treaties and had been adequately mindful of the covenants therein such a situation could have been allowed to develop or that at some stage a solution of their controversies could not have been otherwise achieved.

V. The effect of this development of violence has been to threaten the very existence of the treaties themselves. This has been shown by the following occurrences which have greatly accentuated the concern of the (blank) Governments:

(1) In rejecting a recent proffer of good offices from the British, the American and the French Governments submitted at the request of Japan, the Japanese Government has taken the position that it would not consent to the participation even as observers of any third nations in the discus-

sions of questions arising between Japan and China in regard to that portion of China known as Manchuria. This would seem to deny to any other power even a signatory of the Nine-Power Treaty the right to participate even as an observer in negotiations involving rights and obligations comprised within that Treaty.

(2) Again on February 8, 1932, the Foreign Office of the Japanese Government of Tokyo issued to the press of the world a suggested proposal that there should be created a system of "demilitarized zones" around the principal commercial cities of China, out of which the forces of the Government of China should be excluded. The representative of the Japanese Foreign Office in advancing this proposal frankly affirmed that it was contrary to the Nine-Power Treaty but asserted that ten years' trial had proved that treaty to be ineffective.

VI. The (blank) Governments do not concede that the Nine-Power Treaty is ineffective or inoperative or that it is to be discarded. They do not concede that such a situation as has arisen in Shanghai is inevitable, provided the covenants of the Nine-Power Treaty and the Pact of Paris are faithfully observed by those who have covenanted to observe them. They are unwilling to consent that the enlightened policy which has heretofore marked the efforts of the nations of the earth towards China and towards each other should be repudiated or abandoned without their most earnest reprobation. They do not intend to forego their legitimate prerogative, in view of their treaty rights and obligations, to participate together with the other powers concerned in any negotiations whereby those rights and obligations and the policies which they represent may be affected. They take this occasion to express these views in order that there may be no misunderstanding. They avail themselves of the opportunity afforded by the terms of Article seven of the Nine-Power Treaty to express frankly and without reserve their views upon these occurrences at Shanghai and their belief that if the covenants and policies of the Nine-Power Treaty and the Pact of Paris be allowed to be repudiated or repealed, the loss to all the nations of the world will be immeasurable. For this reason they further notify their fellow signatories and adherents to those treaties that they for themselves and each of them do not propose to recognize as valid any treaty, agreement, arrangement or situation which may be entered into or created in China by means of acts or policies which are in violation of the covenants of those treaties.

COMMUNICATION from Henry L. Stimson, Secretary of State, to the Secretary-General of the League of Nations (Joseph Avenol), February 25, 1933

Transmitted through the American Minister at Berne (Hugh R. Wilson) in a letter dated February 26, 1933. League of Nations, *Official Journal*, Special Supplement No. 112, p. 97

THERE HAS BEEN communicated to me the text of your letter of February 24th, 1933, transmitting to me a copy of the report of the Committee of Nineteen as adopted by the Assembly of the League of Nations on this day.

I note your request that I communicate to you as soon as possible the reply of the Government of the United States.

In response to that request I have the honor to state the views of the American Government as follows:

In the situation which has developed out of the controversy between China and Japan, the purpose of the United States has coincided in general with that of the League of Nations, the common objective being maintenance of peace and settlement of international disputes by pacific means. In pursuance of that objective, while the League of Nations has been exercising jurisdiction over a controversy between two of its members, the Government of the United States has endeavored to give support, reserving to itself independence of judgment with regard to method and scope to the efforts of the League on behalf of peace.

The findings of fact arrived at by the League and the understanding of the facts derived by the American Government from reports made to it by its own representatives are in substantial accord. In the light of its findings of fact, the Assembly of the League has formulated a measured statement of conclusions. With those conclusions, the American Government is in general accord. In their affirmations, respectively of the principle of non-recognition and their attitude in regard thereto, the League and the United States are on common ground. The League has recommended principles of settlement. In so far as appropriate under the treaties to which it is a party, the American Government expresses its general endorsement of the principles thus recommended.

The American Government earnestly hopes that the two nations now engaged in controversy, both of which have long been in friendly relationship with our own and other peoples, may find it possible in the light of world opinion to conform their policies to the need and the desire of the family of nations that disputes between nations shall be settled by none but pacific means.

COMMUNICATION from Joseph C. Grew, American Ambassador to Japan, to the Secretary of State of the United States (Cordell Hull), December 27, 1934

Department of State, *Peace and War,* p. 236; excerpts

Sir:

Now that the London Naval Conversations have terminated, I should like to convey to the Department various thoughts in this general connection to which the Department may desire to give consideration if and when the conversations are renewed or a naval conference convoked. . . .

The thought which is uppermost in my mind is that the United States is faced, and will be faced in future, with two main alternatives. One is to be prepared to withdraw from the Far East, gracefully and gradually perhaps, but not the less effectively in the long run, permitting our treaty rights to be nullified, the Open Door to be closed, our vested economic interests to be dissolved and our commerce to operate unprotected. There are those who advocate this course, and who have advocated it to me personally, on the ground that any other policy will entail the risk of eventual war with Japan. . . . In their opinion, "the game is not worth the candle" because the United States can continue to subsist comfortably even after relinquishing its varied interests in the Far East, thereby eliminating the risk of future war.

The other main alternative is to insist, and to continue to insist, not aggressively yet not the less firmly, on the maintenance of our legitimate rights and interests in this part of the world and, so far as practicable, to support the normal development of those interests constructively and progressively.

There has already been abundant indication that the present Administration in Washington proposes to follow the second of these alternatives. For purposes of discussion we may therefore, I assume, discard the hypothesis of withdrawal and examine the future outlook with the assurance that our Government has not the slightest intention of relinquishing the legitimate rights, vested interests, non-discriminatory privileges for equal opportunity and healthful commercial development of the United States in the Far East.

RELATIONS WITH JAPAN 77

In following this second and logical course, there should be and need be nothing inconsistent, so far as our own attitude is concerned, with the policy of the good neighbor. The determination to support and protect our legitimate interests in the Far East can and should be carried out in a way which, while sacrificing no point of principle, will aim to restrict to a minimum the friction between the United States and Japan inevitably arising from time to time as a result of that determination.

The administration of that policy from day to day becomes a matter of diplomacy, sometimes delicate, always important, for much depends on the method and manner of approach to the various problems with which we have been, are, and will continue to be faced. With the ultra-sensitiveness of the Japanese, arising out of a marked inferiority complex which manifests itself in the garb of an equally marked superiority complex, with all its attendant bluster, chauvinism, xenophobia and organized national propaganda, the method and manner of dealing with current controversies assume a significance and importance often out of all proportion to the nature of the controversy. . . .

It is difficult for those who do not live in Japan to appraise the present temper of the country. An American Senator, according to reports, has recently recommended that we should accord parity to Japan in order to avoid future war. Whatever the Senator's views may be concerning the general policy that we should follow in the Far East, he probably does not realize what harm that sort of public statement does in strengthening the Japanese stand and in reinforcing the aggressive ambitions of the expansionists. The Japanese press of course picks out such statements by prominent Americans and publishes them far and wide, thus confirming the general belief in Japan that the pacifist element in the United States is preponderantly strong and in the last analysis will control the policy and action of our Government. Under such circumstances there is a general tendency to characterize our diplomatic representations as bluff and to believe that they can safely be disregarded without fear of implementation. It would be helpful if those who share the Senator's views could hear and read some of the things that are constantly being said and written in Japan, to the effect that Japan's destiny is to subjugate and rule the world (*sic*), and could realize the expansionist ambitions which lie not far from the surface in the minds of certain elements in the Army and Navy, the patriotic societies and the intense nationalists throughout the country. Their aim is to obtain trade control and eventually predominant political influence in China, the Philippines, the Straits Settlements, Siam and the Dutch East Indies, the Maritime Provinces and Vladivostok, one step at a time, as in Korea and Manchuria, pausing intermittently to consolidate and then continuing as soon as the intervening obstacles can be overcome by diplomacy or force. With such dreams of empire cherished by many, and with an army and navy capable of taking the bit in their own teeth and running away with it regardless of the restraining influence of the saner heads of the Government in Tokyo (a risk which unquestionably exists and of which we have already had ample evidence in the Manchurian affair), we would be reprehensibly somnolent if we were to trust to the security of treaty restraints or international comity to safeguard our own interests or, indeed, our own property.

I may refer here to my despatch No. 608 of December 12, 1933, a re-reading of which is respectfully invited because it applies directly to the present situation. That despatch reported a confidential conversation with the Netherlands Minister, General Pabst, a shrewd and rational colleague with long experience in Japan, in which the Minister said that in his opinion the Japanese Navy, imbued as it is with patriotic and chauvinistic fervor and with a desire to emulate the deeds of the Army in order not to lose caste with the public, would be perfectly capable of descending upon and occupying Guam at a moment of crisis or, indeed, at any other moment, regardless of the ulterior consequences. I do not think that such an insane step is likely, yet the action of the Army in Manchuria, judged from the point of view of treaty rights and international comity, might also have been judged as insensate. The important fact is that under present circumstances, and indeed under circumstances which may continue in future (although the pendulum of chauvinism throughout Japanese history has swung to and fro in periodic cycles of intensity and temporary relaxation) the armed forces of the country are perfectly capable of over-riding the restraining control of the Government and of committing what might well amount to national "hari-kiri" in a mistaken conception of patriotism.

When Japanese speak of Japan's being the "stabilizing factor" and the "guardian of peace" of East Asia, what they have in mind is a Pax Japonica with eventual complete commercial control, and in the minds of some, eventual complete political control of East Asia. While Ambassador Saito may have been misquoted in a recent issue of the Philadelphia *Bulletin* as saying that Japan will be prepared to fight to maintain that conception of peace, nevertheless that is precisely what is in the minds of many Japanese today. There is a swashbuckling temper in the country, largely developed by military propaganda, which can lead Japan during the next few years, or in the next few generations, to any extremes unless the saner minds in the Government prove able to cope with it and to restrain the country from national suicide. . . .

But all this does not make us less sympathetic to the better elements in Japanese life or in any sense "anti-Japanese." Japan is a country of paradoxes and extremes, of great wisdom and of great stupidity, an apt illustration of which may be found in connection with the naval conversations; while the naval authorities and the press have been stoutly maintaining that Japan cannot adequately defend her shores with less than parity, the press and the public, in articles, speeches and interviews, have at the same time been valiantly boasting that the Japanese Navy is today stronger than the American Navy and could easily defeat us in case of war. In such an atmosphere it is difficult, very difficult, for a foreigner to keep a detached and balanced point of view. We in the Embassy are making that effort, I hope with success, and in the meantime about all we can do is to keep the boat from rocking dangerously. Constructive work is at present impossible. Our efforts are concentrated on the thwarting of destructive influences.

Having placed the foregoing considerations on record, I have less hesitation in reiterating and emphasizing with all conviction the potential dangers of the situation and the prime importance of American national preparedness to meet it. As a nation we have taken the lead in international efforts towards the restriction and reduction of armaments. We have had hopes that the movement would be progressive, but the condition of world affairs as they have developed during the past twelve years since the Washington Conference has not afforded fruitful ground for such progress. Unless we are prepared to subscribe to a "Pax Japonica" in the Far East, with all that this movement, as conceived and interpreted by Japan, is bound to entail, we should rapidly build up our navy to treaty strength, and if and when the Washington Naval Treaty expires we should continue to maintain the present ratio with Japan regardless of cost, a peace-time insurance both to cover and to reduce the risk of war. In the meantime every proper step should be taken to avoid or to offset the belligerent utterances of jingoes no less than the defeatist statements of pacifists in the United States, many of which find their way into the Japanese press, because the utterances of the former tend to enflame public sentiment against our country, while the statements of the latter convey an impression of American weakness, irresolution and bluff.

My own opinion, although it can be but guesswork, is that Japan will under no circumstances invite a race in naval armaments, and that having found our position on the ratios to be adamant, further propositions will be forthcoming within the next two years before the Washington Treaty expires, or before our present building program is fully completed. When the United States has actually completed its naval building program to treaty limits, then, it is believed, and probably not before then, Japan will realize that we are in earnest and will seek a compromise. We believe that Japan's naval policy has been formulated on the premise that the United States would never build up to treaty strength, a premise which has been strengthened in the past by the naval policy of the past two Administrations, by the apparent strength of the pacifist element in the United States, and more recently by the effects of the depression.

While it is true that Japan, by sedulously forming and stimulating public opinion to demand parity with the United States in principle if not in fact, has burned her bridges behind her, nevertheless the Japanese leaders are past-masters at remoulding public opinion in the country by skillful propaganda to suit new conditions. Once convinced that parity is impossible, it is difficult to believe that she will allow matters to come to a point where competitive building becomes unavoidable. With a national budget for 1935–1936 totalling 2,193,414,289 yen, or which about 47% is for the Army and Navy, and with an estimated national debt in 1936 of 9,880,000,000 yen, nearly equal to the Cabinet Bureau of Statistics estimate of the national income for 1930, namely 10,635,000,000 yen; with her vast outlay in Manchuria, her already heavily taxed population and the crying need of large sections of her people for relief funds, it is difficult to see how Japan could afford to embark upon a program of maintaining naval parity with the United States and Great Britain.

Having registered our position firmly and unequivocally, we can now afford to await the next move on the part of Japan. I believe that it will come.

So far as we can evaluate here the proceedings of the recent preliminary naval conversations in London, I am of the opinion that the most important and the most valuable result issuing therefrom has been the apparent tendency towards closer Anglo-American cooperation in the Far East. If we can count in future—again as a direct result of Japan's "bungling diplomacy"—on a solid and united front between the United States and Great Britain in meeting Japan's flaunting of treaty rights and her unrestrained ambitions to control East Asia, the future may well assume a brighter aspect for all of us.

Theodore Roosevelt enunciated the policy "Speak softly but carry a big stick." If our diplomacy in the Far East is to achieve favorable results, and if we are to reduce the risk of an eventual war with Japan to a minimum, that is the only way to proceed. Such a war may be unthinkable, and so it is, but the spectre of it is always present and will be present for some time to come. It would be criminally short-sighted to discard it from our calculations, and the best possible way to avoid it is to be adequately prepared, for preparedness is a cold fact which even the chauvinists, the military, the patriots and the ultra-nationalists in Japan, for all their bluster concerning "provocative measures" in the United States, can grasp and understand. The Soviet Ambassador recently told me that a prominent Japanese had said to him that the most important factor in avoiding a Japanese attack on the Maritime Provinces was the intensive Soviet military preparations in Siberia and Vladivostok. I believe this to be true, and again, and yet again, I urge that our own country be adequately prepared to meet all eventualities in the Far East.

The Counselor, the Naval Attaché and the Military Attaché of this Embassy, having separately read this despatch, have expressed to me their full concurrence with its contents both in essence and detail.

TELEGRAM from Cordell Hull, Secretary of State, to the American Ambassador to Japan (Joseph C. Grew), September 2, 1937

Department of State, *Peace and War,* p. 377; paraphrase

187. Reference is made to outline in your telegram No. 321 of August 27, 4 p. m., of the views and estimate of the American Embassy in Japan. I hope that it may be useful for you to have an outline of the general reaction at home to developments taking place and of the Department's present thoughts respecting methods and policy, as a means toward understanding and interpreting the American position.

The United States Government's course, as pursued during recent years in regard to the Far East, has been animated partly by the thought of the advantageousness of encouraging Japanese and Chinese effort at developing toward each other and toward the world attitudes of real cooperativeness. A situation has been produced by the hostilities that have been and are now going on between Japan and China which permits scant hope of any such attitude or practice being reciprocally developed by and between those two countries in the near future.

In view of the methods employed by the Japanese military forces, particularly of their entire lack of responsiveness in their acts to suggestions quietly and patiently made them by the United States and other Governments that reasonable consideration be given by them to the safety, rights, interests, susceptibilities, etc., of individuals and nations which are not parties to the Sino-Japanese conflict, it may be doubted that the elements actually controlling Japan's policies and action value appreciably the friendship of other nations or efforts made by the United States and other Governments to cultivate good will, confidence, and stability in general.

In the current crisis the United States Government has endeavored to follow an absolutely impartial course. It is realized in Washington that hostilities are not likely to be brought to an end by manifestations of disapprobation on moral or legal grounds. It is necessary, however, in shaping the American course, to keep in mind constantly not only the possible serving of that object, not only the possible effects upon Japan, or upon China, or upon both of them, of possible steps, but also the wishes and attitude of the American people, the principles in which the United States believes, the courses which other countries pursue, and various objectives, general and ultimate as well as immediate and particular.

The principles guiding the United States Government were made clear in my statement of July 16, 50 states of the world having since affirmatively expressed themselves in general support thereof. In my subsequent statement of August 23, it is made clear that these principles are regarded as being applicable to the Pacific area. In a well-ordered existence in and of the society of nations, these principles are considered to be fundamental. In their present courses of action it is apparent that neither Japan nor China is acting in accord with these principles, and Japan's course is directly in conflict with many of them.

Of the Japanese feeling that the American course has indicated a desire for fairness and impartiality, I am glad to know. The first solicitude of the United States, however, will have to be, not for the maintenance of unqualified good will by either or both of the combatants toward the United States, but for the welfare of the American people and for the general policies and broad interests of the United States, guided by laws, treaties, public opinion, and other controlling considerations. Your view is shared by me that fundamental American objectives should include (1) the avoidance of involvement and (2) the protection of lives, property, and rights of American citizens. I am in doubt regarding your suggestion that these two objectives might be pursued simultaneously with the third objective, and consequently do not feel that solidifying relations with either combatant nation should be made a definite objective. The United States is opposed to the courses being pursued, particularly

Japan's course. We do not desire to injure China or Japan and wish to be a good neighbor to both, but we do not intend to permit the United States to be hampered in making its decisions by especial solicitude lest its actions displease one or the other, or both, of the combatants.

We do not wish the Japanese to entertain any impression that we look upon the Japanese course with less apprehension or disapproval than does the British Government or of condoning in any sense whatever the course which Japan is pursuing.

American public opinion has been outraged by the methods and strategy employed by the combatants, particularly by the Japanese military, and has become gradually more critical of Japan. Last week's events, particularly the circumstances of the Japanese shooting of the British Ambassador in China and the Japanese Prime Minister's statement that the representations of the powers are of little or no importance, have intensified this divergence from the standard of impartiality in popular feeling and thought. Tending to offset this somewhat has been, of course, the Chinese bombing of the liner *President Hoover*.

In addressing the authorities of either side, I do not intend calling names or making threats. I heartily approve of your tactful and dignified manner of conducting approaches to the Japanese Government. However, I wish the Japanese to understand fully that the United States Government is looking with thorough disapproval upon the present manifestation of Japanese foreign policy and upon the methods employed by the Japanese military in pursuit of that policy. I consider it desirable for you not to overlook any opportunity of impressing upon Japanese officials the importance attached by the United States Government to the principles laid down in my statement of July 16 and to the significance of my statement of August 23, and for you to suggest to Japanese officials that Japan, by the course it is pursuing, is destroying the good will of the world and is laying up for itself among the peoples of the world a liability of distrust, suspicion, popular antipathy, and potential ostracism, the liquidation of which would take many, many years of benevolent endeavor by Japan.

The Roosevelt Administration has not repudiated anything in the record of the efforts made on behalf of principles and of peace by the United States Government at the time of the Manchuria affair. We have in the present crisis endeavored to dissuade Japan and China from entering upon and from continuing hostilities; but mediation has not been offered. I am by no means certain that we wish to assume the responsibilities and role of a mediator. I would not desire, at least for the present, to encourage either side to believe or to expect that, after currently rejecting many American suggestions to exercise restraint, they may rely upon the United States Government serving them as a friendly broker whenever it suits their convenience. I would want both sides to feel that, should they desire good will and any form of impartial assistance from the United States, now is the time for evidence by them of appreciation of American policies and methods through being considerate of American legitimate interests and essential solicitudes.

NOTE from Joseph C. Grew, United States Ambassador to Japan, by instruction of the Department of State, to the Japanese Minister for Foreign Affairs (Koki Hirota), December 14, 1937

Department of State, *Press Releases,* December 18, 1937, p. 448

THE GOVERNMENT and people of the United States have been deeply shocked by the facts of the bombardment and sinking of the U.S.S. *Panay* and the sinking or burning of the American steamers *Meiping, Meian* and *Meisian* by Japanese aircraft.

The essential facts are that these American vessels were in the Yangtze River by uncontested and incontestable right; that they were flying the American flag; that they were engaged in their legitimate and appropriate business; that they were at the moment conveying American official and private personnel away from points where danger had developed; that they had several times changed their position, moving upriver, in order to avoid danger; and that they were attacked by Japanese bombing planes. With regard to the attack, a responsible Japanese naval officer at Shanghai has informed the Commander-in-Chief of the American Asiatic Fleet that the four vessels were proceeding upriver; that a Japanese plane endeavored to ascertain their nationality, flying at an altitude of three hundred meters, but was unable to distinguish the flags; that three Japanese bombing planes, six Japanese fighting planes, six Japanese bombing planes, and two Japanese bombing planes, in sequence, made attacks which resulted in the damaging of one of the American steamers, and the sinking of the U.S.S. *Panay* and the other two steamers.

Since the beginning of the present unfortunate hostilities between Japan and China, the Japanese Government and various Japanese authorities at various points have repeatedly assured the Government and authorities of the United States that it is the intention and purpose of the Japanese Government and the Japanese armed forces to respect fully the rights and interests of other powers. On several occasions, however, acts of Japanese armed forces have violated the rights of the United States, have seriously endangered the lives of American nationals, and have destroyed American property. In several instances, the Japanese Government has admitted the facts, has expressed regrets, and has given assurance that every precaution will be taken against recurrence of such incidents. In the present case, acts of Japanese armed forces have taken place in complete disregard of American rights, have taken American life, and have destroyed American property both public and private.

In these circumstances, the Government of the United States requests and expects of the Japanese Government a formally recorded expression of regret, an undertaking to make complete and comprehensive indemnifications; and an assurance that definite and specific steps have been taken which will ensure that hereafter American nationals, interests and property in China will not be subjected to attack by Japanese armed forces or unlawful interference by any Japanese authorities or forces whatsoever.

ANNOUNCEMENT Issued by the Department of State, April 22, 1938

Department of State, *Press Releases*, April 23, 1938, p. 504

THE American Ambassador to Japan, Mr. Joseph C. Grew, telegraphed the Department today that the American Embassy has received today from the Japanese Government a check for $2,214,007.36 covering indemnification for death and personal injury cases and for property losses sustained as a result of the attack upon the U.S.S. *Panay* and American merchant vessels on December 12, 1937.

NOTE from Joseph C. Grew, American Ambassador to Japan, to the Japanese Minister for Foreign Affairs (Hachiro Arita), December 30, 1938

Department of State, *Press Releases*, December 31, 1938, p. 490; *Foreign Relations of the United States: Japan, 1931–1941*, I, 820

EXCELLENCY,

Acting under the instructions of my Government, I have the honor to address Your Excellency the following note:

The Government of the United States has received and has given full consideration to the reply of the Japanese Government of November 18 to this Government's note of October 6 on the subject of American rights and interests in China.

In the light of facts and experience the Government of the United States is impelled to reaffirm its previously expressed opinion that imposition of restrictions upon the movements and activities of American nationals who are engaged in philanthropic, educational and commercial endeavors in China has placed and will, if continued, increasingly place Japanese interests in a preferred position and is, therefore, unquestionably discriminatory, in its effect, against legitimate American interests. Further, with reference to such matters as exchange control, compulsory currency circulation, tariff revision, and monopolistic promotion in certain areas of China, the plans and practices of the Japanese authorities imply an assumption on the part of those authorities that the Japanese Government or the regimes established and maintained in China by Japanese armed forces are entitled to act in China in a capacity such as flows from rights of sovereignty and, further, in so acting to disregard and even to declare nonexist or abrogated the established rights and interests of other countries, including the United States.

The Government of the United States expresses its conviction that the restrictions and measures under reference not only are unjust and unwarranted but are counter to the provisions of several binding international agreements, voluntarily entered into, to which both Japan and the United States, and in some cases other countries, are parties.

In the concluding portion of its note under reference, the Japanese Government states that it is firmly convinced that "in the face of the new situation, fast developing in East Asia, any attempt to apply to the conditions of today and tomorrow inapplicable ideas and principles of the past neither would contribute toward the establishment of a real peace in East Asia nor solve the immediate issues," and that "as long as these points are understood, Japan has not the slightest inclination to oppose the participation of the United States and other powers in the great work of reconstructing East Asia along all lines of industry and trade."

The Government of the United States in its note of October 6 requested, in view of the oft-reiterated assurances proffered by the Government of Japan of its intention to observe the principle of equality of opportunity in its relations with China, and in view of Japan's treaty obligations so to do, that the Government of Japan abide by these obligations and carry out these assurances in practice.

The Japanese Government in its reply appears to affirm that it is its intention to make its observance of that principle conditional upon an understanding by the American Government and by other governments of a "new situation" and a "new order" in the Far East as envisaged and fostered by Japanese authorities.

Treaties which bear upon the situation in the Far East have within them provisions relating to a number of subjects. In the making of those treaties, there was a process among the parties to them of give and take. Toward making possible the carrying out of some of their provisions, others among their provisions were formulated and agreed upon; toward gaining for itself the advantage of security in regard to certain matters, each of the parties committed itself to pledges of self-denial in regard to certain other matters. The various provisions agreed upon may be said to have constituted collectively an arrangement for safeguarding, for the benefit of all, the correlated principles on the one hand of national integrity and on the other hand of equality of economic opportunity. Experience has shown that impairment of the former of these principles is followed almost invariably by disregard of the latter. Whenever any government begins to exercise political authority in areas beyond the limits of its lawful jurisdiction there develops inevitably a situation in which the nationals of that government demand and are accorded, at the hands of their government, preferred treatment, whereupon equality of opportunity ceases to exist and discriminatory practices, productive of friction, prevail.

The admonition that enjoyment by the nationals of the United States of nondiscriminatory treatment in China—a general and well-established right—is henceforth to be contingent upon an admission by the Government of the United States of the validity of the conception of Japanese authorities of a "new situation" and a "new order" in East Asia, is, in the opinion of this Government, highly paradoxical.

This country's adherence to and its advocacy of the principle of equality of opportunity do not flow solely from a desire to obtain the commercial benefits which naturally result from the carrying out of that principle. They flow from a firm conviction that observance of that principle leads to economic and political stability, which are conducive both to the internal well-being of nations and to mutually beneficial and peaceful relationships between and among nations; from a firm conviction that failure to observe that principle breeds international friction and ill-will, with consequences injurious to all countries, including in particular those countries which fail to observe it; and from an equally firm conviction that observance of that principle promotes the opening of trade channels thereby making available the markets, the raw materials and the manufactured products of the community of nations on a mutually and reciprocally beneficial basis.

The principle of equality of economic opportunity is, moreover, one to which over a long period and on many occasions the Japanese Government has given definite approval. It is one to the observance of which the Japanese Government has committed itself in various international agreements and understandings. It is one upon observance of which by other nations the Japanese Government has of its own accord and upon its own initiative frequently insisted. It is one to which the Japanese Government has repeatedly during recent months declared itself committed.

The people and Government of the United States could not assent to the establishment, at the instance of and for the special purposes of any third country, of a regime which would arbitrarily deprive them of the long-established rights of equal opportunity and fair treatment which are legally and justly theirs along with those of other nations.

Fundamental principles, such as the principle of equality of opportunity, which have long been regarded as inherently wise and just, which have been widely adopted and adhered to, and which are general in their application, are not subject to nullification by a unilateral affirmation.

With regard to the implication in the Japanese Government's note that the "conditions of today and tomorrow" in the Far East call for a revision of the ideas and principles of the past, this Government desires to recall to the Japanese Government its position on the subject of revision of agreements.

This Government had occasion in the course of a communication delivered to the Japanese Government on April 29, 1934, to express its opinion that "treaties can lawfully be modified or be terminated, but only by processes prescribed or recognized or agreed upon by the parties to them."

In the same communication this Government also said, "In the opinion of the American people and the American Government no nation can, without the assent of the other nations concerned, rightfully endeavor to make conclusive its will in situations where there are involved the rights, the obligations and the legitimate interests of other sovereign states."

At various times during recent decades various powers, among which have been Japan and the United States, have had occasion to communicate and to confer with regard to situations and problems

RELATIONS WITH JAPAN

in the Far East. In the conducting of correspondence and of conferences relating to these matters, the parties involved have invariably taken into consideration past and present facts and they have not failed to perceive the possibility and the desirability of changes in the situation. In the making of treaties they have drawn up and have agreed upon provisions intended to facilitate advantageous developments and at the same time to obviate and avert the arising of friction between and among the various powers which, having interests in the region or regions under reference, were and would be concerned.

In the light of these facts, and with reference especially to the purpose and the character of the treaty provisions from time to time solemnly agreed upon for the very definite purposes indicated, the Government of the United States deprecates the fact that one of the parties to these agreements has chosen to embark—as indicated both by action of its agents and by official statements of its authorities—upon a course directed toward the arbitrary creation by that power by methods of its own selection, regardless of treaty pledges and the established rights of other powers concerned, of a "new order" in the Far East. Whatever may be the changes which have taken place in the situation in the Far East and whatever may be the situation now, these matters are of no less interest and concern to the American Government than have been the situations which have prevailed there in the past, and such changes as may henceforth take place there, changes which may enter into the producing of a "new situation" and a "new order," are and will be of like concern to this Government. This Government is well aware that the situation has changed. This Government is also well aware that many of the changes have been brought about by action of Japan. This Government does not admit, however, that there is need or warrant for any one power to take upon itself to prescribe what shall be the terms and conditions of a "new order" in areas not under its sovereignty and to constitute itself the repository of authority and the agent of destiny in regard thereto.

It is known to all the world that various of the parties to treaties concluded for the purpose of regulating contacts in the Far East and avoiding friction therein and therefrom—which treaties contained, for those purposes, various restrictive provisions—have from time to time and by processes of negotiation and agreement contributed, in the light of changed situations, toward the removal of restrictions and toward the bringing about of further developments which would warrant, in the light of further changes in the situation, further removals of restrictions. By such methods and processes, early restrictions upon the tariff autonomy of all countries in the Far East were removed. By such methods and processes, the rights of extraterritorial jurisdiction once enjoyed by occidental countries in relations with countries in the Far East have been given up in relations with all of those countries except China; and in the years immediately preceding and including the year 1931, countries which still possess those rights in China, including the United States, were actively engaged in negotiations—far advanced—looking toward surrender of those rights. All discerning and impartial observers have realized that the United States and other of the "treaty powers" have not during recent decades clung tenaciously to their so-called "special" rights and privileges in countries of the Far East but on the contrary have steadily encouraged the development in those countries of institutions and practices in the presence of which such rights and privileges may safely and readily be given up; and all observers have seen those rights and privileges gradually being surrendered voluntarily, through agreement, by the powers which have possessed them. On one point only has the Government of the United States, along with several other governments, insisted: namely, that new situations must have developed to a point warranting the removal of "special" safeguarding restrictions and that the removals be effected by orderly processes.

The Government of the United States has at all times regarded agreements as susceptible of alteration, but it has always insisted that alterations can rightfully be made only by orderly processes of negotiation and agreement among the parties thereto.

The Japanese Government has upon numerous occasions expressed itself as holding similar views.

The United States has in its international relations rights and obligations which derive from international law and rights and obligations which rest upon treaty provisions. Of those which rest upon treaty provisions, its rights and obligations in and with regard to China rest in part upon provisions in treaties between the United States and China, and in part upon provisions in treaties between the United States and several other powers, including both China and Japan. These treaties were concluded in good faith for the purpose of safeguarding and promoting the interests not of one only but of all of their signatories. The people and the Government of the United States cannot assent to the abrogation of any of this country's rights or obligations by the arbitrary action of agents or authorities of any other country.

The Government of the United States has, however, always been prepared, and is now, to give due and ample consideration to any proposals based on justice and reason which envisage the resolving of problems in a manner duly considerate of the rights and obligations of all parties directly concerned by processes of free negotiation and new commitment by and among all of the parties so concerned. There has been and there continues to be opportunity for the Japanese Government to put forward such proposals. This Government has been and continues to be willing to discuss such proposals, if and when put forward, with representatives of the other powers, including Japan and China, whose rights and interests are involved, at whatever time and in whatever place may be commonly agreed upon.

Meanwhile, this Government reserves all rights of the United States as they exist and does not give assent to any impairment of any of those rights.

TELEGRAM from Joseph C. Grew, American Ambassador to Japan, to the Secretary of State of the United States (Cordell Hull), May 18, 1939

Department of State, *Foreign Relations of the United States: Japan, 1931–1941*, II, 1

235. 1. Before departing tonight on leave and confiding the Embassy to the effective hands of Dooman in whose judgment and analytical ability I have full confidence and whose views on policy and procedure coincide very closely with mine, I wish to submit the following analysis of the political situation in Japan as I estimate it up to date.

2. In a long farewell conversation this morning with the Foreign Minister and in a talk which he had with Dooman yesterday, Arita said that the new agreement now under discussion with Germany and Italy will contain no military or political commitments except such as may apply directly to combating communistic activities. Japan desires to avoid European entanglements. Nevertheless, Japan regards the Soviet Government and the Comintern as identical and if Soviet Russia should become involved in a European war Japan herself might find it impossible to avoid involvement. If Great Britain and France conclude an alliance with Soviet Russia, Japan may be obliged to reconsider her position vis-à-vis the totalitarian states. Apart from the specific field of combating communistic activities, it will be the careful aim of Japan in every other field to maintain an attitude of strict neutrality between the democratic and totalitarian states.

Arita spoke with some bitterness of the efforts of Great Britain to draw Russia into a military alliance. It was all very well to say, as Craigie had said to him, that the proposed British plan would not be applicable in the Far East, but the fact is that Russia straddles both Europe and Asia; even if the British plan were specifically to exclude the Far East, the close association which it would bring about among Great Britain, France, and Russia would inevitably lead to the closest collaboration in the pursuit of their policies in the Far East. Japan, as before stated, has every desire to avoid involvement in every instance and to maintain a neutral position between the two groups, but if the British plan goes through and thus prepares a basis for concerted action in the Far East by the democracies, Japan would necessarily have to reconsider her position vis-à-vis Germany and Italy. In this connection, he went on to say that if war were to break out in Europe—and he believes that there is no immediate danger—and the United States becomes involved, the position which Russia might take might conceivably decide whether peace could be maintained between the United States and Japan.

3. The Minister made to me the following confidential oral statement:

Japan is bound to Germany and Italy by the tie of anti-communism and as we deem it necessary, further strengthening of this bond is being seriously considered. But if any one should regard Japan, because she had taken such a measure, as joining into the camp of totalitarian nations in opposition to the democratic nations, he would surely be misunderstanding the true intention of the Japanese Government. Japan is not a totalitarian, no more than a democratic, state. She has an original constitution of her own which is centered around the Imperial family, and is based on the spirit of levying [allowing?] everything to have its own proper place, surpassing all ideas of antagonism. In joining hands with Germany and Italy we have no other purposes than to combat the destructive activities of Comintern. If the United States, not understanding the true intention of Japan on this point, should base her future policies on such misunderstanding, it would bring about a deplorable situation not only respecting the relations between the United States and Japan but also in respect of the peace of the world.

4. Arita said to me, and I believe his statement to be accurate, that there is now no substantial opposition in the Government to the proposed arrangement with Germany and Italy as now formulated. At the present moment the Cabinet appears to have weathered the recent storm and to be momentarily secure. I do not, however, believe that this present security can be regarded as permanent because [of] many divergent forces active within the country.

5. In my conversation with the Foreign Minister I then turned to the question of America's legitimate rights and interests in China

which are now subject to serious interference by Japan and I stated that Japanese-American relations could not be expected to improve until these interferences were removed. I also emphasized the deplorable effects of the bombing operations. What might I tell my Government on these points?

6. The Minister's reply was ambiguous and vague. He said that most of the interferences of which we complained were temporary and would disappear as military necessity permitted but that certain measures, such as exchange control in North China, might be permanent. There is no intention, he said, to limit American trade beyond the requirements of military necessity or to discriminate against American commerce. There is also no intention to take over the International Settlements in Shanghai or Kulangsu but greater cooperation on the part of the Settlement authorities is hoped for. In connection with the general question of economic rights and interests in China, he said that the feeling of resentment in this country against Great Britain is so strong that it was hopeless to try to improve relations with that country. He would be satisfied if his efforts were successful to prevent these relations from becoming worse than they now are. The position with regard to relations with the United States was an entirely different one, as there is a general call for improvement. He was making a strong effort along those lines and hoped to be able to show concrete results before long.

7. The Minister then made to me the following confidential oral statement:

I have previously stated frankly my opinion regarding the new order in East Asia and we have had occasions of exchanging views on this question. However, I regret to say that Japan's position does not seem to have been fully understood.

I wish to take this opportunity to emphasize once again that the Japanese Government in establishing the new order have no intention of excluding trade and other legitimate economic activities in China of the countries of Europe and America. The establishment of a new order is not exclusive in character as is thought in some quarters, but is the means by which trade and other economic relations between East Asia and the European and American countries will eventually prosper on a sound basis.

As Japan is now carrying on large-scale military operations, and has only recently embarked upon the undertaking of realizing the ideal of the establishment of a new order, the military or economic necessity require some measures which may cause inconveniences to nationals of the third powers and affect their rights and interests. But, since such measures are, as a rule, exceptional and temporary in character, any judgment formed on the basis of the present abnormal conditions is apt to lead to misunderstanding of the real intention of Japan. Such an outcome is much to be regretted as being likely to disturb the foundation of the relations between

Japan and the United States, the two countries which should always remain friendly to each other. Therefore it is earnestly desired that, in dealing with various questions arising between our two countries with regard to China, the United States will understand that large-scale military operations are in progress over an extremely wide area and will at the same time consider the new situation in East Asia on a broader perspective so that she will arrive at a balanced judgment.

He amplified this statement by reverting to one of his favorite themes: National defense has an economic as well as a military aspect. The United States is well equipped in both respects; however, while Japan has an army and navy strong enough to meet any military threat, her economic defense is inadequate; and she cannot enjoy a sense of security until the deficiencies in the latter respect have been made good.

8. The Minister on his own initiative then turned to the subject of the so-called "South Sea advance" and made to me the following confidential oral statement:

We understand that, since the military occupation of Hainan Island by Japan and the placing of the Sinnan Gunto (Spratly Islands) under the jurisdiction of the Formosan Government General, rumors have spread, giving the impression as though Japan entertained some territorial designs toward the South Seas; that as a result certain interested countries are apprehensive, and that even some Americans have a similar apprehension with regard to the Philippines. The Japanese Government consider it regrettable from the standpoint of Japanese-American friendship that such apprehension has been aroused. They are, therefore prepared, if the United States Government should desire that some step be taken by the Japanese Government for the purpose of dispelling such apprehension, to enter into conversation with the United States Government.

Cipher texts by mail to Shanghai, Chungking, Peiping.

NOTE from Cordell Hull, Secretary of State, to the Japanese Ambassador (Kensuke Horinouchi), July 26, 1939

Department of State, *Foreign Relations of the United States: Japan, 1931–1941*, II, 189

Excellency:
During recent years the Government of the United States has been examining the treaties of commerce and navigation in force between the United States and foreign countries with a view to determining what changes may need to be made toward better serving the purposes for which such treaties are concluded. In the course of this sur-

vey, the Government of the United States has come to the conclusion that the Treaty of Commerce and Navigation between the United States and Japan which was signed at Washington on February 21, 1911, contains provisions which need new consideration. Toward preparing the way for such consideration and with a view to better safeguarding and promoting American interests as new developments may require, the Government of the United States, acting in accordance with the procedure prescribed in Article XVII of the treaty under reference, gives notice hereby of its desire that this treaty be terminated, and, having thus given notice, will expect the treaty, together with its accompanying protocol, to expire six months from this date.

MEMORANDUM of Cordell Hull, Secretary of State, Regarding a Conversation with the Japanese Ambassador to the United States (Kensuke Horinouchi), August 26, 1939

Department of State, *Peace and War*, p. 480

THE AMBASSADOR of Japan called at his own request. He proceeded to refer to the reports, already published in the American press, to the effect that American officials were incorrectly attributing anti-American movements and demonstrations in China to Japanese officials or to their influence in thus instigating the Chinese. The Ambassador handed me the attached paper, which I proceeded to read. I thanked him for the attention his Government had given to this matter and the spirit seemingly prompting his Government to seek to clear it up.

I then said that, having seen in the American press the purpose and nature of his contemplated call on me, I had requested the Far Eastern Division to jot down a list of instances of transgressions by Japanese or due to Japanese influence in China to the detriment and injury of Americans and of American interests. I added that this list of incidents had not been elaborated but that I would proceed to read them. I then read the memorandum prepared by the Far Eastern Division, attached hereto and marked "A." The Ambassador appeared somewhat surprised and at a loss for further comment with regard to this paper. He said he would be pleased to have a copy of it. I replied that I would be glad to request the Far Eastern Division to put it in more elaborate form if possible and to send a copy to him at the Japanese Embassy.

The Ambassador then said that, speaking personally, he might say his Government on yesterday had decided to abandon any further negotiations with Germany and Italy relative to closer relations under the anti-Comintern Pact to which they have been parties for some time. He added that the change in affairs in Europe made this course manifest, and, furthermore, it was plain that his Government would find it important to adopt new foreign policy in more or less respects. I might say that he prefaced this general reference to his country by reiterating his personal desire to clear up any misunderstandings or differences between our two countries and to restore the friendly relations heretofore existing. The Ambassador remarked that he hoped there might come about an adjustment of the Japanese-Chinese situation. He just made this general observation and then he passed on to inquire what I knew or thought about the European situation.

I replied that it was very kaleidoscopic; that just now no one could with any satisfaction predict about developments from day to day; that at this time today the British Cabinet was considering the conversation between Mr. Hitler and the British Ambassador at Berlin on yesterday; that no one knows what their decision may be.

I then referred to his comment about Japan and her purpose to adopt a new foreign policy, and I made observations substantially as follows:

The principles and practices of American policy in regard to the world in general and the Far East in particular are well known to all governments everywhere.

During recent years Japanese authorities and/or agencies have been pursuing courses which come into direct conflict with those principles and policies and which involve disregard of principles of international law and of treaties between the United States and Japan and also multilateral treaties to which the United States and Japan are parties.

The United States has made representations over and over and over again in objection to or protest against overt acts of these types. The Japanese Government has given assurances over and over again that it has regard for the principles and the rules and the provisions involved and that it will show its regard for them,—and over and over Japanese authorities have immediately committed other acts in disregard thereof.

We have clear evidence of inspiration by Japanese authorities of action by agencies thereof hostile not only to occidental nationals and interests in general but to American nationals and interests in particular. These courses of action by Japanese have resulted in arousing against Japan feelings of suspicion and attitudes of opposition on the part of almost all of the other powers which have interests in the Far East, especially in China, including the United States.

It should be evident to Japan that there is something wrong with policies and practices on the part of one nation which arouse antagonism on the part of almost all other nations in contact with that nation.

The United States wishes to have amicable relations with every other country in the world. We have in the past had very friendly relations with every country in the Far East, including Japan. Our policy is a policy of "Live and let live." We seek nowhere any special position; but we seek everywhere equality of opportunity under conditions of fair treatment and security.

The world is being given today new object lessons with regard to the futility of policies wherein nations plan to take advantage of other nations by use of armed force in disregard of moral principles and legal principles and generally accepted axioms of friendly and profitable general international intercourse.

The future of American-Japanese relations lies largely in the hands of Japan. American policy is a policy of friendliness and fair dealing toward all nations. It will not change.

The Ambassador seemed appreciative and this ended the conversation.

STATEMENT by Cordell Hull, Secretary of State, March 30, 1940

Issued in response to inquiries with regard to the attitude and position of the United States Government in the light of the setting up at Nanking of a new regime. Department of State, *Bulletin,* March 30, 1940, p. 343

IN THE LIGHT of what has happened in various parts of China since 1931, the setting up of a new regime at Nanking has the appearance of a further step in a program of one country by armed force to impose its will upon a neighboring country and to block off a large area of the world from normal political and economic relationships with the rest of the world. The developments there appear to be following the pattern of other regimes and systems which have been set up in China under the aegis of an outside power and which in their functioning especially favor the interests of that outside power and deny to nationals of the United States and other third countries enjoyment of long-established rights of equal and fair treatment which are legally and justly theirs.

The Government of the United States has noted statements of high officials of that outside power that their country intends to respect the political independence and the freedom of the other country and that with the development of affairs in East Asia this intention will be demonstrated. To this Government the circumstances, both military and diplomatic, which have attended the setting up of the new regime at Nanking do not seem consistent with such an intention.

The attitude of the United States toward use of armed force as an instrument of national policy is well known. Its attitude and position with regard to various aspects of the situation in the Far East have been made clear on numerous occasions. That attitude and position remain unchanged.

This Government again makes full reservation of this country's rights under international law and existing treaties and agreements.

Twelve years ago the Government of the United States recognized, as did other governments, the National Government of the Republic of China. The Government of the United States has ample reason for believing that that Government, with capital now at Chungking, has had and still has the allegiance and support of the great majority of the Chinese people. The Government of the United States of course continues to recognize that Government as the Government of China.

ADDRESS by Sumner Welles, Under Secretary of State, "Our Foreign Policy and National Defense," at Cleveland, September 28, 1940

Department of State, *Foreign Relations of the United States: Japan, 1931–1941*, II, 112; excerpt

UNFORTUNATELY it is not possible for me to refer with any measure of satisfaction to the course of events in the Far East during these past seven years.

The policy of this Government in the Far East has differed in no way from the policies of this country in relation to other regions of the world. It is true, of course, that the problems which have arisen in our relations with the countries of the Far East have had certain peculiarities because of the earlier rights of extraterritorial jurisdiction accorded to the nationals of occidental powers, along with various other special procedures adopted with special reference to special situations, but as situations have changed, the United States has by processes of negotiation and agreement voluntarily assented to the alteration and removal of these special features.

From time to time the nations directly interested in the Far East have entered into treaties and international agreements which have created a network of common interests, as well as common responsibilities and obligations.

In essence the primary requirements of the United States in the Far East may be thus simply set forth: Complete respect by all powers for the legitimate rights of the United States and of its nationals as stipulated by existing treaties or as provided by the generally accepted tenets of international law; equality of opportunity for the trade of all nations; and, finally, respect for those international agreements or treaties concerning the Far East to which the United States is a party, although with the expressed understanding that the United States is always willing to consider the peaceful negotiation of such modifications or changes in these agreements or treaties as may in the judgment of the signatories be considered necessary in the light of changed conditions.

The Government of Japan, however, has declared that it intends to create a "new order in Asia." In this endeavor it has relied upon the instrumentality of armed force, and it has made it very clear that it intends that it alone shall decide to what extent the historic interests of the United States and the treaty rights of American citizens in the Far East are to be observed.

As we here well know, many hundreds of incidents have occurred as a result of which the rights of this country and the rights of our nationals have been violated.

On April 15 of this year, as a result of developments in the European war, the Foreign Minister of Japan, in a public statement, asserted that Japan desired the maintenance of the *status quo* of the Netherlands East Indies. On April 17 the Secretary of State made a statement on behalf of the United States expressing the belief of this Government that the best interests of all nations called for maintenance of the *status quo* in the entire Pacific area. On repeated occasions since then official spokesmen for the Japanese Government have reiterated their desire for the maintenance of the present status of the Netherlands East Indies, and have further specifically declared that this policy applied not only to the Netherlands East Indies, but to French Indochina as well. Nevertheless, and notwithstanding these official declarations, we are all familiar with the events of the past week which have culminated in measures undertaken by the Japanese military forces which threaten the integrity of the French colony.

From the standpoint of reason, of common sense, and of the best practical interests of all of the powers possessing interests in the Far East, there is no problem presented which could not be peacefully solved through negotiation, provided there existed a sincere desire on the part of all concerned to find an equitable and a fair solution which would give just recognition to the rights and to the real needs of all concerned.

MEMORANDUM of Cordell Hull, Secretary of State, Regarding a Conversation with the Japanese Ambassador to the United States (Kensuke Horinouchi), October 8, 1940

Department of State, *Peace and War*, p. 576; excerpts

The Japanese Ambassador called at his request. He first expressed his regret at the unsatisfactory relations existing between our two countries at this time. I replied that, in my opinion, this was not the fault of the Ambassador and myself, who have been untiring in our efforts to promote and preserve satisfactory relations between the United States and Japan.

The Ambassador then said that he was instructed by his Government to hand me a note dated October 7, 1940, . . . relative to our scrap iron and steel embargo which was recently proclaimed.

He read a statement . . . in support of the note mentioned above.

I replied to the effect that I would see what sort of written reply, if any, might be called for.

I then said that I might at this time, and without delay, state that this Government at all times must determine for itself such internal questions as those material to our program of national defense, as we are doing in the instant case, and that it would be impossible for any country engaged in the serious and urgent undertaking of carrying out a program of national defense to allow every other outside nation to come in and pass upon the question of our needs of given commodities; that the embargo, as the Ambassador knows, applies to all nations except Great Britain and the Western Hemisphere. I remarked that for some years this Government had been criticized for not imposing numerous embargoes, primarily from the standpoint of safety and national defense and peace, and that it was only at the height of our national defense preparations that we were imposing a few embargoes on important commodities.

I said that it was really amazing for the Government of Japan, which has been violating in the most aggravating manner valuable

American rights and interests throughout most of China, and is doing so in many instances every day, to question the fullest privilege of this Government from every standpoint to impose the proposed scrap iron and steel embargo, and that to go still further and call it an unfriendly act was still more amazing in the light of the conduct of the Japanese Government in disregarding all law, treaty obligations and other rights and privileges and the safety of Americans while it proceeded at the same time to seize territory by force to an ever-increasing extent. I stated that of all the countries with which I have had to deal during the past eight years, the Government of Japan has the least occasion or excuse to accuse this Government of an unfriendly act. I concluded with the statement that apparently the theory of the Japanese Government is for all other nations to acquiesce cheerfully in all injuries inflicted upon their citizens by the Japanese policy of force and conquest, accompanied by every sort of violence, unless they are to run the risk of being guilty of an unfriendly act. . . .

The Ambassador undertook to repeat the old line of talk about how fair Japan proposed to be with respect to all rights and privileges of foreign nations within its conquered territory. He agreed that no purpose would be served now to go over the many conversations we have had with respect to these matters. . . .

I reiterated the view that it was unheard of for one country engaged in aggression and seizure of another country, contrary to all law and treaty provisions, to turn to a third peacefully disposed nation and seriously insist that it would be guilty of an unfriendly act if it should not cheerfully provide some of the necessary implements of war to aid the aggressor nation in carrying out its policy of invasion. I made it clear that it is the view of this Government that two nations, one in Europe and one in Asia, are undertaking to subjugate both of their respective areas of the world, and to place them on an international order and on a social basis resembling that of 750 years ago. In the face of this world movement, extending itself from day to day, peaceful and interested nations are to be held up to denunciation and threats if they dare to engage in any lawful acts or utterances in opposition to such wide movements of world conquest.

The Ambassador had little to say. He said virtually nothing in attempted extenuation except that his Government would expect everybody to receive considerate and fair treatment throughout the conquered areas. He emphasized equal treatment, and I replied that when the best interests of other nations in peace and law and order were being destroyed, it was not a matter of any concern as to whether there was discrimination between the nations which were victims of such movements.

STATEMENT Issued by the White House, December 10, 1940

The New York Times, December 11, 1940

THE PRESIDENT announced today that national defense requirements for iron and steel have increased to such an extent that it has become necessary to subject, as of December 30, 1940, iron ore, pig iron, ferro alloys, and certain iron and steel manufacturers and semi-manufactures to the licensing requirement. Licenses will be granted for exports to the British Empire and the Western Hemisphere; and for the present, so far as the interests of the national defense permit, for exports to other destinations in quantities approximating usual or prewar exports.

STATEMENT by Cordell Hull, Secretary of State, before the Foreign Affairs Committee of the House of Representatives, January 15, 1941

Department of State, *Foreign Relations of the United States: Japan, 1931–1941,* II, 131; excerpt

WE ARE HERE to consider a bill designed to promote the defense of the United States. I shall not discuss the technical details of the proposed measure, since that will be done by other departments of the Government more directly concerned with these matters. I shall place before you briefly the controlling facts relating to the manner in which the dangers that now confront this Hemisphere and, therefore, this nation have arisen, and the circumstances which render imperative all possible speed in our preparation for meeting these dangers.

During the past eight years, our Government has striven, by every peaceful means at its disposal, to secure the establishment in the world of conditions under which there would be a reasonable hope for enduring peace. We have proceeded in the firm belief that only if such conditions come to exist will there be a certainty that our country will be fully secure and safely at peace. The establishment of such conditions calls for acceptance and application by all nations of certain basic principles of peaceful and orderly international conduct and relations.

Accordingly, in the conduct of our foreign relations, this Government has directed its efforts to the following objectives: (1) Peace and security for the United States with advocacy of peace and limitation and reduction of armament as universal international objectives; (2) support for law, order, justice, and morality and the principle of non-intervention; (3) restoration and cultivation of sound economic methods and relations, based on equality of treatment; (4) development, in the promotion of these objectives, of the fullest practicable measure of international cooperation; (5) promotion of the security, solidarity, and general welfare of the Western Hemisphere.

Observance and advocacy of the basic principles underlying these policies, and efforts toward their acceptance and application, became increasingly important as three nations, one after another, made abundantly clear, by word and by deed, their determination to repudiate and destroy the very foundations of a civilized world order under law and to enter upon the road of armed conquest, of subjugation of other nations, and of tyrannical rule over their victims.

The first step in this fatal direction occurred in the Far East in 1931 with forceful occupation of Manchuria in contravention of the provisions of the Nine Power Treaty and of the Kellogg-Briand Pact. The equilibrium in the Far East which had been established by the Washington Conference treaties of 1921–1922 became seriously disturbed by the setting up by forceful means in a part of China of a regime under Japanese control under the name of "Manchukuo." This control over Manchuria has been marked by the carrying out of a policy of discrimination which has resulted in forcing out American and other foreign interests.

During the years that followed, Japan went steadily forward in her preparations for expansion by force of arms. In December 1934, she gave notice of her intention to terminate the naval treaty of February 6, 1922. She then proceeded with intensified construction of military and naval armaments, at the same time undertaking, from time to time, limited actions directed toward an extension of her domination over China and involving disregard and destruction of the lawful rights and interests of other countries, including the United States.

In July 1937, the armed forces of Japan embarked upon large-scale military operations against China. Invading forces of more than a million men occupied large areas along the seaboard and in the central provinces. In these areas there were set up puppet regimes which instituted systems of controls and monopolies discriminatory in favor of the interests of the invading country.

It has been clear throughout that Japan has been actuated from the start by broad and ambitious plans for establishing herself in a dominant position in the entire region of the Western Pacific. Her leaders have openly declared their determination to achieve and maintain that position by force of arms and thus to make themselves masters of an area containing almost one half of the entire population of the world. As a consequence, they would have arbitrary control of the sea and trade routes in that region.

Previous experience and current developments indicate that the proposed "new order" in the Pacific area means, politically, domination by one country. It means, economically, employment of the resources of the area concerned for the benefit of that country and to the ultimate impoverishment of other parts of the area and exclusion of the interests of other countries. It means, socially, the destruction of personal liberties and the reduction of the conquered peoples to the role of inferiors.

It should be manifest to every person that such a program for the subjugation and ruthless exploitation by one country of nearly one half of the population of the world is a matter of immense significance, importance, and concern to every other nation wherever located.

Notwithstanding the course which Japan has followed during recent years, this Government has made repeated efforts to persuade the Japanese Government that her best interests lie in the development of friendly relations with the United States and with other countries which believe in orderly and peaceful processes among nations. We have at no time made any threats.

[The remainder of the statement deals with conditions resulting from the European War.]

TELEGRAM from Joseph C. Grew, American Ambassador to Japan, to the Secretary of State of the United States (Cordell Hull), January 27, 1941

Department of State, *Peace and War*, p. 618; paraphrase

125. A member of the Embassy was told by my —— colleague that from many quarters, including a Japanese one, he had heard that a surprise mass attack on Pearl Harbor was planned by the Japanese military forces, in case of "trouble" between Japan and the United States; that the attack would involve the use of all the Japanese military facilities. My colleague said that he was prompted to pass this on because it had come to him from many sources, although the plan seemed fantastic.

STATEMENT by Sumner Welles, Acting Secretary of State, July 24, 1941, in Response to Inquiries by Press Correspondents Regarding the Japanese Military Démarche in Indo-China

Department of State, *Bulletin*, July 26, 1941, p. 71

It will be recalled that in 1940 the Japanese Government gave expression on several occasions to its desire that conditions of disturbance should not spread to the region of the Pacific, with special references to the Netherlands East Indies and French Indochina. This desire was expressly concurred in by many other governments, including the Government of the United States. In statements by this Government, it was made clear that any alteration in the existing status of such areas by other than peaceful processes could not but be prejudicial to the security and peace of the entire Pacific area and that this conclusion was based on a doctrine which has universal application.

On September 23, 1940, referring to the events then rapidly happening in the Indochina situation, the Secretary of State stated that it seemed obvious that the existing situation was being upset and that the changes were being achieved under duress. Present developments relating to Indochina provide clear indication that further changes are now being effected under duress.

The present unfortunate situation in which the French Government of Vichy and the French Government of Indochina find themselves is, of course, well known. It is only too clear that they are in no position to resist the pressure exercised upon them.

There is no doubt as to the attitude of the Government and people of the United States toward acts of aggression carried out by use or threat of armed force. That attitude has been made abundantly clear.

By the course which it has followed and is following in regard to Indochina, the Japanese Government is giving clear indication that it is determined to pursue an objective of expansion by force or threat of force.

There is not apparent to the Government of the United States any valid ground upon which the Japanese Government would be warranted in occupying Indochina or establishing bases in that area as measures of self-defense.

There is not the slightest ground for belief on the part of even the most credulous that the Governments of the United States, of Great Britain, or of the Netherlands have any territorial ambitions in Indochina or have been planning any moves which could have been regarded as threats to Japan. This Government can, therefore, only conclude that the action of Japan is undertaken because of the estimated value to Japan of bases in that region primarily for purposes of further and more obvious movements of conquest in adjacent areas.

In the light of previous developments, steps such as are now being taken by the Government of Japan endanger the peaceful use by peaceful nations of the Pacific. They tend to jeopardize the procurement by the United States of essential materials such as tin and rubber which are necessary for the normal economy of this country and the consummation of our defense program. The purchase of tin, rubber, oil, or other raw materials in the Pacific area on equal terms with other nations requiring these materials has never been denied to Japan. The steps which the Japanese Government has taken also endanger the safety of other areas of the Pacific, including the Philippine Islands.

The Government and people of this country fully realize that such developments bear directly upon the vital problem of our national security.

STATEMENT Issued by the White House, July 25, 1941

Department of State, *Bulletin,* July 26, 1941, p. 73

IN VIEW OF the unlimited national emergency declared by the President, he issued, on July 25, an Executive order freezing Japanese assets in the United States in the same manner in which assets of various European countries were frozen on June 14, 1941. This measure, in effect, brings all financial and import and export trade transactions in which Japanese interests are involved under the control of the Government and imposes criminal penalties for violation of the order.

This Executive order, just as the order of June 14, 1941, is designed among other things to prevent the use of the financial facilities of the United States and trade between Japan and the United States in ways harmful to national defense and American interests, to prevent the liquidation in the United States of assets obtained by duress or conquest, and to curb subversive activities in the United States.

At the specific request of Generalissimo Chiang Kai-shek, and for the purpose of helping the Chinese Government, the President has, at the same time, extended the freezing control to Chinese assets in the United States. The administration of the licensing system with respect to Chinese assets will be conducted with a view to strengthening the foreign trade and exchange position of the Chinese Government. The inclusion of China in the Executive order, in accordance with the wishes of the Chinese Government, is a continuation of this Government's policy of assisting China.

COMMUNICATION Presented by Cordell Hull, Secretary of State, to the Japanese Ambassador to the United States (Admiral Kichisaburo Nomura), November 26, 1941

Department of State, *Bulletin*, December 13, 1941, p. 461

ORAL
Strictly confidential
November 26, 1941.

The representatives of the Government of the United States and of the Government of Japan have been carrying on during the past several months informal and exploratory conversations for the purpose of arriving at a settlement if possible of questions relating to the entire Pacific area based upon the principles of peace, law and order and fair dealing among nations. These principles include the principle of inviolability of territorial integrity and sovereignty of each and all nations; the principle of non-interference in the internal affairs of other countries; the principle of equality, including equality of commercial opportunity and treatment; and the principle of reliance upon international cooperation and conciliation for the prevention and pacific settlement of controversies and for improvement of international conditions by peaceful methods and processes.

It is believed that in our discussions some progress has been made in reference to the general principles which constitute the basis of a peaceful settlement covering the entire Pacific area. Recently the Japanese Ambassador has stated that the Japanese Government is desirous of continuing the conversations directed toward a comprehensive and peaceful settlement in the Pacific area; that it would be helpful toward creating an atmosphere favorable to the successful outcome of the conversations if a temporary *modus vivendi* could be agreed upon to be in effect while the conversations looking to a peaceful settlement in the Pacific were continuing. On November 20 the Japanese Ambassador communicated to the Secretary of State proposals in regard to temporary measures to be taken respectively by the Government of Japan and by the Government of the United States, which measures are understood to have been designed to accomplish the purposes above indicated.

The Government of the United States most earnestly desires to contribute to the promotion and maintenance of peace and stability in the Pacific area, and to afford every opportunity for the continuance of discussions with the Japanese Government directed toward working out a broad-gauge program of peace throughout the Pacific area. The proposals which were presented by the Japanese Ambassador on November 20 contain some features which, in the opinion of this Government, conflict with the fundamental principles which form a part of the general settlement under consideration and to which each Government has declared that it is committed. The Government of the United States believes that the adoption of such proposals would not be likely to contribute to the ultimate objectives of ensuring peace under law, order and justice in the Pacific area, and it suggests that further effort be made to resolve our divergences of views in regard to the practical application of the fundamental principles already mentioned.

With this object in view the Government of the United States offers for the consideration of the Japanese Government a plan of a broad but simple settlement covering the entire Pacific area as one practical exemplification of a program which this Government envisages as something to be worked out during our further conversations.

The plan therein suggested represents an effort to bridge the gap between our draft of June 21, 1941 and the Japanese draft of September 25 by making a new approach to the essential problems underlying a comprehensive Pacific settlement. This plan contains provisions dealing with the practical application of the fundamental principles which we have agreed in our conversations constitute the only sound basis for worthwhile international relations. We hope that in this way progress toward reaching a meeting of minds between our two Governments may be expedited.

*Strictly confidential, tentative
and without commitment*

November 26, 1941.

Outline of Proposed Basis for Agreement Between the United States and Japan

Section I

Draft Mutual Declaration of Policy

The Government of the United States and the Government of Japan both being solicitous for the peace of the Pacific affirm that

RELATIONS WITH JAPAN

their national policies are directed toward lasting and extensive peace throughout the Pacific area, that they have no territorial designs in that area, that they have no intention of threatening other countries or of using military force aggressively against any neighboring nation, and that, accordingly, in their national policies they will actively support and give practical application to the following fundamental principles upon which their relations with each other and with all other governments are based:

(1) The principle of inviolability of territorial integrity and sovereignty of each and all nations.

(2) The principle of non-interference in the internal affairs of other countries.

(3) The principle of equality, including equality of commercial opportunity and treatment.

(4) The principle of reliance upon international cooperation and conciliation for the prevention and pacific settlement of controversies and for improvement of international conditions by peaceful methods and processes.

The Government of Japan and the Government of the United States have agreed that toward eliminating chronic political instability, preventing recurrent economic collapse, and providing a basis for peace, they will actively support and practically apply the following principles in their economic relations with each other and with other nations and peoples:

(1) The principle of non-discrimination in international commercial relations.

(2) The principle of international economic cooperation and abolition of extreme nationalism as expressed in excessive trade restrictions.

(3) The principle of non-discriminatory access by all nations to raw material supplies.

(4) The principle of full protection of the interests of consuming countries and populations as regards the operation of international commodity agreements.

(5) The principle of establishment of such institutions and arrangements of international finance as may lend aid to the essential enterprises and the continuous development of all countries and may permit payments through processes of trade consonant with the welfare of all countries.

Section II

Steps To Be Taken by the Government of the United States and by the Government of Japan

The Government of the United States and the Government of Japan propose to take steps as follows:

1. The Government of the United States and the Government of Japan will endeavor to conclude a multilateral non-aggression pact among the British Empire, China, Japan, the Netherlands, the Soviet Union, Thailand and the United States.

2. Both Governments will endeavor to conclude among the American, British, Chinese, Japanese, the Netherland and Thai Governments an agreement whereunder each of the Governments would pledge itself to respect the territorial integrity of French Indochina and, in the event that there should develop a threat to the territorial integrity of Indochina, to enter into immediate consultation with a view to taking such measures as may be deemed necessary and advisable to meet the threat in question. Such agreement would provide also that each of the Governments party to the agreement would not seek or accept preferential treatment in its trade or economic relations with Indochina and would use its influence to obtain for each of the signatories equality of treatment in trade and commerce with French Indochina.

3. The Government of Japan will withdraw all military, naval, air and police forces from China and from Indochina.

4. The Government of the United States and the Government of Japan will not support—militarily, politically, economically—any government or regime in China other than the National Government of the Republic of China with capital temporarily at Chungking.

5. Both Governments will give up all extraterritorial rights in China, including rights and interests in and with regard to international settlements and concessions, and rights under the Boxer Protocol of 1901.

Both Governments will endeavor to obtain the agreement of the British and other governments to give up extraterritorial rights in China, including rights in international settlements and in concessions and under the Boxer Protocol of 1901.

6. The Government of the United States and the Government of Japan will enter into negotiations for the conclusion between the United States and Japan of a trade agreement, based upon reciprocal most-favored-nation treatment and reduction of trade barriers by both countries, including an undertaking by the United States to bind raw silk on the free list.

7. The Government of the United States and the Government of Japan will, respectively, remove the freezing restrictions on Japanese funds in the United States and on American funds in Japan.

8. Both Governments will agree upon a plan for the stabilization of the dollar-yen rate, with the allocation of funds adequate for this purpose, half to be supplied by Japan and half by the United States.

9. Both Governments will agree that no agreement which either has concluded with any third power or powers shall be interpreted by it in such a way as to conflict with the fundamental purpose of this agreement, the establishment and preservation of peace throughout the Pacific area.

10. Both Governments will use their influence to cause other governments to adhere to and to give practical application to the basic political and economic principles set forth in this agreement.

STATEMENT by President Franklin D. Roosevelt, Handed by Sumner Welles, Under Secretary of State, to the Japanese Ambassador (Admiral Kichisaburo Nomura) and the Japanese Special Representative (Saburo Kurusu), December 2, 1941

Department of State, *Foreign Relations of the United States: Japan, 1931–1941*, II, 778

I HAVE RECEIVED reports during the past days of continuing Japanese troop movements to southern Indochina. These reports indicate a very rapid and material increase in the forces of all kinds stationed by Japan in Indochina.

It was my clear understanding that by the terms of the agreement —and there is no present need to discuss the nature of that agreement—between Japan and the French Government at Vichy that the total number of Japanese forces permitted by the terms of that agreement to be stationed in Indochina was very considerably less than the total amount of the forces already there.

The stationing of these increased Japanese forces in Indochina would seem to imply the utilization of these forces by Japan for purposes of further aggression, since no such number of forces could possibly be required for the policing of that region. Such aggression could conceivably be against the Philippine Islands; against the many islands of the East Indies; against Burma; against Malaya or either through coercion or through the actual use of force for the purpose of undertaking the occupation of Thailand. Such new aggression would, of course, be additional to the acts of aggression already undertaken against China, our attitude towards which is well known, and has been repeatedly stated to the Japanese Government.

Please be good enough to request the Japanese Ambassador and Ambassador Kurusu to inquire at once of the Japanese Government what the actual reasons may be for the steps already taken, and what I am to consider is the policy of the Japanese Government as demonstrated by this recent and rapid concentration of troops in Indochina. This Government has seen in the last few years in Europe a policy on the part of the German Government which has involved a constant and steady encroachment upon the territory and rights of free and independent peoples through the utilization of military steps of the same character. It is for that reason and because of the broad problem of American defense that I should like to know the intention of the Japanese Government.

MEMORANDUM of a Conversation between Cordell Hull, Secretary of State, the Japanese Ambassador (Admiral Kichisaburo Nomura), and the Japanese Special Representative (Saburo Kurusu), December 5, 1941

Department of State, *Foreign Relations of the United States: Japan, 1931–1941*, II, 781

THE JAPANESE Ambassador and Mr. Kurusu called at their request at the Department. The Ambassador handed to the Secretary a paper which he said was the Japanese Government's reply to the Presidents inquiry in regard to Japanese troops in French Indochina. The paper reads as follows:

[Here follows text of the statement.]

The Secretary read the paper and asked whether the Japanese considered that the Chinese were liable to attack them in Indochina. He said, so Japan has assumed the defensive against China. He said that he had heard that the Chinese are contending that their massing troops in Yunnan was in answer to Japan's massing troops in Indochina. Mr. Kurusu said that that is all that they have received from their Government in regard to this matter. The Ambassador said that as the Chinese were eager to defend the Burma Road he felt that the possibility of a Chinese attack in Indochina as a means of preventing Japan's attacking the Burma Road from Indochina could not be excluded.

The Secretary said that he had understood that Japan had been putting forces into northern Indochina for the purpose of attacking

China from there. He said that he had never heard before that Japan's troop movements into northern Indochina were for the purpose of defense against Chinese attack. The Secretary added that it was the first time that he knew that Japan was on the defensive in Indochina.

The Ambassador said that the Japanese are alarmed over increasing naval and military preparations of the ABCD powers in the southwest Pacific area, and that an airplane of one of those countries had recently flown over Formosa. He said that our military men are very alert and enterprising and are known to believe in the principle that offense is the best defense. The Secretary asked whether the Ambassador's observations applied to defensive measures we are taking against Hitler. The Ambassador replied that he did not say that, but that it was because of Japan's apprehensions in regard to the situation that they had made their November 20 proposal.

The Secretary asked whether, if the Chinese are about to attack Japan in Indochina, this would not constitute an additional reason for Japan to withdraw her armed forces from Indochina. The Secretary said that he would be glad to get anything further which it might occur to the Japanese Government to say to us on this matter.

The Ambassador said that the Japanese Government was very anxious to reach an agreement with this Government and Mr. Kurusu said that the Japanese Government felt that we ought to be willing to agree to discontinue aid to China as soon as conversations between China and Japan were initiated. The Secretary pointed out that when the Japanese bring that matter up it brings up the matter of the aid Japan is giving to Hitler. He said that he did not see how Japan could demand that we cease giving aid to China while Japan was going on aiding Hitler. Mr. Kurusu asked in what way was Japan aiding Hitler. The Secretary replied that, as he had already made clear to the Japanese Ambassador, Japan was aiding Hitler by keeping large forces of this country and other countries immobilized in the Pacific area. (At this point the Ambassador uttered *sotto voce* an expression in Japanese which in the present context means "this isn't getting us anywhere.") The Secretary reminded the Ambassador of what the Secretary had said to the Ambassador on this point on November 22 as well as on our unwillingness to supply oil to Japan for the Japanese Navy which would enable Japan to operate against us in the southern Pacific and also on our attitude toward continuing aid to China. The Ambassador said that he recalled that the Secretary had said that he would almost incur the danger of being lynched if he permitted oil to go to Japan for her navy. The Ambassador said that he believed that if the Secretary would explain that giving of oil to Japan had been prompted by the desirability of reaching a peaceful agreement such explanation would be accepted. The Secretary replied that senators and others are not even now desisting from criticizing the Secretary for the course that he had hitherto taken.

The Secretary then recapitulated the three points on which he had orally commented to the Japanese Ambassador on November 22, with reference to the Japanese proposal of November 20, namely one, our difficulty with reference to the Japanese request that we discontinue aid to China, two, our feeling that the presence of large bodies of Japanese troops anywhere in Indochina caused among neighboring countries apprehensions for their security, and, three, public attitude in this country toward supplying Japan with oil for military and naval needs. He asked the Ambassador whether he had not set forth clearly his position on these points to the Ambassador on November 22. The Ambassador agreed.

The Ambassador said that this Government blames Japan for its move into Indochina but that if Indochina was controlled by other powers it would be a menace to Japan. The Secretary replied that as the Ambassador was aware we could solve matters without delay if only the Japanese Government would renounce courses of force and aggression. The Secretary added that we were not looking for trouble but that at the same time we were not running away from menaces.

Mr. Kurusu said that he felt that if we could only come to an agreement on temporary measures we could then proceed with our exploration of fundamental solutions. He said that such a fundamental agreement would necessarily take time and that what was needed now was a temporary expedient. The Secretary replied that the Japanese were keeping the situation confused by a malignant campaign conducted through the officially controlled and inspired press which created an atmosphere not conducive to peace. The Secretary said that we knew the Japanese Government could control the press and that therefore we did not understand what the motives are of the higher officials of the Japanese Government in promoting such a campaign. Mr. Kurusu said that on the American side we were not free from injurious newspaper propaganda. He said that for example there was the case of a newspaper report of the Secretary's interview with the press which created an unfortunate impression in Japan. The Secretary replied that he had been seeing for months and months that Japanese officials and the Japanese press had been proclaiming slogans of a bellicose character and that while all this was going on he had kept silent. He pointed out that now he was being jumped on by the Japanese if he said a single word in regard to his Government's principles. Mr. Kurusu then referred to a press report casting aspersions on Kurusu to the effect that he had been sent here to check on the Ambassador, et cetera, et cetera. The Secretary replied that he had heard only good reports in regard to Mr. Kurusu and the Ambassador. At this point the Ambassador and Mr. Kurusu took their leave after making the usual apologies for taking so much of the Secretary's time when he was busy.

J[OSEPH] W. B[ALLANTINE]

MESSAGE from President Franklin D. Roosevelt to Emperor Hirohito of Japan, the Afternoon of December 6, 1941

Department of State, *Bulletin*, December 13, 1941, p. 464

ALMOST A CENTURY ago the President of the United States addressed to the Emperor of Japan a message extending an offer of friendship of the people of the United States to the people of Japan. That offer was accepted, and in the long period of unbroken peace and friendship which has followed, our respective nations, through the virtues of their peoples and the wisdom of their rulers have prospered and have substantially helped humanity.

Only in situations of extraordinary importance to our two countries need I address to Your Majesty messages on matters of state. I feel I should now so address you because of the deep and far-reaching emergency which appears to be in formation.

Developments are occurring in the Pacific area which threaten to deprive each of our nations and all humanity of the beneficial influence of the long peace between our two countries. Those developments contain tragic possibilities.

The people of the United States, believing in peace, and in the right of nations to live and let live, have eagerly watched the conversations between our two Governments during these past months. We have hoped for a termination of the present conflict between Japan and China. We have hoped that a peace of the Pacific could be consummated in such a way that nationalities of many diverse peoples could exist side by side without fear of invasion; that unbearable burdens of armaments could be lifted for them all; and that all peoples would resume commerce without discrimination against or in favor of any nation.

I am certain that it will be clear to Your Majesty, as it is to me, that in seeking these great objectives both Japan and the United States should agree to eliminate any form of military threat. This seemed essential to the attainment of the high objectives.

More than a year ago Your Majesty's Government concluded an agreement with the Vichy Government by which five or six thousand Japanese troops were permitted to enter into Northern French Indo-China for the protection of Japanese troops which were operating against China further north. And this Spring and Summer the Vichy Government permitted further Japanese military forces to enter into Southern French Indo-China for the common defense of French Indo-China. I think I am correct in saying that no attack has been made upon Indo-China, nor that any has been contemplated.

During the past few weeks it has become clear to the world that Japanese military, naval and air forces have been sent to Southern Indo-China in such large numbers as to create a reasonable doubt on the part of other nations that this continuing concentration in Indo-China is not defensive in its character.

Because these continuing concentrations in Indo-China have reached such large proportions and because they extend now to the southeast and the southwest corners of that Peninsula, it is only reasonable that the people of the Philippines, of the hundreds of Islands of the East Indies, of Malaya and of Thailand itself are asking themselves whether these forces of Japan are preparing or intending to make attack in one or more of these many directions.

I am sure that Your Majesty will understand that the fear of all these peoples is a legitimate fear inasmuch as it involves their peace and their national existence. I am sure that Your Majesty will understand why the people of the United States in such large numbers look askance at the establishment of military, naval and air bases manned and equipped so greatly as to constitute armed forces capable of measures of offense.

It is clear that a continuance of such a situation is unthinkable.

None of the peoples whom I have spoken of above can sit either indefinitely or permanently on a keg of dynamite.

There is absolutely no thought on the part of the United States of invading Indo-China if every Japanese soldier or sailor were to be withdrawn therefrom.

I think that we can obtain the same assurance from the Governments of the East Indies, the Governments of Malaya and the Government of Thailand. I would even undertake to ask for the same assurance on the part of the Government of China. Thus a withdrawal of the Japanese forces from Indo-China would result in the assurance of peace throughout the whole of the South Pacific area.

I address myself to Your Majesty at this moment in the fervent hope that Your Majesty may, as I am doing, give thought in this definite emergency to ways of dispelling the dark clouds. I am confident that both of us, for the sake of the peoples not only of our own great countries but for the sake of humanity in neighboring territories, have a sacred duty to restore traditional amity and prevent further death and destruction in the world.

MESSAGE of President Franklin D. Roosevelt to Congress, December 15, 1941, Containing a Summary of United States Past Policy in the Pacific

Department of State, *Bulletin,* December 20, 1941, p. 529

ON DECEMBER 8, 1941, I presented to the Congress a message in person asking for a declaration of war as an answer to the treacherous attack made by Japan the previous day upon the United States. For the information of the Congress, and as a public record of the facts, I am transmitting this historical summary of the past policy of this country in relation to the Pacific area and of the more immediate events leading up to this Japanese onslaught upon our forces and territory. Attached hereto are the various documents and correspondence implementing this history.

I

A little over a hundred years ago, in 1833, the United States entered into its first Far Eastern treaty, a treaty with Siam. It was a treaty providing for peace and for dependable relationships.

Ten years later Caleb Cushing was sent to negotiate and in 1844 there was concluded our first treaty with China.

In 1853, Commodore Perry knocked on Japan's doors. In the next few years those doors began to open; and Japan, which had kept itself aloof from the world, began to adopt what we call Western civilization. During those early years, the United States used every influence it could exert to protect Japan in her transition stage.

With respect to the entire Pacific area, the United States has consistently urged, as it has for all other parts of the globe, the fundamental importance to world peace of fair and equal treatment among nations. Accordingly whenever there has been a tendency on the part of any other nation to encroach upon the independence and sovereignty of countries of the Far East, the United States has tried to discourage such tendency wherever possible.

There was a period when this American attitude was especially important to Japan. At all times it has been important to China and to other countries of the Far East.

At the end of the nineteenth century, the sovereignty of the Philippine Islands passed from Spain to this country. The United States pledged itself to a policy toward the Philippines designed to equip them to become a free and independent nation. That pledge and that policy we have consistently carried out.

At that time there was going on in China what has been called the "scramble for concessions." There was even talk about a possible partitioning of China. It was then that the principle of the "open door" in China was laid down. In 1900, the American Government declared that its policy was to "seek a solution which may bring about permament safety and peace to China . . . protect all rights guaranteed to friendly powers by treaty and international law and safeguard for the world the principle of equal and impartial trade with all parts of the Chinese Empire."

Ever since that day, we have consistently and unfailingly advocated the principles of the open-door policy throughout the Far East.

In the year 1908 the Government of the United States and the Government of Japan concluded an agreement by an exchange of notes. In that agreement, the two Governments jointly declared that they were determined to support "by all pacific means at their disposal the independence and integrity of China and the principle of equal opportunity for commerce and industry of all nations in that Empire"; that it was "the wish of the two Governments to encourage the free and peaceful development of their commerce on the Pacific Ocean"; and that "the policy of both Governments" was "directed to the maintenance of the existing *status quo*" in that region.

The United States has consistently practiced the principles enunciated in that agreement.

In 1921, following the close of the first World War, nine powers having interests in the western Pacific met in conference in Washington. China, Japan, and the United States were there. One great objective of this conference was the maintenance of peace in the Pacific. This was to be achieved by reduction of armament and by regulation of competition in the Pacific and Far Eastern areas. Several treaties and agreements were concluded at that conference.

One of these was the Nine Power Treaty (see Annex 1). It contained pledges to respect the sovereignty of China and the principle of equal opportunity for the commerce and industry of all nations throughout China.

Another was a treaty between the United States, the British Empire, France, Italy, and Japan providing for limitation of naval armament. (See Annex 1.)

The course of events which have led directly to the present crisis began ten years ago. For it was then—in 1931—that Japan undertook on a large scale its present policy of conquest in China. It began by the invasion of Manchuria, which was part of China. The Council and the Assembly of the League of Nations, at once and during many months of continuous effort thereafter, tried to persuade Japan to stop. The United States supported that effort. For example, the Government of the United States on January 7, 1932, specifically stated in notes sent to the Japanese and the Chinese Governments that it would not recognize any situation, treaty, or agreement brought about by violation of treaties. (See Annex 2.)

This barbaric aggression of Japan in Manchuria set the example and the pattern for the course soon to be pursued by Italy and Germany in Africa and in Europe. In 1933 Hitler assumed power in Germany. It was evident that, once re-armed, Germany would embark upon a policy of conquest in Europe. Italy—then still under the domination of Mussolini—also had resolved upon a policy of conquest in Africa and in the Mediterranean.

Through the years which followed, Germany, Italy, and Japan reached an understanding to time their acts of aggression to their common advantage—and to bring about the ultimate enslavement of the rest of the world.

In 1934, the Japanese Minister for Foreign Affairs sent a friendly note to the United States, stating that he firmly believed that no question existed between the two Governments that was "fundamentally incapable of amicable solution." He added that Japan had "no intention whatever to provoke and make trouble with any other Power." (See Annex 3.) Our Secretary of State, Cordell Hull, replied in kind. (See Annex 4.)

But in spite of this exchange of friendly sentiments, and almost immediately thereafter, the acts and utterances of the Japanese Government began to belie these assurances—at least so far as the rights and interests of other nations in China were concerned.

Our Government thereupon expressed to Japan the view of the American people, and of the American Government, that no nation has the right thus to override the rights and legitimate interests of other sovereign states. (See Annex 5.)

The structure of peace which had been founded upon the Washington Conference treaties began to be discarded by Japan. Indeed, in December of 1934, the Japanese Government gave notice of its intention to terminate the Naval Treaty of February 6, 1922, which had limited competition in naval armament. She thereafter intensified and multiplied her rearmament program.

In 1936 the Government of Japan openly associated itself with Germany by entering the Anti-Comintern Pact.

This Pact, as we all know, was nominally directed against the Soviet Union; but its real purpose was to form a league of fascism against the free world, particularly against Great Britain, France, and the United States.

Following this association of Germany, Italy, and Japan, the stage was now set for an unlimited campaign of conquest. In July 1937, feeling themselves ready, the armed forces of Japan opened new large-scale military operations against China. Presently, her leaders, dropping the mask of hypocrisy, publicly declared their intention to seize and maintain for Japan a dominant position in the entire region of eastern Asia, the western Pacific, and the southern Pacific.

They thus accepted the German thesis that seventy or eighty million Germans were by race, training, ability, and might superior in every way to any other race in Europe—superior to about four hundred million other human beings in that area. And Japan, following suit, announced that the seventy or eighty million Japanese people were also superior to the seven or eight hundred million other inhabitants of the Orient—nearly all of whom were infinitely older and more developed in culture and civilization than themselves. Their conceit would make them masters of a region containing almost one-half the population of the earth. It would give them complete control of vast sea lanes and trade routes of importance to the entire world.

The military operations which followed in China flagrantly disregarded American rights. Japanese armed forces killed Americans. They wounded or abused American men, women, and children. They sank American vessels—including a naval vessel, the *Panay*. They bombed American hospitals, churches, schools, and missions. They destroyed American property. They obstructed, and in some cases, drove out American commerce.

In the meantime, they were inflicting incalculable damage upon China, and ghastly suffering upon the Chinese people. They were inflicting wholesale injuries upon other nations—flouting all the principles of peace and good-will among men.

There are attached hereto (see, respectively, Annexes 6, 7, 8, and

9) lists of American nationals killed or wounded by Japanese forces in China since July 7, 1937; of American property in China reported to have been damaged, destroyed, or seriously endangered by Japanese air bombing or air machine-gunning; of American nationals reported to have been assaulted, arbitrarily detained, or subjected to indignities; of interferences with American nationals, rights, and interests. These lists are not complete. However, they are ample evidence of the flagrant Japanese disregard of American rights and civilized standards.

II

Meanwhile, brute conquest was on the rampage in Europe and the Mediterranean.

Hitler and Mussolini embarked upon a scheme of unlimited conquest. Since 1935, without provocation or excuse they have attacked, conquered, and reduced to economic and political slavery some 16 independent nations. The machinery set up for their unlimited conquest included, and still includes, not only enormous armed forces but also huge organizations for carrying on plots, intrigue, intimidation, propaganda, and sabotage. This machine—unprecedented in size—has world-wide ramifications; and into them the Japanese plans and operations have been steadily interlocked.

As the forces of Germany, Italy, and Japan increasingly combined their efforts over these years, I was convinced that this combination would ultimately attack the United States and the Western Hemisphere—if it were successful in the other continents. The very existence of the United States as a great free people, and the free existence of the American family of nations in the New World, would be a standing challenge to the Axis. The Axis dictators would choose their own time to make it clear that the United States and the New World were included in their scheme of destruction.

This they did last year, in 1940, when Hitler and Mussolini concluded a treaty of alliance with Japan deliberately aimed at the United States.

The strategy of Japan in the Pacific area was a faithful counterpart of that used by Hitler in Europe. Through infiltration, encirclement, intimidation, and finally armed attack, control was extended over neighboring peoples. Each such acquisition was a new starting point for new aggression.

III

Pursuing this policy of conquest, Japan had first worked her way into and finally seized Manchuria. Next she had invaded China; and has sought for the past four and one-half years to subjugate her.

Passing through the China Sea close to the Philippine Islands, she then invaded and took possession of Indochina. Today the Japanese are extending this conquest throughout Thailand—and seeking the occupation of Malaya and Burma. The Philippines, Borneo, Sumatra, Java come next on the Japanese timetable; and it is probable that further down the Japanese page, are the names of Australia, New Zealand, and all the other islands of the Pacific—including Hawaii and the great chain of the Aleutian Islands.

To the eastward of the Philippines, Japan violated the mandate under which she had received the custody of the Caroline, Marshall, and Mariana Islands after the World War, by fortifying them, and not only closing them to all commerce but her own but forbidding any foreigner even to visit them.

Japanese spokesmen, after their custom, cloaked these conquests with innocent-sounding names. They talked of the "New Order in Eastern Asia"; and then of the "Co-prosperity sphere in Greater East Asia." What they really intended was the enslavement of every nation which they could bring within their power, and the enrichment—not of all Asia, not even of the common people of Japan—but of the war lords who had seized control of the Japanese State. Here too they were following the Nazi pattern.

By this course of aggression, Japan made it necessary for various countries, including our own, to keep in the Pacific in self-defense large armed forces and a vast amount of material which might otherwise have been used against Hitler. That, of course, is exactly what Hitler wanted them to do. The diversion thus created by Hitler's Japanese ally forced the peace-loving nations to establish and maintain a huge front in the Pacific.

IV

Throughout this course and program of Japanese aggression, the Government of the United States consistently endeavored to persuade the Government of Japan that Japan's best interests would lie in maintaining and cultivating friendly relations with the United States and with all other countries that believe in orderly and peaceful processes. Following the outbreak of hostilities between Japan and China in 1937, this Government made known to the Japanese Government and to the Chinese Government that whenever both those Governments considered it desirable we stood ready to exercise our good offices. During the following years of conflict that attitude on our part remained unchanged.

In October 1937, upon invitation by which the Belgian Government made itself the host, 19 countries which have interests in the Far East, including the United States, sent representatives to Brussels to consider the situation in the Far East in conformity with the Nine Power Treaty and to endeavor to bring about an adjustment of the difficulties between Japan and China by peaceful means. Japan and Germany only of all the powers invited declined to attend. Japan was itself an original signatory of the treaty. China, one of the signatories, and the Soviet Union, not a signatory, attended. After the Conference opened, the countries in attendance made further attempts to persuade Japan to participate in the Conference. Japan again declined.

On November 24, 1937 the Conference adopted a declaration, urging that "hostilities be suspended and resort be had to peaceful processes."

Japan scorned the Conference and ignored the recommendation.

It became clear that, unless this source of affairs in the Far East was halted, the Pacific area was doomed to experience the same horrors which have devastated Europe.

Therefore, in this year of 1941, in an endeavor to end this process by peaceful means while there seemed still to be a chance, the United States entered into discussions with Japan.

For nine months these conversations were carried on, for the purpose of arriving at some understanding acceptable to both countries.

Throughout all of these conversations, this Government took into account not only the legitimate interests of the United States but also those of Japan and other countries. When questions relating to the legitimate rights and interests of other countries came up, this Government kept in appropriate contact with the representatives of those countries.

In the course of these negotiations, the United States steadfastly advocated certain basic principles which should govern international relations. These were:

The principle of inviolability of territorial integrity and sovereignty of all nations.

The principle of non-interference in the internal affairs of other countries.

The principle of equality—including equality of commercial opportunity and treatment.

The principle of reliance upon international cooperation and conciliation for the prevention, and pacific settlement, of controversies.

The Japanese Government, it is true, repeatedly offered qualified statements of peaceful intention. But it became clear, as each proposal was explored, that Japan did not intend to modify in any way her greedy designs upon the whole Pacific world. Although she continually maintained that she was promoting only the peace and greater prosperity of East Asia, she continued her brutal assault upon the Chinese people.

Nor did Japan show any inclination to renounce her unholy alliance with Hitlerism.

In July of this year the Japanese Government connived with Hitler to force from the Vichy Government of France permission to place Japanese armed forces in southern Indochina; and began sending her troops and equipment into that area.

The conversations between this Government and the Japanese Government were thereupon suspended.

But during the following month, at the urgent and insistent request of the Japanese Government, which again made emphatic profession of peaceful intent, the conversations were resumed.

At that time the Japanese Government made the suggestion that the responsible heads of the Japanese Government and of the Government of the United States meet personally to discuss means for bringing about an adjustment of relations between the two countries. I should have been happy to travel thousands of miles to meet the Premier of Japan for that purpose. But I felt it desirable, before so doing, to obtain some assurance that there could be some agreement on basic principles. This Government tried hard—but without success—to obtain such assurance from the Japanese Government.

The various proposals of the Japanese Government and the attitude taken by this Government are set forth in a document which the Secretary of State handed to the Japanese Ambassador on October 2, 1941 (see Annex 10).

Thereafter, several formulas were offered and discussed. But the Japanese Government continued upon its course of war and conquest.

Finally, on November 20, 1941, the Japanese Government presented a new and narrow proposal (see Annex 11) which called for supplying by the United States to Japan of as much oil as Japan might require, for suspension of freezing measures, and for discontinuance by the United States of aid to China. It contained however no provision for abandonment by Japan of her war-like operations or aims.

Such a proposal obviously offered no basis for a peaceful settlement or even for a temporary adjustment. The American Government, in order to clarify the issues, presented to the Japanese Government on November 26, a clear-cut plan for a broad but simple settlement. (See Annex 12.)

The outline of the proposed plan for agreement between the United States and Japan was divided into two parts:

In section one there was outlined a mutual declaration of policy containing affirmations that the national policies of the two countries were directed toward peace throughout the Pacific area, that the two countries had no territorial designs or aggressive intentions in that area, and that they would give active support to certain fundamental principles of peace upon which their relations with each other and all other nations would be based. There was provision for mutual pledges to support and apply in their economic relations with each other and with other nations and peoples liberal economic principles, which were enumerated, based upon the general principle of equality of commercial opportunity and treatment.

In section two there were outlined proposed steps to be taken by the two Governments. These steps envisaged a situation in which there would be no Japanese or other foreign armed forces in French Indochina or in China. Mutual commitments were suggested along lines as follows: (a) to endeavor to conclude a multilateral non-aggression pact among the governments principally concerned in the Pacific area; (b) to endeavor to conclude among the principally interested governments an agreement to respect the territorial integrity of Indochina and not to seek or accept preferential economic treatment therein; (c) not to support any government in China other than the National Government of the Republic of China with capital temporarily at Chungking; (d) to relinquish extraterritorial and related rights in China and to endeavor to obtain the agreement of other governments now possessing such rights to give up those rights; (e) to negotiate a trade agreement based upon reciprocal most-favored-nation treatment; (f) to remove freezing restrictions imposed by each country on the funds of the other; (g) to agree upon a plan for the stabilization of the dollar-yen rate; (h) to agree that no agreement which either had concluded with any third power or powers shall be interpreted by it in a way to conflict with the fundamental purpose of this agreement; and (i) to use their influence to cause other governments to adhere to the basic political and economic principles provided for in this suggested agreement.

In the midst of these conversations, we learned that new contingents of Japanese armed forces and new masses of equipment were moving into Indochina. Toward the end of November these movements were intensified. During the first week of December new movements of Japanese forces made it clear that, under cover of the negotiations, attacks on unspecified objectives were being prepared.

I promptly asked the Japanese Government for a frank statement of the reasons for increasing its forces in Indochina. (See Annex 13.) I was given an evasive and specious reply (see Annex 14). Simultaneously, the Japanese operations went forward with increased tempo.

We did not know then, as we know now, that they had ordered and were even then carrying out their plan for a treacherous attack upon us.

I was determined, however, to exhaust every conceivable effort for peace. With this in mind, on the evening of December sixth last, I addressed a personal message to the Emperor of Japan. (See Annex 15.)

To this Government's proposal of November twenty-sixth the Japanese Government made no reply until December seventh. On that day the Japanese Ambassador here and the Special Representative whom the Japanese Government had sent to the United States to assist in peaceful negotiations, delivered a lengthy document to our Secretary of State, one hour after the Japanese had launched a vicious attack upon American territory and American citizens in the Pacific.

That document (see Annex 16) was a few minutes after its receipt aptly characterized by the Secretary of State as follows:

I must say that in all my conversations with you [the Japanese Ambassador] during the last nine months I have never uttered one word of untruth. This is borne out absolutely by the record. In all my fifty years of public service I have never seen a document that was more crowded with infamous falsehoods and distortions—infamous falsehoods and distortions on a scale so huge that I never imagined until today that any government on this planet was capable of uttering them.

I concur emphatically in every word of that statement.

For the record of history, it is essential in reading this part of my Message always to bear in mind that the actual air and submarine attack in the Hawaiian Islands commenced on Sunday, December 7, at 1:20 p. m., Washington time—7:50 a. m., Honolulu time of same day—Monday, December 8, 3:20 a. m., Tokyo time.

To my message of December 6 (9 p. m. Washington time—December 7, 11 a. m. Tokyo time) to the Emperor of Japan, invoking his cooperation with me in further effort to preserve peace, there has finally come to me on December 10 (6:23 a. m., Washington time—December 10, 8:23 p. m., Tokyo time) a reply, conveyed in a telegraphic report by the American Ambassador at Tokyo dated December 8, 1 p. m. (December 7, 11 p. m., Washington time).

The Ambassador reported that at 7 o'clock on the morning of the eighth (December 7, 5 p. m., Washington time) the Japanese Minister for Foreign Affairs asked him to call at his official residence; that the Foreign Minister handed the Ambassador a memorandum dated December 8 (December 7, Washington time) the text of which had been transmitted to the Japanese Ambassador in Washington to be presented to the American Government (this was the memorandum which was delivered by the Japanese Ambassador to the Secretary of State at 2:20 p. m. on Sunday, December 7—Monday, December 8, 4:20 a. m., Tokyo time); that the Foreign Minister had been in touch with the Emperor; and that the Emperor desired that the memorandum be regarded as the Emperor's reply to my message.

Further, the Ambassador reports, the Foreign Minister made an oral statement. Textually, the oral statement began, "His Majesty has expressed his gratefulness and appreciation for the cordial message of the President." The message further continued to the effect that, in regard to our inquiries on the subject of increase of Japanese forces in French Indochina, His Majesty had commanded his Government to state its views to the American Government. The message concluded, textually, with the statement:

Establishment of peace in the Pacific, and consequently of the world, has been the cherished desire of His Majesty for the realization of which he has hitherto made his Government to continue its earnest endeavors. His Majesty trusts that the President is fully aware of this fact.

Japan's real reply, however, made by Japan's war lords and evidently formulated many days before, took the form of the attack which had already been made without warning upon our territories at various points in the Pacific.

There is the record, for all history to read in amazement, in sorrow, in horror, and in disgust!

We are now at war. We are fighting in self-defense. We are fighting in defense of our national existence, of our right to be secure, of our right to enjoy the blessings of peace. We are fighting in defense of principles of law and order and justice, against an effort of unprecedented ferocity to overthrow those principles and to impose upon humanity a regime of ruthless domination by unrestricted and arbitrary force.

Other countries, too—a host of them—have declared war on Japan. Some of them were first attacked by Japan, as we have been. China has already been valiantly resisting Japan in an undeclared war forced upon her by Japan. After four and one-half years of stubborn resistance, the Chinese now and henceforth will fight with renewed confidence and confirmed assurance of victory.

All members of the great British Commonwealth, themselves fighting heroically on many fronts against Germany and her Allies, have joined with us in the Battle of the Pacific as we have joined with them in the Battle of the Atlantic.

All but three of the governments of nations overrun by German armies have declared war on Japan. The other three are severing relations.

In our own hemisphere many of our sister republics have declared war on Japan and the others have given firm expression of their solidarity with the United States.

The following are the countries which have to date declared war against Japan: Australia, Canada, China, Costa Rica, Cuba, Dominican Republic, Guatemala, Haiti, Honduras, the Netherlands, Nicaragua, New Zealand, Panama, El Salvador, South Africa, United Kingdom, Poland.

These and other peace-loving countries will be fighting as are we, first, to put an end to Japan's program of aggression and, second, to make good the right of nations and of mankind to live in peace under conditions of security and justice.

The people of this country are totally united in their determination to consecrate our national strength and manpower to bring conclusively to an end the pestilence of aggression and force which has long menaced the world and which now has struck deliberately and directly at the safety of the United States.

GERMAN AND ITALIAN AGGRESSIONS

General

ANNUAL MESSAGE of President Franklin D. Roosevelt to Congress, January 3, 1936. Delivered before a Joint Session of the Two Houses of Congress

Department of State, *Press Releases,* January 4, 1936, p. 11; excerpts

MR. PRESIDENT, Mr. Speaker, Members of the Senate and of the House of Representatives: We are about to enter upon another year of the responsibility which the electorate of the United States has placed in our hands. Having come so far, it is fitting that we should pause to survey the ground which we have covered and the path which lies ahead.

On the 4th day of March 1933, on the occasion of taking the oath of office as President of the United States, I addressed the people of our country. Need I recall either the scene or the national circumstances attending the occasion? The crisis of that moment was almost exclusively a national one. In recognition of that fact, so obvious to the millions in the streets and in the homes of America, I devoted by far the greater part of that address to what I called, and the Nation called, critical days within our own borders.

You will remember that on that 4th of March 1933, the world picture was an image of substantial peace. International consultation and wide-spread hope for the bettering of relations between the nations gave to all of us a reasonable expectation that the barriers to mutual confidence, to increased trade, and to the peaceful settlement of disputes could be progressively removed. In fact, my only reference to the field of world policy in that address was in these words: "I would dedicate this Nation to the policy of the good neighbor—the neighbor who resolutely respects himself and, because he does so, respects the rights of others—the neighbor who respects his obligations and respects the sanctity of his agreements in and with a world of neighbors."

Were I today to deliver an inaugural address to the people of the United States, I could not limit my comments on world affairs to one paragraph. With much regret I should be compelled to devote the greater part to world affairs. Since the summer of that same year of 1933, the temper and the purposes of the rulers of many of the great populations in Europe and in Asia have not pointed the way either to peace or to good will among men. Not only have peace and good will among men grown more remote in those areas of the earth during this period, but a point has been reached where the people of the Americas must take cognizance of growing ill will, of marked trends toward aggression, of increasing armaments, of shortened tempers—a situation which has in it many of the elements that lead to the tragedy of general war.

On those other continents many nations, principally the smaller ones, if left to themselves, would be content with their boundaries and willing to solve within themselves and in cooperation with their neighbors their individual problems, both economic and social. The rulers of those nations, deep in their hearts, follow these peaceful and reasonable aspirations of their peoples. These rulers must remain ever vigilant against the possibility today or tomorrow of invasion or attack by the rulers of other peoples who fail to subscribe to the principles of bettering the human race by peaceful means.

Within those other nations—those which today must bear the primary, definite responsibility for jeopardizing world peace—what hope lies? To say the least, there are grounds for pessimism. It is idle for us or for others to preach that the masses of the people who constitute those nations which are dominated by the twin spirits of autocracy and aggression, are out of sympathy with their rulers, that they are allowed no opportunity to express themselves, that they would change things if they could.

That, unfortunately, is not so clear. It might be true that the masses of the people in those nations would change the policies of their governments if they could be allowed full freedom and full access to the processes of democratic government as we understand them. But they do not have that access: lacking it, they follow blindly and fervently the lead of those who seek autocratic power.

Nations seeking expansion, seeking the rectification of injustices springing from former wars, or seeking outlets for trade, for population, or even for their own peaceful contributions to the progress of civilization, fail to demonstrate that patience necessary to attain reasonable and legitimate objectives by peaceful negotiation or by an appeal to the finer instincts of world justice. They have therefore impatiently reverted to the old belief in the law of the sword, or to the fantastic conception that they, and they alone, are chosen to fulfill a mission and that all the others among the billion and a half of human beings must and shall learn from and be subject to them.

I recognize that these words which I have chosen with deliberation will not prove popular in any nation that chooses to fit this shoe to its foot. Such sentiments, however, will find sympathy and understanding in those nations where the people themselves are honestly desirous of peace but must constantly aline themselves on one side or the other in the kaleidoscopic jockeying for position characteristic of European and Asiatic relations today. For the peace-loving nations, and there are many of them, find that their very identity depends on their moving and moving again on the chessboard of international politics.

I suggested in the spring of 1933 that 85 or 90 percent of all the people in the world were content with the territorial limits of their respective nations and were willing further to reduce their armed forces if every other nation in the world would agree to do likewise.

That is equally true today, and it is even more true today that world peace and world good will are blocked by only 10 or 15 percent of the world's population. That is why efforts to reduce armies have thus far not only failed but have been met by vastly increased armaments on land and in the air. That is why even efforts to continue the existing limits on naval armaments into the years to come show such little current success.

But the policy of the United States has been clear and consistent. We have sought with earnestness in every possible way to limit world armaments and to attain the peaceful solution of disputes among all nations.

We have sought by every legitimate means to exert our moral influence against repression, discrimination, intolerance, and autocracy and in favor of freedom of expression, equality before the law, religious tolerance, and popular rule.

In the field of commerce we have undertaken to encourage a more reasonable interchange of the world's goods. In the field of international finance we have, so far as we are concerned, put an end to "dollar diplomacy" money grabbing, and speculation for the benefit of the powerful and rich, at the expense of the small and the poor.

As a consistent part of a clear policy, the United States is following a twofold neutrality toward any and all nations which engage in wars not of immediate concern to the Americas: First, we decline to encourage the prosecution of war by permitting belligerents to obtain arms, ammunition, or implements of war from the United States; second, we seek to discourage the use by belligerent nations of any and all American products calculated to facilitate the prosecution of a war in quantities over and above our normal exports to them in time of peace.

I trust that these objectives, thus clearly and unequivocally stated, will be carried forward by cooperation between this Congress and the President.

I realize that I have emphasized to you the gravity of the situation which confronts the people of the world. This emphasis is justified because of its importance to civilization and therefore to the United States. Peace is jeopardized by the few and not by the many. Peace is threatened by those who seek selfish power. The world has witnessed similar eras—as in the days when petty kings and feudal barons were changing the map of Europe every fortnight, or when great emperors and great kings were engaged in a mad scramble for colonial empire.

We hope that we are not again at the thresholds of such an era. But if face it we must, then the United States and the rest of the Americas can play but one role: through a well-ordered neutrality, to do naught to encourage the contest; through adequate defense, to save ourselves from embroilment and attack; and through example and all legitimate encouragement and assistance, to persuade other nations to return to the ways of peace and good will.

STATEMENT by President Franklin D. Roosevelt, November 15, 1938

Department of State, *Press Releases*, November 19, 1938, p. 338

THE NEWS OF the past few days from Germany has deeply shocked public opinion in the United States. Such news from any part of the world would inevitably produce a similar profound reaction among American people in every part of the Nation.

I myself could scarcely believe that such things could occur in a twentieth-century civilization.

With a view to gaining a first-hand picture of the situation in Germany I asked the Secretary of State to order our Ambassador in Berlin to return at once for report and consultation.

STATEMENT made by Cordell Hull, Secretary of State, at a Press Conference, August 4, 1941

Department of State, *Bulletin*, August 9, 1941, p. 113

I THINK THAT no rational person needs any argument to convince him that during the weeks of my absence the most clinching demonstration has been given of what some of us for some years have insisted was being planned. That is, that there is a world movement of conquest by force, accompanied by methods of governing the conquered peoples that are rooted mainly in savagery and barbarism. That situation calls for ever-increasing preparations for our national defense and ever-increasing production of military supplies both for ourselves and for those who are resisting the would-be world conquerors. On these points there should be absolute unity among the American people, in the first place, and among the other free peoples who have not yet been conquered. With full effort and ever-increasing production and preparation for defense, whenever and wherever such defense is most effective, a successful resistance to the present world movement of invasion and destruction can be made and, in my judgment, undoubtedly will be made. I feel very strongly that with unity of purpose, maximum effort, and firm determination, the remaining free peoples of the world will win and that those who are at present the victims of the forces of barbarism can hope for the restoration of their human rights and liberties.

Against European and African Countries

ETHIOPIA

STATEMENT by Cordell Hull, Secretary of State, September 13, 1935

Department of State, *Press Releases*, September 14, 1935, p. 194

IN VIEW OF the deep concern of this Government and the widespread anxiety of the American people over recent developments which appear to constitute a grave threat to the peace of the world, I consider it desirable to recapitulate the steps thus far taken by this Government in contributing in every practicable way toward a peaceful settlement of the present dispute between Italy and Ethiopia.

On the evening of July 3 the Emperor of Ethiopia summoned the American Chargé d'Affaires *ad interim* at Addis Ababa to the palace and handed the Chargé a communication in which the Emperor stated that he felt it to be his duty to ask the American Government to examine means of securing observance of the Pact of Paris.

The Chargé was instructed to reply to the Emperor as follows:

I have the honor to acknowledge the receipt of Your Imperial Majesty's note of July 3, 1935, and to inform Your Imperial Majesty that I immediately communicated its contents to my Government. I have been instructed by my Government to reply to your note as follows:

"My Government, interested as it is in the maintenance of peace in all parts of the world, is gratified that the League of Nations, with a view to a peaceful settlement, has given its attention to the controversy which has unhappily arisen between your Government and the Italian Government and that the controversy is now in process of arbitration. My Government hopes that, whatever the facts or merits of the controversy may be, the arbitral agency dealing with this controversy may be able to arrive at a decision satisfactory to both of the Governments immediately concerned.

"Furthermore, and of great importance, in view of the provisions of the Pact of Paris, to which both Italy and Abyssinia are parties, in common with 61 other countries, my Government would be loath to believe that either of them would resort to other than pacific means as a method of dealing with this controversy or would permit any situation to arise which would be inconsistent with the commitments of the Pact."

On July 10, during a call of the Italian Ambassador made at the request of the Secretary of State, the Secretary made to the Ambassador a statement as follows:

Although we are not familiar with the facts or the merits of the questions at issue between Italy and Ethiopia, we are deeply interested in the preservation of peace in all parts of the world and we are particularly interested in those international arrangements designed to effect the solution of controversies by peaceable means.

Being convinced that world progress and economic recovery are urgently in need of peaceful conditions, particularly at this time, we feel impelled to impress upon the Italian Ambassador our increasing concern over the situation arising out of Italy's dispute with Ethiopia and our earnest hope that a means may be found to arrive at a peaceful and mutually satisfactory solution of the problem.

On July 11, the Secretary of State conferred with the British and French Ambassadors. He called attention to articles which had appeared in the press wherein there was placed upon the American Government's reply to the Emperor of Ethiopia an interpretation implying that the American Government had abandoned the Kellogg-Briand Pact and the pact therefore was "dead."

The Secretary said he felt this interpretation was entirely contrary to the sense of his note to the Emperor, which had emphasized the principles of the Pact of Paris and had given evidence of this Government's interest in the settlement of this dispute by peaceable means.

On the same day, at his press conference, the Secretary of State pointed out that naturally the American Government, as had frequently been stated previously, is deeply concerned about the preservation of peace in every part of the world and is closely observing conditions and developments.

On July 12, in response to various inquiries of newspaper correspondents, the Secretary of State made a statement as follows:

The Pact of Paris is no less binding now than when it was entered into by the 63 nations that are parties to it. By form and designation it constitutes a treaty by and among those nations. It is a declaration by the governments of the world that they condemn recourse to war for the solution of international controversies, and renounce it as an instrument of national policy in their relations with one another. Furthermore, it is an agreement and a solemn obligation that the settlement or solution of all disputes or conflicts among nations, of whatever nature or of whatever origin, shall never be sought except by pacific means.

The United States and the other nations are interested in the maintenance of the pact and the sanctity of the international commitments assumed thereby for the promotion and maintenance of peace among the nations of the world.

On August 1, the President issued a statement as follows:

At this moment, when the Council of the League of Nations is assembled to consider ways for composing by pacific means the differences that have arisen between Italy and Ethiopia, I wish to voice the hope of the people and the Government of the United States that an amicable solution will be found and that peace will be maintained.

Thereafter, during the month of August, expression of this hope of the people and Government of the United States was communicated in telegrams from the American Government to several other governments.

On September 3, having discovered that an American corporation was a party to a newly granted commercial concession the conclusion of which had added to the perplexities and difficulties confronting the governments and other agencies which are intent upon preservation of peace, the American Government took prompt steps toward removal of this obstacle to peaceful settlement. In connection with that matter, the Secretary of State said at his press conference:

The central point in the policy of this Government in regard to the Italian and Ethiopian controversy is the preservation of peace—to which policy every country throughout the world is committed by one or more treaties —and we earnestly hope that no nations will, in any circumstances, be diverted from this supreme objective.

Now, this Government feels called upon further to express the attitude of this country.

The Government and people of the United States desire peace. We believe that international controversies can and should be settled by peaceful means. We have signed, along with 62 other nations, including Italy and Ethiopia, a treaty in which the signatories have condemned war as an instrument of national policy and have undertaken, each to all, to settle their disputes by none but pacific means.

Under the conditions which prevail in the world today, a threat of hostilities anywhere cannot but be a threat to the interests—political, economic, legal, and social—of all nations. Armed conflict in any part of the world cannot but have undesirable and adverse effects in every part of the world. All nations have the right to ask that any and all issues, between whatsoever nations, be resolved by pacific means. Every nation has the right to ask that no nations subject it and other nations to the hazards and uncertainties that must inevitably accrue to all from resort to arms by any two.

With good will toward all nations, the American Government asks of those countries which appear to be contemplating armed hostilities that they weigh most solicitously the declaration and pledge given in the Pact of Paris, which pledge was entered into by all the signatories for the purpose of safeguarding peace and sparing the world the incalculable losses and human suffering that inevitably attend and follow in the wake of wars.

STATEMENT by President Franklin D. Roosevelt, October 30, 1935

Department of State, *Press Releases*, November 2, 1935, p. 338

IN DEALING with the conflict between Ethiopia and Italy, I have carried into effect the will and intent of the neutrality resolution recently enacted by Congress. We have prohibited all shipments of arms, ammunition, and implements of war to the belligerent governments. By my public statement of October 5, which was emphasized by the Secretary of State on October 10, we have warned American citizens against transactions of any character with either of the belligerent nations except at their own risk.

This Government is determined not to become involved in the controversy and is anxious for the restoration and maintenance of peace.

However, in the course of war, tempting trade opportunities may be offered to our people to supply materials which would prolong the war. I do not believe that the American people will wish for abnormally increased profits that temporarily might be secured by greatly extending our trade in such materials; nor would they wish the struggles on the battlefield to be prolonged because of profits accruing to a comparatively small number of American citizens.

Accordingly, the American Government is keeping informed as to all shipments consigned for export to both belligerents.

CZECHOSLOVAKIA

NOTE from Sumner Welles, Acting Secretary of State, to the German Chargé d'Affaires at Washington (Hans Thomsen), March 20, 1939

Department of State, *Press Releases*, March 25, 1939, p. 221

SIR:

I acknowledge the receipt of your note of March 17 in which, by direction of your Government, you inform the Government of the United States of the terms of the decree issued on March 16 by the Government of the Reich announcing the assumption of a protectorate over the provinces of Bohemia and Moravia.

The Government of the United States has observed that the provinces referred to are now under the *de facto* administration of the German authorities. The Government of the United States does not recognize that any legal basis exists for the status so indicated.

The views of this Government with regard to the situation above referred to, as well as with regard to related facts, were made known on March 17. I enclose herewith for the information of your Government a copy of the statement in which those views were expressed.

[*Enclosure*]

STATEMENT BY THE ACTING SECRETARY OF STATE

The Government of the United States has on frequent occasions stated its conviction that only through international support of a program of order based upon law can world peace be assured.

This Government, founded upon and dedicated to the principles of human liberty and of democracy, cannot refrain from making known this country's condemnation of the acts which have resulted in the temporary extinguishment of the liberties of a free and independent people with whom, from the day when the Republic of Czechoslovakia attained its independence, the people of the United States have maintained specially close and friendly relations.

The position of the Government of the United States has been made consistently clear. It has emphasized the need for respect for the sanctity of treaties and of the pledged word, and for nonintervention by any nation in the domestic affairs of other nations; and it has on repeated occasions expressed its condemnation of a policy of military aggression.

It is manifest that acts of wanton lawlessness and of arbitrary force are threatening world peace and the very structure of modern civilization. The imperative need for the observance of the principles advocated by this Government has been clearly demonstrated by the developments which have taken place during the past 3 days.

ALBANIA

STATEMENT by Cordell Hull, Secretary of State, April 8, 1939

Department of State, *Press Releases*, April 8, 1939, p. 261

THE FORCIBLE and violent invasion of Albania is unquestionably an additional threat to the peace of the world. It would be shortsighted not to take notice of this further development.

Any threat to peace seriously concerns all nations and violates the will of all peoples in the world that their governments shall lead them, not toward war, but along paths of peace.

It is scarcely necessary to add that the inevitable effect of this incident, taken with other similar incidents, is further to destroy confidence and to undermine economic stability in every country in the world, thus affecting our own welfare.

ENTRY OF ITALY INTO THE EUROPEAN WAR

ADDRESS by President Franklin D. Roosevelt, Delivered at the Commencement Exercises of the University of Virginia, at Charlottesville, Virginia, June 10, 1940

Department of State, *Bulletin*, June 15, 1940, p. 635; excerpt

PERCEPTION of danger, danger to our institutions, may come slowly or it may come with a rush and a shock as it has to the people of the United States in the past few months. This perception of danger, danger in a world-wide area—it has come to us clearly and overwhelmingly—we perceive the peril in a world-wide arena, an arena that may become so narrowed that only the Americas will retain the ancient faiths.

Some indeed still hold to the now somewhat obvious delusion that we of the United States can safely permit the United States to become a lone island, a lone island in a world dominated by the philosophy of force.

Such an island may be the dream of those who still talk and vote as isolationists. Such an island represents to me and to the overwhelmingly majority of Americans today a helpless nightmare, the helpless nightmare of a people without freedom; yes, the nightmare of a people lodged in prison, handcuffed, hungry, and fed through the bars from day to day by the contemptuous, unpitying masters of other continents.

It is natural also that we should ask ourselves how now we can prevent the building of that prison and the placing of ourselves in the midst of it.

Let us not hesitate—all of us—to proclaim certain truths. Overwhelmingly we, as a Nation—and this applies to all the other American nations—are convinced that military and naval victory for the gods of force and hate would endanger the institutions of democracy in the western world, and that equally, therefore, the whole of our sympathies lies with those nations that are giving their life blood in combat against these forces.

The people and the Government of the United States have seen with the utmost regret and with grave disquiet the decision of the Italian Government to engage in the hostilities now raging in Europe.

More than 3 months ago the Chief of the Italian Government sent me word that because of the determination of Italy to limit, so far as might be possible, the spread of the European conflict, more than 200 millions of people in the region of the Mediterranean had been enabled to escape the suffering and the devastation of war.

I informed the Chief of the Italian Government that this desire on the part of Italy to prevent the war from spreading met with full sympathy and response on the part of the Government and the people of the United States, and I expressed the earnest hope of this Government and of this people that this policy on the part of Italy might be continued. I made it clear that in the opinion of the Government of the United States any extension of hostilities in the region of the Mediterranean might result in a still greater enlargement of the scene of the conflict, the conflict in the Near East and in Africa, and that if this came to pass no one could foretell how much greater the theater of the war eventually might become.

Again on a subsequent occasion, not so long ago, recognizing that certain aspirations of Italy might form the basis of discussions between the powers most specifically concerned, I offered, in a message addressed to the Chief of the Italian Government, to send to the Governments of France and of Great Britain such specific indications of the desires of Italy to obtain readjustments with regard to her position as the Chief of the Italian Government might desire to transmit through me. While making it clear that the Government of the United States in such an event could not and would not assume responsibility for the nature of the proposals submitted nor for agreements which might thereafter be reached, I proposed that if Italy would refrain from entering the war I would be willing to ask assurances from the other powers concerned that they would faithfully execute any agreement so reached and that Italy's voice in any future peace conference would have the same authority as if Italy had actually taken part in the war, as a belligerent.

Unfortunately, unfortunately to the regret of all of us and to the regret of humanity, the Chief of the Italian Government was unwilling to accept the procedure suggested, and he has made no counter-proposal.

This Government directed its efforts to doing what it could to work for the preservation of peace in the Mediterranean area, and it likewise expressed its willingness to endeavor to cooperate with the Government of Italy when the appropriate occasion arose for the creation of a more stable world order, through the reduction of armaments and through the construction of a more liberal international economic system which would assure to all powers equality of opportunity in the world's markets and in the securing of raw materials on equal terms.

I have likewise, of course, felt it necessary in my communications to Signor Mussolini to express the concern of the Government of the United States because of the fact that any extension of the war in the region of the Mediterranean would inevitably result in great prejudice to the ways of life and government and to the trade and commerce of all of the American republics.

The Government of Italy has now chosen to preserve what it terms its "freedom of action" and to fulfill what it states are its promises to Germany. In so doing it has manifested disregard for the rights and security of other nations, disregard for the lives of the peoples of those nations which are directly threatened by this spread of the war; and has evidenced its unwillingness to find the means through pacific negotiations for the satisfaction of what it believes are its legitimate aspirations.

On this tenth day of June 1940, the hand that held the dagger has struck it into the back of its neighbor.

On this tenth day of June 1940, in this University founded by the first great American teacher of democracy, we send forth our prayers and our hopes to those beyond the seas who are maintaining with magnificent valor their battle for freedom.

In our, in our unity, in our American unity, we will pursue two obvious and simultaneous courses; we will extend to the opponents of force the material resources of this Nation and, at the same time, we will harness and speed up the use of those resources in order that we ourselves in the Americas may have equipment and training equal to the task of any emergency and every defense.

All roads leading to the accomplishment of these objectives must be kept clear of obstructions. We will not slow down or detour. Signs and signals call for speed—full speed ahead.

Yes, it is right that each new generation should ask questions. But in recent months the principal question has been somewhat simplified. Once more the future of the Nation, the future of the American people is at stake.

We need not and we will not, in any way, abandon our continuing effort to make democracy work within our borders. Yes, we still insist on the need for vast improvements in our own social and economic life.

But that, that is a component part of national defense itself.

The program unfolds swiftly, and into that program will fit the responsibility and the opportunity of every man and woman in the land to preserve his and her heritage in days of peril.

I call for effort, courage, sacrifice, devotion. Granting the love of freedom, all of these are possible.

And—and the love of freedom is still fierce, still steady in the Nation today.

GERMAN EXECUTION OF HOSTAGES

STATEMENT by President Franklin D. Roosevelt, October 25, 1941

Department of State, *Bulletin,* October 25, 1941, p. 317

THE PRACTICE of executing scores of innocent hostages in reprisal for isolated attacks on Germans in countries temporarily under the Nazi heels revolts a world already inured to suffering and brutality. Civilized peoples long ago adopted the basic principle that no man should be punished for the deed of another. Unable to apprehend the persons involved in these attacks the Nazis characteristically slaughter fifty or a hundred innocent persons. Those who would "collaborate" with Hitler or try to appease him cannot ignore this ghastly warning.

The Nazis might have learned from the last war the impossibility of breaking men's spirit by terrorism. Instead they develop their *lebensraum* and "new order" by depths of frightfulness which even they have never approached before. These are the acts of desperate men who know in their hearts that they cannot win. Frightfulness can never bring peace to Europe. It only sows the seeds of hatred which will one day bring fearful retribution.

Against the United States

AMERICAN CITIZENS IN GERMANY

NOTE from Prentiss B. Gilbert, American Chargé d'Affaires at Berlin, to the German Minister for Foreign Affairs (Joachim von Ribbentrop), December 14, 1938

Department of State, *Press Releases,* December 17, 1938, p. 450

I HAVE BEEN instructed by my Government to express its disappointment that Your Excellency's Government has not as yet conveyed the assurances which my Government felt confident would be received concerning non-discriminatory treatment in Germany of American citizens without exception based on race or creed.

The attention of Your Excellency's Government was expressly invited to this matter in Mr. Wilson's note of May 9, 1938, and my Government's concern and its desire for the assurances sought therein have been reiterated on several occasions in communications to Your Excellency's Government.

My Government is concerned with the provisions of the decree laws which if made applicable to American citizens would have the effect of arbitrarily dividing them into special classes and subject them to differential treatment on the basis of such classification. It is one of the fundamental principles of my Government to make no distinction between American citizens on the basis of race or creed, and uniformly in its relations with foreign nations it has emphatically declined the right of those nations to apply on their part such discrimination as between American citizens. This principle, furthermore, is applied by my Government to nationals of foreign countries residing in the United States, including Germans. The application to American citizens of the measures referred to would be incompatible with this principle.

My Government believes, therefore, that upon further consideration Your Excellency's Government will decide that American citizens will not be discriminated against in Germany on account of race or creed and that they will not be subjected to provisions of the nature of those embodied in the decree laws in question.

NOTE from Prentiss B. Gilbert, American Chargé d'Affaires at Berlin, to the German Minister for Foreign Affairs (Joachim von Ribbentrop), January 11, 1939

Department of State, *Press Releases*, January 14, 1939, p. 14

I HAVE THE HONOR to acknowledge the receipt of the note signed by Mr. Weizsäcker of December 30, 1938, concerning the treatment in Germany of American citizens, and under instructions of my Government to reply as follows:

My Government, maintaining the position set forth in the note of December 14, 1938 reiterates its fundamental position that it declines to recognize the right of other nations to apply on their part to American citizens measures which would have the effect of arbitrarily dividing them into special classes and subjecting them to differential treatment on the basis of such classification, irrespective of measures applied by other nations to their own citizens on the basis of differential classification of their own citizens.

The treatment accorded in Germany to American citizens, however, is governed not only by the principles of international law but by the prevailing treaties between Germany and the United States, and in this respect my Government has been gratified to note in Your Excellency's declaration that the rights to which American citizens are entitled by virtue of treaties between the two countries would be respected, and that the German Government for its part is prepared to examine and settle on the basis of prevailing treaty provisions cases which in the opinion of my Government are violations of such treaty rights and of which the German Foreign Office is informed by this Embassy.

My Government has accordingly instructed me to present to Your Excellency as they arise such cases of American citizens which heretofore it has been the practice to take up with the competent local authorities and with regard to which formal assurances in general form have repeatedly been sought from Your Excellency's Government that the measures in question would not be applied to American citizens.

I am therefore presenting for examination and settlement certain specific cases of the nature referred to which have already been brought to my attention and I shall pursue this practice should similar cases be brought to my attention in the future.

SINKING OF THE "ROBIN MOOR"

MESSAGE of President Franklin D. Roosevelt to Congress, June 20, 1941

Department of State, *Bulletin*, June 21, 1941, p. 741; see also infra, p. 221

TO THE CONGRESS OF THE UNITED STATES OF AMERICA:

I am under the necessity of bringing to the attention of the Congress the ruthless sinking by a German submarine on May 21 of an American ship, the *Robin Moor*, in the south Atlantic Ocean (25°40′ West, 6°10′ North) while the vessel was on the high seas en route to South Africa.

According to the formal depositions of survivors the vessel was sunk within 30 minutes from the time of the first warning given by the Commander of the submarine to an officer of the *Robin Moor*.

The submarine did not display its flag, and the Commander did not announce its nationality.

The *Robin Moor* was sunk without provision for the safety of the passengers and crew.

It was sunk despite the fact that its American nationality was admittedly known to the Commander of the submarine and that its nationality was likewise clearly indicated by the flag and other markings.

The sinking of this American ship by a German submarine flagrantly violated the right of United States vessels freely to navigate the seas subject only to a belligerent right accepted under international law. This belligerent right, as is known to the German Government, does not include the right deliberately to sink a merchant vessel, leaving the passengers and crew to the mercies of the elements. On the contrary the belligerent is required to place the passengers and crew in places of safety.

The passengers and crew of the *Robin Moor* were left afloat in small lifeboats from approximately two to three weeks when they were accidentally discovered and rescued by friendly vessels. This chance rescue does not lessen the brutality of casting the boats adrift in mid-ocean.

The total disregard shown for the most elementary principles of international law and of humanity brands the sinking of the *Robin Moor* as the act of an international outlaw.

The Government of the United States holds Germany responsible for the outrageous and indefensible sinking of the *Robin Moor*. Full reparation for the losses and damages suffered by American nationals will be expected from the German Government.

Our Government believes that freedom from cruelty and inhuman treatment is a natural right. It is not a grace to be given or withheld at the will of those temporarily in a position to exert force over defenseless people.

Were this incident capable of being regarded apart from a more general background, its implications might be less serious—but it must be interpreted in the light of a declared and actively pursued policy of frightfulness and intimidation which has been used by the German Reich as an instrument of international policy.

The present leaders of the German Reich have not hesitated to engage in acts of cruelty and many other forms of terror against the innocent and the helpless in other countries, apparently in the belief that methods of terrorism will lead to a state of affairs permitting the German Reich to exact acquiescence from the nations victimized.

This Government can only assume that the Government of the German Reich hopes through the commission of such infamous acts of cruelty to helpless and innocent men, women, and children to intimidate the United States and other nations into a course of non-resistance to German plans for universal conquest—a conquest based upon lawlessness and terror on land and piracy on the sea.

Such methods are fully in keeping with the methods of terrorism hitherto employed by the present leaders of the German Reich in the policy which they have pursued toward many other nations subsequently victimized.

The Government of the German Reich may however be assured that the United States will neither be intimidated nor will it acquiesce in the plans for world-domination which the present leaders of Germany may have.

We are warranted in considering whether the case of the *Robin Moor* is not a step in a campaign against the United States analogous to campaigns against other nations. We cannot place reliance on official declarations to the contrary.

Like statements, declarations, and even solemn pledges have been forthcoming in respect of many nations, commencing with the statement that the Government of the German Reich considered its territorial aspirations satisfied when it seized Austria by force. Evidence that the Government of the German Reich continues to plan further conquest and domination is convincing, and, indeed, scarcely disputed.

Viewed in the light of the circumstances the sinking of the *Robin Moor* becomes a disclosure of policy as well as an example of method. Heretofore, lawless acts of violence have been preludes to schemes of land conquest. This one appears to be a first step in assertion of the supreme purpose of the German Reich to seize control of the high seas, the conquest of Great Britain being an indispensable part of that seizure.

Its general purpose would appear to be to drive American commerce from the ocean wherever such commerce was considered a disadvantage to German designs; and its specific purpose would appear to be interruption of our trade with all friendly countries.

We must take it that notice has now been served upon us that no American ship or cargo on any of the seven seas can consider itself immune from acts of piracy. Notice is served on us, in effect, that the German Reich proposes so to intimidate the United States that we would be dissuaded from carrying out our chosen policy of helping Britain to survive.

In brief, we must take the sinking of the *Robin Moor* as a warning to the United States not to resist the Nazi movement of world conquest. It is a warning that the United States may use the high seas of the world only with Nazi consent.

Were we to yield on this we would inevitably submit to world-domination at the hands of the present leaders of the German Reich.

We are not yielding and we do not propose to yield.

NOTE from Cordell Hull, Secretary of State, to the German Chargé d'Affaires at Washington (Hans Thomsen), September 19, 1941
The New York Times, November 4, 1941

SIR:

Reference is made to the Department's communication of June 20, 1941, with which there was transmitted, by direction of the President of the United States, a copy of a message addressed on that date by the President to the Congress of the United States in which it was stated that the German Government would be expected to make full reparation of the losses and damages sustained by American nationals as a consequence of the unlawful sinking of the American vessel, *Robin Moor,* by a German submarine on May 21 1941, in the South Atlantic Ocean.

I now have to inform you that after an investigation undertaken for the purpose of ascertaining the extent of the losses and damages sustained, and with a view to effecting a prompt liquidation of the matter, the Government of the United States is prepared to accept, for appropriate distribution by it, the lump sum of $2,967,092.00, currency of the United States, in satisfaction and full settlement of all claims of the United States and its nationals against the German Government for losses and damages sustained as a consequence of the sinking, subject, however, to the condition that payment of that sum by the German Government be effected at Washington within ninety days from this date.

While the sum mentioned includes an amount representing the value of property of this government which was on board the vessel, no item of punitive damage is included.

APPEALS FOR PEACE

MESSAGE from President Franklin D. Roosevelt Direct to the President of Czechoslovakia (Eduard Beneš) and the Chancellor of Germany (Adolf Hitler), and through the Secretary of State (Cordell Hull) to the Prime Minister of Great Britain (Neville Chamberlain) and the Premier of France (Edouard Daladier), the Morning of September 26, 1938

Department of State, *Press Releases,* October 1, 1938, p. 219

THE FABRIC of peace on the continent of Europe, if not throughout the rest of the world, is in immediate danger. The consequences of its rupture are incalculable. Should hostilities break out the lives of millions of men, women and children in every country involved will most certainly be lost under circumstances of unspeakable horror.

The economic system of every country involved is certain to be shattered. The social structure of every country may well be completely wrecked.

The United States has no political entanglements. It is caught in no mesh of hatred. Elements of all Europe have formed its civilization.

The supreme desire of the American people is to live in peace. But in the event of a general war they face the fact that no nation can escape some measure of the consequences of such a world catastrophe.

The traditional policy of the United States has been the furtherance of the settlement of international disputes by pacific means. It is my conviction that all people under the threat of war today pray that peace may be made before, rather than after, war.

It is imperative that peoples everywhere recall that every civilized nation of the world voluntarily assumed the solemn obligations of the Kellogg-Briand Pact of 1928 to solve controversies only by pacific methods. In addition, most nations are parties to other binding treaties obligating them to preserve peace. Furthermore, all countries have today available for such peaceful solution of difficulties which may arise, treaties of arbitration and conciliation to which they are parties.

Whatever may be the differences in the controversies at issue and however difficult of pacific settlement they may be, I am persuaded that there is no problem so difficult or so pressing for solution that it cannot be justly solved by the resort to reason rather than by the resort to force.

During the present crisis the people of the United States and their Government have earnestly hoped that the negotiations for the adjustment of the controversy which has now arisen in Europe might reach a successful conclusion.

So long as these negotiations continue so long will there remain the hope that reason and the spirit of equity may prevail and that the world may thereby escape the madness of a new resort to war.

On behalf of the 130 millions of people of the United States of America and for the sake of humanity everywhere I most earnestly appeal to you not to break off negotiations looking to a peaceful, fair, and constructive settlement of the questions at issue.

I earnestly repeat that so long as negotiations continue, differences may be reconciled. Once they are broken off reason is banished and force asserts itself.

And force produces no solution for the future good of humanity.

TELEGRAM from Cordell Hull, Secretary of State, to All American Diplomatic Missions Accredited to Governments from Which the United States Government Had Not Already Received Messages or Which Had Not Already Taken Action, on the Afternoon of September 27, 1938

Department of State, *Press Releases,* October 1, 1938, p. 223

PLEASE CALL without delay on the Minister of Foreign Affairs or in his absence on the appropriate official, and express the opinion of this Government that the situation in Europe is today so critical, and the consequences of war would be so disastrous, that no step should be overlooked or omitted that might possibly contribute to the maintenance of peace. The President of the United States has already sent an urgent appeal to the Chancellor of the German Reich, the President of Czechoslovakia, and the Prime Ministers of Great Britain and France urging the importance of keeping negotiations alive and seeking a just settlement of the dispute through peaceful means. If the Chief of State or the Government to which you are accredited were at once to send a comparable message to Germany and Czechoslovakia, emphasizing in his own words the supreme importance of foregoing the use of force in settling the dispute now at issue, we feel that the cumulative effect of such an expression of opinion might possibly even at this late date influence the course of events and contribute to the preservation of peace in Europe. Please make it clear that this suggestion on our part does not in any way imply any opinion as to the points of the dispute at issue.

If the Government to which you are accredited should already have taken such action please express appropriately and with real appreciation of the step taken, the belief of this Government in the cumulative value of this type of international appeal.

For your information the following is the text of the President's appeal referred to above:

[Here follows quoted text of the President's appeal.]

MESSAGE from President Franklin D. Roosevelt to the Chancellor of Germany (Adolf Hitler), the Night of September 27, 1938

Department of State, *Press Releases*, October 1, 1938, p. 224

I DESIRE to acknowledge Your Excellency's reply to my telegram of September 26. I was confident that you would coincide in the opinion I expressed regarding the unforeseeable consequences and the incalculable disaster which would result to the entire world from the outbreak of a European war.

The question before the world today, Mr. Chancellor, is not the question of errors of judgment or of injustices committed in the past. It is the question of the fate of the world today and tomorrow. The world asks of us who at this moment are heads of nations the supreme capacity to achieve the destinies of nations without forcing upon them as a price, the mutilation and death of millions of citizens.

Resort to force in the Great War failed to bring tranquility. Victory and defeat were alike sterile. That lesson the world should have learned. For that reason above all others I addressed on September 26 my appeal to Your Excellency and to the President of Czechoslovakia and to the Prime Ministers of Great Britain and of France.

The two points I sought to emphasize were, first, that all matters of difference between the German Government and the Czechoslovak Government could and should be settled by pacific methods; and, second, that the threatened alternative of the use of force on a scale likely to result in a general war is as unnecessary as it is unjustifiable. It is, therefore, supremely important that negotiations should continue without interruption until a fair and constructive solution is reached.

My conviction on these two points is deepened because responsible statesmen have officially stated that an agreement in principle has already been reached between the Government of the German Reich and the Government of Czechoslovakia, although the precise time, method and detail of carrying out that agreement remain at issue.

Whatever existing differences may be, and whatever their merits may be—and upon them I do not and need not undertake to pass—my appeal was solely that negotiations be continued until a peaceful settlement is found, and that thereby a resort to force be avoided.

Present negotiations still stand open. They can be continued if you will give the word. Should the need for supplementing them become evident, nothing stands in the way of widening their scope into a conference of all the nations directly interested in the present controversy. Such a meeting to be held immediately—in some neutral spot in Europe—would offer the opportunity for this and correlated questions to be solved in a spirit of justice, of fair dealing, and, in all human probability, with greater permanence.

In my considered judgment, and in the light of the experience of this century, continued negotiations remain the only way by which the immediate problem can be disposed of upon any lasting basis.

Should you agree to a solution in this peaceful manner I am convinced that hundreds of millions throughout the world would recognize your action as an outstanding historic service to all humanity.

Allow me to state my unqualified conviction that history, and the souls of every man, woman, and child whose lives will be lost in the threatened war will hold us and all of us accountable should we omit any appeal for its prevention.

The Government of the United States has no political involvements in Europe, and will assume no obligations in the conduct of the present negotiations. Yet in our own right we recognize our responsibilities as a part of a world of neighbors.

The conscience and the impelling desire of the people of my country demand that the voice of their government be raised again and yet again to avert and to avoid war.

MESSAGE from President Franklin D. Roosevelt to the Chancellor of Germany (Adolf Hitler) and *mutatis mutandis* to the Premier of Italy (Benito Mussolini), April 14, 1939

Department of State, *Press Releases*, April 15, 1939, p. 291

YOU REALIZE I am sure that throughout the world hundreds of millions of human beings are living today in constant fear of a new war or even a series of wars.

The existence of this fear—and the possibility of such a conflict—is of definite concern to the people of the United States for whom I speak, as it must also be to the peoples of the other nations of the entire Western Hemisphere. All of them know that any major war, even if it were to be confined to other continents, must bear heavily on them during its continuance and also for generations to come.

Because of the fact that after the acute tension in which the world has been living during the past few weeks there would seem to be at least a momentary relaxation—because no troops are at this moment on the march—this may be an opportune moment for me to send you this message.

On a previous occasion I have addressed you in behalf of the settlement of political, economic, and social problems by peaceful methods and without resort to arms.

But the tide of events seems to have reverted to the threat of arms. If such threats continue, it seems inevitable that much of the world must become involved in common ruin. All the world, victor nations, vanquished nations, and neutral nations will suffer. I refuse to believe that the world is, of necessity, such a prisoner of destiny. On the contrary, it is clear that the leaders of great nations have it in their power to liberate their peoples from the disaster that impends. It is equally clear that in their own minds and in their own hearts the peoples themselves desire that their fears be ended.

It is, however, unfortunately necessary to take cognizance of recent facts.

Three nations in Europe and one in Africa have seen their independent existence terminated. A vast territory in another independent nation of the Far East has been occupied by a neighboring state. Reports, which we trust are not true, insist that further acts of aggression are contemplated against still other independent nations. Plainly the world is moving toward the moment when this situation must end in catastrophe unless a more rational way of guiding events is found.

You have repeatedly asserted that you and the German people have no desire for war. If this is true there need be no war.

Nothing can persuade the peoples of the earth that any governing power has any right or need to inflict the consequences of war on its own or any other people save in the cause of self-evident home defense.

In making this statement we as Americans speak not through selfishness or fear or weakness. If we speak now it is with the voice of strength and with friendship for mankind. It is still clear to me that international problems can be solved at the council table.

It is therefore no answer to the plea for peaceful discussion for one side to plead that unless they receive assurances beforehand that the verdict will be theirs, they will not lay aside their arms. In conference rooms, as in courts, it is necessary that both sides enter upon the discussion in good faith, assuming that substantial justice will accrue to both; and it is customary and necessary that they leave their arms outside the room where they confer.

I am convinced that the cause of world peace would be greatly advanced if the nations of the world were to obtain a frank statement relating to the present and future policy of governments.

Because the United States, as one of the nations of the Western Hemisphere, is not involved in the immediate controversies which have arisen in Europe, I trust that you may be willing to make such a statement of policy to me as the head of a nation far removed from Europe in order that I, acting only with the responsibility and obligation of a friendly intermediary, may communicate such declaration to other nations now apprehensive as to the course which the policy of your Government may take.

Are you willing to give assurance that your armed forces will not attack or invade the territory or possessions of the following independent nations: Finland, Estonia, Latvia, Lithuania, Sweden, Norway, Denmark, The Netherlands, Belgium, Great Britain and Ireland, France, Portugal, Spain, Switzerland, Liechtenstein, Luxemburg, Poland, Hungary, Rumania, Yugoslavia, Russia, Bulgaria, Greece, Turkey, Iraq, the Arabias, Syria, Palestine, Egypt and Iran?

Such an assurance clearly must apply not only to the present day but also to a future sufficiently long to give every opportunity to work by peaceful methods for a more permanent peace. I therefore suggest that you construe the word "future" to apply to a minimum period of assured non-aggression—ten years at the least—a quarter of a century, if we dare look that far ahead.

If such assurance is given by your Government, I will immediately transmit it to the governments of the nations I have named and I will simultaneously inquire whether, as I am reasonably sure, each of the nations enumerated above will in turn give like assurance for transmission to you.

Reciprocal assurances such as I have outlined will bring to the world an immediate measure of relief.

I propose that if it is given, two essential problems shall promptly be discussed in the resulting peaceful surroundings, and in those discussions the Government of the United States will gladly take part.

The discussions which I have in mind relate to the most effective and immediate manner through which the peoples of the world can obtain progressive relief from the crushing burden of armament which is each day bringing them more closely to the brink of economic disaster. Simultaneously the Government of the United States would be prepared to take part in discussions looking towards the most practical manner of opening up avenues of international trade to the end that every nation of the earth may be enabled to buy and sell on equal terms in the world market as well as to possess assurance of obtaining the materials and products of peaceful economic life.

At the same time, those governments other than the United States which are directly interested could undertake such political discussions as they may consider necessary or desirable.

We recognize complex world problems which affect all humanity but we know that study and discussion of them must be held in an atmosphere of peace. Such an atmosphere of peace cannot exist if negotiations are overshadowed by the threat of force or by the fear of war.

I think you will not misunderstand the spirit of frankness in which I send you this message. Heads of great governments in this hour are literally responsible for the fate of humanity in the coming years. They cannot fail to hear the prayers of their peoples to be protected from the foreseeable chaos of war. History will hold them accountable for the lives and the happiness of all—even unto the least.

I hope that your answer will make it possible for humanity to lose fear and regain security for many years to come.

A similar message is being addressed to the Chief of the Italian Government.

GERMAN AND ITALIAN AGGRESSIONS

MESSAGE from President Franklin D. Roosevelt to King Victor Emmanuel of Italy, August 23, 1939, Delivered by the American Ambassador to Italy (William Phillips), August 24, 1939

Department of State, *Bulletin,* August 26, 1939, p. 158

Again a crisis in world affairs makes clear the responsibility of heads of nations for the fate of their own people and indeed of humanity itself. It is because of traditional accord between Italy and the United States and the ties of consanguinity between millions of our citizens that I feel that I can address Your Majesty in behalf of the maintenance of world peace.

It is my belief and that of the American people that Your Majesty and Your Majesty's Government can greatly influence the averting of an outbreak of war. Any general war would cause to suffer all nations whether belligerent or neutral, whether victors or vanquished, and would clearly bring devastation to the peoples and perhaps to the governments of some nations most directly concerned.

The friends of the Italian people and among them the American people could only regard with grief the destruction of great achievements which European nations and the Italian nation in particular have attained during the past generation.

We in America having welded a homogeneous nation out of many nationalities, often find it difficult to visualize the animosities which so often have created crises among nations of Europe which are smaller than ours in population and in territory, but we accept the fact that these nations have an absolute right to maintain their national independence if they so desire. If that be sound doctrine then it must apply to the weaker nations as well as to the stronger.

Acceptance of this means peace, because fear of aggression ends. The alternative, which means of necessity efforts by the strong to dominate the weak, will lead not only to war, but to long future years of oppression on the part of victors and to rebellion on the part of the vanquished. So history teaches us.

On April fourteenth last I suggested in essence an understanding that no armed forces should attack or invade the territory of any other independent nation, and that this being assured, discussions be undertaken to seek progressive relief from the burden of armaments and to open avenues of international trade including sources of raw materials necessary to the peaceful economic life of each nation.

I said that in these discussions the United States would gladly take part. And such peaceful conversations would make it wholly possible for governments other than the United States to enter into peaceful discussions of political or territorial problems in which they were directly concerned.

Were it possible for Your Majesty's Government to formulate proposals for a pacific solution of the present crisis along these lines you are assured of the earnest sympathy of the United States.

The Government of Italy and the United States can today advance those ideals of Christianity which of late seem so often to have been obscured.

The unheard voices of countless millions of human beings ask that they shall not be vainly sacrificed again.

MESSAGE from President Franklin D. Roosevelt to the President of Poland (Ignace Moscicki), August 24, 1939

Department of State, *Bulletin*, August 26, 1939, p. 158

THE MANIFEST gravity of the existing crisis imposes an urgent obligation upon all to examine every possible means which might prevent the outbreak of general war.

With this in mind, I feel justified in suggesting that certain possible avenues of solution be considered.

The controversy between the Government of Poland and the Government of the German Reich might be made the subject of direct discussion between the two governments.

Should this prove impossible or not feasible, a second avenue might be that of submission of the issues to arbitration.

A third method might be conciliation through a disinterested third party, in which case it would seem appropriate that the parties avail themselves of the services of one of the traditionally neutral states, or a disinterested Republic of the Western Hemisphere wholly removed from the area and issues of the present crisis. Should you determine to attempt solution by any of these methods, you are assured of the earnest and complete sympathy of the United States and of its people. During the exploration of these avenues, I appeal to you, as I have likewise appealed to the Government of the German Reich, to agree to refrain from any positive act of hostility.

Both Poland and Germany being sovereign governments, it is understood, of course, that upon resort to any one of the alternatives I suggest, each nation will agree to accord complete respect to the independence and territorial integrity of the other.

It is, I think, well known to you that speaking on behalf of the United States I have exerted and will continue to exert every influence in behalf of peace. The rank and file of the population of every nation, large and small, want peace. They do not seek military conquest. They recognize that disputes, claims, and counter claims will always arise from time to time between nations, but that all such controversies without exception can be solved by peaceful procedure if the will on both sides exists so to do.

I have addressed a communication in similar sense to the Chancellor of the German Reich.

MESSAGE from President Franklin D. Roosevelt to the Chancellor of Germany (Adolf Hitler), August 24, 1939

Department of State, *Bulletin*, August 26, 1939, p. 157

IN THE MESSAGE which I sent to you on April 14 last I stated that it appeared to me that the leaders of great nations had it in their power to liberate their peoples from the disaster that impended, but that unless the effort were immediately made with good will on all sides to find a peaceful and constructive solution of existing controversies, the crisis which the world was confronting must end in catastrophe. Today that catastrophe appears to be very near at hand indeed.

To the message which I sent to you last April I have received no reply, but because of my confident belief that the cause of world peace—which is the cause of humanity itself—rises above all other considerations, I am again addressing myself to you with the hope that the war which impends and the consequent disaster to all peoples everywhere may yet be averted.

I therefore urge with all earnestness—and I am likewise urging the President of the Republic of Poland—that the Governments of Germany and of Poland agree by common accord to refrain from any positive act of hostility for a reasonable and stipulated period, and that they agree likewise by common accord to solve the controversies which have arisen between them by one of the three following methods: first, by direct negotiation; second, by submission of these controversies to an impartial arbitration in which they can both have confidence; or, third, that they agree to the solution of these controversies through the procedure of conciliation, selecting as conciliator or moderator a national of one of the traditionally neutral states of Europe, or a national of one of the American republics which are all of them free from any connection with or participation in European political affairs.

Both Poland and Germany being sovereign governments, it is understood, of course, that upon resort to any one of the alternatives I suggest, each nation will agree to accord complete respect to the independence and territorial integrity of the other.

The people of the United States are as one in their opposition to policies of military conquest and domination. They are as one in rejecting the thesis that any ruler, or any people, possess the right to achieve their ends or objectives through the taking of action which will plunge countless millions of people into war and which will bring distress and suffering to every nation of the world, belligerent and neutral, when such ends and objectives, so far as they are just and reasonable, can be satisfied through processes of peaceful negotiation or by resort to judicial arbitration.

I appeal to you in the name of the people of the United States, and I believe in the name of peace-loving men and women everywhere, to agree to the solution of the controversies existing between your Government and that of Poland through the adoption of one of the alternative methods I have proposed. I need hardly reiterate that should the Governments of Germany and of Poland be willing to solve their differences in the peaceful manner suggested, the Government of the United States still stands prepared to contribute its share to the solution of the problems which are endangering world peace in the form set forth in my message of April 14.

MESSAGE from President Franklin D. Roosevelt to the Chancellor of Germany (Adolf Hitler), August 25, 1939

Department of State, *Bulletin,* August 26, 1939, p. 160

I HAVE THIS HOUR received from the President of Poland a reply to the message which I addressed to Your Excellency and to him last night. The text of President Moszicki's reply is as follows:

I highly appreciate the most important and noble message which Your Excellency was good enough to address to me.

I would like to emphasize that the Polish Government always considered direct negotiations between governments as the most appropriate method of solving difficulties which may arise between states. We consider this method all the more fitting when adopted between neighboring countries. It was with this principle in view that Poland concluded pacts of nonaggression with Germany and the Union of Soviet Republics.

We consider likewise the method of conciliation through a third party as disinterested and impartial as Your Excellency to be a just and equitable method in the solution of controversies arising between nations.

While naturally wishing to avoid even the semblance of availing myself of this occasion to raise the points at issue I nevertheless consider it my duty to point out that in this crisis it is not Poland who is proffering any claims or demanding concessions from any other nation.

It is therefore only natural that Poland agrees to refrain from any positive act of hostility provided the other party also agrees to refrain from any such act direct or indirect.

In conclusion may I express my ardent wish that Your Excellency's appeal for peace may contribute towards general appeasement which the people of the world so sorely need to return once more to the blessed path of progress and civilization.

Your Excellency has repeatedly and publicly stated that the ends and the objectives sought by the German Reich were just and reasonable. In his reply to my message the President of Poland has made it plain that the Polish Government is willing, upon the basis set forth in my messages, to agree to solve the controversy which has arisen between the Republic of Poland and the German Reich by direct negotiation or through the process of conciliation.

Countless human lives can be yet saved and hope may still be restored that the nations of the modern world may even now construct a foundation for a peaceful and a happier relationship if you and the Government of the German Reich will agree to the pacific means of settlement accepted by the Government of Poland.

All the world prays that Germany, too, will accept.

MESSAGE from President Franklin D. Roosevelt to the Premier of Italy (Benito Mussolini), April 29, 1940

Department of State, *Peace and War,* p. 519

My dear Signor Mussolini:

I am requesting my Ambassador in Rome to deliver this message to Your Excellency. Because of the long delays in the transmission of mail, I am conveying to you in this manner a message which under more normal conditions I would have transmitted by means of a personal letter.

During the past days the scope of the conflict in Europe has further widened and two more neutral nations which had done their utmost to avoid involvement in war have been drawn by force into the scene of hostilities.

The people of the United States, as I have already sent you word, have seen with the deepest satisfaction the policy of the Italian Government in exerting every effort to prevent war from spreading to southern and to south-eastern Europe. I fully recognize the profound truth of the statement you made recently to my representative, Mr. Welles, that because of Italy's determination to limit, so far as might be possible, the spread of the conflict, more than 200,000,000 of people in the region of the Mediterranean are still at peace.

A further extension of the area of hostilities, which would bring into the war still other nations which have been seeking to maintain their neutrality, would necessarily have farreaching and unforeseeable consequences, not only in Europe, but also in the Near and the Far East, in Africa, and in the three Americas. No man can today predict with assurance, should such a further extension take place, what the ultimate result might be—or foretell what nations, however determined they may today be to remain at peace, might yet eventually find it imperative in their own defense to enter the war.

I am, as you know, a realist. As occurs inevitably in every contest, the participants themselves are far less able to predict the eventual outcome of the struggle than the onlookers who are near at hand, and these latter perhaps are not in as good a position to determine which may be the winning side as those onlookers who may be still farther away. By reason of its geographic position, this country has a panoramic view of the existing hostilities in Europe. Because of the many imponderables involved, I see no reason to anticipate that any one nation, or any one combination of nations, can successfully undertake to dominate either the continent of Europe or much less a greater part of the world.

I earnestly hope that the powerful influence of Italy and of the United States—an influence which is very strong so long as they remain at peace—may yet be exercised, when the appropriate opportunity is presented in behalf of the negotiation of a just and stable peace which will permit of the reconstruction of a gravely stricken world.

MESSAGE from President Franklin D. Roosevelt to the Premier of Italy (Benito Mussolini), May 14, 1940

Department of State, *Peace and War*, p. 526

I DO NOT KNOW what Your Excellency plans or proposes but reports reaching me from many sources, to the effect that you may be contemplating early entry into the war, have given me great concern.

I send you this appeal as the head of a peaceful nation and as a close friend of twenty other American Republics. All of us in the Americas feel in our hearts that tonight the whole world faces a threat which opposes every teaching of Christ, every philosophy of all the great teachers of mankind over thousands of years.

Forces of slaughter, forces which deny God, forces which seek to dominate mankind by fear rather than by reason seem at this moment to be extending their conquest against a hundred million human beings who have no desire but peace.

You whom the great Italian people call their leader have it in your own hands to stay the spread of this war to another group of 200,000,000 human souls in the Mediterranean Area.

I have sent word to Your Excellency before that I am a realist. As a realist you also will, I know, recognize that if this war should extend throughout the world it would pass beyond the control of heads of States, would encompass the destruction of millions of lives and the best of what we call the liberty and culture of civilization. And no man, no matter how omniscient, how powerful, can foretell the result either to himself or his own people.

Therefore, I make the simple plea that you, responsible for Italy, withhold your hand, stay wholly apart from any war and refrain from any threat of attack. So only can you help mankind tonight and tomorrow and in the pages of history.

TELEGRAM from William Phillips, American Ambassador to Italy, to the Secretary of State of the United States (Cordell Hull), May 27, 1940

Department of State, *Peace and War*, p. 537; paraphrase

420. This morning I was received by Ciano at eleven-thirty. I said to him that I had a message of great importance from President Roosevelt, that I had been ordered to deliver it orally to the Duce, but

that I would be glad for Ciano to read it for his own information. He answered that the Duce could not receive me but that he, Ciano, would take the message and would make, with my permission, a few notes of its text. He thereupon did so with care and attention and I did not feel able to press any further the request that I have an interview with Mussolini. After he had finished I asked him if he could let me have some idea of the general nature of the reply. He answered definitely "It would be a no" and proceeded to explain that the position of the Duce was more than the question of realizing the legitimate aspirations of Italy, that Mussolini was resolved to fulfill his obligations under the alliance with Germany. He said that the Duce was not in at that particular moment but would come back later in the day and Ciano promised that as soon as he was in a position to give me the reply he would send for me.

I asked the Foreign Minister if he had full realization of the seriousness and importance of the message of President Roosevelt. He said that he did but that there was nothing that could now change the situation. In addition he said that he could not give me the exact time of Italy's entrance into the war; it would be impossible for a few days and it might not take place for a few weeks but he did say "it will happen soon."

Finally he asked me about the position of the United States. I called his attention to the program of President Roosevelt for a great defensive armament. Ciano only answered that it was his assumption that the United States sympathized with the Allies in the same manner that Italy sympathized with Germany.

The Foreign Minister called for me at one o'clock and informed me that the statements which he had made to me earlier in the day had been confirmed by Mussolini. Ciano declared that it was the desire of Mussolini to keep his "freedom of action" and that the Duce was not disposed to engage in any negotiations which indeed would not be in accordance with the spirit of Fascism. He laid emphasis on the idea that the Duce was responsible for the "fulfillment of an engagement—of words given" and he said in addition "any attempt to prevent Italy from fulfilling her engagements is not well regarded."

TELEGRAM from Cordell Hull, Secretary of State, to the American Ambassador to Italy (William Phillips), May 30, 1940

Department of State, *Peace and War,* p. 538

BY DIRECTION of the President you are requested to call on Count Ciano and deliver to him orally the following message for the Chief of Government:

The President has received and has of course given the most thoughtful consideration to the reply conveyed by the Chief of Government to the President's last message.

The President feels compelled in the most friendly manner, but at the same time with the utmost frankness, to lay certain very important considerations before Signor Mussolini.

If the war in Europe is now extended through the entrance of Italy into the war, direct interests of the Government of the United States will be immediately and prejudicially affected. The President has already reminded the Chief of Government of the historic and traditional interests of the United States in the Mediterranean. These interests have been upheld over a period of almost one hundred and fifty years. This Government has never asserted any political interests in Europe, but it has asserted its clearly defined interests of an economic and property character. Through the extension of the war to the Mediterranean region and the inevitable destruction of life and property resulting therefrom, the legitimate interests of the American people will be gravely curtailed and such a possibility cannot be viewed with equanimity by their Government.

An extension of the war into the Mediterranean region will almost unquestionably likewise involve a further extension of the war area in the Near East and in other regions of the world. The President has already stated his belief that such further extension of the war might well bring with it the involvement of countries at present remote from the scene of the hostilities. The President feels it necessary to emphasize that possibility. The social and economic relations between the Americas and the whole of Europe are greater than with any other part of the world. These relations are already gravely disturbed as a result of the present hostilities. In the event that there were any further extension of the war, they would obviously be even more seriously disturbed.

In conclusion, the further extension of the war as a result of Italian participation would at once result in an increase in the rearmament program of the United States itself and in a redoubling of the efforts of the Government of the United States to facilitate in every practical way the securing within the United States by the Allied Powers of all the supplies and matériel which they may require.

Signor Mussolini will recognize that arming on an unprecedented scale in the Americas will make difficult the reduction of armaments in Italy,

Europe, and the rest of the world at the conclusion of the present wars. The establishment of normal internal economic and social programs will, therefore, be made infinitely more difficult.

As the Chief of Government well knows, the relations between the Italian and American peoples have always been particularly close and friendly and the President feels sure that the Chief of Government will also recognize that the President has desired and now desires to promote profitable commercial relations between the two countries, as well as a friendly understanding and comprehension of their respective policies and interests between the two Governments. It is for these and the other reasons mentioned that the President believes that entire frankness on his part in these grave moments will be construed by the Chief of Government as an indication of the President's earnest desire to maintain and promote good relations between the two countries.

TELEGRAM from William Phillips, American Ambassador to Italy, to the Secretary of State of the United States (Cordell Hull), June 1, 1940

Department of State, *Peace and War*, p. 544; paraphrase

445. My telegram No. 437, May 31, 2 p.m.

I was sent for by Ciano at 12:15 p.m. and he gave me verbally Mussolini's answer to President Roosevelt's message of May 30. Mussolini, in confirming what Ciano told me yesterday, mentioned particularly that already the decision to enter the war had been made. Mussolini does not agree with the views of the President regarding United States' interests in the Mediterranean maintaining that the interest of the United States in that area is the same as that which Italy has, it might be said, in the Caribbean Sea area.

Regarding the statement of the President that participation by Italy in the war would bring about a redoubling of efforts to aid the Allies on the part of the United States, Mussolini indicated that it was our business and of no concern to him. It was thus proven to him, however, that help is actually being given by the United States to the Allies; that America already has "chosen the Allied side." He desires to fulfill on his part his engagements with Germany and does not believe that an enlargement of the Mediterranean war will necessarily be brought about by the intervention of Italy. As that is not the Italian object, to prevent it, Italy will do everything possible.

In conclusion Ciano said that Mussolini preferred not to receive "any further pressure" as this, I was informed, "would only stiffen his attitude." It was added by Ciano that the President's mind is already known to Mussolini, and of Mussolini's mind, the President is doubtless aware by now.

NATIONAL AND CONTINENTAL DEFENSE, AND AID TO THE DEMOCRACIES

General

MESSAGE of President Franklin D. Roosevelt to Congress, January 28, 1938

Department of State, *Press Releases,* January 29, 1938, p. 190

THE CONGRESS knows that for many years this Government has sought in many capitals with the leaders of many Governments to find a way to limit and reduce armaments and to establish at least the probability of world peace.

The Congress is aware also that while these efforts, supported by the hopes of the American people, continue and will continue they have nevertheless failed up to the present time.

We, as a peaceful Nation, cannot and will not abandon active search for an agreement among the nations to limit armaments and end aggression. But it is clear that until such agreement is reached—and I have not given up hope of it—we are compelled to think of our own national safety.

It is with the deepest regret that I report to you that armaments increase today at an unprecedented and alarming rate. It is an ominous fact that at least one-fourth of the world's population is involved in merciless devastating conflict in spite of the fact that most people in most countries, including those where conflict rages, wish to live at peace. Armies are fighting in the Far East and in Europe; thousands of civilians are being driven from their homes and bombed from the air. Tension throughout the world is high.

As Commander-in-Chief of the Army and Navy of the United States it is my constitutional duty to report to the Congress that our national defense is, in the light of the increasing armaments of other nations, inadequate for purposes of national security and requires increase for that reason.

In spite of the well-known fact that the American standard of living makes our ships, our guns, and our planes cost more for construction than in any other nation and that the maintenance of them and of our Army and Navy personnel is more expensive than in any other nation, it is also true that the proportion of the cost of our military and naval forces to the total income of our citizens or to the total cost of our Government is far lower than in the case of any other great nation.

Specifically and solely because of the piling up of additional land and sea armaments in other countries, in such manner as to involve a threat to world peace and security, I make the following recommendations to the Congress:

(1) That there be authorized for the Army of the United States additions to antiaircraft matériel in the sum of $8,800,000 and that of this sum $6,800,000 be appropriated for the fiscal year 1939.

(2) That there be authorized and appropriated for the better establishment of an enlisted reserve for the Army the sum of $450,000.

(3) That there be authorized the expenditure of $6,080,000 for the manufacture of gauges, dies, and other aids to manufacture of Army matériel, the sum of $5,000,000 thereof to be expended during the fiscal year 1939.

(4) That the sum of $2,000,000 be authorized and appropriated toward the making up of deficiencies in ammunition for the Army.

(5) That the existing authorized building program for increases and replacements in the Navy be increased by 20 percent.

(6) That this Congress authorize and appropriate for the laying down of two additional battleships and two additional cruisers during the calendar year 1938. This will call for the expenditure of a very small amount of Government funds during the fiscal year 1939.

(7) That the Congress authorize and appropriate a sum not to exceed $15,000,000 for the construction of a number of new types of small vessels, such construction to be regarded as experimental in the light of new developments among navies; and to include the preparation of plans for other types of ships in the event that it may be necessary to construct such ships in the future.

I believe also that the time has come for the Congress to enact legislation aimed at the prevention of profiteering in time of war and the equalization of the burdens of possible war. Such legislation has been the subject for many years of full study in this and previous Congresses.

It is necessary for all of us to realize that the unfortunate world conditions of today have resulted too often in the discarding of those principles and treaties which underlie international law and order, and in the entrance of many new factors into the actual conduct of war.

Adequate defense means that for the protection not only of our coasts but also of our communities far removed from the coast, we must keep any potential enemy many hundred miles away from our continental limits.

We cannot assume that our defense would be limited to one ocean and one coast and that the other ocean and the other coast would with certainty be safe. We cannot be certain that the connecting link —the Panama Canal—would be safe. Adequate defense affects therefore the simultaneous defense of every part of the United States of America.

It is our clear duty to further every effort toward peace but at the same time to protect our Nation. That is the purpose of these recommendations. Such protection is and will be based not on aggression but on defense.

MESSAGE of President Franklin D. Roosevelt to Congress, January 12, 1939

Department of State, *Peace and War*, p. 451

In my annual message to this Congress I have spoken at some length of the changing world conditions outside of the American Hemisphere which make it imperative that we take immediate steps for the protection of our liberties.

It would be unwise for any of us to yield to any form of hysteria. Nevertheless, regardless of political affiliations, we can properly join in an appraisal of the world situation and agree on the immediate defense needs of the Nation.

It is equally sensational and untrue to take the position that we must at once spend billions of additional money for building up our land, sea, and air forces on the one hand, or to insist that no further additions are necessary on the other.

What needs to be emphasized is the great change which has come over conflicts between nations since the World War ended, and especially during the past 5 or 6 years.

Those of us who took part in the conduct of the World War will remember that in the preparation of the American armies for actual participation in battle, the United States, entering the war on April 6, 1917, took no part whatsoever in any major engagement until the end of May 1918. In other words, while other armies were conducting the actual fighting, the United States had more than a year of absolute peace at home without any threat of attack on this continent, to train men, to produce raw materials, to process them into munitions and supplies and to forge the whole into fighting forces. It is even a matter of record that as late as the autumn of 1918, American armies

DEFENSE, AND AID TO THE DEMOCRACIES

at the front used almost exclusively French or British artillery and aircraft.

Calling attention to these facts does not remotely intimate that the Congress or the President have any thought of taking part in another war on European soil, but it does show that in 1917 we were not ready to conduct large scale land or air operations. Relatively we are not much more ready to do so today than we were then—and we cannot guarantee a long period, free from attack, in which we could prepare.

I have called attention to the fact that "We must have armed forces and defenses strong enough to ward off sudden attack against strategic positions and key facilities essential to insure sustained resistance and ultimate victory." And I have said, "We must have the organization and location of those key facilities so that they may be immediately utilized and rapidly expanded to meet all needs without danger of serious interruption by enemy attack."

I repeat that "there is new range and speed to offense."

Therefore, it has become necessary for every American to restudy present defense against the possibilities of present offense against us.

Careful examination of the most imperative present needs leads me to recommend the appropriation at this session of the Congress, with as great speed as possible, of approximately $525,000,000, of which sum approximately $210,000,000 would be actually spent from the Treasury before the end of the fiscal year ending June 30, 1940.

The survey indicates that of this sum approximately $450,000,000 should be allocated for new needs of the Army, $65,000,000 for new needs of the Navy, and $10,000,000 for training of civilian air pilots.

The several items will be submitted to the appropriate committees of the Congress by the departments concerned, and I need, therefore, touch only on the major divisions of the total.

In the case of the Army, information from other nations leads us to believe that there must be a complete revision of our estimates for aircraft. The Baker board report of a few years ago is completely out of date. No responsible officer advocates building our air forces up to the total either of planes on hand or of productive capacity equal to the forces of certain other nations. We are thinking in the terms of necessary defenses and the conclusion is inevitable that our existing forces are so utterly inadequate that they must be immediately strengthened.

It is proposed that $300,000,000 be appropriated for the purchase of several types of airplanes for the Army. This should provide a minimum increase of 3,000 planes, but it is hoped that orders placed on such a large scale will materially reduce the unit cost and actually provide many more planes.

Military aviation is increasing today at an unprecedented and alarming rate. Increased range, increased speed, increased capacity of airplanes abroad have changed our requirements for defensive aviation. The additional planes recommended will considerably strengthen the air defenses of the continental United States, Alaska, Hawaii, Puerto Rico, and the Canal Zone. If an appropriation bill can be quickly enacted, I suggest that $50,000,000 of the $300,000,000 for airplanes be made immediately available in order to correct the present lag in aircraft production due to idle plants.

Of the balance of approximately $150,000,000 requested for the Army, I suggest an appropriation of $110,000,000 to provide "critical items" of equipment which would be needed immediately in time of emergency, and which cannot be obtained from any source within the time and quantity desired—matériel such as antiaircraft artillery, semiautomatic rifles, antitank guns, tanks, light and heavy artillery, ammunition, and gas masks. Such purchases would go far to equip existing units of the Regular Army and the National Guard.

I suggest approximately $32,000,000 for "educational orders" for the Army—in other words, to enable industry to prepare for quantity production in an emergency, of those military items which are noncommercial in character and are so difficult of manufacture as to constitute what is known as "bottlenecks" in the problem of procurement.

The balance should be used, I believe, for improving and strengthening the seacoast defenses of Panama, Hawaii, and the continental United States, including the construction of a highway outside the limits of the Panama Canal Zone, important to the defense of the zone.

The estimated appropriation of $65,000,000 for the Navy should be divided into (a) $44,000,000 for the creation or strengthening of Navy bases in both oceans in general agreement with the report of the special board which has already been submitted to the Congress, (b) about $21,000,000 for additional Navy airplanes and air material tests.

Finally, national defense calls for the annual training of additional air pilots. This training should be primarily directed to the essential qualifications for civilian flying. In cooperation with educational institutions, it is believed that the expenditure of $10,000,000 a year will give primary training to approximately 20,000 citizens.

In the above recommendations for appropriations totaling $525,-000,000, I have omitted reference to a definite need, which, however, relates to the implementing of existing defenses for the Panama Canal. The security of the Canal is of the utmost importance. The peace garrison now there is inadequate to defend this vital link. This deficiency cannot be corrected with existing forces without seriously jeopardizing the general defense by stripping the continental United States of harbor defense and antiaircraft personnel. The permanent garrison in the Canal Zone should be increased to provide the minimum personnel required to man the antiaircraft and seacoast armament provided for the defense of the Canal. Such personnel cannot be increased until additional housing facilities are provided—and, in the meantime, additional personnel must be trained. I recommend, therefore, an appropriation of $27,000,000 to provide an adequate peace garrison for the Canal Zone and to house it adequately. Five million dollars of this sum should be made available immediately in order that work on necessary construction can be initiated.

All of the above constitutes a well-rounded program, considered by me as Commander in Chief of the Army and Navy, and by my advisors to be a minimum program for the necessities of defense. Every American is aware of the peaceful intentions of the Government and of the people. Every American knows that we have no thought of aggression, no desire for further territory.

Nevertheless, as the Executive head of the Government, I am compelled to look facts in the face. We have a splendid asset in the quality of our manhood. But without modern weapons, and without adequate training, the men, however splendid the type, would be hopelessly handicapped if we were attacked.

The young men of this Nation should not be compelled to take the field with antiquated weapons. It would be economically unsound to provide in time of peace for all the modern equipment needed in a war emergency. But it would be nationally unsound not to provide the critical items of equipment which might be needed for immediate use, and not to provide for facilities for mass production in the event of war.

Devoid of all hysteria, this program is but the minimum of requirements.

I trust, therefore, that the Congress will quickly act on this emergency program for the strengthening of the defense of the United States.

STATEMENT by Cordell Hull, Secretary of State, August 25, 1940

Department of State, *Bulletin*, August 31, 1940, p. 174

I FEEL CONSTRAINED to re-emphasize the view expressed upon my return from the Habana Conference, that the possibilities of danger to the American republics are real; that a threat to any important part of the Americas means a threat to each and all of the American nations.

The conclusion is therefore inescapable that full and adequate preparations for hemispheric defense cannot be completed too soon. I desire again to appeal for the fullest possible measure of unity on the part of our people in support of such program of defense and of related foreign policies.

RADIO ADDRESS by President Franklin D. Roosevelt, Delivered from the White House over a Nation-wide Network and Broadcast to Foreign Countries, December 29, 1940

Department of State, *Bulletin*, January 4, 1941, p. 3; excerpt

THIS IS NOT A fireside chat on war. It is a talk on national security; because the nub of the whole purpose of your President is to keep you now, and your children later, and your grandchildren much later, out of a last-ditch war for the preservation of American independence and all of the things that American independence means to you and to me and to ours.

Tonight, in the presence of a world crisis, my mind goes back eight years ago to a night in the midst of a domestic crisis. It was a time when the wheels of American industry were grinding to a full stop, when the whole banking system of our country had ceased to function.

I well remember that while I sat in my study in the White House, preparing to talk with the people of the United States, I had before my eyes the picture of all those Americans with whom I was talking. I saw the workmen in the mills, the mines, the factories; the girl behind the counter; the small shopkeeper; the farmer doing his spring plowing; the widows and the old men wondering about their life's savings.

I tried to convey to the great mass of American people what the banking crisis meant to them in their daily lives.

Tonight, I want to do the same thing, with the same people, in this new crisis which faces America.

We met the issue of 1933 with courage and realism.

We face this new crisis—this new threat to the security of our Nation—with the same courage and realism.

Never before since Jamestown and Plymouth Rock has our American civilization been in such danger as now.

For, on September 27, 1940, by an agreement signed in Berlin, three powerful nations, two in Europe and one in Asia, joined themselves together in the threat that if the United States interfered with or blocked the expansion program of these three nations—a program aimed at world control—they would unite in ultimate action against the United States.

The Nazi masters of Germany have made it clear that they intend not only to dominate all life and thought in their own country, but also to enslave the whole of Europe, and then to use the resources of Europe to dominate the rest of the world.

Three weeks ago their leader stated, "There are two worlds that stand opposed to each other." Then in defiant reply to his opponents, he said this: "Others are correct when they say: 'With this world we cannot ever reconcile ourselves.' . . . I can beat any other power in the world." So said the leader of the Nazis.

In other words, the Axis not merely admits but proclaims that there can be no ultimate peace between their philosophy of government and our philosophy of government.

In view of the nature of this undeniable threat, it can be asserted, properly and categorically, that the United States has no right or reason to encourage talk of peace until the day shall come when there is a clear intention on the part of the aggressor nations to abandon all thought of dominating or conquering the world.

At this moment, the forces of the states that are leagued against all peoples who live in freedom are being held away from our shores. The Germans and Italians are being blocked on the other side of the Atlantic by the British, and by the Greeks, and by thousands of soldiers and sailors who were able to escape from subjugated countries. The Japanese are being engaged in Asia by the Chinese in another great defense.

In the Pacific is our fleet.

Some of our people like to believe that wars in Europe and in Asia are of no concern to us. But it is a matter of most vital concern to us that European and Asiatic war-makers should not gain control of the oceans which lead to this hemisphere.

One hundred and seventeen years ago the Monroe Doctrine was

conceived by our Government as a measure of defense in the face of a threat against this hemisphere by an alliance in continental Europe. Thereafter, we stood on guard in the Atlantic, with the British as neighbors. There was no treaty. There was no "unwritten agreement."

Yet, there was the feeling, proven correct by history, that we as neighbors could settle any disputes in peaceful fashion. The fact is that during the whole of this time the Western Hemisphere has remained free from aggression from Europe or from Asia.

Does anyone seriously believe that we need to fear attack while a free Britain remains our most powerful naval neighbor in the Atlantic? Does anyone seriously believe, on the other hand, that we could rest easy if the Axis powers were our neighbor there?

If Great Britain goes down, the Axis powers will control the continents of Europe, Asia, Africa, Australasia, and the high seas—and they will be in a position to bring enormous military and naval resources against this hemisphere. It is no exaggeration to say that all of us in the Americas would be living at the point of a gun—a gun loaded with explosive bullets, economic as well as military.

We should enter upon a new and terrible era in which the whole world, our hemisphere included, would be run by threats of brute force. To survive in such a world, we would have to convert ourselves permanently into a militaristic power on the basis of war economy.

Some of us like to believe that even if Great Britain falls, we are still safe, because of the broad expanse of the Atlantic and of the Pacific.

But the width of these oceans is not what it was in the days of clipper ships. At one point between Africa and Brazil the distance is less than from Washington to Denver—five hours for the latest type of bomber. And at the north of the Pacific Ocean, America and Asia almost touch each other.

Even today we have planes which could fly from the British Isles to New England and back without refueling. And the range of the modern bomber is ever being increased.

During the past week many people in all parts of the Nation have told me what they wanted me to say tonight. Almost all of them expressed a courageous desire to hear the plain truth about the gravity of the situation. One telegram, however, expressed the attitude of the small minority who want to see no evil and hear no evil, even though they know in their hearts that evil exists. That telegram begged me not to tell again of the ease with which our American cities could be bombed by any hostile power which had gained bases in this Western Hemisphere. The gist of that telegram was: "Please, Mr. President, don't frighten us by telling us the facts."

Frankly and definitely there is danger ahead—danger against which we must prepare. But we well know that we cannot escape danger, or the fear of it, by crawling into bed and pulling the covers over our heads.

Some nations of Europe were bound by solemn non-intervention pacts with Germany. Other nations were assured by Germany that they need never fear invasion. Non-intervention pact or not, the fact remains that they were attacked, overrun, and thrown into the modern form of slavery at an hour's notice or even without any notice at all. As an exiled leader of one of these nations said to me the other day: "The notice was a minus quantity. It was given to my government two hours after German troops had poured into my country in a hundred places."

The fate of these nations tells us what it means to live at the point of a Nazi gun.

The Nazis have justified such actions by various pious frauds. One of these frauds is the claim that they are occupying a nation for the purpose of "restoring order." Another is that they are occupying or controlling a nation on the excuse that they are "protecting it" against the aggression of somebody else.

For example, Germany has said that she was occupying Belgium to save the Belgians from the British. Would she hesitate to say to any South American country, "We are occupying you to protect you from aggression by the United States"?

Belgium today is being used as an invasion base against Britain, now fighting for its life. Any South American country, in Nazi hands, would always constitute a jumping-off place for German attack on any one of the other republics of this hemisphere.

Analyze for yourselves the future of two other places even nearer to Germany if the Nazis won. Could Ireland hold out? Would Irish freedom be permitted as an amazing exception in an unfree world? Or the islands of the Azores which still fly the flag of Portugal after five centuries? We think of Hawaii as an outpost of defense in the Pacific. Yet, the Azores are closer to our shores in the Atlantic than Hawaii is on the other side.

There are those who say that the Axis powers would never have any desire to attack the Western Hemisphere. This is the same dangerous form of wishful thinking which has destroyed the powers of resistance of so many conquered peoples. The plain facts are that the Nazis have proclaimed, time and again, that all other races are their inferiors and therefore subject to their orders. And most important of all, the vast resources and wealth of this hemisphere constitute the most tempting loot in all the world.

Let us no longer blind ourselves to the undeniable fact that the evil forces which have crushed and undermined and corrupted so many others are already within our own gates. Your Government knows much about them and every day is ferreting them out.

Their secret emissaries are active in our own and neighboring countries. They seek to stir up suspicion and dissension to cause internal strife. They try to turn capital against labor and vice versa. They try to reawaken long slumbering racial and religious enmities which should have no place in this country. They are active in every group that promotes intolerance. They exploit for their own ends our natural abhorrence of war. These trouble-breeders have but one purpose. It is to divide our people into hostile groups and to destroy our unity and shatter our will to defend ourselves.

There are also American citizens, many of them in high places, who, unwittingly in most cases, are aiding and abetting the work of these agents. I do not charge these American citizens with being foreign agents. But I do charge them with doing exactly the kind of work that the dictators want done in the United States.

These people not only believe that we can save our own skins by shutting our eyes to the fate of other nations. Some of them go much further than that. They say that we can and should become the friends and even the partners of the Axis powers. Some of them even suggest that we should imitate the methods of the dictatorships. Americans never can and never will do that.

The experience of the past two years has proven beyond doubt that no nation can appease the Nazis. No man can tame a tiger into a kitten by stroking it. There can be no appeasement with ruthlessness. There can be no reasoning with an incendiary bomb. We know now that a nation can have peace with the Nazis only at the price of total surrender.

Even the people of Italy have been forced to become accomplices of the Nazis; but at this moment they do not know how soon they will be embraced to death by their allies.

The American appeasers ignore the warning to be found in the fate of Austria, Czechoslovakia, Poland, Norway, Belgium, the Netherlands, Denmark, and France. They tell you that the Axis powers are going to win anyway; that all this bloodshed in the world could be saved; and that the United States might just as well throw its influence into the scale of a dictated peace, and get the best out of it that we can.

They call it a "negotiated peace." Nonsense! Is it a negotiated peace if a gang of outlaws surrounds your community and on threat of extermination makes you pay tribute to save your own skins?

Such a dictated peace would be no peace at all. It would be only another armistice, leading to the most gigantic armament race and the most devastating trade wars in history. And in these contests the Americas would offer the only real resistance to the Axis powers.

With all their vaunted efficiency and parade of pious purpose in this war, there are still in their background the concentration camp and the servants of God in chains.

The history of recent years proves that shootings and chains and concentration camps are not simply the transient tools but the very altars of modern dictatorships. They may talk of a "new order" in the world, but what they have in mind is but a revival of the oldest and the worst tyranny. In that there is no liberty, no religion, no hope.

The proposed "new order" is the very opposite of a United States of Europe or a United States of Asia. It is not a government based upon the consent of the governed. It is not a union of ordinary, self-respecting men and women to protect themselves and their freedom and their dignity from oppression. It is an unholy alliance of power and pelf to dominate and enslave the human race.

The British people are conducting an active war against this unholy alliance. Our own future security is greatly dependent on the outcome of that fight. Our ability to "keep out of war" is going to be affected by that outcome.

Thinking in terms of today and tomorrow, I make the direct statement to the American people that there is far less chance of the United States getting into war if we do all we can now to support the nations defending themselves against attack by the Axis than if we acquiesce in their defeat, submit tamely to an Axis victory, and wait our turn to be the object of attack in another war later on.

If we are to be completely honest with ourselves, we must admit there is risk in *any* course we may take. But I deeply believe that the great majority of our people agree that the course that I advocate involves the least risk now and the greatest hope for world peace in the future.

The people of Europe who are defending themselves do not ask us to do their fighting. They ask us for the implements of war, the planes, the tanks, the guns, the freighters, which will enable them to fight for their liberty and our security. Emphatically we must get these weapons to them in sufficient volume and quickly enough, so that we and our children will be saved the agony and suffering of war which others have had to endure.

Let not defeatists tell us that it is too late. It will never be earlier. Tomorrow will be later than today.

Certain facts are self-evident.

In a military sense Great Britain and the British Empire are today the spearhead of resistance to world conquest. They are putting up a fight which will live forever in the story of human gallantry.

There is no demand for sending an American Expeditionary Force outside our own borders. There is no intention by any member of your Government to send such a force. You can, therefore, nail any talk about sending armies to Europe as deliberate untruth.

Our national policy is not directed toward war. Its sole purpose is to keep war away from our country and our people.

Democracy's fight against world conquest is being greatly aided, and must be more greatly aided, by the rearmament of the United States and by sending every ounce and every ton of munitions and supplies that we can possibly spare to help the defenders who are in the front lines. It is no more unneutral for us to do that than it is for Sweden, Russia, and other nations near Germany to send steel and ore and oil and other war materials into Germany every day.

We are planning our own defense with the utmost urgency; and in its vast scale we must integrate the war needs of Britain and the other free nations resisting aggression.

This is not a matter of sentiment or of controversial personal opinion. It is a matter of realistic military policy, based on the advice of our military experts who are in close touch with existing warfare. These military and naval experts and the members of the Congress and the administration have a single-minded purpose—the defense of the United States.

This Nation is making a great effort to produce everything that is necessary in this emergency—and with all possible speed. This great effort requires great sacrifice.

I would ask no one to defend a democracy which in turn would not defend everyone in the Nation against want and privation. The strength of this Nation shall not be diluted by the failure of the Government to protect the economic well-being of all citizens.

If our capacity to produce is limited by machines, it must ever be remembered that these machines are operated by the skill and the stamina of the workers. As the Government is determined to protect the rights of workers, so the Nation has a right to expect that the men who man the machines will discharge their full responsibilities to the urgent needs of defense.

The worker possesses the same human dignity and is entitled to the same security of position as the engineer or manager or owner.

For the workers provide the human power that turns out the destroyers, the airplanes, and the tanks.

The Nation expects our defense industries to continue operation without interruption by strikes or lock-outs. It expects and insists that management and workers will reconcile their differences by voluntary or legal means, to continue to produce the supplies that are so sorely needed.

And on the economic side of our great defense program, we are, as you know, bending every effort to maintain stability of prices and with that the stability of the cost of living.

Nine days ago I announced the setting up of a more effective organization to direct our gigantic efforts to increase the production of munitions. The appropriation of vast sums of money and a well-coordinated executive direction of our defense efforts are not in themselves enough. Guns, planes, and ships have to be built in the factories and arsenals of America. They have to be produced by workers and managers and engineers with the aid of machines, which in turn have to be built by hundreds of thousands of workers throughout the land.

In this great work there has been splendid cooperation between the Government and industry and labor.

American industrial genius, unmatched throughout the world in the solution of production problems, has been called upon to bring its resources and talents into action. Manufacturers of watches, of farm implements, linotypes, cash registers, automobiles, sewing machines, lawn mowers, and locomotives are now making fuses, bomb-packing crates, telescope mounts, shells, pistols, and tanks.

But all our present efforts are not enough. We must have more ships, more guns, more planes—more of everything. This can only be accomplished if we discard the notion of "business as usual." This job cannot be done merely by superimposing on the existing productive facilities the added requirements for defense.

Our defense efforts must not be blocked by those who fear the future consequences of surplus plant capacity. The possible consequences of failure of our defense efforts now are much more to be feared.

After the present needs of our defense are past, a proper handling of the country's peacetime needs will require all of the new productive capacity—if not more.

No pessimistic policy about the future of America shall delay the immediate expansion of those industries essential to defense.

I want to make it clear that it is the purpose of the Nation to build now with all possible speed every machine and arsenal and factory that we need to manufacture our defense material. We have the men, the skill, the wealth, and above all, the will.

I am confident that if and when production of consumer or luxury goods in certain industries requires the use of machines and raw materials essential for defense purposes, then such production must yield to our primary and compelling purpose.

I appeal to the owners of plants, to the managers, to the workers, to our own Government employees, to put every ounce of effort into producing these munitions swiftly and without stint. And with this appeal I give you the pledge that all of us who are officers of your Government will devote ourselves to the same whole-hearted extent to the great task which lies ahead.

As planes and ships and guns and shells are produced, your Government, with its defense experts, can then determine how best to use them to defend this hemisphere. The decision as to how much shall be sent abroad and how much shall remain at home must be made on the basis of our over-all military necessities.

We must be the great arsenal of democracy. For us this is an emergency as serious as war itself. We must apply ourselves to our task with the same resolution, the same sense of urgency, the same spirit of patriotism and sacrifice, as we would show were we at war.

We have furnished the British great material support and we will furnish far more in the future.

There will be no "bottlenecks" in our determination to aid Great Britain. No dictator, no combination of dictators, will weaken that determination by threats of how they will construe that determination.

The British have received invaluable military support from the heroic Greek Army and from the forces of all the governments in exile. Their strength is growing. It is the strength of men and women who value their freedom more highly than they value their lives.

I believe that the Axis powers are not going to win this war. I base that belief on the latest and best information.

We have no excuse for defeatism. We have every good reason for hope—hope for peace, hope for the defense of our civilization and for the building of a better civilization in the future.

I have the profound conviction that the American people are now determined to put forth a mightier effort than they have ever yet made to increase our production of all the implements of defense, to meet the threat to our democratic faith.

As President of the United States I call for that national effort. I call for it in the name of this Nation which we love and honor and which we are privileged and proud to serve. I call upon our people with absolute confidence that our common cause will greatly succeed.

ANNUAL MESSAGE of President Franklin D. Roosevelt to Congress, January 6, 1941

House Document No. 1, 77th Congress, 1st Session; excerpt

I ADDRESS YOU, the Members of the Seventy-seventh Congress, at a moment unprecedented in the history of the Union. I use the word "unprecedented," because at no previous time has American security been as seriously threatened from without as it is today.

Since the permanent formation of our Government under the Constitution, in 1789, most of the periods of crisis in our history have related to our domestic affairs. Fortunately, only one of these—the 4-year War between the States—ever threatened our national unity. Today, thank God, 130,000,000 Americans, in 48 States, have forgotten points of the compass in our national unity.

It is true that prior to 1914 the United States often had been disturbed by events in other continents. We had even engaged in two wars with European nations and in a number of undeclared wars in the West Indies, in the Mediterranean and in the Pacific for the maintenance of American rights, and for the principles of peaceful commerce. In no case, however, had a serious threat been raised against our national safety or our independence.

What I seek to convey is the historic truth that the United States as a nation has at all times maintained opposition to any attempt to lock us in behind an ancient Chinese wall while the procession of civilization went past. Today, thinking of our children and their children, we oppose enforced isolation for ourselves or for any part of the Americas.

That determination of ours was proved, for example, during the quarter century of wars following the French Revolution.

While the Napoleonic struggles did threaten interests of the United States because of the French foothold in the West Indies and in Louisiana, and while we engaged in the War of 1812 to vindicate our right to peaceful trade, it is, nevertheless, clear that neither France nor Great Britain nor any other nation was aiming at domination of the whole world.

In like fashion, from 1815 to 1914—99 years—no single war in

Europe or in Asia constituted a real threat against our future or against the future of any other American nation.

Except in the Maximilian interlude in Mexico, no foreign power sought to establish itself in this hemisphere; and the strength of the British fleet in the Atlantic has been a friendly strength. It is still a friendly strength.

Even when the World War broke out in 1914, it seemed to contain only small threat of danger to our own American future. But, as time went on, the American people began to visualize what the downfall of democratic nations might mean to our own democracy.

We need not overemphasize imperfections in the Peace of Versailles. We need not harp on failure of the democracies to deal with problems of world reconstruction. We should remember that the peace of 1919 was far less unjust than the kind of "pacification" which began even before Munich, and which is being carried on under the new order of tyranny that seeks to spread over every continent today. The American people have unalterably set their faces against that tyranny.

Every realist knows that the democratic way of life is at this moment being directly assailed in every part of the world—assailed either by arms, or by secret spreading of poisonous propaganda by those who seek to destroy unity and promote discord in nations still at peace.

During 16 months this assault has blotted out the whole pattern of democratic life in an appalling number of independent nations, great and small. The assailants are still on the march, threatening other nations, great and small.

Therefore, as your President, performing my constitutional duty to "give to the Congress information of the state of the Union," I find it necessary to report that the future and the safety of our country and of our democracy are overwhelmingly involved in events far beyond our borders.

Armed defense of democratic existence is now being gallantly waged in four continents. If that defense fails, all the population and all the resources of Europe, Asia, Africa, and Australasia will be dominated by the conquerors. The total of those populations and their resources greatly exceeds the sum total of the population and resources of the whole of the Western Hemisphere—many times over.

In times like these it is immature—and incidentally untrue—for anybody to brag that an unprepared America, single-handed, and with one hand tied behind its back, can hold off the whole world.

No realistic American can expect from a dictator's peace international generosity, or return of true independence, or world disarmament, or freedom of expression, or freedom of religion—or even good business.

Such a peace would bring no security for us or for our neighbors. "Those who would give up essential liberty to purchase a little temporary safety deserve neither liberty nor safety."

As a nation we may take pride in the fact that we are soft-hearted; but we cannot afford to be soft-headed.

We must always be wary of thoses who with sounding brass and a tinkling cymbal preach the "ism" of appeasement.

We must especially beware of that small group of selfish men who would clip the wings of the American eagle in order to feather their own nests.

I have recently pointed out how quickly the tempo of modern warfare could bring into our very midst the physical attack which we must expect if the dictator nations win this war.

There is much loose talk of our immunity from immediate and direct invasion from across the seas. Obviously, as long as the British Navy retains its power, no such danger exists. Even if there were no British Navy, it is not probable that any enemy would be stupid enough to attack us by landing troops in the United States from across thousands of miles of ocean, until it had acquired strategic bases from which to operate.

But we learn much from the lessons of the past years in Europe —particularly the lessons of Norway, whose essential seaports were captured by treachery and surprise built up over a series of years.

The first phase of the invasion of this hemisphere would not be the landing of regular troops. The necessary strategic points would be occupied by secret agents and their dupes—and great numbers of them are already here, and in Latin America.

As long as the aggressor nations maintain the offensive, they—not we—will choose the time and the place and the method of their attack.

That is why the future of all American Republics is today in serious danger.

That is why this annual message to the Congress is unique in our history.

That is why every member of the executive branch of the Government and every Member of the Congress face great responsibility— and great accountability.

The need of the moment is that our actions and our policy should be devoted primarily—almost exclusively—to meeting this foreign peril, for all our domestic problems are now a part of the great emergency.

Just as our national policy in internal affairs has been based upon a decent respect for the rights and dignity of all our fellow men within our gates, so our national policy in foreign affairs has been based on a decent respect for the rights and dignity of all nations, large and small. And the justice of morality must and will win in the end.

Our national policy is this:

First, by an impressive expression of the public will and without regard to partisanship, we are committed to all-inclusive national defense.

Second, by an impressive expression of the public will and without regard to partisanship, we are committed to full support of all those resolute peoples, everywhere, who are resisting aggression and are thereby keeping war away from our hemisphere. By this support, we express our determination that the democratic cause shall prevail; and we strengthen the defense and security of our own Nation.

Third, by an impressive expression of the public will and without regard to partisanship, we are committed to the proposition that principles of morality and considerations for our own security will never permit us to acquiesce in a peace dictated by aggressors and sponsored by appeasers. We know that enduring peace cannot be bought at the cost of other people's freedom.

In the recent national election there was no substantial difference between the two great parties in respect to that national policy. No issue was fought out on this line before the American electorate. Today, it is abundantly evident that American citizens everywhere are demanding and supporting speedy and complete action in recognition of obvious danger.

Therefore, the immediate need is a swift and driving increase in our armament production.

Leaders of industry and labor have responded to our summons. Goals of speed have been set. In some cases these goals are being reached ahead of time; in some cases we are on schedule; in other cases there are slight but not serious delays; and in some cases—and I am sorry to say very important cases—we are all concerned by the slowness of the accomplishment of our plans.

The Army and Navy, however, have made substantial progress during the past year. Actual experience is improving and speeding up our methods of production with every passing day. And today's best is not good enough for tomorrow.

I am not satisfied with the progress thus far made. The men in charge of the program represent the best in training, ability, and patriotism. They are not satisfied with the progress thus far made. None of us will be satisfied until the job is done.

No matter whether the original goal was set too high or too low, our objective is quicker and better results.

To give two illustrations:

We are behind schedule in turning out finished airplanes; we are working day and night to solve the innumerable problems and to catch up.

We are ahead of schedule in building warships; but we are working to get even further ahead of schedule.

To change a whole nation from a basis of peacetime production of implements of peace to a basis of wartime production of implements of war is no small task. And the greatest difficulty comes at the beginning of the program, when new tools and plant facilities and new assembly lines and shipways must first be constructed before the actual matériel begins to flow steadily and speedily from them.

The Congress, of course, must rightly keep itself informed at all times of the progress of the program. However, there is certain information, as the Congress itself will readily recognize, which, in the interests of our own security and those of the nations we are supporting, must of needs be kept in confidence.

New circumstances are constantly begetting new needs for our safety. I shall ask this Congress for greatly increased new appropriations and authorizations to carry on what we have begun.

I also ask this Congress for authority and for funds sufficient to manufacture additional munitions and war supplies of many kinds, to be turned over to those nations which are now in actual war with aggressor nations.

Our most useful and immediate role is to act as an arsenal for them as well as for ourselves. They do not need man power. They do need billions of dollars worth of the weapons of defense.

The time is near when they will not be able to pay for them in ready cash. We cannot, and will not, tell them they must surrender, merely because of present inability to pay for the weapons which we know they must have.

I do not recommend that we make them a loan of dollars with which to pay for these weapons—a loan to be repaid in dollars.

I recommend that we make it possible for those nations to continue to obtain war materials in the United States, fitting their orders into our own program. Nearly all of their matériel would, if the time ever came, be useful for our own defense.

Taking counsel of expert military and naval authorities, considering what is best for our own security, we are free to decide how much should be kept here and how much should be sent abroad to our friends who by their determined and heroic resistance are giving us time in which to make ready our own defense.

For what we send abroad, we shall be repaid, within a reasonable time following the close of hostilities, in similar materials, or, at our option, in other goods of many kinds which they can produce and which we need.

Let us say to the democracies: "We Americans are vitally concerned in your defense of freedom. We are putting forth our energies, our resources, and our organizing powers to give you the strength to regain and maintain a free world. We shall send you, in ever-increasing numbers, ships, planes, tanks, guns. This is our purpose and our pledge."

In fulfillment of this purpose we will not be intimidated by the threats of dictators that they will regard as a breach of international law and as an act of war our aid to the democracies which dare to resist their aggression. Such aid is not an act of war, even if a dictator should unilaterally proclaim it so to be.

When the dictators are ready to make war upon us, they will not wait for an act of war on our part. They did not wait for Norway or Belgium or the Netherlands to commit an act of war.

Their only interest is in a new one-way international law, which lacks mutuality in its observance, and, therefore, becomes an instrument of oppression.

The happiness of future generations of Americans may well depend upon how effective and how immediate we can make our aid felt. No one can tell the exact character of the emergency situations that we may be called upon to meet. The Nation's hands must not be tied when the Nation's life is in danger.

We must all prepare to make the sacrifices that the emergency—as serious as war itself—demands. Whatever stands in the way of speed and efficiency in defense preparations must give way to the national need.

A free nation has the right to expect full cooperation from all groups. A free nation has the right to look to the leaders of business, of labor, and of agriculture to take the lead in stimulating effort, not among other groups but within their own groups.

The best way of dealing with the few slackers or troublemakers in our midst is, first, to shame them by patriotic example, and, if that fails, to use the sovereignty of government to save government.

As men do not live by bread alone, they do not fight by armaments alone. Those who man our defenses, and those behind them who build our defenses, must have the stamina and courage which come from an unshakable belief in the manner of life which they are defending.

The mighty action which we are calling for cannot be based on a disregard of all things worth fighting for.

The Nation takes great satisfaction and much strength from the things which have been done to make its people conscious of their individual stake in the preservation of democratic life in America. Those things have toughened the fiber of our people, have renewed their faith, and strengthened their devotion to the institutions we make ready to protect.

Certainly this is no time to stop thinking about the social and economic problems which are the root cause of the social revolution which is today a supreme factor in the world.

There is nothing mysterious about the foundations of a healthy and strong democracy. The basic things expected by our people of their political and economic systems are simple. They are—

Equality of opportunity for youth and for others.
Jobs for those who can work.
Security for those who need it.
The ending of special privilege for the few.
The preservation of civil liberties for all.
The enjoyment of the fruits of scientific progress in a wider and constantly rising standard of living.

These are the simple and basic things that must never be lost sight of in the turmoil and unbelievable complexity of our modern world. The inner and abiding strength of our economic and political systems is dependent upon the degree to which they fullfill these expectations.

Many subjects connected with our social economy call for immediate improvements.

As examples:

We should bring more citizens under the coverage of old-age pensions and unemployment insurance.

We should widen the opportunities for adequate medical care.

We should plan a better system by which persons deserving or needing gainful employment may obtain it.

I have called for personal sacrifice. I am assured of the willingness of almost all Americans to respond to that call.

A part of the sacrifice means the payment of more money in taxes. In my Budget message I recommend that a greater portion of this great defense program be paid for from taxation than we are paying today. No person should try, or be allowed, to get rich out of this program; and the principle of tax payments in accordance with ability to pay should be constantly before our eyes to guide our legislation.

If the Congress maintains these principles, the voters, putting patriotism ahead of pocketbooks, will give you their applause.

In the future days, which we seek to make secure, we look forward to a world founded upon four essential human freedoms.

The first is freedom of speech and expression—everywhere in the world.

The second is freedom of every person to worship God in his own way—everywhere in the world.

The third is freedom from want—which, translated into world terms, means economic understandings which will secure to every nation a healthy peacetime life for its inhabitants—everywhere in the world.

The fourth is freedom from fear—which, translated into world terms, means a world-wide reduction of armaments to such a point and in such a thorough fashion that no nation will be in a position to commit an act of physical aggression against any neighbor—anywhere in the world.

That is no vision of a distant millennium. It is a definite basis for a kind of world attainable in our own time and generation. That kind of world is the very antithesis of the so-called new order of tyranny which the dictators seek to create with the crash of a bomb.

To that new order we oppose the greater conception—the moral order. A good society is able to face schemes of world domination and foreign revolutions alike without fear.

Since the beginning of our American history we have been engaged in change—in a perpetual peaceful revolution—a revolution which goes on steadily, quietly adjusting itself to changing conditions—without the concentration camp or the quick-lime in the ditch. The world order which we seek is the cooperation of free countries, working together in a friendly, civilized society.

This Nation has placed its destiny in the hands and heads and hearts of its millions of free men and women; and its faith in freedom under the guidance of God. Freedom means the supremacy of human rights everywhere. Our support goes to those who struggle to gain those rights or keep them. Our strength is in our unity of purpose.

To that high concept there can be no end save victory.

RADIO ADDRESS by President Franklin D. Roosevelt, May 27, 1941

Department of State, *Bulletin,* May 31, 1941, p. 647

I AM SPEAKING tonight from the White House in the presence of the Governing Board of the Pan American Union, the Canadian Minister, and their families. The members of this Board are the ambassadors and ministers of the American republics in Washington. It is appropriate that I do this. Now, as never before, the unity of the American republics is of supreme importance to each and every one of us and to the cause of freedom throughout the world. Our future independence is bound up with the future independence of all of our sister republics.

The pressing problems that confront us are military problems. We cannot afford to approach them from the point of view of wishful thinkers or sentimentalists. What we face is cold, hard fact.

The first and fundamental fact is that what started as a European war has developed, as the Nazis always intended it should develop, into a world war for world-domination.

Adolf Hitler never considered the domination of Europe as an end in itself. European conquest was but a step toward ultimate goals in all the other continents. It is unmistakably apparent to all of us that, unless the advance of Hitlerism is forcibly checked now, the Western Hemisphere will be within range of the Nazi weapons of destruction.

For our own defense we have accordingly undertaken certain obviously necessary measures.

First, we joined in concluding a series of agreements with all the other American republics. This further solidified our hemisphere against the common danger.

And then, a year ago, we launched, and are successfully carrying out, the largest armament-production program we have ever undertaken.

We have added substantially to our splendid Navy, and we have mustered our manpower to build up a new Army which is already worthy of the highest traditions of our military service.

We instituted a policy of aid for the democracies—the nations which have fought for the continuation of human liberties.

This policy had its origin in the first month of the war, when I urged upon the Congress repeal of the arms-embargo provisions in the Neutrality Law. In that message of September 1939, I said, "I should like to be able to offer the hope that the shadow over the world might swiftly pass. I cannot. The facts compel my stating, with candor, that darker periods may lie ahead."

In the subsequent months, the shadows deepened and lengthened. And the night spread over Poland, Denmark, Norway, Holland, Belgium, Luxemburg, and France.

In June 1940, Britain stood alone, faced by the same machine of terror which had overwhelmed her allies. Our Government rushed arms to meet her desperate needs.

In September 1940, an agreement was completed with Great Britain for the trade of 50 destroyers for 8 important off-shore bases.

In March 1941, the Congress passed the Lend-Lease Bill and an appropriation of seven billion dollars to implement it. This law realistically provided for material aid "for the government of any country whose defense the President deems vital to the defense of the United States."

Our whole program of aid for the democracies has been based on hard-headed concern for our own security and for the kind of safe and civilized world in which we wish to live. Every dollar of material we send helps to keep the dictators away from our own hemisphere. Every day that they are held off gives us time to build more guns and tanks and planes and ships.

We have made no pretense about our own self-interest in this aid. Great Britain understands it—and so does Nazi Germany.

And now—after a year—Britain still fights gallantly, on a "farflung battle line." We have doubled and redoubled our vast production, increasing, month by month, our material supply of tools of war for ourselves and Britain and China—and eventually for all the democracies.

The supply of these tools will not fail—it will increase.

With greatly augmented strength, the United States and the other American republics now chart their course in the situation of today.

Your Government knows what terms Hitler, if victorious, would impose. They are, indeed, the only terms on which he would accept a so-called "negotiated" peace.

Under those terms, Germany would literally parcel out the world—hoisting the swastika itself over vast territories and populations and setting up puppet governments of its own choosing, wholly subject to the will and the policy of a conqueror.

To the people of the Americas, a triumphant Hitler would say, as he said after the seizure of Austria, and after Munich, and after the seizure of Czechoslovakia: "I am now completely satisfied. This is the last territorial readjustment I will seek." And he would of course add: "All we want is peace, friendship, and profitable trade relations with you in the New World."

And were any of us in the Americas so incredibly simple and forgetful as to accept those honeyed words, what would then happen?

Those in the New World who were seeing profits would be urging that all that the dictatorships desired was "peace." They would oppose toil and taxes for more American armament. Meanwhile, the dictatorships would be forcing the enslaved peoples of their Old-World conquests into a system they are even now organizing—to build a naval and air force intended to gain and hold and be master of the Atlantic and the Pacific as well.

They would fasten an economic stranglehold upon our several nations. Quislings would be found to subvert the governments in our republics; and the Nazis would back their fifth columns with invasion, if necessary.

I am not speculating about all this. I merely repeat what is already in the Nazi book of world-conquest. They plan to treat the Latin American nations as they are now treating the Balkans. They plan then to strangle the United States of America and the Dominion of Canada.

The American laborer would have to compete with slave labor in the rest of the world. Minimum wages, maximum hours? Nonsense! Wages and hours would be fixed by Hitler. The dignity and power and standard of living of the American worker and farmer would be gone. Trade unions would become historical relics and collective bargaining a joke.

Farm income? What happens to all farm surpluses without any foreign trade? The American farmer would get for his products exactly what Hitler wanted to give. He would face obvious disaster and complete regimentation.

Tariff walls—Chinese walls of isolation—would be futile. Freedom to trade is essential to our economic life. We do not eat all the food we can produce; we do not burn all the oil we can pump; we do not use all the goods we can manufacture. It would not be an American wall to keep Nazi goods out; it would be a Nazi wall to keep us in.

The whole fabric of working life as we know it—business, manufacturing, mining, agriculture—all would be mangled and crippled under such a system. Yet to maintain even that crippled independence would require permanent conscription of our manpower; it would curtail the funds we could spend on education, on housing, on public works, on flood control, on health. Instead, we should be permanently pouring our resources into armaments; and, year in and year out, standing day and night watch against the destruction of our cities.

Even our right of worship would be threatened. The Nazi world does not recognize any God except Hitler; for the Nazis are as ruthless as the Communists in the denial of God. What place has religion which preaches the dignity of the human being, of the majesty of the human soul, in a world where moral standards are measured by treachery and bribery and fifth columnists? Will our children, too, wander off, goose-stepping in search of new gods?

We do not accept, and will not permit, this Nazi "shape of things to come." It will never be forced upon us if we act in this present crisis with the wisdom and the courage which have distinguished our country in all the crises of the past.

The Nazis have taken military possession of the greater part of Europe. In Africa they have occupied Tripoli and Libya, and they are threatening Egypt, the Suez Canal, and the Near East. But their plans do not stop there, for the Indian Ocean is the gateway to the East.

They also have the armed power at any moment to occupy Spain and Portugal; and that threat extends not only to French North Africa and the western end of the Mediterranean, but also to the Atlantic fortress of Dakar, and to the island outposts of the New World —the Azores and Cape Verde Islands.

The Cape Verde Islands are only seven hours' distance from Brazil by bomber or troop-carrying planes. They dominate shipping routes to and from the South Atlantic.

The war is approaching the brink of the Western Hemisphere itself. It is coming very close to home.

Control or occupation by Nazi forces of any of the islands of the Atlantic would jeopardize the immediate safety of portions of North and South America and of the island possessions of the United States and of the ultimate safety of the continental United States itself.

Hitler's plan of world-domination would be near its accomplishment today, were it not for two factors: One is the epic resistance of Britain, her Colonies, and the great Dominions, fighting not only to maintain the existence of the Island of Britain, but also to hold the Near East and Africa. The other is the magnificent defense of China, which will, I have reason to believe, increase in strength. All of these, together, prevent the Axis from winning control of the seas by ships and aircraft.

The Axis powers can never achieve their objective of world-domination unless they first obtain control of the seas. This is their supreme purpose today; and to achieve it, they must capture Great Britain.

DEFENSE, AND AID TO THE DEMOCRACIES

They could then have the power to dictate to the Western Hemisphere. No spurious argument, no appeal to sentiment, and no false pledges like those given by Hitler at Munich, can deceive the American people into believing that he and his Axis partners would not, with Britain defeated, close in relentlessly on this hemisphere.

But if the Axis powers fail to gain control of the seas, they are certainly defeated. Their dreams of world-domination will then go by the board; and the criminal leaders who started this war will suffer inevitable disaster.

Both they and their people know this—and they are afraid. That is why they are risking everything they have, conducting desperate attempts to break through to the command of the ocean. Once they are limited to a continuing land war, their cruel forces of occupation will be unable to keep their heel on the necks of the millions of innocent, oppressed peoples on the continent of Europe; and in the end, their whole structure will break into little pieces. And the wider the Nazi land effort, the greater the danger.

We do not forget the silenced peoples. The masters of Germany—those, at least, who have not been assassinated or escaped to free soil—have marked these peoples and their children's children for slavery. But those people, spiritually unconquered: Austrians, Czechs, Poles, Norwegians, Dutch, Belgians, Frenchmen, Greeks, Southern Slavs—yes, even those Italians and Germans who themselves have been enslaved—will prove to be a powerful force in disrupting the Nazi system.

Yes, all freedom—meaning freedom to live, and not freedom to conquer and subjugate other peoples—depends on freedom of the seas. All of American history—North, Central, and South American history—has been inevitably tied up with those words "freedom of the seas."

Since 1799, when our infant Navy made the West Indies and the Caribbean and the Gulf of Mexico safe for American ships; since 1804 and 1805 when we made all peaceful commerce safe from the depredations of the Barbary pirates; since the War of 1812, which was fought for the preservation of sailors' rights; since 1867, when our sea power made it possible for the Mexicans to expel the French Army of Louis Napoleon, we have striven and fought in defense of freedom of the seas—for our own shipping, for the commerce of our sister republics, for the right of all nations to use the highways of world trade—and for our own safety.

During the first World War we were able to escort merchant ships by the use of small cruisers, gunboats, and destroyers; and this type of convoy was effective against submarines. In this second World

War, however, the problem is greater, because the attack on the freedom of the seas is now fourfold: first, the improved submarine; second, the much greater use of the heavily armed raiding cruiser or hit-and-run battleship; third, the bombing airplane, which is capable of destroying merchant ships seven or eight hundred miles from its nearest base; and fourth, the destruction of merchant ships in those ports of the world which are accessible to bombing attack.

The battle of the Atlantic now extends from the icy waters of the North Pole to the frozen continent of the Antarctic. Throughout this huge area, there have been sinkings of merchant ships in alarming and increasing numbers by Nazi raiders or submarines. There have been sinkings even of ships carrying neutral flags. There have been sinkings in the South Atlantic, off West Africa and the Cape Verde Islands; between the Azores and the islands off the American coast; and between Greenland and Iceland. Great numbers of these sinkings have been actually within the waters of the Western Hemisphere.

The blunt truth is this—and I reveal this with the full knowledge of the British Government: the present rate of Nazi sinkings of merchant ships is more than three times as high as the capacity of British shipyards to replace them; it is more than twice the combined British and American output of merchant ships today.

We can answer this peril by two simultaneous measures: First, by speeding up and increasing our great ship-building program; and second, by helping to cut down the losses on the high seas.

Attacks on shipping off the very shores of land which we are determined to protect, present an actual military danger to the Americas. And that danger has recently been heavily underlined by the presence in Western Hemisphere waters of Nazi battleships of great striking-power.

Most of the supplies for Britain go by a northerly route, which comes close to Greenland and the nearby island of Iceland. Germany's heaviest attack is on that route. Nazi occupation of Iceland or bases in Greenland would bring the war close to our continental shores because they are stepping-stones to Labrador, Newfoundland, Nova Scotia, and the northern United States, including the great industrial centers of the North, East, and the Middle West.

Equally, the Azores and the Cape Verde Islands, if occupied or controlled by Germany, would directly endanger the freedom of the Atlantic and our own physical safety. Under German domination they would become bases for submarines, warships, and airplanes raiding the waters which lie immediately off our own coasts and attacking the shipping in the South Atlantic. They would provide a springboard for actual attack against the integrity and independence of Brazil and her neighboring republics.

I have said on many occasions that the United States is mustering its men and its resources only for purposes of defense—only to repel attack. I repeat that statement now. But we must be realistic when we use the word "attack"; we have to relate it to the lightning speed of modern warfare.

Some people seem to think that we are not attacked until bombs actually drop on New York or San Francisco or New Orleans or Chicago. But they are simply shutting their eyes to the lesson we must learn from the fate of every nation that the Nazis have conquered.

The attack on Czechoslovakia began with the conquest of Austria. The attack on Norway began with the occupation of Denmark. The attack on Greece began with occupation of Albania and Bulgaria. The attack on the Suez Canal began with the invasion of the Balkans and North Africa. The attack on the United States can begin with the domination of any base which menaces our security—north or south.

Nobody can foretell tonight just when the acts of the dictators will ripen into attack on this hemisphere and us. But we know enough by now to realize that it would be suicide to wait until they are in our front yard.

When your enemy comes at you in a tank or a bombing plane, if you hold your fire until you see the whites of his eyes, you will never know what hit you. Our Bunker Hill of tomorrow may be several thousand miles from Boston.

Anyone with an atlas and a reasonable knowledge of the sudden striking-force of modern war, knows that it is stupid to wait until a probable enemy has gained a foothold from which to attack. Old-fashioned common sense calls for the use of a strategy which will prevent such an enemy from gaining a foothold in the first place.

We have, accordingly, extended our patrol in north and south Atlantic waters. We are steadily adding more and more ships and planes to that patrol. It is well known that the strength of the Atlantic Fleet has been greatly increased during the past year, and is constantly being built up.

These ships and planes warn of the presence of attacking raiders, on the sea, under the sea, and above the sea. The danger from these raiders is greatly lessened if their location is definitely known. We are thus being forewarned; and we shall be on our guard against efforts to establish Nazi bases closer to our hemisphere.

The deadly facts of war compel nations, for simple self-preservation, to make stern choices. It does not make sense, for instance, to say, "I believe in the defense of all the Western Hemisphere," and in the next breath to say, "I will not fight for that defense until the enemy has landed on our shores." And if we believe in the independence and integrity of the Americas, we must be willing to fight to defend them just as much as we would to fight for the safety of our own homes.

It is time for us to realize that the safety of American homes even in the center of our country has a definite relationship to the continued safety of homes in Nova Scotia or Trinidad or Brazil.

Our national policy today, therefore, is this:

First, we shall actively resist wherever necessary, and with all our resources, every attempt by Hitler to extend his Nazi domination to the Western Hemisphere, or to threaten it. We shall actively resist his every attempt to gain control of the seas. We insist upon the vital importance of keeping Hitlerism away from any point in the world which could be used and would be used as a base of attack against the Americas.

Second, from the point of view of strict naval and military necessity, we shall give every possible assistance to Britain and to all who, with Britain, are resisting Hitlerism or its equivalent with force of arms. Our patrols are helping now to insure delivery of the needed supplies to Britain. All additional measures necessary to deliver the goods will be taken. Any and all further methods or combination of methods, which can or should be utilized, are being devised by our military and naval technicians, who, with me, will work out and put into effect such new and additional safeguards as may be needed.

The delivery of needed supplies to Britain is imperative. This can be done; it must be done; it will be done.

To the other American nations—20 republics and the Dominion of Canada—I say this: The United States does not merely propose these purposes, but is actively engaged today in carrying them out.

I say to them further: You may disregard those few citizens of the United States who contend that we are disunited and cannot act.

There are some timid ones among us who say that we must preserve peace at any price—lest we lose our liberties forever. To them I say: Never in the history of the world has a nation lost its democracy by a successful struggle to defend its democracy. We must not be defeated by the fear of the very danger which we are preparing to resist. Our freedom has shown its ability to survive war, but it would never survive surrender. "The only thing we have to fear is fear itself."

There is, of course, a small group of sincere, patriotic men and women whose real passion for peace has shut their eyes to the ugly realities of international banditry and to the need to resist it at all costs. I am sure they are embarrassed by the sinister support they are receiving from the enemies of democracy in our midst—the Bundists and Fascists and Communists and every group devoted to bigotry and racial and religious intolerance. It is no mere coincidence that all the arguments put forward by these enemies of democracy—all their attempts to confuse and divide our people and to destroy public confidence in our Government—all their defeatist forebodings that Britain and democracy are already beaten—all their selfish promises that we can "do business" with Hitler—all of these are but echoes of the words that have been poured out from the Axis bureaus of propaganda. Those same words have been used before in other countries—to scare them, to divide them, to soften them up. Invariably, those same words have formed the advance guard of physical attack.

Your government has the right to expect of all citizens that they take loyal part in the common work of our common defense—take loyal part from this moment forward.

I have recently set up the machinery for civilian defense. It will rapidly organize, locality by locality. It will depend on the organized effort of men and women everywhere. All will have responsibilities to fulfil.

Defense today means more than merely fighting. It means morale, civilian as well as military; it means using every available resource; it means enlarging every useful plant. It means the use of a greater American common sense in discarding rumor and distorted statement. It means recognizing, for what they are, racketeers and fifth columnists, who are the incendiary bombs of the moment.

All of us know that we have made very great social progress in recent years. We propose to maintain that progress and strengthen it. When the Nation is threatened from without, however, as it is today, the actual production and transportation of the machinery of defense must not be interrupted by disputes between capital and capital, labor and labor, or capital and labor. The future of all free enterprise—of capital and labor alike—is at stake.

This is no time for capital to make, or be allowed to retain, excess profits. Articles of defense must have undisputed right-of-way in every industrial plant in the country.

A nation-wide machinery for condition and mediation of industrial disputes has been set up. That machinery must be used promptly—and without stoppage of work. Collective bargaining will be retained, but the American people expect that impartial recommendations of our Government services will be followed both by capital and by labor.

The overwhelming majority of our citizens expect their Government to see that the tools of defense are built; and for the very purpose of preserving the democratic safeguards of both labor and management, this Government is determined to use all of its power to express the will of its people and to prevent interference with the production of materials essential to our Nation's security.

Today the whole world is divided between human slavery and human freedom—between pagan brutality and the Christian ideal.

We choose human freedom—which is the Christian ideal.

No one of us can waver for a moment in his courage or his faith.

We will not accept a Hitler-dominated world. And we will not accept a world, like the post-war world of the 1920's, in which the seeds of Hitlerism can again be planted and allowed to grow.

We will accept only a world consecrated to freedom of speech and expression—freedom of every person to worship God in his own way—freedom from want—and freedom from terrorism.

Is such a world impossible of attainment?

Magna Charta, the Declaration of Independence, the Constitution of the United States, the Emancipation Proclamation, and every other milestone in human progress—all were ideals which seemed impossible of attainment, yet they were attained.

As a military force, we were weak when we established our independence, but we successfully stood off tyrants, powerful in their day, who are now lost in the dust of history.

Odds meant nothing to us then. Shall we now, with all our potential strength, hesitate to take every single measure necessary to maintain our American liberties?

Our people and our Government will not hesitate to meet that challenge.

As the President of a united and determined people, I say solemnly:

We reassert the ancient American doctrine of freedom of the seas.

We reassert the solidarity of the 21 American republics and the Dominion of Canada in the preservation of the independence of the hemisphere.

We have pledged material support to the other democracies of the world—and we will fulfil that pledge.

We in the Americas will decide for ourselves whether and when and where our American interests are attacked or our security threatened.

We are placing our armed forces in strategic military position.

We will not hesitate to use our armed forces to repel attack.

We reassert our abiding faith in the vitality of our constitutional republic as a perpetual home of freedom, of tolerance, and of devotion to the Word of God.

Therefore, with profound consciousness of my responsibilities to my countrymen and to my country's cause, I have tonight issued a proclamation that an unlimited national emergency exists and requires the strengthening of our defense to the extreme limit of our national power and authority.

The Nation will expect all individuals and all groups to play their full parts without stint and without selfishness and without doubt that our democracy will triumphantly survive.

I repeat the words of the Signers of the Declaration of Independence—that little band of patriots, fighting long ago against overwhelming odds, but certain, as are we, of ultimate victory: "With a firm reliance on the protection of Divine Providence, we mutually pledge to each other our lives, our fortunes, and our sacred honor."

Declarations of National Emergency

PROCLAMATION of National Emergency by President Franklin D. Roosevelt, September 8, 1939

Department of State, *Bulletin*, September 9, 1939, p. 216

PROCLAIMING A NATIONAL EMERGENCY IN CONNECTION WITH THE OBSERVANCE, SAFEGUARDING, AND ENFORCEMENT OF NEUTRALITY AND THE STRENGTHENING OF THE NATIONAL DEFENSE WITHIN THE LIMITS OF PEACE-TIME AUTHORIZATIONS

BY THE PRESIDENT OF THE UNITED STATES OF AMERICA

A Proclamation

WHEREAS a proclamation issued by me on September 5, 1939, proclaimed the neutrality of the United States in the war now unhappily existing between certain nations; and

WHEREAS this state of war imposes on the United States certain duties with respect to the proper observance, safeguarding, and enforcement of such neutrality, and the strengthening of the national defense within the limits of peace-time authorizations; and

WHEREAS measures required at this time call for the exercise of only a limited number of the powers granted in a national emergency:

NOW, THEREFORE, I, FRANKLIN D. ROOSEVELT, President of the United States of America, do proclaim that a national emergency exists in connection with and to the extent necessary for the proper observance, safeguarding, and enforcing of the neutrality of the

United States and the strengthening of our national defense within the limits of peace-time authorizations. Specific directions and authorizations will be given from time to time for carrying out these two purposes.

IN WITNESS WHEREOF I have hereunto set my hand and caused the seal of the United States of America to be affixed.

PROCLAMATION of Unlimited National Emergency by President Franklin D. Roosevelt, May 27, 1941

Department of State, *Bulletin*, May 31, 1941, p. 654

PROCLAIMING THAT AN UNLIMITED NATIONAL EMERGENCY CONFRONTS THIS COUNTRY, WHICH REQUIRES THAT ITS MILITARY, NAVAL, AIR AND CIVILIAN DEFENSES BE PUT ON THE BASIS OF READINESS TO REPEL ANY AND ALL ACTS OR THREATS OF AGGRESSION DIRECTED TOWARD ANY PART OF THE WESTERN HEMISPHERE

BY THE PRESIDENT OF THE UNITED STATES OF AMERICA

A Proclamation

WHEREAS on September 8, 1939 because of the outbreak of war in Europe a proclamation was issued declaring a limited national emergency and directing measures "for the purpose of strengthening our national defense within the limits of peacetime authorizations,"

WHEREAS a succession of events makes plain that the objectives of the Axis belligerents in such war are not confined to those avowed at its commencement, but include overthrow throughout the world of existing democratic order, and a worldwide domination of peoples and economies through the destruction of all resistance on land and sea and in the air, and

WHEREAS indifference on the part of the United States to the increasing menace would be perilous, and common prudence requires that for the security of this nation and of this hemisphere we should pass from peacetime authorizations of military strength to such a basis as will enable us to cope instantly and decisively with any attempt at hostile encirclement of this hemisphere, or the establishment of any base for aggression against it, as well as to repel the threat of predatory incursion by foreign agents into our territory and society.

NOW, THEREFORE, I, FRANKLIN D. ROOSEVELT, President of the United States of America, do proclaim that an unlimited national emergency confronts this country, which requires that its military, naval, air and civilian defenses be put on the basis of readiness to repel any and all acts or threats of aggression directed toward any part of the Western Hemisphere.

I call upon all the loyal citizens engaged in production for defense to give precedence to the needs of the nation to the end that a system of government that makes private enterprise possible may survive.

I call upon all our loyal workmen as well as employers to merge their lesser differences in the larger effort to insure the survival of the only kind of government which recognizes the rights of labor or of capital.

I call upon loyal state and local leaders and officials to cooperate with the civilian defense agencies of the United States to assure our internal security against foreign directed subversion and to put every community in order for maximum productive effort and minimum of waste and unnecessary frictions.

I call upon all loyal citizens to place the nation's needs first in mind and in action to the end that we may mobilize and have ready for instant defensive use all of the physical powers, all of the moral strength and all of the material resources of this nation.

IN WITNESS WHEREOF, [etc.]

Aid to France

MESSAGE from President Franklin D. Roosevelt to the Premier of France (Paul Reynaud), June 13, 1940

Department of State, *Peace and War*, p. 550

YOUR MESSAGE of June 10 has moved me very deeply. As I have already stated to you and to Mr. Churchill, this Government is doing everything in its power to make available to the Allied Governments the material they so urgently require, and our efforts to do still more are being redoubled. This is so because of our faith in and our support of the ideals for which the Allies are fighting.

The magnificent resistance of the French and British armies has profoundly impressed the American people.

I am personally particularly impressed by your declaration that France will continue to fight on behalf of democracy even if it means slow withdrawal, even to North Africa and the Atlantic. It is most important to remember that the French and British fleets continue mastery of the Atlantic and other oceans; also to remember that vital materials from the outside world are necessary to maintain all armies.

I am also greatly heartened by what Prime Minister Churchill said a few days ago about the continued resistance of the British Empire and that determination would seem to apply equally to the great French Empire all over the world. Naval power in world affairs still carries the lessons of history, as Admiral Darlan well knows.

MESSAGE from President Franklin D. Roosevelt to the Premier of France (Paul Reynaud), June 15, 1940

Department of State, *Bulletin*, June 15, 1940, p. 639

I AM SENDING you this reply to your message of yesterday which I am sure you will realize has received the most earnest, as well as the most friendly, study on our part.

First of all, let me reiterate the ever-increasing admiration with which the American people and their Government are viewing the resplendent courage with which the French armies are resisting the invaders on French soil.

I wish also to reiterate in the most emphatic terms that, making every possible effort under present conditions, the Government of the United States has made it possible for the Allied armies to obtain during the weeks that have just passed airplanes, artillery and munitions of many kinds and that this Government so long as the Allied governments continue to resist will redouble its efforts in this direction. I believe it is possible to say that every week that goes by will see additional matériel on its way to the Allied nations.

In accordance with its policy not to recognize the results of conquest of territory acquired through military aggression, the Government of the United States will not consider as valid any attempts to infringe by force the independence and territorial integrity of France.

In these hours which are so heart-rending for the French people and yourself, I send you the assurances of my utmost sympathy and I can further assure you that so long as the French people continue in defense of their liberty which constitutes the cause of popular institutions throughout the world, so long will they rest assured that matériel and supplies will be sent to them from the United States in ever-increasing quantities and kinds.

I know that you will understand that these statements carry with them no implication of military commitments. Only the Congress can make such commitments.

European Possessions in the Western Hemisphere

STATEMENT Issued by the Department of State, June 19, 1940

The Governments of France, Great Britain and the Netherlands were informed in the same sense. Department of State, *Bulletin,* June 22, 1940, p. 681

THE SECRETARY of State, Mr. Cordell Hull, on June 17 instructed the American Chargé at Berlin and the American Ambassador at Rome to send in writing to the Minister for Foreign Affairs of Germany and to the Minister for Foreign Affairs of Italy, respectively, the following communication in the name of the Government of the United States:

The Government of the United States is informed that the Government of France has requested of the German Government the terms of an armistice.

The Government of the United States feels it desirable, in order to avoid any possible misunderstanding, to inform Your Excellency that in accordance with its traditional policy relating to the Western Hemisphere, the United States would not recognize any transfer, and would not acquiesce in any attempt to transfer, any geographic region of the Western Hemisphere from one non-American power to another non-American power.

STATEMENT by Cordell Hull, July 5, 1940, Regarding the German Reply to the United States Note Dated June 18, 1940

Department of State, *Bulletin,* July 6, 1940, p. 3

THE AMERICAN Chargé d'Affaires in Berlin has communicated to the Department the text of a note dated July 1, which he has received from the German Minister of Foreign Affairs.

The note in question refers to the note delivered by the American Chargé d'Affaires under instructions of the Government of the United States on June 18, in which this Government informed the Government of the German Reich that it would not recognize any transfer of a geographical region of the Western Hemisphere from one non-American power to another non-American power, and that it would not acquiesce in any attempt to undertake such transfer.

The German Minister of Foreign Affairs states that the Government of the German Reich is unable to perceive for what reason the Government of the United States of America has addressed this communication to the Reich Government. He states that in contrast with other countries, especially in contrast with England and France, Germany has no territorial possessions in the American Continent, and has given no occasion whatever for the assumption that it intends to acquire such possessions, and he asserts that thus insofar as Germany is concerned, the communication addressed to the Reich Government is without object.

The German Minister of Foreign Affairs continues by remarking that in this case the interpretation of the Monroe Doctrine implicit in the communication of the Government of the United States would amount to conferring upon some European countries the right to possess territories in the Western Hemisphere and not to other European countries. He states that it is obvious that such an interpretation would be untenable. He concludes by remarking that apart from this, the Reich Government would like to point out again on this occasion that the nonintervention in the affairs of the American Continent by European nations which is demanded by the Monroe Doctrine can in principle be legally valid only on condition that the American nations for their part do not interfere in the affairs of the European Continent.

The foregoing is the substance of the German note.

I feel that no useful purpose will be served at this time for this Government to undertake to make any further communication to the Government of the German Reich on the subject matter of the communication above quoted.

The fundamental questions involved are entirely clear to all of the peoples of the American republics, and undoubtedly as well to the majority of the governments and peoples in the rest of the world.

The Monroe Doctrine is solely a policy of self-defense, which is intended to preserve the independence and integrity of the Americas. It was, and is, designed to prevent aggression in this hemisphere on the part of any non-American power, and likewise to make impossible any further extension to this hemisphere of any non-American system of government imposed from without. It contains within it not the slightest vestige of any implication, much less assumption, of hegemony on the part of the United States. It never has resembled, and it does not today resemble, policies which appear to be arising in other geographical areas of the world, which are alleged to be similar to the Monroe Doctrine, but which, instead of resting on the sole policies of self-defense and of respect for existing sovereignties, as does the Monroe Doctrine, would in reality seem to be only the pretext for the carrying out of conquest by the sword, of military occupation, and of complete economic and political domination by certain powers of other free and independent peoples.

The Monroe Doctrine has, of course, not the remotest connection with the fact that certain European nations exercise sovereignty over colonies in the Western Hemisphere and that certain other European nations do not. This situation existed before the Monroe Doctrine was proclaimed. The Doctrine did not undertake to interfere with the existing situation, but did announce that further incursions would not be tolerated. It made clear that the future transfer of existing possessions to another non-American state would be regarded as inimical to the interests of this hemisphere. This has become a basic policy of the Government of the United States. As already stated in the communication addressed to the German Government by this Government under date of June 18, the Government of the United States will neither recognize nor acquiesce in the transfer to a non-American power of geographical regions in this hemisphere now possessed by some other non-American power.

The Government of the United States pursues a policy of non-participation and of non-involvement in the purely political affairs of Europe. It will, however, continue to cooperate, as it has cooperated in the past, with all other nations, whenever the policies of such nations make it possible, and whenever it believes that such efforts are practicable and in its own best interests, for the purpose of promoting economic, commercial, and social rehabilitation, and of advancing the cause of international law and order, of which the entire world stands so tragically in need today.

Lease of British Naval and Air Bases

MESSAGE of President Franklin D. Roosevelt to Congress, September 3, 1940

Department of State, *Bulletin*, September 7, 1940, p. 201. The exchange of notes with Great Britain and the opinion of the Attorney General appear in the same issue on pp. 195 and 201

I TRANSMIT herewith for the information of the Congress notes exchanged between the British Ambassador at Washington and the Secretary of State on September 2, 1940, under which this Government has acquired the right to lease naval and air bases in Newfoundland, and in the islands of Bermuda, the Bahamas, Jamaica, St. Lucia, Trinidad, and Antigua, and in British Guiana; also a copy of an opinion of the Attorney General dated August 27, 1940, regarding my authority to consummate this arrangement.

The right to bases in Newfoundland and Bermuda are gifts—generously given and gladly received. The other bases mentioned have been acquired in exchange for fifty of our over-age destroyers.

This is not inconsistent in any sense with our status of peace. Still less is it a threat against any nation. It is an epochal and far-reaching act of preparation for continental defense in the face of grave danger.

Preparation for defense is an inalienable prerogative of a sovereign state. Under present circumstances this exercise of sovereign right is essential to the maintenance of our peace and safety. This is the most important action in the reinforcement of our national defense that has been taken since the Louisiana Purchase. Then as now, considerations of safety from overseas attack were fundamental.

The value to the Western Hemisphere of these outposts of security is beyond calculation. Their need has long been recognized by our country, and especially by those primarily charged with the duty of charting and organizing our own naval and military defense. They are essential to the protection of the Panama Canal, Central America, the Northern portion of South America, The Antilles, Canada, Mexico, and our own Eastern and Gulf Seaboards. Their consequent importance in hemispheric defense is obvious. For these reasons I have taken advantage of the present opportunity to acquire them.

Lend-Lease Act of March 11, 1941

AN ACT to Promote the Defense of the United States

Public Law 11, 77th Congress, Chapter 11, 1st Session, H.R. 1776. In *International Conciliation*, No. 369, April, 1941

BE IT ENACTED *by the Senate and House of Representatives of the United States of America in Congress assembled.* . . .

SEC. 2. As used in this Act—

(a) The term "defense article" means—

(1) Any weapon, munition, aircraft, vessel, or boat;

(2) Any machinery, facility, tool, material, or supply necessary for the manufacture, production, processing, repair, servicing, or operation of any article described in this subsection;

(3) Any component material or part of or equipment for any article described in this subsection;

(4) Any agricultural, industrial or other commodity or article for defense.

Such term "defense article" includes any article described in this subsection: Manufactured or procured pursuant to section 3, or to which the United States or any foreign government has or hereafter acquires title, possession, or control.

(b) The term "defense information" means any plan, specification, design, prototype, or information pertaining to any defense article.

SEC. 3. (a) Notwithstanding the provisions of any other law, the President may, from time to time, when he deems it in the interest of national defense, authorize the Secretary of War, the Secretary of the Navy, or the head of any other department or agency of the Government—

(1) To manufacture in arsenals, factories, and shipyards under their jurisdiction, or otherwise procure, to the extent to which funds are made available therefor, or contracts are authorized from time to time by the Congress, or both, any defense article for the government of any country whose defense the President deems vital to the defense of the United States.

(2) To sell, transfer title to, exchange, lease, lend, or otherwise dispose of, to any such government any defense article, but no defence article not manufactured or procured under paragraph (1) shall in any way be disposed of under this paragraph, except after consultation with the Chief of Staff of the Army or the Chief of Naval Operations of the Navy, or both. The value of defense articles disposed of in any way under authority of this paragraph, and procured from funds heretofore appropriated, shall not exceed $1,300,000,000. The value of such defense articles shall be determined by the head of the department or agency concerned or such other department, agency or officer as shall be designated in the manner provided in the rules and regulations issued hereunder. Defense articles procured from funds hereafter appropriated to any department or agency of the Government, other than from funds authorized to be appropriated under this Act, shall not be disposed of in any way under authority of this paragraph except to the extent hereafter authorized by the Congress in the Acts appropriating such funds or otherwise.

(3) To test, inspect, prove, repair, outfit, recondition, or otherwise to place in good working order, to the extent to which funds are made available therefor, or contracts are authorized from time to time by the Congress, or both, any defense article for any such

government, or to procure any or all such services by private contract.

(4) To communicate to any such government any defense information, pertaining to any defense article furnished to such government under paragraph (2) of this subsection.

(5) To release for export any defense article disposed of in any way under this subsection to any such government.

(b) The terms and conditions upon which any such foreign government receives any aid authorized under subsection (a) shall be those which the President deems satisfactory, and the benefit to the United States may be payment or repayment in kind or property, or any other direct or indirect benefit which the President deems satisfactory.

(c) After June 30, 1943, or after the passage of a concurrent resolution by the two Houses before June 30, 1943, which declares that the powers conferred by or pursuant to subsection (a) are no longer necessary to promote the defense of the United States, neither the President nor the head of any department or agency shall exercise any of the powers conferred by or pursuant to subsection (a); except that until July 1, 1946, any of such powers may be exercised to the extent necessary to carry out a contract or agreement with such a foreign government made before July 1, 1943, or before the passage of such concurrent resolution, whichever is the earlier.

(d) Nothing in this Act shall be construed to authorize or to permit the authorization of convoying vessels by naval vessels of the United States.

(e) Nothing in this Act shall be construed to authorize or to permit the authorization of the entry of any American vessel into a combat area in violation of section 3 of the Neutrality Act of 1939.

SEC. 4. All contracts or agreements made for the disposition of any defense article or defense information pursuant to section 3 shall contain a clause by which the foreign government undertakes that it will not, without the consent of the President, transfer title to or possession of such defense article or defense information by gift, sale, or otherwise, or permit its use by anyone not an officer, employee, or agent of such foreign government.

SEC. 5. (a) The Secretary of War, the Secretary of the Navy, or the head of any other department or agency of the Government involved shall, when any such defense article or defense information is exported, immediately inform the department or agency designated by the President to administer section 6 of the Act of July 2, 1940 (54 Stat. 714), of the quantities, character, value, terms of disposition, and destination of the article and information so exported.

(b) The President from time to time, but not less frequently than once every ninety days, shall transmit to the Congress a report of operations under this Act except such information as he deems incompatible with the public interest to disclose. Reports provided for under this subsection shall be transmitted to the Secretary of the Senate or the Clerk of the House of Representatives, as the case may be, if the Senate or the House of Representatives, as the case may be, is not in session.

SEC. 6. (a) There is hereby authorized to be appropriated from time to time, out of any money in the Treasury not otherwise appropriated, such amounts as may be necessary to carry out the provisions and accomplish the purposes of this Act.

(b) All money and all property which is converted into money received under section 3 from any government shall, with the approval of the Director of the Budget, revert to the respective appropriation or appropriations out of which funds were expended with respect to the defense article or defense information for which such consideration is received, and shall be available for expenditure for the purpose for which such expended funds were appropriated by law, during the fiscal year in which such funds are received and the ensuing fiscal year; but in no event shall any funds so received be available for expenditure after June 30, 1946.

SEC. 7. The Secretary of War, the Secretary of the Navy, and the head of the department or agency shall in all contracts or agreements for the disposition of any defense article or defense information fully protect the rights of all citizens of the United States who have patent rights in and to any such article or information which is hereby authorized to be disposed of and the payments collected for royalties on such patents shall be paid to the owners and holders of such patents.

SEC. 8. The Secretaries of War and of the Navy are hereby authorized to purchase or otherwise acquire arms, ammunition, and implements of war produced within the jurisdiction of any country to which section 3 is applicable, whenever the President deems such purchase or acquisition to be necessary in the interests of the defense of the United States.

SEC. 9. The President may, from time to time, promulgate such rules and regulations as may be necessary and proper to carry out any of the provisions of this Act; and he may exercise any power or authority conferred on him by this Act through such department, agency, or officer as he shall direct.

SEC. 10. Nothing in this Act shall be construed to change existing law relating to the use of the land and naval forces of the United States, except in so far as such use relates to the manufacture, procurement, and repair of defense articles, the communication of information and other noncombatant purposes enumerated in this Act.

SEC. 11. If any provision of this Act or the application of such provision to any circumstance shall be held invalid, the validity of the remainder of the Act and the applicability of such provision to other circumstances shall not be affected thereby.

Approved, March 11, 1941.

Defense of Greenland

ANNOUNCEMENT by the Department of State, April 10, 1941, of an Agreement between Denmark and the United States

Department of State, *Bulletin,* April 12, 1941, p. 443; text of the agreement, p. 445

THE DEPARTMENT of State announced April 10 the signing on April 9, 1941 of an agreement between the Secretary of State, acting on behalf of the Government of the United States of America, and the Danish Minister, Henrik de Kauffmann, acting on behalf of His Majesty the King of Denmark in his capacity as sovereign of Greenland.

The agreement recognizes that as a result of the present European war there is danger that Greenland may be converted into a point of aggression against nations of the American Continent, and accepts the responsibility on behalf of the United States of assisting Greenland in the maintenance of its present status.

The agreement, after explicitly recognizing the Danish sovereignty over Greenland, proceeds to grant to the United States the right to locate and construct airplane landing fields and facilities for the defense of Greenland and for the defense of the American Continent.

The circumstances leading up to the agreement are as follows.

On April 9, 1940 the German Army invaded and occupied Denmark, and that occupation continues. In condemning this invasion President Roosevelt said:

Force and military aggression are once more on the march against small nations, in this instance through the invasion of Denmark and Norway. These two nations have won and maintained during a period of many generations the respect and regard not only of the American people, but of all peoples, because of their observance of the highest standards of national and international conduct.

The Government of the United States has on the occasion of recent invasions strongly expressed its disapprobation of such unlawful exercise of force. It here reiterates, with undiminished emphasis, its point of view as expressed on those occasions. If civilization is to survive, the rights of the smaller nations to independence, to their territorial integrity, and to the unimpeded opportunity for self-government must be respected by their more powerful neighbors.

This invasion at once raised questions as to the status of Greenland, which has been recognized as being within the area of the Monroe Doctrine. The Government of the United States announces its policy of maintenance of the *status quo* in the Western Hemisphere.

On May 3, 1940 the Greenland Councils, meeting at Godhavn, adopted a resolution in the name of the people of Greenland reaffirming their allegiance to King Christian X of Denmark, and expressed the hope that so long as Greenland remained cut off from the mother country, the Government of the United States would continue to keep in mind the exposed position of the Danish flag in Greenland and of the native and Danish population of Greenland. The Government of the United States expressed its willingness to assure that the needs of the population of Greenland would be taken care of.

On July 25, 1940, the consultation of American Foreign Ministers at Habana declared that any attempt on the part of a non-American state against the integrity or inviolability of the territory, the sovereignty, or the political independence of an American state should be considered an act of aggression, and that they would cooperate in defense against any such aggression. In a further declaration, known as the Act of Habana, it declared that the status of regions in this continent belonging to European powers was a subject of deep concern to all of the governments of the American republics.

During the summer of 1940 German activity on the eastern coast of Greenland became apparent. Three ships proceeding from Norwegian territory under German occupation arrived off the coast of Greenland, ostensibly for commercial or scientific purposes; and at least one of these ships landed parties nominally for scientific purposes, but actually for meteorological assistance to German belligerent operations in the north Atlantic. These parties were eventually cleared out. In the late fall of 1940, air reconnaissance appeared over East Greenland under circumstances making it plain that there had been continued activity in that region.

On March 27, 1941, a German bomber flew over the eastern coast of Greenland and on the following day another German war plane likewise reconnoitered the same territory. Under these circumstances it appeared that further steps for the defense of Greenland were necessary to bring Greenland within the system of hemispheric defense envisaged by the Act of Habana.

The Government of the United States has no thought in mind save that of assuring the safety of Greenland and the rest of the American Continent, and Greenland's continuance under Danish sovereignty. The agreement recognizes explicitly the full Danish sovereignty over Greenland. At the same time it is recognized that so long as Denmark remains under German occupation the Government in Denmark cannot exercise the Danish sovereign powers over Greenland under the Monroe Doctrine, and the agreement therefore was signed between the Secretary of State and the Danish Minister in Washington, acting as representative of the King of Denmark in his capacity as sovereign of Greenland, and with the concurrence of the Governors of Greenland.

The step is taken in furtherance of the traditional friendliness between Denmark and the United States. The policy of the United States is that of defending for Denmark her sovereignty over Greenland, so that she may have a full exercise of it as soon as the invasion is ended. The agreement accordingly provides that as soon as the war is over and the danger has passed, the two Governments shall promptly consult as to whether the arrangements made by the present agreement shall continue or whether they shall then cease.

Freezing of German and Italian Assets in the United States

STATEMENT Issued by the White House, June 14, 1941

Department of State, *Bulletin*, June 14, 1941, p. 718

IN VIEW OF the unlimited national emergency declared by the President, he has today issued an Executive order freezing immediately all German and Italian assets in the United States. At the same time the order also freezes the assets of all invaded or occupied European countries not previously frozen. These include Albania, Austria, Czechoslovakia, Danzig, and Poland. The freezing control will be administered by the Treasury Department.

These measures in effect bring all financial transactions in which German and Italian interests are involved under the control of the Government and impose heavy criminal penalties upon persons failing to comply therewith. The Executive order is designed, among other things, to prevent the use of the financial facilities of the United

States in ways harmful to national defense and other American interests, to prevent the liquidation in the United States of assets looted by duress or conquest, and to curb subversive activities in the United States.

With a view to implementing the control of German and Italian assets in this country and in view of the interrelationship of international financial transactions, the Executive order has also been extended to the remaining countries of continental Europe. However, it is intended that through the medium of general licenses the freezing control will be lifted with respect to Finland, Portugal, Spain, Sweden, Switzerland, and the Union of Soviet Socialist Republics, conditional upon the receipt of adequate assurances from the governments of such countries that the general licenses will not be employed by them or their nationals to evade the purposes of this order. Furthermore, transactions under the general licenses will be subject to reporting and careful scrutiny.

Simultaneously, with the issuance of the Executive order, the President approved regulations ordering a census of all foreign-owned property in the United States. This census will relate not only to property in the United States belonging to countries and nationals subject to freezing control but to all other countries as well.

Under previous Executive orders freezing control has been extended to the assets of Norway, Denmark, Netherlands, Belgium, Luxemburg, France, Latvia, Estonia, Rumania, Bulgaria, Lithuania, Hungary, Yugoslavia, and Greece.

Closing of German and Italian Consular Offices and Other Agencies in the United States

NOTE from Sumner Welles, Under Secretary of State, to the German Chargé d'Affaires at Washington (Hans Thomsen), June 16, 1941

Department of State, *Bulletin*, June 21, 1941, p. 843

S<small>IR</small>:

It has come to the knowledge of this Government that agencies of the German Reich in this country, including German consular establishments, have been engaged in activities wholly outside the scope of their legitimate duties. These activities have been of an improper and unwarranted character. They render the continued presence in the United States of those agencies and consular establishments inimical to the welfare of this country.

I am directed by the President to request that the German Government remove from United States territory all German nationals in anywise connected with the German Library of Information in New York, the German Railway and Tourists Agencies, and the Trans-Ocean News Service, and that each of these organizations and their affiliates shall be promptly closed.

I am also directed to request that all German consular officers, agents, clerks, and employees thereof of German nationality shall be removed from American territory and that the consular establishments likewise be promptly closed.

It is contemplated that all such withdrawals and closures shall be effected before July 10.

NOTE from Sumner Welles, Under Secretary of State, to the Italian Ambassador to the United States (Don Ascanio dei Principi Colonna), June 20, 1941

Department of State, *Bulletin*, June 21, 1941, p. 743

Excellency:

I have the honor to inform Your Excellency that the President has directed me to request that the Italian Government promptly close all Italian consular establishments within United States territory and remove therefrom all Italian consular officers, agents, clerks and employees of Italian nationality. In the opinion of the Government of the United States it is obvious that the continued functioning of Italian consular establishments in territory of the United States would serve no desirable purpose.

I am likewise directed to request the closing of all agencies in this country connected with the Italian Government, together with the cessation of their activities, and, furthermore, the removal of all Italian nationals in any way connected with organizations of the Italian Government in the United States, with the exception of its duly accredited representation in Washington.

It is contemplated that all such withdrawals and closures shall be effected before July 15, 1941.

Defense of Iceland

MESSAGE of President Franklin D. Roosevelt to Congress, July 7, 1941

Department of State, *Bulletin*, July 12, 1941, p. 15

I AM TRANSMITTING herewith for the information of the Congress a message I received from the Prime Minister of Iceland on July first and the reply I addressed on the same day to the Prime Minister of Iceland in response to this message.

In accordance with the understanding so reached, forces of the United States Navy have today arrived in Iceland in order to supplement, and eventually to replace, the British forces which have until now been stationed in Iceland in order to insure the adequate defense of that country.

As I stated in my message to the Congress of September third last regarding the acquisition of certain naval and air bases from Great Britain in exchange for certain over-age destroyers, considerations of safety from overseas attack are fundamental.

The United States cannot permit the occupation by Germany of strategic outposts in the Atlantic to be used as air or naval bases for eventual attack against the Western Hemisphere. We have no desire to see any change in the present sovereignty of those regions. Assurance that such outposts in our defense-frontier remain in friendly hands is the very foundation of our national security and of the national security of every one of the independent nations of the New World.

For the same reason substantial forces of the United States have now been sent to the bases acquired last year from Great Britain in Trinidad and in British Guiana in the south in order to forestall any pincers movement undertaken by Germany against the Western Hemisphere. It is essential that Germany should not be able successfully to employ such tactics through sudden seizure of strategic points in the south Atlantic and in the north Atlantic.

The occupation of Iceland by Germany would constitute a serious threat in three dimensions:

The threat against Greenland and the northern portion of the North American Continent, including the Islands which lie off it.

The threat against all shipping in the north Atlantic.

The threat against the steady flow of munitions to Britain—which is a matter of broad policy clearly approved by the Congress.

It is, therefore, imperative that the approaches between the Americas and those strategic outposts, the safety of which this country regards as essential to its national security, and which it must therefore defend, shall remain open and free from all hostile activity or threat thereof.

As Commander-in-Chief I have consequently issued orders to the Navy that all necessary steps be taken to insure the safety of communications in the approaches between Iceland and the United States, as well as on the seas between the United States and all other strategic outposts.

This Government will insure the adequate defense of Iceland with full recognition of the independence of Iceland as a sovereign state.

In my message to the Prime Minister of Iceland I have given the people of Iceland the assurance that the American forces sent there would in no way interfere with the internal and domestic affairs of that country, and that immediately upon the termination of the present international emergency all American forces will be at once withdrawn, leaving the people of Iceland and their Government in full and sovereign control of their own territory.

The "Black List"

STATEMENT on the Proclaimed List of Certain Blocked Nationals, Issued by the Department of State, July 17, 1941

Department of State, *Bulletin,* July 19, 1941, p. 41

As a further step in view of the unlimited national emergency declared by the President, he has today issued a proclamation authorizing the promulgation of a list of persons which will be known as "The Proclaimed List of Certain Blocked Nationals." The list will consist of certain persons deemed to be acting for the benefit of Germany or Italy or nationals of those countries and persons to whom the exportation, directly or indirectly, of various articles or materials is deemed to be detrimental to the interest of national defense. The list will be prepared by the Secretary of State acting in conjunction with the Secretary of the Treasury, the Attorney General, the Secretary of Commerce, the Administrator of Export Control, and the Coordinator of Commercial and Cultural Relations between the American Republics.

Simultaneously with the issuance of the proclamation, a proclaimed list was issued by the designated Government officials containing the names of more than 1,800 persons and business institutions in the other American republics. This list is the result of long and intensive investigations and studies by the interested governmental agencies. The list will be published in the *Federal Register* and may be obtained in pamphlet form from various governmental institutions and the Federal Reserve banks. From time to time there will be additions to and deletions from the list, which will be made public. The President gave warning that anyone serving as a cloak for a person on the list will have his name added forthwith to the list.

The list will have two principal functions. In the first place, no article covered by the Export Control Act of July 2, 1940 may be exported to persons named in the list except under special circumstances. Secondly, persons on the list will be treated as though they were nationals of Germany or Italy within the meaning of Executive Order 8389, as amended, under which, on June 14, 1941, the freezing control was extended to all of the countries of the continent of Europe and nationals thereof.

At the time of the issuance of the proclamation, it was also announced that in attaining the objectives of Executive Order 8389, as amended, all efforts are being made to cause the least possible interference with legitimate inter-American trade. With that end in view the Treasury Department has issued a general license with respect to inter-American trade transactions and the financial transactions incidental thereto involving persons in the other American republics who may be nationals of a European country designated in the order. This general license will permit such classes of transactions without the necessity of applying for specific licenses.

The general license, however, will not apply to persons so long as their names appear on the proclaimed list. In addition, exporters and importers in the United States may from time to time be advised by their banks, or otherwise, that instructions have been issued by the Secretary of the Treasury requiring specific-license applications for trade transactions involving certain persons in the other American republics who are not named on the proclaimed list.

Furthermore, financial transactions which are not incidental to licensed trade transactions are not covered by the general license. With respect to such purely financial transactions, appropriate specific licenses will have to be obtained from the Treasury Department.

The proclaimed list will also serve as a guide to United States firms in the selections of agents and representatives in the other American republics.

The text of the proclamation follows:

Authorizing a Proclaimed List of Certain Blocked Nationals and Controlling Certain Exports

BY THE PRESIDENT OF THE UNITED STATES OF AMERICA

A Proclamation

I, FRANKLIN D. ROOSEVELT, President of the United States of America, acting under and by virtue of the authority vested in me by Section 5 (b) of the Act of October 6, 1917 (40 Stat. 415) as amended and Section 6 of the Act of July 2, 1940 (54 Stat. 714) as amended and by virtue of all other authority vested in me, and by virtue of the existence of a period of unlimited national emergency and finding that this Proclamation is necessary in the interest of national defense, do hereby order and proclaim the following:

Section 1. The Secretary of State, acting in conjunction with the Secretary of the Treasury, the Attorney General, the Secretary of Commerce, the Administrator of Export Control, and the Coordinator of Commercial and Cultural Relations Between the American Republics, shall from time to time cause to be prepared an appropriate list of

(a) certain persons deemed to be, or to have been acting or purporting to act, directly or indirectly, for the benefit of, or under the direction of, or under the jurisdiction of, or on behalf of, or in collaboration with Germany or Italy or a national thereof; and

(b) certain persons to whom, or on whose behalf, or for whose account, the exportation directly or indirectly of any article or material exported from the United States, is deemed to be detrimental to the interest of national defense.

In similar manner and in the interest of national defense, additions to and deletions from such list shall be made from time to time. Such list and any additions thereto or deletions therefrom shall be filed pursuant to the provisions of the Federal Register Act and such list shall be known as "The Proclaimed List of Certain Blocked Nationals."

Section 2. Any person, so long as his name appears in such list, shall, for the purpose of Section 5 (b) of the Act of October 6, 1917, as amended, and for the purpose of this Proclamation, be deemed to be a national of a foreign country, and shall be treated for all purposes under Executive Order No. 8389, as amended, as though he were a national of Germany or Italy. All the terms and provisions of Executive Order No. 8389, as amended, shall be applicable to any such person so long as his name appears in such list, and to any property in which any such person has or has had an interest, to the same extent that such terms and provisions are applicable to nationals of Germany or Italy, and to property in which nationals of Germany or Italy have or have had an interest.

Section 3. The exportation from the United States directly or indirectly to, or on behalf of, or for the account of any person, so long as his name appears on such list, of any article or material the exportation of which is prohibited or curtailed by any proclamation heretofore or hereafter issued under the authority of Section 6 of the Act of July 2, 1940, as amended, or of any other military equipment or munitions, or component parts thereof, or machinery, tools, or material, or supplies necessary for the manufacture, servicing, or operation thereof, is hereby prohibited under Section 6 of the Act of July 2, 1940, as amended, except (1) when authorized in each case by a license as provided for in Proclamation No. 2413 of July 2, 1940, or in Proclamation No. 2465 of March 4, 1941, as the case may be, and (2) when the Administrator of Export Control under my direction has determined that such prohibition of exportation would work an unusual hardship on American interests.

Section 4. The term "person" as used herein means an individual, partnership, association, corporation or other organization.

The term "United States as used herein means the United States and any place subject to the jurisdiction thereof, including the Philippine Islands, the Canal Zone, and the District of Columbia and any other territory, dependency or possession of the United States.

Section 5. Nothing herein contained shall be deemed in any manner to limit or restrict the provisions of the said Executive Order No. 8389, as amended, or the authority vested thereby in the Secretary of the Treasury and the Attorney General. So far as the said Executive Order No. 8389, as amended, is concerned, "The Proclaimed List of Certain Blocked Nationals," authorized by this Proclamation, is merely a list of certain persons with respect to whom and with respect to whose property interests the public is specifically put on notice that the provisions of such Executive Order are applicable; and the fact that any person is not named in such list shall in no wise be deemed to mean that such person is not a national of a foreign country designated in such order, within the meaning thereof, or to affect in any manner the application of such order to such person or to the property interests of such person.

IN WITNESS WHEREOF [etc.]

Announcement of the "Atlantic Charter"

MESSAGE from President Roosevelt to Congress Concerning His Conferences at Sea with the Prime Minister of Great Britain (Winston Churchill) in August, 1941

Department of State, *Bulletin*, August 23, 1941, p. 147; *see also infra*, pp. 1035-36.

OVER A WEEK AGO I held several important conferences at sea with the British Prime Minister. Because of the factor of safety to British, Canadian, and American ships and their personnel, no prior announcement of these meetings could properly be made.

At the close, a public statement by the Prime Minister and the President was made. . . .

The Congress and the President having heretofore determined through the Lend Lease Act on the national policy of American aid to the democracies which East and West are waging war against dictatorships, the military and naval conversations at these meetings made clear gains in furthering the effectiveness of this aid.

Furthermore, the Prime Minister and I are arranging for conferences with the Soviet Union to aid it in its defense against the attack made by the principal aggressor of the modern world—Germany.

Finally, the declaration of principles at this time presents a goal which is worth while for our type of civilization to seek. It is so clear cut that it is difficult to oppose in any major particular without automatically admitting a willingness to accept compromise with Nazism; or to agree to a world peace which would give to Nazism domination over large numbers of conquered nations. Inevitably such a peace would be a gift to Nazism to take breath—armed breath—for a second war to extend the control over Europe and Asia to the American Hemisphere itself.

It is perhaps unnecessary for me to call attention once more to the utter lack of validity of the spoken or written word of the Nazi government.

It is also unnecessary for me to point out that the declaration of principles includes of necessity the world need for freedom of religion and freedom of information. No society of the world organized under the announced principles could survive without these freedoms which are a part of the whole freedom for which we strive.

Protection of American Vessels

RADIO ADDRESS by President Franklin D. Roosevelt, September 11, 1941

Department of State, *Bulletin*, September 13, 1941, p. 193; *see also supra*, pp. 144-47

THE NAVY DEPARTMENT of the United States has reported to me that on the morning of September fourth the United States destroyer *Greer,* proceeding in full daylight towards Iceland, had reached a point southeast of Greenland. She was carrying American mail to Iceland. She was flying the American flag. Her identity as an American ship was unmistakable.

She was then and there attacked by a submarine. Germany admits that it was a German submarine. The submarine deliberately fired a torpedo at the *Greer,* followed later by another torpedo attack. In spite of what Hitler's propaganda bureau has invented, and in spite of what any American obstructionist organization may prefer to believe, I tell you the blunt fact that the German submarine fired first upon this American destroyer without warning, and with deliberate design to sink her.

Our destroyer, at the time, was in waters which the Government of the United States had declared to be waters of self-defense—surrounding outposts of American protection in the Atlantic.

In the north, outposts have been established by us in Iceland, Greenland, Labrador, and Newfoundland. Through these waters there pass many ships of many flags. They bear food and other supplies to civilians; and they bear matériel of war, for which the people of the United States are spending billions of dollars, and which, by congressional action, they have declared to be essential for the defense of their own land.

The United States destroyer, when attacked, was proceeding on a legitimate mission.

If the destroyer was visible to the submarine when the torpedo was fired, then the attack was a deliberate attempt by the Nazis to sink a clearly identified American warship. On the other hand, if the submarine was beneath the surface and, with the aid of its listening devices, fired in the direction of the sound of the American destroyer without even taking the trouble to learn its identity—as the official German communiqué would indicate—then the attack was even more outrageous. For it indicates a policy of indiscriminate violence against any vessel sailing the seas—belligerent or non-belligerent.

This was piracy—legally and morally. It was not the first nor the last act of piracy which the Nazi Government has committed against the American flag in this war. Attack has followed attack.

A few months ago an American-flag merchant ship, the *Robin Moor,* was sunk by a Nazi submarine in the middle of the South Atlantic, under circumstances violating long-established international law and every principle of humanity. The passengers and the crew were forced into open boats hundreds of miles from land, in direct violation of international agreements signed by the Government of Germany. No apology, no allegation of mistake, no offer of reparations has come from the Nazi Government.

In July 1941, an American battleship in North American waters was followed by a submarine which for a long time sought to maneuver itself into a position of attack. The periscope of the submarine was clearly seen. No British or American submarines were within hundreds of miles of this spot at the time, so the nationality of the submarine is clear.

Five days ago a United States Navy ship on patrol picked up three survivors of an American-owned ship operating under the flag of our sister Republic of Panama—the S.S. *Sessa.* On August seventeenth, she had been first torpedoed without warning and then shelled, near Greenland, while carrying civilian supplies to Iceland. It is feared that the other members of her crew have been drowned. In view of the established presence of German submarines in this vicinity, there can be no reasonable doubt as to the identity of the attacker.

Five days ago, another United States merchant ship, the *Steel Seafarer,* was sunk by a German aircraft in the Red Sea two hundred and twenty miles south of Suez. She was bound for an Egyptian port.

Four of the vessels sunk or attacked flew the American flag and were clearly identifiable. Two of these ships were warships of the American Navy. In the fifth case, the vessel sunk clearly carried the flag of Panama.

In the face of all this, we Americans are keeping our feet on the ground. Our type of democratic civilization has outgrown the thought of feeling compelled to fight some other nation by reason of any single piratical attack on one of our ships. We are not becoming hysterical or losing our sense of proportion. Therefore, what I am thinking and saying does not relate to any isolated episode.

Instead, we Americans are taking a long-range point of view in regard to certain fundamentals and to a series of events on land and on sea which must be considered as a whole—as a part of a world pattern.

It would be unworthy of a great nation to exaggerate an isolated incident or to become inflamed by some one act of violence. But it would be inexcusable folly to minimize such incidents in the face of evidence which makes it clear that the incident is not isolated but part of a general plan.

The important truth is that these acts of international lawlessness are a manifestation of a design which has been made clear to the American people for a long time. It is the Nazi design to abolish the freedom of the seas and to acquire absolute control and domination of the seas for themselves.

For with control of the seas in their own hands, the way can become clear for their next step—domination of the United States and the Western Hemisphere by force. Under Nazi control of the seas, no merchant ship of the United States or of any other American republic would be free to carry on any peaceful commerce, except by the condescending grace of this foreign and tyrannical power. The Atlantic Ocean which has been, and which should always be, a free and friendly highway for us would then become a deadly menace to the commerce of the United States, to the coasts of the United States, and to the inland cities of the United States.

The Hitler Government, in defiance of the laws of the sea and of the recognized rights of all other nations, has presumed to declare, on paper, that great areas of the seas—even including a vast expanse lying in the Western Hemisphere—are to be closed, and that no ships may enter them for any purpose, except at peril of being sunk. Actually they are sinking ships at will and without warning in widely separated areas both within and far outside of these far-flung pretended zones.

This Nazi attempt to seize control of the oceans is but a counterpart of the Nazi plots now being carried on throughout the Western Hemisphere—all designed toward the same end. For Hitler's advance guards—not only his avowed agents but also his dupes among us—have sought to make ready for him footholds and bridgeheads in the New World, to be used as soon as he has gained control of the oceans.

His intrigues, his plots, his machinations, his sabotage in this New World are all known to the Government of the United States. Conspiracy has followed conspiracy.

Last year a plot to seize the Government of Uruguay was smashed by the prompt action of that country, which was supported in full by her American neighbors. A like plot was then hatching in Argentina, and that Government has carefully and wisely blocked it at every point. More recently, an endeavor was made to subvert the Government of Bolivia. Within the past few weeks the discovery was made of secret air-landing fields in Colombia, within easy range of the Panama Canal. I could multiply instances.

To be ultimately successful in world-mastery, Hitler knows that he must get control of the seas. He must first destroy the bridge of ships which we are building across the Atlantic, over which we shall continue to roll the implements of war to help destroy him and all his works in the end. He must wipe out our patrol on sea and in the air. He must silence the British Navy.

It must be explained again and again to people who like to think of the United States Navy as an invincible protection, that this can be true only if the British Navy survives. That is simple arithmetic.

For if the world outside the Americas falls under Axis domination, the shipbuilding facilities which the Axis powers would then possess in all of Europe, in the British Isles, and in the Far East would be much greater than all the shipbuilding facilities and potentialities of all the Americas—not only greater but two or three times greater. Even if the United States threw all its resources into such a situation, seeking to double and even redouble the size of our Navy, the Axis powers, in control of the rest of the world, would have the man-power and the physical resources to outbuild us several times over.

It is time for all Americans of all the Americas to stop being deluded by the romantic notion that the Americas can go on living happily and peacefully in a Nazi-dominated world.

Generation after generation, America has battled for the general policy of the freedom of the seas. That policy is a very simple one—but a basic, fundamental one. It means that no nation has the right to make the broad oceans of the world, at great distances from the actual theater of land war, unsafe for the commerce of others.

That has been our policy, proved time and time again, in all our history.

Our policy has applied from time immemorial—and still applies—not merely to the Atlantic but to the Pacific and to all other oceans as well.

Unrestricted submarine warfare in 1941 constitutes a defiance—an act of aggression—against that historic American policy.

It is now clear that Hitler has begun his campaign to control the seas by ruthless force and by wiping out every vestige of international law and humanity.

His intention has been made clear. The American people can have no further illusions about it.

No tender whisperings of appeasers that Hitler is not interested in the Western Hemisphere, no soporific lullabies that a wide ocean protects us from him can long have any effect on the hard-headed, far-sighted, and realistic American people.

Because of these episodes, because of the movements and operations of German warships, and because of the clear, repeated proof that the present Government of Germany has no respect for treaties or for international law, that it has no decent attitude toward neutral nations or human life—we Americans are now face to face not with abstract theories but with cruel, relentless facts.

This attack on the *Greer* was no localized military operation in the North Atlantic. This was no mere episode in a struggle between two nations. This was one determined step towards creating a permanent world system based on force, terror, and murder.

And I am sure that even now the Nazis are waiting to see whether the United States will by silence give them the green light to go ahead on this path of destruction.

The Nazi danger to our Western World has long ceased to be a mere possibility. The danger is here now—not only from a military enemy but from an enemy of all law, all liberty, all morality, all religion.

There has now come a time when you and I must see the cold, inexorable necessity of saying to these inhuman, unrestrained seekers of world-conquest and permanent world-domination by the sword—"You seek to throw our children and our children's children into your form of terrorism and slavery. You have now attacked our own safety. You shall go no further."

Normal practices of diplomacy—note-writing—are of no possible use in dealing with international outlaws who sink our ships and kill our citizens.

One peaceful nation after another has met disaster because each refused to look the Nazi danger squarely in the eye until it actually had them by the throat.

The United States will not make that fatal mistake.

No act of violence or intimidation will keep us from maintaining intact two bulwarks of defense: first, our line of supply of matériel to the enemies of Hitler; and second, the freedom of our shipping on the high seas.

No matter what it takes, no matter what it costs, we will keep open the line of legitimate commerce in these defensive waters.

We have sought no shooting war with Hitler. We do not seek it now. But neither do we want peace so much that we are willing to pay for it by permitting him to attack our naval and merchant ships while they are on legitimate business.

I assume that the German leaders are not deeply concerned by what we Americans say or publish about them. We cannot bring about the downfall of Nazism by the use of long-range invective.

But when you see a rattlesnake poised to strike, you do not wait until he has struck before you crush him.

These Nazi submarines and raiders are the rattlesnakes of the Atlantic. They are a menace to the free pathways of the high seas. They are a challenge to our sovereignty. They hammer at our most precious rights when they attack ships of the American flag—symbols of our independence, our freedom, our very life.

It is clear to all Americans that the time has come when the Americas themselves must now be defended. A continuation of attacks in our own waters, or in waters which could be used for further and greater attacks on us, will inevitably weaken American ability to repel Hitlerism.

Do not let us split hairs. Let us not ask ourselves whether the Americas should begin to defend themselves after the fifth attack, or the tenth attack, or the twentieth attack.

The time for active defense is now.

Do not let us split hairs. Let us not say—"We will only defend ourselves if the torpedo succeeds in getting home, or if the crew and the passengers are drowned."

This is the time for prevention of attack.

If submarines or raiders attack in distant waters, they can attack equally well within sight of our own shores. Their very presence in any waters which America deems vital to its defense constitutes an attack.

In the waters which we deem necessary for our defense, American naval vessels and American planes will no longer wait until Axis submarines lurking under the water, or Axis raiders on the surface of the sea, strike their deadly blow—first.

Upon our naval and air patrol—now operating in large number over a vast expanse of the Atlantic Ocean—falls the duty of maintaining the American policy of freedom of the seas—now. That means, very simply and clearly, that our patrolling vessels and planes will protect all merchant ships—not only American ships but ships of any flag—engaged in commerce in our defensive waters. They will protect them from submarines; they will protect them from surface raiders.

This situation is not new. The second President of the United States, John Adams, ordered the United States Navy to clean out European privateers and European ships of war which were infesting the Caribbean and South American waters, destroying American commerce.

The third President of the United States, Thomas Jefferson, ordered the United States Navy to end the attacks being made upon American ships by the corsairs of the nations of North Africa.

My obligation as President is historic; it is clear; it is inescapable.

It is no act of war on our part when we decide to protect the seas which are vital to American defense. The aggression is not ours. Ours is solely defense.

But let this warning be clear. From now on, if German or Italian vessels of war enter the waters the protection of which is necessary for American defense they do so at their own peril.

The orders which I have given as Commander-in-Chief to the United States Army and Navy are to carry out that policy—at once.

The sole responsibility rests upon Germany. There will be no shooting unless Germany continues to seek it.

That is my obvious duty in this crisis. That is the clear right of this sovereign Nation. That is the only step possible, if we would keep tight the wall of defense which we are pledged to maintain around this Western Hemisphere.

I have no illusions about the gravity of this step. I have not taken it hurriedly or lightly. It is the result of months and months of constant thought and anxiety and prayer. In the protection of your Nation and mine it cannot be avoided.

The American people have faced other grave crises in their history —with American courage and American resolution. They will do no less today.

They know the actualities of the attacks upon us. They know the necessities of a bold defense against these attacks. They know that the times call for clear heads and fearless hearts.

And with that inner strength that comes to a free people conscious of their duty and of the righteousness of what they do, they will—with Divine help and guidance—stand their ground against this latest assault upon their democracy, their sovereignty, and their freedom.

ADDRESS by President Franklin D. Roosevelt at Washington, D.C., October 27, 1941, Delivered at a Dinner on "Navy and Total Defense-Day"

Department of State, *Bulletin,* November 1, 1941, p. 341; excerpt

F̲ɪᴠᴇ ᴍᴏɴᴛʜs ᴀɢᴏ tonight I proclaimed to the American people the existence of a state of unlimited emergency.

Since then much has happened. Our Army and Navy are temporarily in Iceland in the defense of the Western Hemisphere.

Hitler has attacked shipping in areas close to the Americas throughout the Atlantic.

Many American-owned merchant ships have been sunk on the high seas. One American destroyer was attacked on September fourth. Another destroyer was attacked and hit on October seventeenth. Eleven brave and loyal men of our Navy were killed by the Nazis.

We have wished to avoid shooting. But the shooting has started. And history has recorded who fired the first shot. In the long run, however, all that will matter is who fired the last shot.

America has been attacked. The U.S.S. *Kearny* is not just a Navy ship. She belongs to every man, woman, and child in this Nation.

Illinois, Alabama, California, North Carolina, Ohio, Louisiana, Texas, Pennsylvania, Georgia, Arkansas, New York, Virginia—those are the home States of the honored dead and wounded of the *Kearny*. Hitler's torpedo was directed at every American, whether he lives on our seacoasts or in the innermost part of the Nation, far from the seas and far from the guns and tanks of the marching hordes of would-be conquerors of the world.

The purpose of Hitler's attack was to frighten the American people off the high seas—to force us to make a trembling retreat. This is not the first time he has misjudged the American spirit. That spirit is now aroused.

If our national policy were to be dominated by the fear of shooting, then all of our ships and those of our sister republics would have to be tied up in home harbors. Our Navy would have to remain respectfully—abjectly—behind any line which Hitler might decree on any ocean as his own dictated version of his own war zone.

Naturally we reject that absurd and insulting suggestion. We reject it because of our own self-interest, our own self-respect, and our own good faith. Freedom of the seas is now, as it has always been, the fundamental policy of this Government.

Hitler has often protested that his plans for conquest do not ex-

DEFENSE, AND AID TO THE DEMOCRACIES

tend across the Atlantic Ocean. His submarines and raiders prove otherwise. So does the entire design of his new world-order.

For example, I have in my possession a secret map made in Germany by Hitler's government—by the planners of the new world-order. It is a map of South America and a part of Central America as Hitler proposes to reorganize it. Today in this area there are 14 separate countries. The geographical experts of Berlin, however, have ruthlessly obliterated all existing boundary lines and have divided South America into five vassal states, bringing the whole continent under their domination. And they have also so arranged it that the territory of one of these new puppet states includes the Republic of Panama and our great lifeline—the Panama Canal.

This map makes clear the Nazi design not only against South America but against the United States itself.

Your Government has in its possession another document made in Germany by Hitler's government. It is a detailed plan, which, for obvious reasons, the Nazis did not wish to publicize just yet, but which they are ready to impose on a dominated world—if Hitler wins. It is a plan to abolish all existing religions—Protestant, Catholic, Mohammedan, Hindu, Buddhist, and Jewish alike. The property of all churches will be seized by the Reich. The cross and all other symbols of religion are to be forbidden. The clergy are to be forever silenced under penalty of the concentration camps, where even now so many fearless men are being tortured because they placed God above Hitler.

In the place of the churches of our civilization, there is to be set up an International Nazi Church—a church which will be served by orators sent out by the Nazi government. In the place of the Bible, the words of *Mein Kampf* will be imposed and enforced as Holy Writ. And in place of the cross of Christ will be put two symbols—the swastika and the naked sword.

The God of Blood and Iron will take the place of the God of Love and Mercy.

These grim truths which I have told you of the present and future plans of Hitlerism will of course be hotly denied tomorrow in the controlled press and radio of the Axis Powers. And some Americans will continue to insist that Hitler's plans need not worry us—and that we should not concern ourselves with anything that goes on beyond rifle shot of our own shores.

The protestations of these American citizens—few in number—will, as usual, be paraded with applause through the Axis press and radio during the next few days, in an effort to convince the world that the majority of Americans are opposed to their duly chosen

Government, and in reality are only waiting to jump on Hitler's bandwagon when it comes this way.

The motive of such Americans is not the point at issue. The fact is that Nazi propaganda continues in desperation to seize upon such isolated statements as proof of American disunity.

The Nazis have made up their own list of modern American heroes. It is, fortunately, a short list. I am glad that it does not contain my name.

All of us Americans, of all opinions, are faced with the choice between the kind of world we want to live in and the kind of world which Hitler and his hordes would impose upon us.

None of us wants to burrow under the ground and live in total darkness like a comfortable mole.

The forward march of Hitlerism can be stopped—and it will be stopped.

Very simply and very bluntly—we are pledged to pull our own oar in the destruction of Hitlerism.

And when we have helped to end the curse of Hitlerism we shall help to establish a new peace which will give to decent people everywhere a better chance to live and prosper in security and in freedom and in faith.

Each day that passes we are producing and providing more and more arms for the men who are fighting on actual battlefronts. That is our primary task.

And it is the Nation's will that these vital arms and supplies of all kinds shall neither be locked up in American harbors nor sent to the bottom of the sea. It is the Nation's will that America shall deliver the goods. In open defiance of that will, our ships have been sunk and our sailors have been killed.

I say that we do not propose to take this lying down.

Our determination not to take it lying down has been expressed in the orders to the American Navy to shoot on sight. Those orders stand.

Furthermore, the House of Representatives has already voted to amend part of the Neutrality Act of 1939, today outmoded by force of violent circumstances. The Senate Committee on Foreign Relations has also recommended elimination of other hamstringing provisions in that act. That is the course of honesty and of realism.

Our American merchant ships must be armed to defend themselves against the rattlesnakes of the sea.

Our American merchant ships must be free to carry our American goods into the harbors of our friends.

DEFENSE, AND AID TO THE DEMOCRACIES

Our American merchant ships must be protected by our American Navy.

It can never be doubted that the goods will be delivered by this Nation, whose Navy believes in the tradition of "Damn the torpedoes; full speed ahead!"

Our national will must speak from every assembly line in our vast industrial machine. Our factories and our shipyards are constantly expanding. Our output must be multiplied.

It cannot be hampered by the selfish obstruction of a small but dangerous minority of industrial managers who hold out for extra profits or for "business as usual." It cannot be hampered by the selfish obstruction of a small but dangerous minority of labor leaders who are a menace to the true cause of labor itself, as well as to the Nation as a whole.

The lines of our essential defense now cover all the seas, and to meet the extraordinary demands of today and tomorrow our Navy grows to unprecedented size. Our Navy is ready for action. Indeed, units of it in the Atlantic patrol are in action. Its officers and men need no praise from me.

Our new Army is steadily developing the strength needed to withstand the aggressors. Our soldiers of today are worthy of the proudest traditions of the United States Army. But traditions cannot shoot down dive bombers or destroy tanks. That is why we must and shall provide, for every one of our soldiers, equipment and weapons—not merely as good but better than that of any other army on earth. And we are doing that right now.

For this—and all of this—is what we mean by total national defense.

The first objective of that defense is to stop Hitler. He can be stopped and can be compelled to dig in. And that will be the beginning of his downfall, because dictatorship of the Hitler type can live only through continuing victories—increasing conquests. . . .

NEUTRALITY AND NEUTRALITY LEGISLATION

RADIO ADDRESS by Cordell Hull, Secretary of State, "Our Foreign Policy with Respect to Neutrality," November 6, 1935

Read by Mr. William Phillips, Under Secretary of State, in the absence of the Secretary from Washington. Department of State, *Press Releases,* November 9, 1935, p. 367

BECAUSE OF the generally unsettled world conditions, and the existence of hostilities between two powers with which we are on terms of friendship, the one phase of our foreign policy uppermost in the minds of our people today is that of neutrality. It is being discussed from the platforms, in the press, and in the streets. It is of concern to our people in every walk of life. They have not forgotten the bitter experiences of the World War, the calamitous effects of which will not be erased from their memories during our present generation. Is it therefore any wonder that they should be concerned regarding our policy of neutrality and the steps that their Government is taking to avoid a repetition of those experiences?

Modern neutrality dates from the latter part of the Middle Ages. Prior to that time neutrality was unknown for the reason that belligerents did not recognize an attitude of impartiality on the part of other powers; under the laws of war observed by the most civilized nations of antiquity, the right of one nation to remain at peace while neighboring nations were at war was not admitted to exist. Efforts made by nations from time to time to adopt an attitude of impartiality were successfully resisted by the belligerents, who proceeded on the theory that any country not an ally was an enemy. No intermediate relation was known to the pagan nations of those earlier times, and hence the term "neutrality" did not exist.

During the sixteenth century, however, neutrality as a concept in international law began to be recognized. In 1625 Hugo Grotius, sometimes referred to as "the father of international law," published his celebrated treatise on the laws of peace and war. While his treatment of the subject of neutrality is brief and necessarily so because of the undeveloped status of the law of his time, he nevertheless recognized the possibility of third parties remaining neutral. He did not, however, have that conception of neutrality to which we have been accustomed in more recent times. He stated that it was the duty of those not engaged in a war "to do nothing whereby he who supports a wicked cause may be rendered more powerful, or whereby the movements of him who wages a just war may be hampered."

Since the days of Grotius, neutrality has passed through several stages of evolution. No nation has done more toward its development than has the United States. In 1794 Congress passed our first neutrality act, temporary in character, covering a variety of subjects. In 1818 permanent legislation on these subjects was passed. This legislation formed the basis of the British act of a similar character of 1819, known as the British Foreign Enlistment Act. Other legislation has been passed by Congress from time to time, including that enacted during the World War—I refer particularly to the act of June 15, 1917—and that enacted as recently as the last session of Congress —the joint resolution approved August 31, 1935. This last-mentioned resolution, intended to supplement prior legislation, is designed primarily *to keep the United States out of foreign wars.*

Pursuant to this resolution, the President has issued two proclamations regarding the war now unhappily existing between Ethiopia and Italy. One of these declared the existence of a state of war within the meaning and intent of section 1 of the resolution, thus bringing into operation the embargo on the shipment of arms, ammunition, and implements of war from the United States to either belligerent, and the other declared that American citizens who travel on vessels of the belligerents shall do so at their own risk.

The effect of issuing the proclamation bringing into operation the embargo on the shipment of arms was automatically to bring into operation the provisions of section 3 of the resolution prohibiting American vessels from carrying arms, ammunition, or implements of war to any port of a belligerent country named in the proclamation, or to any neutral port for transshipment to or for the use of the belligerent country.

Any discussion of the avoidance of war, or of the observance of neutrality in the event of war, would be wholly incomplete if too much stress were laid on the part played in the one or the other by the shipment, or the embargoing of the shipment, of arms, ammunition, and implements of war. The shipment of arms is not the only way and, in fact, is not the principal way by which our commerce with foreign nations may lead to serious international difficulties. To assume that by placing an embargo on arms we are making ourselves secure from dangers of conflict with belligerent countries is to close our eyes to manifold dangers in other directions. The imposition of an arms embargo is not a complete panacea, and we cannot assume that when provision has been made to stop the shipment of arms, which as absolute contraband have always been regarded as subject to seizure by a belligerent, we may complacently sit back with the feeling that we are secure from all danger. Attempts by a belligerent to exercise jurisdiction on the high seas over trade with its enemy, or with other neutral countries on the theory that the latter are supplying the enemy, may give rise to difficulties no less serious than those resulting from the exportation of arms and implements of war. So also transactions of any kind between American nationals and a belligerent may conceivably lead to difficulties of one kind or another between the nationals and that belligerent. Efforts of this Government to extend protection to these nationals might lead to difficulties between the United States and the belligerent. It was with these thoughts in mind that the President issued his timely warning that citizens of the United States who engage in transactions of any character with either belligerent would do so at their own risk.

Every war presents different circumstances and conditions which might have to be dealt with differently both as to time and manner. For these reasons, difficulties inherent in any effort to lay down by legislative enactment inelastic rules or regulations to be applied to every situation that may arise will at once be apparent. The Executive should not be unduly or unreasonably handicapped. There are a number of ways in which discretion could wisely be given the President which are not and could not be seriously controversial. These might well include discretion as to the time of imposing an embargo. Moreover, we should not concentrate entirely on means for remaining neutral and lose sight of other constructive methods of avoiding involvement in wars between other countries. Our foreign policy would indeed be a weak one if it began or ended with the announcement of a neutral position on the outbreak of a foreign war. I conceive it to be our duty and in the interest of our country and of humanity, not only to remain aloof from disputes and conflicts with which we have no direct concern, but also to use our influence in any appropriate way to bring about the peaceful settlement of international differences. Our own interest and our duty as a great power forbid that we shall sit idly by and watch the development of hostilities with a feeling of self-sufficiency and complacency when by the use of our influence, short of becoming involved in the dispute itself, we might prevent or lessen the scourge of war. In short, our policy as a member of the community of nations should be twofold: first, to avoid being brought into a war, and second to promote as far as possible the interests of international peace and good will. A virile policy tempered with prudent caution is necessary if we are to retain the respect of other nations and at the same time hold our position of influence for peace and international stability in the family of nations.

In summary, while our primary aim should be to avoid involvement in other people's difficulties and hence to lessen our chances of being drawn into a war, we should, on appropriate occasions and within reasonable bounds, use our influence toward the prevention of war and the miseries that attend and follow in its wake. For after all, if peace obtains, problems regarding neutrality will not arise.

LETTER from Cordell Hull, Secretary of State, to the Chairman of the Committee on Foreign Relations of the Senate (Key Pittman), May 12, 1938

Department of State, *Press Releases*, May 14, 1938, p. 578

My Dear Senator Pittman:

I have received your letter of May 3, 1938, enclosing a copy of S. J. Resolution 288 "repealing the Joint Resolution to prohibit the export of arms, ammunition and implements of war from the United States to Spain, approved January 8, 1937, and conditionally raising the embargo against the Government of Spain," and requesting my comment.

In recent years this Government has consistently pursued a course calculated to prevent our becoming involved in war situations. In August, 1936, shortly after the beginning of the civil strife in Spain, it became evident that several of the great powers were projecting themselves into the struggle through the furnishing of arms and war materials and other aid to the contending sides, thus creating a real danger of a spread of the conflict into a European war, with the possible involvement of the United States. That there was such a real danger was realized by every thoughtful observer the world over. Twenty-seven Governments of Europe took special cognizance of that fact in setting up a committee designed to carry out a concerted policy of non-intervention in the conflict. In view of all these special and unusual circumstances, this Government declared its policy of strict non-interference in the struggle and at the same time announced that export of arms from the United States to Spain would be contrary to such policy.

The fundamental reason for the enactment of the Joint Resolution of January 8, 1937, was to implement this policy by legislation. This

Joint Resolution was passed in the Senate unanimously and in the House of Representatives by a vote of 406 to 1.

In the form in which it is presented, the proposed legislation, if enacted, would lift the embargo, which is now being applied against both parties to the conflict in Spain, in respect to shipments of arms to one party while leaving in effect the embargo in respect to shipments to the other party. Even if the legislation applied to both parties, its enactment would still subject us to unnecessary risks we have so far avoided. We do not know what lies ahead in the Spanish situation. The original danger still exists. In view of the continued danger of international conflict arising from the circumstances of the struggle, any proposal which at this juncture contemplates a reversal of our policy of strict non-interference which we have thus far so scrupulously followed, and under the operation of which we have kept out of involvements, would offer a real possibility of complications. From the standpoint of the best interests of the United States in the circumstances which now prevail, I would not feel justified in recommending affirmative action on the Resolution under consideration.

Our first solicitude should be the peace and welfare of this country, and the real test of the advisability of making any changes in the statutes now in effect should be whether such changes would further tend to keep us from becoming involved directly or indirectly in a dangerous European situation.

Furthermore, if reconsideration is to be given to a revision of our neutrality legislation, it would be more useful to reconsider it in its broader aspects in the light of the practical experience gained during the past two or three years, rather than to rewrite it piecemeal in relation to a particular situation. It is evident that there is not sufficient time to give study to such questions in the closing days of this Congress.

RADIO ADDRESS by President Franklin D. Roosevelt, September 3, 1939

Department of State, *Bulletin,* September 9, 1939, p. 201

TONIGHT MY single duty is to speak to the whole of America.

Until 4:30 this morning I had hoped against hope that some miracle would prevent a devastating war in Europe and bring to an end the invasion of Poland by Germany.

For 4 long years a succession of actual wars and constant crises have shaken the entire world and have threatened in each case to bring on the gigantic conflict which is today unhappily a fact.

It is right that I should recall to your minds the consistent and at times successful efforts of your Government in these crises to throw the full weight of the United States into the cause of peace. In spite of spreading wars I think that we have every right and every reason to maintain as a national policy the fundamental moralities, the teachings of religion, and the continuation of efforts to restore peace—for some day, though the time may be distant, we can be of even greater help to a crippled humanity.

It is right, too, to point out that the unfortunate events of these recent years have been based on the use of force or the threat of force. And it seems to me clear, even at the outbreak of this great war, that the influence of America should be consistent in seeking for humanity a final peace which will eliminate, as far as it is possible to do so, the continued use of force between nations.

It is, of course, impossible to predict the future. I have my constant stream of information from American representatives and other sources throughout the world. You, the people of this country, are receiving news through your radios and your newspapers at every hour of the day.

You are, I believe, the most enlightened and the best informed people in all the world at this moment. You are subjected to no censorship of news; and I want to add that your Government has no information which it has any thought of withholding from you.

At the same time, as I told my press conference on Friday, it is of the highest importance that the press and the radio use the utmost caution to discriminate between actual verified fact on the one hand and mere rumor on the other.

I can add to that by saying that I hope the people of this country will also discriminate most carefully between news and rumor. Do not believe of necessity everything you hear or read. Check up on it first.

You must master at the outset a simple but unalterable fact in modern foreign relations. When peace has been broken anywhere, peace of all countries everywhere is in danger.

It is easy for you and me to shrug our shoulders and say that conflicts taking place thousands of miles from the continental United States, and, indeed, the whole American hemisphere, do not seriously affect the Americas—and that all the United States has to do is to ignore them and go about our own business. Passionately though we may desire detachment, we are forced to realize that every word that comes through the air, every ship that sails the sea, every battle that is fought does affect the American future.

Let no man or woman thoughtlessly or falsely talk of America sending its armies to European fields. At this moment there is being prepared a proclamation of American neutrality. This would have been done even if there had been no neutrality statute on the books, for this proclamation is in accordance with international law and with American policy.

This will be followed by a proclamation required by the existing Neutrality Act. I trust that in the days to come our neutrality can be made a true neutrality.

It is of the utmost importance that the people of this country, with the best information in the world, think things through. The most dangerous enemies of American peace are those who, without well-rounded information on the whole broad subject of the past, the present, and the future, undertake to speak with authority, to talk in terms of glittering generalities, to give to the Nation assurances or prophecies which are of little present or future value.

I myself cannot and do not prophesy the course of events abroad—and the reason is that because I have of necessity such a complete picture of what is going on in every part of the world, I do not dare to do so. And the other reason is that I think it is honest for me to be honest with the people of the United States.

I cannot prophesy the immediate economic effect of this new war on our Nation, but I do say that no American has the moral right to profiteer at the expense either of his fellow citizens or of the men, women, and children who are living and dying in the midst of war in Europe.

Some things we do know. Most of us in the United States believe in spiritual values. Most of us, regardless of what church we belong to believe in the spirit of the New Testament—a great teaching which opposes itself to the use of force, of armed force, of marching armies, and falling bombs. The overwhelming masses of our people seek peace—peace at home, and the kind of peace in other lands which will not jeopardize peace at home.

We have certain ideas and ideals of national safety, and we must act to preserve that safety today and to preserve the safety of our children in future years.

That safety is and will be bound up with the safety of the Western Hemisphere and of the seas adjacent thereto. We seek to keep war from our firesides by keeping war from coming to the Americas. For that we have historic precedent that goes back to the days of the administration of President George Washington. It is serious enough and tragic enough to every American family in every State in the Union to live in a world that is torn by wars on other continents. Today they affect every American home. It is our national duty to use every effort to keep them out of the Americas.

And at this time let me make the simple plea that partisanship and selfishness be adjourned and that national unity be the thought that underlies all others.

This Nation will remain a neutral nation, but I cannot ask that every American remain neutral in thought as well. Even a neutral has a right to take account of facts. Even a neutral cannot be asked to close his mind or his conscience.

I have said not once but many times that I have seen war and that I hate war. I say that again and again.

I hope the United States will keep out of this war. I believe that it will. And I give you assurances that every effort of your Government will be directed toward that end.

As long as it remains within my power to prevent, there will be no blackout of peace in the United States.

MESSAGE of President Franklin D. Roosevelt to Congress, September 21, 1939

Department of State, *Bulletin*, September 23, 1939, p. 275

I HAVE ASKED the Congress to reassemble in extraordinary session in order that it may consider and act on the amendment of certain legislation, which, in my best judgment, so alters the historic foreign policy of the United States that it impairs the peaceful relations of the United States with foreign nations.

At the outset I proceed on the assumption that every member of the Senate and of the House of Representatives, and every member of the executive branch of the Government, including the President and his associates, personally and officially, are equally and without reservation in favor of such measures as will protect the neutrality, the safety, and the integrity of our country and at the same time keep us out of war.

Because I am wholly willing to ascribe an honorable desire for peace to those who hold different views from my own as to what those measures should be, I trust that these gentlemen will be sufficiently generous to ascribe equally lofty purposes to those with whom they disagree. Let no man or group in any walk of life assume exclusive protectorate over the future well-being of America—because I conceive that regardless of party or section the mantle of peace and of patriotism is wide enough to cover us all. Let no group assume the exclusive label of the peace "bloc." We all belong to it.

I have at all times kept the Congress and the American people informed of events and trends in foreign affairs. I now review them in a spirit of understatement.

Since 1931 the use of force instead of the council table has constantly increased in the settlement of disputes between nations—except in the Western Hemisphere, where there has been only one war, now happily terminated.

During these years also the building up of vast armies, navies, and storehouses of war has proceeded abroad with growing speed and intensity. But, during these years, and extending back even to the days of the Kellogg-Briand Pact, the United States has constantly, consistently, and conscientiously done all in its power to encourage peaceful settlements, to bring about reduction of armaments, and to avert threatened wars. We have done this not only because any war anywhere necessarily hurts American security and American prosperity, but because of the more important fact that any war anywhere retards the progress of morality and religion and impairs the security of civilization itself.

For many years the primary purpose of our foreign policy has been that this Nation and this Government should strive to the utmost to aid in avoiding war among other nations. But if and when war unhappily comes, the Government and the Nation must exert every possible effort to avoid being drawn into the war.

The executive branch of the Government did its utmost, within our traditional policy of noninvolvement, to aid in averting the present appalling war. Having thus striven and failed, this Government must lose no time or effort to keep the Nation from being drawn into the war.

In my candid judgment we shall succeed in these efforts.

We are proud of the historical record of the United States and of all the Americans during all these years because we have thrown every ounce of our influence for peace into the scale of peace.

I note in passing what you will all remember—the long debates on the subject of what constitutes aggression, on the methods of determining who the aggressor might be, and, on who the aggressor in past wars had been. Academically this may have been instructive, as it may have been of interest to historians to discuss the pros and cons and the rights and wrongs of the World War during the decade that followed it.

But in the light of problems of today and tomorrow responsibility for acts of aggression is not concealed, and the writing of the record can safely be left to future historians.

There has been sufficient realism in the United States to see how close to our own shores came dangerous paths which were being followed on other continents.

Last January I told the Congress that "a war which threatened to envelop the world in flames has been averted, but it has become increasingly clear that peace is not assured." By April new tensions had developed; a new crisis was in the making. Several nations with whom we had friendly, diplomatic and commercial relations had lost, or were in the process of losing, their independent identity and sovereignty.

During the spring and summer the trend was definitely toward further acts of military conquest and away from peace. As late as the end of July I spoke to members of the Congress about the definite possibility of war. I should have called it the probability of war.

Last January, also, I spoke to this Congress of the need for further warning of new threats of conquest, military and economic; of challenge to religion, to democracy, and to international good faith. I said:

An ordering of society which relegates religion, democracy, and good faith among nations to the background can find no place within it for the ideals of the Prince of Peace. The United States rejects such an ordering and retains its ancient faith. . . .

We know what might happen to us of the United States if the new philosophies of force were to encompass the other continents and invade our own. We, no more than other nations, can afford to be surrounded by the enemies of our faith and our humanity. Fortunate it is, therefore, that in this Western Hemisphere we have, under a common ideal of democratic government, a rich diversity of resources and of peoples functioning together in mutual respect and peace.

Last January, in the same message, I also said: "We have learned that when we deliberately try to legislate neutrality, our neutrality laws may operate unevenly and unfairly—may actually give aid to an aggressor and deny it to the victim. The instinct of self-preservation should warn us that we ought not to let that happen any more."

It was because of what I foresaw last January from watching the trend of foreign affairs and their probable effect upon us that I recommended to the Congress in July of this year that changes be enacted in our neutrality law.

The essentials for American peace in the world have not changed since January. That is why I ask you again to reexamine our own legislation.

Beginning with the foundation of our constitutional government in the year 1789, the American policy in respect to belligerent nations, with one notable exception, has been based on international law. Be it remembered that what we call international law has had as its primary objectives the avoidance of causes of war and the prevention of the extension of war.

The single exception was the policy adopted by this Nation during the Napoleonic Wars, when, seeking to avoid involvement, we acted for some years under the so-called Embargo and Non-Intercourse Acts. That policy turned out to be a disastrous failure—first, because it brought our own Nation close to ruin, and, second, because it was the major cause of bringing us into active participation in European wars in our own War of 1812. It is merely reciting history to recall to you that one of the results of the policy of embargo and nonintercourse was the burning in 1814 of part of this Capitol in which we are assembled.

Our next deviation by statute from the sound principles of neutrality and peace through international law did not come for 130 years. It was the so-called Neutrality Act of 1935—only 4 years ago—an act continued in force by the joint resolution of May 1, 1937, despite grave doubts expressed as to its wisdom by many Senators and Representatives and by officials charged with the conduct of our foreign relations, including myself. I regret that the Congress passed that act. I regret equally that I signed that act.

On July fourteenth of this year I asked the Congress in the cause of peace and in the interest of real American neutrality and security to take action to change that act.

I now ask again that such action be taken in respect to that part of the act which is wholly inconsistent with ancient precepts of the law of nations—the embargo provisions. I ask it because they are, in my opinion, most vitally dangerous to American neutrality, American security, and American peace.

These embargo provisions, as they exist today, prevent the sale to a belligerent by an American factory of any completed implements of war, but they allow the sale of many types of uncompleted implements of war, as well as all kinds of general material and supplies. They, furthermore, allow such products of industry and agriculture to be taken in American-flag ships to belligerent nations. There in itself—under the present law—lies definite danger to our neutrality and our peace.

From a purely material point of view what is the advantage to us in sending all manner of articles across the ocean for final processing there when we could give employment to thousands by doing it here? Incidentally, and again from the material point of view, by such employment we automatically aid our own national defense. And if abnormal profits appear in our midst even in time of peace, as a result of this increase of industry, I feel certain that the subject will be adequately dealt with at the coming regular session of the Congress.

Let me set forth the present paradox of the existing legislation in its simplest terms: If, prior to 1935, a general war had broken out in Europe, the United States would have sold to and bought from belligerent nations such goods and products of all kinds as the belligerent nations, with their existing facilities and geographical situations, were able to buy from us or sell to us. This would have been the normal practice under the age-old doctrines of international law. Our prior position accepted the facts of geography and of conditions of land power and sea power alike as they existed in all parts of the world. If a war in Europe had broken out prior to 1935, there would have been no difference, for example, between our exports of sheets of aluminum and airplane wings; today there is an artificial legal difference. Before 1935 there would have been no difference between the export of cotton and the export of gun cotton. Today there is. Before 1935 there would have been no difference between the shipment of brass tubing in pipe form and brass tubing in shell form. Today there is. Before 1935 there would have been no difference between the export of a motor truck and an armored motor truck. Today there is.

Let us be factual and recognize that a belligerent nation often needs wheat and lard and cotton for the survival of its population just as much as it needs anti-aircraft guns and anti-submarine depth-charges. Let those who seek to retain the present embargo position be wholly consistent and seek new legislation to cut off cloth and copper and meat and wheat and a thousand other articles from all of the nations at war.

I seek a greater consistency through the repeal of the embargo provisions and a return to international law. I seek reenactment of the historic and traditional American policy which, except for the disastrous interlude of the Embargo and Non-Intercourse Acts, has served us well for nearly a century and a half.

It has been erroneously said that return to that policy might bring us nearer to war. I give to you my deep and unalterable conviction, based on years of experience as a worker in the field of international peace, that by the repeal of the embargo the United States will more probably remain at peace than if the law remains as it stands today. I say this because with the repeal of the embargo this Government clearly and definitely will insist that American citizens and American ships keep away from the immediate perils of the actual zones of conflict.

Repeal of the embargo and a return to international law are the crux of this issue.

The enactment of the embargo provisions did more than merely reverse our traditional policy. It had the effect of putting land powers on the same footing as naval powers, so far as sea-borne commerce was concerned. A land power which threatened war could thus feel assured in advance that any prospective sea-power antagonist would be weakened through denial of its ancient right to buy anything anywhere. This, 4 years ago, gave a definite advantage to one belligerent as against another, not through his own strength or geographic position, but through an affirmative act of ours. Removal of the embargo is merely reverting to the sounder international practice and pursuing in time of war as in time of peace our ordinary trade policies. This will be liked by some and disliked by others, depending on the view they take of the present war, but that is not the issue. The step I recommend is to put this country back on the solid footing of real and traditional neutrality.

When and if repeal of the embargo is accomplished, certain other phases of policy reinforcing American safety should be considered. While nearly all of us are in agreement on their objectives, the only question relates to method.

I believe that American merchant vessels should, so far as possible, be restricted from entering danger zones. War zones may change so swiftly and so frequently in the days to come, that it is impossible to fix them permanently by act of Congress; specific legislation may prevent adjustment to constant and quick change. It seems, therefore, more practical to delimit them through action of the State Department and administrative agencies. The objective of restricting American ships from entering such zones may be attained by prohibiting such entry by the Congress; or the result can be substantially achieved by executive proclamation that all such voyages are solely at the risk of the American owners themselves.

The second objective is to prevent American citizens from traveling on belligerent vessels or in danger areas. This can also be accomplished either by legislation, through continuance in force of certain provisions of existing law, or by proclamation making it clear to all Americans that any such travel is at their own risk.

The third objective, requiring the foreign buyer to take transfer of title in this country to commodities purchased by belligerents, is also a result which can be attained by legislation or substantially achieved through due notice by proclamation.

The fourth objective is the preventing of war credits to belligerents. This can be accomplished by maintaining in force existing provisions of law, or by proclamation making it clear that if credits are granted by American citizens to belligerents our Government will take no steps in the future to relieve them of risk or loss. The result of these last two will be to require all purchases to be made in cash and cargoes to be carried in the purchasers' own ships, at the purchasers' own risk.

Two other objectives have been amply attained by existing law, namely, regulating collection of funds in this country for belligerents, and the maintenance of a license system covering import and export of arms, ammunition, and implements of war. Under present enactments, such arms cannot be carried to belligerent countries on American vessels, and this provision should not be disturbed.

The Congress, of course, should make its own choice of the method by which these safeguards are to be attained, so long as the method chosen will meet the needs of new and changing day-to-day situations and dangers.

To those who say that this program would involve a step toward war on our part, I reply that it offers far greater safeguards than we now possess or have ever possessed to protect American lives and property from danger. It is a positive program for giving safety. This means less likelihood of incidents and controversies which tend to draw us into conflict, as they did in the last World War. There lies the road to peace!

The position of the executive branch of the Government is that the age-old and time-honored doctrine of international law, coupled with these positive safeguards, is better calculated than any other means to keep us out of this war.

In respect to our own defense, you are aware that I have issued a proclamation setting forth "A National Emergency in Connection with the Observance, Safeguarding, and Enforcement of Neutrality and the Strengthening of the National Defense Within the Limits of Peace-Time Authorizations." This was done solely to make wholly constitutional and legal certain obviously necessary measures. I have authorized increases in the personnel of the Army, Navy, Marine Corps, and Coast Guard, which will bring all four to a total still below peace-time strength as authorized by the Congress.

I have authorized the State Department to use, for the repatriation of Americans caught in the war zone, $500,000 already authorized by the Congress.

I have authorized the addition of 150 persons to the Department of Justice to be used in the protection of the United States against subversive foreign activities within our borders.

At this time I ask for no other authority from the Congress. At this time I see no need for further executive action under the proclamation of limited national emergency.

Therefore, I see no valid reason for the consideration of other legislation at this extraordinary session of the Congress.

It is, of course, possible that in the months to come unforeseen needs for further legislation may develop, but they are not imperative today.

These perilous days demand cooperation between us without trace of partisanship. Our acts must be guided by one single hard-headed thought—keeping America out of this war. In that spirit, I am asking the leaders of the two major parties in the Senate and in the House of Representatives to remain in Washington between the close of this extraordinary session and the beginning of the regular session on January third. They have assured me that they will do so, and I expect to consult with them at frequent intervals on the course of events in foreign affairs and on the need for future action in this field, whether it be executive or legislative action.

Further, in the event of any future danger to the security of the United States or in the event of need for any new legislation of importance, I will immediately reconvene the Congress in another extraordinary session.

I should like to be able to offer the hope that the shadow over the world might swiftly pass. I cannot. The facts compel my stating, with candor, that darker periods may lie ahead. The disaster is not of our making; no act of ours engendered the forces which assault the foundations of civilization. Yet we find ourselves affected to the core; our currents of commerce are changing, our minds are filled with new problems, our position in world affairs has already been altered.

In such circumstances our policy must be to appreciate in the deepest sense the true American interest. Rightly considered, this interest is not selfish. Destiny first made us, with our sister nations on this hemisphere, joint heirs of European culture. Fate seems now to compel us to assume the task of helping to maintain in the western world a citadel wherein that civilization may be kept alive. The peace, the integrity, and the safety of the Americas—these must be kept firm and serene. In a period when it is sometimes said that free discussion is no longer compatible with national safety, may you by your deeds show the world that we of the United States are one people, of one mind, one spirit, one clear resolution, walking before God in the light of the living.

MESSAGE of President Franklin D. Roosevelt to Congress, October 9, 1941

Department of State, *Bulletin*, October 11, 1941, p. 257

IT IS OBVIOUS to all of us that world conditions have changed violently since the first American Neutrality Act of 1935. The Neutrality Act of 1939 was passed at a time when the true magnitude of the Nazi attempt to dominate the world was visualized by few persons. We heard it said, indeed, that this new European war was not a real war, and that the contending armies would remain behind their impregnable fortifications and never really fight. In this atmosphere the Neutrality Act seemed reasonable. But so did the Maginot Line.

Since then—in these past two tragic years—war has spread from continent to continent; very many nations have been conquered and enslaved; great cities have been laid in ruins; millions of human beings have been killed, soldiers and sailors and civilians alike. Never before has such widespread devastation been visited upon God's earth and God's children.

The pattern of the future—the future as Hitler seeks to shape it—is now as clear and as ominous as the headlines of today's newspapers.

Through these years of war, we Americans have never been neutral in thought. We have never been indifferent to the fate of Hitler's victims. And, increasingly, we have become aware of the peril to ourselves, to our democratic traditions and institutions, to our country, and to our hemisphere.

We have known what victory for the aggressors would mean to us. Therefore, the American people, through the Congress, have taken important and costly steps to give great aid to those nations actively fighting against Nazi-Fascist domination.

We know that we could not defend ourselves in Long Island Sound or in San Francisco Bay. That would be too late. It is the American policy to defend ourselves wherever such defense becomes necessary under the complex conditions of modern warfare.

Therefore, it has become necessary that this Government should not be handicapped in carrying out the clearly announced policy of the Congress and of the people. We must face the truth that the Neutrality Act requires a complete reconsideration in the light of known facts.

The revisions which I suggest do not call for a declaration of war any more than the Lend-Lease Act called for a declaration of war. This is a matter of essential defense of American rights.

In the Neutrality Act are various crippling provisions. The repeal or modification of these provisions will not leave the United States any less neutral than we are today, but will make it possible for us to defend the Americas far more successfully, and to give aid far more effectively against the tremendous forces now marching towards conquest of the world.

Under the Neutrality Act, we established certain areas as zones of combat into which no American-flag ships could proceed. Hitler proclaimed certain far larger areas as zones of combat into which any neutral ship, regardless of its flag or the nature of its cargo, could proceed only at its peril. We know now that Hitler recognizes no limitation on any zone of combat in any part of the seven seas. He has struck at our ships and at the lives of our sailors within the waters of the Western Hemisphere. Determined as he is to gain domination of the entire world, he considers the entire world his own battlefield.

Ships of the United States and of other American republics continue to be sunk, not only in the imaginary zone proclaimed by the Nazis in the North Atlantic, but also in the zoneless South Atlantic.

I recommend the repeal of section 6 of the act of November 4, 1939, which prohibits the arming of American-flag ships engaged in foreign commerce.

The practice of arming merchant ships for civilian defense is an old one. It has never been prohibited by international law. Until 1937 it had never been prohibited by any statute of the United States. Through our whole history American merchant vessels have been armed whenever it was considered necessary for their own defense.

It is an imperative need now to equip American merchant vessels with arms. We are faced not with the old type of pirates but with the modern pirates of the sea who travel beneath the surface or on the surface or in the air destroying defenseless ships without warning and without provisions for the safety of the passengers and crews.

Our merchant vessels are sailing the seas on missions connected with the defense of the United States. It is not just that the crews of these vessels should be denied the means of defending their lives and their ships.

Although the arming of merchant vessels does not guarantee their safety, it most certainly adds to their safety. In the event of an attack by a raider they have a chance to keep the enemy at a distance until help comes. In the case of an attack by air, they have at least a chance to shoot down the enemy or keep the enemy at such height that it cannot make a sure hit. If it is a submarine, the armed merchant ship compels the submarine to use a torpedo while submerged—and many torpedoes thus fired miss their mark. The submarine can no longer rise to the surface within a few hundred yards and sink the merchant ship by gunfire at its leisure.

Already we take many precautions against the danger of mines—and it seems somewhat incongruous that we have authority today to "degauss" our ships as a protection against mines, whereas we have no authority to arm them in protection against aircraft or raiders or submarines.

The arming of our ships is a matter of immediate necessity and extreme urgency. It is not more important than some other crippling provisions in the present act, but anxiety for the safety of our crews and of the almost priceless goods that are within the holds of our ships leads me to recommend that you, with all speed, strike the prohibition against arming our ships from the statute books.

There are other phases of the Neutrality Act to the correction of which I hope the Congress will give earnest and early attention. One of these provisions is of major importance. I believe that it is essential to the proper defense of our country that we cease giving the definite assistance which we are now giving to the aggressors. For, in effect, we are inviting their control of the seas by keeping our ships out of the ports of our own friends.

It is time for this country to stop playing into Hitler's hands, and to unshackle our own.

A vast number of ships are sliding into the water from American shipbuilding ways. We are lending them to the enemies of Hitlerism and they are carrying food and supplies and munitions to belligerent ports in order to withstand Hitler's juggernaut.

Most of the vital goods authorized by the Congress are being delivered. Yet many of them are being sunk; and as we approach full production requiring the use of more ships now being built it will be increasingly necessary to deliver American goods under the American flag.

We cannot, and should not, depend on the strained resources of the exiled nations of Norway and Holland to deliver our goods, nor should we be forced to masquerade American-owned ships behind the flags of our sister republics.

I earnestly trust that the Congress will carry out the true intent of the Lend-Lease Act by making it possible for the United States to help to deliver the articles to those who are in a position effectively to use them. In other words, I ask for congressional action to implement congressional policy. Let us be consistent.

I would not go back to the earlier days when private traders could gamble with American life and property in the hope of personal gain, and thereby embroil this country in some incident in which the American public had no direct interest. But today, under the controls exercised by the Government, no ship and no cargo can leave the United States, save on an errand which has first been approved by governmental authority. And the test of that approval is whether the exportation will promote the defense of the United States.

I cannot impress too strongly upon the Congress the seriousness of the military situation that confronts all of the nations that are combating Hitler.

We would be blind to the realities if we did not recognize that Hitler is now determined to expend all the resources and all the mechanical force and manpower at his command to crush both Russia and Britain. He knows that he is racing against time. He has heard the rumblings of revolt among the enslaved peoples—including the Germans and Italians. He fears the mounting force of American aid. He knows that the days in which he may achieve total victory are numbered.

Therefore, it is our duty, as never before, to extend more and more assistance and ever more swiftly to Britain, to Russia, to all peoples and individuals fighting slavery. We must do this without fear or favor. The ultimate fate of the Western Hemisphere lies in the balance.

I say to you solemnly that if Hitler's present military plans are brought to successful fulfilment, we Americans shall be forced to fight in defense of our own homes and our own freedom in a war as costly and as devastating as that which now rages on the Russian front.

Hitler has offered a challenge which we as Americans cannot and will not tolerate.

We will not let Hitler prescribe the waters of the world on which our ships may travel. The American flag is not going to be driven from the seas either by his submarines, his airplanes, or his threats.

We cannot permit the affirmative defense of our rights to be annulled and diluted by sections of the Neutrality Act which have no realism in the light of unscrupulous ambition of madmen.

We Americans have determined our course.

We intend to maintain the security and the integrity and the honor of our country.

We intend to maintain the policy of protecting the freedom of the seas against domination by any foreign power which has become crazed with a desire to control the world. We shall do so with all our strength and all our heart and all our mind.

ENTRY OF THE UNITED STATES INTO THE WAR, DECEMBER 7–11, 1941

STATEMENT by Cordell Hull, Secretary of State, December 7, 1941

Department of State, *Bulletin,* December 13, 1941, p. 461

JAPAN HAS MADE a treacherous and utterly unprovoked attack upon the United States.

At the very moment when representatives of the Japanese Government were discussing with representatives of this Government, at the request of the former, principles and courses of peace, the armed forces of Japan were preparing and assembling at various strategic points to launch new attacks and new aggressions upon nations and peoples with which Japan was professedly at peace including the United States.

I am now releasing for the information of the American people the statement of principles governing the policies of the Government of the United States and setting out suggestions for a comprehensive peaceful settlement covering the entire Pacific area, which I handed to the Japanese Ambassador on November 26, 1941.

I am likewise releasing the text of a Japanese reply thereto which was handed to me by the Japanese Ambassador today. Before the Japanese Ambassador delivered this final statement from his Government the treacherous attack upon the United States had taken place.

This Government has stood for all the principles that underlie fair-dealing, peace, law and order, and justice between nations and has steadfastly striven to promote and maintain that state of relations between itself and all other nations.

It is now apparent to the whole world that Japan in its recent professions of a desire for peace has been infamously false and fraudulent.

MESSAGE of President Franklin D. Roosevelt to Congress, December 8, 1941, Requesting a Declaration of War against Japan

Department of State, *Bulletin,* December 13, 1941, p. 474

YESTERDAY, DECEMBER 7, 1941—a date which will live in infamy—the United States of America was suddenly and deliberately attacked by naval and air forces of the Empire of Japan.

The United States was at peace with that Nation and, at the solicitation of Japan, was still in conversation with its Government and its Emperor looking toward the maintenance of peace in the Pacific. Indeed, one hour after Japanese air squadrons had commenced bombing in Oahu, the Japanese Ambassador to the United States and his colleague delivered to the Secretary of State a formal reply to a recent American message. While this reply stated that it seemed useless to continue the existing diplomatic negotiations, it contained no threat or hint of war or armed attack.

It will be recorded that the distance of Hawaii from Japan makes it obvious that the attack was deliberately planned many days or even weeks ago. During the intervening time the Japanese Government has deliberately sought to deceive the United States by false statements and expressions of hope for continued peace.

The attack yesterday on the Hawaiian Islands has caused severe damage to American naval and military forces. Very many American lives have been lost. In addition American ships have been reported torpedoed on the high seas between San Francisco and Honolulu.

Yesterday the Japanese Government also launched an attack against Malaya.

Last night Japanese forces attacked Hong Kong.
Last night Japanese forces attacked Guam.
Last night Japanese forces attacked the Philippine Islands.
Last night the Japanese attacked Wake Island.
This morning the Japanese attacked Midway Island.

Japan has, therefore, undertaken a surprise offensive extending throughout the Pacific area. The facts of yesterday speak for themselves. The people of the United States have already formed their opinions and well understand the implications to the very life and safety of our Nation.

As Commander-in-Chief of the Army and Navy I have directed that all measures be taken for our defense.

Always will we remember the character of the onslaught against us. No matter how long it may take us to overcome this premeditated invasion, the American people in their righteous might will win through to absolute victory.

I believe I interpret the will of the Congress and of the people when I assert that we will not only defend ourselves to the uttermost but will make very certain that this form of treachery shall never endanger us again.

Hostilities exist. There is no blinking at the fact that our people, our territory, and our interests are in grave danger.

With confidence in our armed forces—with the unbounded determination of our people—we will gain the inevitable triumph—so help us God.

I ask that the Congress declare that since the unprovoked and dastardly attack by Japan on Sunday, December seventh, a state of war has existed between the United States and the Japanese Empire.

DECLARATION by Congress of a State of War with Japan, December 8, 1941

Department of State, *Bulletin,* December 13, 1941, p. 475

JOINT RESOLUTION declaring that a state of war exists between the Imperial Government of Japan and the Government and the people of the United States and making provisions to prosecute the same.

WHEREAS the Imperial Government of Japan has committed unprovoked acts of war against the Government and the people of the United States of America: THEREFORE BE IT

Resolved by the Senate and House of Representatives of the United States of America in Congress assembled, That the state of war between the United States and the Imperial Government of Japan which has thus been thrust upon the United States is hereby formally declared; and the President is hereby authorized and directed to employ the entire naval and military forces of the United States and the resources of the Government to carry on war against the Imperial Government of Japan; and, to bring the conflict to a successful termination, all of the resources of the country are hereby pledged by the Congress of the United States.

Approved, December 8, 1941, 4:10 p.m., E.S.T.

RADIO ADDRESS by President Franklin D. Roosevelt to the nation, December 9, 1941

Department of State, *Bulletin*, December 13, 1941, p. 476

The sudden criminal attacks perpetrated by the Japanese in the Pacific provide the climax of a decade of international immorality.

Powerful and resourceful gangsters have banded together to make war upon the whole human race. Their challenge has now been flung at the United States of America. The Japanese have treacherously violated the long-standing peace between us. Many American soldiers and sailors have been killed by enemy action. American ships have been sunk; American airplanes have been destroyed.

The Congress and the people of the United States have accepted that challenge.

Together with other free peoples, we are now fighting to maintain our right to live among our world neighbors in freedom and in common decency, without fear of assault.

I have prepared the full record of our past relations with Japan, and it will be submitted to the Congress. It begins with the visit of Commodore Perry to Japan 88 years ago. It ends with the visit of two Japanese emissaries to the Secretary of State last Sunday, an hour after Japanese forces had loosed their bombs and machine guns against our flag, our forces, and our citizens.

I can say with utmost confidence that no Americans today or a thousand years hence need feel anything but pride in our patience and our efforts through all the years toward achieving a peace in the Pacific which would be fair and honorable to every nation, large or small. And no honest person, today or a thousand years hence, will be able to suppress a sense of indignation and horror at the treachery committed by the military dictators of Japan, under the very shadow of the flag of peace borne by their special envoys in our midst.

The course that Japan has followed for the past 10 years in Asia has paralleled the course of Hitler and Mussolini in Europe and Africa. Today, it has become far more than a parallel. It is collaboration so well calculated that all the continents of the world, and all the oceans, are now considered by the Axis strategists as one gigantic battlefield.

In 1931, Japan invaded Manchukuo—without warning.
In 1935, Italy invaded Ethiopia—without warning.
In 1938, Hitler occupied Austria—without warning.
In 1939, Hitler invaded Czechoslovakia—without warning.
Later in 1939, Hitler invaded Poland—without warning.

THE UNITED STATES ENTERS THE WAR

In 1940, Hitler invaded Norway, Denmark, Holland, Belgium, and Luxembourg—without warning.

In 1940, Italy attacked France and later Greece—without warning.

In 1941, the Axis Powers attacked Yugoslavia and Greece and they dominated the Balkans—without warning.

In 1941, Hitler invaded Russia—without warning.

And now Japan has attacked Malaya and Thailand—and the United States—without warning.

It is all of one pattern.

We are now in this war. We are all in it—all the way. Every single man, woman, and child is a partner in the most tremendous undertaking of our American history. We must share together the bad news and the good news, the defeats and the victories—the changing fortunes of war.

So far, the news has all been bad. We have suffered a serious setback in Hawaii. Our forces in the Philippines, which include the brave people of that Commonwealth, are taking punishment, but are defending themselves vigorously. The reports from Guam and Wake and Midway Islands are still confused, but we must be prepared for the announcement that all these three outposts have been seized.

The casualty lists of these first few days will undoubtedly be large. I deeply feel the anxiety of all families of the men in our armed forces and the relatives of people in cities which have been bombed. I can only give them my solemn promise that they will get news just as quickly as possible.

This Government will put its trust in the stamina of the American people, and will give the facts to the public as soon as two conditions have been fulfilled: first, that the information has been definitely and officially confirmed; and, second, that the release of the information at the time it is received will not prove valuable to the enemy directly or indirectly.

Most earnestly I urge my countrymen to reject all rumors. These ugly little hints of complete disaster fly thick and fast in wartime. They have to be examined and appraised.

As an example, I can tell you frankly that until further surveys are made, I have not sufficient information to state the exact damage which has been done to our naval vessels at Pearl Harbor. Admittedly the damage is serious. But no one can say how serious until we know how much of this damage can be repaired and how quickly the necessary repairs can be made.

I cite as another example a statement made on Sunday night that a Japanese carrier had been located and sunk off the Canal Zone. And when you hear statements that are attributed to what they call "an authoritative source," you can be reasonably sure that under these war circumstances the "authoritative source" was not any person in authority.

Many rumors and reports which we now hear originate with enemy sources. For instance, today the Japanese are claiming that as a result of their one action against Hawaii they have gained naval supremacy in the Pacific. This is an old trick of propaganda which has been used innumerable times by the Nazis. The purposes of such fantastic claims are, of course, to spread fear and confusion among us, and to goad us into revealing military information which our enemies are desperately anxious to obtain.

Our Government will not be caught in this obvious trap—and neither will our people.

It must be remembered by each and every one of us that our free and rapid communication must be greatly restricted in wartime. It is not possible to receive full, speedy, accurate reports from distant areas of combat. This is particularly true where naval operations are concerned. For in these days of the marvels of radio it is often impossible for the commanders of various units to report their activities by radio, for the very simple reason that this information would become available to the enemy and would disclose their position and their plan of defense or attack.

Of necessity there will be delays in officially confirming or denying reports of operations, but we will not hide facts from the country if we know the facts and if the enemy will not be aided by their disclosure.

To all newspapers and radio stations—all those who reach the eyes and ears of the American people—I say this: you have a most grave responsibility to the Nation now and for the duration of this war.

If you feel that your Government is not disclosing enough of the truth, you have every right to say so. But—in the absence of all the facts, as revealed by official sources—you have no right to deal out unconfirmed reports in such a way as to make people believe they are gospel truth.

Every citizen, in every walk of life, shares this same responsibility. The lives of our soldiers and sailors—the whole future of this Nation —depend upon the manner in which each and every one of us fulfils his obligation to our country.

Now a word about the recent past—and the future. A year and a half has elapsed since the fall of France, when the whole world first realized the mechanized might which the Axis nations had been building for so many years. America has used that year and a half to great advantage. Knowing that the attack might reach us in all too short a time, we immediately began greatly to increase our industrial strength and our capacity to meet the demands of modern warfare.

Precious months were gained by sending vast quantities of our war material to the nations of the world still able to resist Axis aggression. Our policy rested on the fundamental truth that the defense of any country resisting Hitler or Japan was in the long run the defense of our own country. That policy has been justified. It has given us time, invaluable time, to build our American assembly lines of production.

Assembly lines are now in operation. Others are being rushed to completion. A steady stream of tanks and planes, of guns and ships, of shells and equipment—that is what these 18 months have given us.

But it is all only a beginning of what has to be done. We must be set to face a long war against crafty and powerful bandits. The attack at Pearl Harbor can be repeated at any one of many points in both oceans and along both our coast lines and against all the rest of the hemisphere.

It will not only be a long war, it will be a hard war. That is the basis on which we now lay all our plans. That is the yardstick by which we measure what we shall need and demand; money, materials, doubled and quadrupled production—ever-increasing. The production must be not only for our own Army and Navy and Air Forces. It must reinforce the other armies and navies and air forces fighting the Nazis and the war-lords of Japan throughout the Americas and the world.

I have been working today on the subject of production. Your Government has decided on two broad policies.

The first is to speed up all existing production by working on a seven-day-week basis in every war industry, including the production of essential raw materials.

The second policy, now being put into form, is to rush additions to the capacity of production by building more new plants, by adding to old plants, and by using the many smaller plants for war needs.

Over the hard road of the past months, we have at times met obstacles and difficulties, divisions and disputes, indifference and callousness. That is now all past—and, I am sure, forgotten.

The fact is that the country now has an organization in Washington built around men and women who are recognized experts in their own fields. I think the country knows that the people who are actually responsible in each and every one of these many fields are pulling together with a teamwork that has never before been excelled.

On the road ahead there lies hard work—gruelling work—day and night, every hour and every minute.

I was about to add that ahead there lies sacrifice for all of us.

But it is not correct to use that word. The United States does not consider it a sacrifice to do all one can, to give one's best to our Nation, when the Nation is fighting for its existence and its future life.

It is not a sacrifice for any man, old or young, to be in the Army or the Navy of the United States. Rather is it a privilege.

It is not a sacrifice for the industrialist or the wage-earner, the farmer or the shopkeeper, the trainman or the doctor, to pay more taxes, to buy more bonds, to forego extra profits, to work longer or harder at the task for which he is best fitted. Rather is it a privilege.

It is not a sacrifice to do without many things to which we are accustomed if the national defense calls for doing without.

A review this morning leads me to the conclusion that at present we shall not have to curtail the normal articles of food. There is enough food for all of us and enough left over to send to those who are fighting on the same side with us.

There will be a clear and definite shortage of metals of many kinds for civilian use, for the very good reason that in our increased program we shall need for war purposes more than half of that portion of the principal metals which during the past year have gone into articles for civilian use. We shall have to give up many things entirely.

I am sure that the people in every part of the Nation are prepared in their individual living to win this war. I am sure they will cheerfully help to pay a large part of its financial cost while it goes on. I am sure they will cheerfully give up those material things they are asked to give up.

I am sure that they will retain all those great spiritual things without which we cannot win through.

I repeat that the United States can accept no result save victory, final and complete. Not only must the shame of Japanese treachery be wiped out, but the sources of international brutality, wherever they exist, must be absolutely and finally broken.

In my message to the Congress yesterday I said that we "will make very certain that this form of treachery shall never endanger us again." In order to achieve that certainty, we must begin the great task that is before us by abandoning once and for all the illusion that we can ever again isolate ourselves from the rest of humanity.

In these past few years—and, most violently, in the past few days —we have learned a terrible lesson.

It is our obligation to our dead—it is our sacred obligation to their children and our children—that we must never forget what we have learned.

THE UNITED STATES ENTERS THE WAR 259

And what we all have learned is this:

There is no such thing as security for any nation—or any individual—in a world ruled by the principles of gangsterism.

There is no such thing as impregnable defense against powerful aggressors who sneak up in the dark and strike without warning.

We have learned that our ocean-girt hemisphere is not immune from severe attack—that we cannot measure our safety in terms of miles on any map.

We may acknowledge that our enemies have performed a brilliant feat of deception, perfectly timed and executed with great skill. It was a thoroughly dishonorable deed, but we must face the fact that modern warfare as conducted in the Nazi manner is a dirty business. We don't like it—we didn't want to get in it—but we are in it, and we're going to fight it with everything we've got.

I do not think any American has any doubt of our ability to administer proper punishment to the perpetrators of these crimes.

Your Government knows that for weeks Germany has been telling Japan that if Japan did not attack the United States, Japan would not share in dividing the spoils with Germany when peace came. She was promised by Germany that if she came in she would receive the complete and perpetual control of the whole of the Pacific area—and that means not only the Far East, not only all of the islands in the Pacific, but also a stranglehold on the west coast of North, Central, and South America.

We also know that Germany and Japan are conducting their military and naval operations in accordance with a joint plan. That plan considers all peoples and nations which are not helping the Axis powers as common enemies of each and every one of the Axis powers.

That is their simple and obvious grand strategy. That is why the American people must realize that it can be matched only with similar grand strategy. We must realize for example that Japanese successes against the United States in the Pacific are helpful to German operations in Libya; that any German success against the Caucasus is inevitably an assistance to Japan in her operations against the Dutch East Indies; that a German attack against Algiers or Morocco opens the way to a German attack against South America.

On the other side of the picture, we must learn to know that guerilla warfare against the Germans in Serbia helps us; that a successful Russian offensive against the Germans helps us; and that British successes on land or sea in any part of the world strengthen our hands.

Remember always that Germany and Italy, regardless of any formal declaration of war, consider themselves at war with the United States at this moment just as much as they consider themselves at war with Britain and Russia. And Germany puts all the other republics of the Americas into the category of enemies. The people of the hemisphere can be honored by that.

The true goal we seek is far above and beyond the ugly field of battle. When we resort to force, as now we must, we are determined that this force shall be directed toward ultimate good as well as against immediate evil. We Americans are not destroyers—we are builders.

We are now in the midst of a war, not for conquest, not for vengeance, but for a world in which this Nation, and all that this Nation represents, will be safe for our children. We expect to eliminate the danger from Japan, but it would serve us ill if we accomplished that and found that the rest of the world was dominated by Hitler and Mussolini.

We are going to win the war and we are going to win the peace that follows.

And in the dark hours of this day—and through dark days that may be yet to come—we will know that the vast majority of the members of the human race are on our side. Many of them are fighting with us. All of them are praying for us. For, in representing our cause, we represent theirs as well—our hope and their hope for liberty under God.

MESSAGE of President Franklin D. Roosevelt to Congress, December 11, 1941, Requesting Declarations of War against Germany and Italy

Department of State, *Bulletin,* December 13, 1941, p. 475

ON THE MORNING of December eleventh, the Government of Germany, pursuing its course of world-conquest, declared war against the United States.

The long known and the long expected has thus taken place. The forces endeavoring to enslave the entire world now are moving towards this hemisphere.

Never before has there been a greater challenge to life, liberty, and civilization.

Delay invites greater danger. Rapid and united effort by all of the peoples of the world who are determined to remain free will insure a world victory of the forces of justice and of righteousness over the forces of savagery and of barbarism.

Italy also has declared war against the United States.

I therefore request the Congress to recognize a state of war between the United States and Germany, and between the United States and Italy.

DECLARATIONS by Congress of a State of War with Germany and Italy, December 11, 1941

Department of State, *Bulletin,* December 13, 1941, p. 475

JOINT RESOLUTION Declaring that a state of war exists between the Government of Germany and the Government and the people of the United States and making provision to prosecute the same.

WHEREAS the Government of Germany has formally declared war against the Government and the people of the United States of America: THEREFORE BE IT

Resolved by the Senate and House of Representatives of the United States of America in Congress assembled, That the state of war between the United States and the Government of Germany which has thus been thrust upon the United States is hereby formally declared; and the President is hereby authorized and directed to employ the entire naval and military forces of the United States and the resources of the Government to carry on war against the Government of Germany; and, to bring the conflict to a successful termination, all of the resources of the country are hereby pledged by the Congress of the United States.

Approved, December 11, 1941, 3:05 p.m., E.S.T.

JOINT RESOLUTION Declaring that a state of war exists between the Government of Italy and the Government and the people of the United States and making provision to prosecute the same.

WHEREAS the Government of Italy has formally declared war against the Government and the people of the United States of America: THEREFORE BE IT

Resolved by the Senate and House of Representatives of the United States of America in Congress assembled, That the state of war between the United States and the Government of Italy which has thus been thrust upon the United States is hereby formally declared; and the President is hereby authorized and directed to employ the entire naval and military forces of the United States and the resources of the Government to carry on war against the Government of Italy; and, to bring the conflict to a successful termination, all of the resources of the country are hereby pledged by the Congress of the United States.

Approved, December 11, 1941, 3:06 p.m., E.S.T.

ECONOMIC AND FINANCIAL POLICY

ADDRESS by Cordell Hull, Secretary of State, before the World Monetary and Economic Conference at London, July 27, 1933

Department of State, *Press Releases*, July 29, 1933, p. 63

THE CONFERENCE is now entering the recess stage. The progress of its work has corresponded with the difficulties of its task. Human ingenuity could scarcely have devised a more complete jumble and chaos of business and general economic conditions than those facing the nations and the Conference when it convened and still challenging solution. A multiplicity of other circumstances has further impeded the progress of the Conference, such as the lack of an international public opinion, the malignant opposition of those who blindly or selfishly oppose all international economic cooperation, and the engrossment of many nations with the more or less temporary phases of their domestic programs for the emergency treatment of panic conditions.

It is inevitable in the light of these extremely complicated conditions that the Conference, having reached a few important agreements and concluded a thorough appraisal and understanding of the problems presented, would find it necessary to recess. Time must be afforded for some of these difficulties to be ironed out and for the nations further to broaden their economic plans and policies so as to coordinate them on a gradually increasing scale with the program of international cooperation which this Conference is undertaking to promulgate.

The conditions which defied solution by individual state action and imperatively called for international treatment offered the compelling reason for this Conference. Every rational person knows that since there were international causes of the depression there must be international remedies.

For those either pessimistically or wantonly inclined to attempt further to handicap the Conference in its particular efforts to go forward is virtually to indict and discredit all forms of international cooperation however necessary to deal with international problems which vitally affect the welfare of peoples alike in every part of the world.

It is easy to say that this or that incident or complication or condition has caused a partial failure of the Conference. This has been the experience of past conferences when struggling against many obstacles to solve complicated problems involving human life and human welfare. The very purpose of international cooperative effort is aggressively to override these and all other impediments to the fulfillment of its high mission. To impute failure is to impute the bankruptcy of world statesmanship in the face of unparalleled and universal economic distress and suffering.

Business and economic conditions in every part of the world remain dislocated and disorganized. At the beginning of the Conference the delegates had no adequate conception of the complicated conditions in distant countries and of each other's varying viewpoints. Understanding is the chief basis of all international relationships; and its importance can scarcely be overestimated. Manifestly valuable seed has been sown here already in that we have come to a deeper and more sympathetic comprehension of our common problems.

There are after all only two ways of reaching international agreement. One is by imposing one's will by force—by war. The other is by persuasion—by conference. Even by the violent means of war—which we have all renounced—no one would expect agreement in six weeks. How can it then be said that the Conference—this method which has killed no man—has already failed? Many actual wars of the past growing out of bitter trade controversies would have been averted had there been more peace-time conferences.

My judgment is that just now the world's statesmen cannot sit in conference too often or too long in earnest and patient consideration of all questions calculated to disturb friendly relations and clear understanding between nations and in determined effort to bring about their fair and peaceful adjustment.

Many of those not delegates here who criticize the Conference for not going forward more expeditiously represent the economic leadership in numerous countries which has already failed in repeated attempts since 1929 to cure panic conditions. This group of critics includes the selfish but short-sighted beneficiaries of governmental favoritism and those mock patriots whose constant propaganda would make international finance and commerce almost criminal. These forces are potent in many parts of the world today. They will be very slow to lower a single excessive trade barrier until human distress becomes unbearable. It matters not to them that there ought to be forty billion dollars of additional commerce on the high seas this year, thereby affording employment for labor and markets for surpluses.

In the past there have been spectacular races by nations in military armaments. Their wildest rivalry, however, scarcely exceeds in danger the present mad race between most nations to promote economic armaments which inflict colossal injuries on the masses of people everywhere. At this moment the world is still engaged in wild competition in economic armaments which constantly menace both peace and commerce.

The nations must make up their minds to pursue less extreme economic policies; they must discard artificial expedients to protect industries that are notoriously inefficient or are not justifiable on any practical economic or business grounds.

When some nations undertake to produce every commodity, whatsoever the cost, for purposes of either peace or war, other nations are driven to turn to the adoption of similar policies of unjustifiable production with the result that, as in the case of military armaments, the economic race neutralizes itself to the injury of all who are engaged in it.

I appeal to this Conference and through it to peoples everywhere to demand an end to the ruinous races by nations in either military or economic armaments. It is the duty of statesmanship everywhere to lead the world away from these twin evils of this modern age.

Much has been said about the order in which the subjects on the agenda should be considered. I believe that the membership of the Conference frankly recognizes that both the financial and economic difficulties as listed in the agenda must be visualized as one unified network of obstructions and impediments to international finance and commerce and attacked and dealt with as a whole. It would get nowhere to lower trade barriers without development of stable monetary facilities for the movements of commerce, nor, on the other hand, would commerce move with the aid of complete monetary stabilization if existing insurmountable trade obstructions still continued intact. Substantial progress in dealing with either group depends on corresponding action dealing with the other.

The object of this Conference is to substitute prosperity and good will for panic and trade strife. To relax our efforts in the face of the need and the duty pressing upon us would show an amazing indifference to human welfare. The average citizen must by this time be convinced that those who have opposed sane, practical international economic cooperation have proven to be false prophets. Do the thirty millions of unemployed wage-earners or the many millions of impoverished farmers and producers of raw materials need additional proof of the failure of such leadership? May I again remind you that the domestic economy of more than thirty important countries is primarily dependent upon international finance and commerce, with direct repercussions upon the entire world. The practice of a too narrow policy has choked the entire trade of the world, with disastrous effects upon home production and home prices and markets everywhere.

The processes of exchange and distribution have broken down and their restoration presents the real world problem. Disastrous experience teaches the necessity for a broader economic, social, and political policy. Every country today should first have a comprehensive domestic program calculated most effectively to deal with the existing depression. The United States has launched a constructive program to this end. Indispensable and all-important as domestic programs are, they cannot by themselves restore business to the highest level of permanent recovery. A program of international cooperation is necessary for purposes of a broad basis on which to build the domestic economic structure, to give it stability and to make possible a substantially greater measure of sound and lasting business prosperity.

Let me say, with reference to my own and other countries striving by every available domestic method to extricate themselves from panic conditions, that there is no logic in the theory that such domestic policies are irreconcilable with international cooperation. Each country undoubtedly should invoke every emergency method that would increase commodity prices so that they may gradually be coordinated with international economic action for the common purpose of business recovery. The development of both programs can be proceeded with on a substantial scale from the outset, and to an increasing extent as emergency treatment of panic conditions diminishes.

In harmony with these views I have presented to the Conference a proposal for an agreement among the nations to reduce trade barriers gradually over a period of time, to make the unconditional form of the favored-nation doctrine, with a reasonable exception in favor of broad international efforts for reduction of trade barriers, the universal basis of commercial policy and to extend the life of the tariff truce to a reasonable period beyond the final adjournment of the Conference. This proposal offers a basis upon which a world program might be developed during the course of the recess and the meeting of the Conference to follow.

The American Government therefore hopes that every nation that may not have done so will launch a full domestic program of both ordinary and extraordinary methods and remedies calculated to raise prices, to increase employment, and to improve the business situation.

We must all agree that business conditions in most countries are still at or near a panic level and that their restoration imperatively calls for a program of fundamental policies and methods as outlined in the agenda of this Conference. We know that these conditions have not greatly improved and that the basic features of the Conference agenda remain virtually untouched and unacted upon. We know too that the greatest single step the Conference can take is one that would inspire confidence; and this step can only be taken by a determination of this Conference resolutely to go forward to the solution of each vital problem listed on the agenda.

No nation has ever been able to live unto itself and not become backward and decadent. No people in the past have long remained highly civilized without the continuing benefits of the customs, learning, and culture of other parts of the world, and these are only within the reach of trading nations.

International commerce conducted on a fair basis, as our agenda proposes, is the greatest peacemaker in the experience of the human race. The promotion and preservation of the high ideals and high purposes of economic peace brought this great Conference together, and its failure would be their failures. No governments within my time have faced a graver economic crisis or come together with a higher mission. It would be an unforgivable act if they, through local, regional, or other considerations, should fail to perform this great trust. They should disregard the threats or pleas of minorities selfishly clinging to the excessive tariffs and other favors of their governments. A reasonable combination of the practicable phases of both economic nationalism and economic internationalism—avoiding the extremes of each—should be our objective.

I want to take this opportunity to express to all who have contributed to the work of this assembly—to His Majesty the King who graciously opened the Conference, to the Prime Minister who has so ably presided over this great gathering, and to my other fellow delegates—my own deep satisfaction in the helpful spirit of cooperation which has resulted from our labors so far. We came here beset by our individual problems, compelled by the necessities of special circumstances arising from widely differing conditions in our various countries. We have come to a much clearer understanding of each other's viewpoints and special problems. We have not permitted immediate considerations, no matter how urgent, to divert us from the larger purposes to which we are all committed. We are unitedly resolved to move forward together in a common cause. It cannot fail to be gratifying to all who wish lasting success from this Conference that greater good will and mutual helpfulness, deeper comprehension and renewed determination, have come from our deliberations.

The duty and responsibility of the Conference are well known to us, as they are to every intelligent citizen on the planet. I pray that each of us may be given the light clearly to see and fully to understand. We cannot falter. We will not quit. We have begun and we will go on.

MESSAGE of President Franklin D. Roosevelt to Congress, June 1, 1934

Department of State, *Press Releases,* June 2, 1934, p. 344

IN MY ADDRESS to the Congress January 3 I stated that I expected to report later in regard to debts owed the Government and people of this country by the governments and people of other countries. There has been no formal communication on the subject from the Executive since President Hoover's message of December 19, 1932.

The developments are well known, having been announced to the press as they occurred. Correspondence with debtor governments has been made public promptly and is available in the Annual Report of the Secretary of the Treasury. It is, however, timely to review the situation.

Payments on the indebtedness of foreign governments to the United States which fell due in the fiscal year ended June 30, 1932, were postponed on the proposal of President Hoover announced June 20, 1931, and authorized by the joint resolution of Congress approved December 23, 1931. Yugoslavia alone suspended payment while rejecting President Hoover's offer of postponement.

In the 6 months of July to December 1932, which followed the end of the Hoover moratorium year, payments of $125,000,000 from 12 governments fell due. Requests to postpone the payments due December 15, 1932, were received from Great Britain, France, Belgium, Czechoslovakia, Estonia, Latvia, Lithuania, and Poland. The replies made on behalf of President Hoover through the Department of State declined these requests, generally stating that it was not in the power of the Executive to grant them, and expressing a willingness to cooperate with the debtor government in surveying the entire situation. After such correspondence, Czechoslovakia, Finland, Great Britain, Italy, Latvia, and Lithuania met their contractual obligations, while Belgium, Estonia, France, and Poland made no payment.

In a note of December 11, 1932, after the United States had declined to sanction postponement of the payment due December 15, the British Government, in announcing its decision to make payment of the amount due on December 15, made the following important statement:

For reasons which have already been placed on record His Majesty's Government are convinced that the system of intergovernmental payments in respect of the War Debts as it existed prior to Mr. Hoover's initiative on June 20th, 1931, cannot be revived without disaster. Since it is agreed that the whole subject should be reexamined between the United States and the United Kingdom this fundamental point need not be further stressed here.

In the view of His Majesty's Government therefore the payment to be made on December 15th is not to be regarded as a resumption of the annual payments contemplated by the existing agreement. It is made because there has not been time for discussion with regard to that agreement to take place and because the United States Government have stated that in their opinion such a payment would greatly increase the prospects of a satisfactory approach to the whole question.

His Majesty's Government propose accordingly to treat the payment on December 15th as a capital payment of which account should be taken in any final settlement and they are making arrangements to effect this payment in gold as being in the circumstances the least prejudicial of the methods open to them.

This procedure must obviously be exceptional and abnormal and His Majesty's Government desire to urge upon the United States Government the importance of an early exchange of views with the object of concluding the proposed discussion before June 15th next in order to obviate a general breakdown of the existing intergovernmental agreements.

The Secretary of State, Mr. Stimson, replied to this note on the same day that acceptance by the Secretary of the Treasury of funds tendered in payment of the December 15 installment cannot constitute approval of or agreement to any condition or declaration of policy inconsistent with the terms of the agreement inasmuch as the Executive has no power to amend or to alter those terms either directly or by implied commitment.

No payment was made by France December 15, 1932, as the French Chamber of Deputies by a vote on the morning of December 14 refused authorization to make the payment. The resolution voted by the French Chamber at that time invited the French Government to convoke as soon as possible, in agreement with Great Britain and other debtors, a general conference for the purpose of adjusting all international obligations and putting an end to all international transfers for which there is no compensating transaction. The resolution stated that the Chamber, despite legal and economic considerations, would have authorized settlement had the United States been willing to agree in advance to the convening of the conference for these purposes.

This resolution of the French Chamber is to be read in relation with the public statements of policy made by President Hoover and by myself on November 23, 1932. President Hoover said:

The United States Government from the beginning has taken the position that it would deal with each of the debtor governments separately, as separate and distinct circumstances surrounded each case. Both in the making of the loans and in the subsequent settlements with the different debtors, this policy has been rigidly made clear to every foreign government concerned.

I said:

I find myself in complete accord with the four principles discussed in the conference between the President and myself yesterday and set forth in a statement which the President has issued today.

These debts were actual loans made under distinct understanding and with the intention that they would be repaid.

In dealing with the debts each government has been and is to be considered individually, and all dealings with each government are independent of dealings with any other debtor government. In no case should we deal with the debtor governments collectively.

Debt settlements made in each case take into consideration the capacity to pay of the individual debtor nations.

The indebtedness of the various European nations to our Government has no relation whatsoever to reparations payments made or owed to them.

Of the $125,000,000 due and payable December 15, 1932, the Treasury received $98,750,000, of which $95,550,000 was the British payment made subsequent to the above correspondence, and the other $3,000,000 represented payments by five other debtor nations. The amounts due from Belgium, Estonia, France, Hungary, and Poland which were not received amounted to $25,000,000, of which $19,260,000 was due and payable by France.

In my statement issued November 23, 1932, I had said:

I firmly believe in the principle that an individual debtor should at all times have access to the creditor; that he should have opportunity to lay facts and representations before the creditor and that the creditor always should give courteous, sympathetic and thoughtful consideration to such facts and representations.

This is a rule essential to the preservation of the ordinary relationships of life. It is a basic obligation of civilization. It applies to nations as well as to individuals.

The principle calls for a free access by the debtor to the creditor. Each case should be considered in the light of the conditions and necessities peculiar to the case of each nation concerned.

On January 20, 1933, President Hoover and I agreed upon the following statement:

The British Government has asked for a discussion of the debts. The incoming administration will be glad to receive their representative early in March for this purpose. It is, of course, necessary to discuss at the same time the world economic problems in which the United States and Great Britain are mutually interested, and therefore that representatives should also be sent to discuss ways and means for improving the world situation.

On March 4, 1933, the situation with regard to the indebtedness of other governments to the United States was, in brief, as follows:

France.—The French Parliament had refused to permit payment of $19,261,432.50 interest due on the $3,863,650,000 bonds of France owned by the United States;

Great Britain.—With respect to the British bonded debt held by the Treasury in the principal amount of $4,368,000,000, Great Britain in meeting a due payment of $30,000,000 principal and $65,-550,000 interest had stated that the payment was not to be regarded as a resumption of the annual payments contemplated under the funding agreement of June 19, 1923, but was to be treated, so far as the British Government was concerned, as a capital payment of which account should be taken in any final settlement;

Italy.—With respect to the $2,004,900,000 principal amount of bonds of the Italian Government held by the United States Treasury, the Italian Government had paid the sum of $1,245,437 interest due December 15, 1932; but in doing so it referred to a resolution of the Grand Council of Fascism, adopted December 5, 1932, in which "a radical solution of the 'sponging of the slate' type was declared to be necessary for the world's economic recovery";

Czechoslovakia in making a payment of $1,500,000 principal due December 15, 1932, on its debt of $165,000,000 had stated that "this payment constitutes in the utmost self-denial of the Czechoslovak people their final effort to meet the obligation under such extremely unfavorable circumstances";

Belgium had declined to pay $2,125,000 interest due December 15, 1932, on its bonds of $400,680,000 held by the Treasury of the United States, and in doing so had recited circumstances which it stated "prevent it from resuming, on December 15th, the payments which were suspended by virtue of the agreement made in July, 1931," adding: "Belgium is still disposed to collaborate fully in seeking a general settlement of intergovernmental debts and of the other problems arising from the depression.";

Poland had not paid the $232,000 principal and $3,070,980 interest due December 15, 1932, on its bond in the principal amount of $206,057,000 held by the Treasury of the United States.

Of the nine other governments whose bonds are held by the Treasury of the United States, *Estonia* and *Hungary* had not met payments due December 15, 1932;

Austria is availing itself of a contractual right to postpone payments;

Greece was making only partial payments on its foreign bonded indebtedness, including that held by the United States;

Yugoslavia had declined to sign any Hoover moratorium agreement and had stopped paying;

No payment by *Rumania* had fallen due since the close of the Hoover moratorium;

Finland, Latvia, and *Lithuania* were current in their payments.

Although I had informal discussions concerning the British debt with the British Ambassador even before March 4, 1933, and in April there was further discussion of the subject with the Prime Minister of Great Britain and between experts of the two Governments, it was not possible to reach definitive conclusions. On June 13 the British Government gave notice that in the then existing circumstances it was not prepared to make the payment due June 15, 1933, but would make an immediate payment of $10,000,000 as an acknowledgment of the debt pending a final settlement. To this notice reply was made by the Acting Secretary of State, pointing out that it is not within the discretion of the President to reduce or cancel the existing debt owed to the United States nor to alter the schedule of debt payments contained in the existing settlement. At the same time I took occasion to announce that in view of the representations of the British Government, the accompanying acknowledgment of the debt itself, and the payment made, I had no personal hesitation in saying that I would not characterize the resultant situation as a default. In view of the suggestion of the expressed desire of the British Government to make representations concerning the debt, I suggested that such representations be made in Washington as soon as convenient.

The Agricultural Adjustment Act, approved May 12, 1933, had authorized the President for a period of 6 months from that date to accept silver in payment of installments due from any foreign government, such silver to be accepted at not to exceed a price of 50 cents an ounce. In the payments due June 15, 1933, the Governments of Great Britain, Czechoslovakia, Finland, Italy, Lithuania, and Rumania took advantage of this offer.

On June 15, 1933, payments of about $144,000,000 were due from foreign governments, the larger amounts being about $76,000,000 from Great Britain, almost $41,000,000 from France, and $13,500,000 from Italy. The amounts actually paid into the Treasury were $11,374,000, of which $10,000,000 was paid by Great Britain and $1,000,000 by Italy. Communications were received from most of the debtor governments asking a discussion of the debt question with the United States Government.

In October 1933, representatives of the British Government arrived in Washington and conferred for some weeks with representatives of this Government. These discussions made clear the existing difficulties, and the discussions were adjourned.

The British Government then stated that it continued to acknowledge the debt without prejudicing its right again to present the matter of readjustment and that it would express this acknowledgment tangibly by a payment of $7,500,000 on December 15. In announcing this I stated that in view of the representations, of the payment, and of the impossibility of accepting at that time any of the proposals for a readjustment of the debt, I had no personal hesitation in saying that I should not regard the British Government as in default.

On December 15, 1933, there was due and payable by foreign governments on their debt-funding agreements and Hoover moratorium agreements a total of about $153,000,000. The payments actually received were slightly less than $9,000,000, including $7,500,000 paid by Great Britain, $1,000,000 by Italy, and about $230,000 by Finland.

At the present time Finland remains the only foreign government which has met all payments on its indebtedness to the United States punctually and in full.

It is a simple fact that this matter of the repayment of debts contracted to the United States during and after the World War has gravely complicated our trade and financial relationships with the borrowing nations for many years.

These obligations furnished vital means for the successful conclusion of a war which involved the national existence of the borrowers, and later for a quicker restoration of their normal life after the war ended.

The money loaned by the United States Government was in turn borrowed by the United States Government from the people of the United States, and our Government in the absence of payment from foreign governments is compelled to raise the shortage by general taxation of its own people in order to pay off the original Liberty Bonds and the later refunding bonds.

It is for these reasons that the American people have felt that their debtors were called upon to make a determined effort to discharge these obligations. The American people would not be disposed to place an impossible burden upon their debtors, but are nevertheless in a just position to ask that substantial sacrifices be made to meet these debts.

We shall continue to expect the debtors on their part to show full understanding of the American attitude on this debt question. The people of the debtor nations will also bear in mind the fact that the American people are certain to be swayed by the use which debtor countries make of their available resources—whether such resources would be applied for the purposes of recovery as well as for reasonable payment on the debt owed to the citizens of the United States, or for purposes of unproductive nationalistic expenditure or like purposes.

In presenting this report to you, I suggest that, in view of all existing circumstances, no legislation at this session of the Congress is either necessary or advisable.

I can only repeat that I have made it clear to the debtor nations again and again that "the indebtedness to our Government has no relation whatsoever to reparations payments made or owed to them," and that each individual nation has full and free opportunity individually to discuss its problem with the United States.

We are using every means to persuade each debtor nation as to the sacredness of the obligation and also to assure them of our willingness, if they should so request, to discuss frankly and fully the special circumstances relating to means and method of payment.

Recognizing that the final power lies with the Congress, I shall keep the Congress informed from time to time and make such new recommendations as may later seem advisable.

Trade-Agreements Act of June 12, 1934

AN ACT to amend the Tariff Act of 1930

U.S. Statutes at Large, 73rd Congress, 2nd Session, Vol. 48, Part I, p. 943.

BE IT ENACTED *by the Senate and House of Representatives of the United States of America in Congress assembled,* That the Tariff Act of 1930 is amended by adding at the end of title III the following:

"PART III, PROMOTION OF FOREIGN TRADE, SEC. 350. (a) For the purpose of expanding foreign markets for the products of the United States (as a means of assisting in the present emergency in restoring the American standard of living, in overcoming domestic unemployment and the present economic depression, in increasing the purchasing power of the American public, and in establishing and maintaining a better relationship among various branches of American agriculture, industry, mining, and commerce) by regulating the admission of foreign goods into the United States in accordance with the characteristics and needs of various branches of American production so that foreign markets will be made available to those branches of American production which require and are capable of developing such outlets by affording corresponding market opportunities for foreign products in the United States, the President, whenever he finds as a fact that any existing duties or other import restrictions of the United States or any foreign country are unduly burdening and restricting the foreign trade of the United States and that the purpose above declared will be promoted by the means hereinafter specified, is authorized from time to time—

"(1) To enter into foreign trade agreements with foreign governments or instrumentalities thereof; and

"(2) To proclaim such modifications of existing duties and other import restrictions, or such additional import restrictions, or such continuance, and for such minimum periods, of existing customs or excise treatment of any article covered by foreign trade agreements, as are required or appropriate to carry out any foreign trade agreement that the President has entered into hereunder. No proclamation shall be made increasing or decreasing by more than 50 per centum any existing rate of duty or transferring any article between the dutiable and free lists. The proclaimed duties and other import restriction shall apply to articles the growth, produce, or manufacture of all foreign countries, whether imported directly, or indirectly: *Provided,* That the President may suspend the application to articles the growth, produce or manufacture of any country because of its discriminatory treatment of American commerce or because of other acts or policies which in his opinion tend to defeat the purposes set forth in this section; and the proclaimed duties and other import restrictions shall be in effect from and after such time as is specified in the proclamation. The President may at any time terminate any such proclamation in whole or in part.

"(b) Nothing in this section shall be construed to prevent the application, with respect to rates of duty established under this section pursuant to agreements with countries other than Cuba, of the provisions of the treaty of commercial reciprocity concluded between the United States and the Republic of Cuba on December 11, 1902, or to preclude giving effect to an exclusive agreement with Cuba concluded under this section, modifying the existing preferential customs treatment of any article the growth, produce, or manufacture of Cuba: *Provided,* That the duties payable on such an article shall in no case be increased or decreased by more than 50 per centum of the duties now payable thereon.

"(c) As used in this section, the term 'duties and other import restrictions' includes (1) rate and form of import duties and classification of articles, and (2) limitations, prohibitions, charges, and exactions other than duties, imposed on importation or imposed for the regulation of imports."

SEC. 2. (a) Subparagraph (d) of paragraph 369, the last sentence of paragraph 1402, and the provisos to paragraphs 371, 401, 1650, 1687, and 1803 (1) of the Tariff Act of 1930 are repealed. The provisions of sections 336 and 516 (b) of the Tariff Act of 1930 shall not apply to any article with respect to the importation of which into the United States a foreign trade agreement has been concluded pursuant to this Act, or to any provision of any such agreement. The third paragraph of section 311 of the Tariff Act of 1930 shall apply to any agreement concluded pursuant to this Act to the extent only that such agreement assures to the United States a rate of duty on wheat flour produced in the United States which is preferential in respect to the lowest rate of duty imposed by the country with which such agreement has been concluded on like flour produced in any other country; and upon the withdrawal of wheat flour from bonded manufacturing warehouses for exportation to the country with which such agreement has been concluded, there shall be levied, collected, and paid on the imported wheat used, a duty equal to the amount of such assured preference.

(b) Every foreign trade agreement concluded pursuant to this Act shall be subject to termination, upon due notice to the foreign government concerned, at the end of not more than three years from the date on which the agreement comes into force, and, if not then terminated, shall be subject to termination thereafter upon not more than six months' notice.

(c) The authority of the President to enter into foreign trade agreements under section 1 of this Act shall terminate on the expiration of three years from the date of the enactment of this Act.

SEC. 3. Nothing in this Act shall be construed to give any authority to cancel or reduce, in any manner, any of the indebtedness of any foreign country to the United States.

SEC. 4. Before any foreign trade agreement is concluded with any foreign government or instrumentality thereof under the provisions of this Act, reasonable public notice of the intention to negotiate an agreement with such government or instrumentality shall be given in order that any interested person may have an opportunity to present his views to the President, or to such agency as the President may designate, under such rules and regulations as the President may prescribe; and before concluding such agreement the President shall seek information and advice with respect thereto from the United States Tariff Commission, the Departments of State, Agriculture, and Commerce and from such other sources as he may deem appropriate.

Approved, June 12, 1934, 9.15 p.m.

ADDRESS by Cordell Hull, Secretary of State, "The Foreign Policy of the United States," at Washington, D.C., May 2, 1935

Delivered before the general session of the annual meeting of the Chamber of Commerce of the United States. Published separately by the Department of State as Commercial Policy Series No. 9, Publication No. 733; excerpts

IN THE NINETEENTH century, a closely coordinated world economy was developed based upon the very sound principle that man could conduct his affairs most profitably under conditions of reasonable freedom. It is indeed significant that this period, in which the great advantages of international commerce were generally recognized, witnessed the most rapid growth of population, the most amazing rise in the standard of living, and the broadest increase in the utilization of the earth's natural riches for mankind's benefit and happiness that has ever been experienced.

The industrial technique, together with its handmaidens, commerce and finance, was brought to a high degree of development first in England, from where it spread during the course of the nineteenth century to many other countries, including the United States. In this era we made immense gains in the production of both agricultural and industrial goods, thereby providing employment and a constantly rising standard of living for our rapidly increasing population. No small part of this advance was made possible by the steady expansion of world trade and the increasing demand of other countries for the goods we had to export. Being at that time a debtor and undeveloped country, a policy at times highly protective led to no serious consequences; but shortly after the World War, ignoring the economic transformation which had taken place, we began to erect barriers to our foreign trade not consistent with our newly achieved creditor position nor our efficiency in production. Within the short space of a decade we had raised our tariff rates on three successive occasions, thereby preparing the destruction of our vast foreign trade, upon which a large share of our prosperity rested. This interference, opportunist in spirit, uncoordinated with our other policies, and contrary to our long-term interests, represented a definite break with the ideal of economic liberalism which had made possible this great commercial expansion.

The events of the World War enormously increased the importance of the United States, commercially and financially, in world affairs. Just at the time when the disturbed international relations of the post-war period called for the broadest possible development of world trade as a means of minimizing shocks and creating a new international balance, we adopted an unduly high protectionist policy which played its part in the subsequent world-wide collapse and contributed in so important a measure to the present break-down in international commercial and financial relations. . . .

Extreme high-tariff barriers have been supplemented in many foreign countries by quantitative restrictions, tantamount frequently to embargoes, and by the control of foreign exchange, which is often allotted on a most arbitrary basis. To these a number of other less important but scarcely less burdensome and irritating restrictions have been added, all designed to exclude imports and all having the effect of choking and throttling world trade. As a result, on the one hand surpluses of many kinds of both agricultural and industrial goods have accumulated in the countries which formerly supplied these products to the world, while on the other hand these very goods are being produced uneconomically and consequently at exorbitant prices in the former consumer countries behind their unscalable barriers. Sorry substitutes, absurd synthetic production, and inferior-quality production, virtually worthless, are being attempted.

The international price structure for some time has been dislocated. For many commodities there is no longer any such thing as a world price. In many instances prices are two, three, or four times higher in one country than in the surplus-producing countries. This is true of wheat, lard, and other commodities highly important for our domestic producers and for consuming masses of foreign populations.

The resources of the world needed for modern ways of living and for the development of a higher future civilization are not evenly distributed throughout the globe. Basic raw materials of modern industrialism are highly concentrated in certain countries, notably the United States and western Europe. Even our own great country, with its natural resources of iron ore, coal, petroleum, lead, zinc, copper, and other mineral resources, is deficient in many basic materials which are drawn from all parts of the world, including wood pulp, tin, nickel, manganese ore, rubber, raw silk, jute, hemp, flax and other fibers, hides and skins, and in foods such as sugar, coffee, tea, spices, and certain fruits not obtainable at home. The modern industrial structure depends upon the interchange of products localized in certain areas and which the various countries of the world can enjoy only on the basis of international trade.

One has only to look at the figures of the proportion of domestic production exported by the countries of Central and South America and the Orient to see how highly dependent these areas are upon world trade. No one who has not particularly concerned himself with these problems can realize the degree to which various countries have developed specialties of their own. We in this country have developed such specialties, notably in cotton, lard, tobacco, automobiles, machinery, copper, and petroleum products, fruits, electrical and office appliances, as well as a host of products of smaller value, and these specialties bulk large in our trade with almost every country. Similarly, every other country has specialties with which it reaches out in its contacts with the four corners of the globe.

Whenever this interchange of products, to the extent mutually profitable, is obstructed, the prices of the products that are destined for the world market are seriously depressed. The ensuing economic distress leads to political unrest and sometimes to revolution. The disturbed conditions of the last 6 years incident to the disruption of the world economic system have been chiefly responsible for the political upheavals and the downfall of government after government in almost all parts of the world. Internal distress opens the way for the demagogue and the agitator, stirs up internal class strife, and especially develops international friction, fear, and resentment of foreign peoples and governments, and shatters the very foundations of world peace. The dangerous political situations that exist throughout the world today, the international tension, the recrudescence of the military spirit, the expansion of standing armies, the enormously increased military budgets, the feverish efforts made to invent new instruments of warfare, new weapons for offense and defense—all these have emerged and developed in a world in which the international economic structure has been shattered, in which normal peaceful commercial intercourse has been broken and vast unemployment and human distress has resulted. It is the collapse of the world structure, the development of isolated economies, that has let loose the fear which now grips every nation and which threatens the peace of the world. We cannot have a peaceful world, we cannot have a prosperous world, until we rebuild the international economic structure.

Economic questions and conditions form the basis of international relations now more than at any other time in history. If nations are engaged in discrimination or retaliation or in the practice of irritating trade methods toward one another, the preservation of friendly relations and of that understanding necessary for peace and mutual prosperity is rendered difficult and precarious. Without friendly relations and understanding, nations are little prone to settle questions or controversies by arbitration or other orderly and peaceful means. On the contrary, they are hasty to arm and to institute force for justice in international affairs. We behold that tendency progressed to an alarming extent today.

The desire of the Government to combat this trend, which it is convinced can lead only to the serious deterioration of our civilization, is the controlling reason for the efforts which it is now making to restore international trade on a basis of equality and friendship. This must continue to be the basis for world commercial relations.

The numerous discriminations now practiced by nations in their manipulation of tariff rates, quotas, exchange controls, and other devices designed to exclude foreign products, and in their exclusive bilateral arrangements, have undoubtedly been one of the chief causes which have led to the serious economic and political conditions now prevailing. Not only are nations rapidly impoverishing themselves by these practices, but they are thereby also inviting the enmity and provoking the resentment of other peoples. The irony of bilateral arrangements to the exclusion of triangular and multilateral trade lies in the fact that, while their advantages are soon overcome by the counteractive measures adopted by the states against which they discriminate, the feelings of dislike and distrust which they engender live on. . . .

The tendency to seek special preferences abroad is coupled with the stubborn and frequently unscrupulous resistance encountered by the Government when even the most moderate reduction in a tariff rate is proposed, regardless of how clearly this may be to the advantage of the country as a whole. The pressure which is being currently brought upon both legislators and officials in Washington by those who fear that they are to be deprived of even a small part of the artificial advantage given them by an over-indulgent Government, too often at the expense of efficient producers and consumers in general, would incline one to believe that much of the sturdy self-reliance, hardihood, and vigor of this country are definitely on the decline. Every post which comes to the Department of State brings letters requesting, and frequently demanding, that the Government obtain for their writers some personal or local advantage, often in clear defiance of the general interest. As I suppose is only to be expected, these demands are frequently absurdly conflicting. The Government is asked, on the one hand, to reduce or more often to prevent entirely the importation of this or that article or class of goods, and, on the other, to secure preferences in foreign markets for this or that American product. I have had presented to me time and again schemes for expanding our exports of our agricultural products by means of preferential arrangements, dumping devices, and other measures which involve serious complications of our general trade relations. These same people insist on complete embargoes against industrial and agricultural imports. These people have not yet learned the lesson, which now ought to be evident to everyone, that foreign countries cannot continue to buy our cotton, lard, tobacco, and other surplus commodities unless the exchange with which to pay for these products is made available through imports into the United States. We cannot continue to sell even our most important products abroad unless we are disposed to buy to the extent mutually profitable. I wish to call your attention particularly to the decline in this current year of our exports to many of our best consuming markets in Europe. Thus, our exports to Europe in January and February of this year declined 16 percent in relation to that of January and February of a year ago. If we place embargoes upon our imports, we shall, in the last analysis, witness inevitably the destruction of our export trade. Seized with an unreasoning fear whenever a small driblet of imports of a competitive nature comes over our tariff wall, even when under purely temporary or accidental conditions such as, for example, the drought, action is urged which, if followed too frequently, may lead to retaliation by other countries, so that step by step such actions lead straight toward a complete embargo of imports all around, and, since one country's imports are another country's exports, a like embargo of exports all around.

We oppose exclusive or preferential arrangements the effect of which would be to impose discriminatory tariff rates against other countries. On the other side, this country does not intend to accept discrimination against American commerce in foreign countries. It desires to extend equality of treatment to all nations, and it seeks to obtain fair and equitable treatment from all nations. The unconditional most-favored-nation policy, as already indicated, is the one which almost universal experience since the middle of the last century has demonstrated to be the best suited for the attainment of these purposes. This Government is convinced that only if it makes the most determined attempt to stem the degeneration of international commercial intercourse into a network of bilateral arrangements of an exclusive and restrictive type, with their accompanying discriminations and retaliations, can international trade be restored.

It is my belief that most nations drifted into the condition in which they now find themselves, due primarily to the pressure of the peculiar maladjustments of the post-war period and the wave of extreme economic nationalism incident thereto; that, with possibly a few exceptions, they have not deliberately elected to follow the course to which circumstances have forced them. It is incumbent upon some great nation, certainly the United States as much as any other, to come forward with a broad, constructive program calculated to displace gradually the policies which have proven so futile and so destructive during these past several years. With the sources of information that the organization of the Government places at my disposal, I see not a few evidences of the state of mind of other peoples which give me reason to believe that the program which this administration is following is beginning to supply the inspiration necessary to induce them to alter their course and to hope that the world can shortly expect a general movement in the direction of international economic sanity. . . .

The trade-agreements program, first promulgated and unanimously adopted by the 21 American nations at Montevideo and now actively being carried forward by this Government, is based upon the view that international trade among other things is a material factor in the full and stable business recovery of individual nations; that unreasonable trade barriers can only be effectively reduced by a constructive program carried out over a period of years concurrently by the leading nations of the world; that such liberalized commercial policy will be a vital factor in the reduction of unemployment, the increase in domestic prices, and the improvement of business conditions throughout the world. What we propose in a fair and friendly way, as stated, affords the best possible foundation on which to rebuild sound and worth-while international relations. This program contemplates a simultaneous and continuous attack by all wide-awake nations upon the several well-recognized obstructions to the restoration of international trade and finance.

The opponents of a liberal commercial policy would have every nation, by means of a purely nationalistic program alone, attempt to restore domestic prosperity, while at the same time intensifying the existing network of trade-destroying restrictions and practices. The proponents of a liberal commercial policy, on the other hand, would utilize the most comprehensive domestic and international programs combined, and would cut through these trade restrictions and open the way toward an expansion of world trade as an aid to domestic recovery, thereby combining domestic measures with international measures designed to rehabilitate a full measure of domestic and world prosperity.

This country can and must furnish its fair share of leadership in this great movement. For this it is peculiarly fitted because of its weight and importance in the world economy, and because it is less tied up in the entanglements and restrictive policies in which other countries, frequently against their will, have become enmeshed. The way lies open for new opportunities in world leadership toward peace and prosperity.

STATEMENT by Henry Morgenthau, Jr., Secretary of the Treasury, September 25, 1936, Issued Simultaneously with Similar Statements by the Governments of Great Britain and France

Annual Report of the Secretary of the Treasury . . . for Fiscal Year Ended June 30, 1937, p. 258

By authority of the President, the Secretary of the Treasury makes the following statement:

The Government of the United States, after consultation with the British Government and the French Government, joins with them in affirming a common desire to foster those conditions which safeguard peace and will best contribute to the restoration of order in international economic relations and to pursue a policy which will tend to promote prosperity in the world and to improve the standard of living of peoples.

The Government of the United States must, of course, in its policy towards international monetary relations take into full account the requirements of internal prosperity, as corresponding considerations will be taken into account by the Governments of France and Great Britain; it welcomes this opportunity to reaffirm its purpose to continue the policy which it has pursued in the course of recent years, one constant object of which is to maintain the greatest possible equilibrium in the system of international exchange and to avoid to the utmost extent the creation of any disturbance of that system by American monetary action. The Government of the United States shares with the Governments of France and Great Britain the conviction that the continuation of this two-fold policy will serve the general purpose which all the governments should pursue.

The French Government informs the United States Government that, judging that the desired stability of the principal currencies cannot be insured on a solid basis except after the re-establishment of a lasting equilibrium between the various economic systems, it has decided with this object to propose to its Parliament the readjustment of its currency. The Government of the United States, as also the British Government, has welcomed this decision in the hope that it will establish more solid foundations for the stability of international economic relations. The United States Government, as also the British and French Governments, declares its intention to continue to use appropriate available resources so as to avoid as far as possible any disturbance of the basis of international exchange resulting from the proposed readjustment. It will arrange for such consultation for this purpose as may prove necessary with the other two Governments and their authorized agencies.

The Government of the United States is moreover convinced, as are also the Governments of France and Great Britain, that the success of the policy set forth above is linked with the development of international trade. In particular it attaches the greatest importance to action being taken without delay to relax progressively the present system of quotas and exchange controls with a view to their abolition.

MEMORANDUM Left by Sumner Welles, Under Secretary of State, with Paul Reynaud, French Minister of Finance, in Paris, March 9, 1940

Department of State, *Bulletin*, May 4, 1940, p. 461

THE BASE OF the economic foreign policy of the United States is as follows:

One. Sound international trade relations are an indispensable foundation of economic wellbeing within nations and of enduring peace among nations. International trade can fulfill this vital role satisfactorily only when it enables each nation to have an adequate access to the resources of the entire world, rather than merely to those confined within its frontiers, and to find outlets for its surplus production, on terms of mutual benefit and on the basis of nondiscriminatory treatment.

Two. International trade cannot prosper when its flow is diverted and distorted by attempts at exclusive bilateralism or discriminatory arrangements.

It cannot prosper when its flow is obstructed by the barriers of excessive tariffs, of quantitive regulation, and of controls of foreign exchange transactions. All these are instruments of economic warfare. The world's recent experience has clearly demonstrated their destructive effects on peacetime international commerce—and hence, their depressive influence on standards of living and general economic well-being within nations, as well as their significance as breeders of international ill-will, animosity and conflict.

Three. If, after the termination of present hostilities, the world is to build the foundation of stability and peace, which would eliminate resentments and fears and open the way to economic progress, the process of international trade must be restored to a sound basis.

This will require a gradual elimination of excessive and unreasonable barriers to the flow of goods across national frontiers; the acceptance of the rule of nondiscrimination in commercial treatment through the implementation of the most-favored-nation principle; and the creation of conditions in the fields of foreign exchanges and of credit necessary to a multilateral functioning of the trade process.

PART TWO

GREAT BRITAIN

GENERAL STATEMENTS OF POLICY

ADDRESS by Viscount Cecil, Chief of the British Delegation to the Assembly of the League of Nations, before the Assembly, September 10, 1931

League of Nations, *Official Journal*, Special Supplement No. 93, p. 57; excerpts

THE PERIOD in which this Assembly meets is one in which the purposes for which the League was founded are obviously of a special importance, a special gravity and urgency. Never was it more necessary that the world, and that most cautious and apprehensive section of it, the investing public, should be assured of the continuance of peaceful international relations. Never was the international cooperation which is the second main purpose of the League more needed for the world's current problems. It would be a real tragedy if this Assembly, representing as it does some three-quarters of the world, were to come to an end without contributing anything to the cure of the grave maladies from which the world is now suffering.

The anxiety which is now in all our minds results from the world economic depression which began two years ago, and also from the financial crisis which followed three months ago. Grave as is the economic depression, it is the financial crisis which threatens the more immediate disaster unless urgent action can be taken. . . .

In a sense, the political position is not altogether unfavourable. I do not think that there is the slightest prospect of any war. I know—and history tells us—how rash it is to prophesy as to the future of international affairs; but, nevertheless, I do not believe that there is anyone in this room who will contradict me when I say that there has scarcely ever been a period in the world's history when war seemed less likely than it does at present.

But, nevertheless, there are evils. In the first place, there is prevalent throughout many countries in the world—I was almost going to say every country, but certainly in many countries—a certain atmosphere of internal unrest. That does not only concern those countries; it has its repercussion all over the world. We hear constantly of violent speeches or aggressive demonstrations being made in this country or in that; and I quite realise—for I have been in public affairs all my life—the immense temptation that orators feel in that direction. You see a great multitude before you. That multitude expects to be excited and enthused, and you are led on to make striking and vehement phrases which call forth loud cheers from your audience and cause people to congratulate you on a successful speech. Yet it may well be that such a speech will not only do infinite harm to the foreign relations of your country but will sentence some miserable women and children in far-distant countries to misery and starvation.

If only orators could have before them a picture of people struggling for existence, to whom the economic prosperity of the world means all the difference between life and death, I think they would put a good deal of water in their wine and forego a few of the enthusiastic cheers of their audience. Let us always remember that in this, as in so many other matters, one inflammatory speech cannot be killed even by ten moderate speeches from the same quarter. Unfortunately, moderation is not particularly readable; it does not receive the same publicity as extreme utterances, and for that and other reasons it is very difficult by mere speech to counteract the harm that is done by violent utterances. It is partly due to this, but partly also to many other causes, that there is in the world an atmosphere of international suspicion certainly as great as it has been, perhaps greater than it has been, in recent years, and it is that international suspicion flowing in part from these disturbances and unrest in the countries of the world, and also from other quarters, which it ought to be the special function of the League of Nations to allay.

As I have just said, mere speeches are not enough—not even resolutions or *communiqués*. As you, Sir, so well said in your opening observations, something of the nature of positive action is necessary. I am not suggesting, far from it, that this is a time for a general revision or reconsideration of the treaty position in Europe. That would not promote peace or quietness or tranquility, but I do think we ought to do something; and the obvious thing—as almost every speaker from this tribune has already said—is the promotion of international disarmament. By that means a lot of money could be saved. International disarmament would do more, perhaps, than any other single thing to increase international confidence, and by this great and unmistakable act it would be announced to the world that the nations were turning away from violence and looking to reason for the justification of their aspirations, and were prepared really and genuinely to enthrone justice as the arbiter of international disputes.

Do not let us think that this, which is a very urgent matter, is one that can be left to settle itself. I am not going to attempt to make a disarmament speech, but I do just want to draw your attention to one series of incidents as an illustration of the urgency of this matter. It so happens that quite recently, in the last few months, there have been held what are called "air manœuvres" in a number of countries—in my own country, in France, in Italy and in America, and I dare say in many others. Observe what that means. I am not criticising, I need not say, any of the Governments concerned. These are manœuvres to exercise and perfect an arm which is, perhaps, more essentially than any other an aggressive arm. No doubt if one country has aircraft, another country will say that it is necessary—and perhaps it is—for it also to have aircraft. But these manœuvres show once again that the possession of aircraft by one country is no defence against attack by the aircraft of another. It is not a means of defence; at the most it gives to the country attacked the power of reprisal, but nothing else. That is, I venture to think, the lesson of the manœuvres which have taken place. . . .

I feel that, both for economic reasons and for reasons of world peace and progress and to safeguard everything that is really worth having in the civilisation of the world, this Disarmament Conference must succeed. We cannot afford to let it fail. It must result in a substantial reduction of the armaments of the world, and I am quite sure that that result can be achieved if the spirit in which we come to that Conference is only the right spirit. If each country merely seeks to get off with doing as little as possible, we shall produce no good results; but if we all come here, as I hope and believe we shall, with a desire not to see how little but how much we can do, how large a step we can take towards the ultimate ideal of complete international disarmament—if we come here in that spirit I am satisfied that the Disarmament Conference will be a triumphant success. After all, the Conference meets next year, and, if what I have tried to show you earlier in my observations is right, the crisis is very urgent. What are we doing in the meanwhile? What step can we take to improve the international atmosphere? I believe we can do a good deal.

There are present at this Assembly the representatives of two great and highly respected nations, each in its way a leader of civilisation. If there could be a real *rapprochement* between France and Germany, not only in word but in action, seventy-five per cent of the political unrest of the world would, I believe, thereby be removed.

I have seen it said in the papers and elsewhere that my country is opposed to a *rapprochement;* that for purely selfish reasons we are anxious to see these two great countries in hostility because we thereby have a greater position in the counsels of Europe. That is a gross and scandalous libel on my country; I have never heard Englishmen give vent to any such proposition. I am satisfied that, whether it is the present Government or any future Government of England, it will always be anxious to do its utmost to promote good understanding between its two great neighbours, and nothing would give it greater pleasure or satisfaction than to see a real friendship—I hope there is a real friendship—and a visible friendship, between these two countries. We endeavoured at Locarno to give practical effect to our desire in that direction, and I can only say that, so far as the spirit of Locarno is concerned, it still persists in my country, and we shall always be ready to do anything that we can—I do not know that there is anything we can do—to promote this splendid spirit.

My reason for referring to these two countries is not only because they are in our minds continually; we know how much depends on the policy of each of them. They, however, are not the only countries concerned; my country may very likely itself be doing something which, in the opinion of others, does not help the pacification of the world. If that is so, I only hope it will be pointed out to us, because, as far as I am concerned, I would say that it is the duty of every Government to search its mind at the present crisis in order to see what contribution its country can make towards putting an end to what is, after all, not a normal condition of international life, but an unnatural and diseased condition of the public mind. That seems to me to be the great task to which we should set ourselves in the coming months, and, I may say with absolute confidence, not only on behalf of my Government, but also on behalf of the people on whom that Government depends, that the only real plank in their foreign policy is to contribute to the utmost of their power to the pacification of the world.

ADDRESS by J. Ramsay MacDonald, Prime Minister, Delivered at the Guildhall Banquet, London, November 9, 1934

Royal Institute of International Affairs, *Documents on International Affairs, 1934*, p. 359, citing *The Times* (London), November 10, 1934; excerpts

Peace is the supreme need of the time. If the fears, irritations, provocations, and unsettlement today cannot be controlled by the nations small and great devoted to peace, we may build our houses and our barns on our own soil, but destruction will overwhelm them. No nation in the world challenges our position as the most consistent and dependable of the peacemakers. This Government values and guards that reputation and will cherish it.

In conjunction, I am happy to say, with both France and Italy, every threatening outburst of angry emotion—and there have been not a few—has found us counselling self-control and putting forth every influence we possess for peaceful conditions. We have not changed a shadow in our support for the League of Nations. Buffeted and weakened as it may sometimes be, it nevertheless stands as a check against judgment being sought at the point of the sword. The entrance of the Soviet Republic into the League is an event which we heartily welcomed. Germany's absence from its council chamber we shall continue to deplore. Our Government will never cease to impress upon the German people that by remaining isolated they do not do themselves justice, and that other peoples will continue to apply as an acid test to their declarations of peace the question whether or not they are willing to join us at League deliberations to study the dangers still ahead and devise specific means for meeting them. Alone in one's own citadels fears and grievances become magnified, minds become distorted; the acts of others lose proportion and reality, good judgment becomes warped by vain and unhappy complexes.

. . . If it be said that the international situation is deteriorating, I should not be concerned to dispute the statement; but let us examine it with a sense of proportion. War and peace left many dragon's teeth in European soil. We have reached that point when aggrieved nations ask for more consideration, when other nations in response begin to feel a lack of security, and when statesmen are faced with natural growths in unsettlement which must give anxiety before the final settling down can come. All this belongs to the interplay and sway of cause and effect in history. We must take neither gloomy views nor fussy ones.

. . . What we can foresee in human action we can, as a rule, lead away from its most dire results. In that belief the Government's foreign policy continues to be inspired by a belief in the practicability of a peace policy steadily and wisely pursued on the lines of common sense—a very valuable word.

We are disappointed with the Disarmament Conference thus far. Prolonged and laborious preparations were made for it, and, if some of its most intricate problems were left unsolved by the Preparatory Committee within a month or two of the opening of the Conference, encouraging steps had been taken towards agreement on some key points. That passed. Again and again the British Government came in to try to save the situation. The last attempt which we made, when we boldly produced, for the first time at the Conference, figures for armament strengths, showed that we have pulled our full weight all the time. Our plan, then proposed, was accepted by every nation represented as the basis for a convention. Later we sent Mr. Anthony Eden on special mission to explain our proposals, to find out where they ought to be amended, to enlist support for them. But trouble blew up and darkened the sky. Confidence, on which alone a Disarmament Convention can be based, was damaged, and today the outlook is not so good as many of us hoped and prayed for. But the British Government will continue not only to try to preserve some very useful gains, but to secure agreements in ways that will still be open to it, even if there is no formal Conference sitting.

There is still the League of Nations; there is still the Council of the League of Nations; there will still be opportunities for peaceful countries to bring their influence to bear on the mind of the world. The Government will take every one of these opportunities that present themselves to them. The existence of the League of Nations imposes certain responsibilities upon us. None of these are up our sleeves; all have been disclosed, and every one has been undertaken to safeguard peace. These obligations will be fulfilled. Were they not, the risk of war would be greatly increased, not diminished. But I ask you to believe that the Government is determined not to increase these obligations in a wanton or quixotic way, and certainly not without the knowledge and sanction of Parliament. It has no such added burdens in mind.

... In the meantime we have to take steps to secure that, if we were met by aggression, we should at least be in a position to defend ourselves while we were engaged in attempts to get international agreements on reduced standards of armament. We purposely took the risk of showing an example of disarmament to the rest of the world. We were determined to do nothing which would hamper our work at Geneva, although the equipment of other Powers, both declared and undeclared, would have justified us in expanding our own. We have never overlooked what this example meant for us in diminishing power of protection, and recently we have finished an investigation of our resources for home and imperial defence.

Our experience has proved that, in the present state of mind of the world, disarmament by example is not an effective way to reduce the arms of the world or to increase international confidence and so strengthen peace; under some circumstances it might even tempt an aggressor to attack. I believe with all my heart that the best and the last word on security is an international agreement on scales of national armaments, and, the lower the scales agreed upon, the greater the security of the nations will be. But if these agreements are refused, defence requirements must be met in a way that will put the non-aggressive purpose of that nation beyond question. I believe that the country will trust us to do what we think to be necessary without embarking on an armaments race, on the one hand, or, on the other, forgetting, in providing for our own security, the overriding and far more permanent duty to make war a thing impossible in the future.

STATEMENT by J. Ramsay MacDonald, Prime Minister, March 1, 1935

Issued in connection with a debate regarding national defense in the House of Commons on March 11, 1935. British White Paper, Cmd. 4827; excerpts

I

2. THE ESTABLISHMENT of peace on a permanent footing is the principal aim of British foreign policy. The first and strongest defence of the peoples, territories, cities, overseas trade and communications of the British Empire is provided by the maintenance of peace. If war can be banished from the world, these vast and world-wide interests will remain free from the dangers of attack, and the great work of civilisation and trade will proceed unhampered by the fears that have hindered their progress from the earliest recorded times until to-day. That is why every British Government is bound to use its utmost endeavours to maintain peace.

3. In recent years the chief methods by which His Majesty's Government in the United Kingdom have pursued the establishment of peace on a permanent footing have been as follows:—

(1) By unswerving support of the League of Nations, which His Majesty's Government in the United Kingdom regard as essential machinery for promoting the preservation of peace by facilitating and regularising the means of international co-operation.

(2) By the promotion, in co-operation with other nations, of international instruments designed to produce collective security and a sense of security among the nations. Among the more important may be mentioned:—

(a) The Briand-Kellogg Pact of 1928 for the renunciation by every signatory of war as an instrument of policy.

(b) The Quadruple Pacific Treaty and the Nine-Power Treaty regarding the Far East, both designed to promote peace in that area and in the Pacific.

(c) The Locarno Treaties, designed, by a system of mutual guarantee, to maintain the peace in those countries of Western Europe, to the situation of which this country has never been and can never be indifferent.

The latest development in this direction is the Anglo-French proposal of the 3rd February for regional and mutual arrangements to deter aerial aggression and thereby provide additional security from sudden attacks from the air.

(d) Various proposals for increasing security in Eastern Europe and the Danube Basin, with special reference to the maintenance of the independence and integrity of Austria. These involve no military commitments, direct or indirect, by this country.

(3) By efforts to promote international understanding in general, and in particular to bring back into the comity of nations all the countries which have been enemies in the late war. Successive Governments in the United Kingdom have taken a leading part in such measures as the suspension of the Penalties provisions of the Treaty of Versailles; the election of late enemies to membership of the League of Nations, including, in the case of Germany, permanent membership of the Council; the evacuation of the Rhineland five years in advance of the date fixed by the Treaties; the gradual rationalisation and virtual settlement of reparations at the Lausanne Conference of 1932; the Saar plebiscite; the action in connection with the Disarmament Conference referred to below in (4).

(4) The reduction and limitation of international armaments in order to promote the work of pacification and steadily to reduce the means of making war. The best known instances of disarmament are the Washington Treaty of 1922 and the London Naval Treaty of 1930, both of which, in accordance with their provisions are to form the subject of an International Conference during the present year. After six years of preparation the Disarmament Conference, promoted by the League of Nations, opened at Geneva on the 2nd February, 1932, and ever since the present Government have sought unremittingly to obtain a successful result. In pursuit of this object they have been foremost among the nations in taking the initiative as, for example, to mention only a few instances, their declaration in connection with Germany's claim to equality of rights, of the 17th November, 1932 (Cmd. 4189); the British draft Convention of the 16th March, 1933 (Cmd. 4279), and their proposals of January 1934 (Cmd. 4498).

4. Hitherto, in spite of many setbacks, public opinion in this country has tended to assume that nothing is required for the maintenance of peace except the existing international political machinery, and that the older methods of defence—navies, armies and air forces—on which we have hitherto depended for our security in the last resort

are no longer required. The force of world events, however, has shown that this assumption is premature, and that we have far to go before we can find complete security without having in the background the means of defending ourselves against attack. Nations differ in their temperaments, needs and state of civilisation. Discontent may arise out of various causes, from the recollection of past misfortunes, from a desire to recover past losses or from pressure occasioned by the increase of population. All these are fruitful sources of friction or dispute, and events in various parts of the world have shown that nations are still prepared to use or threaten force under the impulse of what they conceive to be a national necessity; and it has been found that once action has been taken the existing international machinery for the maintenance of peace cannot be relied upon as a protection against an aggressor.

5. The National Government intends to pursue without intermission the national policy of peace by every practicable means and to take advantage of every opportunity, and to make opportunities to make peace more secure. But it can no longer close its eyes to the fact that adequate defences are still required for security and to enable the British Empire to play its full part in maintaining the peace of the world.

II

6. During the years that all parties in this country have been seeking to carry out the policy outlined above, there has been a steady decline in the effective strength of our armaments by sea and land. In the air we virtually disarmed ourselves in 1919, and, subsequently, from time to time postponed attainment of the minimum air strength regarded as necessary to our security in the face of air developments on the Continent. It is not that British Governments have neglected to keep themselves informed of the position. Every year the state of our armaments has been anxiously considered, and if risks have been run they have been accepted deliberately in pursuit of the aim of permanent peace. Again and again, rather than run any risk of jeopardising some promising movement in this direction by increasing expenditure on armaments, Governments have postponed the adoption of measures that were required when considered from the point of view of national defence alone. In this way we have taken risks for peace, but, as intimated by the Secretary of State for Foreign Affairs in the debate on the Address on the 28th November, 1934, "disarming ourselves in advance, by ourselves, by way of an example—has not increased our negotiating power in the Disarmament discussions at Geneva."

7. Parliament and people, however, have been warned again and again that serious deficiencies were accumulating in all the Defence Services, and that our desire to lead the world towards disarmament by our example of unilateral disarmament has not succeeded. We have not contributed thereby to general disarmament, and are approaching a point when we are not possessed of the necessary means of defending ourselves against an aggressor.

III

8. Last midsummer the position was as follows:—

(1) The Disarmament Conference had virtually come to a standstill. Further negotiations, it was clear, would be hampered by the fact that Germany was not only re-arming openly on a large scale, despite the provisions of Part V of the Treaty of Versailles, but had also given notice of withdrawal from the League of Nations and the Disarmament Conference. Japan also had given notice of withdrawal from the League. All the larger Powers except the United Kingdom were adding to their armed forces.

(2) Detailed and prolonged examination had been made into the serious deficiencies that had accumulated in our defence forces and defences. It had been established that, unless a programme was put in hand to re-condition them and to bring them up to date, the country and the Empire would no longer possess an adequate standard of defence. If, therefore, in spite of all our efforts to keep the peace, an aggression should take place directed against ourselves, we should be unable to secure our sea communications, the food of our people or the defence of our principal cities and their population against air attack. Moreover, the great value of the Locarno Treaties to this country is their deterrent effect on would-be aggressors. This is being seriously weakened by the knowledge, shared by all the signatories, that our contribution, in case our obligation is clear to us, could have little decisive effect. The same consideration would, of course, apply to any other method of collective security to which we might be parties.

9. In the above circumstances, His Majesty's Government felt that they would be failing in their responsibilities if, while continuing to the full, efforts for peace by limitation of armaments, they delayed the initiation of steps to put our own armaments on a footing to safeguard us against potential dangers. A co-ordinated programme was drawn up for re-conditioning our defence forces and defences. In the case of the Navy (whose strength is limited by Treaty) and Army, these programmes involve for the most part a process of supplying technical deficiencies, providing up-to-date equipment and adequate

personnel and reserves of war material, without which our forces could not defend our vital interests against an aggressor nor co-operate in any system of collective security.

10. In the case of the Royal Air Force alone was an appreciable increase of units deemed immediately necessary, and for this reason it was announced in Parliament on the 19th July, 1934, and debated by the House of Commons on the 30th July, and by the House of Lords on the 14th November. Increases will also be necessary in the anti-aircraft defences provided by the Army.

11. On the 28th November, 1934, His Majesty's Government drew public attention to the re-armament on which Germany was engaged, and announced a speeding up of the increases in the Air Force already decided upon. The action of His Majesty's Government did not, of course, imply condonation of a breach of the Treaty of Versailles. It merely noted and made public, as a first step, what was known to be proceeding.

12. This re-armament, if continued at its present rate, unabated and uncontrolled, will aggravate the existing anxieties of the neighbours of Germany, and may consequently produce a situation where peace will be in peril. His Majesty's Government have noted and welcomed the declarations of the leaders of Germany that they desire peace. They cannot, however, fail to recognise that not only the forces but the spirit in which the population, and especially the youth of the country, are being organised lend colour to, and substantiate, the general feeling of insecurity which has already been incontestably generated. Nor is the increase of armaments confined to Germany. All over the world, in Russia, in Japan, in the United States of America and elsewhere, armaments are being added to. We could not afford to overlook all these increases, and so have had to begin to meet our deficiencies, but have been anxious not to make the provisions for necessary defence merge into a race in armaments strength. . . .

27. The Government desires to emphasise that the measures now proposed are elastic. They will not only be subject to frequent review in the light of prevailing conditions, but may from time to time be adjusted in either direction if circumstances should, in the opinion of His Majesty's Government, warrant any change.

28. To summarise, peace is the principal aim of British foreign policy. The National Government intend to forward this object not only by methods adopted in past years—support to the League of Nations, security agreements, international understanding and international regulation of armaments—but by any other means that may be available. Notwithstanding their confidence in the ultimate

triumph of peaceful methods, in the present troubled state of the world they realise that armaments cannot be dispensed with. They are required to preserve peace, to maintain security and to deter aggression. The deliberate retardation of our armaments as part of our peace policy has brought them below the level required for the fulfilment of these objects, especially in view of the uncertainty of the international situation and the increase of armaments in all parts of the world. An additional expenditure on the armaments of the three Defence Services can, therefore, no longer be safely postponed.

ADDRESS by Anthony Eden, Secretary of State for Foreign Affairs, before the Assembly of the League of Nations, September 20, 1937

League of Nations, *Official Journal,* Special Supplement No. 169 (1937), p. 62; excerpt

I would like now to turn to the consideration of certain important economic questions which have been emphasised in the admirable reports published by the League. It is clear that we have many good reasons to be satisfied with the economic history of the past year. The disastrous fall in commodity prices which marked the onset of the crisis has been definitely reversed. Production has increased rapidly in many countries but international trade has lagged behind the pace of domestic recovery; and trade barriers have not fallen in the way we could have wished. There has been, nevertheless, an increase in trade, both in quantity and in value, during the last year, and certain contributions have been made to the freeing of trade, and thereby, as I firmly believe, to a more wholesome political atmosphere.

My own country has sometimes been adversely criticised because, under the stress of the crisis of 1931, it adopted a policy of protection. I believe that such criticism is unfair, and that, in point of fact, during these difficult years, the United Kingdom has made no small contribution to the maintenance of international trade.

The United Kingdom import market, which is by far the largest import market in the world, has been kept open to an immense range of raw materials, foodstuffs, semi-manufactured and wholly manufactured goods. During the period of closing markets, we have accepted a steadily increasing percentage of the world's imports, rising from about 16% in 1929 to 17% in 1932 and to 18% last year. From 1933 onwards, the value of our imports has steadily increased. In 1933, it had fallen to £675 million; in 1936, it had risen to £849 million.

Those figures are still increasing and, on the assumption that during the second half of the present year imports continue at the same level as during the first half, the United Kingdom's total imports will be valued at about £967 million. Compared with 1933, the year of our lowest import figures, this represents an increase of 43% in our total imports. This, I am sure, the Assembly will agree, can be considered as a real contribution to the prosperity of international trade and as convincing proof that our economic policy is not narrow, nor exclusive, nor self-sufficient.

Throughout this period, we have taken whatever action has been open to us to assist in the removal of barriers to international trade, and in the pursuit of that policy during the last four years we have negotiated a number of bilateral agreements. It is not, I think, presumptuous to claim that these agreements have helped not a little in the general tendency towards the improvement of international trade.

The second great import market in the world is that of the United States of America, and it is a fact of the greatest importance that, under the leadership of President Roosevelt and of Mr. Cordell Hull, the United States Government has, during these recent years, adopted a vigorous and consistent policy for the reduction of trade barriers. The import markets of our own country and of the United States are the greatest import markets of the world. Together, they represent nearly 30% of the world's total import trade. Last year, we took 18% and the United States over 11%. An agreement on a most-favoured-nation basis between these two countries for the reduction of their Customs duties would, we are convinced, be one of the most effective steps we could take, not only in our own interests, but in those of the whole world.

I desire to refer for a moment to another matter which is before the Assembly for its discussion—the final report and recommendations of the Committee for the study of the problem of raw materials. This enquiry has been of particular interest to us, because it was set up on the initiative of the United Kingdom representative at the Assembly two years ago. We regret that certain countries which have regarded themselves as at a disadvantage in respect to the supply of raw materials should have felt unable to take part.

The Committee in question has done admirable service in presenting the facts and figures of the situation in a manner which would remove all misunderstanding of the essential problem from the minds of those who studied it; and the report and recommendations are deserving of the most careful attention. The facts and figures which the Committee adduces show conclusively that the problem of raw materials is not primarily, or even substantially, one of colonial possessions. In fact—and this is the figure I would leave on the minds of the Assembly—all colonial territories taken together produce only about 3% of the world's supply of raw materials. We have always deliberately refrained from pressing the preferential system beyond a certain limited point; and when last year we became free to introduce a preferential system in Nigeria (which is our largest African colonial market), we did not do so.

Acting in the spirit which prompted our policy in this respect, and wishing to give effect to the recommendation of the Committee on Raw Materials, His Majesty's Government is ready, as part of the efforts now being made to effect economic and political appeasement and to increase international trade—but without prejudice to the principle of colonial preference—His Majesty's Government is ready, I repeat, to enter into discussion with any Powers which may approach it for an abatement of particular preferences in non-self-governing colonial territories where these can be shown to place undue restriction on international trade.

This offer must, of course, be made subject to such reservations as may be necessary to secure reciprocal advantages to colonial products and to meet the competition of excessively low-cost producers. Let me add that this offer is merely an extension of the policy which has guided the United Kingdom in our commercial relations with foreign countries. We have always been ready, and still are ready, to discuss with any country any proposals which that country thinks likely to be of mutual benefit. In making this statement, therefore, I refer not only to the British Colonial Empire but to the United Kingdom itself.

I am afraid, however, that no modification of the British or any other preferential system can provide any adequate remedy for the difficulties of those countries which, by maintaining exchange control, find themselves at a disadvantage in obtaining imports of raw materials and other things which they require. For, as the Committee's report so clearly shows, the principal difficulties of these countries arise, not in obtaining raw materials, whether from colonial areas or elsewhere, but in paying for those raw materials. The whole of that section of the report which is devoted to an examination of complaints expressed and difficulties experienced with regard to the acquisition of and payment for raw materials is of the greatest interest and importance in this respect. It is pointed out that the difficulties —and this is the truth and the heart of our economic problem—in regard to the payment for raw materials are in large part bound up with the solution of wider economic problems which require concerted action to restore freer circulation in capital, goods and labour. Here the lines of the report coincide with those of the Economic Committee in its powerful argument for the relaxation of restriction in trade, especially as regards quotas, clearings and exchange control. The two reports are seen to be two aspects of the same international situation. Starting from different premises, they reach the same conclusion: that only by simultaneous progress in three different directions—economic, financial and political—can normal conditions of trade be restored, and therewith normal and unimpeded access to supplies of raw material.

The task that is before us cannot be confined merely to the sphere of economics. As the report of the Economic Committee so clearly explains, the objectives which all Governments should affirm include, on the one hand, the preservation of peace; on the other, the development of prosperity throughout the world and the improvement in the standard of living of the world's population. These aims are in fact interconnected. They are the three aspects of one and the same objective—a world freed from fear, fear of war, fear of impoverishment, fear of social disintegration and decline.

During the past five years, the country that I represent has succeeded in maintaining and developing relatively prosperous conditions for its people; but we recognise that ultimately the well-being of all countries is linked together, and that our own trade revival will be placed on a more solid basis and can be carried further if a similar revival can be brought about in other countries which are not at present in so fortunate a position.

His Majesty's Government is sincerely anxious to co-operate in a real effort to restore international trade, and for this purpose it is prepared to make its contribution; but any such effort can be effective only if other countries, now in difficulties, are ready to modify their policies in such a way as to resume normal international trading relations and to restore confidence. . . .

ADDRESS by Anthony Eden, Secretary of State for Foreign Affairs, in the House of Commons, November 1, 1937

Parliamentary Debates, House of Commons, Vol. 328, No. 5, p. 577; excerpt

LET ME, THEN, in response to the hon. Gentleman's plea, try to sum up the foundations of our foreign policy in the uncertain conditions which exist to-day. While we are determined, should the necessity arise, to defend our own vital interests and fulfil our international obligations, we will embark on no action which would be contrary to the text or the spirit of the Covenant, or contrary to the Pact of Paris which we have signed. We believe in the principle of the settlement of disputes by peaceful means and we will do our utmost to secure a general acceptance and observance of that principle. While we recognise that the League is at present seriously handicapped by incomplete membership, we believe it still provides the best means for obtaining that result. We shall not be deaf to proposals for League reform, provided they are really calculated to strengthen international confidence and to make the League more capable of fulfilling the aims I have outlined. Such being our object it follows—and here I answer the hon. Gentleman—that we will join no anti-Communist and no anti-Fascist *bloc*. It is nations' foreign policies, not their internal policies, with which we are concerned. We will work wholeheartedly with other nations who are like-minded with us, and there are many such. We offer co-operation to all, but we will accept dictation from none.

In my speech I have failed to make, and I appreciate it, any reference to the task to which I go to-night, and perhaps the House will allow me just to say this. The hon. Gentleman defined the other day in a remarkable speech his desire for co-operation with the United States. He used certain words which were to this effect: "Would we in this dangerous and difficult Far Eastern situation go as far as the United States, in full accord with them, not rushing in front but not being left behind." I wholly accept that definition as our guide. We realise, in conditions as they are in the world to-day we must realise, the difficulties of the Far Eastern situation, and I can only assure the House that it is in that spirit that I go to Brussels to-night, anxious to contribute what little lies in my power in a situation in which nobody can envy the Foreign Secretary of the day.

ADDRESS by Viscount Halifax, Secretary of State for Foreign Affairs, at Chatham House, London, June 29, 1939

The British War Blue Book, p. 78

When I look back to the speech which I delivered at the Chatham House Dinner in June a year ago, I am conscious, as we all are, of the great changes that have taken place. A year ago we had undertaken no specific commitments on the Continent of Europe, beyond those which had then existed for some considerable time and are familiar to you all. To-day we are bound by new agreements for mutual defence with Poland and Turkey: we have guaranteed assistance to Greece and Roumania against aggression, and we are now engaged with the Soviet Government in a negotiation, to which I hope there may very shortly be a successful issue, with a view of associating them with us for the defence of States in Europe whose independence and neutrality may be threatened. We have assumed obligations, and are preparing to assume more, with full understanding of their causes and with full understanding of their consequences. We know that, if the security and independence of other countries are to disappear, our own security and our own independence will be gravely threatened. We know that, if international law and order is to be preserved, we must be prepared to fight in its defence.

In the past we have always stood out against the attempt by any single Power to dominate Europe at the expense of the liberties of other nations, and British policy is, therefore, only following the inevitable line of its own history, if such an attempt were to be made again. But it is not enough to state a policy. What matters is, firstly, to convince the nation that the policy is right, and secondly, to take the steps necessary for that policy to succeed. I believe that at no time since the War has there been such national unity on the main essentials of our foreign policy, and that with this spirit of unity goes a deep and widespread determination to make that policy effective. But I believe, too, that among all classes of our people who, in virtue of their common citizenship, are being called upon to defend their country, and the causes for which it stands, there is an increasing desire to look beyond the immediate present, and to see before them some goal for which they would willingly sacrifice their leisure and, if need be, their lives.

We are already asking for great sacrifices from all ages and classes in the call for national service. In one way and another, every man and woman has a part to play, and I know is prepared to do so. The immense effort that the country is making in equipping itself for defence at sea, in the air and on land is without parallel in peace time. We have an unchallengeable Navy. Our Air Force, still undergoing an expansion which has outstripped all expectations of a few months ago, has now nothing to fear from any other. I have little doubt that its personnel, in spirit and in skill, is superior to all others. Our army, once derided, but which survived to prove its worth so that it made a boast of that derision, is, no doubt, small in comparison with that of some other countries. But, as happened once before, we are creating here also a powerful weapon for the defence of our own liberty and that of other peoples. With every week that passes, that effort gains momentum, and on every side of life, political, administrative, industrial, we have abundant evidence of how firmly this national effort is driven and supported by the people's will. Behind all our military effort stand the British people, more united than ever before, and at their service their wealth and industrial resources. These, again, are the object of contemptuous reference, but they have been earned by the labour, skill and courage of our people. None of this formidable array of strength will be called into play except in defence against aggression. No blow will be struck, no shot fired. Of the truth of that, everyone in this country is convinced. I believe, myself, that most people in other countries really accept it in spite of the propaganda that dins into their ears the contrary. What is also now fully and universally accepted in this country, but what may not even yet be as well understood elsewhere, is that, in the event of further aggression, we are resolved to use at once the whole of our strength in fulfilment of our pledges to resist it.

These great changes in our national life could not, indeed, be brought about, were they not backed by deep conviction, which is immensely strengthened by what we hear and read almost daily from other parts of the world. We are often told that, though once we were a great nation, our ways are now old-fashioned, and that our democracy has no life in it. We read the mischievous misrepresentations of our actions and of our motives, which some people in countries holding a different international philosophy from our own think fit to make. We read them with resentment, knowing that they are false and knowing that those who make them know it, too. These things do not pass unnoticed here, nor, I may say, do provocative insults offered to our fellow-countrymen further afield. I can say at once that Great Britain is not prepared to yield either to calumnies or force. It may afford some satisfaction to those who have pronounced our nation to be decadent to learn that they themselves have found the cure —and one most effective. Every insult that is offered to our people, every rude challenge that is made to what we value and are determined to defend, only unites us, increases our determination and strengthens our loyalty to those others who share our feelings and aspirations. Over a large part of the world the old standards of conduct and of ordinary human decency, which man had laboriously built up, are being set aside. Things are being done to-day which we can hardly read without amazement; so alien are they to our conception of how men should deal with their fellow-men. Rules of conduct between nations are overridden with the same callous indifference as rules of conduct between man and man.

The first thing, therefore, which we have to do is to see that our own standards of conduct do not deteriorate. On that point there must be—and I know there is—complete national unity. We respect our fellow-men. We know that without that there can be no real self-respect either for individuals, or, in the long run, for nations. The day that we lose our respect for our fellow-men, our democracy would have lost something on which its vitality depends, and would justly become what our critics like to think it, moribund, and dead, for it would, indeed, have lost the right to live. If, then we hold fast to these principles, what is the application of them to our foreign policy? At a time when our aims are being constantly misrepresented, it is perhaps well to restate them boldly and with such plainness of speech as I can command. And I would try to deal briefly both with our aims in the immediate present, and our aims in the future; what we are doing now and what we should like to see done as soon as circumstances make it possible.

Our first resolve is to stop aggression. I need not recapitulate the acts of aggression which have taken place, or the effect they have had upon the general trust that European nations feel able to place in words and undertakings. For that reason, and for that reason alone, we have joined with other nations to meet a common danger. These arrangements we all know, and the world knows, have no purpose other than defence. They mean what they say—no more and no less. But they have been denounced as aiming at the isolation—or, as it is called, the encirclement—of Germany and Italy, and as designed to prevent them from acquiring the living space necessary for their national existence. I shall deal with these charges to-night, and I propose to do so with complete frankness.

We are told that our motives are to isolate Germany within a ring of hostile States, to stifle her natural outlets, to cramp and throttle the very existence of a great nation. What are the facts? They are very simple and everybody knows them. Germany is isolating herself, and doing it most successfully and completely. She is isolating herself from other countries economically by her policy of autarchy, politically by a policy that causes constant anxiety to other nations, and culturally by her policy of racialism. If you deliberately isolate yourself from others by your own actions you can blame nobody but yourself, and so long as this isolation continues, the inevitable consequences of it are bound to become stronger and more marked. The last thing we desire is to see the individual German man, or woman, or child suffering privations; but if they do so, the fault does not lie with us, and it depends on Germany and Germany alone whether this process of isolation continues or not, for any day it can be ended by a policy of co-operation. It is well that this should be stated plainly so that there may be no misunderstanding here or elsewhere.

I come next to *Lebensraum*. This word, of which we have not heard the last, needs to be fairly and carefully examined. Every developed community is, of course, faced with the vital problem of living space. But the problem is not solved simply by acquiring more territory. That may indeed only make the problem more acute. It can only be solved by wise ordering of the affairs of a country at home, and by adjusting and improving its relations with other countries abroad. Nations expand their wealth, and raise the standard of living of their people by gaining the confidence of their neighbours, and thus facilitating the flow of goods between them. The very opposite is likely to be the consequence of action by one nation in suppression of the independent existence of her smaller and weaker neighbours. And if *Lebensraum* is to be applied in that sense, we reject it and must resist its application. It is noteworthy that this claim to "living space" is being put forward at a moment when Germany has become an immigration country, importing workers in large numbers from Czecho-Slovakia, Holland and Italy to meet the needs of her industry and agriculture. How then can Germany claim to be over-populated? Belgium and Holland, and to a less extent our own islands, have already proved that what is called over-population can be prevented by productive work. The wide spaces and the natural resources of the British Empire and the United States of America were not able to save them from widespread distress during the great slump of 1929 to 1932. Economically the world is far too closely knit together for any one country to hope to profit itself at the expense of its neighbours, and no more than any other country can Germany hope to solve her economic problems in isolation. It is no doubt impossible at present for us to foresee the day when all trade everywhere will be completely free. But it is possible to make arrangements, given the opportunities, which would greatly enlarge the area of freedom. Through co-operation—and we, for our part, are ready to co-operate —there is ample scope for extending to all nations the opportunity of a larger economic life with all that this means, which is implied in the term *"Lebensraum."*

If the world were organised on such lines, neither Germany nor Italy need fear for her own safety, and no nation could fail to profit from the immense material benefits which the general application of science has brought within universal reach. But no such society of nations can be built upon force, in a world which lives in fear of violence, and has to spend its substance in preparing to resist it. It is idle to cry peace where there is no peace, or to pretend to reach a settlement unless it can be guaranteed by the reduction of warlike preparations, and by the assured recognition of every nation's right to the free enjoyment of its independence. At this moment the doctrine of force bars the way to settlement, and fills the world with envy, hatred, malice and all uncharitableness. But if the doctrine of force were once abandoned, so that the fear of war that stalks the world was lifted, all outstanding questions would become easier to solve. If all the effort which is now devoted to the senseless multiplication of armaments, with the consequent increase of insecurity and distrust, were to be applied to the common peaceful development of resources, the peoples of the world would soon find an incentive to work together for the common good; they would realise that their true interests do not conflict, and that progress and well-being depend upon community of aim and effort. The nations would then be in a position to discuss with real promise of success both political grievances and economic difficulties, whether in the international or colonial field.

This brings me to say something about the principles of our colonial administration. There was a time when in the British Empire, as elsewhere, colonies were regarded merely as a source of wealth and a place of settlement for Europeans. You have only to read any of the colonial literature of those days to see for how little counted the rights and welfare of the natives. But during the last half century a very different view has gained ground, a view which has been finely expressed in Article 22 of the Covenant, namely, that the well-being and development of "people not yet able to stand by themselves under the strenuous conditions of the modern world" is "a sacred trust of civilisation."

That trust has been steadily fulfilled since the War in the case of the Mandated Territories, on which the operation of the provisions of Article 22 of the Covenant has conferred immense benefits. The British Commonwealth is fully aware of the heavy responsibility resting upon it to see that, through respect for these principles, continuity and development is assured to the native populations. The mandatory system, in fact, derives from exactly the same inspiration as that which governs British colonial administrative policy. We have applied the same principles to India and Burma, where they are now steadily at work on a scale that twenty or thirty years ago would have seemed far beyond the bounds of reasonable expectation. Within the last few years we have seen the transformation of Eire into a separate and independent member of the British Commonwealth, enjoying with our other partners of the Empire full Dominion status. For many years we tried, as the phrase went, to hold Ireland, under the mistaken belief, which is to-day invoked to justify the subjection of Czecho-Slovakia, that it was indispensable to our national security. But we have now realised that our safety is not diminished, but immeasurably increased, by a free and friendly Ireland. And so both here and in every country for which we have been responsible we have steadily moved in one direction. The whole picture is a significant and faithful reflection of British thought, projected into political form, and expressing itself, through history and now, in the development of institutions. We recognise, as the United States have recognised, that self-government should be the ultimate goal of colonial policy, a goal which is near or distant, according to the capacity of the peoples concerned to manage their own affairs. In one of your own studies, "The Colonial Problem," the type of research which enhances the name and reputation of Chatham House, you have considered the question whether colonies pay. You drew attention to the benefits of cheap imports which the consumers of a country possessing colonies obtain as the result of the relatively low cost of production of certain commodities in colonial territories. But under an international system, under which the present trade barriers were to a great extent abolished, those benefits, already shared as they are to a considerable extent by many countries not possessing colonies, would be shared still more widely. On all sides there could be more free and ready access to markets and raw materials of the world; wider channels of trade down which would flow the goods which nations require to buy and sell. Such are some of the possibilities within everybody's reach.

How does all this affect our wider problems? One of the most significant facts in world history is the extent to which the principle of trusteeship has come to be adopted in the British Commonwealth during the last thirty years, and there is surely something here that can be used for the great benefit of mankind. Can we not look forward to a time when there may be agreement on common methods and aims of colonial development, which may ensure not only that the universally acknowledged purpose of colonial administration will be to help their inhabitants steadily to raise their level of life, but also that colonial territories may make a growing contribution to the world's resources? On such an agreed foundation of purpose we hope that others might be prepared with us to make their contribution to a better world. If so, I have no doubt that in the conduct of our colonial administration we should be ready to go far upon the economic side, as we have already done on the political side, in making wider application of the principles which now obtain in the mandated territories, including, on terms of reciprocity, that of the open door. Whatever may be the difficulties of the colonial problem, or of any other, I would not despair of finding ways of settlement, once everybody has got the will to settle. But, unless all countries do, in fact, desire a settlement, discussions would only do more harm than good. It is, moreover, impossible to negotiate with a Government whose responsible spokesmen brand a friendly country as thieves and blackmailers and indulge in daily monstrous slanders on British policy in all parts of the world. But if that spirit, which is clearly incompatible with any desire for a peaceful settlement, gave way to something different, His Majesty's Government would be ready to pool their best thought with others in order to end the present state of political and economic insecurity. If we could get so far, what an immense stride the world would have made! We should have exorcised the anxiety which is cramping and arresting business expansion and we should have brought back an atmosphere of confidence among nations and assurance for the future among the youth of this and every other European country. Our next task would be the reconstruction of the international order on a broader and firmer foundation. That is too large a topic for me to embark upon this evening, but I should like to commend it to your thinking.

We must ask ourselves how far the failure of the League was due to shortcomings in the Covenant itself, or how far it was the absence of some of the greatest countries at every stage of its history that has crippled both its moral authority and strength. Is it beyond the political genius of mankind to reconcile national individuality with international collaboration? Can human purpose rise high enough to solve the riddle? An examination of the history of the Covenant may perhaps disclose that some of its obligations were too loose and others too rigid. It has been suggested, for instance, that some system of specific regional guarantees for the preservation of the peace would be more effective than the indefinite but universal obligations of Articles 10 and 16, and it is not impossible that the grouping of the Powers as it exists to-day, instead of dividing Europe, might be so moulded as to become the embryo of a better European system.

That is one side of the problem. But it is not enough to devise measures for preventing the use of force to change the *status quo,* unless there is also machinery for bringing about peaceful change. For a living and changing world can never be held in iron clamps, and any such attempt is the high road to disaster. Changes in the relations, needs, and outlook of nations are going on all the time. And there is no more urgent need, if we are ever to find a workable system of international organisation, than to invent peaceful means by which such changes can be handled. To-day when the European nations, forgetful of their common civilisation, are arming to the teeth, it is more important than ever that we should remind ourselves of the essential unity of European civilisation. European minds meet across political frontiers. With the same background of knowledge, with the same heritage of culture, they study the same problems; the work of the great masters of science, and literature or art is the common property of all peoples and thinkers in every land exchange knowledge on equal and friendly terms. Truly is a divided Europe a house divided against itself. Our foreign policy must, therefore, constantly bear in mind the immediate present and the more distant future, the steps we are now taking and the goal to which they are meant to lead.

I have strained your patience, but if you will allow me a few moments more I will endeavour to pick up the threads of my thought and perhaps make a few points more explicit. British policy rests on twin foundations of purpose. One is determination to resist force. The other is our recognition of the world's desire to get on with the constructive work of building peace. If we could once be satisfied that the intentions of others were the same as our own, and that we all really wanted peaceful solutions—then, I say here definitely, we could discuss the problems that are to-day causing the world anxiety. In such a new atmosphere we could examine the colonial problem, the question of raw materials, trade barriers, the issue of *Lebensraum*, the limitation of armaments, and any other issue that affects the lives of all European citizens.

But that is not the position which we face to-day. The threat of military force is holding the world to ransom, and our immediate task is—and here I end as I began—to resist aggression. I would emphasise that to-night with all the strength at my command, so that nobody may misunderstand it. And if we are ever to succeed in removing misunderstanding and reaching a settlement which the world can trust, it must be upon some basis more substantial than verbal undertakings. It has been said that deeds, not words, are necessary. That also is our view. There must be give and take in practical form on both sides, for there can be no firm bargains on the basis of giving something concrete in return for mere assurances. None of us can in these days see very far ahead in the world in which we live, but we can and must always be sure of the general direction in which we wish to travel. Let us, therefore, be very sure that, whether or not we are to preserve for ourselves and for others the things that we hold dear, depends in the last resort upon ourselves, upon the strength of the personal faith of each one of us, and upon our resolution to maintain it.

DISARMAMENT AND SECURITY

ADDRESS by J. Ramsay MacDonald, Prime Minister, in the House of Commons, June 29, 1931

Royal Institute of International Affairs, *Documents on International Affairs, 1931,* p. 55, citing *Hansard,* June 29, 1931, p. 905; excerpt

For February, 1932, there has been summoned a Conference at Geneva to discuss this question. We hope to settle the question of disarmament, at any rate for the time being, to review the issues revolving round it, and if possible come to an agreement as to the next stage in the operations. We know already that that Conference will be attended by representatives of all the Members of the League of Nations, the United States of America, the Union of Socialist Soviet Republics, Turkey, and Mexico. It will take, I assume, as the basis of discussion, the document which the Preparatory Commission, after some years of hard and efficient work, has produced. But it will attempt to carry that further. The general Convention which one hopes will issue from the Disarmament Conference will not be a declaration of principle, will not be a declaration of intentions, will not be a declaration of method, but it will be something which will be perfectly definite, which will contain standards and schedules, which will bring the question of disarmament into the realm of ascertainable and checkable facts, so that when the work of the Conference has been accomplished we shall not merely have piety, but scales; we shall not merely have principles, but standards; and we shall have something which each nation interested can examine and can see that obligations undertaken by other nations are actually fulfilled.

Our preparation for that Conference, the tremendously great importance of which every one in this House recognizes—not only the Members of one section or one party, but the Members of all parties —has taken the form of the setting up of a sub-committee of the Committee of Imperial Defence, a committee upon which Members of all three parties are represented. The purpose, first of all, has been to have a body of responsible men, Members of this House, sitting in the various quarters of this House, in possession of reliable facts, to give them the information they want so as to enable them to make up their minds regarding their conclusions. This committee and this nation must never get away from the fact which meets them straight in the face as soon as the committee begins to consider disarmament, and that fact is the obligation of disarmament, whether we are going to take an interest in this subject or not. This nation and this House must never forget the specific commitments to which our name has already been placed. I will venture to take up the time of the Committee by quoting these commitments in their specific and precise terms. Article 8 of the Covenant provides:

The members of the League recognize that the maintenance of peace requires a reduction of national armaments to the lowest point consistent with national safety and the enforcement by common action of international obligations.

It goes on:

The Council, taking account of the geographical situation and the circumstances of each State, shall formulate plans of such reduction for consideration and action by the several Governments.

Then the Treaty of Versailles itself, Part V, says:

In order to render possible the initiation of a general limitation of armaments of all nations Germany undertakes strictly to observe the military, naval, and air Clauses which follow.

The section of the reply of the Allied and Associated Powers to the observations of the German delegation on the conditions of peace, dated June 16, 1919, says:

The Allied and Associated Powers wish to make it clear that their requirements in regard to German armaments were not made solely with the object of rendering it impossible for Germany to resume her policy of military aggression. They are also the first steps towards that general reduction and limitation of armaments which they seek to bring about as one of the most fruitful preventives of war, and which it would be one of the first duties of the League of Nations to promote.

Then in the final protocol of the Locarno Conference of October 16, 1925, this further declaration and obligation—it is not merely a declaration, but it is an obligation—is found:

The representatives of the Governments represented here declare their firm conviction that the entry into force of these treaties and conventions will hasten on effectively the Disarmament provided for in Article 8 of the Covenant of the League of Nations. They undertake to give their sincere co-operation to the work relating to Disarmament already undertaken by the League of Nations and to seek realization thereof in a general agreement.

If we were trying to get away from those obligations we could not do it. They are there written definitely, and it is well to remember that yesterday was the anniversary of the signing of the Treaty of Peace which, whatever its defects may have been, certainly at some points glowed with the declaration of pacific faith, and at no points did it offer a greater promise for energetic action and favourable conduct than the declarations that were made in it, and, through its signature, in favour of the disarmament of Europe, not because one nation had abused arms, but because every nation frankly confessed that there was no peace and no security in continued armaments. . . .

How far have we gone in the meantime since the signing of the Treaty? I am going to try a task which I confess I would rather be excused, a task which I always execute very badly, the task of going through a somewhat, it must be on account of the circumstances, intricate series of figures, but I shall do my best. I think it is very essential that these figures should be put on record. I dare say when the figures have been published there will be some controversy about them, and some dispute as to their accuracy. It is a very difficult thing to give figures comparing the expenditure of one nation with another, because there is such a great variety in the value of the coinage used in the various countries. There is, first of all, a difference in the internal value of the coinage compared with its external exchange value in the coinage of another country. There is a constant variation in the value of coinage, not only internally but also externally, and when figures are compared over a series of years, it is discovered that there are all sorts of opportunities for quarrelling with the result. Moreover, there is some difference in what I may call the international art of budgeting, so that some budgets conceal what other budgets reveal. One must use his common sense and, if I may say so, one's experience of the world, in making up one's mind what exactly some of these figures mean, but, roughly, this is the rule which has been followed in making up the figures which I am going to quote. In converting foreign currency into sterling the average annual rates of exchange year by year have been used. I know it is not a meticulously scientific method, and the result may be out by £1,000,000 or even more. I doubt it, but it may be out up to £1,000,000. But when that has been recognized, I venture to say that in no case where I am going to quote figures will the impression be wrong, although it may not be accurate to a hair's breadth.

I will take our own Navy first. In 1914 the total naval expenditure of the United Kingdom was £51,500,000, which, calculated in terms of present-day currency, is equivalent to £76,000,000. That is the figure with which we compare what has happened. In 1924–5 the expenditure was £56,000,000; in 1930 it was £52,400,000. These figures show a reduction of £23,700,000 since 1914, and of £3,500,000 since 1924. Take the figures for the United States. In 1914 the United States spent on its Navy a little over £30,000,000, equal to £42,000,000 valued in present currency. In 1924 the figure was approximately £70,000,000, and in 1930 approximately £78,000,000. These figures, again, show an increase of £36,000,000 as compared with 1914, and £8,700,000 as compared with 1924. If you take France, in 1914 France spent £26,700,000, equal in present-day currency to £29,200,000. In 1924 she spent £13,800,000; in 1930 £24,300,000. These figures show a decrease of nearly £5,000,000 since 1914, but an increase of £10,000,000 since 1924. If we take Italy, before the war she spent £13,300,000 or, in present-day currency, £18,250,000. In 1924 she spent £9,800,000; in 1930 £16,900,000. Here, again, there is a decrease of something like £1,250,000 compared with 1914, but an increase of over £7,000,000 compared with 1924.

Now take Japan. Japan, in 1914, spent £8,500,000 on her Navy, equal in present currency to £15,400,000. In 1924 the figure was just over £23,000,000. In 1930 it was £26,600,000, an increase of over £11,000,000 as compared with 1914, but of only approximately £3,500,000 since 1924. With regard to Germany, the expenditure there has been limited by the Treaty of Versailles. Before the War her naval expenditure was £31,000,000; at the present time, it is in the region of £9,250,000.

Let me turn now to the personnel. In 1914 the naval personnel of the United Kingdom—and I am not at all sure this is not the simplest test for it; it has to be examined and slightly qualified, but, on the whole, I think it is the simplest and most straightforward—in 1914 the naval personnel of the United Kingdom totalled 151,000. In 1924 the figure was 99,453. In 1931 it was 93,630, a reduction of 57,350 since 1914, and of 5,803 since 1924. An examination of the figures of the personnel of other countries will show that they have increased in much the same proportion as ours have decreased.

Then I have in front of me figures regarding the number of ships. In 1914 the British Commonwealth possessed 89 capital ships, and to-day it has 15 capital ships. That is owing to the operation of the Washington Treaty of 1922. The number of cruisers has decreased since 1914 from 131 to 59 built, building, and authorized. The number of destroyers we possessed in 1914 was 298, plus 70 torpedo boats, and these figures will be reduced to about 120 by the London Naval Treaty. We have 40 fewer submarines now than in 1914. In spite of that fact, the number of those vessels has shown a marked increase in other countries. For example, the number held by France has increased by 35; those held by the United States, by 35; Italy, by 38; and Japan, by 49.

DISARMAMENT AND SECURITY

Turning to the Army, as regards the British Army, the expenditure, exclusive of forces maintained at the expense of India and the Colonies, in 1914 was £28,800,000, or in terms of present-day currency, well over £40,000,000. In 1924 the corresponding figure was £45,000,000; and in 1931 £39,000,000, or practically £40,000,000. But these figures require explanation, because they might otherwise be taken as an indication of pure strength. This later figure of £40,000,000, which looks as though it were, from a military point of view, an equivalent expenditure to that of 1914, is not, as a matter of fact. The non-effective charges—the civilian pay, the pay connected with civilians in the War Office service, the maintenance of fabrics and so on—have all substantially increased. The pay of the officers and men has increased, salaries have increased, and the amount, scope, and cost of the amenities of the soldier's life—improved rations, better barracks, canteens, recreational facilities, higher standards of education, improvement in medical and dental treatment—have considerably increased, and have cost money. The cost of mechanization has also increased. These considerations must be taken into account when the military value of the £40,000,000 is being struck. Since 1925 the military expenditure of France has increased by £20,800,000, that of Italy by £15,400,000, and that of the United States by £15,680,000. Then take the man strength. In 1914 ours was 186,420, exclusive of forces maintained at the expense of India and of Colonial Governments. That exclusion still holds good. In 1924 it was 161,600, and in 1931, 148,000. There has, therefore, been a decrease of 37,600 since 1914, and of 12,800 since 1924.

As regards the Air, it is impossible to make comparisons with the Air Service as it is to-day and what it was in 1914. In 1914 the Air Service—I do it no injustice—at the time before the outbreak of war, was, for the purposes we have in view at the moment, somewhat negligible. It was not organized in the way that it has been since, and it is difficult to get out the costs and so on. It is also very difficult to compare our Air Service with foreign Air Services, on account very largely of budgetary methods—of mixing up the Air Service with Naval Services and Army Services, and other considerations—and I can only give one or two figures, which, however, will be striking enough, and will certainly not be misleading. I ought to say that, in the figures of cost which I am going to give, the grants made for civil aviation and the upkeep of aerodromes and so on are included.

If we take France first of all, we find that recently there was a separation of the Air Forces in France from the other forces, so that it is more possible to make a comparison there. Air expenditure in France is at the present moment nearly £21,000,000. That shows an increase of about £4,000,000 from 1929, when her Air Budget was first separated. We have estimated, so far as we can, that the United States has increased her Air expenditure since 1922 by something like £20,000,000, the actual Budget figure this year being, we believe, somewhere in the nature of £34,000,000. Italy, similarly, shows an increase of some £6,000,000 on the 1922 figures. Our own Air expenditure shows no such marked proportionate increase. It is, indeed, only £2,000,000 in excess of the figure of ten years ago, and is actually lower than it was five years ago. It is £18,000,000, which is £2,000,000 more than ten years ago. The figure now is £18,000,000, and the figures I have given are to be added to or taken from that sum. As regards actual numbers, we only possess some 800 first-line aircraft, of which only 400 are permanently available at home. I have already said that comparisons with foreign Powers are very difficult to make, but we know that France has 1,300 aircraft of the first line, and that the United States, Italy, and the Union of Soviet Republics are very well equipped as regards that arm.

The circumstances in which a statement like this is made are perfectly well known. We cannot give accurate figures in some cases. My attention was drawn the other day to a poster—not published in this country—declaring that, in disarmament, again, Great Britain is just the old perfidious diplomatist. That is absolutely and maliciously untrue. I again say that they may take a million here or a million there off these figures, especially the money, but it makes no difference at all; the impression that I have given to the Committee is absolutely accurate, and can be sustained right up to the hilt. This country has been swift, patient, and persistent in carrying out what it believed to be its obligations, and which were obligations which it held in common with other nations.

Let us note that, if that were the whole story, our risks would be far too great, but that is not the whole story. The risk to security which a country runs is not expressed in technical military terms. Indeed, it is very often exactly the opposite that is true—that the strength of armaments is often the measure of war risk. If the figures quoted stood alone, our risks, as I say, would be uncomfortably great, but they do not stand alone. Military security must always be embedded in and subordinate to political security, and it is very often the case that steps taken to produce military security destroy political security—that nations, imagining that they are arming themselves to avoid war, are doing nothing of the kind, but are arming themselves to try and secure victory should war break out. In that case they are doing nothing to avoid war at all, but everything to continue both the psychology and the political conditions which all history has shown to be the fruitful sources, and perhaps the only sources, of war.

Therefore, if the signature of that Treaty on June 28, 1919, twelve years ago, was to any appreciable extent a fulfilling of that oft-quoted dictum during the War, "This is a war to end all wars," nations in the interval should not only have been taking steps to secure victory in the event of war breaking out, but they should have been taking steps to prevent war ever breaking out; and the best way to do that is to improve the relations of the countries one with another. Therefore, we have been acting in that direction. The peace securities of Europe, we have believed, can be weakened by armaments, but there is a corollary to that—that, unless the Disarmament Conference of next year is going to put an end to those expansions which have been so evident in the figures that I have quoted, a declaration is going to be made that disarmament is a failure, and that nations are being doomed to tread the old ruts which have always ended in battles, in ill will, and, cynically, above everything, in a Treaty of Peace that demands war, and war in order to strengthen it.

The reduction must be all round. We have gone pretty nearly to the limit of example. I would appeal to every nation that is interested in peace and in disarmament to study those figures, and to admit and confess that one nation cannot by its own example bring about disarmament, and that it is the duty and responsibility of every one to join together and make that further disarmament possible by international agreements and arrangements.

There is one other point, of course. One cannot overlook the fact that there are dangers in the way. The Pact of Paris, for instance, eliminates war from our diplomacy. It does not seem to eliminate arms. I am sure that is only an oversight, and, when the logical and practical discrepancy is pointed out effectively, the oversight will be admitted by everybody. But still we have to keep our eye upon the oversight. There are certain great forces that we are up against. There is a self-regarding nationalism expressing its nationalist spirit in an exclusive economic policy. There is the nature of peace and there is the problem, the most difficult and intricate of all problems, how you are to readjust, not by force, not by wile, not by guile of any kind whatever, but by just allowing ordinary natural processes—I know that word is a very indefinite one, but the handling must also be indefinite—how we are to enable a readjustment of a Continent settled by force to be made into one settled and enjoying natural relationships—that is one of the most difficult, intricate, and dangerous problems that any generation could have to face. The transition is bound to be marked by apprehension, and when movements are made of the most simple common sense, they are bound to arouse fears.

Here one may say that a country in the position of France is in a peculiarly attackable position in that respect. We are an island. Let us be fair. Let us be just. Fairness and justness do not consist merely of logic. We must be able to use our imagination, to make our fairness a full measure of fairness and our justice a full measure of justice. These people, invaded again and again and again—their fields flattened by the feet of millions of invading soldiers—no Channel, however thin that trickle may be in view of modern invention and the application of science and research—no Channel, but a line drawn upon the ground is their only frontier. What should we feel like if we were in that position? Any one who goes over the Border country between England and Scotland, especially if he has any imagination, can understand modern conditions and the modern psychology of large sections of the people of Europe. Therefore, while we give our figures and ask for our agreements, and beg for our agreements, and negotiate our agreements, do not let us lose that sympathetic touch which is bound to keep France and us together so long as we have the proper imagination to see what a Frenchman feels and, above all, what a French woman feels when war is talked about and disarmament is being negotiated. All that we have been doing has been on the assumption that we are secure in peace for a certain period.

I am not going to say to-day how long that period can be, but I do say this, that assumption, on which the policy of every post-War Government has been founded, ought still to be made. It may be good or it may be bad, but 1932 gives all the nations of the world a chance of laying their heads together and relating their military strengths to their political obligations, and it would be folly on the part of this country, it would be madness on our part, if we did not wait until 1932 came to review the situation as it is then. I hope, in consequence of what has been done both by the reduction of military strength and by the increase of political security, agreement will be come to at that conference. I hope that agreement will enable the Government which will be here to prove by results the justification of the policy which has been revealed by what I have said to the Committee to-day, and that, after the chapter has been closed, the figures agreed to, the columns made, the assignment of this category of strength made, and the assignment of that made, it will be the happy position of the British Government to ask the House of Commons, and the Committee of the House of Commons, to back it in going on to make still further reductions in the cause of international agreement, removing still farther away than we have been able to do up to now the military causes of war, and strengthening and laying deeper and broader the only foundation upon which peace can rest—complete agreement and most friendly relations between all the nations of the world.

DRAFT Disarmament Convention, Submitted by J. Ramsay MacDonald, Prime Minister, to the General Commission of the Conference for the Reduction and Limitation of Armaments, at Geneva, March 16, 1933

British White Paper, Cmd. 4279; excerpts

PART I. SECURITY

ARTICLE 1. The following articles (2–5) are concluded between those of the parties to the present Convention who are parties to the Pact of Paris.

ARTICLE 2. It is hereby declared that any war undertaken in breach of that Pact is a matter of interest to all the High Contracting Parties, and shall be regarded as a breach of the obligations assumed towards each one of them.

ARTICLE 3. In the event of a breach or threat of breach of the Pact of Paris, a conference between the High Contracting Parties shall at once meet at the request of any five of them, provided that at least one of the Governments mentioned by name in article 4 joins in that request. Such request may be addressed to the Secretary-General of the League of Nations, whose duty it will then be to make arrangements for the Conference and to notify the High Contracting Parties accordingly. The meeting shall take place at Geneva, unless any other meeting place is agreed upon.

ARTICLE 4. Any conclusions reached at such meeting shall, to be valid, require the concurrence of the representatives of the Governments of the United States of America, the United Kingdom of Great Britain and Northern Ireland, France, Germany, Italy, Japan and the Union of Soviet Socialist Republics, and of a majority of the representatives of the other Governments participating in the Conference, exclusive in each case of the Parties to the dispute.

ARTICLE 5. It shall be the object of the said Conference, if called in view of a threat of breach of the Pact, to agree upon the steps which could be taken in respect of such threat, and, in the event of a breach of the Pact of Paris being found to have occurred, to determine which party or parties to the dispute are to be held responsible.

ARTICLE 6. Special regional agreements made by certain of the High Contracting Parties for providing information intended to facilitate the decisions to be given under article 5 and for co-ordinating action to be taken by these Parties as a result of such decision are contained in Annexes X and Y.

PART II. DISARMAMENT

ARTICLE 7. The High Contracting Parties agree to limit their respective armaments as provided in the present Convention.

SECTION I. EFFECTIVES

Chapter 1. Provisions as to Numerical Limitation

ARTICLE 8. The average daily effectives in the land, sea and air armed forces of each of the High Contracting Parties shall not exceed the figures laid down for such Party in the Tables annexed to this Chapter.

ARTICLE 9. It is understood that effectives consist of:—
(a) All officers, officer cadets, n.c.o.'s, soldiers, sailors, airmen, reservists, and all other persons (such as military officials of the administrative, sanitary or veterinary services or military agents) of equivalent status, who perform a day's duty in the land, sea and air armed forces.
(b) Persons who perform a day's duty in police forces or similar formations under the conditions prescribed in article 12.
(c) All other persons of at least 18 years of age who receive military training under the control of the State.

ARTICLE 10. The High Contracting Parties undertake to prohibit any military training whatsoever except in organisations under the control of their respective Governments.

ARTICLE 11. The average daily effectives are reckoned by dividing the total number of days' duty performed by actual effectives in each year by the number of days in such year.

In the case of continuous service, every day shall count as a day's duty. A deduction of 5 per cent. may in each case be made from the total average daily effectives on account of persons sick in hospital, persons on leave for two or more days and persons prematurely discharged on leave. Any Party for which the above-mentioned absences represent a greater percentage may make a correspondingly larger deduction after furnishing to the Permanent Disarmament Commission details as to its basis of computation.

In the case of intermittent service or instruction, attendances aggregating six hours may count as the equivalent of one day's duty.

ARTICLE 12. A police force or similar formation may be disregarded for the purpose of calculating effectives unless it has at least one of the following characteristics:—
   (a) Arms other than individual (machine pistols, Lewis guns, machine guns and weapons of accompaniment, etc.).
   (b) Training of a military nature other than close order drill, physical training or technical training in the use of individual arms.
   (c) Transport, signalling or engineer equipment of a suitable nature and on a sufficient scale to enable it to be employed by units in tactical operations.

The procession by a force of one or more of the above characteristics will in principle determine its inclusion in whole or in part in the calculation of effectives of the land armed forces. Doubtful cases should be referred to the Permanent Disarmament Commission, who will give a decision by reviewing the military capacity of the force in the light of all the above characteristics and taking into account in particular the following confirmatory conditions:—
   (i) Quartering in barracks;
   (ii) Training in groups of 100 men or more;
   (iii) Organisation on a military basis;
   (iv) Previous military training.

ARTICLE 13. The following naval effectives should be included among the effectives of the land armed forces:—
   (a) Effectives employed in land coast defence;
   (b) Marines who are normally in excess of those assigned to or destined for service afloat;
   (c) Effectives coming within the classification of similar formations (as defined in article 12).

Naval personnel serving ashore in the fleet services (training, administrative, etc.), as well as those assigned to or destined for service afloat, will be included in the effectives of the sea armed forces.

Table I. Table of Average Daily Effectives Which Are Not to Be Exceeded in the Land Armed Forces

(Note: This Table contains only the figures which are suggested for the countries of Continental Europe. It would, of course, require to be completed by the addition of figures in respect to all the other Parties.)

PARTY	LAND ARMED FORCES	
	Stationed in Home Country	Total including Overseas
Germany	200,000	200,000
Belgium	60,000	75,000

Party	Land Armed Forces	
	Stationed in Home Country	Total including Overseas
Bulgaria	60,000	60,000
Spain	120,000	170,000
France	200,000	400,000
Greece	60,000	60,000
Hungary	60,000	60,000
Italy	200,000	250,000
Netherlands	25,000	75,000
Poland	200,000	200,000
Portugal	50,000	60,000
Roumania	150,000	150,000
Czechoslovakia	100,000	100,000
U.S.S.R.	500,000	500,000
Yugoslavia	100,000	100,000
Each other Continental European State	(No separate figure.)	50,000

Table II. *Table of Average Daily Effectives Which Are Not to Be Exceeded in the Sea Armed Forces*
(The figures will have to be related to the naval material allowed to each Party.)

Table III. *Table of Average Daily Effectives Which Are Not to Be Exceeded in the Air Armed Forces*
(The figures will have to be related to the air material allowed to each Party.)

Chapter 2. Special Provisions as to the Organization of the Land Armed Forces Stationed in Continental Europe

ARTICLE 14. The provisions of this Chapter apply only to the land armed forces stationed in Continental Europe.

ARTICLE 15. Troops whose primary function is to provide drafts or reinforcements for overseas garrisons are excluded from the provisions of this Chapter.

ARTICLE 16. The maximum total period of service for the effectives in the land armed forces stationed in Continental Europe (excluding the troops mentioned in article 15 above and the personnel referred to in article 18) shall not exceed eight months.[a]

ARTICLE 17. For each man the total period of service is the total number of days comprised in the different periods of service to which

[a] In special cases to be decided by the Conference, the maximum total period of service may be extended to twelve months.

he is liable under national law or by the terms of his contract to perform.

ARTICLE 18. In the land armed forces affected by this Chapter, the personnel whose length of service is greater than that prescribed in article 16 shall not at any time exceed the following proportions of the average strength throughout the year of the said forces:—

Officers, officer cadets and persons of equivalent status $\frac{1}{x}$

N.c.o.'s, soldiers and persons of equivalent status . . . $\frac{1}{y}$

Chapter 3. Provisions as to the methods by which the reductions and reorganizations entailed by the preceding Chapters shall be effected

(Note.—A series of articles will be required to deal with this matter.)

SECTION II. MATERIAL

Chapter 1. Land Armaments

ARTICLE 19. The maximum limit for the calibre of mobile land guns for the future shall be 105 mm. Existing mobile land guns up to 155 mm. may be retained, but all replacement or new construction of guns shall be within the maximum limit of 105 mm.

For the purposes of this Section, a gun of 4.5-inch calibre shall be regarded as equivalent to one of 105 mm. in the case of countries whose standard gun is of the former calibre.

The maximum limit for the calibre of coast defence guns shall be 406 mm.

ARTICLE 20. For the purposes of the present Convention, a tank is defined as follows:
"A tank is a fully-armoured, armed, self-propelled vehicle designed to cross broken ground, usually by means of tracks, and to overcome obstacles encountered on the battlefield."

ARTICLE 21. The maximum limit for the weight of tanks shall be 16 tons.

(It will be observed that one important aspect of land war material is not fully dealt with. No proposals are here submitted for tanks under the 16-ton weight limit. In its proposals of the 17th November last the United Kingdom Government drew attention to the different characteristics of the heavy and the light tank. The problem created by the latter evidently requires further international examination, and the question is therefore left open for negotiation in order that agreement may be reached upon the future of this important modern weapon.)

ARTICLE 22. All mobile land guns above 155 mm. and all tanks above 16 tons shall be destroyed in the following stages:—

One-third within 12 months of the coming into force of the Convention.

Two-thirds within 3 years of the coming into force of the Convention.

All guns above 105 mm. shall be destroyed so soon as they are replaced by new guns of or below 105 mm.

Chapter 2. Naval Armaments
Sub-Chapter I

ARTICLE 23. The naval armaments of the Parties to the Treaty of Washington, signed on the 6th February, 1922, and the Treaty of London, signed on the 22nd April, 1930, remain subject to the limitations resulting from the said Treaties.

ARTICLE 24. Articles 25 and 26 constitute the agreement between the Parties to the Treaty of London referred to in article 24, paragraph 4, of that Treaty. France and Italy will ratify the said Treaty not later than the date of their ratification of the present Convention.

ARTICLE 25. Until the 31st December, 1936, the naval combatant vessels of France and Italy, other than capital ships, aircraft carriers and all vessels exempt from limitation under article 8 of the Treaty of London, shall be limited, without prejudice to article 12 of the said Treaty, by the provisions of articles 26 and 27 of the present Convention. The definitions adopted in Annex I for the purposes of the present Chapter will apply.

ARTICLE 26. (a) The completed tonnage in the cruiser, destroyer and submarine categories which is not to be exceeded on the 31st December, 1936, is to be the completed tonnage arrived at in consequence of the provisions of article 27.

(b) France and Italy shall have complete freedom of transfer for the purposes of replacement between cruisers of sub-category (ii) and destroyers.

ARTICLE 27. Until the 31st December, 1936, the programmes of France and Italy in cruisers, destroyers and submarines will be as follows:—

(A) *Cruisers with guns of more than 6.1 inch (155 mm.) calibre.*

No further tonnage shall be laid down or acquired after the date of signing the present Convention.

(B) *Cruisers with guns of 6.1 inch (155 mm.) calibre or less, and destroyers.*

The amount of further construction to be laid down or acquired by France during the period between the 1st January, 1933, and the 31st December, 1936, shall be limited to 34,298 (34,847 metric) standard tons as authorised in the French programme of 1932.

The amount of further construction to be laid down or acquired by Italy during the same period shall be limited to 27,173 (27,608 metric) standard tons.

Tonnage laid down or acquired in accordance with the French programme of 1931 and the Italian programme of 1931-32 and any tonnage laid down or acquired subsequently shall be devoted to the replacement of overage cruisers of this sub-category or of overage destroyers. Upon the completion of any replacement tonnage a corresponding amount of overage tonnage shall be disposed of in accordance with Annex VI to the present Chapter.

(C) *Submarines.*

Until the 31st December, 1936, France and Italy will not lay down or acquire any further submarines. France will arrange her present submarine building and scrapping programme so that on the said date her completed tonnage will not be greater than _____ standard tons.

Any submarine tonnage under construction on that date shall be in anticipation of replacement requirements.

Sub-Chapter II

ARTICLE 28. No High Contracting Party shall lay down or acquire any capital ship during the period up to the 31st December, 1936, except that Italy may lay down one ship not exceeding 26,500 (26,924 metric) standard tons and carrying guns not exceeding 13-inch (330 mm.) calibre.

Except as provided in article 7, paragraph 2, of the Treaty of London, no High Contracting Party shall, until the 31st December, 1936, lay down or acquire any submarine the standard displacement of which exceeds 2,000 (2,032 metric) standard tons or carrying a gun above 5.1 inch (130 mm.) calibre.

Sub-Chapter III

ARTICLE 29. In order to bring about a stabilisation of naval armaments until the 31st December, 1936, the armaments of those High Contracting Parties to whom the Treaties of Washington and London do not apply shall, until the said date, be limited as follows:—

(a) No cruisers carrying guns of a calibre above 6.1 inch (155 mm.) shall be constructed or acquired.

(b) On the 31st December, 1936, the completed tonnage in cruisers of sub-category (ii) destroyers and submaries possessed by each of the said High Contracting Parties shall not exceed the amounts specified for such Party in Annex IV. This provision does not, however, apply to vessels exempt from limitation under Annex II to this Chapter, nor to the special vessels shown in Annex III. These special vessels may not be replaced.

(c) Ships may only be laid down or acquired in accordance with the replacement rules contained in Annex V, and only in replacement of tonnage in the same category or sub-category which is or becomes overage in accordance with these rules.

Nevertheless there shall be complete freedom of transfer for purposes of replacement between the cruisers of sub-category (ii) and destroyers.

Vessels which have to be disposed of as being surplus to the tonnage figures set out in Annex IV shall be disposed of in accordance with the rules set out in Annex VI.

(d) Existing ships of various types which prior to the 1st April, 1933, have been used as stationary training establishments or hulks may be retained in a non-seagoing condition.

ARTICLE 30. The High Contracting Parties assent to the rules laid down in Part IV of the Treaty of London and accept them as established rules of international law.

The present article constitutes, as regards those High Contracting Parties to whom the Treaty of London does not apply, the accession contemplated by article 25 of the said Treaty.

Sub-Chapter IV

ARTICLE 31. It is understood that none of the provisions of the present Chapter shall prejudice the attitude of any of the High Contracting Parties at the conferences referred to in article 32. The present Convention establishes no permanent ratio in any category of ship and creates no precedent as to whether, and if so in what manner, tonnage remaining overage on the 31st December, 1936, for which replacement tonnage has not been laid down, may ultimately be replaced.

ARTICLE 32. Concurrently with the conference in 1935 provided for under article 23 of the Treaty of London, or at least in the same year, there shall be a conference of all the High Contracting Parties possessing naval armaments with a view to the establishment of limitations to be observed after the 31st December, 1936.

ARTICLE 33. The Permanent Disarmament Commission set up under article 64 of the present Convention will take immediate steps to prepare for the conferences of 1935 referred to in article 32, by ascertaining the opinions of the High Contracting Parties concerned. It will also examine, with a view to reporting to the said conferences, technical questions of qualitative reduction in the sizes of vessels of war in the various categories, as well as any other questions relating to the limitation of naval armaments which the Commission may consider could appropriately come before the said conferences.

Chapter 3. Air Armaments

ARTICLE 34. The High Contracting Parties accept the complete abolition of bombing from the air (except for police purposes in certain outlying regions).

ARTICLE 35. The Permanent Disarmament Commission set up under article 64 of the present Convention shall immediately devote itself to the working out of the best possible schemes providing for—
  (a) The complete abolition of military and naval aircraft, which must be dependent on the effective supervision of civil aviation to prevent its misuse for military purposes;
  (b) alternatively, should it prove impossible to ensure such effective supervision, the determination of the minimum number of machines required by each High Contracting Party consistent with his national safety and obligations, and having regard to the particular circumstances of each country.

The schemes prepared by the Permanent Disarmament Commission shall be reported to the second Disarmament Conference. In any case the measures relating to civil aviation set out in Annex II will apply during the period of the present Convention.

ARTICLE 36. With a view to effecting the reductions necessary to facilitate the attainment of the objects referred to in article 35, the number of aeroplanes capable of use in war, in commission in the land, sea and air armed forces of each of the High Contracting Parties who at present possess such aeroplanes, shall, by the end of the period of the present Convention, not exceed the figures laid down for such Party in the table annexed to this chapter; as regards the other High Contracting Parties the *status quo* existing on the 1st January, 1933, shall be maintained during the said period.

Each of the High Contracting Parties mentioned in the table annexed to this chapter may keep a number of aeroplanes in immediate reserve, not exceeding in each case 25 per cent. of the number of aeroplanes in commission in the land, sea and air forces of such Party.

ARTICLE 37. The High Contracting Parties agree that their air armaments will not include aeroplanes exceeding 3 tons unladen weight. Exception, however, may be made in the case of troop-carriers and flying boats. Complete particulars of any such machines exceeding the maximum unladen weight of 3 tons must be returned annually to the Permanent Disarmament Commission.

ARTICLE 38. No dirigible shall be constructed or acquired during the period of the present Convention by any of the High Contracting Parties for commission in their land, sea or air forces. The High Contracting Parties who at present possess such dirigibles, may, however, retain, but not replace, them during the said period.

ARTICLE 39. The definition of unladen weight is given in Annex I.

ARTICLE 40. Aeroplanes, capable of use in war, in commission in the land, sea and air armed forces of any of the High Contracting Parties, in excess of the number indicated for such Party in the Table annexed to this Chapter, must have been put out of commission or otherwise disposed of by the end of the period of the present Convention. At least one-half of such excess must, in the case of each such High Contracting Party, have been so dealt with by the 30th June, 1936.

ARTICLE 41. Aeroplanes exceeding the maximum unladen weight indicated in article 37 and now existing in the armed forces of the High Contracting Parties must all, except in so far as exceptions may be made in accordance with that article, have been destroyed by the end of the period of this convention. At least half of their number must, in the case of each High Contracting Party, have been destroyed by the 30th June, 1936.

Table. Aeroplanes.

[Note.—Figures will have to be inserted subsequently for the other Parties which at present possess military or naval aeroplanes.]

Belgium	150	Norway	75
China	100	Poland	200
Czechoslovakia	200	Portugal	25
Denmark	50	Roumania	150
Estonia	50	Siam	75
Finland	25	Spain	200
France	500	Sweden	75
Greece	75	Switzerland	75
Italy	500	Turkey	100
Japan	500	Union of S.S.R.	500
Latvia	50	United Kingdom	500
Lithuania	50	United States of America	500
Netherlands	150	Yugoslavia	200

ANNEX II

Being convinced of the importance of taking measures designed to prevent the use of civil aviation for military purposes in the event of war, without at the same time hampering its legitimate development and usefulness to mankind in time of peace;

Recognising that to be effective such measures must be framed on a world-wide basis and, therefore, to be generally acceptable, must entail the minimum interference with the existing National and International organisations;

The High Contracting Parties agree as follows:—

. . .

PART III. EXCHANGE OF INFORMATION

ARTICLES 42–46. (The provisions of this part will depend in the main on the limitations and restrictions imposed by the other parts of the Convention. It does not seem necessary, therefore, to attempt to draft them now. It is only necessary to note that articles 34 and 35 of the Draft Convention will have to be reproduced.)

PART V. MISCELLANEOUS PROVISIONS

SECTION I. PERMANENT DISARMAMENT COMMISSION

Chapter 1. Composition

ARTICLE 64. There shall be set up at the seat of the League of Nations a Permanent Disarmament Commission composed of representatives of the Governments of the High Contracting Parties. Each such Government shall appoint one member of the Commission. Each member may be accompanied by substitutes and experts.

. . .

Chapter 2. Functions

ARTICLE 69. It will be the duty of the Commission to watch the execution of the present Convention.

MEMORANDUM of the British Government, January 29, 1934

British White Paper, Cmd. 4512, p. 21. The memorandum was laid before Parliament on January 31, 1934

I

1. On the 22nd November the Bureau of the Disarmament Conference unanimously decided that the work of the conference should be suspended for a period in order to permit of parallel and supplementary efforts being carried on between different States, mainly through the diplomatic channel. In the interval this method has been actively pursued, and bilateral communications have taken place between various capitals. As a result, the points of view of certain Governments have been further defined, and some general propositions which they had previously advanced have taken a more concrete shape. Yet it must be admitted that, on comparing the attitudes thus disclosed, no firm basis of agreement at present emerges; and, while these diplomatic exchanges have undoubtedly cleared the ground and revealed the immensity and difficulty of the problem in their true proportions, the method recently followed cannot in itself produce a unanimous result and is in danger of exhausting its usefulness. On the other hand, a resumption of the discussions at Geneva without any new directive suggestions is only too likely to lead to further disappointment.

2. In these circumstances His Majesty's Government in the United Kingdom consider that the time has arrived when they should make plain their own attitude in the present situation, the gravity of which must be apparent to every thoughtful mind, and should thus make a further positive contribution, so far as lies in their power, to promote a reconciliation of views in a matter upon which the future of the world may depend. If agreement is to be reached and a Convention is to be signed, it is useless for any Power merely to insist on its own ideals and its own requirements or to refuse to depart in any degree from the solution which it deems best. His Majesty's Government are making the present communication, not for the purpose of formulating unattainable ideals, but in order to indicate the lines of a compromise which they believe, after reviewing the history of the discussions and closely studying the recent interchange of views, should be generally acceptable.

3. Before dealing with any specific proposition as to the measure or the regulation of armaments, His Majesty's Government must reassert the main objective to which all proposals on this subject are directed. That objective is, as article 8 of the Covenant declares, the

maintenance of peace. Even though increase of armed strength may be actuated by reasons of defence, it is an index of fear of attack from another quarter, and a measure of the alarm and disquiet existing between peoples. Conversely, a general agreement securing the limitation of armaments at the lowest practicable level would be the most effective and significant proof of international appeasement and an encouragement of the mutual confidence which springs from good and neighbourly relations. Consequently, His Majesty's Government regard agreement about armaments not as an end in itself, but rather as a concomitant of world peace and as an outcome of political amelioration. For this reason, they have always acknowledged the relation between the conception of equality of rights on the one hand, and of security on the other. For this same reason, they welcome the indications that Herr Hitler's recent proposals, whatever may be said of their precise content, are concerned not only with technical questions of armament, but with political guarantees against aggression.

4. It follows from the above considerations that agreement is most likely to be reached on a broad basis which combines regulation of armaments with assurances in the political field. Protracted debates on disarmament in its limited and purely technical aspect can lead to no conclusion, unless wider considerations touching the equality and the security of nations are borne in mind and provided for. Hence the United Kingdom Draft Convention, which was approved at Geneva as a basis of the ultimate agreement by a unanimous vote which included both France and Germany, began with a "Part I" on the subject of Security, proposing methods of consultation for the purpose of determining an appropriate action in the event of a threatened breach of the Briand–Kellogg Pact. The amplification of this proposal is dealt with below (paragraph 9). His Majesty's Government must emphasise that they have never departed from the principles and purposes of the Draft Convention or have sought to substitute a second and contradictory draft for it. If there were any misapprehension in any quarter on this score, the declaration they are now making will finally remove it. The Prime Minister, when presenting the Draft Convention to the Conference in March of last year, plainly intimated that it was not necessarily to be regarded as a final and unalterable text, and subsequent discussion has shown that it requires adjustment in certain respects if general agreement is to be reached. Any suggestions which have since been put forward for consideration have been tentatively advanced with a view to seeing whether they would promote such agreement, and for no other purpose. But the underlying conceptions of the Draft Convention remain

the standpoint of His Majesty's Government, and could only be abandoned if and when a more acceptable alternative were generally agreed.

5. But while His Majesty's Government are not prepared to depart from the lines of the Draft Convention without being assured that there is an alternative which would more readily lead to universal agreement, they have been perfectly prepared to give unprejudiced consideration to new suggestions and to do their utmost to promote their general acceptance. The failure to reach agreement would inflict a fearful blow upon the hopes of all friends of peace throughout the world, whereas the attainment of agreement would create and build up that confidence which is the only secure basis for the limitation of armaments. The importance, therefore, of attaining international agreement by any possible means is so great that no suggestions, from whatever quarter they come, should be rejected merely because of a preference for a better solution which is, in fact, unattainable. An illustration lies ready to hand. It is sometimes urged that the solution of the disarmament problem lies in the immediate abandonment by all the world of all the weapons which the Peace Treaties withheld from certain Powers. But it is manifest that such a solution is in practice unattainable at the present time. That is no reason for abandoning the effort to secure, in this first Convention, all that can be attained. The devotion of the whole British people to the cause of disarmament is deep and sincere, as is sufficiently proved by the present position of its armaments in comparison with those of other leading Powers. They realise that further progress can only be achieved by agreement, and therefore His Majesty's Government would still work for agreement, even though, having regard to the principle of equality of rights, agreement is found to involve alongside of disarmament in some quarters some measure of rearmament in others.

6. It should not be overlooked that the scheme of the Draft Convention itself involves some degree of rearmament for those States whose armaments are at present restricted by treaty. Germany, for example, in view of the numerical increase proposed in her effectives, would need larger quantities of such weapons as she is already entitled to possess. And this is not all. His Majesty's Government have more than once publicly stated that an international agreement based on the admitted principle of equality of rights in a régime of security necessarily involves that, within the stages provided for by such an agreement, the situation must be reached in which arms of a kind permitted to one State cannot continue to be denied to another. His Majesty's Government see no escape from this conclusion, and they

do not seek to escape from it, for they are convinced that the best prospect for the future peace of the world would be afforded by an agreement which recognises and provides for this parity of treatment, while it abolishes or reduces to the lowest possible level all arms of a specially offensive character, and provides by the most appropriate means available for a greater sense of security. So far as Europe is concerned, a reconciliation of the points of view of France and Germany is the essential condition of general agreement. If a way is not found to accommodate their respective points of view, this greater sense of security will not be promoted. And without it, substantial disarmament is impossible. On the other hand, if an agreement is reached, even if the agreement at present attainable falls short of the highest hopes, the gain of reaching and observing such an agreement would be immeasurable, and the fact that it had been reached and observed would form the firm foundation on which a further agreement of more comprehensive character might be based in the future.

7. We must therefore seek a solution where a solution can be found. No agreement is no solution at all, and the world will be thrown back upon unrestricted competition in the supply and manufacture of weapons of destruction, the end of which no man can see. Putting aside, therefore, as not immediately attainable the ideal of universal disarmament to Germany's permitted level, and refusing to acquiesce in the conclusion that agreement cannot be reached, the choice appears to His Majesty's Government to lie between two conceivable courses so far as the future armaments of the heavily armed Powers are concerned. These two choices are:—

(1) To reach agreement in a Convention which will involve the abandonment of certain classes of weapons by the most heavily armed Powers.

(2) To reach agreement on the basis that the most heavily armed Powers, are unable or unwilling to disarm, but that they will undertake not to increase their present armaments.

The second course is the one which is indicated in certain quarters as the most that can be hoped for. But His Majesty's Government cannot contemplate as acceptable a conclusion which, though it would provide for a limitation of armaments, would do nothing whatever to secure their reduction. His Majesty's Government, therefore, would earnestly press upon other Governments that the first course, which they most strongly prefer and regard as more in accord with the main object to be attained, should not be abandoned, but should be actively pursued. The second part of this Memorandum sets out the way in which His Majesty's Government believe this could be accomplished.

II

8. His Majesty's Government conceive that international agreement in the matter of armaments can only be reached by making adequate provision under the three heads of (*a*) security, (*b*) equality of rights, (*c*) disarmament. These three topics were all dealt with in the Draft Convention, and the object of the present document is to explain how, in the light of actual circumstances and of the claims and proposals put forward from various quarters, the contents of that Draft Convention might be modified or expanded in certain particulars with a view to securing general agreement. His Majesty's Government have studied with close attention the points of view advanced by the French, Italian, German and other Governments in the course of recent interchanges. Nearly a year ago His Majesty's Government undertook the responsibility of placing before the General Commission a full Draft Convention. The adjustments now proposed in the text of that Draft are such as subsequent communication and consideration show to be best calculated to bring about concrete results.

9. *Security.*—Part I of the Draft Convention dealt with the subject of security. As the result of a redraft which was unanimously approved on the 24th May, 1933, it now consists of four articles, three of which provide in effect that, in the event of a breach or threat of breach of the Pact of Paris, immediate consultation may be called for and shall take place between signatories to the Convention for the purpose of preserving the peace, of using good offices for the restoration of peace, and, in the event that it proves impossible thus to restore the peace, to determine which party or parties to the dispute should be held responsible. It will be observed therefore that, as at present drafted, the event which brings these provisions into play is the breach or threatened breach of the Pact of Paris. His Majesty's Government regard such provisions as of very great importance. But so vital is the connexion of a feeling of security with the peace of the world that they would add to them yet further details. It is in their view important to extend the principle of consultation in the event of a breach or threat of breach of the Pact of Paris to the event of a breach or threat of breach of the Disarmament Convention itself. They would therefore suggest that three new articles—2 (*a*), 2 (*b*) and 2 (*c*)—should be inserted between the revised articles 2 and 3. The first of these—2 (*a*)—would be article 89 of the present Draft Convention, which declares that the loyal execution of the Convention is a matter of common interest to the High Contracting Parties. Article 2 (*b*) would declare: "The provisions for immediate consultation contained in article 1 will also be applicable in the event of the Permanent Dis-

armament Commission, to be set up in accordance with Part V, Section 1, of the present Convention, reporting the existence of facts which show that any High Contracting Party has failed to execute loyally the present Convention." Article 2 (c) would state: "It shall be the object of such consultation to exchange views as to the steps to be taken for the purpose of restoring the situation and of maintaining in operation the provisions of the present Convention." The insertion of these articles would, in the opinion of His Majesty's Government, emphasise the inescapable duty of all signatories of the Convention to keep in the closest touch with one another, and to do whatever is right and possible to prevent or remedy any violation of so important an international treaty.

A further contribution to the cause of peace and security, by lessening any tension or anxiety which exists between Germany and surrounding States, is provided by the willingness of the German Chancellor to conclude pacts of non-aggression with all Germany's neighbours. Such pacts should in no way weaken, but, on the contrary, should expressly reaffirm existing obligations to maintain peace under such instruments as the Covenant of the League of Nations, the Pact of Paris and the Treaties of Locarno, and His Majesty's Government cannot doubt that if such pacts were expressly entered into in connexion with the Convention (which, like the pacts themselves, His Majesty's Government, for reasons stated below, consider might be made in the first instance for a period of ten years) their practical value for the purpose of creating a sense of security will not be disputed.

His Majesty's Government consider that the suggestions here collected under the head of security constitute a sum total worthy of general acceptance. They have a right to expect that, if these provisions and pledges were solemnly entered into, they would not be lightly violated, and that any violation of them would be met in the most practical and effective way by immediately assembling Governments and States in support of international peace and agreement against the disturber and the violator.

10. *Equality of Rights.*—The Five-Power Declaration of the 11th December, 1932, put on record, in connexion with the problem of disarmament, the principle "of equality of rights in a system which would provide security for all nations" and declared that this principle should find itself embodied in a Disarmament Convention effecting a substantial reduction and limitation of armaments. From this Declaration His Majesty's Government have never withdrawn and they now reaffirm their unqualified adherence to it. The previous paragraph of this Memorandum attempts to define the essential ele-

ments of security without which the necessary conditions for an adequate Disarmament Convention would not be fulfilled. But His Majesty's Government do not hesitate to declare that the principle of equality of rights is no less essential in the matter of armaments than the principle of security—both must have their practical application if international agreement about armaments is to be reached. The proposals which follow, no less than the Draft Convention itself, are conceived in that spirit, and constitute a practical fulfilment of that principle.

11. *Disarmament.*—His Majesty's Government are glad to understand that Chancellor Hitler has declared that Germany voluntarily renounces any claim to possess "offensive" weapons and limits herself to normal "defensive" armaments required for the army with which she would be provided in the Convention. The German Chancellor, moreover, advances this proposition on the assumption that the heavily armed States are not prepared to abandon under the Convention any portion of their existing weapons. As already indicated in paragraph 7 of this Memorandum, His Majesty's Government are entirely unwilling to accept this last assumption, and must insist that the only agreement worthy of the name of a Disarmament Convention will be one which contains reduction as well as limitation of armaments. There is, moreover, a further reason why His Majesty's Government emphasise the fact that the German Chancellor's declaration renouncing offensive armaments and claiming only what is necessary for normal defence, is based upon the assumption that the heavily armed Powers are not prepared to reduce their own armaments in any degree. The measure of Germany's need will necessarily be reduced if this assumption proves incorrect. A positive contribution to disarmament by the heavily armed Powers will therefore help to bring the scale down all round, and should, as His Majesty's Government conceive, reduce the demands which Germany might otherwise be disposed to put forward.

12. The following proposals, in modification of the Draft Convention, are put forward on the assumption that the agreement would last for ten years. They have been framed after giving the fullest and most anxious consideration to suggestions and criticisms from all other quarters, and represent, in the judgment of His Majesty's Government, what might well be agreed in existing circumstances.

13. (a) *Effectives.*—While His Majesty's Government are still in favour, so far as they are concerned, of the figures given in the table they submitted at the end of article 13 of the Draft Convention, they are aware of the recent discussion with the German Government in regard to the proper number of average daily effectives which should

be allotted to Germany. To the figure of 200,000 on a basis of 8 months' service proposed in the Draft Convention, the German Government have suggested the alternative of 300,000 on a basis of 12 months' service. This is one of the outstanding points of difference emerging from the recent exchange of views through the diplomatic channel. Though the point is difficult and serious, His Majesty's Government do not think this divergence ought to raise any insuperable obstacle to an agreed compromise. In the Draft Convention they themselves proposed 200,000 as the figure for the average daily effectives stationed in the home country for France, Germany, Italy and Poland. It is not the figure of 200,000 which in their mind is the essential and unalterable element, but the principle of parity, fairly calculated and applied, in these effectives between the four countries. They are aware that difficult calculations are necessary to establish the right figures for the ten years which, as above suggested, would be the life of the Disarmament Convention, but His Majesty's Government are convinced that the fixing of the proper figure cannot be beyond the power of adjustment between the States principally concerned if the problem was made the subject of frank and conciliatory discussion between them. If the figure of 200,000 was found to be too low, an accommodation could surely be found between this figure (which His Majesty's Government believe to be preferred by the majority of the Powers concerned) and 300,000.

Agreement as to this figure will enable all European continental armies to be reduced to a standard type composed of short-term effectives as proposed in the Draft Convention. His Majesty's Government suggest that this process should be completed in, at most, four years. In article 16 of the Draft Convention, eight months was suggested as the maximum total period of service for these effectives, though, at the same time, it was recognised that in special cases the period might have to be twelve months. His Majesty's Government appreciate that this must necessarily be a matter for the continental Governments to determine, and they are ready to concur in the longer period if such is the general desire.

In regard to land armed forces stationed overseas, His Majesty's Government have no further reductions to propose in addition to those already inserted in the Draft Convention. These, it will be remembered, would entail a considerable reduction of French overseas forces.

A difficult problem has been raised in regard to the so-called "paramilitary training," *i.e.,* the military training outside the army of men of military age. His Majesty's Government suggest that such training outside the army should be prohibited, this prohibition being checked by a system of permanent and automatic supervision, in which the supervising organisation should be guided less by a strict definition of the term "military training" than by the military knowledge and experience of its experts. They are particularly glad to be informed that the German Government have freely promised to provide proof, through the medium of control, that the S.A. and the S.S. are not of a military character, and have added that similar proof will be furnished in respect of the Labour Corps. It is essential to a settlement that any doubts and suspicions in regard to these matters should be set and kept at rest.

14. (b) *Land War Material.*—Certain countries will require, for the increased numbers of their standardised armies, an increased number of such weapons as are at present possessed by their smaller long-service armies. His Majesty's Government accept this view. They would emphasise that, under the Convention, prohibition as to the possession of anti-aircraft guns would disappear. They would suggest that the maximum calibre of guns in permanent frontier and fortress defensive systems should be fixed by international agreement.

Of the types of land war material at present denied by treaty to certain Powers, His Majesty's Government consider two weapons in particular must be dealt with. His Majesty's Government proposed in their Draft Convention that the maximum limit for the weight of tanks should be 16 tons. They recognised, however, that this problem "evidently requires further international examination." They are most anxious, in the interests alike of disarmament and of the realisation of the equality of all countries, that progress should at once be made with the elimination of tanks above the 16-ton limit. They suggest, therefore, that tanks over 30 tons should be destroyed by the end of the first year, over 20 tons by the end of the third year and over 16 tons by the end of the fifth year. These practical steps should help towards the solution of the problem, but "further international examination," as contemplated by Article 21 of the Draft Convention, is obviously necessary. His Majesty's Government propose that his examination should be held by the Permanent Disarmament Commission, and should be completed not later than by the end of the third year. His Majesty's Government understand that the German Government maintain that tanks up to 6 tons are, in their view, necessary for the defence of their country. This view of the German Government was based on the supposition that other countries would make no reduction in respect of tanks at all, whereas His Majesty's Government now propose the reductions set forth above. None the less, His Majesty's Government are, for their part, willing to agree that the new German short-term service army, contemplated

DISARMAMENT AND SECURITY

by the Draft Convention, should be equipped with tanks up to 6 tons. His Majesty's Government would be willing to agree to a similar arrangement in respect of Austria, Hungary and Bulgaria.

As regards mobile land guns, it will be recalled that in the Draft Convention His Majesty's Government made the proposal to secure that the maximum limit of these guns for the future should be 115 mm. They would greatly regret any proposals which tend to increase the size of future construction beyond this calibre, but they are bound to face the fact that the German Government maintain the view that mobile land guns up to 155 mm. are necessary as part of the armament of the proposed new short-term service army. His Majesty's Government, though still preferring the more drastic proposals of their Draft Convention, are willing to acquiesce in this proposal as part of the Convention, if by so doing they can secure prompt and general agreement on all points. His Majesty's Government would be willing to agree to similar proposals in respect of Austria, Hungary and Bulgaria.

But there remains the question whether it is not possible, by means of the proposed Convention, to secure the reduction in the maximum calibre of mobile land guns possessed by any Power. His Majesty's Government propose that such guns over 350 mm. should be destroyed by the end of the first year, those over 220 mm. by the end of the fourth year and those over 155 mm. by the end of the seventh year.

15. (c) *Air Armaments.*—His Majesty's Government have repeatedly emphasised the great importance of agreement in regard to the limitation and reduction of air armaments which may, in the future, prove the most potent military weapons in the possession of mankind. Full reflection has convinced them of the justice of the proposals contained in articles 34–41 of their Draft Convention. Article 35 requires that the Permanent Disarmament Commission shall, immediately, devote itself to the working out of the best possible schemes providing for the complete abolition of military and naval aircraft, which must be dependent on the effective supervision of civil aviation to prevent its misuse for military purposes. His Majesty's Government are aware that the German Delegation at Geneva moved an amendment to this article, proposing the total abolition of military and naval aircraft without, however, making any specific provision for solving the problem of civil aviation. The appropriate occasion to discuss this proposal would be the immediate enquiry provided for in article 35. In their view it would be prejudicial to the prospects of the enquiry that any party not hitherto entitled to possess military aircraft should claim such possession pending the results of

the enquiry. At the same time they frankly recognise that Germany and other States not at present entitled to military aircraft could not be asked to postpone for long their claim. They suggest, therefore, that the maintenance of the *status quo* laid down in article 36 of their Draft Convention should be modified as follows: If the Permanent Disarmament Commission has not decided on abolition at the end of two years, all countries shall be entitled to possess military aircraft. Countries would reduce or increase by stages, as the case might be, in the following eight years so as to attain, by the end of the Convention, the figures in the table annexed to article 41, or some other figures to be agreed on. Germany would acquire parity with the principal air Powers by these stages, and corresponding provisions would be made for other Powers not at present entitled to possess military or naval aircraft.

16. It is, of course, understood that all construction or fresh acquisition of weapons of the kinds which are to be destroyed during the life of the Convention would be prohibited.

17. (d) *Naval Armaments.*—His Majesty's Government, for their part, still stand by the Naval Chapter of the Draft Convention. They appreciate, however, that the time which has passed since they put forward that Draft Convention last March has brought much closer the assembling of the Naval Conference of 1935. Should it be thought, in view of this consideration, that the situation prior to the 1935 Conference could appropriately be dealt with by some simpler arrangement than that contained in the Naval Chapter, His Majesty's Government would be prepared to make proposals to that end in due course. They suggest, however, that prompt agreement on other matters, and embodiment of that agreement in a world-wide convention, would be of great assistance to the naval discussions proposed in article 33 of the Draft Convention.

18. *Supervision.*—His Majesty's Government are well aware of the great importance attached by various Governments to the institution of a system of permanent and automatic supervision to control the observance of the Disarmament Convention. There is obviously a close connection between mutual agreement about levels of armament and a system of adequate international supervision. There are, however, many technical difficulties which arise in this connection and which must be practically met. His Majesty's Government affirm their willingness, if general agreement is reached on all other issues, to agree to the application of a system of permanent and automatic supervision, to come into force with the obligations of the Convention.

19. It will be seen that the adjustments which His Majesty's Gov-

ernment propose are based on a duration of ten years for the Convention. The Draft Convention suggested five years. Continued reflection, however, on the subject and constant discussion with other Governments have convinced His Majesty's Government that any stable system should be founded on a longer period. Only if a longer view is taken can substantial reductions of armaments, and the full realisation of all countries' equality of rights and durable security, be realised. The proposal of the German Chancellor, that undertakings not to resort to force between Germany and other European Powers should be of at least ten years' duration, fits in very closely with the proposal now made by His Majesty's Government that the Disarmament Convention itself should be of ten years' duration. They confidently hope that, if a Convention on the lines now proposed can be accepted, humanity will within the coming ten years acquire such a deep-rooted conviction of the contribution to peace which such a Convention can make that, when the Convention is due to expire, further progress can be achieved in the reduction of armaments. By the successful conclusion of a Convention on such lines, and in the atmosphere of firmer peace and increased mutual confidence which would accompany it, the way will be prepared for a closer and more hopeful approach to the political and economic problems which at present perplex and divide the nations of the world.

20. The object of His Majesty's Government in formulating these proposals and presenting them for consideration is not to describe the terms of an agreement which they themselves would most desire, without regard to the claims or needs of others, but to propound a basis of compromise on which it would appear, in present circumstances, that general agreement could and should now be reached. The proposals, therefore, must be considered as a whole and they are framed in the endeavour fairly to meet essential claims on all sides. The grave consequences which would follow the failure of the Disarmament Conference are realised by all and need no further emphasis. The policy of His Majesty's Government in the international sphere is directed, first and foremost, to contributing to the utmost of their power to the avoidance of these consequences by promoting general agreement. If agreement is secured and the return of Germany to Geneva and to the League of Nations brought about (and this ought to be an essential condition of agreement), the signature of the Convention would open a new prospect of international co-operation and lay a new foundation for international order.

STATEMENT by Viscount Monsell, British Delegate to the Conference for the Limitation of Naval Armament at London, January 15, 1936

Read by Vice Admiral Sir Ernle Chatfield in the First Committee of the Conference. Royal Institute of International Affairs, *Documents on International Affairs, 1936*, p. 608, citing *The Times* (London), January 16, 1936

THE UNITED KINGDOM delegation have examined with great care the proposals laid before the Committee by the Japanese delegation at its first meeting on December 10, 1935, and the subsequent explanations that have been furnished by the Japanese delegation at succeeding meetings of the First Committee. The United Kingdom delegation find themselves in complete agreement with the first part of the Japanese fundamental thesis, which asserts that:

To possess the measure of armaments necessary for national security is a right to which all nations are equally entitled.

2. Throughout the numerous discussions and conversations that have been devoted to the consideration of this thesis we have been actuated solely by the desire to ascertain whether the method of limitation proposed by the Japanese delegation, that is, the establishment of a common upper limit for the naval forces of the leading naval Powers, is in fact based on the above principle, and whether it may reasonably be expected to achieve naval security for the Powers concerned.

3. The presentation of the Japanese case by their principal delegate seems to show that the following points are integral features of the Japanese proposal:

First, that equality of fleets in the area of contact is essential;

Secondly, that in asserting the strengths of these fleets, all the forces of each navy that are capable of taking part in battle, irrespective of where they may be normally located, must be included in their entirety, leaving out of consideration only such small units as are intended for local patrol and defence of harbours;

Thirdly, that while it is recognized that there may be differences between countries as regards their degree of vulnerability, the primary cause of such differences is to be found in different levels of naval strengths, and that it is only after equalization of naval strengths has been postulated that the Japanese delegation are prepared to consider the remaining differences in vulnerability;

Fourthly, that the common upper limit must apply to the fleets of the U.S.A., the British Commonwealth of Nations, and Japan, and may be extended to the fleets of France and Italy should those Powers wish to participate;

DISARMAMENT AND SECURITY

Fifthly, that while the common upper limit should be fixed by the Conference, it should be set as low as possible and preferably below the level of the existing Japanese naval forces.

4. With regard to the first point, the United Kingdom delegation believe that naval strength in the area of contact cannot be measured solely in terms of numbers of fighting ships, but that factors such as remoteness of bases and sources of supply and the vulnerability of long communications must also be taken into consideration. Modern fleets are very dependent on supplies of fuel and stores and on dockyard facilities, and without the latter a damaged ship is likely to be a lost ship. The United Kingdom delegation maintain in fact that a fleet operating far from its own country must inevitably, even though equal in numbers, be far less effective for action than an opposing fleet operating from its home waters. As was stated by the United Kingdom delegation at the sixth meeting of the First Committee:

It is our opinion that a country defending itself in or near its own territory has an inherent advantage over an attacking force and therefore can defend itself with a lesser force than that brought against it.

If, therefore, the fleets in the area of contact are numerically equal, that fleet which is operating in its own home waters will, in effect, possess the advantage in spite of equality in numbers. The conclusion is strengthened by the introduction of aircraft, which add very greatly to the defensive power of a fleet in its own home waters. The position of a Power defending its territories and trade in oceans far from its home bases and factories is equally difficult and disadvantageous if attack on them by a Power with an equal total naval strength is possible. The Japanese delegation has stated to-day that it is generally recognized that there are certain types of warship that are *offensive* and others that are purely *defensive*.

There is, as far as we are aware, no such agreement. On the contrary, although the question is one that has often been discussed, it is a recognized fact that this division of warships into two such categories is wholly impracticable, and is indeed a problem that baffles solution.

5. With regard to the second point of the Japanese exposition, the United Kingdom delegation, while fully recognizing the mobility of naval forces, cannot subscribe to a strategical theory that naval needs are purely relative, and that, in consequence, a Power with greater total naval strength can, whatever the geographical position of its home territories, whatever the dispersion of its interests, or the distribution of the countries for which it is responsible, denude these territories of their essential defences and concentrate its entire fleet in the distant waters of a hypothetical opponent. The United Kingdom

delegation consider that such a theory is neither sound in reasoning nor supported by history. The events of the Russo-Japanese War, for instance, quoted by the Japanese delegate in support of his argument, seem to us to be capable of an opposite interpretation and to demonstrate conclusively the immense handicap imposed on a fleet operating at a great distance from its home bases.

6. A Power with world-wide responsibilities must, in the first place, devote naval forces to the protection of the sea communications between its various parts as well as the long line of communications of its principal naval forces. For this reason alone it is necessary for it to have forces in excess of those of a Power which is able to maintain its whole naval forces in or near its own home waters. Moreover, it must in all equity be admitted that a Power with distant possessions must be able in a time of emergency to despatch an adequate naval force for the defence of those possessions without denuding or seriously impairing its home defences. Apart from these purely strategical necessities, it is clear that political considerations will always prevent the concentration of the whole naval forces in one part of the world. It is not to be supposed that under any conditions the people of the home country would be prepared to permit the whole naval forces of their nation to be despatched to some distant part of the world, leaving them entirely exposed to the lightest attack. They must indeed always insist upon the retention of a substantial naval force in home waters.

7. With regard to the third point, the United Kingdom delegation, for the reasons just given, find themselves quite unable to agree to the proposition that the primary cause of differences in vulnerability is inequality in naval armaments. No substantial argument has been adduced in support of this proposition. Nor do they see any prospect that even such differences in vulnerability could be rectified by the somewhat indefinite procedure suggested by the Japanese delegation.

8. With regard to the fourth and fifth points, the United Kingdom delegation do not find that the proposal to apply a common upper limit either to the British Commonwealth, U.S.A., and Japan alone, or to all the Powers here assembled, is consistent with the defence requirements of the members of the British Commonwealth. In estimating these requirements we have to take into account responsibilities in European waters, in the Atlantic, Indian, and Pacific Oceans. These imply the necessity for a fleet of sufficient strength to be able to dispose simultaneously in more than one area forces adequate to meet all reasonable defensive needs. It has been recognized by most schools of thought that the naval requirements of a country are abso-

DISARMAMENT AND SECURITY

lute as well as relative, and this circumstance alone introduces an element of variation in the naval needs of each Power.

9. The United Kingdom delegation understand that the Japanese delegation claim that equal security amongst the principal Naval Powers would be ensured by the retention by them of equal naval armaments. On this point we find ourselves in complete accord with the principal delegate of the United States, who gave it as his view that:

It is impossible to maintain that equal armaments give equal security.

We ourselves believe that the Washington Treaty itself, with its provisions for maintaining the *status quo* as regards fortifications in those parts of the Pacific Ocean in which Japan is specially interested, offers the best guarantee for that security which is the inalienable right of all nations, and which we conceive to be in accordance with the Japanese principle of "non-menace" and "non-aggression."

10. The Japanese delegation have admitted that, if France and Italy desire to participate in any scheme for a common upper limit, the scope of such a scheme could not be confined to Japan, the United States, and the British Commonwealth of Nations. This being so, it is obvious that the plan would have to be universal in its operation, for by no process of reasoning could it be contended that the plan is suitable to those countries represented at this Conference but inapplicable to those not so represented.

We should therefore be faced with a strange situation in which every country, however slender its resources and however small its responsibilities, would not only have the right to build up its naval strength to equality with its neighbours, but would actually receive an indirect encouragement to do so. For supposing that Power A finds itself prevented by treaty from increasing its existing naval strength, Power B, possessed, let us say, of few responsibilities but much ambition, would be tempted to build up to the level of Power A. In its turn, Power C, concerned at the building of Power B, feels constrained similarly to increase its naval strength to an extent which would otherwise be unnecessary.

Thus the plan for a common upper limit, if adopted, might well furnish an incentive for a general increase in building among the Powers at present possessing smaller navies. It is true that the Japanese plan seems to check such a development by means of "adjustments" between the various Powers. But surely the word "adjustment" is simply a longer, if pleasanter, term for the word "ratio," which it is the purpose of the Japanese delegation to delete from our naval vocabulary. Apart from the Japanese delegation, the French and Italian delegations have demonstrated their strong objection to the reintroduction of the ratio system in any form.

11. The Government and people of this country yield nothing to Japan in their desire to see a general reduction in naval armaments. But such reduction must be achieved by a method which is fair to all and impairs the security of none. Judged by this standard they feel that the plan under discussion not only fails to provide a fair and practicable basis for a general agreement, but would create a position of special disadvantage for the members of the British Commonwealth of Nations. For the country, or countries, which have the greatest needs and which therefore must maintain a navy fully built up to the common upper level would be the only country or countries debarred by the proposal from expanding their naval forces in the event of some development in the world situation making such expansion necessary for their own security. This is a situation which such a country cannot feel to be fair or calculated to produce a sense of security.

12. In expressing their sincere regret that they have been unable to find in the Japanese plan that basis for a reduction and limitation which they so sincerely desire, the United Kingdom delegation nevertheless hope that the Japanese delegation will continue to seek, in cooperation with the other delegations here represented, some alternative method for achieving the end which we all have in view.

ADDRESS by Anthony Eden, Secretary of State for Foreign Affairs, in the House of Commons, March 2, 1937

Parliamentary Debates, House of Commons, Vol. 321, No. 66, p. 205; excerpt

THE POINT WHICH I wished to make was that almost throughout the world this rearmament has been welcomed. The reason is simple. It is because there is nobody abroad who does not realise that this country is not going to engage in a war contrary to our own undertakings under the Covenant. The right hon. Gentleman the Member for Hillsborough (Mr. A. V. Alexander) said the other day that he would not vote for armaments for what he called a national capitalist policy. I am not sure that I understand what that means. A national policy could be quite a good policy, if it is a policy of peace, and a capitalist policy could be a good one, provided, no doubt, that all the capitalists were cooperators. But if by that statement the right hon. Gentleman meant, as I think he did, that he was not prepared to vote for arms to allow this nation to indulge in a war of Imperial aggrandisement for selfish ends, we absolutely agree with it. Nobody has ever asked for arms for that purpose, and nobody in Europe or in the world imagines that this country would employ her arms in that way.

I conclude by saying that we must all regret the necessity for this arms programme, but it is our conviction, and I believe in their hearts the conviction of nearly every Member of the House, that with Europe and the world as they are to-day, for this country to have greater power will aid the forces of peace—on this condition, that we never forget that this rearmament is a means to an end and not an end in itself. There may be fresh opportunities to reach agreement on limitation under our programme and I agree that those opportunities must not be missed. It is even possible that by this route, which none of us wish to take, we shall reach the goal which we all desire to attain, and this at least I claim, that His Majesty's Government in the policy which they are now pursuing, in their statement of their commitments and in their rearmament, are making the best contribution in their power to the preservation of world peace.

RELATIONS WITH GERMANY AND OUTBREAK OF THE WAR

1934–1937

ADDRESS by Stanley Baldwin, Lord President of the Council, in the House of Commons, November 28, 1934

Royal Institute of International Affairs, *Documents on International Affairs, 1934,* p. 352, citing *Hansard,* November 28, 1934, coll. 872–84; excerpts

As I shall show, one of the foundations of the malaise today in Europe is not only fear, but ignorance outside of Germany and secrecy inside. It is only twelve months ago last January that the present régime in Germany came into power. I am not going to criticize that régime. Each country within its own confines must do what seems to itself good in the way of government, but the necessary results of a revolution, whether a great or a less great revolution, whether a more or less peaceful one or a bloody one, are common in this, that you get a dictator or somebody in the position of dictator in power, and it is notoriously more difficult to get contact with a dictator than it is with a democratic government. That is one thing. Secondly, it brings into power, as a rule, a number of new men who have not had experience of dealing for their country in foreign affairs, and whose personalities are not known to the statesmen of other countries. It takes time to get over that difficulty and to re-establish contacts which for many years have been working hopefully in Germany.

What has happened in Europe during last year and this year to illustrate what I have just said? It was only in January that the new régime came into power, and the next month witnessed a strengthening of the constitution of the Little Entente, the first part of Europe to give a response to the new order. Not much later we saw the great perturbation in Austria, largely owing to Nazi propaganda. In October Germany withdrew from the League of Nations and the Disarmament Conference, which had been going on up to that moment. I do not think that any one familiar with Geneva would deny that at that moment we had fairer hopes of accomplishing something substantial than had been the case for many years. Cynics may say that that may not amount to much, but it is a fact that there did look to be a chance of success on the limited armaments which had been suggested not long before by the Prime Minister when he was at Geneva. The team work among European nations was thus broken, and broken for the time to bits, and it was broken in relation to a nation whose presence, to my mind, was of the first importance to any discussions on either disarmament or the limitation of arms.

The harm that that has done in the Concert of Europe is beyond even what we could have imagined at the time. This year we have seen signs of nervousness in countries not generally affected—Switzerland and Scandinavia. We have seen in France credits voted and proposed for increasing the fortifications in the north, for reorganizing in some way the air force, and for expenditure on equipment and munitions. We have seen Italy on the other side of the Alps disturbed by the reaction of the Nazi propaganda of Austria, and we had a speech from Mussolini himself, which, if taken literally, was a very alarmist one. It was the speech in which he pointed out the imminence of war. We must not leave Russia out of account. When Poland made a non-aggression Pact with Germany which followed not long after the introduction of the new régime, Germany rejected the Russian suggestion for a guarantee—a German-Polish guarantee of the Baltic States. Russia is a country which enjoys by her natural position more security than is given to any of us in Europe, yet we can see that she, feeling perhaps some apprehensions in the Far East, at the same time felt nervous of what might be going on—I say might be going on—on her western frontier. Certain *rapprochements* were made by her to France, and there have been conversations, none of which, I guarantee, would have taken place had not Germany left the League of Nations, and had not her internal actions with regard to arms been shrouded from that date in mystery. It was that that led to the proposals for the mutual assistance Pact in Eastern Europe, to which we gave our warm support, and we made suggestions to bring it more into line with Locarno, and generally to make it acceptable among the proposed parties to it. . . .

I have tried to give the House as clearly as I could a statement of facts, and there are two or three words that I desire to say in conclusion. It is my conviction—and I speak with a sense of responsibility—that the state of apprehension that exists throughout Europe, not only as I expressed it, but apprehension over some unknown terror that may come, is an apprehension that has largely been caused by a want of knowledge of what is going on inside Germany. I believe it is right to say that to Germany herself, behind the cloud she has put up of her own will, that apprehension is not unknown. We all share it, just as we all share the industrial anxieties and troubles of Europe. What I feel is happening in Germany is this tragedy, that Germany, by cutting herself off from the comity of nations at Geneva, leaving our discussions, whether on disarmament or whatever they may be, is concentrating all her efforts on trying to recover her industrial position at home. She has vast numbers of men out of work. There is a great deal of poverty in that country. We have all suffered in Europe. We have all endeavoured to help our own country, but we know quite well that there is a point at which that ends. Some of us have been more successful than others and some less successful in dealing with the situation at home and locally.

Situated where Germany is, she is more dependent than most of us on friendship and on trading with her neighbors. When will the day come when she will recognize that? May the opportunity come before long when she will tear this veil of secrecy away and bring to light the things that are alarming Europe, and we may discuss them and see what, even now, may be done. If she does that, she may be able to resume conversations with her neighbors, all of whom are ready to help her in regard to trade and in trying to stabilize the broken exchanges of this old world; but, so long as she stays by herself, having no direct communication with other statesmen in Europe, so more and more these suspicions will grow and, may be, more and more her own troubles will grow. After all, there are periods in the lives of all countries when the greatest perils come to them through not having looked after their own people in time. I hope and believe that this Debate, inaugurated not perhaps with those ideas but with a genuine and rightful desire to get to know the truth in Europe, may have greater consequences and better consequences than any of us could have thought. It may be that an opportunity has been made for a first step once more to bring together the nations of Europe, and it may be that, having learned some wisdom by the deterioration and the degeneration of the conditions of Europe in the last few years, the voice of wisdom and the voice of peace may prevail.

COMMUNICATION from Anthony Eden, Secretary of State for Foreign Affairs, to the British Ambassador to Germany (Sir Eric Phipps), March 26, 1936

British Blue Book, Cmd. 5143, p. 80

S<small>IR</small>,

It may be of assistance to your Excellency if, in the light of the denunciation by the German Government of the Treaty of Locarno, the reoccupation by Germany of the demilitarised zone in the Rhineland and the proposals made by Herr Hitler on the 7th March for a new and comprehensive settlement, I review in a single despatch certain aspects of the diplomatic discussions which have taken place between the summer of 1934 and the 7th March last.

2. These discussions may be considered under five headings:—

    I.—Negotiations for the Eastern Pact and Franco-Soviet Treaty, June 1934 to May 1935.
    II.—Exchange of notes respecting validity of Franco-Soviet Treaty with Treaty of Locarno, May to August 1935.
    III.—Progress of negotiations for Eastern Pact, May to August 1935.
    IV.—Negotiations for an Air Pact and Air Limitation, February 1935 to March 1936.
    V.—Attempts at resumption of negotiations with Germany, November 1935 to March 1936.

I.—*Negotiations for the Eastern Pact and Franco-Soviet Treaty, June 1934 to May 1935*

3. The negotiations which fall for consideration under this heading opened with the French proposal for an Eastern Pact of Non-Aggression and Mutual Assistance. The proposal in its original form was, in the view of His Majesty's Government, inadequate, in that the guarantees of France and Russia were not given on equal terms to Russia and France on the one side, and to Germany on the other. This defect was remedied as a result of an Anglo-French conversation in London on the 11th and 12th July, 1934, and the proposal eventually emerged in the following form: Poland, Russia, Germany, Czechoslovakia, the Baltic States and Finland were to conclude a pact of mutual guarantee, non-aggression and consultation. In addition, Russia was to accept, as towards France and Germany, the obligations of a guarantor Power under the Treaty of Locarno; and France was to accept, as towards Russia and Germany, the commitments under the pact described above in so far as was consistent with her obligations under the Covenant of the League.

4. His Majesty's Government undertook to recommend these proposals, particularly to Poland and Germany; but neither Power approved them, and during the autumn of 1934 Germany made it clear that she preferred the maintenance of peace in Eastern Europe by means of bilateral agreements. When it became apparent that, as the result of the German and Polish attitude, the negotiations had come to a deadlock, a Franco-Russian protocol was signed at Geneva on the 5th December, 1934. Under this the French and Russian Governments agreed not to enter into any negotiations tending towards the

conclusion of any bilateral or multilateral agreements which might compromise the preparation and conclusion of the proposed Eastern Pact; and in the event of a breakdown of the negotiations, to "consult on the new assurances which it should seem to them desirable to give one another."

5. No further progress was made in this matter until the Anglo-French meeting in London on the 3rd February, 1935, when it was agreed that the general settlement to be negotiated between Germany and the other Powers "would make provision for the organisation of security in Europe, particularly by means of the conclusion of pacts, freely negotiated between the interested parties and ensuring mutual assistance in Eastern Europe."

6. During the British Ministers' visit to Berlin on the 25th and 26th March, Herr Hitler communicated to Sir J. Simon an outline of an Eastern Pact providing for bilateral non-aggression pacts supplemented by arbitration, conciliation and consultation arrangements, as well as by an undertaking not to support the aggressor. Herr Hitler explained that the German Government would not object to the inclusion of these bilateral pacts in a multilateral system, but they could not favour giving mutual assistance, or, indeed, being a party to a pact of mutual assistance. This point was further explained during the Stresa Conference when, as the result of a request by Sir E. Phipps, the German Government issued a communiqué stating that they were prepared to enter into an Eastern Pact on the lines indicated in Berlin, notwithstanding the fact that some of the other parties might conclude arrangements for mutual assistance, provided that such arrangements were embodied in separate documents. On learning of this statement the French Government decided that there was no further reason why they should not proceed with the negotiation of a mutual guarantee treaty between themselves and the Soviet Government.

7. A few days later, on the 26th April, His Majesty's Ambassador in Paris was informed that "our Locarno obligations give us a real and direct interest in the terms of the proposed Franco-Soviet Agreement," and that His Majesty's Government were anxious "that France should not subscribe to any agreement which might oblige her to go to war with Germany in circumstances not permitted by article 2 of the Treaty of Locarno." His Majesty's Ambassador was asked to see M. Laval and explain this point to him. He did this on the 27th April, and the reply was that "the French Government had made it an absolute condition that the Franco-Soviet Agreement must be subordinated not only to the working of the Covenant, but also to that of the Locarno Treaty."

RELATIONS WITH GERMANY

8. On the 2nd May the Franco-Soviet Pact was signed. This was followed on the 16th May by the signature of the Russo-Czechoslovak Treaty.

9. Herr Hitler, in his speech of the 21st May, 1935, stated that "we regard the conclusion of these mutual assistance pacts as a development which differs in no way from the formation of the former military alliances. We regret this particularly because an element of legal uncertainty has been introduced into the only clear and really valuable mutual security treaty in Europe, namely, the Locarno Pact. . . . The German Government would be grateful for an authentic interpretation of the effects and results of the Franco-Russian military alliance upon the treaty obligations of the various parties to the Locarno Pact. They also do not wish to allow any doubts to arise as to their opinion that these military alliances are incompatible with the spirit and the letter of the Covenant of the League." A later passage in his speech contained the statement that the German Government "will in particular observe and fulfil all obligations arising out of the Locarno Pact so long as the other parties to the treaty are also willing to adhere to it. The German Government regard the respecting of the demilitarised zone as an extremely difficult contribution for a sovereign State to make to the appeasement of Europe. They consider, however, that they must refer to the fact that the continued increase of troops on the other side is in no way to be regarded as supplementing these endeavours."

II.—Exchange of Notes respecting Validity of Franco-Soviet Treaty with Treaty of Locarno, May to August 1935

10. Herr Hitler's speech of the 21st May was followed by the German Government's memorandum on the alleged incompatibility between the Franco-Soviet Pact and the Treaty of Locarno, communicated to the French Government on the 25th May, 1935, and to His Majesty's Government on the 29th May. The substance of the German complaint was that, while under the treaty the French and Soviet Governments stated that "before undertaking any action which they intend to base upon article 16 of the Covenant, they will address themselves, first of all, to the Council of the League of Nations; they are none the less decided to fulfil the obligations of assistance agreed upon between themselves if for some reason or other the Council of the League does not produce a recommendation or if it does not reach a unanimous decision. . . . The German Government considers that military action undertaken in such conditions would be outside the limits of article 16 of the Covenant and would consequently con-

stitute a flagrant violation of the Treaty of Locarno." The French memorandum rebutting the German contention was communicated to the German Government on the 25th June; and on the 5th July, 1935, Sir S. Hoare handed to the German Ambassador a note in which it was stated that "His Majesty's Government are satisfied that there is nothing in the Franco-Soviet Treaty which either conflicts with the Locarno Treaty or modifies its operation in any way. . . . I hope that, after examining the views thus set forth in the French note of the 25th June and in this communication, the German Government will recognise that the rights and duties of the signatories of the Treaty of Locarno, including those of Germany, have in no way been prejudiced or modified by the conclusion of the Franco-Soviet Treaty." On the 15th July and the 19th July the Italian and Belgian representatives respectively stated that they agreed with the French memorandum. The final development in these negotiations was an oral communication made by the German Ambassador to Sir S. Hoare on the 1st August. This communication states that "the German Government welcome the declarations of the four Governments. They take notice with satisfaction of the declaration of the two guaranteeing Powers that the rights and duties of these Powers cannot be prejudiced or altered by the act of another signatory of the treaty." They "cannot agree with the juridical point of view exposed in the French memorandum and endorsed by the other three Governments. They do not think, however, that any useful purpose would be served by the continuation of an exchange of juridical memoranda, and hold the opinion that there will be sufficient opportunity for the necessary discussions within the framework of the other pending negotiations."

III.—*Progress of Negotiations for Eastern Pact, May to August* 1935

11. The exchange of notes during the summer of 1935 respecting the conformity of the Franco-Soviet Treaty with the Treaty of Locarno did not suspend the negotiations for an Eastern Pact or for an Air Pact and Air Limitation Agreement which had been under discussion since February 1935. On the 3rd June the French Government informed the German Government that it appreciated the value of the communication about the Eastern Pact made by Baron von Neurath to Sir E. Phipps during the Stresa Conference (see paragraph 6 above). The French memorandum stated that "these suggestions seemed likely to be useful as a basis of negotiations, and that the French Government would be happy to know how the discussions could be continued." On a number of occasions, particularly on the 23rd July, the 29th July, the 1st August and the 5th August, His Maj-

esty's Government strongly urged the German Government to continue the negotiation. The only result of these efforts was a statement made by Herr von Bülow to His Majesty's Chargé d'Affaires in Berlin on the 22nd August, which was repeated at the Foreign Office by Prince Bismarck on the following day, that the German Government would not be in a position to make any communication on this matter until after the holidays, *i.e.*, at the beginning of October. Subsequently, on the 18th September, His Majesty's Ambassador at Berlin reported that "Baron von Neurath confirmed that the references to Russia at Nuremberg were merely the reply to anti-German attacks at the Comintern Congress in Moscow. In view of this and of the general situation, he does not propose to reply to our enquiries about an Eastern Pact until quieter times come."

IV.—*Negotiations for an Air Pact and Air Limitation, February 1935 to March 1936*

12. The first proposal for an Air Pact was made at the Anglo-French meeting in London on the 3rd February, 1935. The declaration agreed at that meeting was communicated to the German Government; and on the 14th February they proposed that British Ministers should visit Berlin to discuss particularly the Air Pact. His Majesty's Government pointed out that any such discussion must review all the matters mentioned in the London Declaration. On this understanding the visit of British Ministers to Berlin took place on the 25th and 26th March, 1935; and Herr Hitler expressed the willingness, and, indeed, eagerness, of Germany to conclude an Air Pact at once without burdening the proposal with difficult and complicated conditions such as limitation of air forces and the other parts of the London Declaration. In the Chancellor's view there ought to be first an Air Pact and the fixation of parity in the air between the signatories to the pact. Sir John Simon reminded him that His Majesty's Government thought of the Air Pact not as being an agreement that could be reached quite apart from other agreements, but as forming a portion of that more general settlement which was the object of the Anglo-French Declaration. In the Berlin conversations Herr Hitler also stated that his object was parity with the French air force in France and North Africa provided that developments in Russia did not necessitate a raising of this figure.

13. At Stresa the British, French and Italian Governments "agreed to continue actively the study of the Air Pact . . . and of any bilateral agreements which might accompany it." The question of the Air Pact was taken up with the German Government once more on the

10th May, when Sir John Simon told the German Ambassador that he would be glad to learn more definitely the views of the German Government. Herr von Hoesch, in reply, communicated to the Foreign Office on the 29th May, 1935, a German draft of the Air Pact. The German Government said that this draft might be communicated to the other Locarno Powers; and subsequently, on the 9th July, Herr von Hoesch suggested that there should be circulated in one document to all five Powers the German and British and French drafts which he understood existed. On the 23rd July the German Embassy was informed orally that it was thought that it would only complicate the situation to circulate drafts at that stage. It would be better to agree first on general principles and then try to secure a common draft. Such preliminary drafts as had been prepared were therefore never circulated or discussed, and it is felt that no useful purpose would be served by making them public now.

14. The months of June and July 1935 were spent in an attempt to secure the consent of the French Government to the opening of diplomatic negotiations between the five Powers, the purpose of which would be to agree upon the general principles on which an Air Pact should be based. Once that agreement had been reached, the jurists could meet and prepare a common draft. On the 29th July, 1935, the French Government agreed to the opening of these discussions, on the understanding that His Majesty's Government would secure the agreement of the German Government to the principle of the accompaniment of the Air Pact by such arrangements between any two parties as those two parties might judge necessary to render it effective; and provided that the question of the final conclusion of the Air Pact and of an air limitation agreement, independently of the other matters mentioned in the London Declaration, would be reserved.

15. Sir S. Hoare saw the German Ambassador on the 1st August and explained to him the French Government's position. He told him that His Majesty's Government would not contemplate bilateral arrangements save upon the understanding that they were based upon the spirit and principles of Locarno, and that they would not allow such arrangements to interfere with the Locarno equilibrium or to be used to the disadvantage of the Locarno Powers. Subsequently, on the 13th December, the nature of the arrangements was explained again to the Chancellor himself and Baron von Neurath by your Excellency.

16. On the 23rd August, 1935, the Foreign Office asked the German Embassy when the German Government's reply might be ex-

pected to Sir S. Hoare's communication of the 1st August. No reply could ever be obtained to this enquiry. On the 21st November the French Ambassador in Berlin saw Herr Hitler and emphasised the importance which the French Government attached to the continuance of the negotiations for the Air Pact. He was told that progress was impossible during the continuance of the Italo-Abyssinian dispute. On the 13th December your Excellency urged the Chancellor to continue the negotiations for the Air Pact. The Chancellor referred to the difficulties created by the Franco-Russian Treaty; and when in January Baron von Neurath admitted that that treaty did not affect the Air Pact itself, but only air limitation, he informed your Excellency that to the negotiation of the Air Pact the Italo-Abyssinian difficulty was the obstacle. My disappointment at the check to the Air Pact negotiations was expressed to the Chancellor by your Excellency, through Baron von Neurath, on the 14th January, 1936; and in interviews with the German Ambassador on the 27th February, and again on the 6th March, I pressed yet again for the resumption of negotiations.

V.—*Attempts at Resumption of Negotiations with Germany, November 1935 to March 1936*

17. Herr Hitler's speech of the 21st May, 1935, had contained references to the importance which he attached to good German relations with Great Britain and France. "The German Government," he said, "sincerely intend to do everything to bring about and maintain such relations with the British people and State as will for ever prevent a repetition of the only war which there has as yet been between the two nations." As regards France, he said "We are prepared to do everything on our part to arrive at a true peace and a real friendship with the French nation." Herr von Ribbentrop, in the course of the naval negotiations in the summer of 1935, had gone even further, and stated that the corner-stone of the political conceptions of the German Chancellor was "that ultimately, only an adjustment of the vital interests of our two countries, and a common realistic attitude towards the great European problems can produce a solution of these problems, and in particular a Franco-German settlement which the German people desires and without which Europe will not come to rest."

18. When the question of the Franco-Soviet Pact was about to come up in the French Chambers, M. Laval informed the German Ambassador in Paris on the 15th November that the French Govern-

ment would welcome a decision by the German Government to resume conversations for collective security on the basis of the London Declaration of February 1935.

19. Your Excellency had an interview with Herr Hitler on the 13th December. After explaining that His Majesty's Government would be glad to learn the Chancellor's views on the possibility of further conversations respecting the London Declaration of the 3rd February, and particularly the question of the Air Pact and air limitation, you pointed out the importance which the French Government attached to the accompaniment of the Air Pact by bilateral arrangements for its execution. You added that the arrangements which we contemplated would be based upon the spirit and principles of Locarno and would not interfere with the Locarno equilibrium. Here Hitler expressed strong objection to the bilateral arrangements, though later, on the 17th January, you were informed by Baron von Neurath that bilateral pacts, if discussed at all, must be discussed by all five Powers. Herr Hitler further stated that no air limitation agreement which did not allow him to take into account Russia's enormous strength in the air was possible. He made objection to the Franco-Soviet Treaty; and though from a subsequent interview on the 14th January, 1936, between your Excellency and Baron von Neurath it was clear that the Chancellor did not object in principle to the conclusion of an Air Pact between the Locarno Powers, it became evident from subsequent interviews between your Excellency and Baron von Neurath that the German Government considered the moment inopportune for the discussion of an Air Pact, owing to the strained relations between Italy and Great Britain.

20. On the 8th January, 1936, a further approach was made to the German Government. I instructed you to let the Chancellor know "that I share the views which he has so often expressed regarding the importance of a close and confident understanding and collaboration between Great Britain, France and Germany, and that I hope that our two Governments will keep this objective closely in view notwithstanding the difficulties which Herr Hitler, to my regret, at present sees in the way of any immediate progress along the lines which our two Governments discussed in the early part of last year." Your Excellency made this communication through Baron von Neurath on the 14th January.

21. On the 27th January Baron von Neurath saw me in London, where he had come to attend the Royal Funeral. He stated on this occasion that the German Government fully intended to respect the Treaty of Locarno. All that they asked was that others should observe it in the spirit as well as the letter. The opportunity was taken by me

to tell Baron von Neurath that I still hoped that an Air Pact and an agreement for air limitation might be negotiated.

22. On the 19th February Lord Cranborne asked the German Chargé d'Affaires to come to the Foreign Office, and emphasised to him my view that close collaboration between the three Western Powers was essential to European peace. So far as His Majesty's Government were concerned, it had been made abundantly clear on many occasions that the Franco-Soviet Pact did not affect Great Britain in any way, and that it did not affect the Treaty of Locarno. To this treaty His Majesty's Government still fully subscribed. Lord Cranborne assured the German Chargé d'Affaires that I was most anxious in every way to collaborate both with the French and the German Governments for the preservation of general peace. He gave to Prince Bismarck in this connexion an extract from the message sent through your Excellency to Herr Hitler on the 8th January, already quoted in paragraph 20. Prince Bismarck said that he thought it would be important that this statement should be reaffirmed and he would communicate it to his Government.

23. On the 27th February I saw the German Ambassador, who referred to Prince Bismarck's interview with Lord Cranborne on the 19th February. The Ambassador asked me whether I saw any prospect of making any progress in the improvement of relations between the Western European Powers. I replied that I was particularly anxious to make progress with an Air Pact and air limitation, and had said so more than once. It remained to be considered whether there was any means of doing this in present conditions. The Ambassador, in reply, pointed out the complication created by the Italo-Abyssinian war. How could Italy enter an air limitation agreement at this moment? I replied that these were just the problems which we had to consider. It would not be satisfactory if we merely registered the difficulties and made no attempt to overcome them. I should be seeing M. Flandin in Geneva next week, and no doubt the relations of the western European Powers would form one of the subjects of conversation between us. I would take an early opportunity of giving the Ambassador an account of what had passed between us when I returned to London.

24. On the 28th February the *Paris-Midi* published an interview given to M. Bertrand de Jouvenel by the German Chancellor. In this interview Herr Hitler emphasised the importance which he attached to Franco-German reconciliation, whilst drawing attention to the manner in which the ratification of the Franco-Soviet Treaty was likely to complicate the situation. He stated that the people of France would do well to reflect seriously on his efforts to secure an

understanding. No German leader had ever made such overtures.

25. On the 2nd March the French Ambassador in Berlin saw Herr Hitler and enquired whether the interview which he had given to the *Paris-Midi* implied that he had definite proposals to make to the French Government. If so, the latter would be very glad to know what they were and would carefully consider them. The Chancellor is understood to have asked for time in which to consider the French Ambassador's observations.

26. On the 6th March I myself again sent for the German Ambassador in London, and the important conversation took place which is summarised in my despatch to your Excellency of the 6th March (see No. 57 above). As will be seen, I emphasised to the Ambassador the importance which I attached to an improvement in the relations of the three great Western Powers. It was as a concrete means of improving these relations that I proposed to him the immediate opening of serious discussions on the question of the Air Pact.

27. On the following day the German Ambassador called at the Foreign Office and informed me of the German Government's decision to denounce the Treaty of Locarno and to reoccupy the demilitarised zone.

ADDRESS by Anthony Eden, Secretary of State for Foreign Affairs, in the House of Commons, January 19, 1937

Parliamentary Debates, House of Commons, Vol. 319, No. 36, p. 93; excerpt

AND so I must close this review with a few words about Germany. The future of Germany and the part she is to play in Europe is to-day the main preoccupation of all Europe. Here is a great nation of 65,000,000 people in the very centre of our Continent which has exalted race and nationalism into a creed which is practised with the same fervour as it is preached. All the world is asking at this present time whither these doctrines are to lead Germany, whither they are to lead all of us? Are they to restore to her the position of a great Power in the centre of Europe enjoying the respect of other Powers, both great and small, and using the manifold gifts of her people to restore confidence and prosperity to a world heartily sick of feuds and antagonisms and ardently desiring a return to normal conditions of work and partnership? Or are they to lead her to a sharpening of international antagonisms and to a policy of even greater economic isolation? Europe is to-day seriously asking herself what are the answers to these questions, for Europe cannot go on drifting to a more and more uncertain future. She cannot be torn between acute national rivalries and violently opposed idealogies, and hope to survive, without bearing scars which will last for a generation. Germany has it in her power to influence a choice which will decide not only her fate, but that of Europe. If she chooses co-operation with other nations, full and equal co-operation, there is nobody in this country who will not assist whole-heartedly to remove misunderstandings and to make the way smooth for peace and prosperity.

But it is idle to imagine that we can cure the evils from which we are suffering by mere palliatives; no mere local remedies will suffice. There must be no reserves or evasions on the part of any nation—whatever its ideology, and whatever form of government it prefers itself—in its co-operation with others, and abandoning any form of interference in the affairs of others. We cannot cure the world by pacts or treaties. We cannot cure it by political creeds no matter what they be. We cannot cure it by speeches, however lofty and peace-breathing they may be. There must be the will to co-operate, which is unmistakable. That will can manifest itself in certain very definite ways—by abandoning the doctrine of national exclusiveness and accepting every European State as a potential partner in a general settlement, by bringing armaments down to a level sufficient for the essential needs of defence and no more, and by accepting such international machinery for the settlement of disputes as will make the League of Nations a benefit to all and a servitude to none.

These things must be stated clearly at this time at the beginning of a new year. We ourselves have no greater desire than to co-operate fully with others, and herein we make no exceptions. We shall respond fully to the same desire, wherever it manifests itself, and we shall work for the greatest possible solidarity in the belief that, in their hearts, that is what the vast majority of people in every nation ardently desire.

The Czechoslovakian Crisis, 1938

LETTER from Neville Chamberlain, Prime Minister, to the Chancellor of Germany (Adolf Hitler), September 23, 1938

British White Paper, Cmd. 5847, p. 10

My Dear Reichskanzler,

I think it may clarify the situation and accelerate our conversation if I send you this note before we meet this morning.

I am ready to put to the Czech Government your proposal as to the areas, so that they may examine the suggested provisional boundary. So far as I can see, there is no need to hold a plebiscite for the bulk of the areas, i.e., for those areas which (according to statistics upon which both sides seem to agree) are predominantly Sudeten German areas. I have no doubt, however, that the Czech Government would be willing to accept your proposal for a plebiscite to determine how far, if at all, the proposed new frontier need be adjusted.

The difficulty I see about the proposal you put to me yesterday afternoon arises from the suggestion that the areas should in the immediate future be occupied by German troops. I recognise the difficulty of conducting a lengthy investigation under existing conditions and doubtless the plan you propose would, if it were acceptable, provide an immediate easing of the tension. But I do not think you have realised the impossibility of my agreeing to put forward any plan unless I have reason to suppose that it will be considered by public opinion in my country, in France and, indeed, in the world generally, as carrying out the principles already agreed upon in an orderly fashion and free from the threat of force. I am sure that an attempt to occupy forthwith by German troops areas which will become part of the Reich at once in principle, and very shortly afterwards by formal delimitation, would be condemned as an unnecessary display of force.

Even if I felt it right to put this proposal to the Czech Government, I am convinced that they would not regard it as being in the spirit of the arrangement which we and the French Government urged them to accept and which they have accepted. In the event of German troops moving into the areas as you propose, there is no doubt that the Czech Government would have no option but to order their forces to resist, and this would mean the destruction of the basis upon which you and I a week ago agreed to work together, namely, an orderly settlement of this question rather than a settlement by the use of force.

It being agreed in principle that the Sudeten German areas are to join the Reich, the immediate question before us is how to maintain law and order pending the final settlement of the arrangements for the transfer. There must surely be alternatives to your proposal which would not be open to the objections I have pointed out. For instance, I could ask the Czech Government whether they think there could be an arrangement under which the maintenance of law and order in certain agreed Sudeten German areas would be entrusted to the Sudeten Germans themselves—by the creation of a suitable force, or by the use of forces already in existence, possibly acting under the supervision of neutral observers.

As you know, I did last night, in accordance with my understanding with you, urge the Czech Government to do all in their power to maintain order in the meantime.

The Czech Government cannot, of course, withdraw their forces, nor can they be expected to withdraw the State Police so long as they are faced with the prospect of forcible invasion; but I should be ready at once to ascertain their views on the alternative suggestion I have made and, if the plan proved acceptable, I would urge them to withdraw their forces and the State Police from the areas where the Sudeten Germans are in a position to maintain order.

The further steps that need be taken to complete the transfer could be worked out quite rapidly.

SECOND LETTER from Neville Chamberlain, Prime Minister, to the Chancellor of Germany (Adolf Hitler), September 23, 1938

British White Paper, Cmd. 5847, p. 14

My Dear Reichskanzler,

I have received your Excellency's communication in reply to my letter of this morning and have taken note of its contents.

In my capacity as intermediary, it is evidently now my duty—since your Excellency maintains entirely the position you took last night—to put your proposals before the Czechoslovak Government.

Accordingly, I request your Excellency to be good enough to let me have a memorandum which sets out these proposals, together with a map showing the areas proposed to be transferred, subject to the result of the proposed plebiscite.

On receiving this memorandum, I will at once forward it to Prague and request the reply of the Czechoslovak Government at the earliest possible moment.

In the meantime, until I can receive their reply, I should be glad to have your Excellency's assurance that you will continue to abide by the understanding, which we reached at our meeting on the 14th September and again last night, that no action should be taken, particularly in the Sudeten territory, by the forces of the Reich to prejudice any further mediation which may be found possible.

Since the acceptance or refusal of your Excellency's proposal is now a matter for the Czechoslovak Government to decide, I do not see that I can perform any further service here, whilst, on the other hand, it has become necessary that I should at once report the present situation to my colleagues and to the French Government. I propose, therefore, to return to England.

LETTER from Neville Chamberlain, Prime Minister, to the Chancellor of Germany (Adolf Hitler), September 26, 1938

British White Paper, Cmd. 5847, p. 19

My Dear Reichskanzler,

In my capacity as intermediary I have transmitted to the Czechoslovakian Government the memorandum which your Excellency gave me on the occasion of our last conversation.

The Czechoslovakian Government now inform me that, while they adhere to their acceptance of the proposals for the transfer of the Sudeten-German areas on the lines discussed by my Government and the French Government and explained by me to you on Thursday last, they regard as wholly unacceptable the proposal in your memorandum for the immediate evacuation of the areas and their immediate occupation by German troops, these processes to take place before the terms of cession have been negotiated or even discussed.

Your Excellency will remember that in my letter to you of Friday last I said that an attempt to occupy forthwith by German troops areas which will become part of the Reich at once in principle and very shortly afterwards by formal delimitation, would be condemned as an unnecessary display of force, and that, in my opinion, if German troops moved into the areas that you had proposed, I felt sure that the Czechoslovakian Government would resist and that this would mean the destruction of the basis upon which you and I a week ago agreed to work together, namely, an orderly settlement of this question rather than a settlement by the use of force. I referred also to the effect likely to be produced upon public opinion in my country, in France and, indeed, in the world generally.

The development of opinion since my return confirms me in the views I expressed to you in my letter and in our subsequent conversation.

In communicating with me about your proposals, the Government of Czechoslovakia point out that they go far beyond what was agreed to in the so-called Anglo-French plan. Czechoslovakia would be deprived of every safeguard for her national existence. She would have to yield up large proportions of her carefully prepared defences and admit the German armies deep into her country before it had been organised on the new basis or any preparations had been made for its defence. Her national and economic independence would automatically disappear with the acceptance of the German plan. The whole process of moving the population is to be reduced to panic flight.

I learn that the German Ambassador in Paris has issued a communiqué which begins by stating that as a result of our conversations at Godesberg your Excellency and I are in complete agreement as to the imperative necessity to maintain the peace of Europe. In this spirit I address my present communication to you.

In the first place, I would remind your Excellency that as the Czechoslovakian Government adhere to their acceptance of the proposals for the transfer of the Sudeten-German areas there can be no question of Germany "finding it impossible to have the clear rights of Germans in Czechoslovakia accepted by way of negotiation." I am quoting the words at the end of your Excellency's letter to me of Friday last.

On the contrary, a settlement by negotiation remains possible and, with a clear recollection of the conversations which you and I have had and with an equally clear appreciation of the consequences which must follow the abandonment of negotiation and the substitution of force, I ask your Excellency to agree that representatives of Germany shall meet representatives of the Czechoslovakian Government to discuss immediately the situation by which we are confronted with a view to settling by agreement the way in which the territory is to be handed over. I am convinced that these discussions can be completed in a very short time, and if you and the Czechoslovakian Government desire it, I am willing to arrange for the representation of the British Government at the discussions.

In our conversation, as in the official communiqué issued in Germany, you said that the only differences between us lay in the method of carrying out an agreed principle. If this is so, then surely the tragic consequences of a conflict ought not to be incurred over a difference in method.

A conference such as I suggest would give confidence that the cession of territory would be carried into effect, but that it would be done in an orderly manner with suitable safeguards.

Convinced that your passionate wish to see the Sudeten-German question promptly and satisfactorily settled can be fulfilled without incurring the human misery and suffering that would inevitably follow on a conflict I most earnestly urge you to accept my proposal.

MESSAGE from Neville Chamberlain, Prime Minister, to the Secretary of State of the United States (Cordell Hull), September 26, 1938, in Reply to the Appeal for Peace by President Franklin D. Roosevelt on the Same Day

Department of State, *Press Releases*, October 1, 1938, p. 220

His Majesty's Government hail with gratitude the weighty message that the President of the United States has addressed to them and to certain other Governments in this critical time. It is indeed essential to remember what is at stake and to weigh the issues with all gravity before embarking on a course from which there may be no retreat.

His Majesty's Government have done and are doing their very utmost to secure a peaceful solution of the present difficulties and they will relax no effort so long as there remains any prospect of achieving that object. The Prime Minister is even today making a further earnest appeal for settlement by negotiation in which His Majesty's Government would be ready to lend their good offices. The President's words can but encourage all those who sincerely desire to cooperate in this endeavour. His Majesty's Government for their part respond to the President's appeal in all sincerity and without reserve and they most earnestly hope that the other Governments to which it is addressed will do likewise.

ADDRESS of Neville Chamberlain, Prime Minister, in the House of Commons, September 28, 1938

International Conciliation, November, 1938, p. 446, citing *The New York Times*, September 29, 1938

SHORTLY BEFORE the House adjourned at the end of July, some questions were addressed to me as to the possibility of summoning the House before the time arranged and during the recess in certain eventualities.

Those eventualities referred to possible developments in Spain, but the matter which has brought us together today was one which at that time was already threatening but which we all hoped would find a peaceful solution before we met again.

Unhappily these hopes have not been fulfilled.

Today we are faced with a situation which has had no parallel since 1914. To find the origins of the present controversy it would be necessary to go back to the constitution of the State of Czechoslovakia with all its heterogeneous population. No doubt at the time when it was constituted it seemed to those then responsible that it was the best arrangement that could be made in the light of conditions as they then supposed them to exist.

One cannot help reflecting that if Article XIX of the (League of Nations) Covenant providing for revision of treaties by agreement had been put into operation, as was contemplated by friends of the Covenant, instead of waiting until passions became so exasperated that revision by agreement became impossible, we should have avoided the crisis.

Therefore, for that omission all members of the League must bear their responsibility. I am not here to apportion blame among them. The position we had to face in July was a deadlock. Negotiations had been going on between the Czechoslovak Government and the Sudeten Germans and there were fears that if the deadlock were not speedily broken the German Government might presently interfere.

Before his Majesty's Government there were three alternative courses we might have adopted:

Either we could have threatened to go to war with Germany if she attacked Czechoslovakia; or we could have stood aside and allowed matters to take their course; or, finally, we could attempt to find a peaceful settlement by way of mediation.

The first of these courses was rejected. We had no treaty liabilities to Czechoslovakia. We had always refused to accept any such obligations and indeed this country, which does not readily resort to war, would not have followed us if we had tried to lead it into war to prevent a minority from obtaining autonomy or even from choosing to pass under some other government.

The second alternative was also repugnant. However far this territory may be from Europe, a spark there might give rise to a general conflagration. We felt it our duty to do everything in our power to help the contending parties come to an agreement.

We addressed ourselves to the third course—the task of mediation. We felt that the object was good enough to justify the risk.

And when Lord Runciman had expressed his willingness to undertake our mission, we were happy to think we had secured a mediator of long experience, of well-known qualities of firmness, tact, and sympathy and one that gave us the best hopes of success. That Lord Runciman did not succeed is no fault of his.

We, and indeed all Europe, must ever be grateful to him and his staff for their long and exhausting efforts on the behalf of peace, in course of which they gained the esteem and confidence of both sides.

On the twenty-first of September, Lord Runciman addressed to me a letter reporting the result of his mission. That letter is printed in the White Paper, but I may conveniently mention some of the salient points of the story.

On the seventh of June, the Sudeten German party had put forward certain proposals which embodied eight points of Herr Henlein's speech at Karlsbad on the twenty-fourth of April. The Czechoslovakian Government, on their side, had embodied their proposals in their draft of a nationality statute, language bill, and administrative reform bill. At the middle of August, it had become clear to Lord Runciman that the gap between these two proposals was too wide to permit of negotiations between the parties on that basis.

In his capacity as mediator he was successful in preventing the Sudeten German party from closing the door to further negotiations, and he was largely instrumental in inducing Dr. Beneš, President of Czechoslovakia, to accept new proposals on the twenty-first of August, which appear to have been regarded by Sudeten party leaders as a suitable basis for the continuance of negotiations. Prospects for the negotiations being carried to a successful conclusion were, however, handicapped by a recurrence of incidents in Czechoslovakia involving casualties both on the Czech and Sudeten German sides.

On the first or second of September Herr Henlein went to Berchtesgaden to consult Herr Hitler on the situation. He was the bearer of a message from Lord Runciman to Herr Hitler expressing the hope that he would give his approval and support to the continuance of negotiations going on in Prague. No direct reply was communicated to Lord Runciman by Herr Henlein, but the latter returned convinced of Herr Hitler's desire for a peaceful solution.

It was after he returned that the Sudeten Germans' leaders insisted on the complete satisfaction of the eight Karlsbad points in any solution that might be reached.

The House will see that during August Lord Runciman's efforts had been directed with a considerable degree of success toward bringing the Sudetens and Czechoslovakians closer together. In the meantime, however, developments in Germany itself had been causing considerable anxiety to his Majesty's Government.

On July 28, the Secretary for Foreign Affairs had written a personal letter to the German Minister for Foreign Affairs, Herr von Ribbentrop, expressing his regret on the latter's statement to Sir Nevile Henderson, our Ambassador in Berlin, that the German Government must reserve its attitude towards Lord Runciman's mission, regarding the matter as one of purely British concern.

The Secretary of State had expressed the hope the German Government would collaborate with his Majesty's Government in facilitating a peaceful solution of the Sudeten question and so prepare the way to establishing relations on a basis of mutual confidence and cooperation.

Early in August we received reports of military preparations in Germany on an extensive scale. They included the calling up of reserves, service for the second year of recruits beyond the beginning of October when they would ordinarily have been released, the conscription of labor for the completion of German fortifications on her western frontiers, and measures which empowered the military authorities to conscript civilian goods and services.

These measures, which involved a widespread dislocation of civilian life, could not fail to be regarded abroad as equivalent to partial mobilization and they suggested the German Government was determined to find a settlement of the Sudeten question by autumn.

In these circumstances, his Majesty's Ambassador to Berlin was instructed by the middle of August to point out to the German Government that these abnormal measures could not fail to be interpreted abroad as a threatening gesture towards Czechoslovakia. They must therefore increase the feeling of tension throughout Europe and they might compel the Czechoslovak Government to take precautionary measures on their side.

An almost certain consequence would be to destroy all chance of successful mediation by Lord Runciman's mission, perhaps endanger the peace of every one of the Great Powers of Europe.

This, the Ambassador said, might also destroy the prospects for the resumption of the Anglo-German conversations. In these circumstances it was hoped that the German Government might be able to modify their military measures in order to avoid these dangers.

To these representations, Herr von Ribbentrop replied in a letter in which he refused to discuss military measures and referred to the expressed opinion that the British efforts in Prague had only served to increase Czech intransigence.

In the face of this attitude, his Majesty's Government, through the Chancellor of the Exchequer, who happened to be speaking at Lanark August 22, drew attention again to some words I had used March 24 on this subject when he declared there was nothing he had to add or vary in the statement which I had made.

(Mr. Chamberlain then quoted part of his statement of March 24.)

Toward the end of August, however, events occurred which marked the increasing seriousness of the situation. The French Government, in consequence of information which had reached them about the moving of several German divisions toward their frontier, took certain precautionary measures, including the calling up of reserves to man the Maginot Line.

On the twenty-eighth of August, Sir Nevile Henderson had been recalled to London for consultations and a meeting of Ministers held August 30 to consider his report on the general situation.

On August 31 he returned to Berlin and gave Herr von Kreitzer, the State Secretary, a strong personal warning regarding the probable attitude of his Majesty's Government in the event of German aggression against Czechoslovakia, particularly if France were compelled to intervene. On September 1 our Ambassador saw Herr von Ribbentrop and repeated to him as a personal but most urgent message the warning he had already given the previous day to the State Secretary.

His Majesty's Government desired to impress the seriousness of the situation upon the German Government without the risk of further aggravating the situation by any formal representations which might have been interpreted by the German Government as a public rebuff, as had been the case in regard to our representations of May 21.

His Majesty's Government had also to bear in mind the approach of the Nazi Party Congress. It was to be anticipated that the Chancellor would not fail to make some public statement and, therefore, it appeared necessary, in addition to warning the German Government of the attitude of his Majesty's Government in the United Kingdom, to make every effort in Prague to secure the resumption of negotiations between the Czechoslovak Government and the Sudeten representatives on a basis which would offer a rapid and satisfactory settlement.

Accordingly, his Majesty's Minister in Prague saw Dr. Beneš and emphasized to him that it was vital in the interests of Czechoslovakia to offer immediately and without reservation those concessions without which the Sudeten question could not be considered settled. His Majesty's Government were not in a position to say whether anything less than the full program would suffice.

In Lord Runciman's opinion, what was known as the "Fourth Plan" embodied almost all the requirements of the eight Karlsbad points and formed a basis for negotiations.

The publication of the Fourth Plan, unfortunately, was followed by the serious incident at Moravska-Ostrava [Maehrisch-Ostrau].

It would appear from investigations of the British observer that the importance of this incident was very much exaggerated.

The immediate result was a decision on the part of the Sudeten leader not to resume negotiations until the incident had been liquidated.

Immediately measures were taken by the Czechoslovak Government to liquidate it. Further incidents took place September 11 near Eger, and in spite of Lord Runciman's efforts to bring both parties together negotiations could not be resumed.

In view of the unsatisfactory development of the situation in Czechoslovakia, his Majesty's Government made further efforts to exercise a restraining influence upon the German Government.

The French Government had shown itself particularly insistent that nothing should be left undone to make the attitude of his Majesty's Government clear to the Chancellor himself.

Sir Nevile Henderson was at Nuremberg September 9 and 12 and took every opportunity to impress upon the leading German personalities the attitude of his Majesty's Government as set forth in my speech of March 24 and repeated by Sir John Simon August 27.

It was decided to make personal representations to the Chancellor himself. The French Government were informed of the warning which had been conveyed by Sir Nevile Henderson at Nuremberg.

On September 9 the Cabinet met to consider the situation and decided to take certain precautionary naval measures including the commissioning of mine layers and mine sweepers, and on September 11 I made a statement to the press which received widespread publicity, stressing in particular the close tie uniting Great Britain and France in the probability in certain eventualities of this country going to the assistance of France.

On the morning of September 12 the Cabinet met again. They

decided no further action could usefully be taken before Herr Hitler's speech at Nuremberg that evening. In that speech Hitler laid great stress on the defensive military measures taken on the German western frontier. In his references to Czechoslovakia he reminded the world that on February 22 he had said the Reich would no longer tolerate further oppression and persecution of the Sudeten Germans.

"They demanded the right of self-determination," he said, "and were supported in their demand by the Reich."

Therefore, for the first time, this speech promised the support of the Reich to the Sudeten Germans if they could not obtain satisfaction themselves, and for the first time it publicly raised the issue of self-determination.

It did not, however, close the door on further negotiations in Prague nor demand a plebiscite. The speech also was accompanied by specific references to Germany's frontiers with Poland and France, and the general effect was to leave the situation unchanged, with a slight diminution of tension.

The speech, however, and in particular Herr Hitler's references to support for the cause of the Sudeten Germans, had an immediate and unfortunate effect among these people. Demonstrations took place throughout Sudetenland, resulting in an immediate extension of the incidents which had already begun September 11.

Serious rioting occurred, accompanied by attacks upon Czech police and officials, and by September 14, according to official Czechoslovak figures, there had been twenty-one killed and seventy-five wounded, the majority of whom were Czechs.

An attempt made by Lord Runciman to bring the Sudeten leaders into a discussion with the Czechoslovak Cabinet failed. On September 14 Herr Henlein issued a statement that the Karlsbad points no longer were enough and that the situation called for self-determination.

Thereupon Herr Henlein fled to Germany, where it is understood he has since occupied himself with the formation of a Sudeten legionary organization reported to number 40,000 men.

In these circumstances, Lord Runciman felt no useful purpose could be served by his publishing a plan of his own.

The House will recall that by the evening of September 14 a highly critical situation had developed in which there was an immediate danger of German troops, now concentrated on the frontier, entering Czechoslovakia to prevent further incidents occurring in Sudetenland of fighting between Czech forces and Sudeten Germans, although reliable reports indicated order had been completely restored in those districts by September 14.

On the other hand, the Czechoslovak Government might have felt compelled to mobilize at once and so risk provoking a German invasion. In any event, a German invasion might be expected to bring into operation the French obligation to come to the assistance of Czechoslovakia and so lead to a European war in which this country might well have been involved in support of France.

In these circumstances I decided the time had come to put into operation a plan which I had had in mind for a considerable period as a last resort.

One of the principal difficulties in dealing with a totalitarian government is the lack of any means of establishing contact with the personalities in whose hands lie the final decision.

I, therefore, resolved to go to Germany myself and interview Herr Hitler and find out in a personal conversation whether there was any hope yet of saving peace.

I knew very well that in taking such an unprecedented course I was laying myself open to criticism on the ground that I was detracting from the dignity of the British Prime Minister, and to disappointment, even to resentment, if I failed to bring back a satisfactory agreement.

I felt that in such a crisis where the issues at stake were so vital for a million human beings, considerations of that kind could not be allowed to prevail. Herr Hitler responded to my suggestion with cordiality and on September 15 I made my first flight to Munich, and from there I traveled by train to Herr Hitler's mountain home at Berchtesgaden.

I confess I was astonished at the warmth of approval with which this adventure was everywhere received, but the relief which it brought for the moment was indication of the gravity with which the situation had been viewed.

At this first conversation, which lasted three hours and at which only an interpreter was present besides Herr Hitler and myself, I very soon became aware the situation was much more acute and much more urgent than I had realized.

In courteous but perfectly definite terms, Herr Hitler made it plain he had made up his mind the Sudeten Germans must have the right of self-determination and of returning, if they wished, to the Reich. If they could not achieve this by their own efforts, he said, he would assist them to do so and he declared categorically that, rather than wait, he would be prepared to risk a world war.

At one point, he complained of British threats against Germany, to which I replied he must distinguish between a threat and a warning and that he might have just cause for complaint if I allowed him to think that in no circumstances would this country go to war with Germany when, in fact, there were conditions in which such a contingency might arise.

So strongly did I get the impression that the Chancellor was contemplating an immediate invasion of Czechoslovakia that I asked him why he had allowed me to travel all that way, since I evidently was wasting my time.

He said if I could give him there and then the assurance the British Government accepted the principle of self-determination, he was quite ready to discuss ways and means of carrying it out.

If, on the contrary, I told him such a principle could not be considered by the British Government, then he agreed it was no use to continue our conversations.

I was, of course, in no position to give there and then such a assurance, but I undertook to return at once to consult my colleagues if he would refrain from active hostilities until I had had time to obtain their reply.

That assurance he gave, provided, he said, nothing happened in Czechoslovakia of such a nature as to force his hand and that assurance has remained binding ever since.

I have no doubt now, looking back, that my visit alone prevented an invasion, for which everything had been prepared, and it was clear to me that with German troops in the positions they then occupied, nothing anybody could do would prevent an invasion unless the right of self-determination was granted, and that quickly, to the Sudeten Germans.

And that was the sole hope of a peaceful solution.

I came back to London the next day. That evening the Cabinet met and it was attended also by Lord Runciman who, at my request, had traveled from Prague. Lord Runciman informed us that although in his view responsibility for the final breach in the negotiations at Prague rested upon the Sudeten extremists, nevertheless, in view of recent developments on the frontier, the districts between Czechoslovakia and Germany where the Sudeten population was in the majority should be given the full right of self-determination at once.

He considered the cession of the territories to be inevitable and thought it should be done promptly. Measures for peaceful transfer could be arranged between the two governments. The Germans and Czechs, however, would still have to live side by side in many other parts of Czechoslovakia. In those areas, Lord Runciman thought the basis ought to be sought for local autonomy on the lines of the fourth plan published by the Czechoslovak Government on July 10.

He considered that the dignity and security of Czechoslovakia could only be maintained if her policy, internal and external, were directed to enabling her to live in peace with all her neighbors. For this purpose, in his opinion, her policy should be entirely neutral, as in the case of Switzerland.

His Majesty's Government felt it necessary to consult the French Government before replying to Herr Hitler and, accordingly, M. Daladier and M. Bonnet were invited to London September 18.

(The Prime Minister then quoted the text of the communiqué issued September 19.)

During these conversations the representatives of the two Governments were actuated by the desire to find a solution that would not bring about a European war and therefore a solution which would not automatically compel France to take action in accordance with her obligations. It was agreed the only means of achieving this object was to accept the principle of self-determination.

Accordingly, the British and French Ministers at Prague were instructed to inform the Czechoslovak Government that continuance within Czechoslovakia of districts mainly inhabited by Sudeten Germans would imperil the interests of Czechoslovakia herself and all hopes of peace.

The Czechoslovak Government was asked to agree immediately to direct the transfer to the Reich of areas inhabited by a population more than 50 per cent German.

The Czechoslovak Government were informed that to meet their natural desire for their security in the future, his Majesty's Government would be prepared as a contribution to the pacification of Europe to join in an international guarantee in regard to new boundaries of the Czechoslovak State against unprovoked aggression.

Such a guarantee would safeguard the independence of Czechoslovakia by substituting a general guarantee against unprovoked aggression in place of the existing treaties with France and Russia which involved reciprocal obligations of a military character.

In agreeing to that guarantee, his Majesty's Government were accepting a completely new commitment. We were not previously bound by any obligations toward Czechoslovakia other than those involved by the Covenant of the League.

(The Prime Minister then reviewed the further progress of negotiations, pointing out that the British and French Ministers in Prague were instructed to tell the Czechoslovak Government there was no hope of new proposals.)

This they did immediately and unconditionally September 21. Our Minister in Prague was instructed to inform the Czechoslovak Government September 22 that his Majesty's Government were profoundly conscious of the immense sacrifice which the Czechoslovak Government had agreed to and the immense public spirit which they had shown.

These proposals had been put forward in the hope of averting general disaster and saving Czechoslovakia from invasion.

Her willingness to undertake them won a measure of sympathy which nothing else could have aroused.

The Czechoslovak Government resigned and a government of national concentration under General Syrovy was constituted, but it was emphasized that this government was not a military dictatorship and that it had accepted the Anglo-French proposals.

We had hoped that the immediate problem would not be complicated at this juncture by the claims pressed by Poland and Hungary. They had, however, demanded similar treatment of their minorities as were accorded German minorities.

The Governments of Poland and Hungary have made representations to his Majesty's Government, and we have replied that we take note of those representations but that we are at present concentrating our efforts on the Sudeten problem, on the solution of which the issue of war or peace in Europe depends. While appreciating their position, his Majesty's Government hoped these two Governments would do nothing to add to the present delicate situation.

The Polish Government had expressed considerable dissatisfaction and troop movements had taken place in the direction of Teschen.

The Hungarian Government had been encouraged by conversations of the Regent with Field Marshal Goering and conversations of the Hungarian Prime Minister and Chief of Staff at Berchtesgaden, and mobilization measures had been taken by the Hungarian Army.

On September 22 I went back to Germany to Bad-Godesberg-on-Rhine, where the Chancellor had appointed a meeting place as being more convenient for me.

Once again I had a warm welcome in the streets of villages through which I passed, which demonstrated to me the desire of the German people for peace, and on the afternoon of my arrival I had a second meeting with the Chancellor.

During my stay in London the Government had worked out with the French Government arrangements for effecting the transfer of territory proposed, also for the delimitation of the final frontier.

I explained these to Herr Hitler, who was not previously aware of them, and I also told him about the proposed guarantee against unprovoked aggression.

On that point of guarantee he made no objection, but he said he could not enter into any guarantee unless other Powers, including Italy, were also guarantors.

I said I had not asked them to enter into a guarantee but that I had intended to ask him if he were willing to enter into a pact of non-aggression with a new Czechoslovakia. He said he could not enter into such a compact while the other minorities of Czechoslovakia were not satisfied, but that when they were satisfied he would then be prepared to join an international guarantee.

He said he could not accept other proposals which I described to him, on grounds they were too dilatory and offered too many opportunities for evasion. He insisted a solution was essential on account of the terrorism and oppression with which the Sudeten Germans were faced.

(Mr. Chamberlain said Herr Hitler then gave him an outline of the proposals subsequently embodied in the famous memorandum, "except he did not in this conversation actually name any time limit.")

The honorable members will realize the perplexity in which I found myself in being faced with this totally unexpected situation. I had been told at Berchtesgaden that, if the principle of self-determination were accepted, Herr Hitler would discuss with me ways and means of carrying it out.

He told me afterward he never for one moment supposed I should be able to come back and say that the principle was accepted.

(The Prime Minister added he did not think Herr Hitler deliberately deceived him.)

When I got back to Godesberg, I thought I had only to discuss quietly with him the various proposals already submitted. I was shocked when, at the beginning of the conversations, he (Herr Hitler) said these proposals were not acceptable and that there were other proposals which I had not contemplated at all.

I felt I had to consider what I had to do. Consequently, I withdrew with my mind full of foreboding as to the success of my mission. I have seen speculative accounts of what happened the next day which suggested that long hours passed whilst I remained on one side of the Rhine and Herr Hitler on the other because I had difficulty in obtaining assurances from him about the removal of his troops.

I want to say at once that that is purely imaginary. There was no such difficulty. We had arranged to resume our conversation at 11:30 the next morning, but in view of the difficulty of talking with a man through an interpreter and the fact I could not feel sure that what I had been saying had always been understood and appreciated by him, I thought it would be wise to put down on paper some comments upon these new proposals of his and let him have it some time before the talks began.

Accordingly, I wrote a letter (which is Number IV in the White Paper) which I sent him. I sent that soon after breakfast and in it I declared my readiness to convey the proposals to the Czechoslovak Government, but I pointed out what I thought to be grave difficulties in the way of their acceptance.

On receipt of this letter the Chancellor intimated he would like to say something in reply.

The reply was not received until Wednesday afternoon and contained no more proposals than those which had been described to me the night before. Accordingly, I replied, asking for a memorandum of the proposals and a copy of the map for transmission to Prague, and intimating my intention of returning to England.

The memorandum and map were handed me at my final interview with the Chancellor, which began at 10:30 that night and lasted into the small hours of the morning, and at which the German Foreign Secretary was present as well as Sir Nevile Henderson and Sir Horace Wilson.

For the first time, I found in the memoranda new proposals and I spoke very frankly. I dwelt with all the emphasis at my command upon the risks which would be incurred by insisting on such terms.

I declared the language and manner of the document, which I described as an ultimatum rather than a memorandum, would profoundly shock public opinion in neutral countries and I bitterly reproached the Chancellor on his failure to respond in any way to the efforts which I had made to secure peace.

In spite of those frank words, this conversation was carried on on more friendly terms than that which preceded it.

I think I should add that, before saying farewell to Herr Hitler, I had a few words with him in private which I do not think are without importance.

In the first place, he repeated to me with great earnestness what he had already said at Berchtesgaden—namely, that this was his last territorial ambition in Europe; that he had no wish to have in the Reich people of other races than German.

The next day we received from the Czech Ministers the reply of the Czech Government, which stated they considered Herr Hitler's demands, in their present form, to be absolutely and unconditionally unacceptable.

This reply was communicated to the French Ministers. Conversations were resumed next morning with the French Ministers, and they informed us that if Czechoslovakia were attacked France would fulfil her treaty obligations.

In reply we said if, as a result of these negotiations, the French forces became actively engaged, we should be pledged to support them.

Meanwhile, as a last effort to preserve peace, I sent Sir Horace Wilson to Berlin September 26 with a personal message to Herr Hitler, to be delivered before his speech to be made in Berlin at 8 o'clock that evening; the French Ministers entirely approved of this initiative and we issued a communiqué to that effect.

Sir Horace Wilson took with him a letter from me pointing out that the reception of the German memorandum by Czechoslovakia had confirmed the expectations which I had expressed to him at Godesberg.

I therefore made a further proposal with a view to arriving at a settlement by negotiation rather than by military force—namely, that there should be an immediate discussion between German and Czechoslovak representatives in the presence of British representatives.

Sir Horace Wilson arrived at Berlin on the afternoon of the twenty-sixth and presented this letter to Herr Hitler, who listened to it but expressed the view he could not depart from the procedure of the memorandum since he felt a conference would lead to further intolerable procrastination.

I should tell the House how deeply it was impressed on my mind in my conversations with Herr Hitler, and I see it again in every speech he makes, that he has deep-rooted distrust and disbelief in the sincerity of the Czechoslovak Government. That has been one of the factors in all this difficult story of events.

In the meantime, after reading Herr Hitler's speech in Berlin in which, as I say, he expressed his disbelief in the intentions of the Czech Government to carry out their promises, I offered on behalf of the British Government to guarantee that the promises which they had made to us and the French Government would be carried out.

Yesterday morning Sir Horace resumed his conversations with Herr Hitler but, finding his views unchanged, he, upon my instructions, repeated to him in precise terms what I said a few moments ago, that France would fulfil her obligations to Czechoslovakia and should France become engaged in hostilities with Germany, the British Government would feel obliged to support her.

Now the story which I have told the House brings us up to last night. About 12:30 I received from Herr Hitler the reply to my letter sent by Sir Horace Wilson which is printed in the White Paper. A careful perusal indicates certain indications of his intention. There is a definite statement that troops will not be moved beyond the red line (beyond the Sudeten areas into Czechoslovakia). They are only to preserve order and that a plebiscite will be carried out with a free vote.

It was added he would abide by the results and, finally, he would join in an international guarantee for the remainder of Czechoslovakia, once minority questions were settled.

This was rather a reassuring statement, and I have no hesitation in saying—from the personal contacts I had with him—I believe he means what he says.

But the thing which was uppermost in my mind was that once more the difficulties and obscurities had been narrowed down to points, and it was inconceivable they could not be settled by negotiations. So strongly did I feel this that I felt compelled to send a last appeal.

I sent the following personal message:

After reading your letter, I feel certain that you can get all the essentials without war and without delay, and I will arrange to go to Berlin myself, at once, to discuss the arrangements with you and the representatives of the Czech Government, together with representatives of France and Italy if you desire it.

I cannot believe you will take the responsibility of starting a World War, which might end civilization, for the sake of a few days delay in settling this long-standing problem.

At the same time, I sent the following personal message to Premier Mussolini:

I have today addressed a last appeal to Herr Hitler to refrain from force in the Sudeten problem which I feel sure can be settled by further discussion.

I offered myself to go at once to Berlin to discuss arrangements with the German and Czech representatives—also Italy and France. I trust your Excellency will inform the German Chancellor you are willing to be represented and urge him to agree to my proposal which will keep all our peoples out of war.

I have already promised that the Czech promises should be carried out and feel confident a full agreement can be reached in a week.

In a reply to the message to Signor Mussolini, we were informed that instructions had been sent to the Italian Ambassador in Berlin to see Herr von Ribbentrop at once and to say that, while Italy would fulfil completely her pledges to stand by Germany, in view of the great importance of the request made by his Majesty's Government

Signor Mussolini hoped Herr Hitler would see his way to postpone the action which the Chancellor had told Sir Horace Wilson was to be taken at 2 p. m. today, for at least twenty-four hours to allow him (Premier Mussolini) to reexamine the situation and find a peaceful settlement.

In response, Herr Hitler agreed to postpone mobilization for twenty-four hours.

Whatever views we may have had about Premier Mussolini in the past, I believe everyone will welcome his gesture. He has been willing to work with us—but that is not all!

I have something further to say to the House yet!

I have been informed by Herr Hitler that he invites me to meet him in Munich tomorrow morning.

He has also invited Signor Mussolini and M. Daladier. Signor Mussolini has accepted and no doubt M. Daladier will also accept.

I need not say what my answer will be!

There can be no member in this House who did not feel his heart leap when he heard the crisis had been once more postponed. And now there is to be one more opportunity to try by reason of good will and discussion to find a solution of the problem which already is within sight of settlement.

I cannot say any more. I hope the House will release me now to go and see what I can make of this last effort, and perhaps, in view of this new development, this debate might be adjourned for a few days.

Then, perhaps, we may meet in happier circumstances.

ADDRESS by Neville Chamberlain, Prime Minister, in the House of Commons, October 3, 1938

International Conciliation, November, 1938, p. 466, citing *The New York Times,* October 4, 1938; excerpts

THE HOUSE WILL remember that when I last addressed them I gave them some account of the Godesberg memorandum with the terms of which they are familiar.

They will recollect also that I expressed frankly my view that the terms were such as were likely to shock public opinion generally in the world and bring a prompt rejection by the Czechoslovak Government.

Those views were confirmed by the results.

The immediate and unqualified rejection of that memorandum by the Czechoslovak Government was communicated to us at once by them.

What I think the House will desire to take into consideration first this afternoon is what is the difference between these unacceptable terms and the terms which were included in the agreement signed at Munich, because it is on the difference between those two documents there will depend the judgment as to whether we were successful in what we set out to do.

I say, first of all, that the Godesberg memorandum, although it was cast in the form of proposals, was in fact an ultimatum with a time limit of six days.

On the other hand, the Munich agreement reverts to the Anglo-French plan which lays down the conditions for the abdication and the responsibility of the four Powers and international supervision of the main principles of that memorandum. . . .

I think every fair-minded and every serious-minded man or woman who takes into consideration the modifications of the memoradum must agree that they are of very considerable extent and that they are all in the same direction.

To those who dislike an ultimatum, but who were anxious for a reasonable and orderly procedure every one of these modifications is a step in the right direction.

It is no longer an ultimatum. It is a method which is carried on largely under the supervision of an international body.

Now, in giving a verdict upon the agreement, we should do well to avoid describing it as a personal or a national triumph for anybody.

The real triumph is that it has shown that the representatives of four Great Powers can find it possible to agree on a way of carrying out a difficult and delicate operation by discussion instead of by loss of life.

They have averted a catastrophe which would have ended civilization as we have known it.

Relief at our escape from this great peril of war has everywhere been mingled in this country with profound feelings of—[Labor cries of "Shame! Shame!"]

I have nothing to be ashamed of. [Loud cheers from Government supporters.]

Those who have, may hang their heads.

We must all feel profound sympathy for a small and gallant nation in the hour of their national grief and loss.

I say in the name of this House and of the people of this country that Czechoslovakia has earned our admiration and respect for her restraint, her dignity and her magnificent discipline in the face of such a trial as no nation has been called upon to meet. . . .

Ever since I assumed my present office, my main purpose has been to work for the pacification of Europe, for the removal of those suspicions and animosities which have so long poisoned the air.

The path that leads to peace is a long one and bristles with obstacles.

This question of Czechoslovakia is the latest and perhaps the most dangerous. Now that we have got past it I feel that it may be possible to make further progress along the road to sanity.

Mr. Duff Cooper has alluded in somewhat bitter terms to my conversation last Friday morning with Herr Hitler. I do not know why that conversation should give rise to suspicion, still less to criticism.

I entered into no pact. I made no new commitments. There is no secret understanding. Our conversation was hostile to no other nation.

The object of that conversation for which I asked was to try to extend a little further the personal contact which I had established with Herr Hitler, which I believed to be essential to modern diplomacy. . . .

For a long period now we have been engaged in this country in a great program of rearmament which is daily increasing in pace and volume.

Let no one think because we have signed this agreement between the four Powers at Munich we can afford to relax our efforts or call a halt in our armaments at this moment.

Disarmament on the part of this country will never be unilateral again. We have tried that once and we very nearly brought ourselves into disaster.

If disarmament is to come at all, it must come by steps and it must come with the agreement and active cooperation of other countries. Until we know that we can obtain that cooperation, until we agree on the actual steps which are to be taken, we must remain on guard.

ADDRESS by Lord Halifax, Secretary of State for Foreign Affairs, in the House of Lords, October 3, 1938

International Conciliation, November, 1938, p. 475, citing *The New York Times*, October 4, 1938; excerpt

I SHALL BE ASKED why we consented to the omission of Russia. I would venture to repeat here what I said to the Soviet Ambassador a day or two ago.

Five days ago it seemed to us vital, if war was to be avoided, somehow or other to get matters on a basis of negotiation; but if we were to face the facts—and nothing was to be gained but everything lost by not facing them—we were obliged to recognize that in the present circumstances the heads of the German and Italian Governments would almost certainly—at least not without preliminary discussion, for which there was no time—be reluctant to sit in a conference with a Soviet representative.

Accordingly, if our principal purpose was to insure negotiation, we were bound to have regard for the practical conditions within which alone that purpose could be secured.

But the fact that it was impossible, if we were to talk to the German and Italian Governments in those days at all, to include the Soviet Government directly in the conversations in no way signifies any weakening on our part any more, no doubt, than on that of the French Government to preserve our understanding relations with the Soviet Government.

Nothing has been so persistently pressed upon me during the last two or three months than this: If only Great Britain would say clearly and unmistakably for all to hear that she would resist any unprovoked aggression against Czechoslovakia no such unprovoked aggression would be made.

We never felt able to use that language, but so far as there was force in the argument I do not underrate it. The deterrent value of such a statement will have full force under such a guarantee as we have expressed our willingness to give. To guarantee Czechoslovakia, including within her borders restless and dissatisfied minorities, was one thing; to guarantee Czechoslovakia when those explosive minority questions had been adjusted was quite another.

There are, of course, a great many questions connected with this guarantee that will require more careful consideration than it has yet been possible to give them. Such will be whether these forms should be joined up and, further, what States should be invited to assume those obligations and the circumstances in which these obligations should be held to arise.

These matters and possibly others will be matters for an early exchange of views between the several governments concerned.

There is no one who will not wish at this time to pay his tribute and extend his sympathy to President [Eduard] Beneš [of Czechoslovakia] and his people. Faced with that grim dilemma, Dr. Beneš chose the path of peace, and I cannot but believe the judgment of history will accord him a special place for the wisdom of his choice.

1939

ADDRESS by Neville Chamberlain, Prime Minister, at Birmingham, March 17, 1939
The British War Blue Book, p. 6

I HAD INTENDED to-night to talk to you upon a variety of subjects, upon trade and employment, upon social service, and upon finance. But the tremendous events which have been taking place this week in Europe have thrown everything else into the background, and I feel that what you, and those who are not in this hall but are listening to me, will want to hear is some indication of the views of His Majesty's Government as to the nature and the implications of those events.

One thing is certain. Public opinion in the world has received a sharper shock than has ever yet been administered to it, even by the present régime in Germany. What may be the ultimate effects of this profound disturbance on men's minds cannot yet be foretold, but I am sure that it must be far-reaching in its results upon the future. Last Wednesday we had a debate upon it in the House of Commons. That was the day on which the German troops entered Czecho-Slovakia, and all of us, but particularly the Government, were at a disadvantage because the information that we had was only partial; much of it was unofficial. We had no time to digest it, much less to form a considered opinion upon it. And so it necessarily followed that I, speaking on behalf of the Government, with all the responsibility that attaches to that position, was obliged to confine myself to a very restrained and cautious exposition, on what at the time I felt I could make but little commentary. And, perhaps naturally, that somewhat cool and objective statement gave rise to a misapprehension, and some people thought that because I spoke quietly, because I gave little expression of feeling, therefore my colleagues and I did not feel strongly on the subject. I hope to correct that mistake to-night.

But I want to say something first about an argument which has developed out of these events and which was used in that debate, and has appeared since in various organs of the press. It has been suggested that this occupation of Czecho-Slovakia was the direct consequence of the visit which I paid to Germany last autumn, and that, since the result of these events has been to tear up the settlement that was arrived at at Munich, that proves that the whole circumstances of those visits were wrong. It is said that, as this was the personal policy of the Prime Minister, the blame for the fate of Czecho-Slovakia must rest upon his shoulders. That is an entirely unwarrantable conclusion. The facts as they are to-day cannot change the facts as they were last September. If I was right then, I am still right now. Then there are some people who say: "We considered you were wrong in September, and now we have been proved to be right."

Let me examine that. When I decided to go to Germany I never expected that I was going to escape criticism. Indeed, I did not go there to get popularity. I went there first and foremost because, in what appeared to be an almost desperate situation, that seemed to me to offer the only chance of averting a European war. And I might remind you that, when it was first announced that I was going, not a voice was raised in criticism. Everyone applauded that effort. It was only later, when it appeared that the results of the final settlement fell short of the expectations of some who did not fully appreciate the facts—it was only then that the attack began, and even then it was not the visit, it was the terms of settlement that were disapproved.

Well, I have never denied that the terms which I was able to secure at Munich were not those that I myself would have desired. But, as I explained then, I had to deal with no new problem. This was something that had existed ever since the Treaty of Versailles—a problem that ought to have been solved long ago if only the statesmen of the last twenty years had taken broader and more enlightened views of their duty. It had become like a disease which had been long neglected, and a surgical operation was necessary to save the life of the patient.

After all, the first and the most immediate object of my visit was achieved. The peace of Europe was saved; and, if it had not been for those visits, hundreds of thousands of families would to-day have been in mourning for the flower of Europe's best manhood. I would like once again to express my grateful thanks to all those correspondents who have written me from all over the world to express their gratitude and their appreciation of what I did then and of what I have been trying to do since.

Really I have no need to defend my visits to Germany last autumn, for what was the alternative? Nothing that we could have done, nothing that France could have done, or Russia could have done could possibly have saved Czecho-Slovakia from invasion and destruction. Even if we had subsequently gone to war to punish Germany for her actions, and if after the frightful losses which would have been inflicted upon all partakers in the war we had been victorious in the end, never could we have reconstructed Czecho-Slovakia as she was framed by the Treaty of Versailles.

But I had another purpose, too, in going to Munich. That was to

RELATIONS WITH GERMANY

further the policy which I have been pursuing ever since I have been in my present position—a policy which is sometimes called European appeasement, although I do not think myself that that is a very happy term or one which accurately describes its purpose. If that policy were to succeed, it was essential that no Power should seek to obtain a general domination of Europe; but that each one should be contented to obtain reasonable facilities for developing its own resources, securing its own share of international trade, and improving the conditions of its own people. I felt that, although that might well mean a clash of interests between different States, nevertheless, by the exercise of mutual goodwill and understanding of what were the limits of the desires of others, it should be possible to resolve all differences by discussion and without armed conflict. I hoped in going to Munich to find out by personal contact what was in Herr Hitler's mind, and whether it was likely that he would be willing to co-operate in a programme of that kind. Well, the atmosphere in which our discussions were conducted was not a very favourable one, because we were in the middle of an acute crisis; but, nevertheless, in the intervals between more official conversations I had some opportunities of talking with him and of hearing his views, and I thought that results were not altogether unsatisfactory.

When I came back after my second visit I told the House of Commons of a conversation I had had with Herr Hitler, of which I said that, speaking with great earnestness, he repeated what he had already said at Berchtesgaden—namely, that this was the last of his territorial ambitions in Europe, and that he had no wish to include in the Reich people of other races than German. Herr Hitler himself confirmed this account of the conversation in the speech which he made at the Sportpalast in Berlin, when he said: "This is the last territorial claim which I have to make in Europe." And a little later in the same speech he said: "I have assured Mr. Chamberlain, and I emphasise it now, that when this problem is solved Germany has no more territorial problems in Europe." And he added: "I shall not be interested in the Czech State any more, and I can guarantee it. We don't want any Czechs any more."

And then in the Munich Agreement itself, which bears Herr Hitler's signature, there is this clause: "The final determination of the frontiers will be carried out by the international commission"—the *final* determination. And, lastly, in that declaration which he and I signed together at Munich, we declared that any other question which might concern our two countries should be dealt with by the method of consultation.

Well, in view of those repeated assurances, given voluntarily to me,

I considered myself justified in founding a hope upon them that once this Czecho-Slovakian question was settled, as it seemed at Munich it would be, it would be possible to carry farther that policy of appeasement which I have described. But, notwithstanding, at the same time I was not prepared to relax precautions until I was satisfied that the policy had been established and had been accepted by others, and therefore, after Munich, our defence programme was actually accelerated, and it was expanded so as to remedy certain weaknesses which had become apparent during the crisis. I am convinced that after Munich the great majority of British people shared my hope, and ardently desired that that policy should be carried further. But to-day I share their disappointment, their indignation, that those hopes have been so wantonly shattered.

How can these events this week be reconciled with those assurances which I have read out to you? Surely, as a joint signatory of the Munich Agreement, I was entitled, if Herr Hitler thought it ought to be undone, to that consultation which is provided for in the Munich declaration. Instead of that he has taken the law into his own hands. Before even the Czech President was received, and confronted with demands which he had no power to resist, the German troops were on the move, and within a few hours they were in the Czech capital.

According to the proclamation which was read out in Prague yesterday, Bohemia and Moravia have been annexed to the German Reich. Non-German inhabitants, who, of course, include the Czechs, are placed under the German Protector in the German Protectorate. They are to be subject to the political, military and economic needs of the Reich. They are called self-governing States, but the Reich is to take charge of their foreign policy, their customs and their excise, their bank reserves, and the equipment of the disarmed Czech forces. Perhaps most sinister of all, we hear again of the appearance of the Gestapo, the secret police, followed by the usual tale of wholesale arrests of prominent individuals, with consequences with which we are all familiar.

Every man and woman in this country who remembers the fate of the Jews and the political prisoners in Austria must be filled to-day with distress and foreboding. Who can fail to feel his heart go out in sympathy to the proud and brave people who have so suddenly been subjected to this invasion, whose liberties are curtailed, whose national independence has gone? What has become of this declaration of "No further territorial ambition"? What has become of the assurance "We don't want Czechs in the Reich"? What regard had been paid here to that principle of self-determination on which Herr Hitler argued so vehemently with me at Berchtesgaden when he was asking for the severance of Sudetenland from Czecho-Slovakia and its inclusion in the German Reich?

Now we are told that this seizure of territory has been necessitated by disturbances in Czecho-Slovakia. We are told that the proclamation of this new German Protectorate against the will of its inhabitants has been rendered inevitable by disorders which threatened the peace and security of her mighty neighbour. If there were disorders, were they not fomented from without? And can anybody outside Germany take seriously the idea that they could be a danger to that great country, that they could provide any justification for what has happened?

Does not the question inevitably arise in our minds, if it is so easy to discover good reasons for ignoring assurances so solemnly and so repeatedly given, what reliance can be placed upon any other assurances that come from the same source?

There is another set of questions which almost inevitably must occur in our minds and to the minds of others, perhaps even in Germany herself. Germany, under her present régime, has sprung a series of unpleasant surprises upon the world. The Rhineland, the Austrian *Anschluss,* the severance of Sudetenland—all these things shocked and affronted public opinion throughout the world. Yet, however much we might take exception to the methods which were adopted in each of those cases, there was something to be said, whether on account of racial affinity or of just claims too long resisted—there was something to be said for the necessity of a change in the existing situation.

But the events which have taken place this week in complete disregard of the principles laid down by the German Government itself seem to fall into a different category, and they must cause us all to be asking ourselves: "Is this the end of an old adventure, or is it the beginning of a new?"

"Is this the last attack upon a small State, or is it to be followed by others? Is this, in fact, a step in the direction of an attempt to dominate the world by force?"

Those are grave and serious questions. I am not going to answer them to-night. But I am sure they will require the grave and serious consideration not only of Germany's neighbours, but of others, perhaps even beyond the confines of Europe. Already there are indications that the process has begun, and it is obvious that it is likely now to be speeded up.

We ourselves will naturally turn first to our partners in the British Commonwealth of Nations and to France, to whom we are so closely bound, and I have no doubt that others, too, knowing that we are not disinterested in what goes on in South-Eastern Europe, will wish to have our counsel and advice.

In our own country we must all review the position with that sense of responsibility which its gravity demands. Nothing must be excluded from that review which bears upon the national safety. Every aspect of our national life must be looked at again from that angle. The Government, as always, must bear the main responsibility, but I know that all individuals will wish to review their own position, too, and to consider again if they have done all they can to offer their service to the State.

I do not believe there is anyone who will question my sincerity when I say there is hardly anything I would not sacrifice for peace. But there is one thing that I must except, and that is the liberty that we have enjoyed for hundreds of years, and which we will never surrender. That I, of all men, should feel called upon to make such a declaration—that is the measure of the extent to which these events have shattered the confidence which was just beginning to show its head and which, if it had been allowed to grow, might have made this year memorable for the return of all Europe to sanity and stability.

It is only six weeks ago that I was speaking in this city, and that I alluded to rumours and suspicions which I said ought to be swept away. I pointed out that any demand to dominate the world by force was one which the democracies must resist, and I added that I could not believe that such a challenge was intended, because no Government with the interests of its own people at heart could expose them for such a claim to the horrors of world war.

And, indeed, with the lessons of history for all to read, it seems incredible that we should see such a challenge. I feel bound to repeat that, while I am not prepared to engage this country by new unspecified commitments operating under conditions which cannot now be foreseen, yet no greater mistake could be made than to suppose that, because it believes war to be a senseless and cruel thing, this nation has so lost its fibre that it will not take part to the utmost of its power in resisting such a challenge if it ever were made. For that declaration I am convinced that I have not merely the support, the sympathy, the confidence of my fellow-countrymen and countrywomen, but I shall have also the approval of the whole British Empire and of all other nations who value peace, indeed, but who value freedom even more.

LETTER from Neville Chamberlain, Prime Minister, to the Chancellor of Germany (Adolf Hitler), August 22, 1939

The British War Blue Book, p. 125

Your Excellency,

Your Excellency will have already heard of certain measures taken by His Majesty's Government, and announced in the press and on the wireless this evening.

These steps have, in the opinion of His Majesty's Government, been rendered necessary by the military movements which have been reported from Germany, and by the fact that apparently the announcement of a German-Soviet Agreement is taken in some quarters in Berlin to indicate that intervention by Great Britain on behalf of Poland is no longer a contingency that need be reckoned with. No greater mistake could be made. Whatever may prove to be the nature of the German-Soviet Agreement, it cannot alter Great Britain's obligation to Poland which His Majesty's Government have stated in public repeatedly and plainly, and which they are determined to fulfil.

It has been alleged that, if His Majesty's Government had made their position more clear in 1914, the great catastrophe would have been avoided. Whether or not there is any force in that allegation, His Majesty's Government are resolved that on this occasion there shall be no such tragic misunderstanding.

If the case should arise, they are resolved, and prepared, to employ without delay all the forces at their command, and it is impossible to foresee the end of hostilities once engaged. It would be a dangerous illusion to think that, if war once starts, it will come to an early end even if a success on any one of the several fronts on which it will be engaged should have been secured.

Having thus made our position perfectly clear, I wish to repeat to you my conviction that war between our two peoples would be the greatest calamity that could occur. I am certain that it is desired neither by our people, nor by yours, and I cannot see that there is anything in the questions arising between Germany and Poland which could not and should not be resolved without the use of force, if only a situation of confidence could be restored to enable discussions to be carried on in an atmosphere different from that which prevails today.

We have been, and at all times will be, ready to assist in creating conditions in which such negotiations could take place, and in which it might be possible concurrently to discuss the wider problems affecting the future of international relations, including matters of interest to us and to you.

The difficulties in the way of any peaceful discussion in the present state of tension are, however, obvious, and the longer that tension is maintained, the harder will it be for reason to prevail.

These difficulties, however, might be mitigated, if not removed, provided that there could for an initial period be a truce on both sides—and indeed on all sides—to press polemics and to all incitement.

If such a truce could be arranged, then, at the end of that period, during which steps could be taken to examine and deal with complaints made by either side as to the treatment of minorities, it is reasonable to hope that suitable conditions might have been established for direct negotiations between Germany and Poland upon the issues between them (with the aid of a neutral intermediary, if both sides should think that that would be helpful).

But I am bound to say that there would be slender hope of bringing such negotiations to successful issue unless it were understood beforehand that any settlement reached would, when concluded, be guaranteed by other Powers. His Majesty's Government would be ready, if desired, to make such contribution as they could to the effective operation of such guarantees.

At this moment I confess I can see no other way to avoid a catastrophe that will involve Europe in war.

In view of the grave consequences to humanity, which may follow from the action of their rulers, I trust that Your Excellency will weigh with the utmost deliberation the considerations which I have put before you.

ADDRESS by Neville Chamberlain, Prime Minister, in the House of Commons, August 24, 1939

The British War Blue Book, p. 138

WHEN AT THE beginning of this month Hon. Members separated for the summer recess, I think there can have been few among us who anticipated that many weeks would elapse before we should find ourselves meeting here again. Unfortunately, those anticipations have been fulfilled, and the Government have felt obliged to ask that Par-

RELATIONS WITH GERMANY

liament should be summoned again, in order to take such new and drastic steps as are required by the gravity of the situation. In the last debate which we had upon foreign affairs, which took place on the 31st July, I observed that the Danzig situation required very careful watching. I expressed my anxiety about the pace at which the accumulation of war weapons was proceeding throughout Europe. I referred to the poisoning of public opinion by the propaganda which was going on, and I declared that if that could be stopped and if some action could be taken to restore confidence, I did not believe there was any question which could not be solved by peaceful discussion. I am sorry to say that there has been no sign since of any such action. On the contrary, the international position has steadily deteriorated until to-day we find ourselves confronted with the imminent peril of war.

At the beginning of August a dispute arose between the Polish Government and the Danzig Senate as to the position and functions of certain Polish Customs officials. It was not a question of major importance. Many more acute difficulties have been easily settled in the past under less tense conditions and even in this case discussions had actually begun between the parties last week. While those discussions were in progress, the German Press opened a violent campaign against the Polish Government. They declared that Danzig could not be the subject of any conference or any compromise and that it must come back to the Reich at once and unconditionally. They went further. They linked up with the Danzig question the question of the Corridor. They attacked the whole policy and the attitude of the Polish Government, and they published circumstantial accounts of the alleged ill-treatment of Germans living in Poland. Now we have no means of checking the accuracy of those stories, but we cannot help being struck by the fact that they bear a strong resemblance to similar allegations that were made last year in respect of the Sudeten Germans in Czecho-Slovakia. We must also remember that there is a large Polish minority in Germany and that the treatment of that minority has also been the subject of bitter complaints by the Polish Government.

There is no subject which is calculated to arouse ill-feeling in any country more than statements about the ill-treatment of people of their own race in another country. This is a subject which provides the most inflammable of all materials, the material most likely to cause a general conflagration. In those circumstances one cannot but deeply regret that such incidents, which, if they were established, would naturally excite sympathy for the victims and indignation against the authors of this alleged ill-treatment, should be treated in a way which is calculated still further to embitter the atmosphere and raise the temperature to the danger point. But I think it will be agreed that, in face of this campaign, declarations by Polish statesmen have shown great calm and self-restraint. The Polish leaders, while they have been firm in their determination to resist an attack upon their independence, have been unprovocative. They have always been ready, as I am sure they would be ready now, to discuss differences with the German Government, if they could be sure that those discussions would be carried on without threats of force or violence, and with some confidence that, if agreement were reached, its terms would be respected afterwards permanently, both in the letter and in the spirit. This Press campaign is not the only symptom which is ominously reminiscent of past experience. Military preparations have been made in Germany on such a scale that that country is now in a condition of complete readiness for war, and at the beginning of this week we had word that German troops were beginning to move towards the Polish frontier. It then became evident that a crisis of the first magnitude was approaching, and the Government resolved that the time had come when they must seek the approval of Parliament for further measures of defence.

That was the situation on Tuesday last, when in Berlin and Moscow it was announced that negotiations had been taking place, and were likely soon to be concluded, for a non-aggression pact between those two countries. I do not attempt to conceal from the House that that announcement came to the Government as a surprise, and a surprise of a very unpleasant character. For some time past there had been rumours about an impending change in the relations between Germany and the Soviet Union, but no inkling of that change had been conveyed either to us or to the French Government by the Soviet Government. The House may remember that on the 31st July I remarked that we had engaged upon steps almost unprecedented in character. I said that we had shown a great amount of trust and a strong desire to bring the negotiations with the Soviet Union to a successful conclusion when we agreed to send our soldiers, sailors and airmen to Russia to discuss military plans together before we had any assurance that we should be able to reach an agreement on political matters. Well, Sir, nevertheless, moved by the observation of the Russian Secretary for Foreign Affairs, that if we could come to a successful conclusion of our military discussions, political agreement should not present any insuperable difficulties, we sent the Mission.

The British and French Missions reached Moscow on the 11th August. They were warmly received, in friendly fashion, and discussions were actually in progress and had proceeded on a basis of mutual trust when this bombshell was flung down. It, to say the least of it, was highly disturbing to learn that while these conversations were proceeding on that basis, the Soviet Government were secretly negotiating a pact with Germany for purposes which, on the face of it, were inconsistent with the objects of their foreign policy, as we had understood it. I do not propose this afternoon to pass any final judgment upon this incident. That, I think, would be premature until we have had an opportunity of consulting the French Government as to the meaning and the consequences of this agreement, the text of which was published only this morning. But the question that the Government had to consider when they learned of this announcement was what effect, if any, this changed situation would have upon their own policy. In Berlin the announcement was hailed, with extraordinary cynicism, as a great diplomatic victory which removed any danger of war, since we and France would no longer be likely to fulfil our obligations to Poland. We felt it our first duty to remove any such dangerous illusion.

The House will recollect that the guarantee which we had given to Poland was given before any agreement with Russia was talked of, and that it was not in any way made dependent upon any such agreement being reached. How, then, could we, with honour, go back upon such an obligation, which we had so often and so plainly repeated? Therefore, our first act was to issue a statement that our obligations to Poland and to other countries remained unaffected. Those obligations rest upon agreed statements made to the House of Commons, to which effect is being given in treaties which are at present in an advanced stage of negotiation. Those treaties, when concluded, will formally define our obligations, but they do not in any way alter, they do not add to or subtract from, the obligations of mutual assistance which have already been accepted. The communiqué which we issued to the Press after the meeting of the Cabinet this week spoke also of certain measures of defence which we had adopted. It will be remembered that, as I have said, Germany has an immense army of men already under arms and that military preparations of all kinds have been and are being carried on on a vast scale in that country.

The measures that we have taken up to now are of a precautionary and defensive character, and to give effect to our determination to put this country in a state of preparedness to meet any emergency, but I wish emphatically to repudiate any suggestion, if such a suggestion should be made, that these measures imply an act of menace. Nothing that we have done or that we propose to do menaces the legitimate interests of Germany. It is not an act of menace to prepare to help friends to defend themselves against force. If neighbours wishing to live together peacefully in friendly relations find that one of them is contemplating apparently an aggressive act of force against another of them, and is making open preparations for action, it is not a menace for the others to announce their intention of aiding the one who is the subject of this threat.

There is another action which has been taken to-day in the financial sphere. Hon. Members will have seen the announcement that the Bank Rate, which has remained at 2 per cent. for a long time past, has to-day been raised to 4 per cent., and the House will recognise that this is a normal protective measure adopted for the purpose of defending our resources in a period of uncertainty. There is in this connexion a contribution to be made by British citizens generally. The public can best co-operate in reducing as far as possible any demands which involve directly or indirectly the purchase of foreign exchange; next by scrupulously observing the request of the Chancellor of the Exchequer that capital should not at present be sent or moved out of the country; and, finally, by holding no more foreign assets than are strictly required for the normal purpose of business.

In view of the attitude in Berlin to which I have already referred, His Majesty's Government felt that it was their duty at this moment to leave no possible loophole for misunderstanding, and so that no doubt might exist in the mind of the German Government, His Majesty's Ambassador in Berlin was instructed to seek an interview with the German Chancellor and to hand him a message from me on behalf of the British Government. That message was delivered yesterday and the reply was received to-day. The object of my communication to the German Chancellor was to restate our position and to make quite sure that there was no misunderstanding. His Majesty's Government felt that this was all the more necessary having regard to reports which we had received as to the military movements taking place in Germany and as to the then projected German-Soviet Agreement. I therefore made it plain, as had been done in the communiqué issued after the Cabinet meeting on Tuesday, that if the case should arise His Majesty's Government were resolved and prepared to employ without delay all the forces at their command.

On numerous occasions I have stated my conviction that war between our two countries, admitted on all sides to be the greatest calamity that could occur, is not desired either by our own people or the German people. With this fact in mind I informed the German Chancellor that, in our view, there was nothing in the questions arising between Poland and Germany which could not be, and should not be, resolved without the use of force, if only a situation of confidence could be restored. We expressed our willingness to assist in creating the conditions in which such negotiations could take place. The present state of tension creates great difficulties, and I expressed the view that if there could be a truce on all sides to press polemics and all other forms of incitement suitable conditions might be established for direct negotiations between Germany and Poland upon the points at issue. The negotiations could, of course, deal also with the complaints made on either side about the protection of minorities.

The German Chancellor's reply includes what amounts to a restatement of the German thesis that Eastern Europe is a sphere in which Germany ought to have a free hand. If we—this is the thesis—or any country having less direct interest choose to interfere, the blame for the ensuing conflict will be ours. This thesis entirely misapprehends the British position. We do not seek to claim a special position for ourselves in Eastern Europe. We do not think of asking Germany to sacrifice her national interests, but we cannot agree that national interests can only be secured by the shedding of blood or the destruction of the independence of other States. With regard to the relations between Poland and Germany, the German Chancellor in his reply to me has referred again to the situation at Danzig, drawing attention to the position of that city and of the Corridor, and to the offer which he made early this year to settle these questions by methods of negotiation. I have repeatedly refuted the allegation that it was our guarantee to Poland that decided the Polish Government to refuse the proposals then made. That guarantee was not, in fact, given until after the Polish refusal had been conveyed to the German Government. In view of the delicacy of the situation I must refrain for the present from any further comment upon the communications which have just passed between the two Governments. Catastrophe has not yet come upon us. We must, therefore, still hope that reason and sanity may find a way to reassert themselves. The pronouncement we made recently and what I have said to-day reflects, I am sure, the views of the French Government, with whom we have maintained the customary close contact in pursuance of our well established cordial relations.

Naturally, our minds turn to the Dominions. I appreciate very warmly the pronouncements made by Ministers in other parts of the British Commonwealth. The indications that have been given from time to time, in some cases as recently as yesterday, of their sympathy with our patient efforts in the cause of peace, and of their attitude in the unhappy event of their proving unsuccessful, are a source of profound encouragement to us in these critical times. The House will, I am sure, share the appreciation with which His Majesty's Government have noted the appeal for peace made yesterday by King Leopold in the name of the heads of the Oslo States, after the meeting in Brussels yesterday of the representatives of those States. It will be evident from what I have said that His Majesty's Government share the hopes to which that appeal gave expression, and earnestly trust that effect will be given to it.

The Foreign Secretary, in a speech made on the 29th June to the Royal Institute of International Affairs, set out the fundamental bases of British foreign policy. His observations on that subject were, I believe, received with general approval. The first basis is our determination to resist methods of force. The second basis is our recognition of the world desire to pursue the constructive work of building peace. If we were once satisfied, my noble Friend said, that the intentions of others were the same as our own, and if we were satisfied that all wanted peaceful solutions, then, indeed, we could discuss problems which are to-day causing the world so much anxiety. That definition of the basic fundamental ground of British policy still stands. We want to see established an international order based upon mutual understanding and mutual confidence, and we cannot build such an order unless it conforms to certain principles which are essential to the establishment of confidence and trust. Those principles must include the observance of international undertakings when they have once been entered into, and the renunciation of force in the settlement of differences. It is because those principles, to which we attach such vital importance, seem to us to be in jeopardy that we have undertaken these tremendous and unprecedented responsibilities.

If, despite all our efforts to find the way to peace—and God knows I have tried my best—if in spite of all that, we find ourselves forced to embark upon a struggle which is bound to be fraught with suffering and misery for all mankind and the end of which no man can foresee, if that should happen, we shall not be fighting for the political future of a far away city in a foreign land; we shall be fighting for the preservation of those principles of which I have spoken, the destruction of which would involve the destruction of all possibility of peace and security for the peoples of the world. This issue of peace or war does not rest with us, and I trust that those with whom the responsibility does lie will think of the millions of human beings whose fate depends upon their actions. For ourselves, we have a united country behind us, and in this critical hour I believe that we, in this House of Commons, will stand together, and that this afternoon we shall show the world that, as we think, so will we act, as a united nation.

COMMUNICATION from the British Government to the German Government, August 28, 1939, Replying to the Communication of the German Chancellor (Adolf Hitler) of August 25, 1939

The British War Blue Book, p. 162

His Majesty's Government have received the message conveyed to them from the German Chancellor by His Majesty's Ambassador in Berlin, and have considered it with the care which it demands.

They note the Chancellor's expression of his desire to make friendship the basis of the relations between Germany and the British Empire and they fully share this desire. They believe with him that if a complete and lasting understanding between the two countries could be established it would bring untold blessings to both peoples.

2. The Chancellor's message deals with two groups of questions: those which are the matters now in dispute between Germany and Poland and those affecting the ultimate relations of Germany and Great Britain. In connexion with these last, His Majesty's Government observe that the German Chancellor has indicated certain proposals which, subject to one condition, he would be prepared to make to the British Government for a general understanding. These proposals are, of course, stated in very general form and would require closer definition, but His Majesty's Government are fully prepared to take them, with some additions, as subjects for discussion and they would be ready, if the differences between Germany and Poland are peacefully composed, to proceed so soon as practicable to such discussion with a sincere desire to reach agreement.

3. The condition which the German Chancellor lays down is that there must first be a settlement of the differences between Germany and Poland. As to that, His Majesty's Government entirely agree. Everything, however, turns upon the nature of the settlement and the method by which it is to be reached. On these points, the importance of which cannot be absent from the Chancellor's mind, his message is silent, and His Majesty's Government feel compelled to point out that an understanding upon both of these is essential to achieving further progress. The German Government will be aware that His Majesty's Government have obligations to Poland by which they are bound and which they intend to honour. They could not, for any advantage offered to Great Britain, acquiesce in a settlement which put in jeopardy the independence of a State to whom they have given their guarantee.

4. In the opinion of His Majesty's Government a reasonable solution of the differences between Germany and Poland could and should be effected by agreement between the two countries on lines which would include the safeguarding of Poland's essential interests, and they recall that in his speech of the 28th April last the German Chancellor recognised the importance of these interests to Poland.

But, as was stated by the Prime Minister in his letter to the German Chancellor of the 22nd August, His Majesty's Government consider it essential for the success of the discussions which would precede the agreement that it should be understood beforehand that any settlement arrived at would be guaranteed by other Powers. His Majesty's Government would be ready if desired to make their contribution to the effective operation of such a guarantee.

In the view of His Majesty's Government it follows that the next step should be the initiation of direct discussions between the German and Polish Governments on a basis which would include the principles stated above, namely, the safeguarding of Poland's essential interests and the securing of the settlement by an international guarantee.

They have already received a definite assurance from the Polish Government that they are prepared to enter into discussions on this basis, and His Majesty's Government hope the German Government would for their part also be willing to agree to this course.

If, as His Majesty's Government hope, such discussion led to agreement the way would be open to the negotiation of that wider and more complete understanding between Great Britain and Germany which both countries desire.

5. His Majesty's Government agree with the German Chancellor that one of the principal dangers in the German-Polish situation arises from the reports concerning the treatment of minorities. The present state of tension, with its concomitant frontier incidents, reports of maltreatment and inflammatory propaganda, is a constant danger to peace. It is manifestly a matter of the utmost urgency that all incidents of the kind should be promptly and rigidly suppressed and that unverified reports should not be allowed to circulate, in order that time may be afforded, without provocation on either side, for a full examination of the possibilities of settlement. His Majesty's Government are confident that both the Governments concerned are fully alive to these considerations.

6. His Majesty's Government have said enough to make their own attitude plain in the particular matters at issue between Germany and Poland. They trust that the German Chancellor will not think

that, because His Majesty's Government are scrupulous concerning their obligations to Poland, they are not anxious to use all their influence to assist the achievement of a solution which may commend itself both to Germany and to Poland.

That such a settlement should be achieved seems to His Majesty's Government essential, not only for reasons directly arising in regard to the settlement itself, but also because of the wider considerations of which the German Chancellor has spoken with such conviction.

7. It is unnecessary in the present reply to stress the advantage of a peaceful settlement over a decision to settle the questions at issue by force of arms. The results of a decision to use force have been clearly set out in the Prime Minister's letter to the Chancellor of the 22nd August, and His Majesty's Government do not doubt that they are as fully recognised by the Chancellor as by themselves.

On the other hand, His Majesty's Government, noting with interest the German Chancellor's reference in the message now under consideration to a limitation of armaments, believe that, if a peaceful settlement can be obtained, the assistance of the world could confidently be anticipated for practical measures to enable the transition from preparation for war to the normal activities of peaceful trade to be safely and smoothly effected.

8. A just settlement of these questions between Germany and Poland may open the way to world peace. Failure to reach it would ruin the hopes of better understanding between Germany and Great Britain, would bring the two countries into conflict, and might well plunge the whole world into war. Such an outcome would be a calamity without parallel in history.

COMMUNICATION from the British Government to the German Government, August 30, 1939, Replying to the Communication of the German Chancellor (Adolf Hitler) Dated August 29, 1939

The British War Blue Book, p. 184. The communication was presented by the British Ambassador to Germany (Sir Nevile Henderson) to the German Minister for Foreign Affairs (Joachim von Ribbentrop) at midnight on August 30

His Majesty's Government appreciate the friendly reference in the Declaration contained in the reply of the German Government to the latter's desire for an Anglo-German understanding and to their statement of the influence which this consideration has exercised upon their policy.

2. His Majesty's Government repeat that they reciprocate the German Government's desire for improved relations, but it will be recognised that they could not sacrifice the interests of other friends in order to obtain that improvement. They fully understand that the German Government cannot sacrifice Germany's vital interests, but the Polish Government are in the same position and His Majesty's Government believe that the vital interests of the two countries are not incompatible.

3. His Majesty's Government note that the German Government accept the British proposal and are prepared to enter into direct discussions with the Polish Government.

4. His Majesty's Government understand that the German Government accept in principle the condition that any settlement should be made the subject of an international guarantee. The question of who shall participate in this guarantee will have to be discussed further, and His Majesty's Government hope that to avoid loss of time the German Government will take immediate steps to obtain the assent of the U.S.S.R., whose participation in the Guarantee His Majesty's Government have always assumed.

5. His Majesty's Government also note that the German Government accept the position of the British Government as to Poland's vital interests and independence.

6. His Majesty's Government must make an express reservation in regard to the statement of the particular demands put forward by the German Government in an earlier passage in their reply. They understand that the German Government are drawing up proposals for a solution. No doubt these proposals will be fully examined during the discussions. It can then be determined how far they are compatible with the essential conditions which His Majesty's Government have stated and which in principle the German Government have expressed their willingness to accept.

7. His Majesty's Government are at once informing the Polish Government of the German Government's reply. The method of contact and arrangements for discussions must obviously be agreed with all urgency between the German and Polish Governments, but in His Majesty's Government's view it would be impracticable to establish contact so early as to-day.

8. His Majesty's Government fully recognise the need for speed in the initiation of discussion, and they share the apprehensions of the Chancellor arising from the proximity of two mobilised armies standing face to face. They would accordingly most strongly urge that both parties should undertake that, during the negotiations, no aggressive military movements will take place. His Majesty's Government feel

confident that they could obtain such an undertaking from the Polish Government if the German Government would give similar assurances.

9. Further, His Majesty's Government would suggest that a temporary *modus vivendi* might be arranged for Danzig, which might prevent the occurrence of incidents tending to render German-Polish relations more difficult.

ADDRESS by Neville Chamberlain, Prime Minister, in the House of Commons, September 1, 1939
The British War Blue Book, p. 202

I DO NOT PROPOSE to say many words to-night. The time has come when action rather than speech is required. Eighteen months ago in this House I prayed that the responsibility might not fall upon me to ask this country to accept the awful arbitrament of war. I fear that I may not be able to avoid that responsibility. But, at any rate, I cannot wish for conditions in which such a burden should fall upon me in which I should feel clearer than I do to-day as to where my duty lies. No man can say that the Government could have done more to try to keep open the way for an honourable and equitable settlement of the dispute between Germany and Poland. Nor have we neglected any means of making it crystal clear to the German Government that if they insisted on using force again in the manner in which they had used it in the past we were resolved to oppose them by force. Now that all the relevant documents are being made public we shall stand at the bar of history knowing that the responsibility for this terrible catastrophe lies on the shoulders of one man—the German Chancellor, who has not hesitated to plunge the world into misery in order to serve his own senseless ambitions.

I would like to thank the House for the forbearance which they have shown on two recent occasions in not demanding from me information which they recognised I could not give while these negotiations were still in progress. I have now had all the correspondence with the German Government put into the form of a White Paper. On account of mechanical difficulties I am afraid there are still but a few copies available, but I understand that they will be coming in in relays while the House is sitting. I do not think it is necessary for me to refer in detail now to these documents, which are already past history. They make it perfectly clear that our object has been to try and bring about discussions of the Polish-German dispute between the two countries themselves on terms of equality, the settlement to be one which safeguarded the independence of Poland and of which the due observance would be secured by international guarantees. There is just one passage from a recent communication, which was dated the 30th August, which I should like to quote, because it shows how easily the final clash might have been avoided had there been the least desire on the part of the German Government to arrive at a peaceful settlement. In this document we said:—

His Majesty's Government fully recognise the need for speed in the initiation of discussions and they share the apprehensions of the Chancellor arising from the proximity of two mobilised armies standing face to face. They would accordingly most strongly urge that both parties should undertake that during the negotiations no aggressive military movements should take place. His Majesty's Government feel confident that they could obtain such an undertaking from the Polish Government if the German Government would give similar assurances.

That telegram, which was repeated to Poland, brought an instantaneous reply from the Polish Government, dated the 31st August, in which they said:—

The Polish Government are also prepared on a reciprocal basis to give a formal guarantee in the event of negotiations taking place that Polish troops will not violate the frontiers of the German Reich provided a corresponding guarantee is given regarding the non-violation of the frontiers of Poland by troops of the German Reich.

We never had any reply from the German Government to that suggestion, one which, if it had been followed, might have saved the catastrophe which took place this morning. In the German broadcast last night, which recited the 16 points of the proposals which they have put forward, there occurred this sentence:—

In these circumstances the Reich Government considers its proposals rejected.

I must examine that statement. I must tell the House what are the circumstances. To begin with let me say that the text of these proposals has never been communicated by Germany to Poland at all. The history of the matter is this. On Tuesday, the 29th August, in replying to a Note which we had sent to them, the German Government said, among other things, that they would immediately draw up proposals for a solution acceptable to themselves and

will, if possible, place these at the disposal of the British Government before the arrival of the Polish negotiator.

It will be seen by examination of the White Paper that the German Government had stated that they counted upon the arrival of a plenipotentiary from Poland in Berlin on the 30th that is to say, on the following day. In the meantime, of course, we were awaiting these proposals. The next evening, when our Ambassador saw Herr von Ribbentrop, the German Foreign Secretary, he urged upon the latter that when these proposals were ready—for we had heard no more about them—he should invite the Polish Ambassador to call and should hand him the proposals for transmission to his Government. Thereupon, reports our Ambassador, in the most violent terms Herr von Ribbentrop said he would never ask the Ambassador to visit him. He hinted that if the Polish Ambassador asked him for an interview it might be different.

The House will see that this was on Wednesday night, which according to the German statement of last night, is now claimed to be the final date after which no negotiation with Poland was acceptable. It is plain, therefore, that Germany claims to treat Poland as in the wrong because she had not by Wednesday night entered upon discussions with Germany about a set of proposals of which she had never heard.

Now what of ourselves? On that Wednesday night, at the interview to which I have just referred, Herr von Ribbentrop produced a lengthy document which he read out in German aloud, at top speed. Naturally, after this reading our Ambassador asked for a copy of the document, but the reply was that it was now too late, as the Polish representative had not arrived in Berlin by midnight. And so, Sir, we never got a copy of those proposals, and the first time we heard them—*we* heard them—was on the broadcast last night. Well, Sir, those are the circumstances in which the German Government said that they would consider that their proposals were rejected. Is it not clear that their conception of a negotiation was that on almost instantaneous demand a Polish plenipotentiary should go to Berlin—where others had been before him—and should there receive a statement of demands to be accepted in their entirety or refused? I am not pronouncing any opinion upon the terms themselves, for I do not feel called upon to do so. The proper course, in our view—in the view of all of us—was that these proposals should have been put before the Poles, who should have been given time to consider them and to say whether, in their opinion, they did or did not infringe those vital interests of Poland which Germany had assured us on a previous occasion she intended to respect. Only last night the Polish Ambassador did see the German Foreign Secretary, Herr von Ribbentrop. Once again he expressed to him what, indeed, the Polish Government had already said publicly, that they were willing to negotiate with Germany about their disputes on an equal basis. What was the reply of the German Government? The reply was that without another word the German troops crossed the Polish frontier this morning at dawn and are since reported to be bombing open towns. In these circumstances there is only one course open to us. His Majesty's Ambassador in Berlin and the French Ambassador have been instructed to hand to the German Government the following document:—

Early this morning the German Chancellor issued a proclamation to the German Army which indicated clearly that he was about to attack Poland. Information which has reached His Majesty's Government in the United Kingdom and the French Government indicates that German troops have crossed the Polish frontier and that attacks upon Polish towns are proceeding. In these circumstances it appears to the Governments of the United Kingdom and France that by their action the German Government have created conditions, namely, an aggressive act of force against Poland threatening the independence of Poland, which call for the implementation by the Governments of the United Kingdom and France of the undertaking to Poland to come to her assistance. I am accordingly to inform your Excellency that unless the German Government are prepared to give His Majesty's Government satisfactory assurances that the German Government have suspended all aggressive action against Poland and are prepared promptly to withdraw their forces from Polish territory, His Majesty's Government in the United Kingdom will without hesitation fulfil their obligations to Poland.

If a reply to this last warning is unfavourable, and I do not suggest that it is likely to be otherwise, His Majesty's Ambassador is instructed to ask for his passports. In that case we are ready. Yesterday, we took further steps towards the completion of our defensive preparations. This morning we ordered complete mobilisation of the whole of the Royal Navy, Army and Royal Air Force. We have also taken a number of other measures, both at home and abroad, which the House will not perhaps expect me to specify in detail. Briefly, they represent the final steps in accordance with pre-arranged plans. These last can be put into force rapidly, and are of such a nature that they can be deferred until war seems inevitable. Steps have also been taken under the powers conferred by the House last week to safeguard the position in regard to stocks of commodities of various kinds.

The thoughts of many of us must at this moment inevitably be turning back to 1914, and to a comparison of our position now with that which existed then. How do we stand this time? The answer is that all three Services are ready, and that the situation in all directions is far more favourable and reassuring than in 1914, while behind the fighting Services we have built up a vast organisation of Civil Defence under our scheme of Air Raid Precautions. As regards the immediate man-power requirements, the Royal Navy, the Army and the Royal Air Force are in the fortunate position of having almost as many men as they can conveniently handle at this moment. There are, however, certain categories of service in which men are immediately required, both for Military and Civil Defence. These will be announced in detail through the Press and the B.B.C. The main and most satisfactory point to observe is that there is to-day no need to make an appeal in a general way for recruits such as was issued by Lord Kitchener 25 years ago. That appeal has been anticipated by many months, and the men are already available.

So much for the immediate present. Now we must look to the future. It is essential in the face of the tremendous task which confronts us, more especially in view of our past experiences in this matter, to organise our man-power this time upon as methodical, equitable and economical a basis as possible. We, therefore, propose immediately to introduce legislation directed to that end. A Bill will be laid before you which for all practical purposes will amount to an expansion of the Military Training Act. Under its operation all fit men between the ages of 18 and 41 will be rendered liable to military service if and when called upon. It is not intended at the outset that any considerable number of men other than those already liable shall be called up, and steps will be taken to ensure that the man-power essentially required by industry shall not be taken away.

There is one other allusion which I should like to make before I end my speech, and that is to record my satisfaction, and the satisfaction of His Majesty's Government, that throughout these last days of crisis Signor Mussolini also has been doing his best to reach a solution.

It now only remains for us to set our teeth and to enter upon this struggle, which we ourselves earnestly endeavoured to avoid, with determination to see it through to the end. We shall enter it with a clear conscience, with the support of the Dominions and the British Empire, and the moral approval of the greater part of the world. We have no quarrel with the German people, except that they allow themselves to be governed by a Nazi Government. As long as that Government exists and pursues the methods it has so persistently followed during the last two years, there will be no peace in Europe. We shall merely pass from one crisis to another, and see one country after another attacked by methods which have now become familiar to us in their sickening technique. We are resolved that these methods must come to an end. If out of the struggle we again re-establish in the world the rules of good faith and the renunciation of force, why, then even the sacrifices that will be entailed upon us will find their fullest justification.

ADDRESS by Neville Chamberlain, Prime Minister, in the House of Commons, September 3, 1939

The British War Blue Book, p. 228

When I spoke last night to the House I could not but be aware that in some parts of the House there were doubts and some bewilderment as to whether there had been any weakening, hesitation or vacillation on the part of His Majesty's Government. In the circumstances, I make no reproach, for if I had been in the same position as hon. members not sitting on this Bench and not in possession of all the information which we have, I should very likely have felt the same. The statement which I have to make this morning will show that there were no grounds for doubt. We were in consultation all day yesterday with the French Government and we felt that the intensified action which the Germans were taking against Poland allowed no delay in making our own position clear. Accordingly, we decided to send to our Ambassador in Berlin instructions which he was to hand at 9 o'clock this morning to the German Foreign Secretary and which read as follows:—

Sir,

In the communication which I had the honour to make to you on the 1st September, I informed you, on the instructions of His Majesty's Principal Secretary of State for Foreign Affairs, that unless the German Government were prepared to give His Majesty's Government in the United Kingdom satisfactory assurances that the German Government had suspended all aggressive action against Poland and were prepared promptly to withdraw their forces from Polish territory, His Majesty's Government in the United Kingdom would, without hesitation, fulfil their obligations to Poland.

Although this communication was made more than twenty-four hours ago, no reply has been received but German attacks upon Poland have been continued and intensified. I have accordingly the honour to inform you that, unless not later than 11 A.M., British Summer Time, to-day 3rd September, satisfactory assurances to the above effect have been given by the German Government and have reached His Majesty's Government in London, a state of war will exist between the two countries as from that hour.

That was the final Note. No such undertaking was received by the time stipulated, and, consequently, this country is at war with Germany. I am in a position to inform the House that, according to arrangements made between the British and French Governments, the French Ambassador in Berlin is at this moment making a similar *démarche,* accompanied also by a definite time limit. The House has already been made aware of our plans. As I said the other day, we are ready.

This is a sad day for all of us, and to none is it sadder than to me. Everything that I have worked for, everything that I have hoped for, everything that I have believed in during my public life, has crashed into ruins. There is only one thing left for me to do; that is, to devote what strength and powers I have to forwarding the victory of the cause for which we have to sacrifice so much. I cannot tell what part I may be allowed to play myself; I trust I may live to see the day when Hitlerism has been destroyed and a liberated Europe has been reestablished.

RADIO ADDRESS by Neville Chamberlain, Prime Minister, September 3, 1939

British War Aims (furnished by the British Library of Information, New York), p. 3

I AM SPEAKING to you from the Cabinet Room at 10, Downing Street.

This morning the British Ambassador in Berlin handed the German Government a final Note stating that unless we heard from them by 11 o'clock that they were prepared at once to withdraw their troops from Poland a state of war would exist between us. I have to tell you now that no such undertaking has been received, and that consequently this country is at war with Germany.

You can imagine what a bitter blow it is to me that all my long struggle to win peace has failed. Yet I cannot believe that there is anything more or anything different that I could have done and that would have been more successful.

Up to the very last it would have been quite possible to have arranged a peaceful and honourable settlement between Germany and Poland. But Hitler would not have it. He had evidently made up his mind to attack Poland whatever happened, and although he now says he put forward reasonable proposals which were rejected by the Poles, that is not a true statement.

The proposals were never shown to the Poles, nor to us, and, though they were announced in a German broadcast on Thursday night, Hitler did not wait to hear comments on them, but ordered his troops to cross the Polish frontier. His action shows convincingly that there is no chance of expecting that this man will ever give up his practice of using force to gain his will. He can only be stopped by force.

We and France are to-day, in fulfilment of our obligations, going to the aid of Poland, who is so bravely resisting this wicked and unprovoked attack upon her people. We have a clear conscience. We have done all that any country could do to establish peace, but a situation in which no word given by Germany's ruler could be trusted and no people or country could feel themselves safe had become intolerable. And now that we have resolved to finish it, I know that you will all play your part with calmness and courage.

At such a moment as this the assurances of support that we have received from the Empire are a source of profound encouragement to us.

. . . Now may God bless you all and may He defend the right. For it is evil things that we shall be fighting against, brute force, bad faith, injustice, oppression and persecution. And against them I am certain that the right will prevail.

FINAL REPORT by Sir Nevile Henderson, British Ambassador to Germany, to the Foreign Office, September 20, 1939, on the Circumstances Leading to the Termination of His Mission

British White Paper, Germany No. 1 (1939), *The British War Blue Book*, p. 251; excerpt

My Lord,

Events moved with such rapidity during the last fortnight of my mission to Berlin that it proved impossible at the time to give any consecutive account of them. If I have the honour to do so now, while the facts are still fresh in my memory, it is with the hope that such an account may be both of immediate interest to your Lordship and serve a purpose from the point of view of historical accuracy.

2. Nevertheless, it is not these last minute manoeuvres which have the real importance, except in so far as they confirm the principles and demonstrate the methods and technique of Herr Hitler and of Nazism. A brief description of the background to August 1939 is consequently indispensable, if the events of the last few weeks are to be visualised in their proper perspective.

RELATIONS WITH GERMANY

3. Herr Hitler and National Socialism are the products of the defeat of a great nation in war and its reaction against the confusion and distress which followed that defeat. National Socialism itself is a revolution and a conception of national philosophy. Contrary to democracy, which implies the subordination of the State to the service of its citizens, Nazism prescribes the subordination of its citizens to the service of the State, an all embracing Moloch, and to the individual who rules that State.

4. So long as National Socialism remained an article for internal consumption, the outside world, according to its individual predilection, might criticise or sympathise or merely watch with anxiety. The government of Germany was the affair of the German people. It was not until the theory of German nationalism was extended beyond Germany's own frontiers that the Nazi philosophy exceeded the limits compatible with peace.

5. It would be idle to deny the great achievements of the man who restored to the German nation its self-respect and its disciplined orderliness. The tyrannical methods which were employed within Germany itself to obtain this result were detestable, but were Germany's own concern. Many of Herr Hitler's social reforms, in spite of their complete disregard of personal liberty of thought, word or deed, were on highly advanced democratic lines. The "Strength through Joy" movement, the care for the physical fitness of the nation, and, above all, the organisation of the labour camps, an idea which Herr Hitler once told me that he had borrowed from Bulgaria, are typical examples of a benevolent dictatorship. Nor can the appeal of Nazism with its slogans so attractive to a not over-discerning youth be ignored. Much of its legislation in this respect will survive in a newer and better world, in which Germany's amazing power of organisation and the great contributions which she has made in the past to the sciences, music, literature and the higher aims of civilisation and humanity will again play a leading part.

6. Nor was the unity of Great Germany in itself an ignoble ideal. It had long been the dream of some of the highest-minded of German thinkers, and it must be remembered that even in 1914 Germany was still immature as a political concept. In spite of the potential political danger for its weaker neighbours of a national philosophy which could so easily be distorted and extended beyond its due and legitimate frontiers, the unity of Great Germany was a reality which had to be faced, no less than that other reality, the paramount economic importance of Germany in Eastern, Central and South-Eastern Europe. It was not the incorporation of Austria and the Sudeten Germans in the Reich which so much shocked public opinion in the

world as the unscrupulous and hateful methods which Herr Hitler employed to precipitate an incorporation which would probably have peacefully come in due course of its own volition and in accordance with the established principle of self-determination.

7. Yet even those methods might have been endured in a world which had experienced 1914–1918 and which sought peace as an end in itself, if Herr Hitler had been willing to accord to others the rights which he claimed for Germany. Revolutions are like avalanches, which, once set in motion, cannot stop till they crash to destruction at the appointed end of their career. History alone will determine whether Herr Hitler could have diverted Nazism into normal channels, whether he was the victim of the movement which he had initiated, or whether it was his own megalomania which drove it beyond the limits which civilisation was prepared to tolerate.

8. Be that as it may, the true background to the events of August 1939 was the occupation of Prague on the 15th March of this year, the callous destruction thereby of the hard and newly-won liberty of a free and independent people and Herr Hitler's deliberate violation by this act of the Munich Agreement which he had signed not quite six months before. In 1939, as in 1914, the origin of war with Germany has been due to the deliberate tearing up by the latter of a scrap of paper. To the iniquities of a system which employed the barbarism of the middle ages in its persecution of the Jews, which subjected Roman Catholic priests and Protestant pastors alike to the inhumanities of the concentration camp for obedience to their religious faith, and which crushed out, in a fashion unparalleled in history, all individual liberty within the State itself, was added the violation not only of international agreements freely negotiated, but also of that principle of self-determination which Herr Hitler had invoked with such insistence so long as it suited his own purpose to do so. Up to last March the German ship of State had flown the German national flag, and in spite of the "sickening technique" of Nazism it was difficult not to concede to Germany the right both to control her own destiny and to benefit from those principles which were accorded to others. On the 15th March, by the ruthless suppression of the freedom of the Czechs, its captain hoisted the skull and crossbones of the pirate, cynically discarded his own theory of racial purity and appeared under his true colours as an unprincipled menace to European peace and liberty.

9. Two of the less attractive characteristics of the German are his inability either to see any side of a question except his own, or to understand the meaning of moderation. It would have been understandable to argue that a hostile Bohemia in the centre of Germany

RELATIONS WITH GERMANY

was an untenable proposition. But Herr Hitler could see no mean between rendering the Czechs innocuous as a potential enemy and destroying their liberty as an independent people. There is some surprising reason to believe that Herr Hitler himself was disagreeably and literally astonished at the reaction in Britain and the world generally, which was provoked by the occupation of Prague and his breach of faith with Mr. Chamberlain. But while he may have realised his tactical mistake, it did not deter him from prosecuting his further designs.

10. As I had reported to your Lordship, at the beginning of the year Germany's immediate objectives, apart from the complete political and economic domination of Czecho-Slovakia and the eventual restoration of German colonies, were Danzig and Memel. Her Hitler felt that it would not add much to the general execration of his aggression and ill-faith in March if he settled these two problems simultaneously with Prague. The Democracies were, he thought, so averse to war that they would accept any *fait accompli*. They would be less disturbed if everything was done at once. Thereafter, the agitation would, he anticipated, gradually subside until, after consolidating his gains, he was once more in a position to strike again.

11. With this plan in view the Lithuanian Government was at once browbeaten into surrendering Memel. The same method was employed at Warsaw, but the Poles were made of sterner stuff. Negotiations had been proceeding ever since Munich for a settlement of the Danzig and the Corridor question. After Prague Herr Hitler decided that they must be abruptly concluded, and Herr von Ribbentrop peremptorily dictated to the Polish Ambassador the terms which Herr Hitler would be pleased to impose on the Polish Government. The reply of the latter was given on the 26th March and constituted a refusal to accept a Dictate, while expressing readiness to continue free and equal discussion. Alarmed at the threatening attitude adopted by the German Government in consequence of this refusal, the Polish Government mobilised part of its forces (the German army was already largely mobilised), and the British guarantee to Poland was given on the 31st March.

12. The Ides of March constituted in fact the parting of the ways and were directly responsible for everything which happened thereafter. Thenceforward no small nation in Europe could feel itself secure from some new adaptation of Nazi racial superiority and jungle law. The Polish guarantee was followed by unilateral guarantees on Britain's part to Greece and Roumania as well as by an attempt on the part of the British and French Governments to induce the U.S.S.R. to join in a peace front against aggression, ill-faith and op-

pression. The Nazi Government, for its part and with considerable success in Germany, represented this attempt as a renewal of the alleged pre-war British policy of encirclement. As a war-cry for the German people it was exceedingly effective up to the signature of the Russo-German non-aggression pact on the 23rd August. The rest of Nazi propaganda was on two entirely contradictory lines either of which was destined, according to the development of the situation, to serve Herr Hitler's purpose. The first spread the persistent report that Britain would never go to war for the sake of Danzig. It was calculated to undermine the confidence of the Poles and to shake the faith of the smaller Powers, as well as of the United States of America, in the determination of Britain to resist any further German aggression. The second represented Britain as resolved to make war at the first opportunity on Germany in any case and in order to crush her before she became a too formidable political and economic rival. Both were fallacies, but the Germans are a credulous race and, since the first has failed, it is the latter argumentation which forms the basis of Germany's present war propaganda.

13. Up to the beginning of August, though the clouds were black and the peace front negotiations dragged on interminably, the situation remained serious but not immediately dangerous. Instead, however, of there being any sign of a relaxation of tension at Danzig the position there had gradually become more and more strained. From the end of March till the end of August all personal contact between Warsaw and Berlin was suspended. The remilitarisation of the Free City, alleged by the Germans to be purely defensive, but no less adaptable for offensive purposes, had proceeded apace, and other measures had been taken indicative of a German intention to effect a sudden coup there. The Poles for their part, in view of the great increase in arms smuggling, had been obliged to strengthen their customs inspectors by a number of frontier guards. They had also taken certain economic counter-measures of a nature to prejudice the trade of the Free City.

14. What was, however, even more ominous were the extensive preparations which were being made by the Germans for the twenty-fifth celebration of the battle of Tannenberg on the 27th August, and a German warship was scheduled to visit Danzig at the same time and ostensibly for the same purpose. Early in July I drew your Lordship's attention to the menace involved by these equivocal preparations, which corresponded so closely to Hitler's usual technique of preparing for all eventualities, under cover of a plausible excuse.

15. The first mutterings of the storm were heard on the 4th August. At four posts on the Danzig-East Prussian frontier, the Polish

Customs Inspectors were informed that they would not be permitted henceforward to carry out their duties. Alarmed at the gradual sapping of Polish rights and interests in the Free City, the Polish Commissioner General there was at once instructed to deliver a note to the Danzig Senate, warning the latter that the Polish Government would react in the strongest manner if the work of the inspectors was interfered with. The Senate subsequently denied that it had issued any instructions to the effect alleged, but the German Government replied to what it described as the Polish ultimatum by a verbal note, which was handed by the State Secretary to the Polish Chargé d'Affaires at Berlin on the 9th August. The Polish Government was therein warned that any further demand addressed to the Free City in the nature of an ultimatum or containing threats of reprisals, would at once lead to an aggravation of Polish-German relations, the responsibility for which would fall on the Polish Government. The latter retorted on the following day by a similar verbal note, denying the judicial right of Germany to intervene in the affairs between Poland and the Free City, and warning in its turn the German Government that "any future intervention by the latter to the detriment of Polish rights and interests at Danzig would be considered as an act of aggression."

16. I have little doubt but that the latter phrase served more than anything else to produce that final brainstorm in Herr Hitler's mind on which the peace of the world depended, and upon which it always must have depended so long as the fate, not only of Germany but also of Europe, rested in the hands of a single irresponsible individual.

17. The tragedy of any dictator is that as he goes on, his entourage steadily and inexorably deteriorates. For lack of freedom of utterance he loses the services of the best men. All opposition becomes intolerable to him. All those, therefore, who are bold enough to express opinions contrary to his views are shed one by one, and he is in the end surrounded by mere yes-men, whose flattery and counsels are alone endurable to him. In my report on the events of 1938 I drew your Lordship's special attention to the far reaching and unfortunate results of the Blomberg marriage. I am more than ever convinced of the major disaster which that—in itself—minor incident involved, owing to the consequent elimination from Herr Hitler's entourage of the more moderate and independent of his advisers, such as Field Marshal von Blomberg himself, Baron von Neurath, Generals Fritsch, Beck, &c. After February of last year Herr Hitler became more and more shut off from external influences and a law unto himself.

18. People are apt, in my opinion, to exaggerate the malign influence of Herr von Ribbentrop, Dr. Goebbels, Herr Himmler and the

rest. It was probably consistently sinister, not because of its suggestiveness (since Herr Hitler alone decided policy), nor because it merely applauded and encouraged, but because, if Herr Hitler appeared to hesitate, the extremists of the party at once proceeded to fabricate situations calculated to drive Herr Hitler into courses which even he at times shrank from risking. The simplest method of doing this was through the medium of a controlled Press. Thus what happened in September last year, was repeated in March this year, and again in August. Dr. Goebbels' propaganda machine was the ready tool of these extremists, who were afraid lest Herr Hitler should move too slowly in the prosecution of his own ultimate designs.

19. The 1938 stories of Czech atrocities against its German minority, were rehashed up almost verbatim in regard to the Poles. Some foundation there must necessarily have been for a proportion of these allegations in view of the state of excitable tension which existed between the two peoples. Excess of zeal on the part of individuals and minor officials there undoubtedly was—but the tales of ill-treatment, expropriation and murder were multiplied a hundredfold. How far Herr Hitler himself believed in the truth of these tales must be a matter for conjecture. Germans are prone in any case to convince themselves very readily of anything which they wish to believe. Certainly he behaved as if he did believe, and, even if one may give him the benefit of the doubt, these reports served to inflame his resentment to the pitch which he or his extremists desired.

20. Until the 8th August the campaign against the Poles had been relegated to the more discreet pages of the German press. Up to that date, public enemy No. 1 had been Great Britain and the alleged policy of encirclement. From that date, however, the stories of Polish atrocities began to take the leading place, and by the 17th August the campaign was in full swing. . . .

RELATIONS WITH ITALY

STATEMENT by Anthony Eden, Minister for League of Nations Affairs, in the House of Commons, July 1, 1935

Parliamentary Debates, House of Commons, Vol. 303, No. 123, p. 1524; excerpt

I NOW TURN TO the dispute between Italy and Abyssinia, in regard to which I had conversations with Signor Mussolini on the 24th and 25th June.

I expressed to Signor Mussolini the grave concern of His Majesty's Government at the turn which events were taking between Italy and Abyssinia. Our motives were neither egoistic nor dictated by our interests in Africa, but by our membership of the League of Nations. I said that British foreign policy was founded upon the League. His Majesty's Government could not, therefore, remain indifferent to events which might profoundly affect the League's future. Upon this issue public opinion in this country felt very strongly. It was only through collective security that in our judgment peace could be preserved, and only through the League that Great Britain could play her full part in Europe. It was for this reason that His Majesty's Government had been anxiously studying whether there was any constructive contribution which they could make in order to promote a solution.

I then described to Signor Mussolini the kind of contribution which His Majesty's Government had in mind and which I was authorised to make to him as a tentative suggestion. This suggestion was broadly speaking as follows:

To obtain a final settlement of the dispute between Italy and Abyssinia, His Majesty's Government would be prepared to offer to Abyssinia a strip of territory in British Somaliland giving Abyssinia access to the sea. This proposal was intended to facilitate such territorial and economic concessions by Abyssinia to Italy as might have been involved in an agreed settlement. His Majesty's Government would ask for no concession in return for this arrangement save grazing rights for their tribes in such territory as might be ceded to Italy. This suggestion was not lightly made, and only the gravity of the situation could justify the cession of British territory without equivalent return.

I much regret that this suggestion did not commend itself to Signor

Mussolini, who was unable to accept it as the basis for a solution of the dispute.

On my return to Paris, I gave M. Laval an account of what had passed with Signor Mussolini.

STATEMENT by Anthony Eden, Minister for League of Nations Affairs, in the Committee of Eighteen of the League of Nations, October 12, 1935

League of Nations, *Official Journal,* Special Supplement No. 145, 1935, p. 36

BEFORE ENTERING UPON a detailed discussion of the work which now lies before the Committee, I would like to preface my remarks by an assumption which will, I am sure, be generally endorsed. In view of the delicate nature of the proposals which we are now about to discuss, it is, I assume, universally accepted that the obligation of paragraph 3 of Article 16 is binding upon us all, and, in particular, to quote the article, that members "will mutually support one another in resisting any special measures aimed at one of their number by the Covenant-breaking State."

I think we are all agreed that one of the most essential features of our work should be speed. This is necessary in the interests of humanity, in order to give effect to our obligation under Article 16 to take action "immediately," and in order that the world should realise that the machinery of the League can be made effective.

I would base my observations upon the report of the Sub-Committee of the Committee of Thirteen.

A number of measures other than the arms embargo and financial sanctions were considered by that Sub-Committee. Their report has received the careful consideration of His Majesty's Government, and, in their view, the measure which can be most conveniently and expeditiously taken is to prohibit the importation of goods from Italy. The primary object of this measure would be, by limiting Italy's export trade, to deprive her of a large part of her power to purchase supplies abroad. Doubtless we should suffer inconvenience in not obtaining supplies of those classes of goods which we are accustomed to receive from Italy, but it is inevitable that the application of Article 16 should cause inconvenience to us all. This inconvenience we should have to minimise, and at the same time give effect to our undertaking mutually to support one another, by seeking, as far as possible, to obtain from participating States those commodities which we have hitherto obtained from Italy.

In the view of my Government, this form of pressure should prove very effective, and should have drastic results on Italy's capacity to purchase essential supplies. An embargo by all Members of the League on Italian goods would cut off roughly 70% of Italy's export trade. This measure avoids complications with countries outside the League, since the prohibition is a matter between each participating country and Italy, and does not concern third parties. It is a measure which can be brought into operation immediately in any country where the necessary legislative authority exists. Limitation of imports by quota has unfortunately been only too common for some time past in many countries, and the administrative authorities, therefore, would not be undertaking a task to which they were not accustomed. It would mean that Italian quotas for all classes of goods would be reduced to nil. Some points of detail will, of course, require consideration, such as goods *en route* at the date of application of this sanction, the requirement of certificates of origin for imports from non-participating countries, the proportion of Italian content which would render goods subject to the prohibition, and so on. These are, however, not new questions, and they should be capable of rapid settlement. I am strongly of opinion, therefore, that this is a measure which is not only effective, but can also be brought into operation quickly.

This, however, is not the only form of economic pressure which we must consider. The subject of supplies of essential materials to Italy is an obvious means of exerting pressure if only it can be made effective. Some time, however, must elapse before agreement can be reached as to the particular classes of products, supplies of which should be refused to Italy.

Questions will also arise as to the machinery for making the prohibition effective by securing that goods ostensibly destined for some other country are not in fact ultimately reaching Italy, or replacing in a non-participating country supplies which are being furnished by that country to Italy.

It is these administrative difficulties of rendering the prohibition effective which lead my Government to think that the prohibition of the importation of Italian goods, in which we can all take part, is one which should have priority. We must obviously, however, proceed to examine immediately what measures could be taken to stop the supply of essential commodities to Italy. The compilation of an exhaustive list would probably take considerable time, and I would suggest, therefore, that, in order to enable the members of the Committee to set forth their views, it would be desirable that they should each furnish the Secretariat immediately with a provisional list of those commodities which they think it most essential to prohibit; but the Secretariat should amalgamate these lists into one, which could be circulated forthwith, and that we should then have a general discussion on the practicability of enforcing an embargo on the supply of these commodities to Italy.

In this connection, it would be helpful if the Secretariat could, in respect of each commodity, indicate the sources from which Italy has been accustomed to draw her supplies, and the alternative sources from which substantial supplies are available. I do not suggest an elaborate statistical enquiry, but a brief statement containing some material which would enable us to make a preliminary examination of this question.

There are, of course, other forms of pressure which have been suggested, but I would suggest that the consideration of these might be deferred until we have made some progress in regard to those which I have mentioned.

ADDRESS by Anthony Eden, Secretary of State for Foreign Affairs, in the House of Commons, November 1, 1937

Parliamentary Debates, House of Commons, Vol. 328, No. 5, p. 577; excerpt

THEN, ON ANOTHER matter, the hon. Gentleman who has just sat down gave with some skill an impression which is often given on the public platform. I admit at once, and the world knows it, that the sanctions imposed in the Abyssinian dispute failed of their effect, but the hon. Gentleman gave the impression that the League was most anxious to impose all sorts of further and more serious sanctions and that it was we who held back. That must be known to the House to be an utterly false impression. After all, there were three great Powers in the League at that time. Is the hon. Gentleman going to suggest that it was the France of that day that was so anxious to impose more sanctions? He knows just as well as I do, what were the views of the French Government of that time. If the criticism is, and I admit the force of it, that we took off sanctions, in the view of hon. Gentlemen opposite too soon, then I would remind him of the suggestion which he made himself in that Debate: "Do not take them off now, but go on as you are until September." Surely it is clear to anybody that the continuation of these sanctions from July to September would have made no difference whatever to the result, once the military victory had been gained. If the hon. Gentleman does not agree with my version, let him look up the speech of M. Litvinoff. In an extremely frank speech at the Assembly he told us that there were those who urged the League to put on more sanctions. Then he worked out details to show that even of the sanctions that had been voted a quarter of them had not been applied at all by the nations of the League—that a quarter of the nations had not applied the sanctions which were imposed. . . .

ADDRESS by Neville Chamberlain, Prime Minister, in the House of Commons, November 2, 1938

Royal Institute of International Affairs, *Documents on International Affairs, 1938*, I, 170, citing *Hansard*, November 2, 1938, cols. 207–12; excerpts

I BEG TO MOVE,
"That this House welcomes the intention of His Majesty's Government to bring the Anglo-Italian Agreement into force."

Yesterday, in speaking of the Declaration signed at Munich by Herr Hitler and myself, I said I thought that if it were suitably followed up it might well be found to contain the seed which would ultimately develop into a new era of confidence and peace in Europe. Somewhat the same idea was expressed, in different language, by the right hon. Gentleman the Leader of the Opposition when he asked whether we must always wait for subjects of difference between nations to give rise to threats of war before we considered them ripe for peaceful discussion and negotiation. Since we made an Agreement with Italy on 16th April last, I am glad to think that there are no differences between our two countries [*Interruption*.]—but it is clear that if the improvement in our relations which so markedly followed upon the conclusion of that Agreement is to be maintained, the delay in putting the Agreement into force, which had already lasted for more than six months, cannot be indefinitely prolonged.

It is not necessary for me this afternoon to discuss the merits of the Agreement itself. The terms of the Agreement were debated in this House last May, and on the 2nd of that month, a Motion, which was moved by me, of approval of the Agreement was carried by a large majority. Of course, I am well aware that the Opposition resisted the Motion then, and naturally I do not expect them to have changed their views, but the question we have to consider today is not whether this is a good Agreement or not. That has already been settled as far as this House is concerned. The question we have to consider is whether the time has now come to put it into force, and whether the preliminary condition which I laid down as essential before the Agreement could be put into force has now been fulfilled. The House will remember very well what that condition was. It was that we should be able to consider that the Spanish question was settled, and I explained last July why we had thought it necessary to make that condition. I said then that in our view the justification for the formal recognition of Italian sovereignty over Ethiopia was to be found if we could feel that that recognition would constitute an important advance towards the general appeasement of Europe, and it was because we felt at that time that the conflict which was going on in Spain under the then existing conditions did constitute a perpetual menace to the peace of Europe that we felt that it must be removed from that category before we could ask Parliament to agree to the Agreement being put into force.

Since that time a good many efforts have been made by various Members of the Opposition to get me to say exactly what I meant by a settlement in Spain. I have always refused to give any such definition, not because I wanted to evade any proper duty which fell upon me, but because I did not feel that I could give such a definition in the absence of more knowledge than I possessed of what might be the future developments in the Spanish situation. But perhaps hon. Members may recollect that on 26th July last, in answer to an interruption by the Leader of the Opposition relating to the withdrawal of volunteers from Spain, I used these words:

I would like to see what happens when the volunteers are withdrawn. If His Majesty's Government think that Spain has ceased to be a menace to the peace of Europe, I think we shall regard that as a settlement of the Spanish question. (Official Report, 26th July, 1938; col. 2965, Vol. 338.)

Since then a great deal has happened. Already, even at that date, all the Powers represented on the Non-Intervention Committee, including Italy, of course, had accepted the British plan for the withdrawal of volunteers, and if that plan is not in operation today, it cannot be said that that is the fault of Italy. It cannot properly be said. Again, since then the Spanish Government have announced their intention of withdrawing the International Brigade. When I was at Munich, Signor Mussolini volunteered me the information that he intended to withdraw 10,000 men, or about half the Italian infantry forces from Spain, and since then those men have in fact been withdrawn.

I have no doubt that hon. Members will represent that Italian men, pilots, aircraft and other material still remain in Spain, and so also there remain men and material of other than Italian nationality in Spain on one side or the other; but we have received from Signor Mussolini definite assurances, first of all that the remaining Italian forces of all categories will be withdrawn when the non-intervention plan comes into operation; secondly, that no further Italian troops will be sent to Spain; and thirdly—in case this idea had occurred to anybody—that the Italian Government have never for a moment entertained the idea of sending compensatory air forces to Spain in lieu of the infantry forces which have now been withdrawn. These three assurances, taken in conjunction with the actual withdrawal of this large body of men, in my judgment constitute a substantial earnest of the good intentions of the Italian Government. They form a considerable contribution to the elimination of the Spanish question as a menace to peace.

But these are not the only considerations which weigh with His Majesty's Government. Some hon. Members, with that eternal tendency to suspicion which, I am afraid, only breeds corresponding suspicions on the other side, persist in the view that Germany and Italy have a design of somehow permanently establishing themselves in Spain, and that Spain itself will presently be setting up a Fascist State. I believe both those views to be entirely unfounded. When I was at Munich, I spoke on the subject of the future of Spain with Herr Hitler and Signor Mussolini, and both of them assured me most definitely that they had no territorial ambitions whatever in Spain. I would remind hon. Members that when, in September, Europe was apparently faced with the prospect of a new major war, General Franco made a declaration of his neutrality and stated that he would not violate the French frontier unless he was attacked from that quarter. It seems to us that the events which took place in September put the whole Spanish conflict into a new perspective, and if the nations of Europe escaped a great catastrophe in the acute Czechoslovakian crisis, surely nobody can imagine that, with that recollection fresh in their minds, they are going to knock their heads together over Spain. In my own mind I am perfectly clear that the Spanish question is no longer a menace to the peace of Europe, and, consequently, that there is no valid reason why we should not take a step which, obviously, would contribute to general appeasement.

In the realm of international affairs one thing generally leads to another, and if any justification were required for the policy of the Government in closing our differences with Italy, it surely can be found in the action of Signor Mussolini, when, at my request, he used his influence with Herr Hitler in order to give time for the discussion which led up to the Munich Agreement. By that act, the peace of Europe was saved. Does anybody suppose that my request to Signor Mussolini to intervene would have met with a response from him, or, indeed, that I could even have made such a request if our relations with Italy had remained what they were a year ago?

There is one other point which I ought to mention because it seems to me to weigh heavily, although I think unnecessarily, upon certain minds. That is the propriety of the recognition of Italian sovereignty over Ethiopia. I wonder how far those who hold that view are prepared to carry their reluctance? Are they prepared to withhold recognition in perpetuity? Because, if that really were so, I am afraid they would very speedily find themselves in complete isolation. I would like to remind them that, in the first place the Council of the League of Nations, by a large majority, last May, expressed the unqualified view that it was for each nation to decide for itself whether it should or should not accord this formal recognition. Further, I would remind them that, of all the countries in Europe, there are only two, namely, ourselves and the Government of Soviet Russia, which have restricted themselves to *de facto* recognition. The latest country to recognize formally Italian sovereignty in Ethiopia is France, and their new Ambassador is to be accredited to the King of Italy and the Emperor of Ethiopia. We propose to follow the same course as France, and, accordingly, new credentials will be issued to our Ambassador in Italy on similar lines, thereby according legal recognition to Italian sovereignty.

Perhaps the House may like to know that on being informed of our intention to take this course the French Government not only raised no objection but stated that they welcomed generally anything which could contribute to the improvement of Anglo-Italian relations. It is, perhaps, unnecessary to tell the House that, in accordance with what has now become the usual routine, the Dominions have been kept fully informed of all our intentions, and I am very glad to be able to read to the House a message which I have received from the Prime Minister of Australia who says as follows:

The Commonwealth Government are convinced that the Anglo-Italian agreement should be brought into operation forthwith as a contribution to peace and *de jure* recognition accorded to the Italian conquest of Abyssinia. The withdrawal of 10,000 Italian troops from Spain seems a real contribution. In our opinion, a peaceful and friendly Mediterranean is essential to the present condition of the world. To refuse *de jure* recognition would seem to us to ignore the facts and to risk danger for a matter which is now immaterial,

RELATIONS WITH ITALY

I have also received the following message from the Prime Minister of South Africa:

General Hertzog has noted the contents of this telegram

that is the telegram informing him of our intention to bring the Anglo-Italian Agreement into force—

with much satisfaction, and he feels that the steps that His Majesty's Government in the United Kingdom propose taking are wise and necessary and will materially contribute to appeasement in Europe.

It will be observed how, in both those messages, the Prime Ministers of Australia and South Africa respectively have gone to what, I think, is the root of the matter, and have recognized that, in the action which His Majesty's Government propose to take, they are not concerned solely with the relations between ourselves and Italy, but that the step we are taking must be regarded as a step in the policy which I have described to the House on so many occasions. . . .

I ask the House to approve this Motion, and in doing so I am satisfied that the House will be definitely increasing the prospect of peace as a whole. I say, let us put an end here and now to any idea that it is our desire to keep any State at arm's length, and let us remember that every advance which we may make towards removing possible causes of friction upon one subject, makes it easier and more probable that we can deal satisfactorily with those which remain still unsettled.

RADIO ADDRESS by Winston Churchill, Prime Minister, to the Italian people, December 23, 1940

The New York Times, December 24, 1940

TONIGHT I SPEAK to the Italian people and I speak to you from London, the heart of the British islands and of the British Commonwealth and Empire. I speak to you in what the diplomatists call "words of great truth and respect."

We are at war. That is a very strange and terrible thought. Whoever imagined until the last few melancholy years that the British and Italian nations would be trying to destroy one another. We have always been such friends.

We were the champions of the Italian Resorgimento. We were the partisans of Garibaldi. We were the admirers of Mazzini and Cavour —all that great movement toward the unity of the Italian nation which lighted the nineteenth century was aided and was hailed by the British Parliament and British public.

Our fathers and our grandfathers longed to see Italy freed from the Austrian yoke and to see all minor barriers in Italy swept away so that the Italian people and their fair land might take an honored place as one of the leading powers upon the Continent and as a brilliant and gifted member of the family of Europe and of Christendom.

We have never been your foes till now. In the last war against the barbarous Huns we were your comrades. For fifteen years after that war, we were your friends. Although the institutions which you adopted after that war were not akin to ours and diverged, as we think, from the sovereign impulses which had commanded the unity of Italy, we could still walk together in peace and good-will. Many thousands of your people dwelt with ours in England; many of our people dwelt with you in Italy.

We liked each other. We got on well together. There were reciprocal services, there was amity, there was esteem. And now we are at war—now we are condemned to work each other's ruin.

Your aviators have tried to cast their bombs upon London. Our armies are tearing—and will tear—your African empire to shreds and tatters. We are now only at the beginning of this somber tale. Who can say where it will end? Presently, we shall be forced to come to much closer grips. How has all this come about, and what is it all for?

Italians, I will tell you the truth.

It is all because of one man—one man and one man alone has ranged the Italian people in deadly struggle against the British Empire and has deprived Italy of the sympathy and intimacy of the United States of America.

That he is a great man I do not deny. But that after eighteen years of unbridled power he has led your country to the horrid verge of ruin—that can be denied by none.

It is all one man—one man, who, against the crown and royal family of Italy, against the Pope and all the authority of the Vatican and of the Roman Catholic Church, against the wishes of the Italian people who had no lust for this war; one man has arrayed the trustees and inheritors of ancient Rome upon the side of the ferocious pagan barbarians.

There lies the tragedy of Italian history and there stands the criminal who has wrought the deed of folly and of shame.

What is the defense that is put forward for his action? It is, of course, the quarrel about sanctions and Abyssinia. Let us look at that.

Together after the last war Italy and Britain both signed the covenant of the League of Nations, which forbade all parties to that covenant to make war upon each other or upon fellow-members of the League, and bound all signatories to come to the aid of any member attacked by another.

Presently Abyssinia came knocking at the door, asking to be a member. We British advised against it. We doubted whether they had reached a stage in their development which warranted their inclusion in so solemn a pact. But it was Signor Mussolini who insisted that Abyssinia should become a member of the League and who, therefore, bound himself and bound you and us to respect their covenanted rights.

Thus the quarrel arose; it was out of this that it sprang. And thus, although no blood was shed between us, old friendships were forgotten.

But what is the proportion of this Abyssinian dispute arising out of the covenant of the League of Nations, to which we had both pledged our word; what is it in proportion compared to the death grapple in which Italy and Britain have now been engaged?

I declare—and my words will go far—that nothing that has happened in that Abyssinian quarrel can account for or justify the deadly strife which has now broken out between us.

Time passed. Then the great war between the British and French democracies and Prussian militarism or Nazi overlordship began again.

Where was the need for Italy to intervene? Where was the need to strike at prostrate France? Where was the need to declare war on Britain? Where was the need to invade Egypt, which is under British protection?

We were content with Italian neutrality. During the first eight months of the war we paid great deference to Italian interests. But all this was put down to fear. We were told we were effete, worn out, an old chatterbox people mouthing outworn shibboleths of nineteenth-century liberalism.

But it was not due to fear. It was not due to weakness. The French Republic for the moment is stunned. France will rise again. But the British nation and Commonwealth of Nations across the globe, and indeed I may say the English-speaking world, are now aroused. They are on the march or on the move. All the forces of modern progress and of ancient culture are ranged behind them.

Why have you placed yourselves, you who were our friends and might have been our brothers, why have you placed yourselves in the path of this avalanche, now only just started from its base to roll forward on its predestined track? Why, after all this, were you made to attack and invade Greece? I ask why, but you may ask why, too, because you were never consulted. The people of Italy were never consulted. The Army of Italy was never consulted. No one was consulted.

One man, and one man alone, ordered Italian soldiers to ravage their neighbor's vineyard.

Surely the time has come when the Italian monarchy and people, who guard the sacred center of Christendom, should have a word to say upon these awe-inspiring issues. Surely the Italian Army, which has fought so bravely on many occasions in the past but now evidently has no heart for the job, should take some care of the life and future of Italy.

I can only tell you that I, Churchill, have done my best to prevent this war between Italy and the British Empire, and to prove my words I will read you the message which I sent to Signor Mussolini in the fateful days before it began. Cast your minds back to the 16th of May of this year, 1940. The French front had been broken; the French Army was not yet defeated; the great battle in France was still raging. Here is the message which I sent to Signor Mussolini:

"Now that I have taken up my office as Prime Minister and Minister of Defense, I look back to our meetings in Rome and feel a desire to speak words of goodwill to you, as chief of the Italian nation, across what seems to be a swiftly widening gulf. Is it too late to stop a river of blood from flowing between the British and Italian peoples?

"We can, no doubt, inflict grievous injuries upon one another and maul each other cruelly and darken the Mediterranean with our strife. If you so decree, it must be so. But I declare that I have never been the enemy of Italian greatness, nor ever at heart the foe of the Italian lawgiver. It is idle to predict the course of the great battles now raging in Europe. But I am sure that whatever may happen on the continent, England will go on to the end, even quite alone, as we have done before; and I believe, with some assurance, that we shall be aided in increasing measure by the United States and, indeed, by all the Americas.

"I beg you to believe that it is in no spirit of weakness or of fear that I make this solemn appeal, which will remain on record. Down the ages, above all other calls, comes the cry that the joint heirs of Latin and Christian civilization must not be ranged against one another in mortal strife. Hearken to it, I beseech you in all honor and respect, before the dread signal is given. It will never be given by us."

That is what I wrote upon the 16th day of May. And this is the reply which I received from Signor Mussolini upon the 18th:

"I reply to the message which you have sent me in order to tell you that you are certainly aware of grave reasons of a historical and

RELATIONS WITH ITALY

contingent character which ranged our two countries in opposite camps.

"Without going back very far in time, I remind you of the initiative taken in 1935 by your government to organize at Geneva sanctions against Italy, engaged in securing for herself a small space in the African sun without causing the slightest injury to your interests and territories or those of others. I remind you also of the real and actual state of servitude in which Italy finds herself in her own sea. If it was to honor your signature that your government declared war on Germany, you will understand that the same sense of honor and of respect for engagements assumed in the Italian-German treaty guides Italian policy today and tomorrow in the face of any event whatsoever."

That was the answer; I make no comment upon it. It was a dusty answer; it speaks for itself. Any one can see who it was that wanted peace and who it was that meant to have war.

One man and one man only was resolved to plunge Italy, after all these years of strain and effort, into the whirlpool of war.

And what is the position of Italy today? Where is it that the Duce has led his trusting people after eighteen years of dictatorial power? What hard choice is open to them now?

It is to stand up to the battery of the whole British Empire on sea, in the air and in Africa, and to the vigorous counter-attack of the Greek nation. Or, on the other hand, to call in Attila over the Brenner Pass with his hordes of ravenous soldiery and his gangs of Gestapo policemen to occupy, to hold down and to protect the Italian people, for whom he and his Nazi followers cherish the most bitter and outspoken contempt that is on record between races.

There is where one man, and one man only, has led you. And there I leave this unfolding story until the day comes—as come it will—when the Italian nation will once more take a hand in shaping its own fortunes.

RELATIONS WITH JAPAN

NOTE from the British Government to the Japanese Government, August 29, 1937, Regarding the Wounding of the British Ambassador to China

Royal Institute of International Affairs, *Documents on International Affairs, 1937*, p. 665, citing *The Times* (London), August 30, 1937

The Japanese Government will be aware of the injuries sustained by Sir H. Knatchbull-Hugessen, His Majesty's Ambassador in China, as a result of shooting from Japanese military aeroplanes when motoring with members of his staff from Nanking to Shanghai on August 26 last. The facts were as follows:—

His Majesty's Ambassador was proceeding from Nanking to Shanghai on August 26 accompanied by the Military Attaché and the Financial Adviser to His Majesty's Embassy and a Chinese chauffeur. The party occupied two black saloon cars of obviously private character, each flying the Union Jack, approximately 18 in. by 12 in. in size on the near side of the car, projecting above the roof. At about 2.30 p.m. and about eight miles north-west of Taitsang, i.e., some 40 miles from Shanghai, the cars were attacked by machine-gun fire from a Japanese aeroplane. The aeroplane which fired the machine-gun dived from the off-side of the car at a right angle to it. This was followed by a bomb attack from a second Japanese aeroplane from a height of about 200 ft. The Ambassador was hit by a nickel steel bullet (subsequently found embedded in the car), which penetrated the side of the abdomen and grazed the spine.

His Majesty's Government in the United Kingdom have received with deep distress and concern the news of this deplorable event, in respect of which they must record their emphatic protest and request the fullest measure of redress.

Although non-combatants, including foreigners resident in the country concerned, must accept the inevitable risk of injury resulting indirectly from the normal conduct of hostilities, it is one of the oldest and best-established rules of international law that direct or deliberate attacks on non-combatants are absolutely prohibited, whether inside or outside the area in which hostilities are taking place.

Aircraft are in no way exempt from this rule, which applies as much to attack from the air as to any other form of attack.

Nor can the plea of accident be accepted where the facts are such as to show, at the best, negligence and a complete disregard for the sanctity of civilian life. In the present case the facts which have been recorded above make it clear that this was no accident resulting from any normal hostile operation, and it should have been obvious to the aircraft that they were dealing with non-combatants.

The plea, should it be advanced, that the flags carried on the cars were too small to be visible is irrelevant. There would have been no justification for the attack even had the cars carried no flags at all. The foreign, even the diplomatic, status of the occupants is also irrelevant. The real issue is that they were non-combatants. The aircraft no doubt did not intend to attack His Majesty's Ambassador as such. They apparently did intend to attack non-combatants, and that suffices in itself to constitute an illegality.

It is, moreover, pertinent to observe that in this particular case the Ambassador was travelling in a locality where there were no Chinese troops nor any actual hostilities in progress. No Chinese troops were in fact encountered by the Ambassador's party until about an hour's drive from the scene of the attack.

His Majesty's Government feel that they must take this opportunity to emphasize the wider significance of this event. It is an outstanding example of the results to be expected from indiscriminate attack from the air. Such events are inseparable from the practice, as illegal as it is inhuman, of failing to draw that clear distinction between combatants and non-combatants in the conduct of hostilities which international law, no less than the conscience of mankind, has always enjoined.

The fact that in the present case no actual state of war has been declared or expressly recognized by either party to exist emphasizes the inexcusable nature of what occurred.

His Majesty's Government must therefore request:—

(1) A formal apology, to be conveyed by the Japanese Government to His Majesty's Government;
(2) Suitable punishment of those responsible for the attack;
(3) An assurance by the Japanese authorities that the necessary measures will be taken to prevent the recurrence of incidents of such a character.

NOTE from Sir Robert Leslie Craigie, British Ambassador to Japan, to the Japanese Minister for Foreign Affairs (Koki Hirota), December 16, 1937, Regarding the Bombing of British Vessels

Royal Institute of International Affairs, *Documents on International Affairs, 1937*, p. 767, citing *The Times* (London), December 16, 1937

I HAVE THE HONOUR, on instructions from His Majesty's Government in the United Kingdom, to address Your Excellency on the subject of the attacks made by Japanese aircraft and land forces on British warships and merchant shipping at Wuhu and near Nanking on December 12. These incidents clearly raise grave issues.

At Wuhu a British tug, which had conveyed from Nanking His Majesty's Consul, the British Military Attaché, and the Flag-Captain to the British Rear-Admiral, . . . was attacked by Japanese machine-gun fire after transferring these officers to H.M.S. *Ladybird*. The latter proceeded to join the tug in order to protect her, when she observed a Japanese field-gun battery firing on merchant ships concentrated above the Asiatic Petroleum Company's installation. Firing continued and was directed at H.M.S. *Ladybird* herself. There were four direct hits on this vessel: one naval rating was killed, another was seriously wounded, and there were several minor casualties, including the Flag-Captain. A direct hit was also seen to be sustained by the British merchant ship *Suivo*.

H.M.S. *Bee* then arrived on the scene and was also fired on by the shore battery. The commander of H.M.S. *Bee* landed to protest, and was informed by Colonel Hashimoto, the senior Japanese military officer then at Wuhu, that the firing on the warships was due to a mistake, but that he had orders to fire on every ship on the river. At a later interview, the same officer stated categorically that if any ships moved on the river they would be fired on, and, despite protests, His Majesty's ships *Bee* and *Ladybird,* after berthing, remained covered by guns at point-blank range.

Near Hsiasanshan, above Nanking, where British merchant ships were concentrated in a part of the river previously designated by the Japanese Commander-in-Chief as a safety zone, three separate bombing attacks were made by Japanese aircraft on them and on His Majesty's ships *Cricket* and *Scarab,* which were with them.

His Majesty's Government have now been glad to receive Your Excellency's Note of December 14 offering the profound apology of the Imperial Japanese Government for the attacks on His Majesty's ships, stating that measures were immediately taken to prevent the recurrence of such incidents, and adding that they will deal suitably with those responsible and pay the necessary compensation.

His Majesty's Government observe that Your Excellency's Note makes no mention of the attacks on British merchant vessels, and I am instructed to request that an assurance may be given that all that is said in that Note applies equally to these attacks.

His Majesty's Government take particular note of the statement that those responsible will be suitably dealt with. Adequate punishment of those responsible for the particular attacks under discussion seems indeed to His Majesty's Government to be the only method by which further outrages can be prevented. His Majesty's Government cannot but recall previous incidents in which the Japanese Government have expressed regret for attacks made on British nationals and property, and have given assurances that adequate steps had been taken to prevent any repetition. They call to mind the attack made on His Majesty's Ambassador in China while travelling by road from Nanking to Shanghai, the subsequent attack on motor-cars conveying British officials on a similar journey, the attacks on British civilians and military posts on the defence perimeter at Shanghai, as well as other incidents, and the repeated assurances of the Japanese Government of their intention fully to respect the interests of third Powers in the present conflict with China.

It is clear that the steps hitherto taken by the Japanese Government to prevent such attacks have so far failed in that purpose, and His Majesty's Government must now ask to be informed that measures have actually been taken of a character which will put a definite stop to the incidents of which they complain.

NOTE from Sir Robert Leslie Craigie, British Ambassador to Japan, to the Japanese Minister for Foreign Affairs (Hachiro Arita), January 14, 1939

Royal Institute of International Affairs, *Documents on International Affairs, 1938*, I, 366, citing *The Times* (London), January 16, 1939

I AM INSTRUCTED by His Majesty's Principal Secretary of State for Foreign Affairs to inform your Excellency of the uncertainty and the grave anxiety in which his Majesty's Government in the United Kingdom have been left by a study of Japan's new policy in Far Eastern affairs, as set out in recent statements by the late Prime Minister and other Japanese statesmen. I am to refer more particularly to Prince Konoe's statements of November 3 and December 22 and to the communication made by your Excellency to foreign Press correspondents on December 19. This uncertainty has not been removed by conversations on this subject which I have had with your Excellency from time to time.

From these pronouncements and from other official information issued in Japan, His Majesty's Government infer that it is the intention of the Japanese Government to establish a tripartite combination or *bloc* composed of Japan, China, and Manchuria, in which the supreme authority will be vested in Japan and subordinate rôles will be allotted to China and Manchuria. So far as China is concerned it is understood that the Japanese Government are to exercise control, at least for some time, through the Asia Development Council in Tokyo, which is charged with the formulation and execution of policy connected with political, economic, and cultural affairs in China. Your Excellency's own communication to the Press indicates that the tripartite combination is to form a single economic unit, and the economic activities of other Powers are to be subjected to restrictions dictated by the requirements of national defense and the economic security of the proposed *bloc*.

According to Prince Konoe, the hostilities in China are to continue until the present Chinese Government have been crushed or will consent to enter the proposed combination on Japanese terms. China, he said, will be required to conclude with Japan an anti-Comintern agreement, and Japanese troops are to be stationed at specified points in Chinese territory for an indefinite period, presumably to ensure that Japanese conditions for the suspension of hostilities are observed. Moreover, his Excellency stated that the Inner Mongolian region must be designated as a special anti-Communist area. It is not clear what is meant by this, but in the absence of fuller information it can only be assumed that Inner Mongolia is to be subjected to an even greater degree of Japanese military control than other parts of China.

His Majesty's Government are at a loss to understand how Prince Konoe's assurance that Japan seeks no territory, and respects the sovereignty of China, can be reconciled with the declared intention of the Japanese Government to compel the Chinese people by force of arms to accept conditions involving the surrender of their political, economic, and cultural life to Japanese control, indefinite maintenance in China of considerable Japanese garrisons, and the virtual detachment from China of the territory of Inner Mongolia.

For their part, His Majesty's Government desire to make it clear that they are not prepared to accept or to recognize changes of the nature indicated, which are brought about by force. They intend to adhere to the principles of the Nine-Power Treaty, and cannot agree to the unilateral modification of its terms. They would point out that, until the outbreak of the present hostilities, the beneficial effects which the treaty was expected to produce were steadily being realized. The Chinese people were maintaining and developing for themselves an effective and stable Government, and the principle of equal opportunity for commerce and industry of all nations was bringing prosperity to China and to her international trade, including that with Japan. His Majesty's Government therefore cannot agree, as suggested in Japan, that the treaty is obsolete or that its provisions no longer meet the situation, except in so far as the situation has been altered by Japan in contravention of its terms.

While, however, His Majesty's Government maintain that modifications cannot be effected unilaterally and must be by negotiation between all the signatories, they do not contend that treaties are eternal. If, therefore, the Japanese Government have any constructive suggestions to make regarding the modification of any of the multilateral agreements relating to China, His Majesty's Government for their part will be ready to consider them. In the meantime, His Majesty's Government reserve all their rights under the existing treaties.

I am further instructed to refer to that portion of Prince Konoe's statement of December 22 which states that Japan is prepared to give consideration to the abolition of extraterritoriality and rendition of foreign concessions and settlements in China. This inducement to China to accept Japan's demands would appear to entail but little sacrifice on the part of the Japanese, for if they succeed in their plans for the control of the country they will have no further need for extraterritoriality or concessions. On the other hand, His Majesty's Government would recall that they undertook and nearly completed negotiations with the Chinese Government in 1931 for abrogation of British extraterritorial rights. The negotiations were suspended by the Chinese Government in consequence of the disturbed conditions following the seizure of Manchuria by Japanese forces in that year, but His Majesty's Government have always been ready to resume negotiations at a suitable time, and are prepared to discuss this and other similar questions with a fully independent Chinese Government when peace has been restored.

In conclusion, I am to state that, if, as is possible, His Majesty's Government have in any way misinterpreted the intentions of the Japanese Government, they feel that it is because of the ambiguity with which those intentions have so far been expressed, and they would welcome a more precise and detailed exposition of the Japanese conditions for terminating hostilities and of the Japanese policy towards China.

RADIO ADDRESS by Winston Churchill, Prime Minister, August 24, 1941

Furnished by the British Library of Information, New York City; excerpt

But Europe is not the only continent to be tormented and devastated by aggression. For five long years the Japanese military factions seeking to emulate the style of Hitler and Mussolini, taking all their posturing as if it were a new European revelation, have been invading and harrying the 500,000,000 inhabitants of China. Japanese armies have been wandering about that vast land in futile excursions, carrying with them carnage, ruin and corruption, and calling it "the Chinese incident." Now, they stretch a grasping hand into the southern seas of China. They snatch Indo-China from the wretched Vichy French. They menace by their movements Siam, menace Singapore, the British link with Australasia, and menace the Philippine Islands under the protection of the United States.

It is certain that this has got to stop. Every effort will be made to secure a peaceful settlement. The United States are labouring with infinite patience to arrive at a fair and amicable settlement which will give Japan the utmost reassurance for her legitimate interests. We earnestly hope these negotiations will succeed. But this I must say: that if these hopes should fail we shall, of course, range ourselves unhesitatingly at the side of the United States.

ADDRESS by Winston Churchill, Prime Minister, in the House of Commons, December 8, 1941

The New York Times, December 9, 1941

As soon as I heard last night that Japan had attacked the United States I felt it necessary that Parliament should be immediately summoned.

It is indispensable to our system of government that Parliament should play a full part in all the important acts of state, and at all

RELATIONS WITH JAPAN

crucial moments in the conduct of the war, and I am glad to see so many members have been able to be in their places in spite of the shortness of notice.

With the full approval of the nation and of the Empire I pledged the word of Great Britain about a month ago that should the United States be involved in war with Japan a British declaration of war would follow within the hour.

Therefore I spoke to President Roosevelt on the Atlantic telephone last night with a view to arranging the timing of our respective declarations.

The President told me he would this morning send a message to Congress, which, as is well known, can alone make a declaration of war on behalf of the United States.

I then answered him we would follow immediately. However, it soon appeared that British territory in Malaya had also been the object of Japanese attack and later on it was announced from Tokyo that the Japanese High Command—a curious form, not the Imperial Japanese Government but the Japanese High Command—had declared that a state of war existed between them and Great Britain and the United States.

That being so, there were no need to wait for the declaration of Congress. In any case, American time is nearly six hours behind ours. The Cabinet, which met at 12:30 today, therefore authorized an immediate declaration of war upon Japan. Instructions to this effect were sent to His Majesty's Ambassador in Tokyo and a communication was dispatched to the Japanese Chargé d'Affaires at 1 o'clock today to this effect.

"Sir:

"On the evening of Dec. 7 His Majesty's Government in the United Kingdom learned that the Japanese forces, without a previous warning either in the form of a declaration of war or of an ultimatum with a conditional declaration of war, had attempted a landing on the coast of Malaya and had bombed Singapore and Hong Kong.

"In view of these wanton acts of unprovoked aggression, committed in flagrant violation of international law and particularly by Article I of the Third Hague Convention relative to the opening of hostilities, to which both Japan and the United Kingdom are parties, His Majesty's Ambassador in Tokyo has been instructed to inform the Imperial Japanese Government in the name of His Majesty's Government in the United Kingdom that a state of war exists between the two countries.

"I have the honor to be, with high consideration, your obedient servant."

Meanwhile, hostilities had already begun. The Japanese began a landing on British territory in Northern Malaya at about 6 o'clock yesterday morning, and they were immediately engaged by our forces, which were in readiness.

Home Office measures against Japanese nationals were set in motion at 10:45 last night. The House will see that no time has been lost and that we actually are ahead of our engagements.

The Royal Netherlands Government at once marked their solidarity with Great Britain and the United States. At 3 A. M. the Netherlands Minister informed the Foreign Office his government was telling the Japanese Government that in view of hostile acts perpetrated by Japanese forces against two powers with whom the Netherlands maintained particularly close relations they considered as a consequence that a state of war now existed between the Kingdom of the Netherlands and Japan.

I do not know yet what part Thailand will be called upon to play in this fresh war, but a report has reached us that Japan has landed troops at Singora, in Siamese territory, not far from the landing they have made on the British side of the frontier.

Meanwhile, just before Japan had gone to war with Siam, I had sent the Prime Minister of Siam the following message. It was sent off on Sunday:

"There is a possibility of imminent Japanese invasion of your country. If you are attacked, defend yourself. The preservation of the full independence and sovereignty of Thailand is the British interest and we shall regard an attack on you as an attack on ourselves."

It is worth while looking for a moment at the manner in which the Japanese have begun their assault upon the English-speaking world. Every circumstance of calculated and characteristic Japanese treachery was employed against the United States.

Japanese envoys Nomura and Kurusu were ordered to prolong their missions in the United States in order to keep conversations going while the surprise attack was being prepared to be made before the declaration of war could be delivered.

The President's appeal to the Emperor, which I have no doubt many members have read, reminded him of ancient friendship and of the importance of preserving the peace of the Pacific. This message has received only this base and brutal reply. No one can doubt that every effort to bring about a peaceful solution had been made by the Government of the United States and that an immense patience and composure had been shown in the face of the growing Japanese menace.

RELATIONS WITH JAPAN

Now that the issue is joined in the most direct manner, it only remains for the two great democracies to face their task with whatever strength God may give them.

We may hold ourselves very fortunate, and I think we may rate our affairs not wholly ill-guided, that we were not attacked alone by Japan in our period of weakness after Dunquerque—or at any time in 1940 before the United States had fully realized the dangers which threatened the whole world and had made large advances in its military preparations.

So precarious and narrow was the margin upon which we then lived that we did not dare to express the sympathy we have all along felt for the heroic people of China. We were even forced for a short time in the Summer of 1940 to agree to closing the Burma Road, but later on, at the beginning of this year, as soon as we could regather our strength, we reversed that policy, and the House will remember that both I and the Foreign Secretary have felt able to make increasingly outspoken declarations of friendship for the Chinese people and their great leader, Chiang Kai-shek.

We have always been friends. Last night I cabled to the Generalissimo assuring him that henceforward we would face the common foe together, although imperative demands of the war in Europe and Africa have strained our resources, vast and growing though they are.

The House and the Empire will notice that some of the finest ships in the Royal Navy have reached their stations in the Far East at a very convenient moment. Every preparation on our part has been made, and I do not doubt we shall give a good account of ourselves. The closest accord has been established with powerful American forces, both naval and air, and also with strong and efficient forces belonging to the Royal Netherland Government in the Netherland East Indies. We shall all do our best.

When we think of the insane ambition and insatiable appetite which have caused this vast and melancholy extension of the war we can only feel that Hitler's madness has infected Japanese minds and that the root of the evil and its branch must be extirpated together.

It is of the highest importance that there should be no underrating of the gravity of the new dangers we have to meet, either here or in the United States.

The enemy has attacked with an audacity which may spring from recklessness but which may also spring from a conviction of strength. The ordeal to which the English-speaking world and our heroic Russian allies are being exposed will certainly be hard, especially at the outset, and will probably be long; yet when we look round us upon the somber panorama of the world we have no reason to doubt the justice of our cause or that our strength and will-power will be sufficient to sustain it.

We have at least four-fifths of the population of the world on our side. We are responsible for their safety and for their future.

In the past we have had a light which flickered. In the present we have a light which flames. In the future there will be a light which shines over all the land and sea.

PART THREE

FRANCE

GENERAL STATEMENTS OF POLICY

ADDRESS by Aristide Briand, Minister for Foreign Affairs, before the Assembly of the League of Nations, September 11, 1931

Translation, in League of Nations, *Official Journal*, Special Supplement No. 93, p. 69; excerpts

As FIRST DELEGATE of France, I have come here this year, as in previous years, to make a sincere and ardent declaration of faith in the League of Nations. I was afraid at one time that I might be prevented from doing so, and I can assure you that the prospect caused me the greatest distress. I am glad that circumstances have enabled me to take part in the work of this Assembly.

I am particularly glad to be present at this meeting, since it opened in somewhat disquieting circumstances; the work of the Assembly cannot be said to have begun in any atmosphere of optimism.

The sole talk was of the stagnation of the League, the disappointment it had caused in the minds of the nations; some even went so far as to say that a kind of disaffection was causing men to lose interest in its activities.

Personally, I do not take such rumours or such information at their face value. The League has become powerful and has now acquired a moral standing which makes direct attack difficult. It has very few declared enemies; but no one will be surprised to hear me say that not everyone is its friends; and among those whose habits have been upset by it, whose interests have been threatened, are some who, not daring to attack it openly, allow no occasion to pass for disseminating rumours to its detriment.

Naturally, nations, like individuals, when they are passing through difficult times, when they are ready to take offence at the slightest thing, tend to look for a scapegoat on whom to pronounce sentence, and at such times people are always more ready to lend a willing ear to adverse criticism.

Yet, although it is true that the nations are to-day passing through a difficult period and have great cause for anxiety, it would be extremely unfair to blame the League of Nations. When we examine the position we find, on the contrary, fresh reasons for placing confidence in this institution of ours.

The serious time through which we are passing is primarily, it must be admitted, a consequence of the war. It is one of the last of the tidal waves caused by that terrible upheaval, and it is breaking over the nations and doing terrible damage.

It is only fair to say that there are yet other reasons for this difficult situation. I cannot go into all of them; I have not enough experience to do so, and, moreover, they are too many and too varied. Let us admit, however, that the economic welter in which the world is placed is due also to the fact that, after the war, the nations were seized with a frenzied desire to produce. Nations and individuals threw themselves into their task in a spirit of individualism—I dare not say of egoism, but I am not sure that that description would not be more correct.

They produced without discipline, without method, and without the spirit of co-operation, which was really more necessary at that moment than at any other. Then, suddenly, they found themselves faced with the consequences of this economic anarchy. Some countries are being crushed under the weight of stocks, the disposal of which presents almost insuperable difficulties. They are now looking round for a remedy and, naturally, are at last thinking of co-operation. They say: "But there is a League of Nations! What is it doing? What has it done? Why has it allowed us to be a prey to such anxiety, disquietude and suffering?"

Our President, in a very eloquent speech, warned us against the belief that the League could work miracles. The League can accomplish its task of co-operation, but it is not capable of spontaneous generation in economic and financial matters, and it cannot substitute in individuals or nations the spirit of co-operation for the spirit of individualism and egoism. . . .

When there are in the world nations which not only do not agree, but are opposed to one another, a sort of uneasiness is felt everywhere, and to-day such uneasiness reacts with astonishing rapidity on what is called the business world, which formerly was set on a sort of Olympus, high above peoples and ideas.

We have recently had proof of the importance of these ideological factors. The peoples were passing through a difficult period; already there was talk of a collapse. A meeting of representatives of the European nations was held at Geneva within the League of Nations, and under its auspices. At the close of their work they said to one another: "Is there nothing we can do from the moral point of view to reassure the peoples and restore confidence?" We talked the matter over, and decided to draw up a manifesto in which we most strongly affirmed our confidence in peace—a manifesto in which we said to the nations:

"Do not listen to pessimistic rumours. Do not be discouraged; take comfort. There is no danger of war; here are our signatures as guarantee."

You will remember the effect produced by that manifesto; and yet those were merely ideas, merely phrases. Nevertheless, business men immediately recovered confidence, and the result was a considerable improvement in the economic field. Hence the state of international relations does undoubtedly influence economic life.

It is therefore not a matter of indifference to the League, and it is, moreover, a result of its moral influence that two great nations like Germany and France should, for the last five years, have been seeking opportunities to draw together, to give each other guarantees of peace, to discuss certain questions together. I was one of those responsible for this *rapprochement,* and I am glad of it. Whatever may happen, it will be the act of my public life in which I take the most pride. But such a thing was possible only in this atmosphere. It was possible only owing to you, to your help, to the spirit you have created; otherwise, such an attempt would have been vain.

I must here refer to the very fine speech of my colleague Viscount Cecil, who swept aside with perfectly justifiable scorn certain insinuations to the effect that his country took a kind of fiendish interest in keeping certain nations apart in order to ensure its own supremacy. There is nothing new about that criticism; it has often been made. I consider, however, that Lord Cecil was right to protest on behalf of his country. For my part, I second his protest, and am prepared to bear witness that, in the effort to bring about a *rapprochement,* Great Britain has never ceased to lend her assistance to the two countries. Great Britain collaborated with them in these attempts; it gave them the mark of its approval and reinforced them with the authority of its signature.

I therefore associate myself wholeheartedly with Viscount Cecil's protest. It is untrue to say that England has any secret wish to create difficulty and friction or to do anything liable to cause trouble between two nations like Germany and France.

I affirm, then, that everything that could have been done for the improvement of relations has been done within the framework of the League in accordance with its principles and as the outcome of its efforts, and that the same will be true tomorrow.

At this time, when we are trying to bring about a *rapprochement,* I would scorn to lie to you or try to mislead you. Things have not always been easy for me; I have often come into conflict with the conditions—and the normal conditions too—of public life. I have often been involved in controversies; in both France and Germany our efforts have met with more or less violent resistance, and those who were striving to obtain a better understanding often intercepted and received hard blows. I have received some myself; and on bad days I feel the effects like a return of rheumatism.

But such things cannot deter public men, and it must be placed to the credit of the League that men from different countries have been meeting in Paris and London and in Italy to talk over their problems and dispel misunderstanding; that representatives from Germany have come to Paris, where they were well received—and I am glad of it; that to-morrow French statesmen will be asked to go to Germany; that, in the conversations held there under the eyes of the nation itself, the foundations may be laid of collaboration not merely verbal, but really practical and effective. This is a development which I desire with all my heart and in which I shall be only too glad to take part if I am allowed to do so.

All this took place in an atmosphere of understanding and mutual confidence. To facilitate such contacts and such co-operation we must avoid anything that may shake confidence. We must not hesitate, in a society where confidence is the essential element, to speak of our problems and to give our neighbours full information. We shall thus avoid much misunderstanding and many an unpleasant surprise from the polemics of those whose minds are not attuned to reconciliation or co-operation.

By the creation of such an atmosphere of confidence among the peoples and, when each nation, before acting, remembers that it is not alone and that it is to its advantage to act in a truly international manner, then all mistrust vanishes, cordiality is restored by loyalty and frankness, and the violent controversies which excite the nations, keep them apart and set them against each other have no hold.

From this point of view, much progress and many improvements have taken place. Recently I took a step which caused anxiety to some of my colleagues, and possibly that anxiety is not entirely dispelled even yet. I refer to my invitation, at a difficult moment—a moment which threatened to become even more difficult—to the European nations to get into touch with one another, to form an organisation within the framework of the League, making use of its administrative organs.

The events through which we have passed have shown the importance of such meetings; they enabled the morale of certain nations which were passing through a period of distress, doubt and great hardship to be restored. In Central Europe there were nations which could not employ their harvests to ensure their means of existence or even the continuation of their enterprises. They were vainly seeking the necessary capital; they could not obtain it except at usurious, extortionate, hopelessly high rates of interest.

Our association, if it has not been able to do all it would have liked to do, has provided some relief, created some contacts. Measures have been taken to improve the cereals market; the foundations have been laid of an International Institute of Agricultural Mortgage Credits. I am sure that, in years to come, the nations to which I referred just now will be proud of these results.

I repeat that the Commission of Enquiry for European Union must not be regarded as compromising the universality of the League, for it is the League's own creation. I hope that the Assembly will give it the encouragement which I consider it deserves.

And now, while apologising for having already addressed you at some length, I come to the subject in which you are all chiefly interested, the subject which has occupied the principal place—I might say the place of honour—in the various speeches you have heard, the subject that is bound up with the dominant idea of this institution, with the will to organise peace on increasingly sound lines, that it may be safe from attack in any quarter—I refer to the Conference for the reduction and limitation of armaments which is to meet on February 2nd of next year. You know how difficult it has been to prepare for that Conference, and I must protest that, if there has been any question of delaying it, of adjourning it, such a thought has certainly never been entertained in France.

It is the sad privilege of my country that in such matters people are always ready to think the worst of her. It has been remarked that the Conference had not yet met and that, lurking in the shadows, there is a country on the watch ready to snatch at any favourable opportunity to bring about its adjournment. That is not so. France will not ask for the Conference to be adjourned; France will do nothing to bring about such an adjournment; and I may say that, if any such attempt were made, France would be among the first to oppose it.

The convening of the Conference—I have said it before from this platform, with all the force at my command—represents the fulfilment of a solemn undertaking embodied in the Covenant of the League. If the Conference did not take place, the League would have failed in one of its most solemn undertakings and, I maintain, would thereby have deeply perturbed the conscience of the peoples. But, as things are, I do not think there is a single nation that has any such hidden intention. Moreover, to view things in a fair and reasonable light, we have to admit that, since it first arose, the problem has made headway in the minds of the peoples; the race for armaments, the armaments fever, are things of the past; the mind of the peoples is no longer set on war.

My own country, to mention no other, has lost no opportunity of limiting its armaments; it has reduced the period of military service by two-thirds; it has reduced its effectives by one-half; by a whole series of provisions it has progressed towards the ultimate aim set forth in the Covenant.

For five years, this question has been under discussion in one of your Commissions. You know what difficulties that Commission encountered and you will not have forgotten that sometimes, when it adjourned, it seemed that it would never meet again and that agreement could never be reached on questions of principle, which were apparently incapable of solution.

I may claim, as first delegate of France, that anyone re-reading the Minutes of that Commission will find that at all those difficult functions France boldly intervened with compromise solutions which enabled the Commission to continue towards its goal. Often the solutions she proposed were acceptable; they were adopted, and, thanks to them, it at length became possible last year to contemplate a definite term, a definite purpose, a definite date.

The meeting has been fixed, and we must all be there. Not to be there would be to fail in our undertaking, and it behoves all of us to arrive animated by the spirit of the Covenant. . . .

I now pass to the question of security, a word which my lips hardly dare utter. It is one of those words over which contests have so often raged, which have so often stood as obstacles in the way of certain experiments, that those who employ it appear to do so not in order to act but in order not to act.

This word, however, is written in the Covenant of the League. That is quite natural. If the authors of the Covenant had not kept a place for it, they would have been guilty, for the most generous-minded Members of the League might have been deceived.

As regards security then, has progress been achieved? No one can deny that it has. I who stand on this platform have done all that was in my power to increase the sum total of security. The Paris Pact was conceived with that purpose in view; certain work which you have undertaken and in which you are still engaged is calculated to add to guarantees of this nature.

War is a crime. Such was the dictum of the nations who signed the Paris Pact. Until then, we must not forget, war had actually remained, in certain circumstances, a licit means for settling disputes. It is appalling to think that, in this century, war should have been considered a normal means of putting an end to disputes that might arise between nations. The Paris Pact laid down that it is an impious act to have recourse to war, that war is a crime against mankind. All the nations signed the Pact, thereby declaring that they renounced the possibility of making that fatal gesture—a declaration of war. That is something; morally it is an excellent result.

One fact, however, we cannot disguise: cases still exist in which war may occur. That fact is apt to be forgotten, and it is right not to become obsessed by such an idea; still, it is a contingency that has to be borne in mind. The League of Nations, I willingly admit, had realised this. Lord Cecil will not contradict me if I say that on that point it had thought out a whole system which, had it been adopted, would have obliterated once for all that terrible question-mark. For three whole weeks we met in order to establish that system. I will not discuss the reasons why it was found impossible to put it into application; but it must be admitted that if it had become a living reality, if mutual assistance against the contingency of which I was speaking could actually have been organised, the problem before the coming Conference would have been very much simplified. That system, however, was left standing there, like one of those ever-veiled statues to which I have just referred, those statues of which only the outlines can be discerned. I do not know what Lord Cecil may think about it now; perhaps he will not think I am going too far if I say that like myself he probably would not be sorry if such an institution were ready to function among the nations.

But what was not done, and what perhaps can never be done again in the same way, must be sought in another form. We are drawing near to the conclusion of a term, to a date towards which the peoples are looking with increasing expectation. When, on February 2nd, all the nations of the world, representing the highest ideal, the sum of authority and the sum total of force, are met here solemnly together for that particular purpose, when they are all sitting round the same table and have to consider this twofold problem—the reduction of armaments combined with recourse to juridical guarantees and sanctions relating to security—what will they do? That will be a solemn moment; and I proclaim here and now that never before has such a heavy responsibility lain upon the nations. That will be a decisive moment. Will they, who have power to do anything they choose, leave unanswered, staring them in the face, that terrible question-mark that still haunts us? That is the issue. . . .

ADDRESS by Edouard Daladier, Premier, before the Congress of the Radical-Socialist Party at Vichy, October 8, 1933

Translated from the French text as printed in Royal Institute of International Affairs, *Documents on International Affairs, 1933*, p. 401, citing *Le Temps*, October 9, 1933; excerpts

IF IN PAST months the credit of France has appeared high, particularly abroad, it is because we have followed a foreign policy of foresight and reason. In an anxious and harassed Europe, where so many ringing pleas for violence are often heard, where the worship of force is often celebrated as that of a divinity, our duty is to act in such a way that our country, calm and peaceful, may under all circumstances insure its own freedom. The entire world knows our will for peace. We have spontaneously made sacrifices without precedent in history for the sake of peace. We do not mean to threaten or humiliate any country, no matter what system of government it chooses for itself or endures. That is why we are determined to admit no further reduction of our forces outside of an international agreement, true and honorable, whereby a progressive disarmament may be organized, guaranteed by the establishment of a permanent and automatic control, an agreement whose fulfilment should be effectively assured.

Such is the earnest position which we have adopted. It excludes bargainings, because we have made the matter one of conscience. A period of four years, during which control will be organized and begin to operate, while the various types of armies will be progressively transformed into armies of short-term service excluding paramilitary formations, and while the States which are at present free to arm themselves will submit to the prohibition of manufacturing new heavy war materials, and then, such control having proved effective, the destruction of materials thereafter prohibited for all States. Such are the essential purposes of a disarmament plan which now meets with the approval of Great Britain, the United States, Italy, Russia, and many other countries. It is quite natural that the geographic position of these countries, their history, their own particular spirit should give rise to differences of views. Negotiations are being carried on regarding the guarantees to be required by the agreement. We should feel gratified if this cooperative work could soon bring successful results. Where is there a responsible statesman who could find it possible to recommend to his country in the world as it is today a policy of isolation, or to hurl it into a policy of antagonistic alliances, without being forced to it by necessity? We want dignified and loyal peace

GENERAL STATEMENTS OF POLICY

for all nations, security for all peoples. Such is our thought. In Geneva, before the League of Nations, M. Paul-Boncour expressed it clearly. I am sure that it reflects the will of the country.

I will not go into the negotiations which are being carried on. But at this moment, when the political problems that weigh so heavily on the entire world economy require good will as much as close vigilance on the part of all the nations that have inherited the same civilization, I say that it is comforting to hear the authoritative voice of one of the most eminent members of the British Government rising publicly to re-proclaim his country's solidarity in sharing European responsibilities and at the same time its attitude of full respect for the great international agreements which have been concluded after the war for the maintenance of peace in Europe.

I recognize in that voice the well known voice of a great people ever mindful of the destinies of the western world, such as they are conceived by republican France herself, under an international system of freedom, justice and peace.

At the risk of provoking criticisms, but being anxious to express all my thoughts, I fail to see why, if all the governments are of good faith, progressive and controlled disarmament does not obtain their acceptance.

Europe, in the present crisis, is doomed to ruin if it throws itself into the armament race. Total destruction and the triumph of savagery will be inevitable if it resorts to war again.

But I must ask the question which is in your minds. What does Germany want? She and we have soaked the earth with the best of our blood. In the past all attempts to reach a durable understanding between our two countries have proved unsuccessful. Yet no one questions Germany's right to its existence as a great nation. No one thinks of humiliating Germany. We often hear the German Government publicly professing its will for peace and asserting through diplomatic channels its desire to work in favor of a *rapprochement* between the two countries. Then why is youth beyond the Rhine trained for combat? Why those repeated demonstrations of systematically organized masses? Why the rejection of the first stage towards disarmament? Why demand the right to manufacture today costly war material which must necessarily be destroyed shortly after it goes into service if the agreement is signed?

These are the questions that stand foremost in our minds. France remains faithful to its own spirit, eager for moderation, equity and reason. No one could possibly reproach her for being all the more determined to organize her defense after having repeatedly given proof of her true and faithful devotion to peace. And here I revert to my first words: national defense is inseparable from a balanced budget. There can be no active and free foreign policy unless order prevails in public finances.

ADDRESS by Pierre Laval, Premier, before the Assembly of the League of Nations, September 13, 1935

Translation, in *International Conciliation*, November, 1935, p. 521, citing *The New York Times*, September 14, 1935

IN A DISCUSSION so grave as this, where everybody must assume his responsibility, it is my duty to make heard the voice of my country.

I explained the French position before the Council of the League of Nations. I have done this, I believe, with clearness.

France is faithful to the League Covenant. She cannot fail in her obligations.

The League of Nations was born from the sufferings of men and was erected upon ruins, conceived in order to prevent a return of war.

The adhesion without reservation which we have brought to the League has been enthusiastic and the result of considered opinion. We place our hope in the cooperation of all peoples for the realization of our ideal of peace. Sometimes it has happened in difficult moments that we have known real disappointment at Geneva; yet our faith has never been weakened.

With a perseverance which no difficulty has ever been able to discourage, representatives of France have constantly labored to increase the moral authority of the greatest international institution. They have willed to do this, and they wish always to render this institution stronger and furnish it with means for action.

From the protocol in 1924 to the conference for the limitation of armaments France's representatives have supported with the same fervor the doctrine of collective security. This doctrine remains and will remain the doctrine of France. The Covenant endures as our international law.

How could we ever allow such a law to be weakened? That would be to cast aside all our ideals, and our very interest is opposed to any such step. The policy of France is based in its entirety on the League of Nations.

All our accords with our friends and our allies have been either passed by Geneva or based on Geneva. It suffices for me to recall Locarno, our accords with the Little Entente, the Franco-Soviet pact or the accord with Rome. Any blow struck at the institution at Geneva would be a blow struck at our very security.

In affirming our fidelity to the pact, I renew and confirm the declarations which have been made from this tribune by representatives of my country. If it was necessary to present the circumstances, this would provoke no surprise.

In an address, elevated in its thought, where was found anew the liberal tradition of England and England's sense of the universal, Sir Samuel Hoare told us the day before yesterday of the determination of the United Kingdom to adhere without reservation to the system of collective security.

He affirmed that this determination was and would continue to be the guiding principle of the international policy of Great Britain. No country has welcomed with greater satisfaction the word of the British Secretary of State than France.

No country more than France may appreciate and understand the meaning of such an engagement. This solidarity in responsibilities of all kinds at all times and places which is implied for the future by this declaration marks a date in the history of the League of Nations.

I rejoice with my country, which understands the full necessity of close collaboration with Great Britain for defense of peace and safeguarding Europe.

Already on last February 3 in London our two governments agreed upon a common program which was replete with hope. This news was welcomed throughout the world with real enthusiasm.

Obstacles have surged up which have prevented its realization. I had a beautiful dream. Is it now on the point of being realized?

I speak in the name of a nation which does not fear war but which hates it, in the name of a country which intends to remain strong, which is rich in the highest military virtues and is animated with a ferocious will for peace.

We nourish no ill against any people. We wish for peace for all by the collaboration of all.

It is not without emotion, after having signed the accords at Rome, that I evoke today the difference which weighs so heavily upon our Assembly.

On January 7 last, Premier Benito Mussolini and I, not only in the interests of our two countries, but also for the peace of Europe, definitely settled all those things which might be able to divide us.

Measuring all the value of Franco-Italian friendship, I have neglected nothing to prevent any blow from being struck at the new policy happily inaugurated between France and Italy.

At Stresa, with delegates of the British Government, we found the chief of the Italian Government animated with the same desire and the same determination to preserve the cause of peace. I know he is ready to preserve this collaboration.

That explains sufficiently the price which I attach to maintenance of such solidarity in the very interests of the European community and in the interests of general peace. I have spared no effort at conciliation. In the supreme effort made by the League Council, I shall have the satisfaction of fulfilling simultaneously my duty as a member of the League of Nations and the duty which is dictated by friendship. I conserve hope that the Council will be able within a short space of time to succeed in its rôle of conciliation. Doubtless this task is a rude one, but I persist in believing it is not hopeless.

The committee of five is studying every proposition which is of a nature to satisfy the legitimate aspirations of Italy in a measure compatible with the respect and sovereignty of another State which is a member of the League.

Let all realize that there exists no discord between France and Britain in their effective seeking for the pacific solution. We have had during this year difficulties which seemed insurmountable. Yet they were settled, and because the question of the Saar and the difference between Hungary and Yugoslavia were European problems, must one deduce that because of that they were more easy to solve?

We have succeeded yesterday. Shall we fail tomorrow? In this event the new situation, more poignant still for all of us, will demand our examination.

We are all bound by a solidarity which fixes our duty. Our obligations are inscribed in the Covenant. France will not evade those obligations.

STATEMENT by Léon Blum, Premier, in the French Senate, June 23, 1936

Translation, in *International Conciliation*, September, 1936, p. 432, citing *The New York Times*, June 24, 1936

ON THE EVE OF the international meetings that are about to open the Government owes the Chamber and French opinion explanations of the general principles that will dominate its acts as well as the decisions it has taken regarding problems of immediate import. In the international field as in all others our policy will be a frank one.

We should not fulfil the mandate we have received from the country if we did not proclaim at the outset the country's will for peace. A people that has given so many proofs of its courage can manifest that will without fearing that it may appear as a sign of abandonment.

It can do so all the more because never has it possessed more real and efficacious force with which to assure its defense, uphold its commitments, and collaborate toward the necessary strengthening of collective security.

Fears must now be dissipated that may have been felt momentarily by those who saw nothing but disorder in the gestation of the new order of things. A salutary ferment has come to stimulate our national energies. That great effort of social justice and human emancipation that is in process of accomplishment exalts the patriotism of the laboring masses in that very measure in which the homeland having become more than ever the possession of all, they feel closer solidarity in its destinies.

Such an evolution, pursued in civil peace with the active collaboration of both houses of Parliament, cannot but increase that authority that is necessary for our international action. Is there need for adding that we appeal for support in this task to a unanimous France and Parliament as a whole without class or party distinctions?

The peace that we intend thus to defend is not a conditional peace subordinated to political affinities or antagonisms. We desire that peace for all peoples and with all peoples, knowing that it is indivisible and that none would be safe from the conflagration that would flare up if vigilance on the part of the pacific nations were not ever-present and ever-active. We intend to preach no other crusade than that whose object is a reconciliation of peoples without any exclusion. Propaganda or struggle for or against such and such a political or social system must not become pretexts for war.

Neither do we want a timorous peace under the law of the mightiest nor a passive, egotistical peace based on self-sufficiency. Our will for peace is too sincere not to be active.

For that reason we wish to proclaim very clearly our fidelity to the League of Nations. The trials through which it is passing, far from turning us away from it, stimulate our resolve to strengthen it by a more efficacious organization of collective security, which calls for two conditions—respect for international law and contracts and a restoration of mutual confidence shaken by too many shocks, disappointments, and fears. We desire to contribute to their restoration by evidencing our good faith and loyalty.

It is in that spirit that the Government studied a problem brought to its examination in the most pressing manner—that of the sanctions taken regarding Italy. France associated herself with those sanctions despite the affinities binding her to the Italian people. It is in her traditions always to face her obligations, always to fulfil her duties of justice and humanity.

The League of Nations Council had unanimously recorded an act of aggression; France could not fail in the fidelity she owes to the Geneva Covenant, that common law and common safeguard of nations organized for the maintenance of peace.

Assuredly none expects of us, after the Ethiopian defeat, that we should overwhelm the vanquished by renouncing these sentiments. But in the present state of things, the maintenance of sanctions would be only a symbolical gesture without real efficacy. To what purpose, therefore, perpetuate measures whose character would be aggravated by the very fact that it is no longer possible to set for them any definite objective?

It was in such conditions that last Friday we made public our opinion, assured, as we were, moreover, of being in accord with those friendly peoples from whom we do not wish to separate our action.

The raising of sanctions is accompanied by other problems the solution of which will call for negotiations that should result in the consolidation of peace.

Peace can be consolidated only by strengthening the security of nations. It is to that strengthening that we shall consecrate all our efforts. We do not deem it opportune in the present circumstances to propose too vast or too ambitious a plan. Moreover, general reform of the Covenant is not justified if one takes the trouble to reflect that its failures are attributable much more to mistakes and weaknesses in execution than to the prescriptions that it stipulates. Furthermore, in the present general frame of mind, such reform would risk being carried out on the lines of least resistance.

GENERAL STATEMENTS OF POLICY

Neither do we believe it advisable to have recourse to the interminable procedure provided by amendments. We prefer interpretative texts, bringing without delay precise and efficacious corrections inspired by the lessons of experience.

If the mechanism of collective security has proved insufficient, it is not the Covenant's fault; it is because the Covenant has been applied tardily and in an incomplete manner. You cannot compromise with war; exclusive recourse to economic sanctions progressively applied cannot stop a conflict already in progress.

In order to repress aggression, it is essential to put into operation as soon as possible the maximum means that the international community has at its disposal. In order to assure efficacious application of the Covenant's Article 16 the ideal method would be for all members of the League of Nations to undertake to apply in all circumstances forcible means against an aggressor.

But for the moment it would be chimerical to hope for such total assistance on the part of peoples not directly interested in a conflict.

For this reason collective security must have two aspects. First, a group of Powers—whether that group originates from a given geographical situation or from a community of interests—must be ready itself to employ all its strength against an aggressor. This being assured, the entire collectivity of the League of Nations must obligatorily apply economic and financial sanctions.

Such regional accords of mutual assistance, conceived for the purpose of peace, will constitute threats against no one. They must never become alliances as in the past. Open to all, their workings must always depend on a decision taken by the Council of the League of Nations.

But it is not sufficient to stop an aggressor by the application of Article 16, thus re-enforced. The essential aim of collective organization is to prevent aggression. But the means of prevention at the disposal of the League of Nations are still insufficient.

The manner in which the principle of unanimity inscribed in the Covenant has been interpreted at Geneva paralyzes the application of Article 11. It is not admissible, it is contrary to common sense, that a State whose action has created a threat to peace should by its vote be able to paralyze the action of the community.

So long as Article 11 of the Covenant is interpreted thus, the Council of the League of Nations will be powerless to prevent the preparation of a conflict, and the eventual aggressor will have every leisure to choose his time. The French Government proposes to put an end to this paradoxical situation.

We do not intend for a moment to present a vast program in this domain. What is most urgent must be first attended to, and at this time, when in all Europe the feeling of insecurity is increasing, it is necessary to re-establish among all peoples of good-will confidence in the collective system, which has been so rudely damaged.

During the next months the negotiation of regional pacts should be hastened and this Government will not overlook any effort in this direction.

The reasons that recommend the conclusion of a pact between all the Danubian States, to which perhaps their memories are opposed, but to which their real interests draw them, are more valid than ever. This pact should be open to all the Powers of Central Europe and should be directed against no one of them. We ourselves are interested by the bonds of affection that unite us to the Little Entente.

It is not less necessary to associate all the Mediterranean Powers from Spain to the Balkan Entente in an agreement that will bring them the guarantee that no hegemony can be set up in that sea whose bordering peoples are linked by a common civilization.

As for Western Europe, we wish that an agreement may be reached the conclusion of which will put an end to the crisis precipitated on March 7, but this conclusion does not depend on ourselves alone.

Meanwhile, as the representatives of Belgium, France, Great Britain, and Italy recognized at London on March 19, the Locarno pact continues with its obligations and the guarantees it lays down for our defense and for that of Belgium.

To these tasks we are convinced Italy will lend her necessary collaboration. We shall be happy that her efforts should join cordially with ours and with those of other interested Powers.

In our effort for the reconstruction of collective security we have no doubt as to the unreserved support of the British democracy, which is united with the French democracy by so many common memories and efforts. We hold to this all the more because the close and confident cooperation of our two countries is an essential guarantee of peace in Europe.

France counts beyond the Atlantic on the cordial sentiments of the American democracy, a natural friend of free nations. She is assured of the powerful help of our friends of the Union of Soviet Socialist Republics to whom we are united in a pact of mutual assistance open to all, which has been made in a common concern for peace.

Franco-Polish friendship will receive a new consecration in a cordial and direct search for better formulas of cooperation between the two peoples. With Belgium, Rumania, Czechoslovakia, and Yugoslavia France feels herself united by close intimacy of thought and heart as much as by treaties. Their security constitutes an element of our own security, just as our security is an integral part of theirs.

We count also for the great task that is to be accomplished on the Balkan Entente, on the Spanish democracy and on all the peoples that, from Portugal to the Scandinavian States, with the Netherlands, have given such pledges of fidelity to the League of Nations.

The parties now united in the Popular Front have always fought for a Franco-German entente. Jaurès paid with his life for his passionate action for peace. Briand knew calumny and outrage for having wished that the Rhine should unite instead of separate France and Germany.

We applauded the London accords negotiated by Herriot, which made Locarno possible. We regret nothing of the action we have pursued for fifteen years. We are resolved to continue it further in security and honor to both peoples. On different occasions Chancellor Hitler has proclaimed his wish for an understanding with France. We do not for a moment intend to question the word of a former combatant who during four years experienced the misery of the trenches.

But, however sincere our wish for an entente, how can we forget the lessons of experience and the facts?

German rearmament is developing with a rhythm that is quickening daily. On March 16, 1935, Germany repudiated the military clauses of the Treaty of Versailles in conditions that certain error invoked by her did not suffice to justify. On March 7, 1936, she violated and repudiated the Rhineland pact of Locarno, which had been freely signed by her and which Chancellor Hitler had several times declared constituted an essential guarantee of European peace.

Since that date the situation has remained serious: On March 19 the Locarno Powers submitted to Germany a plan containing concrete proposals that should serve for the inauguration of a new security agreement; on March 24 Germany presented counter propositions that rejected the whole system of agreement founded on mutual assistance in the relations of Germany with her neighbors other than the Locarno Powers; on April 10 the Locarno Powers, anxious to try all means of conciliation, charged the British Government to elucidate a certain number of points contained in the German memorandum. That was the object of the British questionnaire handed to Berlin on May 6.

To that questionnaire the Reich has not yet replied. Will it do so tomorrow? In any case the French Government will examine the German suggestions with a sincere desire of finding in them a basis for agreement. But this agreement cannot be realized unless it accords with the principle of indivisible peace with menace against none.

The evolution of Franco-German relations is closely bound up with the success of the efforts in the international work of disarmament, which is also subordinate to guarantees of collective security. The disappointments that have marked the checks of the Geneva conference have not discouraged the French people. They realize that a race of armaments leads fatally to war; they wish by collective effort to put an end to this rivalry and to make possible progressive, universal disarmament controlled by the community of nations.

It is the duty of the Government without at any time neglecting any necessities of national defense, to draw all nations with it along this road. In that way it would reply to the wishes of the French people and to the deepest and most justified aspirations of mankind; it would, it knows, interpret the ideas of the veterans of the Great War who, after having been faithful to their duty during the struggle, are today fraternally united across their frontiers in the higher duty of trying to spare the world such another dreadful catastophe.

To put an end to the mystery that surrounds the armaments race and to prevent the surprises that it is preparing, the Government will demand first of all preventive publicity and control of the manufacture of war material by a permanent international commission sitting at Geneva. It will propose reconsideration in a second reading of the project voted by a majority of States in April, 1935.

Now in laying before Parliament a bill for the nationalization of the manufacture of war material it will mark its determination to prepare France to assume in the national field all the responsibilities of control that are entailed in this international system.

This control and this preliminary publicity are, however, only the first step, which must be quickly transcended. The Government will join with complete loyalty in all measures taken unanimously for the control, limitation, and reduction of armaments, and it will seize every opportunity to take the initiative.

Since the month of February, 1935, the question of an aerial pact of mutual assistance between the Western Powers, which to be effective should be completed by an agreement for aerial limitation, has been raised by the British and the French Governments acting together.

Despite all our efforts the negotiations have not progressed, the German Government having until now delayed its reply. In its last memorandum it showed that it still in principle was in favor of the conclusion of this pact, but did not say if in its idea the pact should receive the necessary completion of a limitation agreement. A question on this subject has been addressed to it by the British Government and a reply is awaited.

Is it unnecessary to say that to end the armaments race, which in the realm of the air is becoming more and more precipitate and is weighing on the whole European civilization, a limitation agreement is highly desirable? France, on her side, is ready to enter such an agreement, whether only Western air forces or the whole of European air forces are concerned.

To establish a balance sheet of the general economic situation, of the needs of nations and of the measures that should be taken to restart business, we shall ask for the convocation of the Commission of Study for a European union that was created by Aristide Briand. This commission includes all European States, whether members of the League of Nations or not. Germany could therefore participate and make suggestions in the same way as at the beginning the Soviet Union did, although then not a member of the League.

Gentlemen, however tenacious our effort may be, the task set for us is bound to be of long duration. The work accomplished at Geneva will depend first of all on the wills of governments and peoples. We must defend a patrimony that is not only French but human—that of the free expression of those wills, that of the progress of democratic institutions in order and liberty. If these possessions and ideals are not supported by a strong and resolute France, the shadow of doubt will hang over the world.

But all men who today sit on the government bench are united in the common thought that the state of armed peace, which is the generator of catastrophes, should be temporary, that every effort should be made to shorten its duration, and that the security of peoples cannot be assured otherwise than by collective organisms and the international community.

With every indispensable prudence, peoples must be led toward a state of disarmed peace in which the universal conscience will raise automatically against any aggressor all the material and moral forces of pacific peoples, which have been methodically organized in advance.

In drawing up this line of conduct, this government remains faithful to the constant policy of those who at this tribune have always proclaimed that the interests of peace are inseparable from those of France. It wishes to animate this constructive effort with all the force that the French people have given their representatives for the organization in the international domain, as in the national life, of the future of justice and humanity.

To the construction of this future we shall consecrate, with the support that we expect from you, all our activity.

We shall not commit the imprudence of proportioning now to our hopes the state of our defensive forces, which must always be kept at the level of the immediate necessities of national defense. So long as the armaments race has not been stopped, so long as international mechanisms have not given proof of their effectiveness, the duty of France toward herself, as toward her friends, is to remain armed in a measure to discourage all aggression.

But we summon to international collaboration all governments and all peoples who are devoted to peace, who think that it should be founded on respect for freely signed engagements, who wish to substitute for transformation of the world by violence its evolution under the aegis of justice and international morality—all those who, like ourselves, are determined to accept in common all the charges and all the responsibilities of collective security because they see therein, as we do, the best guarantee of national security.

ADDRESS by Yvon Delbos, Minister for Foreign Affairs, in the Chamber of Deputies, November 19, 1937

Translated from the French text as printed in Royal Institute of International Affairs, *Documents on International Affairs, 1937*, p. 130, citing *Journal Officiel—Débats Parlementaires, Chambre des Députés*, November 19, 1937; excerpts

Nothing is more legitimate than the desire manifested by the Chamber, on re-opening its sessions, to call at once for a debate on foreign policy.

In the presence of the circumstances now existing, the Chamber has, indeed, the right and the duty to make pronouncements, without further delay, on the Government's attitude with respect to the events that have occurred since we adjourned.

This attitude, gentlemen, may be defined in a few words: to defend peace, to endeavor to overcome the force of fires already kindled, to prevent others from breaking out that might be the prelude of a universal conflagration, to preserve France and the world from the risks of contagion of war.

That is our immediate program. It assuredly does not exclude the pursuit of greater and deeper constructive efforts, such as those of which my friend M. Elbel spoke yesterday. But the Chamber will not be surprised if I repeat that above all the present condition of Europe and the world requires ceaseless vigilance.

It requires particularly that France be strong. When international law is so disregarded, so badly served by the community, when such an atmosphere of insecurity, uneasiness and menace prevails, it is not the time to appear as a defenseless prey.

GENERAL STATEMENTS OF POLICY 463

Peace cannot be obtained through abdications, the Government said in its ministerial declaration. And it stressed its determination to neglect nothing in order that the greatest possible effort be made to guarantee the security of the nation.

It has kept its word and, feeling assured of the country's unanimous support, it will continue to make these efforts as long as may be necessary, that is, as long as the control and the limitation of armaments of all nations are not attained, as we have proposed, as we persist in proposing and as the safety of mankind requires.

But to want peace, it is not enough merely to place one's self in a position to discourage aggression. It also means striving every hour to diminish the seriousness of conflicts and prevent their extension. It means being in a permanent state of alertness to collaborate with all those nations that share the same ideal and follow the same methods in order to prevent the aggravation of discords existing with other countries by searching for every possibility of reconciliation and understanding.

The task would be easier if the League of Nations were better understood and better supported. But the crisis through which it is passing, due to weakness on the part of its members rather than to the challenges made against it and to obstacles created against it, imposes certain duties on us: the duty to act, which we may fulfil by remaining in the first rank of its upholders, by proposing measures which may most adequately strengthen it; the duty of caution, too, for ideals are not betrayed by taking realities into consideration.

When M. Péri, for example, urges us to act more effectively on behalf of collective security, he forgets that such security is in fact nonexistent and that we cannot constitute it by ourselves or with but very little cooperation.

He admitted, however,—I believe it is the only satisfaction that he has given us—that we have tried to strengthen Article 16 of the Covenant. Yes, but while waiting for it to be strengthened, should we act as if this were already done? . . .

We are ready to contribute towards whatever will break down barriers, increase trade, cause credit to circulate, enable peoples to improve their standard of living by developing their possibilities of work.

It is in that spirit that the tripartite monetary agreement has been signed and that we, with Great Britain, have entrusted to Mr. Van Zeeland the mission which he has kindly accepted.

We are disposed to go further along the path on which President Roosevelt has thrown so much light, because we know very well that it is the only one that can lead to real and lasting peace.

But while waiting to be enabled to establish peace on solid bases, we must be careful that it does not fall from the fragile foundation on which it stands today. That is the drama of our life.

We represent a noble nation which has given enough proofs of its heroism to be able to proclaim that it aims only at fraternity. We would like to meet its aspiration by waiving aside that which separates, by seeking that which unites. We know that peoples, all peoples wish to draw nearer together. Their peaceful aspirations are so earnest that everywhere, in order to find the way to their hearts, it is (only) necessary to speak to them of peace. All those who hold in their hands the fate of men speak the same language.

And yet, instead of the expected action, of the hoped-for results, discord and menace persist, the roar of the cannon is heard in Spain and in the Far East, war breaks out on two continents. It is no longer a question of that general organization of peace which we all aspire to, but of efforts every minute to attenuate and stop the atrocities of war and to prevent war from spreading.

Gentlemen, it is with this will, reflective, earnest, tenacious, that we are participating in the conferences of Brussels and of London.

If, in the war between China and Japan, of which I wish to speak in the first place, it is indeed our duty to watch over the important interests which we have to protect, I need not add that what preoccupies us most is the fate of a nation in which we are doubly interested as a friend and as a victim, it is the problem of international law and morality, so clear in its known quantities and yet so difficult to solve, it is the horror of bloodshed, the will to check its flow and to check the scourge.

I should like to give an account to the Chamber of the efforts that we have made in the various phases of the conflict and of the spirit in which we have desired to collaborate in the international field. I apologize in advance for having to go into certain details. But because I believe that the defense of peace does not consist in general remarks, in words and formulae, but in daily, modest action, sometimes even in secret action, it is the details of our attitude in this problem that I wish to make known to you.

At the beginning, the incident which, in the neighborhood of Peking, during the night of July 8 to 9, brought into contact a detachment of Chinese troops with a regiment of the Japanese occupation corps, could be considered as an incident undoubtedly serious, painful, but local.

It was possible to hope that its development would not spread beyond North China and that it would be possible to reach, on a regional basis, an agreement similar to those agreements which, in the recent past, had put a stop to situations of the same kind.

GENERAL STATEMENTS OF POLICY

France, England and the United States therefore agreed to counsel moderation and to recommend a negotiation in accordance with the provisions of the protocol of 1901.

A few weeks went by. Then, while in the North Japanese military action was launched with fresh violence, the conflict spread to the vicinity of Shanghai with an amplitude which since then has never ceased to grow.

In that great centre of foreign interests in China, there exist in close proximity, next to a Chinese city in full development, an international concession administered by a municipality mostly Anglo-Saxon and a French concession inhabited by more than 500,000 inhabitants, whose orderliness and prosperity are the object of admiration of all visitors.

To re-establish, to protect as far as possible, the interests of all those who are under our jurisdiction and our administration, to insure the defense of the French concession jointly with that of the international concession by having one and then two battalions of Indochinese troops sent there, to neglect nothing in order to preserve all of that immense agglomeration from the ravages of war, such has been our chief duty, the duty which we have been determined to fulfil.

By agreement with the British and American Governments, no step has been spared to try to neutralize the entire agglomeration of Shanghai, and then, following the failure of our efforts, to preserve at least the concessions. The latter result has been practically obtained and I have the satisfaction to declare that today the security of the population which normally inhabits our concession and of thousands of Chinese who have taken refuge in it has been assured.

If we have to deplore that in the last few days, when the battle raged in the very frontiers of our concession, stray bullets caused some casualties, I wish publicly to pay tribute to the effectiveness of the measures taken by our representatives on the spot to protect the lives and the property whose safety was entrusted to them.

But besides this local aspect, the hostilities which are taking place in China have a general aspect, which is much more serious. Three kinds of considerations faced us.

We had to endeavor to fulfil our humanitarian duties, our duties as a member of the League of Nations and as a signatory of the Treaty of Washington.

Then, too, we had to take into account our special situation in the Far East and to look after the preservation in southern China of a situation *de jure* and *de facto* on which the security of our Asiatic possessions depends.

We also had to abide by our determination to maintain a permanent solidarity with Great Britain and the United States, which, with interests similar to ours, have the same lofty conception of their international duty.

These are the considerations which guided the French delegation in Geneva at the meetings of the advisory committee set up by the Assembly. Because of those considerations, I found with the very valuable cooperation of my friends Messrs. de Tessan and Monnerville, inspiration during the debates of the conference at Brussels.

Conscious of the sad experiences to which I referred a moment ago, the Assembly of the League had considered that it would have been useless under the circumstances to propose to the community tasks which, in the present state of things, it would be unable to accomplish.

It thought that before contemplating any other step it was necessary to examine the possibilities of conciliation offered by the operation of the Treaty of Washington, and it was for such an examination that we went to Brussels, not with a feeling of timidity, M. Péri, not unaware of our duties, but because it is the road that has been suggested to us by the entire League of Nations.

The efforts at mediation thus undertaken met with a refusal on the part of Japan to accept such action, despite the rights and obligations which the treaty conferred upon its signatories, despite the precautions taken to render them fully acceptable to both parties.

England, the United States and France then proposed a draft resolution justifying the attitude of the conference and postponing the decision to be reached in common until a further meeting to be held next Monday. The text proposed was approved by fourteen votes to one, three States having abstained.

This lack of unanimity confirms all the more strongly the collapse of collective security of which I have just spoken. When the Government is reproached for not taking sufficient action with a view to collective security, for not taking certain initiatives, I wish it would be borne in mind that decisions of that nature have to be reached unanimously and that when it is evident that not only such unanimity but perhaps even a majority does not exist, it would be vain and even unwise and dangerous to rely too much upon insufficient realities.

It is none the less true that France has done and will do in Brussels, as it did in Geneva, as it always does, all that is in its power to restore peace among nations.

But there is no doubt that in this field, and above all, perhaps, in that very remote Far East, the prerequisite for success is the certainty of international solidarity, not merely moral but effective.

I did not await M. Péri's invitation to realize this and to act accordingly. But before making resounding and spectacular proposals, like those he mentioned, propositions which, moreover, no other country has formulated, it is necessary to consider that to make any such proposals is, in a certain measure, to bind one's self, and in so doing to bind one's self to defend the proposals and in this, as in other matters, we do not wish France to bind itself alone.

Apart from the object itself of the Conference of Brussels, I must stress before the Chamber a fact whose significance will escape no one here or elsewhere: the close and harmonious collaboration of the American, British and French delegations.

In this exchange of views, we have seen how the affinities of free peoples enable them to understand each other easily.

The result is not only a common draft resolution but also three identical declarations in which, in the light of those immortal principles that some people deliberately scorn, we have set forth the attitude assumed in common by the great democracies, their loyalty to international law, their respect for treaties, for the independence of nations that have the right to live as they wish by refusing good offices proffered at the point of the sword.

I also wish to stress the cordial and full concurrence of opinion existing constantly between ourselves and the other delegations animated by the same spirit, particularly our friends of the Union of Soviet Republics and of Belgium.

Now I come to speak of the other Conference, the one which is working in London. I will thus answer certain remarks that were made with some severity at the beginning of this session.

If in the Far East the hour of relief does not seem forthcoming, I do not think I exaggerate the truth in saying that certain favorable signs are visible in the Mediterranean, signs which M. Péri has forgotten in his address and which I am therefore obliged to recall.

The Spanish tragedy is, indeed, as sad as ever and the passions it has stirred in Spain, and also outside of Spain, are unfortunately not about to be appeased.

It seems, however, that after a period of extreme tension, which has imposed on us all the more the duty to maintain our composure, we have reached the point where the powers which were most deeply involved in it see the necessity of stripping the problem of its international aspect.

This was, as you know, one of the essential aims which the French

Government had in view in taking the initiative, which it does not deny, in the policy of non-intervention.

During the past months it may have been thought on numerous occasions, I admit, that this policy was about to disappear. Certain events, certain declarations, which did not pass unnoticed, you may be sure, seemed to contradict that policy only too blatantly.

I said then in Geneva, and I willingly repeat it, that the policy of non-intervention should not turn into dupery and that in any case we would never allow its violation to end by endangering the safety of our frontiers, the freedom of our communications in the Mediterranean and the statute of North Africa.

But instead of proclaiming the end of non-intervention, we have wished in the interest of peace, which stands foremost in our thoughts, to make a supreme effort in order to make that policy a reality.

You know, gentlemen, the difficulties that had to be overcome. The month of August was particularly critical in this respect. It had not been possible at London to reach an agreement for a general withdrawal of foreigners participating in the Spanish struggle; crimes as cowardly as they were cruel were multiplied in the Mediterranean against the peaceful navigation of neutral ships.

The French Government then took the initiative in the matter of the conference which met at Nyon on September 10.

That conference was a success. M. Péri, however, forgot to mention it.

In two days and in spite of a certain absence, an agreement was arrived at to organize vigilance against submarine piracy, Great Britain and France taking full charge of this.

This result, important in itself and because of its moral effect throughout the world, is a proof of what it is possible to accomplish through close and firm Franco-British collaboration, and we would not have achieved this had such Franco-British collaboration failed to be maintained. It also proves that peace would be better assured if similar methods were more often applied by peaceful nations.

It finally proves, M. Péri, that if that is not the case, it is not so much as you say the Government's fault, for when the Government sees the occasion to act effectively it never fails immediately to take advantage of it. In this field too the Government is capable—I do not say this only to you—of initiative and decision.

A few days after the meetings at Nyon and in accordance with the wish expressed by the Nations that met there, Italy entered into the system. Since November 10, its fleet has been participating effectively in the patrol service.

As for submarine piracy, it disappeared almost immediately after

GENERAL STATEMENTS OF POLICY

the announcement of the conference; in all cases, as soon as its success was assured.

It is true that one cannot say as much for air piracy. Attacks have recently occurred in inadmissible circumstances, the authors of which could not be positively identified. The Government is determined not to tolerate their repetition. Notice has been given in categoric terms and every precaution has been taken insofar as it is possible to do so effectively.

These incidents and others show that the success obtained at Nyon has not sufficed to put a stop to the policy of non-intervention; but it has been the starting point for fresh efforts which have not been so useless as I heard stated a few moments ago.

There is no doubt that past disappointments require that we not let ourselves give in to a too great and premature optimism. . . .

I would also like to emphasize that the policy of non-intervention has had the merit, which should not be underestimated in the present serious situation of Europe and the world, of preserving general peace during sixteen months, and that it has never made us lose sight of the vital interests of France. . . .

I would emphasize, in conclusion, that, if we did not intervene in the war, we intervened for the sake of peace by proposing mediation, and that the regret of our failure does not rule out the hope of a better opportunity when hostile brothers who are now fighting will feel tired of killing one another.

Gentlemen, this double duty of non-intervention in war and intervention for peace is all the more imperative because there is no possible respite as long as the Spanish problem remains an international problem.

Ever since it broke out, everything in Europe has been in suspense. The negotiation of the Western Pact intended to replace the Treaty of Locarno has made no progress; the other efforts made with a view to reestablishing a little order and peace have all been doomed to postponement or failures. Anticipating that, once the struggle is over, these hopes may rise again, anticipating that we will thus be enabled to provide fresh guarantees of peace, we must (meanwhile) watch all the closer over the existing ones.

The above are the very reasons for the friendly visit which I will make shortly to Warsaw, Bucharest, Belgrade and Prague following the visits made in France by eminent personages of those countries and of cordial invitations extended to the French Minister for Foreign Affairs . . .

In verifying with them the identity of our international ideas, I will certainly be able to state that they are free not only from hostility but also from exclusivism, for we well know that the collaboration of all is necessary to Europe's welfare.

This is, gentlemen, the spirit in which I am going to make that trip. It is the spirit which animates the Government under the direction of the statesman, in the full sense of the word, close to whom I have the honor to serve. To strengthen the friendships which mutually protect us and which, having no designs against anyone, make for general peace as much as our own security, to prevent aggressions while favoring reconciliation without which Europe is doomed to collective suicide; to dissipate misunderstandings, to harmonize interests, to eliminate the spirit of violence and conquest, thereby preparing a future wherein peoples will at last, under restored international law, under respected international morality, peacefully enjoy the fruits of their intelligence and their labor.

STATEMENT by Georges Bonnet, Minister for Foreign Affairs, in the Council of the League of Nations, May 23, 1939

League of Nations, *Official Journal*, May–June, 1939, p. 265

THE DISCUSSION at the present Council could not continue and be brought to a close without its members having brought before them the very serious anxieties which the international situation continues to inspire. It would, indeed, be a paradox if the League of Nations, which was created essentially for the consideration of, and if possible for the settlement of, disputes, should remain indifferent to the tension that has been produced in the world by events in recent months.

It is true, as Lord Halifax has just stated, that we are bound to note that, in the presence of these successive upheavals, the League has not shown itself to be in a position to supply the necessary remedies. Experience of the past has, in this respect, compelled it to observe an attitude of prudence and expectancy, for which it cannot be blamed. Does that mean, however, that we should therefore abandon the principles that constitute the foundations of the Covenant which unites us? Certainly not! The League of Nations remains the depositary of the great ideas by which the policy of countries which observe and cherish the Covenant is inspired day after day. Security, collaboration, peace—those are the ideals to which the Government of the French Republic remains sincerely attached, and the realisation of which it indefatigably pursues,

GENERAL STATEMENTS OF POLICY

As the French President of the Council of Ministers said recently, nations to-day, as was the case twenty years ago, find themselves confronting an alternative—namely, domination or collaboration. We, who are Members of the League of Nations, have chosen collaboration. We feel ourselves solidly united in the presence of any efforts to bring about the triumph of methods of force.

The French Government, for its part—and it is unnecessary to recall all the earlier efforts of that Government with a view to establishing, within the framework of the Covenant, the necessary guarantees of security—regrets that those efforts have not proved fully successful. Whilst noting their failure, it considers that security, collaboration and peace must be sought by other methods and on a different plane. That is why we also, with a view to maintaining peace, have entered upon a series of negotiations to which the representative of the United Kingdom has just referred. In the opinion of my Government, however, these negotiations are not in contradiction to the principles by which the authors of the Covenant were inspired. On the contrary, they remain in harmony with that ideal of peaceful collaboration and protection which we have always cherished.

For my part, therefore, I can see nothing but advantages to be gained from following the suggestion of the United Kingdom representative that the Council should be informed of the political agreements now being negotiated when they have been concluded.

DISARMAMENT AND SECURITY

COMMUNICATION from the French Government to the German Government, September 11, 1932

Translation, in Royal Institute of International Affairs, *Documents on International Affairs, 1932*, p. 189, citing *The Times* (London), September 13, 1932

THE FRENCH GOVERNMENT has received the document which was delivered to the French Ambassador on August 29 by the German Foreign Minister in the presence of the German Minister of War.

This document attempts to open negotiations on the questions raised at Geneva on July 22 by the German delegation. According to the communication made to our Ambassador, the Berlin Government first wishes to approach us confidentially. It shows a desire for candour to which the French Government intends to answer without reservation or ulterior motive.

I

One point must be settled first and foremost, since it is the basis of the Note of August 29. The German Government invokes the inadequacy of the Disarmament Conference, not only with regard to the methods adopted, but also with regard to the scope of the results achieved. This criticism has been repeated at frequent intervals in the speeches of the Reichswehr Minister. It is recalled in the ninth and final paragraph of the Note.

It is hardly worth while mentioning that this opinion is premature and lacks the authority of a just appreciation of efforts already made. The French Government is strong in the consciousness of having done everything that could have been expected of it to promote a steady evolution of the work of the Conference. When, in the month of June, it was averred that the efforts of the Committees, with only one exception, had led to very inadequate results, it exerted itself to retrace the situation by means of negotiations undertaken under the authority of the General Committee of the Conference. It allowed its exposition on security to stand over to a future date; as the *rapporteur*, M. Beneš, observed, it consented to the same interval for the examination of this exposition as was asked from Germany for the consideration of her claims to equality of rights. It gave proof, moreover, of its will to reduce armaments in contriving that the French Parliament voted a reduction of about 1,500,000,000 francs on military expenses, a reduction corresponding to a reasonable degree with the reparations annuity which it had renounced. And at Geneva the French Government had spared no effort either to allow the first part of the Conference to reach conclusions or to outline the programme of the second part, and facilitate the examination of certain problems such as those put forward in Mr. Hoover's generous proposals.

Against the various interpretations given of our actions we urge these facts. As an instance, the French Government, while reserving the right to internationalize civil aviation, has proposed the total prohibition of aerial bombardment, and has even accepted its abolition in the field of battle.

No one can be surprised by the connexion established between these measures, since it is evident that it would be useless to have suppressed the military bombing squadrons if a so-called civil aeroplane of high power could bombard human habitations with engines of destruction which the armed forces might not use.

As regards the future work of the conference, the Government of the Republic holds similar views. The centre and pivot of its doctrine is the application of Article 8 of the Covenant, which specifies that the maintenance of peace requires the reduction of national armaments to the minimum compatible with national security and the execution of international obligations by common action, and asks for the preparation by the Council of plans for such reduction, with due regard, as the German Government points out in Paragraph 3 of its Note, for the geographical situation and special circumstances of each State.

This text lays down the rules which the French Government accepts. Our doctrine is that we must aim not at individual rearmament, but at general and regulated disarmament. To carry out such a programme effectively successive stages are necessary. The Assembly of the League recognized this in the decisions of 1927, to which the German representatives did not fail to agree.

The Disarmament Conference solemnly proclaimed the fact by its resolution of April 19 last. If, alleging that the result hoped for from the convention now being prepared seemed to it insufficient, the German Government declared that it was entitled to change its own *statut* of armament, it would not only violate the definite engagements of the Treaty it has signed; it would also make impossible, by its attitude, the final achievement of that general disarmament which it professes to desire. Our aim is to arrive at a convention which shall give the nations real guarantees of peace and make it possible to relieve them of their burdens. If Germany wishes to co-operate with France, as with other States, in this work, to negotiate for it, and to discuss it, nothing can be more legitimate and more desirable.

These discussions, in which France means to take part in a sincerely liberal spirit, would make it possible to decide what the *statut* of Germany should be within a general *statut* of peace, placed under the protection of arbitration and supervision

The first aspect of the question is juridical. The German Government itself raises this legal difficulty in its Note when it opposes what it calls the *statut* of Versailles to the final *statut* of the Disarmament Convention. Making a distinction which is worthy of note, it approaches the question both from the legal and from the general point of view.

On the first point the German Government supposes the problem to be solved. It declares that the Disarmament Convention must be substituted *ipso jure* for the Treaty of Versailles, and that no special conditions must be laid down for Germany. On the point of law, the French Government cannot accept these arguments. There is no clause, either in Part V of the Treaty or in the League Covenant, by virtue of which a general limitation of armaments should involve the lapse of the permanent stipulations of the Treaty. With this legal reservation France is ready to take part on the same terms as all the accepted parties in the examination of this problem, with the desire to see due allowance made in the final agreement for the progress made by the work of the Conference.

As to the second point, that is as regards the content, or in other words, as regards the heart of the matter submitted to the Geneva Conference, the French Government has no objection to laying down the rule which it will follow. Wishing to lighten so far as possible the load borne by the nations, and in particular by the French people, it will regulate its progress, allowing the right to disarmament in proportion to the guarantees which it finds in the organization of peace. It withdraws nothing from the declaration which it made at Geneva on July 22 in the following terms:

From the day when, in the spirit of the Covenant, and following its provisions, an international organization is created which assures security to, and imposes identical obligations on, all, the settlement of the question raised by Herr Pflügl will be greatly facilitated.

France has been reproached with her use of the idea and name of security. It must be repeated that this is the expression used in the Covenant. Security is the necessity which the German Government legitimately invokes when it writes, affirming an indisputable truth, that Germany has a right to her national security. It is the guarantee which should be secured for all nations, small and great, by establishing international control of armaments, by making arbitration general, and by securing the effective execution of its decisions. Recent statements, deriving authority from the official position of their author, suggested that France, in her support of this thesis, sought to conceal a disguised impulse towards imperialism.

Nothing is more untrue. France claims no privilege. She asks only for her legitimate share in a general security. She has made positive proposals on the subject in 1924 with the Protocol, and recently by suggesting the organization of an international force. The interest of these proposals is shown by the difficulty of finding other avenues to the desired solutions. This subject, like all subjects connected with the Disarmament Conference, is still open to discussion. Not only is France willing to study any suggestions Germany may make; she invites them as she invites those of all States. Nothing seems to her more fruitful for the pacification of the world than two great countries reconciled in the pursuit of the general good, and to be united later by the gratitude of the nations.

II

Having laid down these principles, the French Government will give its views no less frankly on the second aspect of the German Note of August 29. In its seventh paragraph the Note says that the first question to be considered in Germany is that of changes in the organization of the Army, such as, for instance, the rearrangement of the period of service of long-service troops and the free distribution of effectives. It also refers to training for short periods, and to a special militia compulsorily enrolled and intended to keep order in the country and to protect its coasts and frontiers.

In order to be sure that it does not interpret this text mistakenly, the French Government has referred to the detailed information given by the Reichswehr Minister to the *New York Times* of August 8, to the *Heimatdienst* of September 1, and to the correspondent of the *Resto del Carlino* for its issue of August 31. It finds a clear demand by Germany for aircraft, tanks, and heavy and anti-aircraft artillery for her army, and for submarines, aircraft carriers, and battleships for her navy. There can be no doubt: rearmament is proposed.

It must be pointed out at once that this rearmament would inevitably spread to all the States which are subjected by treaty to a régime similar to that of Germany. Thus the whole problem of central and eastern Europe is raised as an immediate consequence, and competition in armaments would begin again on this broad basis. All

Europe is therefore strictly affected by the question put to France, who cannot undertake to give an isolated answer to so vast a question.

And clearly that is not all. With Germany extending her demands to naval forces by the very terms of the declaration made on August 29 to the French Ambassador by the German Ministers von Neurath and von Schleicher, the whole of the naval *statut* of the Powers would go forward. Thus the imprudence of an isolated answer would undermine the military *statut* of every country in the world. This aspect of the matter cannot go unheeded by responsible statesmen.

If Germany persists in her intentions, concerted action will have to be taken. By what agency? Not by that of the Disarmament Conference. First, because the German demand is directly contrary to the essential aim of this Conference, which is to examine the possibilities of reducing, and not increasing, armaments. Secondly, because nations which were not parties to the Peace Treaty are sitting at the Conference.

The necessary negotiations should certainly not be pursued, or even opened, without consulting the Powers adhering to the Pact of Confidence of July 13, 1932. Germany has expressly adhered to its text. It states in Articles I and II:

I. Acting in the spirit of the Covenant of the League of Nations, they intend, in such an eventuality, to proceed quite frankly to a mutual exchange of views on any possible question of the same origin as that which has been so happily settled at Lausanne, and which concerns the European system. They will, moreover, keep one another informed as to the development of this question. They hope that other Governments will see their way to joining with them in adopting the same procedure.

II. They intend to work together, and with the other Legations at Geneva, to find a solution to the disarmament problem which will be advantageous and equitable for all interested Powers.

Again, the discussion is dominated by the Versailles Treaty, which cannot be modified unilaterally, and by Article 164, the second paragraph of which is in these terms:

Germany agrees that after she has become a member of the League of Nations the armaments fixed in the said Table shall remain in force until they are modified by the Council of the League. Furthermore she hereby agrees strictly to observe the decisions of the Council of the League on this subject.

This text is commented upon by the letter of the President of the Peace Conference in reply to the German observations. After having set out certain changes in the military clauses of the Treaty, this document said: "No change in the constitution of the armaments, as stipulated by the Treaty, will be allowed until Germany is admitted to the League, which may consent to whatever changes it considers desirable."

Thus the League of Nations is the sole judge. France cannot fail to keep the engagements she has taken towards the League, and it is before it that we reserve the right to set forth, if need be, the reasons which prevent us from consenting to the rearmament of Germany.

The survey which France has just undertaken confirms her in the determination, expressed at the beginning of this Note, to remain faithful, whatever may happen, to the Statute of the League of Nations.

Finally, we cannot by isolated negotiations run the risk of infringing upon the rights of the United States. The Peace Treaty signed by the United States with Germany on August 25, 1921, gives it the benefit of the dispositions of Part V of the Treaty.

In a general way, and because the German Government expresses a desire for pacification with which we associate ourselves, the French Government draws attention to the danger which would threaten the re-establishment of the general economy as the result of measures which might cause, at once or in the long run, a revival of competition in armaments and the reawakening of militarism. At Lausanne France consented, for the general good, to sacrifices which impartial judges have justly appreciated. She thinks that it is possible for her within the framework of existing engagements to work with Germany in the search for a new order, not through a return to the old methods of preparing for war, but through progress in the organization of peace.

MEMORANDUM Communicated by Louis Barthou, Minister for Foreign Affairs, to the British Embassy at Paris, April 17, 1934

Translation, in British White Paper, Cmd. 4559, p. 20

1. In a note of the 28th March, supplemented by the communication from His Majesty's Principal Secretary of State for Foreign Affairs of the 10th April, the British Government asked the Government of the Republic to indicate whether it was ready to accept as the basis of a Disarmament Convention the British memorandum of

the 29th January last, as modified in accordance with the German proposals, which Mr. Eden communicated to the French Government on the 1st March.

2. The British Government put forward this question on the hypothesis that agreement might be reached which would make guarantees of execution of the Convention possible. They desired, moreover, to learn the views of the French Government on the nature of such guarantees.

3. Now, the very day on which the British Ambassador made this communication, the *Official Monitor of the Reich* published at Berlin the budget adopted by the German Government on the 22nd March for the financial year 1933–34. A study of this budget showed without possibility of doubt an increase in the expenses of the Ministries of the Army, Navy and Air amounting to 352 million marks.

4. The British Government were no less concerned than the French Government at the size of this increase in expenditure. They drew attention to its gravity by making representations through their Ambassador at Berlin to the Ministry for Foreign Affairs of the Reich. The explanations which they received in return are less a justification than a confirmation.

5. In reality the German Government, without awaiting the results of the negotiations which were in progress, has wished to impose its determination to continue every form of rearmament, within limits of which it claims to be sole judge, in contempt of the provisions of the Treaty, which, in the absence of any other convention, continue to govern the level of its armaments. The German Government intends to increase immediately on a formidable scale not only the strength of its army, but also of its navy and of its aviation. So far as this last is concerned, it is all the less permissible for the neighbours of Germany to disregard the menace that hangs over them, in that numerous aerodromes have recently been organised in the demilitarised zone, also in violation of the Treaty. Side by side with this, the German Government shows less anxiety to suppress the paramilitary organisations or to convert them to civil purposes than to perfect them as an instrument well suited for war. To prove this it is only necessary to read other budgets than that of national defence.

6. Whatever explanation may be advanced after the event, facts of such exceptional gravity can lead to only one observation and conclusion.

7. They prove that the German Government, whether of set purpose or not, has made impossible the negotiations the basis of which it has by its own act destroyed.

8. The duty and the reply of the Government of the Republic are

DISARMAMENT AND SECURITY 479

dictated by recognition of this fact. Even before seeking to discover whether an agreement can be obtained upon a system of guarantees of execution sufficiently efficacious to permit the signature of a Convention which would legalise a substantial rearmament of Germany, France must place in the forefront of her preoccupations the conditions of her own security, which, moreover, she does not separate from that of other interested Powers.

9. The return of Germany to the League of Nations, which she left so abruptly, might have furnished the opportunity and means of dissipating, at least in part, these preoccupations. In its Note of the 17th March the Government of the Republic recorded its agreement with the British Government on the necessity for making the previous return of Germany to the community of States an essential condition of the signature of a disarmament convention. Since then a number of Governments, having the same preoccupation, have expressed the same opinion. The presence of Germany in the Geneva Assembly would be no less indispensable for the realisation of a satisfactory system of guarantees of execution. On this point of capital importance, however, Mr. Eden was not able to bring from Berlin any favourable solution, and the silence observed in this respect in the course of the most recent communications does not permit of better hopes.

10. The Government of the Republic, for its part, cannot abandon in principle this essential and necessary condition which it has formulated. Even less can it assume the responsibility of so dangerous a renunciation at the very moment when German rearmament is being claimed, prepared and developed, without any account being taken of the negotiations entered upon in accordance with the wishes of Germany herself.

11. The experience of the last war, the horrors of which France had to endure more than any other country, imposes upon her the duty of showing prudence. Her will to peace must not be confounded with the abandonment of her defence. She appreciates the friendly action of the British Government in wishing to seek with her an effective system for surrounding with guarantees the execution of a disarmament convention. She regrets that the action of a third party should abruptly have rendered vain the negotiations undertaken by the two countries with equal goodwill and good faith.

12. It will be the duty of the Disarmament Conference to resume its work. That work should not be abandoned, but taken up at the point at which the Conference left it when it invited Governments to proceed to an exchange of views outside the conference, which have not produced a result. Throughout all these negotiations France has remained faithful, and she desires to continue faithful, both to the

principles which have always inspired the General Commission, and to the statutes of the League of Nations, which is the safeguard of the peace of the world. The French Government does not doubt that it will retain at the forthcoming session the co-operation of the British Government, which it always appreciates so highly, in the task of consolidating peace by the guarantees which general security demands.

DRAFT of an Eastern Pact Submitted by the French Government to the British Government in a Memorandum of the French Ambassador at London, June 27, 1934

British Blue Book, Cmd. 5143, p. 7

I.—*Treaty of Regional Assistance to be signed by Poland, Russia, Germany, Czechoslovakia, Finland, Estonia, Latvia, Lithuania*

Part I

(1) THESE COUNTRIES would bind themselves, in conformity with the Covenant of the League of Nations, immediately to lend assistance to one another in the case of attack by one contracting State on another.

(2) No support would be given by any of the signatories to an aggressor country not a party to the treaty.

Part II

(3) In the case of attack or of threatened attack by a contracting country, the other parties would consult together with a view to avoid a conflict and in order to promote a return to peace.

(4) The signatories would undertake the same commitment in the case of attack or of threatened attack by a Power which is not a signatory against a Signatory Power.

(5) The consultations referred to in paragraphs (3) and (4) of Part II could extend to other interested Powers or to Powers entitled to participate in them by virtue of other treaties.

(6) Where one contracting country could benefit from the provisions of articles 10 and 16 of the Covenant of the League, the other signatories would undertake to secure a complete application of such provisions by the League of Nations.

II.—*Agreement between France and Russia*

(1) As towards France,* Russia would accept the obligations arising from the Treaty of Locarno as though the Soviet Union were a signatory of that treaty on the same footing as Great Britain or Italy.

(2) As towards Russia, France would accept the commitments which would arise for her under Part I, paragraphs (1) and (2), of the Regional Treaty if she were a signatory, in cases where it is a question of action in fulfilment of article 16 of the Covenant, or decisive action taken by the Assembly or the Council in fulfilment of paragraph 7 of article 15 of the Covenant.

(3) France would be invited, if the case arose, to participate in the consultations provided for in the Treaty of Regional Assistance under the terms of article (3) of Part II.

III.—*A General Act*

Signatories.—All States signatories of the Treaty of Regional Assistance and, in addition, France:—

(*a*) The two preceding treaties are recognised as being of a character to contribute to the maintenance of peace.

(*b*) They are without prejudice to the obligations and rights of the contracting parties as members of the League of Nations.

(*c*) The entry into force of the three Acts is subject to their ratification and to the entry of Russia into the League of Nations.

STATEMENT by Pierre Laval, Minister for Foreign Affairs, January 7, 1935, Regarding Rapprochement with Italy

Translated from the French text as printed in Royal Institute of International Affairs, *Documents on International Affairs, 1935*, I, 17, citing *L'Europe Nouvelle* (Documents Supplement, No. 9), March 2, 1935; excerpt

THE NEGOTIATIONS which we entered into have led to a positive result. My hopes have not been disappointed: The agreements are signed.

* As a result of an Anglo-French meeting in London on July 11 and 12, 1935, the words "and Germany" were added after "France" in paragraph (1), and after "Russia" in paragraph (2) of the Agreement between France and Russia. The obligations assumed by Russia and France in this Agreement were thereby made to apply not only in relation to France and Russia respectively, but also in relation to Germany. . . . It was further agreed at this meeting that the conclusion of such a pact and Germany's participation in the system of reciprocal guarantees now contemplated would afford the best ground for the resumption of negotiations for the conclusion of a convention such as would provide for a reasonable application of the principle of German equality of rights in armaments within a régime of security for all nations.

In settling our Franco-Italian dispute, we will have facilitated the friendly policy which should hereafter motivate the relations between our two countries.

The conventions which we have signed in connection with African problems are equitable and they will, I hope, be favorably received. M. Mussolini and I have endeavored to show the same spirit of comprehension in seeking the too-long delayed solutions of these delicate problems. Neither of us has sacrificed any of our essential interests. Thus, on both sides, we have removed the obstacles which have hindered the necessary collaboration of our two Governments for too long a time.

Hereafter we will be enabled, without mental reservations and in an atmosphere of mutual trust, to examine freely all the problems which face the statesmen to whom the maintenance of European order is entrusted.

That is how we came to coordinate our views regarding the policy to be followed in Central Europe, and the *procès-verbal* which we have signed will figure among the diplomatic documents of the greatest importance.

We are, indeed, determined to spare no effort in order that the conventions which we have contemplated may become a reality. We have facilitated the task of all the interested countries through a spirit of impartiality and objectiveness, which has been the sole guide of our negotiations.

The policy conceived by us is directed against no one. It extends to all governments, on the same level of moral equality, an offer to associate themselves with an enterprise whose exclusive purpose is to organize peace.

I earnestly hope that our appeal will be heard. By their adherence the interested governments will thus certify their peaceful aspirations.

Our conversations will lead to further happy issues: they will facilitate the necessary rapprochement among all those whose collaboration is indispensable for the safety of peace.

It is with deeds that we will see the realization of the appeasement which is the requisite for the development of the policy that we wish to exercise.

The negotiations at Rome have thus been brought to a successful close. . . .

RELATIONS WITH GERMANY AND OUTBREAK OF THE WAR

LETTER from Pierre Laval, Minister for Foreign Affairs, to the Secretary-General of the League of Nations (Joseph Avenol), April 9, 1935, Transmitting Memorandum Regarding Decisions of the German Government Relating to Armaments

Translation, in League of Nations, *Official Journal*, May, 1935, p. 569

BY MY TELEGRAM of March 20th, I had the honour to request you to arrange for an extraordinary meeting of the Council of the League of Nations to examine, in virtue of Article 11, paragraph 2, of the Covenant, the situation created by the German Law of March 16th, 1935, which has re-established general compulsory military service and has reorganised the German army in twelve army corps and thirty-six divisions.

Following on this communication, I have the honour to send you, in the annexed memorandum, the observations which the French Government desires to present in support of this request. I shall be obliged if you will transmit this communication to the Members of the Council.

MEMORANDUM

1. On March 16th last, the Head of the German State, Chancellor of the Reich, convened the Ambassadors of the European Powers in Berlin, and communicated to them the text of a law re-establishing general compulsory military service in Germany, and providing for the reorganization of the army, bringing it up to twelve army corps and thirty-six divisions. On the same day this law was promulgated. This measure had been preceded, on March 9th, by an official notification of the reconstitution of a German military air force.

Two of the essential provisions of the military clauses of the Peace Treaty have thus been formally repudiated. This is the culmination of long and methodical labours pursued in secret; it bears witness to the scale on which re-armament has already been effected by Germany, apart from the programme now being put into effect; it is not so much the announcement as the definite achievement of a policy.

A year ago Europe was disturbed at the increase in the Reich's military budget for 1934–35. The French Government saw in these estimates of expenditure (that subsequently have been greatly exceeded) a sign of the German Government's determination to continue its re-armament within limits of which it intends to be the sole judge. The Reich authorities protested against this interpretation. In a note handed on April 11th to the British Ambassador in Berlin, the Minister for Foreign Affairs explained the increase in expenditure by the need of preparing for the transformation of the army into a short-term service militia and denied that the budget of the Air Ministry could be regarded as an armament budget. A few days later, on April 27th, he expressed his "stupefaction" that anyone could feel any real alarm at an air budget the expenditure under which was intended solely for the protection of the population against air attack and for the reorganisation of civil aviation. Again, on December 20th, the Air Minister refused to admit that the Reich possessed more than a few experimental craft. Yet three months later, Chancellor Hitler was in a position to inform the British Foreign Secretary that the Reich had, in the matter of aviation, already attained parity with the United Kingdom.

It is surely permissible to point out that such a result could not have been brought about in a few weeks or even a few months. Henceforth the true value of denials and declarations is clear, and the spirit that they reveal assumes its full significance.

2. The acts referred to above are a definite infringement of certain fundamental clauses of Part V of the Treaty of Versailles and of the Agreements concluded subsequently for its application between the German Government and the Governments of the "Principal Allied Powers" represented by the Conference of Ambassadors.

For long it has been impossible to doubt that these articles of the Treaty were being systematically disregarded, but their violation was, as far as possible, concealed. At present their violation is perfectly clear; it is no longer denied. It is the duty of the League of Nations to take cognisance of the matter. Founded as it is on an obligation to respect international undertakings, the guardian of a Covenant, in the Preamble of which it is laid down that States which intend "to promote international co-operation" and "achieve international peace and security" must "scrupulously respect all Treaty obligations in the dealings of organised peoples with one another," the League cannot remain indifferent to the affirmation of a method of policy entirely contrary to the principles on which it rests and the aims assigned to it.

3. On the occasion of Germany's admission to the League, the Assembly expressly referred to Part V of the Treaty in defining the

military, naval and air conditions to which the Reich was bound to conform; it noted a declaration to the effect that Germany would give "effective guarantees of her sincere intention to observe the obligations incumbent on her under the Treaty and acts related thereto."

In treating as null and void the provisions governing its military status, the Government of the Reich has deliberately destroyed one of the bases of its collaboration with the Geneva institution.

4. By so doing, it has seriously compromised the success of the international negotiations for the limitation of armaments pursued under the auspices of the League of Nations and on the basis of Article 8 of the Covenant. The Powers had, however, given many proofs of their will to conform to the provisions of this article. For its part, the French Government must point out that, between 1921 and 1928, the duration of military service was reduced in France from three years to one; that the forces immediately available for the defence of the home country were thus reduced, according to the circumstances, by 42 or 60%; that its overseas forces had also been appreciably reduced; and that only a very small part of the air programme had been carried out.

Certainly, many difficulties had arisen to jeopardise the success of the Geneva Conference; but these difficulties did not release the German Government from its obligations. Even if—and the Government of the Republic formally denies it—the Preamble to Part V was of the nature and scope that it is sometimes sought to attribute to it, one essential fact would nevertheless remain: whatever might be the difficulties of a task further complicated by measures of German rearmament at the very time when the Conference was sitting, the Powers had not renounced their efforts to discover some basis on which an international agreement could be concluded.

The French Government feels bound to refer to the proposals it made as long ago as February 5th, 1932, for limiting bombing aircraft and placing them at the disposal of the League, and for the creation of an international force in connection with a better organisation of security. It must allude to the generous proposals put forward by the French delegation, on November 14th of the same year, for the establishment of a European system of armament reduction and international co-operation. It must allude to the declaration of December 11th, 1932, which indissolubly linked the concession of equality of rights with the establishment of a system of security. Lastly, it must refer to the fact that, in October 1933, at a time when the international situation was already becoming overcast for reasons for which France bears no responsibility whatsoever, it agreed with several other

Governments in proposing a programme of work which would have enabled the Geneva Conference to accomplish something useful and effective. It is true that, when this programme was stated, the Government of the Reich thought fit to leave Geneva and to announce its decision to withdraw from the League of Nations—a violent action, totally unjustified, as the President of the Conference himself observed—but, even after that action had been taken, the enterprise was not abandoned.

On February 3rd last, on the initiative of the French and United Kingdom Governments, a programme was framed which was favourably received by all the Governments attached to the cause of peace.

That programme was accepted by the Government of the Reich itself; but it has been gravely compromised by its decisions of March 16th. It is useless for the German Government to invoke measures which other Governments had found themselves obliged to take in their respective countries; for those measures were justified by the increase in the armaments of the Reich. It is useless for the German Government to invoke in particular the measures which, in order to cope with recruiting difficulties resulting from the war, the French Government has been forced to decide upon in regard to the duration of military service; those measures were acknowledged to be legitimate, as much as five years ago, by the Preparatory Commission for the Disarmament Conference.

Germany has sought to provide a unilateral solution for an international problem. For the method of negotiations, she has substituted the method of the *fait accompli*. Her decisions, incompatible as they are with any system for the reduction of armaments, have raised the problem of general re-armament, in all its gravity, for Europe as a whole.

It is the Council's duty to pronounce upon the responsibility for the situation thus created, and upon the consequences it entails. It is likewise the Council's duty to state the conclusions that must be drawn, for the purposes of their treaty policy, by those Governments which still desire to maintain and consolidate European security.

5. There is a more important question that must be raised; for, in a Europe in which the method of unilaterally denouncing international engagements became general, there would soon be no room for any policy but one of force. No negotiation is possible if, while the conversations are proceeding, one of the parties can arbitrarily possess himself of that which is the subject of those conversations; nor can any negotiation be of service if its results, whatever they may be, can be destroyed at the will of one of the contracting parties. That

is equivalent to abolishing the whole idea of contract and obligation in international relations.

The efforts of the pacific nations are directed towards the establishment of a comprehensive system of collective security among States through the conclusion of pacts of non-aggression, consultation, and mutual assistance. Is it worth while to continue those efforts, if it is to be agreed that the repudiation of a contractual undertaking, however solemnly entered into, involves no consequences other than moral reprobation, if a country runs no risk by releasing itself from its obligations, and if the treaty-breaking State is to be encouraged by impunity to commit further breaches?

The Council would not be carrying out its mission if it looked with indifference upon such a threat to international order. It is its duty to meet that threat by considering the most suitable measures for remedying the situation that has now been created and for preventing its recurrence.

6. Such are the considerations to which the Government of the Republic feels bound to call the Council's attention. Convinced that the observance of undertakings entered into is the duty of every peaceful nation; conscious of the obligations imposed upon the States Members of the League by the various articles of the Covenant; anxious that relations of confidence between peoples should be restored; and declaring itself to be entirely at one with all Governments which desire the consolidation of peace: the French Government confidently expects that the Council will pronounce upon the grave situation to which its attention is drawn, will take decisions concerning the present state of affairs, and will safeguard the future.

STATEMENT by Pierre-Etienne Flandin, Minister for Foreign Affairs, in the Council of the League of Nations, March 14, 1936

League of Nations, *Official Journal*, April, 1936, p. 312

THE FACTS WHICH have given occasion for this special meeting of the Council are too well known for it to be necessary for me to recapitulate them at any length. A week ago to-day, the diplomatic representatives at Berlin of the Powers who signed the Treaty of Locarno with Germany were successively received by the German Chancellor and were told that Germany proclaimed that Treaty to have lapsed and henceforward regarded herself as discharged from its obligations.

In order that there might be no misapprehension as to the reality of that decision, troops entered the demilitarised zone on the same day. These were not, as was first stated, a few "symbolical" detachments, but large forces consisting of over 30,000 regular troops, to mention only those officially reckoned by the German Government.

In bringing these facts before the Council and in denouncing the breach of Article 2 and Article 8 of the Locarno Treaty, the French Government has not so much exercised a right as performed a duty. If it were only a question of rights, the text of the Locarno Treaty would authorise the French Government to take strong and decisive measures forthwith. Being anxious, for its part, not to add any disturbing factor to the European situation, it voluntarily refrained from such action, thus giving expression in its fullest sense to the respect which it pays, and which it hopes all will pay, to international law as the essential means of maintaining peace.

In virtue of Article 4, it was France's duty, as a contracting party, to bring the question immediately before the Council of the League of Nations. She has done so, confident in the Council's impartiality in establishing the fact of a breach and recommending such steps as may be considered desirable, confident also in the readiness of the guarantor Powers to perform the duties devolving on them as a result of that finding, and resolved, finally, to place at the League's disposal all her forces, both material and moral, to help it to overcome one of the most serious crises in the history of peace and of its collective organisation.

To justify her action, Germany has invoked the approval by the French Chamber of Deputies of the Franco-Soviet Pact concluded ten months previously, regarding which there had been an exchange of notes last May and June between the Government of the Reich, the French Government and the Governments guarantors of the Locarno Treaty. In these notes, the legal arguments advanced on the German side were amply refuted. The German Government gave no reply.

But, even if the German Government was not satisfied, it was bound, in virtue of the Arbitration Convention concluded at the same time as the Rhineland Pact, to refer the matter to arbitration. It has not even attempted to do so. Despite the statement I myself made in the Chamber of Deputies before Germany's unilateral denunciation of the Treaties of Locarno and Versailles, to the effect that we would accept the arbitration of the Hague Court of Justice, the German Government has not attempted to initiate such proceedings; nor has it attempted to bring about any common discussion of the problem at a meeting of the Powers signatories of the Locarno

Pact. It has preferred to repudiate a treaty which Chancellor Hitler has repeatedly recognised to have been freely agreed to and on which the signatories intended to confer particular stability, since the contracting parties forwent the right of denunciation and may only ask the Council of the League of Nations to terminate the Treaty if it finds that the League of Nations otherwise provides sufficient guarantees.

That this decision taken by Germany had been prepared long beforehand, and that the argument put forward was merely a pretext, chosen from among several others which had previously been considered, there can be no doubt. But that matters little. I repeat that the French Government is prepared to let the Permanent Court at The Hague decide whether the Treaty of May 2nd, 1935, is incompatible with the Treaty of Locarno.

But not only is there repudiation of a treaty. There is also a definite breach of Article 43 of the Treaty of Versailles, which Article 44 describes as a hostile act.

It is not without good reason that, at Locarno, respect for frontiers and respect for the measures intended to provide a necessary safeguard for Belgium and for France were placed upon the same footing.

There is no doubt that no one could have intended to place a derogation from the principles of demilitarisation on a point of detail on the same footing as the violation of a frontier. But the statements of the authors of the Treaty show that it was not intended to make any difference between an attack on national territory and a deliberate and large-scale violation of the zone. In asking that the violation should be recognised, the French Government simply asks that the law should be applied. Once this has been done, it will be for the guarantors to furnish France and Belgium with the assistance provided for in the Treaty.

But France's rights and her own interests are not alone at stake, nor are the duties of the guarantors alone involved. It is a question—and here I am speaking particularly to the Members of the Council who are not signatories of the Locarno Treaty—of the interests of general peace and, I might say, of the very existence of the League of Nations. The question at issue is whether the practice of the *fait accompli,* the unilateral repudiation of undertakings freely and solemnly accepted, are going to be set up in Europe as a political system; whether treaties are going to be considered as at any moment and immediately capable of modification at the will of their signatories, and whether a Government, in the exercise of its own power, may go back to-day on its promises of yesterday. I ask how such a method can be reconciled with the existence of the League of Nations, whose

Covenant states that, in order to promote international co-operation and to achieve international peace and security, it is necessary to observe strictly all the understandings of international law as the actual rule of conduct among Governments, together with a scrupulous respect for all treaty obligations.

Is such a method compatible with the very notion of collective security, an expression which is meaningless if it does not express the confidence of each member in the undertakings entered into by the others, and the conviction that all the members will contribute to defend each one of them against the breach of its undertakings by another State? Is it likely to encourage the conclusion of fresh international agreements?

The Council gauged these dangers so well that, a year ago, on April 17th, 1935, when condemning the use which Germany had already made of this method, it recognised that, in future, the Members of the League of Nations must oppose by all appropriate means the repudiation of undertakings affecting the security of the nations of Europe and the maintenance of peace.

If, having recognised that necessity a year ago, the Council, which to-day has still more serious facts before it, were to go back on its own decision, I fear that the authority of the League of Nations would suffer irreparable injury in the minds of all peoples.

Such are the facts and such, briefly, are the observations to which they give rise, and which the Council will no doubt desire to consider.

I ask the Council to pronounce that a breach of Article 43 of the Treaty of Versailles has been committed by Germany, and to request the Secretary-General to notify the Powers signatories of the Locarno Treaty in accordance with Article 4 of that Treaty. This notification will enable the guarantor Governments to discharge their obligations of assistance. For its part, the Council will have to consider how it can support that action by recommendations addressed to the Members of the League of Nations.

MESSAGE from Edouard Daladier, Premier, to the President of the United States (Franklin D. Roosevelt), September 26, 1938, in Reply to the Latter's Appeal for Peace the Same Day

Department of State, *Press Releases,* October 1, 1938, p. 220

YOUR MOVING APPEAL has reached me in London at the very moment when, in close co-operation with the British Government France makes a supreme attempt with a view to safeguarding all possibility of an amicable settlement of the conflict that is threatening peace; it is of special value to me that under your high moral authority the devotion of the entire American nation to the principles which have been recognized and publicly acknowledged by all the parties to the Kellogg Pact is now solemnly reaffirmed.

Remaining faithful both to the spirit and the letter of the pledges, we continue with unfailing tenacity to look for any procedure or form of agreement which may be compatible with the dignity and the vital interests of the nations involved.

We trust thus to serve to the last the ideal of justice and peace which has always been a link between our two nations.

ADDRESS by Edouard Daladier, Premier, in the Chamber of Deputies, October 4, 1938

Translation, in *Vital Speeches of the Day,* October 15, 1938, p. 6

DURING THE WEEKS through which we have just lived the world asked with anguish if it was not to be plunged into war. Today, coming before you to render an account of our action, I can tell you that in this crisis we have saved peace.

During recent days I have spoken little because I had to act a great deal. I was reproached with being the most silent man in France. In this moment of quiet, which should mark the point of departure for a new action, I wish to tell you what were these events and how we faced them.

When our government was formed the problem of the Sudetens had already been brought up. The realization of the (Austrian) Anschluss gave it a certain prominence. Already the Czechoslovak Government had announced publication of a nationalities statute and Mr. Henlein formulated in eight points the demands of Sudeten Germans.

The drama had begun. From the first day we tried to stop events from driving us into the irreparable. I then publicly defined on several occasions the position of my government.

We are animated, I said, by two equally strong feelings: the desire to be spared from military action and the will never to denounce our word if through unhappy events this hope was dashed.

At London at the end of April (Foreign Minister) Bonnet and I told the English Government of our preoccupation and how we planned the appeasement of Central Europe. We had the satisfaction of seeing that the British Government was hardly indifferent to these problems. Together we fixed the basis of collaboration in our minds. It was hardly a question of waiting to act until the facts were accomplished and until we should have had to impress them in blood or submit to them in shame. It was a question of forestalling events and trying to prevent them from occurring.

It was thus that of a common accord we acted immediately at the moment of the crisis of May 23, which I now recall was overcome, thanks to the effective aid and peaceful good-will of all interested powers.

From the end of the month of May to the beginning of September there was a sort of international truce, but in the Sudeten region the effervescence of passions prepared new events.

Then, with a sentiment of friendship we advised the Czechoslovak government to give the Sudeten Germans important, just and rapid concessions within the structure of the State.

The action of the English Government was parallel to ours. The mission of Lord Runciman at Prague gave birth to a great hope in bringing direct contacts between Czech statesmen and Sudeten leaders.

It must, however, be admitted there never was parallelism between the propositions of the Czech Government, which ceaselessly made larger concessions, and the Sudeten demands, which became more and more important.

At the beginning of September, after the speech (by Hitler) which closed the Nuremberg conference, and the announcement made by (Konrad) Henlein of the rupture of negotiations between Sudeten delegates and the Prague government, the situation seemed for the first time irremediably compromised.

The German demand was affirmed with violence. It took as a base the right of peoples to dispose of their own destiny. The demands were addressed to the peoples' conscience by descriptions which the

RELATIONS WITH GERMANY

German press gave of the terror which was reported to reign in Sudeten districts.

Were the forces of war going to overcome the forces of peace? At no moment did I think of giving in or abandoning the country to no matter what blind fatality which would have taken the march of events out of the hands of men.

During the night of the 13th to the 14th of September I entered into contact with Mr. Neville Chamberlain. I told him of the utility there would be to substitute for representations and notes direct meetings between responsible men. The English Prime Minister on his side had already had the same feeling and he went to Berchtesgaden.

In a speech to the House of Commons Chamberlain asked his colleagues with emotion if his trip had not seemed incompatible with his dignity of Prime Minister. I wish here to associate the French Parliament with the British Parliament and say simply that, by that courageous initiative and by all his actions during the days and nights which followed, Mr. Neville Chamberlain merits well of peace. What followed the interview at Berchtesgaden you already know. In official publications all documents will be brought together and the representations described as well as the negotiations.

But this document will bring very few unpublished revelations, for perhaps for the first time in the history of the world everything was publicly undertaken and discussed before the people. And I believe I may say that if finally peace was maintained and preserved it was because we did not return to the tricks of secret diplomacy. We acted in the full light of day under control of the people and I wish to affirm here that all the people wish peace.

By his conversation with Mr. Hitler, Mr. Chamberlain could appreciate and get an exact idea of the amplitude of the German demands. On Sunday, September 18, he told us of his impressions and his convictions.

We met again in London, we deliberated, we read maps. The British Government told us of Lord Runciman's opinion. Need I tell you with what emotion we learned that in his soul and conscience the British observer concluded it was an impossibility to make the Czechs and Sudetens live any longer together, while all our efforts had consisted of making Czechoslovakia turn toward a federalism which would have assured the integrity of her territory.

But it was necessary to face realities. We found ourselves faced with the following alternatives:

Either to say "No" to the Sudeten demands and thereby push the Czech Government to an unyielding stand and the German Government to aggression, thereby provoking an armed conflict which would have had for a consequence the rapid destruction of Czechoslovakia, or to try to find a compromise.

If the first hypothesis had been verified, who could have said that the integrity of Czechoslovakia would have been maintained after a terrible war of coalition, even a victorious war.

We chose peace. The Franco-British plan of London came out of that choice, but at the same time as we submitted these sad propositions to Czechoslovakia we brought her an engagement taken by Britain to join with us in an international guarantee, for we were able to get from the British Government the help of her power and her prestige for the maintenance of peace and order in the very heart of Europe.

On leaving London we had the feeling that our plan would bring indignant protests from Prague and receive the agreement of Berlin.

The Czech Government in its heroic devotion to the cause of peace accepted the plan. But at Godesberg Mr. Hitler, in an interview with Mr. Chamberlain, and by his memorandum, formulated under the form of details of application new demands.

And it was thus that the evolution of the negotiations toward a compromise, which had begun with the decision of Mr. Chamberlain and myself to make direct contact with the German Government, stopped in the night of the 23rd to the 24th of September, and during the days which followed Europe slid rapidly toward a rupture.

What then was the situation on the 24th of September at the moment when Mr. Neville Chamberlain, leaving Godesberg, went back to London?

We proposed cession to Germany of territories inhabited by more than 50 per cent of Germans according to a mechanism and a frontier to be fixed by an international commission. We organized the exchange of populations; we brought the new Czechoslovakia an international guarantee.

What did Germany demand? Immediate cession of territories, creation of vast plebiscite zones without giving real guarantees to the populations themselves and without assuring an international guarantee to the new Czechoslovakia.

It might have been thought that for her it was an operation which would have had all the characteristics, all the consequences of conquest except for recourse to arms.

Disaccord between the London plan and the Godesberg memorandum was manifest. It was disaccord on basis as well as on form. Was it going to lead to a European war?

During these anguishing days two great currents were manifest in our country. Both of them were found in the interior of each political party, in the interior of each political tendency, and I may say that they fought for the conscience of each Frenchman. Some put their hope in negotiation, others in unyielding firmness.

As for me, chief of the government, I recognized from the first minute in both movements the infallible instinct of the French people. I felt that the truth was in a mixture of these two currents, not in their contradiction.

What the people of France wanted was to avoid the irreparable. The irreparable was German aggression. The aggression, under the terms of our treaty, would have brought the aid and assistance of France. We would have asked that you face the engagements of France.

So as not to be surprised by force and faced with the development of German preparations, we decided Sept. 24 to take a certain number of military measures, not destined as provocation but to put our country in a position to face any emergency. We did everything to be completely defended. Our military chiefs put our forces in a position to fulfill their supreme duty to the fatherland.

At London, where we again brought our attitude into conformity with the British Government, General Gamelin brought the technical details of the efforts which we had accomplished and efforts which circumstances might call upon us to furnish.

Englishmen, Frenchmen, we each of us were as certain of our common will for peace as of our common will to oppose aggression.

On Sept. 26 in the evening, in an official communication to the press, it was said at London that if Germany attacked Czechoslovakia, France would go to her aid and "Great Britain and Russia would be certainly at the side of France."

And while in the United States of America the great, generous, logical voice of President Roosevelt made a pressing appeal for a peaceful settlement, Mr. Neville Chamberlain, in complete agreement with us, sent a new communication to Chancellor Hitler.

Sir Horace Wilson returned to London carrying the Reichsfuehrer's response. It left little place and little time for negotiation. In the House of Commons Mr. Neville Chamberlain himself has declared that the Chancellor told the British messenger he would resolve and act the next day, Sept. 28, at 2 o'clock in the afternoon. We had only a few hours before us.

The radio speech of Mr. Chamberlain warned the world of the gravity of the situation. We resolved to try a last effort. During the night of the 27th to 28th we asked our Ambassador in Berlin to request a personal audience with Chancellor Hitler and told our Ambassador in London that he might ask Lord Halifax to give instructions to the British Ambassador in Rome to beg Mr. Mussolini to back up the idea of a conference. We thus answered the spirit of the second message of President Roosevelt, who so generously contributed to make possible a peaceful solution.

At 11:15 a.m., Sept. 28, Monsieur (André) François-Poncet (French Ambassador) was received by Chancellor Hitler and told him in the name of the French Government the precise propositions for immediate practical application. Mr. Hitler did not refuse to accept the suggestions. He reserved the right to give them a written answer.

On his side Mr. Chamberlain proposed a last effort for a meeting in Germany of the chiefs of the governments of the four great western powers. Mr. Mussolini backed up this request with force and success. We obtained a decisive result by the twenty-four hour adjournment of German mobilization.

Mr. Hitler immediately issued invitations for the Munich meeting.

I accepted that invitation. It was not a question of procedure or formulating counter-propositions. It was a question of saving peace, which some persons already believed was definitely destroyed. I said "yes" and I don't regret anything. I would have preferred that all of the interested powers were present. But it was necessary to move fast. The least delay might have been fatal. Frank conversation with Mr. Hitler and Mr. Mussolini—was not that worth more than all written propositions or discussions?

You know the result of the interview at Munich which was more a mutual conversation than a formal conference.

We avoided recourse to force and we have, without any doubt being permitted on this subject, provoked in four countries a plebiscite of peace. By the spontaneous warmth of welcome which was reserved at Berlin, Rome, London, and Paris by the peoples of the four capitals for the peace of the four governments, by innumerable evidences which came to them from cities and from the rural districts of their countries, how can we doubt in a single instance of the immense relief of men and of their attachment for peace?

The effective victory for peace was a moral victory for peace: There is the first point which I have been trying to bring out. It was a human victory as well, since the accord at Munich, thanks to reciprocal concessions and the good-will of all, is considerable progress on the memorandum of Godesberg.

It contains stipulations organizing for the individual the right of conscience. It eliminates all dispositions which had figured in the armistice as those which a conqueror imposed upon a conquered.

We have brought to the Czechoslovak State assurances of interna-

RELATIONS WITH GERMANY

tional guarantees. France and Great Britain engaged themselves without reserve or delay to associate themselves with an international guarantee of the new frontiers of the Czechoslovak State against all unprovoked aggression. Germany and Italy engaged themselves moreover to give their guarantee as soon as the question of Polish and Hungarian minorities in Czechoslovakia is regulated.

I am convinced that, thanks to direct conversations, an honorable and just solution may soon be found.

An international committee has been created in order to arbitrate unilateral decisions.

To solutions of force one hopes thereby to substitute practices of law.

If tomorrow German and French contingents are called upon to go into the contested districts with the view of assuring the maintenance of order and regularity of the operation of the plebiscite they will do so with the feeling they are sparing these regions and the entire world from trials of war.

Certainly the Munich accord cut down the territory of Czechoslovakia. But the Czechoslovak Republic can continue its free life and we will aid it. Few States across history have so accepted sacrifices so painful even in the interests of peace.

The Czechs and Slovaks are brave people. We know they would have defended the integrity of their territories with arms and if necessary would have succumbed with honor in desperate resistance.

But their directors, their leaders, President Beneš, Premier Hodza and General Syrovy, had a high conception of the duty toward their nation and toward humanity.

In bringing to the knowledge of the Czech people his acceptance of the Munich accord, General Syrovy showed his duty had been to save the life of a nation, to permit a recovery.

We all have experienced the profoundest admiration for the moving dignity and admirable courage wherewith this noble country has undergone such an unhappy experience.

And now, gentlemen, how have we succeeded in stopping war at the very moment when it seemed ready to break forth? Why, in relation to real sacrifices which we granted, have we been able to add to our balance a certain number of guarantees and advantages, no less real, about which I have just told you?

Because in these difficult negotiations we have always shown our will for justice and for loyalty.

Because we negotiated like men for whom negotiations cannot only be an inevitable phrase in this great international drama but a real road toward peace.

I should add immediately with the same certainty that if our negotiation has succeeded we owe it above all to the fact we supported it with a demonstration of our strength. Let me be understood. I do not wish to say that our force has been a means of intimidation or pressure. One cannot any longer think of intimidating Germany any more than one can think of intimidating France. But to make proof of strength one must be placed in the position of discussing as from equal to equal. One cannot discuss with man or with nation unless one already has conquered his esteem.

As for the esteem of Germany for France, I felt it upon my arrival at Munich. It was founded on the fact one knew France was ready to fight to prevent anything which might attack its vital interests and the interests of justice. What made possible the success of our last negotiation was the determination of which France gave proof and it is necessary here to pay homage to the country which deserves it. At the first call and with admirable energy, when the serious gravity of the situation replaced the former enthusiasm of the young troops, old soldiers of the Great War joined their flags and reconstituted in a few hours that uncrossable barrier which always protects the destinies of the fatherland.

On our frontiers, mixing with the soldiers, the people who would have had most to suffer from war accepted without murmuring all measures of security which were placed upon them by the military authorities.

Let me thank them in the name of France for the esteem which our country upholds these days on all peoples by which it is surrounded, this esteem which found itself on the memory of struggles which already have split us up or united us, this esteem which no veteran can refuse to another veteran no matter what the color of his uniform during the war, this esteem which always imposes itself on a nation which is both virile and pacific, we have a duty to feel it ourselves for the great people which is our neighbor and which was our adversary with whom we desire to be able to establish a durable peace.

Without doubt our conception of life differs greatly from the conception of life now held by Germany and Italy of today. But other countries, whose conception are as different as our own, live with us in good faith. Whatever may be the fault of the regimes which these conceptions give to peoples they can have identical love of peace at the present time and that love of peace reunites all pacific good-will which exists in the world. If I have just recalled the feeling which the French people have for the German people, and from this tribune even many of my predecessors have expressed similar feelings, that does not mean we are thinking of renouncing our present collaborators. For us there is no question of substituting new friends for old friends. In the interests of peace we wish to add to these old and proved friends the support of renewed friendships or new friendships.

I know that in this work we can count on the friendship between France and Great Britain, which recent events have made even more confident and active.

I shall confess to you, gentlemen, that the other day when I arrived at Le Bourget in the middle of this spontaneous joy of the people of Paris, who replied then to the joy of the people of Berlin and Rome and London, I could not prevent myself from feeling a bit uneasy. I thought that peace was not a final conquest but that it should be guarded each day.

I am certainly sensitive to demonstrations of popular joy, but as chief of the government I can only think of the future of the country and the fact that peace has been saved must not be the signal for abandon. It should mark on the contrary a new increase of the energies of the nation.

I say this with all the strength of conviction of which I am capable: If the country should abandon itself and if the maintenance of peace was only a reason for indifference for it, we should immediately turn to even more desperate days. I cannot for my part agree to conduct France toward such days. The most precious good, that which permits all hopes, has been preserved for us and we have peace. Let us keep it and let us establish it on an unshakable basis.

It is possible that at Munich the world's face was changed in the space of a few hours. It is necessary that France reply to this new situation, embracing a new feeling of her own duty. The greatest crime toward the country would be to pass toward polemics before resolutions.

More than any one else I have a right to say that this is what has been worrying me during these last weeks and that has imperiled the efficacy of my action. More than any one else I have the duty of setting an example.

Since the beginning of this speech I have considered the greatest currents that crossed our country during this crisis as convergent demonstrations of the same will. I do not wish to distinguish between one and the other. There were such in this admirable movement, who joined our flag inspired by all the bonds of country, whatever their social condition, their beliefs or their particular convictions.

All Frenchmen who desire the safety of France must consider themselves in a state of permanent mobilization for the service of the nation and of the Fatherland. The first duty of each is to work with all his strength at the job that he is doing. We shall not continue to maintain peace unless our national production permits us to be able to talk as equal to equal with the peoples who surround us.

We cannot maintain peace unless we have healthy finances and a balanced budget and unless we are able to count on the total resources of the nation.

We cannot maintain peace unless we build on a basis of general understanding, unless we organize on the principles of a new Europe and a new world, and unless, after having avoided war in the center of Europe, we make it retreat everywhere where it is still raging.

We cannot continue to maintain peace unless we consolidate the union of heart and spirit that has thus been united in common anguish. Everything that incites hate, everything that makes Frenchmen oppose Frenchmen, cannot constitute anything but treason.

This country must have a moral transformation. Its unity has been remade for several hours. Around it is a mobilized strength that will not permit engaging in vain quarrels.

In order to lead this great task to its best conclusion it is necessary that the government be prepared to act. We have decided to ask you to give us the means to take this action.

You have the power to give it to us or to refuse it to us, but you must know that it is in the interest of the Fatherland itself.

COMMUNICATION from André François-Poncet, French Ambassador to Germany, to the French Minister for Foreign Affairs (Georges Bonnet), October 20, 1938

Translation, in *The French Yellow Book,* p. 20

When on the evening of October 17, the German Chancellor asked me to see him as quickly as possible, he placed one of his private planes at my disposal. I therefore left by air for Berchtesgaden on the next day accompanied by Captain Stehlin. I arrived there towards three in the afternoon. From there a car took me not to the Obersalzberg villa where the Führer lives, but to an extraordinary place where he likes to spend his days when the weather is fine.

From a distance, the place looks like a kind of observatory or small hermitage perched up at a height of 6,000 feet on the highest point of a ridge of rock. The approach is by a winding road about nine miles long, boldly cut out of the rock; the boldness of its construction does as much credit to the ability of the engineer Todt as to the unremitting toil of the workmen who in three years completed this gigantic task. The road comes to an end in front of a long underground passage leading into the mountain, and closed by a heavy double door of bronze. At the far end of the underground passage a wide lift, panelled with sheets of copper, awaits the visitor. Through a vertical shaft of 330 feet cut right through the rock, it rises up to the level of the Chancellor's dwelling-place. Here is reached the astonishing climax. The visitor finds himself in a strong and massive building containing a gallery with Roman pillars, an immense circular hall with windows all round and a vast open fireplace where enormous logs are burning, a table surrounded by about thirty chairs, and opening out at the sides, several sitting-rooms, pleasantly furnished with comfortable arm-chairs. On every side, through the bay-windows, one can look as from a plane high in the air, on to an immense panorama of mountains. At the far end of a vast amphitheatre one can make out Salzburg and the surrounding villages, dominated, as far as the eye can reach, by a horizon of mountain ranges and peaks, by meadows and forests clinging to the slopes. In the immediate vicinity of the house, which gives the impression of being suspended in space, an almost overhanging wall of bare rock rises up abruptly. The whole, bathed in the twilight of an autumn evening, is grandiose, wild, almost hallucinating. The visitor wonders whether he is awake or dreaming. He would like to know where he is—whether this is the Castle of Monsalvat where lived the Knights of the Graal or a new Mount Athos sheltering the meditations of a cenobite, or the palace of Antinea rising up in the heart of the Atlas Mountains. Is it the materialisation of one of those fantastic drawings with which Victor Hugo adorned the margins of his manuscript of Burgraves, the fantasy of a millionaire, or merely the refuge where brigands take their leisure and hoard their treasures? Is it the conception of a normal mind, or that of a man tormented by megalomania, by a haunting desire for domination and solitude, or merely that of a being in the grip of fear?

One detail cannot pass unnoticed, and is no less valuable than the rest for someone who tries to assess the psychology of Adolf Hitler: the approaches, the openings of the underground passage and the access to the house are manned by soldiers and protected by nests of machine-guns. . . .

The Chancellor received me amiably and courteously. He looks pale and tired. It is not one of his excitable days, he is rather in a period of relaxation. Immediately, he draws me towards the bay-windows of the great hall, shows me the landscape and enjoys the surprise and admiration that I make no effort to conceal. We exchange some compliments and a few polite phrases. At his order, the tea is served in one of the adjoining sitting-rooms. When the servants have left and the doors are closed, the conversation begins between the three of us; Herr von Ribbentrop intervenes only at rare intervals, and always to stress and emphasize the Führer's remarks.

Adolf Hitler is disappointed with the sequels of the Munich Agreement. He had believed that the meeting of the Four, which banished the spectre of war, would have marked the beginning of an era of conciliation and improved relations between nations. He cannot see that anything of the kind has occurred. The crisis is not over; it threatens, if the situation does not improve, to become worse within a short time. Great Britain is sonorous with threats and calls to arms. For the Chancellor this is an opportunity to utter, against that country, against her selfishness and her childish belief in the superiority of her rights over those of others, one of those tirades which he has already delivered several times in public.

The Chancellor's irritation calms down fairly quickly. I point out to him that after the joy at the preservation of peace, a reaction was inevitable; the realization of the sacrifices exacted from Czechoslovakia, the harsh treatment meted out to that country could not fail to stir the hearts and even to disturb the conscience of many people; and especially, the Saarbrücken speech had spread the impression that all these sacrifices had been made in vain, that their only effect had been to increase the appetite of the Third Reich. This speech had considerably strengthened the position of the adversaries of the Munich Agreement.

The Führer protests; he had not started the present trouble; the English had done so; he had not uttered a single word against France; and as to Czechoslovakia, it was not true that he had ill-treated her; all that he had done was to insist upon the rights of the German people, which had been trodden underfoot!

I interrupt his self-justification; we must not linger over the past, the future is more important; after the joy at the preservation of peace and the subsequent bitterness aroused by the sacrifices it exacted, a third stage is now reached. The statesmen must now with more self-control consider whether the Munich Agreement is only to be a fruitless episode or whether now that experience has proved that the democracies and the totalitarian states can co-operate in promoting general appeasement, they will attempt to develop this first successful experiment into a larger enterprise and gradually lead back Europe towards more normal and enduring conditions.

Herr Hitler does not raise any objection. He declares that, as far as he is concerned he is quite prepared to do this, and that he had asked me to visit him as much in order to be able to discuss this matter with me as to allow me to take my leave of him.

In my telegram of yesterday, I indicated in a sufficiently explicit manner the course the conversation then took. On the three points that were raised in turn, and which, taken as a whole, form a complete programme starting from Franco-German relations and widening to questions of importance to all the Powers, the Chancellor is full of arguments, objections and suggestions, like a man who has already considered the matter and is not being caught unaware.

As regards the suggestion of a written recognition by France and Germany of their common frontier and an agreement to hold consultations in all cases which might affect the relations of the two countries, Herr Hitler declares that he is ready to accept it immediately; actually, this appears to be the point which makes the greatest appeal to him. He stresses the difficulties which might arise from a formula of non-aggression if it were accompanied by reservations relating to the Covenant of the League of Nations, or to the existence of pacts with a third party. He hopes that these difficulties may be removed, and he does not ask once that France should renounce her pact with Soviet Russia.

As to the problem of a limitation of armaments, he is undecided; he is not opposed to the principle of such a limitation, but he does not see by what means it can be put into practice; he outlines, without dwelling on it, the theory according to which Germany, situated in the centre of Europe and exposed to simultaneous attacks on several fronts, has no true equality of armaments unless she is superior in that respect to any of the States that could attack her; he also fears that if he were to speak of the limitation of armaments, the opposition in Great Britain would say that he was retreating before a display of British energy; his thoughts remain uncertain. On the other hand, he is ready to approach without hesitation the problem of the humanization of war and to go fairly far in this matter. He sees here a good introduction, a happy preface from which might arise a more favourable atmosphere for the ultimate examination of the disarmament question.

As to the monetary and economic problems, he obviously leaves to others the task of dealing with them. That is no business of his. He understands nevertheless that it is important not to leave these matters in abeyance, but to invite experts to take up again the work already begun and to examine the possibilities offered by present conditions.

Concluding the conversation, he gives Herr von Ribbentrop the order, as I have already said, to set his department to work and to make them study the suggestions arising out of our interview with a view to formulating concrete proposals. Paris will then study the drafts and state its own views. I promise that we shall receive his suggestions with earnest sympathy and study them carefully, being moved by the same peaceful intentions that appear to animate the Führer. In the meantime, Germany will approach Italy. France, on her side, can investigate British views. We are not committed, on either side, to anything precise but both sides are agreed to proceed in all good faith to an investigation.

Therefore the utmost discretion should be maintained towards the public until further notice; public opinion must not be informed until the assurance of a positive result has been obtained.

On two other subjects I attempt to persuade the Führer to reveal his views: the claims of Hungary and the war in Spain.

He admits frankly that he considers the pretensions of the Hungarians excessive, although he adds that the cessions and concessions of the Slovaks are insufficient. For him, the only criterion is the ethnographical one, the race; it was the only one on which he based his claims towards the Czechs in tracing the new frontiers; the Hungarians and the Poles had better keep to these principles as well; obviously he has no sympathy with the efforts they are making to obtain a common frontier. The Chancellor boasts that he has brought about the failure of the appeal which Hungary had intended to make to the four Munich Powers. He believes that in so doing, he has avoided a definite danger.

Such a conference [he says], would have placed us before two conflicting theses. I should have been obliged, regardless of my personal opinion, to side with the Hungarians and Poles, because of the political ties that unite them to us; Mussolini would have acted in the same manner. You, however, and the English, for similar reasons, would have defended the Czechs. Thus, three weeks after Munich, we should again have had a conflict, which this time could not have been settled. I rendered a service to Europe in avoiding it. I preferred to exercise pressure on the Hungarians and the Czechs and persuade them to take up the interrupted negotiations, with less intransigence on both sides. Mussolini helped me. I hope that a compromise will take place. But the whole business is dangerous. This occasion shows how wrong France and England were to promise Czechoslovakia to guarantee her frontiers, even before the latter were clearly defined. This may still lead to most unpleasant complications.

With regard to Spain, the Chancellor repeats that he never had any intention of establishing himself there permanently. He had secured some economic advantages, but he would have obtained them in any case. It is far from his thoughts, so he assures me, to use Spain as a perpetual menace against France. Spain herself needs to maintain good relations with France. General Franco's attitude during the September crisis proved this plainly. Let all the foreign volunteers be withdrawn and let the two Spanish factions remain face to face with each other; in these conditions Franco will win in the end, and France will be none the worse for it.

For nearly two hours Herr Hitler has been readily listening to my questions; he has answered them without any embarrassment, with simplicity and—at least apparently—with candour. But the time has come to release him. Antinea's Castle is now submerged in the shadow that spreads over the valley and the mountains. I take my leave. The Führer expresses the wish that I might later return to Germany and come to visit him in a private capacity. He shakes both my hands several times. After going down in the lift and through the underground passage, I find the car waiting for me; passing through Berchtesgaden it takes me back to the airport, from where our plane starts immediately on its night flight to Berlin.

During the whole of our conversation, except for a few outbursts of violence when referring to England, the Führer was calm, moderate, conciliatory. One would have been justified in thinking that one was in the presence of a man with a well-balanced mind, rich in experience and wisdom, and wishing above all things to establish the reign of peace among nations. There were moments when Herr Hitler spoke of Europe, of his feelings as a European, which are, he asserts, more genuine than those expressed so loudly by many people.

He spoke of our "white civilization" as of a very precious possession common to us all, which must be defended. He appeared sincerely shocked at the persistent antagonism which has remained after the Munich Agreement, and which the British attitude revealed to his mind with great clearness. Obviously, the possibility of a coming crisis and the eventual outbreak of a general war are ever present in his mind. Perhaps at heart he himself is sceptical as to his chances of preventing this tragedy? In any case, he seems willing to attempt to do so or he wishes to feel he has made the attempt so as to calm if not his own conscience, at least the conscience of his people. And it is through France that he thinks this attempt must be made.

I have no illusions whatever about Adolf Hitler's character. I know that he is changeable, dissembling, full of contradictions, uncertain. The same man with the debonair aspect, with a real fondness for the beauties of nature, who discussed reasonable ideas on European politics round the tea-table, is also capable of the worst frenzies, of the wildest exaltations and the most delirious ambitions. There are days when, standing before a globe of the world, he will overthrow nations, continents, geography and history, like a demiurge stricken with madness. At other moments, he dreams of being the hero of an everlasting peace, in which he would devote himself to the erection of the most magnificent monuments. The advances that he is prepared to make to France are dictated by a sentiment which he shares, at least intermittently, with the majority of his countrymen, namely the weariness of an age-long contest, and the desire to see it end at last; this feeling is now strengthened by the memories of the Munich interviews, by the sympathy that the person of President Daladier aroused in him, and also by the idea that our country's evolution tends to make it easier for her to understand the Third Reich. But at the same time we may be certain that the Führer remains true to his wish to disintegrate the Franco-British bloc, and to stabilize peace in the west, so as to have a free hand in the east. What plans may be revolving already in his mind? Is it Poland, Russia, the Baltic States which, in his thoughts, will be called upon to pay the cost? Does he himself even know?

Be that as it may, Hitler is one of those men with whom one must never relax one's utmost vigilance, and whom one can only trust with reservations. Personally, I do not draw the conclusion that we should not listen to his suggestions. In these circumstances, as in many other previous ones, I hold that the main thing is that we should know exactly where we stand and with whom we are dealing. But it does not follow that an attitude of abstention and negation is the right one. Dr. Goebbels said recently, and not without reason, that one cannot win in a lottery if one does not take at least the risk of buying a ticket. It is our bounden duty not to neglect a single one of the ways that lead to peace. If it so happens that Herr Hitler, either as a feint or as a deliberate plan, engages himself far enough on that path, it is possible that he will end by not being able to turn back again, even if he wished.

Besides, who could predict the astounding changes of front of which this dictator, impressionable, mutable and abnormal, may be capable, and what will his personal destiny and that of Germany be tomorrow?

After the Munich conference, it was normal and necessary that one should think of expanding the results of an agreement on which public opinion had pinned such high hopes.

As matters stand to-day, Germany is expressing a wish to take the initiative; Germany is trying to work out a formula and a plan.

If we were to turn a deaf ear, we would, to our detriment, be providing her with the alibi which she wishes for perhaps in order to cover her future enterprises.

Besides, the contracts she appears ready to enter into have only a limited scope.

If these promises are kept, they will contribute in a large measure to the lessening of tension in Europe.

If they are broken, the guilty party will assume a moral responsibility which will weigh heavily on his future position.

France should, therefore, undertake to consider the proposals without fear. Perhaps it is not unreasonable to think that the events France has now lived through may have finally convinced her people of the pressing need for national order and cohesion, for a certain moral reform and for rapid and thorough overhauling and improvement of our military organization.

INSTRUCTION from Georges Bonnet, Minister for Foreign Affairs, to the French Ambassadors at London, Berlin, Brussels, Rome and Barcelona, and the French Minister at Prague, December 14, 1938

Translation, in *The French Yellow Book*, p. 39

Herr von Ribbentrop's visit to Paris was undertaken for the express and sufficient object of signing the Franco-German declaration. Nevertheless, it has provided an opportunity for a wide exchange of views between the Foreign Ministers of the two countries. Although these conversations on the whole retained a very general character, they have made it possible to obtain definite information on the German attitude regarding some particularly important international questions.

The anti-French incidents that have recently occurred in Italy naturally gave rise to the question of Franco-Italian and German-Italian relations, and I expressed the wish to see every element incompatible with the pursuance of a policy of Franco-German appeasement disappear from the relations between Paris, Berlin and Rome. Referring to the solidarity between Germany and Italy, similar, he said, to that uniting France and Great Britain, Herr von Ribbentrop was at pains to assure me that nothing in the existence of these two groups appeared to him to prejudice any attempt to bring into harmony the relations between the four Powers, which might eventually extend to an arrangement for co-operation between the two Axes. By indicating that the struggle against Bolshevism is the basis of the common political views of the German and Italian Governments, but without saying so openly, Herr von Ribbentrop wished to convey to us the impression that no other aim could be attributed to it. The recent demonstration in the Italian Chamber of Deputies, which in his opinion involved no government responsibility, appears to have made no particular impression on the German Minister, who affects in the circumstances to consider the Mediterranean questions involved as outside the scope of German interests; in any case he persists in declaring himself convinced that the improvement of Franco-German relations is of a nature to exert a favourable influence on future Franco-Italian relations.

Concerning Spain, he gave us to understand that there again the action of Germany had from the beginning been inspired solely by the struggle against Bolshevism. The German Minister continues to desire the victory of General Franco, as, in his opinion, it would be a guarantee for the re-establishment in Spain of a national order which would favour a general resumption of commercial relations with that country, without prejudice to the interests of France. Moreover, he does not believe in the possibility of mediation. He did not then dispute the propriety of the position maintained by France as well as by Great Britain regarding the application of the decisions of the Non-Intervention Committee.

These considerations incidentally led the Foreign Minister of the Reich to raise the question of French policy toward the U.S.S.R., without however laying any particular stress upon it and only with a view to informing himself of the position. This policy appeared to him to be a survival of the encirclement policy of Versailles. I had to remind him that the Franco-Russian pact was not originally meant to remain only bilateral, that it had been and still was conceived as an element of collective agreement, in which Germany and other Powers had been invited to participate, and that it was the fault neither of France nor of the U.S.S.R., if it had actually developed into an apparently purely Franco-Soviet affair.

With regard to Great Britain, I stressed to Herr von Ribbentrop the part that the improvement of Anglo-German relations must play in any development in the policy of European appeasement, which was considered to be the essential object of any Franco-German action. The Minister was at pains to throw all the blame for the present state of affairs on the British Government. He said that the British Government and especially the British Press, which in the days following the Munich Agreement had appeared to show a certain degree of understanding, had now adopted an attitude that was most disappointing for Berlin; the emphasis placed in London on the urgency of rearmament, the repeated demonstrations in Parliament, under the influence of Mr. Duff Cooper, Mr. Winston Churchill, Mr. Eden and Mr. Morrison, and the articles in the newspapers, had been strongly resented in Germany, where he said it would have been impossible to restrain the action of the Press. I again stressed the fundamental and solid character of Franco-British solidarity, and gave him very clearly to understand that a genuine easing of Franco-German relations could not be conceived as enduring without a corresponding improvement between Great Britain and Germany.

With regard to Czechoslovakia, an exchange of observations was necessary in order to leave no doubt as to the implications of the international agreement of Munich, if executed both in the letter and the spirit. The Minister for Foreign Affairs is to re-examine, as soon as he returns to Berlin, the question of the setting up of the international guarantee, the principle of which was asserted by Germany in protocol No. 1.

Such are the principal political questions mentioned, in very general terms, in the course of the Franco-German conversations of December 6, which never assumed the formal character of a conference. Although they were not embodied in detailed heads of agreement or in any official record, they shed light on certain important points. These explanatory talks were essential at the moment when the Franco-German declaration was signed, which not only aims at promoting peaceful co-operation between the two countries but should also be conducive to a general appeasement in the relations of the principal European Powers.

COMMUNICATION from Robert Coulondre, French Ambassador to Germany, to the French Minister for Foreign Affairs (Georges Bonnet), March 16, 1939, Regarding the Dismemberment of Czechoslovakia

Translation, in *The French Yellow Book,* p. 88

LESS THAN SIX months after the conclusion of the Munich Agreement and hardly four months after the Vienna Award, Germany, treating her own and her partners' signature as negligible quantities, has brought about the dismemberment of Czechoslovakia, occupied with her army Bohemia and Moravia and annexed both these provinces to the Reich. Since yesterday, March 15, the swastika has been flying over the Hradschin, while the Führer, protected by tanks and armoured cars, entered the city among a staggered and thunderstruck population. Slovakia has broken away. A so-called independent state, she has in fact placed herself under the protection of Germany. Sub-Carpathian Russia has been left to Hungary, whose troops have already crossed the frontier. Czechoslovakia, which at Munich agreed to such cruel sacrifices for the sake of peace, no longer exists. The dream of those Nazis who were most eager for her destruction has been realized. Czechoslovakia has vanished from the map of Europe.

The events, which have led up to this result with a lightning speed, are typical of the mentality and the methods of the Nazi rulers. They carry with them certain lessons and practical conclusions which all States anxious for their independence and security should draw without delay, faced as they are with a Germany intoxicated by success and which, abandoning the line of racial claims, is plunging forward into sheer imperialism.

The operation to which Czechoslovakia has just fallen a victim bears to an even greater degree than former coups the characteristic marks of Nazi action: cynicism and treachery in conception, secrecy in preparation and brutality in execution.

At Munich, the Nazi leaders and the Führer himself had laid great stress on the impossibility for Germans and Czechs to live together in the same State; they had urged the implacable and age-long hatred of the Czechs for everything German; they had asserted that the maintenance of peace depended on a line being drawn strictly between the two nationalities; they had managed to convince Lord Runciman of this necessity whilst protesting on the other hand that they had no wish to incorporate alien elements in the Reich. It was in virtue of these principles that the negotiators assembled in the Bavarian capital had compelled the Prague Government to hand over territories in which the German population was predominant. In exchange, Czechoslovakia was to receive an international guarantee of her new frontiers, a guarantee in which Germany herself would take part.

Actually, it very soon appeared, during the work of the International Commission at Berlin at the beginning of October, that the German negotiators were guided far more by strategical than by ethnographical considerations. The numerous interventions of the Wehrmachts Oberkommando during the course of these negotiations showed that the German leaders intended above all to draw a frontier which would deprive Czechoslovakia of all her natural defences and fortifications, and would reduce her to complete military impotence.

Indeed, the boundaries which the Prague Government had to accept in October meant the inclusion of 850,000 Czechs within the Reich.

To-day there is no further question of the separation of Czechs from Germans, which was claimed to be so indispensable to peace in the Danube basin and in Europe. Completely reversing her tactics, Germany has again brought into being that German-Czech amalgamation, the elements of which she had declared last September to be incompatible. Whereas a few months ago, she was saying that the co-existence of these two racial groups was an impossibility, she now claims to show that such a co-existence is entirely natural, that it can be historically justified and that it is the result of certain economic and geographical necessities. There is no further question of the implacable and age-long hatred between Germans and Czechs: on the contrary, it is held that the two peoples can and must live in harmony together inside one political community.

The Munich agreements, therefore, were for the Nazi rulers nothing but a means of disarming Czechoslovakia before annexing it. It would, perhaps, be going rather far to assert that the Führer had conceived this project even at Munich. What is beyond all doubt is that, by annexing under threat of arms the provinces of Bohemia and Moravia, the Government of the Reich, a signatory to the September agreements, is guilty of a breach of trust, of a real act of treachery to the co-signatory States, particularly the Czech Government which, trusting in the word of the Great Powers, had resigned itself to handing over the Sudeten territories.

It was in the name of this ethnographical principle that the Reich had obtained the return of three and a half million Germans in September. It is in contempt of this principle that it annexes eight million Czechs to-day, left defenceless by the handing over of the Sudeten territory.

It is the principle of the right of peoples to self-determination that Germany now invokes in support of the independence (in any case purely illusory) of Slovakia, but this same right is refused to the Carpatho-Ukrainians abandoned to Hungary, and to the Czechs who have been forcibly incorporated in the Reich.

Germany has once again demonstrated her contempt for all written pledges and her preference for methods of brute force and the *fait accompli*. Without scruple she has torn up the Munich Agreement as well as the Vienna Award, proving yet again that her policy has only one guiding principle: to watch for a suitable opportunity and to seize any booty within reach. It is, more or less, the morality common to the gangster and to the denizens of the jungle.

German cynicism has, moreover, been accompanied by consummate skill. With a remarkable control of men and events, the Government of the Reich has been at pains to give an appearance of legality to the violence done to the Czechs.

The official German thesis is that Czechoslovakia fell to pieces of itself. Slovakia, it is declared, in breaking with Prague, split the Federal Republic into three pieces.

As for Bohemia and Moravia, it was freely and of its own volition that the Prague Government, unable to maintain order and to protect the lives of the German minority, placed the care of these provinces—so runs the argument—in the Führer's hands.

Such arguments can deceive no one.

There can be no doubt that Slovak separatism was the work of German agents or of Slovaks controlled directly from Berlin. M. Mach, head of the propaganda department of the Bratislava Government and a most ardent extremist, was well-known for his entire devotion to the Reich. M. Durcansky, Minister of Transport, who made frequent visits to Germany, was also a mere tool in Nazi hands, particularly in those of M. Karmasin, the "Führer" of the 120,000 Germans in Slovakia. As for Mgr. Tiso, a man of little energy, although as a priest he was worried by the growth of Nazi ideology in his country, he was incapable of opposing the separatist tendencies encouraged by Germany. It was on account of this weakness that the Prague Government dismissed him on March 10. This rigorous measure against Mgr. Tiso and the latter's appeal for assistance to the Reich Government supplied the German rulers with the excuse for which they had been waiting to interfere in the quarrel between the Czechs and the Slovaks.

On receipt of the note from the dismissed President, German official circles let it be known that in their view Mgr. Tiso's Government alone had a legal character, and that, by appointing a new Prime Minister, Prague had violated the Constitution. From this moment the Berlin newspapers began to denounce the terror unleashed in Bratislava by the Czechs against the Slovak autonomists and their German comrades.

From the 12th onwards the tone of the Berlin Press became more violent. Now it was not only a question of clashes in Slovakia, but also in Bohemia and Moravia. Within twenty-four hours the Berlin papers had relegated to the background the sufferings of the Slovaks and denounced with every sign of the keenest resentment the brutalities to which Germans in Czechoslovakia were subjected, whether they were members of the racial minority or citizens of the Reich. To judge from the German papers, which used not only the same language but exactly the same expressions as in September last, the lives of the 500,000 Germans in Czechoslovakia were in the most serious danger. The Czechs, in whom the old Hussite spirit and the hatred of Germanism was re-awakening, had once more organized manhunts. The situation was becoming intolerable.

Actually, with the exception of Bratislava, where unrest had been fomented by the German Self-Protection Service and by the Hlinka Guards, who had been armed by Germany, public order had been disturbed neither in Slovakia nor in Bohemia and Moravia. At Brünn, for example, where, according to the German Press, German blood had been shed, the British Consul was able to see and report to his Minister in Prague that there was complete calm. The stories published by the Berlin newspapers under inflammatory titles were, furthermore, very thin in content, much like a few grains of dust whirled along by some infernal bellows.

On the evening of the 13th the German leaders, who had unremittingly counteracted the efforts of Prague to establish a new Slovakian Government, summoned Mgr. Tiso to Berlin. During the night of the 13th–14th, together with M. Durcansky, he had a long interview with the Führer, who expressed his determination to see the creation of "an entirely free Slovakia." The proclamation of Slovak independence should follow without delay. That same evening, the 60 members of the Diet were summoned for the next day at Bratislava, and Slovak independence, decided in Berlin, was unanimously voted by them. From the afternoon of the 14th, the German Press was in a position to declare that Czechoslovakia had fallen to pieces, that she was in a state of complete decay, that the Communists had reappeared and, together with Czech chauvinists, were hunting and ill-treating the Germans, notably at Brünn and Iglau. German blood—so it was reported—was flowing in torrents. Germany—it was said—could no longer tolerate such a state of affairs.

Meanwhile, 14 divisions, composed almost entirely of mechanized units, had been concentrated on the frontiers of Bohemia and Moravia. On the afternoon of the 14th, German troops entered Czech territory and occupied Morawska-Ostrawa.

Before giving the troops the order to march to the invasion of Czech territory, it was necessary to find some semblance of a justification. M. Hacha, President of the Czechoslovak Republic and M. Chvalkovsky, Minister for Foreign Affairs, arrived at Berlin where they were received by the Führer in the presence of Herr von Ribbentrop and Field-Marshal Goering. Brutally, the Führer states that there is no question of negotiation. The Czech statesmen are asked to acquaint themselves with the decisions of Berlin and to bow to them. Any sign of resistance will be crushed. Any opposition to the German troops will be put down by means of aerial bombardment. The Reich has decided to annex Bohemia and Moravia. Prague will be occupied on the following day at 10 o'clock. President Hacha, a man of great age and in failing health, collapses and faints. Field-Marshal Goering's own doctors intervene and bring him round with injections. Then the old man signs the document presented to him, by which the Czech Government places the destiny of Bohemia and Moravia "with full confidence" in the hands of the Führer.

The next day, the 15th, at nine o'clock in the morning, the first mechanized troops reach Prague. During the afternoon, the Führer enters the Imperial Castle of Hradschin and immediately orders the swastika to be hoisted. Czechoslovakia is no more.

The following day, the 16th, the Führer decrees the incorporation of Bohemia and Moravia within the Reich and constitutes them a Protectorate with some sort of self-administration, under the control of a "Protector" representing Germany and residing at Prague.

The same day, Mgr. Tiso, head of the new so-called independent Slovak State, asks the Führer to take Slovakia under his protection. The Chancellor accepts at once. In fact, Slovak independence is at an end. Mutilated by the Vienna Award, robbed of its most fertile lands and reduced to a mountainous region, the country cannot in any case hope for an independent existence.

On March 12 Sub-Carpathian Russia too had proclaimed its independence and solicited the protection of Germany. But the Nazi leaders remained deaf to its appeal, although that country, which for a while had played the role of "Ukrainian Piedmont," had relied entirely upon them.

Sub-Carpathian Ukraine was invaded by Hungarian troops. In despair, the Chust Government offered the country to Rumania. M. Revay, Prime Minister, in a telegram to the French Embassy in Berlin, sought to persuade the French Government to approach the Government in Budapest in the hope that the fate of the country might be decided by diplomatic means and not by force of arms.

Everything seems to point to the conclusion that the Reich has no interest in this State and is abandoning it to Hungary.

One more feature deserves notice. It is the speed with which the operation ending in the partition of Czechoslovakia was decided upon and prepared.

Since the beginning of February, this Embassy had certainly noted numerous indications of Germany's intentions concerning Czechoslovakia. These convergent symptoms left no doubt that the Nazis were only awaiting a favourable opportunity to finish the work begun at Munich and to deal the final blow to a State which, already mortally wounded, was struggling with inextricable internal difficulties.

But it seems that the decision was not taken until March 8 or 9, that is, after the departure of Field-Marshal Goering for Italy, whence he was urgently recalled. Only on March 11 and 12 came the first reports of troop movements. On the 14th, about 200,000 men were massed on the frontiers of Bohemia and Moravia. This concentration took place without any disturbance of the normal life of the country. Once more, bombers played a decisive role. They were the unanswerable argument to which the Czech Ministers bowed, anxious to spare their people the horrors and the destruction of aerial bombardment.

In another letter I point out the repercussions likely to occur in Europe as a result of the new changes brought about in the map of the Continent under the pressure of Nazi Germany.

In conclusion I will simply draw attention to what may be learnt from this new coup committed by the Third Reich.

Nazi Germany has now thrown aside the mask. Until now, she has denied the charge of imperialism. She asserted that her only wish was to re-unite as far as possible all the Germans of Central Europe in one family, to the exclusion of aliens. To-day, it is clear that the Führer's thirst for domination knows no limit.

It is equally clear that all hopes of opposing to the Führer any arguments other than those of force are in vain. The Third Reich has the same contempt as the Empire of Wilhelm II for treaties and pledges. Germany remains the country of "scraps of paper."

National security as well as world peace demand from the French people an immense effort of discipline and the organization of the country's whole energy, which alone will enable France, with the help of her friends, to assert herself and defend her interests in the face of so formidable an adversary as the Germany of Adolf Hitler, plunging forward to the conquest of Europe.

INSTRUCTION from Georges Bonnet, Minister for Foreign Affairs, to the French Ambassador to Germany (Robert Coulondre), March 17, 1939, Regarding the Annexation of Bohemia and Moravia

Translation, in *The French Yellow Book*, p. 95

You should seek an audience with the Minister for Foreign Affairs in order to hand him the note, the text of which you will find herewith. (A similar *démarche* is being made by your British colleague.)

By a letter dated March 15, 1939, His Excellency the German Ambassador, acting on instructions from his Government, has handed to the Minister for Foreign Affairs of the French Republic the text of an agreement reached during the night of March 14–15 between the Führer-Chancellor and the Minister for Foreign Affairs of the Reich on the one side and the President and the Minister for Foreign Affairs of the Czechoslovak Republic on the other side. In the same communication, it was announced that German troops had crossed the Czech frontiers at 6 o'clock in the morning and that all measures had been taken to avoid resistance and bloodshed and to allow the occupation and pacification of the territory to take place in a quiet and orderly way.

The French Ambassador has the honour to convey to the Minister for Foreign Affairs in the Reich the formal Protest made by the Government of the Republic against the measure referred to in Count von Welczeck's communication.

The Government of the Republic considers itself, through the action taken against Czechoslovakia by the German Government, confronted with a flagrant violation of both the letter and the spirit of the Agreement signed in Munich on September 29, 1938.

The circumstances in which the treaty of March 15 was imposed on the leaders of the Czechoslovak Republic could not, in the view of the Government of the French Republic, legalize the position laid down in this treaty.

The French Ambassador has the honour to inform His Excellency the Minister for Foreign Affairs of the Reich that the Government of the Republic cannot in the circumstances recognize the legality of the new situation brought about in Czechoslovakia by the action of the Reich.

COMMUNICATION Handed by Georges Bonnet, Minister for Foreign Affairs, to the German Ambassador to France (Count Johannes von Welczeck), July 1, 1939

Translation, in *The French Yellow Book*, p. 197

I RECEIVED Herr von Ribbentrop in Paris a few months ago, and I signed with him the Franco-German declaration of December 6, 1938.

The personal relations which I formed with him on that occasion make it a duty for me at the present moment to point out to him very definitely the position of the French Government, and to leave no doubt in his mind about the determination of France.

In December last, I clearly specified to Herr von Ribbentrop that the Franco-German declaration—in conformity, for that matter, with the stipulation contained in Article 3—could not be considered as affecting the special relations of France with the countries of Eastern Europe.

In so far as Poland, more particularly, is concerned, events since then have produced a strengthening of the French alliance. M. Daladier definitely indicated in his declaration of April 13 last the scope of the engagements by which the two countries are now linked.

To-day I make a point of recalling these commitments to Herr von Ribbentrop's very special attention, and stressing the unshakeable determination of France to fulfil them by exerting all her strength in support of her pledged word. At a moment when measures of all kinds are being taken in Danzig, whose scope and object it is difficult to appreciate, it is particularly essential to avoid any risk of misunderstanding about the extent of the obligations and about the attitude of the French Government: a misunderstanding whose consequences might be incalculable. I therefore regard it as my duty to state definitely that any action, whatever its form, which would tend to modify the *status quo* in Danzig, and so provoke armed resistance by Poland, would bring the Franco-Polish agreement into play and oblige France to give immediate assistance to Poland.

PERSONAL LETTER from Georges Bonnet, Minister for Foreign Affairs, to the German Minister for Foreign Affairs (Joachim von Ribbentrop), July 21, 1939
Translation, in *The French Yellow Book*, p. 221

Dear Herr von Ribbentrop,

I am in receipt of the letter you wrote to me, marked "Personal," in reply to the communication I myself sent on July 1 to Count von Welczeck.

There is one point which I am anxious to make absolutely clear. At no moment either before or after the declaration of December 6, has it been possible for the German Government to think that France had decided to disinterest herself in the East of Europe.

At the time of the conversations of December 6 I reminded you that since 1921 we had had a treaty of alliance with Poland and since 1935 a pact with the U.S.S.R., both of which we are determined to maintain. I then gave definite assurances on this point to the Ambassadors of Poland and of the U.S.S.R. by communications, which were given the widest publicity in the Press. I remember, moreover, that at the time when I reminded you of the treaties which bound us to Poland, you were good enough to reply that these treaties could not do any harm to Franco-German relations, since your own relations with Poland were at that time excellent.

I was the less surprised at the assurance you gave me since, three months earlier, Herr Hitler had, in his speech at the Sports Palace in Berlin on September 26, referred to the German-Polish agreement as a model of its type:

"Within barely one year we succeeded," he said, "in arriving at an understanding with him (Marshal Pilsudski) which by its very nature has removed the possibility of conflict, at all events for ten years. We are all of us convinced that this understanding will lead to a lasting peace. We appreciate that we have here two peoples who have to live side by side. A country with a population of thirty-three millions will always seek access to the sea; it was therefore necessary to find the way to an agreement. This has been found and is steadily being developed. The decisive factor should be a firm determination on the part of the two Governments, and all reasonable and level-headed men among the two peoples and in the two countries, to work for a constant improvement of their mutual relations."

In addition to this, in the course of our conversation on December 6, one of the most pressing requests which I had to make to Your

RELATIONS WITH GERMANY

Excellency was in respect of our common guarantee to Czechoslovakia in fulfilment of the Munich Agreement. Such a request I could not have addressed to you, if France had no longer been interested in what was happening in Eastern Europe.

Since I was unable to obtain a satisfactory reply on this matter, I sent you a note on February 8, 1939, recalling the agreement signed at Munich on September 29, in order once more to impress upon you the necessity of completing without delay the arrangements for our common guarantee to Czechoslovakia. To this note you replied on March 2, asking me to await the clearing up of internal developments in Czechoslovakia and the improvement of relations between that country and the neighbouring States, before considering a general arrangement between the Munich signatory Powers.

Further, the actual statement which I made from the Tribune of the French Chamber on January 26, 1939, confirmed my attitude in a manner which admitted of no equivocation. This statement, which you may find in our *Journal Officiel* (p. 234), was reproduced in the Press throughout the world.

France has also maintained her traditional friendly relations with Poland. At the time of the Franco-German declaration of December 6, I had, in conformity with the spirit of our agreement, advised the Polish Ambassador of our intentions. In thanking me for keeping them informed, the Polish Government expressed their appreciation of an action, the aim, the significance and the implication of which they fully realized.

Thus, Gentlemen, can we dispose of the legend that our policy had led to the cancellation of our obligations in the East of Europe with the U.S.S.R. or with Poland.

These obligations are still binding and must be honoured in the spirit in which they were entered into.

Thus there is no equivocation whatsoever. You knew the treaty which united France and Poland. You never dreamed of asking me to denounce it on the occasion of the Franco-German declaration of December 6. At the time when we signed that declaration your relations with Poland were excellent, and there was nothing in the Franco-Polish understandings which were likely to arouse susceptibilities on your part.

In the speech he made in the Reichstag on January 30, 1939, Herr Hitler once again expressed his satisfaction at the understanding between Germany and Poland. "At this moment," he declared, "it would be difficult to discover any divergence of opinion amongst the true friends of peace as to the value of this agreement" (the German-Polish pact of non-aggression). These words were the more significant from our point of view because they were uttered some weeks after an important conversation at Berchtesgaden between Herr Hitler and the Polish Foreign Minister, Monsieur Beck.

In the month of March relations between Germany and Poland became strained, and that fact brought about a new situation.

France bears no responsibility for the development of these relations between Berlin and Warsaw. She has in fact always refrained —and will continue to refrain—from any interference in matters bearing upon the special relationships of the two neighbouring countries, and not affecting in any way the general international situation and the maintenance of peace.

In conformity with the statements which I had the honour to make to Count von Welczek, we earnestly hope that a bilateral arrangement between Germany and Poland may prove feasible. But there is one point that I am bound to bring to your notice, particularly in view of the conversations which I had with you on December 6 and 7 in Paris, namely, that France is bound to Poland by a treaty of alliance, and will remain true to her bond, and scrupulously carry out all her promises.

You are good enough, in reminding me of all the efforts which you yourself have made to bring about a *rapprochement* between France and Germany, to call my attention to the fact that Herr Hitler has always desired a Franco-German understanding and has stigmatized as "madness a new war between our two countries."

Such an assurance is in accordance with our sincere wishes. I desire, as you do, the continued maintenance of friendly relations between France and Germany. It is for that reason that, in my communication of July 1, whose validity is maintained with all its implications, I made a point of reminding you, with the frankness called for by the circumstances, of the position of the French Government in respect of Poland, particularly in relation to the situation at Danzig.

France is eagerly desirous of peace. No one can doubt that fact. Moreover, no one can doubt the determination of the French Government to fulfil its obligations. But I cannot permit it to be said that our country would be in any way responsible for war because it remained true to its pledged word.

I beg you, my dear Herr von Ribbentrop, to accept the expression of my sincerest regards.

INSTRUCTION from Georges Bonnet, Minister for Foreign Affairs, to the French Ambassador to Poland, August 24, 1939

Translation, in *The French Yellow Book,* p. 293

You should see M. Beck at the earliest possible moment and tell him that in the new conditions resulting from the Russo-German Pact, the French Government is more anxious than ever that Poland should at all cost avoid laying herself open to the charge of being the aggressor—this being the whole purpose of the German manoeuvre—and thus playing into Germany's hands. The disadvantages arising from such a position would be as grave for Poland as for her allies, on account of the repercussions it might have on the obligations, virtual or actual, which bind the latter to other Powers.

In the same way, the French Government urgently recommends that the Polish Government abstain from all military action in the event of the Danzig Senate proclaiming the City's return to the Reich. To any possible decision of this sort, it is important that Poland should reply only by an action of the same kind, that is to say, by making all reservations and stating her intention of having recourse to all legal remedies which may be afforded to her by diplomatic usage.

The Warsaw Government will understand this counsel all the better since it corresponds to the intentions expressed by Marshal Rydz-Smigly to General Ironside on July 19. As for us, we have all the more grounds for clearly putting forward this advice as it is in harmony with our General Staff's view of the problem: for the Staff considers that, from the strategical point of view, a Polish Army, after advancing into the Free City territory, would be in an extremely delicate position.

You should emphasize to M. Beck that, in our view, the question is one solely of expediency and that, by taking up such a position, the Polish Government would only be safeguarding the full effect of our assistance and would in no way be hampering its liberty of decision, in the event of a definite German military attack; nor would the validity of the French position with regard to Poland, as defined by agreements which it is necessary to recall, be thereby prejudiced.

TELEPHONE COMMUNICATION from Robert Coulondre, French Ambassador to Germany, to the French Minister for Foreign Affairs (Georges Bonnet), August 25, 1939, Transmitting message from the Chancellor of Germany (Adolf Hitler) to the French Premier (Edouard Daladier)

Translation, in *The French Yellow Book*, p. 302

This afternoon I had an interview with Herr Hitler, who had asked to see me at 5:30.

This is the substance of what he told me:

In view of the gravity of the situation [he said], I wish to make a statement which I would like you to forward to M. Daladier. As I have already told him, I bear no enmity whatever towards France. I have personally renounced all claims to Alsace-Lorraine and recognized the Franco-German frontier. I do not want war with your country; my one desire is to maintain good relations with it. I find indeed the idea that I might have to fight France on account of Poland a very painful one. The Polish provocation, however, has placed the Reich in a position which cannot be allowed to continue.

Several months ago I made extremely fair proposals to Poland, demanding the return of Danzig to the Reich and of a narrow strip of territory leading from this German city to East Prussia. But the guarantee given by the British Government has encouraged the Poles to be obstinate. Not only has the Warsaw Government rejected my proposals, but it has subjected the German minority, our blood-brothers, to the worst possible treatment, and has begun mobilization.

At first [pursued Herr Hitler], I forbade the Press of the Reich to publish accounts of the cruelties suffered by the Germans in Poland. But the situation has now become intolerable. Are you aware, [he asked me emphatically,] that there have been cases of castration? That already there are more than 70,000 refugees in our camps? Yesterday seven Germans were killed by the police in Bielitz, and thirty German reservists were machine-gunned at Lodz. Our aeroplanes can no longer fly between Germany and East Prussia without being shot at; their route had been changed, but they are now even attacked over the sea. Thus, the plane which was carrying State Secretary Stuckart was fired at by Polish warships, a fresh incident which I was not yet in a position to bring to the notice of Sir Nevile Henderson this morning.

Raising his voice, Herr Hitler went on:

No nation worthy of the name can put up with such unbearable insults. France would not tolerate it any more than Germany. These things have gone on long enough, and I will reply by force to any further provocations.

I want to state once again: I wish to avoid war with your country. I will not attack France, but if she joins in the conflict, I will see it through to the bitter end. As you are aware, I have just concluded a pact with Moscow that is not only theoretical, but, I may say, practical. I believe I shall win, and you believe you will win: what is certain is that above all French and German blood will flow, the blood of two equally courageous peoples. I say again, it is painful to me to think we might come to that. Please tell this to President Daladier on my behalf.

With these words, Herr Hitler rose to show that the interview was over. Under the circumstances I could make only a brief reply. I told him, first of all, that I knew that all misunderstanding had now been removed; yet that, in a moment as grave as this, I emphatically gave him my word of honour as a soldier that I had no doubt whatever that in the event of Poland's being attacked, France would assist her with all the forces at her command. I was able however to give him my word also that the Government of the Republic would still do all it could to preserve peace and would not spare its counsels of moderation to the Polish Government.

The Chancellor replied: "I believe you; I even believe that men like M. Beck are moderate, but they are no longer in control of the situation."

I added that if French and German blood were to flow, this bloodmoney, however costly, would not be the only payment to be made. The ravages of a war that would certainly be a long one would bring a succession of ghastly miseries in their train. Though I was, as he said, definitely certain of our victory, I feared, at the same time, that at the end of a war, the sole real victor would be M. Trotsky. The Chancellor, interrupting me, exclaimed: "Why, then, did you give Poland a blank cheque?"

I replied by recalling the events of last March and the deep impression they had made on French minds, the feeling of insecurity to which they had given rise and which had led us to strengthen our alliances. I repeated that our most ardent desire was to maintain peace; that we continued to exert a moderating influence in Warsaw; and that I could not believe that it was impossible to bring the incidents complained of to an end.

I had hinted earlier that the German Press seemed to me to have considerably exaggerated the number and importance of these incidents, and I had mentioned in particular the case reported by the *Angriff* on August 15 of the German engineer who was said to have been brutally murdered for political reasons, whereas, in actual fact, he had been on June 15 the victim of an ordinary quarrel whose motives were exclusively passionate. Herr Hitler replied that he had indeed been informed of our moderating influence in Warsaw; yet the incidents were increasing. As for the events of last March, he added, it was true that he had taken the provinces of Bohemia and Moravia under his protection, but he had preserved the liberties of the inhabitants, and anyone who touched a hair of their heads would pay dearly for it; this was a point of honour for the Reich. The Polish minority in these regions were not subjected to any kind of brutalities; in the Saar, too, not a single Frenchman had had any reason for complaint. "It is very painful for me," repeated the Chancellor once again, "to think I might have to fight your country; but the decision does not rest with me. Please tell this to M. Daladier."

I was unable to prolong the interview any further, and after these remarks I took my leave.

MESSAGE from Edouard Daladier, Premier, to the Chancellor of Germany (Adolf Hitler), August 26, 1939, Communicated through the French Foreign Office and the French Ambassador to Germany (Robert Coulondre)

Translation, in *The French Yellow Book*, p. 311

YOUR EXCELLENCY,

The French Ambassador in Berlin has sent me your personal message.

Faced as we are, as you remind me, with the gravest responsibility that can ever be assumed by two heads of government, that of allowing the blood of two great peoples to be shed, when they desire nothing but peace and work, I owe it to you, I owe it to our two peoples to say that the fate of peace still rests solely in your hands.

You cannot doubt my sentiments towards Germany, nor France's pacific dispositions towards your nation. No Frenchman has ever done more than I have to strengthen between our two peoples not merely peace, but a sincere co-operation in their own interest as well as in that of Europe and the whole world.

Unless you attribute to the French people a conception of national honour less high than that which I myself recognize in the German people, you cannot doubt either that France will be true to her solemn promises to other nations, such as Poland, which, I am perfectly sure, wants also to live in peace with Germany.

These two facts are easily reconciled. There is nothing to-day which need prevent any longer the pacific solution of the international crisis with honour and dignity for all peoples, if the will for peace exists equally on all sides.

I can vouch not only for the good will of France, but also for that of all her allies. I can personally guarantee the readiness which Poland has always shown to have recourse to methods of free conciliation, such as may be envisaged between the Governments of two sovereign nations. In all sincerity I can assure you that there is not one of the grievances invoked by Germany against Poland in connection with the Danzig question which might not be submitted to decision by such methods with a view to a friendly and equitable settlement.

I can also pledge my honour that there is nothing in the clear and sincere solidarity of France with Poland and her allies which could modify in any manner whatsoever the peaceful inclinations of my country. This solidarity has never prevented us, and does not prevent us to-day, from helping to maintain Poland in her pacific inclinations.

In so serious an hour I sincerely believe that no man endowed with human feelings could understand that a war of destruction should be allowed to break out without a last attempt at a pacific adjustment between Germany and Poland. Your will for peace may be exercised in all confidence in this direction without the slightest derogation from your sense of German honour. As for myself, the head of the Government of France, a country which, like yours, only desires harmony between the French people and the German people, and which, on the other hand, is united to Poland by bonds of friendship and by the pledged word, I am ready to make all the efforts that an honest man can make in order to ensure the success of this attempt.

Like myself, you were a soldier in the last war. You realize, as I do, how a people's memory retains a horror for war and its disasters, whatever may be its result. My conception of your eminent rôle as leader of the German people, to guide them along the paths of peace towards the full accomplishment of their mission in the common work of civilization, prompts me to ask you for a reply to this proposal. If the blood of France and that of Germany flow again, as they did twenty-five years ago, each of the two peoples will fight with confidence in its own victory, but the most certain victors will be the forces of destruction and barbarism.

COMMUNICATION from Robert Coulondre, French Ambassador to Germany, to the French Minister for Foreign Affairs (Georges Bonnet), August 27, 1939

Translation, in *The French Yellow Book*, p. 317

I REGRET TO HAVE to report to Your Excellency that the proposal of Prime Minister Daladier has not been taken up by Chancellor Hitler. For forty minutes I commented upon the President's moving letter. I said everything that my heart as a man and a Frenchman could prompt to induce the Chancellor to agree to a supreme effort for a pacific settlement of the question of Danzig. I conjured him, in the name of history and for the sake of humanity, not to thrust aside this last chance. For the peace of his conscience, I begged him, who had built an empire without shedding blood, not to shed it now, not to shed the blood of soldiers nor that of women and children, without being absolutely certain that this could not be avoided. I confronted him with the terrible responsibilities that he would assume towards western civilization. I told him that his prestige is great enough outside Germany to remain undiminished even after a gesture of appeasement, the men who feared him would perhaps be astonished, but would admire him, mothers would bless him. Perhaps I moved him; but I did not prevail. His mind was made up.

Herr Hitler, after reading the Prime Minister's letter and paying tribute to the noble thoughts it expressed, told me that ever since Poland had had the English guarantee, it had become vain to seek to lead her to a sound comprehension of the situation. Poland's mind was set in morbid resistance. Poland knew that she was committing suicide, but was doing so telling herself that, thanks to the support of France and England, she would rise once more.

Besides, he added, things have now gone too far. No country having any regard for its honour could tolerate the Polish provocations. France, in Germany's place, would have already gone to war. No doubt there were some reasonable men in Warsaw, but the soldiery of that barbarous country had now broken loose. The central Government no longer had the situation in hand.

I laid stress on the importance of the French proposal: not only did M. Daladier undertake that Poland would agree to seek a solution by free conciliation, but he bound himself, with all the authority vested in his person, to work for the success of an attempt at pacific settlement.

Herr Hitler replied that he did not doubt the sentiments of

M. Daladier and his sincere desire to save peace, but he thought that the advice of the Prime Minister to Warsaw, however pressing it might be, would not be listened to, for Poland was deaf since she had the British guarantee. Moreover, if Poland showed any willingness to talk matters over, it would, doubtless, be in order to gain time for her mobilization.

I returned many times to my point. I pointed out that Poland and Germany had not talked to one another for a long time, that in the course of the crisis the points of view might perhaps have drawn closer, that at any rate it was impossible to find this out unless conversations took place, and that both sides might refrain from taking any military measures while contacts were made.

"It is useless," Herr Hitler replied to me "Poland would not give up Danzig; and it is my will that Danzig, as one of the ports of the Reich, should return to Germany."

In face of the impossibility of breaking down Herr Hitler's resistance, and after having invoked the arguments of sentiment reported at the beginning of this telegram, I thought I ought to leave the door ajar by expressing the hope that the Führer had not said his last word.

As I was taking leave, Herr Hitler announced to me that he would reply in writing to M. Daladier's proposal.

ADDRESS by Edouard Daladier, Premier, in the Chamber of Deputies, September 2, 1939

The address was read to the Senate by M. Camille Chautemps, Vice President of the Council of Ministers. Translation, in *The French Yellow Book*, p. 384

GENTLEMEN,

The Government yesterday decreed general mobilization.

The whole nation is answering the call with serious and resolute calm. The young men have rejoined their regiments. They are now defending our frontiers. The example of dignified courage which they have just set to the world must provide inspiration for our debates. In a great impulse of national brotherliness they have forgotten everything which only yesterday could divide them. They no longer acknowledge any service but the service of France. As we send them the grateful greeting of the nation let us all pledge ourselves together to be worthy of them.

Thus has the Government put France into a position to act in accordance with our vital interests and with national honour.

It has now the duty of setting forth before you the facts as they are, fully, frankly, and clearly.

Peace had been endangered for several days. The demands of Germany on Poland were threatening to provoke a conflict. I shall show you in a moment how—perhaps for the first time in history—all the peaceful forces of the world, moral and material, were leagued together during those days and during those nights to save the world's peace. But just when it could still be hoped that all those repeated efforts were going to be crowned with success, Germany abruptly brought them to naught.

During the day of August 31 the crisis reached its peak. When Germany had at last let Great Britain know that she agreed to hold direct negotiations with Poland, a course which she had, let it be said, refused to me, Poland, in spite of the terrible threat created by the sudden armed invasion of Slovakia by the German forces, at once endeavored to resort to this peaceful method. At one o'clock in the afternoon M. Lipski, the Polish Ambassador to Germany, requested an audience from Herr von Ribbentrop. Peace seemed to be saved. But the Reich Minister for Foreign Affairs would not receive M. Lipski till 7:45 p.m., seven hours later. While the latter was bringing the consent of his Government to direct conversations, the German Minister refused to communicate Germany's claims to the Polish Ambassador, on the pretext that the Ambassador had not full powers to accept or reject them on the spot.

At 9 p.m. the German wireless was communicating the nature and the full extent of these claims; it added that Poland had rejected them. That is a lie. That is a lie, since Poland did not even know them.

And at dawn on September 1 the Führer gave his troops the order to attack. Never was aggression more unmistakable and less warranted; nor for its justification could more lies and cynicism have been brought into play.

Thus was war unleashed at the time when the most noteworthy forces, the authorities who were at the same time the most respected and the most impartial, had ranged themselves in the service of peace; at the time when the whole world had joined together to induce the two sides to come into direct contact so as to settle peacefully the conflict which divides them.

The Head of Christianity had given voice to reason and feelings of brotherhood; President Roosevelt had sent moving messages and proposed a general conference to all countries; the neutral countries had been active in offering their impartial good offices. Need I say that to each of these appeals the French Government gave an immediate welcome and complete assent?

I myself, Gentlemen, if I may be allowed a reference to my own person, thought it my duty as a Frenchman to approach Herr Hitler directly. The Head of the German Government had let me know on August 25, through M. Coulondre, our Ambassador in Berlin, that he deplored the fact that in case of an armed conflict between Germany and Poland, German blood and French blood might be shed. I immediately had a definite proposal put to the Führer, a proposal wholly inspired by the real concern to safeguard without any delay the peace of the world now imperilled.

You were able to read, I think in fact that you must have read these texts. You know the answer I was given; I will not dwell on it.

But we were not disheartened by the failure of this step, and once more we backed up the effort to which Mr. Chamberlain devoted himself with splendid stubbornness. The documents exchanged between London and Berlin have been published. On the one side impartial and persevering loyalty; on the other side, embarrassment, shifty and shirking behaviour. I am also happy at this juncture to pay my tribute to the noble efforts made by the Italian Government. Even yesterday we strove to unite all men of goodwill so as at least to stave off hostilities, to prevent bloodshed and to ensure that the methods of conciliation and arbitration should be substituted for the use of violence.

Gentlemen, these efforts towards peace, however powerless they were and still remain, will at least have shown where the responsibility lies. They insure for Poland, the victim, the effective co-operation and moral support of the nations and of free men of all lands.

What we did before the beginning of this war, we are ready to do once more. If renewed steps are taken towards conciliation, we are still ready to join in.

If the fighting were to stop, if the aggressor were to retreat within his own frontiers, if free negotiations could still be started, you may well believe, Gentlemen, the French Government would spare no effort to ensure, even to-day, if it were possible, the success of these negotiations, in the interests of the peace of the world.

But time is pressing; France and England cannot look on when a friendly nation is being destroyed, a foreboding of further onslaughts, eventually aimed at England and France.

Indeed, are we only dealing with the German-Polish conflict? We are not, Gentlemen; what we have to deal with is a new stage in the advance of the Hitler dictatorship towards the domination of Europe and the world. How, indeed, are we to forget that the German claim to the Polish territories had been long marked on the map of Greater Germany, and that it was only concealed for some years to facilitate other conquests? So long as the German-Polish Pact, which dates back only a few years, was profitable to Germany, Germany respected it; on the day when it became a hindrance to marching towards domination it was denounced unhesitatingly. To-day we are told that, once the German claims against Poland were satisfied, Germany would pledge herself before the whole world for ten, for twenty, for twenty-five years, for all time, to restore or to respect peace. Unfortunately, we have heard such promises before!

On May 25, 1935, Chancellor Hitler pledged himself not to interfere in the internal affairs of Austria and not to unite Austria to the Reich; and on March 11, 1938, the German army entered Vienna; Chancellor Schuschnigg was imprisoned for daring to defend his country's independence, and no one to-day can say what is his real fate after so many physical and moral sufferings. Now we are to believe that it was Dr. Schuschnigg's acts of provocation that brought about the invasion and enslavement of his country!

On September 12, 1938, Herr Hitler declared that the Sudeten problem was an internal matter which concerned only the German minority in Bohemia and the Czechoslovak Government. A few days later he maintained that the violent persecutions carried on by the Czechs were compelling him to change his policy.

On September 26 of the same year he declared that his claim on the Sudeten territory was the last territorial claim he had to make in Europe. On March 14, 1939, Herr Hacha was summoned to Berlin: ordered under the most stringent pressure to accept an ultimatum. A few hours later Prague was being occupied in contempt of the signed pledges given to other countries in Western Europe. In this case also Herr Hitler endeavoured to put on the victims the onus which in fact lies on the aggressor.

Finally, on January 30, 1939, Herr Hitler spoke in loud praise of the non-aggression pact which he had signed five years previously with Poland. He paid a tribute to this agreement as a common act of liberation, and solemnly confirmed his intention to respect its clauses.

But it is Herr Hitler's deeds that count, *not* his word.

What, then, is our duty? Poland is our ally. We entered into commitments with her in 1921 and 1925. These commitments were confirmed.

I, myself, in the Chamber said, on May 11 last:

As a result of the journey of the Polish Minister for Foreign Affairs to London and of the reciprocal pledges of guarantee given by Great Britain and

RELATIONS WITH GERMANY

Poland, by a common agreement with this noble and brave nation we took the measures required for the immediate and direct application of our treaty of alliance.

Parliament approved this policy.

Since then we have never failed both in diplomatic negotiations and in public utterances, to prove faithful to it. Our Ambassador in Berlin has several times reminded Herr Hitler that, if a German aggression were to take place against Poland, we should fulfil our pledges. And on July 1, in Paris, the Minister for Foreign Affairs said to the German Ambassador to France:

> France has definite commitments to Poland. These engagements have been further strengthened as a result of the latest events, and consequently France will at once be at Poland's side as soon as Poland herself takes up arms.

Poland has been the object of the most unjust and brutal aggression. The nations who have guaranteed her independence are bound to intervene in her defence.

Great Britain and France are not Powers that can disown, or dream of disowning, their signatures.

Already last night, on September 1, the French and British Ambassadors were making a joint overturn to the German Government. They handed to Herr von Ribbentrop the following communication from the French Government and the British Government, which I will ask your leave to read out to you:

> Early this morning the German Chancellor issued a proclamation to the German army which clearly indicated that he was about to attack Poland.
>
> Information which has reached His Majesty's Government in the United Kingdom and the French Government indicates that German troops had crossed the Polish frontier and that attacks upon Polish towns are proceeding.
>
> In these circumstances, it appears to the Governments of the United Kingdom and France that, by their action, the German Government have created conditions (viz., an aggressive act of force against Poland threatening the independence of Poland) which call for the implementation by the Governments of the United Kingdom and France of the undertaking to Poland to come to her assistance.
>
> I am accordingly to inform Your Excellency that, unless the German Government are prepared to give the French Government and His Majesty's Government satisfactory assurances that the German Government have suspended all aggressive action against Poland and are prepared promptly to withdraw their forces from Polish territory, the French Government and His Majesty's Government in the United Kingdom will without hesitation fulfil their obligations to Poland.

And indeed, Gentlemen, it is not only the honour of our country: it is also the protection of its vital interests that is at stake.

For a France which should allow this aggression to be carried out would very soon find itself a scorned, an isolated, a discredited France, without allies and without support, and doubtless, would soon herself be exposed to a formidable attack.

This is the question I lay before the French nation, and all nations. At the very moment of the aggression against Poland, what value has the guarantee, once more renewed, given for our eastern frontier, for our Alsace, for our Lorraine, after the repudiation of the guarantees given in turn to Austria, Czechoslovakia, and Poland? More powerful through their conquests, gorged with the plunder of Europe, the masters of inexhaustible natural wealth, the aggressors would soon turn against France with all their forces.

Thus, our honour is but the pledge of our own security. It is not that abstract and obsolete form of honour of which conquerors speak to justify their deeds of violence; it is the dignity of a peaceful people, which bears hatred towards no other people in the world and which never embarks upon a war save only for the sake of its freedom and of its life.

Forfeiting our honour would purchase nothing more than a precarious peace liable to rescission, and when, to-morrow, we should have to fight after losing the respect of our allies and the other nations, we should no longer be anything more than a wretched people doomed to defeat and bondage.

I feel confident that not a single Frenchman harbours such thoughts to-day. But I well know, too, Gentlemen, that it is hard for those who have devoted their whole lives to the cause of peace and who are still prompted by a peaceful ideal to reply, by force if needed, to deeds of violence. As head of the Government, I am not the man to make an apology for war in these tragic hours. I fought before like most of you. I can remember. I shall not utter a single one of those words that the genuine fighters look upon as blasphemous. But I desire to do my plain duty, and shall do it, as an honourable man.

Gentlemen, while we are in session, Frenchmen are rejoining their regiments. Not one of them feels any hatred in his heart against the German people. Not one of them is giving way to the intoxicating call of violence and brutality; but they are ready, unanimously, to discharge their duty with the quiet courage which derives its inspiration from a clear conscience.

Gentlemen, you who know what those Frenchmen are thinking, you who even yesterday were among them in our provincial towns and in our countryside, you who have seen them go off—you will not contradict me if I evoke their feelings here. They are peace-loving men, but they have decided to make every sacrifice needed to defend the dignity and freedom of their country. If they have answered our call, as they have done, without a moment's hesitation, without a murmur, without flinching, that is because they feel, all of them, in the depths of their hearts that it is, in truth, whatever may be said, the very existence of France that is at stake.

You know better than anyone else that no government, no man, would be able to mobilize France merely to launch her into an adventure. Never would the French rise to invade the territory of a foreign country. Theirs is the heroism for defence and not for conquest. When you see France spring to arms it is because she feels herself threatened.

It is not France only that has arisen; it is that whole, far-flung empire under the sheltering folds of our tricolour. From every corner of the globe moving protestations of loyalty from all the protected or friendly races are reaching the mother country to-day. The union of all Frenchmen is thus echoed beyond the seas by the union of all peoples under our protection who in the hour of danger are proffering both their arms and their hearts. And I wish also to salute all the foreigners settled on our soil, who on this very day in their thousands and thousands, as though they were the volunteers of imperilled freedom, are placing their courage and their lives at the service of France.

Our duty is to make an end of aggressive and violent undertakings; by means of peaceful settlement, if we can still do so, and this we shall strive our utmost to achieve, by the wielding of our strength, if all sense of morality as well as all glimmering of reason has died within the aggressors.

If we were not to keep our pledges, if we were to allow Germany to crush Poland, within a few months, perhaps within a few weeks, what could we say to France, if we had to face aggressors once more? Then would those most determined soldiers ask us what we had done with our friends. They would feel themselves alone, under the most dreadful threat, and might lose, perhaps for all time, the confidence which now spurs them on.

Gentlemen, in these hours when the fate of Europe is in the balance, France is speaking to us through the voice of her sons, through the voice of all those who have already accepted, if need be, the greatest sacrifice of all. Let us recapture, as they have done, that spirit which fired all the heroes of our history. France rises with such impetuous impulses only when she feels in her heart that she is fighting for her life and for her independence.

Gentlemen, to-day France is in command.

TELEPHONE COMMUNICATION from Robert Coulondre, French Ambassador to Germany, to the French Minister for Foreign Affairs (Georges Bonnet), September 3, 1939

Translation, in *The French Yellow Book,* p. 400

I HAVE THE HONOUR to confirm as here below the communication which I made to Your Excellency by telephone at 1 p.m.

Herr von Ribbentrop returned at noon. I was received at this hour by the State Secretary, but the latter informed me that he was not in a position to tell me whether a satisfactory reply had been made to my letter of September 1, nor even whether such a reply could be given thereto. He insisted that I should see Herr von Ribbentrop himself. In these circumstances I asked to be received by the Minister for Foreign Affairs at the earliest possible moment.

I was received by Herr von Ribbentrop at 12:30 p.m.

I asked him whether he could give me a satisfactory reply to my letter which I had handed to him on September 1 at 10 p.m.

He replied to me as follows:

After the delivery of your letter, the Italian Government notified the German Government of a proposed compromise, stating that the French Government was in agreement. Later, Signor Mussolini intimated to us that the contemplated compromise had failed owing to British intransigence. This morning the British Ambassador handed us an ultimatum, due to expire two hours later. We rejected it for the reason which is explained in the memorandum which I handed to the British Ambassador to-day and of which I give you a copy.

If the French Government feels bound by its commitments to Poland to enter into the conflict, I can only regret it, for we have no feeling of hostility towards France. It is only if France attacks us that we shall fight her, and this would be on her part a war of aggression.

I then asked the Minister for Foreign Affairs if I was to infer from his utterances that the reply of the Government of the Reich to my letter of September 1 was in the negative. "Yes," he replied.

In these circumstances I must, on behalf of my Government, remind you for the last time of the heavy responsibility assumed by the Government of the Reich by entering, without a declaration of war, into hostilities against Poland and in not acting upon the suggestion made by the Governments of the French Republic and of His Britannic Majesty to suspend all aggressive action against Poland and to declare itself ready to withdraw its forces promptly from Polish territory.

I have the painful duty to notify you that as from to-day, September 3, at 5 P.M., the French Government will find itself obliged to fulfil the obligations that France has contracted towards Poland, and which are known to the German Government.

Well [Herr von Ribbentrop remarked], it will be France who is the aggressor.

I replied to him that history would judge of that.

STATEMENT by Edouard Daladier, Premier, to the Nation, September 3, 1939

Translation, in *The French Yellow Book,* p. 403

MEN AND WOMEN OF FRANCE,

Since daybreak on September 1, Poland has been the victim of the most brutal and most cynical of aggressions. Her frontiers have been violated. Her cities are being bombed. Her army is heroically resisting the invader.

The responsibility for the blood that is being shed falls entirely upon the Hitler Government. The fate of peace was in Hitler's hands. He chose war.

France and England have made countless efforts to safeguard peace. This very morning they made a further urgent intervention in Berlin in order to address to the German Government a last appeal to reason and request it to stop hostilities and to open peaceful negotiations.

Germany met us with a refusal. She had already refused to reply to all the men of goodwill who recently raised their voices in favour of the peace of the world.

She therefore desires the destruction of Poland, so as to be able to dominate Europe quickly and to enslave France.

In rising against the most frightful of tyrannies, in honouring our word, we fight to defend our soil, our homes, our liberties.

I am conscious of having worked unremittingly against the war until the last minute.

I greet with emotion and affection our young soldiers, who now go forth to perform the sacred task which we ourselves did perform before them. They can have full confidence in their chiefs, who are worthy of those who have previously led France to victory.

The cause of France is identical with that of Righteousness. It is the cause of all peaceful and free nations. It will be victorious.

Men and women of France!

We are waging war because it has been thrust on us. Every one of us is at his post, on the soil of France, on that land of liberty where respect of human dignity finds one of its last refuges. You will all co-operate, with a profound feeling of union and brotherhood, for the salvation of the country.

Vive la France!

PART FOUR

*THE UNION OF SOVIET SOCIALIST
REPUBLICS*

GENERAL STATEMENTS OF POLICY

ADDRESS by Maxim Litvinov, People's Commissar for Foreign Affairs, before the Central Executive Committee of the U.S.S.R., December 29, 1933

Translation, in Royal Institute of International Affairs, *Documents on International Affairs, 1933*, p. 425, citing translation published by the Anglo-Russian Parliamentary Committee, London; excerpts

THE GUIDING principle of our foreign policy has been put very briefly, but very expressively, by Comrade Stalin: We desire no foreign land, but we shall not surrender a single inch of our own land to any one. Once we do not desire any foreign lands, then we cannot want war. As for our own land, we have every possibility of defending it and of preventing any attempt at its invasion. Our growing armed forces could teach a lesson to any of our near or distant neighbours which would prevent them for decades from again attempting to invade us, but this would be an unproductive waste of our means and energies. It would distract us for a time from our fundamental work of constructing socialism.

We are therefore doing everything possible to defend our territory by peaceful means, even though this may not be a radical means for removing the threat of aggression against us. We consider that even military activities commenced outside the immediate frontiers of our Union may be a menace to us, hence we not only continue but are intensifying our struggle for peace, which has always been and still is the basic problem of our diplomacy. As Comrade Molotov rightly said: This struggle corresponds with the desire of the masses of the people of all countries.

During the last year we have extended the system of Non-Aggression Pacts. Such pacts are now in force between the U.S.S.R. and not only all our neighbours, with the exception of Japan and China, but also with France and Italy. We have made a further step towards the intensification of the significance and effectiveness of the Non-Aggression Pacts by proposing an exhaustive definition of the idea of aggression itself. This proposal of ours is already contained in agreements with a solid chain of our neighbours from Finland to Afghanistan and with all the three countries of the Little Entente.

The definition of aggression which we have given is generally recognized to be a valuable contribution to the science of international law, and also of international practice; at the same time, it forms an excellent measure for determining the absence or presence in any State of aggressive, annexationist aims. We shall, therefore, continue to struggle for the universal recognition of this definition.

The maintenance of peace cannot depend simply on our efforts, but demands the co-operation of other countries. Endeavouring, therefore, to establish and maintain friendly relations with all countries, we pay special attention to the consolidation of our relations with those countries which, like us, give proof of their sincere endeavour to preserve peace and are ready to oppose those who violate peace. We have never refused and we do not refuse to participate in organized international co-operation aimed at consolidating peace. Not being doctrinaires, we do not refuse to utilize existing or future international organizations and combinations, providing we have or shall have reason to consider that they would serve the purpose of preserving peace.

In the light of all that I have said you will readily understand, Comrades, the significance of the development of our relations with the separate countries.

I shall begin with an event, chronologically the latest in this development, but by its importance at the present moment occupying first place, that is to say, the re-establishment of our diplomatic relations with the great trans-Atlantic Republic. During fifteen years this Republic was the only one of the big Powers who persistently refused, not only formal recognition of the Soviet Union, but acknowledgement of its existence. She refused to recognize the fact of the October (November) Revolution and the changes brought about by it. For the U.S.A. there still existed somewhere in space the Provisional Government of Kerensky, with whose agents she continued to have official relations.

The reason for this persistence in ignoring the U.S.S.R. was not that the U.S.A. had more serious disputes with us than had other countries or because she had suffered any more from our revolutionary legislation. No, in essence she simply continued the struggle declared by the whole capitalist world after the October Revolution against the new Soviet State which had declared as its aim the creation of a Socialist country. This was a struggle against the peaceful coexistence of two social systems. . . .

Having ceased to act as the champion of the whole capitalist world, and having come into contact with us, the U.S.A. at once became convinced that there were no national or State antagonisms between her and our Union, and that outstanding questions could be readily settled. Moreover, being herself interested in the preservation of peace, the U.S.A. has recognized relations with us as a powerful factor in the preservation of this peace and has correspondingly valued cooperation with us in this direction.

We, on our part, also estimate the establishment of relations with America primarily from the standpoint of its significance in the cause of peace. I may remark, in passing, that in re-establishing relations with the U.S.A. we have maintained the fundamental principle underlying our restoration of relations with all capitalist countries. The fact that there have been no sacrifices on either side is, indeed, an important guarantee for further consolidation of our relations with the U.S.A.

The frank exchange of opinions between President Roosevelt and myself has convinced us both of the possibility of the closest relations between our two countries. It is but just to mention the far-sightedness of President Roosevelt who, immediately he came to power and perhaps even before, realized the fruitlessness of any further struggle against us on behalf of capitalism, and envisaged the advantage of relations with us in the interest of the U.S.A. and of world peace.

We consider our relations with the great Turkish Republic as a model of relations with foreign States. For over ten years these relations have improved from year to year and have attained real friendship, rendering complete satisfaction to both sides and instilling in them a feeling of complete security for the section of the frontier between the two countries. The policy of friendship and mutual confidence has provided the basis for fruitful co-operation on the international arena. . . .

In discussing the gradual considerable improvement of our relations with other countries, we must before all mention France. After the signature of the Pact of Non-Aggression, our relations with France, during the past year, have improved rapidly. This is due partly to the absence of any State political antagonisms between us, and also to our common desire to work actively for the preservation of world peace.

We have the advantage of the continuity of our Government and foreign policy, whilst in France Governments change frequently with a possible change in political orientation; inasmuch as the French people sincerely desire peace, and it is this that unites us with France, we need not fear very much that any change in Government will hinder the successful development of friendly relations.

The recent visit to the U.S.S.R. of M. Herriot, one of the most outstanding and brilliant representatives of the French nation, and one who reflects their peace-loving sentiments, as well as the official visit of representatives of French aviation, led by the Minister for Air, M. Pierre Cot, have given a new impulse to Franco-Soviet *rapprochement*. I certainly hope that all this is but an introductory step towards the further development of Franco-Soviet relations, and I am sure that this development will become all the more rapid as the elements menacing peace accumulate. It is, however, necessary to note that our relations with France still require a certain economic strengthening which, I hope, will be effected by the Trade Agreement about to be concluded.

Our relations with Italy continue to be characterized by their stability. In the course of ten years, there have been no fluctuations, no conflicts, either political or economic. During this period we have had not a few instances of valuable diplomatic co-operation on the part of Italy. We have also utilized Italian technical aid in various branches of our construction, and economic relations between the two countries have developed to our mutual advantage.

My recent visit to Italy, and my reception there, demonstrate the endeavour of both countries to develop their relations in all branches, and we have come to this conclusion with the head of the Italian Government, M. Mussolini, after an exchange of opinion on questions of current policy and of the best methods of preserving universal peace. Our efforts to maintain and develop simultaneously relations with all the large countries is a not unimportant contribution to the maintenance of general peace.

Unfortunately, this endeavour has not yet been realized, or completely realized, in regard to Great Britain. Our relations with the latter cannot boast either of stability or continuity. There are no objective reasons for this, and I am certain that the British people, as a whole, desire to live in peace and friendship with us. But there are elements there who are still rapt in the sweet dream of a general capitalist struggle against the socialist country—a dream from which the U.S.A. has just shaken free.

They will be unable to destroy or even to shake our socialist country, and, consequently, in view of the well-known practical character and common sense of the British, one cannot help being astonished that amongst them there should still be such Quixotic snipers and partisans. In so far as it depends upon us we are ready, and we should like to have as good relations with Great Britain as with other countries.

We are convinced that sincere and good relations between the Great Powers are not only a necessary condition, but are a guarantee, for general peace. It is expected that a temporary Trade Agreement will be signed shortly which, removing as it will certain misunderstandings, we may hope will make possible better relations between ourselves and Great Britain.

We, of course, attach very great importance to our relations with our nearest neighbours, particularly with the largest of these—with Poland. Here, too, we note very considerable progress. The conclusion of a Pact of Non-Aggression and of the Convention Defining an Aggressor could not but result in a strengthening of our mutual confidence and understanding. The political perturbations which have occurred in Europe during the past year, resulting in our common danger and common anxieties, have created a community of interests between ourselves and Poland. . . .

What I have said regarding the influence of the treaties of Non-Aggression and of the Definition of an Aggressor on our relations with Poland are equally applicable to our relations with the other neighbouring States on our western frontier, namely, Finland, Estonia, Latvia, and Lithuania. These countries are becoming more and more convinced of the absolute sincerity of our aspirations for peace, of our good will towards them, and of our interest in the preservation of their full economic and political independence. . . .

In giving a review of our relations with the outside world, I have certainly not lost sight of such big States as Germany and Japan. I devote to them a special place in my review precisely because they occupy a very important place in the foreign policy of the Soviet Union. The latest phase of the development in the relationships between these two countries permits me to hope that they will have no grievance against me for singling them out for special attention.

If I am not mistaken they have even recognized that they are of common race. This has become quite possible since the idea of race has ceased to be regarded as an ethnological and anthropological conception, and has become something in the nature of the designation of a militant organization.

For ten years we had the closest economic and political relations with Germany. We were the only great country which wished to have nothing to do with the Versailles Treaty and its consequences. We renounced the rights and advantages which this treaty reserved for us.

Germany occupied first place in our foreign trade, and Germany, like ourselves, gained considerable advantages from the political and economic relations which were established between us. With these relations as a support, Germany could speak with her former victors in a bolder and more assured manner. She succeeded in freeing herself from certain of the more burdensome consequences of the Versailles Treaty. She sought closer relations with all the former victors, although she did not always succeed in this.

She concluded the Locarno Treaty with France, a treaty which is nothing other than a Pact of Non-Aggression, and even more than that, since it also provides for outside guarantors. In Locarno, she also concluded with Poland an Arbitration Treaty, which is also nothing but a Pact of Non-Aggression. Germany entered into the League of Nations, accepting the Covenant, which is also a Pact of Non-Aggression, providing in addition, for sanctions.

We, on our side, as soon as we found it possible, also concluded a Pact of Non-Aggression with France and Poland. These treaties and pacts on both sides should not, and in fact did not, worsen our relations with Germany, which were in no way based on hostility to other countries. Nevertheless, our relations with Germany during the last year have become, it may be said, unrecognizable.

In Germany speeches and declarations were made, and acts took place, which were not only not in consonance with our former relations, but rather gave one cause to think that these relations had been transformed into their very opposite. The causes for this have been as follows: With the change of Government in Germany which took place in 1932, a political leader obtained office and subsequently took the helm who, at the time of our very best relations with Germany, openly opposed these relations and advocated a *rapprochement* with the West for a joint attack upon the Soviet Union.

He organized a new political club where this idea was propagated, and he worked zealously for its realization. On coming to power he made an attempt, true unsuccessful, to realize this idea formally. Subsequently, a *coup d'état* occurred in Germany which brought a new party into power which propagated the most extreme anti-Soviet ideas. The founder of this party developed in detail his conception of the foreign policy of Germany in a literary work.

According to this conception, Germany had to reconquer not only everything she had lost by the Versailles Treaty, not only had she to conquer lands where there were German minorities, but by fire and sword she had to carve a way for herself for expansion eastwards, without stopping at the frontiers of the Soviet Union, and subject to her will the peoples of the U.S.S.R. . . .

There have been, in addition, not a few anti-Soviet negotiations and proposals with the above ideas at their base entered into by people, not indeed occupying State posts, but, nevertheless, in very responsible positions. . . . All this is what has made our former relations with Germany unrecognizable.

I considered it necessary to say this openly since, on the German side, attempts are often made to ascribe to us the initiative for the change in our relations and to explain it as the result of our displeasure at the present régime which persecutes Communists, and others. We, of course, have our own opinion about the German régime. We, of course, sympathize with the sufferings of our German comrades, but we Marxists are the last who can be reproached with allowing our feelings to dictate our policy.

The whole world knows that we can and do maintain good relations with capitalist States of any régime, including the Fascist. We do not interfere in the internal affairs of Germany, as we do not interfere in that of other countries, and our relations with her are conditioned not by her internal but by her external policy. . . .

I am asked by representatives of the German Government what exactly is it that we want from Germany and what she must do to set our doubts at rest regarding her loyalty. To this I generally reply, let her not do what she is doing. Let the German Government look into what her numerous agents and emissaries are doing, and let her tell them that they should not do it.

But we also make the following declaration: We desire to have with Germany, as with other States, the best of relations. Nothing but good can result from such relations, both for the Soviet Union and Germany. We on our side are not striving to expand either on the west, or on the east, or in any other direction. We have no feelings of hostility towards the German people and are not preparing to attack either their territory or their rights, and whatever we may do we shall never encourage other States to make such attacks.

We should be glad if Germany could say the same to us and if there were no facts which could contradict them. We would desire to be assured that such declarations referred, not only to the present moment, but also to that time when she will have stronger forces for realizing those aggressive ideas which her present leaders preached before their rise to power, and which some of them preach even now.

I shall not be mistaken, Comrades, if I assume that you are most of all interested at the present time in regard to our relations with Japan. These relations are arresting the attention, not only of the Soviet Union, but of the whole world, since the policy of Japan is, at the present time, the heaviest storm cloud on the international political horizon. I shall permit myself, therefore, to deal in brief with the development of our relations with Japan.

Since the conclusion of the Peking Agreement, right up to the end of 1931, the best of neighbourly relations existed between Japan and ourselves. There were no conflicts, no serious misunderstandings, and when such arose they were resolved by peaceful diplomatic means. There was no talk about threats from one side or the other. Our attitude to Japan was so trustful (since at that time there was no occasion for mistrust) that we left our Far Eastern frontier almost without any defence. The position began to change when Japan started her military operations in Manchuria. Together with the whole world, we could not but consider these operations as a violation on the part of Japan of numerous obligations which she had voluntarily undertaken in her international treaties.

The Japanese Government, as you will remember, then offered explanations for her operations which explained nothing and convinced nobody. She simultaneously gave us official assurances that her troops would not proceed beyond a definite line in Manchuria itself, and that, in any case, our interests, in particular the interests of the Chinese Eastern Railway, would under no circumstances suffer.

These assurances were then continuously repeated as the Japanese troops advanced farther, right up to the complete occupation of the whole of Manchuria and to the formation of the so-called independent Manchukuo. These actions, as you know, were characterized by the entire external world, including also the League of Nations, to which Japan herself belonged, as a violation of such agreements as the Washington Nine-Power Pact, the League of Nations Covenant, and the Kellogg Pact.

The occupation of Manchuria was, however, also a violation of the Portsmouth Treaty, confirmed by the Peking Agreement, in virtue of which Japan had no right to maintain troops in Manchuria beyond a defined very small number. We refused to participate in international action at that time, firstly because we did not believe in the sincerity and consistency of the States which participated in these actions and, above all, because we did not seek, as we do not seek now, an armed conflict with Japan. We were only trying to obtain from Japan one thing: the observance of our commercial interests in the Chinese Eastern Railway, since we have no other interests in Manchuria.

Despite all the solemn promises and assurances, the representatives of Japan in Manchuria, nevertheless, soon began a direct attack on our interests, endeavouring to render impossible the management of the Chinese Eastern Railway jointly with the Chinese or Manchurians, as provided for in our agreements. They disrupted the work of the line itself, resorted for this purpose to provocative, violent acts, and submitted to the Soviet side of the administration quite unfounded arbitrary claims.

The whole world was surprised at our composure and our long patience, but we had firmly decided not to digress from our policy of peace, refraining from any hostile acts and confining ourselves to protests, which remained, however, without any effect. But the more calm and patient our attitude, the more insolent and provocative became the actions of the Japanese forces in Manchuria. A definite impression was created that they were consciously trying to provoke us to stronger action than protests.

Not desiring to lend ourselves to such provocation, we proposed to Japan, on May 2, 1933, that she should purchase from us the Chinese Eastern Railway. The entire railway, track, rolling stock, station premises and other accessories of the line were built with the hard-earned money of the peoples of our Union and thus formed their inalienable property. We only desired one thing, that the present value of the line should be returned to its real owners.

It seemed as though Japan accepted our proposal for the purchase of the railway. When, however, we entered upon the concrete negotiations regarding the conditions of sale, it turned out that Japan did not want to buy the railway, but wanted to receive it as a present. She offered a paltry ridiculous sum, naïvely assuming that we wished to sell the railway just as a matter of form, but that in reality we were prepared to give it away for nothing. Such negotiations could not, of course, lead to anything concrete, although we fixed a minimum price for the line. . . .

The negotiations have not been resumed since that time, but the unlawful acts on the railway continue, and the work of the line is being paralysed. Moreover, our declarations and protests against these unlawful acts remain without a reply from Japan, who is vainly trying to convince us that she is in no way involved in these deeds, for which only "independent" Manchukuo is ostensibly responsible. We have our own opinion of the "independence" of Manchukuo. So, by the way, has the whole world. Manchukuo is not yet recognized by a single State, and is considered by everybody exclusively as a puppet of the Japanese Government and the Japanese command in Manchuria.

If any perfectly objective proofs thereof were needed, it was recently provided by Tass, which published the well-known documents, the authenticity of which is not open to doubt. It is clear from these documents that the forcible measures against Soviet employees of the railway, ostensibly taken by the Manchurian courts of justice, were dictated by the Japanese military and administrative agents, who, in this way, hoped to secure the railway for next to nothing.

We, therefore, declared to the Japanese Government that we could not recognize her references to the Manchurian authorities, nor could we recognize the responsibility of any one but the Japanese Government for the violation of our rights and interests in the Chinese Eastern Railway.

What is in question, however, is not the Chinese Eastern Railway alone. Side by side with the infringement of our rights on the line, the question of war against the Soviet Union for the seizure of the Maritime Provinces and the entire Far Eastern Region is being discussed by statesmen, including official representatives of the Japanese Government, as well as by the Press.

The matter is not merely confined to conversations, but a considerable number of Japanese troops have been concentrated in Manchuria, near our frontier, war material is being brought up, roads and railways are being built. Thus, not only is the violent seizure of our line threatened by Japan, but there is a direct threat to our frontiers.

In such a state of affairs there was nothing left for our Government to do except to start strengthening our frontiers, transferring thereto the necessary forces and taking other military measures. But while we are taking exclusively defensive measures, Japan, as is known, is feverishly preparing for war, which can be no other than aggressive, since no one is threatening the safety of Japan. . . .

Our policy is clear. We do not aspire to make use of a favourable situation, we do not aspire to wage war under any circumstances. We say to Japan:

We do not threaten you, we do not want your land or other territories lying on your side of our frontiers, we want to live in peace with you as we have done up to the present, respecting your rights and interests and asking only that you adopt the same attitude toward our rights and interests. Your first step to prove your peaceful disposition should be a cessation of repressive police measures on the Chinese Eastern Railway, the restoration of our violated rights, and then a calm continuation of the negotiations for a fair commercial price for the railroad.

The second step in demonstrating Japan's desire for peace should be the signing of the Pact of Non-Aggression which we proposed two years ago. We should like to entertain the hope that Japan will act in accordance with the counsel of her level-headed patriots and not with that of the militarist adventurers.

After my exposition of the relations of the Soviet Union with other countries, it remains for me to say a few words about our relation to an international organization of which the Soviet Union is a member—the Disarmament Conference. This Conference is still formally reckoned among the living. The appellation of corpse, which I applied to it in America, is nevertheless no exaggeration. The question now is whether to sign its death certificate or to try and galvanize the corpse. Such galvanization is possible and the Conference may come to life again, but it will no longer be a disarmament conference, but a conference for additional armaments.

We went to the Conference to take part in the framing of guarantees of peace, of common safety, but the rearmament of any State whatever can in no sense be considered such a guarantee. When they tell us additional armaments for some and disarmament for others, we fear that only the first part of this formula will be carried out, without the second; for it is quite clear that they will not succeed in disarming to any extent precisely those nations which are already making practical use of their arms and openly threatening to employ them on a still larger scale in the near future. It will be impossible to demand that only those Governments shall disarm against which such threats are directed.

It will again be possible to talk seriously of disarmament only when the Governments of the world cease to treat Pacts of Non-Aggression like scraps of paper, cynically suggesting that "The more the better," and when they sincerely give up war as a method of settling international disputes. Then from the dusty archives of the League of Nations will be hauled out the Soviet proposals on disarmament, and the discussions will indeed deal with real disarmament, complete and universal, and not with quotas of armaments.

Comrades, in my report I have tried to acquaint you with the present tendencies in international relations, with the alignment of forces around the pressingly real question "war or peace?" and to set forth the rôle of the U.S.S.R. in the struggle of these forces. The creatively peaceful character of this rôle is hardly doubted by any one now. But not all other countries have yet declared their position in this struggle and their attitude towards the Soviet Union. A characteristic feature of the situation is that the peaceful intentions of other Governments have come to be estimated according to their attitude towards the Soviet Union. . . .

Whilst agreeing to co-operate with other countries, and bearing in mind that the continuity of our policy provides the highest guarantee for the fulfilment of our international obligations, we must not forget, however, that we are dealing with capitalist States, with Governments which are unstable and subject to frequent change; we must remember that we are faced with the possibility of the advent to power of groups and people who, in order to vent their class hatred toward our country, are sometimes prepared to sacrifice even their own national State interests.

Being compelled to be on the alert in our defence, we will strengthen and perfect, to an even greater degree than formerly, our

Red Army, Red Navy, and Red Air Force, the chief means of defending our security. We must bear in mind that, in the event of the failure of the combined forces of the friends of peace, violation of the peace may be directed against us in the first place.

We shall, therefore, remember that, against our will, a time may arrive when we may have to justify the declaration of Comrade Stalin that we will not give up a single inch of our territory. In defence of every inch of our Soviet land, be it in the West or in the East, not only the Red military forces but also the Red peoples of our immense Union will participate. That they are led by the Red Party, the Communist Party of the U.S.S.R., and its inspirer and leader, Comrade Stalin, guarantees them the same successes in war as they have had in peace.

LETTER from Maxim Litvinov, People's Commissar for Foreign Affairs, to the President of the Assembly of the League of Nations (R. J. Sandler), Regarding Membership in the League, September 15, 1934

Translation, in League of Nations, Fifteenth Ordinary Session of the Assembly, *Verbatim Record,* September 17, 1934, p. 2

THE SOVIET GOVERNMENT has received a telegram signed by a great many Members of the League of Nations—namely, South Africa, Albania, Australia, Austria, Great Britain, Bulgaria, Canada, Chile, China, Spain, Estonia, Abyssinia, France, Greece, Haiti, Hungary, India, Iraq, Italy, Latvia, Lithuania, Mexico, New Zealand, Persia, Poland, Roumania, Czechoslovakia, Turkey, Uruguay and Yugoslavia—in which, pointing out both that the mission of the League of Nations is the organisation of peace, and that this necessitates the general co-operation therein of all nations, they invite the Union of Soviet Socialist Republics to join the League of Nations and add its co-operation. Simultaneously, the Soviet Government has been officially informed by the Governments of Denmark, Finland, Norway and Sweden of their favourable attitude to the entry of the Union of Soviet Socialist Republics into the League.

The Soviet Government, which has made the organisation and consolidation of peace the main task of its foreign policy, and has never been deaf to proposals for international co-operation in the interests of peace, considering that, coming as it does from an overwhelming majority of Members of the League, this invitation represents the real will to peace of the League of Nations, and their recognition of the necessity of co-operation with the Union of Soviet Socialist Republics is willing to respond to it, and become a Member of the League, occupying therein the place due to itself, and undertaking to observe all the international obligations and decisions binding upon members in conformity with Article 1 of the Covenant.

The Soviet Government is especially glad to be coming into the League at a moment when the question of the amendment of the Covenant in order to bring it into harmony with the Briand-Kellogg Pact, and to banish completely international warfare, is being considered by it.

Since Articles 12 and 13 of the Covenant leave it open to States to submit disputes to arbitration or judicial settlement, the Soviet Government considers it necessary to make it clear that, in its opinion, such methods should not be applicable to conflicts regarding questions arising before its entry into the League.

I venture to express the hope that this declaration will be accepted by all Members of the League in that spirit of sincere desire for international co-operation and for ensuring peace to all nations in which it is made.

REPORT by Vyacheslav M. Molotov, President of the Soviet of People's Commissars, to the Seventh All-Union Soviet Congress at Moscow, January 28, 1935

Translation, in Royal Institute of International Affairs, *Documents on International Affairs, 1934,* p. 405, citing official translation; excerpts

BUT ALSO the relations between these (capitalist) countries are becoming more and more strained, are developing towards an intensification of the struggle for foreign markets, turning ever more frequently into a trade and currency war. Pacifist talks are receding into the background. Pacifists are no longer in fashion. In bourgeois countries the extreme imperialist wirepullers, who are more and more openly talking of new predatory wars, of the way out of the crisis by means of war, are coming nearer to power.

Notwithstanding all the danger of the unleashing of a new imperialist war for these very dominant classes of capitalist countries, certain countries have already passed over to active deeds. Thus, Japan did not stop before war with China, occupied Manchuria and is making herself at home generally in the country of the great Chinese people.

Not only Japan, but also Germany withdrew from the League of Nations, the meaning of this policy being understood by all. This was done in order to untie their hands in the matter of armaments and war preparations. Just recently the famous Washington agreement on naval armaments, concluded thirteen years ago between America, England, Japan, and other States, collapsed, since this agreement began to be a hindrance to some one in the race in naval armaments and in the preparation of new military conquests for the Pacific Ocean. The diplomacy and foreign policy of bourgeois countries is more and more serving those who are already now choosing their allies in a war for a new re-division of the world among imperialist powers at the expense of the weaker countries.

We have to take into consideration that the immediate danger of war has increased for the U.S.S.R. Certain influential circles in Japan have already long since openly been speaking about war against the Soviet Union. It must not be forgotten that there is now in Europe a ruling party openly declaring its historical task to be the seizure of territory in the Soviet-Union.

Not to see a new war approaching means to close one's eyes to the chief danger.

To all this the Soviet Union replied, above all, by strengthening activities in the struggle for peace.

All know the broad initiative of the U.S.S.R. in the question of non-aggression pacts. For the period under review the Soviet Union concluded pacts with neighbouring Baltic States and with a number of European countries. Through no fault of the U.S.S.R. she did not succeed in concluding a non-aggression pact with Japan.

Great importance was attached to the proposal of the U.S.S.R. on the definition of the aggressor. At international conferences and in a number of international agreements can be found references for the need of special measures against an attacking side, against an aggressive state unleashing war. But, notwithstanding this, the Governments of bourgeois countries did not show any haste to state clearly whom it is necessary to consider the attacking side, i. e. the country responsible for beginning war. Soviet diplomacy, particularly interested in the defence of peace and in measures against military attacks, had to take up this matter. Soviet diplomacy has fulfilled this task with honour.

Such a proposal was introduced by us for discussion at an international conference. In order immediately to put this matter forward in a practical manner, we proposed that a number of countries should sign such a pact, i. e., an agreement on the definition of an attacking side. As is known, such a pact was signed by all European States bordering on us, also by Turkey, Persia, and Afghanistan, and, in addition, by Czechoslovakia and Yugoslavia.

Our Government always attached great significance to openly putting the question of disarmament, or at least, of the maximum reduction of armaments. Precisely in this sense did Soviet diplomacy work at the international disarmament conference. It can be said that numerous meetings of the international conference on disarmament were fruitless. But no one can say that the Soviet Union did not do everything it possibly could to insist on universal or at least maximum disarmament.

It is not for us to defend the Geneva disarmament conference, but we do not doubt that the efforts of Soviet diplomacy at this conference, which became widely known in many countries, were not without results.

A logical continuation of this policy is our proposal to transform the disarmament conference, from which some wish to dissociate themselves as soon as possible, into a permanent peace conference, into an organ permanently concerning itself with preventing war. This proposal will still be discussed by other countries at an international conference, and we will insist on it.

During the recent period we were again confronted with the question of our attitude to the League of Nations. It is known that the League of Nations in its time was created by States then still not desirous of recognizing the right of the new Worker-Peasant State to exist, but instead, participating in anti-Soviet military intervention. Strong efforts were made in its time to transform the League of Nations into a weapon directing the mouth of the cannon on the Soviet Union. For this it had to ensure agreement among the imperialists. But this undertaking did not succeed.

Since then much water has flowed under the bridge. Events of recent times have emphasized those changes which have taken place in the situation of the League of Nations. The most belligerent aggressive elements have begun to leave the League of Nations. The League of Nations has become for them in the given circumstances confining, inconvenient. But the majority of participants in the League of Nations are now for one or another consideration not interested in the unleashing of war.

We had to draw from this situation our concrete Bolshevist conclusions. Therefore we regarded with sympathy the proposal of thirty States for the entry of the U.S.S.R. into the League of Nations. In so far as in the question of guaranteeing peace the League of Nations can now play a certain positive rôle, the Soviet Union could not but recognize the expediency of co-operation with the League of Nations in this matter, although it is not characteristic of us to over-estimate the rôle of such organizations. Needless to say, the invitation by thirty States to the U.S.S.R. to join the League of Nations by no means lessens the international authority of the Soviet Union, but bespeaks the reverse. We enter this fact in our assets.

The Soviet Government not only showed initiative, but supported the steps of other Governments directed to the defence of peace and international security. In connexion with this it is worth while noting the active support we gave to the proposal of France of the so-called Eastern Pact of mutual assistance. This pact should also embrace, besides the U.S.S.R., countries such as France, Germany, Czechoslovakia, Poland, Lithuania, Esthonia, Latvia.

The signatories of this agreement should render each other every kind of support, including military, in the event of an attack by one of the countries signatory to the pact. During a number of months there have been negotiations among the said countries on the conclusion of this pact. I will not dwell now on those reasons why Germany and, with her, Poland, till now refuse to give consent to signing it. But the importance of the Eastern Pact for all advocates of peace in Europe is understood. And, therefore, notwithstanding the obstacles that still exist and the objections of the countries referred to, the Soviet Government considers its attitude to this question unchanged. We will regard success in this matter as a step forward in the cause of guaranteeing peace in Europe.

From all this it has seen what is the basis of the foreign policy of the Soviet Union. The basis of our foreign policy is supporting peace and developing peaceful relations with all countries. . . .

The rôle of the U.S.S.R. as a firm factor in universal peace is now widely recognized. It has become a rule for other countries to appeal to the Soviet Union in those cases when it is a question of guaranteeing peace. And this is understandable.

Not a single country, not even one of the smallest States on the borders of the U.S.S.R., has grounds for entertaining a feeling of unrest in relation to the Soviet Union, which is far from what can be said of certain other big States. The authority and might of the Worker-Peasant State in international relations now serves one cause—the cause of universal peace. The Soviet Union has become the one to express the vital interests of the toilers of all countries in the realm of international relations. Whatever our class enemies may say, the political meaning of the dictatorship of the proletariat in the U.S.S.R. in the given conditions, when the danger of war becomes more and more acute, consists in the fact that throughout the world there is not a more reliable bulwark in the cause of peace than our worker-peasant power.

Our relations with other countries depend not only upon us but upon the foreign policies of these States. And all of you know how many contradictions there are in the policies of the bourgeois States. . . .

An example of the best development of friendly relations are our relations with Turkey. The last years have constituted not only a period of development of Soviet-Turkish economic and cultural relations, but a striking political demonstration of Soviet-Turkish friendship. Only recently, before the Soviet Revolution, Turkey, with her Constantinople and Straits, was the object of predatory imperialist aspirations of Russian reactionaries and liberals of all shades, representing the Russia of merchants, landlords, and manufacturers.

Between that epoch and Soviet Power an abyss has developed. The Soviet Power, as the power of workers and peasants, has proceeded and still proceeds from another policy which excludes the policy of plans of conquest.

Our relations with Great Britain have on the whole developed normally. . . .

In our relations with France there must be noted considerable improvement during the past period. The entire international situation, and especially the changes which have taken place in Europe, made most real the problem of insuring peace and security, in regard to which both the Soviet Union and France showed special interest. It must be emphasized that for the immediate future the significance of this problem has by no means decreased, and therefore the intended *rapprochement* has a favourable soil for development. Things will depend mostly on the consistency of the parties interested in carrying out the intended line.

As concerns Poland, we have in sufficient and evident form shown our desire for the further development of Soviet-Polish relations. However, we cannot say that we are satisfied with the results already achieved in this connexion. But we can firmly say that we intend to continue the course for the development of Soviet-Polish good neighbourly relations.

It is impossible to close our eyes to the changes that have taken place in Soviet-German relations with the coming to power of National-Socialism. As for ourselves we can say that we have not had and do not have any other wish than to continue further good relations with Germany also. In the path of Soviet-German relations, however, serious difficulties have arisen during the past period. . . .

Of course, it is not the super-nationalistic racial theories of the German nation as "masters" of the whole world which are the hindrance to the development of Soviet-German relations. Although we have not a high opinion of these "theories" we do not hide our deep respect for the German people, as one of the great nations of the modern epoch. We—internationalists—have proved in fact the deep respect of the Soviet power both for large and small nations, both for the nations of the Soviet Union and also for the nations of other countries. In this lies one of the signs of the great strength of the principles of the Soviet power. On the contrary, in reactionary racial theories we see a sign of doom. . . .

And so it is not a matter of these "theories," but of that which lies at the base of the foreign policy of modern Germany. We are forced to put this question directly, as clarity in our mutual relations can only be of benefit. One circumstance draws our special attention. I have in mind the statement of Herr Hitler on Russia in his book *My Struggle,* which is now being especially widely spread through Germany. . . .

And we ask after this—does Hitler's statement on Russia, which is now being repeated in newer and newer editions of his book, remain in force? Does there remain in force the statement made by Herr Hitler on the necessity of passing to a "policy of territorial conquest" in the East of Europe and of "when we (National-Socialists) speak of new lands in Europe, then we can in the first place have in mind only Russia and the border states subordinate to her?" Evidently this statement remains in force, as only on this surmise does a great deal become clear in the present relations of the German Government to the Soviet Union and also to the project of the Eastern Pact.

That is just why we do not consider it possible to pass these statements of Herr Hitler by. Let the toilers of the Soviet Union know how matters stand. All we want is clarity on this question. And as the above statements of Herr Hitler apparently remain in force, we will reckon with this fact and from it draw conclusions for ourselves.

Finally, about our relations with Japan.

Throughout the whole of this period we displayed in these relations patience and the requisite compliance, aiming at avoiding each and every cause for sharpening Soviet-Japanese relations. Such was our attitude towards the solution of disputed questions in the economic sphere, when the question was one of the areas and the methods of fishing in Soviet waters by Japanese citizens, when the question was one of Japanese concessions in Sakhalin, and so on. All know that, guided by its peace policy, the Soviet Government made a proposal to sell the Chinese Eastern Railway in Manchuria to Japan and Manchukuo, having it in view to remove in this way excuses for all kinds of conflicts. In this question the Soviet Government maintained a dignified yet flexible position and secured from the other side a withdrawal of the original inacceptable proposals. The negotiations for the sale of the Chinese Eastern Railway are now, apparently, approaching a near conclusion. We hope that our exertions towards improvement of Soviet-Japanese relations and the insuring of peace in the Far East will yield positive results.

But we have no ground whatever for complacency. The aggressive militant elements in Japan are not putting away their weapons. . . .

In all its foreign policy, the Soviet Government has proceeded from peace-loving aims and the desire to have normal relations and necessary commercial ties with other states. As a result of this policy we have secured the strengthening of our international position and an indisputable growth in the international authority of the Soviet Union.

In contradistinction to certain other countries, our foreign policy has been distinguished by perfect clarity and consistency. Our participation in international agreements has always been distinguished by the fact that our signature can be depended on. We have a right to expect the same clarity on the part of other states as well.

ADDRESS by Vyacheslav M. Molotov, President of the Soviet of People's Commissars, before the Central Executive Committee of the U.S.S.R., January 11, 1936

Translation, in Royal Institute of International Affairs, *Documents on International Affairs, 1935*, I, 222, citing official translation; excerpts

I SHALL NOW pass to the relations with Germany and Japan, which, for obvious reasons, attract the particular attention of the toilers of our country.

I shall begin with Germany.

I must say quite frankly that the Soviet Government would have desired the establishment of better relations with Germany than exist at present. This seems to us unquestionably expedient from the standpoint of the interests of the peoples both of the U.S.S.R. and of Germany. But the realization of such a policy depends not only on us, but also on the German Government.

And what is the foreign policy of the present German Government? I spoke of the principal trend of this foreign policy at the Seventh

Congress of Soviets, when I quoted from Herr Hitler's book *My Struggle,* which is in a sense a programme, and which is being distributed in Germany in millions of copies. In this book Herr Hitler definitely speaks of the necessity of adopting a "policy of territorial conquest." And in this connexion Herr Hitler makes no bones about declaring: "When we speak of new lands in Europe to-day we can only think in the first instance of Russia and her border States."

Since the time these statements of Herr Hitler's were read from the rostrum of the Congress of Soviets, the German Government has not made any attempt to deny these plans of aggrandizement at the expense of the Soviet Union, but, on the contrary, by its silence has fully confirmed that Herr Hitler's statements referred to still retain their validity. For us this was not unexpected. Carrying their plans to extremes, Messieurs the National Socialists, as we all know, are driving their preparations precisely in the direction of such aggrandizement, although not in this direction alone.

This criminal propaganda for the seizure of foreign territory has now found new followers outside Germany. . . .

Everybody knows that German Fascism is not merely confining itself to elaborating plans of conquest, but is preparing to act in the immediate future. The German Fascists have, in the sight of all, turned the country which has fallen into their hands into a military camp, which, owing to its position in the very centre of Europe, constitutes a menace not only to the Soviet Union. Even if we do not mention countries, who does not know that over Czechoslovakia, for instance, which is not threatening any of her neighbours and is engaged in peaceful toil, the dark clouds of German Fascism have gathered, bristling with soldiers' bayonets and mouths of guns, supplied with every known, and yesterday still unknown, chemical for poisoning and infecting people, and with swift and silent war-planes, for the purpose of unexpected attack, and armed with everything which converts modern warfare into a mass slaughter not only of soldiers at the front, but also of simple, peaceful citizens, women and children?

All this constitutes a growing menace to the peace of Europe, and not of Europe alone.

How contradictory the situation in present-day Germany is can be seen from the following:

Side by side with the desperate anti-Soviet foreign policy of definite ruling circles in Germany, at the initiative of the German Government an agreement between Germany and the U.S.S.R. was proposed and concluded on April 9, 1935, for a credit of 200,000,000 marks for a period of five years. On the whole, this credit is being successfully utilized by us just as is the five-year credit of 250,000,000 kroner accorded to us last year by Czechoslovakia. During the past few months representatives of the German Government have offered us a new and larger credit, this time for a period of ten years. Although we are not chasing after foreign credits and, in contradistinction to past days, are now to a large extent purchasing abroad for cash and not on credit, we have not refused, and are not now refusing, to consider also this business proposal of the German Government. . . .

Finally, as regards relations with Japan.

The Soviet Union has demonstrated its peaceable and accommodating spirit by concluding an agreement for the sale of the Chinese Eastern Railway in Manchuria. The agreement for the sale of the Chinese Eastern Railway was signed last March. The railway has been handed over to the Japanese-Manchurian authorities. The payments to the Soviet Union of the sums due for the Chinese Railway and the purchase of goods with these sums in Japan and Manchuria are proceeding normally. On all other practical questions the Soviet Union has also hitherto found ways of reaching agreement with Japan.

However, the principal question in the relations between the U.S.S.R. and Japan remains unsettled. Japan, so far, has evaded the proposal we made three years ago for the conclusion of a Soviet-Japanese treaty of non-aggression. Such conduct cannot be regarded otherwise than as suspicious.

On the other hand, there is no cessation or reduction in the number of attempts made by Japanese-Manchurian troops to violate our frontiers. . . .

We must continue to strengthen our Red Army, and at the same time utilize every opportunity of maintaining peace and of explaining to the toilers of all countries the special line of principle we are pursuing in the international policy of peace.

The fact that we have joined the League of Nations does not mean that there is no longer a fundamental difference in principle between Soviet foreign policy and the policy of the foreign Powers. The Italo-Abyssinian War shows that the contrary is the case. . . .

ADDRESS by Maxim Litvinov, People's Commissar for Foreign Affairs, before the Assembly of the League of Nations, September 21, 1938

League of Nations, *Official Journal*, Special Supplement No. 183, p. 74; excerpts

THE SUBJECT before us is the annual report of the Secretary-General on the League's work during the past twelve months. Quite naturally and rightly, however, the speakers so far have dealt, not with what the League has done during this year, but with what it has not done this year or in previous years. Evidently everyone recognises that the League of Nations was not set up for the activity recounted in the report presented by the League's Secretary-General.

It must not be forgotten that the League was created as a reaction to the world war and its countless horrors; that its object was to make that the last war, to safeguard all nations against aggression, and to replace the system of military alliances by the collective organisation of assistance to the victim of aggression. In this sphere the League has done nothing. Two States—Ethiopia and Austria—have lost their independent existence in consequence of violent aggression. A third State, China, is now a victim of aggression and foreign invasion for the second time in seven years, and a fourth State, Spain, is in the third year of a sanguinary war, owing to the armed intervention of two aggressors in its internal affairs. The League of Nations has not carried out its obligations to these States.

At the present time, a fifth State, Czechoslovakia, is suffering interference in its internal affairs at the hands of a neighbouring State, and is publicly and loudly menaced with attack. One of the oldest, most cultured, most hardworking of European peoples, which acquired its independence as a State after centuries of oppression, to-day or to-morrow may decide to take up arms in defence of that independence.

I am sure that the sympathies, if not of all Governments, then at any rate of all peoples represented at the Assembly, go out to the Czechoslovak people in this its terrible hour of trial; that we all remember the most active part played by Czechoslovakia and its present President, M. Beneš, in the organisation and development of the League of Nations; and that all our thoughts are so occupied with the events in Czechoslovakia and around it that we delegates find it difficult to give the necessary attention to the Assembly's agenda—in which Czechoslovakia is not mentioned. There is nothing surprising, therefore, in the fact that the general discussion has centred on what the League of Nations ought to have done, but did not do.

Unfortunately, our discussion has not been limited to the recording and explanation of the League's blunders and mistakes, but has included attempts retrospectively to justify them, and even to legalise them for the future. Various arguments have been used, among them the most favoured being a reference to the absence of universality. The shallowness of this argument has been pointed out more than once. The League of Nations was not any more universal during the first twelve years of its existence than it is to-day. From the outset it lacked three of the largest Powers and a multitude of smaller States. Furthermore, some States left it; others joined it; and up to the time of the first case of aggression it never crossed anyone's mind—or, at all events, no one expressed such views in the League—that the League could not fulfil its principal functions, and that therefore its Constitution should be altered and those functions, the functions of guardianship of peace, withdrawn.

No one has yet proved, and no one can prove, that the League of Nations refused to apply sanctions to the aggressor in this case or in that because States were absent from its ranks, and that this was the reason why sanctions, applied in one case, were prematurely brought to an end. Even composed as it is to-day, the League of Nations is still strong enough by its collective action to avert or arrest aggression. All that is necessary is that the obligatory character of such actions be confirmed, and that the machinery of the League of Nations be at least once brought into action in conformity with the Covenant. This requires only the goodwill of the States Members, for there are no objective reasons of such a character as to prevent the normal functioning of the League: at any rate, no such reasons as could not be foreseen by the founders of the League and by those States which later joined it. . . .

At a moment when the mines are being laid to blow up the organisation on which were fixed the great hopes of our generation, and which stamped a definite character on the international relations of our epoch; at a moment when, by no accidental coincidence, decisions are being taken outside the League which recall to us the international transactions of pre-war days, and which are bound to overturn all present conceptions of international morality and treaty obligations; at a moment when there is being drawn up a further list of sacrifices to the god of aggression, and a line is being drawn under the annals of all post-war international history, with the sole conclusion that nothing succeeds like aggression—at such a moment, every State must define its rôle and its responsibility before its contemporaries and before history. That is why I must plainly declare here that the Soviet Government bears no responsibility whatsoever for the events now taking place, and for the fatal consequences which may inexorably ensue.

After long doubts and hesitations, the Soviet Union joined the League in order to add the strength of a people of a hundred and seventy millions to the forces of peace. In the present hours of bitter disillusionment, the Soviet Union is far from regretting this decision, if only because there would undoubtedly have otherwise been attempts to attribute the alleged impotence and collapse of the League to its absence.

Having entered the League, the Soviet Union has been unfailingly loyal to the League obligations which it undertook, and has faithfully carried out, and expressed its readiness to perform, all the decisions and even recommendations of the League which were directed to preserving peace and combating the aggressors, irrespective of whether those decisions coincided with its immediate interests as a State.

Such was its attitude during the attack on Ethiopia. The Soviet delegation invariably insisted that the League should do its duty to Spain, and it is not the fault of the Soviet Union that the Spanish problem was withdrawn from the League of Nations and transferred to the so-called London Non-Intervention Committee, which, as we now all know, considers its object to be to avoid intervening in the intervention of the aggressive countries in Spanish affairs. The activity of the Soviet Government in relation to the Spanish events, both in the London Committee and outside it, has been permeated with the spirit of League of Nations principles and the established standards of international law. The same can be said likewise of the Chinese question. The Soviet delegation always insisted that the League of Nations should afford the maximum support to the victim of Japanese aggression, and those modest recommendations which the League of Nations adopted are being fulfilled more than loyally by the Soviet Government.

Such an event as the disappearance of Austria passed unnoticed by the League of Nations. Realising the significance of this event for the fate of the whole of Europe, and particularly of Czechoslovakia, the Soviet Government, immediately after the Anschluss, officially approached the other European Great Powers with a proposal for an immediate collective deliberation on the possible consequences of that event, in order to adopt collective preventive measures. To our regret, this proposal, which, if carried out, could have saved us from the alarm which all the world now feels for the fate of Czechoslovakia, did not receive its just appreciation.

Bound to Czechoslovakia by a pact of mutual assistance, the Soviet

Union abstained from any intervention in the negotiations of the Czechoslovak Government with the Sudeten Germans, considering this to be the internal business of the Czechoslovak State. We abstained from all advice to the Czechoslovak Government, considering quite inadmissible that it should be asked to make concessions to the Germans, to the detriment of its interests as a State, in order that we should be set free from the necessity of fulfilling our obligations under the treaty bearing our signature. Neither did we offer any advice in the contrary direction. We valued very highly the tact of the Czechoslovak Government, which did not even enquire of us whether we should fulfil our obligations under the pact, since obviously it had no doubt of this, and had no grounds for doubt. When, a few days before I left for Geneva, the French Government for the first time enquired as to our attitude in the event of an attack on Czechoslovakia, I gave in the name of my Government the following perfectly clear and unambiguous reply.

We intend to fulfil our obligations under the pact and, together with France, to afford assistance to Czechoslovakia by the ways open to us. Our War Department is ready immediately to participate in a conference with representatives of the French and Czechoslovak War Departments, in order to discuss the measures appropriate to the moment. Independently of this, we should consider desirable that the question be raised at the League of Nations if only as yet under Article 11, with the object, first, of mobilising public opinion and, secondly, of ascertaining the position of certain other States, whose passive aid might be extremely valuable. It was necessary, however, to exhaust all means of averting an armed conflict, and we considered one such method to be an immediate consultation between the Great Powers of Europe and other interested States, in order if possible to decide on the terms of a collective *démarche*.

This is how our reply was framed. It was only two days ago that the Czechoslovak Government addressed a formal enquiry to my Government as to whether the Soviet Union is prepared, in accordance with the Soviet-Czech pact, to render Czechoslovakia immediate and effective aid if France, loyal to her obligations, will render similar assistance, to which my Government gave a clear answer in the affirmative.

I believe it will be admitted that both were replies of a loyal signatory of an international agreement and of a faithful servant of the League. It is not our fault if no effect was given to our proposals, which, I am convinced, could have produced the desired results, both in the interests of Czechoslovakia, and in those of all Europe and of general peace. Unfortunately, other steps were taken, which have led, and which could not but lead, to such a capitulation as is bound sooner or later to have quite incalculable and disastrous consequences.

To avoid a problematic war to-day and receive in return a certain and large-scale war to-morrow—moreover, at the price of assuaging the appetites of insatiable aggressors and of the destruction or mutilation of sovereign States—is not to act in the spirit of the Covenant of the League of Nations. To grant bonuses for sabre-rattling and recourse to arms for the solution of international problems—in other words, to reward and encourage aggressive super-imperialism—is not to act in the spirit of the Briand-Kellogg Pact.

The Soviet Government takes pride in the fact that it has no part in such a policy, and has invariably pursued the principles of the two pacts I have mentioned, which were approved by nearly every nation in the world. Nor has it any intention of abandoning them for the future, being convinced that in present conditions it is impossible otherwise to safeguard a genuine peace and genuine international justice. It calls upon other Governments likewise to return to this path.

ADDRESS by Vyacheslav M. Molotov, President of the Council of People's Commissars and People's Commissar for Foreign Affairs, before the Supreme Soviet, May 31, 1939

Translation, in *The New York Times,* June 1, 1939; excerpts. Reprinted by permission of the Associated Press

THE MOTION of the Deputies that the session of the Supreme Soviet should hear a statement of the People's Commissariat of Foreign Affairs is quite understandable. Recently serious changes have taken place in the international situation. These changes, from the point of view of peace-loving powers, have considerably worsened the international situation.

We now have to deal with certain results of the policy of the aggressive powers, on the one hand, and of the policy of non-intervention on the part of the democratic countries, on the other hand. Representatives of aggressive countries are not averse to boasting about the results of their policy of aggression already achieved. Whatever one may say, there is no want of boasting observed here.

Representatives of the democratic countries, which have turned away from the policy of collective security and have conducted a policy of non-resistance to aggression, are endeavoring to belittle the significance of the worsening that has taken place in the international situation. They still continue to occupy themselves in the main with "soothing" public opinion and pretending that nothing substantial has taken place in the recent period.

The position of the Soviet Union in appraising current events of international life differs from that of both the one and the other party. As everybody understands, it can under no circumstances be suspected of any sympathy whatsoever for aggressors. It is also alien to all glossing over of the really worsened international situation.

To us it is clear that attempts to hide from public opinion the real changes that have taken place in the international situation must be countered by the facts. It will then become obvious that "soothing" speeches and articles are only needed by those who have no desire to hinder the further development of aggression, in the hope of turning aggression, so to speak, in a more or less "acceptable" direction.

Just recently authoritative representatives of Britain and France endeavored to soothe the public opinion of their countries by glorifying the successes of the ill-starred Munich agreement. They said that the September agreement in Munich averted European war by means of concessions on the part of Czecho-Slovakia that comparatively were not so big after all.

It seemed to many people already at that time that the representatives of Britain and France went further in Munich in their concessions at the expense of Czecho-Slovakia than they had a right to do. The Munich agreement was, so to speak, a culminating point of the policy of non-intervention, the culminating point of compromise with the aggressive countries.

And what were the results of this policy? Did the Munich agreement put a stop to aggression? Not at all. On the contrary, Germany did not rest content with the concessions she received in Munich—that is, with obtaining the Sudeten areas populated by Germans. Germany went farther and just simply put an end to one of the large Slav States—Czecho-Slovakia. Not much time passed after September, 1938, when the Munich conference took place, before Germany put an end to the existence of Czecho-Slovakia in March, 1939.

Germany succeeded in carrying this through without resistance from any side whatsoever, and so smoothly that the question arises, What in reality was the true aim of the conference in Munich?

In any case the elimination of Czecho-Slovakia, despite the Munich agreement, showed the whole world where the policy of non-intervention had led, a policy which in Munich, it can be said, reached its acme. The collapse of this policy was obvious. Yet the aggressor countries continued to adhere to their policy. Germany deprived the

Lithuanian republic of Memel and the Memel region. As we know, Italy was not behindhand. In April Italy put an end to the independent State of Albania.

After this there is nothing surprising in the fact that at the end of April the head of the German State in one speech abolished two important international treaties—namely, the naval agreement between Germany and Great Britain, and the non-aggression pact between Germany and Poland.

There was a time when great international significance was attached to these treaties. Germany, however, made away with these treaties very simply, disregarding all formalities. Such was Germany's reply to United States President Roosevelt's proposal, a proposal permeated with a peace-loving spirit.

Matters did not end with the tearing up of two international treaties. Germany and Italy went farther. The other day a military and political treaty concluded between them was published. This treaty is basically of an offensive character. According to this treaty, Germany and Italy are to support one another in any hostilities begun by one of these countries, including any aggression, any offensive war.

It is not so long since *rapprochement* between Germany and Italy was camouflaged by the alleged need for a joint struggle against communism. To this end quite a lot of noise was made about the so-called "anti-Comintern pact." The hullabaloo, in its time, played a certain part in distracting attention. Now aggressors no longer consider it necessary to use as a screen.

There is not a murmur about the struggle against the Comintern in the military and political treaty between Germany and Italy. On the other hand, the statesmen and the press of Germany and Italy definitely state that this treaty is directed precisely against the chief European democratic countries.

It seems clear that the facts mentioned testify to a grave change for the worse in the international situation. In this connection certain changes in the direction of resisting aggression are also to be observed in the policy of the non-aggressive countries of Europe. How serious these changes are is still to be seen. As yet it cannot even be said whether these countries are seriously desirous of abandoning the policy of non-intervention, the policy of non-resistance to the further development of aggression.

Will it not happen that the existing endeavor of these countries to restrict aggression in some regions will not serve as an obstacle to the unloosing of aggression in other regions? Such questions are being raised in certain bourgeois periodicals abroad, too. We must, therefore, be vigilant.

We stand for peace and for preventing the further development of aggression. But we must remember Comrade Stalin's precept: "To be cautious and not to allow our country to be drawn into conflicts by warmongers who are accustomed to have others pull chestnuts out of the fire for them."

Only thus will we succeed in defending to the end the interests of our country and the interests of universal peace.

There are, however, a number of signs showing that the democratic countries of Europe are increasingly coming to realize that the non-intervention policy has collapsed, to realize the need for a more serious search for ways and means to establish a united front of peaceable powers against aggression. In a country like Great Britain the people are beginning to talk loudly of the need for a sharp change of foreign policy.

We, of course, understand the difference between verbal declarations and real policy. Nevertheless, one cannot but note that this talk is not accidental. Here are a few facts. There was no mutual assistance pact between Great Britain and Poland. Now a decision has been reached about such a pact. The significance of this pact is only enhanced by the fact that Germany has torn up her non-aggression pact with Poland. It must be admitted that the mutual assistance pact between Britain and Poland alters the European situation.

Further, there was no mutual assistance pact between Great Britain and Turkey, but recently a certain agreement regarding mutual assistance between Great Britain and Turkey was arrived at. And this fact, too, alters the international situation.

In connection with these new facts it must be regarded as one of the characteristics of the recent period that non-aggressive European powers have been endeavoring to get the U.S.S.R. to collaborate in resisting aggression. Naturally this endeavor deserves attention.

Accordingly, the Soviet Government accepted the proposal of Great Britain and France to enter negotiations with the purpose of strengthening political relations between the U.S.S.R., Great Britain and France and establishing a peace front against the further development of aggression.

How do we define our tasks in the present international situation? We consider they are in line with the interests of other non-aggressive countries. They consist in checking the further development of aggression, and to this end of establishing a reliable and effective defensive front of non-aggressive powers.

In connection with the proposals made by the British and French Governments, the Soviet Government entered into negotiations with them regarding the measures necessary for combating aggression.

This was as far back as the middle of last April. Negotiations then begun are not yet ended.

But even at that time it was apparent that if there was a real wish to create an effective front of peaceable countries against the advance of aggression the following minimum conditions were necessary:

Conclusion of an effective pact of mutual assistance against aggression, a pact of exclusively defensive character between Great Britain, France and the U.S.S.R.;

A guarantee against attack by aggressors on the part of Great Britain, France and the U.S.S.R., to the States of Central and Eastern Europe, including all European countries bordering on the U.S.S.R., without exception;

Conclusion of a concrete agreement by Great Britain, France and the U.S.S.R. regarding the form and extent of immediate and effective assistance to be given to each other and to the guaranteed States in event of attack by aggressors.

Such is our opinion, an opinion we force upon nobody, but to which we adhere. We do not demand acceptance of our point of view and do not ask anybody to do so. We consider, however, that this point of view really answers the interests of the security of peaceable States.

It would be an agreement of exclusively defensive character, operating against attack on the part of aggressors, and fundamentally differing from the military and offensive alliance recently concluded between Germany and Italy. Naturally the basis of such an agreement is the principle of reciprocity and equality of obligations. . . .

I shall dwell very briefly on Far Eastern questions and our relations with Japan. Here the most important event of this year was our negotiation with Japan on the fisheries question. As you know, the Japanese have a large number of fisheries in our waters in the Maritime Province, in the Sea of Okhotsk, in Sakhalin and Kamchatka. Toward the end of last year they had 384 fishing lots. Meanwhile the term of the convention, on the basis of which the Japanese received these lots, had already expired. In the case of many of the lots the previously established terms of lease had also expired.

The Soviet Government, therefore, entered into negotiations with Japan on the fisheries question. We declared that a certain number of lots whose established term lease had expired could no longer be placed at the disposal of the Japanese because of strategic considerations.

Despite the obvious justification of our position, the Soviet point of view met with great resistance on the part of the Japanese. After protracted negotiations, thirty-seven fishing lots were withdrawn from the Japanese and ten new lots were granted to them in other places.

Following this, the convention was extended for another year. This agreement with Japan on the fisheries question is of great political importance, the more so that Japanese reactionary circles did everything to stress the political aspect of this affair, even to the extent of using all sorts of threats.

However, Japanese reactionaries have had another opportunity to convince themselves that threats to the Soviet Union miss their aim and that the rights of the Soviet State are securely protected.

Now as regards frontier questions. It seems that by now those concerned should realize that the Soviet Government will not tolerate any provocation on the part of Japanese-Manchurian troops on its borders. We must now remind them of this with regard to the frontiers of the Mongolian People's Republic as well.

In accordance with the pact of mutual assistance between the U.S.S.R. and the Mongolian People's Republic, we deem it our duty to render the Mongolian People's Republic the necessary help in protecting her borders. We take seriously such things as a pact of mutual assistance signed by the Soviet Government. I must warn that, on the strength of the pact of mutual assistance concluded between us, we will defend the frontiers of the Mongolian People's Republic with the same determination as our own frontiers.

It is time to realize that accusations of aggression leveled by Japan against the government of the Mongolian People's Republic are ridiculous and absurd. It is also time to realize that there is a limit to all patience. It would therefore be best for them to drop in good time the constantly recurring provocative violations of the frontiers of the U.S.S.R. and the Mongolian People's Republic by Japanese and Manchurian military units.

We have given warning to this effect through the Japanese Ambassador in Moscow as well.

There is no need for me to deal with our attitude toward China. You are well acquainted with Stalin's statement regarding the support for nations which have become victims of aggression and are fighting for the independence of their countries.

This fully applies to China and her struggle for national independence. We are consistently carrying out this policy in practice. It is fully in line with the task that faces us in Europe—namely, establishment of a united front of peaceful powers against the further extension of aggression.

The U.S.S.R. today is not what it was, say, in 1921, when it was just starting its peaceful constructive work.

We must remind people of this because even to this day some of our neighbors are apparently unable to realize this. The fact must also be recognized that the U.S.S.R. is no longer what it was only five or ten years ago, that the U.S.S.R. has grown in strength.

The foreign policy of the Soviet Union must reflect the changes in the international situation and the greater role of the U.S.S.R. as a powerful factor of peace. There is no need to show that the foreign policy of the Soviet Union is fundamentally peaceful and opposed to aggression. Aggressor countries themselves are best aware of this.

Some of the Democratic powers very belatedly and hesitatingly are coming to realize this plain truth. Yet the Soviet Union cannot but occupy a foremost place in a united front of peaceable States that are really opposing aggression.

ADDRESS by Vyacheslav M. Molotov, President of the Council of People's Commissars and People's Commissar for Foreign Affairs, before the Supreme Soviet, October 31, 1939

Translation, in *The New York Times,* November 1, 1939; excerpts. Reprinted by permission of the Associated Press

COMRADE DEPUTIES:

There have been important changes in the international situation during the past two months. This applies above all to Europe, but also to countries far beyond the confines of Europe. In this connection mention must be made of three principal circumstances which are of decisive importance.

First, mention should be made of the changes that have taken place in the relations between the Soviet Union and Germany. Since the conclusion of the Soviet-German non-aggression pact on Aug. 23, an end has been put to the abnormal relations that have existed between the Soviet Union and Germany for a number of years.

Instead of the enmity that was fostered in every way by certain European powers, we now have a *rapprochement* and the establishment of friendly relations between the U.S.S.R. and Germany. Further improvement of these new relations, good relations, found its reflection in the German-Soviet treaty on amity and frontier signed in Moscow Sept. 28.

This radical change in relations between the Soviet Union and Germany, the two biggest States in Europe, was bound to have its affect on the entire international situation. Furthermore, events have entirely confirmed the estimate of the political significance of the

GENERAL STATEMENTS OF POLICY

Soviet-German *rapprochement* given at the last session of the Supreme Soviet.

Second, mention must be made of such a fact as the defeat of Poland in war and the collapse of the Polish State. The ruling circles of Poland boasted quite a lot about the "stability" of their State and the "might" of their army. However, one swift blow to Poland, first by the German Army and then by the Red Army, and nothing was left of this ugly offspring of the Versailles treaty which had existed by oppressing non-Polish nationalities.

The "traditional policy" of unprincipled manoeuvring between Germany and the U.S.S.R., and the playing of one against the other has proved unsound and has suffered complete bankruptcy.

Third, it must be admitted that the big war that has flared up in Europe has caused radical changes in the entire international situation. It is a war begun as a war between Germany and Poland and turned into a war between Germany on the one hand and Britain and France on the other.

The war between Germany and Poland ended quickly owing to the utter bankruptcy of the Polish leaders. As we know, neither the British nor the French guarantees were of help to Poland. To this day, in fact, nobody knows what these "guarantees" were.

The war between Germany and the Anglo-French bloc is only in its first stage and has not yet been really developed. It is nevertheless clear that a war like this was bound to cause radical changes in the situation in Europe and not only in Europe. In connection with these important changes in the international situation, certain old formulas, which we employed but recently and to which many people are so accustomed, are now obviously out of date and unapplicable.

We must be quite clear on this point so as to avoid making gross errors in judging the new political situation that has developed in Europe.

We know, for example, that in the past few months such concepts as "aggression" and "aggressor" have acquired a new concrete connotation, a new meaning. It is not hard to understand that we can no longer employ these concepts in the sense we did, say, three or four months ago.

Today, as far as the European great powers are concerned, Germany is in the position of a State that is striving for the earliest termination of the war and for peace, while Britain and France, which but yesterday were declaiming against aggression, are in favor of continuing the war and are opposed to the conclusion of peace. The roles, as you see, are changing.

Efforts of the British and French Governments to justify their new position on the grounds of their undertakings to Poland are, of course, obviously unsound. Everybody realizes that there can be no question of restoring the old Poland.

It is, therefore, absurd to continue the present war under the flag of the restoration of the former Polish State. Although the Governments of Britain and France understand this they do not want the war stopped and peace restored but are seeking new excuses for continuing the war with Germany.

The ruling circles of Britain and France have been lately attempting to depict themselves as champions of the democratic rights of nations against Hitlerism and the British Government has announced that its aim in the war with Germany is nothing more nor less than "the destruction of Hitlerism." It amounts to this, that the British, and with them the French supporters of the war, have declared something in the nature of an "ideological" war on Germany, reminiscent of the religious wars of olden times.

In fact, religious wars against heretics and religious dissenters were once the fashion. As we know, they led to direst results for the masses, to economic ruin and the cultural deterioration of nations.

These wars could have no other outcome. But they were wars of the Middle Ages. Is it back to the Middle Ages, to the days of religious wars, superstition and cultural deterioration that the ruling classes of Britain and France want to drag us?

In any case under an "ideological" flag has now been started a war of even greater dimensions and fraught with even greater danger for the peoples of Europe and the whole world. But there is absolutely no justification for a war of this kind. One may accept or reject the ideology of Hitlerism as well as any other ideological system; that is a matter of political views.

But everybody would understand that an ideology cannot be destroyed by force, that it cannot be eliminated by war. It is, therefore, not only senseless but criminal to wage such a war as the war for "the destruction of Hitlerism," camouflaged as a fight for "democracy." And, indeed, you cannot give the name of a fight for democracy to such action as the banning of the Communist party in France, arrests of the Communist Deputies in the French Parliament, or the curtailing of political liberties in England or the unremitting national oppression in India, etc.

Is it not clear that the aim of the present war in Europe is not what it is proclaimed to be in the official statements intended for the public in France and England? That is, it is not a fight for democracy but something else of which these gentlemen do not speak openly.

The real cause of the Anglo-French war with Germany was not that Britain and France had vowed to restore old Poland and not, of course, that they decided to undertake a fight for democracy. The ruling circles of Britain and France have, of course, other and more actual motives for going to war with Germany. These motives do not lie in any ideology but in their profoundly material interests as mighty colonial powers.

Great Britain, with a population of 47,000,000, possesses colonies with a population of 480,000,000. The colonial empire of France, whose population does not exceed 42,000,000, embraces a population of 72,000,000 in the French colonies. The possession of these colonies, which makes possible the exploitation of hundreds of millions of people, is the foundation of the world supremacy of Great Britain and France. It is the fear of Germany's claim to these colonial possessions that is at the bottom of the present war of England and France with Germany, who has grown substantially stronger lately as the result of the collapse of the Versailles treaty.

It is fear of losing world supremacy that dictates to the ruling circles of Great Britain and France the policy of fomenting war with Germany. Thus the imperialist character of this war is obvious to any one who wants to face realities and does not close his eyes to facts.

One can see from all this who is interested in this war which is being waged for world supremacy. Certainly not the working class. This war promises nothing to the working class but bloody sacrifice and hardships.

Well, now, judge for yourselves whether the meaning of such concepts as "aggression" and "aggressor" has changed recently or not. It is not difficult to see that the use of these words in their old meaning, that is, the meaning attached to them before the recent decisive turn in the political relations between the Soviet Union and Germany and before the outbreak of the great imperialist war in Europe, can only create confusion in the people's minds and must inevitably lead to erroneous conclusions.

To avoid this we must not allow an uncritical attitude toward the old concepts, which are no longer applicable in the new international situation. That has been the course of international affairs in the recent period.

I shall now pass the changes that have taken place in the international position of the Soviet Union itself. Here the changes have been no mean ones; but, if we confine ourselves to essentials, the following must be admitted, namely, that thanks to our consistently pursued peaceful foreign policy we have succeeded in considerably strengthening our position and the international weight of the Soviet Union.

As I have said, our relations with Germany have radically improved. Here development has proceeded along the line of strengthening our friendly relations, extending our practical co-operation and rendering Germany political support in her efforts for peace.

The non-aggression pact concluded between the Soviet Union and Germany bound us to maintain neutrality in case of Germany's participating in war. We have consistently pursued this course, which was in no wise contradicted by the entry of our troops into territory of the former Poland, which began Sept. 17.

It will be sufficient to recall the fact that on that same day, Sept. 17, the Soviet Government sent a special note to all the States with which it maintains diplomatic relations, declaring that the U.S.S.R. will continue its policy of neutrality in its relations with them.

It is known that our troops entered the territory of Poland only after the Polish State had collapsed and actually ceased to exist. Naturally, we could not remain neutral toward these facts, since as a result of these events we were confronted with urgent problems concerning the security of our State.

Furthermore, the Soviet Government could not but reckon with the exceptional situation created for our brothers in Western Ukraine and Western White Russia, who had been abandoned to their fate as a result of the collapse of Poland.

Subsequent events fully confirmed that the new Soviet-German relations are based on the firm foundation of mutual interests. After Red Army units entered the territory of the former Polish State serious questions arose relating to the delimitation of the State interests of the U.S.S.R. and Germany. These questions were promptly settled by mutual agreement.

The German-Soviet treaty on amity and frontier between the U.S.S.R. and Germany, concluded at the end of September, has consolidated our relations with the German State. Relations between Germany and the other West European bourgeois States have in the past two decades been determined primarily by Germany's efforts to break the fetters of the Versailles treaty, whose authors were Great Britain and France with the active participation of the United States. This, in the long run, led to the present war in Europe.

The relations between the Soviet Union and Germany have been based on a different foundation which had no interest whatever in perpetuating the post-war Versailles system. We have always held that a strong Germany is an indispensable condition for a durable peace in Europe.

It would be ridiculous to think that Germany could be "simply put out of commission" and struck off the books. The powers that cherish this foolish and dangerous dream ignore the deplorable experience of Versailles, do not realize Germany's increased might, and fail to see that any attempt at repetition of Versailles in the present state of international affairs, which radically differ from that of 1914, may end in disaster for them. . . .

I shall now pass on to our relations with the Baltic countries. As you know, important changes have taken place in this sphere as well.

The relations of the Soviet Union with Estonia, Latvia and Lithuania are based on peace treaties concluded with the respective countries in 1920. By these treaties Estonia, Latvia and Lithuania became independent States, and ever since then the Soviet Union has invariably pursued a friendly policy toward these newly created small States.

This was the reflection of a radical difference between the policy of the Soviet Government and the policy of Czarist Russia, which brutally oppressed the small nations, denied them every opportunity of independent national and political development and left them with the most painful memories of it.

It must be admitted that the experience of the past two decades of the development of Soviet-Estonian, Soviet-Latvian and Soviet-Lithuanian friendly relations created favorable conditions for the further consolidation of political and all other relations between the U.S.S.R. and its Baltic neighbors. This has been revealed, too, in the recent diplomatic negotiations with representatives of Latvia, Estonia and Lithuania and in treaties that were signed in Moscow as a result of these negotiations.

As you know, the Soviet Union has concluded pacts of mutual assistance with Estonia, Latvia and Lithuania that are of major political significance. The principles underlying all these pacts are identical. They are based on mutual assistance between the Soviet Union, on the one hand, and Estonia, Latvia and Lithuania on the other, and they include military assistance in case any of these countries is attacked.

In view of the special geographic position of these countries, which are, in a way, approaches to the U.S.S.R., particularly from the Baltic, these pacts allow the Soviet Union to maintain naval bases and airfields in specified parts of Estonia and Latvia, and, in the case of Lithuania, the pact provides for defense of Lithuanian borders jointly with the Soviet Union. . . .

The special character of these mutual assistance pacts in no way implies any interference by the Soviet Union in the affairs of Estonia,

Latvia or Lithuania, as some foreign newspapers are trying to make out. On the contrary, all these pacts of mutual assistance strictly stipulate the inviolability of the sovereignty of the signatory States and the principle of non-interference in each other's affairs.

These pacts are based on mutual respect for the political, social and economic structure of the contracting parties, and are designed to strengthen the basis for peaceful, neighborly cooperation between our peoples. We stand for the scrupulous and punctilious observance of pacts on a basis of complete reciprocity, and we declare that all nonsense about sovietizing the Baltic countries is only to the interest of our common enemies and of all anti-Soviet provocateurs. In view of the improvement in our political relations with Estonia, Latvia and Lithuania, the Soviet Union has gone a long way to meet the economic needs of these States and has concluded trade agreements with them.

Thanks to these economic agreements, trade with the Baltic countries will increase several fold, and there are favorable prospects for its further growth. At a time when all European countries, including neutral States, are experiencing tremendous trade difficulties, these economic agreements between the U.S.S.R. and Estonia, Latvia and Lithuania are of great and positive importance to them.

Thus the rapprochement between the U.S.S.R. on the one hand and Estonia, Latvia and Lithuania on the other will contribute to more rapid progress of agriculture, industry and transport and in general to the national well-being of our Baltic neighbors.

The principles of Soviet policy toward small countries have been demonstrated with particular force by the treaty providing for the transfer of the city of Vilna and the Vilna region to the Lithuanian Republic. Thereby the Lithuanian State, with its population of 2,500,000, considerably extends its territory, increases its population by 550,000 and receives the city of Vilna, whose population is almost double that of the present Lithuanian capital.

The Soviet Union agreed to transfer the city of Vilna to the Lithuanian Republic not because Vilna has a predominantly Lithuanian population. No, the majority of the inhabitants of Vilna are non-Lithuanian. But the Soviet Government took into consideration the fact that the city of Vilna, which was forcibly wrested from Lithuania by Poland, ought to belong to Lithuania as a city with which are associated on the one hand the historical past of the Lithuanian State and on the other hand the national aspirations of the Lithuanian people.

It has been pointed out in the foreign press that there has never been a case in world history of a big country's handing over such a big city to a small State of its own free will. All the more strikingly, therefore, does this act of the Soviet State demonstrate its goodwill.

Our relations with Finland are of a special character. This is to be explained chiefly by the fact that in Finland there is a greater amount of outside influence on the part of third powers. An impartial person must admit, however, that the same problems concerning the security of the Soviet Union and particularly of Leningrad which figured in the negotiations with Estonia also figure in the negotiations with Finland. In a certain sense it may be said that in this case the problem of the Soviet Union's security is even more acute inasmuch as Leningrad, which after Moscow is the most important city of the Soviet State, is situated at a distance of only thirty-two kilometers from the Finnish border. This means that the distance of Leningrad from the border of a foreign State is less than that required for modern long-range guns to shell it. On the other hand, the approaches to Leningrad from the sea also depend to a large extent on whether Finland, which owns the entire northern shore of the Gulf of Finland and all the islands along the central part of the Gulf of Finland, is hostile or friendly toward the Soviet Union. In view of this, as well as in view of the present situation in Europe, it may be expected that Finland will display necessary understanding.

What has been the basis of the relations between the Soviet Union and Finland during all these years? As you know, the basis of these relations has been the peace treaty of 1920, which was on the pattern of our treaties with our other Baltic neighbors. Of its own free will the Soviet Union insured the separated and independent existence of Finland.

There can be no doubt that only the Soviet Government, which recognizes the principle of the free development of nationalities, could make such a step. It must be said that none but the Soviet Government in Russia could tolerate the existence of an independent Finland at the very gates of Leningrad.

This is eloquently testified by Finland's experience with the "democratic" government of Kerensky and Tsereteli, not to mention the government of Prince Lvov and Milyukoff, let alone the Czarist government. Doubtless this important circumstance might serve as a sound premise for the improvement in Soviet-Finnish relations, in which, as may be seen, Finland is no less interested than the Soviet Union.

Soviet-Finnish negotiations were begun recently on our initiative. What is the subject of these negotiations? It is not difficult to see that in the present state of international affairs, when in the center of Europe war is developing between some of the biggest States, a war fraught with great surprises and dangers for all European States, the Soviet Union is not only entitled but obliged to adopt serious measures to increase its security.

It is natural for the Soviet Government to display particular concern with regard to the Gulf of Finland, which is the approach to Leningrad from the sea, and also with regard to the land border which hangs over Leningrad some thirty kilometers away.

I must remind you that the population of Leningrad has grown to 3,500,000, which almost equals the entire population of Finland, amounting to 3,650,000.

There is scarcely any need to dwell on the tales spread by the foreign press about the Soviet Union's proposals in the negotiations with Finland. Some assert the U.S.S.R. "demands" the city of Vyborg and the northern part of Lake Ladoga. Let us say for our part that this is a sheer fabrication and lie.

Others assert that the U.S.S.R. demands the cession of the Aland Islands. This is also a fabrication and lie.

There is also nonsensical talk about some allegedly existing claims of the Soviet Union against Sweden and Norway. But these irresponsible lies are not even worth refuting.

Actually our proposals in the negotiations with Finland are extremely modest and are confined to that minimum without which it is impossible to safeguard the security of the U.S.S.R. and to put on a firm footing the friendly relations with Finland.

We have begun negotiations with Finnish representatives. [Juho] Paasikivi and [V. A.] Tanner were sent for this purpose by the Finnish Government to Moscow, proposing the conclusion of a Soviet-Finnish pact of mutual assistance approximately on the lines of our pacts of mutual assistance with other Baltic States, but inasmuch as the Finnish Government declared that the conclusion of such a pact would contradict its position of absolute neutrality we did not insist on our proposal.

We then proposed that we proceed to discuss concrete questions in which we are interested from the standpoint of safeguarding the security of the U.S.S.R. and especially of Leningrad, both from the sea—in the Gulf of Finland—and from the land in view of the extreme proximity of the border to Leningrad.

We have proposed that an agreement be reached to shift the Soviet-Finnish border on the Isthmus of Karelia several dozen kilometers further to the north of Leningrad. In exchange for this we have proposed to transfer to Finland part of Soviet Karelia double the size of the territory which Finland is to transfer to the Soviet Union.

We have further proposed that an agreement be reached for Finland to lease to us for a definite term a small section of her territory near the entrance to the Gulf of Finland where we might establish a naval base. With a Soviet naval base at the southern entrance to the Gulf of Finland, namely at Baltic Port, as provided for by the Soviet-Estonian pact of mutual assistance, the establishment of a naval base at the northern entrance to the Gulf of Finland would fully safeguard the Gulf of Finland against hostile attempts on the part of other states.

We have no doubt that the establishment of such a base would not only be in the interests of the Soviet Union but also of the security of Finland herself.

Our other proposals, in particular our proposal as regards the exchange of certain islands in the Gulf of Finland as well as parts of the Rybachi and Sredni peninsulas for territory twice as large in Soviet Karelia evidently do not meet with any objections on the part of the Finnish Government. Differences with regard to certain of our proposals have not yet been overcome, and concessions made by Finland in this respect, as for instance the cession of part of the territory of the Isthmus of Karelia obviously do not meet the purpose.

We have further made a number of new steps to meet Finland half way. We declared that if our main proposals are accepted we shall be prepared to drop our objections to the fortification of the Aland Islands, on which the Finnish Government has been insisting for a long time. We only made one stipulation. We said that we would drop our objection to fortification of the Aland Islands on condition that the fortification is done by Finland's own national forces without the participation of any third country, inasmuch as the U.S.S.R. will take no part in it.

We have also proposed to Finland to disarm the fortified zones along the entire Soviet-Finnish border on the Isthmus of Karelia, which should fully accord with the interests of Finland. We have further expressed our desire to reinforce the Soviet-Finnish pact of non-aggression with additional mutual guarantees.

Lastly, consolidation of Soviet-Finnish political relations would undoubtedly form a splendid basis for the rapid development of economic relations between the two countries. Thus we are ready to meet Finland in matters in which she is particularly interested.

In view of all this we do not think that Finland will seek a pretext to frustrate the proposed agreement. . . .

A few words about our negotiations with Turkey. All kinds of tales are being spread abroad regarding the substance of these negotiations. Some allege that the U.S.S.R. demanded cession of the district of Ardagan and Kars. Let us say for our part that this is a sheer fabrication and lie.

Others allege that the U.S.S.R. has demanded changes in the international convention concluded at Montreux and a privileged position as regards the Straits. That is also a fabrication and lie.

As a matter of fact the subject at issue was the conclusion of a bilateral pact of mutual assistance limited to the regions of the Black Sea and the Straits. The U.S.S.R. considered: First, that the conclusion of such a pact could not induce it to actions which might draw it into armed conflict with Germany; second, that the U.S.S.R. should have a guarantee that in view of a war danger Turkey would not allow warships of non-Black Sea powers through the Bosporus to the Black Sea.

Turkey rejected both these stipulations of the U.S.S.R. and thereby made the conclusion of a pact impossible.

The Soviet-Turkish negotiations did not lead to the conclusion of a pact but they did help to clear up or at least to explore a number of political questions that interest us. In the present international situation it is particularly important to know the true fact and policy of States, relations with whom are of serious importance.

Many things pertaining to the policy of Turkey have now become much clearer to us, both as a result of the Moscow negotiations and as a result of recent acts of the Turkish Government in the sphere of foreign policy. As you know, the Government of Turkey has preferred to tie up its destinies with a definite group of European powers, belligerents in the present war. It has concluded a pact of mutual assistance with Great Britain and France, who for the past two months have been waging war on Germany.

Turkey has thereby definitely discarded her cautious policy of neutrality and has entered the orbit of the developing European war. This is highly pleasing to both Great Britain and France, who are bent on drawing as many neutral countries as possible into their sphere of war.

Whether Turkey will not come to regret it we shall not try to guess. It is only incumbent on us to take note of these new factors in the foreign policy of our neighbor and to keep a watchful eye on the developments of events.

If Turkey has now to some extent tied her hands and has taken the hazardous line of supporting one group of belligerents, the Turkish Government evidently realizes the responsibility it has thereby assumed. But that is not the foreign policy the Soviet Union is pursuing, thanks to which it has secured not a few successes in the sphere of foreign policy.

GENERAL STATEMENTS OF POLICY

The Soviet Union prefers to keeps its hands free in the future as well, to go on consistently pursuing its policy of neutrality and not only not to help the spread of war but to help strengthen whatever strivings there are for the restoration of peace.

We are confident that the policy of peace the U.S.S.R. has been consistently pursuing holds out the best prospects for the future as well. And this policy we will pursue in the region of the Black Sea, too, confident that we shall fully insure its proper application as the interests of the Soviet Union and of the States friendly to the Soviet Union demand.

Now, as regards our relations with Japan. There has recently been certain improvement in Soviet-Japanese relations. The symptoms of this improvement have been observable since the recent conclusion of the Moscow agreement, as the result of which the well-known conflict on the Mongolian-Manchurian border was liquidated. . . .

While the example of luckless Poland has recently demonstrated how little pacts of mutual assistance signed by some of the European great powers are sometimes worth, what happened on the Mongolian-Manchurian border has demonstrated something quite different. It has demonstrated the value of pacts of mutual assistance to which is appended the signature of the Soviet Union.

As for the conflict in question, it was liquidated by the Soviet-Japanese agreement concluded in Moscow on Sept. 15 and peace has been fully restored on the Mongolian-Manchurian border. Thus the first step was made toward improvement of Soviet-Japanese relations.

The next step is the formation of a joint frontier commission, consisting of representatives of the Soviet-Mongolian and Japanese-Manchurian sides. This commission will have to examine certain disputed frontier questions. There is no doubt that if good will is displayed, not only on our part, the method of businesslike examination of frontier questions will yield good results.

In addition, the possibility has been established of starting Soviet-Japanese trade negotiations. It must be admitted that the development of Soviet-Japanese trade is in the interests of both countries.

Thus we have reason to speak of the beginnings of improvement in our relations with Japan. It is difficult as yet to judge how far we may reckon on rapid development of this tendency. We have not yet been able to ascertain how far the ground for it has been prepared in Japanese circles. For our part I must say that we look with favor on Japanese overtures of this kind and we approach them from the viewpoint of our fundamental political position and our concern for the interests of peace.

DISARMAMENT AND SECURITY

MINUTES of Meeting of the General Commission of the Conference for the Reduction and Limitation of Armaments, February 25, 1932

League of Nations, *Records of the Conference for the Reduction and Limitation of Armaments, Series B, Minutes of the General Commission,* I, 6; excerpt

M. LITVINOFF (Union of Soviet Socialist Republics) moved the following draft resolution:

Animated by the firm desire for an effective and solidly organised peace;

Actuated by the determination to create genuine security for all States and all peoples by preventing the possibility of future wars;

Convinced that the very existence of armaments and the tendency they show constantly to increase inevitably lead to armed international conflicts which tear the workers from their peaceful occupations and bring innumerable calamities in their train;

Considering that military expenditure, which imposes an intolerable burden upon the masses of the people, fosters and enhances the economic crisis with all its consequences;

Noting that the States which it represents have renounced war as an instrument of national policy;

Believing that the only effective means of contributing to the organisation of peace and the establishment of security against war is the general, complete and rapid abolition of all armed forces, setting out from the principle of equality for all;

Convinced that the idea of general and complete disarmament answers to the sincere aspirations of the masses towards peace:

The Conference decides to base its work on the principle of general and complete disarmament.

M. Litvinoff said he was glad to respond to the invitation of the previous day to speak again in favour of total disarmament. He was particularly gratified that it came from M. Tardieu, the Prime Minister of France. He would not abuse the invitation, however, by repeating all the arguments in detail, but would merely summarise them.

The main arguments were as follows: The threat of war was at present more actual than it had ever been, if it were permissible to speak of a threat when war was already going on. In a new war, mankind would be threatened with more appalling disasters than it had ever before experienced. In the present acute crisis, the workers in particular would be threatened. The utmost security must be created against war, and this could only be achieved by the total abolition of all armed forces.

Although the Soviet proposal had been rejected by the Preparatory Commission, M. Litvinoff ventured to submit it to the Conference, because the delegates attending the latter had in many cases wider powers and fuller instructions than those attending the Commission.

The proposal, moreover, was first made five years previously and since then much might have been learned from the events which had since occurred. Five years previously, the capitalist world was passing through an epoch of so-called pacifism, and many people believed that, with the lessons of the Great War fresh in the minds of all, the likelihood of another war was decreasing, that public opinion would not allow a new war, that all that was required to eliminate war completely from international practice was an extension of the network of international treaties and pacts. When, in view of the relations existing, and still more those not existing, between itself and other countries, the Soviet Union expressed fears of attack by capitalist States, it was thought to be suffering from a kind of persecution mania. As for war between non-Soviet States, that was regarded as quite out of the question. The possibility of a new war had, however, been clearly demonstrated by its occurrence, and the probability that it would spread or be repeated on a bigger scale was undeniable, in view of the increasing differences between States.

War was at present discussed in the capitalist Press as a problem of actual policy, a way out of the present economic crisis. Modern economists had even told a select audience of economists in Washington as recently as December 29th, 1931, that as yet no Government had ever put an end to a crisis in any way but by war; such a way out of a crisis might have its dangers, but there were also dangers in not trying it. Other quotations from recent periodicals were as follows: "From the point of view of the sober economist, war is an economic undertaking on a big scale . . . Paraphrasing Klausewitz's well-known aphorism, it might be said that war is the continuation of business management by other means . . ." "No country would gain anything but advantage from a war." "During war, business always improves in some countries. The majority of countries are at present so dissatisfied with the existing conditions of business that it would be worth their while to risk the prospect of war." Again, "We have spent millions of dollars on first-class armaments, and it is extremely disagreeable to see these investments lying idle without bringing in any dividends." The writer of these words considered over-population as the principal cause of the present crisis, and suggested that it should be overcome by the cannibalism of war.

Such articles were a sign of the times and a symptom of the spirit bred by increasing international differences. In view of that spirit, it was no wonder that, while the League Council was appealing to the States at war in the Far East to put a stop to hostilities, and the delegates at the Disarmament Conference were expressing sorrow at the bloodshed which was occurring in the Far East, shipment after shipment of military supplies was being openly and freely sent from other countries to the belligerent States, with the consent of their Governments. Did not that show that international differences, together with the vested interests behind war industries, were stronger than the desires and resolutions of pacifists? Was it not obvious that such a state of affairs could only be ended by the total abolition and destruction of armaments, by general and total disarmament?

He might limit his arguments in favour of total disarmament to those he had just mentioned, leaving it to other delegates to point out the obstacles. He feared, however, that the objections raised in the Preparatory Commission would again be put forward, and wished therefore to save time by recalling them immediately, together with the replies then given.

He had already mentioned the formal objections. Among them should be included references to Article 8 of the League Covenant, which was said to impose upon Members of the League the obligation to reduce their armaments only to a level consistent with national safety. The Soviet proposal for total disarmament, however, was not based on the obligations of the States taking part in the Conference. They were asked to do, not what they were obliged to do, but what they were ready to do. They were asked, if they were ready, together with the Soviet Union, to disarm completely, in order to banish war from international practice, abandoning the idea of war as a business proposition. The Soviet Union by no means ignored the factor of security, but felt that security, and security for all countries, could only be attained through total disarmament.

But serious, as well as merely formal, objections had been put forward at the Preparatory Commission. It had been said, for example, that even should permanent armies and navies be abolished, frontier guards would be necessary to keep down smuggling, as well as a police force, fire-brigades, forest guards, convoy troops, and so on, and that such armed forces would enable countries to attack one another. Undoubtedly, if total disarmament were adopted, States could not be allowed to maintain, at their own sweet will and without limitation, potential armed forces in the form of police, frontier or other guards. That question would have to be regulated in an international convention.

Under such a convention, two neighbouring States would probably be entitled to maintain an equal number of guards on either side of the frontier. As for the police, these might represent a potential army if it were considered necessary to arm them with machine-guns, tanks, artillery, poison gas, bomb-carriers and so on. The Soviet Union, however, did not admit that that would be necessary. Besides, it was hard to believe that any State could mobilise all its police, collecting them from the towns and villages and assembling them at the frontiers, in order to hurl them at a neighbouring country. In fact, States strengthened their forces in war time for the maintenance of internal order and never ventured to withdraw the police forces from their everyday duties. The same applied to the mobilisation of convoy troops, while the idea of mobilising fire-brigades might safely be dismissed.

It had also been said that, even if armies and modern armaments were destroyed, human nature would be constitutionally unable to refrain from fighting, and nations would attack one another with the most primitive weapons, even resorting to fisticuffs. Even admitting that—which he did not—a very small frontier guard would suffice to ward off such attacks, and civilisation would not suffer much if in the Far East, for example, fighting with bare fists took place, instead of the exchange of shells from heavy artillery and the dropping of bombs from the air, involving the destruction of human life and incalculable loss to property.

What would appear to be a more serious objection had also been made. Even after total disarmament, it had been said, the more industrially developed countries would be able themselves to manufacture new armaments for attacking their unarmed neighbours. But the possibility that it would be infringed was an argument which could be used against any international convention. Undoubtedly, if it were to be supposed that some States would stick loyally to the convention while others infringed it by secretly increasing their armed forces, the security of the former would be jeopardised. But such a fear would render useless the conclusion of any international agreement.

As he had already pointed out, it would be much easier effectively to supervise the observation of a convention for total disarmament than of one on reduction. The re-establishment of war industries once they had been stopped, the mobilisation of considerable troops after the mobilisation records had been destroyed, their arming and equipment, would take too long to pass unnoticed. A dreadnought could not be built, a submarine equipped or long-range guns or gas-throwers manufactured undiscovered. There might be first-class metal and chemical industries in a densely populated country, but complicated and prolonged processes would be required to convert those potential forces into armed forces. Military units must be formed and trained, and time was required to bring the elaborate mechanism of war into operation. In the present state of military technique, systematically and regularly trained reserves alone were of any value in an army. Technique was making such strides that the rank and file, the non-commissioned officers, and even the officers required a thorough re-training every few years. The abolition of conscription and the complete destruction of mobilisation records would therefore remove any possibility of using organised masses for military purposes at short notice.

Finally, the potential forces in modern States differed greatly, and from this point of view there was no such thing as equality of security. Would not industrially developed States, by mobilising industry, gain enormous superiority, on the outbreak of war, over the forces of less industrially developed countries, to say nothing of agrarian countries? Was it not obvious that it was much easier to develop and expand existing war industries and military units than to create destroyed war industries and to establish an army from among the untrained masses? Was the mobilisation of the masses for military purposes conceivable, if they did not see before them an armed opponent from whom they feared attack? Even at the present time, the creation of armies and mobilisation for war were only possible when the imagination of a nation was aroused through fictitious or actual threats or attacks on their country. With total disarmament, it would be impossible to create such false impressions, and that alone would make preparations for war impossible. For that reason, too, it would be impossible to mobilise even those reserves who had received military training before total disarmament had been introduced.

The Soviet Government was profoundly convinced that the only guarantee of security for all nations was equality in disarmament—reduction to zero. The feeling of security would then be so strong that no Government would be able, even if it desired, to mobilise its people to attack another country.

These were the most important criticisms of total disarmament made in the Preparatory Commission, and the Soviet Government was prepared to consider any further criticisms. It was convinced, however, that the advantages of its scheme completely outweighed any defects that might be found in it. There was no alternative, no other guarantee against war. No such guarantee was offered by the reduction of armaments, let alone by their limitation and the abolition of certain types of armaments.

The Soviet State valued its independence not less, and in all probability more, than other States; it needed security not less but more than other States. The workers and peasants of the Soviet Union, who by their heroic efforts had won true freedom, had been forced, after a devastating world war, to take up arms for three years to protect that freedom against attacks from within and without. Since then, they had worked for twelve years with unbounded enthusiasm, laying the foundations of a new life.

They had carried out vast economic plans described outside the Soviet Union, only a few years previously, as Utopian. They knew that foreign invasion, the violation of the security of their State, might threaten to overthrow the foundations they had already laid and destroy their hopes for the speedy realisation of a new life. Nevertheless, they would not feel the slightest threat to themselves in the abolition of armed forces in the Soviet Union, provided the same action were taken in other countries. On the contrary, their feeling of security would be increased; they would not be afraid of attack by the unarmed masses of other countries, even though the Soviet Union had on its borders countries so numerically superior as China and India. Nor would total and general disarmament constitute a threat to the security of other nations.

Whatever attitude the other States adopted towards its proposal for total disarmament, however, the Soviet Government felt bound to use the opportunity afforded by a world conference to raise the problem. Where else could it be raised? Whatever the outcome, the vote on this question would be of the greatest historic significance, and could not but affect international relations. For that reason, he ventured to commend his resolution to the Conference.

MINUTES of a Meeting of the General Commission of the Conference for the Reduction and Limitation of Armaments, May 29, 1934

League of Nations, *Records of the Conference for the Reduction and Limitation of Armaments, Series B, Minutes of the General Commission*, III, 657; excerpts

M. LITVINOFF (Union of Soviet Socialist Republics) observed that there were two questions before the present session of the General Commission. In the first place, the Commission had to state whether the direct purpose of the Conference—namely, to solve the problem of disarmament—could be achieved or not, and, in the latter event, to establish the causes of failure. He might be permitted to doubt whether all the delegations represented could arrive at a common opinion as to the causes of failure, but in his view it would be necessary and very valuable for individual delegations, at any rate, to make their observations on that subject.

The second question, which would probably give greater concern to the Commission, was that of the fate of the Conference itself. The Commission would have to decide whether the Conference should continue at all, and, if so, for what purpose, or whether the Conference should voluntarily pass out of existence.

Without wishing to anticipate the discussion, he would permit himself to start, in his remarks, from the premise that it would be impossible at present to find a solution of the problem of disarmament, on account of the irreconcilable differences which had come to light. For the sake of brevity, he would enumerate only the fundamental differences. From the very beginning of the work, not only of the Conference itself, but also of the Preparatory Commission, two basic tendencies had made their appearance—one represented by the Soviet delegation, and the other by nearly all the other delegations. The Soviet delegation refused to consider disarmament as an independent or self-sufficient objective, serving merely economic, budgetary, propagandist or other ends. It desired to see in disarmament the most effective means for abolishing the institution of war, and the concrete realisation of that idea which had later become the foundation of the Briand-Kellogg Pact, accepted by every State in the world, for the renunciation of war as an instrument for the settlement of international differences. It had considered, and still considered, that a genuine renunciation of war could not be effective without a complete renunciation of armaments, and that, so long as armaments existed, peace could not be ensured; that only one kind of peace was possible—a disarmed peace; and that an armed peace was only an armistice, an interval between wars, the sanctioning of war in principle and *de facto*, and the negation of the principle embodied in the Briand-Kellogg Pact.

The Soviet delegation therefore had begun by proposing total universal disarmament. The acceptance of that proposal would have eliminated beforehand the numerous differences which arose at the Conference on the subject of dividing weapons into defensive and offensive, on the criteria of security, on various formulae for the reduction of armaments, on equality in armaments and particularly on the subject of control. Nothing was easier than to control the com-

DISARMAMENT AND SECURITY 589

plete absence of armaments, and nothing more difficult than to ascertain the reduction or limitation of armaments.

The adoption of the Soviet proposal, he would add, might have prevented a number of regrettable political events which had occurred since that time in various countries, with the rising tide of nationalism, jingoism and militarism, and might have left its mark on the international economic situation as well. The Soviet delegation had made its proposal at a time when the so-called pacifist ideology was in full bloom, leading many to believe that war was impossible, at all events in the immediate future. The Soviet delegation, however, had even then foreseen and foretold that the coming of an era of new wars was inevitable and close at hand, and it had therefore insisted on the most speedy adoption of radical measures to avert those dangers. He believed that, if the peoples of the world, who had at that time had more influence over the policy of their Governments than they possessed to-day, had seen as clearly beforehand the development of international political life, they would not have allowed the Conference to get away so easily from the Soviet proposal for total disarmament.

Unfortunately, the Soviet proposal had aroused the opposition of all the other delegations, with the exception, if his memory was correct, of the Turkish, and the basis of their opposition was the view that the question of war and peace was not pressing, and that history had placed decades at the disposal of the States, in which the problem of the guarantees of peace might be solved by easy stages and homeopathic doses.

The Soviet delegation was convinced now as before, nay, still more firmly than before, that, if the peoples—after possibly a further painful, disastrous experience—returned once again to the idea of seeking out international methods for averting wars by means of disarmament, they could not fail to recall the Soviet proposal for total disarmament, and this time take it up with all seriousness, since that guarantee for peace was the most effective of all while the present social and economic system was maintained in the non-Soviet States.

The difference of principle just mentioned could not, however, bring the work of the Conference to a standstill. The Soviet delegation had not put forward its proposals in the form of an ultimatum, but had declared its readiness to co-operate with the other delegations also in working out a system for the partial reduction of armaments. But it was just at that point that real difficulties had begun. While the Soviet delegation declared its readiness to accept any measures of reduction applying to any forms of weapons, differences had arisen among the other delegations. The primary conflict was whether to reduce existing armaments or to limit them to the present level. Although it had seemed at one time that this dispute had been settled, by a vote of the Conference in favour of a considerable reduction of armaments, the Commission now had before it once again a proposal for nothing more than their limitation.

As to the reduction of armaments, there was, up to the present, no unanimity regarding the degree, the principles or the criteria of such a reduction. There was no common opinion as to whether reduction should embrace all forms of armaments—by land, sea and air—or only some of those forms. A decision had appeared at one moment to be near for the complete prohibition of aerial bombardment, from which there logically followed the necessity of abolishing the instruments of bombardment themselves. But here, too, the Conference had come up against a proposal for the maintenance of these instruments, but with a limitation of their activity to definite regions and particular objects, as though it were possible to be satisfied with fixing destination-boards to bombing-planes, such as were fixed to railway carriages—for example, "Ostend-Interlaken." The question of supervision was also in a far from satisfactory state. He would abstain from enumerating the many other differences. It was sufficient to say that on no one question raised at the Conference were there either concrete decisions or even general formulae on which all the delegations had come to agreement. . . .

He did not want to be misunderstood. The Soviet delegation had not altered its attitude to the cause of disarmament in the very least. It continued to attribute the greatest importance to disarmament. It did not in any way propose to abandon the further discussion of the problem of disarmament. Even less did it raise any objection to such schemes of disarmament as might be put forward. On the contrary, it declared in advance its consent to any scheme of disarmament acceptable to the other States, and, in particular, to its nearest neighbours. Let anyone produce such a scheme likely to receive the support of all the delegations. But there was none. Neither the President of the Conference nor the previous speaker had given any indication of a scheme of that kind. M. Litvinoff had no reason to expect that later speakers would introduce new schemes or new proposals, or that such proposals would meet with a better fate than those already discussed. He was therefore obliged to record that the futility of such a discussion on disarmament, in the absence of any proposals whatsoever which had a chance of securing universal acceptance, had been sufficiently demonstrated. After all, the Conference could not engage in discussion for the sake of discussion, or offer up prayers for disarmament. The Soviet delegation could not, therefore, close its eyes to facts, however unpleasant, and it drew the inevitable conclusions from the situation which had been created.

From what he had said, it would seem logically to follow that the Conference itself should close down. That would be very well, if the question were to be approached only from the formal or pedantic point of view, taking into account merely its title. But the Soviet delegation, as he had already mentioned, continued to have in mind a wider conception of the Conference, as being intended by means of disarmament to bring into being one of the guarantees of world peace. Consequently, the question was not that of disarmament itself, since that was only a means to an end, but that of guaranteeing peace. And, since that was so, the question naturally arose, could not the Conference feel its way towards other guarantees for peace; or, at any rate, might it not increase the measure of security for at least those States which, cherishing no aggressive designs, were not interested in war, and which, in the event of war, might become only the objects of attack?

He might be asked what guarantees there were that the Conference would be more unanimous on such questions than it had been on the question of disarmament, and that the new activity which he was suggesting for the Conference would therefore be any more fruitful or successful. He would reply that, in order to achieve any degree whatsoever of reduction in armaments, the unconditional agreement of nearly every State was essential, and that the whole cause might be frustrated by the disagreement of even one more or less important Power, let alone one of the great Powers. But unanimity was not required to realise other measures of security. The Conference must, of course, do everything in its power to induce every State to accede to such measures. He hoped that that would be the case and that consideration for their own interest would induce even States which did not sympathise with these measures not to stand aloof from the general system that would be set up. But, even if there should be dissident States, that should by no means prevent the remainder from coming still more closely together to take steps which would strengthen their own security.

Questions of security were far from unknown to the Conference. The Conference had even created a special political commission for these questions. More than that, it had already discussed these questions, without, it was true, carrying the discussion to its conclusion. He would recall, first, the Soviet proposal for the definition of aggression, which had already been approved by one of the Commissions of the Conference, and which had since been embodied in a number of international treaties. The further increase in the number of supporters of the Soviet definition of aggression would considerably facilitate the application of other proposals dealing with security which had been made at the Conference.

Finally, there might be new proposals of a similar character—as, for example, proposals for sanctions of various kinds against an aggressor, in the meaning of the Briand-Kellogg Pact. A graduated scale of such sanctions might be established, without pursuing it to the point of military measures not acceptable to all States. Independently of a more or less universal or European pact, there might be concluded, in addition, separate regional pacts of mutual assistance, as proposed on a former occasion by the French delegation. There was no question of military alliances, or of the division of States into mutually hostile camps, or still less of a policy of encirclement. Care must be taken not to create universal pacts which would exclude any State wishing to participate, or such regional pacts as would not admit all those interested in the security of the particular region concerned. In measures of security of this kind, the principle of equality of all States, without exception, could not arouse any doubts or hesitation.

If the work proceeded along these lines, the time and energy spent on the Conference would not have been lost, and the delegations would not return empty-handed to the peoples who had sent them to Geneva. And who could say whether the reinforcement of security, and the effect which it would have on aggressively inclined Governments, would not create conditions enabling the Conference to take up once more the problem of disarmament with greater chances of success?

As the delegates would see, M. Litvinoff was not by any means speaking of security in contrast to disarmament. Nor did he propose to exclude disarmament from the Conference's programme of work. Everything that bore upon a system of guarantees of peace, and, consequently, disarmament in particular, must receive the careful attention of the Conference. But every question ought to be taken up when it had some chance of a satisfactory solution. To-day, it might be security; to-morrow, disarmament. He apologised for so frequently using the word "security," which, in the eyes of so many, was an antonym of disarmament. But he could find no more suitable term to express that which was understood by the word "security."

He was, however, far from wishing to put a limit to the Conference, either in scope or in time. He was proposing something much more, much wider—namely, the transformation of the Conference into a permanent body, concerned to preserve by every possible means the security of all nations and to safeguard universal peace. In other words, he proposed that the Conference be transformed into a permanent and regularly assembling Conference of Peace.

Hitherto, peace conferences had mostly been called on the termination of wars, and had had as their object the division of the spoils of war, the imposition on the vanquished of painful and degrading conditions, the redistribution of territories, the refashioning of States, thus hatching out the germs of future wars. But the Conference which he had in mind should sit for the prevention of war and its terrible consequences. It should work out, extend and perfect the measures for strengthening security, it should give a timely response to warnings of impending danger of war and to appeals for aid, to S.O.S.s from threatened States, and it should afford the latter timely aid within its power, whether such be moral, economic, financial or otherwise.

He could foresee objections pointing to the existence of the League of Nations, which was bound by Articles 12, 15, 16, and others, of its Covenant to pursue the same objects as those to which he would like to see the work of the Conference directed. But, in the first place, the League of Nations had a multitude of tasks; it was occupied with a great deal of business, both great and small; it had been created at a time when the peril of war seemed to many to be eliminated for years to come. To-day, when the peril of war stood before men's very eyes, it was feasible to consider the creation of a special body with all its activity concentrated upon one objective—the preventing or the lessening of the danger of war. Secondly, the League of Nations was too straitly bound by its statutes; appeals to its authority and the taking of decisions were too stringently regulated, while the tribune of the Conference might be made more accessible, more free, more responsive to the needs of the moment. Let the Conference continue to be considered an organ of the League, using the services of the League; let it continue to maintain the closest contact with the League; let it be far from replacing the League, which would maintain its prerogatives in their entirety. He was fully aware of the difficulty of setting up a new international organisation entirely divorced from, or competing with, the League of Nations; and such a proposal was foreign to his intentions. But, after all, the very summoning of the present international Disarmament Conference proved that the framework of the League was inadequate for such great problems as disarmament, whereas his proposal treated of a still greater problem —the permanent safeguarding of peace.

M. Litvinoff saw no other alternative. The Disarmament Conference had been called at a time when, to many, war seemed only a theoretical or an historical possibility. Could the Conference, must the Conference, close down completely and disappear without a trace? Could the delegations peacefully disperse to their homes with the consciousness that they had not done their duty—just now of all times, when the peril of a most bloody war, or rather of a series of such wars, overhung every continent and the whole of humanity? There were few States at present which could consider themselves removed from such a peril. It might affect some earlier, others later, but it was not to be escaped. . . .

STATEMENT by Maxim Litvinov, People's Commissar for Foreign Affairs, regarding the German Denunciation of the Treaty of Locarno, in the Council of the League of Nations, March 17, 1936

Translation, in League of Nations, *Official Journal,* April, 1936, p. 319; excerpts

THIS IS the third time, in the short period of eighteen months during which the Soviet Union has been a Member of the League of Nations, that its representative on the Council of the League has had to speak on the subject of a breach of international obligations.

The first time was in connection with the infringement by Germany of the military clauses of the Versailles Treaty. The second time was on the occasion of the Italo-Abyssinian conflict. The third, to-day, is in consequence of the unilateral infringement by Germany of both the Versailles Treaty and the Locarno Pact.

In all three cases the Soviet Union was either formally disinterested because it took no part in the treaties which had been infringed, as in the case of those of Versailles and Locarno, or, as in the case of the Italo-Abyssinian conflict, its own interests were not in the least affected.

These circumstances have not in the past prevented, and will not in the present case prevent, the representative of the Soviet Union from taking his place among those members of the Council who register in the most decisive manner their indignation at a breach of international obligations, condemn it, and support the most effective measures to avert similar infringements in the future.

This attitude of the Soviet Union is predetermined by its general policy of struggling for peace, for the collective organisation of security and for the maintenance of one of the instruments of peace—the existing League of Nations. We consider that one cannot struggle for peace without at the same time defending the integrity of

DISARMAMENT AND SECURITY

international obligations, particularly such as have direct bearing on the maintenance of existing frontiers, on armaments and on political or military aggression. One cannot struggle for the collective organisation of security without adopting collective measures against breaches of international obligations.

We do not, however, class among such measures collective capitulation in face of the aggressor, in face of an infringement of treaties, or collective encouragement of such infringements, and still less collective agreement to a bonus for the aggressor by adopting a basis of agreement, or other plans, acceptable or profitable to the aggressor.

We cannot preserve the League of Nations, founded on the sanctity of international treaties (including the Covenant of the League itself), if we turn a blind eye to breaches of those treaties, or confine ourselves to verbal protests, and take no more effective measures in defence of international undertakings.

We cannot preserve the League of Nations if it does not carry out its own decisions and pledges, but, on the contrary, accustoms the aggressor to ignore its recommendations, its admonitions or its warnings.

Such a League of Nations will never be taken seriously by anyone. The resolutions of such a League will only become a laughing-stock. Such a League is not required, and I will go further and say that such a League may even be harmful, because it may lull the vigilance of the nations and give rise to illusions among them which will prevent them from themselves adopting the necessary measures of self-defence in good time.

The responsibility of the League of Nations and of its directing body, the Council, is all the greater the more simple is the breach of international obligations under discussion. The characteristic feature of all the three cases I have just mentioned is their simplicity—simplicity in the sense that the establishment of the very fact of a breach of international obligations represented no difficulty and could arouse no disputes and differences. When I speak of the absence of disputes and differences, I do not, of course, have in mind the particular State which is accused of breaking treaties. Such a State will naturally always either deny the breach or, at any rate, invent all kinds of arguments to justify its action. One cannot conceive of a case in which such a State would openly declare that it has no justification and that it alone is to blame, and no one else.

The question under discussion at the present session of the Council even surpasses the preceding cases by its simplicity, in the sense I have indicated. Here we find, not only a substantial infringement of treaties, but the ignoring of a particular clause in a treaty, providing a method of settling disputes which may arise in the event of an alleged or actual infringement of the treaty.

Before drawing final conclusions as to the German Government's actions, I think it only just to take into account all that has been said by Mr. Hitler in justification of these actions, or in deprecation of their significance.

The German Government asserts that France was the first to break the Locarno Treaty in the spirit and the letter, by concluding a Pact of Mutual Assistance with the Soviet Union. It applied for an explanation to the other Locarno Powers—namely, Great Britain and Italy. One must imagine that, if these Powers had agreed with the German thesis that the Franco-Soviet Pact is incompatible with the Locarno Treaty, Germany would have utilised their conclusions to the utmost. But, as these Powers came to a different conclusion, Germany peremptorily declares that France, Great Britain, Belgium and Italy—*i.e.*, the other Locarno Powers—are interpreting the Locarno Treaty incorrectly, and that the only correct interpretation is her own. Without doubt this is an extremely convenient method of resolving disputed international questions—when a country, convinced of the injustice of its case, confers upon itself, first the functions of a judge in its own cause, and then those of sheriff's officer.

That the German assertion of the incompatibility of the Franco-Soviet Pact and the Locarno Treaty will not hold water follows with absolute clarity from the entirely defensive character of the Pact. The whole world knows that neither the Soviet Union nor France has any claims to German territory, and that they are not striving to change the frontiers of Germany. If Germany undertakes no aggression against either France or the Soviet Union, the Pact will not begin to operate. But if the Soviet Union becomes the victim of an attack by Germany, the Locarno Treaty gives France, as any other Member of the League, the unquestionable right to come to the assistance of the Soviet Union. In this event, an unmistakable definition of the aggressor is facilitated by the absence of a common frontier between Germany and the Soviet Union. If the German armed forces cross the boundaries of their own country, and pass through the States and the seas dividing the two countries in order to invade the territory of the Soviet Union, the German aggression will be quite apparent, and *vice versa*. . . .

I know that there are people who really do see a particular expression of Germany's love for peace in the offer to France and Belgium of a pact of non-aggression for twenty-five years, to be guaranteed by Great Britain and Italy. These people forget that the Locarno Treaty which Germany has just torn up represented just such a pact of non-

DISARMAMENT AND SECURITY

aggression, with the same guarantees, and its validity was not for twenty-five years, but for an indefinite period. The other difference was that the Locarno Treaty included supplementary guarantees for France and Belgium, in the shape of a demilitarised zone in the Rhineland. Thus the alleged new proposal made by Germany amounts to the maintenance of that same Locarno Treaty, but with a reduction in its period of validity, and with a diminution of the guarantees for Belgium and France which they enjoyed in virtue of the old Locarno Treaty. But these limited guarantees which Mr. Hitler is now proposing might be offered to France and Belgium by the guarantors of Locarno, if they so desire, even without Germany's consent and participation. Thus, Mr. Hitler's proposal amounts to this: that, while depriving France and Belgium of certain guarantees with which they were provided by the Locarno Treaty, he wants to retain for Germany all the benefits of that treaty in their totality.

But Mr. Hitler's "love of peace" does not stop at this. He is ready to sign pacts of non-aggression, not only with France and Belgium, but with his other neighbours—true, without anybody else's guarantee. The Soviet Union has itself signed pacts of non-aggression with all its neighbours (excepting Japan, which rejects such a pact up to this day). But the Soviet Union has always attached great importance to the point that these pacts should not facilitate aggression against third parties. We therefore always included in these pacts a special clause, freeing either of the contracting parties from any obligations under the pact if the other party commits an act of aggression against a third State. Such a clause, however, will be absent from the pacts proposed by Mr. Hitler, according to the model which he has indicated. And, without such a clause, the proposed system of pacts reduces itself to the principle of localisation of war which is preached by Mr. Hitler. Every State which has signed such a pact with Germany is immobilised by her in the event of Germany attacking a third State.

This proposal of Mr. Hitler's gives me the impression that we are faced with a new attempt to divide Europe into two or more parts, with the object of guaranteeing non-aggression for one part of Europe in order to acquire a free hand for dealing with other parts. As I have already had to point out at Geneva, such a system of pacts can only increase the security of the aggressor and not the security of peace-loving nations.

Presuming, however, that the "peace-loving" proposals I have enumerated will not be reckoned sufficient compensation for a breach of international laws, Germany expresses her readiness to return to the League of Nations. In common with other Members of the League, we sincerely regret the incompleteness of the League, and the absence from it of some great countries, particularly Germany. We shall welcome the return into its midst of Hitler's Germany as well, if and when we are convinced that she has recognised those fundamental principles on which the League rests, and without which it would not only cease to be an instrument of peace, but eventually might be transformed into its opposite. Among these principles, in the first place, are the observance of international treaties, respect for the inviolability of existing frontiers, recognition of the equality of all Members of the League, support of the collective organisation of security and renunciation of the settlement of international disputes by the sword. . . .

Before concluding, let me express the hope that I shall not be misunderstood, and that the conclusion will not be drawn from what I have said that the Soviet Union is proposing only registration, condemnation, severe measures and nothing else; that it declares itself against negotiations and a peaceful settlement of the serious dispute which has arisen. Such a conclusion would present a completely false picture of our conception. We are not less, but, on the contrary, more, interested than others in the maintenance of peace, both to-day and for decades to come, and not only in one area of Europe, but throughout the whole of Europe and all over the world. We are resolutely against anything that might bring a war nearer by even a single month. But we are also against hasty decisions, dictated rather by excessive fear and other emotions than by a sober reckoning of realities—decisions which, while represented as eliminating the causes of an imaginary war to-day, create all the premises for an actual war to-morrow. We stand for an international agreement which would not only consolidate the existing foundations of peace, but, if possible, would likewise create new foundations. We stand for the participation in such an agreement of all the countries which so desire. But we object to the idea that withdrawal from the League of Nations, brutal infringement of international treaties and sabre-rattling should confer upon a State the privilege of dictating to the whole of Europe its conditions for negotiations, of selecting the participants in those negotiations to suit its convenience, and of imposing its own scheme for an agreement. We are against negotiations proceeding on a basis which disorganises the ranks of the sincere partisans of peace, and which must inevitably lead to the destruction of the only inter-State political organisation—the League of Nations. We are of the opinion that the sincere partisans of peace are no less entitled than the breakers of treaties to propose their scheme for the organisation of European peace. We are for the creation of security for all the nations of Europe, and against a half-peace which is not peace at all but war,

But, at whatever new international agreements we might desire to arrive, we must first of all ensure their loyal fulfilment by all those who participate in them, and the Council of the League must declare its attitude towards unilateral infringements of such agreements, and how it intends and is able to react against them. From this standpoint the greatest possible satisfaction of the complaint made by the French and Belgian Governments becomes of exceptional importance. Taking cognisance of this, I declare in the name of my Government its readiness to take part in all measures which may be proposed to the Council of the League by the Locarno Powers and will be acceptable to the other Members of the Council.

OTHER SUBJECTS BEFORE 1941

Responsibility for Acts of the Communist International

NOTE from N. Krestinski, Acting People's Commissar for Foreign Affairs, to the American Ambassador to the Union of Soviet Socialist Republics (William C. Bullitt), August 27, 1935

Translation, in Department of State, *Press Releases,* August 31, 1935, p. 149

Mr. Ambassador:

By note of August 25 of this year you invited my attention to the activity of the Congress of the Communist International which took place at Moscow and, referring to the note of the People's Commissar for Foreign Affairs Litvinov to the President of the United States of America, Mr. Roosevelt, under date of November 16, 1933, protested against this activity, considered by your Government as a violation of the obligations of the Government of the Union of Soviet Socialist Republics concerning noninterference in the internal affairs of the United States provided for in the note of November 16, 1933.

In connection therewith I consider it necessary to emphasize with all firmness that the Government of the Union of Soviet Socialist Republics has always regarded and still regards with the greatest respect all obligations which it has taken upon itself including naturally the mutual obligation concerning noninterference in internal affairs provided for in the exchange of notes of November 16, 1933, and discussed in detail in the conversations between the President of the United States of America, Mr. Roosevelt, and the People's Commissar Litvinov. There are contained no facts of any kind in your note of August 25 which could be considered as a violation on the part of the Soviet Government of its obligations.

On the other hand it is certainly not new to the Government of the United States that the Government of the Union of Soviet Socialist Republics cannot take upon itself and has not taken upon itself obligations of any kind with regard to the Communist International.

Hence the assertion concerning the violation by the Government of the Union of Soviet Socialist Republics of the obligations contained in the note of November 16, 1933, does not emanate from obligations accepted by both sides, in consequence of which I cannot accept your protest and am obliged to decline it.

The Government of the Union of Soviet Socialist Republics, sincerely sharing the opinion of the Government of the United States of America that strict mutual noninterference in internal affairs is an essential prerequisite for the maintenance of friendly relations between our countries, and steadfastly carrying out this policy in practice, declares that it has as its aim the further development of friendly collaboration between the Union of Soviet Socialist Republics and the United States of American responding to the interests of the people of the Soviet Union and the United States of America and possessing such great importance for the cause of universal peace.

Taking advantage of the occasion, I invite you to accept the assurances of my high esteem.

Czechoslovakian Crisis, 1938

ADDRESS by Maxim Litvinov, People's Commissar for Foreign Affairs, before the Assembly of the League of Nations, September 21, 1938 (excerpt)

International Conciliation, November, 1938, p. 421, citing *The New York Times*, September 22, 1938; excerpt

BOUND TO Czechoslovakia by a pact of mutual assistance, the Soviet Union abstained from any intervention in the negotiations of the Czechoslovak Government with the Sudeten Germans, considering this to be the internal business of the Czechoslovak State.

We have refrained from all advice to the Czechoslovak Government, considering it quite inadmissible that it should be asked to make concessions to the Germans, to the detriment of its interests as a State, in order that we should be set free from the necessity of fulfilling our obligations under the treaty bearing our signature. Neither did we offer any advice in the contrary direction.

We value very highly the fact that the Czechoslovak Government up to the last few days did not even inquire of us whether we would fulfil our obligations on the pact, since obviously it had no doubt of this. It had no grounds for doubt. But when, a few days before I left for Geneva, the French Government for the first time inquired of my Government as to its attitude in the event of an attack on

Czechoslovakia, I gave the French representative in Moscow, in the name of my Government, the following perfectly clear and unambiguous reply:

We intend to fulfil our obligations under the pact, together with France, to afford assistance to Czechoslovakia by the way open to us; our War Department is ready immediately to participate in a conference with representatives of the French and Czechoslovak War Departments in order to discuss measures appropriate to the moment. In an event like this, we shall consider desirable that the question be raised in the League of Nations, if only as yet under Article XI, with the object, first, of mobilizing public opinion, and, secondly, ascertaining the position of certain other States whose passive aid might be extremely valuable.

We said further that it was necessary to exert all means of avoiding an armed conflict and we considered one such method to be immediate consultation between the Great Powers of Europe and other interested States, in order, if possible, to decide on the terms for a collective démarche. This is how our reply was framed. . . .

War with Finland, 1939–1940

RADIO ADDRESS by Vyacheslav M. Molotov, President of the Council of People's Commissars and People's Commissar for Foreign Affairs, November 29, 1939

Translation, in the League of Nations, *Official Journal,* November–December, 1939, Part II, p. 541; a press release of the Tass Agency, November 30, 1939

MEN AND WOMEN, citizens of the Soviet Union, the hostile policy pursued by the present Finnish Government towards our country obliges us to take immediate steps to ensure the external security of the State. As you know, during these last two months, the Soviet Government has patiently carried on negotiations with the Finnish Government on proposals which, in the present alarming international situation, it regarded as an indispensable minimum to ensure the safety of the country, and particularly that of Leningrad. During those negotiations, the Finnish Government has adopted an uncompromising and hostile attitude towards our country. Instead of amicably seeking a basis of agreement, those who at present govern Finland, out of deference to the foreign imperialists who stir up hatred against the Soviet Union, have followed a different path. Despite all our concessions, the negotiations have led to no result. Now we see the consequences. During the last few days, on the frontier between the U.S.S.R. and Finland, the Finnish military clique has begun to indulge in revolting provocations, not stopping short of artillery fire upon our troops near Leningrad, which has caused serious casualties among the Red troops.

The attempts made by our Government to prevent the renewal of these provocations by means of practical proposals addressed to the Finnish Government have not merely met with no support but have again been countered by the hostile policy of the governing circles in Finland. As you have learnt from the Soviet Government's note of yesterday, they have replied to our proposals by a hostile refusal, by an insolent denial of the facts, by an attitude of mockery towards the casualties we have suffered, and by an unconcealed desire to continue to hold Leningrad under the direct threat of their troops. All this has definitely shown that the present Finnish Government, embarrassed by its anti-Soviet connections with the imperialists, is unwilling to maintain normal relations with the U.S.S.R. It continues to adopt a hostile position towards our country and will take no heed of the stipulations of the Treaty of Non-aggression concluded between the two countries, being anxious to keep our glorious Leningrad under a military menace. From such a Government and from its insensate military clique nothing is now to be expected but fresh insolent provocations.

For this reason, the Soviet Government was compelled yesterday to declare that it now considered itself released from the engagements which it had undertaken under the Treaty of Non-aggression concluded between the U.S.S.R. and Finland and which had been irresponsibly violated by the Finnish Government. In view of the fresh attacks made by Finnish troops against Soviet troops on the Soviet-Finnish frontier, the Government now finds itself compelled to take new decisions. The Government can no longer tolerate the situation created, for which the Finnish Government is entirely responsible. The Soviet Government has come to the conclusion that it could no longer maintain normal relations with the Finnish Government, and for this reason has found it necessary to recall immediately its political and economic representatives from Finland. Simultaneously, the Government gave the order to the Supreme Command of the Red Army and Navy to be prepared for all eventualities and to take immediate steps to cope with any new attacks on the part of the Finnish military clique.

The foreign Press hostile to us declares that our action is aimed at seizing and annexing to the U.S.S.R. Finnish territory. This is a malicious slander. The Soviet Government never did, and does not now, cherish any such intentions. Nay, more, had Finland herself pursued a friendly policy towards the U.S.S.R., the Soviet Government, which has always desired to maintain friendly relations with Finland, would willingly have taken the initiative in making territorial concessions. On that condition, the Soviet Government would have been prepared to discuss favourably even such questions as that of the reunion of the Karelians inhabiting the chief districts of present-day Soviet Karelia with their Finnish kinsmen in a single independent Finnish State. For that, however, it is essential that the Finnish Government should adopt towards the U.S.S.R., not a hostile, but a friendly attitude which would correspond to the vital interests of both States. There are some who say that the steps we have taken are directed against the independence of Finland or constitute interference in her internal and external affairs. That is also a malicious slander. We look on Finland, whatever regime prevails there, as an independent sovereign State in the whole of its foreign and domestic policy. It is our steadfast wish that the Finnish people should settle their own internal and external questions as they think fit. The peoples of the U.S.S.R. did everything that could be done at the time to create an independent Finland. Our peoples are equally ready in the future to help the Finnish people achieve their free and independent development.

Nor does the U.S.S.R. intend to infringe in any way the interests of other States in Finland. Questions concerning the relations between Finland and other States are the affair of Finland alone, and the U.S.S.R. does not consider itself entitled to interfere in the matter. We are solely concerned to ensure the safety of the U.S.S.R., and in particular of Leningrad, with its population of three-and-a-half million inhabitants. In the present atmosphere of white heat generated by the war, we cannot allow the solution of this vital and urgent problem to depend on the ill-will of the present rulers of Finland. This problem will have to be solved by the efforts of the U.S.S.R. itself in friendly collaboration with the Finnish people. We are sure that a favourable solution of this problem of the safety of Leningrad will be the foundation for a solid friendship between the U.S.S.R. and Finland.

TELEGRAM from Vyacheslav M. Molotov, President of the Council of People's Commissars and People's Commissar for Foreign Affairs, to the Secretary-General of the League of Nations (Joseph Avenol), December 5, 1939

Translation, in League of Nations, *Official Journal,* November–December, 1939, Part II, p. 512

IN ACCORDANCE with instructions from the U.S.S.R. Government, I have the honour to inform you that that Government considers unjustified proposal to convene December 9th Council League of Nations and December 11th Assembly League of Nations on the initiative of M. Rodolphe Holsti and in virtue of Article 11, paragraph 1, of the League Covenant.

The U.S.S.R. is not at war with Finland and does not threaten the Finnish nation with war. Consequently, reference to Article 11, paragraph 1, is unjustified. Soviet Union maintains peaceful relations with the Democratic Republic of Finland, whose Government signed with the U.S.S.R. on December 2nd Pact of Assistance and Friendship. This Pact settled all the questions which the Soviet Government had fruitlessly discussed with delegates former Finnish Government now divested of its power.

By its declaration of December 1st, the Government of the Democratic Republic of Finland requested the Soviet Government to lend assistance to that Republic by armed forces with a view to the joint liquidation at the earliest possible moment of the very dangerous seat of war created in Finland by its former rulers. In these circumstances, appeal of M. Rodolphe Holsti to the League cannot justify convocation of the Council and the Assembly, especially as the persons on whose behalf M. Rodolphe Holsti has approached the League cannot be regarded as mandatories of the Finnish people.

If, notwithstanding considerations set out above, Council and Assembly are convened to consider the appeal of M. Rodolphe Holsti, U.S.S.R. Government would be unable to take part in these meetings. This decision is also based on the fact that the communication from the Secretary-General of the League concerning convocation Council and Assembly reproduces the text of the letter from M. Rodolphe Holsti, which is full of insults and calumnies against the Soviet Government, this being incompatible with the respect due to the U.S.S.R.

PART FIVE

GERMANY

GENERAL STATEMENTS OF POLICY

ADDRESS by Julius Curtius, Minister for Foreign Affairs, before the Assembly of the League of Nations, September 12, 1931

Translation, in League of Nations, *Official Journal,* Special Supplement No. 93, p. 88; excerpts

THE GENERAL discussion shows that the position of the Assembly of the League of Nations this year has been determined in the main by two facts—the terrible economic depression from which most countries are suffering, and the approach of the Disarmament Conference. These two facts we must bear in mind in any appreciation of the League's work during the past year, or in any attempt to estimate the extent of the assistance which the League is likely to be able to give in present circumstances and the importance of the decisions which we shall be called upon to take this year.

It has often been said, in the last few years—no one, I think, will contest this—that the fate of the Disarmament Conference will be of decisive importance in determining the fate of the League itself. An equally potent factor in shaping the opinion of nations in regard to the League will be the extent to which the latter can help to overcome the crisis from which nearly the whole world is suffering. For this reason I will, like many of the speakers before me on this platform, confine myself in the main to questions relating to the economic and financial problems which are causing us such anxiety and to the problem of disarmament.

The German delegation, I need hardly say, will co-operate fully in the discussions on the other questions on the agenda and will take the opportunity of expounding its views in the competent committees—more particularly, its views on the question of bringing the Pact of Paris into harmony with the Covenant of the League, the question of European Union and the minorities question. I consider, however, that the nations, whose attention is now riveted on Geneva, will desire above all things to know whether the statesmen assembled here are capable of finding, or at least of helping to find, some way out of the crisis, and whether we are able to offer them reasonable grounds for hoping that, in the burning question of disarmament, tangible results will be obtained by the Conference which is to meet in February.

We are all acquainted with the events which, since our last Assembly, have done so much to aggravate the depression from which we were already suffering then. To the collapse of production and markets has, in many countries, been added financial catastrophe. The dangers of the economic situation have assumed alarming proportions; on the one hand, congestion of raw materials and foodstuffs; on the other, want and famine; concentration of capital and accumulation of gold in a small number of countries and shortage of capital and a crushing burden of interest in others; and then the most terrible manifestation of the collapse of the international economy; unemployment in the industrial countries, which next winter will increase to an extent which it is impossible to see at present, with the resulting army of despairing and desperate men who will be only too ready to lend an ear to extremist and revolutionary influences. No one can deny that the whole foundation of our economic and financial system and, indeed, the whole basis of our civilisation is tottering. . . .

All attempts to re-establish the normal movement of commodities and capital are doomed to ultimate failure directly the principles of justice and equality in political relations are neglected. The League is called upon also to guarantee those principles even in cases in which the practical solution of the various economic and financial problems has not been expressly entrusted to it. If such an attitude could spread from Geneva and really be endorsed by Governments, it would extend from the latter to public opinion in every country; and thus the impatience, the excitability and ready irritation, which are very comprehensible in present conditions, would give place to a calmer, more confident outlook.

We must not try to disguise from ourselves a fact that should be frankly admitted—namely, that in many countries profound scepticism reigns and—what is perhaps worse still—growing indifference to the Geneva institutions. The circles in which this phenomenon is observed are by no means those which do not understand the idea of the League or are hostile to it. On the contrary, it is precisely those people who put their faith in the League that are becoming increasingly disillusioned owing to the absence of tangible results. It would, of course, be absurd to hope for miracles or to expect that our deliberations should provide an immediate remedy for the present distress. What people of common sense want are measures designed to get at the root of the evil and to effect an improvement in the situation. This difficult period of world depression can be turned to account, if it results in the realisation and the strengthening of the conception of real solidarity and of the need for co-operation on a basis of equality.

The German Government will certainly do everything in its power to promote such international co-operation. It is well aware that German interests and the general interest alike imperatively demand such an attitude. Indeed, it was this conception of present-day problems that took us successively to Chequers, Paris, London and Rome. I entirely concur in the view that the League has no reason to be jealous of these direct efforts of responsible statesmen, but has, on the contrary, every reason to encourage them.

The British delegate emphasised the importance which, at every stage in the evolution of international relations, attaches to Franco-German *rapprochement*, which, as he says, should not be confined to words, but should find expression in acts. Lord Cecil may be sure that the German Government fully appreciates the importance of this point. I am happy to say that the coming visit of French statesmen to Berlin will furnish an opportunity for a direct exchange of views, and I trust that results may be obtained in this way which will be of advantage to both countries and, in addition, serve the general interests of the world.

I now come to the second of the great problems with which the League is faced—and it is an urgent problem—disarmament. While the economic depression of which I have spoken is attributable mainly to events that have occurred outside the League, the latter has, on the contrary, been solely responsible from the outset for the manner in which the disarmament problem has been dealt with. Disarmament was proclaimed to the world in the League Covenant, and that was the principal task assigned to the League on its foundation. On that issue the League's fate depends, and that is the issue to be decided by the Conference convened for next February.

Following the example of many speakers who have preceded me on this platform, I also consider it desirable to explain once more before this Assembly—the last before the Conference—views of my country on the essential points. The preparation and work of the Conference is bound to be facilitated if the opinions of the various Governments are explained now as clearly as possible. Why disguise the fact that divergent opinions still exist? Let me state frankly from the outset that I can associate myself with many of the views expressed here up to the present, but not with all of them.

I should like to refer to the speech of the Italian delegate. I listened with the greatest satisfaction to his statements of principle on the relations between the pacific settlement of disputes, disarmament and security. I cannot but entirely agree with M. Grandi when he said that the pacific settlement of disputes and disarmament together constitute the decisive means of strengthening security.

All efforts designed to secure the final and complete abolition of war are bound to remain incomplete until the League has extended the system of the pacific settlement of disputes so as to guarantee a just and equitable settlement of even the most serious conflicts in the political field.

As regards the importance of disarmament as a factor in increasing security, the statements made in the Assembly in 1928 concerning the relationship between the reduction of armaments and increased international security are as true now as they were then. The conviction that not armaments but disarmament furnishes the real element of security is the essential characteristic of the community of States organised into the League of Nations, as opposed to the old methods of international policy. The security of States is a guarantee of peace only if all States participate to the same degree. The Covenant knows only one kind of national security for all its Members. Security based on preponderance of armaments will always imply a state of insecurity and constitute a danger for the other countries which are less strongly armed. It engenders distrust and inevitably revives the idea of the race for armaments, the complete suppression of which was one of the main objects for which the League was created. The feeling of being left without military defences in the face of strongly armed neighbours weighs on a nation and cripples it throughout, as any German who has had an opportunity of observing the effects of that state of affairs on his nation will be prepared to to tell you. . . .

The task assigned to the Disarmament Conference is to effect a real and effective reduction of armaments. At the same time the method of achieving the final object enunciated in Article 8 of the Covenant must be clearly established.

In view of the tremendous inequality of armaments, mere limitation at the present level would be equivalent to sanctioning those inequalities, would be tantamount to the failure of the Conference. More than ten years ago, as the result of a lost war, the obligation to reduce their armaments to a minimum was imposed on certain States, including my own country. That obligation has long been fulfilled. I would refer here to the tables showing the position with regard to German armaments, which the German Government forwarded in reply to the League's questionnaire and which have been distributed during the last few days. Those tables show how far Germany has disarmed; she no longer possesses any heavy artillery, any military aircraft, any tanks or submarines. They even show that Germany has, in some respects, kept below the figures authorised by the Treaty of Versailles.

In this connection I must again emphasise one point of primary importance. The counterpart of the obligations assumed by Germany in 1919 is a formal undertaking on the part of the other States that disarmament by Germany should be simply a prelude to general disarmament by the other Powers. German disarmament was to be the first step in a scheme of general disarmament. Twelve years have elapsed since then, and Germany has been a Member of the League for five years, without that undertaking having been fulfilled. If the Disarmament Conference does now at last meet, the German people cannot be asked to agree to any act which would imply the sanctioning of the present armaments position. A large and effective reduction of the armaments of the strongly armed Powers thus constitutes for Germany a preliminary condition for the success of the Conference.

If the Disarmament Conference is to arrive at a result which is politically acceptable, it must put an end, as regards the limitation of armaments, to the existence of different rules of international law for those who were victorious and those who were defeated in the world war. Equality of all States must be the starting-point. There cannot be two standards of weights and measures in the community of nations. The same methods must apply to all as regards the reduction and limitation of the various categories of armaments. Otherwise, the Convention will not fulfil the psychological and moral conditions necessary for the accession of the German people.

I was extremely interested in the suggestion put forward by the first delegate of Italy to the effect that, pending the Conference and while it is sitting, the States should declare their readiness to postpone the execution of new armaments programmes. The German Government as it were anticipated this suggestion in its statement on the occasion of the negotiations concerning President Hoover's plan. I entirely associate myself with M. Grandi's views, and am convinced that the idea of an armaments truce would improve the chances of success at the Conference and facilitate its work. I warmly congratulate M. Grandi on his idea, and trust that it may be possible for all the States concerned to put it into practice. I for my part regard it as self-evident that the mere limitation of armaments as thus contemplated must only be a temporary measure of limited duration.

I cannot conclude my remarks on disarmament without saying that I associate myself with Lord Cecil's appeal to Governments. Let us give our delegates to the Conference the fullest and widest powers. It is the maximum and not the minimum of disarmament that we must aim at in our negotiations. Only if the States—especially the powerfully armed States—make sacrifices in the interests of a courageous, resolute and far-sighted policy of disarmament and peace, can the world be delivered from the nightmare by which it is haunted and which is obstructing it in the performance of its manifold international functions.

It is not merely a matter of saving in the national budgets or of the degrees of security in the different countries. No; I repeat, the fate of the League itself hangs in the balance. If the League fails in this task, it will fall short of the nations' expectations and of our united hopes. The failure of the Disarmament Conference would rob the League of its moral authority in a world of political tension, which is crying out for a solution, a peaceful and harmonious solution.

RADIO ADDRESS by Adolf Hitler, Chancellor of the Reich, October 14, 1933

Translation, in Royal Institute of International Affairs, *Documents on International Affairs, 1933*, p. 289, citing *Frankfurter Zeitung*, October 15, 1933; excerpts

WHEN THE German nation laid down its arms in November 1918, placing its trust in the assurances contained in President Wilson's Fourteen Points, the end came to a terrible struggle, the responsibility for which might be cast upon a few statesmen, but certainly not on the peoples. The German nation fought so heroically only because it was firmly convinced that it had been unjustly attacked, and was, therefore, fighting in a just cause. Other countries had hardly any idea of the sacrifices which the German nation—standing as it did almost alone—had to make at that time. If the world had during these months held out a hand to the vanquished opponent, humanity would have been spared much misery and endless disappointment.

The German nation has suffered the bitterest disappointment; never has a vanquished nation tried so honestly to co-operate in healing the wounds of its former enemies, as the German nation during the long years in which it fulfilled the dictated conditions imposed upon it.

The fact that all these sacrifices have not led to any real reconciliation between the nations has been due solely to the nature of a treaty which, in its attempt to perpetuate a situation of victor and vanquished, necessarily perpetuated hatred and hostility. The nations might have been justified in hoping that this, the greatest war in the history of the world, would have shown that, particularly for European nations, no possible gain could compare with the immensity of the sacrifices made. When, therefore, this treaty compelled the German nation to destroy its armaments in order to render possible general world disarmament, innumerable people believed that this demand was to be regarded as a sign of growing enlightenment.

The German nation destroyed its arms.

Believing that its former enemies would fulfill their part of the treaty obligations, the German people honoured their side of the bargain with almost fanatical sincerity; land, naval, and air material was destroyed, scrapped, and dismantled in countless numbers. In place of an army which had once numbered a million, a small professional army, with equipment which was utterly inadequate from a military point of view, was established in accordance with the demands of the dictating Powers. The political destinies of the German nation were at this time in the hands of men whose outlook was limited to the world of the conquering States. The German nation had every right to expect that, if only for this reason, the rest of the world would keep its word, in the same way that the German people were fulfilling their treaty obligations by the sweat of their brow and in deep distress and unendurable privation.

No war can be a permanent state of mankind. No peace could perpetuate a state of war. A time must come when victor and vanquished must find their way to common understanding and mutual trust. For fifteen years the German people have waited in the hope that when the war ended an end might also come to hatred and hostility. The object of the Peace Treaty of Versailles appears to be not to bring lasting peace to mankind, but rather to perpetuate hatred forever.

The results were inevitable. When right definitely yields to might, a permanent state of insecurity results which destroys and hinders all normal functions in the life and intercourse of nations. When the Treaty was concluded it was forgotten that the reconstruction of the world could not be effected by the forced labour of an oppressed nation, but only by the trustful co-operation of all, and that the primary condition for this co-operation was the destruction of the war psychosis. It is clear that the problematical question of war guilt cannot be settled historically by the victor compelling the vanquished to sign a confession of guilt in the Preamble of a Peace Treaty, but that the ultimate war guilt can better be established from the contents of the dictated treaty itself.

The German nation is firmly convinced of its innocence in respect of the outbreak of the war. The other actors in that tragedy probably have the same conviction, but this makes it all the more necessary that all should strive that this general conviction of innocence should not be the cause of permanent hostility, that the memories of this catastrophe should not be artificially conserved for the purpose, and that the unnatural perpetuation of the situation of "victor" and "vanquished" should not lead to a permanent state of inequality which fills one side with comprehensible pride and the other with bitter fury. . . .

I welcome as a sign of a nobler sense of justice, for which countless millions of Germans will be grateful, that the French Premier, M. Daladier, in his last speech used words showing a spirit of conciliation and understanding. National-Socialist Germany has no other desire than that the competition of the nations of Europe should again be directed into the channels in which they have given mankind both an example of honourable rivalry and those invaluable possessions of civilization, culture, and art, which at present enrich and beautify the world. We also welcome hopefully the assurance which the French Government under its present leader has given; that it does not desire intentionally to offend or "humiliate the German nation. We are moved at the reference to the fact—unfortunately only too true—that these two great nations have so often in the course of their history poured out the blood of their best youth and manhood on the field of battle. I speak in the name of the whole German people when I affirm that we sincerely desire to end a feud which has resulted in the loss of so many lives, a loss so disproportionate to anything that has been gained by it. The German people is convinced that the honour of its arms has remained unsullied and unsmirched, just as we see in the French soldier only our ancient, but glorious, opponent. We and the whole German nation would rejoice at the thought that we might spare our children and children's children what we as honourable men had to watch and suffer in the long years of bitterness. The history of the last one hundred and fifty years should in its changing course have taught the two nations that essential and enduring changes are no more to be gained by the sacrifice of blood. As a National-Socialist, I, with all my followers, refuse by reason of our national principles to acquire by conquest the members of other nations, who will never love us, at the cost of the blood and lives of those who are dear to us.

It would be a great day for all humanity if these two nations of Europe would banish, once and for all, force from their common life. The German people is ready to do so. While claiming boldly those rights which the Treaties themselves have given us, I will say as boldly that there are for Germany no grounds for territorial conflict. When the Saar territory has been restored to Germany only a madman would consider the possibility of war between the two States, for which, from our point of view, there is no rational or moral ground. For no one could demand that millions of men in the flower of youth should be annihilated for the sake of a readjustment, indefinite in scope, of our present frontier.

When the French Premier asks why German youth is marching and drilling, then I reply that it is not in order to demonstrate against France, but to give effect to that political training of the will which was necessary for the overthrow of Communism and which will be necessary to keep Communism in check. In Germany there is only one body that bears arms and that is the Army. On the other hand, National-Socialist organizations know only one enemy and that is Communism. But the world must accept the fact that in order to protect our people from this danger, the German nation chooses for its internal organization those forms which alone can provide a guarantee of success.

When the French Premier, M. Daladier, goes on to ask why Germany is demanding arms which would have to be subsequently abolished, he is under a misapprehension. The demand of the German nation and the German Government has not been for weapons, but for equality of rights. If the world decides that all weapons are to be abolished down to the last machine gun, we are ready to join at once in such a Convention.

If the world decides that certain weapons are to be destroyed, we are ready to dispense with them immediately. But if the world grants to each nation certain weapons, we are not prepared to let ourselves be excluded from this concession as a nation with inferior rights. If we thus honourably maintain our conviction, we are, for other nations more reliable partners than if we were prepared, against our conviction, to accept humiliating and dishonourable conditions; for we, with our signature, pledge the word of a whole nation, whilst negotiators without honour or character are only disowned by their own people.

. . . Former German Governments entered the League of Nations confidently and with the hope of finding there a forum for the fair adjustment of national interests, and above all for honourable reconciliation between former opponents. But the essential condition was the recognition of the equality of rights of the German people. With the same condition Germany participated in the Disarmament Conference. For an honour-loving nation of 65,000,000 people and a Government with no less a sense of honour, this degradation to the rank of a member without equal rights, in such an institution and such a conference, is a humiliation not to be borne. The German Government has more than fulfilled its disarmament obligations. It is now the turn of the armed States to carry out their pledges to the same degree. The German Government did not take part in the Conference in order to haggle for a few guns or machine-guns, but to co-operate as a member with equal rights in the general pacification of the world.

Germany has no less a right to security than other nations. If the British Minister, Mr. Baldwin, maintained it as self-evident that, for England, disarmament could be understood only to mean the disarmament of the more highly armed Powers simultaneously with the rearmament of England up to a common level, then it would be unfair to overwhelm Germany with reproaches if she decided to stand out for the same point of view as a member of the Conference with equal rights. Germany's demand in this respect constituted no threat to the other Powers. The defensive means of other nations are constructed to withstand the most powerful aggressive weapons; Germany on the other hand does not demand any offensive weapons, but only those defensive weapons which are not forbidden in future, but are to be allowed to all nations. Further, Germany is prepared from the outset to be content with minimum figures which are out of proportion to the gigantic armament of offensive and defensive weapons with which she is surrounded by her former opponents.

Germany cannot tolerate the deliberate degradation of the nation by the perpetuation of a discrimination which consists in withholding the rights which are granted as a matter of course to other nations. In my peace speech last May, I stated that under such conditions we should to our regret no longer be in a position to belong to the League of Nations or take part in international conferences. The men who are at present the leaders of Germany have nothing in common with the traitors of November 1918. Like every decent Englishman and every decent Frenchman, we all had our duty to our Fatherland and placed our lives at its service. We are not responsible for the war or for what occurred in it, but we feel responsible for what every honest man must do in the time of his country's distress and for what we have done. We have such infinite love for our people that we desire wholeheartedly an understanding with other nations, and whenever it is possible we shall try to attain it, but, as representatives of an honourable nation and as men of honour, it is impossible for us to be members of institutions under conditions which are only bearable to those who are devoid of a sense of honour. . . .

Since it has been made clear to us from the declarations of the official representatives of certain great Powers that they were not prepared to consider real equality of rights for Germany at present, we have decided that it is impossible, in view of the indignity of her position, for Germany to continue to force her company upon other nations. Threats of force could, if put into practice, only amount to breaches of international law. The German Government is profoundly convinced that its appeal to the whole German nation will prove that the Government's desire for peace, as also its conception of honour, represents the views of the whole nation.

In order to prove this assertion, I have decided to request the President of the Reich to dissolve the German Reichstag and by means of fresh elections, combined with a referendum, to give the German people the opportunity of making an historic declaration, not only in the sense of approving the Government's principles, but also in that of an unconditional association with them. May the world be convinced by this declaration that, in the struggle for equality of rights and honour, the German nation stands with the Government, and that both are inspired by no other desire than to co-operate in putting an end to an era of tragic errors and regrettable disputes and conflicts between those who, as inhabitants of a continent which in cultural importance is the greatest of all, have a common mission to fulfil in future towards the whole of mankind. May this great demonstration by our nation in favour of peace and honour be successful in bringing to the relations between European states the condition which is essential, if the quarrels and disputes of centuries are to be ended and if a better community of nations is to be built up, that is to say, the recognition of a nobler common duty arising, out of common and equal rights.

ADDRESS by Baron Konstantin von Neurath, Minister for Foreign Affairs, before the Seventh International Road Congress at Berlin, October 12, 1934

Translation, in Royal Institute of International Affairs, *Documents on International Affairs, 1934*, p. 331, citing *Völkerbund*, October 12, 1934; excerpts

THE AIMS WHICH we are following in the sphere of foreign policy are limited from the very beginning. When nation and government are exerting their whole strength to bring about a revival at home, to such an extent as is the case in Germany, the pursuit of all imperialistic aims abroad must naturally be given up. The foundation on which the German Government rest is not such that, in order to stabilize their power at home, they must have recourse to a successful foreign policy. In the case of a régime which, like the German régime, is rooted in, and must be rooted in, the profound will of the people, such a procedure cannot be considered for a moment. Not because we have neither the time nor the strength, but because such a procedure would be contrary to the entire sense and nature of the political events in the new Germany. We know that in order to secure the permanency of the work which we have begun, we need peace and the friendship of other nations, and our entire foreign policy is governed by this consideration.

There are only two basic points in this programme which require that we should present positive demands to the other governments and on the fulfilment of which we must insist; while in other respects our foreign policy can be characterized—if I may use somewhat commonplace phraseology—by the wish that we should be left in peace to carry out our plans at home. These two points are: the demand that we should be treated as a country with equal rights in the question of armaments, and the demand that the coming settlement of the Saar question shall be carried out in a manner which is in conformity with political reason and the provisions of the treaties. These two demands have one thing in common; they do not aim at fresh power and possessions abroad, but only at the closing of open wounds in the German body corporate.

I do not need to go again into that distressing chapter of the negotiations concerning the problem of disarmament. The course and the failure of these negotiations are known to all the world. The German Government can say with a clear conscience that they have done their very best to bring about a just and practicable solution of the armaments question, and I believe that there can no longer be any real doubt about this abroad. We still, however, hear from public and official quarters different opinions on this question, and that is largely the reason why the political atmosphere is now so oppressive, so that there is a danger of every sound and reasonable development being prevented. If this or that government still believes that Germany's right to equality can be doubted, or made dependent upon especial performances in advance and guarantees, that is a question which we cannot discuss. Such an attitude in reality only implies the desire still to treat Germany as a state of inferior rights, and to force her to admit that her desire for equality of rights is a source of unrest and possibly even a menace to peace. The exact contrary is the case. A state which cannot defend its frontiers is not only not an independent and autonomous state, but, when its frontiers are open and it is surrounded by highly armed states, an incentive to other countries to pursue a dangerous policy. We claim equality of rights for

Germany in the matter of armaments as a guarantee of peace and in order that we ourselves may be a real factor for peace in Europe. The reproach that, by proclaiming our peaceful intentions, we only wish to gain a short breathing space in order, subsequently, after having sufficiently strengthened ourselves, to proceed with the realization of our real aggressive plans is, after all our declarations and offers in the matter of disarmament, and after all we have otherwise said and done for the political pacification of Europe, so absurd that we can only interpret it as a deliberate and intentional calumny. In the political arrangements which we have made or proposed already, for instance in our reaffirmation of the principles of Locarno or in our last political agreement with Poland, where are any time-limits or other justifications for such suspicions?

Is it not absolute political nonsense to make concrete statements as to what a government might intend to do in ten or more years in the domain of foreign policy? And does not the only actual possibility of preparing for the maintenance of peace for a long time to come consist in treating the acute problems of the present time with understanding and making an honest endeavour to get rid of the tension existing at present? General and abstract constructions which go farther may be suited, as I have already hinted, to promote certain systems of idealogy, or also to disguise certain very actual political tendencies of special nature, but in our opinion they are not, as a rule, an actual help in securing general peace.

When the German Government decided a year ago to leave the League of Nations, they did not do so, as I should like to repeat to you to-day once more, because they wished to obtain greater freedom of movement in political matters for themselves, or because they were disinclined to co-operate politically with other states. They merely did so because the indispensable foundation for such co-operation, namely, our equality, was lacking. Of course what matters in this respect is not only words and theory, but political practice. That also constitutes a definition of the point of view which is decisive for any discussion of the question of our possible return to the League of Nations. That is by no means a standpoint based on one-sided special interests. Germany is certainly not the only country to consider that the League of Nations as an institution has been shaken to its foundations by its complete failure in the question of disarmament. It is also certainly an important symptom that quite recently a fresh dangerous crack has become visible in the building at Geneva owing to the development in the important question of minorities, which is so closely connected with the system of the Treaty of Versailles. We believe that far-reaching reforms would be necessary if the League of

Nations is to be made what it ought to be according to its statutes, namely a really practical instrument for maintaining peace. Its serious deficiencies will not be made good by the mere return of former members or the mere adhesion of new ones. That also applies to the Soviet Union's admission to the League of Nations, which has now taken place, and which is certainly a highly interesting act in the course of political developments, but which, however, we no longer claim the right to discuss, now that we have left the League of Nations, although we have always regarded it as the right thing to obtain the co-operation of all the states in international tasks.

The fundamental point of view of equality has, of its very nature, also exerted influence on our attitude with regard to another problem which has been much discussed in recent weeks. That is the Franco-Russian project for an Eastern Pact, or, as many wish to call it, a North-Eastern Pact. Even if in this case our point of view, which we recently communicated with detailed reasons to the Governments concerned and of which the principal points have already been made public, has been used as a ground for attacks on Germany and for casting suspicion on her will to peace, it is hard for us to attribute that to reasonably practical, not to mention objective, considerations. It is proposed that we should participate in a system of pacts under which ten states are to undertake to support each other at once in the event of war with their entire military resources. At the same time it is stated perfectly openly and decisively that our joining this system of pacts would, of course, not include the recognition of Germany's equality in the sphere of armaments, but that at most it would be a matter for consideration, after the system had come into force, whether and in what way it might be possible to resume the international discussion of the armaments question. We are, therefore, asked to enter into a special political community with other Powers entailing the assumption of far-reaching obligations, while at the same time our claim to equality is expressly disputed in a question which is most intimately connected with the aim of this community, namely, in the question of the state of military armaments. Could the Governments concerned really seriously assume that Germany is in a position to accept such a presumption? And further, ought not the other Powers to have asked themselves from the start what it would mean for Germany, in her central position in the midst of highly armed States, if she allowed herself to be drawn once for all into conflicts between other States of which the consequences cannot be foreseen, and which would make her the probable battlefield in the event of any conflagrations in Europe, while the only assurance given in return is that in this case her territory would, if necessary, be defended by Soviet Russian troops against an attack from the west, and by French troops against an attack from the east? It is not quite easy for us, when faced by such a project, to believe that its authors really had nothing in view but the mutual assurance of peace for the benefit of all States. We have not been able to avoid the impression that this project was rather due to special political tendencies. If the assumption which has been reported from various quarters abroad is correct that, in the event of the breakdown of their plan for a pact, France and Russia would decide on a dual alliance, that would only confirm this impression.

I openly admit that I am unable to regard the constant succession of plans for pacts of all kinds, which might well be described as pactomania, as a good symptom of the spirit in which the business of European politics is now being to a great extent conducted. It is impossible that the salvation of Europe should depend on alliances and groupings of Powers which change according to the circumstances of the moment. The political tendencies which run in such a direction are merely a proof of the deficiencies in the political system imposed upon Europe by the treaties of 1919, which are constantly becoming more evident. In the long run it is dangerous and also useless to decline to recognize and openly admit the existence of these deficiencies. As long as people have not the courage to look the indisputable facts and necessities in the face, and to seek an adjustment of the divergent interests in an open discussion between the States concerned, on the basis of mutual respect and equality, an improvement in the general political situation is inconceivable. . . .

I have now come to the end of my remarks. I should be glad if what I have said to you could contribute to completing the picture you are taking home of the new Germany, of its hopes and desires, and of the final aim of its policy. We have nothing to keep quiet about and nothing to conceal. We are sure that the direct knowledge of facts and ideas obtained by visitors to Germany can only turn out to our advantage, and can only serve to remove the mistakes and misunderstandings still disseminated abroad. In so far as foreign countries are not willing to sympathize with the plans and methods of our home policy, we can do nothing about it. But as regards our foreign policy, we have a right to demand that an end should be made of the misrepresentations and suspicions which still constantly make their appearance, and that the fact should be taken into account that the National-Socialist Government is a partner who combines a determination to protect the indispensable and vital interests and values of the German people with an equally firm determination to be a stable factor in the peace of Europe.

ADDRESS by Adolf Hitler, Chancellor of the Reich, at the Party Congress at Nuremberg, September 13, 1937

Translation, in Royal Institute of International Affairs, *Documents on International Affairs, 1937*, p. 180, citing the *Frankfurter Zeitung*, September 15, 1937; excerpts

As YOU KNOW, this Jewish Bolshevism (of which I have been speaking), following the usual procedure of a *détour* by way of democracy, has set its hand to open revolution in Spain. It would be a serious distortion of the facts to believe that the Bolshevist oppressors in that country were the holders of legal power, while those who fought for nationalist Spain were illegal revolutionaries. Far from it! We see in the men who surround General Franco the true and eternal Spain, and in the usurpers of Valencia the revolutionary mercenaries of Moscow, whose object is Spain to-day, but to-morrow will perhaps be another State. Can we remain indifferent in the face of these events?

I should like now to make a brief declaration: In the press of our western democracies and in the speeches of many of their politicians we are always hearing how important the natural spheres of interest of these Powers are. It appears to be taken for granted by the representatives of these States that their interests, including every sea as well as every State in Europe and also outside Europe, have been bestowed on them by Nature. On the other hand, we notice outbursts of annoyance whenever a country, which does not belong to this exclusive circle of international owners, speaks of definite interests outside its own frontiers. To this assumption I should like to reply as follows:

We are always hearing from England and France that they possess sacred rights in Spain. What kind of interests are these? Are they political or economic? If it is a case of political interests, then we understand such a claim as little as if some one were to claim political interests in Germany. It is no concern of others who rules in Germany, so long as the régime does not carry out or contemplate hostilities against other nations. If it is economic interests which people in England and France have in mind, then we are prepared to admit them without further ado, on the understanding, of course, that we claim for ourselves equal economic interests. In other words, National-Socialist Germany is watching the attempts of the Jewish world revolution to gain a footing in Spain with intense interest, and in two directions:

(1) Just as England and France desire that the balance of power in Europe should not be shifted, either in favour of Germany or Italy,

so we are equally anxious that the balance of power should not be altered by an increase in the power of Bolshevism. If Fascism rules in Italy, that is purely a national affair of Italy. It would be foolish to imagine that directions or orders could be given to this Fascist Italy from a centre lying outside the country. It would be still more foolish to regard this Fascist Italy as a part of a great international Fascist organization. Far from it. It is fundamental in Fascism and National-Socialism that the ideology and sphere of activity of these political philosophies lie only within their own frontiers. In the same way it is clear that a nationalist Spain will be national, that is to say, Spanish, just in the same way as there can be no doubt that Bolshevism is internationally conscious, has only one Centre, and recognizes elsewhere only branches of this Centre. Just as, on the one hand, people in England and France tend to be anxious for fear lest Spain should be occupied by Italy or Germany, so, on the other, we are disturbed by the possibility that Spain might be conquered by Soviet Russia. This conquest need not be carried out in the form of an occupation by Soviet troops, but it will nevertheless be an accomplished fact the moment a Bolshevized Spain becomes a section, that is to say, an integral part, of the Bolshevist Moscow Centre—an affiliation receiving its political instructions as well as its material subventions from Moscow. To sum up: we see in any attempt of Bolshevism to spread farther in Europe a shifting of the European balance of power. And just as England is concerned with the prevention of any such change in her own interest, so we adopt the same attitude where our own interests are at stake. We must refuse to take advice, regarding the nature of the change in the balance of power by the Bolshevists, from statesmen who have not the knowledge that we have in this matter and who have not had the same painful opportunities as we have had of gathering experience.

(2) No less important is the fact that a Bolshevist-political change in the balance of power would amount to an economic change which could not fail to involve catastrophic consequences for European States whose economics are so closely inter-related. The first visible sign of the success of any Bolshevist revolution is a fall in production and the total destruction of economic values as well as of the economic structure of the country affected. . . .

As soon as Bolshevism appeared in Spain, the entire national production was so injured that an immediate reduction in a really valuable exchange of goods took place; when it is argued, on the other hand, that other countries still can do good business with Spain, it must be forgotten that payment for deliveries is being made in gold, which has not acquired its value through Spanish Bolshevism but only as a symbol of former national Spanish work and service, and which has been stolen, seized, and brought abroad by Spanish Bolshevism. It is not possible to build up permanent and solid trade on such a basis; it can rest only on the exchange of real values and not on the activities of thieves and swindlers.

Perhaps England is only thinking politically about this Spanish question. For us Germans, who cannot base our trade on a world empire of our own, Europe is, especially as it is to-day, one of the essential conditions of our existence. A Bolshevistic Europe would destroy the trade of our country, not because we do not wish to engage in trade, but because we should find nobody to trade with. This is not a matter of theoretical observation or moral reproach for us, and certainly not a problem for international lamentation—because we have not so much respect for international institutions as to imagine for a second that we can get any help from them apart from phrases —but a matter of vital importance. We have no doubt that if Spain were finally to become Bolshevik, and if this flood perhaps were to spread over the rest of Europe or even spread at all—and Bolshevism itself declares this to be certain and it is at all events what it intends —this would be a severe economic catastrophe for Germany. For we must maintain a mutual exchange of goods with these countries in sheer defence of the life of the German people. This exchange is only possible when these countries are producing goods under orderly normal conditions. Should this cease through a Bolshevik catastrophe, Germany would also have to face very hard times economically.

We are all conscious that in such an event the Geneva League of Nations would probably show as much power to help as our own Inter-German Federal Parliament at Frankfurt. How little is to be expected from such a form of international assistance we already see to-day. The Bolshevik rising once begun in Spain, not only did trade with Germany immediately fall, but more than 15,000 German nationals had to leave this harassed land. Their businesses were plundered, German schools destroyed, the community houses partly burned, and the property of all these industrious men destroyed at one blow. They have been robbed of the fruits of years of honourable work. I scarcely believe that the League of Nations will compensate them. Even in the light of these happenings we address no appeal to it; we know it has its own problems and tasks. It has had to occupy itself, for example, for years in supporting the various Marxist and Jewish emigrants in order to keep them alive. . . .

I would like to take this opportunity of replying to those who insist on the necessity of international economic relations and their permanent improvement, who talk about international solidarity in this

GENERAL STATEMENTS OF POLICY

connexion, and who now think that they must complain that in their opinion National-Socialist Germany has deliberately tried to isolate herself. I have already emphasized what a great mistake has been made by statesmen and leading-article writers who seriously believe this. It is strikingly contradicted by facts. We have neither the wish nor the intention to be hermits. Germany has not isolated herself either politically or economically. Certainly she has not isolated herself politically, because, on the contrary, it has been our endeavour to work with all who have a really European aim in view. We categorically refuse to be united with those whose programme means the destruction of Europe and make no secret of it. . . .

We are witnessing the comedy of the Press of just those countries in which it is believed that we must be lectured upon greater participation in world economy, publishing immediately it became known that, for example, we are doing business with Nationalist Spain—that we are delivering machinery and such goods to them, and that they in return are sending us raw materials and foodstuffs. But surely we are doing exactly what these apostles of world economy so earnestly desire! Why, then suddenly all this fuss? As a matter of fact we know only too well the inner reasons for it. It is annoyance that we are in no circumstances prepared to import into Germany as commercial goods those Marxist contagious goods (*Infektionsstoffe*) which once brought us to the edge of the abyss; it is annoyance not only that we isolate ourselves but also that we absolutely refuse to have anything to do with countries with the same ideals as the Marxists or with an administration which thinks or acts as they do. I can only repeat that for Germany a different orientation is simply impossible, for we are more interested in Europe than perhaps some other nations need to be. Our country, our people, our civilization, our economy have developed out of the general limitations of Europe. We must, therefore, be the enemy of any attempt to introduce in part or in whole into this European family of nations an element of disintegration and destruction. . . .

ADDRESS by Adolf Hitler, Chancellor of the Reich, before the Reichstag, February 20, 1938

Translation, in *Vital Speeches of the Day*, March 1, 1938, p. 297; excerpts

From year to year the demand will grow stronger for those colonial possessions which Germany never took away from another power and which are for their possessors today as good as worthless, though for our own nation they appear indispensable.

I wish at this juncture to repel the hope expressed that it will be possible to haggle away our claims by the offer of credits. We desire not credits, but the fundamentals of life which would enable us, through our diligence, to insure the existence of the nation. . . .

After profound changes in the world map, both in territorial and ethnographic aspects, had been made in such brutal fashion, the League of Nations was founded with the task of establishing these crazy and irresponsible actions as final in the political and economic development of nations—with the task of establishing these results as an unalterable basis for the life and boundaries of human society on this planet. It was to be forbidden in the future to change by force what had been established by force.

In order somewhat to alleviate such a hair-raising ravishment of humanity, it was at least left open that this situation, the result of the force of thousands of years, should in the future be corrected along the path of justice and understanding. This somewhat difficult task was then incidentally intrusted to the League of Nations. Germany itself had absolutely no right to join this higher company for the defense of earlier acts of force, but first received this gracious permission under the unforgettable Chancellor Gustav Stresemann.

You know, my delegates, how greatly this institution has failed. It was neither a League of Nations in the beginning—and through later resignations two of the most powerful nations were missing from its ranks—nor was it an instrument of justice or, as it is claimed with a brazen front today, of the principles of justice.

It was the institution for the maintenance of the results of a thousand years of injustice. Then, either force is justice or force is injustice. If force today is unjust, then it was unjust in earlier times. When, therefore, the situation at the present time has been brought about by force, then has this situation been made possible by injustice. The League of Nations, therefore, does not maintain a just state of affairs, but one that has been born of a thousand years of injustice.

GENERAL STATEMENTS OF POLICY

We now hear that all this will be changed. We notice very often, for instance, that English statesmen would joyfully give us back our colonial possessions were they not bothered by the thought of the injustice and force which would be visited upon the natives. . . . If one were to apply the noble fundamental that a colony may only be owned by some one when the natives have manifested their express desires in this respect to the colonial acquisition of the past, the colonial possessions of our world powers would probably shrink appreciably in size.

All these colonial empires came into being not through a plebiscite, least of all through democratic plebiscites among the natives, but through stark and brutal violence. The colonies today, of course, are inseparable parts of the respective states and as such form a part of that order of the world which democratic politicians persist in describing as "an order of law," of a law which the League of Nations is now intrusted with preserving.

I completely understand that those interested in maintaining order consider the League of Nations as an agreeable moral forum serving to maintain it and if necessary to defend possessions which had been gained by violence. I do not understand that somebody who has just been robbed should on his part join such illustrious company.

And I must protest against the conclusion that we are not willing to protect the principles of right only because we do not belong to the League of Nations. On the contrary, we do not belong to the League of Nations because we believe it is no organ of right but rather an institution defending the wrong done at Versailles. Thereto a number of factual considerations must be added:

First, we left the League of Nations because, true to its origin and purpose, it denied us the right of equal armaments, and consequent equality security.

Second, we would never enter it again because we do not intend to allow ourselves to be impelled by a majority decision of the League to defend a wrong done in any part of the world.

Third, we believe we thereby render service to all peoples who have the misfortune to believe they can expect real help from the League. For we should have considered it a better course if, in the Ethiopian conflict, the League had shown a better understanding of Italian necessities and awakened less hopes and made fewer promises to the Ethiopians. This might have made possible a more simple and more reasonable solution of the entire problem.

Fourth, we do not think for a moment of allowing the German nation to be implicated in conflicts in which it is not interested. We are not willing to fight for territorial or economic interests of others without obtaining the slightest advantage for Germany. Moreover, we also do not expect such assistance from other nations. . . .

Fifth, we will in the future not allow our attitude to be prescribed by an institution which, by declining recognition of obvious facts, indulges in behavior less familiar in reasonable men than in a well known large bird. Should the League of Nations exist for 100 years it would lead to comical results inasmuch the League obviously is unable to understand historical or economic necessities and fulfill exigencies following from them. . . .

Germany will recognize Manchukuo. In deciding this measure, I do so in order to draw here the final line between a policy of fantastic absurdities and one of sober realization of facts.

Concluding, I want to state again that Germany, especially after Italy's resignation from the League, no longer thinks of ever returning to this institution. This does not mean a refusal to cooperate with other powers. Quite the contrary. It means a refusal to assume responsibilities which cannot be foreseen and which, in most cases, cannot be fulfilled.

To this cooperation with other nations, Germany made many and, we believe, valuable contributions. The Reich today cannot be considered as isolated, either economically or politically. On the contrary, ever since I assumed power in the Reich I have strived to establish the best possible relations with most states. Only with one state have we not sought relations: Soviet Russia. More than ever we see Bolshevism as the incarnation of human destructiveness.

We do not hold the Russian people, as such, responsible for this gruesome ideology of destruction. We know it is the small Jewish intellectual uppercrust which has brought this great people into this crazy frame of mind. If this teaching would limit itself territorially to Russia, then one might ignore it, because Germany has no intention to impose upon the Russian people our conceptions of life. Unfortunately, Jewish international Bolshevism from the Soviet breeding place tries to undermine the spirit of the people of the world, cause collapse of the social order and put chaos in place of culture. . . .

From this follows also our relationship with Japan. . . . I cannot share the opinion of certain statesmen that a service will be rendered to the European world through the harming of Japan. I fear that a Japanese defeat in the Far East would never benefit Europe or America, but would solely be to the advantage of Bolshevistic Soviet Russia. I do not consider China to be spiritually or materially strong enough to be able to stand up alone against the Bolshevist aggression.

I believe that even the most complete victory of Japan would be infinitely less dangerous for the culture and general peace of the world than a victorious Bolshevism would be. Germany has a treaty with Japan for the combating of the machinations of the Communist Internationale. She has always had friendly relations with China. I think that we are able before all to assume the role of really neutral spectators of this drama.

I do not have to express the assurance that we all had, and have, the desire to see the re-establishment of a condition of calm and finally of peace between the two great Far Eastern nations. We even believe that peace would long since have been established had it not been that certain powers, as in the case of Abyssinia, have added too much to one side of the scale with their advice and possibly with the promise of moral assistance.

The taking of this position, as things stand now, has only a purely platonic significance. The drowning man clutches at every straw. It would have been better to apprise China of the earnestness of her position than, as has happened so often, to cite the League of Nations as the sure guarantor of peace and security.

Irrespective of the time and the manner in which the situation in the Far East will finally be decided, Germany in its determination to ward off Communism will always consider and value Japan as a factor for the freedom and the safeguarding of human culture. We have no doubt that even the most complete Japanese victory will not in the slightest affect the culture of the white peoples, nor do we doubt that a victory of Bolshevism would mean the end of the thousand-year-old culture of the white race. . . .

Germany has no territorial interests in the Far East. Germany has the understandable wish to promote trade and commerce. This does not obligate us to enter the lists on behalf of either of the opposing forces. It does, however, obligate us to recognize that a triumph of Bolshevism would destroy the last possibilities there.

Incidentally, Germany once had possessions in the Far East. That did not prevent a coalition of white and yellow races from driving the German Reich from those possessions.

We certainly do not wish to receive an invitation to return to the Far East. Nor does Germany entertain territorial interests in regard to the frightful civil war now raging in Spain. The situation there is similar to that which Germany once experienced. The attack, personally and materially inspired and directed by Moscow against a national independent state, led to resistance on the part of the national population, which did not wish to let itself be massacred.

And just as in Germany, the democratic internationalists also stand in this instance on the side of the Bolshevist incendiaries. The German government saw in a Bolshevization of Spain not only an unsettling element in Europe but also a disturbance of the European balance of power, for as soon as that land becomes a branch of the Moscow headquarters a danger would arise for a further extension of this pestilence of ruin and destruction, which under no circumstances could we contemplate with indifference. We are, therefore, happy that our anti-Bolshevist attitude is shared also by a third state.

German-Italian relations are based on the existence of identical conceptions of life and of the state, as well as upon joint defense against international dangers menacing us. How much this conviction has become the common possession of the entire German nation was most strikingly shown by the enthusiasm with which the creator of Fascist Italy was welcomed in the Reich.

All European statesmen ought to realize one thing: Had Mussolini not assumed power in Italy through the victory of the Fascist movement in 1922, that country would probably have fallen prey to Bolshevism. The consequences of such a collapse for European culture would have been simply unimaginable. Hence, German sympathy for Mussolini is a tribute to a phenomenon of an epochal significance.

Italy's situation in many respects is similar to that of Germany. Under such circumstances it is inevitable that we, suffering from similar overpopulation, showed understanding for the acts of a regime and of a man who is not willing to let a nation perish for the sake of fantastic ideals of the League of Nations, but on the contrary were determined to save it. This is more obvious, as the pretended ideals of the League of Nations largely coincide with the extremely realistic interests of leading powers.

In the Spanish conflict as well, Germany and Italy have the same views and have adopted the same stand. Their goal is to secure existence of a fully independent national Spanish state.

From specific motives, the German-Italian friendship has gradually developed into an element for stabilization of Europe and peace. Agreement between these two states and Japan constitutes the most powerful obstacle in the way of the further spread of Bolshevism.

During recent years there has been frequent talk of differences between France and England, on the one hand, and Germany on the other. It is not quite clear to me what the substance of these differences is supposed to be. Germany has no territorial claims on France in Europe, as I have stressed more than once. We hope the period of territorial rivalry between Germany and France was closed by the return of the Saar district.

Germany also has no dispute with England, except over colonies. However, there is not the slightest symptom indicating the possibility

GENERAL STATEMENTS OF POLICY

of any conflict. The only thing poisoning, and thereby affecting, their relations is the well-nigh intolerable press campaign conducted in those countries under the motto of "personal opinion." . . .

Germany, at any rate, has the most sincere desire to establish trustful relations with all European big powers as well as other states. If this is not accomplished, it will not have been our fault. We believe, however, that in view of the press attitude, little may be expected for the time being from conferences or individual discussions.

For it is impossible to have any disillusion about the following fact —this international press campaign against peace will know immediately how to sabotage any attempt to arrive at an understanding among nations. It will forthwith misinterpret every discussion or twist it into the opposite. It will immediately falsify every agreement. Under these circumstances it cannot be conceived that good can come of such conversations and meetings as long as governments generally are not in a position to take decisive steps without considering their public opinion.

We believe, therefore, that for the time being a normal diplomatic exchange of notes is the only feasible means from which to take a base, at least from too flagrant falsifications of this international press.

If Germany itself limits its interests, this is not to mean that we are disinterested in what is happening around us. We are happy to have normal and partly friendly relations with most states bordering Germany. We feel that everywhere a feeling of relaxation exists. The striving for real neutrality, which we can note in a number of European states, fills us with sincere satisfaction. We believe we may perceive in this an element of increasing calm and increased security. We also see, however, on the other hand, the painful results on the European map and the European economic and political situation brought about by lunatic Versailles' action.

Two of the states bordering Germany alone include a mass of 10,000,000 Germans. Until 1866 they were united with the German people in a federation, on a constitutional basis. In the World War they fought until 1918 shoulder to shoulder with German soldiers of the Reich. Against their will, they were prevented by peace treaties from joining the Reich. This was painful enough.

About one thing, however, there should be no doubt. Separation from state sovereignty of the Reich cannot lead to the loss of racial or political rights. That is to say, the general rights of racial and political self-determination solemnly assured us in Wilson's fourteen points as a prerequisite of the Armistice must not be disregarded simply because the people in question are Germans.

We know perfectly well no completely satisfactory delineation of frontiers is possible in Europe. More important it seems to be to avoid unnecessary tormenting of national minorities, thus adding suffering of persecution because of racial allegiance to suffering of separation. . . .

In the fifth year after conclusion of the Reich's first great foreign political settlement, it fills us with sincere satisfaction to see that in our relations with the country with which we had perhaps the gravest differences there is not only a lessening of tension but ever more amiable *rapprochement* in recent years. I know perfectly well that this is due to the fact that at the time no western parliamentarianism ruled in Warsaw, but instead a Polish marshal who was a towering personality and realized the significance for Europe of such a Polish-German agreement.

Work questioned by many since then has proved its worth. And may I say that since the League discontinued its incessant attempts at interference in Danzig and sent there a new commissioner who is a man of outstanding personality, this point—perhaps a most dangerous one for European peace—completely lost its menacing character. The Polish state respects the national status of Danzig as well as Germany respects Polish rights. Thus it was possible to pave the way for an understanding which, starting with Danzig, was able to clear completely the poisoned atmosphere between Germany and Poland and to initiate sincerely amiable co-operation despite attempts by many disturbers of the peace.

I am happy, my deputies, to announce that during these last days another understanding has been reached with a country which is particularly close to us for many reasons. It is not only its people, but above all its long common history and common culture which links us to German Austria.

Difficulties emerging in enforcement of the July 11 (1936) agreement forced us to try to eliminate misunderstandings and obstacles in the way of final reconciliation. Then it was clear that a situation that had grown unbearable could one day, whether desired or not, develop the prerequisites for a very severe catastrophe. It lies outside the power of mankind to halt that destiny which carelessness or unintelligence has started rolling. I am happy to be able to state that this realization was also the opinion of the Austrian Chancellor, whom I asked to visit me.

The thought and the intention were present to ease the tension of our relations by giving that part of the German-Austrian people which is National Socialistic in its convictions and world view equality before the law as it exists at present, in the same measure as is enjoyed by the rest of the population.

In accordance with this, a great peace action was to take place in the form of a general amnesty and a better understanding of the two countries through closer friendly relations in the various fields of a possible political, personal and material economic co-operation. This is a supplementation of the agreement of the eleventh of July.

I would like at this time, before the German people, to express my sincere thanks to the Austrian Chancellor for the great understanding and warm-hearted readiness with which he accepted my invitation and endeavored with me to find a way in accord with the interest of both countries and in the interest of the entire German race —that entire German race whose sons we all are, irrespective of where the crib of our homeland stood. I believe that we have herewith made a contribution to European peace.

The best proof for the correctness of this assumption is the furious rage of those democratic world citizens who, although otherwise always talking about peace, let no opportunity go by without inciting to war.

They are peeved and infuriated by this work for understanding. It may therefore justly be assumed that it is good and opportune. This example may perhaps help bring about more extensive and gradual European relaxation. Germany supported by its friendships, at any rate will leave no stone unturned to rescue what also in the future is prerequisite to our work—peace.

I may here again assure you, my party comrades, that our relations with other European and also overseas states are good and normal or even very friendly. I need only to point to our exceedingly friendly relations with Hungary, Bulgaria, Yugoslavia and many other states. About the extent of our economic co-operation with other nations, our foreign trade balance has afforded you an impressive picture.

But above all stands the co-operation with those two great powers which, like Germany, have recognized in Bolshevism a world menace and are therefore determined to oppose Communist Internationale in a united defense. That this co-operation with Italy and Japan may become ever more intense is my most sincere wish.

For the rest, I am happy about every possible relaxation in the political situation. . . .

At this hour I should only like to pray to the Lord God also in years to come to bestow his blessing upon our work, our acts, our insight and our resolution to preserve us from overbearing as well as cowardly subservience, guiding us on the right path which His providence mapped out for the German people and that He always will give us the courage to do what is right and never waver or shrink before any violence or any danger.

Long live Germany and the German nation.

DISARMAMENT AND SECURITY

ADDRESS by Julius Curtius, Minister for Foreign Affairs, in the Council of the League of Nations, January 20, 1931

Royal Institute of International Affairs, *Documents on International Affairs, 1931*, p. 50; excerpt

THE COUNCIL is aware of German opinion regarding the draft Convention. Since the creation of the Preparatory Commission we have been forced to realize each year more clearly that the path followed by the Preparatory Commission was leading it farther and farther away from its original aim. We have given continual warnings and we have reminded you in what real disarmament must consist. Nevertheless, in spite of the objections raised by us, the essential factors of any real *land* disarmament have been eliminated one after the other from the draft Convention. The scheme for disarmament prepared by the Commission represents, at most, the stabilization of the existing armaments and would even permit of an increase in those armaments. That is why the German representative, acting on the instructions of his Government, was obliged, in the spring of 1929, to dissociate himself from the majority of the Commission. But even this clear warning was not heeded by the Commission. The latter even went so far in the end as to place in the draft, which in itself is entirely inadequate, a new confirmation of the disarmament imposed upon Germany by the Treaties. It was therefore quite natural that Germany could not accept the results of the Preparatory Commission's work.

The Disarmament Conference can only achieve acceptable results if, before the figures are entered, it thoroughly revises the methods at present proposed. It should, moreover, be guided by the fundamental principle of the League of Nations—that is to say, the equality of all its Members, and should not set security against insecurity and threats against powerlessness.

COMMUNICATION from Baron Konstantin von Neurath, Minister for Foreign Affairs, to the President of the Conference for the Reduction and Limitation of Armaments (Arthur Henderson), September 14, 1932

Royal Institute of International Affairs, *Documents on International Affairs, 1932*, p. 198, citing *The Times* (London), September 17, 1932

SIR:

On behalf of the German Government I have the honor to communicate to you the following:

In the course of the discussions of the General Committee (of the Disarmament Conference), which led up to the adoption of the Resolution of July 23, 1932, the head of the German delegation indicated the reasons for which the German Government was unable to accept the Resolution in question. He pointed out that in view of the stage reached by the discussions of the Conference the question of equality of rights of the disarmed States could no longer remain without a solution. On that occasion he accordingly declared that the German Government could not take part in the further labors of the Conference before the question of Germany's equality of rights had been satisfactorily cleared up.

The Resolution having been adopted, nevertheless, it is clear even now that the future Disarmament Convention will fall far short of the system of disarmament laid down by the Versailles Treaty, and will differ therefrom essentially as regards both the form and the manner of the disarmament. The question of how the future régime is to be applied to Germany thus becomes a matter of direct and immediate importance. It is obvious that unless this question is answered no settlement of individual concrete points of the disarmament problem is possible.

In the German Government's view only one solution can be considered—namely, that all States should be subject to the same rules and principles in respect of disarmament, and that no discriminatory exceptional system should exist in the case of any one of them. Germany cannot be expected to take part in the negotiations with regard to the measures of disarmament to be laid down in the Convention, until it is established that the solutions which may be found are also to apply to Germany.

With a view to the earliest possible realization of the condition for the future co-operation of Germany with the Conference, the German Government has in the interval endeavored to clear up the question of equality of rights through diplomatic channels. Unfortunately, it must be stated that the German efforts have not hitherto led to any satisfactory result. In these circumstances I find myself compelled, to my regret, to inform you that the German Government is unable to avail itself of the invitation to the session of the Bureau of the Conference which is to begin on September 21, 1932.

The German Government is now, as ever, convinced that thoroughgoing general disarmament is urgently necessary for the purpose of ensuring peace. It will follow the labors of the Conference with interest, and will determine its further attitude by the course which they may take.

COMMUNICATION Telegraphed by Baron Konstantin von Neurath, Minister for Foreign Affairs, to the President of the Conference for the Reduction and Limitation of Armaments (Arthur Henderson), October 14, 1933

British White Paper, Cmd. 4437, p. 11

ON BEHALF OF the German Government, I have the honour to make to you the following communication:—

In the light of the course which recent discussions of the Powers concerned have taken in the matter of disarmament, it is now clear that the Disarmament Conference will not fulfil what is its sole object, namely, general disarmament. It is also clear that this failure of the conference is due solely to the unwillingness on the part of the highly-armed States to carry out their contractual obligation to disarm. This renders impossible the satisfaction of Germany's recognised claim to equality of rights, and the condition on which the German Government agreed at the beginning of this year again to take part in the work of the conference thus no longer exists.

The German Government is accordingly compelled to leave the Disarmament Conference.

DISARMAMENT AND SECURITY

PROCLAMATION by Adolf Hitler, Chancellor of the Reich, to the German Nation, October 14, 1933, Regarding the Withdrawal of Germany from the Disarmament Conference and the League of Nations

Translation, in Royal Institute of International Affairs, *Documents on International Affairs, 1933*, p. 287, citing *Völkerbund*, October 20, 1933

FILLED WITH the sincere desire to accomplish the work of the peaceful internal reconstruction of our nation and of its political and economic life, former German Governments, trusting in the grant of a dignified equality of rights, declared their willingness to enter the League of Nations and to take part in the Disarmament Conference.

In this connexion Germany suffered a bitter disappointment.

In spite of our readiness to carry through German disarmament at any time, if necessary, to its ultimate consequence, other Governments could not decide to redeem the pledges signed by them in the Peace Treaty.

By the deliberate refusal of real moral and material equality of rights to Germany, the German nation and its Governments have been profoundly humiliated.

After the German Government had declared, as a result of the equality of rights expressly laid down on December 11, 1932, that it was again prepared to take part in the Disarmament Conference, the German Foreign Minister and our delegates were informed by the official representatives of other States in public speeches and direct statements that this equality of rights could no longer be granted to present-day Germany.

As the German Government regards this action as an unjust and humiliating discrimination against the German nation, it is not in a position to continue, as an outlawed and second-class nation, to take part in negotiations which could only lead to further arbitrary results.

While the German Government again proclaims its unshaken desire for peace, it declares to its great regret that, in view of these imputations, it must leave the Disarmament Conference. It will also announce its departure from the League of Nations.

It submits this decision, together with a fresh statement of its adherence to a policy of sincere love of peace and readiness to come to an understanding, to the judgement of the German nation, and awaits from it a declaration of the same love of peace and readiness for peaceful relations, but also of the same conception of honour and the same determination.

As Chancellor of the German Reich, I have therefore proposed to the President of the Reich, as a visible expression of the united will of Government and people, to submit this policy of the Government to the nation in a referendum, and to dissolve the German Reichstag in order to give the German people an opportunity of electing those deputies who, as sworn representatives of this policy and of peace and honour, can give the nation the guarantee of an unswerving representation of its interests in this respect.

As Chancellor of the German nation and leader of the National Socialist movement, I am convinced that the entire nation stands united to a man behind a declaration and a decision which arise as much from love of our people and regard for its honour, as from the conviction that the ultimate world reconciliation, which is so necessary for all, can only be attained when the conceptions of victor and vanquished give way to the nobler view of equal rights of existence.

STATEMENT Issued by the German Government, April 16, 1934, Regarding the British Memorandum on Disarmament of January 29, 1934

British White Paper, Cmd. 4559, p. 18

THE German Government are ready to accept the United Kingdom memorandum of the 29th January, 1934, as the basis of a convention, subject to certain important modifications. The German Government find it impossible to wait two years for appropriate means of aerial defence. They wish to possess a defensive air force of short-range machines not including bombing planes from the beginning of the convention, the numerical strength of which would not exceed 30 per cent. of the combined air forces of Germany's neighbours or 50 per cent. of the military aircraft possessed by France (in France itself and in the French North African territories), whichever figure was the less. This claim the German Government make without prejudice to the result of the air enquiry proposed in the United Kingdom memorandum, which would be held as proposed therein and which should at least abolish bombers. Germany does not ask for higher numbers of military aircraft than these during the first five years of a ten years' convention, but after those five years she claims that the necessary reductions and increases should be made so that she should attain full equality of numbers with the principal air Powers at the end of the ten years of the convention. The German Government would be prepared to agree, on the basis of reciprocity, to the institution of the new regulations mentioned by the German Chancellor to Mr. Eden on the 21st February to ensure the non-military character of the S.A. and S.S., such character to be verified by a system of supervision. These regulations would provide that the S.A. and S.S. would (1) possess no arms; (2) receive no instruction in arms; (3) not be concentrated or trained in military camps; (4) not be, directly or indirectly, commanded or instructed by officers of the regular army; (5) not engage in or take part in field exercises. The German Government are also prepared to agree to the postponement of the reductions of armaments of other Powers until the end of the fifth year of the convention, the measure of disarmament laid down in the United Kingdom memorandum being carried out during the second five years of the convention. All the other proposals made in the United Kingdom memorandum, which would be unaffected by these modifications, such, for example, as supervision, are accepted by the German Government. The German Government continue to recognise the Treaties of Locarno. They consider that Germany's return to the League can only be dealt with after the solution of the question of disarmament and above all of their equality of rights.

PROCLAMATION by Adolf Hitler, Chancellor of the Reich, Denouncing Part V of the Treaty of Versailles, March 16, 1935

Translation, in Royal Institute of International Affairs, *Documents on International Affairs, 1935*, I, 58, citing *The New York Times*, March 17, 1935

TO THE GERMAN PEOPLE:

When in November, 1918, the German people, trusting in the promises given in President Wilson's Fourteen Points, grounded arms after four and a half years' honourable resistance in a war whose outbreak they had never desired, they believed they had rendered a service not only to tormented humanity, but also to a great idea *per se*.

Themselves the most serious sufferers from the result of this insane struggle, the millions composing our people trustingly seized upon the idea of a new order in the relations between peoples, an order which was to be ennobled on one hand by doing away with the secrecy of diplomatic cabinet policies and on the other hand by abandoning the terrible methods of war. The historically severest result of the defeat seemed to many Germans to be the only sacrifice necessary in order once and for all to save the world from similar terrors.

The idea of the League of Nations has perhaps in no nation awakened more fervent acclaim than in Germany, stripped as she was of all earthly happiness. Only thus it was conceivable that the German people not only accepted but also fulfilled the conditions, verily senseless in many respects, for the destruction of every condition and possibility of defence.

The German people, and especially their Governments of that time, were convinced that, by fulfilment of the conditions of disarmament laid down in the Versailles Treaty and in accordance with the promises of that Treaty, the beginning of international general disarmament would be marked and guaranteed.

For, only in a two-sided fulfilment of the task by the Treaty could there lie a moral and sensible justification for a demand which, one-sidedly imposed and executed, had necessarily to lead to an eternal discrimination, and thereby to a declaration of inferiority of a great nation.

Under such conditions, however, a peace treaty of this sort could never create the conditions for a true inward reconciliation of peoples, nor for the pacification of the world achieved in this manner, but could only set up a hatred that would gnaw eternally.

Germany has, according to the investigation of the Inter-Allied Control Commission, fulfilled the disarmament conditions imposed upon her. Following is the work of destruction of the German power of resistance and the means necessary therefor, as was certified by this commission.

Army: 59,897 cannon and heavy gun barrels, 130,558 machine guns, 31,470 mine throwers and barrels, 6,007,000 guns and carbines, 243,937 machine-gun bores, 28,001 cannon carriages, 4,390 machine-gun carriages, 38,750,000 bullets, 16,550,000 hand- and gun-grenades, 60,400,000 fuses, 491,000,000 rounds of ammunition for hand weapons, 335,000 tons of shell cases, 23,515 tons of cartridge cases, 37,600 tons of powder, 79,500 ammunition empties, 212,000 telephones, 1,072 flame throwers, 31 armoured cars, 59 tanks, 1,762 observation cars, 8,982 wireless stations, 1,240 field-bakeries, 2,199 pontoons, 981.7 tons of equipment for soldiers, 8,230,350 sacks of equipment for soldiers, 7,300 pistols and revolvers, 180 machine-gun sleds, 21 transportable workshops, 12 anti-aircraft gun carriages, 11 limbers, 64,000 steel helmets, 174,000 gas masks, 2,500 machines of the former war industry, 8,000 gun barrels.

Air forces: 15,714 chasing and bombing planes, 2,757 airplane motors.

Navy: Material that was either destroyed, scrapped, sunk, or handed over—26 first-class battleships, 4 coastal cruisers, 4 armoured cruisers, 18 small cruisers, 21 schooling and other ships, 83 torpedo boats, 315 submarines.

In addition there had to be destroyed vehicles of all sorts, utensils for gas attacks and partly for gas protection, fuel of various kinds, explosives, searchlights, gun-sighting appliances, instruments for measuring distance in sound, optical instruments of all kinds, harness for horses, equipment for narrow-gauge railways, printeries, field-kitchens, workshops, cut and thrust weapons, steel helmets, material for transporting munitions, normal and special machines belonging to war industry, mounting frames, drawings for the latter, and hangars for airplanes and airships, etc.

After this historically unexampled fulfilment of a treaty, the German people had the right to expect the redemption also by the other side of obligations undertaken. For, firstly, Germany had disarmed; secondly, in the Peace Treaty the demand had been expressly made that Germany must be disarmed in order thereby to create the precondition for general disarmament; that is, it was contended that Germany's armaments alone furnished the reason for the armaments of the other countries; thirdly, the German people at that time were filled both as regards their Government and their parties with a spirit that corresponded exactly with the pacifist-democratic ideals of the League of Nations and its founders.

But while Germany as one party to the Treaty had fulfilled its obligations, the redemption of the obligation on the part of the second partner to the Treaty failed to become a fact. That means; the High Contracting Parties of the former victor States have one-sidedly divorced themselves from the obligations of the Versailles Treaty.

Not alone did they refrain from disarming in a manner that could by any stretch be comparable with the destruction of German arms. No. Not even was there a halt in the armaments race; on the contrary, the increase of armaments on the part of a whole group in States became evident. Whatever had during the war been invented in the way of new engines of destruction was now in peacetime brought to final perfection by methodically scientific labour.

In the realm of creating mighty armoured cars, as well as in that of new fighting and bombing planes, continuous and terrible improvements resulted. New gigantic cannon were constructed, new explosive fire and gas bombs were developed.

The world, however, since then has again resumed its cries of war, just as though there never had been a World War nor the Versailles Treaty. In the midst of these highly-armed, warlike States, which were more and more making use of the most modern motorized equipment, Germany was, militarily speaking, in a vacuum, defencelessly at the mercy of every threatening danger.

The German people recall the misfortune and suffering of fifteen years' economic misery and political and moral humiliation. It was, therefore, understandable that Germany began loudly to demand the fulfilment of the promises made by other States to disarm, for this is clear: the world would not only stand for one hundred years of peace, but such a period would be an unmeasured boon. It cannot, however, stand for one hundred years of division into victor and vanquished.

The conviction that international disarmament was morally justified and necessary gained ground, not only in Germany, but also among many other peoples. From the insistence of these forces there resulted attempts through conferences to give direction to the reduction of armaments, and thereby to a general equalization on a low level. Thus there developed the first proposals for an international agreement on armaments, of which we remember the MacDonald plan as significant.

Germany was ready to accept this plan and adopt it as the foundation for arrangements to be arrived at. It failed because the other States declined to accept it, and was finally abandoned.

Inasmuch as in these circumstances the equality which was solemnly promised to the German people and Reich in the declaration of December, 1932, failed of realization, the new Reich's Government, as guardian of the honour and right to live of the German people, was unable to continue to take part in conferences of that sort or to continue membership in the League of Nations. However, even after leaving Geneva, Germany still was ready, not only to examine the other States' proposals, but herself to make practical proposals.

In that connexion she identified herself with the viewpoint which other States themselves had expressed; namely, that the creation of armies with short enlistments is not suited to the purposes of attack, and is therefore recommendable for peaceful defence. Germany was therefore ready to transform the Reichswehr with its long service period into an army with short enlistments, consonantly with the wishes of the other States.

Her proposals, made during the winter of 1933-4, were practical and executable. The fact that they were declined, as well as the fact that Italian and English proposals along similar lines were finally declined, justified the conclusion that on the other side of the contracting parties there no longer existed any inclination for a belated and honest fulfilment of the disarmament clauses of Versailles.

In these circumstances, the German Government saw itself compelled of its own accord to take those necessary measures which could ensure the end of a condition of impotent defencelessness of a great people and Reich, which was as unworthy as in the last analysis it was menacing. In so doing it proceeded from the same premises which Mr. Baldwin in his last speech so truthfully expressed:

A country which shows itself unwilling to make what necessary preparations are requisite for its own defence will never have power, moral or material, in this world.

The Government of the present-day German Reich, however, desires but one single moral and material power—namely the power to safeguard peace for the Reich and thereby, really also, for all Europe.

The Government, therefore, continued to do what it could and what served the advancement of peace.

Firstly, it proposed a long time ago the conclusion of non-aggression pacts to all its neighbour States.

Secondly, it has sought for and found the adjustment laid down in the treaty with its eastern neighbour which, thanks to the great understanding shown on the other side, has, as it hopes, forever taken the poison out of the threatening atmosphere which it found on seizing power, and which will lead to lasting reconciliation and friendship between the two peoples.

Thirdly, it has finally given France the solemn assurance that Germany, after the adjustment of the Saar question, now no longer will make territorial demands upon France.

It believes thereby, in a manner rare in history, to have created the precondition for ending the century-old strife between the two great nations by making a heavy political and material sacrifice.

The German Government must, however, to its regret, note that for months the rest of the world has been rearming continuously and increasingly. It sees in the creation of a Soviet Russian Army of 101 divisions, that is, in an admitted present peace strength of 960,000 men, an element that at the time of the conclusion of the Versailles Treaty could not have been divined. It sees in the forcing of similar measures in other States further proofs of the refusal to accept the disarmament idea as originally proclaimed.

Far be it from the German Government to raise complaint against any other State. It must point out, however, today that by France's introduction of a two-year service period as now decided, the idea upon which the creation of armies with short enlistment had been tested has been abandoned in favour of an organization with long enlistments. This, however, was one of the arguments advanced at the time for demanding that Germany give up her Reichswehr.

In these circumstances the German Government considers it impossible still longer to refrain from taking the necessary measures for the security of the Reich or even to hide the knowledge thereof from the other nations.

If, therefore, it now fulfils the wish for enlightening the world on Germany's intentions, as expressed in the speech by the British Minister Stanley Baldwin, on November 28, 1934, it does so: firstly in order to give the German people the conviction and other States the knowledge that the safeguarding of the honour and security of the German Reich henceforth will be again entrusted to the [sole charge] of the German nation; secondly, in order, by fixing the extent of German measures, to devitalize those claims which attempt to ascribe to the German people a striving for a position of military hegemony in Europe.

What the German Government, as the guardian of the honour and interests of the German nation, desires is to make sure that Germany possesses sufficient instruments of power not only to maintain the integrity of the German Reich, but also to command international respect and value as co-guarantor of general peace.

For in this hour the German Government renews before the German people, before the entire world, its assurance of its determination never to proceed beyond the safeguarding of German honour and the freedom of the Reich, and especially does it not intend in rearming Germany to create any instrument for warlike attack, but on the contrary, exclusively for defence and thereby for the maintenance of peace.

In so doing, the German Reich's Government expresses the confident hope that the German people, having again reverted to their own honour, may be privileged in independent equality to make their contribution for the pacification of the world in free and open cooperation with other nations and their Governments.

With this in view, the German Reich's Government today passed the following law:

German Law of March 16, 1935

(1) Service in defensive forces is predicated on universal military service.

(2) The German peace army, including police units which have been incorporated in the army, shall comprise twelve corps commands and thirty-six divisions.

(3) Supplementary laws for regulating universal military service will be drafted and submitted to the Reich Cabinet by the Reich Minister of Defence.

ADDRESS by Adolf Hitler, Chancellor of the Reich, before the Reichstag, May 21, 1935

Translation, in British Blue Book, Cmd. 5143, p. 32; excerpt

THE German Government reject the decision reached at Geneva on the 17th April. It was not Germany who unilaterally infringed the Treaty of Versailles, but the dictated peace of Versailles was unilaterally infringed in the points known and thus rendered invalid by those Powers which could not decide to follow the disarmament demanded from Germany by themselves disarming as contemplated by treaty.

The fresh discrimination made against Germany at Geneva by this resolution makes it impossible for the German Government to return to that institution before the conditions for a real legal equality of all participants have been created. For this purpose the German Government consider it necessary to make a clear line of demarcation between the Treaty of Versailles, which is built upon the division of the nations into victors and vanquished, and the League of Nations, which must be built upon the estimation of all its members as being of equal value and possessing equal rights.

This equality of rights must extent to all functions and all rights of property in international life.

2. The German Government have, as a result of the nonfulfilment of the undertakings to disarm on the part of the other States, for their part renounced the articles which, as a result of the one-sided burden laid upon Germany contrary to the treaty, constitute a discrimination against the German nation for an unlimited period. They hereby, however, most solemnly declare that these measures of theirs apply only to the points mentioned, which discriminate morally and practically against the German nation. The German Government will therefore unconditionally respect the remaining articles regarding international relations, including the territorial provisions, and will only carry out by means of peaceable understandings such revisions as will be inevitable in the course of time.

3. The German Government do not intend to sign any treaty which seems to them incapable of fulfilment, but they will scrupulously observe every treaty voluntarily signed by them, even if it was drawn up before they took over the Government and power. They will therefore, in particular, observe and fulfil all obligations arising out of the Locarno Pact so long as the other parties to the treaty are also willing to adhere to the said pact. The German Government

regard the respecting of the demilitarised zones as an extremely difficult contribution for a sovereign State to make to the appeasement of Europe. They consider, however, that they must refer to the fact that the continued increase of troops on the other side are in no way to be regarded as supplementing these endeavours.

4. The German Government are ready at any time to take part in a system of collective co-operation to secure peace in Europe, but consider it necessary to give play to the law of continuous development by allowing for the possibility of the revision of treaties. They regard the possibility of a regulated development of treaties as an element for the securing of peace, but regard the suppression of any necessary changes as only too liable to result in an explosion in the future.

5. The German Government are of opinion that the reconstruction of a system of European co-operation cannot be brought about by conditions which have been forced upon one party. They believe that it is right, in view of often conflicting interests, always to be content with a minimum, rather than to allow this co-operation to founder upon an unattainable maximum of demands. They are further convinced that this attempt to arrive at an understanding, with a big aim in view, can only be achieved step by step.

6. The German Government are ready on principle to conclude pacts on non-aggression with their various neighbouring States, and to supplement them by all provisions which aim at isolating the combatants and localising the war-makers. They are, in particular, prepared to undertake all obligations which may result therefrom with regard to the delivery of materials and arms in time of peace or war and which are respected by all the parties concerned.

7. The German Government are ready to agree to an air convention to supplement the Locarno Pact and to enter into discussions regarding the same.

8. The German Government have made known the size of the new German army. Under no circumstances will they depart from this. They do not regard the fulfilment of their programme on land, in the air or at sea as constituting any threat to another nation. They are, however, prepared at any time to limit their armaments to the extent which is also adopted by the other States.

The German Government have already voluntarily made known certain limitations of their intentions. In this way they have done their best to show their goodwill to avoid an unrestricted world armaments race. Their limitations of the German air arm to a condition of parity with the various other Western Great Powers renders possible at any time the fixing of a maximum, which Germany will then undertake to observe scrupulously.

The limitation of the German navy to 35 per cent. of the British navy is still 15 per cent. below the total tonnage of the French fleet. As the various press commentaries have voiced the opinion that this demand is only a beginning and would be increased especially with the possession of colonies, the German Government declare definitely that this is Germany's final and fixed demand.

Germany neither intends nor regards it as necessary, nor is she in a position, to take part in any new naval rivalry. The German Government voluntarily recognise the supreme vital importance, and thus the justification, for a dominating protection of the British world Empire at sea, just as we ourselves, on the land, are determined to do everything necessary for the protection of our existence and freedom on the continent. The German Government sincerely intend to do everything to bring about and maintain such relations with the British people and State as will for ever prevent a repetition of the only war which there has as yet been between the two nations.

9. The German Government are ready to take an active part in all endeavours which can result in a practical limitation of unbounded armaments. They regard a return to the order of ideas of the former Geneva Red Cross Convention as the sole possible way to achieve this. They believe that for the present the only way is the abolition and outlawry, step by step, of means and methods of warfare which by their very nature are at variance with the Geneva Red Cross Convention already in force.

They believe in that connexion that just as the use of dum-dum bullets was once forbidden and thus to a large extent prevented in practice, so the use of certain other weapons should be forbidden and thus also prevented in practice. Among such weapons they include those which are principally designed less to bring death and destruction to the fighting soldiers than to the women and children who take no part in the fighting.

The German Government regard the idea of abolishing aeroplanes but leaving bombardment unrestricted as being mistaken and ineffective. They consider it, however, possible to ban the use of certain weapons internationally as being contrary to international law, and to outlaw those nations which nevertheless employ such weapons as standing outside humanity and its rights and laws.

They believe that here, too, progress step by step will soonest lead to success. In short, prohibition of gas, inflammable and explosive bombs outside an actual area of warfare. This limitation can be so extended to result in a complete international prohibition of bomb-dropping. So long, however, as bomb-dropping as such is permitted, any limitation of the number of bombing planes is of doubtful value in view of the possibility of rapidly replacing losses.

If bomb-dropping as such is branded as a barbarism contrary to international law, the construction of bombing planes will automatically soon cease as being superfluous and pointless. If it was once possible as a result of the Geneva Red Cross Convention gradually to prevent the killing of defenceless wounded or prisoners—a thing possible in itself—it must also be possible by means of an analogous convention to forbid the bombing of an equally defenceless civilian population and finally to bring it to an end altogether.

Germany sees in such a fundamental conception of this problem greater appeasement and security for the nations than in all the pacts of mutual assistance and military conventions.

10. The German Government are ready to agree to any limitation leading to the abolition of the heaviest weapons which are especially suitable for aggression. Such are, above all, the heaviest artillery, and secondly, the heaviest tanks. In view of the enormous fortifications on the French frontier, such an international abolition of the heaviest offensive weapons would automatically give France a 100 per cent. security at once.

11. Germany declares herself ready to agree to any limitation of the calibre of artillery, of battleships, cruisers and torpedo-boats. Similarly, the German Government are ready to accept any international limitation of naval tonnage. Finally, they are ready to agree to the limitation of the tonnage of submarines, or even to their complete abolition, in the event of an international agreement to that effect.

The German Government furthermore reiterate the assurance that they are ready to join in any international scheme for the limitation or abolition of arms which shall take effect for all countries at the same time.

12. The German Government are of opinion that all attempts to achieve an effective alleviation of the certain items of tensions between various States by means of international or multilateral agreements are doomed to failure unless suitable measures are successfully taken to prevent a poisoning of public opinion among the nations by irresponsible individuals in speech and in writing, on the film and in the theatre.

13. The German Government are ready at any time to agree to an international arrangement which will effectively prevent and render

impossible all attempts to interfere from outside in the affairs of other States. They must, however, demand that such an arrangement should be internationally effective and benefit all States. As there is a danger that in countries with Governments which do not possess the confidence of the nation, internal revolts brought about by interested parties may only too easily be attributed to foreign interference, it seems to be necessary that the term "interference" should be internationally defined. . . .

MEMORANDUM Presented by Leopold von Hoesch, German Ambassador to Great Britain, to the British Secretary of State for Foreign Affairs (Anthony Eden), March 7, 1936, Regarding the Franco-Soviet Treaty, the Treaty of Locarno and the Demilitarized Zone in the Rhineland

Translation, in British White Paper, Cmd. 5118

IMMEDIATELY after being informed of the Pact between France and the Union of Socialist Soviet Republics, concluded on the 2nd May, 1935, the German Government drew the attention of the other signatory Powers of the Locarno Rhine Pact to the fact that the obligations, which France has undertaken in the new Pact, are not compatible with her obligations arising out of the Rhine Pact. The German Government then explained their point of view in full detail and in both its legal and political aspects—in its legal aspect in the German Memorandum of the 25th May, 1935, in its political aspect in the many diplomatic conversations which followed on that Memorandum. It is also known to the Governments concerned that neither their written replies to the German Memorandum, nor the arguments brought forward by them through the diplomatic channel or in public declarations, were able to invalidate the German Government's point of view.

In fact, all the diplomatic and public discussions which have taken place since May 1935 regarding these questions, have only been able to confirm on all points the view expressed by the German Government at the outset.

1. It is an undisputed fact that the Franco-Soviet Pact is exclusively directed against Germany.

2. It is an undisputed fact that in the Pact France undertakes, in the event of a conflict between Germany and the Soviet Union, obligations which go far beyond her duty as laid down in the Covenant of

the League of Nations, and which compel her to take military action against Germany even when she cannot appeal either to a recommendation or to an actual decision of the Council of the League.

3. It is an undisputed fact that France, in such a case, claims for herself the right to decide on her own judgment who is the aggressor.

4. It is thereby established that France has undertaken towards the Soviet Union obligations which practically amount to undertaking in a given case to act as if neither the Covenant of the League of Nations, nor the Rhine Pact, which refers to the Covenant, were valid.

This result of the Franco-Soviet Pact is not removed by the fact that France, in the Pact, makes the reservation that she does not wish to be bound to take military action against Germany if by such action she would expose herself to a sanction on the part of the guarantor Powers, Italy and Great Britain. As regards this reservation, the decisive fact remains that the Rhine Pact is not based only on the obligations of Great Britain and Italy as guarantor Powers, but primarily on the obligations established in the relations between France and Germany. Therefore it matters only whether France, in undertaking these treaty obligations, has kept herself within the limits imposed on her so far as Germany is concerned by the Rhine Pact.

This, however, the German Government must deny.

The Rhine Pact was intended to achieve the object of securing peace in Western Europe by providing that Germany on the one hand and France and Belgium on the other hand, in their relation to one another, should renounce for all future time the use of military force. If at the time of the conclusion of the pact certain exceptions to this renunciation of war going beyond the right of self-defence were admitted, the political reason for this, as is generally known, lay solely in the fact that France had already undertaken certain obligations towards Poland and Czechoslovakia, which she did not wish to sacrifice to the conception of absolute security in the West. Germany, with her own clear conscience in regard to the matter, at the time accepted these limitations on the renunciation of war. She did not raise objections to the treaties with Poland and Czechoslovakia, laid by France on the table at Locarno, solely on the obvious condition that these treaties were in conformity with the construction of the Rhine Pact, and contained no sort of provisions regarding the application of article 16 of the Covenant of the League of Nations, such as those contained in the new Franco-Soviet agreements. The contents of these special agreements, as then notified to the German Government, fulfilled this condition. The exceptions admitted in the Rhine Pact were not, it is true, specifically confined to Poland and Czechoslovakia, but were formulated as an abstract principle. Nevertheless, the intention of all the negotiations relating to these questions was merely to find a compromise between the renunciation of war by Germany and France, and the wish of France to maintain the obligations which she had already undertaken towards her allies. If, therefore, France now utilises the abstract provisions of the Rhine Pact, which permit the possibility of war, in order to conclude a fresh alliance against Germany with a Power highly armed in a military sense; if she thus further, and in so decisive a manner, restricts the scope of the renunciation of war agreed upon with Germany; and if in this connexion, as shown above, she does not even observe the fixed formal legal limits, she has created an entirely new situation, and has destroyed the political system of the Rhine Pact, not only in theory but also in fact.

The latest debates and decisions of the French Parliament have shown that France, in spite of the German representations, is determined to put the pact with the Soviet Union definitively into force. A diplomatic conversation has even revealed that France already regards herself as bound by her signature of this pact on the 2nd May, 1935. In the face of such a development of European politics, the German Government, if they do not wish to neglect or to abandon the interests of the German people which they have the duty of safeguarding, cannot remain inactive.

The German Government have continually emphasised during the negotiations of the last years their readiness to observe and fulfil all the obligations arising from the Rhine Pact as long as the other contracting parties were ready on their side to maintain the pact. This obvious and essential condition can no longer be regarded as being fulfilled by France. France has replied to the repeated friendly offers and peaceful assurances made by Germany by infringing the Rhine Pact through a military alliance with the Soviet Union exclusively directed against Germany. In this manner, however, the Locarno Rhine Pact has lost its inner meaning and ceased in practice to exist. Consequently, Germany regards herself for her part as no longer bound by this dissolved treaty. The German Government are now constrained to face the new situation created by this alliance, a situation which is rendered more acute by the fact that the Franco-Soviet Treaty has been supplemented by a Treaty of Alliance between Czechoslovakia and the Soviet Union exactly parallel in form. In accordance with the fundamental right of a nation to secure its frontiers and ensure its possibilities of defence, the German Government have to-day restored the full and unrestricted sovereignty of Germany in the demilitarised zone of the Rhineland.

In order, however, to avoid any misinterpretation of their intentions and to establish beyond doubt the purely defensive character of these measures, as well as to express their unchangeable longing for a real pacification of Europe between States which are equals in rights and equally respected, the German Government declare themselves ready to conclude new agreements for the creation of a system of peaceful security for Europe on the basis of the following proposals:—

(1) The German Government declare themselves ready to enter at once into negotiations with France and Belgium with regard to the creation of a zone demilitarised on both sides, and to give their agreement in advance to any suggestion regarding the depth and nature thereof on the basis of full parity.

(2) The German Government propose, for the purpose of ensuring the sanctity and inviolability of the boundaries in the West, the conclusion of a non-aggression pact between Germany, France and Belgium, the duration of which they are ready to fix at twenty-five years.

(3) The German Government desire to invite Great Britain and Italy to sign this treaty as guarantor Powers.

(4) The German Government agree, in case the Netherlands Government should so desire and the other Contracting Parties consider it appropriate, to bring the Netherlands into this treaty system.

(5) The German Government are prepared, in order to strengthen further these security agreements between the Western Powers, to conclude an air pact calculated to prevent in an automatic and effective manner the danger of sudden air attacks.

(6) The German Government repeat their offer to conclude with the States bordering Germany in the East non-aggression pacts similar to that with Poland. As the Lithuanian Government have in the last few months corrected their attitude towards the Memel Territory to a certain extent, the German Government withdraw the exception which they once made regarding Lithuania and declare their readiness, on condition that the guaranteed autonomy of the Memel Territory is effectively developed, to sign a non-aggression pact of this nature with Lithuania also.

(7) Now that Germany's equality of rights and the restoration of her full sovereignty over the entire territory of the German Reich have finally been attained, the German Government consider the chief reason for their withdrawal from the League of Nations to be

removed. They are therefore willing to re-enter the League of Nations. In this connexion they express the expectation that in the course of a reasonable period the question of colonial equality of rights and that of the separation of the League Covenant from its Versailles setting may be clarified through friendly negotiations.

MEMORANDUM Presented by Joachim von Ribbentrop, German Ambassador-at-Large, to the British Secretary of State for Foreign Affairs (Anthony Eden), April 1, 1936

Translation, in British White Paper, Cmd. 5175, p. 4; excerpt

21. THE German Government believe, then, that the task confronting the statesmen of Europe should be divided into three parts as follows:—

(a) A period (during which the atmosphere would gradually be calming down) for elucidating the procedure for the negotiations to be initiated.
(b) A period of actual negotiations for securing the peace of Europe.
(c) A later period for dealing with such supplementary aspects of the European peace settlement as are desirable, and the content and scope of which cannot or should not be precisely laid down or defined in advance (disarmament, economic questions, &c.).

22. To this end the German Government propose the following peace plan:—

(1) In order to give to the future agreements to ensure the peace of Europe the character of inviolable treaties, the nations participating in them shall do so only on a footing of absolute equality and equal respect. The only compelling reason for signing these treaties must lie in their generally recognised and obvious suitability for ensuring the peace of Europe, and thus the social happiness and economic prosperity of the nations.

(2) In order to shorten, as far as possible, the period of uncertainty (in the economic interests of the European nations) the German Government propose a limit of four months for the first period until the signature of the proposed non-aggression pacts, and the consequent guaranteeing of European peace.

(3) The German Government give the assurance that they will not proceed to any reinforcement whatsoever of the troops in the

Rhineland during this period, always provided that the Belgian and French Governments act similarly.

(4) The German Government give the assurance that they will not, during this period, move the troops in the Rhineland closer to the Belgian and French frontiers.

(5) The German Government propose to set up a commission composed of representatives of the two guarantor Powers, England and Italy, and of a disinterested third neutral Power, to guarantee the execution of these reciprocal assurances.

(6) Germany, Belgium and France shall each be entitled to send a representative to this commission. If Germany, Belgium and France think, for any particular reason, that they can point to a change in the military situation within this period of four months, they have the right to communicate what they have observed to the Guarantee Commission.

(7) Germany, Belgium and France declare their willingness, in such a case, to permit the Commission to make the necessary investigations, through the British and Italian Military Attachés, and to report thereon to the participating Powers.

(8) Germany, Belgium and France give the assurance that they will take fully into consideration the objections arising therefrom.

(9) Moreover, the German Government are willing, on the basis of complete reciprocity, to agree with their two Western neighbours to any military limitations on the German Western frontier.

(10) Germany, Belgium and France and the two guarantor Powers shall agree, at once or at the latest after the French elections, to enter into discussions, under the leadership of the British Government, for the conclusion of a twenty-five years' non-aggression pact or security pact between France and Belgium, on the one hand, and Germany, on the other.

(11) Germany agrees that England and Italy shall once again sign this security pact as guarantor Powers.

(12) Should special obligations to render military assistance arise out of these security agreements, Germany for her part declares her willingness to assume such obligations also.

(13) The German Government hereby repeat their proposal for the conclusion of an air pact to supplement and reinforce these security agreements.

(14) The German Government repeat that, should the Netherlands so desire, they are willing to include this country also in the proposed Western European security agreement.

(15) In order to give to this covenant of peace, voluntarily entered into between Germany, on the one hand, and France, on the other,

the character of a reconciliation and of a settlement of their centuries-old feud, Germany and France shall pledge themselves to take steps, in connexion with the education of the young in both countries, and in publications, to avoid everything which might be calculated to poison the relationship between the two peoples, whether it be the adoption of a derogatory or contemptuous attitude, or improper interference in the internal affairs of the other country. They shall agree to set up, at the headquarters of the League of Nations in Geneva, a joint commission whose function it shall be to submit to the two Governments, for their information and investigation, all complaints received.

(16) In pursuance of their intention to give this agreement the character of a sacred covenant, Germany and France shall undertake to ratify it by means of a plebiscite of the two peoples.

(17) Germany declares her willingness, for her part, to enter into communication with the States on her south-eastern and north-eastern frontiers, with a view to extending to them a direct invitation to conclude the non-aggression pacts proposed.

(18) Germany expresses her willingness to re-enter the League of Nations either at once or after the conclusion of these agreements. At the same time, the German Government again express their expectation that, within a reasonable time and by means of friendly negotiations, the question of colonial equality of rights as well as that of the separation of the Covenant of the League of Nations from its basis in the Treaty of Versailles setting will be cleared up.

(19) Germany proposes the constitution of an international court of arbitration, which shall have competence in respect of the observance of the various agreements concluded, and whose decisions shall be binding on all parties.

23. After the conclusion of this great work of securing European peace, the German Government consider it urgently necessary to endeavour by practical measures to attempt to check unlimited competition in armaments. This they would regard not merely as an alleviation of the financial and economic position of the nations, but above all as leading to a psychological *détente*.

24. The German Government have, however, no faith in an attempt to bring about settlements of a universal kind, which would be doomed to failure from the outset, and can therefore be proposed only by those who have no interest in achieving practical results. They believe, on the contrary, that the negotiations conducted and the results achieved in the sphere of the limitation of naval armaments can have an instructive and stimulating effect.

25. The German Government therefore propose that conferences

be convened in the future having each time only one clearly defined objective.

26. They consider that the task of most immediate importance is to impart to aerial warfare the moral and humane atmosphere of, and the protection afforded by, the Geneva Convention, as far as non-combatants or wounded are concerned. Just as the killing of defenceless wounded, or prisoners, or the use of dum-dum bullets, or the waging of submarine warfare without warning, have been regulated or forbidden by international conventions, so it must be possible for civilised humanity to prevent the senseless abuse of new types of weapons without running counter to the object for which war is waged.

27. The German Government therefore propose as the immediate practical objectives of these conferences—
  (1) The prohibition of the dropping of gas, poisonous or incendiary bombs.
  (2) The prohibition of dropping bombs of any kind whatsoever on open localities outside the range of the medium artillery of the fighting fronts.
  (3) The prohibition of the bombardment with long-range guns of places more than 20 km. distant from the battle zone.
  (4) The abolition and prohibition of the construction of tanks of the heaviest type.
  (5) The abolition and prohibition of artillery of the heaviest calibre.

28. As and when possibilities of further limitation of armaments emerge from such discussions and agreements, attention shall be given to them.

29. The German Government hereby declare themselves prepared now to accede to every such arrangement, in so far as it is internationally valid.

30. The German Government believe that if only a first step is taken on the road to disarmament, this will have an enormous effect on the relations between nations, and consequently on the return of that atmosphere of confidence which is the prior condition for the development of trade and prosperity.

31. In order to meet the general desire for the restoration of favourable economic conditions, the German Government are therefore prepared, immediately after the conclusion of the political treaties, to enter into an exchange of views on economic problems with the other countries concerned, in the spirit of the proposals made, and to contribute as far as lies in their power to the improve-

ment of the economic situation in Europe and of the world economic situation, which is inseparable from it.

32. The German Government believe that in the peace plan set forth above they have made their contribution to the creation of a new Europe on a basis of mutual respect and confidence between sovereign States. Many opportunities for such a pacification of Europe, to which Germany has so often, in the last few years, offered to contribute, have been neglected. May this effort to achieve a European understanding at last succeed.

33. The German Government confidently believe that by submitting the peace plan outlined above they have paved the way to this goal.

ADDRESS by Adolf Hitler, Chancellor of the Reich, at the Party Congress at Nuremberg, September 9, 1936

Translation, in *International Conciliation*, November, 1936, citing *Völkischer Beobachter*, September 10, 1936; excerpt

JUST AS we in Germany can solve the problems before us only if internal peace is preserved, we are convinced that the European peoples and States can approach a happier future only through the preservation of European peace. It is our grim determination, however, not to let Germany become the unarmed victim of any foreign military power.

We have learned from the last eighteen years. We know the fate of a nation which without a force of its own must depend on foreign justice and help. We see around us signs of evil times to come. What we preached for years about the great world-danger at the end of this second thousand years of our Christian era has become a grim reality. Everywhere has begun the undermining work of Bolshevist wirepullers.

In a period in which bourgeois statesmen are discussing non-intervention, the Jewish revolutionary headquarters in Moscow are using the radio and every available financial and other agent to accomplish revolution on this continent. Do not tell us that by constant reference to these dangers we are creating a fear psychosis within Germany. We are National Socialists. We have never been afraid of Bolshevism.

We are not, however, members of that absurd bourgeois guild who sing "Who's afraid of the big bad wolf?" on the edge of a catastrophe; who close their eyes and are unable to distinguish between white and red until, when their eyes are finally opened by brutal facts, they jump under the bed, teeth chattering.

We National Socialists have never been afraid of Communism. We only recognized the real character of this shameful Jewish doctrine of world-incitement. We studied its abominable methods and warned against its results. Besides, however, have I as the leader of the Nazi movement, when it had only one hundred members to place against the million of followers of Communism, never doubted that we would be able to overthrow them and root them out of Germany. We warned against this party for fifteen years in Germany while the bourgeoisie laughed. We are not afraid today of a Bolshevist invasion of Germany, not, however, because we think it impossible, but because we are determined to make the nation so strong that it will be able, like National Socialism within our boundaries, to face this doctrine of world hate and to resist viciously every foreign attack.

That is the reason for the military measures we have taken. These German measures will be larger or smaller in proportion to the dangers surrounding us. It is for us no pleasure to lock up these forces of our people in armaments and barracks. We are simply men enough to look these facts coolly in the face.

I want to state in this proclamation before the whole German people that I am profoundly convinced that it is necessary to preserve Germany's external peace in the same manner as I guaranteed its internal peace. I will not avoid any measure calculated to give the nation a sense of security, and above all to secure for ourselves the sense that the complete independence of the Reich is guaranteed.

The Moscow Communist propagandists, Neumann, Béla Kun and their associates, who today are destroying Spain in the interest of the Communist movement, will play no rôle in Germany, and the summons of Moscow radio senders to transform Spain into a heap of ashes will not be repeated in Germany. That the National Socialist party and the National Socialist army of the third Reich guarantee. The German people, however, have no other wish than to live in peace with those who wish to live in peace and friendship with us.

I, therefore, after discussions with the Reich War Minister, decreed the immediate introduction of a two-year term of military service. I know that the young German without moving an eyelash, will obey this necessity. The present German régime has the right to ask this of Germans, for we all served in the greatest war of all times, not for two but for four years. We did it for Germany, for the German nation, for our German homeland. The National Socialist movement fought fifteen years and required great sacrifices from its followers for the salvation of Germany from the internal Bolshevist enemy. In this love for our people, and in this readiness to sacrifice ourselves for the freedom and independence of our nation, we feel ourselves bound to all nations with similar principles and ideals. Germany can be happy, however, to know that her internal and external peace are guaranteed and insured by her own strength. The more turbulent the world grows about us, the greater will be the loyalty of the German people to the National Socialist movement to which Germany owes her rebirth. Germany will recognize more and more in the National Socialist party the strong leadership which freed her from her own inner disunion, and transformed her into a strong, self-confident nation. She will recognize that National Socialism has at the last hour unified the nation for the mastery of its political, cultural, and economic problems. And the more the heavens about our fatherland grow red with Bolshevist uprisings, with a greater love and sacrifice will National Socialist Germany stand true to her army, to which we owe the greatest and proudest tradition of our people.

The army has at one time also educated us. We have all come from the army; we who organized and became the S.A. (Storm Troops), the S.S. (Special Guards), and the N.S.K.K. (Motor Corps). The army gave us the men with which we formed our first storm troops, the old guard of our movement. And to the army shall belong for two years the young sons of our people, in order that they may secure the strength and the capacity to fight for the independence of our Fatherland, for the protection of the German nation. Because I am able to make this open declaration on this eighth Reich Party Day, I regard with profound joy this proudest accomplishment of the National Socialist Government and the National Socialist soldiery. Now generation after generation will make the most noble sacrifices that can be demanded of man. The German people have in the year 1936, in the fourth year of the National Socialist régime, ended the period of their historic dishonor. Long live the National Socialist movement! Long live our National Socialist army! Long live our Germany!

MEMORANDUM Communicated by the German Government to the British Government on April 27, 1939, Denouncing the Anglo-German Naval Agreement of 1935, the Supplementary Declaration of 1937, and Part III of the Anglo-German Naval Agreement of 1937

Translation, in *British War Blue Book*, p. 68

WHEN in the year 1935 the German Government made the British Government the offer to bring the strength of the German fleet to a fixed proportion of the strength of the naval forces of the British Empire by means of a treaty, it did so on the basis of the firm conviction that for all time the recurrence of a warlike conflict between Germany and Great Britain was excluded. In voluntarily recognising the priority of British interests at sea through the offer of the ratio 100:35 it believed that, by means of this decision, unique in the history of the Great Powers, it was taking a step which would lead to the establishment of a friendly relationship for all time between the two nations. This step on the part of the German Government was naturally conditional on the British Government for their part also being determined to adopt a political attitude which would assure a friendly development of Anglo-German relations.

On this basis and under these conditions was the Anglo-German Naval Agreement on the 18th June, 1935, brought into being. This was expressed in agreement by both parties on the conclusion of the agreement. Moreover, last autumn after the Munich Conference the German Chancellor and the British Prime Minister solemnly confirmed in the declaration, which they signed, that they regarded the agreement as symbolical of the desire of both peoples never again to wage war on one another.

The German Government has always adhered to this wish and is still to-day inspired by it. It is conscious of having acted accordingly in its policy and of having in no case intervened in the sphere of English interests or of having in any way encroached on these interests. On the other hand it must to its regret take note of the fact that the British Government of late is departing more and more from the course of an analogous policy towards Germany. As is clearly shown by the political decisions made known by the British Government in the last weeks as well as by the inspired anti-German attitude of the English press, the British Government is now governed by the opinion that England, in whatever part of Europe Germany might be involved in warlike conflict, must always take up an attitude hostile to Germany, even in a case where English interests are not touched in any way by such a conflict. The British Government thus regards war by England against Germany no longer as an impossibility, but on the contrary as a capital problem of English foreign policy.

By means of this encirclement policy the British Government has unilaterally deprived the Naval Agreement of the 18th June, 1935, of its basis, and has thus put out of force this agreement as well as the complementary declaration of the 17th July, 1937.

The same applies to Part III of the Anglo-German Naval Agreement of the 17th July, 1937, in which the obligation is laid down to make a mutual Anglo-German exchange of information. The execution of this obligation rests naturally on the condition that a relationship of open confidence should exist between two partners. Since the German Government to its regret can no longer regard this relationship as existing, it must also regard the provisions of Part III referred to above as having lapsed.

The qualitative provisions of the Anglo-German Agreement of the 17th July, 1937, remain unaffected by these observations which have been forced upon the German Government against its will. The German Government will abide by these provisions also in the future and so make its contribution to the avoidance of a general unlimited race in the naval armaments of the nations.

Moreover, the German Government, should the British Government desire to enter into negotiations with Germany, in regard to the future problems here arising, is gladly ready to do so. It would welcome it if it then proved possible to reach a clear and categorical understanding on a sure basis.

ACQUISITION OF AUSTRIA

MANIFESTO Broadcast by Theo Habicht, "Inspector for Austria," July 5, 1933

Translation, in Royal Institute of International Affairs, *Documents on International Affairs, 1933*, p. 387, citing the *Völkischer Beobachter*, July 7, 1933; excerpts

THE PROHIBITION of the German National-Socialist movement in Austria by the Dollfuss Government was a stab in the back, and in its consequences, both political and economic, a crime not only against the future of Austria but against the whole German people. . . . It is thought possible to foster Austrian separatism within the National-Socialist movement. The attempts which are being made in this direction and in particular the declarations of the Federal Chancellor that he is prepared to hold out the hand of friendship to a new Austrian national front, though only after it has completely cut adrift from the National-Socialist movement in the Reich and if it is under new and independent leaders, have been emphatically denounced by the headquarters of the N.S.D.A.P. Hitler Movement in Austria as an intolerable presumption.

The movement itself alone decides who are to be its leaders in the National-Socialist movement and who its plenipotentiaries. Any attempt to include its members and adherents in a new organization or under new leadership will be regarded by headquarters in Austria as a betrayal of the national movement; and any one who supports or furthers any efforts in this direction will be expelled from the ranks and be branded as a traitor to the National movement. As far as the outward form of organization is concerned, the N.S.D.A.P. Hitler Movement in Austria has ceased to exist as a result of the prohibition of the Dollfuss Government; its spiritual unity, however, remains unimpaired and will carry the struggle to its inevitable successful conclusion.

National-Socialists! Comrades of the Styrian *Heimatschutz!* German men and women in Austria! The Dollfuss Government, in contravention of law and justice, has prohibited our speakers from carrying the word to hundreds and thousands at demonstrations and meetings. It is therefore the duty of every individual in every district, in every place, and at all times, to spare no effort in the service of the Movement, and in winning over the whole nation to our idea.

The Dollfuss Government has suppressed or silenced our press; see to it, then, that whatever can take its place is distributed, by all means available, as widely as possible, from hand to hand, from man to man, and from house to house. The Dollfuss Government has prohibited the wearing of our badges; get to work and plaster the Swastika on walls and fences, on rocks and trees or wherever else possible. The whole of Austria, the whole world, shall see and understand that National-Socialism is a living force in Austria and that no power on earth can remove it. We would not be worthy of the name of Hitler's warriors if the clash with this terror did not make us mightier than before and if we cannot ultimately triumph over it. Our brothers in the Reich have successfully battled with and overcome similar slanderous campaigns; if we should fail, we can but appear weaklings in their eyes.

The organization in its new form is complete. Let us take up the struggle which the Dollfuss Government has thrust upon us and carry it through, ruthlessly and relentlessly, to victory. With us are a thousand years of German history, behind us stands the whole German people, but before us lie, as our goal, the liberation of Austria and the establishment of the German nation.

Long live Adolf Hitler, long live the greater Germany!

COMMUNIQUÉ of the German Government Broadcast by Joseph Goebbels, Minister of Propaganda, July 11, 1936

Royal Institute of International Affairs, *Documents on International Affairs, 1936*, p. 320, citing *The Times* (London), July 13, 1936

I HAVE BEEN authorized by the Reich Government to make known the following *communiqué* about an agreement which was concluded yesterday between the German and Austrian Governments. It represents a considerable practical step towards a peaceful disentanglement of and relaxation of tension in the European situation. I will now read the text of the official *communiqué*:

Convinced that they are thereby rendering a valuable contribution towards the peaceful development of Europe, and believing that they are thereby doing the best service to the various common interests of the two German States, the Government of the German Reich and the Government of the Austrian Federal State have decided to restore normal and friendly mutual relations.

It is therefore declared:

(1) In the sense of the statement made by the *Führer* and Reich Chancellor on May 21, 1935, the German Government recognizes the full sovereignty of the Federal State of Austria;

(2) Each of these two Governments shall regard the internal political conditions of the other country, including the question of Austrian National-Socialism, as a domestic concern of that country, upon which it will exert neither direct nor indirect influence;

(3) The Austrian Federal State Government's general policy and its policy towards Germany in particular shall be constantly guided by the principle that Austria recognizes herself to be a German State. The Rome Protocol of 1934, together with its additional clauses of 1936, and the relations of Austria to Italy and Hungary as partners in the said Protocol are not hereby affected.

Recognizing that the relaxation of tension desired by both parties can be brought about only if in addition certain preliminary conditions are established by the Governments of both countries, the Reich Government and the Austrian Federal Government shall in a series of detailed measures create these required preliminary conditions.

ADDRESS by Adolf Hitler, Chancellor of the Reich, at Linz, Austria, March 12, 1938, Delivered Following the Entry of German Military Forces into Austria on March 11 and 12

Translation, in Raoul de Roussy de Sales, *My New Order* (1941), p. 466; *see also ante*, pp. 634-35

I THANK YOU for your words of greeting. Above all I thank all of you assembled here who have borne witness that it is not the will and the wish of some few only to found this great Reich of the German people, but that it is the wish and the will of the German people. Would that on this evening some of our international seekers after truth whom we know so well could not only see the facts but later admit them to be facts. When years ago I went forth from this town, I bore within me precisely the same profession of faith which today fills my heart. Judge of the depth of my emotion when after so many years I have been able to bring that profession of faith to its fulfillment.

If Providence once called me forth from this town to be the leader of the Reich, it must, in so doing, have given to me a commission, and that commission could be only to restore my dear homeland to the German Reich. I have believed in this commission, I have lived and fought for it, and I believe I have now fulfilled it. You all are witnesses and sureties for that. I know not on what day you will be summoned, I hope it will not be far distant. Then you must make good your pledge with your own confession of faith, and I believe that then before the whole German people I shall be able to point with pride to my own homeland. And this must then prove to the world that every further attempt to tear this people asunder will be in vain.

And just as then it will be your duty to make your contribution to this German future, so all Germany is ready for its part to make its contribution and it is already making it today. In the German soldiers who now from all the shires of the Reich are marching into Austria you must see those who are ready and willing to make sacrifices in their fight for the unity of the whole great German people, for the power of the Reich, for its greatness and its glory now and evermore—Germany, Sieg Heil!

ACQUISITION OF CZECHOSLOVAKIA

MEMORANDUM by the Foreign Office, Regarding a Conversation between Field Marshal Hermann Goering and the Hungarian Minister (Döme Sztójay), September 16, 1938

From files of the German Government. Translation, in Department of State, *Bulletin*, June 9, 1946, p. 984

THE Hungarian Minister informed me on his visit of today that Field Marshal Göring had invited him to come today to Karinhall. The principal reason for this invitation was the Field Marshal's impression that Hungary was not doing enough in the present crisis. The Hungarian press was keeping comparatively silent. In the Hungarian minority areas in Czechoslovakia it was completely calm in contrast to the situation in the Sudeten German areas, and the Hungarian Ministers in the various capitals were not, in contrast to their Czechoslovakian colleagues, going to visit the Foreign Minister two or three times a day. Finally neither the Hungarian Government nor the leaders of the Hungarian minorities had clearly demanded the surrender of the Hungarian areas by Czechoslovakia. The Hungarian Minister defended himself against these charges, but had by his own admission acknowledged that they were partially true by presenting, at the same time, certain reasons for the Hungarian conduct.

The Field Marshal then returned to the matter of Hungarian-Yugoslav relations. He told the Hungarian Minister that he, the Field Marshal, as the second ranking personage in the state, could give him the definite assurance that Yugoslavia would remain quiet if Hungary took no military action on the first day, but only after three or four days. He, Herr Sztójay, indicated that he was skeptical of this view. He could not see why Yugoslavia would, in case of a Hungarian attack, on the first day regard it as a case under the treaty of alliance and take military steps, but, on the contrary, would not do so on the third or fourth day. The Field Marshal told him, however, that in a conversation with a Yugoslav personality—whom he did not name—he had gotten complete assurance on the point. In this connection I informed the Hungarian Minister in strict confidence that according to a telegram from our Ambassador at Rome, the Yugoslav Minister in that capital, on orders of Stojadinovitch, had expressed himself in a similar fashion to the Italian Government concerning which Budapest had already been informed by Count Ciano.

The Field Marshal finally gave Herr Sztójay almost as complete information about the Berchtesgaden conference as had been set forth in the information telegrams to our own missions. The Field Marshal seemed to have given Herr Sztójay no information beyond that.

The Hungarian Minister, after the conversation, telephoned to Budapest and talked with Herr Csáky and, in the course of the afternoon, received orders from Herr Kanya to make the following statement to the Field Marshal and at the same time to the Foreign Ministry:

1. The Hungarian press and the Hungarian national elements in Czechoslovakia would, from then on, be more active, especially the Hungarian press would, in the next few days, express itself in much different terms than previously.

2. The Hungarian Ministers in Prague and London would be ordered to inform the Governments there that Hungary demanded a popular decision in the Hungarian minority areas. He, Sztójay, had received the same orders for Berlin, and he made use of the interview with me to carry out this commission. He was also ordered to bring up the point both with the Field Marshal and also at the Foreign Ministry, of whether the Führer could not do something to indicate that he regarded the Hungarian demands as his own also. Thereupon I told the Minister that it would naturally be difficult for the Führer to speak for other national elements in the same way as for the Germans.

3. Between Hungary and Poland complete understanding prevailed. In that connection Herr Sztójay remarked, in the course of the conversation, that Poland was making no demands for Slovakia, but only for the territory of Teschen and for certain limited frontier adjustments in Slovakian territory, concerning which agreements could be made regarding the details. It was assumed that Slovakia would receive a considerable degree of autonomy within the framework of the Hungarian state.

The Hungarian Minister will carry out this commission in an interview with the Field Marshal tomorrow (Saturday). It was his intention to travel to Budapest Saturday night and to arrive here again on Monday.

WOERMANN

MEMORANDUM by the Foreign Office, Regarding a Conversation between Adolf Hitler, Chancellor of the Reich, the Premier of Hungary (Béla Imredy) and the Hungarian Minister for Foreign Affairs (Kálmán de Kánya), September 20, 1938

From files of the German Government. Translation, in Department of State, *Bulletin*, June 9, 1946, p. 984

COUNSELOR of Legation Brücklmeier just informed me by telephone about yesterday's interview between the Führer, Premier Imredy and Foreign Minister Kánya.

The Führer first made objection to the Hungarians about the undecided attitude of Hungary in the present crisis. He, the Führer, was determined to settle the Czech question, even at the risk of a world war. Germany demanded all German territories. He was convinced that England and France would not move. It was now the last minute for Hungary to join in, as otherwise he would not be in a position to look out for Hungarian interests. In his opinion it would be best to destroy Czechoslovakia. Certainly this airplane mother ship in the heart of Europe could not be endured permanently. He urged the Hungarians (1) to demand a plebiscite in the territories requested by Hungary, (2) to give no guaranty of any sort for the possible new boundaries of Czechoslovakia. If necessary Hungary should threaten to withdraw from the League of Nations and to create irregular troops (Freikorps). The Czechoslovakian question would be settled by the Führer in three weeks at the most. Premier Imredy answered that the pace of the settlement surprised Hungary. In Hungary a solution within one or two years had been expected. In the meantime the Hungarian minorities had already asked for a plebiscite and the Hungarian Government would back up this request. In addition, Hungary would start military preparations at once, but these could be only partially completed within two weeks. Regarding the attitude of Yugoslavia Premier Imredy declared the present régime there was weak, but the Francophile military class would have to be taken very seriously. Perhaps something could be accomplished there by money and threats.

The Führer declared further that he had made the German demands on Chamberlain with brutality. In his opinion the only satisfactory solution would be military action. There remained the danger that the Czechs might accept everything.

Prime Minister Imredy declared that Hungary would only guarantee a new Czechoslovakian boundary if all Hungarian demands were met. The Führer declared that Germany would give no guaranty unless all the states concerned agreed. In the further course of the conversation, the Führer amplified the German position by explaining that such a possibility could exist only after the solution of all problems, including that of the Iglau language enclave. The Führer then again declared that he had presented the German demands at Godesberg in the most brutal manner. In case disorder should break out in Czechoslovakia over the question, he would take military action. It would be better, however, if the pretext should be given by Czechoslovakia.

ERICH KORDT

LETTER from Adolf Hitler, Chancellor of the Reich, to the British Prime Minister (Neville Chamberlain), September 23, 1938

Translation, in British White Paper, Cmd. 5847, p. 11

YOUR EXCELLENCY,

A thorough examination of your letter, which reached me to-day, as well as the necessity of clearing up the situation definitely, led me to make the following communication:—

For nearly two decades the Germans, as well as the various other nationalities in Czechoslovakia, have been maltreated in the most unworthy manner, tortured, economically destroyed, and, above all, prevented from realising for themselves also the right of the nations to self-determination. All attempts of the oppressed to change their lot failed in the face of the brutal will to destruction of the Czechs. The latter were in possession of the power of the State and did not hesitate to employ it ruthlessly and barbarically. England and France have never made an endeavour to alter this situation. In my speech before the Reichstag of the 22nd February, I declared that the German Reich would take the initiative in putting an end to any further oppression of these Germans. I have in a further declaration during the Reich Party Congress given clear and unmistakable expression to this decision. I recognise gratefully that at last, after twenty years, the British Government, represented by your Excellency, has now decided for its part also to undertake steps to put an end to a situation which from day to day, and, indeed, from hour to hour, is becoming more unbearable. For if formerly the behaviour of the Czechoslovak Government was brutal, it can only be described during recent weeks and days as madness. The victims of this madness are innumerable Germans. In a few weeks the number of refugees who have been driven out has risen to over 120,000. This situation, as stated above, is unbearable, and will now be terminated by me.

Your Excellency assures me now that the principle of the transfer of the Sudeten territory to the Reich has, in principle, already been accepted. I regret to have to reply to your Excellency that as regards this point, the theoretical recognition of principles has also been formerly granted to us Germans. In the year 1918 the Armistice was concluded on the basis of the 14 points of President Wilson, which in principle were recognised by all. They were, however, in practice broken in the most shameful way. What interests me, your Excellency, is not the recognition of the principle that this territory is to go to Germany, but solely the realisation of this principle, and the realisation which both puts an end in the shortest time to the sufferings of the unhappy victims of Czech tyranny, and at the same time corresponds to the dignity of a Great Power. I can only emphasise to your Excellency that these Sudeten Germans are not coming back to the German Reich in virtue of the gracious or benevolent sympathy of other nations, but on the ground of their own will based on the right of self-determination of the nations, and of the irrevocable decision of the German Reich to give effect to this will. It is, however, for a nation an unworthy demand to have this recognition made dependent on conditions which are not provided for in treaties nor are practical in view of the shortness of the time.

I have, with the best intentions and in order to give the Czech nation no justifiable cause for complaint, proposed—in the event of a peaceful solution—as the future frontier, that nationalities frontier which I am convinced represents a fair adjustment between the two racial groups, taking also into account the continued existence of large language islands. I am, in addition, ready to allow plebiscites to be taken in the whole territory which will enable subsequent corrections to be made, in order—so far as it is possible—to meet the real will of the peoples concerned. I have undertaken to accept these corrections in advance. I have, moreover, declared myself ready to allow this plebiscite to take place under the control either of international commissions or of a mixed German-Czech commission. I am finally ready, during the days of the plebiscite, to withdraw our troops from the most disputed frontier areas, subject to the condition that the Czechs do the same. I am, however, not prepared to allow a territory which must be considered as belonging to Germany, on the ground of the will of the people and of the recognition granted even by the Czechs, to be left without the protection of the Reich. There is here no international power or agreement which would have the right to take precedence over German right.

The idea of being able to entrust to the Sudeten Germans alone the maintenance of order is practically impossible in consequence of the obstacles put in the way of their political organisation in the course of the last decade, and particularly in recent times. As much in the interest of the tortured, because defenceless, population as well as with regard to the duties and prestige of the Reich, it is impossible for us to refrain from giving immediate protection to this territory.

Your Excellency assures me that it is now impossible for you to propose such a plan to your own Government. May I assure you for my part that it is impossible for me to justify any other attitude to the German people. Since, for England, it is a question at most of political imponderables, whereas, for Germany, it is a question of primitive right of the security of more than 3 million human beings and the national honour of a great people.

I fail to understand the observation of your Excellency that it would not be possible for the Czech Government to withdraw their forces so long as they were obliged to reckon with possible invasion, since precisely by means of this solution the grounds for any forcible action are to be removed. Moreover, I cannot conceal from your Excellency that the great mistrust with which I am inspired leads me to believe that the acceptance of the principle of the transfer of Sudeten Germans to the Reich by the Czech Government is only given in the hope thereby to win time so as, by one means or another, to bring about a change in contradiction to this principle. For if the proposal that these territories are to belong to Germany is sincerely accepted, there is no ground to postpone the practical resolution of this principle. My knowledge of Czech practice in such matters over a period of long years compels me to assume the insincerity of Czech assurances so long as they are not implemented by practical proof. The German Reich is, however, determined by one means or another to terminate these attempts, which have lasted for decades, to deny by dilatory methods the legal claims of oppressed peoples.

Moreover, the same attitude applies to the other nationalities in this State. They also are the victims of long oppression and violence. In their case, also, every assurance given hitherto has been broken. In their case, also, attempts have been made by dilatory dealing with their complaints or wishes to win time in order to be able to oppress them still more subsequently. These nations, also, if they are to achieve their rights, will, sooner or later, have no alternative but to secure them for themselves. In any event, Germany, if—as it now appears to be the case—should find it impossible to have the clear rights of Germans in Czechoslovakia accepted by way of negotiation, is determined to exhaust the other possibilities which then alone remain open to her.

MEMORANDUM Presented by Adolf Hitler, Chancellor of the Reich, to the British Prime Minister (Neville Chamberlain), September 23, 1938

Translation, in British White Paper, Cmd. 5847, p. 14. A copy of the memorandum was presented to the Czechoslovakian Government by the British Minister at Prague

REPORTS WHICH are increasing in number from hour to hour regarding incidents in the Sudetenland show that the situation has become completely intolerable for the Sudeten German people and, in consequence, a danger to the peace of Europe. It is therefore essential that the separation of the Sudetenland agreed to by Czechoslovakia should be effected without any further delay. On the attached map the Sudeten German area which is to be ceded is shaded red. The areas in which, over and above the areas which are to be occupied, a plebiscite is also to be held are drawn in and shaded green.

The final delimitation of the frontier must correspond to the wishes of those concerned. In order to determine these wishes, a certain period is necessary for the preparation of the voting, during which disturbances must in all circumstances be prevented. A situation of parity must be created. The area designated on the attached map as a German area will be occupied by German troops without taking account as to whether in the plebiscite there may prove to be in this or that part of the area a Czech majority. On the other hand, the Czech territory is occupied by Czech troops without regard to the question whether, within this area, there lie large German language islands, the majority of which will without doubt avow their German nationality in the plebiscite.

With a view to bringing about an immediate and final solution of the Sudeten German problem the following proposals are now made by the German Government:—

1. Withdrawal of the whole Czech armed forces, the police, the gendarmerie, the customs officials and the frontier guards from the area to be evacuated as designated on the attached map, this area to be handed over to Germany on the 1st October.

2. The evacuated territory is to be handed over in its present

condition (see further details in appendix). The German Government agree that a plenipotentiary representative of the Czech Government or of the Czech Army should be attached to the headquarters of the German military forces to settle the details of the modalities of the evacuation.

3. The Czech Government discharges at once to their homes all Sudeten Germans serving in the military forces or the police anywhere in Czech State territory.

4. The Czech Government liberates all political prisoners of German race.

5. The German Government agrees to permit a plebiscite to take place in those areas, which will be more definitely defined, before at latest the 25th November. Alterations to the new frontier arising out of the plebiscite will be settled by a German-Czech or an international commission. The plebiscite itself will be carried out under the control of an international commission. All persons who were residing in the areas in question on the 28th October, 1918, or were born there prior to this date will be eligible to vote. A simple majority of all eligible male and female voters will determine the desire of the population to belong to either the German Reich or to the Czech State. During the plebiscite both parties will withdraw their military forces out of areas which will be defined more precisely. The date and duration will be settled by the German and Czech Governments together.

6. The German Government proposes that an authoritative German-Czech commission should be set up to settle all further details.

Godesberg, *September 23, 1938.*

Appendix

The evacuated Sudeten German area is to be handed over without destroying or rendering unusable in any way military, commercial or traffic establishments (plants). These include the ground organisation of the air service and all wireless stations.

All commercial and traffic materials, especially the rolling-stock of the railway system, in the designated areas, are to be handed over undamaged. The same applies to all utility services (gas-works, power stations, etc.)

Finally, no food-stuffs, goods, cattle, raw material, etc., are to be removed.

RADIO ADDRESS by Adolf Hitler, Chancellor of the Reich, September 26, 1938

Translation, in Raoul de Roussy de Sales, *My New Order* (1941), p. 517; excerpts

GERMAN fellow-countrymen and fellow-countrywomen, on February 20 before the members of the German Reichstag I expressed for the first time a fundamental demand of an absolute character. At that time the whole nation heard me and it understood me. One statesman failed to share in this understanding. He has been removed and the promise which I made at that time has been fulfilled. Then for the second time I spoke on this same demand before the Parteitag of the Reich. And again the nation heard this demand. Today I now come before the nation and for the first time I speak before the people itself, just as I did in the time of our great fight, and you know what that means. For the world there is no longer room for any doubt: now it is not a leader or one man who speaks: now the German people speaks.

If I am now the spokesman of this German people, then I know: At this second the whole people in its millions agrees word for word with my words, confirms them, and makes them its own oath! Let the other statesmen ask themselves whether that is also true in their case!

The question which in these last months and weeks has moved us so profoundly has long been familiar to us: it is not so much Czechoslovakia: it is rather Mr. Benes. In this name is concentrated all that which today moves millions, which causes them to despair or fills them with a fanatical resolution.

But why was it that this question could rise to such significance? I wish, my fellow-countrymen, quite briefly to explain to you once again the character and the aims of German foreign policy.

In contradistinction to the many democratic States, German foreign policy is fixed and conditioned by a *Weltanschauung*. The *Weltanschauung* of this new Reich is directed to maintaining and to securing the existence of our German people. We have no interest in oppressing other peoples. We wish to seek our blessedness after our own fashion: the others can do so in their own way. This view, which in our *Weltanschauung* is racially conditioned, leads to a limitation of our foreign policy: that is to say, the aims of our foreign policy are not unlimited, they are not determined by chance, but they are grounded on the determination to serve the German people alone, to maintain it in our world and to safeguard its existence.

What is then the position today? You know that formerly under the watchword "The Right of the Peoples to Self-Determination" the German people, as well as others, was filled with a belief in super-State help and therefore allowed itself to the last extreme to renounce any resort to its own strength. . . . You know that this trust of those days was most shamefully betrayed! The result was the Treaty of Versailles, and of the frightful consequences of this Treaty you are all aware. . . .

Although now today through our own efforts we have once more become free and strong, yet we are not moved by any hatred against other nations. We bear no grudge. What happened we know: the peoples are not to be held responsible for that, but only a small conscienceless clique of international profit-makers seeking their business ends, who do not hesitate, if necessary, to let whole nations go to ruin if only their despicable interests are served. Therefore we nurse no hatred against neighboring peoples, and that we have also proved.

We had hardly begun the restoration of Germany to equality of rights when, as the clearest sign of our renunciation of a policy of *"Revanche"* upon the rest of the world, I proposed a series of agreements which were intended to lead to a limitation of armaments. . . .

When thus for two years I had made to the world offer on offer, and these offers always met with rejection and then once more rejection, I gave orders that the German Army should be brought to the best attainable condition. And now I can proudly admit: we did then certainly complete an armament such as the world has never yet seen. I have offered disarmament as long as it was possible. But when that was rejected then I formed, I admit, no half-hearted decision. I am a National Socialist and an old German front-line soldier!

If they do not wish the world to be without arms, good: then, German people, do you, too, now carry your arms!

I have in fact armed in these five years. I have spent milliards on this armament: that the German people must now know! I have seen to it that a new army should be provided with the most modern armament known. I have given to my friend Goering the order: Make me now an air-arm which can protect Germany in the face of any conceivable attack. Thus we have built up a military force of which today the German people can be proud and which the world will respect if at any time it makes its appearance.

We have created for our protection the best air-defense, the best tank-defense which is to be found on earth. In these five years, day and night, work has been carried on. Only in one single sphere have

I succeeded in bringing about an understanding. To this subject I shall return. But in spite of this I have continued to follow up the ideas of the limitation of armaments and of a policy of disarmament. I have really in these years pursued a practical peace policy. I have approached all the apparently impossible problems with the firm resolve to solve them peacefully even when there was the danger of making more or less serious renunciations on Germany's part. I myself am a front-line soldier and I know how grave a thing war is. I wanted to spare the German people such an evil. Problem after problem I have tackled with the set purpose to make every effort to render possible a peaceful solution.

The most difficult problem which faced me was the relation between Germany and Poland. There was a danger that the conception of a "hereditary enmity" might take possession of our people and of the Polish people. That I wanted to prevent. I know quite well that I should not have succeeded if Poland at that time had had a democratic constitution. For these democracies which are overflowing with phrases about peace are the most bloodthirsty instigators of war. But Poland at that time was governed by no democracy but by a man. In the course of barely a year it was possible to conclude an agreement which, in the first instance for a period of ten years, on principle removed the danger of a conflict. We are all convinced that this agreement will bring with it a permanent pacification. We realize that here are two peoples which must live side by side and that neither of them can destroy the other. A State with a population of thirty-three millions will always strive for an access to the sea. A way to an understanding had therefore to be found. It has been found and it will be ever further developed. The decisive point is that both Governments and all reasonable and intelligent folk in both peoples and countries should have the firm determination continuously to improve relations. It was a real achievement in the cause of peace which is of more value than all the chatter in the Palace of the League of Nations at Geneva.

At this time I have also sought gradually to establish good and lasting relations with the other nations. We have given guarantees for the States in the West, and to all those States bordering on our frontiers we have given assurances of the inviolability of their territory so far as Germany is concerned. These are no mere words. That is our sacred determination. We have no interest in breaking the peace.

These German offers also met with a growing understanding. Gradually ever more peoples are freeing themselves from that insane infatuation of Geneva which, I might say, serves no policy of an obligation to peace but rather a policy of obligation to war. They are freeing themselves, and they begin to see the problems soberly: they are ready for understanding and for peace.

I went further and offered the hand to England. I have voluntarily renounced the idea of ever again entering upon a competition in fleet-building in order to give to the British Empire the feeling of security. And that I have not done because I was not able to build above the limit fixed: let no one have any illusions on that score: I acted thus solely in order to maintain a lasting peace between the two peoples. But it must be admitted that here one condition must be observed; it will not do that one party should say: I am determined never again to wage war and to this end I offer you a voluntary limitation of my armaments at 35 per cent, while the other party declares: If it suits me I shall wage war again from time to time. Such an agreement is morally justified only when both peoples solemnly promise that they are determined never again to wage war with each other. Germany has this determination. We all desire to hope that amongst the English people those who share this determination may gain the upper hand!

I went further. Directly after the restoration of the Saar territory which was decided by a plebiscite. I declared to France that there were now absolutely no differences outstanding between us. I said that for us the Alsace-Lorraine question no longer existed. It is a frontier district. The people of this country during the most recent decades has never really been asked for its own opinion. We have the feeling that the inhabitants of this province will be happiest if they are not fought over again. All of us do not wish for any war with France. We want nothing from France—positively nothing! And when the Saar territory had returned to the Reich thanks to the loyal execution of the treaties by France—that I desire to reaffirm in this place—I solemnly declared: for the future all territorial differences between France and Germany have been removed. Today I cannot any longer see any difference between us. Here are two great peoples who both wish to work and live. And they will live their lives best if they work together.

After this irrevocable renunciation, made once for all, I turned to a further problem which was easier to solve than others because here the common *weltanschaulich* basis forms a favorable condition for a readier mutual understanding—the problem of the relation of Germany to Italy.

It is true that the solution of this problem is only in part to be put to my credit, in part it is due to the rare genius of that great man whom the Italian people has the good fortune to be able to possess as its leader. This relation has long ago overstepped the sphere of a pure economic or political expediency: it has passed beyond treaties and alliances and has become a true, strong union of hearts. Here an axis has been formed represented by two peoples who both have come to be united, alike in ideology and in politics, in a close indissoluble friendship.

Here, too, I have taken a final step—once and for all—fully conscious of my responsibility before my fellow-countrymen. I have banished from the world a problem that from henceforth simply does not exist for us. However bitter that may be for the individual, with us in the last resort it is the interest of the people as a whole which stands above everything. And this interest is: to be able to work in peace! This whole work for peace, my fellow-countrymen, is no mere empty phrase, but this work is reinforced through deeds which no lying mouth can destroy.

Two problems still remained. Here I was bound to make a reservation. Ten million Germans found themselves beyond the frontiers of the Reich in two great closed areas of settlement, Germans who wished to return to their Reich as their homeland. This number—ten millions—is no small affair: here it is a question of a quarter as many people as make up the population of France. And if for over forty years France never gave up her claim to the few millions of the French population of Alsace-Lorraine, then we had a right before God and the world to maintain our claim to these ten million Germans. My fellow-countrymen, there is a point at which concession must cease because otherwise it would become ruinous weakness. I should have no right to take my stand before the history of Germany had I been willing in simple indifference to sacrifice these ten millions. I should then also have no moral right to be the leader of this people. I have taken upon myself sacrifices and renunciations enough: here was the limit beyond which I could not go!

How true that was has been proved through the plebiscite in Austria. At that time a glowing profession of faith was made, a profession of faith such as the rest of the world had certainly not expected. But we know by experience: a plebiscite for the democracies is superfluous or even harmful the moment it does not lead to the result that they themselves expect. In spite of this, this problem was solved to the satisfaction of the whole great German people.

And now before us stands the last problem that must be solved and will be solved. It is the last territorial claim which I have to make in Europe, but it is the claim from which I will not recede and which, God willing, I will make good.

The history of the problem is as follows: in 1918 under the watchword "The Right of the Peoples to Self-Determination" Central

Europe was torn in pieces and was newly formed by certain crazy so-called "statesmen." Without regard for the origin of the peoples, without regard for either their wish as a nation or for economic necessities, Central Europe at that time was broken up into atoms and new so-called States were arbitrarily formed. To this procedure Czechoslovakia owes its existence. This Czech State began with a single lie and the father of this lie was named Benes. This Mr. Benes at that time appeared in Versailles and he first of all gave the assurance that there was a Czechoslovak nation. He was forced to invent this lie in order to give to the slender number of his own fellow-countrymen a somewhat greater range and thus a fuller justification. And the Anglo-Saxon statesmen, who were, as always, not very adequately versed in respect of questions of geography or nationality, did not at that time find it necessary to test these assertions of Mr. Benes. Had they done so, they could have established the fact that there is no such thing as a Czechoslovak nation but only Czechs and Slovaks and that the Slovaks did not wish to have anything to do with the Czechs. . . .

So in the end, through Mr. Benes, these Czechs annexed Slovakia. Since this State did not seem fitted to live, out of hand three and a half million Germans were taken in violation of their right to self-determination and their wish for self-determination. Since even that did not suffice, over a million Magyars had to be added, then some Carpathian Russians, and at last several hundred thousand Poles.

That is this State which then later proceeded to call itself Czechoslovakia—in violation of the right of the peoples to self-determination, in violation of the clear wish and will of the nations to which this violence had been done. When I speak to you here it goes without saying that I should sympathize with the fate of all these oppressed peoples, with the fate of Poles, Hungarians, and Ukrainians. I am naturally spokesman only for the fate of my Germans.

At the time Mr. Benes lied this State into being, he gave a solemn pledge to divide it on the model of the Swiss system into cantons, for amongst the democratic statesmen there were some who still had some twinges of conscience. We all know how Mr. Benes has redeemed his pledge to introduce this cantonal system. He began his reign of terror. Even at that time the Germans already attempted to protest against this arbitrary violence. They were shot down. After that a war of extermination began. In these years of the "peaceful" development of Czechoslovakia nearly 600,000 Germans had to leave Czechoslovakia. This happened for a very simple reason: otherwise they would have had to starve!

The whole development from the year 1918 up to 1938 showed one thing clearly: Mr. Benes was determined slowly to exterminate the German element. And this to a certain extent he has achieved. He has hurled countless people into the profoundest misery. He has managed to make millions of people fearful and anxious. Through the continuous employment of his methods of terrorism he has succeeded in reducing to silence these millions, while at the same time it also became clear what were the "international" duties of this State. . . .

And now, my fellow-countrymen, I believe that the time has come when one must mince matters no longer. If anyone for twenty years has borne such a shame, such a disgrace, such a misfortune as we have done, then in very truth it cannot be denied that he is a lover of peace. When anyone has the patience which we have shown then in very truth it cannot be said that he is bellicose. For in the last resort Mr. Benes has seven million Czechs, but here there stands a people of over seventy-five millions.

I have now placed a memorandum containing a last and final German proposal in the hands of the British Government. This memorandum contains nothing save the putting into effect of what Mr. Benes has already promised. The content of this proposal is very simple:

That area which in its people is German and has the wish to be German comes to Germany and that, too, not only when Mr. Benes has succeeded in driving out perhaps one or two million Germans, but now, and that immediately! I have here chosen that frontier which on the basis of the material which has existed for decades on the division of people and language in Czechoslovakia is the just frontier-line. But in spite of this I am more just than Mr. Benes and I have no wish to exploit the power which we possess. I have therefore laid it down from the outset that this area will be placed under German supremacy because it is essentially settled by Germans. The final delimitation of the frontier, however, I then leave to the vote of our fellow-countrymen themselves who are in the area! I have therefore laid down that in this area there must then be held a plebiscite. And in order that no one can say that the procedure of the plebiscite might be unjust, I have chosen as the basis for this plebiscite the Statute that governed the Saar Plebiscite.

Now I am and was prepared, so far as I am concerned, to allow a plebiscite to be held throughout the area. But Mr. Benes and his friends objected. They wished that a plebiscite should be allowed only in certain parts of the area. Good, I have yielded the point. I was even prepared to allow the plebiscite to be subject to the inspection of international Commissions of Control.

I went even further and agreed to leave the delimitation of the frontier to a German-Czech Commission. Mr. Chamberlain suggested: might it not be an international Commission? To this, too, I agreed. I even wished during this period of the plebiscite to withdraw again the troops, and I have today declared my readiness to invite for this period the British Legion, which offered me its services, to go into these districts and there maintain calm and order. And I was further ready to allow the international Commission to fix the final frontier and to hand over all details of procedure to a Commission composed of Germans and Czechs.

The content of this memorandum is nothing else than the practical execution of what Mr. Benes has already promised, and that, too, under the most complete international guarantees. Mr. Benes now says that this memorandum is "a new situation." And in what, in fact, does this "new situation" consist? It consists in this: that this time—exceptionally—the promise made by Mr. Benes must also be kept! That is for Mr. Benes the "new situation." What is there that Mr. Benes has not promised at some time in his life? And no promise had been kept! Now for the first time he has got to keep to something.

Mr. Benes says: "We cannot go back from this area." Mr. Benes has then understood the transfer of this area to mean that the legal title is recognized as belonging to the German Reich but the area is still to be subject to the violence of the Czechs. That is now past!

I have demanded that now after twenty years Mr. Benes should at last be compelled to come to terms with the truth. On October 1 he will have to hand over to us this area.

Mr. Benes now places his hopes on the world! And he and his diplomats make no secret of the fact. They state: it is our hope that Chamberlain will be overthrown, that Daladier will be removed, that on every hand revolutions are on the way. They place their hope on Soviet Russia. He still thinks then that he will be able to evade the fulfillment of his obligations.

And then I can say only one thing: now two men stand arrayed one against the other: there is Mr. Benes, and here stand I. We are two men of a different make-up. In the great struggle of the peoples, while Mr. Benes was sneaking about through the world, I as a decent German soldier did my duty. And now today I stand over against this man as the soldier of my people!

I have only a few statements still to make: I am grateful to Mr. Chamberlain for all his efforts. I have assured him that the German people desires nothing else than peace, but I have also told him that I cannot go back behind the limits set to our patience. I have further assured him, and I repeat it here, that when this problem is solved there is for Germany no further territorial problem in Europe. And I have further assured him that at the moment when Czechoslovakia solves her problems, that means when the Czechs have come to terms with their other minorities, and that peaceably and not through oppression, then I have no further interest in the Czech State. And that is guaranteed to him! We want no Czechs!

But in the same way I desire to state before the German people that with regard to the problem of the Sudeten Germans my patience is now at an end! I have made Mr. Benes an offer which is nothing but the carrying into effect of what he himself has promised. The decision now lies in his hands. Peace or War! He will either accept this offer and now at last give to the Germans their freedom, or we will go and fetch this freedom for ourselves. The world must take note that in four and a half years of war and through the long years of my political life there is one thing which no one could ever cast in my teeth: I have never been a coward!

Now I go before my people as its first soldier and behind me—that the world should know—there marches a people and a different people from that of 1918!

If at that time a wandering scholar was able to inject into our people the poison of democratic catchwords—the people of today is no longer the people that it was then. Such catchwords are for us like wasp-stings: they cannot hurt us: we are now immune.

In this hour the whole German people will unite with me! It will feel my will to be its will. Just as in my eyes it is its future and its fate which give me the commission for my action. And we wish now to make our will as strong as it was in the time of our fight, the time when I, as a simple unknown soldier, went forth to conquer a Reich and never doubted of success and final victory. Then there gathered close about me a band of brave men and brave women, and they went with me. And so I ask you, my German people, take your stand behind me, man by man, and woman by woman.

In this hour we all wish to form a common will and that will must be stronger than every hardship and every danger. And if this will is stronger than hardship and danger then one day it will break down hardship and danger.

We are determined!

Now let Mr. Benes make his choice!

MESSAGE from Adolf Hitler, Chancellor of the Reich, to the President of the United States (Franklin D. Roosevelt), September 26, 1938, in Reply to the Latter's Appeal for Peace of the Same Date

Translation, in Department of State, *Press Releases,* October 1, 1938, p. 221

IN YOUR TELEGRAM received by me on September 26, Your Excellency addressed to me an appeal in the name of the American people, in the interest of the maintenance of peace not to break off the negotiations regarding the dispute which has arisen in Europe and to strive for a peaceful, honorable and constructive settlement of this question. Be assured that I can fully appreciate the lofty intent on which your remarks are based, and that I share in every respect your opinion regarding the unforeseeable consequences of a European war. Precisely for this reason, however, I can and must refuse all responsibility of the German people and their leaders, if the further development, contrary to all my efforts up to the present, should actually lead to the outbreak of hostilities. In order to arrive at a fair judgment regarding the Sudeten-German problem under discussion, it is indispensable to consider the incidents, in which, in the last analysis, the origin of this problem and its dangers has its cause. In 1918, the German people laid down their arms, in the firm confidence that by the conclusion of peace with their enemies at that time the principles and ideals would be realized which had been solemnly announced by President Wilson and had been just as solemnly accepted as binding by all the belligerent powers. Never in history has the confidence of a people been more shamefully betrayed than it was then. The peace conditions imposed on the conquered nations in the Paris suburbs treaties have fulfilled nothing of the promises given. Rather have they created a political regime in Europe which made of the conquered nations world pariahs without rights and which must be recognized in advance by every discerning person as untenable. One of the points in which the character of the dictates of 1919 was the most openly revealed was the founding of the Czechoslovak state, and the establishment of its boundaries without any consideration of history and nationality. The Sudeten land was also included therein, although this area had always been German, and although its inhabitants, after the destruction of the Hapsburg monarchy, had unanimously declared their desire for annexation to the German Reich. Thus the right of self-determination, which had been proclaimed by President Wilson as the most important basis of national life, was simply denied to the Sudeten Germans. But that was not enough. In the treaties of 1919, certain obligations, with regard to the German people, which, according to the text, were far reaching, were imposed on the Czechoslovak state. These obligations also were disregarded from the first. The League of Nations has completely failed to guarantee the fulfillment of these obligations in connection with the task assigned to it. Since then the Sudeten land has been engaged in the severest struggle for the maintenance of its Germanism. It was a natural and inevitable development that after the recovery of strength by the German Reich and after the reunion of Austria with it, the urge of the German Sudetens for maintenance of their culture and for closer union with Germany increased. Despite the loyal attitude of the Sudeten German party and its leaders, the difference with the Czechs became ever stronger. From day to day it became ever clearer that the Government in Prague was not disposed really to consider seriously the most elementary rights of the Sudeten Germans. Rather did it attempt with ever more violent methods the Czechization of the Sudetenland. It was inevitable that this procedure would lead to ever greater and more serious tensions. The German Government at first did not intervene in any way in this development of things, and maintained its calm restraint, even when the Czechoslovak Government, in May of this year, proceeded to a mobilization of its army, under the purely fictitious pretext of German troop concentrations. The renunciation of military countermeasures at that time in Germany, however, only served to strengthen the uncompromising attitude of the Government of Prague. This has been clearly shown by the course of the negotiations of the Sudeten German party with the Government regarding a peaceful adjustment. These negotiations produced the conclusive proof that the Czechoslovak Government was far from thoroughly grasping the problem of the Sudeten Germans and bringing about an equitable solution. Consequently conditions in the Czechoslovak state, as is generally known, have in the last few weeks become utterly intolerable. Political persecution and economic oppression have plunged the Sudeten Germans into extreme misery. To characterize these circumstances it is enough to refer to the following. There are at present 214,000 Sudeten German refugees who had to leave their house and home in their ancestral country and flee across the German border, as they saw therein the last and only possibility to escape from the revolting Czechoslovak regime of violence and bloodiest terror. Countless dead, thousands of injured, ten thousands of persons arrested and imprisoned, desolated villages are the accusing witnesses before world opinion of an outbreak of hostilities carried out for a long time by the

Prague Government, which you in your telegram rightly fear. Entirely aside from the German economic life in the Sudeten German territory, for 20 years systematically destroyed by the Czech Government, which already shows all the signs of ruin, which you anticipate as the result of an outbreak of war, these are the facts which compelled me in my Nuremberg speech of September 13 to state before the whole world that the deprivation of rights of the three and one-half millions of Germans in Czechoslovakia must be stopped and that these people, if they of themselves cannot find justice and help, must receive both from the German Reich. However, to make a last attempt, to reach the goal in a peaceful way, I made concrete proposals for the solution of the problem in a memorandum delivered on September 23 to the British Premier, which in the meantime has been made public. Since the Czechoslovak Government had previously declared itself already to be in agreement with the British and French Governments that the Sudeten German settlement area would be separated from the Czechoslovak state and joined to the German Reich, the proposals of the German memorandum contemplate nothing else than to bring about a prompt and equitable fulfillment of that Czechoslovak promise. It is my conviction that you, Mr. President, when you realize the whole development of the Sudeten German problem from its inception to the present day, will recognize that the German Government has truly not been lacking either in patience or a sincere desire for a peaceful understanding. It is not Germany who is to blame for the fact that there is any Sudeten German problem at all, and that the present unjustifiable circumstances have arisen from it. The terrible fate of the people affected by the problem no longer admits of a further postponement of its solution. The possibilities of arriving at a just settlement by agreement, are therefore exhausted with the proposals of the German memorandum. It does not rest with the German Government, but with the Czechoslovak Government alone, to decide whether it wants peace or war.

LETTER from Adolf Hitler, Chancellor of the Reich, to the British Prime Minister (Neville Chamberlain), September 27, 1938

Translation, in British White Paper, Cmd. 5847, p. 21

DEAR MR. CHAMBERLAIN,

I have in the course of the conversations once more informed Sir Horace Wilson, who brought me your letter of the 26th September, of my final attitude. I should like, however, to make the following written reply to certain details in your letter:—

The Government in Prague feels justified in maintaining that the proposals in my memorandum of the 23rd September went far beyond the concession which it made to the British and French Governments and that the acceptance of the memorandum would rob Czechoslovakia of every guarantee for its national existence. This statement is based on the argument that Czechoslovakia is to give up a great part of her prepared defensive system before she can take steps elsewhere for her military protection. Thereby the political and economic independence of the country is automatically abolished. Moreover, the exchange of population proposed by me would turn out in practice to be a panic-stricken flight.

I must openly declare that I cannot bring myself to understand these arguments or even admit that they can be regarded as seriously put forward. The Government in Prague simply passes over the fact that the actual arrangement for the final settlement of the Sudeten German problem, in accordance with my proposals, will be made dependent not on a unilateral German petition or on German measures of force, but rather, on the one hand, on a free vote under no outside influence, and, on the other hand, to a very wide degree on German-Czech agreement on matters of detail to be reached subsequently. Not only the exact definition of the territories in which the plebiscite is to take place, but the execution of the plebiscite and the delimitation of the frontier to be made on the basis of its result, are in accordance with my proposals to be met independently of any unilateral decision by Germany. Moreover, all other details are to be reserved for agreement on the part of a German-Czech commission.

In the light of this interpretation of my proposals and in the light of the cession of the Sudeten population areas, in fact agreed to by Czechoslovakia, the immediate occupation by German contingents demanded by me represents no more than a security measure which is intended to guarantee a quick and smooth achievement of the final settlement. This security measure is indispensable. If the German Government renounced it and left the whole further treatment of the problem simply to normal negotiations with Czechoslovakia, the present unbearable circumstances in the Sudeten German territories which I described in my speech yesterday would continue to exist for a period, the length of which cannot be foreseen. The Czechoslovak Government would be completely in a position to drag out the negotiations on any point they liked, and thus to delay the final settlement. You will understand after everything that has passed that I cannot place such confidence in the assurances received from the Prague Government. The British Government also would surely not be in a position to dispose of this danger by any use of diplomatic pressure.

That Czechoslovakia should lose a part of her fortifications is naturally an unavoidable consequence of the cession of the Sudeten German territory agreed to by the Prague Government itself. If one were to wait for the entry into force of the final settlement in which Czechoslovakia had completed new fortifications in the territory which remained to her, it would doubtless last months and years. But this is the only object of all the Czech objections. Above all, it is completely incorrect to maintain that Czechoslovakia in this manner would be crippled in her national existence or in her political and economic independence. It is clear from my memorandum that the German occupation would only extend to the given line, and that the final delimitation of the frontier would take place in accordance with the procedure which I have already described. The Prague Government has no right to doubt that the German military measures would stop within these limits. If, nevertheless, it desires such a doubt to be taken into account the British and, if necessary, also the French Government can guarantee the quick fulfilment of my proposal. I can, moreover, only refer to my speech yesterday in which I clearly declared that I regret the idea of any attack on Czechoslovak territory, and that under the condition which I laid down I am even ready to give a formal guarantee for the remainder of Czechoslovakia. There can, therefore, be not the slightest question whatsoever of a check to the independence of Czechoslovakia. It is equally erroneous to talk of an economic rift. It is, on the contrary, a well-known fact that Czechoslovakia after the cession of the Sudeten German territory would constitute a healthier and more unified economic organism than before.

If the Government in Prague finally evinces anxiety also in regard to the state of the Czech population in the territories to be occupied, I can only regard this with surprise. It can be sure that, on the German side, nothing whatever will occur which will preserve for those Czechs a similar fate to that which has befallen the Sudeten Germans consequent on the Czech measures.

In these circumstances, I must assume that the Government in Prague is only using a proposal for the occupation by German troops in order, by distorting the meaning and object of my proposal, to mobilise those forces in other countries, in particular in England and France, from which they hope to receive unreserved support for their aim and thus to achieve the possibility of a general warlike conflagration. I must leave it to your judgment whether, in view of these facts, you consider that you should continue your effort, for which I should like to take this opportunity of once more sincerely thanking you, to spoil such manoeuvres and bring the Government in Prague to reason at the very last hour.

NOTE from Hans Thomsen, German Chargé d'Affaires at Washington, to the Secretary of State of the United States (Cordell Hull), March 17, 1939

Department of State, *Press Releases,* March 25, 1939, p. 220

Mr. Secretary of State:

By direction of the German Government, I have the honor to notify the Government of the United States of America of the following decree of March 16 of the Government of the Reich on the Prtectorate of Bohemia and Moravia:

Article 1. The areas of the former Czechoslovak Republic occupied by German troops belong from now on to the domain of the Greater German Reich and come under its protection as the Protectorate of Bohemia and Moravia.

Article 2. The German inhabitants of the Protectorate become nationals and, under the provisions of the Reich Citizens Law of September 1935, citizens of the Reich. With respect to them, therefore, the provisions for the protection of the German blood and the German honor also apply. They are subject to the jurisdiction of German courts. The other inhabitants become nationals of the Protectorate of Bohemia and Moravia.

Article 3. The Protectorate is autonomous and administers its own affairs. It exercises its right of sovereignty granted it within the framework of the Protectorate in harmony with the political, military, and economic requirements of the Reich. The rights of sovereignty will be exercised by its own organs and its own authorities with officials of its own.

Article 4. The head of the autonomous government of the Protectorate enjoys the protection and the honors of the head of a state. The head of the Protectorate must have the confidence of the Fuehrer and the Chancelor of the Reich for the exercise of his office.

Article 5. As protector of the interests of the Reich, the Fuehrer and Chancelor of the Reich appoints the Reich Protector in Bohemia and Moravia, whose seat is Praha. The Reich Protector has the duty of seeing to the observance of the political policies of the Fuehrer and Chancelor of the Reich. The members of the Protectorate government are confirmed by the Reich Protector. The latter is empowered to have himself informed regarding all measures of the government of the Protectorate and to give it advice. He may veto measures capable of injuring the Reich, and, in case there is danger in delay, he may take the measures necessary for the common interest. The promulgation of laws, regulations, and other legal prescriptions, as well as the execution of administrative measures and court orders having the force of law is to be suspended if the Reich Protector interposes a veto.

Article 6. The Reich takes charge of the foreign affairs of the Protectorate, and in particular of the protection of its nationals in foreign countries. The Reich will conduct foreign affairs in accordance with the common interests. The Protectorate is given a representative near the Reich Government with the official designation of minister.

Article 7. The Reich grants military protection to the Protectorate. In the exercise of this protection, the Reich maintains garrisons and military establishments in the Protectorate. For maintaining internal security and order, the Protectorate may organize its own units. Their organization, strength, number, and armament are determined by the Government of the Reich.

Article 8. The Reich exercises direct supervision over transportation, mail, and tele-communications.

Article 9. The Protectorate belongs to the customs territory of the Reich and is under its customs sovereignty.

Article 10. Until further notice, the crown is legal tender together with the reichsmark. The relation of the two currencies to each other is determined by the Reich Government.

Article 11. The Reich can issue legal regulations valid for the Protectorate, in so far as the common interests so require. In so far as a common need exists, the Reich can transfer administrative branches to its own administration and provide the officials belonging to the Reich who are needed therefor. The Government of the Reich can take the measures necessary for the maintenance of security and order.

Article 12. The law now in effect in Bohemia and Moravia remains in force, in so far as it does not contradict the sense of the assumption of protection by the German Reich.

Article 13. The Reich Minister of the Interior issues, in agreement with the Reich ministers concerned, the legal and administrative regulations necessary for the execution and supplementing of this decree.

Under Article 6 of this decree the German Reich takes charge of the foreign affairs of the Protectorate, in particular, of the protection of its nationals in foreign countries. The former diplomatic representatives of Czechoslovakia in foreign countries are no longer qualified for official acts.

RELATIONS WITH FRANCE, GREAT BRITAIN AND POLAND; OUTBREAK OF THE WAR

STATEMENT by Joachim von Ribbentrop, Minister for Foreign Affairs, December 6, 1938, Regarding the Franco-German Declaration of the Same Date

Translation, in *The French Yellow Book*, p. 37; for The Declaration *see infra*, p. 1024; see also *supra*, 636 ff., 668 ff.

WITH TO-DAY's declarations, France and Germany, taking into consideration the solid foundation constituted by the friendship uniting them to other States, have agreed to put an end to the age-long conflicts concerning their frontier, and, by mutually recognizing their territories, hope to facilitate the course of reciprocal understanding, and of consideration for the vital national interest of both countries.

As partners with equal rights, two great nations declare themselves prepared, after serious differences in the past, to establish good neighbourly relations in the future. With this declaration of good will, they express the conviction that no opposition of a vital nature exists between them, which could justify a serious conflict. The economic interests of the two countries complement each other. German art and the spiritual life of Germany owe valuable inspirations to France, just as Germany, on her side, has often enriched French art.

The mutual esteem which arose from the courage shown by the French and the German peoples during the World War can find its natural complement in peace, and still increase, thanks to the courageous effort of each nation in its daily work.

I am therefore convinced that the Franco-German declaration of to-day will help to remove historical prejudices and that the *détente* in our neighbourly relations which finds expression in this declaration will meet with unanimous approval not only from the leaders, but also from the peoples of our States.

The feelings of the German people towards a new orientation in the relations between the two States were manifested by the warm welcome given at Munich to the French Prime Minister, M. Edouard Daladier. The marks of sympathy which I have received during the few hours of my stay in Paris prove how these feelings are also shared by the French population.

I hope and trust that the declaration of to-day will initiate a new era in the relations between our two peoples.

ADDRESS by Adolf Hitler, Chancellor of the Reich, before the Reichstag, January 30, 1939

Translation, in *British War Blue Book*, p. 6; excerpt

We have just celebrated the fifth anniversary of the conclusion of our non-aggression pact with Poland. There can scarcely be any difference of opinion to-day among the true friends of peace with regard to the value of this agreement. One only needs to ask oneself what might have happened to Europe if this agreement, which brought such relief, had not been entered into five years ago. In signing it, this great Polish marshal and patriot rendered his people just as great a service as the leaders of the National Socialist State rendered the German people. During the troubled months of the past year the friendship between Germany and Poland was one of the reassuring factors in the political life of Europe.

PERSONAL LETTER from Joachim von Ribbentrop, Minister for Foreign Affairs, to the French Minister for Foreign Affairs (Georges Bonnet), July 13, 1939

Translation, in *The French Yellow Book*, p. 213

My dear M. Bonnet,

On July 1 you handed to Count von Welczeck a note personally intended for me, which obliges me now to make known to you, clearly and in a manner free from any misunderstanding, the attitude of the German Government with regard to Franco-German relations in general, and the question of Danzig in particular.

On December 6, 1938, the French and German Governments signed a declaration in accordance with which they solemnly recognized the existing frontiers between France and Germany as finally fixed, and according to which also they desired to use all their efforts for the establishment of peaceful and good neighbourly relations between the two countries.

On the side of the Government of the Reich, this declaration was the logical sequel to the policy of understanding with France continually followed ever since that Government came into power; a policy which, in principle, it would still wish to maintain.

As to your remark about the reservation recorded in Article 3 of the Franco-German declaration concerning the special relations of

France and of Germany with regard to third Powers, it is unquestionably not correct to say that this reservation implies a recognition of France's special relations with Poland. In the conversations which took place in Berlin and Paris at the time of the preliminary negotiations on the subject of the declaration, and on the occasion of the signature, it was on the contrary perfectly clear that the reservation referred to the special relations of friendship of France towards Great Britain and of Germany towards Italy. We were in agreement, in particular, at the time of our conversations in Paris on December 6, 1938, in considering that respect for vital reciprocal interests must be the prior condition and the principle of the future development of good Franco-German relations.

On that occasion, I expressly pointed out that Eastern Europe constituted a sphere of German interests, and, contrary to what is stated in your note, you then stressed on your part, that, in France's attitude with regard to the problems of Eastern Europe, a radical change had taken place since the Munich conference.

In direct contradiction to this attitude established by us at the beginning of December stands the fact that France has taken advantage of the Führer's generous proposal to Poland for the settlement of the question of Danzig and of Poland's somewhat peculiar reaction, in order to contract with that country fresh commitments, strengthened and aimed at Germany. At the end of your note, these commitments are defined in such a way that any military intervention by Poland, on the occasion of any departure from the *status quo* in Danzig, would lead France to give immediate military assistance to Poland.

With regard to this policy of the French Government, I have the following comments to make:

(1) Germany, just as it has never interfered in France's vital interests, must reject, once for all and categorically, any interference by France in its spheres of vital interest. Germany's relations with its Eastern neighbours, whatever form they assume, in no way affect French interests; they are a matter which only concerns German policy. Accordingly the Government of the Reich does not find itself in a position to discuss with the French Government questions concerning German-Polish relations, or to recognize its right to exercise any influence upon questions dealing with the future settlement of the destiny of the German city of Danzig.

(2) For your personal guidance, I beg to make the following statement about the German point of view in the Polish question:

The Polish government has replied to the Führer's historic and unique offer, aiming at the settlement of the question of Danzig and at a definitive consolidation of German-Polish relations, by threats of war which can only be described as strange. At the present moment it is impossible to say whether the Polish Government will depart from this peculiar position and return to reason. But, as long as it maintains the unreasonable attitude which it has taken up one can only say that any violation of Danzig soil by Poland, or any Polish provocation incompatible with the prestige of the German Reich, would meet in reply with an immediate march by the Germans and the total destruction of the Polish army.

(3) The statement already mentioned, which is contained in the final sentence of your note, would, if taken literally, mean that France recognizes Poland's right to oppose by arms any departure in any respect from the *status quo* in Danzig, and that, if Germany declines to tolerate that violence should thus be done to German interests, France will attack Germany. If such was in fact the purpose of French policy, I would beg you to consider that such threats could only further strengthen the Führer in his resolve to ensure the safeguarding of German interests by all the means at his disposal. The Führer has always desired Franco-German understanding and described as madness a fresh war between the two countries, which are no longer separated by any conflict of vital interests. But, if we have reached a point where the French Government wants war, it will find Germany ready at any moment. It would then be the French Government alone which would have to bear before its people and before the world the responsibility for such a war.

Because of the pleasant personal relations which I was able to form with Your Excellency on the occasion of the signature of the declaration of December 6, 1938, I regret that your note constrains me to make this reply. I should not like to abandon the hope that in the end, reason will prevail and that the French people will recognize where its real interests are to be found. Since I have devoted myself for more than twenty years to Franco-German understanding, this would also represent to me personally the fulfilment of a deeply felt wish.

COMMUNICATION from Adolf Hitler, Chancellor of the Reich, to the Prime Minister of Great Britain (Neville Chamberlain), August 23, 1939

Translation, in *British War Blue Book,* p. 132

Your Excellency,
The British Ambassador has just handed to me a communication in which your Excellency draws attention in the name of the British

Government to a number of points which in your estimation are of the greatest importance.

I may be permitted to answer your letter as follows:—

1. Germany has never sought conflict with England and has never interfered in English interests. On the contrary, she has for years endeavoured—although unfortunately in vain—to win England's friendship. On this account she voluntarily assumed in a wide area of Europe the limitations on her own interests which from a national-political point of view it would have otherwise been very difficult to tolerate.

2. The German Reich, however, like every other State possesses certain definite interests which it is impossible to renounce. These do not extend beyond the limits of the necessities laid down by former German history and deriving from vital economic pre-requisites. Some of these questions held and still hold a significance both of a national-political and a psychological character which no German Government is able to ignore.

To these questions belong the German City of Danzig, and the connected problem of the Corridor. Numerous statesmen, historians and men of letters even in England have been conscious of this at any rate up to a few years ago. I would add that all these territories lying in the aforesaid German sphere of interest and in particular those lands which returned to the Reich eighteen months ago received their cultural development at the hands not of the English but exclusively of the Germans and this, moreover, already from a time dating back over a thousand years.

3. Germany was prepared to settle the questions of Danzig and of the Corridor by the method of negotiation on the basis of a proposal of truly unparalleled magnanimity. The allegations disseminated by England regarding a German mobilisation against Poland, the assertion of aggressive designs towards Roumania, Hungary, &c., as well as the so-called guarantee declarations which were subsequently given had, however, dispelled Polish inclination to negotiate on a basis of this kind which would have been tolerable for Germany also.

4. The unconditional assurance given by England to Poland that she would render assistance to that country in all circumstances regardless of the causes from which a conflict might spring, could only be interpreted in that country as an encouragement thenceforward to unloosen, under cover of such a charter, a wave of appalling terrorism against the one and a half million German inhabitants living in Poland. The atrocities which since then have been taking place in that country are terrible for the victims, but intolerable for a Great Power

such as the German Reich which is expected to remain a passive onlooker during these happenings. Poland has been guilty of numerous breaches of her legal obligations towards the Free City of Danzig, has made demands of the character of ultimata, and has initiated a process of economic strangulation.

5. The Government of the German Reich therefore recently caused the Polish Government to be informed that it was not prepared passively to accept this development of affairs, that it will not tolerate further addressing of notes in the character of ultimata to Danzig, that it will not tolerate a continuance of the persecutions of the German minority, that it will equally not tolerate the extermination of the Free City of Danzig by economic measures, in other words, the destruction of the vital bases of the population of Danzig by a kind of Customs blockade, and that it will not tolerate the occurrence of further acts of provocation directed against the Reich. Apart from this, the questions of the Corridor and of Danzig must and shall be solved.

6. Your Excellency informs me in the name of the British Government that you will be obliged to render assistance to Poland in any such case of intervention on the part of Germany. I take note of this statement of yours and assure you that it can make no change in the determination of the Reich Government to safeguard the interests of the Reich as stated in paragraph 5 above. Your assurance to the effect that in such an event you anticipate a long war is shared by myself. Germany, if attacked by England, will be found prepared and determined. I have already more than once declared before the German people and the world that there can be no doubt concerning the determination of the new German Reich rather to accept, for however long it might be, every sort of misery and tribulation than to sacrifice its national interests, let alone its honour.

7. The German Reich Government has received information to the effect that the British Government has the intention to carry out measures of mobilisation which, according to the statements contained in your own letter, are clearly directed against Germany alone. This is said to be true of France as well. Since Germany has never had the intention of taking military measures other than those of a defensive character against England or France, and, as has already been emphasized, has never intended, and does not in the future intend, to attack England or France, it follows that this announcement as confirmed by you, Mr. Prime Minister, in your own letter, can only refer to a contemplated act of menace directed against the Reich. *I therefore inform your Excellency that, in the event of these military*

announcements being carried into effect, I shall order immediate mobilisation of the German forces.

8. The question of the treatment of European problems on a peaceful basis is not a decision which rests on Germany but primarily on those who since the crime committed by the Versailles dictate have stubbornly and consistently opposed any peaceful revision. Only after a change of spirit on the part of the responsible Powers can there be any real change in the relationship between England and Germany. I have all my life fought for Anglo-German friendship; the attitude adopted by British diplomacy—at any rate up to the present—has, however, convinced me of the futility of such an attempt. Should there be any change in this respect in the future nobody could be happier than I.

VERBAL COMMUNICATION Made by Adolf Hitler, Chancellor of the German Reich, to the British Ambassador to Germany (Sir Nevile Henderson) at an Interview, August 25, 1939

Translation, in *British War Blue Book*, p. 155

BY WAY OF introduction the Führer declared that the British Ambassador had given expression at the close of the last conversation to the hope that, after all, an understanding between Germany and England might yet be possible. He (the Führer) had therefore turned things over in his mind once more and desired to make a move as regards England which should be as decisive as the move as regards Russia which had led to the recent agreement. Yesterday's sitting in the House of Commons and the speeches of Mr. Chamberlain and Lord Halifax had also moved the Führer to talk once more to the British Ambassador. The assertion that Germany affected to conquer the world was ridiculous. The British Empire embraced 40 million square kilometres, Russia 19 million square kilometres, America 9½ million square kilometres, whereas Germany embraced less than 600,000 square kilometres. It is quite clear who it is who desires to conquer the world.

The Führer makes the following communication to the British Ambassador:—

1. Poland's actual provocations have become intolerable. It makes no difference who is responsible. If the Polish Government denies responsibility, that only goes to show that it no longer itself possesses

any influence over its subordinate military authorities. In the preceding night there has been a further twenty-one new frontier incidents; on the German side the greatest discipline had been maintained. All incidents had been provoked from the Polish side. Furthermore, commercial aircraft had been shot at. If the Polish Government stated that it was not responsible, it showed that it was no longer capable of controlling its own people.

2. Germany was in all the circumstances determined to abolish these Macedonian conditions on her eastern frontier and, what is more, to do so in the interests of quiet and order, but also in the interests of European peace.

3. The problem of Danzig and the Corridor must be solved.—The British Prime Minister had made a speech which was not in the least calculated to induce any change in the German attitude. At the most, the result of this speech could be a bloody and incalculable war between Germany and England. Such a war would be bloodier than that of 1914 to 1918. In contrast to the last war, Germany would no longer have to fight on two fronts. Agreement with Russia was unconditional and signified a change in foreign policy of the Reich which would last a very long time. Russia and Germany would never again take up arms against each other. Apart from this, the agreements reached with Russia would also render Germany secure economically for the longest possible period of war.

The Führer had always wanted an Anglo-German understanding. War between England and Germany could at the best bring some profit to Germany but none at all to England.

The Führer declared that the German-Polish problem must be solved and will be solved. He is, however, prepared and determined after the solution of this problem to approach England once more with a large comprehensive offer. He is a man of great decisions, and in this case also he will be capable of being great in his action. He accepts the British Empire and is ready to pledge himself personally for its continued existence and to place the power of the German Reich at its disposal if—

(1) His colonial demands which are limited and can be negotiated by peaceful methods are fulfilled and in this case he is prepared to fix the longest time limit.

(2) His obligations towards Italy are not touched; in other words, he does not demand that England gives up her obligations towards France and similarly for his own part he cannot withdraw from his obligations towards Italy.

(3) He also desires to stress the irrevocable determination of Germany never again to enter into conflict with Russia. The Führer is

ready to conclude agreements with England which, as has already been emphasised, would not only guarantee the existence of the British Empire in all circumstances as far as Germany is concerned, but also if necessary an assurance to the British Empire of German assistance regardless of where such assistance should be necessary. The Führer would then also be ready to accept a reasonable limitation of armaments which corresponds to the new political situation, and which is economically tolerable. Finally, the Führer renewed his assurances that he is not interested in Western problems and that a frontier modification in the West does not enter into consideration. Western fortifications which have been constructed at a cost of milliards were final Reich frontier on the West.

If the British Government would consider these ideas a blessing for Germany and also for the British Empire might result. If it rejects these ideas there will be war. In no case would Great Britain emerge stronger; the last war proved this.

The Führer repeats that he is a man of *ad infinitum* decisions by which he himself is bound and that this is his last offer. Immediately after solution of the German-Polish question he would approach the British Government with an offer.

PERSONAL LETTER from Adolf Hitler, Chancellor of the Reich, to the French Premier (Edouard Daladier), August 27, 1939

Transmitted through the French Ambassador to Germany (Robert Coulondre) and the French Foreign Office. Translation, in *The French Yellow Book*, p. 321

M<small>Y DEAR</small> P<small>RESIDENT OF THE</small> C<small>OUNCIL</small>,

I can understand the thoughts that you have expressed. Nor have I, for my part, ever minimized the high duties devolving on those on whom the fate of peoples rests. As an ex-Serviceman I am as aware as you are of the frightfulness of war. Owing to this outlook and to this experience, I have likewise made sincere efforts to eliminate all cause of conflict between our two peoples. Some time ago I gave a public assurance to the French people that the return of the Saar territory was the preliminary condition of such an appeasement. As soon as this return had been effected, I solemnly confirmed my renunciation of any other claim that might affect France.

The German people has approved my attitude.

As you were able to ascertain on the occasion of our last meeting, the German people, fully conscious of their own attitude, did not and do not harbour any kind of bitterness or of hatred towards their old and gallant opponent. Quite the contrary. The appeasement on our Western Frontier engendered a growing sympathy, at least on the part of the German people, a sympathy which on numerous occasions showed itself particularly demonstrative. The building of great fortifications in the West, which has absorbed and absorbs many millions of marks, amounts at the same time for Germany to an official act of acceptance and fixation of the final frontier of the Reich. The German people has consequently renounced the two provinces which belonged in the past to the German Empire, and were conquered afresh with much blood and defended a last time with yet more blood. This renunciation does not represent, as your Excellency will certainly agree, any tactical attitude for external consumption, but a decision which was strictly confirmed by all the measures that we have taken.

You could not, Mr. Prime Minister, mention one instance in which, either by a line or a speech, I have ever acted contrary to this final fixation of the Western frontier of the German Reich. By this renunciation and this attitude, I thought to have eliminated every conceivable element of conflict between our two peoples, which might lead to a repetition of the tragedy of 1914–1918. But this voluntary limitation of the vital aspirations of Germany on the West cannot be considered as an acceptance, valid in all other spheres, of the *Diktat* of Versailles. I therefore year by year sought to obtain, by means of negotiation, the revision of at least the most incredible and most intolerable clauses of this *Diktat*. I found this impossible. That this revision ought to take place many far-seeing people in all countries considered to be obvious. Whatever reproaches might be levelled at my methods, however much you might feel obliged to oppose them, no one has the right to overlook or to deny that, thanks to them, it has been possible, in numerous cases, without fresh shedding of blood, not only to find a solution satisfactory for Germany, but also that, by such methods, the statesmen of other nations have been freed from the obligation (which it was often impossible for them to fulfil) of assuming before their own peoples the responsibility for this revision. For, in any case, it is a point upon which your Excellency will agree with me: the revision was inevitable. The *Diktat* of Versailles was intolerable. No Frenchman of honour, you least of all, M. Daladier, would have acted, in a similar situation, differently from me. I have, therefore, in this spirit, endeavoured to wipe out from the world the most unreasonable of the provisions of the *Diktat* of Versailles. I made to the Polish Government a proposal which alarmed the German people. No one but I myself could have attempted to bring such a proposal to the light of day. And therefore it could be made only once. I am now convinced, in my innermost conscience, that if England in particular, instead of launching a savage Press campaign against Germany, and of spreading rumours of German mobilization, had by one means or another induced Poland to show herself reasonable, Europe would be enjoying to-day and for twenty-five years the profoundest peace. But on the contrary, through the mendacious allegation of German aggression, Polish public opinion was alarmed, it became more difficult for the Polish Government to take of their own accord the clear-cut decisions required, and above all their appreciation of the actual limits of what was possible was thereby obscured when we made our offer of a promise of guarantee. The Polish Government rejected my proposals. Polish public opinion, convinced that England and France would henceforth fight for Poland, then started to advance demands which could be treated as ludicrous follies if they were not infinitely dangerous as well. Then began an intolerable reign of terror, a physical and economic oppression of the million and a half Germans still to be numbered in the territories separated from the Reich. I do not want to speak here of the horrors that have been perpetrated. But Danzig itself, following the incessant encroachments of the Polish authorities, has become increasingly aware of being subjected, with no hope of redemption, to the arbitrary exactions of a force alien to the national character of the city and of its population.

May I be allowed, M. Daladier, to inquire how you would act, as a Frenchman, if, as the unhappy result of a courageous struggle, one of your provinces was separated by a corridor occupied by a foreign Power; if a great city—let us say Marseilles—were forcibly prevented from proclaiming itself French, and if Frenchmen residing in this territory were at the present moment beset, beaten, maltreated, nay bestially done to death? You are a Frenchman, M. Daladier; I know therefore how you would act. I am a German. Have no doubt, M. Daladier, as to my feeling of honour and as to my conviction that it is my duty to act precisely thus. If you suffered what we are suffering, would you accept, M. Daladier, that Germany should want to intervene without any motive so that the corridor should continue to cut across France?—so as to prevent the return of the stolen territories to the mother country?—so as to prohibit the return of Marseilles to France? In any case, the idea would never occur to me, M. Daladier, that Germany should embark on a struggle with you for this reason. For I and all of us have renounced Alsace-Lorraine to avoid a fresh shedding of blood. And still less should we shed blood in order to maintain a state of affairs which would be intolerable for you and which would be of no value to us. All that you express in your letter, M. Daladier, I feel exactly as you do. Perhaps, just because we are ex-Servicemen, we are able to understand each other more easily in many spheres. But I beg of you, do understand this equally well; it is not possible for a nation of honour to give up nearly two millions of human beings and to see them ill-treated on its frontiers. I have therefore formulated a precise demand; Danzig and the Corridor must return to Germany. The Macedonian situation must be liquidated on our eastern frontier. I do not see the possibility of bringing to a pacific solution a Poland who now feels herself inviolable under the protection of her guarantees. But I should despair of an honourable future for my people if, under such circumstances, we had not decided to settle the question in one way or another. If, consequently, fate compels our two peoples to fight afresh, there would nevertheless be a difference between the motives of the one and the others. I, M. Daladier, should then be fighting with my people for the reparation of an injustice which was inflicted upon us, while the others would fight for maintenance of that injustice. This is the more tragic, since many of the most important personalities of your own nation have recognized the insanity of the solution of 1919, as well as the impossibility of its indefinite prolongation. I perfectly realize the heavy consequences which such a conflict would involve. But I believe that the heaviest would fall on Poland, for it is a fact that, whatever the issue of a war born of this question, the Polish State of to-day would be lost anyhow. That for this result our two peoples must engage in a new and bloody war of extermination, is a matter of the deepest sorrow not only for you, M. Daladier, but also for me. But, as already indicated, I fail to see any possibility for us to obtain any result from Poland by reasonable means so as to redress a situation which is intolerable for the German people and for the German nation.

COMMUNICATION from Adolf Hitler, Chancellor of the Reich, to the British Government, Handed to the British Ambassador to Germany (Sir Nevile Henderson) during the Evening of August 29, 1939, in Reply to the British Government's Communication of August 28, 1939

Translation, in *British War Blue Book*, p. 175

The British Ambassador in Berlin has submitted to the British Government suggestions which I felt bound to make in order—
(1) to give expression once more to the will of the Reich Government for sincere Anglo-German understanding, co-operation and friendship;
(2) to leave no room for doubt as to fact that such an understanding could not be bought at the price of a renunciation of vital German interests, let alone the abandonment of demands which are based as much upon common human justice as upon the national dignity and honour of our people.

The German Government have noted with satisfaction from the reply of the British Government and from the oral explanations given by the British Ambassador that the British Government for their part are also prepared to improve the relationship between Germany and England and to develop and extend it in the sense of the German suggestion.

In this connexion, the British Government are similarly convinced that the removal of the German-Polish tension, which has become unbearable, is the pre-requisite for the realisation of this hope.

Since the autumn of the past year, and on the last occasion in March, 1939, there were submitted to the Polish Government proposals, both oral and written, which, having regard to the friendship then existing between Germany and Poland, offered the possibility of a solution of the questions in dispute acceptable to both parties. The British Government are aware that the Polish Government saw fit, in March last, finally to reject these proposals. At the same time, they used this rejection as a pretext or an occasion for taking military measures which have since been continuously intensified. Already in the middle of last month Poland was in effect in a state of mobilisation. This was accompanied by numerous encroachments in the Free City of Danzig due to the instigation of the Polish authorities; threatening demands in the nature of ultimata, varying only in degree, were addressed to that City. A closing of the frontiers, at first in the form of a measure of customs policy but extended later in a military sense affecting also traffic and communications, was imposed with the object of bringing about the political exhaustion and economic destruction of this German community.

To this were added barbaric actions of maltreatment which cry to Heaven, and other kinds of persecution of the large German national group in Poland which extended even to the killing of many resident Germans or to their forcible removal under the most cruel conditions. This state of affairs is unbearable for a Great Power. It has now forced Germany, after remaining a passive onlooker for many months, in her turn to take the necessary steps for the safeguarding of justified German interests. And indeed the German Government can but assure the British Government in the most solemn manner that a condition of affairs has now been reached which can no longer be accepted or observed with indifference.

The demands of the German Government are in conformity with the revision of the Versailles Treaty in regard to this territory which has always been recognised as being necessary: viz., return of Danzig and the Corridor to Germany, the safeguarding of the existence of the German national group in the territories remaining to Poland.

The German Government note with satisfaction that the British Government also are in principle convinced that some solution must be found for the new situation which has arisen.

They further feel justified in assuming that the British Government too can have no doubt that it is a question now of conditions, for the elimination of which there no longer remain days, still less weeks, but perhaps only hours. For in the disorganised state of affairs obtaining in Poland, the possibility of incidents intervening, which it might be impossible for Germany to tolerate, must at any moment be reckoned with.

While the British Government may still believe that these grave differences can be resolved by way of direct negotiations, the German Government unfortunately can no longer share this view as a matter of course. For they have made the attempt to embark on such peaceful negotiations, but, instead of receiving any support from the Polish Government, they were rebuffed by the sudden introduction of measures of a military character in favour of the development alluded to above.

The British Government attach importance to two considerations: (1) that the existing danger of an imminent explosion should be eliminated as quickly as possible by direct negotiation, and (2) that the existence of the Polish State, in the form in which it would then continue to exist, should be adequately safeguarded in the economic and political sphere by means of international guarantees.

On this subject the German Government makes the following declaration:—

Though sceptical as to the prospects of a successful outcome, they are nevertheless prepared to accept the English proposal and to enter into direct discussions. They do so, as has already been emphasised, solely as the result of the impression made upon them by the written statement received from the British Government that they too desire a pact of friendship in accordance with the general lines indicated to the British Ambassador.

The German Government desire in this way to give the British Government and the British nation a proof of the sincerity of Germany's intentions to enter into a lasting friendship with Great Britain.

The Government of the Reich felt, however, bound to point out to the British Government that in the event of a territorial rearrangement in Poland they would no longer be able to bind themselves to give guarantees or to participate in guarantees without the U.S.S.R. being associated therewith.

For the rest, in making these proposals the German Government have never had any intention of touching Poland's vital interests or questioning the existence of an independent Polish State. The German Government, accordingly, in these circumstances agree to accept the British Government's offer of their good offices in securing the despatch to Berlin of a Polish Emissary with full powers. They count on the arrival of this Emissary on Wednesday, the 30th August, 1939.

The German Government will immediately draw up proposals for a solution acceptable to themselves and will, if possible, place these at the disposal of the British Government before the arrival of the Polish negotiator.

COMMUNICATION from the German Government to the British Government, Handed by the German State Secretary (Baron Ernst von Weizsäcker) to the British Ambassador (Sir Nevile Henderson) at 9:15 P.M. on August 31, 1939 (translation)

Translation, in *British War Blue Book*, p. 192

His Majesty's Government informed the German Government, in a note dated the 28th August, 1939, of their readiness to offer their mediation towards direct negotiations between Germany and Poland over the problems in dispute. In so doing they made it abundantly clear that they, too, were aware of the urgent need for progress in view of the continuous incidents and the general European tension. In a reply dated the 29th August, the German Government, in spite of being sceptical as to the desire of the Polish Government to come to an understanding, declared themselves ready in the interests of peace to accept the British mediation or suggestion. After considering all the circumstances prevailing at the time, they considered it necessary in their note to point out that, if the danger of a catastrophe was to be avoided, then action must be taken readily and without delay. In this sense they declared themselves ready to receive a personage appointed by the Polish Government up to the evening of the 30th August, with the proviso that the latter was, in fact, empowered not only to discuss but to conduct and conclude negotiations.

Further, the German Government pointed out that they felt able to make the basic points regarding the offer of an understanding available to the British Government by the time the Polish negotiator arrived in Berlin.

Instead of a statement regarding the arrival of an authorised Polish personage, the first answer the Government of the Reich received to their readiness for an understanding was the news of the Polish mobilisation, and only towards 12 o'clock on the night of the 30th August, 1939, did they receive a somewhat general assurance of British readiness to help towards the commencement of negotiations.

Although the fact that the Polish negotiator expected by the Government of the Reich did not arrive removed the necessary condition for informing His Majesty's Government of the views of the German Government as regards possible bases of negotiation, since His Majesty's Government themselves had pleaded for direct negotiations between Germany and Poland, the German Minister for Foreign Affairs, Herr von Ribbentrop, gave the British Ambassador on the occasion of the presentation of the last British note precise information as to the text of the German proposals which would be regarded as a basis of negotiation in the event of the arrival of the Polish plenipotentiary.

The Government of the German Reich considered themselves entitled to claim that in these circumstances a Polish personage would immediately be nominated, at any rate retroactively.

For the Reich Government cannot be expected for their part continually not only to emphasise their willingness to start negotiations, but actually to be ready to do so, while being from the Polish side merely put off with empty subterfuges and meaningless declarations.

It has once more been made clear as a result of a *démarche* which has meanwhile been made by the Polish Ambassador that the latter himself has no plenary powers either to enter into any discussion, or even to negotiate.

The Führer and the German Government have thus waited two days in vain for the arrival of a Polish negotiator with plenary powers.

In these circumstances the German Government regard their proposals as having this time too been to all intents and purposes rejected, although they consider that these proposals, in the form in which they were made known to the British Government also, were more than loyal, fair and practicable.

The Reich Government consider it timely to inform the public of the bases for negotiation which were communicated to the British Ambassador by the Minister for Foreign Affairs, Herr von Ribbentrop.

The situation existing between the German Reich and Poland is at the moment of such a kind that any further incident can lead to an explosion on the part of the military forces which have taken up their position on both sides. Any peaceful solution must be framed in such a way as to ensure that the events which lie at the root of this situation cannot be repeated on the next occasion offered, and that thus not only the East of Europe, but also other territories shall not be brought into such a state of tension. The causes of this development lie in: (1) the impossible delineation of frontiers, as fixed by the Versailles dictate; (2) the impossible treatment of the minority in the ceded territories.

In making these proposals, the Reich Government are, therefore, actuated by the idea of finding a lasting solution which will remove the impossible situation created by frontier delineation, which may assure to both parties their vitally important line of communication, which may—as far as it is at all possible—remove the minority problem and, in so far as this is not possible, may give the minorities the assurance of a tolerable future by means of a reliable guarantee of their rights.

The Reich Government are content that in so doing it is essential that economic and physical damage done since 1918 should be exposed and repaired in its entirety. They, of course, regard this obligation as being binding for both parties.

These considerations lead to the following practical proposals:—

(1) The Free City of Danzig shall return to the German Reich in view of its purely German character, as well as of the unanimous will of its population;

(2) The territory of the so-called Corridor which extends from the Baltic Sea to the line Marienwerder-Graudenz-Kulm-Bromberg (in-

clusive) and thence may run in a westerly direction to Schönlanke, shall itself decide as to whether it shall belong to Germany or Poland;

(3) For this purpose a plebiscite shall take place in this territory. The following shall be entitled to vote: all Germans who were either domiciled in this territory on the 1st January, 1918, or who by that date have been born there, and similarly of Poles, Kashubes, &c., domiciled in this territory on the above day (the 1st January, 1918) or born there up to that date. The Germans who have been driven from this territory shall return to it in order to exercise their vote with a view to ensuring an objective plebiscite, and also with a view to ensuring the extensive preparation necessary therefor. The above territory shall, as in the case of the Saar territory, be placed under the supervision of an international commission to be formed immediately, on which shall be represented the four Great Powers—Italy, the Soviet Union, France and England. This commission shall exercise all the rights of sovereignty in this territory. With this end in view, the territory shall be evacuated within a period of the utmost brevity, still to be agreed upon, by the Polish armed forces, the Polish police, and the Polish authorities;

(4) The Polish port of Gdynia, which fundamentally constitutes Polish sovereign territory so far as it is confined territorially to the Polish settlement, shall be excluded from the above territory. The exact frontiers of this Polish port should be determined between Germany and Poland, and, if necessary, delimited by an international committee of arbitration;

(5) With a view to assuring the necessary time for the execution of the extensive work involved in the carrying out of a just plebiscite, this plebiscite shall not take place before the expiry of twelve months;

(6) In order to guarantee unrestricted communication between Germany and East Prussia and between Poland and the sea during this period, roads and railways shall be established to render free transit traffic possible. In this connexion only such taxes as are necessary for the maintenance of the means of communication and for the provision of transport may be levied;

(7) The question as to the party to which the area belongs is to be decided by simple majority of the votes recorded;

(8) In order to guarantee to Germany free communication with her province of Danzig–East Prussia, and to Poland her connexion with the sea after the execution of the plebiscite—regardless of the results thereof—Germany shall, in the event of the plebiscite area going to Poland, receive an extra-territorial traffic zone, approximately in a line from Bütow to Danzig or Dirschau, in which to lay down an autobahn and a 4-track railway line. The road and the railway

shall be so constructed that the Polish lines of communication are not affected, *i.e.,* they shall pass either over or under the latter. The breadth of this zone shall be fixed at 1 kilometre, and it is to be German sovereign territory. Should the plebiscite be favourable to Germany, Poland is to obtain rights, analogous to those accorded to Germany, to a similar extra-territorial communication by road and railway for the purpose of free and unrestricted communication with her port to Gdynia;

(9) In the event of the Corridor returning to the German Reich, the latter declares its right to proceed to an exchange of population with Poland to the extent to which the nature of the Corridor lends itself thereto;

(10) Any special right desired by Poland in the port of Danzig would be negotiated on a basis of territory against similar rights to be granted to Germany in the port of Gdynia;

(11) In order to remove any feeling in this area that either side was being threatened, Danzig and Gdynia would have the character of exclusively mercantile towns, that is to say, without military installations and military fortifications;

(12) The peninsula of Hela, which as a result of the plebiscite might go either to Poland or to Germany, would in either case have similarly to be demilitarised;

(13) Since the Government of the German Reich has the most vehement complaints to make against the Polish treatment of minorities, and since the Polish Government for their part feel obliged to make complaints against Germany, both parties declare their agreement to have these complaints laid before an international committee of enquiry, whose task would be to examine all complaints as regards economic or physical damage, and any other acts of terrorism. Germany and Poland undertake to make good economic or other damage done to minorities on either side since the year 1918, or to cancel expropriation as the case may be, or to provide complete compensation to the persons affected for this and any other encroachments on their economic life;

(14) In order to free the Germans who may be left in Poland and the Poles who may be left in Germany from the feeling of being outlawed by all nations, and in order to render them secure against being called upon to perform action or to render services incompatible with their national sentiments, Germany and Poland agree to guarantee the rights of both minorities by means of the most comprehensive and binding agreement, in order to guarantee to these minorities the preservation, the free development and practical application of their nationality (Volkstum), and in particular to permit for this

purpose such organisation as they may consider necessary. Both parties undertake not to call upon members of the minority for military service;

(15) In the event of agreement on the basis of these proposals, Germany and Poland declare themselves ready to decree and to carry out the immediate demobilisation of their armed forces;

(16) The further measures necessary for the more rapid execution of the above arrangement shall be agreed upon by both Germany and Poland conjointly.

COMMUNICATION from Hans Thomsen, German Chargé d'Affaires at Washington, to the Secretary of State of the United States (Cordell Hull), August 31, 1939, Replying to President Roosevelt's Appeals for Peace on August 25 and 26, 1939

Translation, in Department of State, *Bulletin*, September 2, 1939, p. 183

Mr. Secretary of State:

By order of my Government, I wish to use your kind intermediary for the purpose of stating to the President of the United States that his messages of August 25 and 26 addressed to the German Fuehrer and Reich Chancellor have been greatly appreciated by the latter.

The German Fuehrer and Reich Chancellor has also, on his side, left nothing untried for the purpose of settling the dispute between Germany and Poland in a friendly manner. Even at the last hour he accepted an offer from the Government of Great Britain to mediate in this dispute. Owing to the attitude of the Polish Government, however, all these endeavors have remained without result.

PROCLAMATION by Adolf Hitler, Chancellor of the Reich, to the German Army, September 1, 1939

Translation, in *British War Blue Book*, p. 214

The Polish State has refused the peaceful settlement of relations which I desired, and has appealed to arms. Germans in Poland are persecuted with bloody terror and driven from their houses. A series of violations of the frontier, intolerable to a great Power, prove that Poland is no longer willing to respect the frontier of the Reich.

In order to put an end to this lunacy, I have no other choice than to meet force with force from now on. The German Army will fight the battle for the honour and the vital rights of reborn Germany with hard determination. I expect that every soldier, mindful of the great traditions of eternal German soldiery, will ever remain conscious that he is a representative of the National-Socialist Greater Germany. Long live our people and our Reich!

ADDRESS by Adolf Hitler, Chancellor of the Reich, before the Reichstag, September 1, 1939

Translation, in *British War Blue Book*, p. 207

FOR MONTHS we have been suffering under the torture of a problem which the Versailles *Diktat* created—a problem which has deteriorated until it becomes intolerable for us. Danzig was and is a German city. The Corridor was and is German. Both these territories owe their cultural development exclusively to the German people. Danzig was separated from us, the Corridor was annexed by Poland. As in other German territories of the East, all German minorities living there have been ill-treated in the most distressing manner. More than 1,000,000 people of German blood had in the years 1919–20 to leave their homeland.

As always, I attempted to bring about, by the peaceful method of making proposals for revision, an alteration of this intolerable position. It is a lie when the outside world says that we only tried to carry through our revisions by pressure. Fifteen years before the National Socialist Party came to power there was the opportunity of carrying out these revisions by peaceful settlements and understanding. On my own initiative I have, not once but several times, made proposals for the revision of intolerable conditions. All these proposals, as you know, have been rejected—proposals for limitation of armaments and even, if necessary, disarmament, proposals for the limitation of war-making, proposals for the elimination of certain methods of modern warfare. You know the proposals that I have made to fulfil the necessity of restoring German sovereignty over German territories. You know the endless attempts I made for a peaceful clarification and understanding of the problem of Austria, and later of the problem of the Sudetenland, Bohemia, and Moravia. It was all in vain.

It is impossible to demand that an impossible position should be cleared up by peaceful revision and at the same time constantly reject peaceful revision. It is also impossible to say that he who undertakes to carry out these revisions for himself transgresses a law, since the Versailles *Diktat* is not law to us. A signature was forced out of us with pistols at our head and with the threat of hunger for millions of people. And then this document, with our signature, obtained by force, was proclaimed as a solemn law.

In the same way, I have also tried to solve the problem of Danzig, the Corridor, &c., by proposing a peaceful discussion. That the problems had to be solved was clear. It is quite understandable to us that the time when the problem was to be solved had little interest for the Western Powers. But that time is not a matter of indifference to us. Moreover, it was not and could not be a matter of indifference to those who suffer most.

In my talks with Polish statesmen I discussed the ideas which you recognise from my last speech to the Reichstag. No one could say that this was in any way an inadmissible procedure or undue pressure. I then naturally formulated at last the German proposals, and I must once more repeat that there is nothing more modest or loyal than these proposals. I should like to say this to the world. I alone was in the position to make such proposals, for I know very well that in doing so I brought myself into opposition to millions of Germans. These proposals have been refused. Not only were they answered first with mobilisation, but with increased terror and pressure against our German compatriots and with a slow strangling of the Free City of Danzig—economically, politically, and in recent weeks by military and transport means.

Poland has directed its attacks against the Free City of Danzig. Moreover, Poland was not prepared to settle the Corridor question in a reasonable way which would be equitable to both parties, and she did not think of keeping her obligations to minorities.

I must here state something definitely; Germany has kept these obligations; the minorities who live in Germany are not persecuted. No Frenchman can stand up and say that any Frenchman living in the Saar territory is oppressed, tortured, or deprived of his rights. Nobody can say this.

For four months I have calmly watched developments, although I never ceased to give warnings. In the last few days I have increased these warnings. I informed the Polish Ambassador three weeks ago that if Poland continued to send to Danzig notes in the form of ultimata, if Poland continued its methods of oppression against the Germans, and if on the Polish side an end was not put to Customs measures destined to ruin Danzig's trade, then the Reich could not remain inactive. I left no doubt that people who wanted to compare the Germany of to-day with the former Germany would be deceiving themselves.

An attempt was made to justify the oppression of the Germans by claiming that they had committed acts of provocation. I do not know in what these provocations on the part of women and children consist, if they themselves are maltreated, in some cases killed. One thing I do know—that no great Power can with honour long stand by passively and watch such events.

I made one more final effort to accept a proposal for mediation on the part of the British Government. They proposed, not that they themselves should carry on the negotiations, but rather that Poland and Germany should come into direct contact and once more to pursue negotiations.

I must declare that I accepted this proposal, and I worked out a basis for these negotiations which are known to you. For two whole days I sat with my Government and waited to see whether it was convenient for the Polish Government to send a plenipotentiary or not. Last night they did not send us a plenipotentiary, but instead informed us through their Ambassador that they were still considering whether and to what extent they were in a position to go into the British proposals. The Polish Government also said that they would inform Britain of their decision.

Deputies, if the German Government and its Leader patiently endured such treatment Germany would deserve only to disappear from the political stage. But I am wrongly judged if my love of peace and my patience are mistaken for weakness or even cowardice. I, therefore, decided last night and informed the British Government that in these circumstances I can no longer find any willingness on the part of the Polish Government to conduct serious negotiations with us.

These proposals for mediation have failed because in the meanwhile there, first of all, came as an answer the sudden Polish general mobilisation, followed by more Polish atrocities. These were again repeated last night. Recently in one night there were as many as twenty-one frontier incidents: last night there were fourteen, of which three were quite serious. I have, therefore, resolved to speak to Poland in the same language that Poland for months past has used towards us. This attitude on the part of the Reich will not change.

The other European States understand in part our attitude. I should like here above all to thank Italy, which throughout has supported us, but you will understand that for the carrying on of this struggle we do not intend to appeal to foreign help. We will carry out this task ourselves. The neutral States have assured us of their neutrality, just as we had already guaranteed it to them.

When statesmen in the West declare that this affects their interests, I can only regret such a declaration. It cannot for a moment make me hesitate to fulfil my duty. What more is wanted? I have solemnly assured them, and I repeat it, that we ask nothing of these Western States and never will ask anything. I have declared that the frontier between France and Germany is a final one. I have repeatedly offered friendship and, if necessary, the closest co-operation to Britain, but this cannot be offered from one side only. It must find response on the other side. Germany has no interests in the West, and our western wall is for all time the frontier of the Reich on the west. Moreover, we have no aims of any kind there for the future. With this assurance we are in solemn earnest, and as long as others do not violate their neutrality we will likewise take every care to respect it.

I am happy particularly to be able to tell you of one event. You know that Russia and Germany are governed by two different doctrines. There was only one question that had to be cleared up. Germany has no intention of exporting its doctrine. Given the fact that Soviet Russia has no intention of exporting its doctrine to Germany, I no longer see any reason why we should still oppose one another. On both sides we are clear on that. Any struggle between our people would only be of advantage to others. We have, therefore, resolved to conclude a pact which rules out for ever any use of violence between us. It imposes the obligation on us to consult together in certain European questions. It makes possible for us economic co-operation, and above all it assures that the powers of both these powerful States are not wasted against one another. Every attempt of the West to bring about any change in this will fail.

At the same time I should like here to declare that this political decision means a tremendous departure for the future, and that it is a final one. Russia and Germany fought against one another in the World War. That shall and will not happen a second time. In Moscow, too, this pact was greeted exactly as you greet it. I can only endorse word for word the speech of the Russian Foreign Commissar, Molotov.

I am determined to solve (1) the Danzig question; (2) the question of the Corridor; and (3) to see to it that a change is made in the relationship between Germany and Poland that shall ensure a peaceful co-existence. In this I am resolved to continue to fight until either the present Polish Government is willing to bring about this change or until another Polish Government is ready to do so. I am resolved to remove from the German frontiers the element of uncertainty, the everlasting atmosphere of conditions resembling civil war. I will see to it that in the East there is, on the frontier, a peace precisely similar to that on our other frontiers.

In this I will take the necessary measures to see that they do not contradict the proposals I have already made known in the Reichstag itself to the rest of the world, that is to say, I will not war against women and children. I have ordered my air force to restrict itself to attacks on military objectives. If, however, the enemy thinks he can from that draw *carte blanche* on his side to fight by the other methods he will receive an answer that will deprive him of hearing and sight.

This night for the first time Polish regular soldiers fired on our own territory. Since 5.45 A.M. we have been returning the fire, and from now on bombs will be met with bombs. Whoever fights with poison gas will be fought with poison gas. Whoever departs from the rules of humane warfare can only expect that we shall do the same. I will continue this struggle, no matter against whom, until the safety of the Reich and its rights are secured.

For six years now I have been working on the building up of the German defences. Over 90 milliards have in that time been spent on the building up of these defence forces. They are now the best equipped and are above all comparison with what they were in 1914. My trust in them is unshakable. When I called up these forces and when I now ask sacrifices of the German people and if necessary every sacrifice, then I have a right to do so, for I also am to-day absolutely ready, just as we were formerly, to make every personal sacrifice.

I am asking of no German man more than I myself was ready throughout four years at any time to do. There will be no hardships for Germans to which I myself will not submit. My whole life henceforth belongs more than ever to my people. I am from now on just first soldier of the German Reich. I have once more put on that coat that was the most sacred and dear to me. I will not take it off again until victory is secured, or I will not survive the outcome.

Should anything happen to me in the struggle then my first successor is Party Comrade Göring; should anything happen to Party Comrade Göring my next successor is Party Comrade Hess. You would then be under obligation to give to them as Führer the same blind loyalty and obedience as to myself. Should anything happen to Party Comrade Hess, then by law the Senate will be called, and will choose from its midst the most worthy—that is to say the bravest —successor.

As a National Socialist and as German soldier I enter upon this struggle with a stout heart. My whole life has been nothing but one long struggle for my people, for its restoration, and for Germany.

There was only one watchword for that struggle: faith in this people. One word I have never learned: that is, surrender.

If, however, anyone thinks that we are facing a hard time, I should ask him to remember that once a Prussian King, with a ridiculously small State, opposed a stronger coalition, and in three wars finally came out successful because that State had that stout heart that we need in these times. I would, therefore, like to assure all the world that a November 1918 will never be repeated in German history. Just as I myself am ready at any time to stake my life—anyone can take it for my people and for Germany—so I ask the same of all others.

Whoever, however, thinks he can oppose this national command, whether directly or indirectly, shall fall. We have nothing to do with traitors. We are all faithful to our old principle. It is quite unimportant whether we ourselves live, but it is essential that our people shall live, that Germany shall live. The sacrifice that is demanded of us is not greater than the sacrifice that many generations have made. If we form a community closely bound together by vows, ready for anything, resolved never to surrender, then our will will master every hardship and difficulty. And I would like to close with the declaration that I once made when I began the struggle for power in the Reich. I then said: "If our will is so strong that no hardship and suffering can subdue it, then our will and our German might shall prevail."

COMMUNICATION from the German Government to the British Government, Handed by Joachim von Ribbentrop, Minister for Foreign Affairs, to the British Ambassador (Sir Nevile Henderson) at 11:20 A.M., September 3, 1939

Translation, in *British War Blue Book*, p. 225

The German Government have received the British Government's ultimatum of the 3rd September, 1939. They have the honour to reply as follows:—

1. The German Government and the German people refuse to receive, accept, let alone to fulfil, demands in the nature of ultimata made by the British Government.

2. On our eastern frontier there has for many months already reigned a condition of war. Since the time when the Versailles Treaty first tore Germany to pieces, all and every peaceful settlement was refused to all German Governments. The National Socialist Gov-

ernment also has since the year 1933 tried again and again to remove by peaceful negotiations the worst rapes and breaches of justice of this treaty. The British Government have been among those who, by their intransigent attitude, took the chief part in frustrating every practical revision. Without the intervention of the British Government—of this the German Government and German people are fully conscious—a reasonable solution doing justice to both sides would certainly have been found between Germany and Poland. For Germany did not have the intention nor had she raised the demands of annihilating Poland. The Reich demanded only the revision of those articles of the Versailles Treaty which already at the time of the formulation of that Dictate had been described by understanding statesmen of all nations as being in the long run unbearable, and therefore impossible for a great nation and also for the entire political and economic interests of Eastern Europe. British statesmen, too, declared the solution in the East which was then forced upon Germany as containing the germ of future wars. To remove this danger was the desire of all German Governments and especially the intention of the new National Socialist People's Government. The blame for having prevented this peaceful revision lies with the British Cabinet policy.

3. The British Government have—an occurrence unique in history—given the Polish State full powers for all actions against Germany which that State might conceivably intend to undertake. The British Government assured the Polish Government of their military support in all circumstances, should Germany defend herself against any provocation or attack. Thereupon the Polish terror against the Germans living in the territories which had been torn from Germany immediately assumed unbearable proportions. The Free City of Danzig was, in violation of all legal provisions, first threatened with destruction economically and by measures of customs policy, and was finally subjected to a military blockade and its communications strangled. All these violations of the Danzig Statute, which were well known to the British Government, were approved and covered by the blank cheque given to Poland. The German Government, though moved by the sufferings of the German population which was being tortured and treated in an inhuman manner, nevertheless remained a patient onlooker for five months, without undertaking even on one single occasion any similar aggressive action against Poland. They only warned Poland that these happenings would in the long run be unbearable, and that they were determined, in the event of no other kind of assistance being given to this population, to help them themselves. All these happenings were known in every detail to the Brit-

ish Government. It would have been easy for them to use their great influence in Warsaw in order to exhort those in power there to exercise justice and humaneness and to keep to the existing obligations. The British Government did not do this. On the contrary, in emphasising continually their obligation to assist Poland under all circumstances, they actually encouraged the Polish Government to continue in their criminal attitude which was threatening the peace of Europe. In this spirit, the British Government rejected the proposal of Signor Mussolini, which might still have been able to save the peace of Europe, in spite of the fact that the German Government had declared their willingness to agree to it. The British Government, therefore, bear the responsibility for all the unhappiness and misery which have now overtaken and are about to overtake many peoples.

4. After all efforts at finding and concluding a peaceful solution had been rendered impossible by the intransigence of the Polish Government covered as they were by England, after the conditions resembling civil war, which had existed already for months at the eastern frontier of the Reich, had gradually developed into open attacks on German territory, without the British Government raising any objections, the German Government determined to put an end to this continual threat, unbearable for a great Power, to the external and finally also to the internal peace of the German people, and to end it by those means which, since the Democratic Governments had in effect sabotaged all other possibilities of revision, alone remained at their disposal for the defence of the peace, security and honour of the Germans. The last attacks of the Poles threatening Reich territory they answered with similar measures. The German Government do not intend, on account of any sort of British intentions or obligations in the East, to tolerate conditions which are identical with those conditions which we observe in Palestine, which is under British protection. The German people, however, above all do not intend to allow themselves to be ill-treated by Poles.

5. The German Government, therefore, reject the attempts to force Germany, by means of a demand having the character of an ultimatum, to recall its forces which are lined up for the defence of the Reich, and thereby to accept the old unrest and the old injustice. The threat that, failing this, they will fight Germany in the war, corresponds to the intention proclaimed for years past by numerous British politicians. The German Government and the German people have assured the English people countless times how much they desire an understanding, indeed close friendship, with them. If the British Government hitherto always refused these offers and now answer them with an open threat of war, it is not the fault of the

German people and of their Government, but exclusively the fault of the British Cabinet or of those men who for years have been preaching the destruction and extermination of the German people. The German people and their Government do not, like Great Britain, intend to dominate the world, but they are determined to defend their own liberty, their independence and above all their life. The intention, communicated to us by order of the British Government by Mr. King-Hall, of carrying the destruction of the German people even further than was done through the Versailles Treaty is taken note of by us, and we shall therefore answer any aggressive action on the part of England with the same weapons and in the same form.

PROCLAMATION by Adolf Hitler, Chancellor of the Reich, to the German People, September 3, 1939

Translation, in *British War Blue Book*, p. 230

GREAT BRITAIN has for centuries pursued the aim of rendering the peoples of Europe defenceless against the British policy of world conquest by proclaiming a balance of power, in which Great Britain claimed the right to attack on threadbare pretexts and destroy that European State which at the moment seemed most dangerous. Thus, at one time, she fought the world power of Spain, later the Dutch, then the French, and, since the year 1871, the German.

We ourselves have been witnesses of the policy of encirclement which has been carried on by Great Britain against Germany since before the war. Just as the German nation had begun, under its National Socialist leadership, to recover from the frightful consequences of the *Diktat* of Versailles, and threatened to survive the crisis, the British encirclement immediately began once more.

The British war inciters spread the lie before the War that the battle was only against the House of Hohenzollern or German militarism; that they had no designs on German colonies; that they had no intention of taking the German mercantile fleet. They then oppressed the German people under the Versailles *Diktat* the faithful fulfilment of which would have sooner or later exterminated 20 million Germans.

I undertook to mobilise the resistance of the German nation against this, and to assure work and bread for them. But as the peaceful revision of the Versailles *Diktat* of force seemed to be succeeding, and the German people again began to live, the new British encirclement policy was resumed. The same lying inciters appeared as in 1914. I have many times offered Great Britain and the British people the understanding and friendship of the German people. My whole policy was based on the idea of this understanding. I have always been repelled. I had for years been aware that the aim of these war inciters had for long been to take Germany by surprise at a favourable opportunity.

I am more firmly determined than ever to beat back this attack. Germany shall not again capitulate. There is no sense in sacrificing one life after another and submitting to an even worse Versailles *Diktat*. We have never been a nation of slaves and will not be one in the future. Whatever Germans in the past had to sacrifice for the existence of our realm, they shall not be greater than those which we are to-day prepared to make.

This resolve is an inexorable one. It necessitates the most thorough measures, and imposes on us one law above all others: If the soldier is fighting at the front, no one shall profit by the war. If the soldier falls at the front no one at home shall evade his duty.

As long as the German people was united it has never been conquered. It was the lack of unity in 1918 that led to collapse. Whoever offends against this unity need expect nothing else than annihilation as an enemy of the nation. If our people fulfils its highest duty in this sense, that God will help us who has always bestowed His mercy on him who was determined to help himself.

RELATIONS WITH CERTAIN OTHER COUNTRIES

Italy

OFFICIAL COMMUNIQUÉ Issued after the Visit to Germany of Count Galeazzo Ciano, Italian Minister for Foreign Affairs, October 25, 1936

Translation, in Royal Institute of International Affairs, *Documents on International Affairs, 1936*, p. 341, citing *The Times* (London), October 26, 1936

IN THE COURSE of the visit of the Italian Foreign Minister, Count Ciano, to Germany, the current political, economic, and social questions of major importance, especially those which affect both countries directly, were discussed in his conversation with the *Führer* and in his various talks with leading German personalities. The conversations took place in an atmosphere of friendly cordiality. To the satisfaction of both parties there have been established a concurrence of views and the intention of the two Governments to devote their joint activities to the promotion of general peace and reconstruction. The two Governments have decided to remain in touch for the accomplishment of these aims.

ADDRESS by Adolf Hitler, Chancellor of the Reich, at Berlin, September 28, 1937, Delivered during the Visit to Berlin of Premier Benito Mussolini

Translation, in *Vital Speeches of the Day,* October 15, 1937, p. 18

WE HAVE just witnessed an historic event, the significance of which has no parallel. More than a million people have gathered here, participating in a demonstration which is being closely followed by the national communities of two countries, numbering 115,000,000, besides hundreds of millions more in other parts of the world who are following the proceedings over the radio as more or less interested listeners.

What moves us the most at this moment is the deep-rooted joy to see in our midst a guest (Premier Benito Mussolini of Italy) who is one of the lonely men in history, who are not put to trial by historic events but who determine the history of their country themselves.

Secondly, we realize that this demonstration is not one of those meetings which we can experience anywhere. It is the avowal of common ideals and common interests. It is the avowal pronounced by two men and it is heard by a million people assembled before us, an avowal which is expected and confirmed by 115,000,000 with a burning heart.

That is why the present demonstration is more than a public meeting. It is a manifestation of nations. The true meaning of this public gathering consists of the sincere desire to guarantee peace to our two countries which is not the reward for resigned cowardice but the result of a responsible policy safeguarding the racial, intellectual, and physical fitness of the nation as well as its cultural possessions. In doing this we hope to serve the interests of two nations and, more than that, the interests of the European continent.

The fact that we are in a position today to hold this meeting reminds us of the changes that have taken place in the period which we have left behind us. There is no nation in the world which longs more for peace than Germany, and no country has suffered more from the terrible consequences of misplaced blind confidence than our nation. We recall a period of fifteen years before National Socialism came into power, a time which was marked by oppression, exploitation, the denial of equal rights with other nations, and an unutterable mental torture and material distress. The ideals of liberalism and democracy have not preserved the German nation from the worst depression history has ever seen. National Socialism was thus forced to create a new ideal and a more effective one, according all human rights to our people which had been denied the nation for fifteen long years.

During this time of bitter experience, Italy, and Fascist Italy, especially, has refused to take part in the humiliation Germany was subjected to. I must make it a point to say this tonight before the German people and the whole world. In the course of these years, Italy has shown understanding for the demands of a great nation claiming equal rights with other peoples in the endeavor to provide the means of subsistence, and, above all, to save its honor. We are only too glad that the hour has come, in which we are given the opportunity to recall the past and, as I believe, in which we have remembered our debt of gratitude.

The common trend of ideas expressed in the Fascist and National

Socialist revolutions has developed today into a similar course of action. This will have a salutary influence on the world, in which destruction and deformation are trying to win the upper hand. Fascist Italy has been transformed into a new *Imperium Romanum* by the ingenious activities of a compelling personality.

You, Benito Mussolini, will have realized the fact that in these days, due to the National Socialist State, Germany has become a Great Power, thanks to her racial attitude and her military strength. The inherent strength of the two countries is the best guaranty for the preservation of Europe which is inspired by a sense of responsibility in the discharge of its cultural mission. It is not willing to allow destructive elements to cause its decline and dissolution.

You who are present at this very hour and those who are listening to us in other parts of the world must acknowledge that two sovereign national régimes have come into contact at a time in which the democratic and Marxist international revels in demonstrations of hatred which must result in dissension.

Every attempt to interfere with the understanding between the two nations or to play one up against the other, by casting suspicion and by obscuring the real aims in order to dissolve the ideal partnership, will be of no avail because of the innermost desire of 115,000,000 people, who are united at the manifestation of this very hour, and because of the determination of the two men who are standing here to address you.

The United States

NOTE from the German Foreign Office to the American Chargé d'Affaires at Berlin (Prentiss B. Gilbert), December 30, 1938

Department of State, *Press Releases*, January 14, 1939, p. 13

IN REPLY to your note of December 14, 1938, No. 2, relative to the treatment of American citizens in Germany, I have the honor to state as follows:

According to your note, the Government of the United States only feels it may expect a general assurance from the German Government to the effect that American citizens will not be subjected to differential treatment due to their race or creed. It believes that it can base this expectation on the assertion that it is one of its fundamental principles to make no distinction between American citizens on the basis of race or creed and that in its relations with other countries has always contested the right of the latter to apply on their part such discrimination to American citizens.

Naturally the Government of the United States of America, like any sovereign Government, has a right to set up political principles of one kind or another regarding measures to be adopted within its own country in the questions here involved. It is an entirely different question however whether such principles are also legally binding on other Governments regarding measures falling within their sovereignty. Obviously that would only be the case if such principles either corresponded with universally accepted rules of international law or if they had been made the subject of special agreements between separate states.

There is, however, no general principle in international law according to which a state would be bound to refrain from discriminatory treatment of foreign citizens residing in its country based on race or creed or other characteristics. The American Government is probably aware that the German Government is not the first, nor is it the only, Government that has considered such differential treatment necessary in specific cases. In no case has it done so, however, on the basis of the foreign citizenship of the persons affected; it has applied special measures of the kind in question to certain categories of foreign citizens only when its own citizens of the same categories were likewise subjected to these measures. Beyond that, out of special consideration and where it proved to be technically feasible, the German Government even legally conceded more favorable treatment in this connection to foreign citizens than to its own citizens.

Therefore the only question remaining to be answered is whether and to what extent any special treaty agreements between Germany and the United States of America may stand in the way of the application to American citizens of the German measures challenged by the American Government. In this respect the Foreign Office has repeatedly declared to the American Embassy, orally and in writing, that the German Government would of course respect rights to which American citizens were entitled by virtue of treaties between the two countries. To date the American Embassy has not informed the Foreign Office of a single case in which, in its opinion, such treaty rights had been violated by German measures. If such cases should be brought to its attention by the American Embassy, the German Government for its part is prepared to examine and settle them on the basis of prevailing treaty provisions.

MEMORANDUM of a Conversation between Adolf Hitler, Chancellor of the Reich, and the Chief of the Spanish State (General Francisco Franco) at Hendaye, October 23, 1940

From files of the German Government. Translation, in Department of State, *The Spanish Government of the Axis, Official German Documents*, p. 21

THE FÜHRER replied that he was glad to see the Caudillo personally for the first time in his life after he had so often been with him in spirit during the Spanish Civil War. He knew precisely how difficult the struggle in Spain had been, since he himself since 1918–19 had had to go through similar grave conflicts, until he had helped the National Socialist movement to victory. Spain's enemies had been his enemies, too. The struggle which was raging in Europe today would be decisive for the fate of the Continent and the world for a long time to come. Militarily, this struggle in itself was decided. Germany had established a front against the British Islands from the North Cape to the Spanish border and would no longer allow the English a landing on the Continent. The military actions were now taking place right in English motherland. In spite of that, England had certain hopes: Russia and America. With Russia, Germany had treaties. Aside from this, however, he (the Führer) immediately after conclusion of the French campaign had undertaken a reorganization of the German Army so that, beginning with March of the coming year, the latter would present itself in the following strength: of a total of 230 divisions, 186 were attacking divisions. The rest consisted of defense and occupation troops. Of the 186 attacking divisions, 20 were armored divisions equipped with German material, while 4 additional armored brigades possessed captured material in part. In addition to this there were 12 motorized divisions. With this Army strength Germany was grown ready for any eventuality. He (the Führer) believed that England was wrong too in placing her hope on Russia. If the latter country were aroused at all from its inactivity, it would, at the most, be active on the German side. It was therefore a matter of misspeculation on the part of England.

With respect to America, there was no need to be afraid of an active attack during the winter. There would therefore be no change in the present military situation. Until America's military power would be fully armed, at least 18 months to two years would pass.

There would arise, nevertheless, a considerable danger if America and England entrenched themselves on the islands stretching out off Africa in the Atlantic Ocean. The danger was all the greater because it was not certain whether the French troops stationed in the colonies would under all circumstances remain loyal to Pétain. The greatest threat existing at the moment was that a part of the Colonial Empire would, with abundant material and military resources, desert France and go over to De Gaulle, England, or the United States. Moreover, the war of Germany against England was continuing. The difficulty was that the operations had to be carried on across an ocean which Germany at sea did not control. She had only air supremacy. Of course the weather over the Channel for exercising it had, up to then, been extremely unfavorable. Since the middle of August there had not even been five fair days, and the major attack against England had as yet not been able to begin since an attack against the British naval forces, on the part of Germany, could only be carried out from the air, whereby, under good atmospheric conditions, the British fleet had always been forced to yield, according to previous experiences.

According to meteorological forecasts which prophesied with certainty a period of fair weather for seven to eight days, a great air attack had been started on a fixed day. Of course it had to be broken off again after lasting half a day because of a sudden change in the weather.

Germany had, up to this point, carried off very great victories. But for this very reason, he (the Führer) wanted to guard against suffering a failure by some thoughtless move. In this connection, the Führer mentioned as an example of his tactics, the events of the great offensive in France. Originally he had had the plan of striking the great blow as early as October of the previous year, but had constantly been hindered from doing this by the weather. He had suffered because of not being able to act but he had been really determined not to begin the offensive in bad weather, but on the contrary had preferred to wait until the weather conditions became better. When the meteorologists had then reported to him that on May 10 the normal period of clear weather for the summer would begin, he had, on May 8, issued the order for attack. The result of this attack was known, and in the battle against England he would act precisely as in the French offensive. He would begin the great attack only when the weather conditions permitted absolute success. In the meantime, England, and especially London, was being bombarded day and night. On London alone, 3,500,000 kilograms of bombs had been dropped. Many harbor installations, factories, and armament works were thus being shattered; England's approaches were being mined; and an increasing U-boat activity was contributing to the further isolation of the Islands. At the moment, the number of U-boats being finished every month was 10. In spring, it would rise to 17; in July to 25; and after that up to 34 per month. He hoped the concentrated activity of the air-arm, mine-layers and destroyers, U-boats, and speed boats would do so much damage and harm to England that in the end attrition would set in. In spite of this, he was lying in wait in order to carry out the great blow during fair weather, even if this could not happen until spring. It is self-evident that the time during which such vast masses of troops were lying inactive would continue to be exploited.

Naturally Germany had an interest in ending the war in a short time if possible, since every additional month cost money and sacrifice. In the attempt to bring about the end of the war as soon as possible and to render the entry of the United States into the war more difficult, Germany had concluded the Tripartite Pact. This Pact was compelling the United States to keep its Navy in the Pacific Ocean and to prepare herself for a Japanese attack from that direction. In Europe as well, Germany was attempting to expand her base. He could confidentially report that several other nations had announced their intention of joining the Tripartite Pact.

COMMUNIQUÉ Issued by the Official German News Agency, September 6, 1941, Regarding the Attack on the U.S.S. *Greer*

Translation, in *The New York Times*, September 7, 1941

ON THE FOURTH of September a German submarine was attacked with depth bombs and continuously pursued in the German blockade zone at a point charted at Lat. 62 degrees 31 minutes N. and Long. 27 degrees 6 minutes W. The German submarine was unable to establish the nationality of the attacking destroyer.

In justified defense against the attack, the submarine thereupon at 14:39 o'clock fired two torpedoes at the destroyer, both of which missed aim. The destroyer continued its pursuit and attacks with depth bombs until midnight, then abandoned them.

If official American quarters, namely the Navy Department, assert the attack was initiated by the German submarine, such charge can only have the purpose of giving the attack of an American destroyer on a German submarine, which was undertaken in complete violation of neutrality, a semblance of legality. This attack is evidence that President Roosevelt, despite his previous assertions to the contrary, has commanded American destroyers not only to report the location of German U-boats and other German craft, as violating neutrality, but also to proceed to attack them.

Roosevelt thereby is endeavoring with all the means at his disposal to provoke incidents for the purpose of baiting the American people into the war.

NOTE from Hans Thomsen, German Chargé d'Affaires at Washington, to the Secretary of State of the United States (Cordell Hull), September 26, 1941, Regarding the Sinking of the *Robin Moor*

The New York Times, November 4, 1941

MR. SECRETARY OF STATE:

On the nineteenth day of this month you sent me a new note with reference to your communication of June 20 of this year concerning the American steamer "Robin Moor." I have the honor to reply to you herewith that the two communications made are not such as to lead to an appropriate reply by my government. In this regard I refer to my note of June 25 (June 24) of this year.

Accept, Mr. Secretary of State, the renewed assurances of my most distinguished consideration.

COMMUNIQUÉ Issued by the German Government from the Military Headquarters of Adolf Hitler, Chancellor of the Reich, November 1, 1941, Referring to the Address of President Franklin D. Roosevelt on October 28, 1941

Translation, in *New York Herald Tribune*, November 2, 1941

THE PRESIDENT of the United States of America made the following allegations in his speech of October the 28th last:

First, that the government of the United States had in their possession a secret map which had been drawn up in Germany by the Reich government. This map was purported to depict Central and South America as the Fuehrer wished to reorganize them, by turning the fourteen countries in this area into five vassal states, thus putting the whole of the South American continent under his domination. One of these five states was to include the Republic of Panama, as well as the Panama Canal.

Secondly, that the American government was in possession of a second document of which the Reich government was also the author. This document contained a plan to do away with all existing religions throughout the world after Germany had won the war. The Roman Catholic, Protestant, Mahometan, Buddhist and Jewish religions, were all to be abolished, all church property confiscated, the cross and all other religious symbols forbidden and all ecclesiastical orders silenced under penalty of the concentration camp.

In the place of existing churches an international National Socialist church was to be established in which speakers, appointed by the National Socialist Reich government, would officiate. The Bible was to be replaced by the words from the Fuehrer's "Mein Kampf," the crucifix by the swastika and the drawn sword and, finally, the Fuehrer was to take the place of God.

In reply to these assertions the Reich government points out:

First, there is no such thing as a map prepared in Germany by the Reich government concerning the partition of Central and South America, nor does there exist a document drawn up by the Reich government concerning the partition of Central and South America. Nor does there exist a document drawn up by the Reich government concerning the abolition of religion throughout the world. In both cases therefore the documents in question must be forgeries of the worst order.

Secondly, the allegations concerning a conquest of the South American continent by Germany, and the abolition of religion and churches throughout the world, and their replacement by a National Socialist church, are so absurd and so irrational that the Reich government considers it unnecessary to go into them.

[The official communique concludes with the statement that all neutral governments including those of the Central and South American countries have been informed to the above effect through diplomatic channels.]

SECOND COMMUNIQUÉ Issued by the German Government from the Military Headquarters of Adolf Hitler, Chancellor of the Reich, November 1, 1941, Referring to the Address of President Franklin D. Roosevelt on October 28, 1941

Translation, in *New York Herald Tribune,* November 2, 1941

THE PRESIDENT of the United States of America declared in his speech of October the 28th, that on September the 4th one American destroyer, and on October the 17th another American destroyer had been attacked by German naval forces. The American government had wished to avoid the shooting, but the shooting had begun, and history had established who had fired the first shot, America had been attacked.

In reality, however, the reports of the German submarine commanders and official statements published by the American naval authorities give the facts. The American destroyer *Greer* was involved in the incident of Sept. 4 and the American destroyer *Kearny* in the incident of Oct. 17. Co-operating closely with British naval forces, the destroyer *Greer* had chased a German submarine for hours. During the pursuit the German submarine, which had submerged, was attacked with depth charges. It was not until this attack had taken place that the German submarine went into action. The destroyer kept up the chase with depth charges for several hours, but without success.

The destroyer *Kearny* was acting as an escort to a convoy, when she picked up distress calls from a second convoy in another part of the Atlantic, which was engaged with German naval forces. The *Kearny,* thereupon, changed her course, proceeded to the scene of the engagement and attacked a German submarine with depth charges. The American Secretary of the Navy, Mr. Knox, himself has confirmed that the *Kearny* had dropped depth charges and that not until some time after were three torpedoes fired at her, one of which struck the destroyer. The Reich government, therefore, declares that, first, the version given President Roosevelt in his speech, that American destroyers had been attacked by German naval forces and that, therefore, Germany had attacked America, is not in accordance with the facts, and is, indeed contradicted by the official statements of the American naval authorities themselves.

Secondly, that quite on the contrary, the two American destroyers had attacked German submarines, and that therefore the United

States had attacked Germany, a fact which has also been confirmed by the American naval authorities.

NOTE from Joachim von Ribbentrop, Minister for Foreign Affairs, to the American Chargé d'Affaires at Berlin (Leland B. Morris), Delivered the Morning of December 11, 1941

Department of State, *Bulletin*, December 13, 1941, p. 481. A copy of the note was presented at the same time by Hans Thomsen, German Chargé d'Affaires at Washington, to the Chief of the European Division of the Department of State (Ray Atherton), the Secretary of State being unable at the time to receive Herr Thomsen

Mr. Chargé d'Affaires:

The Government of the United States having violated in the most flagrant manner and in ever increasing measure all rules of neutrality in favor of the adversaries of Germany and having continually been guilty of the most severe provocations toward Germany ever since the outbreak of the European war, provoked by the British declaration of war against Germany on September 3, 1939, has finally resorted to open military acts of aggression.

On September 11, 1941, the President of the United States publicly declared that he had ordered the American Navy and Air Force to shoot on sight at any German war vessel. In his speech of October 27, 1941, he once more expressly affirmed that this order was in force. Acting under this order, vessels of the American Navy, since early September 1941, have systematically attacked German naval forces. Thus, American destroyers, as for instance the *Greer*, the *Kearney* and the *Reuben James*, have opened fire on German sub-marines according to plan. The Secretary of the American Navy, Mr. Knox, himself confirmed that American destroyers attacked German sub-marines.

Furthermore, the naval forces of the United States, under order of their Government and contrary to international law have treated and seized German merchant vessels on the high seas as enemy ships.

The German Government therefore establishes the following facts:

Although Germany on her part has strictly adhered to the rules of international law in her relations with the United States during every period of the present war, the Government of the United States from initial violations of neutrality has finally proceeded to open acts of war against Germany. The Government of the United States has thereby virtually created a state of war.

The German Government, consequently, discontinues diplomatic relations with the United States of America and declares that under these circumstances brought about by President Roosevelt Germany too, as from today, considers herself as being in a state of war with the United States of America.

ADDRESS by Adolf Hitler, Chancellor of the Reich, before the Reichstag, December 11, 1941

Translation, in *The New York Times,* December 12, 1941; excerpts

... Two MEN only were responsible for this enmity between the United States and Germany—Woodrow Wilson and Franklin Delano Roosevelt.

It was a broken pledge, as history since has proved; a pledge broken by Woodrow Wilson that in its consequences led to untold misery both for the victors and the vanquished in the last World War. And it was this broken pledge that made Versailles possible.

At that time German people certainly paid dearly for being credulous and believing in President Wilson's assurances, and today we have more or less the same picture of an American president inciting the world to go to war against Germany.

I can well understand that there is a world-wide gulf between the outlook of President Roosevelt and myself.

Roosevelt, of course, comes from a wealthy family and has had all advantages of upbringing in that circle.

I, myself, come from a small, very poor family and have always had to work for myself.

During the first World War Roosevelt was able to go into politics and to see to it that he made money. I, of course, became a soldier and simply took orders for four years. I tried to do nothing but my duty.

In fact, I shared my fate with millions and Roosevelt shared his fate with the upper 10,000.

During inflation Roosevelt went on earning money, whereas I remained in hospitals.

Then we both developed in politics. Roosevelt became boss of a City Council, a position to which he had risen by his money, and I became Chancellor because I was leader of a popular movement. One thing, of course, we both have in common. Our coming into power was closely connected with democracy—that is, with the failure of States which had relied on democracy.

In both countries there was ruin and nobody had any work. While in Germany, during the next years an immense regeneration of labor, trade and art took place, Roosevelt did not succeed in altering anything in spite of the fact that in America there were only eighteen people to the square kilometer compared to 145 in Germany.

This can only be due to total incompetence. In five years it has been possible in Germany to find work for every one. During the same period in America Roosevelt has succeeded in undermining American economy, in devaluating the dollar and in keeping up the figure of unemployed. Jews, of course, have flourished.

In fact, in Europe it seems inconceivable that Roosevelt should not have ended up before a State court. In fact, he would presumably —before a civil court—have received a term of imprisonment for sharp practice in business.

For what possible reason could such enmity against the German people have arisen?

First—Germany practically is the only country in Europe which never possessed any colonies whatsoever on the soil of the North American Continent. Apart from German emigrants to the United States, Germany has never interfered in the affairs of America. . . .

Second—Germany has never adopted any antagonistic attitude toward the United States, but, in fact, the Germans who emigrated gave their blood fighting for the liberty of the United States.

Third—Germany never has taken part in any war waged against the United States.

Fourth—In 1917 the United States on their part entered the war against Germany for reasons which since have been proved to be entirely spurious. They have been proved to be such by an investigation committee set up by none other than President Roosevelt himself. This committee has proved that only vested interests of a small capitalistic clique were benefited.

There have been no territorial claims or any other differences of opinion standing in the way of an understanding between the United States and Germany.

Under various influences Roosevelt has tried to create conflicts everywhere, to deepen existing conflicts and to prevent a peaceful settlement of existing conflicts.

For years he wished there might arise in Europe a conflict in which by taking sides he might engage American industry.

From 1937 onward he took all the opportunities which he could possibly seize to act against the Reich. In his speech of October 5, 1937, he began his campaign of hatred against us by talking of a quarantine which he would establish against the dictatorships.

Then he recalled his Ambassador, so from that moment onward the two countries were only represented by chargés d'affaires in their respective capitals.

In November, 1938, he checked every possibility of peaceful settlement by giving the impression that he himself was in favor of peace, but at the same time threatening all those countries who were trying to settle their own affairs peacefully with economic reprisals, financial measures and other acts.

About that also we have very clear reports from the Polish embassies in Washington, London and Paris.

In 1939 he went on with his work of hatred and warmongering. He interfered in internal European affairs which were none of his business, which were just as little his business as the affairs of one of the American States are of the head of the German State.

He did not recognize certain governments which had established themselves in Europe. He failed to recognize the new order. On the contrary, he recognized and upheld puppet governments . . . and with the representative of one of these governments even made treaty to secure a foothold in territory which was not American.

President Roosevelt addressed an appeal to me and to the Duce on April 5, 1939, which was a mixture of arrogance and ignorance of the geographic conditions of our continent.

When I had given President Roosevelt a very polite but firm answer, he ceased to talk for the time, but, instead, Mrs. Roosevelt began a campaign. She and her son refused to live in the world as we National Socialists understand it, . . . a world of work and not a world of falsehood.

Then, on April 11, 1939, President Roosevelt obtained an amendment to the Neutrality Act by repealing the arms exportation embargo unilaterally. . . .

Roosevelt froze Norwegian and Danish assets, though it was well known that they were not subject to German control or interference. Then the Norwegian, Dutch and Belgian puppet governments were recognized by Roosevelt, and finally, on June 15, Roosevelt sent a telegram to the then Prime Minister of France, M. Reynaud, promising to double American aid to France if France only continued her resistance against Germany.

He also assured France he would not recognize in the name of the United States any territorial changes such as return of Alsace-Lorraine to Germany. It goes without saying that such recognition from America is of no consequence whatever to Germany and the German Government.

These examples I have only cited in order to show up the activities of this warmonger in their proper light.

Roosevelt was afraid even then of a European peace because it might interfere with his plans. He was afraid that Europe might realize peace, after all, was possible and in her best interests.

He froze French assets, but only in order to get hold of gold which had been transported from Casablanca to the United States on board a United States cruiser.

Then, in August, 1940, Roosevelt made a further step toward war, announcing a joint military program between the United States and Canada. He continually invented crises and interrupted journeys on week-ends, rapidly returning to Washington to make these crises more credible.

Finally, he drew still closer to war in November, 1940, lending fifty destroyers to England, although he received in return British bases of considerable value. It is not quite certain whether it was hate or a desire to take over the British Empire which was the primary driving force in this act.

Then, when British assets in the United States had become exhausted, he concluded the lease-lend agreement, and in the meantime a whole series of incidents had been directed by Roosevelt against Germany.

Then Roosevelt declared the Red Sea open to American shipping. He had shortly before that confiscated German ships in the United States and German subjects had been interned and treated contrary to international law in a most despicable manner.

Of all such incidents the fate meted out to two escaped German prisoners who reached the United States territory from Canada was particularly despicable—they were handcuffed and handed back to Canadian authorities contrary to all international agreement and custom.

Roosevelt also interfered in the Balkans. He sent the notorious Colonel Donovan to incite a revolt there.

He gave Yugoslavia and Greece guarantees, he recognized the exiled governments and froze their assets.

On April 26, America delivered twenty motor speed boats to England; on April 6, American troops landed in Greenland for the first time, and soon after a German submarine was attacked with depth charges.

On June 17, all German Consulates, the German Library of Information and other official German bureaus were closed at the demand of the American Government, while on June 20, American troops landed in Iceland, a move by which Roosevelt hoped to render ineffective the operations of German submarines.

On July 10, American Secretary of State for Navy Knox ordered the American Navy to fire on Axis ships.

As a result, a great number of incidents occurred, such as when, on Sept. 26, depth charges were fired on a German submarine, a feat which was repeated on October 6 in the case of the American destroyer *Kearny*.

A few weeks later the American Navy even went so far as to seize the harmless German merchant ship *Odenwald,* which was crossing to an American port. The crew was imprisoned.

It does not impress me very much if Roosevelt sees fit to call me a gangster. After all, one would do well to remember that "gangster" is an American term, and apparently gangsters prevail in that country. On the other hand, I cannot feel insulted by Roosevelt because, just as with President Wilson, I consider Roosevelt to be insane.

Against Japan, Roosevelt resorted to similar methods, making hypocritical demands. The world must have been relieved to see at last a State rise up to tell Roosevelt to mind his own business, and he cannot very well complain this was not called for. That Japan took this step and decided to defend her freedom must fill all decent people with profound satisfaction.

We know, of course, that the eternal Jew is behind all this. Roosevelt himself may not realize it, but then that only shows his own limitations.

Indeed, we all know the intention of the Jews to rule all civilized States in Europe and America. We know this is a time when for nations it is the question of "to be or not to be."

When President Roosevelt sees fit to give me good advice, he is like the bald hairdresser recommending a famous hair tonic to his clients.

Economically, countries like the United States and Great Britain are so backward that we will not accept gifts from them; we merely demand our rights.

These countries have done everything to prevent both Germany and Italy from creating conditions essential to their existence. . . . I have therefore given to the American Chargé d'Affaires his passports today.

In pursuing a policy of world dictatorship President Roosevelt has refrained from no step to prevent Germany and Italy from creating conditions that could secure their existence.

Both he and England have opposed every revision, and, in flagrant contradiction of international law, America has attacked our ships, interned the crews and, in the end, went even so far as to give its

Navy, contrary to all international law, the order to attack and sink German and Italian ships.

Since then a plan prepared by President Roosevelt has been revealed in the United States, according to which his intention was to attack Germany by 1943 with all the resources at the disposal of the United States. Thus our patience has come to the breaking point. . . .

Japan

MEMORANDUM of a Conversation between Baron Ernst von Weizsäcker, State Secretary, and the Japanese Ambassador (Hiroshi Oshima), September 18, 1939

From files of the German Government. Translation, in Department of State, *Bulletin*, June 16, 1946, p. 1038

St. S. Nr. 734

THE Japanese Ambassador was given considerable information about the situation today by me. He referred to the visit of Take Ushi [*sic*]. He congratulated us on the success of the Polish campaign, etc. In conclusion, he came out in a somewhat ashamed manner with the attached document, which is dated August 26 and in connection with which he had the following to say:

Admittedly I had, at the end of August, talked him—Oshima—out of the idea of lodging the earnest protest of the Japanese Government on account of the inconsistency of the German-Russian non-aggression pact with the secret agreement between Germany and Japan. Out of consideration for the German Government at that critical stage, he had followed my advice. However, it was impossible for him to go directly contrary to the orders of his Government. He had, therefore, simply telegraphed his Government that he had followed their directions. In reality he, Oshima, had postponed carrying out the step until now. He had waited for the conclusion of the Polish campaign and he declared that now the step was no longer of so much consequence, especially since he had, on his own account, taken all the bitterness out of the orders from Tokyo. He asked that I understand the accompanying note in that light.

I read the note, which really is no longer of very great consequence, but I received it from him for study only in my personal capacity and not officially. Oshima will explain the matter further himself if he sees the Reich Foreign Minister soon. He will then suggest that this document, with our consent, be allowed to disappear in the archives. He did not consider a discussion, especially one of a legalistic nature, to be desirable or timely.

I said to the Ambassador, in conclusion, that his view did not agree entirely with ours and that I had hoped that the matter could be finally disposed of. I was, however, ready to inform the Reich Foreign Minister in advance to the effect that he, Oshima, considered that he was bound to bring the matter to a formal conclusion in some way.

I did not consider it correct to refuse to receive the note from the Ambassador for consideration, since Oshima was apparently honestly concerned about disposing of the matter completely.

WEIZSÄCKER

[Enclosure]

THE JAPANESE EMBASSY IN BERLIN TO THE GERMAN FOREIGN OFFICE

The Japanese Embassy has the honor, on instructions from the Japanese Government, to inform the Foreign Office of the views of the Japanese Government in connection with the non-aggression and consultative pact recently concluded between the German Government and the Government of the Union of Soviet Socialist Republics, as follows:

"The Japanese Government regards the non-aggression and consultative pact, recently concluded between the German Government and the Government of the Union of Soviet Socialist Republics, as in contradiction to the secret annex to the agreement against the Communist International."

BERLIN, *August 26, 1939.*

TELEGRAM from Eugen Ott, German Ambassador to Japan, to the German Foreign Office, June 19, 1940, with Foreign Office Notation

From files of the German Government. Translation, in Department of State, *Bulletin,* June 16, 1946, p. 1038

No. 594 of June 19.

Urgent.   For the Reich Chancellery.   Secret.

THE Chief of the European Bureau of the Foreign Ministry informed me confidentially that the Japanese Ambassador in Berlin today received instructions to express to the German Government the congratulations of the Japanese Government on the German victory, and on this occasion to call attention to the special interest of Japan in the future fate of French Indochina. The Ambassador was to repeat the thanks of Japan for the friendly attitude of Germany in the Chinese conflict, and, at the same time, to indicate that Japan believed that she had furnished substantial assistance to Germany during the European war by holding the American forces in the Pacific Ocean. The Ambassador was instructed to suggest to the German Government, in return for this attitude of Japan, a friendly gesture with respect to Indochina. To the question of what form such a gesture should take, the Chief replied that the Foreign Ministry had in mind a German declaration to the effect that Japan would have a free hand in Indochina. According to the press the Japanese Ambassador to Rome has received similar instructions.

Since, in the course of the French collapse, the pressure of popular opinion urging the Government to action has become stronger, the Foreign Minister decided on this step to save his policy and his cabinet from an otherwise unavoidable fall. There was danger, however, that the Foreign Minister would make tactical use of the German free hand with respect to Indochina in negotiations for an agreement with America. Characteristic of the unaltered basic position of the Foreign Minister is the fact reported elsewhere that, on the same day, he came to a friendly agreement with England and France on [the question of] Tientsin.

As seen from Tokyo, the strengthening of Japanese power in East Asia through the addition of Indochina would be likely to be in the German interest. Thereby, on the one hand, the prospects for a speedy conclusion of the China conflict would be heightened and, on the other hand, the tension between Japan and the Anglo-Saxon powers would be so increased that danger of agreement would be eliminated for some time. If, therefore, it is intended to comply with the Japanese desire, a formula must be found which will bind Japan finally and unreservedly to our side. This could be accomplished especially if Japan had to pledge herself to take immediate possession of Indochina.

I learn confidentially from Army circles that in those circles the idea of occupation of the strategically important Yunnan Road is being agitated. If the Government should evade a similarly expressed demand for the occupation of Indochina, in case the matter should become public, it would have to expect at least that its position would be shaken and possibly that it would be dissolved and replaced by a cabinet closer to us.

Foreign Office Notation on Telegram No. 594 of June 19 from Tokyo on the Subject of Indochina

The thanks of Japan for the friendly attitude of Germany in the China conflict come rather late. The sacrifice which we have made on behalf of Japan (shutting off of delivery of war materials to China and the loss thereby of important Chinese raw materials) have so far received no recognition on the Japanese side, far less has any economic compensation been made. The Japanese request for a friendly gesture on the part of Germany is, in view of the attitude adopted by Japan toward Germany during the war in economic relations, somewhat surprising.

In case this is mentioned to the Japanese Ambassador in the course of the forthcoming discussion, the following examples may be cited:

1. Japanese shipping has, from the beginning, and in a most comprehensive manner, submitted itself to the English and French blockade controls.

2. The Japanese Government for a long time did not accede to the German desires for transit of goods through Japan and only in the last few months has she displayed some evidence of becoming more accommodating. Thus a shipment of wolfram from Canton and a shipment of tin from Colombia were transmitted to Germany. The Japanese Government also recently offered us, from its own supply, 100 tons each of wolfram and tin to be delivered without charge. There continue to be, however, requests that are still not complied with; for instance, increase of Japanese sea trade with Vladivostok, which route is covered only three times per month by a Japanese steamer. Also, further shipment of tin from Colombia has so far been impossible on account of the refusal of the Japanese shipping line.

3. Japan, in January of this year, concluded a monopoly agreement with Manchukuo for her supply of soy beans without saying anything about it to us, although previously we were the largest importer; in 1938—for example—to the extent of 800,000 tons. After representations were made, Japan so far has only allotted 70,000 tons for delivery to us from Manchukuo.

4. Japan continues to refuse the return transportation from America in small groups of the crew of almost 500 men of the *Columbus*, since the members of the crew are regarded, from the English point of view, as participants in the war, although according to the American view they are regarded as shipwrecked individuals.

5. Japan, it is true, is delivering to us her entire production of whale oil from the last catch, some 75,000 tons. We know, however, from confidential sources, that she first offered half of it to England

and decided to make delivery to us only when she got no satisfactory English offer.

For transmittal to the Secretary of State.

BERLIN, *June 20, 1940.*

WIEHL

MEMORANDUM of a Conversation between Joachim von Ribbentrop, Minister for Foreign Affairs, the Premier of Italy (Benito Mussolini), and the Italian Minister for Foreign Affairs (Count Galeazzo Ciano), at the Palazzo Venezia, Rome, May 13, 1941

From files of the German Government. Translation, in Department of State, *Bulletin*, June 30, 1946, p. 1103

IN THE further course of the conversation the subject of Japan was touched on and especially the Japanese-American exchange of views. The Reich Foreign Minister stated that the principle that Japan shared a common destiny with Germany and Italy had been so clearly understood by the Japanese that he did not think that Japan would pursue a policy that would not in the end align itself once more with the policy pursued by Germany and Italy. The Reich Foreign Minister referred in this connection to the remark of Matsuoka that he was frequently forced as a result of internal politics into maneuvering and perhaps into doing some things which might not be readily understood in Germany. He trusted Matsuoka, though he could not, of course, see what was in his heart. He was not pleased that the conversations with President Roosevelt were carried on by Admiral Nomura, for Nomura was inclined at heart toward the Anglo-Saxons. Matsuoka had first put the following further inquiries: (1) whether the United States were willing to enter into an undertaking not to enter the European conflict; (2) what was the attitude of the United States on the problem of the Philippines. If, contrary to expectations, Japanese policy followed a course contrary to the spirit of the Three Power Pact, general opposition on a large scale would certainly arise in Japan and Ambassador Oshima would probably become the soul of a real revolution. These matters must be handled carefully so as to avoid causing Matsuoka unnecessary difficulties.

The whole affair showed that Roosevelt was beginning to become alarmed, probably because he was gradually realizing that in case of warlike complications he could accomplish nothing because of America's bad armament position and therefore wished to keep his back free.

The Duce remarked that it would certainly be advantageous for Germany and Italy if Matsuoka in this way kept the United States from entry into the war. On the other hand the basis for his course could also be the desire of Japan herself to remain out of the war.

The Reich Foreign Minister remarked that if a strong attitude were adopted and the declaration made that American protective convoys meant war, the Americans would probably hesitate, for American rearmament was the biggest bluff in the world's history.

The Duce referred in this connection to the division which had arisen in the United States and cited the speeches of Hoover and Lindbergh as those of the most prominent opponents of the Roosevelt policy. On the other hand, however, were the Jews, and their propaganda was so strong that they had gotten the whole of America under their influence. However, if a struggle arose in a country between a war party and a peace party, the war party generally won, since war was closer to the souls of men than peace.

The Reich Foreign Minister replied that the same naturally held good for Japan and he expressed the conviction that Japan sooner or later would enter the war on the side of the Axis powers, in order to seize the best opportunities open to her. He was absolutely sure that Japan would honor her treaty obligations.

TELEGRAM from Joachim von Ribbentrop, Minister for Foreign Affairs, to the German Ambassador to Japan (Eugen Ott), July 1, 1941

From files of the German Government. Translation, in Department of State, *Bulletin*, June 16, 1946, p. 1038

Priority.   Urgent.   Secret.

REQUEST you to deliver to the Foreign Minister as speedily as possible the following telegram from me addressed to him personally. The telegram is to be drawn up there on white paper, without heading, and with my signature. The text of the telegram follows:

TO HIS EXCELLENCY THE JAPANESE FOREIGN MINISTER, HERR MATSUOKA, TOKYO

Personal. At the time of Your Excellency's visit in Berlin it was our intention that on the occasion of events which were of especial importance for the welfare of both our countries, we would get into communication personally. Such a moment has now arrived and I have the honor to inform Your Excellency as follows:

1. By the mighty blows of the German Armed Forces we have succeeded, in the first eight days of the German-Russian campaign, in breaking the backbone of the Russian Army. A considerable part of the best combat divisions of the enemy have been in part annihilated, in part captured, in part so shattered that the remnants will scarcely be able to appear again as effectives during the course of this war. The enemy air force is almost completely defeated, so that on the principal fighting front, since yesterday, German mastery of the air has become complete. Incalculable stores of material have been captured or destroyed. Detailed information about the quantities of such material will be given in the German Army communiqué.

Meanwhile the German armies are continuing to push farther east along the whole front. The coming operations of the German Army will, I have no doubt, destroy the remaining forces of the enemy in the same manner and it can be counted on, that perhaps even in only a few weeks Russian resistance over the whole European area of the Soviet Union will be broken. It is very likely, as I already told Your Excellency a few days ago through Ambassador Ott, that this in turn will result shortly in the total collapse of the Bolshevist régime.

2. From this military success, unparalleled in history, for which we have to thank first of all the valor of the German soldiery, and by which the great military threat to which Europe was exposed has been eliminated, arises the obligation on the part of the German leadership to create for the future a political situation in the East which would prevent for all time a repetition of such events. It is also our conviction that as long as Russia continues to exist as the nucleus of Bolshevism, neither Europe, nor East Asia, nor the world at large will ever have quiet. Germany is determined to draw the necessary consequences from this knowledge. She hopes to have the collaboration of Japan, since a final solution of the Russian question could be brought about most speedily and completely by Japan and Germany together.

3. The approaching collapse of the military power of Russia and the probable fall of the Bolshevist régime itself offers to Japan the unique opportunity to free herself from the Russian threat and to give the Japanese Empire security in the north, which is a necessary prerequisite to her expansion in the south in accordance with her vital needs. It seems to me, therefore, the requirement of the hour that the Japanese Army should, as quickly as possible, get into possession of Vladivostok and push as far as possible toward the west. The aim of such an operation should be that, before the coming of cold weather, the Japanese Army advancing westward should be able to shake hands at the half-way mark with the German troops advancing to the east, that both by way of the Trans-Siberian Railroad and by air uninterrupted communication should be established between Germany and Japan by way of Russian territory, and that finally the

whole Russian question should be solved by Germany and Japan in common in a way which would eliminate the Russian threat to both Germany and Japan for all time.

4. The defeat of the Soviet Union by Germany and Japan would allow us to bring the actual power of the states allied in the Three Power Pact into effective cooperation for the first time. Germany and Italy would then be the completely controlling elements in the entire European-African Hemisphere. They would then be in a position to strengthen their pressure on England enormously by bombardments from the air and by U-boats, and by appropriate operations bring about the final destruction of England. Japan, on her part, with her back free, would be able to devote her whole force to the final solution of the problems affecting her in the south. That the elimination of the Soviet régime would also ease the solution of the Chinese conflict is mentioned only in passing.

In respect to America, I hope that, after the defeat of Russia, the weight of the Three Power states, Germany, Italy, and Japan, and the powers allied to them, to whom I hope a considerable number of additional European states will soon be added, will suffice to paralyze any rising tendency in the United States to participate in the war.

Summing up I would like to state that:

I am convinced that with the triumph of German arms in the past weeks the historic opportunity has now come, perhaps never to recur, for Japan, together with Germany, to solve the Russian question and to free our peoples for a long time from every threat arising from that vast expanse, either as a consequence of its political philosophy or of a military nature. That our countries together, in pursuance of the Anti-Comintern policy hitherto carried on by them in common, can give the decisive blow for the elimination of Bolshevism, that greatest enemy of mankind, will be for both our peoples and their leaders the classic justification of their common political ideas, and their greatest claim to eternal fame.

In addition, I believe that the defeat of Russia will materially hasten the conquest of England by the Axis powers. Thereby there will be provided the prerequisites for the New Order in Europe and East Asia so desired by both our peoples, and no one in the world will be able to dispute any longer the right of the states united in the Three Power Pact and now more closely joined than ever in their struggle in Bolshevism, to set up a new and just world order.

The Union of Soviet Socialist Republics

ADDRESS by Adolf Hitler, Chancellor of the Reich, before the Reichstag, October 6, 1939

Translation, in *Vital Speeches of the Day*, October 15, 1939, p. 2; excerpt

IN MY SPEECH at Danzig I already declared that Russia was organized on principles which differ from those held in Germany. However, since it became clear that Stalin found nothing in the Russian-Soviet principles which should prevent him from cultivating friendly relations with States of a different political creed, National Socialist Germany sees no reason why she should adopt another criterion. The Soviet Union is the Soviet Union, Nationalist Socialist Germany is National Socialist Germany.

But one thing is certain: from the moment when the two States mutually agreed to respect each other's distinctive regime and principles, every reason for any mutually hostile attitude had disappeared. Long periods in the history of both nations have shown that the inhabitants of these two largest States in Europe were never happier than when they lived in friendship with each other. The Great War, which once made Germany and Russia enemies, was disastrous for both countries.

It is easy to understand that the capitalist States of the West are interested today in playing off these two States and their principles against each other. For this purpose, and until it is realized, they certainly regard the Soviet Union as a sufficiently respectable partner for the conclusion of a useful military pact. But they regard it as perfidy that their honorable approaches were rejected and in their place *rapprochement* took place between those two very powers who had every reason for seeking happiness for their respective peoples in developing their economic relationship along the lines of peaceful cooperation.

Months ago I stated in the Reichstag that the conclusion of the German-Russian non-aggression pact marked the turning point in the whole German foreign policy. The new pact of friendship and mutual interest since signed between Germany and the Soviet Union will insure not only peace but a constant satisfactory cooperation for both States.

Germany and Russia together will relieve one of the most acute danger spots in Europe of its threatening character and will, each in her own sphere, contribute to the welfare of the peoples living there, thus aiding to European peace in general. If certain circles today see in this pact either the breakdown of Russia or Germany—as suits them best—I should like to give them my answer.

For many years imaginary aims were attributed to Germany's foreign policy which at best might be taken to have arisen in the mind of a schoolboy.

At a moment when Germany is struggling to consolidate her own living space, which only consists of a few hundred thousand square kilometers, insolent journalists in countries which rule over 40,000,000 square kilometers state Germany is aspiring to world domination!

German-Russian agreements should prove immensely comforting to these worried sponsors of universal liberty, for do they not show most emphatically that their assertions as to Germany's aiming at domination of the Urals, the Ukraine, Rumania, etc., are only excrescences of their own unhealthy war-lord fantasy?

In one respect it is true Germany's decision is irrevocable, namely in her intention to see peaceful, stable and thus tolerable conditions introduced on her eastern frontiers; also it is precisely here that Germany's interests and desires correspond entirely with those of the Soviet Union. The two States are resolved to prevent problematical conditions arising between them which contain germs of internal unrest and thus also of external disorder and which might perhaps in any way unfavorably affect the relationship of these two great States with one another.

Germany and the Soviet Union have therefore clearly defined the boundaries of their own spheres of interest with the intention of being singly responsible for law and order and preventing everything which might cause injury to the other partner.

The aims and tasks which emerge from the collapse of the Polish State are, in so far the German sphere of interest is concerned, roughly as follows:

1. Demarcation of the boundary for the Reich, which will do justice to historical, ethnographical and economic facts.
2. Pacification of the whole territory by restoring a tolerable measure of peace and order.
3. Absolute guarantees of security not only as far as Reich territory is concerned but for the entire sphere of interest.
4. Re-establishment and reorganization of economic life and of trade and transport, involving development of culture and civilization.
5. As the most important task, however, to establish a new order of ethnographic conditions, that is to say, resettlement of nationali-

ties in such a manner that the process ultimately results in the obtaining of better dividing lines than is the case at present. In this sense, however, it is not a case of the problem being restricted to this particular sphere, but of a task with far wider implications, for the east and south of Europe are to a large extent filled with splinters of the German nationality, whose existence they cannot maintain.

In their very existence lie the reason and cause for continual international disturbances. In this age of the principle of nationalities and of racial ideals, it is Utopian to believe that members of a highly developed people can be assimilated without trouble.

It is therefore essential for a far-sighted ordering of the life of Europe that a resettlement should be undertaken here so as to remove at least part of the material for European conflict. Germany and the Union of Soviet Republics have come to an agreement to support each other in this matter.

The German Government will, therefore, never allow the residual Polish State of the future to become in any sense a disturbing factor for the Reich itself and still less a source of disturbance between the German Reich and Soviet Russia. . . .

PROCLAMATION by Adolf Hitler, Chancellor of the Reich, June 22, 1941

Translation, in Raoul de Roussy de Sales, *My New Order* (1941), p. 977; for other documents on German-Soviet relations, 1939–41, *see infra*, Appendix I, and *supra*, under General Statements of Policy, pp. 609 ff.

GERMAN PEOPLE!
NATIONAL SOCIALISTS!

Weighted down with heavy cares, condemned to months-long silence, the hour has now come when at last I can speak frankly.

When on September 3, 1939, the German Reich received the English declaration of war there was repeated anew a British attempt to render impossible every beginning of a consolidation and thereby of Europe's rise, by fighting whatever power on the Continent was strongest at any given time.

That is how of yore England ruined Spain in many wars. That is how she conducted her wars against Holland. That is how later she fought France with the aid of all Europe and that is how at the turn of the century she began the encirclement of the then German Reich and in 1914 the World War. Only on account of its internal dissension was Germany defeated in 1918. The consequences were terrible.

After hypocritical declarations that the fight was solely against the

Kaiser and his regime, the annihilation of the German Reich began according to plan after the German Army had laid down its arms.

While the prophecies of the French statement, that there were 20,000,000 Germans too many—in other words, that this number would have to be exterminated by hunger, disease or emigration—were apparently being fulfilled to the letter, the National Socialist movement began its work of unifying the German people and thereby initiating resurgence of the Reich. This rise of our people from distress, misery and shameful disregard bore all the signs of a purely internal renaissance. Britain especially was not in any way affected or threatened thereby.

Nevertheless, a new policy of encirclement against Germany, born as it was of hatred, recommenced immediately. Internally and externally there resulted that plot familiar to us all between Jews and democrats, Bolshevists and reactionaries, with the sole aim of inhibiting the establishment of the new German people's State, and of plunging the Reich anew into impotence and misery.

Apart from us the hatred of this international world conspiracy was directed against those peoples which like ourselves were neglected by fortune and were obliged to earn their daily bread in the hardest struggle for existence.

Above all, the right of Italy and Japan to share in the goods of this world was contested just as much as that of Germany and in fact was formally denied.

The coalition of these nations was, therefore, only an act of self-protection in the face of the egoistic world combination of wealth and power threatening them. As early as 1936 Prime Minister Churchill, according to statements by the American General Wood before a committee of the American House of Representatives, declared Germany was once again becoming too powerful and must therefore be destroyed. In the Summer of 1939 the time seemed to have come for England to begin to realize its intended annihilation by repetition of a comprehensive policy of encirclement of Germany.

The plan of the campaign of lies staged for this purpose consisted in declaring that other people were threatened, in tricking them with British promises of guarantees and assistance, and of making them march against Germany just as it did preceding the Great War. Thus Britain from May to August, 1939, succeeded in broadcasting to the world that Lithuania, Estonia, Latvia, Finland and Bessarabia as well as the Ukraine were being directly threatened by Germany.

A number of these States allowed themselves to be misled into accepting the promise of guarantee proffered with these assertions, thus joining the new encirclement front against Germany. Under these circumstances I considered myself entitled to assume responsibility before my own conscience and before the history of the German people not only of assuring these countries or their governments of the falseness of British assertions, but also of setting the strongest power in the east, by especially solemn declarations, at rest concerning the limits of our interests.

National Socialists! At that time you probably all felt that this step was bitter and difficult for me. Never did the German people harbor hostile feeling against the peoples of Russia. However, for over ten years Jewish Bolshevist rulers had been endeavoring from Moscow to set not only Germany but all Europe aflame. At no time ever did Germany attempt to carry her National Socialist *Weltanschauung* into Russia, but on the contrary Jewish Bolshevist rulers in Moscow unswervingly endeavored to foist their domination upon us and other European peoples, not only by ideological means but above all with military force.

The consequences of the activity of this regime were nothing but chaos, misery and starvation in all countries. I, on the other hand, have been striving for twenty years with a minimum of intervention and without destroying our production, to arrive at a new socialist order in Germany which not only eliminates unemployment but also permits the worker to receive an ever greater share of the fruits of his labor.

The success of this policy of economic and social reconstruction of our people, consisting of systematically eliminating differences of rank and class, has a true people's community as the final aim of the world.

It was therefore only with extreme difficulty that I brought myself in August, 1939, to send my foreign minister to Moscow in an endeavor there to oppose the British encirclement policy against Germany. I did this only from a sense of all responsibility toward the German people, but above all in the hope after all of achieving permanent relief of tension and of being able to reduce sacrifices which might otherwise have been demanded of us.

While Germany solemnly affirmed in Moscow that the territories and countries enumerated—with the exception of Lithuania—lay outside all German political interests, a special agreement was concluded in case Britain were to succeed in inciting Poland actually into war with Germany. In this case, too, German claims were subject to limitations entirely out of proportion to the achievement of German forces.

National Socialists! The consequences of this treaty which I myself desired and which was concluded in the interests of the German nation were very severe, particularly for Germans living in the countries concerned.

Far more than 500,000 German men and women, all small farmers, artisans and workmen, were forced to leave their former homeland practically overnight in order to escape from a new regime which at first threatened them with boundless misery and sooner or later with complete extermination.

Nevertheless, thousands of Germans disappeared. It was impossible ever to determine their fate, let alone their whereabouts. Among them were no fewer than 160 men of German citizenship. To all this I remained silent because I had to. For, after all, it was my one desire to achieve final relief of tension and, if possible, a permanent settlement with this State.

However, already during our advance in Poland, Soviet rulers suddenly, contrary to the treaty, also claimed Lithuania.

The German Reich never had any intention of occupying Lithuania and not only failed to present any such demand to the Lithuanian Government, but on the contrary refused the request of the then Lithuania to send German troops to Lithuania for that purpose as inconsistent with the aims of German policy.

Despite all this I complied also with this fresh Russian demand. However, this was only the beginning of continually renewed extortions which kept on repeating ever since.

Victory in Poland which was won by German troops exclusively caused me to address yet another peace offer to the Western Powers. It was refused owing to efforts of international and Jewish warmongers.

At that time already the reason for such refusal lay in the fact that Britain still had hopes of being able to mobilize a European coalition against Germany which was to include the Balkans and Soviet Russia. It was therefore decided in London to send Mr. Cripps as ambassador to Moscow. He received clear instructions under all circumstances to resume relations between the English and Soviet Russia and develop them in a pro-British direction. The British press reported on the progress of this mission as long as tactical reasons did not impose silence.

In the autumn of 1939 and spring of 1940 the first results actually made themselves felt. As Russia undertook to subjugate by armed force not only Finland but also the Baltic States she suddenly motivated this action by the assertion, as ridiculous as it was false, that she must protect these countries from an outside menace or forestall it. This could only be meant to apply to Germany, for no other power could even gain entrance into the Baltic area, let alone go to war there. Still I had to be silent. However, those in power in the Kremlin immediately went further.

Whereas in the spring of 1940 Germany, in accordance with the so-called pact of friendship, withdrew her forces from the Far Eastern frontier and, in fact, for the most part cleared these areas entirely of German troops, a concentration of Russian forces at that time was already beginning in a measure which could only be regarded as a deliberate threat to Germany.

According to a statement that Molotov personally made at that time, there were twenty-two Russian divisions in the Baltic States alone already in the spring of 1940. Since the Russian Government itself always claimed it was called in by the local population, the purpose of their presence there could only be a demonstration against Germany.

While our soldiers from May 5, 1940, on had been breaking Franco-British power in the west, Russian military deployment on our eastern frontier was being continued to a more and more menacing extent. From August, 1940, on I therefore considered it to be in the interest of the Reich no longer to permit our eastern provinces, which moreover had already been laid waste so often, to remain unprotected in the face of this tremendous concentration of Bolshevist divisions.

Thus there resulted British-Soviet Russian co-operation intended mainly at the tying up of such powerful forces in the east that radical conclusion of the war in the west, particularly as regards aircraft, could no longer be vouched for by the German High Command. This, however, was in line with the objects not only of the British but also of the Soviet Russian policy, for both England and Soviet Russia intended to let this war go on for as long as possible in order to weaken all Europe and render it progressively more impotent.

Russia's threatened attack on Rumania was in the last analysis equally intended to gain possession of an important base, not only of Germany's but also of Europe's, economic life, or at least destroy it. The Reich, especially since 1933, sought with unending patience to gain States in Southeast Europe as trading partners. We therefore also had the greatest interest in their internal constitutional consolidation and organization. Russia's advance into Rumania and Greece's tie-up with England threatened to turn these regions, too, within a short time into a general theater of war.

Contrary to our principles and customs, and at the urgent request of the then Rumanian Government, which was itself responsible for this development, I advised acquiescence to the Soviet Russian demands for the sake of peace and the cession of Bessarabia. The Rumanian Government believed, however, that it could answer for this before its own people only if Germany and Italy in compensation would at least guarantee the integrity of what still remained of Rumania. I did so with heavy heart, principally because when the German Reich gives a guarantee, that means it also abides by it. We are neither Englishmen nor Jews.

I still believe at this late hour to have served the cause of peace in that region, albeit by assuming serious personal obligation. In order, however, finally to solve these problems and achieve clarity concerning the Russian attitude toward Germany, as well as under pressure of continually increasing mobilization on our Eastern frontier, I invited Mr. Molotov to come to Berlin.

The Soviet Minister for Foreign Affairs then demanded Germany's clarification of or agreement to the following four questions:

Point one was Molotov's question: Was the German guarantee for Rumania also directed against Soviet Russia in case of attack by Soviet Russia on Rumania?

My answer: The German guarantee is a general one and is unconditionally binding upon us. Russia, however, never declared to us that she had other interests in Rumania beyond Bessarabia. The occupation of Northern Bukovina had already been a violation of this assurance. I did not therefore think that Russia could now suddenly have more far-reaching intentions against Rumania.

Molotov's second question: That Russia again felt menaced by Finland. Russia was determined not to tolerate this. Was Germany ready not to give any aid to Finland and above all immediately to withdraw German relief troops marching through to Kirkenes?

My answer: Germany continued to have absolutely no political interests in Finland. A fresh war by Russia against the small Finnish people could not, however, be regarded any longer by the German Government as tolerable, all the more so as we could never believe Russia to be threatened by Finland. Under no circumstances did we want another theater of war to arise in the Baltic.

Molotov's third question: Was Germany prepared to agree that Russia give a guarantee to Bulgaria and send Soviet Russian troops to Bulgaria for this purpose in connection with which he—Molotov—was prepared to state that the Soviets did not intend on that account, for example, to depose the King?

My answer: Bulgaria was a sovereign State and I had no knowledge that Bulgaria had ever asked Soviet Russia for any kind of guarantee such as Rumania had requested from Germany. Moreover, I would have to discuss the matter with my allies.

Molotov's fourth question: Soviet Russia required free passage through the Dardanelles under all circumstances and for her protection also demanded occupation of a number of important bases on the Dardanelles and Bosphorus. Was Germany in agreement with this or not?

My answer: Germany was prepared at all times to agree to alteration of the Statute of Montreux in favor of the Black Sea States. Germany was not prepared to agree to Russia's taking possession of bases on the Straits.

National Socialists! Here I adopted the only attitude that I could adopt as the responsible leader of the German Reich but also as the representative of European culture and civilization and conscious of my responsibility. The consequence was to increase in Soviet Russia the activity directed against the Reich, above all, however, the immediate commencement of undermining the new Rumanian state from within and an attempt to remove the Bulgarian Government by propaganda.

With the help of the confused and immature leaders of the Rumanian Legion (Iron Guard) a coup d'état was staged in Rumania whose aim was to overthrow Chief of State General Antonescu and produce chaos in the country so as to remove all legal power of the government and thus the precondition for an implement of the German guarantee. I nevertheless still believed it best to remain silent.

Immediately after the failure of this undertaking, renewed reinforcement of concentrations of Russian troops on Germany's eastern frontier took place. Panzer detachments and parachutists were transferred in continually increasing numbers to dangerous proximity to the German frontier. German fighting forces and the German nation know that until a few weeks ago not a single tank or mechanized division was stationed on our eastern frontier.

If any final proof was required for the coalition meanwhile formed between England and Soviet Russia despite all diversion and camouflage, the Yugoslav conflict provided it. While I made every effort to undertake a final attempt to pacify the Balkans and in sympathetic co-operation with Il Duce invited Yugoslavia to join the Tripartite Pact, England and Soviet Russia in a joint conspiracy organized that coup d'état which in one night removed the then government which had been ready to come to agreement.

For we can today inform the German nation that the Serb putsch against Germany did not take place merely under the British, but primarily under Soviet Russian auspices. As we remained silent on this matter also, the Soviet leaders now went still one step further. They not only organized the putsch, but a few days later also concluded that well-known friendship pact with the Serbs in their will to resist pacification of the Balkans and incite them against Germany. And this was no platonic intention: Moscow demanded mobilization of the Serb Army.

Since even now I still believed it better not to speak, those in power in the Kremlin went still further: The Government of the German Reich today possesses documentary evidence which proves that Russia, in order finally to bring Serbia into the war, gave her a promise to supply her via Salonika with arms, aircraft, munitions and other war materials against Germany. And this happened almost at the very moment when I myself advised Japanese Foreign Minister Matsuoka that eased tension with Russia always was in hope, thereby to serve the cause of peace.

Only the rapid advance of our incomparable divisions to Skoplje as well as the capture of Salonika itself frustrated the aims of this Soviet Russian–Anglo-Saxon plot. Officers of the Serb air force, however, fled to Russia and were there immediately received as allies.

The victory of the Axis Powers in the Balkans in the first instance thwarted the plan to involve Germany this Summer in months-long battles in Southeastern Europe while meantime steadily completing the alignment of Soviet Russian armies and increasing their readiness for war in order, finally, together with England and supported by American supplies anticipated, to crush the German Reich and Italy.

Thus Moscow not only broke but miserably betrayed the stipulations of our friendly agreement. All this was done while the rulers in the Kremlin, exactly as in the case of Finland and Rumania, up to the last moment pretended peace and friendship and drew up an ostensibly innocent démenti.

Although until now I was forced by circumstances to keep silent again and again, the moment has now come when to continue as a mere observer would not only be a sin of omission but a crime against the German people—yes, even against the whole of Europe.

Today something like 160 Russian divisions are standing at our frontiers. For weeks constant violations of this frontier have taken place, not only affecting us but from the far north down to Rumania. Russian airmen consider it sport nonchalantly to overlook these frontiers, presumably to prove to us that they already feel themselves masters of these territories. During the night of June 17 to June 18 Russian patrols again penetrated into the Reich's territory and could only be driven back after prolonged firing. This has brought us to the hour when it is necessary for us to take steps against this plot devised by the Jewish–Anglo-Saxon warmongers and equally the Jewish rulers of the Bolshevist center in Moscow.

RELATIONS WITH OTHER COUNTRIES

German people! At this moment a march is taking place that, as regards extent, compares with the greatest the world hitherto has seen. United with their Finnish comrades, the fighters of the victory of Narvik are standing in the Northern Arctic. German divisions commanded by the conqueror of Norway, in co-operation with the heroes of Finnish freedom, under their marshal, are protecting Finnish soil. Formations of the German eastern front extend from East Prussia to the Carpathians. German and Rumanian soldiers are united under Chief of State Antonescu from the banks of the Pruth along the lower reaches of the Danube to the shores of the Black Sea. The task of this front, therefore, no longer is the protection of single countries, but the safeguarding of Europe and thereby the salvation of all.

I therefore decided today again to lay the fate and future of the German Reich and our people in the hands of our soldiers.

May God help us especially in this fight!

INVASIONS OF VARIOUS COUNTRIES

Denmark and Norway

MEMORANDUM of the German Government Presented to the Norwegian Government and *mutatis mutandis* to the Danish Government, April 9, 1940

Translation, in *The New York Times*, April 10, 1940; excerpt. Reprinted by permission of the Associated Press

IN THIS decisive phase of war for existence, forced upon the German people by England and France, the Reich's Government can under no circumstances tolerate that Scandinavia be converted by the Western Powers into a theatre of war against Germany and that the Norwegian people be directly or indirectly misused for war against Germany.

Germany is unwilling to stand by idly or take lying down such a realization of enemies' plans. The Reich's Government therefore has, beginning today, set in motion certain military operations which will lead to the occupation of strategic points on Norwegian soil.

The Reich's Government thereby assumes protection of the Kingdom of Norway for the duration of this war. It is determined from now on, with its instruments of force, to protect peace in the north against every English-French attack and definitely to render it secure.

The Reich's Government has not desired this development. The responsibility, therefore, lies solely with England and France. To be sure, both States hypocritically proclaim the protection of small States, but in reality they violate these in the hope thereby to be able to translate into reality their will to destroy Germany, as proclaimed more openly each day.

German troops, therefore, enter Norwegian soil not in hostile spirit. The German Supreme Command does not intend to use the points occupied by German troops as operations bases for fighting England as long as not forced to do so through acts of England and France.

German military operations are aimed at the exclusive goal of safeguarding the Norse against the intended occupation of Norwegian strategic points by English and French forces.

The Reich's Government is convinced that it serves Norway's best interests also by this action. For this act of rendering them secure through Germany's armed forces gives the sole guarantee to the Scandinavian peoples that their countries will not after all become a battlefield, and perhaps the scene of the most terrible acts of force during this war.

The Reich's Government, therefore, expects the Royal Norwegian Government and the Norwegian people to have full understanding for Germany's procedure and not to resist in any way. All resistance would have to be and would be broken by every available means by the German armed forces deployed here, and therefore lead only to utterly useless bloodshed. The Royal Norwegian Government is therefore requested to take all measures with the greatest speed which are necessary to render certain that the advance of German troops can progress without friction and difficulties.

In the spirit, long existing, of good German-Norwegian relations, the Reich's Government declares to the Royal Norwegian Government that Germany has no intention through her measures now or in the future of touching upon the territorial integrity and political independence of the Kingdom of Norway.

Dated April 9, 1940.

Belgium and the Netherlands

MEMORANDUM of the German Government Presented to the Governments of Belgium and the Netherlands, May 10, 1940

Translation, in *The New York Times*, May 10, 1940; excerpt

IN THE life-and-death struggle thrust upon the German people, the government does not intend to await an attack by Britain and France inactively allowing the war to be carried through Belgium and Holland onto German soil. The government, therefore, has issued orders to safeguard the neutrality of the two countries with all the military means of the Reich.

Yugoslavia

ORDER of the Day Issued by Adolf Hitler, Chancellor of the Reich, to the Soldiers of the Southeast Front, April 6, 1941

Translation, in *The New York Times,* April 6, 1941, citing text as read over the Berlin radio early on April 6 and heard by the National Broadcasting Company's station in New York.

Soldiers of the Southeast Front:

Since early this morning the German people are at war with the Belgrade government of intrigue. We shall only lay down arms when this band of ruffians has been definitely and most emphatically eliminated, and the last Briton has left this part of the European Continent, and that these misled people realize that they must thank Britain for this situation, they must thank England, the greatest warmonger of all time.

The German people can enter into this new struggle with the inner satisfaction that its leaders have done everything to bring about a peaceful settlement.

We pray to God that He may lead our soldiers on the path and bless them as hitherto.

In accordance with the policy of letting others fight for her, as she did in the case of Poland, Britain again tried to involve Germany in the struggle in which Britain hoped that she would finish off the German people once and for all, to win the war, and if possible to destroy the entire German Army.

In a few weeks long ago the German soldiers on the Eastern Front, Poland, swept aside this instrument of British policy. On April 9, 1940, Britain again attempted to reach its goal by a thrust on the German north flank, the thrust at Norway.

In an unforgettable struggle the German soldiers in Norway eliminated the British within a period of a few weeks.

What the world did not deem possible the German people have achieved. Again, only a few weeks later, Churchill thought the moment right to make a renewed thrust through the British Allies, France and Belgium, into the German region of the Ruhr. The victorious hour of our soldiers on the West Front began.

It is already war history how the German Armies defeated the legions of capitalism and plutocracy. After forty-five days this campaign in the West was equally and emphatically terminated.

Then Churchill concentrated the strength of his Empire against our ally, Italy, in Africa. Now the danger has also been banned from the African theater of the war through the cooperation of Italian and German units.

The new aim of the British warmongers now consists of the realization of a plan that they had already hatched at the outbreak of the war and only postponed because of the gigantic victories of the German Army. The memory of the landing of British troops at Salonika in the course of the first world War also caught little Greece in the spider web of British intrigue.

I have repeatedly warned of the attempt by the British to land troops in Southeastern Europe, and I have said that this constitutes a threat to the German Reich. Unfortunately this warning went unheeded by the Yugoslav nation. I have further tried, always with the same patience, to convince Yugoslav statesmen of the absolute necessity for their cooperation with the German Reich for restoration of lasting peace and order within Yugoslavia.

After long effort we finally succeeded in securing the cooperation of Yugoslavia by its adherence to the tripartite pact without having demanded anything whatsoever of the Yugoslav nation except that it take its part in the reconstruction of a new order in Europe.

At this point the criminal usurpers of the new Belgrade government took the power of the State unto themselves, which is a result of being in the pay of Churchill and Britain. As in the case of Poland, this new Belgrade government has mobilized decrepit and old people into their inner Cabinet. Under these circumstances I was forced immediately to recall the German national colony within Yugoslav territory.

Members and officers of the German Embassy, employés of our consulates in Yugoslavia, were daily being subjected to the most humiliating attacks. The German schools, exactly as in Poland, were laid in ruins by bandits. Innumerable German nationals were kidnapped and attacked by Yugoslavs and some even were killed.

In addition, Yugoslavia for weeks has planned a general mobilization of its army in great secrecy. This is the answer to my eight-year-long effort to bring about closer cooperation and friendship with the Yugoslav people, a task that I have pursued most fastidiously.

When British divisions were landed in Greece, just as in World War days, the Serbs thought the time was ripe for taking advantage of the situation for new assassinations against Germany and her allies.

Soldiers of the Southeast Front: Now your zero hour has arrived. You will take the interests of the German Reich under your protection as your comrades did a year ago in Norway and on the West Front. You will do just as well on the Southeast Front.

In doing this, your duty, you will not be less courageous than the men of those German divisions who in 1915, on the same Balkan soil, fought so victoriously. You will be humane only in those places where the enemy is humane toward you. Where the enemy confronts you with utter brutality you will beat them back with the same weapon.

The fight on Greek soil is not a battle against the Greek people, but against that archenemy, England, which is again trying to extend the war far into the Southeast Balkans, the same as he tried far in the north last year. For this reason, on this very spot in the Balkans, we shall fight shoulder to shoulder with our ally until the last Briton has found his Dunkerque in Greece.

If any Greeks support this British course, then those Greeks will fall at the same time as the British.

When the German soldier shall have proved himself, shall have proved that he is capable of beating the British in the Balkans, in the midst of snow and mountains, then also he will have proved that he can beat the British in the heat of the desert of Africa.

However, we will pursue no other ultimate aim than to win freedom for our German people and to secure a living-space for the German family.

The prayers and the thoughts, the very life of all Germans, are again in the heart of every German soldier.

Berlin, April 6, 1941.

ADOLF HITLER,
Commander in Chief.

ECONOMIC AND FINANCIAL POLICY

ADDRESS by Hjalmar Schacht, President of the Reichsbank, at Bad Eilsen, August 30, 1934. Given before the International Conference of Agricultural Science

Translation, in Royal Institute of International Affairs, *Documents on International Affairs, 1934,* p. 265, citing the *Frankfurter Zeitung,* August 31, 1934; excerpts.

IN THE COURSE of about three years Germany has paid back Rm. 11 milliards out of a total foreign indebtedness of more than Rm. 25 milliards, that is to say more than her total non-political indebtedness. This figure includes a reduction of Rm. 4 milliards through the depreciation of foreign currencies. The effective repayment of more than Rm. 7 milliards was made possible:

(1) by the complete surrender of the Reichsbank's gold and foreign exchange reserves to the amount of about Rm. 3 milliards;
(2) by the liquidation of all foreign credit balances in any way realizable and of other property still available or rebuilt belonging to German undertakings abroad or private persons;
(3) by rigorous import restrictions and a simultaneous stimulation of exports;
(4) by a deflationary policy which the Basle experts described as "unparalleled."

It was achieved:

(1) In spite of a rise in the internal interest level through capital losses during and after the War;
(2) in spite of the fact that whole branches of production, particularly agriculture, were hopelessly unremunerative;
(3) in spite of an increase in unemployment to a third of those employable;
(4) in spite of the restrictions placed by nearly the whole world against German exports without consideration for her difficulties;
(5) in spite of the currency depreciation of two-thirds of the world to the extent of from 40 to 60 per cent. of their original parity, which severely reduced the competitive power of German goods;
(6) in spite of the further reduction of exports as a result of boycott movements;

(7) in spite of the fact that the burden of foreign indebtedness was increased through the fall in prices to a greater extent than the gain resulting from foreign currency depreciation.

Today Germany's transfer capacity is completely exhausted; Germany has paid back her economic debts at the expense of immense sacrifices. She can no longer pay reparations, which today are unfortunately owed no longer to Governments but to private creditors, from her own resources. There is now no doubt in the world that interest and amortization on foreign debts can only be paid in the form of goods and services. In these circumstances it is useless, even ridiculous, to force payments from Germany by any kind of pressure; any form of pressure can only cause serious injury and affect adversely not only German economy, but also that of any State engaged in world trade, for a country of the importance of Germany cannot simply be withdrawn from world economy without the most severe repercussions upon other countries engaged in world trade. . . .

The world, therefore, is confronted today with two alternatives: either it can remain passive in regard to the debts problem and write off Germany as a purchaser as well as a debtor and throw world trade back some decades, or alter its credit policy, assist in settling the German transfer problem and clear the way for a world trade revival. Germany's position is clear: she cannot retreat from her demand that not only her own economy but also world economy today be freed from the crippling effects of one-sided political pressure. . . .

She recognizes that the debt problem has been complicated by the substitution of private creditors for the reparations Powers; she knows that German debtors have recognized their signature of agreements with private creditors. She recognizes the binding nature of these signatures without reserve; she is prepared to pay whatever she can and beyond this whatever the world is ready to take from her in goods and services at reasonable prices. . . .

Theoretically there are two solutions: (1) German goods should be freed from all restrictions; (2) German debts should be cancelled. Actually neither way is practicable: the first is blocked by the opposition of foreign industries and the second by the opposition of foreign capitalists. The only way practically possible must therefore lie in the middle, that is to say that the Governments of creditor States should be prepared to take more German goods and the creditors themselves agree to reduce their claims. . . .

A year or two ago such a middle way might have offered a chance of success, today it is no longer adequate. Germany's deficiency of foreign exchange forces her to a drastic reduction of imports. . . .

Germany can pay the service on her debt only through a considerable increase in the volume of world trade. Under the pressure of international deflationist policy there can be no hope of this enlarged volume of world trade. Nothing, therefore, remains but to grant her a full moratorium of many years' duration to enable her to recuperate. At the same time the burden of her foreign indebtedness must be reduced to such dimensions that after the lapse of the moratorium it can be borne. If these two conditions are fulfilled in an international agreement the decisive obstacle to revival of world trade will have been removed. . . .

ANNOUNCEMENT of the "New Plan" by Hjalmar Schacht, President of the Reichsbank, in September, 1934

As explained by the Berlin Correspondent of *The Economist* (London), in the issue of September 15, 1934, p. 488; excerpts

THE NEW "PLAN" for foreign trade control recently announced by the Ministry of Economy, to be based on the Law for Trade in Industrial Raw and Half-Finished Materials of March 22nd (the first general import control statute), consists essentially in an extension of the control system to numerous industrial commodities hitherto excluded and to agricultural products. Import and internal distribution of all these will be regulated on the principle (to be applied to each individual transaction) that only such goods shall be imported as can be paid for in view of the current reserve position. To the already existing eleven import control boards for different classes of industrial materials are added ten new ones, plus four for agricultural products, so that henceforth there will be 25 boards. The older control system is also defined further and in altered detail. The new system is embodied in an "Ordinance for Trade in Commodities," which contains the general and wide empowering clause: "The Reich Minister of Economy is authorised to supervise and regulate trade in commodities, and in particular to issue regulations concerning their provision, distribution, storage, sale and consumption." For such purposes the Minister may require the reporting of transactions and the keeping of books. The Minister of Economy will appoint a Reich Commissioner to direct and represent each board. . . .

The effect of all these measures is to subject imported goods of every kind to public control both as regards their purchase from abroad and their distribution at home. There is no limit to the Ministry of Economy's power to take measures for ensuring the distribution it desires. From September 24th the control boards will replace the present exchange boards (Devisenstellen) in regulating payment (supply of foreign exchange) for import. The general import exchange rationing will cease. The boards will issue "exchange certificates" for import payments, which must be produced to the Customs authorities; and only these certificates, together with a Customs certificate of the actual import, will authorise payment to the foreign seller. The import of goods for which exchange certificates are refused is not prohibited; but the purchaser will not be able to count on his ability to pay within a reasonable time; and in order to prevent evasion of the exchange law, imports of this last class must be reported to the competent board. The present free limit for import payments is reduced from 50 to 10 marks. While in general the "exchange certificates" will authorise immediate payment, certificates guaranteeing payment at a later time will also be granted. The Ministries of Economy and Food and the Reichsbank will from time to time jointly determine the amount of exchange certificates to be issued. Certificates will also be necessary for payment in reichsmarks. In considering applications for certificates, a sufficient supply of materials for the export industries will in all circumstances be ensured. The new regulations, it is officially added, will be used in order to further the conclusion of compensation agreements. . . .

ADDRESS by Adolf Hitler, Chancellor of the Reich, at the Party Congress at Nuremberg, September 9, 1936

Translation, in *International Conciliation,* November, 1936, citing *Völkischer Beobachter,* September 10, 1936; excerpt

LIKE EVERY healthy national economy, German economy has first of all the desire to utilize as far as possible its own economic possibility for the maintenance of its people, in order to use the secondary consideration and participate with its own healthy economy in world economy.

Inasmuch as the National Socialist State is under no circumstances willing to restrict the numbers of its population, but is rather determined to increase the natural fertility of the nation, we are forced to consider and weigh the consequences of such a development for the future. A substantial increase in the production of our soil is impossible, and a substantial increase in exports in the near future is improbable.

It is therefore the task of the National Socialist State and its economic leadership to investigate thoroughly what essential raw materials, fuel, etc., can be produced within Germany. The foreign exchange we can thus save will serve in the future as an additional safeguard for our food supply and the purchase of those materials which cannot be found in our territory under any circumstances.

I therefore announce this today as our new four-year program:

In four years Germany must be wholly independent of foreign countries in respect to all those materials which can in any way be produced through German capability, through German chemistry, our machine and mining industries. The creation of this great German raw material industry will employ productively those masses freed by the completion of rearmament. We hope thus to increase national production in many fields so as to reserve the proceeds of our exports first of all for food and for raw materials, which we still lack.

I have just issued necessary orders for carrying out this tremendous German economic plan. Its execution will take place with National Socialist energy and force.

Independent of this, Germany cannot, however, relinquish her demand for the solution of her colonial demands. The right of the German people to live is just as great as that of the people of any other nation.

I know, my National Socialist countrymen, that this new program represents a mighty task, but scientifically it is already solved in many fields; the production methods are being already partly tried and fixed. It will, therefore, be but a question of our energy and determination to translate this program into reality.

ADDRESS by Adolf Hitler, Chancellor of the Reich, before the Reichstag, January 30, 1939

Translation, in Raoul de Roussy de Sales, *My New Order* (1941), p. 559; excerpts

WHAT IS the root cause of all our economic difficulties? It is the overpopulation of our territory. And in this connection there is only one fact and one question which I can hold up to the Western and the extra-European democracies.

The fact is this: In Germany there are 135 people to the square kilometer, living entirely without their former reserve; for fifteen years a prey to all the rest of the world, burdened with tremendous debts, without colonies, but the German people are nevertheless fed and clothed, and, moreover, there are no unemployed among them.

... If certain methods of our economic policy appear injurious to the rest of the world, it should recognize that a hatred on the part of the former victor States, which was irrational and purposeless from an economic point of view, was chiefly responsible for making these efforts necessary. On this occasion again, as so often before, I wish to make clear in a few words to you, gentlemen, and thus to the entire German people, an existing situation which we must either accept or alter.

Before the war Germany was a flourishing economic power. She participated in international trade and observed the economic laws which had general validity at that time as well as the methods of that trade. I need say nothing here with regard to the compulsion to participate in this trade activity since it is presumptuous to assume that God created the world only for one or two peoples. Every people has the right to ensure its existence on this earth. ...

The war in which Germany found herself involved, purely as a result of a mistaken interpretation of loyalty to an ally, ended after over four years with that fantastic proclamation of the famous American President Wilson. These fourteen points, which were then supplemented by four additional ones, represent the solemn commitments of the Allied powers, on the basis of which Germany laid down her arms. After the Armistice these undertakings were broken in the most infamous manner.

There then began the insane efforts of the victor States to transform the sufferings of the war into a permanent state of warfare during times of peace. For the most part an end has been put to this condition today. This has not happened because the democratic statesmen have displayed insight or even merely a sense of equity but solely through the strength of the reawakened German nation. ...

Any benefits one can possibly imagine from this war have been completely canceled, not merely by the tremendous sacrifices of human lives and goods but also by the continuing burden on all production, and above all on the budgets of the States. This, however, was a fact which was evident and could be seen immediately after the war. If it had been taken into consideration, the peace treaties would certainly have been drawn up on a different basis.

For example, proof for all time to come of an extraordinarily limited insight in judging economic possibilities was furnished by the sums proposed in the years 1919 and 1920 as possible reparations payments. They are so far beyond the bounds of any economic reason that one can only assume a general desire for world destruction as the sole intelligible cause for this procedure, which otherwise can only be characterized as insanity. . . .

But this was not all: in order to prevent or hamper any autarchic activity by Germany, the Reich was even deprived of its own colonial possessions which had been acquired by purchases and treaty. This means that the strongest people of Central Europe was forced through a series of truly brilliant maneuvers to work much harder than before as an exporting nation regardless of cost. For German exports had to be large enough not only to satisfy German requirements, but also to provide additional insanely high reparations, which, of course, meant that, in order to pay 1 mark, 3 or 4 marks' worth of goods had to be exported, since in the long run these gigantic sums could only be paid from profits and not from capital. Since Germany was not in a position to fulfill these obligations the victor nations by means of loans subsidized German trade competition on the world market, after ten or twelve million men had given their lives on the battlefield to eliminate the trade enemy from the world market.

I will only mention parenthetically that this insane procedure finally led to exaggerated developments and in the end upset all national economies and caused serious currency crises. The entire conduct of the so-called victor powers after the end of the war was completely irrational and irresponsible. The theft of the German colonies was morally an injustice. Economically it was utter insanity! The political motives advanced were so mean that one is tempted merely to call them silly. . . .

In actual fact the problem at the end of the war had become still more critical than it was before the war. Quite briefly, the problem was as follows:

How can a just and sensible share in the world's wealth be assured to all great nations? For surely no one can seriously assume that, as in the case of Germany, a mass of 80,000,000 intelligent persons, can be permanently condemned as pariahs, or be forced to remain passive forever by having some ridiculous legal title, based solely on former acts of force, held up before them. And this is true not only of Germany but of all nations in a similar position, for it is quite clear that: either the wealth of the world is divided by force, in which case this division will be corrected from time to time by force, or else the division is based on the ground of equity and therefore, also, of common sense, in which case equity and common sense must also really serve the cause of justice and ultimately of expedience.

But to assume that God has permitted some nations first to acquire a world by force and then to defend this robbery with moralizing theories is perhaps comforting and above all comfortable for the "haves," but not for the "have nots." It is just as unimportant as it is uninteresting and lays no obligation upon them. Nor is the problem solved by the fact that a most important statesman simply declares with a scornful grin that there are nations which are "haves" and that the others on that account must always be "have nots." . . .

As far as Germany is concerned the situation is very simple. The Reich has 80,000,000 inhabitants; that means over fifteen persons to the square kilometer. The great German colonial possessions, which the Reich once acquired peacefully by treaties and by paying for them, have been stolen—contrary indeed to the solemn assurance given by President Wilson, which was the basic condition on which Germany laid down her arms.

The objection that these colonial possessions are of no importance in any case should only lead to their being returned to us with an easy mind. But the objection that this is not possible because Germany would not know what to do with them since she did not do anything with them before is ridiculous. Germany, which was late in acquiring her colonial possessions, was able to develop them in a relatively short time and before the war was not faced by the same acute needs as today. This objection is consequently just as foolish as if anybody were to question a nation's capacity to build a railway because it had no railway 100 years ago.

The further objection that her colonial possessions cannot be returned to her because Germany would thus acquire a strategic position is a monstrous attempt to deny general rights to a nation and a people a priori. For this can be the only answer: Germany was in any case the only State which set up no colonial army since she trusted to the terms of the Congo Act which were afterward broken by the Allies.

Germany does not require her colonial possessions at all in order to set up armies there—she has a sufficiently large German population for this purpose at home—but to relieve her economic difficulties. . . .

As she lacks a sphere of economic development for herself, Germany is forced to satisfy her own requirements by an increasing participation in world trade and in exchanges of goods. For on one point those very nations must be agreed, which themselves have immense economic possibilities at their disposal, either because they themselves occupy large territories or because they have great additional colonial possessions—namely, that the economic existence of a nation cannot be maintained without a sufficient supply of foodstuffs or without independent raw materials. If both are lacking a nation is forced to participate in world trade under all circumstances and perhaps to an extent which may even be undesirable to other countries. Only a few years ago, when conditions forced Germany to adopt her Four-Year

Plan, we could to our great astonishment hear from the lips of British politicians and statesmen the reproach—which at that time sounded so sincere—that Germany was withdrawing from the sphere of international economics, even from world economic contacts, and was thus retiring into regrettable isolation.

I replied to Mr. Eden that this apprehension was perhaps a little exaggerated and if it was meant at all sincerely was not admissible. Conditions today make it quite impossible for Germany to withdraw from world trade. They simply compel us by the mere force of necessity to participate in it under all circumstances even when the form of our participation perhaps does not suit one country or another. . . .

At one point, however, nature sets the limit to any further intensification of effort. That means, if some change does not take place, that German consumption power would find its natural limitation in the maximum of production of food supplies. The situation which would then arise could only be overcome in two ways:

First, by means of additional imports of foodstuffs and increased exports of German products, which would necessitate the importation of at least some of the raw materials necessary for their manufacture, with the result that only a proportion of imports received would be available for the purchase of foodstuffs, or,

Second, the extension of our nation's living space so that in our domestic economy the problem of Germany's food supplies can be solved.

As the second solution is for the time being not yet feasible, by reason of the continued blindness of the one-time victorious powers, we are forced to occupy ourselves with the first; in other words, we have to export in order to buy foodstuffs and, moreover, as these exports require raw materials, all of which we do not possess, we are forced to export still more in order to assure ourselves of these extra raw materials. This necessity is consequently not of a capitalistic kind, as perhaps may be the case in other countries, but arises out of the uttermost need a nation can meet with, namely, the need for its daily bread. And when in this matter statesmen of other countries threaten us with I do not know what kinds of economic counter-measures, I can only give the assurance that in such a case a desperate economic struggle would ensue, which would be easy for us to carry out, easier for us than for the ever-satiated nations because our leading idea would be a very simple one: the German nation must live; that means export or die. And I assure all the international skeptics that the German nation will not die, least of all for this reason, but that it will live. If need be it will place all the production resources of our new

National Socialist community at the disposal of its leaders to begin such a struggle, and to see it through. . . .

In 1933 and 1934 I made one offer after another to set reasonable limits to armaments. They were coldly rejected as was the claim for the return of the stolen German colonial possessions. If these gifted statesmen and politicians in the other countries draw up an account of the net profits which have accrued to them from the military and colonial inequality, and therefore the general legal inequality for which they have so persistently contended, then they will perhaps hardly be able to contest that they have already paid far too much for their supposed military superiority, and the wonderful colonial possessions they took from Germany.

Economically it would have been wiser to have reached a reasonable and prudent agreement with Germany in regard to the colonies and European politics, rather than to have taken a course, which perhaps yields enormous dividends to the international armament profiteers, but at the same time forces the gravest burdens on the nations. I estimate that the 3,000,000 square kilometers of the German colonial possessions which have fallen to England and France, together with the refusal to accept Germany on a basis of political and military equality, will in a short time have cost England alone 20,000,000,000 gold marks; and I am afraid that in the not too distant future this sum will increase at an even greater rate with the result that, far from yielding golden profits, the former German colonies will cost a great deal. The objection could be raised that this would also apply to Germany. Granted that it is no great pleasure for us either, there is one difference between us: We are struggling for a vital right, without which we cannot in the long run live, whereas the others are struggling to uphold an injustice which is only a burden to them and yields no profit whatsoever.

Under the present circumstances the only way open to us is to continue our economic policy of trying to produce the utmost from the territory at our disposal. This compels us to intensify our efforts in all branches, in order to expand production. This, in turn, forces us to carry out the Four-Year Plan more resolutely than ever. This means we must further utilize our labor resources, and here we are approaching a new period in Germany's economic policy. . . .

To this purpose, trade and industry, and finance must necessarily be more closely concentrated. . . .

PART SIX

ITALY

GENERAL STATEMENTS OF POLICY

ADDRESS by Dino Grandi, Minister for Foreign Affairs, before the Assembly of the League of Nations, September 8, 1931

Translation, in League of Nations, *Official Journal*, Special Supplement No. 93, p. 38; excerpts

I HAVE NO intention of theorising on the structure of the Covenant; but, to illustrate my remarks, I might mention certain ideas which the Italian delegation has repeatedly put forward here. These may perhaps be pertinent now, when we are preparing for the Disarmament Conference—that is, on the eve of complex negotiations which cannot begin in the necessary atmosphere of clarity, and under favourable conditions unless, from the outset, each one of us frankly states his country's policy.

Since we regard the problem of disarmament as an integral part of the League system, that system must obviously be our starting-point. One principle stands out clearly from the stipulations of the Covenant,—namely, that peace can rest only on the security of nations, and security can be found only in the harmonious evolution of two factors: the peaceful settlement of disputes and a general reduction of armaments.

Disarmament and arbitration, the rejection of all solutions based on force, and the relative equalising of the military strength of States at the lowest possible level—that is not just a theory or dogmatic assertion. It lies at the root of the system which the League Covenant has evolved with a view to the reduction of armaments; it corresponds essentially to real and pressing demands. Indeed, there is no problem of security distinct from disarmament and arbitration.

If, in international relations, solutions could not be reached by the use of force, if there were no excess of armaments, the problem of security would not even arise. It has arisen because the legal organisation of the association of nations which we have been laboriously constructing during the last few years still leaves the door open to the race for armaments, a factor that undermines its structure and jeopardises its efficacy. It is not merely because the excess of armaments has the effect of blunting the sense of justice among the nations, but because no nation can hope to live in peace and security under a system of international justice which, however perfect in theory, is in practice menaced by the pressure that armaments may bring to bear on inter-State relations. . . .

. . . In any case, work is being done, ideas are being clarified and—let us be frank—the interests served by international solidarity are being proclaimed and defined. Our business now is to organise, to safeguard and to clear the way, and that we cannot do so long as our efforts at collective organisation are paralysed by the race for armaments.

In this connection, one of the most delicate questions of international policy—the financial obligations arising out of the war—is not without some bearing on the disarmament problem. There is, of course, no diplomatic connection between disarmament, reparations and debts; but nobody will deny the moral connection between them.

Before nations sacrifice their rights, they must be persuaded of the usefulness of the sacrifices demanded of them, and it is difficult to see the usefulness of any fresh settlement of the financial obligations arising out of the war, as long as the race for armaments continues.

We cannot deny the justice of an observation put forward more than once—the sacrifices made must not, by permitting the increase of armaments, be allowed to aggravate the present state of insecurity, which, more than anything, is militating against a general economic recovery, and is one of the fundamental causes, if not the main cause, of the present unsettled situation.

One other observation is relevant in connection with this general economic problem. All countries are suffering as the result of the continual increase in Customs barriers, a protectionist policy which means that the economic development of the various countries is proceeding on individual lines, and prevents the sound development of the process of integration which alone can secure effective economic collaboration between States. One of the immediate causes of the retention and strengthening of these Customs barriers, which have the effect of dividing the world into often extremely small commercial units, and which have had, and still have, the effect of dispersing the efforts of the nations, is the general state of political insecurity which drives nations to organise a system of economic security and to snatch at all costs at some independent means of defence for possible use against dangers that may threaten them from without.

I am well aware that the protectionist fever from which the world is suffering to-day has other more general causes; but, in Europe, undoubtedly one of those causes is an obscure sentiment of danger—possibly a vague and distant danger—which we must do our best to allay. What the countries of Europe want is tranquillity. Let the more powerful States give the less powerful ones a feeling of general security, and let that feeling of general security rest, not only on their avowed will to peace, but on a definite and equitable adjustment of the relations between them, and we shall see the disappearance—as if by magic—of all the special political reasons for what I might describe as economic armaments. Let us lay down our arms, and we shall see the reduction of those barriers, sometimes ridiculously high, which separate the economic systems of our nations.

In my Government's view, therefore, disarmament is the starting-point of many things—the putting into execution of the system of security and peace created by the Covenant, the establishment of greater confidence between States, and the re-establishment of laws of economic integration which have suffered such ruthless violation.

That is the most urgent item in the League's programme; that is the task most closely in keeping with the League's essential purpose. . . .

The Disarmament Conference has been convened and will begin work on February 2nd. My observations may therefore appear superfluous; indeed, I hope that they will prove so. Naturally, they do not refer to the convening of the Conference, but to the policy that may be adopted by the Governments represented there, to the ideas they may bring to it, and to the methods they intend to follow. Now is the time for courage, moderation and above all, common sense. Each one of us must realise the difficulties of the others, must state his own requirements frankly, limiting them to what is really essential, and must reduce his armaments to the lowest point consistent with national safety, and the enforcement by common action of international obligations, within the meaning of Article 8 of the Covenant.

I am, however, inclined to think that, during the actual period of preparation for the Disarmament Conference, States which have definitely undertaken to participate in the Conference might adopt provisional measures. The Council of the League, as you know, suggested preliminary discussions. Acting on that recommendation, we might do really useful work by adopting practical measures without delay. My own feeling is that we ought to try immediately to arrive at a really effective armaments truce, at least for the period of the Conference, and I should like to ask you seriously to consider my suggestion.

A general and immediate agreement between States to suspend the execution of programmes for fresh armaments would not only set our peoples an example of goodwill, but would create a psychological and political atmosphere of greater calm and confidence, which would do more than any declaration of principles to further the work of the Conference and lead to tangible results.

In this connection I may inform you that His Majesty the King of Italy has just signed the General Act for the Pacific Settlement of International Disputes, and I have received from my Government instructions with a view to the accession of Italy to the General Convention to strengthen the Means of preventing War, should that Convention be approved by the Assembly.

I have already had occasion to explain to the Council the importance attached by Italy to the General Act, an instrument which we regard as a welcome addition to the technical machinery of international justice.

Our present duty is to create the conditions for the functioning of international justice. I have no wish unduly to stress my point of view, nor was it my desire, in directing your attention to the disarmament problem, to exclude other questions which call for consideration, or to pass over the fact that disarmament is only one element in the much more complex problem of the international situation. It does, however, seem to me to be the most urgent problem, and a problem which must be settled before we can hope to solve the others.

I do not propose now to go into the economic questions affecting international relations at this difficult period of the life of the peoples. The Italian delegation will certainly have occasion, in the course of our proceedings, to explain its attitude towards these questions, the technical nature of which necessitates careful and detailed study.

The further we get away from the great war, the more keenly do we realise the terrible wounds which it inflicted on all countries without distinction—wounds which we should find it impossible to heal were it not for the fact that the spirit of sacrifice which the war brought out in all the belligerent countries itself engendered powers of resistance which have enabled countries to defend their civilisation—reserves which encourage them to face the future with greater confidence.

We are all counting upon that spirit now, and Europe can count on the spirit of the Italian people. Still, as I said, individual national action is not enough, while the creation of exclusive groups might injure, rather than further, the cause of co-operation, security and peace.

As a matter of fact, since the war, European policy has been distracted by the conflict between two great forces which it has not yet been possible to adjust: on the one hand, the collective movement towards establishing a regime of more systematic and stable co-operation than any which has existed before, and, on the other, the tendency of particular States to form themselves into independent groups for the defence of their national interests—in our opinion, a very doubtful solution of the problem of international co-operation.

A collective effort on the part of European and non-European nations, whether Members of the League or not, is necessary to correct these conflicting tendencies, and to discourage the idea of creating exclusive groups in Europe. Such groups are not, in our opinion, in accordance with the conception embodied in the Covenant of regional understandings for securing the maintenance of peace. On the contrary, they have the effect of creating divisions highly prejudicial to the peace and tranquillity of nations. It is a mistake to think that it represents a first stage towards the formation of a larger group. The formation of *blocs,* in the form either of military alliances or agreements for the furtherance of particular interests or special regimes, inevitably leads to the creation of other *blocs.* This automatically entails the establishment of powerful associations of interests which tend to form separate centres of action and watch one another.

If we desire to establish a real system of peace, it must be based on real international interests. That is a delicate problem of adjustment as between the particular interests of individual States and the organic system of international co-operation. The Covenant provides us with a happy solution of the problem, and we ought not only to respect that solution but to deduce from it general rules of conduct applicable in our international relations.

We all form one single group, and our dearest hope is to see it expand rather than disintegrate. We trust that the League of Nations may become a true reflection of the solidarity of nations, of all States, great and small, European and non-European, all helping to further their common civilisation, a civilisation which it is our duty not only to protect, but to strengthen and extend. . . .

ADDRESS by Benito Mussolini, Premier, before the General Staff of the Italian Army, August 24, 1934

Translation, in Royal Institute of International Affairs, *Documents on International Affairs, 1934,* p. 362, citing *The Times* (London), August 28, 1934; excerpt

NOBODY IN present-day Europe deliberately seeks war. Least of all does Italy, and of this fact she has given innumerable positive proofs. None the less, war is a possibility and may break out unexpectedly from one minute to the next. In some distant countries it has already done so. In Europe also at the end of July there arose, unforeseen and dramatically, a situation recalling in a particular manner 1914. It may be added that, if we had not as a precautionary step promptly sent divisions to our eastern and northern frontiers, there would have been a danger of those complications arising which at a given moment are not to be solved except by armed intervention. I would also add that these divisions marched magnificently in stages of 37 and even of 66 miles with a high morale which evoked the admiration and respect of our frontier populations.

It is, therefore, necessary to be prepared for war not to-morrow but to-day. We are becoming—and shall become so increasingly because this is our desire—a military nation. A militaristic nation, I will add, since we are not afraid of words. To complete the picture, warlike—that is to say, endowed ever to a higher degree with the virtues of obedience, sacrifice, and dedication to country. This means that the whole life of a nation, political, economic, and spiritual, must be systematically directed towards our military requirements. War has been described as the Court of Appeal between nations. And since the peoples do not become crystallized but pursue the course dictated by their strength and by their historical dynamic nature, it follows that, in spite of all conferences, all protocols, and all the more or less highest and good intentions, the hard fact of war may be anticipated to accompany the human kind in the centuries to come just as it stands on record at the dawn of human history.

To-day all those called back to the colours resume their arms and grey-green uniforms with enthusiasm. What is still more important, the whole people if called upon to-morrow will answer like a single man. I recall to you that military forces represent the essential element in the hierarchy of the nation. Nothing has yet been discovered which can take the place of that which is the clearest, most tangible, most decisive expression of the total strength of an entire people—that is to say, the size, the prestige, the power of its arms on land, on the sea, and in the air.

ADDRESS by Benito Mussolini, Premier, at Milan, October 6, 1934

Translation, in Royal Institute of International Affairs, *Documents on International Affairs, 1934,* p. 363, citing *Corriere della Sera,* October 6, 1934; excerpt

I WOULD NOW give you a rapid survey of the international horizon, limiting it to the countries whose frontiers march with ours and whose relations with us can never be one of indifference: either we must be friends or foes.

Let us begin in the East. It is evident that there are no great possibilities of the improvement of our relations with our neighbours beyond the snows and on the other side of the Adriatic while they continue the press polemics which wound us so deeply.

A first condition of a policy of friendship which does not rest frigidly correct within the terms of diplomatic protocols but descends a little to the heart of the people—a first condition is that the valour of the Italian army should not in the slightest way be called in question—that army which has fought on through thick and thin, which has left its mangled bodies in the trenches of the Carso, in those of Macedonia and of Bligny, which has contributed more than 600,000 dead to the common victory, a victory which began to be "common" only in June and upon the banks of the Piave. Nevertheless we, since we feel and are strong, can once more offer the possibility of an agreement for which precise *de facto* conditions exist. We have defended and will defend the independence of the Austrian Republic, an independence which has been consecrated by the blood of a Chancellor who may have been small in stature but whose spirit and soul were great.

Those who assert that Italy has any aggressive aims, or that she wishes to establish some kind of protectorate over that Republic, are either ignorant of the facts or are consciously lying.

This gives me a chance to say that the development of European history without Germany is inconceivable, but it is equally necessary that certain circles in Germany should not give the impression that it is Germany who wishes to withdraw herself from the course of European history.

Our relations with Switzerland are of the best and will remain so, not only for the next ten years but for a longer period than can at present be foreseen. We desire only that Italian culture should be preserved and strengthened in *Canton Ticino,* not only in our own interest but above all in the interest and for the future of the Swiss Republic.

It is clear that within less than a year our relations with France have ameliorated . . . the atmosphere has improved and, if we reach an agreement which we strongly desire, this will be very useful and very fruitful for both countries and in the general interest of Europe. All this will be seen between the end of October and the beginning of November.

The improvement in relations between the peoples of Europe is all the more important in that the Disarmament Conference has failed. No one doubts that Citizen Henderson, like any other self-respecting Englishman, is a tenacious man, but nevertheless he will not succeed in any way in bringing to life again the "disarmist Lazarus" crushed and buried under the weight of cruisers and cannons. In this state of affairs you will not be surprised that we have decided definitely upon the complete and military preparation of the Italian people.

ADDRESS by Benito Mussolini, Premier, in the Chamber of Deputies, May 25, 1935

Translation, in Royal Institute of International Affairs, *Documents on International Affairs, 1935,* I, 175, citing *Corriere della Sera,* May 26, 1935; excerpt

THE TIME has not yet come for me to give a general outline of the activities of the Fascist Government in the field of foreign policy, such as I gave before the Senate in June 1928. Many problems are still unsolved, certain important diplomatic conversations are still in progress, even the relative positions of the Powers are continually shifting according as their interests coincide more, or less, or not at all, with regard to such questions as may arise.

Our actions must be founded on political realism, that is to say, on an accurate valuation of international forces, their interrelated interests and their inevitable transformations. This is, of course, the case with all States worthy of the name. Having laid down this principle, I will confine my speech to the events nearest to us in time. Together with the budget of the Ministry for Foreign Affairs, the whole group of Franco-Italian agreements signed last January has been laid before you for approval. These agreements form a systematic compromise for the settlement of certain questions connected with Article 13 of the Treaty of London, an article drafted in an "excessively" conditional form, as any one who reads it again will notice. Such agreements, which, taken as a whole, may be considered satisfactory, mean the turning over of a new page in the post-War history of Franco-Italian relations, and they establish the necessary conditions for an effective collaboration between the two countries, as was explicitly stated in the general declaration.

Some people have asked why such agreements have only been concluded seventeen years after the end of the War. I answer that the delay has been caused by the complexity of the interests involved, by the new situations which have arisen in Europe, and also by the existence of pitiful illusions, piously cultivated nevertheless in certain circles in France, with regard to the stability of the Fascist régime.

My duty to take an objective view compels me to add that such illusions seem to have vanished once and for all into thin air.

In the same way I wish to lay stress on the fact that the state of feeling between the two peoples has for some time been much improved; let us hope that nothing in future will happen to trouble it again.

After the signing of the Franco-Italian agreements in January, the British and French Governments met together in London in February, and laid down certain points of fundamental importance for what was then the political situation in Europe.

The Franco-British Conference in London may be considered as a continuation of the Franco-Italian Conference in Rome. Optimists were led to foresee a normal development of the European situation when, on the following March 16, this normal development was shattered by Germany's unilateral denunciation of Part V, the disarmament chapter, of the Versailles Treaty.

The world was faced with an accomplished fact, which was commented upon by three diplomatic protests. This happened during a series of explorations. Every one was at once convinced that such an accomplished fact was irrevocable.

At this point there is some interest, if only in retrospect, in letting it be known that, in January 1934, Germany was disposed to accept an infinitely more limited realization of her equality of rights, a realization which consisted in an army of 300,000 men, with armaments which, at least for a certain period of years, would be defensive only and subject to control on the lines of the Italian memorandum.

But what has not happened is no subject for history, and recriminations are useless, even as it is useless to go on talking about disarmament.

It is very difficult for us to believe in the possibility of a limitation of armaments or the prohibition of certain methods of warfare. Nevertheless, if anything definite is going to be done, it is not we who will put difficulties in the way.

The waters were still very troubled, and with them the spirit of the nations, when the April Conference was convened at Stresa.

Without exaggerating its intrinsic importance, the Conference was sufficiently decisive in that it established the solidarity of the three Western Powers in the face of certain urgent problems.

It is certain that, with such an effective, constant, and omnipresent solidarity, political action is possible on a large scale, with the aim of eliminating the principal obstacles which hinder the races of Europe from living together in that peace which is an increasingly necessary condition of the existence and future of our continent.

At Stresa the decision was taken to convene another conference to deal with the problems of the Danubian basin; such a conference cannot now be held early in June as was previously stated; I may add that it will not be convened unless the ground has been prepared, and prepared very diligently. The Italo-Austro-Hungarian meeting at Venice was intended to serve, and has served, this purpose; I also wish to say that the Austro-Hungarian requests are not such as to hinder the attainment of the desirable objectives which the conference has set itself to reach.

With regard to Germany, our proposal, already communicated to Berlin, is that she should be invited to the conference and kept informed of the successive phases of its preparation.

After the Franco-Russian and Russo-Czechoslovak conventions, conventions which have upset the balance of forces, the German Chancellor's speech was awaited with great interest.

His thirteen points cannot be either accepted or rejected as a whole; it would be preferable to define them more clearly and study them more deeply. It is not out of the question that diplomacy will undertake this task in the next few weeks.

With regard to Italo-German relations, it is true that there is only one problem which compromises them, that of Austria. This problem, however, is of the greatest importance.

It may therefore not be out of place, now that we have reached this subject, to address a few words to those who would like to fossilize us on the Brenner to prevent us from moving in any other part of the world.

It must also be stated once and for all, and with no possibility of doubt, that the problem of Austrian independence is an Austrian and European problem. In so far as it is European it is a particularly, but not exclusively, Italian problem.

In other words Fascist Italy does not mean to limit her historic mission to a single political problem, or to a single military sector such as the defence of a frontier, even such an important one as the

Brenner, because all our frontiers, at home and in the colonies, are indistinguishably sacred, and must be vigilantly defended against any threat whatsoever, even if it is only a potential one. . . .

ADDRESS by Benito Mussolini, Premier, at Avellino, Italy, August 30, 1936

Delivered before 20,000 soldiers, Fascists, and peasants, at the annual war games, and broadcast. Translation, in *Vital Speeches of the Day*, October 1, 1936, p. 824

OFFICERS, non-commissioned officers, soldiers, Black Shirts, and people of Hirpinia:

Listen to me while I speak to you and to the Italian people.

The grand manoeuvres of the fourteenth year of Fascism have ended. They have developed, from the first to the last day, in an atmosphere vibrant with enthusiasm.

The generous hospitality of the Hirpinian people has enveloped the participating units in its atmosphere.

Your fervent patriotism and your dedication to the régime make you worthy, O comrades of Hirpinia, of having had take place in your magnificent territory the grand manoeuvres of the first year of the Fascist empire.

Tomorrow on the plains of Volturara, before His Majesty Victor Emmanuel, King of Italy and Emperor of Ethiopia, will pass more than 60,000 men, 200 tanks, 400 pieces of heavy artillery, 400 mortars, 3,000 machine guns, and 2,800 armored cars.

This aggregation of men and means is imposing, but it represents at most a modest and almost insignificant total in comparison to the total of men and means on which Italy can surely count.

I invite Italians to take absolutely to heart this declaration of mine.

Not despite the African war, but as a consequence of the African war all the armed forces of Italy today are more efficient than ever.

We always, in the course of a few hours and after a simple order, can mobilize 8,000,000 men.

It is a formidable bloc that fourteen years of Fascist régime have prepared at white heat with great sacrifice.

The Italian people should know that their internal peace and that abroad will be protected and, with it, the peace of the world.

With the most crushing of victories in one of the most just wars, Italy, with war in Africa, has acquired an immense, rich, imperial territory where for many decades she will be able to carry out the achievements of her labors and of her creative ability.

For this reason, but only for this reason, will we reject the absurdity of eternal peace, which is foreign to our creed and to our temperament.

We desire to live a long time at peace with all; we are determined to offer our lasting, concrete contribution to the project of collaboration among peoples. But after the catastrophic failure of the disarmament conference, in the face of an armaments race already under way and irresistible from this time on, and in the face of certain political situations which now are in the course of uncertain development, the order of the day for Italians, for Fascist Italians, can be only this:

We must be strong. We must be always stronger. We must be so strong that we can face any eventualities and look directly in the eye whatever may befall.

To this supreme principle must be subordinated and will be subordinated all the life of the nation.

The conquest of the empire was not obtained by compromises on that table of diplomacy. It was obtained by fine, glorious, and victorious battle, fought with the spirit which has overcome enormous material difficulties and an almost world-wide coalition of nations.

It is the spirit of the Black Shirt revolution, the spirit of this Italy, the spirit of this populous Italy, warlike and vigilant on sea, on land, and in the heavens.

It is the spirit I have seen shining in the eyes of the soldiers who have manoeuvred in these past days, the spirit we shall see shine when King and country call them.

Since the manoeuvres last year, twelve months have passed: twelve months only, but how many events, how much history, has passed in these twelve months! They have been rich in events the influence of which is felt today but will be felt still more in the course of time.

Before concluding this meeting I ask you:

Were old accounts settled? [The crowd shouted "Yes!"]

And have we marched straight ahead up to now? [The crowd: "Yes!"]

I tell you, I promise you, we will do likewise tomorrow and always.

STATEMENT by Count Galeazzo Ciano, Minister for Foreign Affairs, at the End of His Visit to Germany, October 25, 1936

Translation, in Royal Institute of International Affairs, *Documents on International Affairs, 1936*, p. 341, citing *The Times* (London), October 26, 1936

During the last few days in conversations with the Führer at Berchtesgaden, and with Baron von Neurath in Berlin, I have had a thorough exchange of views on the political situation in general, and this exchange of views has emphasized the determination of our two Governments to cooperate in the interests of peace and reconstruction. This joint activity finds a solid basis not only in the common interests of our two countries but in the supreme obligation assumed by Germany and Italy to defend the great institutions of Europe.

In this connection we examined the negotiations now proceeding to replace the Treaty of Locarno. As you know, the German Government, as well as the Italian, have already sent their reply to the British memorandum, and both Governments have emphasized their specific desire to collaborate in establishing such conditions of security as may arise from a guarantee pact for Western Europe.

We also examined with Baron von Neurath various aspects of the problem of the League of Nations. As in the past our two Governments will continue to remain in close and friendly contact.

As regards the situation in the Danube Basin I can say that, after examining this situation in the light of the Protocol of Rome and the Austro-German Agreement of July 11, we were able to state to our mutual satisfaction the practical and positive results to the benefit of Austria which this policy has already brought about. Both Governments will treat the problems concerning the Danubian Basin in a spirit of friendly collaboration.

We have also taken into consideration the situation in Spain and have agreed to recognize the fact that the National Government of General Franco is supported by the firm will of the Spanish population in the larger part of the national area, where it has succeeded in re-establishing order and civil discipline in contrast with the anarchical conditions prevailing there hitherto. At the same time we have once more confirmed the principle of non-intervention in Spanish affairs, as well as the maintenance of the international obligations entered into in that spirit. It is superfluous to add that we have agreed in affirming that Italy and Germany have no other wish than that Spain shall as soon as possible resume, with absolute national and colonial integrity, her due place in the community of nations.

With regard to the serious dangers which threaten the social structure of Europe, the Führer and Baron von Neurath on the one side and I on the other have renewed the firm determination of the Italian and German peoples to defend with all energy the sacred inheritance of European civilization in its great institutions based on family and nation. In this spirit we have decided with Baron von Neurath to further the cultural relations between Germany and Italy, and, immediately after my return to Rome, we shall initiate conversations which will lead to an agreement for cultural exchanges between the two countries.

As was announced yesterday, the Führer has decided to recognize the Italian Empire of Ethiopia. I need not tell you with what satisfaction I have taken cognizance of this decision. We have now regulated Italo-German trade relations with regard to Ethiopia, and the various unsettled questions will be solved to the mutual satisfaction of both countries. All these points were laid down verbatim in a *procès-verbal* which was drafted after the conclusion of the conversations.

I return to Italy with a feeling of sincere admiration for everything I have seen in Germany, a feeling which, in the first place, is directed towards the Führer, to whom I convey the greetings of the Duce and of Fascist Italy.

I did not know Germany, and therefore, as you can well imagine, I have in recent years and almost day by day followed the Nazi movement and the great work of national reconstruction carried out under the guiding inspiration and creative impulse of the Führer. All that I have seen has given me a vivid and clear impression, and the contacts which I have made with your statesmen, the institutions which I have visited, and the demonstrations at which I have been present, have completed in my mind the general picture of Nazi Germany, to which go out my deep and sincere good wishes. The cordial contacts between our two Governments will be maintained, and our collaboration for the general peace and reconstruction of Europe will be continued, in Rome as well as in Berlin, in the same spirit and with the same determination with which we have begun it during these last few days.

ADDRESS by Benito Mussolini, Premier, at Milan, November 1, 1936

Translation, in *International Conciliation,* January, 1937, p. 122

BLACK SHIRTS OF MILAN:

By means of the speech which I am about to make to you and for which I ask, and you will give me, a few dozen minutes of your attention, I intend to lay down the position of Fascist Italy with regard to its relations with other peoples in this so turgid and disquieting moment.

The high level of your political education allows me to lay before you these problems which elsewhere are debated in so-called parliaments or after so-called democratic banquets.

I shall be extremely brief, but I add that every one of my words has been weighed.

If one wishes to clarify the European atmosphere it is first necessary to clear the table of all illusions, of all commonplaces, of all conventional lies that still constitute relics of the great shipwreck of Wilsonian ideology.

One of these illusions that is already flat is the illusion of disarmament. No one wishes to disarm first, and for all to disarm together is impossible and absurd. And still, when the conference for disarmament meets in Geneva, the illusion functions in full. The result is a mountain of bombastic oratory. On this mountain is concentrated for some days all the glare of the projectors of world publicity. Then, at a certain moment, out from the mountain comes a tiny mouse, which finally is lost in a labyrinth of procedure which for fertile invention has no precedent in history.

For us Fascisti, in the habit of examining with cool eye the reality of life and of history, another illusion we reject is that which passed by the name of collective security. Collective security never existed, does not exist, and will never exist. A virile people provides within its own borders its collective security and refuses to confide its destiny to uncertain hands of third persons.

Another platitude which it is necessary to reject is indivisible peace. Indivisible peace could have only this meaning: indivisible war. But peoples refuse, and justly so, to fight for interests that do not concern them.

The very League of Nations is based upon an absurdity which consists of the criterion of absolute juridical parity among all States;

whereas the States are different from one another, at least from the viewpoint of their historic responsibility.

For the League of Nations the dilemma is expressed in very clear terms, either to reform itself or to perish.

Since it is extremely difficult for the League to reform itself, as far as we are concerned it can perish in peace.

In any event, we have not forgotten and we shall not forget that the League of Nations by diabolical methods has organized an iniquitous siege against the people of Italy, has tried to starve these people, men, women, and children, has sought to shatter our military force and the work of civilization being carried on 2,500 to 5,000 miles distant in another land. It did not succeed: not because it did not want to, but because it found itself faced by the compact unity of the Italian people, capable of all sacrifices and also of fighting the fifty-two coalition States.

Now, in order to make a policy of peace it is not necessary to pass through the corridors of the League of Nations. Here, O comrades, I made what in navigation is called the ship's position. After seventeen years of polemics, recrimination, and misunderstandings of problems left in suspense, accords with France were reached in January, 1935.

These accords could and should have opened a new epoch of truly friendly relations between the two countries. But sanctions came along. Naturally, friendship experienced its first freezing.

We were then on the eve of winter. Winter passed; spring came and with spring our triumphant victories. Sanctions continued to be applied with truly meticulous vigor.

For almost two months after we were in Addis Ababa sanctions still continued.

It is a classical case of the letter which kills the spirit; of formalism which strangles the living, concrete reality of life!

France today still holds her finger pointed at the yellowing ledgers of Geneva, saying:

"The empire of the lion of Judah is still alive."

But beyond the masters of Geneva, what in reality does our victory mean? That the empire of the ex-Negus is more than dead.

And it is quite evident that as long as the French Government maintains toward us an attitude of waiting and reserve we cannot but do the same toward her.

One of the countries bordering Italy, with whom our relations were and are and always will be extremely friendly, is Switzerland. It is a little country but of very great importance both for its ethnical composition and for its geographical position, which it occupies at the crossroads of Europe.

By the accords of July 11 a new epoch was opened in the history of modern Austria. The accords of July 11—let all hurried and badly informed commentators take note—were known and approved by me as of June 5, and it is my conviction that such accords strengthened the governmental make-up of this State, giving greater guarantee for its independence.

Until justice shall be rendered to Hungary there cannot be a definite systematization of interests in the Danubian Basin.

Hungary is a truly great but disabled veteran. Four million Magyars live beyond her present borders. By desiring to follow the dictate of too abstract justice, one fell into an injustice that is perhaps greater.

The sentiments of the Italian people toward the Magyar people are marked by thorough recognition—which, moreover, is reciprocal—of their military qualities, their courage, and their spirit of sacrifice.

There will perhaps come soon a solemn occasion in which the sentiments of the Italian people will find public, clamorous manifestation.

The fourth country bordering Italy is Yugoslavia. Recently the atmosphere between the two countries was greatly improved. You will remember that about two years ago in this same square I made a clear reference to the possibility of establishing relations of cordial friendship between the two countries. Speaking again on this same subject today, I declare that necessary conditions, moral, political, and economic, exist today for putting relations between these two countries on a new basis of true and concrete friendship.

In addition to these four countries bordering Italy, a great country recently aroused vast sympathy from the masses of the Italian people: I speak of Germany.

The meetings at Berlin had as a result an understanding between the two countries on definite problems, some of which are particularly troublesome these days.

But these understandings which have been consecrated and duly signed—this Berlin-Rome protocol—is not a barrier, but is rather an axis around which all European States animated by the will for collaboration and for peace may collaborate.

Germany, although surrounded and solicited, did not adhere to sanctions. By the accord of July 11 an element of dissension between Berlin and Rome disappeared. May I remind you, even before the meeting in Berlin, Germany had practically recognized the Empire of Rome.

It is no wonder if we today raise the banner of anti-Bolshevism. This is our old banner!

We were born under this sign! We have fought against this enemy! We have conquered him through our sacrifices of blood!

This is because what is called Bolshevism and communism is today —listen well to me—only super-capitalism of a State carried to its most ferocious extreme. It is not, therefore, the negation of a system, but the development and sublimation of this system, and the time has come to put an end to it. This might be by opposing Fascism and democracy to it. Truly, one can say that this, our great Italy, is still the great unknown.

If many of those Ministers and Deputies and such who speak in order to listen to themselves decided just once to cross the frontiers of Italy they would be convinced that if there is a country where concrete, real, and substantial democracy has been realized this country is Italy of the Fascist era. We are not like reactionaries of other countries. We are not embalmers of the past: we are anticipators of the future.

We do not carry to its extreme consequences the capitalistic civilization, above all in its mechanical, almost inhuman aspect. We create a new synthesis through which fascism opens the road to a human, true civilization of work.

I have concerned myself up to this point with the Continent. But Italy is an island. It is necessary for Italians little by little to take on an insular mentality, because it is the only method for taking all problems of naval defense of the nation in their true light.

Italy is an island which emerges from the Mediterranean.

This sea—I address myself here also toward the English, who perhaps at this moment are listening by radio—this sea for Great Britain is a highroad, one of the many highroads or, rather, short cuts through which the British Empire reaches its outlying territory more rapidly.

Let it be said between parentheses that when the Italian Negrelli projected the cutting of the Isthmus of Suez he was considered— above all, in England—as scatterbrained.

If the Mediterranean is for others a highroad, for us Italians it is life.

We have said a thousand times, and I repeat before this magnificent multitude, that we do not intend to menace this road, we do not intend to interrupt it. But we demand on the other hand that our rights and vital interests be also respected. There are no other alternatives. The reasoning brains of the British Empire must realize the thing is done and is irrevocable. The sooner the better. Bilateral conflicts are not to be thought of, and even less a conflict which from bilateral would become immediately European.

There is, therefore, only one solution: direct, rapid, and complete understanding on the basis of recognition of reciprocal interests.

But if this does not come about, if in fact—and I refuse to believe it from today on—one is really thinking of suffocating the life of the Italian people in that sea which was the sea of Rome, very well! Let it be known that the Italian people would spring to their feet like one man, ready for combat with a determination which would have scarce precedence in history.

Milan Comrades, let us turn to our own affairs: Marching orders for the fifteenth year of fascism are the following: Peace with all, with those near and afar. Armed peace!

Therefore, our program of armaments for land, sea, and sky will be regularly developed.

Acceleration of all productive energies of the nation, in agricultural and industrial fields. Development of the corporative system to its definite realization.

But here is a duty I confide to you, O Milanese of this most ardent and most Fascist Milan which has revealed its great soul these days. I confide to you, O Milanese of this generous working and untiring Milan, this duty:

You must place yourselves, as you will place yourselves, as an advance guard for the development of the empire so as to make it in the shortest possible period an element of well being, of power, of glory for the nation.

ADDRESS by Count Galeazzo Ciano, Minister for Foreign Affairs, before the Fascist Chamber, May 13, 1937

Translation, in Royal Institute of International Affairs, *Documents on International Affairs, 1937*, p. 271, citing *Corriere della Sera*, May 14, 1937; excerpts

IN GIVING a report to the Fascist Chamber of activity in the realm of foreign policy I think it would be useful, in the interests of clarity and brevity, to recapitulate chronologically the principal events of recent months, in order to facilitate a better orientation in regard to the present situation.

On July 15, 1936, Year XIV of the Fascist era, the sanctions experiment of Geneva terminated with the final surrender of the besiegers—an experiment sterile, but instructive not only because it gave a striking proof of Italian military and civic virtue but also because, when first put to the test, certain ideologies which had found favour and supporters in the world, if not with us, were shown up in their true light as artificial and dangerous. It was necessary to refer to this at once in order to clarify the general situation in Europe at the end of the Ethiopian campaign. Upon all international relations and also upon the internal situation of many States the failure of the collective policy had repercussions of singular importance. It cannot be overlooked in examining subsequent events and developments in European policy.

As soon as Italy issued from her great trial of strength she gave clear proof of a desire to collaborate with others by communicating to the League of Nations on June 29, 1936, the full and fruitful programme of work which was assigned to present and future generations in the land of the new conquest. Even those who are always ready to sound the alarm when we make any gesture of this nature had to admit on this occasion that Fascist Italy had given proof of great balance and exceptional moderation. There were also those, whose consciences were less sensitive after all that had happened, who felt vaguely uneasy in regard to our country. Everything, taking into account certain explicit statements, which had, however, not been solicited by us, led one to believe that with a gesture of courageous and dutiful loyalty the justice and the good cause of Rome would be recognized in the new reality of the Italian Empire.

I must emphasize at once, in order to avoid any misunderstanding or false interpretation of my words, that we have neither demanded nor solicited the recognition of the Empire. Our policy is based too solidly on a sound realism to attribute substantial value to a gesture which is, after all, purely formal, and a matter of reciprocal interest. Further, it is no new thing that the recognitions are slow in coming. But history does not for this reason stay her course. . . .

The absence of so-called *de jure* recognition—and the difference between it and what is described as *de facto* recognition is so subtle as often to put the tired-out jurists in doubt—does not rob the crown of our victory of one laurel leaf or prevent the tricolor from fluttering in the sky of an Empire conquered, pacified and at work.

But I will add at once that this recognition has been highly acceptable when it has come as a spontaneous manifestation from those nations, and they are now many, which have thereby wished to signify their friendship for Italy and to offer her their collaboration.

One often hears the question asked: What is the position of Italy in the League of Nations? What will be her future attitude? Sometimes even these questions are put in such an ambiguous manner as to make one suspect that they conceal within them warning or blandishment.

To this we reply comprehensively that our present and future attitude is bound up with what the League of Nations will do and what it will become.

In his speech at Milan, the *Duce* expressed his view of the League of Nations with laconic brevity and sculptural clearness, when he said: "Either it must renew itself or perish."

Today even the most fervent supporters of the League idea admit that the old ship is leaking in every plank; but instead of establishing the fault in the system, instead of recognizing that the institution has shown itself to be unequal to the task which it has assumed, when faced with the many tests which it has been compelled to undergo, they still attempt to save the essence of it by attributing the various failures which it has suffered to a lack of League spirit on the part of its various Members.

Does not, however, the very fact that the League fails to inspire complete confidence even in its most active Members prove that it is ineffective and that its life is artificial?

Nevertheless, even in regard to the problem of the reform of the League, Italy preserves an attitude of waiting, which, though not over-confident, is still not dogmatically sceptical.

I will state—for the contrary rumour frequently circulates—that we have no plan of reform to launch at the appropriate moment. Motives of gratitude towards the League, such as might induce us to rescue it in its extremity, frankly, we lack. If our country's history has followed its great course, we owe it to the genius of a chief and to the faith of a people. Geneva, on her side, has done her best to give a very different turn to the affair.

Therefore, we shall take no initiative, either now or in the future. But if a real occasion were to arise for rendering service to the cause of peace, which we desire with firm, realistic and objective will, the Fascist Government would not fail to offer their constructive collaboration.

In July last, in a European atmosphere that was already complex, the Spanish revolution began. The movement broke out in consequence of a series of crimes and political vendettas which induced General Franco and the other heads of the army, in whom were vested the honour and the prestige of Spain, to cease temporizing and to declare open hostilities against a Government which was preparing to subject the country to the ideologies and to the systems of international Bolshevism.

During the development of the conflict international sympathy tended towards one side or the other, according to the internal régime of each country. Europe threatened to divide into two opposing camps. In the face of this danger the well-known decision was taken to form the Non-Intervention Committee. From the beginning, Italy, inspired by a constant and firm spirit of realism, offered her contribution. As far back as August 3, 1936, we saw the problem as a whole and pointed out the necessity of assuming definite undertakings also as regarded the prohibition of public subscriptions and the dispatch of volunteers to either side in the conflict. Our suggestion was not accepted. The struggle continued and assumed ever greater proportions. As was to be foreseen, volunteers flocked in numbers to join the two opposing sides.

The measures adopted by the London Committee in order to limit the conflict are known; others are still under examination. Although in the practical application of the measures of control certain gaps have been discovered, such as to make us slightly sceptical of the complete efficacy of the control system, nevertheless, we declare and confirm that for our part we shall respect the undertakings that we have given with Fascist loyalty and scrupulousness.

The formal recognition given on November 18, 1936, by the Fascist Government, together with that of the Reich, to the Government of General Franco finds its justification in the incontrovertible fact that the delivered area of Spain consists of more than three-fifths of its territory, inhabited by a clear numerical majority of the population; it is also a token of sympathy for the valorous soldier who had inspired and led the national revival of his people.

Having thus defined with precision the elements of Italy's loyal collaboration in the policy of non-intervention, I feel it my duty to point to the grave danger represented by the periodical attacks of a section of the international press, which in its attitude towards Italy continues to be inspired solely by feelings of resentment, hate, and falsehood.

When recent events are recorded with the objectivity of history and not with the partisanship of certain newspapers, it will be definitely proved that the victorious courage of the Italian volunteers in Spain in their struggle against the Red tyranny has proved itself, in every place and occasion, worthy of its heroic traditions.

I have already referred to the danger that Europe might be divided into two opposing *blocs* as a result of the Spanish conflict. And since there has been much talk and discussion on this subject, and since the responsibility for such an occurrence is being potentially placed to the debit of a number of countries, I think it well to recall that ever since the *Duce* has directed our foreign policy, he has always strenuously sought to prevent Europe being divided into two hostile camps, and that the wide and deep gap which the Treaty of Versailles had already created between the Great Powers should not become incapable of being filled. For fifteen years Italy has endeavoured to facilitate a policy of conciliation and cooperation between those countries which the War had divided, and with this object Europe has been reminded several times of the necessity of meeting the material and moral needs of Germany, who of her own right, as well as in the international interest, should resume her proper position in the work of European reconstruction. It was not possible to expect an effective and sincere contribution from the German people as long as they were crushed under the burden of the reparations, penalized and restricted in their activities as a Sovereign State. Fascism has always proclaimed this truth, and we were the first to assert the need of putting an end to a paradoxical position which prevented Germany from being restored to her full rights and her historic functions.

No one can read into our policy an intention to create dangerous and threatening divisions. On more than one occasion the policy of Fascist Italy and that of Nazi Germany were found to be advancing on parallel lines.

This was particularly evident as regards the Western Pact, Belgian security, policy towards Austria and the Basin of the Danube in general, the stand against Bolshevism, and the Spanish affair and, more particularly, the question of non-intervention in the territorial integrity of Spain and the recognition of General Franco's National Government—all questions on which the international activity of Europe has been centered in recent months.

The parallelism of policy, which already existed and which has become ever more clearly marked, was confirmed and regularized by personal contact on the occasion of my journey to Berlin. The recent visits of the Minister for Foreign Affairs of the Reich and of other Nazi authorities have strengthened and brought continually up to date this fruitful collaboration.

It is no *bloc* that we have formed. It has already been stated that the political system between Rome and Berlin is an axis and not a diaphragm. It draws its inspiration from a desire to collaborate with every nation and does not hide anything mysterious or obscure. On the contrary, the practice of recent months has shown that the political parallelism of two great authoritarian States of Europe constitutes a highly useful factor of security and peace, and a goal towards which all the forces which mean to save civilization from the Bolshevist threat and to accomplish a profitable and lasting work of reconstruction already turn naturally and will continue to turn.

The friendship between Italy and Germany has already deeply impermeated every class of society in the two countries. This is of great importance, for if international friendships do not penetrate from intention of the two Governments into the heart of the people's conscience, they are inevitably bound to break up. Italo-German collaboration will be continued in this spirit, which does not ask for protocols other than those signed on the occasion of my visit to Germany. Besides the political sphere, it will continue to be exercised with equal effectiveness in the economic sphere, wherever the two great nations are able to show their keen sense of international responsibility.

An international instrument which, after what is now a sufficiently long period of working, has shown itself to be both vital and efficient, is the understanding between Italy, Austria, and Hungary. On the basis of the Rome Protocols, our collaboration with the two neighboring States gives clear results and represents a sure element of equilibrium in Central Europe.

At the recent meeting at Venice, as is shown by the document published at the end of the conversations, Italy confirmed her policy of friendship as regards Austria, who, in turn, continues to hold the Rome Protocols and the Austro-German Agreement of July 11 as fundamental and immutable bases of her international activity.

No change, therefore, in the friendship between us and Austria. Those who hoped that such a friendship would be anti-German in working may undeceive themselves. This was not, and is not, part of our intention, nor was it desired by or even possible for Austria. Let those take note who hastily assumed the task of spreading an alarm which was by no means disinterested. And since there are still some who, at every rustling of the leaves, feel compelled to announce unexpected changes in Italian policy, it is well to proclaim, once and for all, that Fascism does not care for the policy of waltzing each turn with a different partner. It is true that we are most cautious and reflect for a long time before choosing a path or fixing an aim, but it is equally true that, once a decision is taken, we do not easily allow ourselves to be turned aside.

Our friendship with Hungary strikes its roots ever deeper and more strongly, with the passage of time and of events, in the hearts of the two peoples, and in a few days the Magyar capital will be able to open its heart enthusiastically to the august person of His Majesty the King Emperor.

The signature of the Mediterranean Agreement between Italy and Great Britain which took place at Rome on January 2 of this year was welcomed by international public opinion as an event which was destined to prove one of the principal elements of European pacification. The fact that, after a long period of tension, Great Britain and Italy had decided that the moment had come to reach a loyal understanding by recognizing their reciprocal rights and interests in the Mediterranean, appeared to be of singular importance. The origin, the development of the negotiations, and finally the text of the agreement are too well known to need further illustration. In brief, the declaration confirms the vital importance to both countries of freedom to enter, leave and pass through the Mediterranean; it repeats that Italian and British interests are not conflicting, excludes the intention to modify the *status quo* in the Mediterranean Basin, and binds the two countries to respect their reciprocal interests and rights in that zone. The agreement was completed by an exchange of letters regarding the respecting, in every circumstance, of the territorial integrity of Spain, which, however, I must be allowed to add, we have never even distantly thought of violating. At the moment of signature the British Government expressed to us their satisfaction and the hope that the agreement would mark the beginning of further collaboration between the two Governments in the cause of peace and of international security. We, on our side, replied that this satisfaction and these intentions were fully shared by the Fascist Government.

In effect, in the new atmosphere which followed immediately the conclusion of the agreement, and despite the fact that on the British side juridical recognition of the Empire had not taken place, it was possible, during January, to conclude certain agreements concerning the Empire itself, regulating the grazing and watering rights of the border tribes, as well as the transit trade to and from Italian East Africa through the ports of Berbera and Zeila and the roads leading from these two places to the Italian frontier. These agreements proved useful and satisfactory to both parties.

It was somewhat discouraging, however, to be obliged to note that, after a short interval, certain unexpected obstacles had delayed, to say the least, the process of *rapprochement* which, with reciprocal goodwill, seemed to be already initiated.

By way of explanation, it has been said in some quarters that Italy had adopted a stiffer attitude towards the British Empire as a result of the decision taken by the Government in London as regards rearmament. This is entirely inexact. These decisions on the part of England have not disturbed us in the least. We do not refuse to others the right which, after the failure of the Disarmament Conference, we have claimed in full measure for ourselves and which we are now methodically engaged in translating into reality.

As regards our relations with France, we did not think it necessary, at the time of the accord with England, to conclude agreements of any kind, since we did not think, and we still do not think, that the atmosphere had ever been so strained as to render necessary a public clarification. The abnormal position of French diplomatic representation at Rome, on which discussion often arises, is due to a decision by the Fascist Government of a general character according to which foreign plenipotentiaries who have the honour of representing their country at the Quirinal must present their letters of credence to the Sovereign with his titles of King and Emperor, to which he is entitled by our laws, and which no guest, even though he be a diplomat, may assume the right to ignore or overlook. This is a general measure and is not aimed at any one in particular, nor does it discriminate against any particular country. If any diplomat has presented his credentials in the old form, and if they have been accepted by us, this is because the *agrément* for the appointment had been granted several months beforehand, while the decision taken by us applied to the future and logically did not contemplate the past.

There are no essential questions between us and France which separate us deeply. For our part, we are awaiting, without impatience, but also without useless recrimination, a rectification which will signify on the French side an intention to bring relations between the two countries on to a new footing.

A field in which the collaboration of Italy and Germany with the Great Western Powers has been carried out recently with regularity and assiduity, though so far without tangible results, has been that of the negotiations for the renewal of the Treaty of Locarno. . . .

Italy's present position towards a new Locarno is as follows: We are ready to renew the agreement, to resume in full the old guarantees on condition that the original and determining structure of the Treaty of Locarno is not substantially changed. This is the practical proposal which we have made to the Powers; instead of entering into doctrinal disputes, perhaps with no outcome, regarding the structure of new security pacts, we propose to take the old Treaty, which, after all, has given good results, and modernize it so that it corresponds to the conditions which have arisen since 1925. . . .

The fact that we intend to revive the Treaty of Locarno in its essential elements as a Western Pact does not mean that we wish to ignore the vital interests of other nations, in other geographical zones of Europe, and above all else those of Poland, with whom our relations have always been most cordial and who abolished sanctions even before the decision at Geneva. We are conscious of these interests in their full and urgent reality, but we consider that the first aim to which our work and our will should be directed is that of re-establishing a system of security for Western Europe which, if it is to be solid, must have a definite object and clearly defined character.

In this direction we shall continue to labour. But we make it clear that we shall not agree to the meeting of a conference until the preparatory work has been diligently carried out and gives the most absolute assurance that the conference will lead to positive results.

A recent diplomatic act, which has made a great impression on the world, is the Pact of Belgrade. The vicissitudes of our relations with our neighbor, the Kingdom of Yugoslavia, since the immediate postwar period are well known. . . .

The Italo-Yugoslav Treaty, which, as you know, possesses a solid structure and is of wide scope, without being in the least aimed at any one else, is a new proof of the part which Fascist Italy is playing actively and realistically in the work of reconstruction, in accordance with her fashion, which makes her oppose to the empty sound of words the convincing eloquence of facts.

In general, our relations with the States of the Balkan peninsula can be called very satisfactory.

My recent visit to Albania gave me an opportunity of seeing with interest and pleasure the rapid progress made by that country, and also of appreciating the depth and sincerity of the sentiments which unite us with the Albanian people, to whom we have given proof of loyal friendship, especially in times of difficulty.

With Turkey, after our conversations in Milan, relations have returned to the original atmosphere of cordiality which found its expression in the Italo-Turkish Treaty of March 30, 1928, and which had been disturbed only by an unnecessary distrust, not of spontaneous origin. I may state with satisfaction that after a frank clarification sentiments of reciprocal confidence have been restored between Turkey and Italy and that even the various questions still in suspense will find an early solution.

With Greece, Rumania, and Bulgaria our relations are cordial and are, in our opinion, capable of further and fruitful development. . . .

Our friendly policy with regard to the Arab Moslem world possesses a lengthy and sound tradition. . . .

We possess in the Arab countries of the Mediterranean and the Red Sea sincere and precious friends whom we intend to cultivate with every care, and who have received a concrete proof of our friendship during the visit of the *Duce* to Libya. Every day there reaches us from the most distant lands evidence of the impression produced by that event in the whole boundless Islamic world, which, in accordance with its traditions, loves in the *Duce* the wisdom of the statesman united to the action of the warrior. . . .

Towards Asia our work has been carried on with particular interest and in a cordial spirit of collaboration. Our relations with Japan had been advanced by the spontaneous recognition accorded by the Empire of the Rising Sun of Italian sovereignty over Ethiopia.

Friendship with Japan is of ancient date and is based, not only upon respect and reciprocal admiration for the qualities of both peoples as soldiers and hard workers, but also upon the attitude adopted by the Japanese Government towards Bolshevism and in defence of order. Much has been done also in the sphere of commercial and cultural exchanges, and further developments are planned for the immediate future.

Relations of equal cordiality exist between us and the Chinese Republic. . . .

Our relations with the Republics of the two Americas are followed with equally active interest. With the United States, after the denunciation of the Treaty of Commerce and Navigation, negotiations are in progress for a new treaty, and a new project for a consular convention is also being examined through the channel of the Embassy with the United States Government. Although it could not be said that in recent times events have brought about particularly close political relations between the two countries, the Fascist Government follows with sympathy the efforts of American statesmen to forward world economic reconstruction and is ready, as soon as occasion offers, to contribute actively thereto.

For their part, Italians would be glad if, as a result of a better understanding of Italian ideals and achievements, the American public would not allow themselves to be misled so frequently by a propaganda of which it was easy to recognize the origin and the purpose.

The countries of Latin America offer a vast field for Italian commercial and cultural expansion. In every one of them there have been possibilities in this direction in recent months, and the growing interest which they take in Fascist Italy is shown by the number of requests for military and civil missions received by the Italian Government.

Political and commercial relations with Brazil deserve special mention in view of the fact that the latter, not being a Member of the League of Nations, did not apply sanctions, but maintained towards us throughout the Ethiopian conflict an attitude of cordial friendship which we have not forgotten. . . .

. . . allow me to speak for a moment on developments in the realm of commercial policy.

During the sanctions period the channels of our trade were suddenly stopped, except for those with non-sanctionist States and Switzerland, who, faithful to her tradition of unalterable friendship, excused herself from interrupting business relations with us.

When the end of the sanctions régime was announced there were those who had calculated that they would find an Italy anxious to resume old obligations and ready to accept any conditions which might be imposed, in order not to lose a minute after the stroke of midnight which marked the end of sanctions. A fresh disillusionment awaited them. Certain conditions were forthwith laid down by us for the realization of a programme which had been elaborated with calm and decision.

In the future we should be prepared, and indeed anxious, to resume trade, but imports would be limited to necessary goods, and these goods would be paid for with Italian wares and without the expenditure of foreign exchange. In fact, a rule as elementary as it was equitable: to buy only from those who bought from us.

With this object in view we declared all our previous quota and clearing agreements to have lapsed through the failure of the sanctionist States to fulfil them, and made the following principles the absolute basis of all new commercial treaties:

(1) No money payment would be made to unfreeze commercial debts, but Italy would offer a proportion of her active trade balance with individual countries to go to the gradual liquidation of her arrears due to those countries.

(2) A proportion between imports and exports should be established in order to make this possible.

(3) Imports from abroad should be limited to raw materials and to certain manufactured and semi-manufactured goods of special importance, while all imports not of vital necessity should be rigorously cut down.

The resulting negotiations led to the conclusion of twenty-three temporary agreements or treaties and settled the new trade network.

Only with Russia, of all the countries with which we were in contact, was it impossible to conclude our negotiations successfully, because that country demanded a balance in her favour of many tens of millions and we were unable to see why such exceptionally favourable treatment should be accorded to the Soviet Union.

The development of Fascist Italy, as a result of the foundation of the Empire—a great event of contemporary history—has enlarged the horizon of our interests and of our activities, not only because an intensification of trade and relations corresponding with our new greatness has resulted, but also because the struggle which we carried on and the victory which we won have focused international interest upon our country. If, on the one hand, we have found arrayed against us a coalition of countries moved by jealousy or lack of understanding, we have, on the other, attracted to our side the sympathy and solidarity of all those forces in the world which stand for youth, revival, and the future. . . .

ADDRESS by Benito Mussolini, Premier, at Berlin, September 28, 1937

Translation, in *Vital Speeches of the Day,* October 15, 1937, p. 17

Comrades, my visit to this country must not be judged by the standards of an ordinary diplomatic or political visit. The fact that I have come to Germany today does not imply that I shall travel to some other city tomorrow. I have not come here in the capacity of chief of the Italian government. I am standing here as the leader of a national revolution giving proof of the strong ties uniting me with your revolutionary movement. There are no ulterior motives connected with my journey, and no secret intentions. There will be no scheming here which might tend to menace divided Europe still further. The confirmation of the unshaken Rome-Berlin axis is not directed against other states.

In answer to the question posed by the whole world, "What will be the outcome of the meeting in Berlin, war or peace?" We—the Fuehrer and myself—reply in a loud voice, "Peace."

If people would take the trouble to study the national revolutions in Germany and in Italy there would be far less prejudice and many points for argument would soon be eliminated. We share many of the fundamental principles in our respective ideologies. National Socialism and Fascism do not only have the same enemies in the world who serve the same master, the Third International, but they share an elevated conception of life and history.

Germany and Italy likewise pursue the same policy in the economic sphere, a policy of economic autarchy, for the political freedom of a nation can only be guaranteed by its economic independence. A nation, strong from the military point of view, might easily become the victim of an economic blockade. We Italians were threatened by that great danger last year when fifty-two nations at Geneva decided to impose economic sanctions against us which, although they finally failed, were nevertheless a great threat to our very existence, and in the end only showed the world what Fascist Italy was able to achieve.

We shall never forget that Germany was not amongst the nations which imposed sanctions against us. That was the time when the first signs of the necessity for cooperation between Fascist Italy and National Socialist Germany appeared on the political horizon. What is nowadays generally known by the term "the Axis Rome-Berlin" actually came into existence in autumn, 1935, and ever since then the

Italo-German solidarity has been constantly strengthened and has done everything to promote peace in Europe.

Fascism has its own ethics, and we intend to adhere thereto in any circumstances, and these ethics of ours oblige us always to be frank and outspoken with everybody and, once we have made real friends with any one, to remain faithful to him to the last.

All arguments which our opponents employ against us are of no avail because there exists no dictatorships, either in Germany or in Italy, but there exist organizations which really serve the good of the peoples.

No government in the whole world enjoys the confidence of their peoples as much as do the Italian and German governments.

The greatest and soundest democracies which exist in the world today are Italy and Germany. Elsewhere, politics is dominated by the great powers of capitalism, by secret societies and political groups which work against each other under pretext of the so-called "inalienable rights of humanity." In Germany and Italy it is absolutely impossible that politics be interfered with or influenced by private persons.

Everything that Germany and Italy have in common is most clearly expressed in their joint struggle against Bolshevism, which is the modern counterpart of the darkest Byzantine tyranny—that unparalleled exploitation of the trustfulness of lower races, that régime of starvation, bloodshed and slavery.

Since the war, fascism has fought against this form of human depravity, which is nourished from falsehood, fought against it with all its might by word and deed.

Thus did we fight in Spain, where thousands of Italian Fascist volunteers have fallen for the sake of Europe's culture, a culture which may yet see a revival if it will turn a deaf ear on the false prophets in Geneva and Moscow and turn to the burning realities of our revolutions.

Comrades, beyond the frontiers of our countries we, like you, make no propaganda in the ordinary sense of the word in order to gain adherents. We believe that truth by itself is powerful enough to penetrate all barriers and that truth will finally conquer.

The Europe of tomorrow will be Fascist by the logical consequence of events but not by our propaganda.

It is nearly twenty years ago since your great leader sent forth to the masses his appeal for a revolution—that appeal which was destined to become the battle cry of the entire German nation, "Deutschland Erwache!" ("Germany Awake!"). The Third Reich is an accomplished fact.

I do not know whether and when Europe will awake, for secret forces not unknown to us are at work striving to transform a civil war into a world conflagration.

It is of the utmost importance that our two peoples, which together count no less than 115,000,000 souls, stand firm and united with the same unswerving confidence. Today's tremendous demonstration has given the world proof of this.

STATEMENT by Count Galeazzo Ciano, Minister for Foreign Affairs, November 6, 1937, Referring to Italy's Accession of the Same Date to the German-Japanese Agreement of November 25, 1936

Translation, in Royal Institute of International Affairs, *Documents on International Affairs, 1937*, p. 307, citing *Corriere della Sera*, November 7, 1937

As a result of the signature of the Tripartite Pact three Great Powers, Italy, Germany, and Japan, are arrayed together against the insidious attacks of Bolshevism. With them the sound and constructive forces of all civilized countries will be solid. The pact has no secret aims. It is not directed against any other country, and any other States which wish to associate themselves with this common action are free to join it. It is an instrument placed at the service of peace and civilization, which Fascism intends to defend and preserve against all dangers.

ADDRESS by Benito Mussolini, Premier, at Rome, December 11, 1937

Given from a balcony of the Palazzo Venezia. Translation, in Royal Institute of International Affairs, *Documents on International Affairs, 1937*, p. 290, citing *The Times* (London), December 13, 1937

The historic decision which the Grand Council has acclaimed and which you have received with your most enthusiastic shouts could not be longer postponed. We have wished, for long years, to offer to the world a spectacle of unheard-of patience. We had not forgotten, and shall not forget, the opprobrious attempt at economic strangulation of the Italian people perpetrated at Geneva.

But some people had thought that at a certain moment the League of Nations would have made a gesture of dutiful reparation. It has not done so. It has not wished to do so. The good intentions of certain Governments vanish as soon as their delegates come into contact with that destructive environment represented by the Geneva Council of fools, manoeuvred by turbid occult forces, enemies of our Italy and of our revolution.

In these circumstances our presence at the door of Geneva could not be tolerated any longer: it wounded our doctrine, our style, and our martial temperament. The hour came when a choice had to be made in the dilemma: either inside or outside. Inside? [A shout from the crowd of "No!"] Outside? [A shout from the crowd, this time of "Yes!"] So now we shout "Enough!" and turn our backs without regret on the tottering temple where men do not work for peace but prepare for war.

It is simply grotesque to believe, or to profess, that pressure has been brought to bear to determine our attitude; there has been none, nor could there be any. Our comrades of the Berlin and Tokyo axis have, in very truth, shown the most complete discretion.

The exit of Italy from the League of Nations is an event of great historical significance which has attracted the attention of the world, and its consequences cannot yet be completely foreseen. But it does not mean that we shall abandon our fundamental lines of policy, directed towards collaboration and peace. We have, in the past few days, given a conspicuous proof of this by setting the seal on peace in the waters of the Adriatic.

The threatening voices which from time to time arise and which perhaps will again arise from the herds of the great Democracies leave us completely indifferent. Nothing can be done against a people such as the Italian people, which is capable of any sacrifice whatsoever. We stand armed in the air, on the land, and on the sea, strong and tempered by two victorious wars. But, above all, we have the heroic spirit of our revolution which no human force in the world will ever be able to bend.

ADDRESS by Benito Mussolini, Premier, at Rome, March 26, 1939, in Commemoration of the 20th Anniversary of the Founding of the First Fascist Squad

Translation, in *Vital Speeches of the Day*, April 15, 1939, p. 389

COMRADES OF the vigil [founding of Fascism]! Faithful Squadristi of the first and all hours: It is with profound emotion that I speak to you twenty years after the founding of the Italian Fascist combat squad.

While looking you squarely in the eye, I see again so many days that we have lived together—sad, stormy, dramatic days but always unforgettable.

On March 23, 1919, we raised the black banner of the Fascist revolution, forerunner of European renaissance. Around this banner your squadrons gathered, formed of veterans of the trenches and of the very young. We decided to march against cowardly government, against disintegrating oriental theories, to free the people from the nefarious influx of principles of the world of '89. [An apparent reference to Italy's ideological aversion to the democratic principles of the French Revolution.]

Around this banner there fell fighting like heroes in the most Roman sense of the word thousands of comrades in streets and squares of Italy, in Africa and in Spain—comrades whose memory is ever alive and present in our hearts.

There may be some one who has forgotten the very hard years of the founding, but the men of these squads have not forgotten them, cannot forget them. It may be that in the meantime some have sat down, but the men of these squads are on foot ready to take up musket and to jump on the trucks as you did in the expeditions of that time.

The men of these squads can say to him who stays at home too much that the revolution is not finished, but from the point of view of customs, character and social distances, it has scarcely begun.

I leave to others the task of striking a balance of our labor in this first twenty-year period of fascism. The balance sheet is gigantic.

What we have done is destined to remain and will remain through the centuries.

Nor do I waste time comparing the Italy of 1919—deluded, restless, disorganized, infected with Bolshevism as a nation not victorious but defeated—with the Italy of 1939, orderly, disciplined, creative, warlike, imperial.

But it might be worth while to remember how many times the demo-plutocratic factory of liars announced to the now scattered flocks of their beaten sheep the approaching, imminent, certain ruin of Fascist Italy on the fiction that it was bled in Africa and still more in Spain and, therefore, had urgent need of a loan which naturally could come only from the British.

That is not true.

What really is true is that this Fascist Italy is still as unknown even in the age of radio as the farthest and most remote regions of the earth.

What we have done is important but for us what we shall do is more important. And we shall do it because my will knows no obstacles and because your enthusiasm and your spirit of sacrifice are intact.

You are not my bodyguard. You are, above all, and you wish to be the bodyguard of the revolution and the Fascist regime.

Comrade Squadristi, your gathering which is the culminating manifestation of the celebrations of the first twenty years of Fascism, takes place in a serious moment in the life of Europe.

We are not carried away and we will not be carried away by that which now is known as the war psychosis, a mixture of hysteria and fear.

Our course of navigation is definite and our principles are clear. Listen with necessary attention and discretion:

First, as regards the professional pacifists, they are particularly detestable individuals. And as regards the word peace, it is by now virtually worn out from much use and rings falsely like counterfeit money.

However well it may be known that we consider a perpetual peace as a catastrophe for human civilization, we also consider a long period of peace necessary to safeguard Europe and the development of European civilization.

Further, as regards recent solicitations, we shall take no initiative whatsoever until our sacred rights are recognized.

Second, the period of waiting, if it ever existed, is definitely closed. The memory of it is offensive to us and to all Italians.

The attempts to crack and break the Rome-Berlin axis are childish. The axis is not only a relationship between two States. It is a meeting between two revolutions which have shown themselves as opposed to all other conceptions of contemporary civilization. Here is the strength of the axis. And here are the conditions of its duration.

But since in every action there is always a share of superficial motives which sometimes replace reason, I am here to tell you in the most explicit manner that what happened in Central Europe was fated to happen.

I declare that if the great democracies weep bitterly over the premature and somewhat dishonorable end of what was their dearest creature, this is a perfect reason for us not to associate ourselves with their more or less decent tears.

I add that if the problem be placed on the level of morals, nobody —I say nobody—has the right to throw the first stone as the ancient and modern history of Europe abundantly demonstrates. I say that when a people, which had very many men and immense arsenals, is not capable of a gesture, this demonstrates that it is overripe for its new fate.

And I say that if the longed-for constitution of a coalition against the authoritarian regimes should come about, these regimes would take up the challenge and would pass from defense to counter-attack at all points.

In my Genoa speech, I spoke of a barricade which separated Italy from France. This barricade may be considered sufficiently demolished and within a few days, perhaps a few hours, the magnificent infantry of Nationalist Spain will deliver the last blow and that Madrid, where the Leftists expected the tomb of Fascism, will be, instead, the tomb of Bolshevism.

Third, we do not ask the world's judgment, but we desire the world to be informed. Well, then, in the Italian note of December 17, 1938, the Italian problems with France were clearly set forth, problems of a colonial character. These problems have a name. They are called Tunisia, Jibuti and the Suez Canal.

The French Government is perfectly free to refuse us even the simplest discussion of these problems as it has done up to now through its too-often-repeated and too-categorical "jamais" (never).

But it cannot complain later if the ditch which now separates the two countries becomes so deep that filling it becomes hard work, if not impossible.

No matter how things go we wish to hear no more about brotherhood, sisterhood, cousins and such other bastard relationships because relationships between States are relations of force and these relations of force are the determining elements of their policy.

Fourth, geographically, historically, politically and militarily, the Mediterranean is a vital spot for Italy. When we say the Mediterranean we naturally include the gulf which is called the Adriatic and in which Italy's interests are preeminent but not exclusive as regards the Slavs. It is for that reason that peace has reigned there for two years.

Fifth, last but fundamental and damaging: we must arm. The watchword is this: more cannon, more ships, more airplanes, at whatever cost, with whatever means, even if it should mean wiping out all that is called civil life.

When one is strong one is dear to one's friends and feared by one's enemies. Since prehistoric times one shout has come down on the waves of the centuries and the series of generations: "Woe to the weak!"

Comrades Squadristi, the glorious blackshirt with which we have fought and will fight is adorned today with a decoration of which you should be particularly proud, a decoration red in color, the red of our blood and of others which we are ready to shed when the interests of Italy are at stake.

This is your day—your great day. Now, then, with your courage and your sacrifice, with your faith you have given a powerful impulse to the wheel of history.

Now I ask you:

Do you wish honors?

Rewards?

A comfortable life?

Does the impossible exist for you?

What are three words which form your dogma? Believe, obey, fight!

In these three words was, is and will be the secret of every victory!

DISARMAMENT AND SECURITY

MEMORANDUM of the Italian Government, Published in Rome, January 31, 1934

Translation, in British White Paper, Cmd. 4512, p. 15; *see also supra*, pp. 775, 787, 789

IN THE CONVERSATIONS which took place in Rome on the 3rd and 4th January between the Head of the Government and the British Minister for Foreign Affairs, the Head of the Government communicated to Sir John Simon the Italian point of view regarding the disarmament situation and the prospects of disarmament on the lines of the following document:—

1. The Italian Government are convinced that an examination of the problem of "disarmament" with reference to the position of Germany as well as to the general situation, cannot but show that we have well-nigh reached the extreme limit of time available for overcoming the deadlock in which we have found ourselves since June last.

The Italian Government think it unnecessary to dwell on this premise. It will be enough to mention the existence of clear and numerous indications which go to prove that if the solution be further delayed rearmament, instead of a debated question, will become a question which may or might be practically solved in a unilateral manner. The gravity of such a fact is self-evident, in view of the increased difficulties which it would create for a peaceful international and juridical solution of the problem of equality, for a European *détente* and for the possibilities of reaching a reasonable convention of effective disarmament in a not too distant future. It is on the other hand certain that the results will be a renewed spirit of mutual suspicion, the division of Europe into hostile groups and a race in armaments.

From this premise the Italian Government deduce that each Government must now assume their own responsibilities, decide to adopt a definite attitude and be prepared to make it known publicly.

2. The experience of the discussions that have taken place during the past two years at the Disarmament Conference, the course of the diplomatic negotiations, and the public declarations made by responsible statesmen, have brought the Italian Government to harbour well-grounded doubts whether the armed Powers desire or are able to agree on such measures of disarmament as would permit a

DISARMAMENT AND SECURITY

solution of the present situation limiting the demands of Germany within the modest dimensions envisaged at a previous stage.

It is further necessary to bear in mind that Germany by excluding from her demands for equality the heavier types of war materials, and confining her claim to the so-called defensive weapons—that is to say the weapons that even on the most optimistic hypothesis would be retained by the armed Powers at least for the duration of a first period, or for that of a first convention—has been able in a measure to dissociate the problem of equality of rights from that of effective disarmament. Such disarmament is therefore now presented as the task of the armed Powers exclusively, Germany having long ago completely done her part.

It follows that the undertaking to bring pressure upon her to make her recede from or moderate her claims for defensive material, becomes all the more difficult, even if the armed Powers were willing to consent to an important and immediate reduction of their offensive armaments; for the German position consists in denying the correlation between the two kinds of armaments, the first representing equality of rights and the second disarmament, which does not bind her as she is not armed.

The Italian Government desire, however, to state that their policy has been, is and intends to remain, a policy of disarmament; and only recently by their unconditional acceptance of the British plan of the 16th March, 1933, they afforded the most convincing proof of this. They continue therefore to consider a solution in this sense as the most desirable. If, therefore, within a reasonable time, the negotiations which are being pursued should afford justifiable grounds for hoping that the armed Powers have unanimously resolved to undertake substantial measures of disarmament, Italy, in accordance with her own interests, would not only adhere to this decision, but would not fail to join, with the utmost goodwill, in the attempt to turn it to immediate advantage in order to obtain from Germany greater limitations to her rearmament than, in the contrary event, it seems possible to secure by agreements.

The Italian Government desire, however, to declare in all frankness that only clear intentions, clearly defined without delay, not subordinated to clauses or conditions that are already *a priori* unacceptable to other Powers, and of such a scope as to create a technically, juridically and morally sound position for the negotiators, would offer any hope of success. In the contrary event, we shall only have a renewal of academic declarations and counter-declarations, of discussions and of recriminations which will not and cannot do anything to avoid the regrettable events to which allusion has been made.

3. Leaving such a possibility still open, therefore, but turning, as indeed the urgency of the moment requires, to the situation as it appears at present, the Italian Government appeal to three principal criteria: that is to say, to a condition of fact, to a juridical point and to an estimate of probabilities, that in their aggregate seem to them to restrict the field of possible solutions and combinations within limits as clear as they are compact and, having regard to the circumstances, satisfactory.

(a) *Condition of Fact*.—The danger that, if no agreement is reached, the question of equality may, in fact, be solved independently of agreements tending to sanction it and to regulate the method of its achievement. This consideration naturally carries with it an examination of the possibilities and the scope of the sanctions, and of the willingness to apply them, designed to hinder or suppress movements which do not take the treaties into account; but the mere consideration of such an eventuality affords a measure of the gravity of the situation which would arise in the event of no agreement being reached, and emphasises, if indeed that were necessary, the necessity of arriving at such an agreement in a prompt and satisfactory manner.

(b) *Juridical Point*.—It is undeniable that equality of rights has been solemnly recognised to Germany and to the other States disarmed by the Treaties of Peace. The impossibility in which the armed Powers, signatories of the said treaties, find themselves of immediately reducing their armaments to a level reasonably approaching the level of German disarmament gives to the German claim for rearmament a juridical and moral force, of which it is not easy to deny the evident truth. And if it is possible to demonstrate, as will be shown below, that the condition of security is also found to have been reasonably met, the argument in favour of Germany assumes a content not easy to refute.

(c) *Estimate of Probabilities*.—The Italian Government cannot but give the utmost weight to the pacific declarations of President Hindenburg and Chancellor Hitler. Apart from the fact that it is not possible to base agreements on suspicion, one must admit that the repeated and uniform declarations of the Head of the German Government afford confidence that well-defined agreements, freely accepted, would not only not be lightly broken, but would not, for the whole term of their duration, be compromised in the diplomatic field by demands for further concessions and modifications.

And inasmuch as scrutiny of what may be in the interests and within the power of a contracting party undoubtedly invests the sincerity of its pledges with a greater certainty, the Italian Government express their considered opinion that the Germany of Hitler is at present taken up with a work of far-reaching transformation and internal readjustment with which it would be difficult to reconcile designs for warlike enterprises beyond the frontiers. It is understood in this connexion that the Italian Government are naturally aware of other and more material aspects of the problem of security; but these will be referred to later.

4. Admitting what has been said above, the Italian Government are of opinion that it is still possible to conclude a convention such as to satisfy—perhaps partially, but none the less positively—public opinion, especially if the latter was suitably enlightened. In considering this point it should be remarked that we have clear indications that even in neutral countries directly interested, public opinion is adapting itself to the idea that the principal and practical question is no longer how to prevent German rearmament, but how to avoid that such rearmament should take place unregulated and uncontrolled.

5. With regard, more especially, to the convention which the Italian Government think might be attained, and which might remain in force up to the 31st December, 1940, it should, in particular, provide for—

(1) The abolition of chemical warfare, with every necessary measure of supervision to prevent preparation and training.

(2) Prohibition of the bombardment of civil populations, bearing in mind that in the field of prohibition of bombardment from the air more radical measures will be possible where the rule of the interdependence of land, sea and air armaments permits; it should be noted that such a measure ought greatly to facilitate the solution of the problem of equality of rights with regard to German air armaments.

(3) Limitation to the present level of military expenditure by the Powers not bound by the Treaties of Peace, with a proviso for expenditure on replacements and completion of defensive works.

(4) Limitation to the present level of land war material of the Powers not bound by the said treaties, but provision for the replacement of material.

6. *Effectives.*—It should be borne in mind that the German claim for an average daily effective of 300,000 men is governed by the hypothesis that the other armed Powers do not reduce their effectives to the figures put forward in the MacDonald plan, but keep to their present figures. If it were found preferable to face the problem of reduction, Germany declares herself ready to rediscuss the figures given above.

This being so, the Italian Government, considering the present level of effectives of, for instance, France, Poland and Czechoslovakia, doubt whether it can plausibly be argued that the ratios resulting from the MacDonald plan have been altered in favour of Germany in the German proposals.

As to the particular problem of the reduction and standardisation of effectives, the Italian Government wish to point out that it would entail so many delicate problems between other contracting Powers, that facing it might cause damaging delays in the conclusion of the agreement. Further, they are bound to admit that, at least as particularly concerns them, the abandonment of the present organisation of land effectives in the sense of the MacDonald plan would certainly entail a heavy burden of expenditure not compensated by corresponding economies with regard to war material.

They are therefore prepared to negotiate on the basis of the *status quo* and of limitation as envisaged by the German proposals. As to the stages in which the transformation of the German forces and their increase would take place, the Italian Government are of opinion that technical requirements impose such stages upon Germany, and that therefore an opportunity is offered to make them the subject of contractual obligations. It is to be noted that the work of transformation could not take place without the conspicuous incapacity for action not only offensive but also defensive that usually accompanies such periods of radical change in military organisation.

Whilst it seems difficult to reject in principle the German claim for defensive armaments—guns up to 155 mm. or the equivalent, anti-aircraft guns, tanks up to 6 tons, scouting and fighting planes—if we hope to see them realised under a régime of convention and supervision, the limits and the measure of the ratio between the defensive war materials and the effectives to be granted might form the object of negotiations.

7. In regard to naval armaments, apart from the examination of precise explanations which Germany might give in this field, eventual revision of the conditions applying to German naval armaments ought in principle to be postponed until the next naval conference.

8. To the concessions which an agreement on those lines would entail France would find an immediate and effective counterpart in the maintenance intact of her armaments. There seems to be no doubt that, from the technical military point of view, this would suffice to guarantee her an undoubted security for the whole duration of the convention, so that this problem from the material point of view might be said to be favourably solved. This argument acquires still greater validity if the efficacy of modern systems of permanent

defence of the frontiers is taken into consideration, as well as the assistance ensured by existing treaties.

9. As to security based on treaties, it is unnecessary for the Italian Government to refer to the Pact of Rome, the Pact of Locarno and the significance and value of the undertakings contained therein. It is not so much the formal and treaty aspect of security which gives weight to the Four-Power Pact, as the continual and methodical collaboration between the great Western Powers which its clauses contemplate, and this both in the field of disarmament and in other fields.

Italy considers herself loyally bound by the Locarno Pact, which assigns a special position to the Italian and British Governments, and precisely on account of her unwavering loyalty considers that she cannot diverge from the view of the London Government in holding that further diplomatic guarantees against aggressions are not only not indispensable, but, if multiplied, would tend to lose their value.

The German Government have, further, recently offered the conclusion of ten-year non-aggression pacts to all neighbouring States.

10. A final and fundamental counterpart to the acceptance of Germany's demands—representing in itself a new contribution to security—might be an undertaking on the part of Germany to return to Geneva, not only with a view to signing the general Disarmament Convention there, but to resume her place in the League of Nations. The Italian Government are particularly anxious to call attention to the first-rate importance of such an event.

11. Finally, the Italian Government cannot lay too much stress upon the necessity that the exchanges of view which are at present taking place should at last lead to sufficient progress to enable the entire question to emerge from the present deadlock, thus justifying a meeting of the Foreign Ministers or of the Heads of the Governments of the four Western Powers, a meeting to which the representatives of the other principal Powers concerned might be invited.

STATEMENT by Dino Grandi, Italian Delegate to the Conference for the Limitation of Naval Armament at London, March 25, 1936

Royal Institute of International Affairs, *Documents on International Affairs, 1936,* p. 615, citing *The Times* (London), March 26, 1936; excerpts

It is with the most sincere regret that Italy finds herself prevented from being among the Powers who are today signing the Naval Treaty, towards the technical elaboration of which the Italian delegation have so willingly and actively cooperated. . . . You will, however, recall that at the opening of the Conference I frankly stated that my Government was compelled to take carefully into account the position in which my country had been placed by the attitude of many States in regard to the Italo-Abyssinian dispute.

I may add that at that time my Government sincerely hoped that before the conclusion of the Naval Conference the abnormal situation in which Italy found herself would have been clarified, and that consequently my country would have been in a position to proceed in the work which had been undertaken with such sincere good will and with every hope of success.

Unfortunately this has not happened. Only a few weeks after the beginning of the Naval Conference Italy found herself confronted with agreements of mutual naval assistance in the Mediterranean which were openly designed to give military support to those very sanctions, the iniquity and injustice of which the Italian people so deeply resent, and which have only had a pernicious effect—that of disrupting the political solidarity between the Great Powers, of crushing the efforts at economic reconstruction, of increasing disorder and political confusion in Europe.

These agreements have deeply wounded the Italian people, who find themselves today in the unquestionable necessity of considering the problem of my country's naval security in relation to the new situation in which they have been placed. In these circumstances the Italian Government find themselves compelled to maintain unprejudiced their freedom in the field of naval construction, and to provide, in the manner which they consider more appropriate, for the safeguard of the supreme interests in the country's naval defence.

You will surely appreciate that an agreement for the limitation of armaments and, above all, the contents and the technical clauses of such an agreement, cannot be disembodied from the framework of the political relations between the States, nor can it likewise ignore the problems connected with their respective security. . . .

WAR WITH ETHIOPIA

RADIO ADDRESS by Benito Mussolini, Premier, October 2, 1935

Translation, in Royal Institute of International Affairs, *Documents on International Affairs, 1935*, II, 169, citing *The Times* (London), October 3, 1935

BLACKSHIRTS of the revolution, men and women of all Italy, Italians scattered throughout the world, across the mountains and across the oceans, listen.

A solemn hour is about to strike in the history of the Fatherland. Twenty million Italians are at this moment gathered in the squares throughout the whole of Italy. It is the most gigantic demonstration which the history of mankind records. Twenty millions, a single heart, a single will, a single decision. This manifestation is to signify that the identity between Italy and Fascism is perfect, absolute, and unchangeable. Only brains weakened by puerile illusions or benumbed in a crass ignorance can think the contrary, because they do not know what this Fascist Italy of 1935 is. For many months the wheel of destiny, under the impulse of our calm determination, has been making towards the goal. In these last hours the rhythm has become more speedy and cannot now be arrested.

Not only is an army marching towards its objectives, but 40,-000,000 Italians are marching in unison with this army, all united because there is an attempt to commit against them the blackest of all injustices, to rob them of a place in the sun. When in 1915 Italy united its lot with those of the Allies, how many shouts of admiration and how many promises! But after the common victory, to which Italy had brought the supreme contribution of 670,000 dead, 400,000 disabled, 1,000,000 wounded, when it came to sitting around the table of the mean peace, to us were left only the crumbs from the sumptuous colonial booty of others. During 20 years we have been patient while there tightened round us ever more rigidly the ring which wanted to suffocate our overflowing vitality. With Ethiopia we have been patient for 40 years. Now, enough!

At the League of Nations, instead of recognizing the just rights of Italy, they dared to speak of sanctions. Now, until there is a proof to the contrary, I refuse to believe that the true people of France can associate themselves with sanctions against Italy. The dead of Bligny, who perished in a heroic attack which drew admiration even from the enemy, would turn in their graves. Until there is proof to the contrary I refuse to believe that the true people of Great Britain want to spill blood and push Europe on the road to catastrophe in order to defend an African country universally stamped as a barbarous country and unworthy of taking its place with the civilized peoples.

At the same time, we must not pretend not to know the eventualities of to-morrow. To sanctions of an economic character we will reply with our discipline, with our sobriety, and with our spirit of sacrifice. To sanctions of a military character we will reply with orders of a military character. To acts of war we will reply with acts of war.

Let nobody delude himself that he can deflect us. A people which is proud of its name and of its future cannot adopt a different attitude. But let it be said once again in the most categorical manner, as a sacred pledge which I take at this moment before all the Italians who are listening to me, that we will do everything possible to avoid a colonial conflict assuming the character and bearing of a European conflict. This may be the wish of those who see in a new war revenge for fallen temples, but it cannot be our wish.

Never more than in this historic epoch has the Italian people revealed the force of its spirit and the power of its character. And it is against this people to which humanity owes the greatest of its conquests, it is against this people of heroes, poets, artists, navigators, and administrators, that they dare to speak of sanctions.

Italy, proletarian and Fascist Italy, Italy of Vittorio Veneto and of the Revolution, to your feet! To your feet!

Let the cry of your firm and unshakable decision reach the sky and be a comfort to the soldiers who are about to fight in Africa, and let this be a spur to them and a warning to enemies in all parts of the world, a cry of justice and a cry of victory.

STATEMENT by Baron Pompeo Aloisi, Representative of Italy in the Council of the League of Nations, October 5, 1935

Translation, in Royal Institute of International Affairs, *Documents on International Affairs, 1935*, II, 173, citing League of Nations, *Official Journal*, November, 1935, pp. 1210–12

The Italian delegation has been instructed by its Government to make the following declarations to the Council:

To-day's meeting has been convened in consequence of the communications sent by the Italian and Ethiopian Governments to the

League in the last few days. So far as it is concerned, the Italian Government can only refer to its telegram of October 3, in which it described the most recent phases of a situation that had been set forth with ample documentary evidence in the Italian memorandum of September 4.

Had the League Council given that memorandum, together with the Italian Government's declarations accompanying it, all the attention it deserved, had it made a thorough study of all the factors involved, it would have realized that the situation in Ethiopia was such that there could be no illusion as to the possibility of modifying it by any proposals which failed to take account of the evil itself and consequently could not reach it at its source.

The Italian Government has appreciated the efforts which in all goodwill the Council has made, but it has been unable to comprehend, and still does not comprehend, the reasons for which the Council did not see fit, before attempting conciliation, to make a realistic investigation of the conditions of Ethiopia, both within the country and in its capacity as a State belonging to the League.

It is on these conditions, and therefore on the contents of its memorandum, that the Italian Government must still insist to-day. The recent developments of the situation may be readily understood, and will be seen to be even inevitable, when it is considered that it is not only now that Italy has fallen a victim to Ethiopian aggression, but that a state of aggression—concerning which ample documentary proof has been supplied—has been continuing for several years, that Ethiopia has been intensifying her armaments since 1928—under the shelter of the Treaty of Friendship concluded with Italy and thanks, even to large supplies of arms liberally granted to her by the Italian Government to help her maintain order in the interior of the country—and that these armaments, on the contrary, were not and could not be designed for use against any countries except the adjacent Italian colonies.

By neglecting to make a detailed and thorough inquiry into this situation and by causing the discussion to be diverted to theoretical arguments, the facts have been forgotten, and involuntarily the position has arisen where Ethiopia has been enabled to come before the League in the guise of victim, as if the measures which Italy found it necessary to adopt in order to put her colonies in a state of defence had been determined solely by a situation that had arisen suddenly and without well-established historical antecedents.

Furthermore, Ethiopia has not been viewed as she really is—that is to say, a State in which a dangerous situation exists in consequence of the anarchical conditions prevailing there, of the absence of any effective central authority, and of any control of the military forces, which are still largely based on the feudal system.

It is precisely this state of affairs that has constituted in the past, and still constitutes for Italy, a perpetual and steadily growing menace which she has been obliged to meet with appropriate measures of defence.

Ethiopia has also been viewed as if she were a unified State, whereas the greater part of her territory consists of recently conquered colonies, in the strict and true sense of the term. On this point, too, although the position was universally known, insufficient attention has been paid to the ample documentary evidence in the Italian memorandum, and it is for that reason that, even in this matter, the proposals put forward as a remedy are divorced from all reality.

Upon this deviation from the true reasons for the Italo-Ethiopian dispute has been artificially grafted an alarmist agitation in international public opinion, encouraged by certain factors that are entirely alien to the question itself. This has led to the unimaginable and absurd result that the constant Ethiopian menace to Italy has been transformed into an Italian menace to Ethiopia. It has been claimed that Italy should be refused the right to take the necessary defensive measures; an attempt has even been made to qualify them as arbitrary and illegal.

It is against this distortion of the truth that the Italian Government is obliged to protest, partly because it is conscious of its own responsibilities, and partly because Italy's measures of legitimate defence have been provoked by the increasingly threatening attitude of Ethiopia. Italy remained in the positions she had taken up in her territory until the moment when the general mobilization order issued by the Negus gave final proof of the imminent peril of Ethiopia's intentions. The aggressive character of that mobilization and the aims which it has in view have been openly avowed and proclaimed.

These are the actual words addressed by the Negus himself to his troops, as reproduced by American and French correspondents at Addis Ababa: "When with God's help this war has been brought to a victorious conclusion, the warriors will be given Eritrea and Italian Somaliland as a reward for their services to the King of Kings."

The facts I have just stated definitely refute the arguments which the Ethiopian Government reiterates once again in its Note of to-day, and show that those arguments can only be regarded as an attempt to distort, by invoking the letter of certain articles in the Covenant, the historical truth as it exists in fact and as it is proved by the documentary evidence supplied by the Italian Government.

The claim that, after this general mobilization, Italy should have awaited, without action, the attack of over a million armed men is more than good faith can endure, even if account is not taken of the conditions in which Italy is ensuring the defence of her colonies, which are several thousand kilometres away from the home-country.

No State has ever been able to disregard—no State could ever disregard—the requirements of military security of that kind.

The operations carried out by the Italian troops after the Ethiopian mobilization are therefore quite legitimate, even within the framework of the Covenant, as they are merely an immediate and necessary reply to an act of provocation.

In bad faith Ethiopia had no hesitation in combining the mobilization order with an announcement that the troops were being withdrawn thirty kilometres. The sole object of this latter measure was really to veil the other. Ethiopia desired, by this withdrawal, to set up a convenient screen behind which she could assemble troops at her own time and complete her preparations for aggression. Moreover, it does not appear from the latest information that this withdrawal actually took place, but all these various manoeuvres once more confirm the fact that the measures taken by the Italian forces could not be delayed longer.

The responsibility for this situation must be attributed to the encouragement which Ethiopia thought she could find in the discussions at Geneva and in the attempts made to distort them before international public opinion.

The Italian nation cannot understand, and will never be able to understand, why the truth should be distorted only in regard to it and why an attempt is made to set in motion, against Italy alone, procedures which were inoperative in other cases.

These attempts and the obstacles raised against the acceptance of the good reasons advanced by Italy have so encouraged Ethiopia that she felt sure the time had come to take advantage of the situation and to carry out her hostile projects against Italy. It only remained for the Italian Government to use its own means to circumvent a manoeuvre of that kind, since sufficient consideration has hitherto not been given to the real state of affairs.

If, on the contrary, the starting-point had been the plain fact that Ethiopia is unworthy to belong to the League of Nations, that country would certainly not have dared to order general mobilization against Italy.

The Italian Government must therefore emphasize its declaration that the dangers of the present situation could have been removed if the action undertaken had been based on the actual conditions in

Ethiopia, instead of this country being still considered as having equal rights with the other States Members of the League.

In circumstances far less serious than those with which we are faced to-day, I remember having heard it strongly maintained in the Council that expulsion from the League, as provided in Article 16 of the Covenant, might have been decided upon in respect of an original State Member which was accused of not having fulfilled its engagements under Article 23 of the Covenant—namely, the obligation that it should secure just treatment of the native inhabitants subject to its control.

May I venture in this connexion to quote the words of the United Kingdom representative, Mr. Eden, during the Council's meeting on May 18, 1934:

The Council would recall that, under Article 23 (b) of the League Covenant, the Members of the League undertook to secure just treatment of the native inhabitants of the territories under their control. It was the view of the United Kingdom Government, and he stated it with the utmost earnestness—that Liberia had so grossly failed to observe this obligation attaching to her as a Member of the League of Nations that the League would be quite entitled to consider her expulsion under paragraph 4 of Article 16.

Though the representative of the United Kingdom did not then think it desirable to make a formal proposal for expulsion, it is none the less true that he admitted, in principle, that such a measure was applicable in a far less serious case than that of Ethiopia.

So long as the various factors that have led Ethiopia to take up an aggressive attitude towards Italy are not removed, and so long as she is still encouraged by the distortion of the facts relating to the Italo-Ethiopian dispute, no equitable solution can be found for the dispute between Italy and Ethiopia.

FROM THE OUTBREAK OF THE WAR IN EUROPE

COMMUNICATION from King Victor Emmanuel to the President of the United States (Franklin D. Roosevelt), August 30, 1939, in Reply to the Latter's Appeal for Peace of August 23, 1939

Translation, in Department of State, *Bulletin*, September 2, 1939, p. 183

I AM GRATEFUL to you for your interest. I have immediately transmitted your message to my Government. As is known to all, there has been done and there is being done by us whatever is possible to bring about a peace with justice.

ADDRESS by Benito Mussolini, Premier, before leaders of the Fascist Party at Rome, September 23, 1939

Translation, in *Vital Speeches of the Day*, October 15, 1939, p. 15

I DESIRED THAT my contact with the leaders of the Fascist party should be renewed with you, my comrades from Bologna, first because you have made the most blood sacrifices to the cause of the Fascist revolution, second because you are worthy of your name—the Tenth Legion, the most faithful of the legions which Caesar could always count on—and third for the importance which in the political, economic and moral life of the nation Bologna and Milan have.

After this meeting others will follow for leaders of other regions and the Fascist party thus will proceed to its complete mobilization from the center of the nation to all its frontiers.

We meet in a stormy moment which brings not only the map of Europe into play but perhaps even that of continents. It is only natural that these great events and their repercussions cause emotion even among our leaders.

But small groups of miserable human dregs who have been reduced to living in slums, hidden places and dark corners, have taken advantage of our special and understandable feelings.

This riffraff is responsible for the circulation of rumors, the most ridiculous of which refer to me. This situation was destined to come to an end. Aroused with deep shame, I would have been forced to know one thing in which I have always firmly believed, namely, that the Italian people are one of the most intelligent on earth.

I do not want to dramatize the situation because it is not worth while, but it is necessary to clean up the human residue living in dark corners where Masonic and Jewish riffraff and anti-fascist foreign sympathizers have taken refuge. We will not allow them nor others to undermine the physical and moral health of the Italian people.

The Italian people have realized that the pilot must not be disturbed, especially when he is engaged in stormy navigation, nor must he be asked questions about the course.

If and when I shall appear on the balcony of the Palazzo Venezia and convoke the Italian people to hear me, it will not be to discuss the situation but to announce decisions of historic importance such as that of October 2, 1935, or May 9, 1936.

[On October 2, 1935, Premier Mussolini announced the state of the conquest of Ethiopia. On May 9, 1936, he announced the occupation of Addis Ababa and the revival of the Italian Empire.]

Now, this is not the moment. My policy was fixed in the (Cabinet) declaration of September 1 and there is no reason to change it.

This answers to our national interests, to our political pacts and the desire of all peoples, including the Germans. The policy is that of at least localizing the conflict.

For the rest, with Poland liquidated, Europe is not yet actually at war. The masses of the armies have not yet clashed. The clash can be avoided by recognizing that it is a vain illusion to try to maintain or, worse still, to reconstitute positions which history and the natural dynamism of peoples have condemned.

It has been with wise intention not to enlarge the conflict that the governments of London and Paris have not done more to face the Russian *fait accompli,* but the consequence is that these governments have compromised their moral justification in taking action against the German *fait accompli.*

In this present moment of uncertainties the ruling voice which spontaneously has arisen from the Italian masses says, "Strengthen our army in preparation for any eventualities and support every possible peace effort while working in silence."

This is the style of Fascism, this must be and is the style of the Italian people.

COMMUNICATION from Benito Mussolini, Premier, to the President of the United States (Franklin D. Roosevelt), May 2, 1940

Translation, in Department of State, *Peace and War*, p. 522

1. If two nations, Denmark and Norway, have been involved in the war, the responsibility does not fall upon Germany, but upon the initiatives of the Allies.

2. Italy's non-belligerency has effectively insured peace for two hundred millions of men, but notwithstanding, Italian merchant traffic is subjected to a constant surveillance that is vexatious and harmful.

3. As far as I know, Germany is opposed to a further extension of the conflict, and Italy likewise. We must learn whether this is also the Franco-British aim.

4. The only European nation that dominates a large part of the world and possesses a monopoly on many basic raw materials is Great Britain. Italy has no programs of that kind, but declares that no peace is possible without the fundamental problems of Italian liberty being settled.

5. As to the repercussions which an extension of the war fronts might have on the three Americas, I call attention to the fact that Italy has never concerned itself with the relations of the American republics with each other and with the United States (thereby respecting the Monroe Doctrine), and might therefore ask for "reciprocity" with regard to European affairs.

6. Whenever conditions permit, and always starting with the recognition of the actual and accomplished facts, Italy is ready to make her contribution to a better order of the world.

COMMUNICATION from Benito Mussolini, Premier, to the President of the United States (Franklin D. Roosevelt), May 18, 1940

Department of State, *Peace and War*, p. 536

I reply to the message which you sent me at noon on the fourteenth instant. I understand perfectly the motives by which it was inspired and I consider it worthy of much respect and of the greatest consideration but there are two fundamental motives which cannot escape your spirit of political realism and those are that Italy is and intends to remain allied with Germany and that Italy cannot remain absent at a moment in which the fate of Europe is at stake. I cannot therefore but reconfirm the substance of my first message.

RADIO ADDRESS by Benito Mussolini, June 10, 1940

Translation, in *The New York Times*, June 11, 1940. Reprinted by permission of the Associated Press

FIGHTERS OF land, sea and air, Blackshirts of the revolution and of the legions, men and women of Italy, of the Empire and of the Kingdom of Albania, listen!

The hour destined by fate is sounding for us. The hour of irrevocable decision has come. A declaration of war already has been handed to the Ambassadors of Great Britain and France.

We take the field against the plutocratic and reactionary democracies who always have blocked the march and frequently plotted against the existence of the Italian people.

Several decades of recent history may be summarized in these words: Phrases, promises, threats of blackmail, and finally, crowning that ignoble edifice, the League of Nations of fifty-two nations.

Our conscience is absolutely clear.

With you, the entire world is witness that the Italy of Fascism has done everything humanly possible to avoid the tempest that envelops Europe, but all in vain.

It would have sufficed to revise treaties to adapt them to changing requirements vital to nations and not consider them untouchable for eternity.

It would have sufficed not to begin the stupid policy of guarantees, which proved particularly deadly for those who accepted them.

It would have sufficed not to reject the proposal the Fuehrer made last Oct. 6 after the campaign in Poland ended.

Now all that belongs to the past.

If today we have decided to take the risks and sacrifices of war, it is because the honor, interests and future firmly impose it since a great people is truly such if it considers its obligations sacred and does not avoid the supreme trials that determine the course of history.

We are taking up arms, after having solved the problem of our continental frontiers, to solve our maritime frontiers. We want to

AFTER WAR BEGINS IN EUROPE

break the territorial and military chains that confine us in our sea because a country of 45,000,000 souls is not truly free if it has not free access to the ocean.

This gigantic conflict is only a phase of the logical development of our revolution. It is the conflict of poor, numerous peoples who labor against starvers who ferociously cling to a monopoly of all riches and all gold on earth.

It is a conflict of fruitful, useful peoples against peoples who are in a decline. It is a conflict between two ages, two ideas.

Now the die is cast and our will has burned our ships behind us.

I solemnly declare that Italy does not intend to drag other peoples bordering on her by sea or land into the conflict. Switzerland, Yugoslavia, Greece, Turkey and Egypt, take note of these words of mine. It depends on them and only on them if these words are rigorously confirmed or not.

Italians, in a memorable mass meeting in Berlin, I said that according to the rules of Fascist morals when one has a friend one marches with him to the end. This we have done and will continue to do with Germany, her people and her victorious armed forces.

On this eve of an event of import for centuries, we turn our thoughts to His Majesty, the King and Emperor, who always has understood the thought of the country.

Lastly, we salute the new Fuehrer, the chief of great allied Germany.

Proletarian, Fascist Italy has arisen for the third time, strong, proud, compact as never before.

There is only one order. It is categorical and obligatory for every one. It already wings over and enflames hearts from the Alps to the Indian Ocean: Conquer!

And we will conquer in order, finally, to give a new world of peace with justice to Italy, to Europe and to the universe.

Italian people, rush to arms and show your tenacity, your courage, your valor.

COMMUNICATION from Emmanuele Grazzi, Italian Minister at Athens, to the Greek Government, October 28, 1940, Regarding the Occupation of Strategic Points in Greek Territory by Italian Armed Forces

Translation, in *The New York Times*, October 29, 1940. Reprinted by permission of the Associated Press

THE Italian Government has repeatedly noted how, in the course of the present conflict, the Greek Government assumed and maintained an attitude which was contrary not only with that of formal, peaceful, good neighborly relations between two nations but also with the precise duties which were incumbent on the Greek Government in view of its status as a neutral country.

On various occasions the Italian Government has found it necessary to urge the Greek Government to observe these duties and to protest against their systematic violation, particularly serious since the Greek Government permitted its territorial water, its coasts and its ports to be used by the British fleet in the course of its war operations, aided in supplying the British air forces and permitted organization of a military information service in the Greek archipelago to Italy's damage.

The Greek Government was perfectly aware of these facts, which several times formed the basis of diplomatic representations on the part of Italy to which the Greek Government, which should have taken consideration of the grave consequences of its attitude, failed to respond with any measure for the protection of its own neutrality, but, instead, intensified its activities favoring the British armed forces and its cooperation with Italy's enemies.

The Italian Government has proof that this cooperation was foreseen by the Greek Government and was regulated by understandings of a military, naval and aeronautical character. The Italian Government does not refer only to the British guarantee accepted by Greece as a part of the program of action against Italy's security but also to explicit, precise engagements undertaken by the Greek Government to put at the disposal of powers at war with Italy important strategic positions on Greek territory, including air bases in Tessaglia and Macedonia designed for attack on Albanian territory.

In this connection the Italian Government must remind the Greek Government of the provocative activities carried out against the Albanian nation, together with the terroristic policy it has adopted toward the people of Ciamuria and the persistent efforts to create disorders beyond its frontiers.

For these reasons, also, the Italian Government has accepted the necessity, even though futilely, of calling the attention of the Greek Government to the inevitable consequences of its policy toward Italy. This no longer can be tolerated by Italy.

Greek neutrality has been tending continuously toward a mere shadow. Responsibility for this situation lies primarily on the shoulders of Great Britain and its aim to involve ever more countries in war.

But now it is obvious that the policy of the Greek Government has been and is directed toward transforming Greek territory, or at least permitting Greek territory to be transformed, into a base for war operations against Italy.

This could only lead to armed conflict between Italy and Greece, which the Italian Government has every intention of avoiding.

The Italian Government, therefore, has reached the decision to ask the Greek Government, as a guaranty of Greek neutrality and as a guaranty of Italian security, for permission to occupy with its own armed forces several strategic points in Greek territory for the duration of the present conflict with Great Britain.

The Italian Government asks the Greek Government not to oppose this occupation and not to obstruct the free passage of the troops carrying it out.

These troops do not come as enemies of the Greek people and the Italian Government does not in any way intend that the temporary occupation of several strategic points, dictated by special necessities of a purely defensive character, should compromise Greek sovereignty and independence.

The Italian Government asks that the Greek Government give immediate orders to military authorities that this occupation may take place in a peaceful manner. Wherever the Italian troops may meet resistance this resistance will be broken by armed force, and the Greek Government would have the responsibility for the resulting consequences.

ADDRESS by Benito Mussolini, Premier, at the Palazzo Venezia, Rome, December 11, 1941

Translation, in *The New York Times,* December 12, 1941. Reprinted by permission of the Associated Press

This is another day of solemn decision in Italy's history and of memorable events destined to give a new course to the history of continents.

The powers of the steel pact, Fascist Italy and National Socialist Germany, ever closely linked, participate from today on the side of heroic Japan against the United States of America.

The Tri-partite Pact becomes a military alliance which draws around its colors 250,000,000 men determined to do all in order to win.

Neither the Axis nor Japan wanted an extension of the conflict.

One man, one man only, a real tyrannical Democrat, through a series of infinite provocations, betraying with a supreme fraud the population of his country, wanted the war and had prepared for it day by day with diabolical obstinacy.

The formidable blows that on the immense Pacific expanse have been already inflicted to American forces show how prepared are the soldiers of the Empire of the Rising Sun.

I say to you, and you will understand, that it is a privilege to fight with them.

Today, the Tri-partite Pact, with the plentitude of its forces and its moral and material resources, is a formidable instrument for the war and a certainty for victory.

Tomorrow the Tri-partite Pact will become an instrument of just peace between the peoples.

Italians! Once more arise and be worthy of this historical hour!

We shall win.

PART SEVEN

JAPAN

GENERAL STATEMENTS OF POLICY

ADDRESS by Kenkichi Yoshizawa, Japanese Ambassador to France and Chief of the Japanese Delegation to the Assembly of the League of Nations, before the Assembly, September 9, 1931

Translation, in League of Nations, *Official Journal*, Special Supplement No. 93, p. 50

AMONG THE important international questions which, since the constitution of the League, have called for its watchful attention and indefatigable efforts, the problem of the reduction of armaments undoubtedly occupies the first place. After unavoidably lengthy preparatory work, we are now in the happy position of being able to look forward to the coming conference for the reduction of armaments as the crowning of our efforts, and I must warmly congratulate the Preparatory Commission for the Conference, which has thus brilliantly achieved its task after heavy work extending over a period of five years.

Thanks to the Commission, we now have before us a draft Convention for the limitation and reduction of armaments, which may usefully be taken as a basis for the work of the Conference in 1932.

I need hardly say here that it is the earnest wish of the Japanese Government to consolidate world peace and to further the welfare of humanity by means of an equitable agreement on the reduction of armaments. My Government is willing to participate in the coming Conference and to do all in its power to contribute to its success. As everyone knows, the Japanese Government, acting always in the spirit underlying the work of disarmament, endeavoured to bring about a reduction in naval armaments at the successive Conferences held at Washington, Geneva and London, and the agreements concluded are being loyally carried out. In the field of land disarmament also, it has, on its own initiative, already effected considerable reductions. Indeed, whereas before the war there were in Japan twenty-one army divisions, apart from certain independent units, in 1922 the effectives of each division were greatly reduced and in 1925 four divisions were disbanded. Consequently, there are at present only seventeen divisions, with effectives representing not more than 65 per cent of the pre-war effectives, a figure which corresponds to 0.28 per cent of the population,

On the other hand, as our army did not participate in the operations on the European battlefields, its war material and air force are not adequate for the requirements of national defence, and my Government has therefore been obliged to readjust that state of affairs. While willing to do all in its power, in full agreement with the participating Governments, to make a success of the general Conference, the Japanese Government earnestly desires that the Powers whose situation is closely bound up with the national defence of Japan should make similar efforts for the conclusion and loyal execution of the Disarmament Convention.

In view of these considerations, the Japanese Government intends to put forward at the coming Conference such proposals as seem to it most equitable, in accordance with the spirit of Article 8 of the League Covenant, and having regard also to the present position of our armaments and our peculiar situation in the Far East.

It is particularly desirable that the Disarmament Conference should yield positive results at a time like the present, when the world is passing through a period of general economic depression of exceptional gravity. Opinions may differ as to the causes of that depression, but it can hardly be denied that one of its causes is to be found in the fact that numbers of countries have, in their overanxiety to protect themselves economically, one after the other adopted a policy incompatible with the principle of liberty of trade based on a rational division of international work.

Immediately after the world war, a tendency to erect Customs barriers was observed in nearly every country. In order to combat this tendency, the League convened the Economic Conference of 1927, which exhorted the States to abolish all obstacles to liberty of trade. Subsequently, by means of a Convention for the Abolition of Import and Export Prohibitions, a Convention for a Customs Truce, and other attempts to solve various problems affecting world economic co-operation, the League endeavoured to create an international atmosphere essentially favourable to liberty of trade between the members of the international community.

Those efforts on the part of the League should certainly not be under-estimated. Nevertheless, we must admit that, when the world crisis came—that is, in the course of the last few years—there was revealed more and more clearly a tendency to restrict or prohibit the import of foreign commodities or to prevent their import in actual fact by increasing Customs duties on the pretext that such were necessary to protect the home trade and industry, make good a budget deficit or remedy unemployment. There are even signs of nations going further still and ignoring or restricting the application of the most-favoured-nation clause in commercial treaties, or other similar guarantees.

There is thus a risk of serious interference with the principle of equality of opportunity or non-discrimination which had hitherto been accepted by the nations. Moreover, that tendency not only jeopardises international obligations, but constitutes a serious obstacle to the development of the productive resources of each country, causing international trade depression and aggravating the economic crisis from which the whole world is now suffering.

At the present time, the various countries have become so interdependent economically that any policy of economic isolation pursued by certain countries inevitably entails tremendous difficulties for all the other countries which, in their international trade, adopt the principle of freedom of trade. If an increasing number of States strike out on a line which must inevitably lead to the abandonment of a liberal policy, such a tendency can only be described as deplorable from the standpoint of international economic peace.

I wish to take this opportunity of drawing the attention of all countries to these grave considerations and to express the sincere hope that the League will use every means at its disposal and exert its prestige in order to mitigate, as far as possible, this highly regrettable tendency.

As regards the question of the amendment of the Covenant of the League of Nations in order to bring it into harmony with the Pact of Paris, the Japanese delegation last year expressed certain doubts as to the desirability of such a measure. My Government sees no reason to modify its original view, but I am glad to be able to tell you that it is prepared to accede, in principle, to the draft amendments embodied in the report of the First Committee of the last Assembly, it being understood that those amendments shall in no way affect the legitimate exercise of the right of self-defence.

In conclusion, I should like to take this opportunity of expressing our great satisfaction that the League of Nations has responded to the appeal of our neighbour, China, and that a plan has been prepared and put into execution under the supervision of the Council—a manifest demonstration of the League spirit of universality and solidarity.

More than ever before, the League must mobilise its full resources to secure cordial collaboration and must prevail upon all States to collaborate in eradicating, as far as possible, the evils from which the whole world is suffering. I for one earnestly hope for the progress and success of all the League's activities.

ADDRESS by Koki Hirota, Minister for Foreign Affairs, in the Imperial Diet, January 23, 1934

Translation, in Royal Institute of International Affairs, *Documents on International Affairs, 1933*, p. 493, citing *The New York Times*, January 23, 1934

The Japanese Government was obliged to serve notice of withdrawal from the League of Nations on March 27 last year because the Manchurian incident and question regarding the State of Manchukuo showed that there was no agreement between Japan and the League on fundamental principles of preserving the peace in eastern Asia.

At the time when the decisive step was taken, His Majesty the Emperor graciously issued a rescript pointing out clearly and precisely the path this nation should henceforth pursue.

It reads:

Now that Manchukuo has been founded, our empire deems it essential to respect the independence of the new State and to encourage its healthy development in order that sources of evil in the Far East may be eradicated and enduring peace thereby established.

However, the advancement of international peace is what, as evermore, we desire, and our attitude toward the enterprises of peace shall sustain no change. By quitting the League and embarking on a course of its own, our empire does not mean that it will stand aloof in the Extreme Orient, nor that it will isolate itself thereby from the fraternity of nations.

It is our desire to promote mutual confidence between our empire and all other Powers and to make known the justice of its cause throughout the world.

I am convinced that, if we all unite in our endeavours to act in accordance with the wishes of our august sovereign, the world will surely come to realize the fairness and justice of Japan's position, and bright will be the future of our empire.

Personally speaking, in obedience to the Imperial message, I am determined to use every ounce of my energy to "carry out our national policy by diplomatic means in the interest of world peace."

Fortunately to-day, after our withdrawal from the League, commercial as well as diplomatic relations between Japan and friendly Powers in general have become even closer and more cordial than before. I wish to avail myself of this occasion to dwell somewhat on recent phases of our relations with those countries which are situated in our immediate neighbourhood.

Manchukuo, thanks to the tireless labour of His Excellency the Regent and of Government authorities, and also to the whole-hearted assistance and collaboration extended to her by this country, true to the spirit of the Japan-Manchukuo protocol, has been making steady progress along all lines of her constructive work.

In ordering various governmental institutions, especially in the maintenance of law and order, in developments of industry and communication, in consolidation of the national finance and in the advancement of education and culture, signal success has been achieved.

Moreover, a decision is about to be made on the establishment of a monarchical régime which has been so eagerly awaited by all her people, and which will go far to solidify the foundations of Manchukuo as a young independent nation.

This is a matter of congratulation, not for Manchukuo alone, but for the peace of the Orient and the peace of the world. I think it behooves our Government and people, always mindful of the Imperial rescript, to exert their efforts unremittingly in assisting the healthy growth of the new State.

The Japanese Government has serious responsibilities for the maintenance of peace in eastern Asia and has a firm resolve in that regard. But what is more essential in the matter is the stabilization of China herself.

Our government sincerely hopes for the political and economic rehabilitation of China. It hopes that she will be enabled to unite with Japan in performing the obvious mission of both Japan and China—to contribute through mutual aid and co-operation to peaceful development of their part of the globe.

Unfortunately the actual situation of present-day China belies all such hopes. It has been reported that of late the Chinese Government, realizing the mistake of persisting in its anti-Japanese attitude, has decided to take steps towards the rectification of Sino-Japanese relations, but so far no concrete evidence has come to our notice to confirm the truth of the report.

Should China appreciate our true motives and give tangible signs of sincerity on her part, Japan would be glad to reciprocate and meet her more than half-way in a spirit of good will. It is gratifying to note that North China, under control of the Peiping political committee, remains comparatively quiet.

In view of the important rights and interests of Japan in that region and of its territorial contiguity with Manchukuo, and also from the standpoint of the Tangku truce agreement, the question of maintenance of peace and order in North China is of special concern to Japan. She expects China to see to it that nothing will happen that may bring chaos to that area.

Meanwhile we are watching, not without grave misgivings, the activities of the Communist party and the increasing rampancy of "Red" armies in China.

Regarding Japan's relations with the Soviet Union, it may be recalled that, subsequent to the conclusion of the Peking basic treaty in 1925, normal contact was maintained between the two countries, and that even after the Manchurian incident there was thorough mutual understanding between the two Powers of their respective positions, so that no difficult question was encountered.

However, more recently the attitude of the Soviet Union toward Japan seems to have undergone a change of some sort. It is most surprising and regrettable that the Soviet Union should now take to broadcasting at home and abroad, through the press and other channels, unwarranted criticisms directed against Japan, and circulate exaggerated stories about aggravations of this or that situation, evidently for political and diplomatic purposes which such rumours are calculated to serve.

Japan has consistently preserved her fair and equitable attitude toward the Soviet Union throughout the years past, before and after the Manchurian incident. Despite the fundamental differences in both the theory and constitution of the State that divide the two countries, we have always endeavoured to keep on good neighbourly terms with Soviet Russia and sought the solution of all questions by pacific means.

Especially since the establishment of Manchukuo, the Japanese Government has been acting solely upon its conviction that a proper adjustment of the tripartite relationship among Japan, Manchukuo, and the Soviet Union was of paramount importance for the tranquillity of eastern Asia. Japan certainly is setting up no new military establishments along the Manchukuo-Soviet frontiers, Moscow propaganda notwithstanding.

Indeed, it is only as a part of the above-mentioned friendly policy that Japan has undertaken since last June to act as an intermediary between Manchukuo and the Soviet Union in their negotiations on the proposed transfer of the North Manchuria Railway. Such being the case, I am sure that before long the Soviet Union must come to appreciate fully the true intentions of Japan.

It is earnestly hoped that the North Manchuria Railway negotiations, which have unfortunately been at a standstill for some time past, will soon be resumed.

It may be definitely stated that between Japan and the United States of America there exists no question that is intrinsically difficult of solution. Far from having any thought of picking a quarrel with America, Japan fervently desires American friendship. At the same

GENERAL STATEMENTS OF POLICY   841

time I am confident that the United States will not fail to appraise correctly Japan's position in eastern Asia.

Only for a time following the outbreak of the Manchurian incident, public opinion in America was aroused against Japan, bringing about something like temporary estrangement of the two peoples. It is hardly necessary to reiterate that Japan is actuated by no ulterior motive other than her desire to establish enduring peace in eastern Asia.

Therefore, if only America will clearly perceive the actual condition of the Orient and realize Japan's role as a stabilizing force in eastern Asia, whatever emotional tension may yet linger between the two peoples is bound to disappear.

I sincerely hope that the two great nations across the Pacific will, in view of their important relations, commercial and otherwise, continue to join forces in cultivating their historical friendship and good understanding so as to keep the ocean for ever true to its name.

Japan's traditional amity with the British Empire remains unshaken, even in these times. I believe the two sea powers occupying geographically similar key positions, one in the East and the other in the West, can effectively serve the cause of universal peace through sympathetic appreciation of their respective standpoints and wholehearted collaboration in all quarters of the world.

It is in this sense that our Government is seeking to readjust whatever conflict of interests relating to questions of trade there may be and to strengthen further the ties of friendship that bind our empires. That our negotiations with India, an important member of the British Empire, over knotty problems of commerce, have now been substantially concluded is a source of gratification on both sides.

Now a survey of the world as a whole reveals a sorry situation in which economic disorder, political unrest and confusion, and conflict of ideas threaten to destroy international equilibrium at any moment, while the mutual confidence of nations in one another appears to have wilted not a little.

I consider that no insuperable difficulties need be anticipated in settling any question, if the nations manifest their sincerity and with true comprehension of one another's position meet in a genuine and generous spirit of universal brotherhood.

What is wanted is the abandonment of bootless jealousy and antagonism, and reinforcement of the sense of unity and mutual interdependence. However, international trade barriers, instead of decreasing, are fast multiplying. The World Economic Conference was forced to adjourn without having achieved the desired results.

Of late our industries have made marked strides with corresponding expansion in our oversea trade, although, owing to the prevailing economic nationalism, one country after another has begun to set up fresh obstacles against the advance of our export industries. Our Government is making earnest efforts to deal effectively with the situation.

Since mutual understanding of one another's unique national culture is of no small value in fostering good will between nations, our Government is planning to take suitable measures in concert with private institutions for facilitating the cultural intercourse of our nation with the outside world.

In the light of what I have already stated, it is impossible for me to deny that our foreign relations are now, and will be in the future, beset with many serious problems. However, the path of a rising nation is always strewn with problems.

As long as our people are united and well prepared to face courageously whatever difficulties may arise, and as long as we retain our composure and sobriety and "stray not from the path of rectitude, and in action always embrace the golden mean," I am confident that Japan has nothing to fear and her future will be full of hope. We should not forget that Japan, serving as only a corner-stone for the edifice of peace of eastern Asia, bears the entire burden of responsibilities.

It is this important position and these vast responsibilities in which Japan's diplomacy and national defence are rooted. Our national defence is organized in its very nature for defensive and self-protective purposes. At the same time our diplomacy has no claims to put forth, save what is legitimate and rational and consonant with our national mission.

That eventually this position in which Japan naturally and actually finds herself will be rightly understood by other Powers is, I believe, a foregone conclusion.

ADDRESS by Koki Hirota, Minister for Foreign Affairs, in the Imperial Diet, January 21, 1936

Translation, in Royal Institute of International Affairs, *Documents on International Affairs, 1937*, p. 632, citing text furnished by the Japanese Embassy in London

I HAVE THE HONOUR to report and state my views on the latest developments in Japan's foreign relations.

With the further advance of this country's international position in recent years the greater have grown its responsibilities. Fortunately the world is being brought, though gradually, to recognize Japan's sincere desire to contribute towards the establishment of world peace and more particularly our whole-hearted endeavours towards the stabilization of East Asia, while our friendly relations with neighbouring countries are being by degrees put on a solid basis.

In view of the most gratifying progress of Manchukuo, it has been decided to abolish by stages Japan's extraterritorial rights in that country and concurrently to readjust our administrative rights in the railway zone and to contribute thereby towards her development as an independent nation. Whereas the close and inseparable relationship between our two countries is rooted in the fundamental fact of the alliance for common defence concluded at the time of the establishment of Manchukuo, the natural circumstance of our mutual interdependence in the economic field has led to the establishment of the Japan-Manchukuo Joint Economic Commission. The unchallenged independence of Manchukuo and her healthy growth now actually constitute an indispensable postulate for the stability of East Asia. It is most desirable that she should continue to enhance her international prestige and promote her friendly relations with her neighbours. In other words, best efforts must be put forth for the readjustment of the relationships between Japan, Manchukuo, and China, on the one hand, and for the proper adjustment of the relations between Japan, Manchukuo, and the Soviet Union on the other.

As for the relations between Japan, Manchukuo, and China, though some improvements have been effected, an urgent necessity is felt to regulate further the tripartite relations and put them upon a normal footing so as to strengthen the foundations of the peace of East Asia. The Japanese Government have therefore formulated, after careful deliberations, a definite programme for their policy towards China. This programme consists mainly of the following three points.

The first point is concerned with the basic readjustment of Sino-Japanese relations, by which we aim to bring about the cessation by China of all unfriendly acts and measures, such as have been hitherto adopted. In fact, what we want is not only such a negative attitude on the part of China but her active and effective collaboration with Japan. Antagonism between Japan and China, which obviously works to the disadvantage of both, is a thing intolerable from the larger viewpoint of East Asia. It would be most regrettable should China resort to unfriendly actions or to her habitual policy of playing off a third Power against this country, thus undermining the stability of East Asia. On the other hand, if she should come to a full realization of this point we would, of course, be ready to extend to her our moral and material support for her advancement. Taking a long view of the situation, we have remained patient and forbearing, inviting China's self-reflection and her realization of her own responsibilities in East Asia, and waiting for a change in her policy towards our country. It is within the past year or so that China has shown her willingness to improve Sino-Japanese relations. At the last session of the Diet we declared our policy of non-aggression and non-menace towards the neighbouring countries, and set out to regularize the relations between Japan and China and to readjust the mutual interests of the two countries. Nevertheless, I am sorry that our endeavours in this direction have not brought forth fully satisfactory results so far.

The rehabilitation of Sino-Japanese relations must necessarily be attended by the regularization of the relations between Manchukuo and China, because in North China particularly the interests of these two countries and of Japan are directly and closely bound up. Owing to the fact that the Chinese Government has not recognized Manchukuo, which is contiguous with North China, and also to the singular local circumstances that have prevailed in North China itself for long years, a situation arose in that region last year which appeared disquieting for some time. More recently, however, the tension has been considerably relaxed through the establishment of the Hopei-Chahar Political Council. At any rate, it is plain that no stability can ever be attained without the adjustment of the relations between Japan, Manchukuo, and China. In the fulfilment of this purpose lies the second point of our programme. We are convinced that as the first step to a complete and final adjustment of the relations between Japan, Manchukuo, and China, the Chinese Government should recognize Manchukuo, and the two countries should open diplomatic intercourse and harmonize their interests. It is hoped that the day will soon arrive when this is done. In the meantime we believe a temporary measure should be devised in order to prevent any untoward eventuality in the relations between the three countries.

The greatest of all difficulties confronting China to-day is, I believe, Communism, which has found a ready soil for propagation in the unsettled conditions of East Asia, and which has affected China most seriously, endangering not only her border regions but her internal social order. The rampancy of Communism in China seems to surpass all our knowledge. The Red menace is, of course, not confined to East Asia, which has been selected as a field of action just at this time. The suppression of the Communist activities in our part of the globe and the liberation of China from the Red menace is, therefore, a matter of vital importance not only for China but for the stabilization of East Asia and of the world. Herein lies the third point. It is the desire of the Japanese Government to co-operate with China in various ways for the eradication of Communism.

These, then, are the three points of our programme. They involve no new or startling principles. In fact they are nothing but the most obvious and elemental concepts that must underlie the great undertaking of insuring the stability of East Asia, and as such they should, I do not hesitate to say, constitute a common cause of all nations in East Asia. The Chinese Government not only has indicated its concurrence with our views, but has proposed recently to open negotiations on Sino-Japanese *rapprochement* along the lines stated above. Although, much to our regret, there are at this moment student agitations in China which contravene the very spirit of our programme, it is expected that the present situation will soon be rectified by the Chinese authorities and an auspicious atmosphere for the opening of the said negotiations will prevail. The Japanese Government have communicated their acceptance of the Chinese proposal, and are awaiting notice from the Chinese Government of the completion of its preparations. With the progress of these negotiations we shall be able, I am confident, to lay the foundation for a thorough readjustment of Sino-Japanese relations.

Turning next to the relations between Japan, Manchukuo, and the Soviet Union, I must say that the Japanese Government have always done their best to secure peace and friendship among them. We have succeeded in eliminating a long-standing obstacle to that purpose through the conclusion of the agreement for the transference of the North Manchuria Railway. In the light of the fact that Japan, being committed to the common defence of Manchukuo, is automatically and directly affected by the political and military relations of that country with its neighbouring States, we are obliged to pay special attention to the tripartite relations of our country and Manchukuo and the Soviet Union. Along the extended common frontier between the two latter countries, there are spots where the border line is not clear, giving rise to frequent troubles. With a view to settling such frontier disputes, there is now the question of setting up a mixed commission, while the Manchukuo Government insists upon clarifying first the obscure points in the border line. With regard to the relations between the three countries, what we are most concerned about is the excessive military works which the Soviet Union is erecting in her outlying possession—namely, in East Siberia—arousing thereby public feeling strongly not only in Manchukuo but also in this country. We are calling the attention of the Soviet authorities to this matter whenever we have an opportunity to do so.

The Japanese Government attached a great importance to the developments of the Naval Conference at London which was opened on December 9 last year, and from which our delegation has now been withdrawn. The fundamental policy of the Japanese Government at the Conference was the same as at the time of the preliminary conversations held at London two years ago. Last October, when the British Government, engaged in the preparations for the Conference, sought the views of our Government regarding the plan for the declaration of building programmes and the question of qualitative limitation, we took occasion to make clear our stand by stating:

The true key to the maintenance and the promotion of world peace can be discovered only when the Powers mutually give full consideration to one another's vital needs and natural requirements and when they carry out a thorough limitation of armaments in such a way as to make a state of non-aggression and non-menace prevail among them, and the Great Powers, therefore, should be the first to strive unremittingly in these directions in order to forward the cause of peace. The fundamental policy of the Japanese Government regarding naval disarmament has no other object than the realization of such a thorough-going limitation.

It is in this spirit that the Japanese delegation proposed at the present Conference a plan for setting up a common upper limit at the lowest possible level and for the abolition of or a drastic reduction in such vessels of offensive type as capital ships, aircraft carriers, and "A" class cruisers. Despite the earnest efforts of our delegation, this just and fair proposal of Japan was not accepted by the Powers. Moreover, since it became evident that the proposals submitted by the other delegations did not meet our fundamental policy, our delegation proposed as the last resort to terminate the Conference in an amicable manner after settling such questions as could be settled and concluding agreements thereon. That proposal was also rejected, whereupon our delegation had no other alternative than to withdraw from the Conference.

A survey of the present world situation reveals the existence of much unrest and friction in many quarters and a tendency on the part of the Powers to expand rather than to curtail their armaments —which is so detrimental to the cause of disarmament. Therein lies, perhaps, one of the reasons why Japan's proposal for a sweeping reduction has not been accepted. However, it is scarcely necessary to say that, regardless of whether or not there is a disarmament treaty, the Japanese Government, devoted to the principle of non-aggression and non-menace, have no intention of doing anything to stimulate a naval competition, or of altering their policy of co-operation with the Powers in arms reduction for the cause of world peace.

Whatever may be the outcome of the present Conference, the friendly policy of this country towards the great naval Powers will undergo no change, especially towards Great Britain and the United States, with whom we have enjoyed a historic friendship for many past decades. Since Japan and America are geographically so situated that they possess each a special sphere of activity of her own, it is impossible that the two nations should ever be brought into collision. With Great Britain, we would most naturally seek to adjust our interests in various parts of the globe, and to further our traditional amity. Our intercourse with the British Dominion States is steadily growing in intimacy, with corresponding increase in trade. To Australia we sent last year Ambassador Debuchi as a goodwill envoy who went there to return the visit of Sir John Latham on a similar mission, and who also made a tour of New Zealand to promote Japan's friendly intercourse with that nation. In the South Seas countries we are endeavouring to cultivate peace and friendships for the sole purpose of the development of trade and economic relations. It is with this purpose in view that we sincerely hope for a smooth progress of the newly inaugurated Commonwealth of the Philippines.

The uninterrupted expansion of our foreign trade from year to year, coupled with the steady growth of the productive power of our industries, is a most encouraging aspect of these times. Our trade, expanding both in exports and in imports, may be said to exemplify the principle of mutual benefits in international commerce. It goes without saying that the healthy development of trade among the nations is indispensable to the promotion of international goodwill and economic well-being of the world. In spite of this evident truth, many countries are still, I regret to say, continuing their restrictive measures of various kinds which obstruct the freedom of trade. To a modern nation, particularly such as our own, with a vast population but meagre natural resources, the assurance of the sources of raw material and of a market for finished products is the condition of prime necessity to its economic existence. I really believe that such assurance alone can render possible the maintenance of political stability among nations. To cramp the world by the reckless erection of high trade barriers will only serve to invite complications and conflicts, and mean a retrogression of civilization. On the other hand, freedom of movement of men and goods throughout the world, and the Open Door and equal opportunity to natural resources, if that should be realized, would automatically create an atmosphere of freedom and mutual confidence, and no doubt contribute vastly towards the furtherance of universal peace and brotherhood.

The Japanese Government are carrying on friendly negotiations with the Governments of other countries for the purpose of adjusting our mutual interests and promoting trade and commerce as much as possible. During the past year we were unfortunately forced to invoke the Trade Protection Law against Canadian imports for some months, but I am happy to state that the application of that law has since been stopped as a result of the amicable agreement concluded between the two countries.

It is to be regretted that there are abroad statesmen of repute who seem determined to impose upon others their private convictions as to how the world should be ordered, and who are apt to denounce those who oppose their dictates as if they were disturbers of peace. No one is qualified to talk world peace unless he not only knows the national aspirations and obligations of his country but also understands and appreciates the standpoints of other countries. The understanding and appreciation of another country's standpoint is often attainable through the understanding and appreciation of that country's culture and civilization. We have succeeded in building up our national strength and prestige by adding and adapting to our civilization Occidental arts and science which we have imported during the past years. Now it is time for us, I believe, to try to introduce our arts and culture to other lands, and thus contribute towards international good understanding and to the enrichment of world civilization and the promotion of the peace and happiness of mankind.

In conclusion, let me say that the future of our foreign relations is, as I have stated, extremely complicated and complex, while at the same time our country's international position continues to rise. It behooves us well that, in conformity with the Imperial Rescript issued on this country's withdrawal from the League of Nations, we should strive to cultivate abroad good faith among nations and perform at home each his appointed task and go forth together with courage and determination to meet the world situation of to-day.

ADDRESS by Koki Hirota, Minister for Foreign Affairs, in the Imperial Diet, January 22, 1938

Translation, in Royal Institute of International Affairs, *Documents on International Affairs, 1938*, I, 342, citing *Contemporary Japan*, March, 1938, pp. 785–89; excerpts

JAPAN HAS no territorial ambitions in China, nor has she any intention of separating North China from the rest of the country. All she wants is that China, taking a broad view of the situation, will collaborate with Japan towards the fulfilment of the ideal of Sino-Japanese co-operation for the common prosperity and well-being of the two countries. Accordingly, even after the outbreak of the present affair, we eagerly look forward to joining forces with China for the purpose of securing peace in East Asia as soon as the Nationalist Government should have discarded their policy of opposition to Japan and Manchukuo and evinced a sincere desire to work together for this ideal of Japan. However, the Nationalist Government failed to understand our true intentions, and they were caught, so to speak, in the trap set by themselves, being bound by their commitments to the anti-Japanism that they had fostered for such long years. Unable to act wisely and well with a calm judgment, but relying upon third Powers, or allying themselves with Communists, they are even now calling for a prolonged resistance, regardless of the plight of the 400 million people of China whom they have plunged into the depth of suffering and misery. Now the heroic operations of our loyal and valiant forces in the north and in the south have forced the Nationalist Government to abandon Nanking, their capital, and to flee far up the Yangtze River. Still unrepentant, they persist in their desperate opposition. It is a most lamentable thing for the sake of East Asia as a whole as well as for the people of China.

Some time ago when the Japanese Government received a proffer of good offices by the German Government to act as an intermediary for bringing about direct negotiations between Japan and China, they proposed . . . the following four points as the basic conditions for the solution of the affair:

1. China to abandon her pro-Communist and anti-Japanese and anti-Manchukuo policies to collaborate with Japan and Manchukuo in their anti-Comintern policy.

2. Establishment of demilitarized zones in the necessary localities, and of a special régime for the said localities.

3. Conclusion of an economic agreement between Japan, China, and Manchukuo.

4. China to pay Japan the necessary indemnities.

The items summarized the minimum requirements which were considered absolutely indispensable by the Japanese Government. It was my earnest hope that the Nationalist Government would sue for peace on the basis of these fundamental conditions. However, that Government, blind to the larger interests of East Asia, and ignoring both our magnanimity and Germany's friendly intention, exhibited no readiness to ask frankly for peace, but only sought to delay the matter and ultimately failed to send a reply that could be regarded in any way as sincere. The Nationalist Government having thus wilfully thrown away the last chance placed at their disposal by the Japanese Government, it became clear that there would be no hope of ever arriving at a solution by waiting indefinitely for any reconsideration on the part of the Nationalist Government. It is because of these circumstances that the Japanese Government issued on the 16th of this month a statement that they would from thenceforward cease to deal with the Nationalist Government. As is made plain in that statement, our Government now look forward to the establishment and the growth of a new Chinese régime capable of genuine cooperation with Japan, which it is their intention to assist in the building up of a new and rehabilitated China. . . .

I desire to avail myself of this occasion to say that in Europe and America there are some who are apt to entertain misgivings regarding Japan's intentions as though she were trying to close the Chinese door, and expel the interests of the Powers from China. Let me state explicitly that not only will Japan respect to the fullest extent the rights and interests of the Powers in the occupied areas, but she is prepared, for the purpose of promoting the welfare of the Chinese people, to leave the door wide open to all Powers and to welcome their economic and cultural cooperation there. It is earnestly to be hoped that the Powers, by recognizing the new conditions prevailing in China, and by appreciating the propriety of such Japanese demands for necessary and national adjustments as have been submitted, or may be submitted hereafter, in order to meet those conditions, will cooperate for the establishment of a new order in the Far East. . . .

Japan's policy towards the Soviet Union has always been guided by our conviction of the urgent need of placing the relations of the two countries upon a normal footing for the sake of the peace of East Asia. It is in accordance with this policy that we endeavored within the past year to solve the long pending issue of the revision of the Fishery Treaty; but unfortunately, owing to the attitude of the Soviet authorities, we were obliged to conclude a *modus vivendi* at the year end as in the year before last. . . .

This Government attach great importance to a smooth operation of the Japanese concession enterprises in North Sakhalin. Let me say that the Japanese Government will never allow these rights and interests derived from the Soviet-Japanese Basic Treaty to be nullified through unreasonable pressure. Again, the relations between the Soviet Union and China are attracting the special attention of our nation. China concluded in August last a non-aggression pact with the Soviet Union, while members of the Communist International have penetrated all classes of the Chinese, destroying the social order of the country and endangering the stability of East Asia. Japan, ever solicitous for the civilization of East Asia and the welfare of its people, cannot but view the situation with the gravest concern. . . .

Since the outbreak of the present affair, the United States has always maintained a fair and just attitude, acting on all occasions with such careful regard for the cause of Japanese-American friendship that, despite such mishaps as the *Panay* incident, the relations of the two countries, I am happy to say, have suffered no impairment. The importance to the conduct of our foreign affairs of American understanding needs scarcely to be mentioned. We shall continue to do our best towards the furtherance of Japanese-American amity and good will.

As regards Great Britain, there has been no change in the policy of the Japanese Government, which aims at the maintenance of the traditional friendship between the two countries. I hope that the British Government and people, grasping fully the importance of Anglo-Japanese relations, will endeavor to comprehend correctly Japan's position in East Asia and to cooperate with Japan for the furtherance of peace and good understanding between the two nations. At the same time, I desire to urge upon our own people to stand solidly behind this policy of the Government, in view of the seriousness of the general situation.

I am glad to say that Japan and Germany have been brought closer together than ever. . . . Especially do this Government appreciate the friendly and most sympathetic attitude Germany has taken in consonance with the spirit of the German-Japanese Anti-Comintern Agreement. We will strive to strengthen further the cooperation between the two countries.

From the beginning of the present affair, Italy, understanding our true motives, has collaborated with us along all lines. It is well known to you how consistently and how energetically the Italian Government supported our country in November last year at the Brussels Conference of the Signatory Powers to the Nine-Power Treaty. In connection with the question already mentioned of the settlement of the present affair, the Italian Government again manifested their sympathetic concern. This Government are most grateful for these proofs of good will on the part of Italy, which had taken actually the same position as Japan in the matter of combating the Comintern, and joined in the German-Japanese Anti-Comintern Agreement in November last. It is a subject for congratulation from the standpoint of securing world peace that Japan, Germany, and Italy have come to join forces under the Anti-Comintern banner. This Government will seek to extend further the effective operation of this agreement in concert with Germany and Italy.

In Spain . . . the Franco Government is identified with the Government of this country in the policy adopted against the Comintern. In the light of these facts we have decided to recognize that Government, and the necessary steps to that end were taken early in December last year. . . .

ADDRESS by Hachiro Arita, Minister for Foreign Affairs, in the Imperial Diet, February 1, 1940

Translation, in *The New York Times*, February 1, 1940, citing text as made public by the Japanese Consulate General in New York

1. I AM particularly glad to have this opportunity of speaking of Japan's foreign policy and international relations before the Diet, for this year marks the 2,600th anniversary of the founding of our empire.

2. It is unnecessary to say that the key to Japan's foreign policy lies in the large spirit in which our empire was founded. It aims first at stabilizing East Asia, after which every effort will be made to bring about peace, based upon international justice. In pursuance of this fundamental policy the Japanese Government are doing everything in their power to settle the China affair and to adjust international relations from an independent standpoint of their own.

3. As is well known, our basic policy for settlement of the China affair is to join forces with New China, which shall be purged of all anti-Japanese and pro-Comintern influence; to unite with her in the common purpose of establishing a new order in East Asia and to realize neighborly amity and common defense against the Comintern and full economic cooperation.

4. It is a source of profound satisfaction to both countries that the so-called peace and national salvation movement is now well under way and that a Central Chinese Government under the leadership of Wang Ching-wei is to be established in the near future. With regard to our attitude toward the proposed new government, we intend to continue the declared policy of the previous Cabinet; that is to say, we shall do all in our power to assist its formation and growth, since its aims are largely in accord with our own.

5. In connection with the new order in East Asia I should like to add that although there are some who suspect Japan of the intention to eliminate the rights and interests of third powers in China the Japanese Government, as has been repeatedly enunciated, have absolutely no desire to do away with the rights and interests of third pow-

ers in China. We are, in fact, anxious to see the development of China's trade with other powers and welcome foreign investments in China as long as they are of a purely economic character. And that, I am confident, is also the wish of the new Central Government of China that is about to be established.

There will at first, owing to the fact that military operations are still being carried out, be restrictions of one kind or another, but these restrictions will be modified or removed as soon as local conditions are restored to normal.

Manchukuo, to which our country is bound by neighborly and inseparable ties of relationship, having made swift and splendid progress, is now ready to emerge as a great power of East Asia, a fact which is most gratifying for the sake of general peace and prosperity in this part of the globe.

6. The Japanese Government have always desired to adjust relations with the Soviet Union and so contribute toward ensuring the peace of East Asia as a whole. More recently the international feeling between the two countries took a turn for better. We are planning to seek concrete and practical solutions of the principal questions now pending and a consequent general adjustment of Soviet-Japanese relations.

With regard to boundary questions a truce agreement was signed last Autumn in connection with the Nomonhan incident; and since last December the temporary Manchukuoan-Mongolian boundary commission, representing the countries concerned, has been set up for the purpose of delimiting the precise boundary line in the disputed areas. The Japanese Government is now negotiating for the early establishment of commissions with the view to delimiting boundaries not only in the Nomonhan area but also all along the frontier between Manchukuo and Soviet territory for the prevention of boundary disputes and for a peaceful solution of all possible international contentions in frontier districts so as to bring tranquillity to all sectors of the Manchukuoan-Mongolian and Manchukuoan-Soviet frontiers.

7. Negotiations for a treaty of commerce between Japan and the Soviet Union are now in progress at Moscow and we are looking to a satisfactory culmination of the negotiations. With regard to the long-pending question of concluding a fisheries treaty it is our intention to settle this matter as soon as possible in accordance with the stipulation provided for in the modus vivendi which was concluded in December last. It is hoped that the Soviet Government will cooperate fully with the view to solving these specific questions and, moreover, that they will cease interfering with our concession in-

dustries in China and collaborate in securing the peace of East Asia as a whole.

8. Japan's relations with Germany and Italy have grown increasingly cordial ever since the conclusion of the anti-Comintern agreement. Our nation is profoundly grateful to the governments and peoples of those countries for the sympathy and support they extended to Japan since the beginning of the China affair. Our policy of defense against the Comintern remains unaltered. We will, moreover, continue to cultivate, in accordance with that policy, our intimate relations with all signatory powers of the Anti-Comintern agreement.

Since the beginning of the China affair the Japanese Government have done all in their power to bring the British Government to a correct appreciation of the reality of the situation. More recently we have attempted to solve the Tientsin question and to effect a general adjustment of British-Japanese relations.

It is most unfortunate that on January 21 a British man-of-war searched the Japanese ship *Asama Maru* and seized twenty-one of the German passengers on board. In view of the unprecedented fact that this incident occurred in our home waters it is deeply regretted by our government as well as by the entire nation. Negotiations are now in progress with the British authorities and we are doing our utmost to arrive at a satisfactory settlement.

9. Last year on July 26 the United States Government suddenly gave notice of their intention to abrogate the treaty of commerce and navigation which had been for thirty years, since 1911, a pledge of friendship between Japan and America. The reason which prompted the American Government to take this step is believed to be that by so doing it would serve in a solution of the various questions which have arisen between Japan and America in connection with the China affair. We endeavored therefore to conclude a new treaty or at least to prevent the advent of a treatyless situation by making the American Government understand more thoroughly the attitude and aims of Japan. Unfortunately, the commercial relations between the two countries have nevertheless fallen into a treatyless status as from January 26 of this year.

10. On the other hand, in December the American Government took steps internally in order to accord Japanese ships and goods after the lapse of the treaty the same treatment as before; they further declared their intention to make no change in the treatment of Japanese subjects residing in or entering the United States as so-called treaty merchants. Thus, despite the treatyless situation, Japanese-American trade relations have in practice undergone no change.

Although the policy of the Japanese Government in the present

China affair is not to eliminate the legitimate rights and interests of the United States and other third powers, but on the contrary to invite their active participation in the construction of a new order in East Asia it is inevitable that trade and other economic activities of third powers should be affected at times by military operations which are being conducted on so vast a scale.

11. In these circumstances our government have resorted to all possible means to protect the rights and interests of third powers while our military forces have frequently endured even strategic disadvantages on that account. Moreover, we are making it a point to give due consideration to damages suffered by third-power nationals in consequence of our military operations. I firmly believe that with the establishment and development of the new order America will come to learn the absence of a desire on our part for either exclusion or monopoly in both economic and commercial fields.

A treatyless situation which deprives trade of stability and makes relations in general difficult is not desirable for either Japan or America. We propose to exert further efforts in the confident hope that Japanese-American relations will be restored to a normal status, that is to say on a treaty basis.

12. With regard to South Seas regions the Japanese Government are desirous of maintaining with them a relationship of co-existence and co-prosperity through economic cooperation and collaboration in the development of natural resources. We intend to put forth every effort along this line toward enhancing the existing close relations between Japan and those regions.

13. Under prevailing conditions Japan must do her utmost for the promotion of her export trade and the assurance of a supply of necessary goods. The various organs concerned with trade are doing everything in their power to realize these purposes by maintaining close coordination among them. Economic cooperation with all other countries is being expedited by removing obstacles to trade, developing new markets, strengthening economic cooperation between Japan, Manchukuo and China, concluding trade agreements on principles of reciprocity and compensation and in various other ways.

14. There are many countries with which we are conducting trade negotiations. The United States of America and the Soviet Union I have already mentioned, but included among them are France, Italy, India and various countries of Central and South America.

Since the outbreak of the European war it has been noted that not only are there many instances in which economic policies adopted by belligerent powers tend to obstruct our importation of essential goods or to interfere with development of our export trade, but also that some of these measures, exceeding belligerent rights recognized under international law, are destructive of the freedom of trade and of freedom of the seas. The government have, therefore, presented vigorous protests to the powers concerned and they are taking other appropriate steps for the protection of our trade rights.

15. On the outbreak of the European war last September the Japanese Government made known, both at home and abroad, our intention not to be involved in that war, but to concentrate our efforts on settlement of the China affair. The government has since strictly adhered to this non-involvement policy.

It is believed, however, that the present war is destined to bring about drastic changes in the general situation of Europe regardless of how it may end and consequently its effects on settlement of the China affair and the stabilization of East Asia are likely to be tremendous. The government, while watching the development of the war with grave concern are, however, determined to take appropriate steps to meet any changes in the situation.

16. International peace fails to be maintained for various reasons. But, after all, is this not largely due to the fact that some nations insist upon trying to maintain an irrational and unjust international *status quo* relative to race, religion, territory, resources, trade, immigration and other matters by adopting exclusionist policies or by abusing their superior positions? Real world peace, based on justice, can not therefore be expected to prevail unless and until these causes are thoroughly examined and the root of the evil is eliminated, after which all countries would be enabled to find its proper place in the family of nations.

17. Now that in Europe also a growing demand is heard for a new order, while steady progress is being made in East Asia for its realization, it seems that a rare opportunity is afforded mankind for self-examination. At such a time as this we feel more keenly than ever the importance of the ethical aspect of diplomacy. With this conviction the Japanese Government have hitherto devoted their efforts toward the establishment of peace based on justice. I hope, then, that our nation, with united and inflexible determination, will go forward to establish a new order in East Asia and will contribute thereby to the happiness and welfare of all mankind.

GENERAL STATEMENTS OF POLICY 857

ADDRESS by Shigenori Togo, Minister for Foreign Affairs, in the Imperial Diet, November 17, 1941

Translation, in *The New York Times*, November 17, 1941. Reprinted by permission of the Associated Press

WITH HEAVY responsibilities for the conduct of foreign affairs having unexpectedly devolved upon me, it is a great pleasure for me to avail myself of this opportunity today of speaking on the foreign policy of the imperial government.

Japan, engaged for the past four years in military operations for the construction of a new order in East Asia, is now marching forward to surmount current difficulties with the unity of the entire nation. First of all, I wish good fortune and success to officers and men of our gallant fighting services who are distinguishing themselves on the front under the august virtue of His Imperial Majesty, paying at the same time my humble and sincere tribute to the honored spirits of these who have fallen.

It needs no reiteration that the fundamental principle of Japan's foreign policy aims at establishment of peace in East Asia based on justice, thereby contributing toward promotion of the general welfare of mankind. It is by nothing other than the fruit of constant efforts exerted in the espousal of this great principle that our country has witnessed the unceasing development of her national fortune since the Meiji Restoration.

It may be recalled that in the past seventy odd years Japan has, on more than one occasion, successfully overcome national crises. Especially noteworthy is the Russian-Japanese War, in which Japan staked her national existence in order to eliminate an obstacle to the peace of East Asia. She has since been advancing her position as a stabilizing force in East Asia and is now endeavoring with unflinching courage to accomplish the great task of inaugurating a new order in East Asia on the basis of justice as a contribution toward the peace of the world.

Fortunately, Germany and Italy having similar views with Japan, the three-power pact was brought into being. In little more than a year of its existence, as is well known, the pact has made, as intended, a great contribution toward the construction of a new order in East Asia and Europe as well as toward the prevention of the spread of war.

The Empire of Manchukuo has become increasingly strong in her foundation since her establishment. No less than thirteen countries have already recognized Manchukuo, and her international status, together with her national prosperity, is being enhanced.

In China, Japan is conducting military operations to subjugate the

Chungking regime. The basic policy of Japan toward the China affair consists in establishing cooperation between Japan and China, thereby securing the stability of East Asia and the advancement of common prosperity in this region.

A basic treaty regulating relations between Japan and the national government [the Wang Ching-Wei puppet regime] of China. It is the determination of the Imperial Government to extend their cooperation toward further strengthening of the national government of China.

Along with successful conclusion of the China affair, Japan takes a great interest in the region of the north, and also in the South Seas. Following the outbreak of the European war Japan has exerted every effort to prevent the conflict from spreading to the east from the standpoint of maintaining the peace of East Asia in general.

The Japanese-Soviet neutrality pact, concluded in April this year, is also intended to secure safety in the north in conformity with the said policy. Although hostilities subsequently broke out between Germany and the Soviet Union, our government have steadfastly maintained this policy of preserving security in the north.

It is, in a word, Japan's determination to prevent by all means not only the causation of factors likely to disturb peace in the north, but also the development of such a situation as will menace the rights and interests of Japan.

As regards the South Seas region, the imperial government successfully mediated in the settlement of a border dispute between Thailand and French Indo-China, and also established close political and economic relations with French Indo-China. They further concluded with France a protocol for the joint defense of French Indo-China to meet the international situation confronting the latter when it began to threaten seriously the security of French Indo-China and consequently the tranquillity of East Asia and the security of Japan.

They have dispatched Mr. Yoshizawa as special Ambassador to French Indo-China to draw still closer the bonds of friendship between Japan and that country. They have also strengthened economic relations with Thailand and are endeavoring to promote cooperation between the two countries by exchanging Ambassadors.

It is extremely deplorable, however, that malicious propaganda should be let loose by some third powers representing Japan as harboring aggressive designs toward those regions. I have not the slightest doubt that the peoples of East Asia, understanding the real intentions of Japan, will cooperate with our country for the establishment of a new order in East Asia.

Japan is thus concentrating her sincere and utmost efforts on successful termination of the China affair and initiation of the new order in East Asia. But when our troops entered the southern part of French Indo-China this Summer in accordance with the protocol for joint defense referred to above, Great Britain and the United States chose to regard it as a menace to their territories and froze Japan's assets in their countries, which constitutes a measure tantamount to rupturing economic relations.

The British dominions and colonies have all followed suit and the Netherlands East Indies, too, has joined in similar steps. Great Britain and the United States have even gone to the length of establishing encircling positions against Japan by inducing Australia, the Netherlands East Indies and the Chungking regime to join in.

The international situation confronting Japan has thus become increasingly tense day after day, and pressure of the kind above referred to from Great Britain and the United States toward our country constitutes a really serious question, affecting as it deeply does the very existence of our empire.

In this connection I should like to call the attention of every one here and abroad to the fact that despite such developments the imperial government, prompted by the high motive to preserve peace in the world and particularly in the Pacific, and also to avert the worst eventuality, have hitherto devoted their utmost efforts in order to overcome the difficult situation.

Since the outbreak of the China affair Japanese-American relations have progressively deteriorated, steadily gathering force, so that if they were left to drift without timely check there was no knowing whether the situation would not ultimately end in catastrophe.

Should such an eventuality occur it would entail great suffering not only in countries in the Pacific basin, but on all of mankind as well.

Solicitous for peace as ever, the Japanese Government have, since April last, carried on conversations with the government of the United States, with a view to bringing about a fundamental adjustment of Japanese-American relations. The former Cabinet endeavored earnestly to reach a successful conclusion of negotiations, in view particularly of the tension in the situation which had been accentuated since Summer this year, but agreement of views was not reached between the two countries.

The present Cabinet, in order to avert an international crisis and preserve the peace of the Pacific, decided also to continue negotiations, which are still in progress. I regret to say that I have not the liberty of revealing, at this juncture, the details of the negotiations.

But I think an amicable conclusion is by no means impossible if the Government of the United States are, on the one hand, as genuinely solicitous for world peace as are the Imperial Government, and on the other understand Japan's natural requirements and her position in East Asia and consider the situation as it exists there in the light of realities.

Moreover, the views of the two countries have generally been made clear through conversations which have now lasted more than six months, and consequently I believe it must be evident to the United States Government that, viewed even from the technical angle, there is no necessity of spending much time on negotiations hereafter.

Such being the circumstances, the Japanese Government are bending their best efforts to a successful conclusion of the negotiations, but there is naturally a limit to our conciliatory attitude. Should an occasion arise such as might menace the very existence of the empire or compromise the prestige of Japan as a great power, it goes without saying that Japan must face it with a firm and resolute attitude.

For my part, I am taking charge of negotiations with a firm resolve regarding this point.

Japan is now confronted with an unprecedentedly difficult situation and it is necessary that the entire nation should unite and join forces to overcome it. National defense and diplomacy are inseparable while internal politics and external policy are a counterpart of each other.

At no time is the need for mobilization of the nation's total strength, with the government and the people uniting, felt more acutely than at the present juncture. In concluding the frank statement of my views and opinions, I earnestly hope that the 100,000,000 of my fellow-countrymen will extend their full support and cooperation.

DISARMAMENT

NOTE VERBALE from Hirosi Saito, Japanese Ambassador to the United States, to the Secretary of State of the United States (Cordell Hull), December 29, 1934

Department of State, *Foreign Relations of the United States: Japan, 1931–1941*, I, 274; see also supra, p. 835

I HAVE BEEN telegraphically instructed by Mr. Hirota to say to you, on the occasion of handing you the written notice of the intention of the Japanese Government to terminate the Washington Naval Treaty of 1922, in the following sense with suitable amplifications:—

As has already been made known to the American Delegation in London, the basic policy of the Japanese Government in the present disarmament negotiations consists in the discontinuance of the ratio system and the total abolition or the utmost limitation of aggressive war vessels. From that point of view, the Japanese Government considers it inadmissible to have the Treaty continue in force.

The Japanese Government entertains the desire that the preliminary negotiations shall be conducted in the friendliest spirit possible and, to that end, wished that all Powers concerned would conjointly make the notification of treaty termination. The proposal has not been accepted by any of the Powers, and the Japanese Government has been constrained to act singly in giving notice in accordance with the provisions of Article 23 of the Treaty itself.

It is, however, a matter of course that the Japanese Government has no intention whatever to proceed to naval aggrandisement or to disturb international peace. It will continue in its sincere endeavors to strengthen the relationships of peace and amity among all Powers, by participating as heretofore in the friendly negotiations with the other Powers concerned in which it will strive for the conclusion with them of a new agreement, just, fair and adequate in conception and consonant with the spirit of disarmament, to replace the Washington Treaty.

STATEMENT by Admiral Osami Nagano, Chairman of the Japanese Delegation to the Conference for the Limitation of Naval Armament at London, in the First Committee of the Conference, January 15, 1936

Royal Institute of International Affairs, *Documents on International Affairs, 1936*, p. 606, citing *The Times* (London), January 17, 1936

I WISH TO STATE—and this I do with all due deference to the lofty aims of the other Powers—that Japan is second to no country in her sincere and zealous desires for world peace. We have taken as our primary objective the elimination of the menace of war and the assurance of equality of security for all Powers concerned.

The disarmament question should be considered on the basis of "one Power versus one Power" relationship. If two Powers are to conclude such an agreement on the strengths of their naval forces as will give them equal standing and guarantee their mutual security, the most rational principle to be applied is that of equality of armaments. We believe, in fact, that there is no other method which would be at once fair and just. And this is especially true as between two Powers which are separated by ocean and whose defence is wholly dependent on their navies.

It is a peculiar characteristic of naval forces that they can be moved about at will with great facility. It follows, therefore, that when discussing naval relations between two countries, it is only reasonable that at least all vessels capable of participating in naval engagements should be taken into consideration.

In order to establish as complete a state of non-aggression and non-menace as possible, we advocate the complete abolition or drastic reduction of offensive armaments. We advocate the abolition of aircraft carriers and a drastic reduction in capital ships and A-class cruisers. As regards armaments which are essentially defensive in character and purpose, we believe that each Power should be permitted to equip itself in the manner best suited to its conditions and circumstances.

I would undertake to set forth the framework of our formula:

(1) There would first of all be fixed a maximum global tonnage which none of the Powers concerned may exceed, and which must be fixed at as low a level as possible so as not to be contrary to the spirit of disarmament.

(2) There would be fixed for those categories which are generally recognized to be predominantly offensive in character—namely, capital ships, aircraft carriers (in the event of their non-abolition), and

DISARMAMENT

A-class cruisers—a common maximum tonnage and number of units to be allowed to each Power in respect of each of the three categories separately.

(3) As regards B-class cruisers and vessels of lesser type, which are generally recognized to be essentially defensive, it should be sufficient to fix a common maximum global tonnage for all of the said categories.

(4) Any Power which may deem it necessary to do so for reasons of its special circumstances may voluntarily reduce its tonnage in A-class cruisers, and increase its tonnage in any of the defensive categories.

(5) The Japanese plan would not necessarily preclude the adoption of such a formula, for instance, as the declaration of naval building programmes.

(6) If there should be any Power which claims the necessity of effecting modifications even beyond the adjustments contemplated in the foregoing paragraphs, such claim would be carefully examined by the Powers concerned, and if it is found to be reasonable and well-founded Japan would not refuse its recognition. But we could in no circumstances consent to an increase in the combatant strength of a navy such as would jeopardize the state of non-menace and non-aggression.

May I be permitted at this point to consider, in the light of the basic conception underlying the Japanese proposal, a few of the points raised by the other delegations in the course of their observations on our plan? We can readily understand that the possession of greater and more numerous oversea possessions and lines of communication may well justify a demand for a greater strength than other Powers in small and purely defensive types of vessels which have no combatant capacity at sea but which are suitable for coast patrol, defence of harbours, and other similar purposes. But if, for the same reason, a Power should demand superiority in naval force as a whole, the sense of security of other Powers would thereby be disturbed. In any case, I believe it is a well-known fact that the conditions of nations whose naval forces are now on a basis of parity are not the same as regards their oversea possessions and lines of communications.

Japan is wholly dependent on the sea. She is poor in natural resources, and, with her population exceeding in density that of any other country in the world, is forced to look to countries beyond the seas for the greater part of the supplies necessary to her existence, as well as for the raw materials for her industries.

By way of conclusion, I desire to say that while Japan will never cease to hope for the conclusion of a comprehensive agreement on naval disarmament, that is not to say that she is going to insist on obtaining the impossible. It is our conviction that through the adoption of the principles embodied in the Japanese proposal the Conference would succeed in achieving a comprehensive agreement on naval disarmament without serious difficulties.

LETTER from Admiral Osami Nagano, Chairman of the Japanese Delegation to the Conference for the Limitation of Naval Armament at London, to the Chairman of the Conference (Lord Monsell), January 15, 1936

Royal Institute of International Affairs, *Documents on International Affairs, 1936*, p. 614, citing *The Times* (London), January 16, 1936; *see also supra*, pp. 842, 846

I HAVE THE HONOUR to notify your lordship that, as it has become sufficiently clear at today's session of the First Committee that the basic principles embodied in our proposal for a comprehensive limitation and reduction of naval armaments cannot secure general support, our delegation have now come to the conclusion that we can no longer usefully continue our participation in the deliberations of the present Conference.

We remain, nevertheless, firmly convinced that our proposal is one best calculated to attain an effective disarmament, and we regret to state that we cannot subscribe, for the reasons we have repeatedly set forth, to the plans of quantitative limitation submitted by the other delegations.

I desire to assure you, on this occasion, that we most sincerely appreciate the cordial manner in which you have been good enough to conduct the Conference; at the same time, I should like to tender our deepest thanks, on behalf of our delegation, for the hearty cooperation of all the delegations to this Conference.

NOTE from Koki Hirota, Minister for Foreign Affairs, to the American Ambassador to Japan (Joseph C. Grew), February 12, 1938

"Unofficial translation," which accompanied the note, in Department of State, *Press Releases*, February 12, 1938, p. 255

YOUR EXCELLENCY:

I have the honor to acknowledge the receipt of Your Excellency's letter number 875 dated 5th February 1938 in which you set forth your Government's desire regarding the communication of information on the matter of naval construction.

It may be recalled that at the last London Naval Conference the Japanese Government proposed, in the earnest desire to bring about a drastic reduction of naval armament, the total abolition of capital ships and aircraft-carriers, which are aggressive in their nature, and at the same time contended that qualitative limitation, if not accompanied by quantitative limitation, would not be calculated to achieve any fair and equitable measure of disarmament. Unfortunately the views of the Japanese Government were not shared by your Government and the other governments concerned. This fundamental principle entertained by the Japanese Government was, as your Government will be aware, made clear again last year in their reply to the proposal of your Government regarding the limitation of gun calibers. The Japanese Government, always prompted by the spirit of nonmenace and nonaggression, have no intention whatever of possessing an armament which would menace other countries. At this juncture, when, as a result of the nonacceptance by other countries of the reasonable desires of Japan in the matter of disarmament, there is as yet in existence no fair disarmament treaty to which Japan is a party, the Japanese Government are of opinion that the mere communication of information concerning the construction of vessels will, in the absence of quantitative limitation, not contribute to any fair and equitable measure of disarmament and regret that they are unable to comply with the desire of your Government on this point.

The Japanese Government fail to see any logical reasoning in an assumption on the part of your Government that this Government must be deemed to entertain a scheme of constructing vessels which are not in conformity with the limits provided in the London Naval Treaty of 1936, from the mere fact that they do not despatch a reply giving the desired information; and they are of opinion that it is not a matter which should concern this Government if your Government, on the basis of whatever reason or rumor, should exercise the right of escalation provided in any treaty to which Japan is not a party.

Your Government are good enough to intimate that, should the Japanese Government hereafter be prepared to agree to some limitation in respect of the tonnage of vessels and the caliber of guns, they would also be prepared to discuss the matter. The Japanese Government still holding the firm conviction that qualitative limitation, if not accompanied by quantitative limitation, would by no means contribute to the attainment of any fair and equitable measure of disarmament, cannot but consider that the discussion suggested by your Government would not conduce in any measure to the realization of their desires concerning disarmament. It is to be added, however, that as the Japanese Government do not fall behind other Governments in their ardent desire for disarmament, they will be ready at any moment to enter into any discussions on the matter of disarmament which give primary importance to a fair quantitative limitation.

INVASIONS OF CHINA AND RELATIONS WITH THE UNITED STATES

STATEMENT Issued by the Japanese Government after an Extraordinary Cabinet Meeting, September 24, 1931

As presented by the Japanese Embassy at Washington to the Department of State, September 25, 1931. Department of State, *Foreign Relations of the United States: Japan, 1931–1941*, I, 11

(1) THE Japanese Government has constantly been exercising honest endeavors in pursuance of its settled policy to foster friendly relations between Japan and China and to promote the common prosperity and well-being of the two countries. Unfortunately, the conduct of officials and individuals of China, for some years past, has been such that our national sentiment has frequently been irritated. In particular, unpleasant incidents have taken place one after another in regions of Manchuria and Mongolia in which Japan is interested in especial degree until an impression has gained strength in the minds of the Japanese people that Japan's fair and friendly attitude is not being reciprocated by China in like spirit. Amidst an atmosphere of perturbation and anxiety thus created a detachment of Chinese troops destroyed tracks of the South Manchurian Railway in the vicinity of Mukden and attacked our railway guards at midnight of September 18th. A clash between Japanese and Chinese troops then took place.

(2) The situation became critical as the number of Japanese guards stationed along the entire railway did not then exceed ten thousand four hundred while there were in juxtaposition some two hundred twenty thousand Chinese soldiers. Moreover, hundreds of thousands of Japanese residents were placed in jeopardy. In order to forestall imminent disaster the Japanese army had to act swiftly. The Chinese soldiers, garrisoned in neighboring localities, were disarmed and the duty of maintaining peace and order was left in the hands of the local Chinese organizations under the supervision of the Japanese troops.

(3) These measures having been taken, our soldiers were mostly withdrawn within the railway zone. There still remain some detachments in Mukden and Kirin and small number of men in a few other places. But nowhere does a state of military occupation as such exist.

Reports that Japanese authorities have seized customs or salt gabelle office at Yingkou or that they have taken control of Chinese railways between Supingkai and Chengchiatun or between Mukden and Sinmintun are entirely untrue, nor has the story of our troops having ever been sent north of Changchun or into Chientao any foundation in fact.

(4) The Japanese Government at a special cabinet meeting September 19th took decision that all possible efforts should be made to prevent aggravation of the situation and instructions to that effect were given to the commander of the Manchurian garrison. It is true that a detachment was despatched from Changchun to Kirin September 21st, but it was not with a view to military occupation but only for the purpose of removing the menace to the South Manchuria Railway on flank. As soon as that object has been attained the bulk of our detachment will be withdrawn. It may be added that while a mixed brigade of four thousand men was sent from Korea to join the Manchurian garrison the total number of men in the garrison at present still remains within the limit set by the treaty and that fact cannot therefore be regarded as having in any way added to the seriousness of the international situation.

(5) It may be superfluous to repeat that the Japanese Government harbors no territorial designs in Manchuria. What we desire is that Japanese subjects shall be enabled to safely engage in various peaceful pursuits and be given an opportunity for participating in the development of that land by means of capital and labor. It is the proper duty of a government to protect the rights and interests legitimately enjoyed by the nation or individuals. The endeavors of the Japanese Government to guard the South Manchurian Railway against wanton attacks would be viewed in no other light. The Japanese Government, true to established policy, is prepared to cooperate with the Chinese Government in order to prevent the present incident from developing into a disastrous situation between the two countries and to work out such constructive plans as will once for all eradicate causes for future friction. The Japanese Government would be more than gratified if the present difficulty could be brought to a solution which will give a new turn to mutual relations of the two countries.

NOTE from Kenkichi Yoshizawa, Minister for Foreign Affairs, to the American Ambassador to Japan (W. Cameron Forbes), January 16, 1932

Department of State, *Press Releases*, January 16, 1932, p. 68

I HAVE THE HONOR to acknowledge the receipt of Your Excellency's note dated the 8th January, which has had the most careful attention of this Government.

The Government of Japan were well aware that the Government of the United States could always be relied on to do everything in their power to support Japan's efforts to secure the full and complete fulfillment in every detail of the treaties of Washington and the Kellogg Treaty for the Outlawry of War. They are glad to receive this additional assurance of the fact.

As regards the question which Your Excellency specifically mentions of the policy of the so-called "open door," the Japanese Government, as has so often been stated, regard that policy as a cardinal feature of the politics of the Far East, and only regret that its effectiveness is so seriously diminished by the unsettled conditions which prevail throughout China. In so far as they can secure it, the policy of the open door will always be maintained in Manchuria, as in China proper.

They take note of the statement by the Government of the United States that the latter can not admit the legality of matters which might impair the treaty rights of the United States or its citizens or which might be brought about by means contrary to the treaty of 27 August 1928. It might be the subject of an academic doubt, whether in a given case the impropriety of means necessarily and always avoids the ends secured; but as Japan has no intention of adopting improper means, that question does not practically arise.

It may be added that the treaties which relate to China must necessarily be applied with due regard to the state of affairs from time to time prevailing in that country, and that the present unsettled and distracted state of China is not what was in the contemplation of the high contracting parties at the time of the Treaty of Washington. It was certainly not satisfactory then: but it did not display that disunion and those antagonisms which it does to-day. This can not affect the binding character of the stipulations of treaties: but it may in material respects modify their application, since they must necessarily be applied with reference to the state of facts as they exist.

My Government desire further to point out that any replacement which has occurred in the personnel of the administration of Manchuria has been the necessary act of the local population. Even in cases of hostile occupation—which this was not—it is customary for the local officials to remain in the exercise of their functions. In the present case they for the most part fled or resigned: it was their own behavior which was calculated to destroy the working of the apparatus of government. The Japanese Government can not think that the Chinese people, unlike all others, are destitute of the power of self-determination and of organizing themselves in order to secure civilized conditions when deserted by the existing officials.

While it need not be repeated that Japan entertains in Manchuria no territorial aims or ambitions, yet, as Your Excellency knows, the welfare and safety of Manchuria and its accessibility for general trade are matters of the deepest interest and of quite extraordinary importance to the Japanese people. That the American Government are always alive to the exigencies of Far Eastern questions has already been made evident on more than one occasion. At the present juncture, when the very existence of our national policy is involved, it is agreeable to be assured that the American Government are devoting in a friendly spirit such sedulous care to the correct appreciation of the situation.

I shall be obliged if Your Excellency will transmit this communication to your Government, and I avail myself, etc.

STATEMENT Issued by the Japanese Government, September 15, 1932

Translation, in League of Nations, *Official Journal,* Special Supplement No. 111, p. 79

MANCHURIA is the land for the preservation of whose integrity Japan, on one memorable occasion, set her national destinies at stake. For twenty-seven years which have elapsed since, our people have participated in the development of Manchuria. Their untiring efforts have rendered it the prosperous land that it is to-day, and it has now come to have inescapable bearing upon our national defence and the very existence of our people. Of recent years, however, the anti-foreign revolutionary diplomacy which has been adopted by China under the influence of radical ideology has steadily encroached upon our all-important rights and interests there, and, finally, the incident of September 18th last compelled Japan to resort to necessary measures of self-defence.

Upon the downfall of all the north-eastern regime consequent upon the occurrence of the Manchurian affair, leading personalities in the province of Mukden, Kirin, Heilung-kiang and Jehol, Tungsheng Special District and the League of Mongolian Banners, assembled in consultation, and on March 1st of this year promulgated a Declaration of Independence, by which they proclaimed severance as from that date of all relations with the Republic of China and the establishment of the independent State of Manchukuo. The declaration set forth a constructive programme of the new State in which, *inter alia*, it has made clear its intention internally to abolish the political corruption of the old regime and to carry out a policy characteristic of the "Kingly Way," and externally to honour a sense of justice, to seek international goodwill and friendship, to take over existing obligations and to respect the principle of the open door and equal opportunity—domestic and foreign policies which are all very fair and above-board. On March 10th, the Manchukuo Government sent a communication to Japan and sixteen other countries, in which they repeated the above programme and requested them to establish normal diplomatic relations with Manchukuo.

With serious concern and minute attention, the Imperial Japanese Government have closely followed the development of conditions in Manchukuo during the last half year and have come to recognise that Manchukuo's sincerity and determination to carry out the above policies can be relied upon. For instance, Manchukuo has established a special committee in order to prepare for the abolition of extra-territoriality, for the opening up of the interior to all foreigners alike and for other treaty revisions, and in this regard its attitude, directed as it has been to the attainment of desired revision through the agreement with the Powers concerned and without resorting to any unilateral measure of termination, has been particularly notable.

Measures which have been taken for the reform of financial and other systems have also obtained appreciable results. Thus, Manchukuo is now steadily developing into full maturity as an independent State and is assured of a future full of promise.

In consideration of the attitude of Manchukuo to the domestic and foreign problems above referred to and of Japan's interest in Manchuria in regard to the vital importance of her national defence and existence of her people, the Imperial Japanese Government have set out to secure tranquillity in this region as soon as possible and to guarantee for all time to come foundations of security of the Empire and peace of the Far East. With these purposes in view, the Government instructed General Muto, His Majesty's Ambassador, to sign on this date a Protocol recording agreement concluded with Manchukuo authorities and thus accorded formal recognition to that country. That Japan's action in this connection is not derogatory to any treaty to which she is party has been made clear in the address of the Minister for Foreign Affairs made at the Imperial Diet on August 25th last.

The Protocol confirms the fact that Manchukuo is an independent State organised in accordance with the free will of its inhabitants, and it stipulates that all rights and interests which Japan and her subjects possess within the territory of Manchukuo by virtue of treaties and other agreements are to be confirmed and respected, thus doing away once for all with all pending disputes concerning these rights and interests. Recognising the fact that any menace to Manchuria constitutes at the same time a threat to the safety and existence of the Empire, the Protocol further provides that Japan and Manchukuo are to co-operate in the maintenance of their national security and that the Japanese forces necessary for this purpose are to be stationed in Manchukuo. It is the object of the Protocol thus to establish perpetual relationship of good neighbourhood between the two countries and to secure the peace of the Far East. On several occasions the Japanese Government have declared that they harbour no territorial designs in Manchuria and the preamble of the Protocol reaffirms that both contracting Powers will mutually respect each other's territorial rights.

As regards the economic activities of foreigners, the Manchukuo Government made clear in their communication of March 10th above alluded to that they would observe the principle of the open door. What Japan desires in Manchuria is to do away with all anti-foreign policies there, so that the region may become a safe place of abode for natives and foreigners alike, while at the same time guaranteeing her legitimate rights and interests there; and, therefore, it is hardly necessary to repeat the assurance that Japan sincerely hopes that all peoples of the world will pursue their economic activities in Manchuria on the footing of equal opportunity and will thereby contribute to the development and prosperity of that region.

It is safely to be expected that the entire world will come to have ever-increasing understanding of and confidence in the sincere desire and the earnest effort of Manchukuo to carry out its foreign and domestic policies and that Powers will make no long delay in establishing diplomatic relations with it. In according formal recognition to Manchukuo, the Japanese Government desire to express hearty wishes for the future of the country and a fervent hope that our people will spare no effort in fulfilling the duty of a friendly neighbour, so that two countries may live and flourish together in common prosperity.

STATEMENT by Yosuke Matsuoka, Chief of the Japanese Delegation to the Special Session of the Assembly of the League of Nations Convened at the Request of the Chinese Government, February 24, 1933

League of Nations, *Official Journal*, Special Supplement No. 112, p. 23; for report adopted by the League, February 24, 1933, see *infra*, p. 923

ON BEHALF OF my Government, I wish to make a declaration.

It is a source of profound regret and disappointment to the Japanese delegation and to the Japanese Government that the draft report has now been adopted by this Assembly.

Japan has been a Member of the League of Nations since its inception. Our delegates to the Versailles Conference of 1919 took part in the drafting of the Covenant. We have been proud to be a Member of the League, associated with the leading nations of the world in one of the grandest purposes in which humanity could unite. It has always been our sincere wish and pleasure to co-operate with the fellow-Members of the League in attaining the great aim held in common and long cherished by humanity. I deeply deplore the situation we are now confronting, for I do not doubt that the same aim, the desire to see a lasting peace established, is animating all of us in our deliberations and our actions.

It is a matter of common knowledge that Japan's policy is fundamentally inspired by a genuine desire to guarantee peace in the Far East and to contribute to the maintenance of peace throughout the world. Japan, however, finds it impossible to accept the report adopted by the Assembly, and, in particular, she has taken pains to point out that the recommendations contained therein could not be considered such as would secure peace in that part of the world.

The Japanese Government now finds itself compelled to conclude that Japan and the other Members of the League entertain different views on the manner of achieving peace in the Far East, and the Japanese Government is obliged to feel that it has now reached the limit of its endeavours to co-operate with the League of Nations in regard to the Sino-Japanese differences.

The Japanese Government will, however, make the utmost efforts for the establishment of peace in the Far East and for the maintenance and strengthening of good and cordial relations with other Powers. I need hardly add that the Japanese Government persists in its desire to contribute to human welfare and will continue its policy of co-operating in all sincerity in the work dedicated to world peace, in so far as such co-operation is possible in the circumstances created by the unfortunate adoption of the report.

On behalf of the Japanese delegation, before leaving the room, let me tender its sincerest appreciation of the efforts ungrudgingly made to find a solution of the Sino-Japanese dispute before you, for the past seventeen months, by the President and Members of the Council, as well as by the President and Members of the General Assembly to whom we offer our sincere thanks.

(The Japanese delegation withdrew.)

STATEMENT Issued by the Japanese Government in Virtue of Paragraph 5 of Article 15 of the Covenant of the League of Nations, February 25, 1933

Transmitted by Yosuke Matsuoka, Chief of the Japanese Delegation to the Special Session of the Assembly of the League, to the Secretary-General of the League (Joseph Avenol) in a letter dated February 24, 1933. League of Nations, *Official Journal*, Special Supplement No. 112 (1933), p. 90

PART I.—JAPAN'S CO-OPERATION WITH THE LEAGUE OF NATIONS

JAPAN has taken the greatest interest in the development and success of the League from the days of its inception. Her successive Governments have extended to it, for nearly fourteen years, their hearty co-operation, and her statesmen have devoted their best efforts to the extension of its influence and the enhancement of its prestige. Japan takes pride in recalling the active participation of her representatives in the work of the League. As an original and permanent Member of the Council, she has had many opportunities of co-operating in its beneficent activities, and, of these opportunities, she has fully availed herself. She regards the League as a most powerful instrument for the good of humanity, and she is only anxious in the interest of this great experiment in the establishment of universal peace that the Members of the League shall fully appreciate the situation in the Far East and deal with it in a practical way rather than by formulæ and principles.

The present dispute was first brought by China to the consideration of the Council of the League of Nations under Article 11 of the Covenant in September 1931. In spite of the fact that Japan in this case was obliged to act solely in self-defence against aggression on the part of China, Japan, from the very beginning, has spared no effort in explaining to the League the facts and background of this unfortunate incident, and, at the same time, she has constantly, and without waiting for the resolution passed by the Council on September 30th, endeavoured, as far as possible, not to aggravate the situation. Japan has also, from time to time, communicated to the League all information relative to the development of the situation, so that the League might be enabled to understand the actual conditions prevailing in the Far East.

Unfortunately, however, the condition of Manchuria showed no immediate improvement, in the matter of peace and order, owing to the continued activities of Chang Hsueh-Liang, while the feelings of the Chinese and the Japanese peoples became further strained, with the result that there was no possibility of withdrawing the Japanese troops within the railway zone under the then existing circumstances. When the Council met again in October, Japan realised the importance of allaying the excited national feeling of the two peoples, as the first essential condition of securing the safety of the lives and property of Japanese subjects and of making possible the withdrawal of the Japanese troops. She was convinced that, for this purpose, it was necessary for the two parties concerned to pave the way for direct negotiations, with the object of restoring normal relations between the two countries. Japan took pains to explain this view to the President and certain Members of the Council, but the proposal to initiate direct negotiations was not accepted.

Moreover, the Council formed a plan to invite a representative of the United States of America, a non-member State of the League, to participate in its deliberations as an observer. To this proposition, Japan raised an objection, contending that participation in the proceedings of the Council by a State not a member of the League is contrary to its constitution, but the other Members of the Council insisted on regarding the step as a mere matter of procedure, and they invited a United States observer to the Council. Japan remained convinced that this was a matter which concerned the constitution of the League and that the action of the majority constituted a clear case of violation of the Covenant. It became apparent that if the opinion of her fellow-Members was that such an important matter of substance could be decided by a majority as a mere matter of procedure, she had ratified the Covenant under an error. However, owing to her strong desire to uphold the cause of the League, she continued to participate in the activities of the Council.

The discrepancy between the views of the other Members of the League and those entertained by Japan arose from a lack of understanding of the Far-Eastern situation on the part of the League. In her desire to assist the League and to maintain its legitimate influence and usefulness, Japan proposed, at the Council meeting held in November 1931, that the League should despatch a Commission of Enquiry to China, so that its Members might be able to understand fully the actual conditions prevailing in that country. This proposal was adopted by the Council in its resolution of December 10th.

The Commission of Enquiry, headed by Lord Lytton, reached China in March 1932, by way of Japan, and entered Manchukuo in April. Japan rendered every facility to the Commission in order to assist its investigations. Through the establishment of the new State of Manchukuo, especial difficulty was encountered in the matter of the entrance of the Chinese Assessor into the territory of that State. Japan therefore exerted her good offices with Manchukuo in order to smooth over this difficulty, and enabled the Commission to carry out its investigations.

The report of the Commission of Enquiry was made public on October 1st, 1932. On account of the brief period allowed for the investigation of the Commission, much remained to be desired for the report to claim to present a true picture of the actual condition of China. Accordingly, Japan, on November 18th last, handed to the League her observations on the Lytton report, in order to provide it with accurate material for coming to a fair conclusion on the questions involved.

The Lytton report was the subject of deliberation by the Council from November 21st, and by the Assembly from December 6th, 1932. The Committee of Nineteen, appointed by the Assembly, without the concurrence of Japan, drafted, on December 15th, a resolution and a statement of reasons concerning the procedure to be followed in performing the duty of conciliation which devolved upon that body in accordance with paragraph 3, Article 15 of the Covenant. Japan proposed the deletion from the draft resolution of passages regarding the participation of States which were not members of the League, and also the modification of certain points relating to the competence of the proposed Committee of Conciliation as well as the entire deletion of the last paragraph of the statement of reasons, which declared in particular that the maintenance and recognition of the present regime in Manchuria could not be considered as a solution. At the same time, considering that paragraph 3 of Article 15 represents the final resort provided for in the Covenant for the conciliatory solution of a dispute, Japan endeavoured to discover some compromise which would enable her to continue her co-operation with the League.

As stated in part II, section 13, of the report, the President of the Committee and the Secretary-General were authorised to enter into conversations with both the Japanese and Chinese delegations. The conversations between the Japanese delegation and the Secretary-General were carried on from the first part of January 1933. As a result of these conversations, a draft was drawn up and it was referred, with the knowledge of the President of the Committee, to the Japanese Government for its approval. Subsequently, when the amendments of the Japanese Government to this draft were communicated to the Committee of Nineteen, it was made known to the Japanese delegation that the said draft could not be taken up as a basis of further negotiation. This caused a great surprise to the Japanese Government, as it had every reason to believe that the President of the Committee, who together with the Secretary-General was authorised to conduct negotiations with both delegations, was also fully aware of the conversations and raised no objection to the preparation of the draft.

The Committee finally agreed to the deletion from the draft resolution of passages relating to the participation of non-member States in the work of the proposed Committee of Conciliation, but proposed that the Japanese Government should accept the rest of the text of the resolutions and the statement of reasons of December 15th, and make a reservation in regard to the last paragraph of the statement of reasons, to which Japan had taken objection. The declaration contained in this paragraph would, as is stated elsewhere in the present statement, not only constitute an action *ultra vires* on the part of the League, but prejudice the whole question and imply a direct attack on the policy followed by the Japanese Government with respect to the existence of Manchukuo. Furthermore, such an attitude on the part of the League was in no way in accord with the idea of conciliation advocated by the Committee of Nineteen, as well as by the Japanese Government. For these reasons, Japan found it impossible to accept the proposal of the Committee.

Upon the refusal of the Japanese delegation to agree to the Committee's proposal in this regard, the latter set to the procedure of drafting a report under paragraph 4 of Article 5.

However, the Japanese Government refused to give up the hope for conciliation, and, in its final efforts to achieve this end, agreed to withdraw the various amendments which it had presented when the text of December 15th was communicated to it, and consented to accept as the basis of conciliation the principles and conclusions of Chapter IX of the Lytton report, in so far as they were applied in a way to "harmonise with the events which have taken place"—which phrase is an almost literal quotation from that report itself. Further, they agreed to the maintenance of the last paragraph of the President's declaration (formerly called the "statement of reasons") on the condition that its wording be modified in such a way that it would not appear to constitute a prejudgment and an attack directed against the policy of the Japanese Government *vis-à-vis* Manchukuo.

The Committee of Nineteen found this final proposal likewise unacceptable. Thus the Committee rejected all the Japanese proposals and came to the conclusion that conciliation under paragraph 3 was impossible. The Committee forthwith proceeded with the drafting of a report under paragraph 4 of Article 15 of the Covenant. The draft report thus prepared was submitted to the Assembly on February 21st, and, in spite of the negative vote on the part of Japan, it was adopted by the Assembly on February 24th.

Part II.—Errors in the Report concerning Chief Characteristics of the Dispute

The report sets forth in part III what are termed "Chief Characteristics of the Dispute." It is most regrettable that this part of the report is substantially based upon the report of the Commission of Enquiry. As stated in that report, "the issues involved in this conflict are not as simple as they are often represented to be. They are, on the contrary, exceedingly complicated and only an intimate knowledge of all the facts, as well as of their historical background, should entitle anyone to express a definite opinion upon them." It must be remembered that the Commission of Enquiry spent only six weeks in Manchuria and fifteen in China, most of which was passed in Peiping, and their trip covered only a very limited area of China—a few open ports where the real condition of China could not have thoroughly been studied. In these circumstances, it was impossible for them to acquire "an intimate knowledge of all the facts, as well as their historical background." Hence, the document is not as complete and impartial as it should be. It is quite natural that there should be not a few errors in the report of the Assembly which was drafted upon the basis of the Lytton report. These errors might have been avoided if the Committee of Nineteen had taken into due consideration the observations of the Japanese Government, presented to the Council on November 18th, 1932. At any rate, it must be said that the Lytton report, admirable and praiseworthy as it is, is not a document which one can look upon as containing all the facts as well as all the historical background, upon which alone final judgment should be based. The errors in the report of the Assembly are numerous. Let only the most salient be cited:

1. The report appears to cling in part III to the fiction that China exists to-day as a single organised State to be dealt with on the same

footing as any country in Europe or America. The fiction happens to be merely a convenient formula which embodies in a concise form the generous aspiration of the Powers for the recovery of China as a unified and orderly State. Japan has worked hard to act upon that formula during these many years, and she is prepared to continue on the same lines, in cases where ordinary matters alone are concerned. But where her vital necessities come into play, as in Manchuria, she is forced to reconsider the fiction, and to ask herself what are the actual facts, and who are the actual rulers. States which are Members of the League of Nations and have little interest in China can afford to preserve the convenient fiction intact without serious difficulty. But Japan, in a totally different position, economically and strategically, is compelled, however reluctantly, to examine and set a limit to the fiction, and to direct her course according to realities.

It is the view of the Japanese Government that the erstwhile Chinese State ceased to rule in Manchuria when "the fall of the United Republic, after the death of Yuan Shi-kai in 1916, signalised the break-up of all unity of government in China." (Observations of the Japanese Government, page 15.)

As a matter of fact, none of the Governments, including the Nanking Government, maintains authority over China, save over the limited areas which it actually controls. That is why the Japanese Government in their observations insist that Manchuria is not naturally and necessarily an integral part of China. It will then be asked, as it has been asked: Why did Japan invoke the Nanking Government at the outset of the Manchurian incident? Why did Japan negotiate with Peking in 1915? Why did she declare Manchuria to be a part of China in 1922? The answer is that Japan clung until the last moment to the fiction of Manchuria being an integral part of China. She had many excellent opportunities of departing from it, if she had wished, afforded by the chaotic state of the country. She steadily refrained from availing herself of the opportunities. But when chaos came to threaten her whole position in Manchuria, it became necessary for her to take measures to protect her vast interests and important rights.

It should be observed at this point that Japan is not setting a precedent for defying the existence of a neighbour State merely because it is weak or disturbed by internal disruption. It is needless to say that so long as the Government of a State, which had actually ruled the whole area, maintains its authority in any part of its territory, so long does the State continue to subsist and to remain inviolable. The peculiar circumstances of China do not reside in the fact that its common government is weak or distracted by disruption. They reside in the unique fact that no authority which now exists has ever been a common government of China at all, and none, therefore, has title to rule the entire country.

The League of Nations should not forget that fact overrides form, and that a State must possess a single and continuous government.

2. The report, in agreeing that the Chinese boycott against Japan, imposed after the September 18th incident, falls within the province of retaliatory measures, sows the seeds of incalculable future trouble for each and every Power interested in China. All the major Powers conduct military operations in China under certain circumstances, and maintain armed forces in Chinese territory for that specific purpose. If the adoption by the Powers of any forcible measure for the protection of their rights and interests is on each occasion to be the subject of a retaliatory boycott, the application of force will of necessity be extended without limit.

By their acceptance in the resolutions of September 30th and of December 10th, 1931, China and Japan agreed that they should take the necessary measures to prevent any aggravation of the situation. The Japanese Government desire to call the attention of the League to the fact that it was the conspicuous failure on the part of China to take such proper measures that led to the regrettable Shanghai incident. It should also be added that, in any discussion of the boycott, the fact of anti-foreign education in schools and the "revolutionary foreign policy" (admitted by the Nanking Government) should not be left out of consideration, as these three subjects are inseparably bound together.

3. The report quotes and adopts from the Lytton report the reference to the possibility of an arbitral settlement of the Sino-Japanese dispute. But arbitration presupposes a normal organised State with a government supreme throughout its territory and capable of enforcing an award. China, as has been stated above, has not for years been in such a state, at any rate, so far as to render it possible to arbitrate with her in vital matters concerning Manchuria. With whom would the arbitration have proceeded? With Chang Hsueh-Liang, whom the League does not recognise? Or with the Nanking Government, whose authority (as the report of the Commission of Enquiry showed) he did not obey? Japan, with her vital interests at stake, could not and cannot possibly resort to arbitration in such a matter with such a country as China.

4. The report, again, quotes and adopts the refusal of the Commission of Enquiry to recognise as measures of self-defence the military operations of the Japanese army on the night of September 18th, although it does not exclude the possibility that the Japanese officers

on the spot might have thought they were acting in self-defence. This is simply another case of a facile and uncritical acceptance of the opinion of the Commission of Enquiry, utterly ignoring the emphatic contradiction contained in the observations of the Japanese Government. On what grounds can the League or any other third party pronounce a verdict on the case contrary to the judgment of the Japanese officers on the spot? The right of self-defence is one of those inalienable rights of State which may be duly exercised in certain specific circumstances, and the question of on what occasion and to what extent that right should be exercised is a matter which can be determined only by the State concerned. In this connection, the Japanese Government in their observations have referred to the reservations made by both France and the United States in concluding the Pact of Paris, a reference which the Assembly found it possible to pass over in silence. The report, in stating that the operations of the Japanese army, viewed as a whole as they developed through the entire period of the conflict, cannot be regarded as an act of self-defence, fails to take into cognisance the tension which existed, overwhelming forces by which the Japanese were faced, and the utter uncertainty which prevailed as to the probable action of those forces. Above all, it fails to take into account the vital rights and interests of Japan in Manchuria, which are not confined to the Leased Territory and the railways, but involve mining and forestry, consular police and consular jurisdiction, residence and trade throughout the entire region. When these rights and interests are threatened, the measures for their protection may have to be extended throughout Manchuria. But never have Japanese military operations exceeded the bounds of necessity for self-protection. In order that it may not be supposed to have been passed over *sub silentio,* the Japanese Government take this opportunity of explicitly denying the specific conclusions reached in the report that no question can arise of Chinese responsibility for the development of events since September 18th, 1931, and that the use of boycotts by China subsequent to that date falls under the category of reprisals. Even if the theory that the Japanese military action did not constitute lawful self-defence should be accepted, that clearly would not invest the Chinese with an unlimited licence to behave as they chose to and to enter upon a career of unrestricted violence and wrong. Much more is this the case if, as Japan contends, the actions of her troops were urgently called for by the necessities of self-defence. How can reprisals possibly be exercised against a lawful act? The proper reply to acts of self-defence is negotiation and explanation and not reprisals, which generally lead to war. Had the United States exercised reprisals in the *Caroline* case, war with England must have ensued. Again, it must be noted that the resolution of September 30th 1931 precludes either party from aggravating the situation; and it would seem strange to hold that this meant that China might take steps which would certainly aggravate it, leaving Japan alone responsible for any untoward development.

What appears to be a most curious statement is found in part III of the report, which reads:

"Adoption of measures of self-defence does not exempt a State from complying with the provisions of Article 12 of the Covenant."

As has already been observed by the Japanese Government, the right of self-defence is exercised upon the occasion "of an urgent [to quote Webster's definition] and overwhelming necessity allowing no choice of means and no instant for deliberation." To require the observance, upon such occasion, of Article 12 of the Covenant, which stipulates that the right of self-defence may be exercised three months after the award by the arbitrators or the judicial decision or the report by the Council of the League has been made public, is to deny the right of self-defence itself.

5. The report says that the declaration of independence by Manchukuo was not spontaneous. Since the statement is based upon no fresh investigation conducted at a later date, it may be readily gathered that the report has here again adopted the erroneous conclusions of the Commission of Enquiry contained in Chapter VI of the latter's report, the baselessness of which has been fully exposed in the observations of the Japanese Government. It must strike an impartial observer as extraordinary that the Assembly repeats this finding of the Commission of Enquiry in face of the emphatic denials of Japan. There are two factors which may partly account for this. First, the movement during the tyrannous regime of the Changs for the keeping of Manchuria aloof from all participation in the affairs of China Proper was subterranean, and had no repercussion in the outside world, and the authors of the report may therefore have been sceptical of its existence. Secondly, they appear to be misled by giving implicit credence to the legend of the so-called "continental policy" of Japan and her supposed plan to seek a political solution of the Manchurian issue as a step towards the execution of that policy. It is unnecessary to repeat that the Japanese "continental policy" is a mere Chinese fabrication, and that Japan harbours no territorial designs in any part of the world. But all this, though it may explain the rejection by the Assembly of the uncompromising denial made by Japan, can hardly be thought to excuse it.

The simple fact is that, as has so often been explained, on the disappearance of all the administrative organisations, such as they were,

CHINA INVADED; RELATIONS WITH THE U.S.   883

which had existed under the Changs, spontaneous local organisations naturally sprang up, and the Japanese troops, which were responsible for the maintenance of order, necessarily co-operated with them. It was a proper and necessary step, and, in the circumstances, an unavoidable one. Such was the whole significance of the presence of Japanese troops, and such was the sole aim of the activities of Japanese civil and military officers. Unfortunately, the Commission of Enquiry, and consequently the Assembly, in their implicit reliance on the assumption that there had never existed any independence movement in Manchuria, have been obliged to attribute to the activities of Japanese civil and military officers the independence which was actually proclaimed—and to do so upon no solid grounds whatever.

As to the assertion that the people of Manchuria are hostile to the new State, again there is no valid evidence beyond fifteen hundred letters of dubious origin received by the Commission of Enquiry. The Japanese Government desire to point out the fact that, within less than a year since its foundation, Manchukuo has achieved a marked and healthy progress in the restoration of law and order, and that no criticism or complaint has been heard of regarding its conduct of affairs, whether domestic or foreign.

Regardless of the attitude of the Assembly towards the new State of Manchukuo, she has gone forward steadily on the road of progress. Freed from the yoke of misgovernment under the tyrannous rule of the Changs, the thirty million inhabitants of Manchuria,—Manchus, Mongols and Chinese, all alike,—have already begun to reap the benefits of their labours, which were denied them in former days. Throughout most of the country, banditry has been suppressed. Those hostile elements, largely composed of the remnants of Chang Hsueh-Liang's troops and receiving not inconsiderable assistance from their former warlord, had constituted an obstacle to the establishment of peace throughout the territory. Thanks, however, to the combined efforts of the Japanese and Manchukuo forces, they have been practically cleared out of the provinces of Fengtien, Kirin and Heilungkiang, and the security of life and property have been re-established in these provinces. It is only in the Province of Jehol that the organised opposition still continues.

In the domain of finance, something entirely unknown in the history of China has been realised in Manchukuo. Though the State is still in its infancy, a sound budgetary system has been initiated and is being carried out with utmost satisfaction. The establishment of the Central Bank, which is functioning on the same lines as those of the advanced countries of the world, has contributed much to the stabilisation of State finances and to the economic and industrial development of the country. A similar progress has also been noted in the domain of railway administration, commerce and industry, and, with the abundant resources with which she is endowed, there is every prospect of this country achieving in days to come a still greater progress along these lines, to the benefit of her inhabitants and foreigners alike.

All this could not have been the case had the population of the country been hostile or even sullenly submissive. It is to be regretted, therefore, that the Assembly should have, without referring to the observations submitted by Japan, accepted the assumption of the Commission of Enquiry, which, here again, has no foundation in fact.

6. The report dwells upon the need of international co-operation in the reconstruction of China, and mentioned the provision of technical assistance as one form of that international co-operation. Obviously, the reconstruction of China cannot be accomplished by any such superficial and inadequate means. It could only be rendered possible by some forceful international intervention of such a nature as would at once prove incompatible with the stipulation of the Nine-Power Treaty regarding the administrative integrity and political independence of China. That is another proof that it is necessary to allow ample elasticity by taking due account of changing conditions in the application of the Nine-Power Treaty and the Covenant of the League, as far as China is concerned.

Part III.—Impracticabilities of the Recommendations

1. Japan recognises that the Covenant of the League of Nations and the Pact of Paris constitute the basic principles of the settlement of international disputes, in so far as international relations in general are concerned. But a certain degree of elasticity must be allowed in the application of these principles to such special and entirely abnormal conditions as prevail in China.

2. As to the proposal for the withdrawal of troops contained in section II, 1, A, of part IV of the report, it is to be noted that the presence of Japanese troops outside the railway zone, so far from being incompatible with legal principles, has, from the very beginning, been due entirely to the sheer necessities of lawful self-defence and is in no way derogatory to the accepted principles regarding the settlement of international disputes. It is further to be noted that these Japanese troops are now responsible, in accordance with the Japan-Manchukuo Protocol, for the maintenance of peace and order in Manchukuo.

It is true that, by the resolutions of September 30th and of December 10th, 1931, Japan undertook to withdraw her troops within the railway zone, in so far as the safety of the lives and property of her subjects was assured, but the condition attaching to that undertaking—namely, the assurance of safety of life and property—has never been satisfied, and the undertaking itself has now become inapplicable on account of the independence of Manchukuo and the conclusion of the agreements embodied in the Protocol signed on September 15th last. Should the Japanese troops be withdrawn within the railway zone in accordance with the recommendation contained in the report, it would be inevitable that unrest and disturbances would ensue in the evacuated territory. Those Members of the League that have but little direct interest in the affairs of the Far East can afford to maintain that the upholding of abstract formulæ is more important than the maintenance of the peace in this part of the world. But Japan, vitally concerned in the maintenance of peace and order in Manchuria, cannot tolerate that that region should again be plunged into disorder. It cannot be supposed that a gendarmerie system, as proposed by the Lytton report, would remove all apprehensions on this score. There is no precedent in the history of the world in which the security of such a vast territory was secured by gendarmerie. The proposition is absurd and cannot be put into practice. If the Japanese troops were withdrawn, the country would be quickly overrun by bandits and by Chang Hsueh-Liang's troops, resulting in anarchy and disorder.

3. As to section II, 1, of part IV of the report, where it is stated that the sovereignty over Manchuria belongs to China, it has to be noted that, at any rate, since the year 1916, Manchuria has never been subject to the authority of China, and that, in the final analysis, the present difficulty has been caused by the supposition that the sovereignty of China actually extended and extends to that region. It is entirely superfluous to say that the enforcement of this fiction will never ensure the protection of Japan's rights and interests and the maintenance of peace in the Far East. Inasmuch as the report repudiates the restoration of the old regime as leading merely to a repetition of disorder and friction, so any return to the fiction in question must equally be repudiated. Nor is it possible for Japan to admit any policy which is incompatible with the simple fact of the existence of the State of Manchukuo and the provisions of the Japan-Manchukuo Protocol.

4. With regard to the ten principles set out in the Lytton report and cited in section I of part IV of the report, apart from the observa-

tions made above, the Japanese Government deem it sufficient to quote the following passages from their observations presented to the League in November last:

"Certain of these principles, to which the Japanese Government have no fundamental objection, have already found concrete application in the Protocol signed by Japan and Manchukuo. But, in any view of the matter, it must evidently be impossible, so long as the anarchical state of things in China persists, to arrive at a satisfactory solution of the questions at issue on the basis of the first nine of these principles, especially principles 4 to 9 inclusive. As is sustained in principle 10, these nine principles cannot be practically applied 'without a strong central government in China.'"

5. In section II, 3, part IV of the report, the Assembly contemplates the establishment of a Committee to assist in the negotiations which are to be opened between the two parties in accordance with the method specified in the report. This, however, is directly contrary to the insistence of Japan not to allow any third party to intervene in the Manchurian problem, and Japan finds it absolutely impossible to accept such a proposal. As, moreover, the recommendations referred to as 1 A and 1 B of section II, part IV of the report, must be dismissed as unpractical, and those made under 2 of the said section II are equally inapplicable in the present state of China, there would seem to be no scope left for the activities of the proposed Committee.

6. The report states, in effect, in section III of part IV that the maintenance and recognition of the existing regime in Manchuria is no solution and that the Members of the League should, after having adopted the report, abstain from recognising the present regime either *de jure* or *de facto*. Further, it expresses the hope that the States non-members of the League, who are signatories of the Pact of Paris and the Nine-Power Treaty, will associate themselves with the views set forth in the report in this regard. The Japanese Government cannot but consider that the Assembly, in proposing in such a manner to influence or to bind, if only morally, both Member and non-member States, in the matter of recognising or not recognising another State, is exceeding its powers conferred upon it by Article 15 of the Covenant. In any case, in making a proposition of this nature, the League of Nations, whose primary duty is the preservation of peace throughout the world, could not surely contribute to the maintenance of peace and security, not only in Manchukuo, but also in the Far East. Such an action on the part of the League would prove to be an obstacle to the good understanding and friendly relations between nations, upon which peace depends.

Conclusion

The Japanese Government is fully convinced that the action of the Japanese army on the night of September 18th, 1931, and thereafter, has never exceeded the limits appropriate to measures of self-defence, and that Manchukuo has been founded by the spontaneous will of the people of Manchuria. Accordingly, they consider that neither the action of the Japanese army in Manchuria, nor the conclusion of the Japan-Manchukuo Protocol, is in violation of the Covenant of the League of Nations, the Nine-Power Treaty, the Pact of Paris, or any other international treaties.

The Japanese Government maintain that, in view of the quite abnormal condition of China, where no existing authority has ever ruled the entire country, and particularly in view of the unparalleled complexity and peculiarity of the Manchurian problem, and also having regard to the anti-foreign character of the policy of the National Government, it is impossible to think of applying to the present dispute the general formulæ applicable to an ordinary international question, and they maintain, moreover, that neither any procedure which may be adopted for such an exceptional case, nor any solution thereby attained, can ever establish a precedent for ordinary cases of international dispute.

Were it possible to apply ordinary formulæ, the plans adumbrated by the Assembly would themselves be ruled out of consideration as interferences with what the Assembly regards as Chinese sovereign rights.

Unfortunately, the Assembly, through the refusal of its Members to face facts, and their uncritical acceptance of the report of the Commission of Enquiry, has only indulged in academic and inadequate principles. The Assembly stands, if it may so be said, for mere formulæ, Japan for solid realities. Japan takes her stand on established principles, the Assembly on preconceived hypotheses. It results from the refusal of the Assembly to go beyond the Lytton report. As pointed out in the preceding part of the present statement, the new State of Manchukuo has made rapid progress. Peace and order are superseding banditry. Commerce and industry have responded to improved situation, to the benefit of foreigners and the people of Manchukuo alike. This is a concrete proof of the truth of Japanese contention that recognition and encouragement of the Manchurian State is the only road to a satisfactory solution of the Manchurian question and to the maintenance of a lasting peace in the Orient.

On the other hand, it appears impossible to look for any improvement in the Chinese situation in the near future, and China is likely to remain a chronic anxiety to the rest of the world. Communism has already invaded China, and the alarming extent and success of the invasion is far too seldom realised. A communised China would constitute a problem for Europe and America beside which other questions would pale into insignificance. But a Manchuria free from all Chinese connection constitutes a barrier to communistic danger in the Far East. Its value ought surely to be apparent to every statesman. It is earnestly hoped that the League of Nations will soon be led to change its attitude, to discard reliance on academic and inapplicable doctrine, and to respect and recognise the forces that are actually rendering possible the maintenance of peace in the various regions of the world. The Covenant of the League of Nations itself provides in Article 21 for due recognition of regional understandings, and the Japan-Manchukuo Protocol of September 15th, 1932, falls incontestably within the category of understandings such as these, as the special interests of Japan in Manchuria have again and again been recognised. At the same time, Japan takes this opportunity of repeating her disclaimer of all desire for territorial gains or commercial advantages.

TELEGRAM from Count Yasuya Uchida, Minister for Foreign Affairs, to the Secretary-General of the League of Nations (Sir Eric Drummond), March 27, 1933, Regarding the Japanese Withdrawal from the League

League of Nations, *Official Journal*, May, 1933, p. 657

THE Japanese Government believe that the national policy of Japan, which has for its aim to ensure the peace of the Orient and thereby to contribute to the cause of peace throughout the world, is identical in spirit with the mission of the League of Nations, which is to achieve international peace and security. It has always been with pleasure, therefore, that this country has for thirteen years past, as an original Member of the League and a permanent Member of its Council, extended a full measure of co-operation with her fellow-Members towards the attainment of its high purpose. It is, indeed, a matter of historical fact that Japan has continuously participated in the various activities of the League with a zeal not inferior to that exhibited by any other nation. At the same time, it is and has always been the conviction of the Japanese Government that, in order to render possible the maintenance of peace in various regions of the world, it is necessary in existing circumstances to allow the operation of the Covenant of the League to vary in accordance with the actual conditions prevailing in each of those regions. Only by acting on this just and equitable principle can the League fulfil its mission and increase its influence.

Acting on this conviction, the Japanese Government, ever since the Sino-Japanese dispute was, in September 1931, submitted to the League, have, at meetings of the League and on other occasions, continually set forward a consistent view. This was that, if the League was to settle the issue fairly and equitably, and to make a real contribution to the promotion of peace in the Orient, and thus enhance its prestige, it should acquire a complete grasp of the actual conditions in this quarter of the globe and apply the Covenant of the League in accordance with these conditions. They have repeatedly emphasised and insisted upon the absolute necessity of taking into consideration the fact that China is not an organised State; that its internal conditions and external relations are characterised by extreme confusion and complexity and by many abnormal and exceptional features; and that, accordingly, the general principles and usages of international law which govern the ordinary relations between nations are found to be considerably modified in their operation so far as China is concerned, resulting in the quite abnormal and unique international practices which actually prevail in that country.

However, the majority of the Members of the League evinced, in the course of its deliberations during the past seventeen months, a failure either to grasp these realities or else to face them and take them into proper account. Moreover, it has frequently been made manifest in these deliberations that there exist serious differences of opinion between Japan and these Powers concerning the application and even the interpretation of various international engagements and obligations, including the Covenant of the League and the principles of international law. As a result, the report adopted by the Assembly at the special session of February 24th last, entirely misapprehending the spirit of Japan, pervaded as it is by no other desire than the maintenance of peace in the Orient, contains gross errors both in the ascertainment of facts and in the conclusions deduced. In asserting that the action of the Japanese army at the time of the incident of September 18th and subsequently did not fall within the just limits of self-defence, the report assigned no reasons and came to an arbitrary conclusion, and in ignoring alike the state of tension which preceded, and the various aggravations which succeeded, the incident—for all of which the full responsibility is incumbent upon China—the report creates a source of fresh conflict in the political arena of the Orient. By refusing to acknowledge the actual circumstances that led to the foundation of Manchukuo, and by attempting to challenge the position taken up by Japan in recognising the new State, it cuts away the ground for the stabilisation of the Far-Eastern situation. Nor can the terms laid down in its recommendations—as was fully explained in the statement issued by this Government on February 25th last—ever be of any possible service in securing enduring peace in these regions.

The conclusion must be that, in seeking a solution of the question, the majority of the League have attached greater importance to upholding inapplicable formulæ than to the real task of assuring peace, and higher value to the vindication of academic theses than to the eradication of the sources of future conflict. For these reasons, and because of the profound differences of opinion existing between Japan and the majority of the League in their interpretation of the Covenant and of other treaties, the Japanese Government have been led to realise the existence of an irreconcilable divergence of views, dividing Japan and the League on policies of peace, and especially as regards the fundamental principles to be followed in the establishment of a durable peace in the Far East. The Japanese Government, believing that, in these circumstances, there remains no room for further co-operation, hereby give notice, in accordance with the provisions of Article 1, paragraph 3, of the Covenant, of the intention of Japan to withdraw from the League of Nations.

REPLY of the Japanese Government, October 27, 1937, to the Invitation of the Belgian Government to Hold a Conference at Brussels

Department of State, *The Conference of Brussels* . . . , p. 9

THE Japanese Government have the honor to acknowledge the receipt of the *note verbale* under the date of the 20th instant, by which the Royal Government, in accordance with the request of the Government of Great Britain, and with the approbation of the Government of the United States of America, propose to the powers signatory to the treaty of February 6, 1922, to meet at Brussels on the 30th of this month in order to examine, in conformity with the article VII of the said treaty, the situation in the Far East and to study amicable means of hastening the end of the regrettable conflict which is taking place there.

The League of Nations, in a report adopted on October 6th, has declared, on the basis of the declarations of only one of the two parties, that the military operations carried out by Japan in China are in violation of the Nine-power Treaty. The action of Japan in China is a measure of self-defense which she has been compelled to take in the face of China's fierce anti-Japanese policy and practice, and especially by her provocative action in resorting to force of arms; and consequently it lies as has been declared already by the Imperial Government, outside the purview of the Nine-power Treaty.

The Assembly of the League of Nations has even gone to the length of assuring China of its moral support, and of recommending its members to abstain from any action that might weaken that country's power of resistance and add to its difficulties in the present conflict, and also to study how they might actively give aid to China. This seems to take no account of the just intention of the Imperial Government, who propose to bring about a sincere cooperation between Japan and China, to assure enduring peace in East Asia, and to contribute thereby to the peace of the world. This is to take sides with one of the parties and to encourage its hostile disposition, but in no way to contribute to an early settlement.

The Royal Government make in their invitation no mention of this connection between the proposed Conference and the League of Nations. However, in view of the fact that in its resolution the League of Nations suggested a meeting of those of its members who were party to the Nine-power Treaty, and that the Government of the United States, who have acquiesced in the request of the Government of Great Britain for the convocation of the Conference, have declared, on October 6, their approval of the resolution, the Imperial Government cannot but conclude that the convocation of the Conference is linked to the resolution of the League of Nations.

Now the League of Nations, as mentioned above, has expressed its view casting reflection upon the honor of Japan, and it has adopted a resolution which is incontestably unfriendly towards her. In these circumstances the Imperial Government are constrained to believe that frank and full discussion to bring about a just, equitable and realistic solution of the conflict between Japan and China cannot be expected between the powers concerned at the proposed Conference.

Moreover the present Sino-Japanese conflict, arising from the special situation of East Asia, has a full bearing upon the very existence of the two countries. The Imperial Government are firmly convinced that an attempt to seek a solution at a gathering of so many powers whose interests in East Asia are of varying degree, or who have practically no interests there at all, will only serve to complicate the situation still further, and to put serious obstacles in the path of a just and proper solution.

For the reasons explained above the Imperial Government regret their inability to accept the invitation of the Royal Government.

The present conflict has been caused by none other than the Chinese Government, who for these many years have been engaged as a matter of national policy in disseminating anti-Japanese sentiments and encouraging anti-Japanese movements in China, and who, in collusion with Communist elements, have menaced the peace of East Asia by their virulent agitation against Japan.

Consequently, what is most urgently needed for a solution of the conflict is a realization on the part of the Chinese Government of the common responsibility of Japan and China respecting the stability of East Asia, a revision of their attitude, and a change of their policy to that of cooperation between the two countries. What Japan asks of the powers is that they comprehend fully this need. Such cooperation, based upon such comprehension, can alone, she believes, contribute effectively towards the stabilization of East Asia.

STATEMENT Issued by the Japanese Foreign Office, October 28, 1937, Regarding the Convoking of the Conference of Brussels

Department of State, *The Conference of Brussels* . . . , p. 11

THE Japanese Government, having replied to the invitation of the Belgian Government to the Conference signatories of the Nine-power Treaty, 1922, take this opportunity of making public at home and abroad a statement of their views.

1. China has witnessed the rise and fall of countless regimes since the revolution of 1912, but her foreign policy has been consistently one of anti-foreignism. Especially since 1924, when the Kuomintang set up the Nationalist Government in Canton and entered into an alliance with the Communists as a means of winning control of the central administration, the anti-foreign policy then began to be pursued with unprecedented vigor and ruthlessness, and anti-foreign sentiments were kindled ablaze among the populace. The memory is still fresh of the way in which foreign powers, one after another, were victimized and deprived of their vested rights and interests. It hap-

pens that Japan has been made for the past 10 years the principal target of this anti-foreign policy of China.

Japan has always striven to promote friendship and cooperation among the nations of East Asia, in the firm conviction that therein lies the key to the stability of that region. Japan welcomed the deepening of Chinese national consciousness which followed upon the revolution, believing that it would conduce to intimate Sino-Japanese collaboration, and she adopted the policy of meeting the legitimate national aspirations of China to the utmost possible extent.

For instance, in 1926 Japan took the lead in assisting China to recover her customs autonomy, and took a firm stand in favor of China on the question of the abolition of extraterritoriality. Japan, so cultivating Chinese good-will, looked patiently and eagerly forward to a favorable response that would consort with her ideal of friendship and cooperation. However, China showed no signs of appreciation of this sympathetic attitude on the part of Japan. On the contrary, she hoisted still higher the banner of anti-Japanism, and seemed resolved to annihilate all Japanese rights and interests in China.

The Nanking Government employed anti-Japanism as a convenient tool in domestic politics for the mobilization of public opinion in support of their regime, and resorted to the unheard-of tactics of making it the foundation of moral education in the army and in the schools, so that even innocent children and youths were taught to look upon their friendly neighbor country as an enemy. As a result, not only were the peaceful trade and economic activities of Japan interrupted, but even the very lives of Japanese nationals were jeopardized.

This anti-Japanese campaign finally took the form of organized terrorism as in the cases of the killing of a Japanese bluejacket at Shanghai in November 1935 and of the subsequent murderous attacks upon Japanese subjects at Swatow, Chengtu, Pakhoi, Hankow and Shanghai, and the bombing of Japanese residents at Changsha and Swatow.

In the face of the alarming situation, Japanese Government remained calm and forbearing. Urgent demands were repeatedly made upon the Nanking Government for the reversal of their disastrous policy, but to no avail. Then, towards the end of last year, there occurred the Sian incident, in which General Chiang Kai-shek was held captive for some days. Though the exact circumstances surrounding that sensational incident remain a mystery, it is an indisputable fact that shortly afterwards Communist elements, gaining the ascendancy in the Nanking Government, began to conduct campaigns of disturbance in North China and Manchukuo under the banner of the "Anti-Japanese People's Front," which finally led to the Lukouchiao incident of July 7 of this year, in which Japanese soldiers were unlawfully fired upon by Chinese troops in the outskirts of Peking.

2. Upon the occurrence of the Lukouchiao incident the Japanese Government, desirous of averting possible Sino-Japanese crisis, immediately formulated a policy of non-aggravation and local settlement, and devoted their best efforts towards bringing about an amicable solution, in spite of the intolerable situations that were created, one after another, by the Chinese on the spot.

On the other hand the Nanking Government, in violation of the Umezu-Ho agreement, moved north the vast forces under their direct command, to threaten the Japanese garrisons, and also instigated local Chinese armies against Japan. The situation was thus aggravated until a general clash between the two countries became inevitable.

It should be recalled that the Nanking Government, which employ anti-Japanism as an instrument of internal unification, had been conducting for some years a militaristic propaganda aimed at Japan, and that at the same time, by importing vast quantities of munitions, constructing fortifications, and giving intensive training to the troops, she had succeeded in building up strong armaments, so that their military men grew overconfident of their own strength and the people themselves were deluded into putting an exaggerated estimate upon their country's fighting-power.

A belligerent spirit towards Japan came to prevail throughout the land. Long before the present outbreak, Chinese newspapers and magazines were accustomed to call Japan the "enemy country" and the Japanese their enemies. At the time of the Lukouchiao incident— the Nanking Government being driven to action against Japan by the internal situation they themselves had created—Japan's cautious attitude and her policy of local settlement were both doomed to utter failure.

With aggravation of the situation all Japanese residents, not only in North China but also in Central and South China, became exposed to imminent danger, and were compelled to evacuate *en masse,* abandoning the enterprises that they had toilsomely built up during long years in the past. At the same time, the Chinese in Shanghai, in contravention of the 1932 truce agreement, secretly set out to construct military works in the demilitarized zone and to perfect their war preparations. Accordingly in June last the Japanese Government made a request for a special conference of the powers concerned, and called the attention of the Chinese Government to the matter.

The Chinese refused to alter their attitude, and upon the outbreak of the armed conflict in North China, they moved troops into the prohibited zone in flagrant violation of the truce agreement, and finally following upon the murder of an officer and a man belonging to the Japanese landing party, on August 9, they launched an attack upon the International Settlement. While the Japanese authorities were still engaged in negotiation with the representatives of the powers concerned, in a desperate attempt to prevent hostilities with extreme patience and forbearance and bearing serious strategical disadvantages, the Chinese began to shell and bomb the Japanese quarter of the Settlement as well as the Japanese garrison defending it, with a view to annihilating the 30,000 Japanese residents as well as the Japanese forces, who were hopelessly outnumbered by the Chinese Army. Thereupon Japan was compelled to take counter measures in self-defense.

As is clear from the foregoing accounts, the fundamental cause of the aggravation of the present affair is to be found in the policy of the Nanking Government, who moved large, threatening forces into North China in contravention of the Umezu-Ho agreement, and also tore up the truce agreement by marching troops on the International Settlement. Japan was compelled to take up arms in self-defense, and she has chosen this opportunity to make the Nanking Government revise their attitude for the sake of the permanent peace of East Asia. Therefore, the present affair can never be settled until the Nanking Government mend their ways, abandon once for all their anti-Japanese policy, and accept Japan's policy of cooperation and collaboration between the two countries.

It should be remembered that one of the important factors underlying Nanking's feverish agitations of more recent years against Japan is the action taken by the League of Nations at the time of the Manchurian incident. That body then adopted a resolution framed in utter disregard of the realities of the situation in East Asia, which strongly stimulated China in her anti-Japanese policy.

Now the League has once more taken up the appeal of the Nanking Government. Without going fully into the real causes of the present affair, it has concluded, on the basis of false report, that the bombing of the military works in the strongly fortified Nanking and Canton was an attack upon defenseless cities, and adopted the resolution of September 27 condemning Japan.

Again on October 6 the General Assembly of the League not only concluded that Japan's action constituted a violation of the Anti-war Pact and the Nine-power Treaty but also adopted a resolution which openly calls for assistance to China. Such proceedings on the part of the League only fall in with the cunning scheme of the Nanking

Government to exert pressure upon Japan by inviting the intervention of third powers, and serves no useful end but to encourage China in her resolve to oppose Japan to the last and to render a settlement of the affair more difficult than ever.

It must be said that the League of Nations is repeating the error that it committed only a few years ago. Japan's action is a measure of self-defense taken in the face of China's challenge, and obviously there can be no question of violation of the Nine-power Treaty. Moreover, as compared with the time when the treaty was concluded, the situation in East Asia today has been rendered totally different, owing to the infiltration of Communist influence and the changes of internal conditions prevailing in China.

In any case, as regards the Conference that has been convened by the signatories of the Nine-power Treaty, it is a foregone conclusion that a majority of the participants will hold themselves bound by the above-mentioned resolutions of the League of Nations, and even if Japan took part in its deliberations, no fair and just result could ever be expected therefrom as in the case of the League of Nations meeting at the time of the Manchurian incident. Especially as this conference is to be attended by powers which are not directly interested in East Asia, it is calculated to arouse popular feeling both in Japan and China, thereby complicating the situation still further but contributing nothing towards a solution. The Japanese Government have therefore decided to decline the invitation.

The Japanese nation, rising as one man, is united in the determination to surmount all obstacles for the purpose of effecting a speedy settlement. Japan is by no means indifferent towards international cooperation. But the Sino-Japanese difficulties can be solved only through direct negotiations between the two powers on whom falls the common burden of responsibility for the stability of East Asia. What is needed is the elimination of Nanking's anti-Japanese policy and the Communist elements which are identified with it, so that there may be established an enduring peace based upon Sino-Japanese unity and cooperation.

Japan never looks upon the Chinese people as an enemy, nor does she harbor any territorial designs. It is rather her sincere wish to witness the material and spiritual advancement of the Chinese nation. And it is her desire to promote cultural and economic cooperation with foreign powers regarding China, while at the same time she will respect fully their rights and interests there.

Accordingly, as soon as the powers understand the true intention of Japan, and take suitable steps to make the Nanking Government reconsider their attitude and policy, then, and only then, a way will have been paved for their cooperation with Japan respecting the settlement of the present conflict.

NOTE from Koki Hirota, Minister for Foreign Affairs, to the American Ambassador to Japan (Joseph C. Grew), December 14, 1937

Translation, in Department of State, *Press Releases,* December 18, 1937, p. 450

MONSIEUR L'AMBASSADEUR:

Regarding the incident of the 12th December in which the United States gunboat *Panay* and three steamers belonging to the Standard Oil Company were sunk by the bombing of the Japanese naval aircraft on the Yangtze River at a point about 26 miles above Nanking, I had the honor, as soon as unofficial information of the incident was brought to my knowledge, to request Your Excellency to transmit to the Government of the United States the apologies of the Japanese Government. From the reports subsequently received from our representatives in China, it has been established that the Japanese naval air force, acting upon information that the Chinese troops fleeing from Nanking were going up the river in steamers, took off to pursue them, and discovered such vessels at the above mentioned point. Owing to poor visibility, however, the aircraft, although they descended to fairly low altitudes, were unable to discern any mark to show that any one of them was an American ship or man of war. Consequently the United States gunboat *Panay* and the vessels of the Standard Oil Company, being taken for Chinese vessels carrying the fleeing Chinese troops, were bombed and sunk.

While it is clear, in the light of the above circumstances, that the present incident was entirely due to a mistake, the Japanese Government regret most profoundly that it has caused damages to the United States man of war and ships and casualties among those on board, and desire to present hereby sincere apologies. The Japanese Government will make indemnifications for all the losses and will deal appropriately with those responsible for the incident. Furthermore, they have already issued strict orders to the authorities on the spot with a view to preventing the recurrence of a similar incident.

The Japanese Government in the fervent hope that the friendly relations between Japan and the United States will not be affected by this unfortunate affair, have frankly stated as above their sincere attitude which I beg Your Excellency to make known to your Government.

STATEMENT by Prince Konoe, Prime Minister, January 18, 1938

Translation, in Royal Institute of International Affairs, *Documents on International Affairs, 1938*, I, 341, citing *The Times* (London), January 20, 1938

1. WE no longer regard the National Government as one with which we can negotiate for the regulation of our relations with China. We will not abandon the use of military and all other means to crush the National Government.

2. It is conceivable that the National Government may repaint their signboard, "Abandon anti-Japanism and compromise with the Peking Provisional Government." If so, well and good, but that is their concern and not ours. All that we want is a Government that will cooperate with us for the peace of East Asia and the development of Oriental culture.

3. The birth of a new Chinese Government may resemble that of Manchukuo, but their relations with Japan will be different. It is significant that any connection between our national defense and Manchukuo's is absent. We do not consider that the Peking Government must become the Central Government of China, but probably they will form a nucleus in which other similar régimes will be incorporated. We have minutely studied the conditions on which we should make peace with the National Government. Our efforts have been futile. If the new Government prove one on which we can rely we will agree to far more generous terms than those offered to the National Government.

4. Economic reconstruction in the occupied areas must be effected by practical means. State control to some extent is inevitable, but capitalist enterprise and foreign capital must not be antagonized.

5. To make an enemy of everybody is bad diplomacy. We must avoid words and actions likely to irritate foreign Powers. Great Britain is a realistic nation, which changes her policy as situations change. The same is true of Russia. Internal conditions indicate that Russia will make no move at present.

6. A new political party is necessary, but the Government have no intention of forming it. Reform of the Diet is necessary, but the China Affair will not be settled soon or easily, and the situation which

will arise afterwards will be even graver. The Government at present have no choice but to proceed with measures for the prosecution of the struggle with China.

NOTE from Hachiro Arita, Minister for Foreign Affairs, to the American Ambassador to Japan (Joseph C. Grew), November 18, 1938

Translation, in Department of State, *Press Releases,* November 19, 1938, p. 350

EXCELLENCY:

I have the honour to acknowledge the receipt of Your Excellency's note, No. 1076 dated October sixth, addressed to the then Minister for Foreign Affairs Prince Konoye, concerning the rights and interests of the United States in China.

In the note are cited various instances based on information in the possession of the Government of the United States that the Japanese authorities are subjecting American citizens in China to discriminatory treatment and violating the rights and interests of the United States.

I have now the honour to state hereunder the opinions of the Japanese Government with regard to these instances.

One. The circumstances which led to the adoption of the present measures concerning export exchange in Tsingtao and the present situation being, so far as the Japanese Government are aware, as set forth below, they consider that those measures can not be construed as constituting any discrimination against American citizens.

A short time ago the Federal Reserve Bank of China was established in North China whose notes with an exchange value fixed at one shilling and two pence against one yuan, have been issued thus far to the amount of more than one hundred million yuan, and are widely circulated. These bank notes being the compulsory currency of the Provisional Government, the maintenance of their value and their smooth circulation is regarded as an indispensable basis for the conduct and the development of economic activities in North China. Consequently the Japanese Government have taken a cooperative attitude; and all Japanese subjects are using the said notes, and in their export trade are exchanging them at the rate of one shilling and two pence. On the other hand, the old *FA–PI* still circulating in these areas had depreciated in exchange value to about eight pence per yuan. Consequently those who are engaged in export trade and are using this currency are enjoying illegitimate profits, as compared with those who use the Federal Reserve notes and carry on legitimate transactions at the legitimate rate of exchange: that is to say, Japanese subjects who use the Federal Reserve notes have been suffering unreasonable disadvantages as compared with persons who while residing and carrying on their business in the areas under the jurisdiction of the Provisional Government of North China, use nevertheless, the old *FA–PI* exclusively.

Furthermore, the existence of the before-mentioned disparity in exchange value between the new notes and the old *FA–PI,* which the Federal Reserve Bank has been exchanging at a rate not very much below par, is bound to exert an unfavourable effect upon the exchange value of the new notes, and eventually upon the exchange value of the Japanese yen.

The Japanese Government feel that it is incumbent upon them not to remain indifferent to such a situation.

The export exchange measures adopted in Tsingtao are calculated to place the users of old Chinese currency who have been obtaining unfair profits, on an equal footing with those who are using the Federal Reserve notes. These measures are also intended to protect the exchange value of the Federal Reserve Bank notes. Inasmuch as the application of the measures makes no differentiation according to nationality they cannot be considered as discriminatory measures. As a matter of fact, it is through these measures that those users of the Federal Reserve notes who had in a sense been discriminated against, have been placed on an equal footing with the others, and thus enabled to compete on a fair basis.

Two. In North and Central China the new Chinese regimes some time ago effected revisions of the customs tariff in an attempt to secure a rational modification of the former tariff enforced by the Kuomintang Government, which was unduly high and illcalculated to promote the economic recovery and general welfare of the Chinese people. However, the schedule actually adopted for the time being is the one that was approved by the powers in nineteen hundred thirty-one, so that no complaint has been heard from foreign residents of any nationality on the spot. The Japanese Government are of course in favour of the purpose of the said revision, believing that it will serve to promote effectively the trade of all countries with China.

Three. As for the organization of certain promotion companies in China, the restoration and development of China's economic, financial and industrial life after the present affair is a matter of urgent necessity for the welfare of the Chinese. Moreover, the Japanese Government are deeply solicitous for the early inauguration and progress of work having for its object this restoration and development, for the sake of the realization of a new order in East Asia, and are doing all in their power in that direction. The North China Development Company and the Central China Development Company were established with a view to giving China the necessary assistance toward the said restoration and also with the aim of contributing toward the development of China's natural resources. It is far from the thoughts of the Japanese Government to impair the rights and interests of American citizens in China or to discriminate against their enterprises. The Japanese Government therefore do not oppose, but welcome heartily, the participation of third powers on the basis of the new situation that has arisen.

The telecommunication companies in North and Central China and of the Inland Navigation Steamship Company at Shanghai and the wharfage company at Tsingtao have also been established to meet the imperative need of an early restoration of communications, transportation, and harbor facilities. With the exception of the telecommunications enterprise, which, because of its obvious relation to the maintenance of peace and order and to the national defense, as well as because of its public character, has been placed in the hands of special companies, all these enterprises are turned over to concerns that are ordinary Chinese or Japanese juridical persons, without any intention of allowing them to reap monopolistic profits by discriminating against America or any other power. As regards the wool trade, while the control of purchasing agencies was enforced for a time in the Mongolian region, it has since been discontinued. There is no plan at present of any sort for establishing a monopoly in tobacco.

Four. Concerning the return of American citizens to the occupied areas, Your Excellency is aware that in North China there is no restriction, excepting in very special cases where the personal safety of those who return would be endangered, while in the Yangtze Valley large numbers of Americans have already returned. The reason why permission to return has not yet been made general is, as has been repeatedly communicated to Your Excellency, due to the danger that persists because of the imperfect restoration of order and also to the impossibility of admitting nationals of third powers on account of strategic necessities such as the preservation of military secrets. Again, the various restrictions enforced in the occupied areas concerning the residence, travel, enterprise and trade of American citizens, constitute the minimum regulations possible consistent with military necessities and the local conditions of peace and order. It is the intention of the Japanese Government to restore the situation to normal as soon as circumstances permit.

Five. The Japanese Government were surprised at the allegation that there exists a fundamental difference between the treatment accorded to Japanese in America and the treatment accorded to Americans in Japan. While it is true that in these days of emergency Americans residing in this country are subject to various economic restrictions, yet these are, needless to say, restrictions imposed not upon Americans alone but also on all foreigners of all nationalities as well as upon the subjects of Japan. I beg to reserve for another occasion a statement of the views of the Japanese Government concerning the treatment of Japanese subjects in American territory, referred to in Your Excellency's note.

As has been explained above, the Japanese Government, with every intention of fully respecting American rights and interests in China, have been doing all that could possibly be done in that behalf. However, since there are in progress at present in China military operations on a scale unprecedented in our history, it may well be recognized by the Government of the United States that it is unavoidable that these military operations should occasionally present obstacles to giving full effect to our intention of respecting the rights and interests of American citizens.

Japan at present is devoting her energy to the establishment of a new order based on genuine international justice throughout East Asia, the attainment of which end is not only an indispensable condition of the very existence of Japan, but also constitutes the very foundation of the enduring peace and stability of East Asia.

It is the firm conviction of the Japanese Government that in the face of the new situation, fast developing in East Asia, any attempt to apply to the conditions of today and tomorrow inapplicable ideas and principles of the past neither would contribute toward the establishment of a real peace in East Asia nor solve the immediate issues.

However, as long as these points are understood, Japan has not the slightest inclination to oppose the participation of the United States and other powers in the great work of reconstructing East Asia along all lines of industry and trade; and I believe that the new regimes now being formed in China are prepared to welcome such foreign participation.

STATEMENT by Prince Konoe, Prime Minister, December 22, 1938

Translation, in Royal Institute of International Affairs, *Documents on International Affairs, 1938*, I, 353, citing *The Times* (London), December 23, 1938

THE JAPANESE GOVERNMENT are resolved to carry on military operations for the complete extermination of the anti-Japanese Kuomintang régime, and at the same time to proceed with the work of establishing a new order in East Asia together with those far-sighted Chinese who share our ideals and aspirations. A spirit of renaissance is now spreading over all parts of China and enthusiasm for reconstruction is mounting ever higher. The Japanese Government desire to make public their basic policy for adjusting relations between China and Japan in order that their intentions may be thoroughly understood at home and abroad.

Japan, China, and Manchukuo will be united by the common aim of establishing a new order in East Asia and realizing a relationship of neighborly amity, common defense against Communism, and economic cooperation. For that purpose it is necessary first that China should cast aside all narrow and prejudiced views of the past and do away with the folly of anti-Japanism and resentment regarding Manchukuo. In other words Japan frankly desires China to enter of her own free will into complete diplomatic relations with Manchukuo.

The existence of Comintern influence in East Asia cannot be tolerated. Japan therefore considers it an essential condition of the adjustment of Sino-Japanese relations that there should be concluded an anti-Comintern agreement between the two countries in consonance with the spirit of the Anti-Comintern Agreement between Japan, Germany, and Italy. In order to ensure the full accomplishment of this purpose Japan demands, in view of the actual circumstances prevailing in China, that Japanese troops shall be stationed, as an anti-Communist measure, at specified points during the time the Agreement is in force, and that the Inner Mongolian region be designated a special anti-Communist area.

As regards economic relations between the two countries, Japan does not intend to exercise an economic monopoly in China, nor does she intend to demand that China shall limit the interests of those third Powers which grasp the meaning of the new East Asia and are willing to act accordingly. Japan seeks only to render effective cooperation and collaboration between the two countries. That is to say, Japan demands that China, in accordance with the principle of equality between the two countries, shall recognize freedom of residence and trade on the part of Japanese subjects in the interior of China with a view to promoting the economic interests of both peoples, and that in the light of historical and economic relations between the two nations China should extend to Japan facilities for the development of China's natural resources, especially in the regions of North China and Inner Mongolia.

The above gives the general lines of what Japan demands. If Japan's true object in conducting the present vast military campaign be fully understood it will be plain that what she seeks is neither territory nor indemnity for the cost of military operations. Japan demands only minimum guarantees for the execution of her function as a participant in the establishing of a new order. Japan not only respects China's sovereignty, but is prepared to give positive consideration to the questions of the abolition of extraterritoriality and the rendition of foreign concessions and settlements—matters which are necessary for the full independence of China.

STATEMENT by Admiral Kichisaburo Nomura, Minister for Foreign Affairs, at a Meeting of the Japanese Cabinet, October 27, 1939, as Published in the Japanese Press

Translation, in Department of State, *Foreign Relations of the United States: Japan, 1931–1941*, II, 30; excerpt

RECENT OPINION in the United States toward the China affair, both official and unofficial, is extremely unfavorable and in the course of the coming negotiations looking toward the adjustment of Japanese-American relations it is doubtful whether Japan's wishes can be realized. Accordingly, the Imperial Government must anticipate that with the expiration on January 25 next year of the Treaty of Commerce and Navigation between Japan and the United States, Japanese-American relations may reach the worst state possible and must take into consideration at once counter-measures with respect to imports and exports, plans for commodity mobilization and similar problems.

PRO-MEMORIA from Admiral Kichisaburo Nomura, Minister for Foreign Affairs, to the American Ambassador (Joseph C. Grew), December 18, 1939

Department of State, *Foreign Relations of the United States: Japan, 1931–1941*, II, 49

1. ON TWO previous occasions I have had the opportunity of consulting with Your Excellency on the problem of opening the way for improvement in the existing condition of relations between Japan and the United States. Today is our third meeting. On the occasion of our first interview, November 4, Your Excellency expressed the hope that in order to open the way for the improvement of existing conditions in the relations between Japan and the United States, Japan would on its part take such measures as would directly indicate to the American people that Japan desires improved diplomatic relations. These measures were to be not only of a negative but also of a positive nature. The summarized table which you presented at our meeting on November 4 has been carefully analyzed, the true conditions of the pending problems and questions have been made clear and a policy for their solution has been set forth. It is desired in the first place to present an outline of the progress, based on this policy, which has been made toward a solution.

I should like to call to Your Excellency's attention the following facts with regard to the so-called negative measures of which you have spoken:

(1) Bombings. An examination of the number of recent cases reveals one during September, two during October and none during November.

(2) Indignities. No cases have been heard of recently.

(3) Questions concerning commercial rights and interests. While two or three cases have recently been reported by your Embassy, it is our policy to take appropriate and just measures for each case as soon as circumstances have been carefully examined.

Further, as it has been frequently stated, Japan is not in a position requiring it to assume responsibility for so-called compensation in such cases as are given under (*a*) on table B which was presented to Your Excellency last December 4. Nevertheless I am in a position again to declare that it is our policy to reimburse, as a solatium and token of sympathy, nationals of third countries promptly and in just and appropriate relation to the actual losses. If there is not complete agreement with regard to this point there is the possibility of further consideration. Among the items listed under (*b*), I can inform you that it is expected in the not distant future a settlement will be reached on the Western Roads Areas question which you seemed to view with particular seriousness in connection with the problems of the International Settlement at Shanghai. There are also prospects of readjustment at the same time of the question of the opening of the area north of Soochow Creek. I am sure that Your Excellency has also been informed by local Government [sic] reports that the question of the purchase of leaf tobacco in Shantung by the Universal Leaf Tobacco Company has been provisionally settled.

With respect to customs, currency, Salt Administration and other general problems relating to China, while exhaustive study must be given these matters in view of changing situations and future effects, in so far as the adjustment of these points with the interested countries is concerned, full consideration is being given to their interests, and a practical, fair settlement should be reached. Study is now being undertaken to this end.

2. The second point I should like to mention is the problem of navigation of the Yangtze River which has long been under consideration by the Japanese military. It is the intention of the military to open the lower reaches of the Yangtze River as far as Nanking. While military operations continue in that area, and opening of the river will cause various difficulties and inconveniences, it is possible gradually to moderate military requirements. Moreover, with the inauguration of the period for gradual building up of China, it is the intention of the military to open up a portion of China despite the military inconveniences which will have to be endured. However in dealing with the opening of the military [river] to navigation, consideration must be given to the need for consolidating various military establishments in that area and to the continued carrying on of military operations even at the present time along the banks of the river as far as Nanking, not to mention the upper reaches of the river; it therefore follows that there will be restrictions based upon military necessity. However, these restrictions should gradually be relaxed with the passage of time.

While it is desired to effect the opening of the river as early as possible in order to prevent any disturbances to the economic life of the area and to forestall any adverse effects upon the building up of the area, it is a matter [sic] anticipated, in the light of the preparation mentioned above and the necessity of consultation with various powers, that about two months will be required. The matter of the Pearl River is also being considered along the above lines.

3. On the occasion of my conversation with Your Excellency on

November 4, I stated that in order to improve international relations a precise understanding on the part of one side of the views and position of the other was essential and Your Excellency concurred. In so far as we are concerned, we are doing all that we can along the lines above indicated to improve Japanese-American relations and we intend to continue this policy. In our previous conversation Your Excellency spoke of the utterances by certain types of persons in American official life and of the difficulty of suppressing these utterances or newspaper comment. As you are aware there occur in Japan as well statements criticizing or opposing the actions of the Government, and when the public is moved by these statements, the Government is unable to restrain it.

With special reference to the question of reopening the Yangtze River, the view is held in certain quarters that the Japanese forces having made enormous sacrifices to reopen the river after it had been closed by the Chinese, no obligation rests on the Japanese to throw the river open to all. Consequently, as above stated, if at a time when progress is being made toward the adjusting of pending questions and concrete preparations are being made for the throwing open of the Yangtze River, no effective results are seen from the standpoint of improving international relations, the Government would be attacked by public opinion. In such contingency, adverse criticisms and attacks would certainly arise not only in connection with the reopening of the river but with the settlement of other pending questions, and difficulties would develop in putting such plans of settlement into effect. The result would be that relations between Japan and the United States, instead of improving would, it is feared, tend toward the opposite direction and so proceed to a point which it would be difficult to estimate. I earnestly hope that Your Excellency will appreciate these considerations.

During our conversation on November 4, Your Excellency referred to measures both negative and positive and I recall Your Excellency's observation that "In my view it is possible to bring about a speedy reversal of public opinion in the United States and there is possibility of improvement in our relations if these measures can be taken immediately." It is my expectation that the American Government will especially appreciate the fact that the Imperial Government is overcoming innumerable difficulties and as above stated is exerting its utmost efforts with a view to opening the way for improvement in American-Japanese relations, and that the American Government will in the same spirit reciprocate the efforts being put forward on our side. It goes without saying that more than anything else the termination of the Treaty of Commerce and Navigation casts the darkest shadow over American-Japanese relations. There remains but a little more than one month before the treaty expires. On the occasion of our previous conversation I said I personally hope that if it is to be that the treaty must expire, commerce between the two countries may continue in a normal manner so that there may occur nothing which will cause the peoples of the two countries to be penalized. To meet this situation some means must be devised; formalities of various kinds must first be taken, but we cannot afford to postpone due [*giving thought*] to the time required for these formalities and nearly [*other*] related matters. I therefore believe that there is need for arranging to enter into negotiations before the Christmas holidays begin and request Your Excellency's consideration of this point.

DRAFT Proposal Handed by Admiral Kichisaburo Nomura, Japanese Ambassador to the United States, to the Secretary of State of the United States (Cordell Hull), September 6, 1941

Department of State, *Peace and War*, p. 735

THE GOVERNMENT of Japan undertakes:

(a) that Japan is ready to express its concurrence in those matters which were already tentatively agreed upon between Japan and the United States in the course of their preliminary informal conversations;

(b) that Japan will not make any military advancement from French Indo-China against any of its adjoining areas, and likewise will not, without any justifiable reason, resort to military action against any regions lying south of Japan;

(c) that the attitudes of Japan and the United States towards the European War will be decided by the concepts of protection and self-defense, and, in case the United States should participate in the European War, the interpretation and execution of the Tripartite Pact by Japan shall be independently decided;

(d) that Japan will endeavor to bring about the rehabilitation of general and normal relationship between Japan and China, upon the realization of which Japan is ready to withdraw its armed forces from China as soon as possible in accordance with the agreements between Japan and China;

(e) that the economic activities of the United States in China will not be restricted so long as pursued on an equitable basis;

(f) that Japan's activities in the Southwestern Pacific Area will be carried on by peaceful means and in accordance with the principle of non-discrimination in international commerce, and that Japan will cooperate in the production and procurement by the United States of natural resources in the said area which it needs;

(g) that Japan will take measures necessary for the resumption of normal trade relations between Japan and the United States, and in connection with the above-mentioned, Japan is ready to discontinue immediately the application of the foreigners' transactions control regulations with regard to the United States on the basis of reciprocity.

The Government of the United States undertakes:

(a) that, in response to the Japanese Government's commitment expressed in point (d) referred to above, the United States will abstain from any measures and actions which will be prejudicial to the endeavor by Japan concerning the settlement of the China Affair;

(b) that the United States will reciprocate Japan's commitment expressed in point (f) referred to above;

(c) that the United States will suspend any military measures in the Far East and in the Southwestern Pacific Area;

(d) that the United States will immediately [upon settlement] reciprocate Japan's commitment expressed in point (g) referred to above by discontinuing the application of the so-called freezing act with regard to Japan and further by removing the prohibition against the passage of Japanese vessels through the Panama Canal.

DRAFT Proposal Handed by Admiral Kichisaburo Nomura, Japanese Ambassador to the United States, to the Secretary of State of the United States (Cordell Hull), November 20, 1941

Department of State, *Bulletin,* December 20, 1941, p. 540

1. BOTH THE Governments of Japan and the United States undertake not to make any armed advancement into any of the regions in the South-eastern Asia and the Southern Pacific area excepting the part of French Indo-China where the Japanese troops are stationed at present.

2. The Japanese Government undertakes to withdraw its troops now stationed in French Indo-China upon either the restoration of peace between Japan and China or the establishment of an equitable peace in the Pacific area.

In the meantime the Government of Japan declares that it is prepared to remove its troops now stationed in the southern part of French Indo-China to the northern part of the said territory upon the conclusion of the present arrangement which shall be embodied in the final agreement.

3. The Governments of Japan and the United States shall cooperate with a view to securing the acquisition of those goods and commodities which the two countries need in Netherlands East Indies.

4. The Governments of Japan and the United States mutually undertake to restore their commercial relations to those prevailing prior to the freezing of the assets.

The Government of the United States shall supply Japan a required quantity of oil.

5. The Government of the United States undertakes to refrain from such measures and actions as will be prejudicial to the endeavors for the restoration of general peace between Japan and China.

MEMORANDUM Presented by Admiral Kichisaburo Nomura, Japanese Ambassador to the United States, to the Secretary of State of the United States (Cordell Hull), December 7, 1941

Department of State, *Bulletin*, December 13, 1941, p. 466

1. The Government of Japan, prompted by a genuine desire to come to an amicable understanding with the Government of the United States in order that the two countries by their joint efforts may secure the peace of the Pacific Area and thereby contribute toward the realization of world peace, has continued negotiations with the utmost sincerity since April last with the Government of the United States regarding the adjustment and advancement of Japanese-American relations and the stabilization of the Pacific Area.

The Japanese Government has the honor to state frankly its views concerning the claims the American Government has persistently maintained as well as the measures the United States and Great Britain have taken toward Japan during these eight months.

2. It is the immutable policy of the Japanese Government to insure the stability of East Asia and to promote world peace and thereby to enable all nations to find each its proper place in the world.

Ever since China Affair broke out owing to the failure on the part of China to comprehend Japan's true intentions, the Japanese Government has striven for the restoration of peace and it has consistently exerted its best efforts to prevent the extension of war-like disturbances. It was also to that end in September last year Japan concluded the Tripartite Pact with Germany and Italy.

However, both the United States and Great Britain have resorted to every possible measure to assist the Chungking régime so as to obstruct the establishment of a general peace between Japan and China, interfering with Japan's constructive endeavours toward the stabilization of East Asia. Exerting pressure on the Netherlands East Indies, or menacing French Indo-China, they have attempted to frustrate Japan's aspiration to the ideal of common prosperity in cooperation with these regions. Furthermore, when Japan in accordance with its protocol with France took measures of joint defence of French Indo-China, both American and British Governments, wilfully misinterpreting it as a threat to their own possessions, and inducing the Netherlands Government to follow suit, they enforced the assets freezing order, thus severing economic relations with Japan. While manifesting thus an obviously hostile attitude, these countries have strengthened their military preparations perfecting an encirclement of Japan, and have brought about a situation which endangers the very existence of the Empire.

Nevertheless, to facilitate a speedy settlement, the Premier of Japan proposed, in August last, to meet the President of the United States for a discussion of important problems between the two countries covering the entire Pacific area. However, the American Government, while accepting in principle the Japanese proposal, insisted that the meeting should take place after an agreement of view had been reached on fundamental and essential questions.

3. Subsequently, on September 25th the Japanese Government submitted a proposal based on the formula proposed by the American Government, taking fully into consideration past American claims and also incorporating Japanese views. Repeated discussions proved of no avail in producing readily an agreement of view. The present cabinet, therefore, submitted a revised proposal, moderating still further the Japanese claims regarding the principal points of difficulty in the negotiation and endeavoured strenuously to reach a settlement. But the American Government, adhering steadfastly to its original assertions, failed to display in the slightest degree a spirit of conciliation. The negotiation made no progress.

Therefore, the Japanese Government, with a view to doing its utmost for averting a crisis in Japanese-American relations, submitted on November 20th still another proposal in order to arrive at an equitable solution of the more essential and urgent questions which, simplifying its previous proposal, stipulated the following points:

(1) The Governments of Japan and the United States undertake not to dispatch armed forces into any of the regions, excepting French Indo-China, in the Southeastern Asia and the Southern Pacific area.
(2) Both Governments shall cooperate with the view to securing the acquisition in the Netherlands East Indies of those goods and commodities of which the two countries are in need.
(3) Both Governments mutually undertake to restore commercial relations to those prevailing prior to the freezing of assets.
The Government of the United States shall supply Japan the required quantity of oil.
(4) The Government of the United States undertakes not to resort to measures and actions prejudicial to the endeavours for the restoration of general peace between Japan and China.
(5) The Japanese Government undertakes to withdraw troops now stationed in French Indo-China upon either the restoration of peace between Japan and China or the establishment of an equitable peace in the Pacific Area; and it is prepared to remove the Japanese troops in the southern part of French Indo-China to the northern part upon the conclusion of the present agreement.

As regards China, the Japanese Government, while expressing its readiness to accept the offer of the President of the United States to act as "introducer" of peace between Japan and China as was previously suggested, asked for an undertaking on the part of the United States to do nothing prejudicial to the restoration of Sino-Japanese peace when the two parties have commenced direct negotiations.

The American Government not only rejected the above-mentioned new proposal, but made known its intention to continue its aid to Chiang Kai-shek; and in spite of its suggestion mentioned above, withdrew the offer of the President to act as so-called "introducer" of peace between Japan and China, pleading that time was not yet ripe for it. Finally on November 26th, in an attitude to impose upon the Japanese Government those principles it has persistently maintained, the American Government made a proposal totally ignoring Japanese claims, which is a source of profound regret to the Japanese Government.

4. From the beginning of the present negotiation the Japanese Government has always maintained an attitude of fairness and moderation, and did its best to reach a settlement, for which it made all possible concessions often in spite of great difficulties. As for the China question which constitutes an important subject of the negotiation, the Japanese Government showed a most conciliatory attitude. As for the principle of non-discrimination in international commerce, advocated by the American Government, the Japanese Government expressed its desire to see the said principle applied throughout the world, and declared that along with the actual practice of this principle in the world, the Japanese Government would endeavour to apply the same in the Pacific area including China, and made it clear that Japan had no intention of excluding from China economic activities of third powers pursued on an equitable basis. Furthermore, as regards the question of withdrawing troops from French Indo-China, the Japanese Government even volunteered, as mentioned above, to carry out an immediate evacuation of troops from Southern French Indo-China as a measure of easing the situation.

It is presumed that the spirit of conciliation exhibited to the utmost degree by the Japanese Government in all these matters is fully appreciated by the American Government.

On the other hand, the American Government, always holding fast to theories in disregard of realities, and refusing to yield an inch on its impractical principles, caused undue delay in the negotiation. It is difficult to understand this attitude of the American Government and the Japanese Government desires to call the attention of the American Government especially to the following points:

1. The American Government advocates in the name of world peace those principles favorable to it and urges upon the Japanese Government the acceptance thereof. The peace of the world may be brought about only by discovering a mutually acceptable formula through recognition of the reality of the situation and mutual appreciation of one another's position. An attitude such as ignores realities and imposes one's selfish views upon others will scarcely serve the purpose of facilitating the consummation of negotiations.

Of the various principles put forward by the American Government as a basis of the Japanese-American Agreement, there are some which the Japanese Government is ready to accept in principle, but in view of the world's actual condition it seems only a utopian ideal on the part of the American Government to attempt to force their immediate adoption.

Again, the proposal to conclude a multilateral non-aggression pact between Japan, United States, Great Britain, China, the Soviet Union, the Netherlands and Thailand, which is patterned after the old concept of collective security, is far removed from the realities of East Asia.

2. The American proposal contained a stipulation which states— "Both Governments will agree that no agreement, which either has concluded with any third power or powers, shall be interpreted by it in such a way as to conflict with the fundamental purpose of this agreement, the establishment and preservation of peace throughout the Pacific area." It is presumed that the above provision has been

proposed with a view to restrain Japan from fulfilling its obligations under the Tripartite Pact when the United States participates in the war in Europe, and, as such, it cannot be accepted by the Japanese Government.

The American Government, obsessed with its own views and opinions, may be said to be scheming for the extension of the war. While it seeks, on the one hand, to secure its rear by stabilizing the Pacific Area, it is engaged, on the other hand, in aiding Great Britain and preparing to attack, in the name of self-defense, Germany and Italy, two Powers that are striving to establish a new order in Europe. Such a policy is totally at variance with the many principles upon which the American Government proposes to found the stability of the Pacific Area through peaceful means.

3. Whereas the American Government, under the principles it rigidly upholds, objects to settle international issues through military pressure, it is exercising in conjunction with Great Britain and other nations pressure by economic power. Recourse to such pressure as a means of dealing with international relations should be condemned as it is at times more inhumane than military pressure.

4. It is impossible not to reach the conclusion that the American Government desires to maintain and strengthen, in coalition with Great Britain and other Powers, its dominant position it has hitherto occupied not only in China but in other areas of East Asia. It is a fact of history that the countries of East Asia for the past hundred years or more have been compelled to observe the *status quo* under the Anglo-American policy of imperialistic exploitation and to sacrifice themselves to the prosperity of the two nations. The Japanese Government cannot tolerate the perpetuation of such a situation since it directly runs counter to Japan's fundamental policy to enable all nations to enjoy each its proper place in the world.

The stipulation proposed by the American Government relative to French Indo-China is a good exemplification of the above-mentioned American policy. Thus the six countries,—Japan, the United States, Great Britain, the Netherlands, China, and Thailand,—excepting France, should undertake among themselves to respect the territorial integrity and sovereignty of French Indo-China and equality of treatment in trade and commerce would be tantamount to placing that territory under the joint guarantee of the Governments of those six countries. Apart from the fact that such a proposal totally ignores the position of France, it is unacceptable to the Japanese Government in that such an arrangement cannot but be considered as an extension to French Indo-China of a system similar to the Nine Power Treaty structure which is the chief factor responsible for the present predicament of East Asia.

5. All the items demanded of Japan by the American Government regarding China such as wholesale evacuation of troops or unconditional application of the principle of non-discrimination in international commerce ignored the actual conditions of China, and are calculated to destroy Japan's position as the stabilizing factor of East Asia. The attitude of the American Government in demanding Japan not to support militarily, politically or economically any régime other than the régime at Chungking, disregarding thereby the existence of the Nanking Government, shatters the very basis of the present negotiation. This demand of the American Government falling, as it does, in line with its above-mentioned refusal to cease from aiding the Chungking régime, demonstrates clearly the intention of the American Government to obstruct the restoration of normal relations between Japan and China and the return of peace to East Asia.

5. In brief, the American proposal contains certain acceptable items such as those concerning commerce, including the conclusion of a trade agreement, mutual removal of the freezing restrictions, and stabilizing of yen and dollar exchange, or the abolition of extra-territorial rights in China. On the other hand, however, the proposal in question ignores Japan's sacrifices in the four years of the China Affair, menaces the Empire's existence itself, and disparages its honour and prestige. Therefore, viewed in its entirety, the Japanese Government regrets that it cannot accept the proposal as a basis of negotiation.

6. The Japanese Government, in its desire for an early conclusion of the negotiation, proposed simultaneously with the conclusion of the Japanese-American negotiation, agreements to be signed with Great Britain and other interested countries. The proposal was accepted by the American Government. However, since the American Government has made the proposal of November 26th as a result of frequent consultation with Great Britain, Australia, the Netherlands and Chungking, and presumably by catering to the wishes of the Chungking régime in the questions of China, it must be concluded that all these countries are at one with the United States in ignoring Japan's position.

7. Obviously it is the intention of the American Government to conspire with Great Britain and other countries to obstruct Japan's efforts toward the establishment of peace through the creation of a new order in East Asia, and especially to preserve Anglo-American

rights and interests by keeping Japan and China at war. This intention has been revealed clearly during the course of the present negotiation. Thus, the earnest hope of the Japanese Government to adjust Japanese-American relations and to preserve and promote the peace of the Pacific through cooperation with the American Government has finally been lost.

The Japanese Government regrets to have to notify hereby the American Government that in view of the attitude of the American Government it cannot but consider that it is impossible to reach an agreement through further negotiations.

DECEMBER 7, 1941.

PART EIGHT

INTERNATIONAL AGREEMENTS AND RESOLUTIONS, JOINT COMMUNIQUÉS

ACTION BY THE LEAGUE OF NATIONS IN CERTAIN CASES

Japanese Invasion of Manchuria in 1931

RESOLUTION Adopted by the Council of the League of Nations, September 30, 1931

Department of State, *Foreign Relations of the United States: Japan, 1931–1941*, I, 29

THE COUNCIL,

1. Notes the replies of the Chinese and Japanese Governments to the urgent appeal addressed to them by its President and the steps that have already been taken in response to that appeal;
2. Recognises the importance of the Japanese Government's statement that it has no territorial designs in Manchuria;
3. Notes the Japanese representative's statement that his Government will continue, as rapidly as possible, the withdrawal of its troops, which has already been begun, into the railway zone in proportion as the safety of the lives and property of Japanese nationals is effectively assured and that it hopes to carry out this intention in full as speedily as may be;
4. Notes the Chinese representative's statement that his Government will assume responsibility for the safety of the lives and property of Japanese nationals outside that zone as the withdrawal of the Japanese troops continues and the Chinese local authorities and police forces are re-established;
5. Being convinced that both Governments are anxious to avoid taking any action which might disturb the peace and good understanding between the two nations, notes that the Chinese and Japanese representatives have given assurances that their respective Governments will take all necessary steps to prevent any extension of the scope of the incident or any aggravation of the situation;
6. Requests both parties to do all in their power to hasten the restoration of normal relations between them and for that purpose to continue and speedily complete the execution of the above-mentioned undertakings;
7. Requests both parties to furnish the Council at frequent intervals with full information as to the development of the situation;

8. Decides, in the absence of any unforeseen occurrence which might render an immediate meeting essential, to meet again at Geneva on Wednesday, October 14th, 1931, to consider the situation as it then stands;

9. Authorises its President to cancel the meeting of the Council fixed for October 14th should he decide, after consulting his colleagues, and more particularly the representatives of the two parties, that, in view of such information as he may have received from the parties or from other members of the Council as to the development of the situation, the meeting is no longer necessary.

RESOLUTION Adopted by the Council of the League of Nations, October 24, 1931

Department of State, *Foreign Relations of the United States: Japan, 1931–1941*, I, 29

THE COUNCIL,

In pursuance of the resolution passed on September 30th;

Noting that in addition to the invocation by the Government of China, of Article 11 of the Covenant, Article 2 of the Pact of Paris has also been invoked by a number of the Governments;

(1) Recalls the undertakings given to the Council by the Governments of China and Japan in that resolution, and in particular the statement of the Japanese representative that the Japanese Government would continue as rapidly as possible the withdrawal of its troops into the railway zone in proportion as the safety of the lives and property of Japanese nationals is effectively assured, and the statement of the Chinese representative that his Government will assume the responsibility for the safety of the lives and property of Japanese nationals outside that zone—a pledge which implies the effective protection of Japanese subjects residing in Manchuria;

(2) Recalls further that both Governments have given the assurance that they would refrain from any measures which might aggravate the existing situation, and are therefore bound not to resort to any aggressive policy or action and to take measures to suppress hostile agitation;

(3) Recalls the Japanese statement that Japan has no territorial designs in Manchuria, and notes that this statement is in accordance with the terms of the Covenant of the League of Nations, and of the Nine-Power Treaty, the signatories of which are pledged "to respect

the sovereignty, the independence, and the territorial and administrative integrity of China";

(4) Being convinced that the fulfilment of these assurances and undertakings is essential for the restoration of normal relations between the two parties:

(*a*) Calls upon the Japanese Government to begin immediately and to proceed progressively with the withdrawal of its troops into the railway zone, so that the total withdrawal may be effected before the date fixed for the next meeting of the Council;

(*b*) Calls upon the Chinese Government, in execution of its general pledge to assume the responsibility for the safety of the lives and property of all Japanese subjects resident in Manchuria, to make such arrangements for taking over the territory thus evacuated as will ensure the safety of the lives and property of Japanese subjects there, and requests the Chinese Government to associate with the Chinese authorities designated for the above purpose representatives of other Powers in order that such representatives may follow the execution of the arrangements;

(5) Recommends that the Chinese and Japanese Governments should immediately appoint representatives to arrange the details of the execution of all points relating to the evacuation and the taking over of the evacuated territory so that they may proceed smoothly and without delay;

(6) Recommends the Chinese and Japanese Governments, as soon as the evacuation is completed, to begin direct negotiations on questions outstanding between them, and in particular those arising out of recent incidents as well as those relating to existing difficulties due to the railway situation in Manchuria. For this purpose, the Council suggests that the two parties should set up a conciliation committee, or some such permanent machinery;

(7) Decides to adjourn till November 16th, at which date it will again examine the situation, but authorises its President to convoke a meeting at any earlier date should it in his opinion be desirable.

RESOLUTION Adopted by the Council of the League of Nations, December 10, 1931

Department of State, *Foreign Relations of the United States: Japan, 1931–1941*, I, 59

THE COUNCIL,

(1) Reaffirms the resolution passed unanimously by it on September 30th, 1931, by which the two parties declare that they are solemnly bound; it therefore calls upon the Chinese and Japanese Governments to take all steps necessary to assure its execution, so that the withdrawal of the Japanese troops within the railway zone may be effected as speedily as possible under the conditions set forth in the said resolution;

(2) Considering that events have assumed an even more serious aspect since the Council meeting of October 24th;

Notes that the two parties undertake to adopt all measures necessary to avoid any further aggravation of the situation and to refrain from any initiative which may lead to further fighting and loss of life;

(3) Invites the two parties to continue to keep the Council informed as to the development of the situation;

(4) Invites the other Members of the Council to furnish the Council with any information received from their representatives on the spot;

(5) Without prejudice to the carrying out of the above-mentioned measures,

Desiring, in view of the special circumstances of the case, to contribute towards a final and fundamental solution by the two Governments of the questions at issue between them:

Decides to appoint a Commission of five members to study on the spot and to report to the Council on any circumstance which, affecting international relations, threatens to disturb peace between China and Japan, or the good understanding between them, upon which peace depends;

The Governments of China and of Japan will each have the right to nominate one assessor to assist the Commission.

The two Governments will afford the Commission all facilities to obtain on the spot whatever information it may require;

It is understood that, should the two parties initiate any negotiations, these would not fall within the scope of the terms of reference of the Commission, nor would it be within the competence of the

Commission to interfere with the military arrangements of either party.

The appointment and deliberations of the Commission shall not prejudice in any way the undertaking given by the Japanese Government in the resolution of September 30th as regards the withdrawal of the Japanese troops within the railway zone.

(6) Between now and its next ordinary session, which will be held on January 25th, 1932, the Council, which remains seized of the matter, invites its President to follow the question and to summon it afresh if necessary.

REPORT Adopted by the Assembly of the League of Nations, February 24, 1933

Department of State, Publication No. 449 (*Sino-Japanese Dispute*, a photographic reprint of the document as published by the League of Nations); excerpt

PART III.——CHIEF CHARACTERISTICS OF THE DISPUTE

It will be seen from this review that for more than sixteen months the Council or Assembly has continuously tried to find a solution for the Sino-Japanese dispute. Numerous resolutions have been adopted based on various articles of the Covenant and other international agreements. The complexity, to which reference has already been made, of the historical background of the events; the special legal situation of Manchuria, where Japan, as will be noted later, exercised within Chinese territory extensive rights; finally, the involved and delicate relations existing in fact between the Chinese and Japanese authorities in certain parts of Manchuria justified and rendered necessary the prolonged efforts of negotiation and enquiry made by the League. However, the hopes entertained by the Council and the Assembly of an improvement in the situation, arising from the declarations of the parties and the resolutions adopted with their participation, were disappointed. The situation, on the contrary, tended to grow constantly worse. In Manchuria, or other parts of the territory of a Member of the League, military operations, which the report of the Commission of Enquiry has described as "war in disguise," continued and still continue.

Having considered the principal features of the dispute, the Assembly has reached, in particular, the following conclusions and noted the following facts:

1. The dispute between China and Japan which is submitted to the Assembly originated in Manchuria, which China and foreign Powers have always regarded as an integral part of China under Chinese sovereignty. In its observations on the report of the Commission of Enquiry, the Japanese Government contests the argument that the rights conferred on Russia and subsequently acquired by Japan "in the extremely limited area known as the Southern Manchuria Railway zone" conflict with Chinese sovereignty. "They were, on the contrary, derived from the sovereignty of China."

The rights conferred by China on Russia and subsequently on Japan derive from the sovereignty of China. Under the Treaty of Pekin in 1905, "the Imperial Chinese Government consented to all the transfers and assignments made by Russia to Japan" under the Treaty of Portsmouth. In 1915, it was to China that Japan addressed demands for the extension of her rights in Manchuria and it was with the Government of the Chinese Republic that, following on these demands, the Treaty of May 25th, 1915, was concluded concerning South Manchuria and Eastern Inner Mongolia. At the Washington Conference, the Japanese delegation stated, on February 2nd, 1922, that Japan renounced certain preferential rights in South Manchuria and Eastern Inner Mongolia and explained that, "in coming to this decision, Japan had been guided by a spirit of fairness and moderation, having always in view China's sovereign rights and the principle of equal opportunity." The Nine-Power Treaty, concluded at the Washington Conference, applies to Manchuria as to every other part of China. Finally, during the first phase of the present conflict, Japan never argued that Manchuria was not an integral part of China.

2. Past experience shows that those who control Manchuria exercise a considerable influence on the affairs of the rest of China—at least of North China—and possess unquestionable strategic and political advantages. To cut off these provinces from the rest of China cannot but create a serious irredentist problem likely to endanger peace.

3. The Assembly, in noting these facts, is not unmindful of the tradition of autonomy existing in Manchuria. That tradition, in one extreme case, and in a period of particular weakness on the part of the Central Government of China, made it possible, for instance, for the plenipotentiaries of Marshal Chang Tso-lin to conclude, in the name of the "Government of the autonomous three Eastern Provinces of the Republic of China," the agreement of September 20th, 1924, with the Union of Soviet Socialist Republics concerning the Chinese Eastern Railway, navigation, the delimitation of frontiers, etc. It is obvious from the provisions of that agreement, however, that the Government of the autonomous three Eastern Provinces did not regard

itself as the Government of a State independent of China, but believed that it might itself negotiate with the Union of Soviet Socialist Republics on questions affecting the interests of China in the three provinces, though the Central Government had, a few months previously, concluded an agreement on these questions with the self-same Power.

This autonomy of Manchuria was also shown by the fact that, first, Marshal Chang Tso-lin and later Marshal Chang Hsueh-liang were the heads both of the civil and military administration and exercised the effective power in the three provinces through their armies and their officials. The independence proclaimed by Marshal Chang Tso-lin at different times never meant that either he or the people of Manchuria wished to be separated from China. His armies did not invade China as if it were a foreign country but merely as participants in the civil war. Through all its wars and periods of "independence," Manchuria remained an integral part of China. Further, since 1928, Marshal Chang Hsueh-liang has recognised the authority of the Chinese National Government.

4. During the quarter of a century ending in September 1931, the political and economic ties uniting Manchuria with the rest of China grew stronger, while, at the same time, the interests of Japan in Manchuria did not cease to develop. Under the Chinese Republic, the "three Eastern Provinces" constituting Manchuria were thrown wide to the immigration of Chinese from the other provinces who, by taking possession of the land, have made Manchuria in many respects a simple extension of China north of the Great Wall. In a population of about 30 millions, it is estimated that the Chinese or assimilated Manchus number 28 millions. Moreover, under the administration of Marshals Chang Tso-lin and Chang Hsueh-liang, the Chinese population and Chinese interests have played a much more important part than formerly in the development and organisation of the economic resources of Manchuria.

On the other hand, Japan had acquired or claimed in Manchuria rights the effect of which was to restrict the exercise of sovereignty by China in a manner and to a degree quite exceptional. Japan governed the leased territory of Kwantung, exercising therein what amounted in practice to full sovereignty. Through the medium of the South Manchuria Railway, she administered the railway zones, including several towns and important parts of populous cities, such as Mukden and Changchun. In these areas, she had control of the police, taxes, education, and public utilities. She maintained armed forces in certain parts of the country: the army of Kwantung in the leased territory; railway guards in the railway zones; consular police in the various districts. Such a state of affairs might perhaps have continued without leading to complications and incessant disputes if it had been freely desired or accepted by both parties and if it had been the expression and manifestation of a well-understood policy of close economic and political co-operation. But, in the absence of such conditions, it was bound to lead to mutual misunderstandings and conflicts. The interconnection of respective rights, the uncertainty at times of the legal situation, the increasing opposition between the conception held by the Japanese of their "special position" in Manchuria, and the claims of Chinese nationalism were a further source of numerous incidents and disputes.

5. Before September 18th, 1931, each of the two parties had legitimate grievances against the other in Manchuria, Japan taking advantage of rights open to question and the Chinese authorities putting obstacles in the way of the exercise of rights which could not be contested. During the period immediately preceding the events of September 18th, various efforts were made to settle the questions outstanding between the two parties by the normal method of diplomatic negotiations and pacific means, and these means had not been exhausted. Nevertheless, the tension between Chinese and Japanese in Manchuria increased, and a movement of opinion in Japan advocated the settlement of all outstanding questions—if necessary, by force.

6. The present period of transition and national reconstruction in China, despite the efforts of the Central Government and the considerable progress already achieved, necessarily involves political disturbances, social disorder, and disruptive tendencies inseparable from a state of transition. It calls for the employment of a policy of international co-operation. One of the methods of that policy would be that the League of Nations would continue to afford China the technical assistance in modernising her institutions which her Government might request with a view to enabling the Chinese people to reorganise and consolidate the Chinese State.

The full application of the policy of international co-operation initiated at the Washington Conference, the principles of which are still valid, has been delayed, chiefly by the violence of the anti-foreign propaganda carried on in China from time to time. In two respects —the use of the economic boycott and anti-foreign teaching in schools —this propaganda has been pushed to such lengths that it has contributed to creating the atmosphere in which the present dispute broke out.

7. The use of the boycott by the Chinese previous to the events of September 18th, 1931, to express their indignation at certain inci-

dents or to support certain claims could not fail to make a situation which was already tense still more tense.

The use of the boycott by China, subsequent to the events of September 18th, 1931, falls under the category of reprisals.

8. The object of the provisions of the Covenant of the League of Nations regarding the settlement of disputes is to prevent the tension between nations becoming such that a rupture appears to be inevitable. The Commission of Enquiry found that each of the issues between China and Japan was in itself capable of settlement by arbitral procedure. It is precisely because the accumulation of these issues increased the tension between the two nations that it was incumbent on the nation which regarded itself as injured to draw the attention of the League of Nations to the situation when diplomatic negotiations were unduly protracted.

Article 12 of the Covenant contains formal obligations as regards the pacific settlement of disputes.

9. Without excluding the possibility that, on the night of September 18th–19th, 1931, the Japanese officers on the spot may have believed that they were acting in self-defence, the Assembly cannot regard as measures of self-defence the military operations carried out on that night by the Japanese troops at Mukden and other places in Manchuria. Nor can the military measures of Japan as a whole, developed in the course of the dispute, be regarded as measures of self-defence. Moreover, the adoption of measures of self-defence does not exempt a State from complying with the provisions of Article 12 of the Covenant.

10. Since September 18th, 1931, the activities of the Japanese military authorities, in civil as well as in military matters, have been marked by essentially political considerations. The progressive military occupation of the Three Eastern Provinces removed in succession all the important towns in Manchuria from the control of the Chinese authorities, and, following each occupation, the civil administration was reorganised. A group of Japanese civil and military officials conceived, organised, and carried through the Manchurian independence movement as a solution to the situation in Manchuria as it existed after the events of September 18th, and, with this object, made use of the names and actions of certain Chinese individuals and took advantage of certain minorities and native communities that had grievances against the Chinese administration. This movement, which rapidly received assistance and direction from the Japanese General Staff, could only be carried through owing to the presence of the Japanese troops. It cannot be considered as a spontaneous and genuine independence movement.

11. The main political and administrative power in the "Government" of "Manchukuo," the result of the movement described in the previous paragraph, rests in the hands of Japanese officials and advisers, who are in a position actually to direct and control the administration; in general, the Chinese in Manchuria, who, as already mentioned form the vast majority of the population, do not support this "Government" and regard it as an instrument of the Japanese. It should also be noted that, after the Commission of Enquiry completed its report and before the report was considered by the Council and the Assembly, "Manchukuo" was recognised by Japan. It has not been recognised by any other State, the Members of the League in particular being of opinion that such recognition was incompatible with the spirit of the resolution of March 11th, 1932.

* * *

The situation which led up to the events of September 18th, 1931, presents certain special features. It was subsequently aggravated by the development of the Japanese military operations, the creation of the "Manchukuo Government" and the recognition of that "Government" by Japan. Undoubtedly the present case is not that of a country which has declared war on another country without previously exhausting the opportunities for conciliation provided in the Covenant of the League of Nations; neither is it a simple case of the violation of the frontier of one country by the armed forces of a neighbouring country, because in Manchuria, as shown by the circumstances noted above, there are many features without an exact parallel in other parts of the world. It is, however, indisputable that, without any declaration of war, a large part of Chinese territory has been forcibly seized and occupied by Japanese troops and that, in consequence of this operation, it has been separated from and declared independent of the rest of China.

The Council, in its resolution of September 30th, 1931, noted the declaration of the Japanese representative that his Government would continue, as rapidly as possible, the withdrawal of its troops, which had already been begun, into the railway zone in proportion as the safety of the lives and property of Japanese nationals was effectively ensured, and that it hoped to carry out this intention in full as speedily as might be. Further, in its resolution of December 10th, 1931, the Council, re-affirming its resolution of September 30th, noted the undertaking of the two parties to adopt all measures necessary to avoid any further aggravation of the situation and to refrain from any initiative which might lead to further fighting and loss of life.

It should be pointed out in connection with these events that, under Article 10 of the Covenant, the Members of the League undertake to respect the territorial integrity and existing political independence of all Members of the League.

Lastly, under Article 12 of the Covenant, the Members of the League agree that, if there should arise between them any dispute likely to lead to a rupture, they will submit the matter either to arbitration or judicial settlement or to enquiry by the Council.

While at the origin of the state of tension that existed before September 18th, 1931, certain responsibilities would appear to lie on one side and the other, no question of Chinese responsibility can arise for the development of events since September 18th, 1931.

PART IV.——STATEMENT OF THE RECOMMENDATIONS

This part sets forth the recommendations which the Assembly deems just and proper in regard to the dispute.

SECTION I

The recommendations of the Assembly take into account the very special circumstances of this case and are based on the following principles, conditions and considerations:

(*a*) The settlement of the dispute should observe the provisions of the Covenant of the League, the Pact of Paris, and the Nine-Power Treaty of Washington.

Article 10 of the Covenant of the League provides that "the Members of the League undertake to respect and preserve as against external aggression the territorial integrity and existing political independence of all Members of the League."

According to Article II of the Pact of Paris, "the High Contracting Parties agree that the settlement or solution of all disputes or conflicts of whatever nature, or of whatever origin they may be, which may arise among them, shall never be sought except by pacific means."

According to Article 1 of the Nine-Power Treaty of Washington, "the Contracting Powers, other than China, agree to respect the sovereignty, the independence, and the territorial and administrative integrity of China."

(*b*) The settlement of the dispute should observe the provisions of Parts I and II of the Assembly resolution of March 11th, 1932.

In that resolution, which has already been quoted in this report, the Assembly considered that the provisions of the Covenant were entirely applicable to the present dispute, more particularly as regards:

(1) The principle of a scrupulous respect for treaties;
(2) The undertaking entered into by Members of the League of

Nations to respect and preserve as against external aggression the territorial integrity and existing political independence of all the Members of the League;

(3) Their obligation to submit any dispute which may arise between them to procedures for peaceful settlement.

The Assembly has adopted the principles laid down by the President-in-Office of the Council in his declaration of December 10th, 1931, and has recalled the fact that twelve Members of the Council had again invoked those principles in their appeal to the Japanese Government on February 16th, 1932, when they declared that no infringement of the territorial integrity and no change in the political independence of any Member of the League brought about in disregard of Article 10 of the Covenant ought to be recognised as valid and effectual by Members of the League.

The Assembly has stated its opinion that the principles governing international relations and the peaceful settlement of disputes between Members of the League above referred to are in full harmony with the Pact of Paris. Pending the steps which it might ultimately take for the settlement of the dispute which had been referred to it, it has proclaimed the binding nature of the principles and provisions referred to above and declared that it was incumbent upon the Members of the League not to recognise any situation, treaty or agreement which might be brought about by means contrary to the Covenant of the League of Nations or to the Pact of Paris.

Lastly, the Assembly has affirmed that it is contrary to the spirit of the Covenant that the settlement of the Sino-Japanese dispute should be sought under the stress of military pressure on the part of either party, and has recalled the resolutions adopted by the Council on September 30th and December 10th, 1931, in agreement with the parties.

(c) In order that a lasting understanding may be established between China and Japan on the basis of respect for the international undertakings mentioned above, the settlement of the dispute must conform to the principles and conditions laid down by the Commission of Enquiry in the following terms:

1. *Compatibility with the interests of both China and Japan.*

Both countries are Members of the League and each is entitled to claim the same consideration from the League. A solution from which both did not derive benefit would not be a gain to the cause of peace.

2. *Consideration for the interests of the Union of Soviet Socialist Republics.*

To make peace between two of the neighbouring countries without regard for the interests of the third would be neither just nor wise, nor in the interests of peace.

3. *Conformity with existing multilateral treaties.*

Any solution should conform to the provisions of the Covenant of the League of Nations, the Pact of Paris, and the Nine-Power Treaty of Washington.

4. *Recognition of Japan's interests in Manchuria.*

The rights and interests of Japan in Manchuria are facts which cannot be ignored, and any solution which failed to recognise them and to take into account also the historical associations of Japan with that country would not be satisfactory.

5. *The establishment of new treaty relations between China and Japan.*

A restatement of the respective rights, interests and responsibilities of both countries in Manchuria in new treaties, which shall be part of the settlement by agreement, is desirable if future friction is to be avoided and mutual confidence and co-operation are to be restored.

6. *Effective provisions for the settlement of future disputes.*

As a corollary to the above, it is necessary that provision should be made for facilitating the prompt settlement of minor disputes as they arise.

7. *Manchurian autonomy.*

The Government in Manchuria should be modified in such a way as to secure, consistently with the sovereignty and administrative integrity of China, a large measure of autonomy designed to meet the local conditions and special characteristics of the Three Provinces. The new civil regime must be so constituted and conducted as to satisfy the essential requirements of good government.

8. *Internal order and security against external aggression.*

The internal order of the country should be secured by an effective local gendarmerie force, and security against external aggression should be provided by the withdrawal of all armed forces other than gendarmerie, and by the conclusion of a treaty of non-aggression between the countries interested.

9. *Encouragement of an economic* rapprochement *between China and Japan.*

For this purpose a new commercial treaty between the two countries is desirable. Such a treaty should aim at placing on an equitable basis the commercial relations between the two countries and bringing them into conformity with their improved political relations.

10. *International co-operation in Chinese reconstruction.*

Since the present political instability in China is an obstacle to friendship with Japan and an anxiety to the rest of the world (as the maintenance of peace in the Far East is a matter of international concern), and since the conditions enumerated above cannot be fulfilled without a strong Central Government in China, the final requisite for a satisfactory solution is temporary international co-operation in the internal reconstruction of China, as suggested by the late Dr. Sun Yat-sen.

Section II

The provisions of this section constitute the recommendations of the Assembly under Article 15, paragraph 4, of the Covenant.

Having defined the principles, conditions and considerations applicable to the settlement of the dispute,

The Assembly recommends as follows:

1. Whereas the sovereignty over Manchuria belongs to China,

A. Considering that the presence of Japanese troops outside the zone of the South Manchuria Railway and their operations outside this zone are incompatible with the legal principles which should govern the settlement of the dispute, and that it is necessary to establish as soon as possible a situation consistent with these principles,

The Assembly recommends the evacuation of these troops. In view of the special circumstances of the case, the first object of the negotiations recommended hereinafter should be to organise this evacuation and to determine the methods, stages and time-limits thereof.

B. Having regard to the local conditions special to Manchuria, the particular rights and interests possessed by Japan therein, and the rights and interests of third States,

The Assembly recommends the establishment in Manchuria, within a reasonable period, of an organisation under the sovereignty of, and compatible with the administrative integrity of, China. This organisation should provide a wide measure of autonomy, should be in harmony with local conditions and should take account of the multilateral treaties in force, the particular rights and interests of Japan, the rights and interests of third States, and, in general, the principles and conditions reproduced in Section I (*c*) above; the determination of the respective powers of and relations between the Chinese Central Government and the local authorities should be made the subject of a Declaration by the Chinese Government having the force of an international undertaking.

2. Whereas, in addition to the questions dealt with in the two recommendations 1*A* and 1*B,* the report of the Commission of Enquiry mentions in the principles and conditions for a settlement of the dispute set out in Section I (*c*) above certain other questions affecting the good understanding between China and Japan, on which peace in the Far East depends,

The Assembly recommends the parties to settle these questions on the basis of the said principles and conditions.

3. Whereas the negotiations necessary for giving effect to the fore-

going recommendations should be carried on by means of a suitable organ,

The Assembly recommends the opening of negotiations between the two parties in accordance with the method specified hereinafter.

Each of the parties is invited to inform the Secretary-General whether it accepts, so far as it is concerned, the recommendations of the Assembly, subject to the sole condition that the other party also accepts them.

The negotiations between the parties should take place with the assistance of a Committee set up by the Assembly as follows: The Assembly hereby invites the Governments of Belgium, Great Britain, Canada, Czechoslovakia, France, Germany, the Irish Free State, Italy, The Netherlands, Portugal, Spain and Turkey each to appoint a member of the Committee as soon as the Secretary-General shall have informed them that the two parties accept the Assembly's recommendations. The Secretary-General shall also notify the Governments of the United States of America and of the Union of Soviet Socialist Republics of this acceptance and invite each of them to appoint a member of the Committee should it so desire. Within one month after having been informed of the acceptance of the two parties, the Secretary-General shall take all suitable steps for the opening of negotiations.

In order to enable the Members of the League, after the opening of negotiations, to judge whether each of the parties is acting in conformity with the Assembly's recommendations:

(*a*) The Committee will, whenever it thinks fit, report on the state of the negotiations, and particularly on the negotiations with regard to the carrying out of recommendations 1*A* and *B* above; as regards recommendation 1*A*, the Committee will in any case report within three months of the opening of negotiations. These reports shall be communicated by the Secretary-General to the Members of the League and to the non-member States represented on the Committee;

(*b*) The Committee may submit to the Assembly all questions relating to the interpretation of Section II of Part IV of the present report. The Assembly shall give this interpretation in the same conditions as those in which the present report is adopted, in conformity with Article 15, paragraph 10, of the Covenant.

Section III

In view of the special circumstances of the case, the recommendations made do not provide for a mere return to the *status quo* existing before September, 1931. They likewise exclude the maintenance and recognition of the existing regime in Manchuria, such maintenance and recognition being incompatible with the fundamental principles of existing international obligations and with the good understanding between the two countries on which peace in the Far East depends.

It follows that, in adopting the present report, the Members of the League intend to abstain, particularly as regards the existing regime in Manchuria, from any act which might prejudice or delay the carrying out of the recommendations of the said report. They will continue not to recognise this regime either *de jure* or *de facto*. They intend to abstain from taking any isolated action with regard to the situation in Manchuria and to continue to concert their action among themselves as well as with the interested States not members of the League. As regards the Members of the League who are signatories of the Nine-Power Treaty, it may be recalled that, in accordance with the provisions of that Treaty: "Whenever a situation arises which, in the opinion of any one of them, involves the application of the stipulations of the present Treaty and renders desirable discussion of such application, there shall be full and frank communication between the contracting Powers concerned."

In order to facilitate as far as possible the establishment in the Far East of a situation in conformity with the recommendations of the present report, the Secretary-General is instructed to communicate a copy of this report to the States non-members of the League who are signatories of or have acceded to the Pact of Paris or of the Nine-Power Treaty, informing them of the Assembly's hope that they will associate themselves with the views expressed in the report, and that they will, if necessary, concert their action and their attitude with the Members of the League.

RESOLUTION Adopted by the Assembly of the League of Nations, February 24, 1933

Department of State, *Foreign Relations of the United States: Japan, 1931-1941*, I, 113

WHEREAS, in virtue of Article 3, paragraph 3, of the Covenant, the Assembly may deal at its meetings with any matter affecting the peace of the world, and therefore cannot regard with indifference the development of the Sino-Japanese dispute;

And whereas, according to Part IV, Section III of the report adopted by the Assembly in virtue of Article 15, paragraph 4, the Members of the League "intend to abstain from taking any isolated action with regard to the situation in Manchuria and to continue to concert their action among themselves as well as with the interested States not Members of the League" and, "in order to facilitate as far as possible the establishment in the Far East of a situation in conformity with the recommendations of the present report, the Secretary-General is instructed to communicate a copy of this report to the States non-members of the League who are signatories of or have acceded to the Pact of Paris or the Nine-Power Treaty, informing them of the Assembly's hope that they will associate themselves with the views expressed in the report, and that they will, if necessary, concert their action and their attitude with the Members of the League":

The Assembly decides to appoint an Advisory Committee to follow the situation, to assist the Assembly in performing its duties under Article 3, paragraph 3, and, with the same objects, to aid the Members of the League in concerting their action and their attitude among themselves and with the non-member States.

The Committee will consist of the representatives of the Members of the Committee of Nineteen and the representatives of Canada and the Netherlands.

The Committee will invite the Governments of the United States of America and the Union of Soviet Socialist Republics to co-operate in its work.

It shall report and make proposals to the Assembly whenever it thinks fit. It shall also communicate its reports to the Governments of the States non-members of the League which are co-operating in its work.

The Assembly shall remain in session and its President, after consulting the Committee, may convene it whenever he thinks fit.

Return of the Saar to Germany

RESOLUTION Adopted by the Council of the League of Nations, January 17, 1935

<small>Royal Institute of International Affairs, *Documents on International Affairs, 1934*, p. 69, citing League of Nations, *Official Journal*, February, 1935, p. 134</small>

HAVING REGARD to Articles 49 and 50 of the Treaty of Versailles and Chapter III of the Annex to those articles,

And to the Council's decision of June 4, 1934,

And to the regulations for the plebiscite in the Territory of the Saar Basin, dated July 7, 1934,

And to the report dated January 15, 1935, whereby the Plebiscite Commission has informed the Council of the result of the plebiscite which was held on January 13, 1935,

And to the undertakings entered into by Germany and France,

The Council,

1. Decides in favour of union with Germany of the whole of the Territory of the Saar Basin, as defined in Article 48 of the Treaty of Versailles, under the conditions resulting from that Treaty and from the special undertakings entered into in connexion with the plebiscite.

2. Fixes March 1, 1935, as the date for the re-establishment of Germany in the government of the Territory of the Saar Basin.

3. Instructs its Committee to decide, in consultation with the French Government, the German Government, and the Governing Commission of the Saar Territory, upon the arrangements necessary for the change of régime in the Territory and upon the manner in which the undertakings mentioned above shall be carried out. Should these arrangements not have been decided upon by February 15, 1935, the Committee will submit its proposals to the Council, which will take the necessary decisions, in conformity with paragraphs 35 (c), 39 (c), and 39 of the Annex to Article 50, and with the special undertakings entered into by the two Governments on the occasion of the plebiscite.

German Denunciation of Part V of the Treaty of Versailles

RESOLUTION Submitted by the Governments of France, Great Britain, and Italy, and Adopted by the Council of the League of Nations, April 17, 1935

League of Nations, *Official Journal*, May, 1935, p. 551

THE COUNCIL,
Considering,
(1) That the scrupulous respect of all treaty obligations is a fundamental principle of international life and an essential condition of the maintenance of peace;
(2) That it is an essential principle of the law of nations that no Power can liberate itself from the engagements of a treaty nor modify the stipulations thereof unless with the consent of the other contracting parties;
(3) That the promulgation of the Military Law of March 16th, 1935, by the German Government conflicts with the above principles;
(4) That, by this unilateral action, the German Government confers upon itself no right;
(5) That this unilateral action, by introducing a new disturbing element into the international situation, must necessarily appear to be a threat to European security;
Considering, on the other hand,
(6) That the British Government and the French Government, with the approval of the Italian Government, had communicated to the German Government as early as February 3rd, 1935, a plan for a general settlement, to be freely negotiated, for the organisation of security in Europe and for a general limitation of armaments in a system of equality of rights, while ensuring the active co-operation of Germany in the League of Nations;
(7) And that the unilateral action of Germany above referred to was not only inconsistent with this plan, but was taken at a time when negotiations were actually being pursued:
I. Declares that Germany has failed in the duty which lies upon all the Members of the international community to respect the undertakings which they have contracted, and condemns any unilateral repudiation of international obligations.
II. Invites the Governments which took the initiative in the plan

of February 3rd, 1935, or which gave their approval to it, to continue the negotiations so initiated, and in particular to promote the conclusion, within the framework of the League of Nations, of the agreements which may appear necessary to attain the object defined in this plan, due account being taken of the obligations of the Covenant, with a view to assuring the maintenance of peace;

III. Considering that the unilateral repudiation of international obligations may endanger the very existence of the League of Nations as an organisation for maintaining peace and promoting security;

Decides:

That such repudiation, without prejudice to the application of the measures already provided in international agreements, should, in the event of its having relation to undertakings concerning the security of peoples and the maintenance of peace in Europe, call into play all appropriate measures on the part of Members of the League and within the framework of the Covenant;

Requests a Committee composed of . . . to propose for this purpose measures to render the Covenant more effective in the organisation of collective security and to define in particular the economic and financial measures which might be applied, should in the future a State, whether a Member of the League of Nations or not, endanger peace by the unilateral repudiation of its international obligations.

Italian-Ethiopian War

MINUTES of Meeting of the Council of the League of Nations, October 7, 1935

Royal Institute of International Affairs, *Documents on International Affairs, 1935*, II, 183, citing League of Nations, *Official Journal*, November, 1935, pp. 1225–26, and British White Paper, Cmd. 5071; excerpt

THE PRESIDENT:

In the name of the members of the Council, I am obliged to repeat the declaration which I made from the chair at the private meeting. It is as follows:

The report of the committee which is before the Council describes facts from official sources and draws attention to the provisions of the Covenant.

To-day, October 7, five days after the opening of hostilities, the establishment of the existence of a state of war, in relation to the obligations of the Covenant, compels the members of the Council to face their responsibilities. This obligation does not in any way prejudice the rights of the parties to make known their observations subsequently at another meeting of the Council. However anxious the members of the Council may be courteously to take account of the convenience of one of their colleagues, they cannot allow that anxiety to take precedence over a primary duty.

I take note of the protest made by the representative of Italy, and, in the name of the Council, I declare, as its President and as its mandatory—with, therefore, the unanimous consent of my colleagues other than the parties—that the members of the Council will be called upon at to-day's meeting to state their views as to the conclusions of the Council Committee, and that the Council will hear the representative of Italy, should he so desire, at another meeting.

We will proceed by roll-call to the consultation of the members of the Council and of the two parties.

I will begin by consulting the members of the Council other than the parties.

The Members of the Council other than the parties, consulted by roll-call, declared themselves in agreement with the conclusions of the report.

The President:

I will now consult the parties.

Baron Aloisi:

While making every reservation as to the procedure which is now being followed, I state, for all useful purposes, that I do not approve the conclusion of the report.

I also reserve my right to submit, at a later meeting, any observations I may have to offer on the document before us.

M. Teclé-Hawariate:

I accept the report.

The President:

I take note that fourteen members of the League of Nations represented on the Council consider that we are in presence of a war begun in disregard of the obligations of Article 12 of the Covenant.

Accordingly, the report of the Council Committee and the minutes of the present meeting will be sent to all the members of the League of Nations. As the Assembly stated in its resolution of October 4, 1921, "the fulfilment of their duties under Article 16 is required from the members of the League by the express terms of the Covenant, and they cannot neglect them without a breach of their treaty obligations."

The Council has now to assume its duty of co-ordination in regard to the measures to be taken. Since the Assembly of the League of Nations is convened for the day after tomorrow, October 9, 1935, my colleagues will doubtless feel it desirable to associate the Assembly with their task.

The report of the Council Committee and the minutes of the present meeting will therefore be communicated to the President of the Assembly.

MINUTES of Meeting of the Assembly of the League of Nations, October 11, 1935

Royal Institute of International Affairs, *Documents on International Affairs, 1935,* II, 199, citing League of Nations, *Official Journal,* Special Supplement No. 138, pp. 100–114; excerpt

THE PRESIDENT:

Before terminating this meeting and the present phase of our work, I feel it my duty briefly to summarize the results of the Assembly's proceedings.

The Assembly's task has been discharged. The minutes of the Council's meeting of October 7, 1935, and the report of the Council Committee concerning the events in Ethiopia, noting that there has been a resort to war in disregard of engagements under Article 12 of the Covenant—which report fourteen members of the Council approved—were communicated by the President of the Council to the President of the Assembly. They were submitted to the Assembly, which has considered them at its last three meetings. Of the fifty-four members present at the Assembly, three States expressed a contrary opinion; a fourth, this morning, has spoken against the application of sanctions, and fifty States members of the League have expressed an opinion in accordance with that of the fourteen States members of the Council, by conveying, either explicitly by their declarations or tacitly, their Government's acquiescence in the report and documents in question.

That is the first conclusion.

With regard to the question of the co-ordination of the measures to be taken under Article 16 which was brought up in the Assembly by the fact of the President of the Council having transmitted to the President of the Assembly the minutes of the Council's meeting of October 7, 1935, the Assembly recommended that the States members of the League, acting severally—without the parties to the dispute—should set up a Committee of Co-ordination; that committee met this morning, and, immediately getting to work, considered its role and its terms of reference and decided to continue its proceedings as soon as our meetings are over.

That is the second conclusion.

As I have said, the Assembly's task in the present phase of its session has thus been completed.

Before terminating this meeting I have one more duty to fulfil. Being all in agreement with the several members of the Assembly who, in touching and even heartbreaking words, referring to the great merits of Italy and the rights of Ethiopia, urged the need of securing rapid conciliation and peace, we are bound to tell the two parties how much we all hope that peace will rapidly be restored. As the President of the Council pointed out at the meeting of October 7, Article II of the Covenant stipulates that, even in case of war, the Council must take any action that may be deemed wise and effectual to safeguard the peace of nations. The Council has consequently stated that it will remain at the disposal of the parties in order to aid them in establishing the conditions under which hostilities might be brought to an end.

The Assembly can only hope that this statement will be accepted by the two parties in the spirit in which it was made by the Council —that is to say, in a spirit of collaboration.

As there are no more items on the agenda of this morning's meeting or of the present phase of the session, I declare the session adjourned and the meeting closed.

RESOLUTIONS Recommended by the Committee of Seventeen (later the Committee of Eighteen) and Adopted by the Coordination Committee of the League of Nations, October 11–19, 1935

With the exception of the "Declaration concerning Mutual Support" and "Steps to Be Taken by Members of the League in Respect of Their Public Law," these resolutions were submitted as Proposals I–V in the order that they here appear. League of Nations, *Official Journal*, Special Supplement No. 145, pp. 14–27

Export of Arms, Ammunition and Implements of War

With a view to facilitating for the Governments of the Members of the League of Nations the execution of their obligations under Article 16 of the Covenant, the following measures should be taken forthwith:

(1) The Governments of the Members of the League of Nations which are enforcing at the moment measures to prohibit or restrict

the exportation, re-exportation or transit of arms, munitions and implements of war to Ethiopia will annul these measures immediately;

(2) The Governments of the Members of the League of Nations will prohibit immediately the exportation, re-exportation or transit to Italy or Italian possessions of arms, munitions and implements of war enumerated in the attached list;

(3) The Governments of the Members of the League of Nations will take such steps as may be necessary to secure that arms, munitions and implements of war, enumerated in the attached list, exported to countries other than Italy will not be re-exported directly or indirectly to Italy or to Italian possessions;

(4) The measures provided for in paragraphs (2) and (3) are to apply to contracts in process of execution.

Each Government is requested to inform the Committee, through the Secretary-General of the League, within the shortest possible time of the measures which it has taken in conformity with the above provisions.

Declaration Concerning Mutual Support

With a view to facilitating for the Governments of the members of the League of Nations the execution of their obligations under Article 16 of the Covenant, it is recognised that any proposals for action under Article 16 are made on the basis of the following provisions of that article:

The Members of the League agree, further, that they will mutually support one another in the financial and economic measures which are taken under this article, in order to minimise the loss and inconvenience resulting from the above measures, and that they will mutually support one another in resisting any special measures aimed at one of their number by the Covenant-breaking State.

With a view to facilitating for the Governments of the Members of the League of Nations the execution of their obligations under Article 16 of the Covenant, the following measures should be taken forthwith:

The Governments of the Members of the League of Nations will forthwith take all measures necessary to render impossible the following operations:

(1) All loans to or for the Italian Government and all subscriptions to loans issued in Italy or elsewhere by or for the Italian Government;

(2) All banking or other credits to or for the Italian Government and any further execution by advance, overdraft or otherwise of ex-

isting contracts to lend directly or indirectly to the Italian Government;

(3) All loans to or for any public authority, person or corporation in Italian territory and all subscriptions to such loans issued in Italy or elsewhere;

(4) All banking or other credits to or for any public authority, person or corporation in Italian territory and any further execution by advance, overdraft or otherwise of existing contracts to lend directly or indirectly to such authority, person or corporation;

(5) All issues of shares or other capital flotations for any public authority, person or corporation in Italian territory and all subscriptions to such issues of shares or capital flotations in Italy or elsewhere;

(6) The Governments will take all measures necessary to render impossible the transactions mentioned in paragraphs (1) to (5), whether effected directly or through intermediaries of whatsoever nationality.

The Governments are invited to put in operation at once such of the measures recommended as can be enforced without fresh legislation, and to take all practicable steps to secure that the measures recommended are completely put into operation by October 31st, 1935. Any Governments which find it impossible to secure the requisite legislation by that date are requested to inform the Committee, through the Secretary-General, of the date by which they expect to be able to do so.

Each Government is requested to inform the Committee, through the Secretary-General of the League, within the shortest possible time of the measures which it has taken in conformity with the above provisions.

Steps to Be Taken by Members of the League in Respect of Their Public Law

The Committee of Co-ordination,

Considering that it is important to ensure rapid and effective application of the measures which have been and may subsequently be proposed by the Committee;

Considering that it rests with each country to apply these measures in accordance with its public law and, in particular, the powers of its Government in regard to execution of treaties:

Calls attention to the fact that the Members of the League, being bound by the obligations which flow from Article 16 of the Covenant, are under a duty to take the necessary steps to enable them to carry out these obligations with all requisite rapidity.

Prohibition of Importation of Italian Goods

With a view to facilitating for the Governments of the Members of the League of Nations the execution of their obligations under Article 16 of the Covenant, the following measures should be taken:

(1) The Governments of the Members of the League of Nations will prohibit the importation into their territories of all goods (other than gold or silver bullion and coin) consigned from or grown, produced or manufactured in Italy or Italian possessions, from whatever place arriving;

(2) Goods grown or produced in Italy or Italian possessions which have been subjected to some process in another country, and goods manufactured partly in Italy or Italian possessions and partly in another country will be considered as falling within the scope of the prohibition unless 25% or more of the value of the goods at the time when they left the place from which they were last consigned is attributable to processes undergone since the goods last left Italy or Italian possessions;

(3) Goods the subject of existing contracts will not be excepted from the prohibition;

(4) Goods *en route* at the time of imposition of the prohibition will be excepted from its operation. In giving effect to this provision, Governments may, for convenience of administration, fix an appropriate date, having regard to the normal time necessary for transport from Italy, after which goods will become subject to the prohibition;

(5) Personal belongings of travellers from Italy or Italian possessions may also be excepted from its operation.

Having regard to the importance of collective and, so far as possible, simultaneous action in regard to the measures recommended, each Government is requested to inform the Co-ordination Committee, through the Secretary-General, as soon as possible, and not later than October 28th, of the date on which it could be ready to bring these measures into operation. The Co-ordination Committee will meet on October 31st for the purpose of fixing, in the light of the replies received, the date of the coming into force of the said measures.

Embargo on Certain Exports to Italy

With a view to facilitating for the Governments of the Members of the League of Nations the execution of their obligations under Article 16 of the Covenant, the following measures should be taken:

(1) The Governments of the Members of the League of Nations

will extend the application of paragraph (2) of Proposal I of the Co-ordination Committee to the following articles as regards their exportation and re-exportation to Italy and Italian possessions, which will accordingly be prohibited:

(a) Horses, mules, donkeys, camels and all other transport animals;

(b) Rubber;

(c) Bauxite, aluminium and alumina (aluminium-oxide), iron-ore and scrap-iron;

Chromium, manganese, nickel, titanium, tungsten, vanadium, their ores and ferro-alloys (and also ferro-molybdenum, ferro-silicon, ferro-silico-manganese and ferro-silicon-manganese-aluminium);

Tin and tin-ore.

List (c) above includes all crude forms of the minerals and metals mentioned and their ores, scrap and alloys;

(2) The Governments of the Members of the League of Nations will take such steps as may be necessary to secure that the articles mentioned in paragraph (1) above exported to countries other than Italy or Italian possessions will not be re-exported, directly or indirectly, to Italy or to Italian possessions;

(3) The measures provided for in paragraphs (1) and (2) above are to apply to contracts in course of execution;

(4) Goods *en route* at the time of imposition of the prohibition will be excepted from its operation. In giving effect to this provision, Governments may, for convenience of administration, fix an appropriate date, having regard to the normal time necessary for transport to Italy or Italian possessions, after which goods will become subject to the prohibition.

Having regard to the importance of collective and, so far as possible, simultaneous action in regard to the measures recommended, each Government is requested to inform the Co-ordination Committee, through the Secretary-General, as soon as possible, and not later than October 28th, of the date on which it could be ready to bring these measures into operation. The Committee of Co-ordination will meet on October 31st for the purpose of fixing, in the light of the replies received, the date of the coming into force of the said measures.

The attention of the Co-ordination Committee has been drawn to the possible extension of the above proposal to a certain number of other articles. It entrusts the Committee of Eighteen with the task of making any suitable proposals to Governments on this subject.

Organisation of Mutual Support

The Co-ordination Committee draws the special attention of all Governments to their obligations under paragraph 3 of Article 16 of the Covenant, according to which the Members of the League undertake mutually to support one another in the application of the economic and financial measures taken under this article.

I. With a view to carrying these obligations into effect, the Governments of the Members of the League of Nations will:

(a) Adopt immediately measures to assure that no action taken as a result of Article 16 will deprive any country applying sanctions of such advantages as the commercial agreements concluded by the participating States with Italy afforded it through the operation of the most-favoured-nation clause;

(b) Take appropriate steps with a view to replacing, within the limits of the requirements of their respective countries, imports from Italy by the import of similar products from the participating States;

(c) Be willing, after the application of economic sanctions, to enter into negotiations with any participating country which has sustained a loss with a view to increasing the sale of goods so as to offset any loss of Italian markets which the application of sanctions may have involved;

(d) In cases in which they have suffered no loss in respect of any given commodity, abstain from demanding the application of any most-favoured-nation clause in the case of any privileges granted under paragraphs (b) and (c) in respect of that commodity.

II. With the above objects, the Governments will, if necessary with the assistance of the Committee of Eighteen, study, in particular, the possibility of adopting, within the limits of their existing obligations, and taking into consideration the annexed opinion of the Legal Sub-Committee of the Co-ordination Committee, the following measures:

(1) The increase by all appropriate measures of their imports in favour of such countries as may have suffered loss of Italian markets on account of the application of sanctions;

(2) In order to facilitate this increase, the taking into consideration of the obligations of mutual support and of the advantages which the trade of certain States Members of the League of Nations, not participating in the sanctions, would obtain from the application of these sanctions, in order to reduce by every appropriate means and to an equitable degree imports coming from these countries;

(3) The promotion, by all means in their power, of business relations between firms interested in the sale of goods in Italian markets which have been lost owing to the application of sanctions and firms normally importing such goods;

(4) Assistance generally in the organisation of the international marketing of goods with a view to offsetting any loss of Italian markets which the application of sanctions may have involved.

They will also examine, under the same conditions, the possibility of financial or other measures to supplement the commercial measures, in so far as these latter may not ensure sufficient international mutual support.

III. The Co-ordination Committee requests the Committee of Eighteen to afford, if necessary, to the Governments concerned the assistance contemplated at the beginning of Part II of the present proposal.

RESOLUTIONS Recommended by the Committee of Eighteen and Adopted by the Coordination Committee of the League of Nations, November 2, 1935

League of Nations, *Official Journal*, Special Supplement No. 146, pp. 8 and 12

THE Co-ordination Committee notes that thirty-nine Governments of Members of the League of Nations have taken or are taking measures with a view to rendering impossible those financial operations with Italy and Italian possessions defined in Proposal II adopted by the Committee on October 14th, and that ten other Governments have expressed their willingness to take such measures.

It requests all Governments to take steps in order that the measures contemplated in Proposal II may take full legal effect by or before November 18th.

Each Government which has not already sent a communication to this effect is requested to inform the Committee, through the Secretary-General of the League, within the shortest possible time, of the measures which it has taken in conformity with this resolution.

The Co-ordination Committee,
Taking note of the facts:
(1) That forty-three Governments of States Members of the League have already expressed their willingness to accept Proposal III and forty-four Proposal IV adopted by the Committee on October 19th,

and that six others which, owing to their distance from the seat of the League, did not immediately receive the full text of these proposals have expressed their readiness to consider them favourably;

(2) That nearly all these Governments have declared themselves ready to put the proposed measures into force by the middle of November or by such date as may be fixed by the Co-ordination Committee:

Decides to fix November 18th as the date for the entry into force of these measures;

Invites all Governments of Members of the League to take the necessary steps so that these measures may be effectively applied throughout their territories by November 18th;

Requests each Government to inform the Committee through the Secretary-General of the League, within the shortest possible time, of the measures which it has taken in conformity with the above provisions.

The Members of the League of Nations participating in the measures taken in regard to Italy under Article 16 of the Covenant,

Having regard, in particular, to Proposal III, under which they have agreed to prohibit as from November 18th all imports consigned from Italy or her possessions:

I. Consider that the debts now payable by Italy to them, under clearing agreements or any other arrangements, the payment of which becomes impossible by reason of the aforesaid prohibition, will remain valid at their present value notwithstanding any offers of payment in kind that may be made by Italy or any action that might be taken by her against the creditor States;

II. Recognise:

(a) That, on the discontinuance of the measures taken in regard to Italy under Article 16 of the Covenant, they should support one another in order to ensure that Italy discharges her obligations to the creditor States as she should have done if she had not incurred the application of Article 16 of the Covenant;

(b) Furthermore, that, if in the meantime particularly serious losses are sustained by certain States owing to the suspension by Italy of the payment of the aforesaid debts, the mutual support provided for by paragraph 3 of Article 16 will be specially given in order to make good such losses by all appropriate measures.

The Committee on Mutual Support will draw up a list of the debts referred to in paragraph I above and will examine the measures contemplated in paragraph II (b) above.

RESOLUTION Adopted by the Assembly of the League of Nations, July 4, 1936

Royal Institute of International Affairs, *Documents on International Affairs, 1935*, II, 234, citing *Verbatim Record* of the 16th League Assembly, July 4, 1936

II. THE ASSEMBLY, taking note of the communications and declarations which have been made to it on the subject of the situation arising out of the Italo-Ethiopian dispute; recalling the previous findings and decisions in connexion with this dispute: recommends that the Co-ordination Committee should make all necessary proposals to the Governments in order to bring to an end the measures taken by them in execution of Article 16 (Sanctions) of the Covenant.

MINUTES of the Final Meeting of the Coordination Committee, July 6, 1936

League of Nations, *Official Journal*, Special Supplement No. 149, p. 56; excerpts

THE CHAIRMAN [Augusto de Vasconcellos, of Portugal] stated that, a short while ago, he had received a letter from the Chilian representative requesting the convocation of the Co-ordination Committee to consider a proposal for raising sanctions, and adding that Chile would, in any event, conform to the decisions of the League. As the Council at the moment had postponed any decision in the matter, he had not hitherto been in a position to take any action in respect of the Chilian representative's request. But the Assembly had now recommended the Co-ordination Committee to make the requisite proposals with a view to terminating the action taken in execution of Article 16 of the Covenant. . . .

The purpose of the present meeting was to take stock of this recommendation and to pass a resolution on that subject.

He did not propose to make any political comments on the Committee's work. That, the Committee would remember, had been his attitude from the first. Comment and criticism there had been in the Assembly for all to hear. He proposed only to make a brief impartial statement, and to submit a draft resolution for the Committee's consideration.

The moment had arrived at which it was possible to draw certain general conclusions with regard to the Committee's work and the results achieved; and it would be as well, therefore, to begin by recalling the precise circumstances in which the Committee was set up, as also the principles by which it had been governed and the limits to the effective exercise of its activities.

The Co-ordination Committee was set up by a recommendation approved by the Assembly on October 10th, 1935, and began work on October 11th, 1935. It was in effect a conference of delegates of sovereign States met to study the co-ordination of the measures to be taken in reference to a State regarded by the other Members of the Council as having violated its obligations under the Covenant.

The obligations of the Members of the League derived directly from the Covenant and their fulfilment followed as a consequence of the respect of treaties.

The Committee had not therefore been called upon itself to take decisions, but merely to adopt proposals for submission to the different Governments for their consideration.

The measures to be recommended by the Co-ordination Committee were those provided in Article 16 of the Covenant; but, from the outset, political and military sanctions were eliminated for reasons on which it was not for him to express an opinion.

The Committee, when it met some nine months ago, had no precedents for its guidance. It was called upon to make a first experiment in the application of Article 16.

The Assembly resolutions of 1921 recognised that it might be necessary to exercise a certain measure of choice in respect of the economic and financial measures required in each particular case, and that these measures might not all necessarily admit of immediate simultaneous application.

The Co-ordination Committee had felt bound to consider a number of possible measures and to make a thorough study of each.

In view of the fact that the League of Nations was not universal, it was obvious from the first that the system of sanctions to be applied under Article 16 could not be complete.

It was noticeable, however, that the attitude of certain non-member States, to which all the Committee's proposals were communicated for information, was in a number of cases encouraging.

One of the States in question associated itself with the Members of the League for the purposes of the application of the proposed measures. Other States, without associating themselves directly with the measures proposed, took certain steps which facilitated the Committee's work.

From the outset of the Committee's work, stress was laid on the fact that the measures taken should be such as to admit of rapid enforcement.

In this connection, the Committee could not fail to note that all the States Members of the League had not complied with the invitation in the Assembly resolutions of 1921 to the Governments of the different States to "take the necessary preparatory measures, above all of a legislative character, to enable them to enforce at short notice the necessary measures of economic pressure."

While certain countries, it is true, when faced for the first time with the practical issue of applying Article 16, were able to take the requisite practical steps at short notice, other Governments encountered in that connection considerable difficulties of a constitutional character. This fact had its effect, up to a point, on the progress of the Committee's work and the results ultimately attained.

Apart from all matters relating to paragraph 2 of Article 16 (military measures), the proposals worked out by the Co-ordination Committee did not purport to be, and were not, a complete system of sanctions. The economic and financial measures proposed in the Covenant were not, in the present case, applied in their entirety.

It could not be said that, taken as a whole, the proposals adopted were equivalent to that complete severance of all commercial or financial relations which Article 16 contemplated. Moreover, the Committee did not make any proposal for a general restriction, as contemplated in Article 16, of commercial and other relations with persons residing in the State violating the Covenant.

In one of its main proposals—namely, that for the prohibition of Italian imports—the Committee in large measure respected vested rights in respect of orders actually paid for and consignments *en route*. In addition, the interval of one month between the adoption of the proposal and its enforcement—which was doubtless inevitable, in view of the fact that these important measures were being applied for the first time by some fifty States—made it possible, not only for legitimate traders, but also for speculators, to increase their purchases from Italy. The effective results of the prohibition of importation were thus considerably delayed.

It was possible that the hesitation to apply other measures was due in part to practical reasons; but it was due also in part to the desire not to take any steps calculated to prevent the continuance of efforts with a view to a satisfactory settlement of the difference by conciliation. At the Council meeting on April 20th, 1936, the Spanish representative drew attention to what he described as the "contradictory procedure" due to the overlapping of attempts at conciliation by the Council and the development of measures under Article 16 of the Covenant.

The foregoing observations related to the circumstances in which the Co-ordination Committee had to work, as well as to some of the motives for the proposals submitted by the Committee to Governments.

In conclusion, the Chairman proposed to say something of the results actually achieved.

As regards the financial measures taken (Proposal II), it was obviously difficult to give precise details. But all the information available went to show that that proposal had been applied in a highly effective manner.

The clearest proof of the results of the economic measures was contained in the Italian trade figures. He had asked the Secretariat to prepare a document embodying the latest figures available.

In spite of the circumstances already referred to, which had led to a certain delay in the enforcement of this Proposal by a number of States, the results were considerable. Apart from the figures for November and December 1935, which reflected the heavy imports before the enforcement of the Proposal and the completion of orders paid for before November 18th, the table which had been distributed gave the figures at present available for the period January to April 1936 with the corresponding figures for 1935.

Imports from Italy to countries for which figures were available to the end of April—representing, in normal years, some 90% of the total of Italian exports—showed a reduction of nearly 50%. Omitting from the calculation the figures for countries which did not apply Proposal III, the percentage was as large as 90.7%.

Another indication of the aggregate effect of Proposals II and III was to be found in the figures showing Italy's losses of gold. On October 20th, 1935, the gold and foreign-exchange reserve of the Banca d'Italia amounted to 4,316 million lire. According to published statements by the Governor of the Bank, the Bank lost 909 million lire between October 20th and December 31st, 1935. In the period January–April 1936, the countries for which information was available showed gold imports from Italy to a total of 1,282 million lire. There was therefore a total loss in six months and ten days of 2,091 million lire, or half the original reserve.

Here was clear proof that the results of this initial attempt to apply Article 16 had not been negligible. As the President of the Assembly so rightly said two days before in his admirable closing speech, in another conflict, in which the opposing forces happened to be less unequal, the assistance given by such measures of an economic and financial character might be of the greatest importance to the State victim of aggression. . . .

The Committee decided upon July 15th as the date on which sanctions would be raised.

German Violation of Article 43 of the Treaty of Versailles

RESOLUTION Adopted by the Council of the League of Nations, March 19, 1936

League of Nations, *Official Journal*, April, 1936, Part I, p. 340

THE COUNCIL of the League of Nations,

On the application of Belgium and France, made to it on March 8th, 1936:

Finds that the German Government has committed a breach of Article 43 of the Treaty of Versailles by causing, on March 7th, 1936, military forces to enter and establish themselves in the demilitarised zone referred to in Article 42 and the following articles of that Treaty and in the Treaty of Locarno;

Instructs the Secretary-General, in application of Article 4, paragraph 2, of the Treaty of Locarno, to notify this finding of the Council without delay to the Powers signatories of that Treaty.

German Denunciation of the Locarno Treaty

RESOLUTION Adopted by the Council of the League of Nations, March 24, 1936

League of Nations, *Official Journal*, April, 1936, Part I, p. 347. The "Treaty of Mutual Guarantee" was signed at Locarno on October 16, 1925

THE COUNCIL,

Thanks the representative of the United Kingdom for his communication, dated March 20th, 1936, transmitting the text of proposals drawn up on March 19th, 1936, by the representatives of the Members of the League who are signatories of the Treaty of Locarno, and which are now under consideration by the respective Governments;

Considers that any further action on its part should remain in abeyance for the present, in view of the conversations which are being carried on;

Invites the said Governments to keep it advised of the progress of the said conversations;

Decides to meet again as soon as circumstances render further consideration of the question desirable.

Japanese Aggressions against China, 1937–1939

FIRST REPORT of the Sub-Committee of the Far-East Advisory Committee of the League of Nations, Adopted by the Committee, October 5, 1937, and by the Assembly of the League, October 6, 1937

League of Nations, *Official Journal*, Special Supplement No. 177, p. 37; excerpt

Conclusions

It is clear that the two countries take very different views as to the underlying grounds of the dispute and as to the incident which led to the first outbreak of hostilities.

It cannot, however, be challenged that powerful Japanese armies have invaded Chinese territory and are in military control of large areas, including Peiping itself; that the Japanese Government has taken naval measures to close the coast of China to Chinese shipping; and that Japanese aircraft are carrying out bombardments over widely separated regions of the country.

After examination of the facts laid before it, the Committee is bound to take the view that the military operations carried on by Japan against China by land, sea and air are out of all proportion to the incident that occasioned the conflict; that such action cannot possibly facilitate or promote the friendly co-operation between the two nations that Japanese statesmen have affirmed to be the aim of their policy; that it can be justified neither on the basis of existing legal instruments nor on that of the right of self-defence, and that it is in contravention of Japan's obligations under the Nine-Power Treaty of February 6th, 1922, and under the Pact of Paris of August 27th, 1928.

SECOND REPORT of the Sub-Committee of the Far-East Advisory Committee of the League of Nations, Adopted by the Committee, October 5, 1937, and by the Assembly of the League, October 6, 1937

League of Nations, *Official Journal*, Special Supplement No. 177, p. 43

1. IN THE REPORT which the Sub-Committee has already submitted to the Advisory Committee, the facts of the present situation in China and the treaty obligations of Japan have been examined. That report shows that the action taken by Japan is a breach of Japan's treaty obligations and cannot be justified.

2. The establishment of the understandings of international law as the actual rule of conduct among Governments and the maintenance of respect of treaty obligations in the dealings of organised peoples one with another are matters of vital interest to all nations.

3. The present situation in China is a matter of concern not only to the two States in conflict but, to a greater or lesser degree, to all States. Many Powers are already directly affected in the lives of their nationals and in their material interests. But even more important than this is the interest which all States must feel in the restoration and maintenance of peace. This, indeed, is the fundamental purpose for which the League exists. It has thus the duty as well as the right to attempt to bring about a speedy restoration of peace in the Far East, in accordance with existing obligations under the Covenant and the treaties.

4. The Sub-Committee has considered in the first place the obligations which the Covenant places in such circumstances upon Members of the League.

5. The Advisory Committee has been set up under the wide terms of Article 3 (3) of the Covenant, which authorises the Assembly to deal at its meetings with any matter within the sphere of action of the League or affecting the peace of the world.

6. This Article places no limit upon the action of the Assembly, and Article 11 which, *inter alia,* has been invoked by China provides that "the League shall take any action that may be deemed wise and effectual to safeguard the peace of nations."

7. The Sub-Committee has examined the situation with a view to determining what action would be "wise and effectual."

8. It cannot be admitted that the present conflict in the Far East, which has been shown to involve an infringement of Japan's treaty obligations, is one which can as of right only be settled by direct

methods between the Chinese and Japanese Governments. On the contrary, the whole situation must be taken into the fullest consideration and in particular any appropriate means by which peace may be re-established, in conformity with the principles of the Covenant and of international law and with the provisions of existing treaties, must be examined.

9. The Sub-Committee is convinced that even at this stage of the conflict, before examining other possibilities, further efforts must be made to secure the restoration of peace by agreement.

10. In attempting a settlement, by negotiation, of the present conflict, the League cannot lose sight of the fact that one party is not a member of the League and has, in relation to the work of the Advisory Committee, explicitly declined to co-operate in political matters with the League.

11. The Sub-Committee notes that under the Nine-Power Treaty signed at Washington, the contracting Powers, other than China, agreed, *inter alia,* to respect the sovereignty, the independence, and the territorial and administrative integrity of China, and that all contracting Powers, including China, agreed that, whenever a situation should arise which involved the application of the stipulations of the Treaty and rendered desirable the discussion of such application, there should be full and frank communication between the Powers concerned. It appears, therefore, to the Sub-Committee that the first step which the Assembly should take, in the name of the League, would be to invite those Members of the League who are parties to the Nine-Power Treaty to initiate such consultation at the earliest practicable moment. The Sub-Committee would suggest that these Members should meet forthwith to decide upon the best and quickest means of giving effect to this invitation. The Sub-Committee would further express the hope that the States concerned will be able to associate with their work other States which have special interests in the Far East to seek a method of putting an end to the conflict by agreement.

12. The States thus engaged in consultation may at any stage consider it desirable to make proposals through the medium of the Advisory Committee to the Assembly. The Sub-Committee recommends that the Assembly should not close its session and should declare the League's willingness to consider co-operation to the maximum extent practicable in any such proposals. The Advisory Committee should in any case hold a further meeting (whether at Geneva or elsewhere) within a period of one month.

13. Pending the results of the action proposed, the Advisory Committee should invite the Assembly to express its moral support

for China and to recommend that Members of the League should refrain from taking any action which might have the effect of weakening China's power of resistance and thus of increasing her difficulties in the present conflict, and should also consider how far they can individually extend aid to China.

RESOLUTION Adopted by the Assembly of the League of Nations, October 6, 1937

League of Nations, *Official Journal*, Special Supplement No. 169, p. 148; for action by the Conference of Brussels, see *infra*, p. 1012

THE ASSEMBLY:

Adopts as its own the reports submitted to it by its Advisory Committee on the subject of the conflict between China and Japan (documents A.78, A.79 and A.80. 1937.VII);

Approves the proposals contained in the second of the said reports (document A.80.1937.VII) and requests its President to take the necessary action with regard to the proposed meeting of the Members of the League which are Parties to the Nine-Power Treaty signed at Washington on February 6th, 1922;

Expresses its moral support for China, and recommends that Members of the League should refrain from taking any action which might have the effect of weakening China's power of resistance and thus of increasing her difficulties in the present conflict, and should also consider how far they can individually extend aid to China;

Decides to adjourn its present session and to authorise the President to summon a further meeting if the Advisory Committee so requests.

RESOLUTION Adopted by the Council of the League of Nations, February 2, 1938

Royal Institute of International Affairs, *Documents on International Affairs, 1938,* I, 369, citing League of Nations, *Official Journal*, February, 1938, p. 120

THE COUNCIL,

Having taken into consideration the situation in the Far East:

Notes with regret that hostilities in China continue and have been intensified since the last meeting of the Council;

Deplores this deterioration in the situation the more in view of the efforts and achievements of the National Government of China in her political and economic reconstruction;

Recalls that the Assembly, by its resolution of October 6, 1937, has expressed its moral support for China and has recommended that Members of the League should refrain from taking any action which might have the effect of weakening China's power of resistance and thus of increasing her difficulties in the present conflict, and should also consider how far they can individually extend aid to China;

Calls the most serious attention of the Members of the League to the terms of the above-mentioned resolution;

Is confident that those States represented on the Council for whom the situation is of special interest, will lose no opportunity of examining, in consultation with other similarly interested Powers, the feasibility of any further steps which may contribute to a just settlement of the conflict in the Far East.

RESOLUTION Adopted by the Council of the League of Nations, May 14, 1938

Royal Institute of International Affairs, *Documents on International Affairs, 1938,* I, 370, citing League of Nations, *Official Journal,* May–June, 1938, p. 378

THE COUNCIL,

Having heard the statement by the representative of China on the situation in the Far East and on the needs of the national defense of China:

I

Earnestly urges Members of the League to do their utmost to give effect to the recommendations contained in the previous resolutions of the Assembly and Council in this matter, and to take into serious and sympathetic consideration requests they may receive from the Chinese Government in conformity with the said resolutions;

Expresses its sympathy with China in her heroic struggle for the maintenance of her independence and territorial integrity, threatened by the Japanese invasion, and in the suffering which is thereby inflicted on her people.

II

Recalls that the use of toxic gases is a method of war condemned by international law, which cannot fail, should recourse be had to it, to meet with the reprobation of the civilized world; and requests the

Governments of States who may be in a position to do so to communicate to the League any information that they may obtain on the subject.

RESOLUTIONS Adopted by the Council of the League of Nations, May 22, 1939

League of Nations, *Official Journal*, May–June, 1939, p. 277

I

THE COUNCIL,
(1) Referring to the resolutions and reports hitherto adopted by the Assembly and the Council relating to the appeal of the Chinese Government;
(2) Having heard the statement of the Chinese representative at the Council's meeting on May 22nd, 1939;
(3) Continuing to view with great concern the grave situation in the Far East created by Japanese aggression;
(4) Renewing its expression of profound sympathy with China in her heroic struggle for the maintenance of her independence and territorial integrity threatened by the Japanese invasion, and in the suffering which it thereby inflicted on her people;
(5) Deeming it desirable that measures of aid to China, including relief measures and such other measures as may from time to time be found practicable, should be made as effective as possible;
(6) Following with interest the growing solidarity of action on the part of several States directly concerned in dealing with recent developments in the Far East;
(7) Noting with satisfaction that a number of States have taken certain measures in aiding China:
(8) Expresses the hope that such measures will be continued, and that the resolutions previously adopted by the Assembly and the Council will be further implemented;
(9) Invites the Members of the League, particularly those directly concerned in the Far East, in consultation with the Far East Advisory Committee, to examine the possibilities of the practical application of the measures above referred to.

II

THE COUNCIL,
(1) Having regard to the resolution of the Assembly of September

28th, 1937, solemnly condemning the aerial bombardment of open towns in China by Japanese aircraft;

(2) Taking note of the statement of the Chinese representative relating to the recent cases of ruthless attacks by Japanese aircraft on Chinese civilian populations resulting in an appalling loss of life;

(3) Recalling the resolution adopted by the Assembly on September 30th, 1938, by which the Assembly, taking note of the Chinese Government's request for the despatch of an international committee to examine cases of the bombing from the air of civilian populations in China, recommends that the Council should take any such appeal into consideration:

(4) Takes note with interest of the statement of the Chinese representative that a number of States, not all of them Members of the League, have taken steps to discourage or prevent the supply of aircraft to Japan;

(5) Invites the Governments of the States represented on the Council and on the Far East Advisory Committee having official representatives in China to inform themselves as fully as possible as to cases of bombing by Japanese aircraft of civilian populations in China and to furnish without delay to the Council information so obtained.

Withdrawal of Non-Spanish Combatants from Spain

RESOLUTION Adopted by the Council of the League of Nations, September 30, 1938

League of Nations, *Official Journal*, February, 1939, p. 126

THE COUNCIL,

Bearing in mind the statements made by Government representatives during the discussions in the Sixth Committee and the Assembly concerning the question submitted by the Spanish Government with regard to the withdrawal of non-Spanish combatants;

Noting that the Non-Intervention Committee has drawn up a plan for the withdrawal from Spain of the foreign nationals taking part in the conflict in that country;

Being anxious not to prejudice in any way the execution of this plan, which has already been accepted by the Spanish Government:

(*a*) Adopts the present report;

(*b*) Decides to despatch to Spain an international commission, whose duty it will be, making use of the facilities provided by the Spanish Government, to note the measures of withdrawal taken by that Government, and report on their effectiveness, on the disposal of the persons thus withdrawn and on the extent to which it considers that the withdrawal is complete;

(c) Declares that no responsibility is assumed by the Council either for the method of withdrawal or for the evacuation of the persons withdrawn;

(d) Takes note of the Spanish Government's statement that it undertakes to afford the commission every guarantee, facility and assistance that the latter may think needful for the performance of its duty;

(e) Appoints a Committee of three members, consisting of the representatives of the United Kingdom, France and Iran, whose duty it will be to constitute, despatch and, so far as necessary, direct the working of the commission;

(f) For this purpose, authorises the Secretary-General to draw the necessary funds from the 1938 budget—item 2 (c) (i): "Unforeseen Expenditure (Political)"—up to a maximum of 250,000 Swiss francs;

(g) Authorises the Secretary-General, in agreement with the Committee of Three, to take such other action or measures as may be necessary to give effect to the present resolution.

Expulsion of the U.S.S.R. from the League

RESOLUTIONS Adopted by the Assembly of the League of Nations, December 14, 1939

League of Nations, *Official Journal*, November–December, 1939, Part II, p. 540

THE ASSEMBLY:

I

Whereas, by the aggression which it has committed against Finland, the Union of Soviet Socialist Republics has failed to observe not only its special political agreements with Finland but also Article 12 of the Covenant of the League of Nations and the Pact of Paris;

And whereas, immediately before committing that aggression, it denounced, without legal justification, the Treaty of Non-aggression which it had concluded with Finland in 1932, and which was to remain in force until the end of 1945:

Solemnly condemns the action taken by the Union of Soviet Socialist Republics against the State of Finland;

Urgently appeals to every Member of the League to provide Finland with such material and humanitarian assistance as may be in its power and to refrain from any action which might weaken Finland's power of resistance;

Authorises the Secretary-General to lend the aid of his technical services in the organisation of the aforesaid assistance to Finland;

And likewise authorises the Secretary-General, in virtue of the Assembly resolution of October 4th, 1937, to consult non-member States with a view to possible co-operation.

II

Whereas, notwithstanding an invitation extended to it on two occasions, the Union of Soviet Socialist Republics has refused to be present at the examination of its dispute with Finland before the Council and the Assembly;

And whereas, by thus refusing to recognise the duty of the Council and the Assembly as regards the execution of Article 15 of the Covenant, it has failed to observe one of the League's most essential covenants for the safeguarding of peace and the security of nations;

And whereas it has vainly attempted to justify its refusal on the ground of the relations which it has established with an alleged Government which is neither *de jure* nor *de facto* the Government recognised by the people of Finland in accordance with the free working of their institutions;

And whereas the Union of Soviet Socialist Republics has not merely violated a covenant of the League, but has by its own action placed itself outside the Covenant;

And whereas the Council is competent under Article 16 of the Covenant to consider what consequences should follow from this situation;

Recommends the Council to pronounce upon the question.

RESOLUTION Adopted by the Council of the League of Nations, December 14, 1939

League of Nations, *Official Journal*, November–December, 1939, Part II, p. 506

The Council,

Having taken cognisance of the resolution adopted by the Assembly on December 14th, 1939, regarding the appeal of the Finnish Government;

1. Associates itself with the condemnation by the Assembly of the action of the Union of Soviet Socialist Republics against the Finnish State; and
2. For the reasons set forth in the resolution of the Assembly,
   In virtue of Article 16, paragraph 4, of the Covenant,
   Finds that, by its act, the Union of Soviet Socialist Republics has placed itself outside the League of Nations. It follows that the Union of Soviet Socialist Republics is no longer a Member of the League.

REDUCTION AND LIMITATION OF ARMAMENTS

RESOLUTION Adopted by the Assembly of the League of Nations, September 29, 1931

League of Nations, *Official Journal*, Special Supplement No. 93, pp. 158–61

CONVINCED THAT the crisis which at the present time is creating such profound disturbance among the nations of the world is due to a number of economic and political causes originating principally in the lack of mutual confidence between the nations; and,

Convinced that a renewal of the competition in armaments would necessarily lead to an international and social catastrophe:

The Assembly addresses a solemn appeal to all those who are desirous that practical effect should be given to the principles of peace and justice upon which the Covenant is based and urges them to devote all their efforts towards creating a world opinion strong enough to enable the General Disarmament Conference to achieve positive results, including, in particular, a gradual reduction of armaments to be continued until such time as the object laid down in Article 8 of the Covenant is attained.

In view of the fact that an undertaking on the part of all States not to increase their armaments would help to create an atmosphere of confidence, to prevent competition in armaments and to prepare the ground for the success of the forthcoming Conference:

The Assembly,

Requests the Governments invited to the Disarmament Conference to prepare for this event by means of an armaments truce, and, accordingly,

Requests the Council to urge the Governments convened to the said Conference to give proof of their earnest desire for the successful issue of the efforts to ensure and organise peace and, without prejudging the decisions of the Conference or the programmes or proposals submitted to it by each Government, to refrain from any measure involving an increase in their armaments;

Likewise requests the Council to ask the Governments to state, before November 1st, 1931, whether they are prepared for a period of one year as from that date to accept this truce in armaments.

RESOLUTION Adopted by the General Commission of the Conference for the Reduction and Limitation of Armaments, July 23, 1932

League of Nations, *Records of the Conference for the Reduction and Limitation of Armaments, Series B, Minutes of the General Commission*, I, 153–205

I

THE CONFERENCE for the Reduction and Limitation of Armaments:
Profoundly convinced that the time has come when all nations of the world must adopt substantial and comprehensive measures of disarmament in order to consolidate the peace of the world, to hasten the resumption of economic activity, and to lighten the financial burdens which now weigh upon the peoples of the world;

Desirous of avoiding a competition in the power of armaments which would be both ruinous to the peoples and threatening to their national defence;

Recalling its resolutions of April 19th, 20th, and 22nd, 1932;

Firmly determined to achieve a first decisive step involving a substantial reduction of armaments, on the basis of Article 8 of the Covenant of the League of Nations, and as a natural consequence of the obligations resulting from the Briand-Kellogg Pact;

Welcoming heartily the initiative taken by the President of the United States of America in formulating concrete proposals for a substantial reduction of armaments by the prohibition of certain methods of warfare, by the abolition of certain material, and by reductions varying in magnitude and amounting for certain armaments to the proportion of one-third;

Bearing in mind also the draft Convention of the Preparatory Commission, the statements and proposals made to the Conference by a number of delegations, and the reports and resolutions of the various Commissions of the Conference:

Decides forthwith and unanimously, guided by the general principles underlying President Hoover's declaration:

1. That a substantial reduction of world armaments shall be effected, to be applied by a general Convention alike to land, naval and air armaments;

2. That a primary objective shall be to reduce the means of attack.

II. CONCLUSIONS OF THE FIRST PHASE OF THE CONFERENCE

The Conference, noting that agreement has now been reached on a certain number of important points, decides, without prejudice to more far-reaching agreements hereafter, to record forthwith the following concrete measures of disarmament, which should form part of the General Convention to be concluded. The Conference also decides to establish certain principles as the basis for further reductions of armaments, and to determine the procedure necessary for the active prosecution of its work.

1. Air Forces

The Conference, deeply impressed with the danger overhanging civilisation from bombardment from the air in the event of future conflict, and determined to take all practicable measures to provide against this danger, records at this stage of its work the following conclusions:

1. Air attack against the civilian population shall be absolutely prohibited;
2. The High Contracting Parties shall agree as between themselves that all bombardment from the air shall be abolished, subject to agreement with regard to measures to be adopted for the purpose of rendering effective the observance of this rule;

These measures should include the following:

(*a*) There shall be effected a limitation by number and a restriction by characteristics of military aircraft;

(*b*) Civil aircraft shall be submitted to regulation and full publicity. Further, civil aircraft not conforming to the specified limitations shall be subjected to an international regime (except for certain regions where such a regime is not suitable) such as to prevent effectively the misuse of such civil aircraft.

2. Land Armaments

(a) *Land artillery*

1. All heavy land artillery of calibres between any maximum limit as determined in the succeeding paragraph and a lower limit to be defined shall be limited in number;
2. The limitation of calibre of land artillery shall be fixed by the Convention;

Subject to an effective method being established to prevent the rapid transformation of guns on fixed mountings into mobile guns, different maxima for the calibre of land guns may be fixed as follows:

(*a*) A maximum limit for the calibre of coastal guns, which shall not be less than the maximum calibre of naval guns;

(*b*) A maximum limit for the calibre of guns in permanent frontier or fortress defensive systems;

(*c*) A maximum limit for the calibre of mobile land guns (other than guns employed for coastal defence).

(b) *Tanks*

The maximum unit tonnage of tanks shall be limited.

3. *Chemical, Bacteriological and Incendiary Warfare*

Chemical, bacteriological and incendiary warfare shall be prohibited under the conditions unanimously recommended by the Special Committee.

4. *Supervision*

There shall be set up a Permanent Disarmament Commission with the constitution, rights and duties generally as outlined in Part VI of the draft Convention submitted by the Preparatory Commission for the Disarmament Conference, with such extension of its powers as may be deemed by the Conference necessary to enable the Convention to be effectively applied.

III. Preparation of the Second Phase of the Conference

The Conference requests the Bureau to continue its work during the period of adjournment of the General Commission, with a view to framing, with the collaboration (if necessary) of a Drafting Committee, draft texts concerning the questions on which agreement has already been reached. Such texts will be communicated to all delegations as soon as they are drafted, and will then be submitted to the Commission.

Points which call for detailed examination will be examined by the Bureau or by the appropriate committees, with the assistance of the Governments concerned, in order that definite conclusions may be reached as soon as the General Commission meets again.

The questions which will form the subject of such examination are the following:

1. *Effectives*

A strict limitation and a real reduction of effectives shall be brought about.

For this purpose, the Conference invites the Bureau to examine, with the collaboration of such delegations as it considers necessary, the proposal of President Hoover relating to effectives. These studies should take into consideration, in the case of each country, the actual conditions of defence and the number and character of its forces.

2. *Limitation of National Defence Expenditure*

(*a*) The Conference shall decide on the resumption of its labours, taking into account the special conditions of each State, what system of limitation and publicity of expenditure on national defence will provide the peoples with the best guarantee of an alleviation of their financial burdens, and will prevent the measures of qualitative and quantitative disarmament to be inserted in the Convention from being neutralised by increases or improvements in authorised armaments.

(b) With a view to the decisions to be taken under this head, the Conference requests the Committee on National Defence Expenditure and its technical committee to continue and to complete the work entrusted to its organs and to submit their report as soon as possible. The Conference requests its Bureau to draw up, on the basis of this report, a plan accomplishing the purpose aimed at and taking into consideration the special conditions of the various States.

3. *Trade in and Manufacture of Arms*

The Bureau will set up a special Committee to submit proposals to the Conference, immediately on the resumption of its work, in regard to the regulations to be applied to the trade in, and private and State manufacture of, arms and implements of war.

4. *Naval Armaments*

As regards the proposals made by President Hoover and other related proposals concerning naval armaments, the Conference invites the Powers parties to the Naval Treaties of Washington and London, which have already produced important results, to confer together and to report to the General Commission, if possible before the resumption of its work, as to the further measures of naval reduction which might be feasible as a part of the general programme of disarmament.

The Conference further invites the naval Powers other than the Powers parties to the above Treaties to make arrangements for determining the degree of naval limitation they are prepared to accept in view of the Washington and London Treaties and the general programme of disarmament envisaged in the present resolution.

The Bureau will be kept informed of the progress of these negotiations, which it will be its duty to co-ordinate within the framework of the General Convention in preparation for the comprehensive decisions of the General Commission.

5. *Violations*

Rules of international law shall be formulated in connection with the provisions relating to the prohibition of the use of chemical, bacteriological and incendiary weapons and bombing from the air, and shall be supplemented by special measures dealing with infringement of these provisions.

6. *Future Work of the Conference: Procedure*

Pending the resumption of the meetings of the General Commission, the Bureau will keep the delegations informed of the progress of the work.

It will be for the Bureau to fix the date of the next meeting of the General Commission with one month's notice. The meeting of the General Commission shall take place not later than four months after the resumption of the work of the Bureau, which will meet during the week beginning September 19th, 1932.

IV. GENERAL PROVISIONS

The present resolution in no way prejudges the attitude of the Conference towards any more comprehensive measures of disarmament or towards the political proposals submitted by various delegations.

V. ARMAMENTS TRUCE

In order to ensure that, pending the resumption of the meetings of the General Commission and during the second phase of its work, no steps shall be initiated by any Power which might prejudice the preparation of the General Disarmament Convention, the Conference decides to recommend to the Governments to renew for a period of four months from November 1st, 1932, the truce provided for by the resolution of the Assembly of the League of Nations of September 29th, 1931.

COMMUNICATION from Arthur Henderson, President of the Conference for the Reduction and Limitation of Armaments, to the German Minister for Foreign Affairs (Baron Konstantin von Neurath), September 18, 1932

Royal Institute of International Affairs, *Documents on International Affairs, 1932*, p. 199, citing *The Times* (London), September 20, 1932

YOUR EXCELLENCY,

I have the honor to acknowledge Your Excellency's letter of September 14.

Need I say how much I regret the information which you convey to me that the German Government has decided not to participate in the session of the Bureau of the Disarmament Conference which

I have summoned for September 21, in accordance with the resolution of the General Commission.

The German Government apparently bases that decision on the assumption that, the Resolution of the General Commission of July 23 having been adopted, it is clear that the future Disarmament Conference will fall far short of the system of disarmament laid down by the Versailles Treaty, and will differ therefrom essentially, both as regards the form and manner of disarmament.

It would be outside my competence as President to enter into any discussion as to "the system of disarmament laid down by the Versailles Treaty." Since, however, I do not believe that the form and extent of disarmament to be brought about through the Convention are already determined, I feel bound to express my doubts as to the construction placed by the German Government on the bearing of the Resolution of July 23. May I call Your Excellency's attention to certain provisions of that Resolution?

First, in the preamble it is stated that "a substantial reduction of world armaments shall be effected, to be applied by a General Convention alike to land, naval, and air armaments." Second, in the part concerning the conclusions of the first phase of the Conference (I would beg Your Excellency to notice these words "the *first* phase"), the following passage occurs:

> The Conference, noting that agreement has now been reached on a certain number of important points, decides without prejudice to more far-reaching agreements hereafter, to record forthwith the following concrete measures of disarmament which should form part of the General Convention to be concluded.

Third, Part 4 of the Resolution, General Provisions:

> The present Resolution in no way prejudices the attitude of the Conference towards any more comprehensive measures of disarmament, or towards the political proposals submitted by various delegations.

I trust Your Excellency will therefore agree that the form, extent and scope of the ultimate Convention are still undetermined, and remain to be treated at the forthcoming sessions of the Conference and its Committees.

So much for the Resolution itself. But further, may I ask Your Excellency to read the speech which I made as President of the Conference at the meeting of the General Commission on July 23, when the Resolution was under consideration.

After quoting certain passages of the Resolution, I said that a time would come when all the preparations in which we had been engaged month after month for six long months would produce a great gathering-in, and I added that if I thought that that gathering-in would not come in the second stage of the Conference, I should have to ask the Commission to excuse me from again coming to Geneva for a further six months; and lastly, that I trusted that all the representatives would vote for the resolution and come to Geneva in the autumn with the determination that we should have a great gathering-in, and that our work would terminate in a General Convention which would secure a substantial reduction of world armaments, to be applied to land, naval and air armaments.

This is still my firm and honest conviction, and after weighing the reasons set out in this letter I sincerely trust that the German Government may reconsider its decision, and resume its participation at the earliest possible moment in the work of the Bureau, particularly as the prolonged absence of Germany from our deliberation may seriously affect the cause of general disarmament. I make this appeal the more confidently in view of the closing sentence of the letter which Your Excellency has been good enough to address to me.

I am naturally communicating to the members of the Bureau copies of Your Excellency's letter and of this reply.

DECLARATIONS by the Governments of the United States, Great Britain, France, Germany and Italy (Sometimes Known as the "Five-Power Agreement"), Regarding the Work of the Disarmament Conference, Communicated to the President of the Conference (Arthur Henderson), December 11, 1932

League of Nations, *Records of the Conference for the Reduction and Limitation of Armaments, Series B, Minutes of the General Commission*, III, 653

1. THE GOVERNMENTS OF the United Kingdom, France and Italy have declared that one of the principles that should guide the Conference for the Reduction and Limitation of Armaments should be the grant to Germany, and to the other Powers disarmed by treaty, of equality of rights in a system which would provide security for all nations, and that this principle should find itself embodied in the Convention containing the conclusions of the Conference for the Reduction and Limitation of Armaments.

This declaration implies that the respective limitations of the armaments of all States should be included in the proposed Disarmament Convention. It is clearly understood that the methods of application of such equality of rights will be discussed by the Conference.

2. On the basis of this declaration, Germany has signified its willingness to resume its place at the Conference for the Reduction and Limitation of Armaments.

3. The Governments of the United Kingdom, France, Germany and Italy are ready to join in a solemn reaffirmation to be made by all European States that they will not in any circumstances attempt to resolve any present or future differences between the signatories by resort to force. This shall be done without prejudice to fuller discussions on the question of security.

4. The five Governments of the United States of America, the United Kingdom, France, Germany and Italy declare that they are resolved to co-operate in the Conference with the other States there represented in seeking without delay to work out a Convention which shall effect a substantial reduction and a limitation of armaments, with provision for future revision with a view to further reduction.

COMMUNICATION Telegraphed by Arthur Henderson, President of the Conference for the Reduction and Limitation of Armaments, to the German Minister for Foreign Affairs (Baron Konstantin von Neurath), October 16, 1933, Regarding the German Withdrawal from the Conference

British White Paper, Cmd. 4437, p. 11

I HAVE now communicated to the General Commission your Excellency's telegram of the 14th October announcing the decision of the German Government to discontinue participation in the work of the Conference for the Reduction and Limitation of Armaments and indicating the reasons for that decision.

The German Government took this step at a moment when the Bureau had just decided to submit to the General Commission a definite programme. This programme, to be completed within a limited period, provided for the realisation progressively, in accordance with Resolutions of the Conference in which Germany herself concurred, of reductions of armaments comparable to those contemplated in the Draft Convention submitted to the General Commission.

This programme provided also, with corresponding measures of security, for the realisation of Equality of Rights, which the Germans have always placed in the forefront of their demands.

I regret therefore that this grave decision should have been taken by your Government for reasons which I am unable to accept as valid.

RESOLUTION Adopted by the General Commission of the Conference for the Reduction and Limitation of Armaments, June 8, 1934

League of Nations, *Records of the Conference for the Reduction and Limitation of Armaments, Series B, Minutes of the General Commission*, III, 682–88

THE GENERAL COMMISSION,

Taking into consideration the resolutions submitted to it by the delegations of the six Powers, the Turkish delegation and the delegation of the Union of Soviet Socialist Republics respectively;

Taking account of the clarification of its work resulting from the French memorandum of January 1st, 1934, the Italian memorandum of January 4th, 1934, the United Kingdom memorandum of January 29th, 1934, and the German declaration of April 16th, 1934;

Convinced of the necessity of the Conference continuing its work with a view to arriving at a general Convention for the reduction and limitation of armaments;

Resolved to continue without delay the investigations already undertaken;

I

Invites the Bureau to seek, by whatever means it deems appropriate and with a view to the general acceptance of a Disarmament Convention, a solution of the outstanding problems, without prejudice to the private conversations on which Governments will desire to enter in order to facilitate the attainment of final success by the return of Germany to the Conference.

II

Having regard to the peculiar importance presented by the study and solution of certain problems to which attention was drawn at the beginning of the general discussion,

Takes the following decisions:

(1) *Security*

(a) Since the results of the earlier work of the Conference have enabled certain regional security agreements to be concluded in Europe during the past year, the General Commission decides to appoint a special committee to conduct such preliminary studies as it may consider appropriate in order to facilitate the conclusion of further agreements of the same nature which may be negotiated outside the Conference. It would be for the General Commission to determine the relationship, if any, of these agreements to the General Convention.

(b) The General Commission decides to appoint a special committee to study the question of guarantees of execution, and to resume the work relating to supervision.

(2) *Air Forces*

The General Commission instructs its Air Committee to resume forthwith the study of the questions mentioned in its resolution of July 23rd, 1932, under the heading: "1. Air Forces."

(3) *Manufacture of and Trade in Arms*

The General Commission requests its special Committee on questions relating to the manufacture of and trade in arms to resume its work forthwith and, in the light of the statements made by the United States delegate at the meeting of May 29th, 1934, to report to it as early as possible on the solutions it recommends.

These Committees will carry on their work on parallel lines; and it will be coordinated by the Bureau.

III

The General Commission leaves it to the Bureau to take the necessary steps at the proper time to ensure that, when the President convenes the General Commission, it will have before it, as far as possible, a complete draft Convention.

IV

Recognising that the proposal of the Soviet delegation that the Conference be declared a permanent institution under the title of the Peace Conference calls for careful study, the General Commission requests the President to submit that proposal (document Conf.D/C.G.163) to the Governments.

Anglo-German Naval Agreement, June 18, 1935

NOTE from Sir Samuel Hoare, Secretary of State for Foreign Affairs, to Joachim von Ribbentrop, German Ambassador-at-Large, June 18, 1935

British White Paper, Cmd. 4953

YOUR EXCELLENCY,

During the last few days the representatives of the German Government and His Majesty's Government in the United Kingdom have been engaged in conversations, the primary purpose of which has been to prepare the way for the holding of a general conference on the subject of the limitation of naval armaments. I have now much pleasure in notifying your Excellency of the formal acceptance by His Majesty's Government in the United Kingdom of the proposal of the German Government discussed at those conversations that the future strength of the German navy in relation to the aggregate naval strength of the Members of the British Commonwealth of Nations should be in the proportion of 35:100. His Majesty's Government in the United Kingdom regard this proposal as a contribution of the greatest importance to the cause of future naval limitation. They further believe that the agreement which they have now reached with the German Government, and which they regard as a permanent and definite agreement as from to-day between the two Governments, will facilitate the conclusion of a general agreement on the subject of naval limitation between all the naval Powers of the world.

2. His Majesty's Government in the United Kingdom also agree with the explanations which were furnished by the German representatives in the course of the recent discussions in London as to the method of application of this principle. These explanations may be summarised as follows:—

(a) The ration of 35:100 is to be a permanent relationship, i.e., the total tonnage of the German fleet shall never exceed a percentage of 35 of the aggregate tonnage of the naval forces, as defined by treaty, of the Members of the British Commonwealth of Nations, or, if there should in future be no treaty limitations of this tonnage, a percentage of 35 of the aggregate of the actual tonnages of the Members of the British Commonwealth of Nations.

(b) If any future general treaty of naval limitation should not adopt the method of limitation by agreed ratios between the Fleets of different Powers, the German Government will not insist on the incorporation of the ratio mentioned in the preceding sub-paragraph in such future general treaty, provided that the method therein adopted for the future limitation of naval armaments is such as to give Germany full guarantees that this ratio can be maintained.

(c) Germany will adhere to the ratio 35:100 in all circumstances, e.g., the ratio will not be affected by the construction of other Powers. If the general equilibrium of naval armaments, as normally maintained in the past, should be violently upset by any abnormal and exceptional construction by other Powers, the German Government reserve the right to invite His Majesty's Government in the United Kingdom to examine the new situation thus created.

(d) The German Government favour, in the matter of limitation of naval armaments, that system which divides naval vessels into categories, fixing the maximum tonnage and/or armament for vessels in each category, and allocates the tonnage to be allowed to each Power by categories of vessels. Consequently, in principle, and subject to (f) below, the German Government are prepared to apply the 35 per cent. ratio to the tonnage of each category of vessel to be maintained, and to make any variation of this ratio in a particular category or categories dependent on the arrangements to this end that may be arrived at in a future general treaty on naval limitation, such arrangements being based on the principle that any increase in one category would be compensated for by a corresponding reduction in others. If no general treaty on naval limitation should be concluded, or if the future general treaty should not contain provision creating limitation by categories, the manner and degree in which the German Government will have the right to vary the 35 per cent. ratio in one or more categories will be a matter for settlement by agreement between the German Government and His Majesty's Government in the United Kingdom, in the light of the naval situation then existing.

(e) If, and for so long as, other important naval Powers retain a single category for cruisers and destroyers, Germany shall enjoy the right to have a single category for these two classes of vessels, although she would prefer to see these classes in two categories.

(f) In the matter of submarines, however, Germany, while not exceeding the ratio of 35:100 in respect of total tonnage, shall have the right to possess a submarine tonnage equal to the total submarine tonnage possessed by the Members of the British Commonwealth of Nations. The German Government, however, undertake that, except in the circumstances indicated in the immediately following sentence, Germany's submarine tonnage shall not exceed 45 per cent. of the total of that possessed by the Members of the British Commonwealth of Nations. The German Government reserve the right, in the event of a situation arising which in their opinion makes it necessary for Germany to avail herself of her right to a percentage of submarine tonnage exceeding the 45 per cent. above mentioned, to give notice to this effect to His Majesty's Government in the United Kingdom, and agree that the matter shall be the subject of friendly discussion before the German Government exercise that right.

(g) Since it is highly improbable that the calculation of the 35 per cent. ratio should give for each category of vessels tonnage figures exactly divisible by the maximum individual tonnage permitted for ships in that category, it may be necessary that adjustments should be made in order that Germany shall not be debarred from utilising her tonnage to the full. It has consequently been agreed that the German Government and His Majesty's Government in the United Kingdom will settle by common accord what adjustments are necessary for this purpose, and it is understood that this procedure shall not result in any substantial or permanent departure from the ratio 35:100 in respect of total strengths.

3. With reference to sub-paragraph (c) of the explanations set out above, I have the honour to inform you that His Majesty's Government in the United Kingdom have taken note of the reservation and recognise the right therein set out, on the understanding that the 35:100 ratio will be maintained in default of agreement to the contrary between the two Governments.

4. I have the honour to request your Excellency to inform me that the German Government agree that the proposal of the German Government has been correctly set out in the preceding paragraphs of this note.

NOTE from Joachim von Ribbentrop, German Ambassador-at-Large, to the British Secretary of State for Foreign Affairs (Sir Samuel Hoare), June 18, 1935

Translation, in British White Paper, Cmd. 4953

Your Excellency,

I have the honour to acknowledge the receipt of your Excellency's note of to-day's date, in which you were so good as to communicate to me on behalf of His Majesty's Government in the United Kingdom the following:—

[Here follows a German translation of paragraphs 1 to 3 of the British Note.]

I have the honour to confirm to your Excellency that the proposal of the German Government is correctly set forth in the foregoing note, and I note with pleasure that His Majesty's Government in the United Kingdom accept this proposal.

The German Government, for their part, are also of the opinion that the agreement at which they have now arrived with His Majesty's Government in the United Kingdom, and which they regard as a permanent and definite agreement with effect from to-day between the two Governments, will facilitate the conclusion of a general agreement on this question between all the naval Powers of the world.

TREATY for the Limitation of Naval Armament between the United States, France, Great Britain, Canada, Australia, New Zealand, and India, Signed at London, March 25, 1936

Department of State, Treaty Series, No. 919 (1937); excerpts

THE PRESIDENT of the United States of America, the President of the French Republic and His Majesty the King of Great Britain, Ireland and the British Dominions beyond the Seas, Emperor of India;

Desiring to reduce the burdens and prevent the dangers inherent in competition in naval armament;

Desiring, in view of the forthcoming expiration of the Treaty for the Limitation of Naval Armament signed at Washington on the 6th February, 1922, and of the Treaty for the Limitation and Reduction of Naval Armament signed in London on the 22nd April, 1930 (save for Part IV thereof), to make provision for the limitation of naval armament, and for the exchange of information concerning naval construction;

Have resolved to conclude a Treaty for these purposes and have appointed as their Plenipotentiaries:— . . .

PART II: LIMITATION

ARTICLE 2

After the date of the coming into force of the present Treaty, no vessel exceeding the limitations as to displacement or armament prescribed by this Part of the present Treaty shall be acquired by any High Contracting Party or constructed by, for or within the jurisdiction of any High Contracting Party.

ARTICLE 3

No vessel which at the date of the coming into force of the present Treaty carries guns with a calibre exceeding the limits prescribed by this Part of the present Treaty shall, if reconstructed or modernised, be rearmed with guns of a greater calibre than those previously carried by her.

Article 4

(1) No capital ship shall exceed 35,000 tons (35,560 metric tons) standard displacement.

(2) No capital ship shall carry a gun with a calibre exceeding 14 in. (356 mm.); provided however that if any of the Parties to the Treaty for the Limitation of Naval Armament signed at Washington on the 6th February, 1922, should fail to enter into an agreement to conform to this provision prior to the date of the coming into force of the present Treaty, but in any case not later than the 1st April, 1937, the maximum calibre of gun carried by capital ships shall be 16 in. (406 mm.).

(3) No capital ship of sub-category (*a*), the standard displacement of which is less than 17,500 tons (17,780 metric tons), shall be laid down or acquired prior to the 1st January, 1943.

(4) No capital ship, the main armament of which consists of guns of less than 10 in. (254 mm.) calibre, shall be laid down or acquired prior to the 1st January, 1943.

Article 5

(1) No aircraft carrier shall exceed 23,000 tons (23,368 metric tons) standard displacement or carry a gun with a calibre exceeding 6.1 in. (155 mm.).

(2) If the armament of any aircraft carrier includes guns exceeding 5.25 in. (134 mm.) in calibre, the total number of guns carried which exceed that calibre shall not be more than ten.

Article 6

(1) No light surface vessel of sub-category (*b*) exceeding 8,000 tons (8,128 metric tons) standard displacement, and no light surface vessel of sub-category (*a*) shall be laid down or acquired prior to the 1st January, 1943.

(2) Notwithstanding the provisions of paragraph (1) above, if the requirements of the national security of any High Contracting Party are, in His opinion, materially affected by the actual or authorised amount of construction by any Power of light surface vessels of sub-category (*b*), or of light surface vessels not conforming to the restrictions of paragraph (1) above, such High Contracting Party shall, upon notifying the other High Contracting Parties of His intentions and the reasons therefor, have the right to lay down or acquire light sur-

face vessels of sub-categories (*a*) and (*b*) of any standard displacement up to 10,000 tons (10,610 metric tons) subject to the observance of the provisions of Part III of the present Treaty. Each of the other High Contracting Parties shall thereupon be entitled to exercise the same right.

(3) It is understood that the provisions of paragraph (1) above constitute no undertaking expressed or implied to continue the restrictions therein prescribed after the year 1942.

Article 7

No submarine shall exceed 2,000 tons (2,032 metric tons) standard displacement or carry a gun exceeding 5.1 in. (130 mm.) in calibre.

Article 8

Every vessel shall be rated at its standard displacement, as defined in Article 1A of the present Treaty.

Article 9

No preparations shall be made in merchant ships in time of peace for the installation of warlike armaments for the purpose of converting such ships into vessels of war, other than the necessary stiffening of decks for the mounting of guns not exceeding 6.1 in. (155 mm.) in calibre.

Article 10

Vessels which were laid down before the date of the coming into force of the present Treaty, the standard displacement or armament of which exceeds the limitations or restrictions prescribed in this Part of the present Treaty for their category or sub-category, or vessels which before that date were converted to target use exclusively or retained exclusively for experimental or training purposes under the provisions of previous treaties, shall retain the category or designation which applied to them before the said date.

PART III: ADVANCE NOTIFICATION AND EXCHANGE OF INFORMATION

Article 11

(1) Each of the High Contracting Parties shall communicate every year to each of the other High Contracting Parties information, as hereinafter provided, regarding His annual programme for the construction and acquisition of all vessels of the categories and sub-categories mentioned in Article 12 (*a*), whether or not the vessels con-

cerned are constructed within His own jurisdiction, and periodical information giving details of such vessels and of any alterations to vessels of the said categories or sub-categories already completed.

(2) For the purposes of this and the succeeding Parts of the present Treaty, information shall be deemed to have reached a High Contracting Party on the date upon which such information is communicated to His Diplomatic Representatives accredited to the High Contracting Party by whom the information is given.

(3) This information shall be treated as confidential until published by the High Contracting Party supplying it. . . .

PART IV: GENERAL AND SAFEGUARDING CLAUSES

Article 22

No High Contracting Party shall, by gift, sale or any mode of transfer, dispose of any of His surface vessels of war or submarines in such a manner that such vessel may become a surface vessel of war or a submarine in any foreign navy. This provision shall not apply to auxiliary vessels.

Article 23

(1) Nothing in the present Treaty shall prejudice the right of any High Contracting Party, in the event of loss or accidental destruction of a vessel, before the vessel in question has become over-age, to replace such vessel by a vessel of the same category or sub-category as soon as the particulars of the new vessel mentioned in Article 12 (*b*) shall have reached all the other High Contracting Parties.

(2) The provisions of the preceding paragraph shall also govern the immediate replacement, in such circumstances, of a light surface vessel of the sub-category (*b*) exceeding 8,000 tons (8,128 metric tons) standard displacement, or of a light surface vessel of sub-category (*a*), before the vessel in question has become over-age, by a light surface vessel of the same sub-category of any standard displacement up to 10,000 tons (10,160 metric tons).

Article 24

(1) If any High Contracting Party should become engaged in war, such High Contracting Party may, if He considers the naval requirements of His defence are materially affected, suspend, in so far as He is concerned, any or all of the obligations of the present Treaty, provided that He shall promptly notify the other High Contracting Parties that the circumstances require such suspension, and shall specify the obligations it is considered necessary to suspend.

(2) The other High Contracting Parties shall in such case promptly consult together, and shall examine the situation thus presented with a view to agreeing as to the obligations of the present Treaty, if any, which each of the said High Contracting Parties may suspend. Should such consultation not produce agreement, any of the said High Contracting Parties may suspend, in so far as He is concerned, any or all of the obligations of the present Treaty, provided that He shall promptly give notice to the other High Contracting Parties of the obligations which it is considered necessary to suspend.

(3) On the cessation of hostilities, the High Contracting Parties shall consult together with a view to fixing a date upon which the obligations of the Treaty which have been suspended shall again become operative, and to agreeing upon any amendments in the present Treaty which may be considered necessary.

Article 25

(1) In the event of any vessel not in conformity with the limitations and restrictions as to standard displacement and armament prescribed by Articles 4, 5 and 7 of the present Treaty being authorised, constructed or acquired by a Power not a party to the present Treaty, each High Contracting Party reserves the right to depart if, and to the extent to which, He considers such departures necessary in order to meet the requirements of His national security;

(a) during the remaining period of the Treaty, from the limitations and restrictions of Articles 3, 4, 5, 6 (1) and 7, and

(b) during the current year, from His Annual Programmes of construction and declarations of acquisition.

This right shall be exercised in accordance with the following provisions:—

(2) Any High Contracting Party who considers it necessary that such right should be exercised, shall notify the other High Contracting Parties to that effect, stating precisely the nature and extent of the proposed departures and the reasons therefor.

(3) The High Contracting Parties shall thereupon consult together and endeavour to reach an agreement with a view to reducing to a minimum the extent of the departures which may be made.

(4) On the expiration of a period of three months from the date of the first of any notifications which may have been given under paragraph (2) above, each of the High Contracting Parties shall, subject to any agreement which may have been reached to the contrary, be entitled to depart during the remaining period of the present Treaty from the limitations and restrictions prescribed in Articles 3, 4, 5, 6 (1) and 7 thereof.

(5) On the expiration of the period mentioned in the preceding

paragraph, any High Contracting Party shall be at liberty, subject to any agreement which may have been reached during the consultations provided for in paragraph (3) above, and on informing all the other High Contracting Parties, to depart from His Annual Programmes of construction and declarations of acquisition and to alter the characteristics of any vessels building or which have already appeared in His Programmes or declarations.

(6) In such event, no delay in the acquisition, the laying of the keel, or the altering of any vessel shall be necessary by reason of any of the provisions of Part III of the present Treaty. The particulars mentioned in Article 12 (*b*) shall, however, be communicated to all the other High Contracting Parties before the keels of any vessels are laid. In the case of acquisition, information relating to the vessel shall be given under the provisions of Article 14.

Article 26

(1) If the requirements of the national security of any High Contracting Party should, in His opinion, be materially affected by any change of circumstances, other than those provided for in Articles 6 (2), 24 and 25 of the present Treaty, such High Contracting Party shall have the right to depart for the current year from His Annual Programmes of construction and declarations of acquisition. The amount of construction by any Party to the Treaty, within the limitations and restrictions thereof, shall not, however, constitute a change of circumstances for the purposes of the present Article. The above mentioned right shall be exercised in accordance with the following provisions:—

(2) Such High Contracting Party shall, if He desires to exercise the above mentioned right, notify all the other High Contracting Parties to that effect, stating in what respects He proposes to depart from His Annual Programmes of construction and declarations of acquisition, giving reasons for the proposed departure.

(3) The High Contracting Parties will thereupon consult together with a view to agreement as to whether any departures are necessary in order to meet the situation.

(4) On the expiration of a period of three months from the date of the first of any notifications which may have been given under paragraph (2) above, each of the High Contracting Parties shall, subject to any agreement which may have been reached to the contrary, be entitled to depart from His Annual Programmes of construction and declarations of acquisition, provided notice is promptly given to the other High Contracting Parties stating precisely in what respects He proposes so to depart.

(5) In such event, no delay in the acquisition, the laying of the

keel, or the altering of any vessel shall be necessary by reason of any of the provisions of Part III of the present Treaty. The particulars mentioned in Article 12 (b) shall, however, be communicated to all the other High Contracting Parties before the keels of any vessels are laid. In the case of acquisition, information relating to the vessel shall be given under the provisions of Article 14.

PART V: FINAL CLAUSES

Article 27

The present Treaty shall remain in force until the 31st December, 1942.

Article 28

(1) His Majesty's Government in the United Kingdom of Great Britain and Northern Ireland will, during the last quarter of 1940, initiate through the diplomatic channel a consultation between the Governments of the Parties to the present Treaty with a view to holding a conference in order to frame a new treaty for the reduction and limitation of naval armament. This conference shall take place in 1941 unless the preliminary consultations should have shown that the holding of such a conference at that time would not be desirable or practicable.

(2) In the course of the consultation referred to in the preceding paragraph, views shall be exchanged in order to determine whether, in the light of the circumstances then prevailing and the experience gained in the interval in the design and construction of capital ships, it may be possible to agree upon a reduction in the standard displacement or calibre of guns of capital ships to be constructed under future annual programmes and thus, if possible, to bring about a reduction in the cost of capital ships. . . .

In faith whereof the above-named Plenipotentiaries have signed the present Treaty and have affixed thereto their seals.

Done in London the 25th day of March, nineteen hundred and thirty-six.

[*Signatures*]

PROCÈS-VERBAL Relating to the Rules of Submarine Warfare as Set Forth in Part IV of the Treaty of London of April 22, 1930, Signed by Representatives of the United States, Australia, Canada, France, Great Britain, India, the Irish Free State, Italy, Japan, New Zealand, and the Union of South Africa, at London, November 6, 1936

British White Paper, Cmd. 5302

WHEREAS the Treaty for the Limitation and Reduction of Naval Armaments signed in London on the 22nd April, 1930, has not been ratified by all the signatories;

And whereas the said Treaty will cease to be in force after the 31st December, 1936, with the exception of Part IV thereof, which sets forth rules as to the action of submarines with regard to merchant ships as being established rules of international law, and remains in force without limit of time;

And whereas the last paragraph of Article 22 in the said Part IV states that the High Contracting Parties invite all other Powers to express their assent to the said rules;

And whereas the Governments of the French Republic and the Kingdom of Italy have confirmed their acceptance of the said rules resulting from the signature of the said Treaty;

And whereas all the signatories of the said Treaty desire that as great a number of Powers as possible should accept the rules contained in the said Part IV as established rules of international law;

The Undersigned, representatives of their respective Governments, bearing in mind the said Article 22 of the Treaty, hereby request the Government of the United Kingdom of Great Britain and Northern Ireland forthwith to communicate the said rules, as annexed hereto, to the Governments of all the Powers which are not signatories of the said Treaty, with an invitation to accede thereto definitely and without limit of time.

RULES

(1) In their action with regard to merchant ships, submarines must conform to the rules of International Law to which surface vessels are subject.

(2) In particular, except in the case of persistent refusal to stop on being duly summoned, or of active resistance to visit or search, a warship, whether surface vessel or submarine, may not sink or render incapable of navigation a merchant vessel without having first placed passengers, crew

and ship's papers in a place of safety. For this purpose the ship's boats are not regarded as a place of safety unless the safety of the passengers and crew is assured, in the existing sea and weather conditions, by the proximity of land, or the presence of another vessel which is in a position to take them on board.

Signed in London, the 6th day of November, nineteen hundred and thirty-six.

[Signatures]

PROTOCOL of June 30, 1938, Modifying the Treaty for the Limitation of Naval Armament, signed March 25, 1936

Royal Institute of International Affairs, *Documents on International Affairs, 1938*, I, 515, citing British White Paper, Cmd. 5781

WHEREAS by Article 4 (1) of the Treaty for the Limitation of Naval Armaments signed in London on the 25th March, 1936, it is provided that no capital ship shall exceed 35,000 tons (35,560 metric tons) standard displacement;

And WHEREAS by reason of Article 4 (2) of the said treaty the maximum calibre of gun carried by capital ships is 16 inches (406 mm.);

And WHEREAS on the 31st March, 1938, the Government of the United States of America and the Government of the United Kingdom of Great Britain and Northern Ireland gave notice under paragraph (2) of Article 25 of the said Treaty of their decision to exercise the right provided for in paragraph (1) of the said Article to depart from the limitations and restrictions of the treaty in regard to the upper limits of capital ships of sub-category (a);

And WHEREAS consultations have taken place as provided in paragraph (3) of Article 25, with a view to reaching agreement in order to reduce to a minimum the extent of the departures from the limitations and restrictions of the treaty;

The undersigned, duly authorized by their respective Governments, have agreed as follows:

1. As from this day's date the figure of 35,000 tons (35,560 metric tons) in Article 4 (1) of the said treaty shall be replaced by the figure of 45,000 tons (45,720 metric tons).

2. The figure of 16 inches (406 mm.) in Article 4 (2) remains unaltered.

3. The present protocol, of which the French and English texts shall both be equally authentic, shall come into force on this day's date.

In faith whereof the undersigned have signed the present protocol. Done in London the 30th day of June, 1938.

    For the Government of the United States of America:
        HERSCHEL V. JOHNSON
    For the Government of the French Republic:
        ROBERT CAMBON
    For the Government of the United Kingdom of Great Britain and Northern Ireland:
        ALEXANDER CADOGAN

ROME-BERLIN-TOKYO AXIS AGREEMENTS

GERMAN-JAPANESE AGREEMENT and Supplementary Protocol, Signed at Berlin, November 25, 1936

Translation, in Department of State, *Foreign Relations of the United States: Japan, 1931–1941*, II, 153

AGREEMENT GUARDING AGAINST THE COMMUNISTIC INTERNATIONAL

THE Imperial Government of Japan and the Government of Germany,

In cognizance of the fact that the object of the Communistic International (the so-called Komintern) is the disintegration of, and the commission of violence against, existing States by the exercise of all means at its command,

Believing that the toleration of interference by the Communistic International in the internal affairs of nations not only endangers their internal peace and social welfare, but threatens the general peace of the world,

Desiring to co-operate for defence against communistic disintegration, have agreed as follows:

ARTICLE I

The High Contracting States agree that they will mutually keep each other informed concerning the activities of the Communistic International, will confer upon the necessary measures of defence, and will carry out such measures in close co-operation.

ARTICLE II

The High Contracting States will jointly invite third States whose internal peace is menaced by the disintegrating work of the Communistic International, to adopt defensive measures in the spirit of the present Agreement or to participate in the present Agreement.

ARTICLE III

The Japanese and German texts are each valid as the original text of this Agreement. The Agreement shall come into force on the day of its signature and shall remain in force for the term of five years. The High Contracting States will, in a reasonable time before the expiration of the said term, come to an understanding upon the further manner of their co-operation.

In witness whereof the undersigned, duly authorized by their respective Governments, have affixed hereto their seals and signatures.

Done in duplicate at Berlin, November 25th, 11th year of Showa, corresponding to November 25th, 1936.

[SEAL]   (Signed)   VISCOUNT KINTOMO MUSHAKOJI
Imperial Japanese Ambassador Extraordinary and Plenipotentiary

[SEAL]   (Signed)   JOACHIM VON RIBBENTROP
German Ambassador Extraordinary and Plenipotentiary

SUPPLEMENTARY PROTOCOL TO THE AGREEMENT GUARDING AGAINST THE COMMUNISTIC INTERNATIONAL

On the occasion of the signature this day of the Agreement guarding against the Communistic International the undersigned plenipotentiaries have agreed as follows:

(a) The competent authorities of both High Contracting States will closely co-operate in the exchange of reports on the activities of the Communistic International and on measures of information and defence against the Communistic International.

(b) The competent authorities of both High Contracting States will, within the framework of the existing law, take stringent measures against those who at home or abroad work on direct or indirect duty of the Communistic International or assist its disintegrating activities.

(c) To facilitate the co-operation of the competent authorities of the two High Contracting States as set out in (a) above, a standing committee shall be established. By this committee the further measures to be adopted in order to counter the disintegrating activities of the Communistic International shall be considered and conferred upon.

Done at Berlin, November 25th, 11th year of Showa, corresponding to November 25th, 1936.

(Signed)   VISCOUNT KINTOMO MUSHAKOJI
Imperial Japanese Ambassador Extraordinary and Plenipotentiary

(Signed)   JOACHIM VON RIBBENTROP
German Ambassador Extraordinary and Plenipotentiary

PROTOCOL Concluded by Italy, Germany, and Japan, at Rome, November 6, 1937

Translation, in Department of State, *Foreign Relations of the United States: Japan, 1931-1941*, II, 159

THE Italian Government, the Government of the German Reich, and the Imperial Government of Japan,

Considering that the Communist International continues constantly to imperil the civilized world in the Occident and Orient, disturbing and destroying peace and order,

Considering that only close collaboration looking to the maintenance of peace and order can limit and remove that peril,

Considering that Italy—who with the advent of the Fascist regime has with inflexible determination combated that peril and rid her territory of the Communist International—has decided to align herself against the common enemy along with Germany and Japan, who for their part are animated by like determination to defend themselves against the Communist International,

Have, in conformity with Article 2 of the Agreement against the Communist International concluded at Berlin on November 25, 1936, by Germany and Japan, agreed upon the following:

ARTICLE 1

Italy becomes a party to the Agreement against the Communist International and to the Supplementary Protocol concluded on November 25, 1936, between Germany and Japan, the text of which is included in the annex to the present Protocol.

ARTICLE 2

The three powers signatory to the present Protocol agree that Italy will be considered as an original signatory to the Agreement and Supplementary Protocol mentioned in the preceding article, the signing of the present Protocol being equivalent to the signature of the original text of the aforesaid Agreement and Supplementary Protocol.

ARTICLE 3

The present Protocol shall constitute an integral part of the abovementioned Agreement and Supplementary Protocol.

ARTICLE 4

The present Protocol is drawn up in Italian, Japanese, and German, each text being considered authentic. It shall enter into effect on the date of signature.

In testimony whereof, etc. . . .

Ciano—Von Ribbentrop—Hotta

SUMMARY of the Three-Power Pact between Germany, Italy, and Japan, signed at Berlin, September 27, 1940

Tentative translation as received by the American Embassy at Tokyo from the Japanese Ministry for Foreign Affairs, September 27, 1940; in Department of State, *Foreign Relations of the United States: Japan, 1931-1941*, II, 165

The Governments of Japan, Germany and Italy, considering it as the condition precedent of any lasting peace that all nations of the world be given each its own proper place, have decided to stand by and cooperate with one another in regard to their efforts in Greater East Asia and the regions of Europe respectively wherein it is their prime purpose to establish and maintain a new order of things calculated to promote mutual prosperity and welfare of the peoples concerned. Furthermore it is the desire of the three Governments to extend cooperation to such nations in other spheres of the world as may be inclined to put forth endeavours along lines similar to their own, in order that their ultimate aspirations for world peace may thus be realized. Accordingly the Governments of Japan, Germany and Italy have agreed as follows:

Article 1

Japan recognizes and respects the leadership of Germany and Italy in the establishment of a new order in Europe.

Article 2

Germany and Italy recognize and respect the leadership of Japan in the establishment of a new order in Greater East Asia.

Article 3

Japan, Germany and Italy agree to cooperate in their efforts on the aforesaid lines. They further undertake to assist one another with all political, economic and military means when one of the three Contracting Parties is attacked by a power at present not involved in the European War or in the Sino-Japanese Conflict.

Article 4

With a view to implementing the present Pact, Joint Technical Commissions the members of which are to be appointed by the respective Governments of Japan, Germany and Italy will meet without delay.

Article 5

Japan, Germany and Italy affirm that the aforesaid terms do not in any way affect the political status which exists at present as between each of the three Contracting Parties and Soviet Russia.

Article 6

The present Pact shall come into effect immediately upon signature and shall remain in force for ten years from the date of its coming into force.

At proper time before the expiration of the said term the High Contracting Parties shall, at the request of any one of them, enter into negotiations for its removal [*renewal?*].

AMERICAN SOLIDARITY

DECLARATION of the Principles of the Solidarity of America (the "Declaration of Lima"), Adopted at the Eighth International Conference of American States, at Lima, December 24, 1938

Department of State, *Report of the Delegation of the United States of America to the Eighth International Conference of American States*, p. 189.

CONSIDERING:

That the peoples of America have achieved spiritual unity through the similarity of their republican institutions, their unshakeable will for peace, their profound sentiment of humanity and tolerance, and through their absolute adherence to the principles of international law, of the equal sovereignty of States and of individual liberty without religious or racial prejudices;

That on the basis of such principles and will, they seek and defend the peace of the continent and work together in the cause of universal concord;

That respect for the personality, sovereignty, and independence of each American State constitutes the essence of international order sustained by continental solidarity, which historically has been expressed and sustained by declarations and treaties in force; and

That the Inter-American Conference for the Maintenance of Peace, held at Buenos Aires, approved on December 21, 1936, the Declaration of the Principles of Inter-American Solidarity and Cooperation and approved, on December 23, 1936, the Protocol of Non-intervention,

THE GOVERNMENTS OF THE AMERICAN STATES DECLARE:

First. That they reaffirm their continental solidarity and their purpose to collaborate in the maintenance of the principles upon which the said solidarity is based.

Second. That faithful to the above-mentioned principles and to their absolute sovereignty, they reaffirm their decision to maintain them and to defend them against all foreign intervention or activity that may threaten them.

Third. And in case the peace, security or territorial integrity of any American Republic is thus threatened by acts of any nature that may impair them, they proclaim their common concern and their determination to make effective their solidarity, coordinating their respective sovereign wills by means of the procedure of consultation, established by conventions in force and by declarations of the Inter-American Conferences, using the measures which in each case the circumstances may make advisable. It is understood that the Governments of the American Republics will act independently in their individual capacity, recognizing fully their juridical equality as sovereign states.

Fourth. That in order to facilitate the consultations established in this and other American peace instruments, the Ministers for Foreign Affairs of the American Republics, when deemed desirable and at the initiative of any one of them, will meet in their several capitals by rotation and without protocolary character. Each Government may, under special circumstances or for special reasons, designate a representative as a substitute for its Minister for Foreign Affairs.

Fifth. This Declaration shall be known as the "Declaration of Lima."

THE "Declaration of Panama," Adopted at the Meeting of the Ministers for Foreign Affairs of the American Republics at Panama, October 3, 1939

Department of State, *Report of the Delegate of the United States of America to the Meeting of the Foreign Ministers of the American Republics Held at Panama*, p. 62

THE GOVERNMENTS OF the American republics meeting at Panamá, have solemnly ratified their neutral status in the conflict which is disrupting the peace of Europe, but the present war may lead to unexpected results which may affect the fundamental interests of America and there can be no justification for the interests of the belligerents to prevail over the rights of neutrals causing disturbances and suffering to nations which by their neutrality in the conflict and their distance from the scene of events, should not be burdened with its fatal and painful consequences.

During the World War of 1914–18 the Governments of Argentina, Brazil, Chile, Colombia, Ecuador and Peru advanced, or supported, individual proposals providing in principle a declaration by the American republics that the belligerent nations must refrain from committing hostile acts within a reasonable distance from their shores.

The nature of the present conflagration, in spite of its already lamentable proportions, would not justify any obstruction to inter-

American communications which, engendered by important interests, call for adequate protection. This fact requires the demarcation of a zone of security including all the normal maritime routes of communication and trade between the countries of America.

To this end it is essential as a measure of necessity to adopt immediately provisions based on the above-mentioned precedents for the safeguarding of such interests, in order to avoid a repetition of the damages and sufferings sustained by the American nations and by their citizens in the war of 1914–1918.

There is no doubt that the governments of the American republics must foresee those dangers and as a measure of self-protection insist that the waters to a reasonable distance from their coasts shall remain free from the commission of hostile acts or from the undertaking of belligerent activities by nations engaged in a war in which the said governments are not involved.

For these reasons the governments of the American republics

Resolve and hereby Declare

1. As a measure of continental self-protection, the American republics, so long as they maintain their neutrality, are as of inherent right entitled to have those waters adjacent to the American Continent, which they regard as of primary concern and direct utility in their relations, free from the commission of any hostile act by any non-American belligerent nation, whether such hostile act be attempted or made from land, sea, or air.

Such waters shall be defined as follows. All waters comprised within the limits set forth hereafter except the territorial waters of Canada and of the undisputed colonies and possessions of European countries within these limits:

    Beginning at the terminus of the United States–Canada boundary in Passamaquoddy Bay, in 44°46′36″ north latitude, and 66°54′11″ west longitude;

    Thence due east along the parallel 44°46′36″ to a point 60° west of Greenwich;

    Thence due south to a point in 20° north latitude;

    Thence by a rhumb line to a point in 5° north latitude, 24° west longitude;

    Thence due south to a point in 20° south latitude;

    Thence by a rhumb line to a point in 58° south latitude, 57° west longitude;

    Thence due west to a point in 80° west longitude;

    Thence by a rhumb line to a point on the equator in 97° west longitude;

Thence by a rhumb line to a point in 15° north latitude, 120° west longitude;

Thence by a rhumb line to a point in 48°29′38″ north latitude, 136° west longitude;

Thence due east to the Pacific terminus of the United States–Canada boundary in the Strait of Juan de Fuca.

2. The governments of the American republics agree that they will endeavor, through joint representation to such belligerents as may now or in the future be engaged in hostilities, to secure the compliance by them with the provisions of this declaration, without prejudice to the exercise of the individual rights of each state inherent in their sovereignty.

3. The governments of the American republics further declare that whenever they consider it necessary they will consult together to determine upon the measures which they may individually or collectively undertake in order to secure the observance of the provisions of this declaration.

4. The American republics, during the existence of a state of war in which they themselves are not involved, may undertake, whenever they may determine that the need therefor exists, to patrol, either individually or collectively, as may be agreed upon by common consent, and in so far as the means and resources of each may permit, the waters adjacent to their coasts within the area above defined.

JOINT DECLARATION by the American Republics, May 19, 1940

The declaration, which had been proposed by the Uruguayan Government and agreed to by the other American Republics, was released by the President of Panama. Department of State, *Bulletin*, May 25, 1940, p. 568

THE AMERICAN REPUBLICS in accord with the principles of international law and in application of the resolutions adopted in their inter-American conferences, consider unjustifiable the ruthless violation by Germany of the neutrality and sovereignty of Belgium, Holland and Luxemburg.

In paragraphs four and five of the Ninth Resolution of the Meeting of Foreign Ministers held at Panama in 1939 entitled "Maintenance of International Activities in accordance with Christian Morality," it was established that the violation of the neutrality or the invasion of weaker nations as a measure in the conduct and success of war warrants the American Republics in protesting against this infraction of international law and the requirements of justice.

The American Republics therefore resolve to protest against the military attacks directed against Belgium, Holland and Luxemburg, at the same time making an appeal for the reestablishment of law and justice in the relations between countries.

DECLARATION XV, "Reciprocal Assistance and Cooperation for the Defense of the Nations of the Americas," Adopted at the Meeting of the Ministers for Foreign Affairs of the American Republics at Habana, July 30, 1940

Department of State, *Report of the Secretary of State of the United States of America on the Second Meeting of the Ministers of Foreign Affairs of the American Republics,* p. 71

THE Second Meeting of the Ministers of Foreign Affairs of the American Republics

DECLARES

That any attempt on the part of a non-American state against the integrity or inviolability of the territory, the sovereignty or the political independence of an American state shall be considered as an act of aggression against the states which sign this declaration.

In case acts of aggression are committed or should there be reason to believe that an act of aggression is being prepared by a non-American nation against the integrity or inviolability of the territory, the sovereignty or the political independence of an American nation, the nations signatory to the present declaration will consult among themselves in order to agree upon the measure it may be advisable to take.

All the signatory nations, or two or more of them, according to circumstances, shall proceed to negotiate the necessary complementary agreements so as to organize cooperation for defense and the assistance that they shall lend each other in the event of aggressions such as those referred to in this declaration.

DECLARATION I, "Breaking of Diplomatic Relations," Adopted at the Meeting of the Ministers for Foreign Affairs of the American Republics at Rio de Janeiro, January 28, 1942

Department of State, *Bulletin*, February 7, 1942

I

THE American Republics reaffirm their declaration to consider any act of aggression on the part of a non-American State against one of them as an act of aggression against all of them, constituting as it does an immediate threat to the liberty and independence of America.

II

The American Republics reaffirm their complete solidarity and their determination to cooperate jointly for their mutual protection until the effects of the present aggression against the Continent have disappeared.

III

The American Republics, in accordance with the procedures established by their own laws and in conformity with the position and circumstances obtaining in each country in the existing continental conflict, recommend the breaking of their diplomatic relations with Japan, Germany and Italy, since the first-mentioned State attacked and the other two declared war on an American country.

IV

Finally, the American Republics declare that, prior to the reestablishment of the relations referred to in the preceding paragraph, they will consult among themselves in order that their action may have a solidary character.

OTHER AGREEMENTS AND JOINT COMMUNIQUÉS

GERMAN-POLISH AGREEMENT of January 26, 1934

Translation, in *British War Blue Book*, p. 1

THE GERMAN GOVERNMENT and the Polish Government consider that the time has come to introduce a new phase in the political relations between Germany and Poland by a direct understanding between State and State. They have, therefore, decided to lay down the principles for the future development of these relations in the present declaration.

The two Governments base their action on the fact that the maintenance and guarantee of a lasting peace between their countries is an essential pre-condition for the general peace of Europe.

They have therefore decided to base their mutual relations on the principles laid down in the Pact of Paris of the 27th August, 1928, and propose to define more exactly the application of these principles in so far as the relations between Germany and Poland are concerned.

Each of the two Governments, therefore, lays it down that the international obligations undertaken by it towards a third party do not hinder the peaceful development of their mutual relations, do not conflict with the present declaration, and are not affected by this declaration. They establish, moreover, that this declaration does not extend to those questions which under international law are to be regarded exclusively as the internal concern of one of the two States.

Both Governments announce their intention to settle directly all questions of whatever sort which concern their mutual relations.

Should any disputes arise between them and agreement thereon not be reached by direct negotiation, they will in each particular case, on the basis of mutual agreement, seek a solution by other peaceful means, without prejudice to the possibility of applying, if necessary, those methods of procedure in which provision is made for such cases in other agreements in force between them. In no circumstances, however, will they proceed to the application of force for the purpose of reaching a decision in such disputes.

The guarantee of peace created by these principles will facilitate the great task of both Governments of finding a solution for problems of political, economic and social kinds, based on a just and fair adjustment of the interests of both parties.

Both Governments are convinced that the relations between their countries will in this manner develop fruitfully, and will lead to the establishment of a neighbourly relationship which will contribute to the well-being not only of both their countries, but of the other peoples of Europe as well.

The present declaration shall be ratified, and the instruments of ratification shall be exchanged in Warsaw as soon as possible.

The declaration is valid for a period of ten years, reckoned from the day of the exchange of the instruments of ratification.

If the declaration is not denounced by one of the two Governments six months before the expiration of this period, it will continue in force, but can then be denounced by either Government at any time on notice of six months being given. Made in duplicate in the German and Polish languages.

Berlin, January 26, 1934.

For the German Government:
FREIHERR VON NEURATH.
For the Polish Government:
JOSEF LIPSKI.

JOINT COMMUNIQUÉ Issued by the French, British and Italian Governments, Regarding the Independence of Austria, February 17, 1934

Royal Institute of International Affairs, *Documents on International Affairs, 1933*, p. 394, citing *The Times* (London), February 19, 1934

THE AUSTRIAN GOVERNMENT has inquired of the Governments of France, Great Britain, and Italy as to their attitude with regard to the *dossier* which it has prepared with a view to establishing German interference in the internal affairs of Austria and communicated to them.

The conversations which have taken place between the three Governments on this subject have shown that they take a common view as to the necessity of maintaining Austria's independence and integrity in accordance with the relevant treaties.

COMMUNIQUÉ Issued by the Premier of Italy and the Minister for Foreign Affairs of France at Rome, January 7, 1935

Translated from the French text as printed in Royal Institute of International Affairs, *Documents on International Affairs, 1935*, I, 18, citing *L'Europe Nouvelle* (Documents Supplement, No. 9), March 2, 1935

M. Mussolini and M. Pierre Laval have concluded the Franco-Italian negotiations by signing agreements relating to the interests of both countries in Africa and documents recording the community of views of their Governments regarding problems of a European character. They have confirmed the agreement of the two Governments on the need for a multilateral understanding on Central European problems. They are agreed that the conclusion which they have reached (in this regard) should be submitted as soon as possible to the consideration of the various interested nations. They are agreed that pending the conclusion of this *entente* they will examine jointly, in the spirit of this *entente*, all measures which the situation may call for.

JOINT RESOLUTION of Representatives of the Governments of France, Great Britain, and Italy at the Conference of Stresa, Including the Anglo-Italian Declaration and the Final Declaration, April 14, 1935

British White Paper, Cmd. 4880

The Representatives of the Governments of Italy, France and the United Kingdom have examined at Stresa the general European situation in the light of the results of the exchanges of views which have taken place in recent weeks, of the decision taken on the 16th March by the German Government, and of the information obtained by British Ministers during the visits recently paid by them to several European capitals. Having considered the bearing of this situation on the policy defined in the arrangements reached respectively in Rome and in London, they found themselves in complete agreement on the various matters discussed.

1. They agreed upon a common line of conduct to be pursued in the course of the discussion of the request presented to the Council of the League of Nations by the French Government.
2. The information which they have received has confirmed their

view that the negotiations should be pursued for the development which is desired in security in Eastern Europe.

3. The Representatives of the three Governments examined afresh the Austrian situation.

They confirmed the Anglo-Franco-Italian declarations of the 17th February and the 27th September, 1934, in which the three Governments recognised that the necessity of maintaining the independence and integrity of Austria would continue to inspire their common policy.

Referring to the Franco-Italian protocol of the 7th January, 1935, and to the Anglo-French declarations of the 3rd February, 1935, in which the decision was reaffirmed to consult together as to the measures to be taken in the case of threats to the integrity and independence of Austria, they agreed to recommend that Representatives of all the Governments enumerated in the protocol of Rome should meet at a very early date with a view to concluding the Central European agreement.

4. As regards the proposed Air Pact for Western Europe, the Representatives of the three Governments confirmed the principles and procedure that should be followed as envisaged in the London communiqué of the 3rd February, and agreed to continue actively the study of the question with a view to the drafting of a pact between the five Powers mentioned in the London communiqué and of any bilateral agreements which might accompany it.

5. In approaching the problem of armaments, the Representatives of the three Powers recalled that the London communiqué envisaged an agreement to be freely negotiated with Germany to take the place of the relevant clauses of Part V of the Treaty of Versailles, and took into careful and anxious consideration the recent action of the German Government and the report furnished by Sir John Simon of his conversations with the German Chancellor on this subject.

It was regretfully recognised that the method of unilateral repudiation adopted by the German Government, at a moment when steps were being taken to promote a freely negotiated settlement of the question of armaments, had undermined public confidence in the security of a peaceful order. Moreover, the magnitude of the declared programme of German rearmament, already well in process of execution, had invalidated the quantitative assumptions upon which efforts for disarmament had hitherto been based and shaken the hopes by which those efforts were inspired.

The Representatives of the three Powers, nevertheless, reaffirm their earnest desire to sustain peace by establishing a sense of security, and declare for themselves that they remain anxious to join in every practicable effort for promoting international agreement on the limitation of armaments.

6. The Representatives of the three Governments took into consideration the desire expressed by the States, whose military status was respectively determined by the Treaties of Saint-Germain, Trianon and Neuilly, to obtain the revision of this status.

They decided that the other States concerned should be informed of this desire through the diplomatic channel.

They agreed to recommend the other States concerned to examine this question with a view to its settlement by mutual agreement within the framework of general and regional guarantees of security.

Anglo-Italian Declaration

The following joint Declaration was made by the Representatives of Italy and the United Kingdom in reference to the Treaty of Locarno:—

The Representatives of Italy and of the United Kingdom, the Powers which participate in the Treaty of Locarno only in the capacity of guarantors, formally reaffirm all their obligations under that Treaty, and declare their intention, should the need arise, faithfully to fulfil them.

Inasmuch as the two Powers have entered into these obligations in relation to all the other parties to the Treaty of Locarno, this joint declaration, which has been made at the Stresa Conference in which France is participating, will also be formally communicated to the Governments of Germany and Belgium.

Final Declaration

The three Powers, the object of whose policy is the collective maintenance of peace within the framework of the League of Nations, find themselves in complete agreement in opposing, by all practicable means, any unilateral repudiation of treaties which may endanger the peace of Europe, and will act in close and cordial collaboration for this purpose.

TREATY of Mutual Assistance between France and the Union of Soviet Socialist Republics, Signed at Paris, May 2, 1935

Translation, in League of Nations, Treaty Series, 1936, p. 404

THE CENTRAL EXECUTIVE COMMITTEE OF
THE UNION OF SOVIET SOCIALIST REPUBLICS
and
THE PRESIDENT OF THE FRENCH REPUBLIC,

Being desirous of strengthening peace in Europe and of guaranteeing its benefits to their respective countries by securing a fuller and stricter application of those provisions of the Covenant of the League of Nations which are designed to maintain the national security, territorial integrity and political independence of States;

Determined to devote their efforts to the preparation and conclusion of a European agreement for that purpose, and in the meantime to promote, as far as lies in their power, the effective application of the provisions of the Covenant of the League of Nations;

Have resolved to conclude a Treaty to this end and have appointed as their Plenipotentiaries:

[Here follow the names of the plenipotentiaries.]

Who, having exchanged their full powers, found in good and due form, have agreed upon the following provisions:

ARTICLE 1

In the event of France or the Union of Soviet Socialist Republics being threatened with or in danger of aggression on the part of any European State, the Union of Soviet Socialist Republics and reciprocally France undertake mutually to proceed to an immediate consultation as regards the measures to be taken for the observance of the provisions of Article 10 of the Covenant of the League of Nations.

ARTICLE 2

Should, in the circumstances specified in Article 15, paragraph 7, of the Covenant of the League of Nations, France or the Union of Soviet Socialist Republics be the object, notwithstanding the sincerely peaceful intentions of both countries, of an unprovoked aggression on the part of a European State, the Union of Soviet Socialist Republics and reciprocally France shall immediately come to each other's aid and assistance.

Article 3

In consideration of the fact that under Article 16 of the Covenant of the League of Nations any Member of the League which resorts to war in disregard of its covenants under Articles 12, 13 or 15 of the Covenant is *ipso facto* deemed to have committed an act of war against all other Members of the League, France and reciprocally the Union of Soviet Socialist Republics undertake, in the event of one of them being the object, in these conditions and notwithstanding the sincerely peaceful intentions of both countries, of an unprovoked aggression on the part of a European State, immediately to come to each other's aid and assistance in application of Article 16 of the Covenant.

The same obligation is assumed in the event of France or the Union of Soviet Socialist Republics being the object of an aggression on the part of a European State in the circumstances specified in Article 17, paragraphs 1 and 3, of the Covenant of the League of Nations.

Article 4

The undertakings stipulated above being consonant with the obligations of the High Contracting Parties as Members of the League of Nations, nothing in the present Treaty shall be interpreted as restricting the duty of the latter to take any action that may be deemed wise and effectual to safeguard the peace of the world or as restricting the obligations resulting for the High Contracting Parties from the Covenant of the League of Nations.

Article 5

The present Treaty, both the French and the Russian texts whereof shall be equally authentic, shall be ratified and the instruments of ratification shall be exchanged at Moscow as soon as possible. It shall be registered with the Secretariat of the League of Nations.

It shall take effect as soon as the ratifications have been exchanged and shall remain in force for five years. If it is not denounced by either of the High Contracting Parties giving notice thereof at least one year before the expiry of that period, it shall remain in force indefinitely, each of the High Contracting Parties being at liberty to terminate it at a year's notice by a declaration to that effect.

In faith whereof the Plenipotentiaries have signed the present Treaty and have thereto affixed their seals.

Done at Paris, in duplicate, this 2nd day of May, 1935.

(L. S.) (Signed) V. POTEMKINE.
(L. S.) (Signed) PIERRE LAVAL.

Protocol of Signature

Upon proceeding to the signature of the Franco-Soviet Treaty of Mutual Assistance of to-day's date, the Plenipotentiaries have signed the following Protocol, which shall be included in the exchange of ratifications of the Treaty.

I

It is agreed that the effect of Article 3 is to oblige each Contracting Party immediately to come to the assistance of the other by immediately complying with the recommendations of the Council of the League of Nations as soon as they have been issued in virtue of Article 16 of the Covenant. It is further agreed that the two Contracting Parties will act in concert to ensure that the Council shall issue the said recommendations with all the speed required by the circumstances and that, should the Council nevertheless, for whatever reason, issue no recommendation or fail to reach a unanimous decision, effect shall none the less be given to the obligation to render assistance. It is also agreed that the undertakings to render assistance mentioned in the present Treaty refer only to the case of an aggression committed against either Contracting Party's own territory.

II

It being the common intention of the two Governments in no way to contradict, by the present Treaty, undertakings previously assumed towards third States by France and by the Union of Soviet Socialist Republics in virtue of published treaties, it is agreed that effect shall not be given to the provisions of the said Treaty in a manner which, being incompatible with treaty obligations assumed by one of the Contracting Parties, would expose that Party to sanctions of an international character.

III

The two Governments, deeming it desirable that a regional agreement should be concluded aiming at organising security between Contracting States, and which might moreover embody or be accompanied by pledges of mutual assistance, recognise their right to become parties by mutual consent, should occasion arise, to similar agreements in any form, direct or indirect, that may seem appropriate, the obligations under these various agreements to take the place of those assumed under the present Treaty.

IV

The two Governments place on record the fact that the negotiations which have resulted in the signature of the present Treaty were originally undertaken with a view to supplementing a Security Agreement embracing the countries of North-Eastern Europe, namely, the Union of Soviet Socialist Republics, Germany, Czechoslovakia, Poland and the Baltic States which are neighbours of the Union of Soviet Socialist Republics; in addition to that Agreement, there was to have been concluded a Treaty of Assistance between the Union of Soviet Socialist Republics, France and Germany, by which each of those three States was to have undertaken to come to the assistance of any one of them which might be the object of aggression on the part of any other of those three States. Although circumstances have not hitherto permitted of the conclusion of those Agreements, which both Parties continue to regard as desirable, it is none the less the case that the undertakings stipulated in the Franco-Soviet Treaty of Assistance are to be understood as intended to apply only within the limits contemplated in the three-party Agreement previously planned. Independently of the obligations assumed under the present Treaty, it is further recalled that, in accordance with the Franco-Soviet Pact of Non-Aggression signed on November 29th, 1932, and moreover, without affecting the universal character of the undertakings assumed in that Pact, in the event of either Party becoming the object of aggression by one or more third European Powers not referred to in the above-mentioned three-party Agreement, the other Contracting Party is bound to abstain, during the period of the conflict, from giving any aid or assistance, either direct or indirect, to the aggressor or aggressors, each Party declaring further that it is not bound by any Assistance Agreement which would be contrary to this undertaking.

Done at Paris, this 2nd day of May, 1935.

(Signed) V. POTEMKINE.
(Signed) PIERRE LAVAL.

DECLARATION by the British and Italian Governments Regarding the Mediterranean, January 2, 1937

British White Paper, Cmd. 5348

His Majesty's Government in the United Kingdom and the Italian Government:

Animated by the desire to contribute increasingly, in the interests of the general cause of peace and security, to the betterment of relations between them and between all the Mediterranean Powers, and resolved to respect the rights and interests of those Powers;

Recognise that the freedom of entry into, exit from, and transit through, the Mediterranean is a vital interest both to the different parts of the British Empire and to Italy, and that these interests are in no way inconsistent with each other;

Disclaim any desire to modify or, so far as they are concerned, to see modified the *status quo* as regards national sovereignty of territories in the Mediterranean area;

Undertake to respect each other's rights and interests in the said area;

Agree to use their best endeavours to discourage any activities liable to impair the good relations which it is the object of the present declaration to consolidate.

This declaration is designed to further the end of peace and is not directed against any other Power.

                            Eric Drummond.   G. Ciano.

Rome, January 2, 1937

THE NYON ARRANGEMENT between Great Britain, Bulgaria, Egypt, France, Greece, Rumania, Turkey, the Union of Soviet Socialist Republics, and Yugoslavia, Signed at Nyon, September 14, 1937

League of Nations, Treaty Series, 1937–1938, p. 137

Whereas arising out of the Spanish conflict attacks have been repeatedly committed in the Mediterranean by submarines against merchant ships not belonging to either of the conflicting Spanish parties; and

Whereas these attacks are violations of the rules of international law

OTHER AGREEMENTS

referred to in Part IV of the Treaty of London of April 22nd, 1930, with regard to the sinking of merchant ships and constitute acts contrary to the most elementary dictates of humanity, which should be justly treated as acts of piracy; and

Whereas without in any way admitting the right of either party to the conflict in Spain to exercise belligerent rights or to interfere with merchant ships on the high seas even if the laws of warfare at sea are observed and without prejudice to the right of any Participating Power to take such action as may be proper to protect its merchant shipping from any kind of interference on the high seas or to the possibility of further collective measures being agreed upon subsequently, it is necessary in the first place to agree upon certain special collective measures against piratical acts by submarines:

In view thereof the undersigned, being authorised to this effect by their respective Governments, have met in conference at Nyon between the 9th and the 14th September 1937, and have agreed upon the following provisions which shall enter immediately into force:

I. The Participating Powers will instruct their naval forces to take the action indicated in paragraphs II and III below with a view to the protection of all merchant ships not belonging to either of the conflicting Spanish parties.

II. Any submarine which attacks such a ship in a manner contrary to the rules of international law referred to in the International Treaty for the Limitation and Reduction of Naval Armaments signed in London on April 22nd, 1930, and confirmed in the Protocol signed in London on November 6th, 1936, shall be counter-attacked and, if possible, destroyed.

III. The instruction mentioned in the preceding paragraph shall extend to any submarine encountered in the vicinity of a position where a ship not belonging to either of the conflicting Spanish parties has recently been attacked in violation of the rules referred to in the preceding paragraph in circumstances which give valid grounds for the belief that the submarine was guilty of the attack.

IV. In order to facilitate the putting into force of the above arrangements in a practical manner, the Participating Powers have agreed upon the following arrangements.

1. In the western Mediterranean and in the Malta Channel, with the exception of the Tyrrhenean Sea, which may form the subject of special arrangements, the British and French fleets will operate both on the high seas and in the territorial waters of the Participating Powers, in accordance with the division of the area agreed upon between the two Governments.

2. In the eastern Mediterranean,

(a) Each of the Participating Powers will operate in its own territorial waters;

(b) On the high seas, with the exception of the Adriatic Sea, the British and French fleets will operate up to the entrance to the Dardanelles, in those areas where there is reason to apprehend danger to shipping in accordance with the division of the area agreed upon between the two Governments. The other Participating Governments possessing a sea border on the Mediterranean undertake, within the limit of their resources, to furnish these fleets any assistance that may be asked for; in particular, they will permit them to take action in their territorial waters and to use such of their ports as they shall indicate.

3. It is further understood that the limits of the zones referred to in sub-paragraphs 1 and 2 above, and their allocation shall be subject at any time to revision by the Participating Powers in order to take account of any change in the situation.

V. The Participating Powers agree that, in order to simplify the operation of the above-mentioned measures, they will for their part restrict the use of their submarines in the Mediterranean in the following manner:

(a) Except as stated in (b) and (c) below, no submarine will be sent to sea within the Mediterranean.

(b) Submarines may proceed on passage after notification to the other Participating Powers, provided that they proceed on the surface and are accompanied by a surface ship.

(c) Each Participating Power reserves for purposes of exercises certain areas defined in Annex I hereto in which its submarines are exempt from the restrictions mentioned in (a) or (b).

The Participating Powers further undertake not to allow the presence in their respective territorial waters of any foreign submarines except in case of urgent distress, or where the conditions prescribed in sub-paragraph (b) above are fulfilled.

VI. The Participating Powers also agree that, in order to simplify the problem involved in carrying out the measures above described, they may severally advise their merchant shipping to follow certain main routes in the Mediterranean agreed upon between them and defined in Annex II hereto.

VII. Nothing in the present agreement restricts the right of any Participating Power to send its surface vessels to any part of the Mediterranean.

VIII. Nothing in the present agreement in any way prejudices existing international engagements which have been registered with the Secretariat of the League of Nations.

OTHER AGREEMENTS

IX. If any of the Participating Powers notifies its intention of withdrawing from the present Arrangement, the notification will take effect after the expiry of thirty days and any of the other Participating Powers may withdraw on the same date if it communicates its intention to this effect before that date.

Done at Nyon, this fourteenth day of September nineteen hundred and thirty-seven, in a single copy, in the English and French languages, both texts being equally authentic, and which will be deposited in the archives of the Secretariat of the League of Nations.

[Signatures]

AGREEMENT Supplementary to the Nyon Arrangement, between Great Britain, Bulgaria, Egypt, France, Greece, Rumania, Turkey, the Union of Soviet Socialist Republics, and Yugoslavia, Signed at Geneva, September 17, 1937

League of Nations, Treaty Series, 1937-1938, p. 151

WHEREAS under the Arrangement signed at Nyon on the 14th September, 1937, whereby certain collective measures were agreed upon relating to piratical acts by submarines in the Mediterranean, the Participating Powers reserved the possibility of taking further collective measures; and

Whereas it is now considered expedient that such measures should be taken against similar acts by surface vessels and aircraft;

In view thereof, the undersigned, being authorised to this effect by their respective Governments, have met in conference at Geneva on the seventeenth day of September and have agreed upon the following provisions which shall enter immediately into force:

I. The present Agreement is supplementary to the Nyon Arrangement and shall be regarded as an integral part thereof.

II. The present Agreement applies to any attack by a surface vessel or an aircraft upon any merchant vessel in the Mediterranean not belonging to either of the conflicting Spanish parties, when such attack is accompanied by a violation of the humanitarian principles embodied in the rules of international law with regard to warfare at sea, which are referred to in Part IV of the Treaty of London of April 22nd, 1930, and confirmed in the Protocol signed in London on November 6th, 1936.

II. Any surface war vessel, engaged in the protection of merchant shipping in conformity with the Nyon Arrangement, which witnesses an attack of the kind referred to in the preceding paragraph shall:

(a) If the attack is committed by an aircraft, open fire on the aircraft;

(b) If the attack is committed by a surface vessel, intervene to resist it within the limits of its powers, summoning assistance if such is available and necessary.

In territorial waters each of the Participating Powers concerned will give instructions as to the action to be taken by its own war vessels in the spirit of the present Agreement.

Done at Geneva, this seventeenth day of September 1937, in the English and French languages, both texts being equally authentic, in a single copy which will be deposited in the archives of the Secretariat of the League of Nations.

[Signatures]

REPORT Adopted by the Conference of Brussels, November 24, 1937, and Declaration of the Conference of the Same Date

Department of State, *Press Releases*, November 27, 1937, p. 396; for action by the League of Nations, *see supra*, pp. 919-935 and 954-960

THE CONFERENCE at Brussels was assembled pursuant to an invitation extended by the Belgian Government at the request of His Majesty's Government in the United Kingdom with the approval of the American Government. It held its opening session on November 3, 1937. The Conference has now reached a point at which it appears desirable to record the essential phases of its work.

In the winter of 1921-22 there were signed at Washington a group of inter related treaties and agreements of which the Nine Power Treaty regarding principles and policies to be followed in matters concerning China constituted one of the most important units. These treaties and agreements were the result of careful deliberation and were entered into freely. They were designed primarily to bring about conditions of stability and security in the Pacific area.

The Nine Power Treaty stipulates in Article one that

The Contracting Powers, other than China, agree:

(1) To respect the sovereignty, the independence, and the territorial and administrative integrity of China;

(2) To provide the fullest and most unembarrassed opportunity to China to develop and maintain for herself an effective and stable government;

(3) To use their influence for the purpose of effectually establishing and

OTHER AGREEMENTS

maintaining the principle of equal opportunity for the commerce and industry of all nations throughout the territory of China;

(4) To refrain from taking advantage of conditions in China in order to seek special rights or privileges which would abridge the rights of subjects or citizens of friendly States, and from countenancing action inimical to the security of such States.

Under and in the light of these undertakings and of the provisions contained in the other treaties, the situation in the Pacific area was for a decade characterized by a substantial measure of stability, with considerable progress towards the other objectives envisaged in the treaties. In recent years there have come a series of conflicts between Japan and China, and these conflicts have culminated in the hostilities now in progress.

The Conference at Brussels was called for the purpose, as set forth in the terms of the invitation, "of examining in conformity with Article seven of that treaty, the situation in the Far East and of studying peaceable means of hastening an end of the regrettable conflict which prevails there." With the exception of Japan, all of the signatories and adherents to the Nine Power Treaty of February 6, 1922 accepted the invitation and sent representatives to Brussels for the purpose stated in the invitation.

The Chinese Government, attending the Conference and participating in its deliberations, has communicated with the other parties to the Nine Power Treaty in conformity with Article 7 of that treaty. It has stated here that its present military operations are purely in resistance to armed invasion of China by Japan. It has declared its willingness to accept a peace based upon the principles of the Nine Power Treaty and to collaborate wholeheartedly with the other powers in support of the principle of the sanctity of treaties.

The Japanese Government in replying with regret that it was not able to accept the invitation to the Conference affirmed that "the action of Japan in China is a measure of self defense which she has been compelled to take in the face of China's fierce anti-Japanese policy and practice and especially by her provocative action in resorting to force of arms; and consequently it lies, as has been declared already by the Imperial Government, outside the purview of the Nine Power Treaty"; and advanced the view that an attempt to seek a solution at a gathering of so many powers "would only serve to complicate the situation still further and to put serious obstacles in the path of a just and proper solution."

On November 7, 1937 the Conference sent through the Belgian Government to the Japanese Government a communication in the course of which the Conference inquired whether the Japanese Government would be willing to depute a representative or representatives to exchange views with representatives of a small number of powers to be chosen for that purpose, the exchange of views to take place within the framework of the Nine Power Treaty and in conformity with the provisions of that treaty, toward throwing further light on points of difference and facilitating a settlement of the Sino-Japanese conflict. In that communication the representatives of the states met at Brussels, expressed their earnest desire that peaceful settlement be achieved.

To that communication the Japanese Government replied in a communication of November 12, 1937 stating that it could not do otherwise than maintain its previously expressed point of view that the present action of Japan in her relations with China was a measure of self defense and did not come within the scope of the Nine Power Treaty; that only an effort between the two parties would constitute a means of securing the most just and the most equitable settlement, and that the intervention of a collective organ such as the Conference would merely excite public opinion in the two countries and make it more difficult to reach a solution satisfactory to all.

On November 15 the Conference adopted a declaration in the course of which it affirmed that the representatives of the Union of South Africa, the United States of America, Australia, Belgium, Bolivia, Canada, China, France, the United Kingdom, India, Mexico, Netherlands, New Zealand, Portugal, and the Union of Socialist Soviet Republics ". . . consider this conflict of concern in fact to all countries party to the Nine Power Treaty of Washington of 1922 and to all countries party to the Pact of Paris of 1928 and of concern in fact to all countries members of the family of nations."

In the presence of this difference between the views of the Conference and of the Japanese Government there now appears to be no opportunity at this time for the Conference to carry out its terms of reference insofar as they relate to entering into discussions with Japan towards bringing about peace by agreement. The Conference therefore is concluding this phase of its work and at this moment of going into recess adopts a further declaration of its views.

The text of the communication sent to the Japanese Government on November 7, 1937 reads as follows:

> The representatives of the states met in Brussels on November 3, last, have taken cognizance of the reply which the Japanese Government sent in of October 27 to the invitation of the Belgian Government, and the statement which accompanied this reply.
>
> In these documents the Imperial Government states that it cherishes no territorial ambitions in respect of China and that on the contrary it sin-

OTHER AGREEMENTS

cerely desires "to assist in the material and moral development of the Chinese nation," that it also desires "to promote cultural and economic cooperation" with the foreign powers in China and that it intends furthermore scrupulously "to respect foreign rights and interest in that country."

The points referred to in this declaration are among the fundamental principles of the Treaty of Washington of February 6, 1922 (The Nine Power Treaty). The representatives of the states parties to this treaty have taken note of the declarations of the Imperial Government in this respect.

The Imperial Government moreover denies that there can be any question of a violation of the Nine Power Treaty by Japan and it formulates a number of complaints against the Chinese Government. The Chinese Government for its part contends that there has been violation, denies the charges of the Japanese Government and, in turn, makes complaint against Japan.

The treaty has made provision for just such a situation. It should be borne in mind that the exchange of views taking place in Brussels is based essentially on these provisions and constitutes "full and frank communication" as envisaged in Article VII. This Conference is being held with a view to assisting in the resolving by peaceful means of a conflict between parties to the treaty.

One of the parties to the present conflict, China, is represented at the Conference and has affirmed its willingness fully to cooperate in its work.

The Conference regrets the absence of the other party, Japan, whose cooperation is most desirable.

The Imperial Government states that it is "firmly convinced that an attempt to seek a solution at a gathering of so many powers whose interests in East Asia are of varying degree, or who have practically no interests there at all, will only serve to complicate the situation still further and to put serious obstacles in the path of a just and proper solution."

It should be pointed out that all of these powers which are parties to the treaty are, under the terms of this instrument, entitled to exercise the rights which the treaty confers upon them; that all powers which have interests in the Far East are concerned regarding the present hostilities; and that the whole world is solicitous with regard to the effect of these hostilities on the peace and security of the members of the family of nations.

However, the representatives of the states met at Brussels believe that it may be possible to allay Japan's misgivings referred to above; they would be glad to know whether the Imperial Government would be disposed to depute a representative or representatives to exchange views with representatives of a small number of powers to be chosen for that purpose. Such an exchange of views would take place within the framework of the Nine Power Treaty and in conformity with the provisions of that treaty. Its aims would be to throw further light on the various points referred to above and to facilitate a settlement of the conflict. Regretting the continuation of hostilities, being firmly convinced that a peaceful settlement is alone capable of insuring a lasting and constructive solution of the present conflict, and having confidence in the efficacy of methods of conciliation, the representatives of the states met at Brussels earnestly desire that such a settlement may be achieved.

The states represented at the Conference would be very glad to know as soon as possible the attitude of the Imperial Government towards this proposal.

The text of the declaration adopted by the Conference on November 15, 1937 reads as follows: [Text follows here].

The text of the declaration adopted by the Conference November 24, 1937 reads as follows:

THE NINE POWER TREATY is a conspicuous example of numerous international instruments by which the nations of the world enunciate certain principles and accept certain self denunciatory rules in their conduct with each other solemnly undertaking to respect the sovereignty of other nations, to refrain from seeking political or economic domination of other nations, and to abstain from interference in their internal affairs.

These international instruments constitute a framework within which international security and international peace are intended to be safeguarded without resort to arms and within which international relationships should subsist on the basis of mutual trust, good will and beneficial trade and financial relations.

It must be recognized that whenever armed force is employed in disregard of these principles the whole structure of international relations based upon the safeguards provided by treaties is disturbed. Nations are then compelled to seek security in ever increasing armaments. There is created everywhere a feeling of uncertainty and insecurity. The validity of these principles cannot be destroyed by force, their universal applicability cannot be denied and indispensability to civilization and progress cannot be gainsaid.

It was in accordance with these principles that this Conference was called in Brussels for the purpose, as set forth in the terms of the invitation issued by the Belgian Government "of examining in conformity with article seven of the Nine Power Treaty, the situation in the Far East and of studying peaceable means of hastening an end of the regrettable conflict which prevails there."

Since its opening session on November 3rd the Conference has continuously striven to promote conciliation and has endeavored to secure the cooperation of the Japanese Government in the hope of arresting hostilities and bringing about a settlement.

The Conference is convinced that force can provide not just and lasting solution for disputes between nations. It continues to believe that it would be to the immediate and the ultimate interest of both parties to the present dispute to avail themselves of the assistance of others in an effort to bring hostilities to an early end as a necessary preliminary to the achievement of a general and lasting settlement. It further believes that a satisfactory settlement cannot be achieved by direct negotiation between the parties to the conflict alone and that only by consultation with other powers principally concerned can there be achieved an agreement the terms of which will be just, generally acceptable and likely to endure.

This Conference strongly reaffirms the principles of the Nine Power Treaty as being among the basic principles which are essential to world peace and orderly progressive development of national and international life.

The Conference believes that a prompt suspension of hostilities in the Far East would be in the best interests not only of China and Japan but of all nations. With each day's continuance of the conflict the loss in lives and property increases and the ultimate solution of the conflict becomes more difficult.

The Conference therefore strongly urges that hostilities be suspended and resort be had to peaceful processes.

The Conference believes that no possible step to bring about by peaceful processes a just settlement of the conflict should be overlooked or omitted.

In order to allow time for participating governments to exchange views and further explore all peaceful methods by which a just settlement of the dispute may be attained consistently with the principles of the Nine Power Treaty and in conformity with the objectives of that treaty the Conference deems it advisable temporarily to suspend its sittings. The conflict in the Far East remains, however, a matter of concern to all of the powers assembled at Brussels—by virtue of commitments in the Nine Power Treaty or of special interest in the Far East—and especially to those most immediately and directly affected by conditions and events in the Far East. Those of them that are parties to the Nine Power Treaty have expressly adopted a policy designed to stabilize conditions in the Far East and, to that end, are bound by the provisions of that treaty, outstanding among which are those of articles 1 and 7.

The Conference will be called together again whenever its chairman or any two of its members shall have reported that they consider that its deliberations can be advantageously resumed.

AGREEMENT between Great Britain and Italy, Signed at Rome, April 16, 1938

The agreement consisted of a protocol with annexes, as indicated, several exchanges of notes, and a *Bon Voisinage* agreement. Royal Institute of International Affairs, *Documents on International Affairs, 1938*, I, 141, citing British White Paper, Cmd. 5726

PROTOCOL

THE GOVERNMENT of the United Kingdom of Great Britain and Northern Ireland and the Italian Government, animated by the desire to place the relations between the two countries on a solid and lasting basis and to contribute to the general cause of peace and security, have decided to undertake conversations in order to reach agreement on questions of mutual concern;

And the said conversations having taken place;

His Excellency the Right Honorable the Earl of Perth, G.C.M.G., C.B., His Majesty's Ambassador Extraordinary and Plenipotentiary at Rome, and

His Excellency Count Galeazzo Ciano di Cortellazzo, Minister for Foreign Affairs,

duly authorized for that purpose by their respective Governments, have drawn up the present Protocol and have signed the Agreements and Declarations annexed hereto, each of which shall be regarded as a separate and self-contained instrument:—

(1) Reaffirmation of the Declaration of the 2nd January, 1937, regarding the Mediterranean, and of the Notes exchanged on the 31st December 1936;
(2) Agreement regarding the Exchange of Military Information;
(3) Agreement regarding certain Areas in the Middle East;
(4) Declaration regarding Propaganda;
(5) Declaration regarding Lake Tsana;
(6) Declaration regarding the Military Duties of Natives of Italian East Africa;
(7) Declaration regarding the free Exercise of Religion and the Treatment of British religious Bodies in Italian East Africa;
(8) Declaration regarding the Suez Canal.

The said instruments shall take effect on such date as the two Governments shall together determine. Except in so far as any of them contain provisions with regard to their revision or duration, each of the said instruments shall remain in force indefinitely, but should either Government at any time consider that a change of circumstances renders the revision of any of these instruments necessary, the two Governments will consult together with a view to such a revision.

The two Governments agree that, immediately after the taking effect of the said instruments, negotiations will be opened, in which the Egyptian Government will be invited to participate so far as all questions affecting Egypt or the Anglo-Egyptian Sudan are concerned, with a view to a definitive agreement on the boundaries between the Sudan, Kenya and British Somaliland on the one side and Italian East Africa on the other; and with regard to other questions affecting reciprocally (a) Italian interests on the one hand and British, Egyptian or Sudan interests on the other hand in the above-mentioned territories, and (b) the relations between those territories.

These negotiations will also include the question of commercial relations between the Sudan and Italian East Africa.

It is also agreed that negotiations between the Government of the United Kingdom and the Italian Government will take place as soon as possible on the subject of commercial relations between Italian East Africa and the United Kingdom, India, and British colonies, overseas territories, protectorates and mandated territories administered by the Government of the United Kingdom, including the subject of the application, on conditions to be established, to the whole of Italian East Africa of the Treaty of Commerce and Navigation signed at Rome on the 15th June, 1883. These negotiations will be inspired by the common desire to further commercial relations between these territories and to ensure adequate facilities for trade.

Done at Rome, in duplicate, the 16th April, 1938, in the English and Italian languages, both of which shall have equal force.

(Signed) PERTH   CIANO

PROPOSALS Presented by the French and British Governments to the Czechoslovakian Government, September 19, 1938

British White Paper, Cmd. 5847, p. 8

THE REPRESENTATIVES of the French and British Governments have been in consultation to-day on the general situation, and have considered the British Prime Minister's report of his conversation with Herr Hitler. British Ministers also placed before their French colleagues their conclusions derived from the account furnished to them of the work of his Mission by Lord Runciman. We are both convinced that, after recent events, the point has now been reached where the further maintenance within the boundaries of the Czechoslovak State of the districts mainly inhabited by Sudeten Deutsch cannot, in fact, continue any longer without imperilling the interests of Czechoslovakia herself and of European peace. In the light of these considerations, both Governments have been compelled to the conclusion that the maintenance of peace and the safety of Czechoslovakia's vital interests cannot effectively be assured unless these areas are now transferred to the Reich.

2. This could be done either by direct transfer or as the result of a plebiscite. We realise the difficulties involved in a plebiscite, and

we are aware of your objections already expressed to this course, particularly the possibility of far-reaching repercussions if the matter were treated on the basis of so wide a principle. For this reason we anticipate, in the absence of indication to the contrary, that you may prefer to deal with the Sudeten Deutsch problem by the method of direct transfer, and as a case by itself.

3. The area for transfer would probably have to include areas with over 50 per cent. of German inhabitants, but we should hope to arrange by negotiations provisions for adjustment of frontiers, where circumstances render it necessary, by some international body, including a Czech representative. We are satisfied that the transfer of smaller areas based on a higher percentage would not meet the case.

4. The international body referred to might also be charged with questions of possible exchange of population on the basis of right to opt within some specified time-limit.

5. We recognise that, if the Czechoslovak Government is prepared to concur in the measures proposed, involving material changes in the conditions of the State, they are entitled to ask for some assurance of their future security.

6. Accordingly, His Majesty's Government in the United Kingdom would be prepared, as a contribution to the pacification of Europe, to join in an international guarantee of the new boundaries of the Czechoslovak State against unprovoked aggression. One of the principal conditions of such a guarantee would be the safeguarding of the independence of Czechoslovakia by the substitution of a general guarantee against unprovoked aggression in place of existing treaties which involve reciprocal obligations of a military character.

7. Both the French and British Governments recognise how great is the sacrifice thus required of the Czechoslovak Government in the cause of peace. But because that cause is common both to Europe in general and in particular to Czechoslovakia herself they have felt it their duty jointly to set forth frankly the conditions essential to secure it.

8. The Prime Minister must resume conversations with Herr Hitler not later than Wednesday, and earlier if possible. We therefore feel we must ask for your reply at the earliest possible moment.

AGREEMENTS between Germany, Great Britain, France, and Italy, Signed at Munich, September 29, 1938

British White Paper, Cmd. 5848

GERMANY, the United Kingdom, France and Italy, taking into consideration the agreement, which has been already reached in principle for the cession to Germany of the Sudeten German territory, have agreed on the following terms and conditions governing the said cession and the measures consequent thereon, and by this agreement they each hold themselves responsible for the steps necessary to secure its fulfilment:—

1. The evacuation will begin on the 1st October.
2. The United Kingdom, France and Italy agree that the evacuation of the territory shall be completed by the 10th October, without any existing installations having been destroyed and that the Czechoslovak Government will be held responsible for carrying out the evacuation without damage to the said installations.
3. The conditions governing the evacuation will be laid down in detail by an international commission composed of representatives of Germany, the United Kingdom, France, Italy and Czechoslovakia.
4. The occupation by stages of the predominantly German territory by German troops will begin on the 1st October. The four territories marked on the attached map will be occupied by German troops in the following order: the territory marked No. I on the 1st and 2nd of October, the territory marked No. II on the 2nd and 3rd of October, the territory marked No. III on the 3rd, 4th and 5th of October, the territory marked IV on the 6th and 7th of October. The remaining territory of preponderantly German character will be ascertained by the aforesaid international commission forthwith and be occupied by German troops by the 10th of October.
5. The international commission referred to in paragraph 3 will determine the territories in which a plebiscite is to be held. These territories will be occupied by international bodies until the plebiscite has been completed. The same commission will fix the conditions in which the plebiscite is to be held, taking as a basis the conditions of the Saar plebiscite. The commission will also fix a date, not later than the end of November, on which the plebiscite will be held.
6. The final determination of the frontiers will be carried out by the international commission. This commission will also be entitled to recommend to the four Powers, Germany, the United Kingdom, France and Italy, in certain exceptional cases minor modifications in

the strictly ethnographical determination of the zones which are to be transferred without plebiscite.

7. There will be a right of option into and out of the transferred territories, the option to be exercised within six months from the date of this agreement. A German-Czechoslovak commission shall determine the details of the option, consider ways of facilitating the transfer of population and settle questions of principle arising out of the said transfer.

8. The Czechoslovak Government will within a period of four weeks from the date of this agreement release from their military and police forces any Sudeten Germans who may wish to be released, and the Czechoslovak Government will within the same period release Sudeten German prisoners who are serving terms of imprisonment for political offenses.

Munich, September 29, 1938.

ADOLF HITLER
NEVILLE CHAMBERLAIN
EDOUARD DALADIER
BENITO MUSSOLINI

ANNEX TO THE AGREEMENT

His Majesty's Government in the United Kingdom and the French Government have entered into the above agreement on the basis that they stand by the offer, contained in paragraph 6 of the Anglo-French proposals of the 19th September, relating to an international guarantee of the new boundaries of the Czechoslovak State against unprovoked aggression.

When the question of the Polish and Hungarian minorities in Czechoslovakia has been settled, Germany and Italy for their part will give a guarantee to Czechoslovakia.

Munich, September 29, 1938.

ADOLF HITLER
NEVILLE CHAMBERLAIN
EDOUARD DALADIER
BENITO MUSSOLINI

DECLARATION

The Heads of the Governments of the four Powers declare that the problems of the Polish and Hungarian minorities in Czechoslovakia, if not settled within three months by agreement between the respective Governments, shall form the subject of another meeting of

the Heads of the Governments of the four Powers here present.
Munich, September 29, 1938.

ADOLF HITLER
NEVILLE CHAMBERLAIN
EDOUARD DALADIER
BENITO MUSSOLINI

SUPPLEMENTARY DECLARATION

All questions which may arise out of the transfer of the territory shall be considered as coming within the terms of reference to the international commission.
Munich, September 29, 1938.

ADOLF HITLER
NEVILLE CHAMBERLAIN
EDOUARD DALADIER
BENITO MUSSOLINI

COMPOSITION OF THE INTERNATIONAL COMMISSION

The four Heads of Governments here present agree that the international commission provided for in the agreement signed by them today, shall consist of the Secretary of State in the German Foreign Office, the British, French and Italian Ambassadors accredited in Berlin, and a representative to be nominated by the Government of Czechoslovakia.
Munich, September 29, 1938.

ADOLF HITLER
NEVILLE CHAMBERLAIN
EDOUARD DALADIER
BENITO MUSSOLINI

JOINT COMMUNIQUÉ Issued by Adolf Hitler, Chancellor of Germany, and Neville Chamberlain, Prime Minister of Great Britain, at Munich, September 30, 1938

International Conciliation, November, 1938 (No. 344), p. 466, citing *The New York Times,* October 1, 1938

WE, the German Fuehrer and Chancellor and the British Prime Minister, have had a further meeting today and are agreed in recognizing the question of Anglo-German relations as of the first importance for the two countries and for Europe.

We regard the agreement signed last night and the Anglo-German naval agreement as symbolic of the desire of our two peoples never to go to war with one another again.

We are resolved that the method of consultation shall be the method adopted to deal with any other questions that may concern our two countries, and we are determined to continue our efforts to remove probable sources of difference and thus contribute to assure the peace of Europe.

DECLARATION by the French and German Governments, Signed at Paris, December 6, 1938

Translation, in *The French Yellow Book*, p. 35

M. GEORGES BONNET, Minister for Foreign Affairs of the French Republic and M. Joachim von Ribbentrop, Minister for Foreign Affairs of the German Reich,

Acting in the name and by order of their respective Governments, have agreed on the following points at their meeting in Paris on December 6, 1938:

(1) The French Government and the German Government fully share the conviction that pacific and neighborly relations between France and Germany constitute one of the essential elements of the consolidation of the situation in Europe and of the preservation of general peace. Consequently both Governments will endeavor with all their might to assure the development of the relations between their countries in this direction.

(2) Both Governments agree that no question of a territorial nature remains in suspense between their countries and solemnly recognize as permanent the frontier between their countries as it is actually drawn.

(3) Both Governments are resolved, without prejudice to their special relations with third Powers, to remain in contact on all questions of importance to both their countries and to have recourse to mutual consultation in case any complications arising out of these questions should threaten to lead to international difficulties.

In witness whereof the Representatives of the two Governments have signed the present Declaration, which comes into force immediately.

Executed in duplicate in the French and German languages at Paris, on December 6, 1938.

[*Signatures*]

OTHER AGREEMENTS

COMMUNIQUÉ Issued by the British and Polish Governments, April 6, 1939

The British War Blue Book, p. 49

THE CONVERSATIONS with M. Beck have covered a wide field and shown that the two Governments are in complete agreement upon certain general principles.

It was agreed that the two countries were prepared to enter into an agreement of a permanent and reciprocal character to replace the present temporary and unilateral assurance given by His Majesty's Government to the Polish Government. Pending the completion of the permanent agreement, M. Beck gave His Majesty's Government an assurance that the Polish Government would consider themselves under an obligation to render assistance to His Majesty's Government under the same conditions as those contained in the temporary assurance already given by His Majesty's Government to Poland.

Like the temporary assurance, the permanent agreement would not be directed against any other country but would be designed to assure Great Britain and Poland of mutual assistance in the event of any threat, direct or indirect, to the independence of either. It was recognized that certain matters, including a more precise definition of the various ways in which the necessity for such assistance might arise, would require further examination before the permanent agreement could be completed.

It was understood that the arrangements above mentioned should not preclude either Government from making agreements with other countries in the general interest of the consolidation of peace.

TREATY of Non-Aggression between Germany and the Union of Soviet Socialist Republics, Signed at Moscow, August 23, 1939 (translation)

Department of State, *Bulletin*, August 26, 1939, p. 172

THE GOVERNMENTS OF the German Reich and the Union of Soviet Socialist Republics directed by the wish to strengthen the cause of peace between Germany and the Union of Soviet Socialist Republics and proceeding upon the basic provisions of the treaty of neutrality concluded between Germany and the Union of Soviet Socialist Republics in April 1926 have reached the following agreement:

Article I

The two contracting parties undertake to refrain from any act of violence, any aggressive action or any attack against one another whether individually or jointly with other powers.

Article II

In case one of the contracting parties should become the object of war-like acts on the part of a third power the other contracting party will not support that third power in any form.

Article III

The Governments of the two contracting parties will in future remain in contact with each other through continuous consultations in order to inform each other concerning questions affecting their mutual interests.

Article IV

Neither of the two contracting parties will participate in any grouping of powers which is indirectly or directly aimed against the other party.

Article V

Should disputes or conflicts arise between the contracting parties regarding questions of any kind whatsoever, the two parties would clear away these disputes or conflicts solely by means of friendly exchanges of views or if necessary, by arbitration commissions.

Article VI

The present treaty is concluded for a period of ten years with the provision that unless one of the contracting parties denounces it one year before the end of this period the duration of the validity of this treaty is to be regarded as automatically prolonged for another five years.

Article VII

The present treaty is to be ratified within the shortest possible time. The documents of ratification are to be exchanged in Berlin. The treaty becomes effective immediately upon signature.

Drawn up in duplicate texts in the German and Russian languages.

Moscow, August 23, 1939.

RIBBENTROP
MOLOTOV

AGREEMENT of Mutual Assistance between Great Britain and Poland, August 25, 1939

The British War Blue Book, p. 49

THE GOVERNMENT OF the United Kingdom of Great Britain and Northern Ireland and the Polish Government:

Desiring to place on a permanent basis the collaboration between their respective countries resulting from the assurances of mutual assistance of a defensive character which they have already exchanged:

Have resolved to conclude an Agreement for that purpose and have appointed as their Plenipotentiaries:

The Government of the United Kingdom of Great Britain and Northern Ireland:

The Rt. Hon. Viscount Halifax, K.G., G.C.S.I., G.C.I.E., Principal Secretary of State for Foreign Affairs;

The Polish Government:

His Excellency Count Edward Raczyński, Ambassador Extraordinary and Plenipotentiary of the Polish Republic in London;

Who, having exchanged their Full Powers, found in good and due form, have agreed on the following provisions:—

Article 1

Should one of the Contracting Parties become engaged in hostilities with a European Power in consequence of aggression by the latter against that Contracting Party, the other Contracting Party will at once give the Contracting Party engaged in hostilities all the support and assistance in its power.

Article 2

(1) The provisions of Article 1 will also apply in the event of any action by a European Power which clearly threatened, directly or indirectly, the independence of one of the Contracting Parties, and was of such a nature that the Party in question considered it vital to resist it with its armed forces.

(2) Should one of the Contracting Parties become engaged in hostilities with a European Power in consequence of action by that Power which threatened the independence or neutrality of another European State in such a way as to constitute a clear menace to the security of that Contracting Party, the provisions of Article 1 will apply, without prejudice, however, to the rights of the other European State concerned.

Article 3

Should a European Power attempt to undermine the independence of one of the Contracting Parties by processes of economic penetration or in any other way, the Contracting Parties will support each other in resistance to such attempts. Should the European Power concerned thereupon embark on hostilities against one of the Contracting Parties, the provisions of Article 1 will apply.

Article 4

The methods of applying the undertakings of mutual assistance provided for by the present Agreement are established between the competent naval, military and air authorities of the Contracting Parties.

Article 5

Without prejudice to the foregoing undertakings of the Contracting Parties to give each other mutual support and assistance immediately on the outbreak of hostilities, they will exchange complete and speedy information concerning any development which might threaten their independence and, in particular, concerning any development which threatened to call the said undertakings into operation.

Article 6

(1) The Contracting Parties will communicate to each other the terms of any undertakings of assistance against aggression which they have already given or may in future give to other States.

(2) Should either of the Contracting Parties intend to give such an undertaking after the coming into force of the present Agreement, the other Contracting Party shall, in order to ensure the proper functioning of the Agreement, be informed thereof.

(3) Any new undertaking which the Contracting Parties may enter into in future shall neither limit their obligations under the present Agreement nor indirectly create new obligations between the Contracting Party not participating in these undertakings and the third State concerned.

Article 7

Should the Contracting Parties be engaged in hostilities in consequence of the application of the present Agreement, they will not conclude an armistice or treaty of peace except by mutual agreement.

Article 8

(1) The present Agreement shall remain in force for a period of five years.

(2) Unless denounced six months before the expiry of their period it shall continue in force, each Contracting Party having thereafter the right to denounce it at any time by giving six months' notice to that effect.

(3) The present Agreement shall come into force on signature.

In faith whereof the above-named Plenipotentiaries have signed the present Agreement and have affixed thereto their seals.

Done in English in duplicate, at London, the 25th August, 1939. A Polish text shall subsequently be agreed upon between the Contracting Parties and both texts will then be authentic.

(L.S.) HALIFAX.
(L.S.) EDWARD RACZYŃSKI.

AGREEMENTS between Germany and the Union of Soviet Socialist Republics, Signed at Moscow, September 28, 1939

Translation, in *The New York Times*, September 29, 1939

FRONTIER AND FRIENDSHIP AGREEMENT

THE German Reich Government and the Government of Soviet Russia, after the disintegration of the former Polish State, consider it their task to restore in this region law and order and to insure nationals living there an existence corresponding to their national character. With this aim in view they have agreed as follows:

Article I

The German Reich Government and the Government of the Soviet Republics lay down as the frontier of their respective spheres of interests in the region of the former Polish State the line which is drawn on the attached map and which will be described in detail in a supplementary protocol.

Article II

Both parties recognize the frontier laid down in Article I of the interest spheres of both States as definite and will decline interference of any kind by a third power with this settlement.

Article III

The necessary new political regulation is undertaken by the German Reich Government in districts west of the line laid down in Article I and by the Government of the Soviet Republic in districts east of this line.

Article IV

The German Reich Government and the Government of the Soviet Republic regard the before-mentioned settlement as a foundation for progressing development of friendly relations between their peoples.

Article V

This treaty will be ratified, and ratification documents will be exchanged in Berlin as soon as possible. The agreement comes into force on the day of its signature.

VON RIBBENTROP
MOLOTOFF

PROTOCOL STATEMENT

The following statement by the German Reich Government and the Government of the Soviet Russian Republic of Sept. 28, 1939, is attached to the protocol:

After the German Reich Government and the Government of the Soviet Russian Republic have definitely settled by the treaty signed today the question resulting from disintegration of the Polish State, thus creating a safe foundation for lasting peace in Eastern Europe, they unanimously express the opinion that it would correspond to the true interests of all peoples and make an end to the war existing between Germany on the one hand and England and France on the other hand. Therefore, both governments, if necessary in conjunction with one of the befriended nations, will direct their joint efforts toward searching this aim as soon as possible. But should the efforts of both governments fail, then the fact would be established that England and France are responsible for continuation of the war, and in case of continuation of the war the Governments of Germany and Soviet Russia will consult each other regarding the necessary measures.

Sept. 28, 1939.

VON RIBBENTROP.
MOLOTOFF.

Supplementary Protocol

The frontier line begins at the southern point of Lithuania, running from there in a generally western direction north of Augustow to the German Reich's frontier.

It follows the Reich's frontier to the River Pisa. From there, following the course of the River Pisa to Ostroleka, it then runs southeast until reaching the River Bug near the River Nurec.

Following the route River Bug to Krystynopol, it then turns westward, running north of Rawa Ruska and Lubaczow to the River Sabuop. From here it follows the course of the River San to its head.

Letter from Mr. Vyacheslav M. Molotov, President of the Council of People's Commissars and Commissar for Foreign Affairs, to Herr Joachim von Ribbentrop, Minister for Foreign Affairs of Germany

Referring to our conversations, I have the honor to confirm that the Soviet Russian Government, based on the general political understanding reached and in this spirit, is ready to develop with all means economic relations and exchange of goods between Germany and Soviet Russia.

With this aim in view, an economic program will be drafted according to which the Soviet Union supplies Germany with materials for which Germany will compensate her by industrial supplies stretched over a long time. Both partners will see that this economic program is carried out in such a manner that the German-Soviet Russian exchange of goods, as regards volume, again reaches the maximum level of the past.

For carrying out the pending measures, both governments will take the necessary steps immediately and see that the negotiations shall be begun as speedily as possible and be concluded.

AGREEMENTS between the Union of Soviet Socialist Republics and Japan, Signed at Moscow, April 13, 1941

Translation, in *The New York Times,* April 14, 1941. Reprinted by permission of the Associated Press

Neutrality Pact

THE PRESIDIUM of the Supreme Soviet of the U.S.S.R. and His Majesty the Emperor of Japan, guided by a desire to strengthen peaceful and friendly relations between the two countries, decided to conclude a pact on neutrality, for the purpose of which they appointed as their representatives:

For the Presidium of the Supreme Soviet of the U.S.S.R., Vyacheslaff Molotoff, Chairman of the Council of People's Commissars and People's Commissar for Foreign Affairs.

For His Majesty the Emperor of Japan, Yosuke Matsuoka, Minister of Foreign Affairs, Ju San Min, Cavalier of the Order of the Sacred Treasure, First Class; and Yoshitsugu Tatekawa, Ambassador Extraordinary and Plenipotentiary in the U.S.S.R., Lieut. Gen., Ju San Min, Cavalier of the Order of the Rising Sun, First Class, and the Order of the Golden Kite, Fourth Class.

Who, after the exchange of their credentials, which were found in due and proper form, agreed on the following:

Article I

Both contracting parties undertake to maintain peaceful and friendly relations between them and mutually respect the territorial integrity and inviolability of the other contracting party.

Article II

Should one of the contracting parties become the object of hostilities on the part of one or several third Powers, the other contracting party will observe neutrality throughout the duration of the conflict.

Article III

The present pact comes into force from the day of its ratification by both contracting parties and remains valid for five years. In case neither of the contracting parties denounces the pact one year before expiration of the term, it will be considered automatically prolonged for the next five years.

Article IV

The present pact is subject to ratification as soon as possible. Instruments of ratification shall be exchanged in Tokyo also as soon as possible.

In confirmation whereof the above-named representatives signed the present pact in two copies, drawn up in the Russian and Japanese languages, and affixed thereto their seals.

Done in Moscow April 13, 1941, which corresponds to the 13th Day of the Fourth Month of the 16th Year of Showa.

Signed by:

MOLOTOFF,
YOSUKE MATSUOKA,
YOSHITSUGU TATEKAWA.

Frontier Declaration

In conformity with the spirit of the neutrality pact concluded April 13, 1941, between the U.S.S.R. and Japan, the Governments of the U.S.S.R. and Japan, in the interests of ensuring peaceful and friendly relations between the two countries, solemnly declare that the U.S.S.R. pledges to respect the territorial integrity and inviolability of Manchukuo, and Japan pledges to respect the territorial integrity and inviolability of the Mongolian People's Republic.

Moscow, April 13, 1941.

Signed on behalf of the Government of the U.S.S.R. by:

MOLOTOFF.

On behalf of the Government of Japan by:

YOSUKE MATSUOKA,
YOSHITSUGU TATEKAWA.

JOINT DECLARATION of President Franklin D. Roosevelt, of the United States, and Winston Churchill, Prime Minister of Great Britain, at Sea, August 14, 1941 (the "Atlantic Charter")

Department of State, *Bulletin*, August 16, 1941, p. 125

THE PRESIDENT of the United States and the Prime Minister, Mr. Churchill, representing His Majesty's Government in the United Kingdom, have met at sea.

They have been accompanied by officials of their two Governments, including high-ranking officers of their Military, Naval, and Air Services.

The whole problem of the supply of munitions of war, as provided by the Lease-Lend Act, for the armed forces of the United States and for those countries actively engaged in resisting aggression has been further examined.

Lord Beaverbrook, the Minister of Supply of the British Government, has joined in these conferences. He is going to proceed to Washington to discuss further details with appropriate officials of the United States Government. These conferences will also cover the supply problems of the Soviet Union.

The President and the Prime Minister have had several conferences. They have considered the dangers to world civilization arising from the policies of military domination by conquest upon which the Hitlerite government of Germany and other governments associated therewith have embarked, and have made clear the stress which their countries are respectively taking for their safety in the face of these dangers.

They have agreed upon the following joint declaration:

Joint declaration of the President of the United States of America and the Prime Minister, Mr. Churchill, representing His Majesty's Government in the United Kingdom, being met together, deem it right to make known certain common principles in the national policies of their respective countries on which they base their hopes for a better future for the world.

First, their countries seek no aggrandizement, territorial or other;

Second, they desire to see no territorial changes that do not accord with the freely expressed wishes of the peoples concerned;

Third, they respect the right of all peoples to choose the form of government under which they will live; and they wish to see sovereign rights and self-government restored to those who have been forcibly deprived of them;

Fourth, they will endeavor, with due respect for their existing obligations, to further the enjoyment by all States, great or small, victor or vanquished, of access, on equal terms, to the trade and to the raw materials of the world which are needed for their economic prosperity;

Fifth, they desire to bring about the fullest collaboration between all nations in the economic field with the object of securing, for all, improved labor standards, economic advancement, and social security;

Sixth, after the final destruction of the Nazi tyranny, they hope to see established a peace which will afford to all nations the means of dwelling in safety within their own boundaries, and which will afford assurance that all the men in all the lands may live out their lives in freedom from fear and want;

Seventh, such a peace should enable all men to traverse the high seas and oceans without hindrance;

Eighth, they believe that all of the nations of the world, for realistic as well as spiritual reasons, must come to the abandonment of the use of force. Since no future peace can be maintained if land, sea, or air armaments continue to be employed by nations which threaten, or may threaten, aggression outside of their frontiers, they believe, pending the establishment of a wider and permanent system of general security, that the disarmament of such nations is essential. They will likewise aid and encourage all other practicable measures which will lighten for peace-loving peoples the crushing burden of armaments.

FRANKLIN D. ROOSEVELT
WINSTON S. CHURCHILL

JOINT DECLARATION by Twenty-six United Nations, January 1, 1942, Regarding Cooperative War Efforts against the Axis Countries

Department of State, *Bulletin,* January 3, 1942, p. 3

DECLARATION BY UNITED NATIONS:

A JOINT *Declaration by the United States of America, The United Kingdom of Great Britain and Northern Ireland, The Union of Soviet Socialist Republics, China, Australia, Belgium, Canada, Costa Rica, Cuba, Czechoslovakia, Dominican Republic, El Salvador, Greece, Guatemala, Haiti, Honduras, India, Luxembourg, Netherlands, New Zealand, Nicaragua, Norway, Panama, Poland, South Africa, Yugoslavia.*

The Governments signatory hereto,

Having subscribed to a common program of purposes and principles embodied in the Joint Declaration of the President of the United States of America and the Prime Minister of the United Kingdom of Great Britain and Northern Ireland dated August 14, 1941, known as the Atlantic Charter,

Being convinced that complete victory over their enemies is essential to defend life, liberty, independence and religious freedom, and to preserve human rights and justice in their own lands as well as in other lands, and that they are now engaged in a common struggle against savage and brutal forces seeking to subjugate the world, *Declare:*

(1) Each Government pledges itself to employ its full resources, military or economic, against those members of the Tripartite Pact and its adherents with which such government is at war.

(2) Each Government pledges itself to cooperate with the Governments signatory hereto and not to make a separate armistice or peace with the enemies.

The foregoing declaration may be adhered to by other nations which are, or which may be, rendering material assistance and contributions in the struggle for victory over Hitlerism.

Done at WASHINGTON,
January First, 1942.

[*Signatures*]

APPENDIX I

Selected Documents from NAZI-SOVIET RELATIONS, 1939–1941, *Published by the Department of State in 1948*

With one exception, the following are translations of documents taken from the archives of the German Foreign Office; the exception (Hitler's Military Directive of December 18, 1940, for "Operation Barbarossa") was taken from the archives of the German Wehrmacht

SECRET ADDITIONAL PROTOCOL to the Treaty of Non-Aggression between Germany and the Union of Soviet Socialist Republics, Signed at Moscow, August 23, 1939

Nazi-Soviet Relations, 1939–1941, p. 78; for the previously published Treaty, *see supra*, p. 1025

On the occasion of the signature of the Nonaggression Pact between the German Reich and the Union of Socialist Soviet Republics the undersigned plenipotentiaries of each of the two parties discussed in strictly confidential conversations the question of the boundary of their respective spheres of influence in Eastern Europe. These conversations led to the following conclusions:

1. In the event of a territorial and political rearrangement in the areas belonging to the Baltic States (Finland, Estonia, Latvia, Lithuania), the northern boundary of Lithuania shall represent the boundary of the spheres of influence of Germany and the U.S.S.R. In this connection the interest of Lithuania in the Vilna area is recognized by each party.

2. In the event of a territorial and political rearrangement of the areas belonging to the Polish state the spheres of influence of Germany and the U.S.S.R. shall be bounded approximately by the line of the rivers Narew, Vistula, and San.

The question of whether the interests of both parties make desirable the maintenance of an independent Polish state and how such a state should be bounded can only be definitely determined in the course of further political developments.

In any event both Governments will resolve this question by means of a friendly agreement.

3. With regard to Southeastern Europe attention is called by the

Soviet side to its interest in Bessarabia. The German side declares its complete political disinterestedness in these areas.*

4. This protocol shall be treated by both parties as strictly secret.

Moscow, August 23, 1939.

<table><tr><td>For the Government
of the German Reich:
v. RIBBENTROP</td><td>Plenipotentiary of the
Government of the U.S.S.R.:
V. MOLOTOV</td></tr></table>

TELEGRAM from Joachim von Ribbentrop, German Minister for Foreign Affairs, to the German Ambassador to the Union of Soviet Socialist Republics (Count Friedrich Werner von der Schulenburg), September 15, 1939

Nazi-Soviet Relations, 1939–1941, p. 93

VERY URGENT
STRICTLY SECRET
No. 360 of September 15

For the Ambassador personally.

I request that you communicate the following to Herr Molotov at once:

1) The destruction of the Polish Army is rapidly approaching its conclusion, as appears from the review of the military situation of September 14 which has already been communicated to you. We count on the occupation of Warsaw in the next few days.

2) We have already stated to the Soviet Government that we consider ourselves bound by the definition of spheres of influence agreed upon in Moscow, entirely apart from purely military operations, and the same applies of course to the future as well.

3) From the communication made to you by Molotov on September 14, we assume that the Soviet Government will take a hand militarily, and that it intends to begin its operation now. We welcome this. The Soviet Government thus relieves us of the necessity of annihilating the remainder of the Polish Army by pursuing it as far as the Russian boundary. Also the question is disposed of in case a Russian intervention did not take place, of whether in the area lying to the east of the German zone of influence a political vacuum might not occur. Since we on our part have no intention of undertaking any political or

* The German text of this article of the Protocol is as follows: "Hinsichtlich des Südostens Europas wird von sowjetischer Seite das Interesse an Bessarabien betont. Von deutscher Seite wird das völlige politische Desinteressement an diesen Gebieten erklärt."

administrative activities in these areas, apart from what is made necessary by military operations, without such an intervention on the part of the Soviet Government there might be the possibility of the construction of new states there.

4) For the political support of the advance of the Soviet Army we propose the publication of a joint communiqué of the following content:

"In view of the complete collapse of the previous form of government in Poland, the Reich Government and the Government of the U.S.S.R. consider it necessary to bring to an end the intolerable political and economic conditions existing in these territories. They regard it as their joint duty to restore peace and order in these areas which are naturally of interest to them and to bring about a new order by the creation of natural frontiers and viable economic organizations."

5) We assume in proposing such a communiqué that the Soviet Government has already given up the idea, expressed by Molotov in an earlier conversation with you, of taking the threat to the Ukrainian and White Russian populations by Germany as a ground for Soviet action. The assignment of a motive of that sort would be out of the question in practice. It would be directly contrary to the true German intentions, which are confined exclusively to the realization of well-known German spheres of interest. It would also be in contradiction to the arrangements made in Moscow and, finally, would—in opposition to the desire for friendly relations expressed on both sides—expose the two States before the whole world as enemies.

6 Since the military operations must be concluded as soon as possible because of the advanced season of the year, we would be gratified if the Soviet Government would set a day and hour on which their army would begin their advance, so that we on our part might govern ourselves accordingly. For the purpose of the necessary coordination of military operations on either side, it is also necessary that a representative of each Government, as well as German and Russian officers on the spot in the area of operations, should have a meeting in order to take the necessary steps, for which meeting we propose to assemble at Bialystok by air.

I request an immediate reply by telegraph. The change in text agreed upon by Gaus with Hilger has already been taken care of.

TELEGRAM from Count Friedrich Werner von der Schulenburg, German Ambassador to the Union of Soviet Socialist Republics, to the German Foreign Office, September 20, 1939

Nazi-Soviet Relations, 1939–1941, p. 101

STRICTLY SECRET
No. 395 of September 19

Molotov stated to me today that the Soviet Government now considered the time ripe for it, jointly with the German Government, to establish definitively the structure of the Polish area. In this regard, Molotov hinted that the original inclination entertained by the Soviet Government and Stalin personally to permit the existence of a residual Poland had given way to the inclination to partition Poland along the Pissa-Narew-Vistula-San Line. The Soviet Government wishes to commence negotiations on this matter at once, and to conduct them in Moscow, since such negotiations must be conducted on the Soviet side by persons in the highest positions of authority, who cannot leave the Soviet Union. Request telegraphic instructions.

TELEGRAM from Joachim von Ribbentrop, German Minister for Foreign Affairs, to the German Ambassador to the Union of Soviet Socialist Republics (Count Friedrich Werner von der Schulenburg), September 23, 1939

Nazi-Soviet Relations, 1939–1941, p. 102

STRICTLY SECRET
No. 417 of September 22

Reference your telegram No. 295 [395?]. For the Ambassador personally.

We, too, consider the time now ripe to establish by treaty jointly with the Soviet Government the definitive structure of the Polish area. The Russian idea of a border line along the well-known Four-Rivers Line coincides in general with the view of the Reich Government. It was my original intention to invite Herr Molotov to Germany in order to formulate this treaty. In view of your report that the leading personages there cannot leave the Soviet Union, we agree to negotiations in Moscow. Contrary to my original purpose of entrusting you with these negotiations, I have decided to fly to Moscow myself. This particularly because—in view of the full powers granted me by the Führer, thus making it possible to dispense with counterinquiries, etc.—negotiations can be brought to a speedier conclusion. In view of the general situation, my sojourn in Moscow will have to be limited to one or two days at the most. Please call on Herren Stalin and Molotov and wire me earliest proposed date.

CONFIDENTIAL and Secret Protocols to the Boundary and Friendship Treaty between Germany and the Union of Soviet Socialist Republics, Signed at Moscow, September 28, 1939

Nazi-Soviet Relations, 1939–1941, p. 106; for the previously-published Treaty and Protocols, see supra, p. 1029

Confidential Protocol

The Government of the U.S.S.R. shall place no obstacles in the way of Reich nationals and other persons of German descent residing in the territories under its jurisdiction, if they desire to migrate to Germany or to the territories under German jurisdiction. It agrees that such removals shall be carried out by agents of the Government of the Reich in cooperation with the competent local authorities and that the property rights of the emigrants shall be protected.

A corresponding obligation is assumed by the Government of the German Reich in respect to the persons of Ukrainian or White Russian descent residing in the territories under its jurisdiction.

Moscow, September 28, 1939.

For the Government of the German Reich:	By authority of the Government of the U.S.S.R.:
J. RIBBENTROP	W. MOLOTOW

Secret Supplementary Protocol

The undersigned Plenipotentiaries declare the agreement of the Government of the German Reich and the Government of the U.S.S.R. upon the following:

The Secret Supplementary Protocol signed on August 23, 1939, shall be amended in item 1 to the effect that the territory of the Lithuanian state falls to the sphere of influence of the U.S.S.R., while, on the other hand, the province of Lublin and parts of the province of Warsaw fall to the sphere of influence of Germany (cf. the map attached to the Boundary and Friendship Treaty signed today). As soon as the Government of the U.S.S.R. shall take special measures on Lithuanian territory to protect its interests, the present German-Lithuanian border, for the purpose of a natural and simple boundary delineation, shall be rectified in such a way that the Lithuanian territory situated to the southwest of the line marked on the attached map should fall to Germany.

Further it is declared that the economic agreements now in force between Germany and Lithuania shall not be affected by the measures of the Soviet Union referred to above.

Moscow, September 28, 1939.

*For the Government
of the German Reich:*
J. RIBBENTROP

*By authority of the
Government of the U.S.S.R.:*
W. MOLOTOW

Secret Supplementary Protocol

The undersigned plenipotentiaries, on concluding the German-Russian Boundary and Friendship Treaty, have declared their agreement upon the following:

Both parties will tolerate in their territories no Polish agitation which affects the territories of the other party. They will suppress in their territories all beginnings of such agitation and inform each other concerning suitable measures for this purpose.

Moscow, September 28, 1939.

*For the Government
of the German Reich:*
J. RIBBENTROP

*By authority of the
Government of the U.S.S.R.:*
W. MOLOTOW

MEMORANDUM of a Conversation between Adolf Hitler, Chancellor of the German Reich, and Vyacheslav M. Molotov, Chairman of the Council of People's Commissars and Commissar for Foreign Affairs of the Union of Soviet Socialist Republics, at Berlin, November 12, 1940

Nazi-Soviet Relations, 1939–1941, p. 226; the conversation was in the presence of the German Minister for Foreign Affairs (Joachim von Ribbentrop) and other officials

STATE SECRET
Füh. 32/40 g. Rs.

After some words of welcome, the Führer stated that the idea that was uppermost in his mind in the conversations now taking place was this: In the life of peoples it was indeed difficult to lay down a course for development over a long period in the future and the outbreak of conflicts was often strongly influenced by personal factors; he believed, nevertheless, that an attempt had to be made to fix the development of nations, even for a long period of time, in so far as that was possible, so that friction would be avoided and the elements of conflict precluded as far as humanly possible. This was particularly in order when two nations such as the German and Russian nations had at their helm men who possessed sufficient authority to commit their countries to a development in a definite direction. In the case of Russia and Germany, moreover, two very great nations were involved which need not by nature have any conflict of interests, if each nation understood that the other required certain vital necessities without the guarantee of which its existence was impossible. Besides this, both countries had systems of government which did not wage war for the sake of war, but which needed peace more than war in order to carry out their domestic tasks. With due regard for vital needs, particularly in the economic field, it should really be possible to achieve a settlement between them, which would lead to peaceful collaboration between the two countries beyond the life span of the present leaders.

After Molotov had expressed his entire agreement with these arguments, the Führer continued that it was obviously a difficult task to chart developments between peoples and countries over a long period. He believed, however, that it would be possible to elaborate clearly and precisely certain general points of view quite independently of personal motives and to orient the political and economic interests of peoples in such a manner as to give some guarantee that conflicts would be avoided even for rather long periods. The situation in which the conversation of today was taking place was characterized by the fact that Germany was at war, while Soviet Russia was not. Many of the measures taken by Germany had been influenced by the fact of her belligerency. Many of the steps that were necessary in the course of the war had developed from the conduct of the war itself and could not have been anticipated at the outbreak of war. By and large, not only Germany but also Russia had gained great advantages. On further consideration, the political collaboration during the one year of its existence had been of considerable value to both countries.

Molotov stated that this was quite correct.

The Führer declared further that probably neither of the two peoples had realized its wishes 100 percent. In political life, however, even a 20–25 percent realization of demands was worth a good deal. He believed that not every wish would be fulfilled in the future either, but that the two greatest peoples of Europe, if they went along together, would, in any case, gain more than if they worked against each other. If they stood together, some advantage would always accrue to both countries. If they worked against each other, however, third countries would be the sole gainers.

Molotov replied that the argument of the Führer was entirely correct and would be confirmed by history; that it was particularly applicable to the present situation, however.

The Führer then went on to say that proceeding from these ideas he had again quite soberly pondered the question of German-Russian collaboration, at a time when the military operations were in effect concluded.

The war had, moreover, led to complications which were not intended by Germany, but which had compelled her from time to time to react militarily to certain events. The Führer then outlined to Molotov the course of military operations up to the present, which had led to the fact that England no longer had an ally on the continent. He described in detail the military operations now being carried out against England, and he stressed the influence of atmospheric conditions on these operations. The English retaliatory measures were ridiculous, and the Russian gentlemen could convince themselves at first hand of the fiction of alleged destruction in Berlin. As soon as atmospheric conditions improved, Germany would be poised for the great and final blow against England. At the moment, then, it was her aim to try not only to make military preparations for this final struggle, but also to clarify the political issues which would be of importance during and after this showdown. He had, therefore, re-examined the relations with Russia, and not in a negative spirit, but with the intention of organizing them positively—if possible, for a long period of time. In so doing he had reached several conclusions:

1. Germany was not seeking to obtain military aid from Russia;
2. Because of the tremendous extension of the war, Germany had been forced, in order to oppose England, to penetrate into territories remote from her and in which she was not basically interested politically or economically;
3. There were nevertheless certain requirements, the full importance of which had become apparent only during the war, but which were absolutely vital to Germany. Among them were certain sources of raw materials which were considered by Germany as most vital and absolutely indispensable. Possibly Herr Molotov was of the opinion that in one case or another they had departed from the conception of the spheres of influence which had been agreed upon by Stalin and the Reich Foreign Minister. Such departures had already occurred in some cases in the course of Russian operations against Poland. In a number of cases, on calm consideration of the German and Russian interests, he (the Führer) had not been ready to make concessions, but he had realized that it was desirable to meet the needs of Russia half-way, as, for instance, in the case of Lithuania. From an economic point of view, Lithuania had, it is true, had a certain importance for us, but from a political point of view, we had understood the necessity of straightening out the situation in this whole field in order thereby to prevent in the future the spiritual revival of tendencies that were capable of causing tension between the two countries of Germany and Russia. In another case, namely, that of the South Tyrol, Germany had taken a similar position. However, in the course of the war, factors had arisen for Germany which could not have been anticipated at the outbreak of the war, but which had to be considered absolutely vital from the standpoint of military operations.

He (the Führer) now had pondered the question how, beyond all petty momentary considerations, further to clarify in bold outline the collaboration between Germany and Russia and what direction future German-Russian developments should take. In this matter the following viewpoints were of importance for Germany:

1. Need for *Lebensraum* [*Raumnot*]. During the war Germany had acquired such large areas that she would require one hundred years to utilize them fully.
2. Some colonial expansion in Central Africa was necessary.
3. Germany needed certain raw materials, the supply of which she would have to safeguard under all circumstances. And

4. She could not permit the establishment by hostile powers of air or naval bases in certain areas.

In no event, however, would the interests of Russia be affected. The Russian empire could develop without in the least prejudicing German interests. (Molotov said this was quite correct.) If both countries came to realize this fact, they could collaborate to their mutual advantage and could spare themselves difficulties, friction, and nervous tension. It was perfectly obvious that Germany and Russia would never become one world. Both countries would always exist separate from each other as two powerful elements of the world. Each of them could shape its future as it liked, if in so doing it considered the interests of the other. Germany herself had no interests in Asia other than general economic and commercial interests. In particular, she had no colonial interests there. She knew, furthermore, that the possible colonial territories in Asia would probably fall to Japan. If by any chance China, too, should be drawn into the orbit of the awakening [*erwachenden*] nations, any colonial aspirations would be doomed to disappointment from the start in view of the masses of people living there.

There were in Europe a number of points of contact [*Berührungsmomenten*] between Germany, Russia, and Italy. Each one of these three countries had an understandable desire for an outlet to the open sea. Germany wanted to get out of the North Sea, Italy wanted to remove the barrier of Gibraltar, and Russia was also striving toward the ocean. The question now was how much chance there was for these great countries really to obtain free access to the ocean without in turn coming into conflict with each other over the matter. This was also the viewpoint from which he looked upon the organization of European relations after the war. The leading statesmen of Europe must prevent this war from becoming the father of a new war. The issues to be settled had, therefore, to be settled in such a manner that, at least in the foreseeable future, no new conflict could arise.

In this spirit, he (the Führer) had talked with the French statesmen and believed that he had found among them some sympathy for a settlement which would lead to tolerable conditions for a rather long period and which would be of advantage to all concerned, if only to the extent that a new war did not again have to be feared immediately. Referring to the preamble of the Armistice Treaty with France, he had pointed out to Pétain and Laval that, as long as the war with England lasted, no step might be taken which would in any way be incompatible with the conditions for ending this war against Great Britain.

Elsewhere, too, there were problems such as these, but ones which arose only for the duration of the war. Thus, for instance, Germany had no political interests whatsoever in the Balkans and was active there at present exclusively under the compulsion of securing for herself certain raw materials. It was a matter of purely military interests, the safeguarding of which was not a pleasant task, since, for instance, a German military force had to be maintained in Rumania, hundreds of kilometers away from the supply centers.

For similar reasons the idea was intolerable to Germany that England might get a foothold in Greece in order to establish air and naval bases there. The Reich was compelled to prevent this under any circumstances.

The continuation of the war under such circumstances was of course not desirable. And that is why Germany had wanted to end the war after the conclusion of the Polish campaign. At that time England and France could have had peace without personal sacrifices; they had, however, preferred to continue the war. Of course, blood also creates rights, and it was inadmissible that certain countries should have declared and waged war without afterward paying the cost. He (the Führer) had made this clear to the French. At the present stage of developments, however, the question was which of the countries responsible for the war had to pay more. At any rate, Germany would have preferred to end the war last year and to have demobilized her army in order to resume her peacetime work, since from an economic point of view any war was bad business. Even the victor had to incur such expenses before, during, and after the war that he could have reached his goal much more cheaply in a peaceful development.

Molotov concurred in this idea, stating that in any case it was vastly more expensive to attain a goal by military measures than by peaceful means. The Führer pointed out further that under the present circumstances Germany had been forced by wartime developments to become active in areas in which she was politically disinterested but had at most economic interests. Self-preservation, however, absolutely dictated this course. Nevertheless, this activity of Germany—forced upon her in the areas in question—represented no obstacle to any pacification of the world which would later be undertaken, and which would bring to the nations working toward the same end that for which they hoped.

In addition, there was the problem of America. The United States was now pursuing an imperialistic policy. It was not fighting for England, but only trying to get the British Empire into its grasp. They were helping England, at best, in order to further their own rearmament and to reinforce their military power by acquiring bases. In the distant future it would be a question of establishing a great solidarity among those countries which might be involved in case of an extension of the sphere of influence of this Anglo-Saxon power, which had a more solid foundation, by far, than England. In this case, it was not a question of the immediate future; not in 1945, but in 1970 or 1980, at the earliest, would the freedom of other nations be seriously endangered by this Anglo-Saxon power. At any rate, the Continent of Europe had to adjust itself now to this development and had to act jointly against the Anglo-Saxons and against any of their attempts to acquire dangerous bases. Therefore, he had undertaken an exchange of ideas with France, Italy, and Spain, in order with these countries to set up in the whole of Europe and Africa some kind of Monroe Doctrine and to adopt a new joint colonial policy by which each of the powers concerned would claim for itself only as much colonial territory as it could really utilize. In other regions, where Russia was the power in the foremost position, the interests of the latter would, of course, have to come first. This would result in a great coalition of powers which, guided by sober appraisal of realities, would have to establish their respective spheres of interest and would assert themselves against the rest of the world correspondingly. It was surely a difficult task to organize such a coalition of countries; and yet, to conceive it was not as difficult as to carry it out.

The Führer then reverted to the German-Russian efforts. He understood thoroughly Russia's attempts to get ice-free ports with absolutely secure access to the open sea. Germany had enormously expanded her *Lebensraum* in her present eastern provinces. At least half of this area, however, must be regarded as an economic liability. Probably both Russia and Germany had not achieved everything they had set out to do. In any case, however, the successes had been great on both sides. If a liberal view were taken of the remaining issues and due regard were taken of the fact that Germany was still at war and had to concern herself with areas which, in and for themselves, were of no importance to her politically, substantial gains for both partners could be achieved in the future, too. In this connection the Führer again turned to the Balkans and repeated that Germany would at once oppose by military action any attempt by England to get a foothold in Salonika. She still retained unpleasant memories from the last war of the then Salonika Front.

To a question of Molotov's as to how Salonika constituted a danger, the Führer referred to the proximity of the Rumanian petroleum fields, which Germany wished to protect under all circumstances. As soon as peace prevailed, however, the German troops would immediately leave Rumania again.

In the further course of the conversation, the Führer asked Molotov how Russia planned to safeguard her interests in the Black Sea and in the Straits. Germany would also be prepared at any time to help effect an improvement for Russian in the régime of the Straits.

Molotov replied that the statements of the Führer had been of a general nature and that in general he could agree with his reasoning. He was also of the opinion that it would be in the interest of Germany and the Soviet Union if the two countries would collaborate and not fight each other. Upon his departure from Moscow, Stalin had given him exact instructions, and everything that he was about to say was identical with the views of Stalin. He concurred in the opinion of the Führer that both partners had derived substantial benefits from the German-Russian agreement. Germany had received a secure hinterland that, as was generally known, had been of great importance for the further course of events during the year of war. In Poland, too, Germany had gained considerable economic advantages. By the exchange of Lithuania for the Voivodeship of Lublin, all possible friction between Russia and Germany had been avoided. The German-Russian agreement of last year could therefore be regarded as fulfilled, except for one point, namely, Finland. The Finnish question was still unsolved, and he asked the Führer to tell him whether the German-Russian agreement, as far as it concerned Finland, was still in force. In the opinion of the Soviet Government, no changes had occurred here. Also, in the opinion of the Soviet Government, the German-Russian agreement of last year represented only a partial solution. In the meanwhile, other issues had arisen that also had to be solved.

Molotov then turned to the matter of the significance of the Tripartite Pact. What was the meaning of the New Order in Europe and in Asia, and what role would the U.S.S.R. be given in it? These issues must be discussed during the Berlin conversations and during the contemplated visit of the Reich Foreign Minister to Moscow, on which the Russians were definitely counting. Moreover, there were issues to be clarified regarding Russia's Balkan and Black Sea interests with respect to Bulgaria, Rumania, and Turkey. It would be easier for the Russian Government to give specific replies to the questions raised by the Führer, if it could obtain the explanations just requested. It would be interested in the New Order in Europe, and particularly in the tempo and the form of this New Order. It would also like to have an idea of the boundaries of the so-called Greater East Asian Sphere.

The Führer replied that the Tripartite Pact was intended to regulate conditions in Europe as to the natural interests of the European countries and, consequently, Germany was now approaching the

Soviet Union in order that she might express herself regarding the areas of interest to her. In no case was a settlement to be made without Soviet Russian cooperation. This applied not only to Europe, but also to Asia, where Russia herself was to cooperate in the definition of the Greater East Asian Sphere and where she was to designate her claims there. Germany's task in this case was that of a mediator. Russia by no means was to be confronted with a *fait accompli*.

When the Führer undertook to try to establish the above-mentioned coalition of powers, it was not the German-Russian relationship which appeared to him to be the most difficult point, but the question of whether a collaboration between Germany, France, and Italy was possible. Only now that he believed this problem could be solved, and after a settlement in broad outlines had in effect been accepted by the three countries, had he thought it possible to contact Soviet Russia for the purpose of settling the questions of the Black Sea, the Balkans, and Turkey.

In conclusion, the Führer summed up by stating that the discussion, to a certain extent, represented the first concrete step toward a comprehensive collaboration, with due consideration for problems of Western Europe, which were to be settled between Germany, Italy, and France, as well as for the issues of the East, which were essentially the concern of Russia and Japan, but in which Germany offered her good offices as mediator. It was a matter of opposing any attempt on the part of America to "make money on Europe." The United States had no business either in Europe, in Africa, or in Asia.

Molotov expressed his agreement with the statements of the Führer regarding the role of America and England. The participation of Russia in the Tripartite Pact appeared to him entirely acceptable in principle, provided that Russia was to cooperate as a partner and not be merely an object. In that case he saw no difficulties in the matter of participation of the Soviet Union in the common effort. But the aim and the significance of the Pact must first be more closely defined, particularly because of the delimitation of the Greater East Asian Sphere.

In view of a possible air raid alarm the talk was broken off at this point and postponed until the following day, the Führer promising Molotov that he would discuss with him in detail the various issues which had come up during the conversation.

SCHMIDT

Berlin, November 16, 1940.

MEMORANDUM of a Conversation between Adolf Hitler, Chancellor of the German Reich, and Vyacheslav M. Molotov, Chairman of the Council of People's Commissars and Commissar for Foreign Affairs of the Union of Soviet Socialist Republics, at Berlin, November 13, 1940, in the Presence of the German Minister for Foreign Affairs (Joachim von Ribbentrop) and other officials

Nazi-Soviet Relations, 1939–1941, p. 234

Füh. 33/40

The Führer referred to the remarks of Molotov during yesterday's conversation, according to which the German-Russian agreement was fulfilled "with the exception of one point: namely, of Finland."

Molotov explained that this remark referred not only to the German-Russian agreement itself, but in particular to the Secret Protocols too.

The Führer replied that, in the Secret Protocol, zones of influence and spheres of interest had been designated and distributed between Germany and Russia. In so far as it had been a question of actually taking possession, Germany had lived up to the agreements, which was not quite the case on the Russian side. At any rate, Germany had not occupied any territory that was within the Russian sphere of influence.

Lithuania had already been mentioned yesterday. There could be no doubt that in this case the changes from the original German-Russian agreement were essentially due to Russian initiative. Whether the difficulties—to avoid which the Russians had offered their suggestion—would actually have resulted from the partition of Poland, could be left out of the discussion. In any case, the Voivodeship of Lublin was no compensation, economically, for Lithuania. However, the Germans had seen that in the course of events a situation had resulted which necessitated revision of the original agreement.

The same applied to Bucovina. Strictly speaking, in the original agreement Germany had declared herself disinterested only in Bessarabia. Nevertheless, she had realized, in this case too, that revision of the agreement was in certain respects advantageous for the other partner.

The situation regarding Finland was quite similar. Germany had no political interest there. This was known to the Russian Government. During the Russo-Finnish War Germany had meticulously fulfilled all her obligations in regard to absolute benevolent neutrality.

Molotov interposed here that the Russian Government had had no cause for criticism with regard to the attitude of Germany during that conflict.

In this connection the Führer mentioned also that he had even detained ships in Bergen which were transporting arms and ammunition to Finland, for which Germany had actually had no authority. Germany had incurred the serious opposition of the rest of the world, and of Sweden in particular, by her attitude during the Russo-Finnish War. As a result, during the subsequent Norwegian campaign, itself involving considerable risks, she had to employ a large number of divisions for protection against Sweden, which she would not have needed otherwise.

The real situation was as follows: In accordance with the German-Russian agreements, Germany recognized that, politically, Finland was of primary interest to Russia and was in her zone of influence. However, Germany had to consider the following two points:

1. For the duration of the war she was very greatly interested in the deliveries of nickel and lumber from Finland, and
2. She did not desire any new conflict in the Baltic Sea which would further curtail her freedom of movement in one of the few merchant shipping regions which still remained to her. It was completely incorrect to assert that Finland was occupied by German troops. To be sure, troops were being transported to Kirkenes via Finland, of which fact Russia had been officially informed by Germany. Because of the length of the route, the trains had to stop two or three times in Finnish territory. However, as soon as the transit of the troop contingents to be transported had been completed, no additional troops would be sent through Finland. He (the Führer) pointed out that both Germany and Russia would naturally be interested in not allowing the Baltic Sea to become a combat zone again. Since the Russo-Finnish War, the possibilities for military operations had shifted, because England had available long-range bombers and long-range destroyers. The English thereby had a chance to get a foothold on Finnish airports.

In addition, there was a purely psychological factor which was extremely onerous. The Finns had defended themselves bravely, and they had gained the sympathies of the world—particularly of Scandinavia. In Germany too, during the Russo-Finnish War, the people were somewhat annoyed at the position which, as a result of the agreements with Russia, Germany had to take and actually did take. Germany did not wish any new Finnish war because of the aforementioned considerations. However, the legitimate claims of Russia were not affected by that. Germany had proved this again and again by her attitude on various issues, among others, the issue of the fortification of the Aaland Islands. For the duration of the war, however, her economic interests in Finland were just as important as in Rumania. Germany expected consideration of these interests all the more, since she herself had also shown understanding of the Russian wishes in the issues of Lithuania and Bucovina at the time. At any rate, she had no political interest of any kind in Finland, and she fully accepted the fact that that country belonged to the Russian zone of influence.

In his reply Molotov pointed out that the agreement of 1939 had referred to a certain stage of the development which had been concluded by the end of the Polish War, while the second stage was brought to an end by the defeat of France, and that they were really in the third stage now. He recalled that by the original agreement, with its Secret Protocol, the common German-Russian boundary had been fixed and issues concerning the adjacent Baltic countries and Rumania, Finland, and Poland had been settled. For the rest, he agreed with the remarks of the Führer on the revisions made. However, if he drew up a balance sheet of the situation that resulted after the defeat of France, he would have to state that the German-Russian agreement had not been without influence upon the great German victories.

As to the question of the revision of the original agreement with regard to Lithuania and the Voivodeship of Lublin, Molotov pointed out that the Soviet Union would not have insisted on that revision if Germany had not wanted it. But he believed that the new solution had been in the interest of both parties.

At this point the Reich Foreign Minister interjected that, to be sure, Russia had not made this revision an absolute condition, but at any rate had urged it very strongly.

Molotov insisted that the Soviet Government would not have refused to leave matters as provided in the original agreement. At any rate, however, Germany, for its concession in Lithuania, had received compensation in Polish territory.

The Führer interjected here that in this exchange one could not, from the point of view of economics, speak of adequate compensation.

Molotov then mentioned the question of the strip of Lithuanian territory and emphasized that the Soviet Government had not received any clear answer yet from Germany on this question. However, it awaited a decision.

Regarding Bucovina, he admitted that this involved an additional territory, one not mentioned in the Secret Protocol. Russia had at first confined her demands to Northern Bucovina. Under the present circumstances, however, Germany must understand the Russian interest in Southern Bucovina. But Russia had not received an answer to her question regarding this subject either. Instead, Germany had guaranteed the entire territory of Rumania and completely disregarded Russia's wishes with regard to Southern Bucovina.

The Führer replied that it would mean a considerable concession on the part of Germany, if even part of Bucovina were to be occupied by Russia. According to an oral agreement, the former Austrian territories were to fall within the German sphere of influence. Besides, the territories belonging to the Russian zone had been mentioned by name: Bessarabia, for example. There was, however, not a word regarding Bucovina in the agreements. Finally, the exact meaning of the expression "sphere of influence" was not further defined. At any rate, Germany had not violated the agreement in the least in this matter. To the objection of Molotov that the revisions with regard to the strip of Lithuanian territory and of Bucovina were not of very great importance in comparison with the revision which Germany had undertaken elsewhere by military force, the Führer replied that so-called "revision by force of arms" had not been the subject of the agreement at all.

Molotov, however, persisted in the opinion previously stated: that the revisions desired by Russia were insignificant.

The Führer replied that if German-Russian collaboration was to show positive results in the future, the Soviet Government would have to understand that Germany was engaged in a life and death struggle, which, at all events, she wanted to conclude successfully. For that, a number of prerequisites depending upon economic and military factors were required, which Germany wanted to secure for herself by all means. If the Soviet Union were in a similar position, Germany on her part would, and would have to, demonstrate a similar understanding for Russian needs. The conditions which Germany wanted to assure did not conflict with the agreements with Russia. The German wish to avoid a war with unforeseeable consequences in the Baltic Sea did not mean any violation of the German-Russian agreements according to which Finland belonged in the Russian sphere of influence. The guarantee given upon the wish and request of the Rumanian Government was no violation of the agreements concerning Bessarabia. The Soviet Union had to realize that in the framework of any broader collaboration of the two countries advantages of quite different scope were to be reached than the insignificant revisions which were now being discussed. Much greater successes could then be achieved, provided that Russia did not now seek successes in territories in which Germany was interested for the duration of the war. The future successes would be the greater, the more Germany and Russia succeeded in fighting back to back against the outside world, and would become the smaller, the more the two countries faced each other breast to breast. In the first case there was no power on earth which could oppose the two countries.

In his reply Molotov voiced his agreement with the last conclusions of the Führer. In this connection he stressed the viewpoint of the Soviet leaders, and of Stalin in particular, that it would be possible and expedient to strengthen and activate the relations between the two countries. However, in order to give those relations a permanent basis, issues would also have to be clarified which were of secondary importance, but which spoiled the atmosphere of German-Russian relations. Finland belonged among these issues. If Russia and Germany had a good understanding, this issue could be solved without war, but there must be neither German troops in Finland nor political demonstrations in that country against the Soviet-Russian Government.

The Führer replied that the second point could not be a matter for debate, since Germany had nothing whatsoever to do with these things. Incidentally, demonstrations could easily be staged, and it was very difficult to find out afterward who had been the real instigator. However, regarding the German troops, he could give the assurance that, if a general settlement were made, no German troops would appear in Finland any longer.

Molotov replied that by demonstrations he also understood the dispatch of Finnish delegations to Germany or receptions of prominent Finns in Germany. Moreover, the circumstance of the presence of German troops had led to an ambiguous attitude on the part of Finland. Thus, for instance, slogans were brought out that "nobody was a Finn who approved of the last Russo-Finnish Peace Treaty," and the like.

The Führer replied that Germany had always exerted only a moderating influence and that she had advised Finland and also Rumania, in particular, to accept the Russian demands.

Molotov replied that the Soviet Government considered it as its duty definitively to settle and clarify the Finnish question. No new agreements were needed for that. The old German-Russian agreement assigned Finland to the Russian sphere of influence.

In conclusion the Führer stated on this point that Germany did not desire any war in the Baltic Sea and that she urgently needed Finland as a supplier of nickel and lumber. Politically, she was not interested and, in contrast to Russia, had occupied no Finnish territory. Incidentally, the transit of German troops would be finished within the next few days. No further troop trains would then be sent. The decisive question for Germany was whether Russia had the intention of going to war against Finland.

Molotov answered this question somewhat evasively with the statement that everything would be all right if the Finnish Government would give up its ambiguous attitude toward the U.S.S.R., and if the agitation against Russia among the population (bringing out of slogans such as the ones previously mentioned) would cease.

To the Führer's objection that he feared that Sweden might intervene in a Russo-Finnish War the next time, Molotov replied that he could not say anything about Sweden, but he had to stress that Germany, as well as the Soviet Union, was interested in the neutrality of Sweden. Of course, both countries were also interested in peace in the Baltic, but the Soviet Union was entirely able to assure peace in that region.

The Führer replied that they would perhaps experience in a different part of Europe how even the best military intentions were greatly restricted by geographical factors. He could, therefore, imagine that in the case of a new conflict a sort of resistance cell would be formed in Sweden and Finland, which would furnish air bases to England or even America. This would force Germany to intervene. He (the Führer) would, however, do this only reluctantly. He had already mentioned yesterday that the necessity for intervention would perhaps also arise in Salonika, and the case of Salonika was entirely sufficient for him. He had no interest in being forced to become active in the North too. He repeated that entirely different results could be achieved in future collaboration between the two countries and that Russia would after all, on the basis of the peace, receive everything that in her opinion was due her. It would perhaps be only a matter of six months or a year's delay. Besides, the Finnish Government had just sent a note in which it gave assurance of the closest and friendliest cooperation with Russia.

Molotov replied that the deeds did not always correspond with the words, and he persisted in the opinion which he had previously expressed: that peace in the Baltic Sea region could be absolutely insured, if perfect understanding were attained between Germany and Russia in the Finnish matter. Under those circumstances he did not understand why Russia should postpone the realization of her wishes for six months or a year. After all, the German-Russian agreement contained no time limits, and the hands of none of the partners were tied in their spheres of influence.

With a reference to the changes made in the agreement at Russia's request, the Führer stated that there must not be any war in the Baltic. A Baltic conflict would be a heavy strain on German-Russian relations and on the great collaboration of the future. In his opinion, however, future collaboration was more important than the settlement of secondary issues at this very moment.

Molotov replied that it was not a matter of war in the Baltic, but of the question of Finland and its settlement within the framework of the agreement of last year. In reply to a question of the Führer, he declared that he imagined this settlement on the same scale as in Bessarabia and in the adjacent countries, and he requested the Führer to give his opinion on that.

When the Führer replied that he could only repeat that there must be no war with Finland, because such a conflict might have far-reaching repercussions, Molotov stated that a new factor had been introduced into the discussion by this position, which was not expressed in the treaty of last year.

The Führer replied that during the Russo-Finnish War, despite the danger that in connection with it Allied bases might be established in Scandinavia, Germany had meticulously kept her obligations toward Russia and had always advised Finland to give in.

In this connection the Reich Foreign Minister pointed out that Germany had even gone so far as to deny to the Finnish President the use of a German cable for a radio address to America.

Then the Führer went on to explain that just as Russia at the time had pointed out that a partition of Poland might lead to a strain on German-Russian relations, he now declared with the same frankness that a war in Finland would represent such a strain on German-Russian relations, and he asked the Russians to show exactly the same understanding in this instance as he had shown a year ago in the issue of Poland. Considering the genius of Russian diplomacy, ways and means could certainly be found to avoid such a war.

Molotov replied that he could not understand the German fear that a war might break out in the Baltic. Last year, when the international situation was worse for Germany than now, Germany had not raised this issue. Quite apart from the fact that Germany had occupied Denmark, Norway, Holland, and Belgium, she had completely defeated France and even believed that she had already conquered England. He (Molotov) did not see where under those circumstances the danger of war in the Baltic Sea should come from. He would have to request that Germany take the same stand as last year. If she did that unconditionally, there would certainly be no complications in connection with the Finnish issue. However, if she made reservations, a new situation would arise which would then have to be discussed.

In reply to the statements of Molotov regarding the absence of military danger in the Finnish question, the Führer stressed that he too had some understanding of military matters, and he considered it entirely possible that the United States would get a foothold in those regions in case of participation by Sweden in a possible war. He (the Führer) wanted to end the European War, and he could only repeat that in view of the uncertain attitude of Sweden a new war in the Baltic would mean a strain on German-Russian relations with unforeseeable consequences. Would Russia declare war on the United States, in case the latter should intervene in connection with the Finnish conflict?

When Molotov replied that this question was not of present interest, the Führer replied that it would be too late for a decision when it became so. When Molotov then declared that he did not see any indication of the outbreak of war in the Baltic, the Führer replied that in that case everything would be in order anyway and the whole discussion was really of a purely theoretical nature.

Summarizing, the Reich Foreign Minister pointed out that

(1) the Führer had declared that Finland remained in the sphere of influence of Russia and that Germany would not maintain any troops there;

(2) Germany had nothing to do with demonstrations of Finland against Russia, but was exerting her influence in the opposite direction, and

(3) the collaboration of the two countries was the decisive problem of long-range importance, which in the past had already resulted in great advantages for Russia, but which in the future would show advantages compared with which the matters that had just been discussed would appear entirely insignificant. There was actually no reason at all for making an issue of the Finnish question. Perhaps it was a misunderstanding only. Strategically, all of Russia's wishes had been satisfied by her peace treaty with Finland. Demonstrations in a conquered country were not at all unnatural, and if perhaps the transit of German troops had caused certain reactions in the Finnish population they would disappear with the end of those troop transits. Hence, if one considered matters realistically, there were no differences between Germany and Russia.

The Führer pointed out that both sides agreed in principle that Finland belonged to the Russian sphere of influence. Instead, therefore, of continuing a purely theoretical discussion, they should rather turn to more important problems.

After the conquest of England the British Empire would be apportioned as a gigantic world-wide estate in bankruptcy of 40 million square kilometers. In this bankrupt estate there would be for Russia access to the ice-free and really open ocean. Thus far, a minority of 45 million Englishmen had ruled 600 million inhabitants of the British Empire. He was about to crush this minority. Even the United States was actually doing nothing but picking out of this bankrupt estate a few items particularly suitable to the United States. Germany, of course, would like to avoid any conflict which would divert her from her struggle against the heart of the Empire, the British Isles. For that reason, he (the Führer) did not like Italy's war against Greece, as it diverted forces to the periphery instead of concentrating them against England at one point. The same would occur during a Baltic war. The conflict with England would be fought to the last ditch, and he had no doubt that the defeat of the British Isles would lead to the dissolution of the Empire. It was a chimera to believe that the Empire could possibly be ruled and held together from Canada. Under those circumstances there arose world-wide perspectives. During the next few weeks they would have to be settled in joint diplomatic negotiations with Russia, and Russia's participation in the solution of these problems would have to be arranged. All the countries which could possibly be interested in the bankrupt estate would have to stop all controversies among themselves and concern themselves exclusively with the partition of the British Empire. This applied to Germany, France, Italy, Russia, and Japan.

Molotov replied that he had followed the arguments of the Führer with interest and that he was in agreement with everything that he had understood. However, he could comment thereon less than the Führer, since the latter had surely thought more about these problems and formed more concrete opinions regarding them. The main thing was first to make up their minds regarding German-Russian collaboration, in which Italy and Japan could be included later on. In this connection nothing should be changed that had been started; rather, they should only contemplate a continuation of what had been begun.

The Führer mentioned here that the further efforts in the sense of the opening up of great prospects would not be easy and emphasized in this connection that Germany did not want to annex France, as the Russians appeared to assume. He wanted to create a world coalition of interested powers which would consist of Spain, France, Italy, Germany, Soviet Russia, and Japan and would to a certain degree represent a coalition—extending from North Africa to Eastern Asia—of all those who wanted to be satisfied out of the British bankrupt estate. To this end all internal controversies between the members of this coalition must be removed or at least neutralized. For this purpose the settlement of a whole series of questions was necessary. In the West, i. e. between Spain, France, Italy, and Germany, he believed he had now found a formula which satisfied everybody alike. It had not been easy to reconcile the views of Spain and France for instance, in regard to North Africa; however, recognizing the greater future possibilities, both countries finally had given in. After the West was thus settled, an agreement in the East must now be reached. In this case it was not a matter of relations between Soviet Russia and Turkey only, but also of the Greater Asian Sphere. The latter consisted not only of the Greater East Asian Sphere, but also of a purely Asiatic area oriented toward the south, that Germany even now recognized as Russia's sphere of influence. It was a matter of determining in bold outlines the boundaries for the future activity of peoples and of assigning to nations large areas where they could find an ample field of activity for fifty to a hundred years.

Molotov replied that the Führer had raised a number of questions which concerned not only Europe but, beyond that, other territories too. He wanted to discuss first a problem closer to Europe, that of Turkey. As a Black Sea power, the Soviet Union was tied up with a number of countries. In this connection there was still an unsettled question that was just now being discussed by the Danube Commission. Moreover, the Soviet Union had expressed its dissatisfaction to Rumania that the latter had accepted the guarantee of Germany and Italy without consultation with Russia. The Soviet Government had already explained its position twice, and it was of the opinion that the guarantee was aimed against the interests of Soviet Russia, "if one might express oneself so bluntly." Therefore, the question had arisen of revoking this guarantee. To this the Führer had declared that for a certain time it was necessary and its removal therefore impossible. This affected the interests of the Soviet Union as a Black Sea power.

Molotov then came to speak of the Straits, which, referring to the Crimean War and the events of the years 1918–19, he called England's historic gateway for attack on the Soviet Union. The situation was all the more menacing to Russia, as the British had now gained a foothold in Greece. For reasons of security the relations between Soviet Russia and other Black Sea powers were of great importance. In this connection Molotov asked the Führer what Germany would say if Russia gave Bulgaria, that is, the independent country located closest to the Straits, a guarantee under exactly the same conditions as Germany and Italy had given one to Rumania. Russia, however, intended to agree beforehand on this matter with Germany and, if possible, with Italy too.

To a question by Molotov regarding the German position on the question of the Straits, the Führer replied that the Reich Foreign Minister had already considered this point and that he had envisaged a revision of the Montreux Convention in favor of the Soviet Union.

The Reich Foreign Minister confirmed this and stated that the Italians also took a benevolent attitude on the question of this revision.

Molotov again brought up the guarantee to Bulgaria and gave the assurance that the Soviet Union did not intend to interfere in the internal order of the country under any circumstances. "Not a hairsbreadth" would they deviate from this.

Regarding Germany's and Italy's guarantee to Rumania, the Führer stated that this guarantee had been the only possibility of inducing Rumania to cede Bessarabia to Russia without a fight. Besides, because of her oil wells, Rumania represented an absolute German-Italian interest, and, lastly, the Rumanian Government itself had asked that Germany assume the air and ground protection of the oil region, since it did not feel entirely secure from attacks by the English. Referring to a threat of invasion by the English at Salonika, the Führer repeated in this connection that Germany would not tolerate such a landing, but he gave the assurance that at the end of the war all German soldiers would be withdrawn from Rumania.

In reply to Molotov's question regarding Germany's opinion on a Russian guarantee to Bulgaria, the Führer replied that if this guarantee was to be given under the same conditions as the German-Italian guarantee to Rumania, the question would first arise whether Bulgaria herself had asked for a guarantee. He (the Führer) did not know of any request by Bulgaria. Besides, he would, of course, have to inquire about the position of Italy before he himself could make any statement.

However, the decisive question was whether Russia saw a chance to gain sufficient security for her Black Sea interests through a revision of the Montreux Convention. He did not expect an immediate answer to this question, since he knew that Molotov would first have to discuss these matters with Stalin.

Molotov replied that Russia had only one aim in this respect. She wanted to be secure from an attack by way of the Straits and would like to settle this question with Turkey; a guarantee given to Bulgaria would alleviate the situation. As a Black Sea power Russia was entitled to such security and believed that she would be able to come to an understanding with Turkey in regard thereto.

The Führer replied that this would conform approximately with Germany's views, according to which only Russian warships might pass freely through the Dardanelles, while the Straits would be closed to all other warships.

Molotov added that Russia wanted to obtain a guarantee against an attack on the Black Sea via the Straits not only on paper but "in reality" and believed that she could reach an agreement with Turkey in regard thereto. In this connection he came back again to the question of the Russian guarantee to Bulgaria and repeated that the internal regime of the country would remain unaffected, whereas on the other hand Russia was prepared to guarantee Bulgaria an outlet to the Aegean Sea. He was again addressing to the Führer—as the one who was to decide on the entire German policy—the question as to what position Germany would take with regard to this Russian guarantee.

The Führer replied with a counter-question as to whether the Bulgarians had actually asked for a guarantee, and he again stated that he would have to ask the Duce for his opinion.

Molotov stressed that he was not asking the Führer for a final decision, but that he was asking only for a provisional expression of opinion.

The Führer replied that he could not under any circumstances take a position before he had talked with the Duce, since Germany was interested in the matter only secondarily. As a great Danubian power, she was interested only in the Danube River, but not in the passage into the Black Sea. For if she were perchance looking for sources of friction with Russia, she would not need the Straits for that.

The talk then turned again to the great plans for collaboration between the powers interested in the British Empire's bankrupt estate. The Führer pointed out that he was not, of course, absolutely sure whether these plans could be carried out. In case it was not possible, a great historical opportunity would be missed, at any rate. All these questions would perhaps have to be examined again in Moscow by the Foreign Ministers of Germany, Italy, and Japan together with Herr Molotov, after they had been appropriately prepared through diplomatic channels.

At this point in the conversation the Führer called attention to the late hour and stated that in view of the possibility of English air attacks it would be better to break off the talk now, since the main issues had probably been sufficiently discussed.

Summarizing, he stated that subsequently the possibilities of safeguarding Russia's interests as a Black Sea power would have to be examined further and that in general Russia's further wishes with regard to her future position in the world would have to be considered.

In a closing remark Molotov stated that a number of important and new questions had been raised for Soviet Russia. The Soviet Union, as a powerful country, could not keep aloof from the great issues in Europe and Asia.

Finally he came to speak of Russo-Japanese relations, which had recently improved. He anticipated that the improvement would continue at a still faster pace and thanked the Reich Government for its efforts in this direction.

Concerning Sino-Japanese relations, it was certainly the task of Russia and Germany to attend to their settlement. But an honorable solution would have to be assured for China, all the more since Japan now stood a chance of getting "Indonesia."

SCHMIDT

Berlin, November 15, 1940.

MEMORANDUM of a Conversation between Joachim von Ribbentrop, German Minister for Foreign Affairs, and Vyacheslav M. Molotov, Chairman of the Council of People's Commissars and Commissar for Foreign Affairs of the Union of Soviet Socialist Republics, at Berlin, November 13, 1940

Nazi-Soviet Relations, 1939–1941, p. 247

SECRET
RM 42/40

Duration of conversation: 9:45 p. m. until 12 midnight.

Because of the air raid alert that had been ordered, Reich Minister for Foreign Affairs von Ribbentrop and Herr Molotov went into the Reich Foreign Minister's air raid shelter after the supper at the Embassy of the U. S. S. R. at 9:40 p. m. on November 13, 1940, in order to conduct the final conversation.

The Reich Foreign Minister opened the conversation with the statement that he wanted to take the opportunity to supplement and give more specific form to what had been discussed thus far. He wanted to explain to Herr Molotov his conception of the possibility of establishing a joint policy of collaboration between Germany and the Soviet Union for the future and to enumerate the points which he had in mind in this connection. He had to stress explicitly, however, that this was merely a matter of ideas which were still rather rough, but which might perhaps be realized at some time in the future. By and large, it was a matter of achieving future collaboration between the countries of the Tripartite Pact—Germany, Italy, and Japan—and the Soviet Union, and he believed that first a way must be found to define in bold outlines the spheres of influence of these four countries and to reach an understanding on the problem of Turkey. From the very beginning it was clear in this connection that the problem of the delimitation of the spheres of influence concerned all four countries, whereas only the Soviet Union, Turkey, Italy, and Germany were interested in the settlement of the Straits question. He conceived the future developments as follows: Herr Molotov would discuss with Herr Stalin the issues raised in Berlin; then, by means of further conversations, an agreement could be reached between the Soviet Union and Germany; thereupon the Reich Foreign Minister would approach Italy and Japan in order to find out how their interests with respect to the delimitation of spheres of influence could be reduced to a common formula. He had already approached Italy as to Turkey. The further *modus procedendi* between Italy, the Soviet Union, and Germany would be to exert influence upon Turkey in the spirit of the wishes of the three countries. If they succeeded in reducing the interests of the four countries concerned to a common denominator—which, given good will, was entirely possible—it would undoubtedly work to the advantage of all concerned. The next step would consist in attempting to record both sets of issues in confidential documents. If the Soviet Union entertained a similar view, that is, would be willing to work against the extension, and for the early termination of the war (the Reich Foreign Minister believed that Herr Molotov had indicated his willingness in the previous discussions), he had in mind as the ultimate objective an agreement for collaboration between the countries of the Tripartite Pact and the Soviet Union. He had drafted the contents of this agreement in outline form and he would like to inform Herr Molotov of them today, stressing in advance that he had not discussed these issues so concretely either with Japan or with Italy. He considered it necessary that Germany and the Soviet Union settle the issues first. This was not by any means a matter of a German proposal, but—as already mentioned—one of still rather rough ideas, which would have to be deliberated by both parties and discussed between Molotov and Stalin. It would be advisable to pursue the matter further, particularly in diplomatic negotiations with Italy and Japan, only if the question had been settled as between Germany and the Soviet Union.

Then the Reich Foreign Minister informed Herr Molotov of the contents of the agreement outlined by him in the following words:

The Governments of the states of the Three Power Pact, Germany, Italy, and Japan, on the one side, and the Government of the U.S.S.R. on the other side, motivated by the desire to establish in their natural boundaries an order serving the welfare of all peoples concerned and to create a firm and enduring foundation for their common labors toward this goal, have agreed upon the following:

Article 1

In the Three Power Pact of September 27, 1940, Germany, Italy, and Japan agreed to oppose the extension of the war into a world conflict with all possible means and to collaborate toward an early restoration of world peace. They expressed their willingness to extend their collaboration to nations in other parts of the world which are inclined to direct their efforts along the same course as theirs. The Soviet Union declares that it concurs in these aims and is on its part determined to cooperate politically in this course with the Three Powers.

Article 2

Germany, Italy, Japan, and the Soviet Union undertake to respect each other's natural spheres of influence. In so far as these spheres of influence come into contact with each other, they will constantly consult each other in an amicable way with regard to the problems arising therefrom.

Article 3

Germany, Italy, Japan, and the Soviet Union undertake to join no combination of powers and to support no combination of powers which is directed against one of the Four Powers.

The Four Powers will assist each other in economic matters in every way and will supplement and extend the agreements existing among themselves.

The Reich Foreign Minister added that this agreement was intended for a period of ten years, with the provision that the Governments of the Four Powers, before the expiration of this term, were to reach an understanding regarding the matter of an extension of the agreement.

The agreement itself would be announced to the public. Beyond that, with reference to the above-mentioned agreement, a confidential (secret) agreement could be concluded—in a form still to be determined—establishing the focal points in the territorial aspirations of the Four Countries.

As to Germany, apart from the territorial revisions to be made in Europe at the conclusion of the peace, her territorial aspirations centered in the Central African region.

The territorial aspirations of Italy, apart from the European territorial revisions to be made at the conclusion of the peace, centered in North and Northeast Africa.

The aspirations of Japan would still have to be clarified through diplomatic channels. Here too, a delimitation could easily be found, possibly by fixing a line which would run south of the Japanese home islands and Manchukuo.

The focal points in the territorial aspirations of the Soviet Union would presumably be centered south of the territory of the Soviet Union in the direction of the Indian Ocean.

Such a confidential agreement could be supplemented by the statement that the Four Powers concerned, except for the settlement of individual issues, would respect each other's territorial aspirations and would not oppose their realization.

The above-mentioned agreements could be supplemented by a second secret protocol, to be concluded between Germany, Italy, and the Soviet Union. This second secret protocol could perhaps read that Germany, Italy, and the Soviet Union, on the occasion of the signing of the agreement between Germany, Italy, Japan, and the Soviet Union, were agreed that it was in their common interest to release Turkey from her previous ties and win her progressively to a political collaboration with them.

They declare that they would pursue this aim in close contact with each other, in accordance with a procedure to be established.

Germany, Italy, and the Soviet Union would jointly exert their influence to the end that the Straits Convention of Montreux, presently in force, would be replaced by another convention which would accord to the Soviet Union the unrestricted right of passage through the Straits for her warships at any time, whereas all other powers except the other Black Sea countries, but including Germany and Italy, would renounce in principle the right of passage through the Straits for their warships. Transit through the Straits for merchant ships would, of course, have to remain free in principle.

In this connection, the Reich Foreign Minister stated as follows:

The German Government would welcome it if the Soviet Union were prepared for such collaboration with Italy, Japan, and Germany. This matter was to be clarified in the near future by the German Ambassador in Moscow, Count von der Schulenburg, and the Soviet Ambassador in Berlin. In conformity with the statement contained in Herr Stalin's letter, that he was not adverse to a fundamental examination of the question, which had been confirmed by Herr Molotov during his stay in Berlin, a conference of the Foreign Ministers of Germany, Italy, and Japan for the purpose of signing such an agreement might be envisaged as the ultimate goal. He, the Reich Foreign Minister, was of course aware that such questions required careful examination; he did not, therefore, expect any answer from Herr Molotov today, but he was happy to have had the opportunity to inform Herr Molotov in this slightly more concrete form of the thoughts that had recently been motivating Germany. Furthermore, he wished to tell Herr Molotov the following:

As Herr Molotov knew, he (the Reich Foreign Minister) had always shown a particular interest in the relations between Japan and the Soviet Union. He would appreciate it if Herr Molotov could say what the state of these relations was at the present time. As far as the German Government was informed, Japan was anxious to conclude a nonaggression treaty. It was not his intention to interfere in matters which did not directly concern him, but he believed that it would be useful if this question were also discussed between him and Molotov. If a mediating influence on the part of Germany were desired, he would be glad to undertake this office. To be sure, he still clearly recalled Herr Stalin's remark, when Herr Stalin said that he knew the Asiatics better than Herr von Ribbentrop did. Nevertheless, he wished to mention that the willingness of the Japanese Government to come to a broad understanding with the Soviet Union was known to him. He also had the impression that if the nonaggression pact materialized the Japanese would be prepared to settle all other issues in a generous manner. He wished to stress explicitly that Japan had not asked the German Government to mediate. He, the Reich Foreign Minister, was, however, informed of the state of affairs, and he knew that, in case of the conclusion of a nonaggression pact, Japan would be willing to recognize the Russian spheres of influence in Outer Mongolia and Sinkiang, provided an understanding with China were reached. An agreement could also be reached on possible Soviet aspirations in the direction of British India, if an understanding were reached between the Soviet Union and the Tripartite Pact. The Japanese Government was disposed to meet the Soviet wishes half-way in regard to the oil and coal concessions on Sakhalin Island, but it would first have to overcome resistance at home. This would be easier for the Japanese Government if a nonaggression pact were first concluded with the Soviet Union. Thereafter, the possibility would undoubtedly arise for an understanding on all other points also.

The Reich Foreign Minister concluded by requesting Herr Molotov to inform him of his views on the issues presented by him.

Herr Molotov replied that, concerning Japan, he had the hope and conviction that they would now make more progress on the road to understanding than had previously been the case. Relations with Japan had always been fraught with difficulties and reverses. Nevertheless, there now seemed to be prospects of an understanding. The Japanese Government had suggested the conclusion of a nonaggression treaty to the Soviet Government—in fact, even before the change of government in Japan—in which connection the Soviet Government had put a number of questions to the Japanese Government. At present, the answer to these questions had not yet been received. Only when it arrived could negotiations be entered into—negotiations which could not be separated from the remaining complex of questions. The solution of the problem would therefore require some time.

As for Turkey, the Soviet Union assumed that they would have to reach an understanding with Turkey on the Straits question first of all. Germany and the Soviet Union were agreed that the Convention of Montreux was worthless. For the Soviet Union, as the most important Black Sea power, it was a matter of obtaining effective guarantees of her security. In the course of her history, Russia had often been attacked by way of the Straits. Consequently paper agreements would not suffice for the Soviet Union; rather, she would have to insist on effective guarantees of her security. Therefore, this question had to be examined and discussed more concretely. The questions which interested the Soviet Union in the Near East, concerned not only Turkey, but Bulgaria, for instance, about which he, Molotov, had spoken in detail in his previous conversation with the Führer. But the fate of Rumania and Hungary was also of interest to the Soviet Union and could not be immaterial to her under any circumstances. It would further interest the Soviet Government to learn what the Axis contemplated with regard to Yugoslavia and Greece, and, likewise, what Germany intended with regard to Poland. He recalled the fact that, regarding the future form of Poland, a Protocol existed between the Soviet Union and Germany for the implementation of which an exchange of opinion was necessary. He asked whether from the German viewpoint this Protocol was still in force. The Soviet Government was also interested in the question of Swedish neutrality, and he wanted to know whether the German Government still took the stand that the preservation of Swedish neutrality was in the interest of the Soviet Union and Germany. Besides, there existed the question of the passages out of the Baltic Sea (Store Belt, Lille Belt, Oeresund, Kattegat, Skagerrak). The Soviet Government believed that discussions must be held regarding this question similar to those now being conducted concerning the Danube Commissions. As to the Finnish question, it was sufficiently clarified during his previous conversations with the Führer. He would appreciate it if the Reich Foreign Minister would comment on the foregoing questions, because this would facilitate the clarification of all other questions which Herr von Ribbentrop had previously raised.

In his answer the Reich Foreign Minister stated that he had no comment to make on the Bulgarian question, other than what the Führer had already told Herr Molotov; that, first, it would have to be determined whether Bulgaria desired a guarantee at all from the

Soviet Union, and that, moreover, the German Government could not take a stand on this question without previously consulting Italy. On all other questions he felt he had been "queried too closely" ["*überfragt*"], by Herr Molotov. As to the preservation of Sweden's neutrality, we were just as much interested in it as the Soviet Union. As to the passages out of the Baltic Sea, the Baltic Sea was at present an inland sea, where we were interested in the maintenance of the free movement of shipping. Outside of the Baltic Sea, however, there was war. The time was not yet ripe for discussing the new order of things in Poland. The Balkan issue had already been discussed extensively in the conversations. In the Balkans we had solely an economic interest, and we did not want England to disturb us there. The granting of the German guarantee to Rumania had apparently been misconstrued by Moscow. He wanted to repeat again, therefore, that at that time it was a matter of averting a clash between Hungary and Rumania through quick action. If he, the Reich Foreign Minister, had not intervened at that time, Hungary would have marched against Rumania. On the other hand, Rumania could not have been induced to cede so much territory, if the Rumanian Government had not been strengthened by the territorial guarantee. In all its decisions, the German Government was guided solely by the endeavor to preserve peace in the Balkans and to prevent England from gaining a foothold there and from interfering with supplies to Germany. Thus our action in the Balkans was motivated exclusively by the circumstances of our war against England. As soon as England conceded her defeat and asked for peace, German interests in the Balkans would be confined exclusively to the economic field, and German troops would be withdrawn from Rumania. Germany had—as the Führer had repeatedly declared—no territorial interests in the Balkans. He could only repeat again and again that the decisive question was whether the Soviet Union was prepared and in a position to cooperate with us in the great liquidation of the British Empire. On all other questions we would easily reach an understanding if we could succeed in extending our relations and in defining the spheres of influence. Where the spheres of influence lay had been stated repeatedly. It was therefore—as the Führer had so clearly put it—a matter of the interests of the Soviet Union and Germany requiring that the partners stand not breast to breast but back to back, in order to support each other in the achievement of their aspirations. He would appreciate it if Herr Molotov would comment on this matter. Compared to the great basic issues, all others were completely insignificant and would be settled automatically as soon as an over-all understanding was reached. In conclusion, he wished to remind Herr Molotov that the latter owed him an answer to the question of whether the Soviet Union was in principle sympathetic to the idea of obtaining an outlet to the Indian Ocean.

In his reply Molotov stated that the Germans were assuming that the war against England had already actually been won. If, therefore, as had been said in another connection, Germany was waging a life and death struggle against England, he could only construe this as meaning that Germany was fighting "for life" and England "for death." As to the question of collaboration, he quite approved of it, but he added that they had to come to a thorough understanding. This idea had also been expressed in Stalin's letter. A delimitation of the spheres of influence must also be sought. On this point, however, he (Molotov) could not take a definitive stand at this time, since he did not know the opinion of Stalin and of his other friends in Moscow in the matter. However, he had to state that all these great issues of tomorrow could not be separated from the issues of today and the fulfillment of existing agreements. The things that were started must first be completed before they proceeded to new tasks. The conversations which he—Molotov—had had in Berlin had undoubtedly been very useful, and he considered it appropriate that the questions raised should now be further dealt with through diplomatic channels by way of the ambassadors on either side.

Thereupon Herr Molotov cordially bade farewell to the Reich Foreign Minister, stressing that he did not regret the air raid alarm, because he owed to it such an exhaustive conversation with the Reich Foreign Minister.

HILGER

Moscow, November 18, 1940.

CIRCULAR TELEGRAM from Baron Ernst von Weizsäcker, State Secretary of the German Foreign Office, to All German Diplomatic Missions and the Offices in Paris and Brussels, November 15, 1940

Nazi-Soviet Relations, 1939–1941, p. 255

Multex 425

The conversations between the German and the Soviet-Russian Governments on the occasion of the presence of Molotov in Berlin were conducted on the basis of the treaties concluded last year and resulted in complete agreement regarding the firm determination of both countries to continue in the future the policy inaugurated by these treaties. Beyond that, they served the purpose of coordinating the policy of the Soviet Union with the policy of the Tripartite Pact. As already expressed in the final communiqué regarding the visit of Molotov, this exchange of views took place in an atmosphere of mutual confidence and resulted in agreement by both sides on all important questions of interest to Germany and the Soviet Union. This result clearly proves that all conjectures regarding alleged German-Russian conflicts are in the realm of fantasy and that all speculations of the foe as to a disturbance in the German-Russian relationship of trust and friendship are based on self-deception.

This is particularly stressed by the friendly visit of Molotov in Berlin. [This sentence added in Ribbentrop's handwriting.]

    Same text to all missions.
    Please acknowledge receipt.

TELEGRAM from Count Friedrich Werner von der Schulenburg, German Ambassador to the Union of Soviet Socialist Republics, to the German Foreign Office, November 26, 1940

Nazi-Soviet Relations, 1939–1941, p. 258

VERY URGENT
STRICTLY SECRET
No. 2362 of November 25

    For the Reich Minister in person.
    Molotov asked me to call on him this evening and in the presence of Dekanosov stated the following:

The Soviet Government has studied the contents of the statements of the Reich Foreign Minister in the concluding conversation on November 13 and takes the following stand:

The Soviet Government is prepared to accept the draft of the Four Power Pact which the Reich Foreign Minister outlined in the conversation of November 13, regarding political collaboration and reciprocal economic [support *] subject to the following conditions:

1) Provided that the German troops are immediately withdrawn from Finland, which, under the compact of 1939, belongs to the Soviet Union's sphere of influence. At the same time the Soviet Union undertakes to en-

* "*Unterstützung*" in Moscow Embassy draft; garbled in text as received in Berlin.

sure peaceful relations with Finland and to protect German economic interests in Finland (export of lumber and nickel).

2) Provided that within the next few months the security of the Soviet Union in the Straits is assured by the conclusion of a mutual assistance pact between the Soviet Union and Bulgaria, which geographically is situated inside the security zone of the Black Sea boundaries of the Soviet Union, and by the establishment of a base for land and naval forces of the U.S.S.R. within range of the Bosporus and the Dardanelles by means of a long-term lease.

3) Provided that the area south of Batum and Baku in the general direction of the Persian Gulf is recognized as the center of the aspirations of the Soviet Union.

4) Provided that Japan [renounces *] her rights to concessions for coal and oil in Northern Sakhalin.

In accordance with the foregoing, the draft of the protocol concerning the delimitation of the spheres of influence as outlined by the Reich Foreign Minister would have to be amended so as to stipulate the focal point of the aspirations of the Soviet Union south of Batum and Baku in the general direction of the Persian Gulf.

Likewise, the draft of the protocol or agreement between Germany, Italy, and the Soviet Union with respect to Turkey should be amended so as to guarantee a base for light naval and land forces of the U.S.S.R. on [am] the Bosporus and the Dardanelles by means of a long-term lease, including—in case Turkey declares herself willing to join the Four Power Pact—a guarantee of the independence and of the territory of Turkey by the three countries named.

This protocol should provide that in case Turkey refuses to join the Four Powers, Germany, Italy, and the Soviet Union agree to work out and to carry through the required military and diplomatic measures, and a separate agreement to this effect should be concluded.

Furthermore there should be agreement upon:

a) a third secret protocol between Germany and the Soviet Union concerning Finland (see Point 1 above).

b) a fourth secret protocol between Japan and the Soviet Union concerning the renunciation by Japan of the oil and coal concession in Northern Sakhalin (in return for an adequate compensation).

c) a fifth secret protocol between Germany, the Soviet Union, and Italy, recognizing that Bulgaria is geographically located inside the security zone of the Black Sea boundaries of the Soviet Union and that it is therefore a political necessity that a mutual assistance pact be concluded between the Soviet Union and Bulgaria, which in no way shall affect the internal regime of Bulgaria, her sovereignty or independence.

In conclusion Molotov stated that the Soviet proposal provided for five protocols instead of the two envisaged by the Reich Foreign Minister. He would appreciate a statement of the German view.

* *"Verzichtet"* in Moscow Embassy draft; omitted in text as received in Berlin.

MILITARY DIRECTIVE for "Operation Barbarossa" of Adolf Hitler, Chancellor of the Reich, December 18, 1940

Nazi-Soviet Relations, 1939–1941, p. 260

The Führer and Commander-in-Chief of the German Armed Forces
OKW/WFSt/Abt.L (I) Nr. 33 408/40 gK Chefs.
Military Secret [Geheime Kommandosache]

TOP SECRET [CHEF SACHE] Führer's Headquarters,
BY OFFICER ONLY December 18, 1940

Directive No. 21
Operation Barbarossa

The German Armed Forces must be prepared *to crush Soviet Russia in a quick campaign* (Operation Barbarossa) even before the conclusion of the war against England.

For this purpose the *Army* will have to employ all available units, with the reservation that the occupied territories must be secured against surprise attacks.

For the *Air Force* it will be a matter of releasing such strong forces for the eastern campaign in support of the Army that a quick completion of the ground operations may be expected and that damage to Eastern German territory by enemy air attacks will be as slight as possible. This concentration of the main effort in the East is limited by the requirement that the entire combat and armament area dominated by us must remain adequately protected against enemy air attacks and that the offensive operations against England, particularly her supply lines, must not be permitted to break down.

The main effort of the *Navy* will remain unequivocally directed against *England* even during an eastern campaign.

I shall order the *concentration* against Soviet Russia possibly eight weeks before the intended beginning of operations.

Preparations requiring more time to start are to be started now—if this has not yet been done—and are to be completed by May 15, 1941.

It is to be considered of decisive importance, however, that the intention to attack is not discovered.

The preparations of the High Commands are to be made on the following basis:

I. *General Purpose:*

The mass of the Russian *Army* in Western Russia is to be destroyed in daring operations, by driving forward deep armored wedges, and the retreat of units capable of combat into the vastness of Russian territory is to be prevented.

In quick pursuit a line is then to be reached from which the Russian Air Force will no longer be able to attack German Reich territory. The ultimate objective of the operation is to establish a defense line against Asiatic Russia from a line running approximately from the Volga River to Archangel. Then, in case of necessity, the last industrial area left to Russia in the Urals can be eliminated by the Luftwaffe.

In the course of these operations the Russian *Baltic Sea Fleet* will quickly lose its bases and thus will no longer be able to fight.

Effective intervention by the Russian *Air Force* is to be prevented by powerful blows at the very beginning of the operation.

II. *Probable Allies and their Tasks:*

1. On the flanks of our operation we can count on the active participation of *Rumania* and *Finland* in the war against Soviet Russia.

The High Command will in due time concert and determine in what form the armed forces of the two countries will be placed under German command at the time of their intervention.

2. It will be the task of *Rumania,* together with the forces concentrating there, to pin down the enemy facing her and, in addition, to render auxiliary services in the rear area.

3. *Finland* will cover the concentration of the redeployed German *North Group* (parts of the XXI Group) coming from Norway and will operate jointly with it. Besides, Finland will be assigned the task of eliminating Hangö.

4. It may be expected that *Swedish* railroads and highways will be available for the concentration of the German North Group, from the start of operations at the latest.

III. *Direction of Operations:*

A. *Army* (hereby approving the plans presented to me):

In the zone of operations divided by the Pripet Marshes into a southern and northern sector, the main effort will be made *north* of this area. Two Army Groups will be provided here.

The southern group of these two Army Groups—the center of the entire front—will be given the task of annihilating the forces of the enemy in White Russia by advancing from the region around and north of Warsaw with especially strong armored and motorized units. The possibility of switching strong mobile units to the North must thereby be created in order, in cooperation with the Northern Army Group operating from East Prussia in the general direction of Leningrad, to annihilate the enemy forces fighting in the Baltic. Only after having accomplished this most important task, which must be followed by the occupation of Leningrad and Kronstadt, are the offensive operations aimed at the occupation of the important traffic and armament center of Moscow to be pursued.

Only a surprisingly fast collapse of Russian resistance could justify aiming at both objectives simultaneously.

The most important assignment of the XXI Group, even during the eastern operations, will still be the protection of Norway. The additional forces available are to be employed in the north (mountain corps), first to secure the Petsamo Region and its ore mines as well as the Arctic Ocean route, and then to advance jointly with Finnish forces against the Murmansk railroad and stop the supply of the Murmansk region by land.

Whether such an operation with *rather strong* German forces (two or three divisions) can be conducted from the area of and south of Rovaniemi depends upon Sweden's willingness to make the railroads available for such a concentration.

The main body of the Finnish Army will be assigned the task, in coordination with the advance of the German northern flank, of pinning down strong Russian forces by attacking west of or on both sides of Lake Ladoga and of seizing Hangö.

The Army Group employed south of the Pripet Marshes is to make its main effort in the area from Lublin in the general direction of Kiev, in order to penetrate quickly with strong armored units into the deep flank and rear of the Russian forces and then to roll them up along the Dnieper River.

The German-Rumanian groups on the right flank are assigned the task of:

(a) protecting Rumanian territory and thereby the southern flank of the entire operation.

(b) pinning down the opposing enemy forces while Army Group South is attacking on its northern flank and, according to the progressive development of the situation and in conjunction with the Air Force, preventing their orderly retreat across the Dniester during the pursuit,

[and,] *in the North,* of reaching Moscow quickly.

The capture of this city means a decisive success politically and economically and, beyond that, the elimination of the most important railway center.

B. *Air Force:*

Its task will be to paralyze and to eliminate as far as possible the intervention of the Russian Air Force as well as to support the Army at its main points of effort, particularly those of Army Group Center and, on the flank, those of Army Group South. The Russian railroads, in the order of their importance for the operations, will be cut or the most important near-by objectives (river crossings) seized by the bold employment of parachute and airborne troops.

In order to concentrate all forces against the enemy Air Force and to give immediate support to the Army the armament industry will not be attacked during the main operations. Only after the completion of the mobile operations may such attacks be considered—primarily against the Ural Region.

C. *Navy:*

The Navy's role against Soviet Russia is, while safeguarding our own coast, to prevent an escape of enemy naval units from the Baltic Sea. As the Russian Baltic Sea Fleet, once we have reached Leningrad, will be deprived of its last base and will then be in a hopeless situation, any larger naval operations are to be avoided before that time.

After the elimination of the Russian Fleet it will be a question of protecting all the traffic in the Baltic Sea, including the supply by sea of the northern flank of the Army (mine clearance!).

IV. All orders to be issued by the commanders-in-chief on the basis of this directive must clearly indicate that they are *precautionary measures* for the possibility that Russia should change her present attitude toward us. The number of officers to be assigned to the preparatory work at an early date is to be kept as small as possible; additional personnel should be briefed as late as possible and only to the extent required for the activity of each individual. Otherwise, through the discovery of our preparations—the date of their execution has not even been fixed—there is danger that most serious political and military disadvantages may arise.

V. I expect reports from the commanders-in-chief concerning their further plans based on this directive.

The contemplated preparations of all branches of the Armed Forces, including their progress, are to be reported to me through the High Command [*OKW*].

ADOLF HITLER

* The document also bears four sets of initials, apparently those of Keitel, Jodl, Warlimont, and one unidentified.

TELEGRAM from Count Friedrich Werner von der Schulenburg, German Ambassador to the Union of Soviet Socialist Republics, to the German Foreign Office, January 17, 1941

Nazi-Soviet Relations, 1939–1941, p. 270

VERY URGENT
STRICTLY SECRET
No. 122 of January 17

For the Reich Foreign Minister.

1. Molotov asked me to call on him this afternoon and stated the following:

Since the most important economic questions in the relations between Germany and the Soviet Union had been settled by the recently concluded treaties, it would now be in order to turn to purely political issues again. The Soviet Government was surprised that it had not yet received from Germany any answer to its statement of position of November 25 (cf. telegraphic report No. 2562 [2362] of November 25) concerning the issues raised during the Berlin discussions, and he would appreciate it if I would bring that fact to the attention of the Government of the German Reich with the remark that the Soviet Government was counting on an early German reply.

I replied to Herr Molotov that there was not the slightest cause for any surprise, since this was a matter of issues which must first be thoroughly discussed with Italy and Japan. As soon as these deliberations had been concluded the Soviet Government would certainly be informed of our position with regard to their reply.

2. Molotov then touched upon the Balkans and in that connection stated word for word as follows:

According to all reports available here, German troops in great numbers were concentrated in Rumania and ready to march into Bulgaria with the aim of occupying Bulgaria, Greece, and the Straits. There was no doubt that England would try to forestall the operations of the German troops, to occupy the Straits, to open military operations against Bulgaria in alliance with Turkey, and turn Bulgaria into a theater of war. The Soviet Government had repeatedly called the attention of the Government of the German Reich to the fact that it considered the territory of Bulgaria and the Straits as a security zone of the U.S.S.R. and that it could therefore not remain indifferent in the face of events which menaced the security interests of the U.S.S.R. Consequently the Soviet Government regarded it as its duty to call attention to the fact that it would consider the appearance of any foreign armed forces on the territory of Bulgaria and of the Straits as a violation of the security interests of the U.S.S.R.

Molotov added that he had instructed Dekanosov to make an identical *démarche* in Berlin. In my reply I confined myself to the statements prescribed by telegraphic instructions No. 36 of January 7 and No. 57 of January 10.

TELEGRAM from Joachim von Ribbentrop, German Minister for Foreign Affairs, to the State Secretary of the German Foreign Office (Baron Ernst von Weizsäcker), January 21, 1941

Nazi-Soviet Relations, 1939–1941, p. 271

No. 38   Fuschl, January 21, 1941—11:30 p. m.

Teletype through Office of Reich Foreign Minister to State Secretary von Weizsäcker, No. 31.

1. I request that you ask the Russian Ambassador to call on you Wednesday evening and that you give him in oral form the following reply to the statement made to you on January 17. Thereupon the text of the reply is to be handed to him in the form of a memorandum.

Text of the reply:

1. The Reich Government has not received any reports that England contemplates occupying the Straits. Nor does the Reich Government believe that Turkey will permit English military forces to enter her territory. However, the Reich Government is informed that England intends and is about to gain a foothold on Greek territory.

2. The Führer pointed out repeatedly to Chairman Molotov during his visit to Berlin in November that Germany would prevent by all military means any attempt by England to gain a foothold on Greek soil.

It is the inalterable intention of the Reich Government not under any circumstances to permit English military forces to establish themselves on Greek territory, which would mean a threat to vital interests of Germany in the Balkans. It is therefore carying out certain troop concentrations in the Balkans, which have the sole purpose of preventing the British from gaining any foothold on Greek soil.

3. Germany does not intend to occupy the Straits. She will respect the territory under Turkish sovereignty unless Turkey on her part commits a hostile act against German troops. On the other hand, however, the German Army will march through Bulgarian territory should any military operations be carried out against Greece. The Reich Government has, of course, no intention of violating any Soviet Russian security interests nor

would this by any means be the case if German troops march through Bulgaria.

4. For the action which may have to be undertaken against England in Greece, Germany is carrying on a troop concentration in the Balkans on such a scale that it will enable her to checkmate any English attempt at building up a front in those regions.

The Reich Government believes that in so doing it is also serving Soviet interests, which would be opposed to England's gaining a foothold in these regions.

5. The Reich Government—as it indicated on the occasion of the Berlin visit of Chairman Molotov—has an understanding of the Soviet interest in the Straits question and is prepared to endorse a revision of the Montreux Convention at the proper time. Germany on her part is politically not interested in the Straits question and will withdraw her troops from there after having carried out her operations in the Balkans.

6. As to the stand requested by Chairman Molotov concerning the question of continuing the political discussion begun some time ago in Berlin, the following may be stated:

The Reich Government still adheres to the ideas explained to Chairman Molotov during his presence in Berlin. The Soviet Government on the other hand made certain counterproposals at the end of November. At the present time the Reich Government is in touch with the Governments of its allies, Italy and Japan, concerning all those issues, and it hopes that after having further clarified the whole problem it will be able to resume the political discussion with the Soviet Government in the near future.

End of the reply.

2. Ambassador Schulenburg is receiving instructions from here to take corresponding action with Herr Molotov on Wednesday evening or Thursday morning.

3. Furthermore, I request that, after the call of the Russian Ambassador, you hand Ambassador Alfieri a copy of the statement given to you by Herr Dekanosov on January 17, as well as a copy of our reply, for the confidential information of the Italian Government. The Duce and Count Ciano have already been informed by me here.

TELEGRAM from Joachim von Ribbentrop, German Minister for Foreign Affairs, to the German Ambassador to the Union of Soviet Socialist Republics (Count Friedrich Werner von der Schulenburg), February 27, 1941

Nazi-Soviet Relations, 1939–1941, p. 276

VERY URGENT
No. 144 of February 27
Transmitted to Moscow as No. 403, February 27—10:58 p. m.

For the Ambassador personally.
Please go to see Herr Molotov on Friday, February 28, toward evening and communicate to him verbally the following:

1. As the Soviet Government knows, negotiations have for some time been in progress between the Government of the Reich and the Italian Government on the one hand and the Bulgarian Government on the other, regarding the accession of Bulgaria to the Three Power Pact. These negotiations have now been concluded, and it has been agreed that Bulgaria will accede to the Three Power Pact, and the Protocol regarding this accession will be signed on March 1. The Government of the Reich is anxious to inform the Soviet Government of this in advance.

2. I would ask you to go to see Herr Molotov again on March 1, toward evening, and to tell him the following:

Reports in our possession concerning British intentions in Greece have forced the Government of the Reich to take further security measures forthwith, making necessary the shifting of German troops to Bulgarian soil. Referring to the statement made to the Soviet Government on January 23d, please add that this is a precautionary measure taken to prevent the British from gaining a firm foothold in Greece. Should Herr Molotov go into the subject in any further detail, we remind you—for your guidance—that, in the first place, these security measures are taken exclusively to prevent British entrenchment on Greek territory; secondly, that the measures are not directed at Turkey, and that we shall respect Turkish sovereignty unless Turkey commits a hostile act against us; that, thirdly, these German troop concentrations are war measures, and that the elimination of the British danger in Greece will automatically result in the withdrawal of the German troops.

Please inform me by wire how Herr Molotov receives your communications.

For your personal information, you are further informed that the

Bulgarian Minister in Moscow will also make similar communications from his Government on February 28th and on March 1.

TELEGRAM from Count Friedrich Werner von der Schulenburg, German Ambassador to the Union of Soviet Socialist Republics, to the German Foreign Office, March 1, 1941 (12:25 a.m.)

Nazi-Soviet Relations, 1939–1941, p. 277

VERY URGENT
No. 444 of February 28

In reference to your telegram of the 27th, No. 403.

I called on Herr Molotov this evening and carried out instruction (1).

Molotov received my communication with obvious concern and stated that the German Reich Government had been informed of the viewpoint of the Soviet Government on November 25, 1940 (see telegraphic report of November 25, No. 2562 [2362]). The position of the Soviet Government in the matter was still determined by the communication of that date. Then, the future position of Bulgaria was considered within the framework of certain particular circumstances. In the meantime, events had taken a different turn. The view of the Soviet Government, on the other hand, that Bulgaria came within the security zone of the Soviet Union, remained unchanged.

Despite my objections that the accession of Bulgaria was in no way prejudicial to the interests of the Soviet Union, Molotov held to his view, stating that the accession of Bulgaria was taking place under circumstances quite different than had been anticipated, and that it was unfortunately not evident to him that events were unfolding within the framework of the Soviet Government's *démarche* of November 25.

TELEGRAM from Count Friedrich Werner von der Schulenburg, German Ambassador to the Union of Soviet Socialist Republics, to the German Foreign Office, March 1, 1941 (10:15 p.m.)

Nazi-Soviet Relations, 1939–1941, p. 278

VERY URGENT
SECRET
No. 453 of March 1

Reference your telegram of the 27th, No. 403.

Instruction under (2) carried out at 6:30 p. m., Moscow time, today.

Molotov, who received my communication with great gravity, stated first of all that he was informed regarding the German decision, since the Bulgarian Minister had today already appraised Herr Vishinsky. Molotov thereupon expressed his deep concern that the German Government had, in a matter of such importance to the Soviet Government, made decisions contrary to the Soviet Government's conception of the security interests of the Soviet Union. The Soviet Government had repeatedly stressed its special interest in Bulgaria to the German Government, both during the Berlin conferences and later. Consequently it could not remain indifferent in the face of Germany's last measures in Bulgaria and would have to define its attitude with regard thereto. It hoped that the German Reich Government would attach the proper significance to this attitude. Molotov in my presence drafted in his own hand a rough memorandum setting forth the position of the Soviet Government, had it copied, and handed it to me. The text of the note is as follows:

1. It is to be regretted that despite the caution contained in the *démarche* of November 25, 1940, on the part of the Soviet Government, the German Reich Government has deemed it possible to take a course that involves injury to the security interests of the U.S.S.R. and has decided to effect the military occupation of Bulgaria.

2. In view of the fact that the Soviet Government maintains the same basic position as in its *démarche* of November 25, the German Government must understand that it cannot count on support from the U.S.S.R. for its acts in Bulgaria.

In my reply, I confined myself to your instructions, and stressed particularly that there could be no question of an impairment of Soviet security interests.

MEMORANDUM of a Conversation between Adolf Hitler, Chancellor of the German Reich, and Yosuke Matsuoka, Japanese Minister for Foreign Affairs, at Berlin, March 27, 1941, in the Presence of the German Minister for Foreign Affairs (Joachim von Ribbentrop) and Other Officials

Nazi-Soviet Relations, 1939–1941, pp. 289, 294, 297 (excerpts)

Matsuoka declared—after referring to the reports of Ambassador Ott and the Reich Foreign Minister, through which the Führer would certainly be informed about the current situation in Japan—that he would personally set forth the situation in the frankest fashion. There were in Japan, as in other countries, certain intellectual circles which only a powerful individual could hold firmly under control. He meant by that the sort of person who would like to capture the tiger cub, but who was not prepared to go into the den and take it away from its mother. He had used this line of thought in making the same point in the presence of two princes of the Imperial Family in a conference at headquarters. It was regrettable that Japan had not yet eliminated those elements and that some of these people were even occupying influential positions. Confidentially, he could state that in the interview at headquarters, after an earnest discussion, his point of view had prevailed. Japan would take action, and in a decisive form, if she had the feeling that otherwise she would lose a chance which could only occur once in a thousand years; and in fact Japan would act without consideration of the state of her preparations, since there were always some people who claimed that preparations were insufficient. Matsuoka had also made this point with the two princes. The hesitant politicians in Japan would always delay and act partly from a pro-British or pro-American attitude.

Matsuoka declared that he had come out for the alliance long before the outbreak of the European war. He had been very active at that time to this end, but unfortunately he had had no success. After the outbreak of the European war he personally had held the opinion that Japan should first attack Singapore and bring to an end the British influence in that area and should then join the Three Power Pact, since he did not favor the idea that Japan should join the alliance without having made some contribution toward bringing about the collapse of England. While Germany had been engaged in a titanic struggle against England for a year, Japan, up to the conclusion of the alliance, had contributed nothing. He had therefore come out very strongly for the plan of an attack on Singapore, but he had not prevailed and, under the force of events, had then reversed his program and had come around to the entry into the alliance first.

He had not the slightest doubt that the South Sea problem could not be solved by Japan without the capture of Singapore. They would have to press into the tiger's den and drag out the young by force.

It was only a question of the time when Japan would attack. According to his idea the attack should come as soon as possible. Unfortunately he did not control Japan, but had to bring those who were in control around to his point of view. He would certainly be successful in this some day. But at the present moment he could under these circumstances make no pledge on behalf of the Japanese Empire that it would take action.

He would, after his interviews with the Führer and the Reich Foreign Minister, and after he had examined the situation in Europe, give his closest attention to these matters on his return. He could make no definite commitment, but he would promise that he personally would do his utmost for the ends that had been mentioned.

Matsuoka then requested urgently that the representations which he had made be treated as strictly confidential, since, if they became known in Japan, those among his Cabinet colleagues who thought differently from him would probably become alarmed and would seek to get him out of office.

In connection with his efforts to bring about the treaty of alliance he had maintained strict secrecy up to the last minute and in order to deceive his opponents he had oftentimes intentionally given the impression of having a pro-American or pro-British attitude.

Shortly before the conclusion of the treaty of alliance it had been reported to him that the British Ambassador was conducting a strong propaganda campaign among the Japanese to the effect that Japan was taking a very risky step in adhering to the Three Power Pact. The American Ambassador also had been active in the same direction. A few days after the conclusion of the treaty of alliance he had asked the American Ambassador whether the reports about these propaganda activities were correct. The latter had admitted everything and had stated as well that every Japanese whom he had met, since the adherence to the treaty of alliance had become known, had expressed the opinion that Germany would win the war. In the opinion of the American Ambassador that was false; Germany had no chance to win the war and therefore in the Ambassador's opinion it actually was a very risky step for Japan if the alliance had been concluded in the expectation of a possible German victory.

Matsuoka continued that he had answered the American Ambassador that only the good God knew who would finally win the war.

He (Matsuoka) had, however, not concluded the alliance on the basis of the victory of this or the other power, but he had based his action on his vision of the New Order. He had heard with interest the statements of the Führer on the subject of the New Order and had been fully and completely convinced by them. If, however, he assumed entirely hypothetically that the fortune of war at some period would turn against Germany, he must tell the American Ambassador that in such a case Japan would come at once to the assistance of her ally.

His vision of the New Order had been set forth in the preamble to the Three Power Pact. There was at stake an ideal, which had been handed down from one generation to another from time immemorial. For him personally the realization of this ideal was his life's aim, to which up to the present day he had dedicated his fullest efforts, in order to make on his own part a slight contribution toward its realization. The Berlin-Rome-Tokyo Three Power Pact was also a contribution to such a realization. The consummation of this idea, so Matsuoka went on, would be realized under the slogan: "No conquest, no oppression, and no spoliation." This would not be understood in all quarters in Japan. If, however, Japan seemed likely to depart from this line he would be the first to attempt to prevent it.

In this connection Matsuoka referred to still another principle of the preamble to the Three Power Pact, according to which every people must assume the place they deserved. Although Japan, in the creation of the New Order, if it was necessary, would proceed by force, and although she must sometimes lead with a strong hand the peoples who would be affected by this New Order, nevertheless she had always before her the slogan which he had previously quoted: "No conquest, no oppression, no spoliation." . . .

Matsuoka then continued that he had discussed with Stalin his ideas about the New Order and had stated that the Anglo-Saxon represented the greatest hindrance to the establishment of this order and that Japan therefore was compelled to fight against them. He had told Stalin that the Soviets on their part also were coming out for something new and that he believed that after the collapse of the British Empire the difficulties between Japan and Russia could be eliminated. He had represented the Anglo-Saxons as the common foe of Japan, Germany, and Soviet Russia.

Stalin had arranged to give him an answer when he passed through Moscow again on his return journey to Japan; he had, however, after some reflection stated that Soviet Russia had never gotten along well with Great Britain and never would.

MEMORANDUM of a Conversation between Joachim von Ribbentrop, German Minister for Foreign Affairs, and Yosuke Matsuoka, Japanese Minister for Foreign Affairs, at Berlin, March 29, 1941

Nazi-Soviet Relations, 1939–1941, p. 303; excerpt

The Reich Foreign Minister referred to the earlier discussion with Matsuoka concerning the latter's impending conversations with the Russians in Moscow. He expressed the opinion that in view of the general situation it might be best not to go into things too deeply with the Russians. He did not know how the situation would develop. But one thing was certain: if Russia should ever attack Japan, Germany would strike immediately. He could give this firm assurance to Matsuoka, so that Japan could push southward toward Singapore without fear of any complications with Russia. As it was, the greater part of the German Army was on the eastern boundary of the Reich and was ready to attack at any time. He (the Reich Foreign Minister) believed, however, that Russia would not occasion any military action. But if Germany should become involved in a conflict with Russia, the Soviet Union would be finished within a few months. In that case, Japan would, of course, not have anything at all to fear, if she wanted to advance toward Singapore. So, in any case, she need not be kept from that undertaking by any fears of Russia.

Of course, we could not tell how matters would develop with Russia. It was uncertain whether or not Stalin would accentuate his present policy of unfriendliness toward Germany. He (the Reich Foreign Minister) in any event wanted to point out to Matsuoka that a conflict with Russia was always within the realm of possibility. At any rate, Matsuoka could not report to the Japanese Emperor, upon his return, that a conflict between Germany and Russia was inconceivable. On the contrary, as matters stood, such a conflict, though not probable, still would have to be designated as possible.

With regard to Russian adherence to the Three Power Pact, as had been offered to Molotov by Germany, the Reich Foreign Minister remarked that there had been no question of the direct admission of Russia into the Pact, but rather of a different grouping. As already stated, however, the Russians had set conditions for their adherence which Germany could not accept, so that matters were now in suspense.

In reply to a question interpolated by Matsuoka, whether that meant that Germany would perhaps again seek, after the lapse of some time, to get Russia to adhere to the Three Power Pact, the Reich Foreign Minister replied that an attempt of that kind would probably not be made for some time, since the conditions submitted by Russia were irreconcilable with the German view, particularly those concerning Finland and Turkey.

In reply to an inquiry by Matsuoka for further details on the Russian conditions, the Reich Foreign Minister responded that German resistance to the Soviet demands with respect to Finland was based on economic considerations, and also on sentiment. Germany had fought on the side of the Finns in the World War. Matsuoka put in here that the Finns apparently laid great stress on being considered as belonging on the German side. The Japanese Minister in Helsinki, whom he had recalled in connection with the recent shifting of diplomats, told a newspaperman at Manchuli on the trip homeward that Finland now appeared to have placed herself on Russia's side. Some time later, the Finnish Minister in Tokyo protested officially to Matsuoka against that statement and declared that Finland would never place herself on Russia's side.

The Reich Foreign Minister pointed out that the Social-Democratic governments in Finland had always been against the Führer, so that there was no reason for Germany to help them during the Russo-Finnish War. Besides, Germany had to assume an absolutely neutral position, because in the conversations with Molotov and Stalin, Finland had been designated as not lying within the German sphere of interest. But when the Finns defended themselves so valiantly against the Russians, strong feeling for them sprang up in Germany, so that it was now impossible to give up Finland, since an occupation by Russia would lead to complete destruction of the country, as was shown by the example of the Baltic States.

The second Russian condition dealt with the guarantee to Bulgaria, together with occupation of the country by Russian troops, concerning which he had already been informed in detail in the earlier conversations.

The third condition had as its subject the establishment of bases on the Dardanelles. Matsuoka was already informed on that point too. At any rate, Germany preferred the Dardanelles to remain in the hands of the Turks. Besides, she could not permit a penetration of the Russians into the Balkans. However, Russia kept trying to push forward in that direction. Thus, in connection with recent happenings in Yugoslavia, activity was now increasing partly with the aid of the Sokol organization or through direct Communist influence. At any rate, the discussions with the Russians on those conditions had not been taken up again. We had merely told the Soviet Union that

Germany could not allow any new conflict in Finland or the Balkans. Since then all these questions were, as stated, in suspense, and no favorable development was to be expected.

During the further course of the conversation, the Reich Foreign Minister imparted to the Japanese Foreign Minister, in confidence, his view of the true Russian interest. The Soviet Union wanted the war to last as long as possible. It knew that it could not itself gain anything by military attacks. Therefore the exceedingly rapid defeat of France did not suit that sly politician Stalin very well. He wanted a long war that would tire out the peoples and make them ripe for Bolshevik influence. That was the true aim of Russian policy, which should never be lost sight of.

Matsuoka agreed with these ideas and cited the situation in China as an example. Chiang Kai-shek, with whom he was in personal touch, who knew him and trusted him, was greatly alarmed as to the further increase of the influence of the Red Army in China.

The Reich Foreign Minister said that it was entirely possible that the conditions previously described would lead rather rapidly to a conflict between Germany and Russia. If Germany should feel herself endangered, she would immediately attack and put an end to Bolshevism.

To a suggestion by Matsuoka, not to allow the Anti-Comintern Pact to expire, but to renew it, the Reich Foreign Minister replied that he could not take a definitive position on the matter yet, since the situation as it would appear in the autumn, at the expiration of the Pact, could not be foreseen at the present time. As a matter of principle, however, Germany's stand was always in the sense of the Anti-Comintern Pact.

When Matsuoka asked the Reich Foreign Minister to inform him in good time, before the expiration of the Anti-Comintern Pact, regarding the German stand with respect to a possible extension of the Pact, the Reich Foreign Minister rejoined that by October the situation would certainly have been clarified to such an extent that a definite stand by Germany would be possible.

Thereupon the Reich Foreign Minister spoke once more of the question of Singapore. In view of the fears expressed by Japan of possible submarine attacks from the Philippines and of the intervention of the British Mediterranean Fleet and Home Fleet, he had discussed the situation once again with Admiral Raeder. The latter had told him that the British Fleet would be so fully occupied this year in British home waters and in the Mediterranean that it could not send a single ship to the Far East. The American submarines were designated by Admiral Raeder as so poor that Japan need not concern herself about them at all.

Matsuoka at once rejoined that the Japanese Navy considered the danger from the English Navy as very slight, and was also of the opinion that in case of a clash with the American Navy it could destroy the latter without trouble. It did fear, however, that the Americans would not give battle with their fleet, and that in that way the conflict with the United States would perhaps last for five years. They were very uneasy over that in Japan.

The Reich Foreign Minister replied that America could not do anything at all against Japan in case of the capture of Singapore. For that very reason Roosevelt would perhaps think twice before deciding actually to move against Japan. For while he could not do anything against Japan, there was the probability that the Philippines would be taken by Japan; this would naturally entail great loss of prestige for the American President, since, as a result of insufficient American military preparation, he could not retaliate.

Matsuoka pointed out in this connection that he was doing everything to soothe the British with regard to Singapore. He was acting as if Japan had no designs whatsoever on this key point of England in the East. It might therefore be that in his words and acts he would assume a friendly manner toward the English. But Germany should not be misled by that. He was assuming that manner not only in order to soothe the British, but to mislead the pro-British and pro-American elements in Japan, until he should one day suddenly attack Singapore.

With regard to this, the Reich Foreign Minister stated that in his opinion the declaration of war by Japan against England should follow from an attack on Singapore.

Matsuoka remarked in this connection that his tactics were based upon the safe assumption that the whole Japanese Nation would be united at one stroke by the sudden attack on Singapore. ("Nothing succeeds like success," the Reich Foreign Minister interjected here.) He (Matsuoka) was here following the words of a famous Japanese statesman addressed to the Japanese Navy at the outbreak of the Russo-Japanese War: "Open fire, and the Nation will then be united." The Japanese had to be shaken up to rouse them. Lastly, as an Oriental he also believed in fate, which comes whether we want it or not.

MEMORANDUM of a Conversation between Adolf Hitler, Chancellor of the German Reich, and Yosuke Matsuoka, Japanese Minister for Foreign Affairs, at Berlin, April 4, 1941, in the Presence of the German Minister for Foreign Affairs (Joachim von Ribbentrop) and Other Officials

Nazi-Soviet Relations, 1939–1941, pp. 311, 313

Matsuoka then advanced the request that the Führer should instruct the appropriate authorities in Germany to meet the desires of the Japanese Military Commission as fully as possible. Especially in the field of U-boat warfare, Japan required German help in the way of furnishing the latest operational experience and the newest technical improvements and discoveries. Japan would do everything in her power to avoid a war with the United States. In case his country determined on a stroke against Singapore, the Japanese Navy must, of course, also make preparations against the United States, for in such a case America might possibly come out on the side of Great Britain. Personally, he (Matsuoka) believed that the entry of the United States into the war on the side of Great Britain could be avoided. The army and navy must, however, prepare for the worst, i. e., for a war against America. They believed that such a war would last over five years and would be fought out as a guerrilla war in the Pacific Ocean and South Seas. For this reason the experience derived by Germany in her guerrilla war would be most important for Japan. It was a matter of how such a war could best be carried on and how all the technical improvements of the U-boats, down to individual parts, such as periscopes and the like, could be made useful by Japan.

Summing up, Matsuoka asked the Führer to see to it that the improvements and discoveries in the naval and military fields should be made available to the Japanese by the competent German authorities.

The Führer agreed to this and added that Germany also considered a war with the United States to be undesirable, but that it had already been included in his calculations. In Germany the viewpoint was that America's performance depended upon her transport capabilities, which in turn would be limited by the tonnage available. Germany's warfare against shipping tonnage represented an appreciable weakening not only of England but of America also. Germany had made her preparations so that no American could land in Europe. She would wage a vigorous war against America with the U-boats and the Luftwaffe, and with her greater experience, which the United States had still to achieve, would be more than a match for America, entirely apart from the fact that the German soldiers were, obviously, far superior to the Americans.

In the further course of the conversation the Führer declared that if Japan got into a conflict with the United States, Germany on her part would take the necessary steps at once. It made no difference with whom the United States first came into conflict, whether it was with Germany or with Japan. They would always be intent upon disposing of one country first, not with the idea of then coming to an agreement with the other country, but with the idea of disposing of it next. Therefore Germany would, as he had said, promptly take part in case of a conflict between Japan and America, for the strength of the allies in the Three Power Pact lay in their acting in common. Their weakness would be in allowing themselves to be defeated separately.

Matsuoka again repeated his request that the Führer should give the necessary instructions, so that the competent German authorities would make available to the Japanese the latest inventions and improvements of interest to them, for the Japanese Navy must make preparations at once for a conflict with the United States.

With regard to Japanese-American relations Matsuoka continued that in his own country he had always declared that if Japan continued in the same fashion as at present, a war with the United States sooner or later would be unavoidable. In his view this conflict might better occur sooner than later. Accordingly, so his argument had run, should not Japan decide to act with determination at the proper moment and take the risk of a war against America? Exactly by such means the war might perhaps be postponed for generations, especially if Japan secured domination in the South Seas. In Japan, however, many people refused to follow this line of thought. In those circles Matsuoka was considered to be a dangerous man with dangerous ideas. He declared, however, that if Japan proceeded further along the present course she would some day have to fight and that this might happen under more unfavorable circumstances then than at present.

The Führer replied that he had much sympathy for Matsuoka's position, since he had found himself in similar situations (the occupation of the Rhineland, and the resumption of full military independence). He had also come to the conclusion that in a period when he was still young and vigorous he should make use of favorable circumstances and take upon himself the risk of a war which was eventually unavoidable. That he had been right in taking this position had been demonstrated by events. Europe was now free. He would not hesitate a moment to reply at once to any extension of the war, whether by Russia or by America. Providence favored those who did not let perils overtake them, but who confronted them courageously.

Matsuoka replied that the United States, or rather the statesmen who were in control there, had lately undertaken a last maneuver with respect to Japan, in which they declared that America would not fight Japan on account of China or the South Pacific, on condition that Japan should permit shipments of rubber and tin from these areas to proceed unhindered to their points of destination in America. America would, however, fight Japan the moment she felt that Japan intended to enter the war with the intention of assisting in the destruction of Great Britain. With the English-oriented education which many Japanese had received, this sort of argument naturally was not without effect on the Japanese.

The Führer declared in this connection that this attitude of America meant no more than that, as long as the British Empire remained, the United States would cherish the hope of one day being able to proceed together with Great Britain against Japan, while, with a collapse of the Empire they would be completely isolated as against Japan and could accomplish nothing against her.

The Reich Foreign Minister here interjected that the Americans under any circumstances would seek to uphold the English power position in East Asia; that, however, this attitude showed how much they feared joint action on the part of Japan and Germany.

Matsuoka continued that it seemed important to him to give the Führer the true story about the actual situation in Japan. Therefore he must inform him of the regrettable circumstances that he (Matsuoka), as Japanese Foreign Minister, in Japan itself did not dare to say a word about the plans which he had set forth to the Führer and the Reich Foreign Minister. In political and financial circles it would do him much harm. He had once, previously, before he had become Japanese Foreign Minister, made the mistake of telling a close friend something about his intentions. The latter had apparently spread the matter about, so that every kind of rumor arose, which, although he always otherwise spoke the truth, as Foreign Minister he was bound energetically to contradict. Also, under these circumstances, he could not state how soon he would be able to hold a conference with the Japanese Prime Minister or with the Emperor about the questions which had been discussed. He would first have to go into developments in Japan closely and carefully, in order to determine a favorable occasion on which to give Prince Konoye and the Emperor the true picture about his real plans. The decision would then have to follow in a few days, for otherwise the problems would be talked to pieces. If he were not able to put through his plans, it would be an indication that he lacked sufficient influence, power of persuasion and tactical ability. But if he could put them through, it would show that he had attained great influence in Japan. He personally believed that he would be able to put them through.

On his return he would admit to the Emperor, the Prime Minister, and the Navy and War Ministers, if they asked, that the matter of Singapore had been discussed. He would, however, declare that this had only been done in a hypothetical way.

In addition Matsuoka expressly requested that nothing be cabled on the subject of Singapore, since he feared that by use of telegrams something might slip out. In case of necessity, he would send a courier.

The Führer agreed and assured him that he could rely fully and completely on German discretion.

Matsuoka replied that he had confidence in German discretion, but he could not, unfortunately, say the same thing for Japan.

After some personal farewell greetings the conversation came to a close.

SCHMIDT

Berlin, April 4, 1941.

LETTER from Adolf Hitler, Chancellor of the German Reich, to Benito Mussolini, Premier of Italy, June 21, 1941

Nazi-Soviet relations, 1939–1941, p. 349

June 21, 1941.

DUCE!

I am writing this letter to you at a moment when months of anxious deliberation and continuous nerve-racking waiting are ending in the hardest decision of my life. I believe—after seeing the latest Russian situation map and after appraisal of numerous other reports—that I cannot take the responsibility for waiting longer, and above all, I believe that there is no other way of obviating this danger—unless it be further waiting, which, however, would necessarily lead to disaster in this or the next year at the latest.

The situation: England has lost this war. With the right of the drowning person, she grasps at every straw which, in her imagination might serve as a sheet anchor. Nevertheless, some of her hopes are naturally not without a certain logic. England has thus far always conducted her wars with help from the Continent. The destruction of France—in fact, the elimination of all west-European positions—is directing the glances of the British warmongers continually to the place from which they tried to start the war: to Soviet Russia.

Both countries, Soviet-Russia and England, are equally interested in a Europe fallen into ruin, rendered prostrate by a long war. Behind these two countries stands the North American Union goading them on and watchfully waiting. Since the liquidation of Poland, there is evident in Soviet-Russia a consistent trend, which, even if cleverly and cautiously, is nevertheless reverting firmly to the old Bolshevist tendency to expansion of the Soviet State. The prolongation of the war necessary for this purpose is to be achieved by tying up German forces in the East, so that—particularly in the air—the German Command can no longer vouch for a large-scale attack in the West. I declared to you only recently, Duce, that it was precisely the success of the experiment in Crete that demonstrated how necessary it is to make use of every single airplane in the much greater project against England. It may well happen that in this decisive battle we would win with a superiority of only a few squadrons. I shall not hesitate a moment to undertake such a responsibility if, aside from all other conditions, I at least possess the one certainty that I will not then suddenly be attacked or even threatened from the East. The concentration of Russian forces—I had General Jodl submit the most recent map to your Attaché here, General Maras—is tremendous. Really, all available Russian forces are at our border. Moreover, since the approach of warm weather, work has been proceeding on numerous defenses. If circumstances should give me cause to employ the German air force against England, there is danger that Russia will then begin its strategy of extortion in the South and North, to which I would have to yield in silence, simply from a feeling of air inferiority. It would, above all, not then be possible for me, without adequate support from an air force, to attack the Russian fortifications with the divisions stationed in the East. If I do not wish to expose myself to this danger, then perhaps the whole year of 1941 will go by without any change in the general situation. On the contrary. England will be all the less ready for peace for it will be able to pin its hopes on the Russian partner. Indeed, this hope must naturally even grow with the progress in preparedness of the Russian armed forces. And behind this is the mass delivery of war material from America which they hope to get in 1942.

Aside from this, Duce, it is not even certain whether we shall have this time, for with so gigantic a concentration of forces on both sides— for I also, was compelled to place more and more armored units on the eastern border, and also to call Finland's and Rumania's attention to the danger—there is the possibility that the shooting will start spontaneously at any moment. A withdrawal on my part would, however, entail a serious loss of prestige for us. This would be particularly unpleasant in its possible effect on Japan. I have, therefore, after constantly racking my brains, finally reached the decision to cut the noose before it can be drawn tight. I believe, Duce, that I am hereby rendering probably the best possible service to our joint conduct of the war this year. For my over-all view is now as follows:

1) *France* is, as ever, not to be trusted. Absolute surety that North Africa will not suddenly desert does not exist.

2) *North Africa* itself, insofar as your colonies, Duce, are concerned, is probably out of danger until fall. I assume that the British, in their last attack, wanted to relieve Tobruk. I do not believe they will soon be in a position to repeat this.

3) *Spain* is irresolute and—I am afraid—will take sides only when the outcome of the war is decided.

4) In *Syria,* French resistance can hardly be maintained permanently either with or without our help.

5) An attack on *Egypt* before Autumn is out of the question altogether. I consider it necessary, however, taking into account the whole situation, to give thought to the development of an operational unit in Tripoli itself which can, if necessary, also be launched against the West. Of course, Duce, the strictest silence must be maintained with regard to these ideas, for otherwise we cannot expect France to continue to grant permission to use its ports for the transportation of arms and munitions.

6) Whether or not *America* enters the war is a matter of indifference, inasmuch as she supports our opponent with all the power she is able to mobilize.

7) The situation in England itself is bad; the provision of food and raw materials is growing steadily more difficult. The martial spirit to make war, after all, lives only on hopes. These hopes are based solely on two assumptions: Russia and America. We have no chance of eliminating America. But it does lie in our power to exclude Russia. The elimination of Russia means, at the same time, a tremendous relief for Japan in East Asia, and thereby the possibility of a much stronger threat to American activities through Japanese intervention.

I have decided under these circumstances, as I already mentioned, to put an end to the hypocritical performance in the Kremlin. I assume, that is to say, I am convinced, that Finland, and likewise Rumania, will forthwith take part in this conflict, which will ultimately free Europe, for the future also, of a great danger. General Maras informed us that you, Duce, wish also to make available at least one corps. If you have that intention, Duce—which I naturally accept with a heart filled with gratitude—the time for carrying it out will still be sufficiently long, for in this immense theater of war the troops cannot be assembled at all points at the same time anyway. You, Duce, can give the decisive aid, however, by strengthening your forces in North Africa, also, if possible, looking from Tripoli toward the West, by proceeding further to build up a group which, though it be small at first, can march into France in case of a French violation of the treaty; and finally, by carrying the air war and, so far as it is possible, the submarine war, in intensified degree, into the Mediterranean.

So far as the security of the territories in the West is concerned, from Norway to and including France, we are strong enough there—so far as army troops are concerned—to meet any eventuality with lightning speed. So far as the air war on England is concerned, we shall, for a time, remain on the defensive,—but this does not mean that we might be incapable of countering British attacks on Germany; on the contrary, we shall, if necessary, be in a position to start ruthless bombing attacks on British home territory. Our fighter defense, too, will be adequate. It consists of the best squadrons that we have.

As far as the war in the East is concerned, Duce, it will surely be difficult, but I do not entertain a second's doubt as to its great success. I hope, above all, that it will then be possible for us to secure a common food-supply base in the Ukraine for some time to come, which will furnish us such additional supplies as we may need in the future. I may state at this point, however, that, as far as we can tell now, this year's German harvest promises to be a very good one. It is conceivable that Russia will try to destroy the Rumanian oil region. We have built up a defense that will—or so I think—prevent the worst. Moreover, it is the duty of our armies to eliminate this threat as rapidly as possible.

If I waited until this moment, Duce, to send you this information, it is because the final decision itself will not be made until 7 o'clock tonight. I earnestly beg you, therefore, to refrain, above all, from making any explanation to your Ambassador at Moscow, for there is no absolute guarantee that our coded reports cannot be decoded. I, too, shall wait until the last moment to have my own Ambassador informed of the decisions reached.

The material that I now contemplate publishing gradually, is so exhaustive that the world will have more occasion to wonder at our forbearance than at our decision, except for that part of the world which opposes us on principle and for which, therefore, arguments are of no use.

Whatever may now come, Duce, our situation cannot become worse as a result of this step; it can only improve. Even if I should be obliged at the end of this year to leave 60 or 70 divisions in Russia, that is only a fraction of the forces that I am now continually using on the eastern front. Should England nevertheless not draw any conclusions from the hard facts that present themselves, then we can, with our rear secured, apply ourselves with increased strength to the dispatching of our opponent. I can promise you, Duce, that what lies in our German power, will be done.

Any desires, suggestions, and assistance of which you, Duce, wish to inform me in the contingency before us, I would request that you either communicate to me personally or have them agreed upon directly by our military authorities.

In conclusion, let me say one more thing, Duce. Since I struggled through to this decision, I again feel spiritually free. The partnership with the Soviet Union, in spite of the complete sincerity of the efforts to bring about a final conciliation, was nevertheless often very irksome to me, for in some way or other it seemed to me to be a break with my whole origin, my concepts, and my former obligations. I am happy now to be relieved of these mental agonies.

With hearty and comradely greetings,
    Your
                                                          [ADOLF HITLER]

APPENDIX II

CHRONOLOGY of International Events, March 1938 to December 1941, Issued by the Department of State, December 18, 1941

Department of State, *Bulletin*, December 27, 1941, p. 590

1938

March 11
German troops crossed Austrian frontier. *The Times* (London), March 12, 1938, p. 12.

March 13
Austro-German Union proclaimed at Vienna: "Austria is a state (land) of the German Reich." Text of Anschluss law, Department of State *Press Releases,* March 19, 1938, Vol. XIX, p. 374.

April 16
British-Italian agreement signed, whereby Great Britain recognized the conquest of Ethiopia and Italy promised to withdraw all troops from Spain at the conclusion of the civil war. Great Britain, Foreign Office *Treaty Series,* No. 31 (1938).

April 27–29
Three-day Anglo-French conference at London. Arrangement concluded whereby the British and French general staffs would collaborate more closely henceforth in military and naval defense. *New York Times,* April 29, 1938, p. 1; April 30, p. 1.

July 21
Chaco Peace Pact signed, ending the long conflict between Bolivia and Paraguay. Department of State *Press Releases,* July 23, 1938, Vol. XIX, p. 44.

September 15
Chamberlain-Hitler talk at Berchtesgaden. *New York Times,* September 16, 1938, p. 1.

September 22–23
Chamberlain-Hitler talks at Godesberg. *New York Times,* September 23, 1938, p. 1; September 24, 1938, p. 1.

September 26
President Roosevelt appealed for peace directly to Hitler and President Beneš, Department of State *Press Releases,* October 1, 1938, Vol. XIX, p. 219.

APPENDIX II 1099

September 29
  Chamberlain, Daladier, Hitler, and Mussolini signed Munich Pact. Great Britain, Cmd. 5848, *Further Documents Respecting Czechoslovakia, Including the Agreement Concluded at Munich on September 29, 1938*, Miscellaneous No. 8 (1938).
September 30
  Chamberlain-Hitler peace declaration signed. Great Britain, House of Commons *Parliamentary Debates*, Vol. 339, col. 49.
October 1–10
  Sudeten areas occupied by Germany. See Great Britain, Cmd. 5848.
October 1
  Czechoslovakia yielded to Poland. *New York Times*, October 2, 1938, p. 1.
October 2
  Polish troops occupied the Teschen area. *New York Times*, October 3, 1938, p. 1.
December 6
  Franco-German peace declaration signed. *New York Times*, December 7, 1938, p. 1.

1939

March 14
  German, Hungarian, and Rumanian troops invaded Czechoslovakia. Slovakia proclaimed independence. *New York Times*, March 15, 1939, p. 1.
March 16
  German Government officially proclaimed Bohemia and Moravia protectorates: Decree of March 16 of the Government of the Reich on the Protectorate of Bohemia and Moravia. Department of State *Press Releases*, March 25, 1939, Vol. XX, p. 220.
  Slovakia taken over as a protectorate by Germany. *New York Times*, March 17, 1939, p. 1.
  Hungary announced annexation of Carpatho-Ukraine. *New York Times*, March 17, 1939, p. 1.
March 22
  Memel ceded to Germany by Lithuania: Reunion completed with the signature at Berlin of a five-point non-aggression pact. *New York Times*, March 23, 1939, p. 4.
March 31
  Prime Minister Chamberlain in the House of Commons announced a British and French pledge to come to the assistance of Poland with all the power at their command "in the event of any action which clearly threatened Polish independence and which the Polish

Government accordingly considered it vital to resist with their national forces . . ." Great Britain, House of Commons *Parliamentary Debates,* Vol. 345, col. 2415.

April 1

Spanish civil war ended: "After having made prisoner and disarmed the Red Army, the National troops have attained their final military objective. In consequence, the civil war is over."—*Communiqué* by General Franco. *The Times* (London), April 3, 1939, p. 13.

April 6

Prime Minister Chamberlain announced in the House of Commons a Polish-British agreement, bringing into existence a triple alliance —France, Great Britain, and Poland. The agreement was a provisional mutual-aid pact, pending the elaboration of a formal treaty of alliance. Great Britain, House of Commons *Parliamentary Debates,* Vol. 345, col. 2996.

April 7

Italian troops invaded Albania. Great Britain, House of Commons *Parliamentary Debates,* Vol. 346, col. 6.

April 13

Prime Minister Chamberlain made statement in House of Commons which guaranteed borders of Rumania and Greece: ". . . in the event of any action being taken which clearly threatened the independence of Greece or Rumania . . . His Majesty's Government would feel themselves bound at once to lend . . . all the support in their power." Similar assurances were given by France. Great Britain, House of Commons *Parliamentary Debates,* Vol. 346, col. 13.

April 14

Communication of President Roosevelt to Chancelor Hitler and Premier Mussolini: Plea for 10-year guaranty of peace. Department of State *Press Releases,* April 15, 1939, Vol. XX, p. 527.

April 28

German note notified Great Britain of denunciation of the Naval Agreement of June 18, 1935. *New York Times,* April 29, 1939, p. 6. German note to Poland denounced the 10-year non-aggression treaty of January 26, 1934 between the two countries and requested the return of Danzig as well as an extraterritorial railway and highway connection to East Prussia. *New York Times,* April 29, 1939, p. 7.

July 26

United States gave notice of intention to abrogate its commercial treaty of 1911 with Japan in note from the Secretary of State to the

APPENDIX II

Japanese Ambassador. Department of State *Bulletin,* July 29, 1939, Vol. I, p. 81.

August 23
German-U.S.S.R. non-aggression pact signed. Department of State *Bulletin,* August 26, 1939, Vol. I, p. 172.

August 24
President Roosevelt sent appeals for peace to Chancelor Hitler, President Moscicki, and King Victor Emmanuel. Department of State *Bulletin,* August 26, 1939, Vol. I, pp. 157–159.

August 25
Great Britain and Poland signed formal treaty of mutual assistance. Great Britain, Cmd. 6101, *Agreement Between the Government of the United Kingdom and the Polish Government, London, August 25, 1939,* Poland No. 1 (1939).

September 1
German troops invade Poland; Danzig joined Germany. *New York Times,* September 1, 1939, p. 1.

September 3
Great Britain declared a state of war existed with Germany. Great Britain, Cmd. 6106, *Documents Concerning German-Polish Relations and the Outbreak of Hostilities Between Great Britain and Germany on September 3, 1939, Miscellaneous* No. 9 (1939), pp. 175, 178.

France declared a state of war existed with Germany. *Journal Officiel de la République Française, Lois et Décrets,* September 4, 1939, p. 11086.

September 16
Soviet troops invaded Poland. *New York Times,* September 17, 1939, p. 1.

September 28
German-U.S.S.R. border and friendship treaty signed, resulting in partitioning of Poland. *New York Times,* September 29, 1929, p. 1.

Estonian-U.S.S.R. 10-year mutual-assistance pact signed at Moscow: Gave U.S.S.R. bases for aviation and artillery. Department of State *Bulletin,* November 11, 1939, Vol. I, p. 543.

October 3
Declaration of Panamá signed. Department of State *Bulletin,* October 7, 1939, Vol. I, p. 331.

October 5
Latvian-U.S.S.R. 10-year mutual-assistance pact signed at Moscow. Department of State *Bulletin,* November 11, 1939, Vol. I, p. 542.

October 10
Lithuanian-U.S.S.R. 15-year mutual-assistance treaty signed at Mos-

cow. Department of State *Bulletin,* December 16, 1939, Vol. I, p. 705.

October 19

Anglo-French-Turkish 15-year mutual-assistance pact signed at Ankara. Department of State *Bulletin,* November 11, 1939, Vol. I, p. 544.

November 1

Polish Corridor, Posen, and Upper Silesia annexed by Germany. Department of State *Bulletin,* November 4, 1939, p. 458.

November 3

U.S.S.R. incorporated Polish Western Ukraine and Western White Russia. *New York Times,* November 4, 1939, p. 5.

November 4

United States Neutrality Act of 1939 approved. *U.S. Statutes at Large,* Vol. 54, pt. 1, p. 4.

November 21

German-Slovak treaty signed at Berlin, ceding to Slovakia 225 square miles of territory annexed by Poland in 1920, 1924, and 1938. *New York Times,* November 22, 1939, p. 8.

November 30

Soviet troops invaded Finland. Department of State *Bulletin,* December 2, 1939, Vol. I, p. 610.

1940

March 12

Soviet-Finnish peace treaty and protocol signed at Moscow. Department of State *Bulletin,* April 27, 1940, Vol. II, p. 453.

April 8

Great Britain and France announced that three areas of Norwegian waters had been mined in the attempt to prevent shipment of Scandinavian ore to Germany. *New York Times,* April 8, 1940, p. 1.

April 9

German troops invaded Denmark. Department of State *Bulletin,* April 13, 1940, Vol. II, p. 374.

Germany attacked Norway. Department of State *Bulletin,* April 13, 1940, Vol. II, p. 374.

April 17

Secretary of State Hull issued a formal statement declaring any change in *status quo* "would be prejudicial to the cause of stability, peace, and security" in the entire Pacific Area. Department of State *Bulletin,* April 20, 1940, Vol. II, p. 411.

APPENDIX II

May 9–10
   Germany invaded Belgium, Luxembourg, and the Netherlands. Department of State *Bulletin,* May 11, 1940, Vol. II, p. 485.
May 10
   Winston Churchill became Prime Minister of Great Britain following resignation of Neville Chamberlain. *New York Times,* May 11, 1940, p. 1.
   British occupation of Iceland announced in London. *New York Times,* May 10, 1940, p. 1.
May 15
   The Netherlands Army surrendered. *New York Times,* May 15, 1940, p. 1.
May 19
   Chancelor Hitler issued a proclamation decreeing the re-incorporation into the Reich of Eupen, Malmédy, and Moresnet. *New York Times,* May 20, 1940, p. 1.
May 28
   Belgian Army under King Leopold surrendered. *New York Times,* May 29, 1940, p. 1.
June 9
   Norwegian high command ordered army to cease hostilities at midnight. *New York Times,* June 11, 1940, p. 16.
June 10
   Italy declared war on Great Britain and France. *New York Times,* June 11, 1940, p. 2.
June 14
   German troops entered Paris. *New York Times,* June 15, 1940, p. 1.
June 15
   Soviet troops marched into Lithuania. *New York Times,* June 16, 1940, p. 1.
June 17
   U.S.S.R. announced Estonia and Latvia had agreed to free passage of Soviet troops and to formation of new governments. *New York Times,* June 17, 1940, p. 1.
June 22
   Franco-German armistice signed. *New York Times,* June 26, 1940, p. 4.
June 24
   Franco-Italian armistice signed. *New York Times,* June 25, 1940, p. 1.

June 27
Rumania agreed to cede Bessarabia to U.S.S.R. *New York Times,* June 28, 1940, p. 1.
June 28
British Government recognized Gen. Charles de Gaulle as leader of group to maintain French resistance. *New York Times,* June 29, 1940, p. 9.
July 3
British sank or seized major part of French fleet. Great Britain, House of Commons *Parliamentary Debates,* Vol. 362, col. 1043.
July 5
French Government of Marshal Pétain broke off diplomatic relations with Great Britain as result of British attack on French warships at Oran. *New York Times,* July 6, 1940, p. 1.
July 18
British Prime Minister announced terms of a temporary agreement for stoppage of war supplies to China through Burma and Hong Kong. Great Britain, House of Commons *Parliamentary Debates,* Vol. 363, col. 399.
August 25
Estonia, Latvia, and Lithuania ratified U.S.S.R. incorporation. *New York Times,* August 27, 1940, p. 4.
September 2
United States-British notes on lease of British bases in return for 50 United States destroyers. Department of State *Bulletin,* September 7, 1940, Vol. III, p. 199; March 29, 1941, Vol. IV, p. 387.
September 7
Bulgarian-Rumanian agreement ceding the Dobrudja to Bulgaria signed at Craiova, Bulgaria. *New York Times,* September 8, 1940, p. 45.
September 22
Japanese-French agreement regarding concessions in Indochina to Japan. *New York Times,* September 23, 1940, p. 1.
September 27
German-Italian-Japanese 10-year military-economic alliance pact signed at Berlin. *New York Times,* September 28, 1940, p. 3.
October 28
Italy attacked Greece prior to expiration of ultimatum, creating state of war. *New York Times,* October 29, 1940, p. 1; Department of State *Bulletin,* March 1, 1941, Vol. IV, p. 224; November 16, 1940, Vol. III, p. 426.

APPENDIX II

November 4
  Spanish incorporation of international zone of Tangier. *New York Times,* November 5, 1940, p. 7.

November 20
  Hungary signed protocol of adherence to Axis tripartite pact at Vienna. *New York Times,* November 21, 1940, p. 6.

November 23
  Rumania signed protocol of adherence to Axis tripartite pact at Vienna. *New York Times,* November 24, 1940, p. 2.

November 24
  Slovakia signed protocol of adherence to Axis tripartite pact at Berlin. *New York Times,* November 25, 1940, p. 1.

November 26
  Governor-General of Belgian Congo declared state of war with Italy. *New York Times,* November 27, 1940, p. 4.

November 30
  Japanese peace treaty signed with the Wang Ching-wei regime at Nanking, China. *New York Times,* December 1, 1940, p. 5; *China Weekly Review* (Shanghai), December 7, 1940, pp. 8, 24.

December 6
  Japanese-Thai pact of amity signed. *New York Times,* December 12, 1940, p. 10.

December 12
  Hungarian-Yugoslav treaty of friendship signed. *New York Times,* December 13, 1940, p. 5.

1941

January 10
  German-Soviet agreements on barter and border matters signed at Moscow. *New York Times,* January 11, 1941, p. 8.

January 30
  French Indochinese-Thai armistice signed at Saigon. *New York Times,* February 3, 1941, p. 5.

February 10
  Great Britain severed diplomatic relations with Rumania. *New York Times,* February 11, 1941, p. 1.

February 17
  Bulgarian-Turkish declaration of non-aggression signed at Ankara. *New York Times,* February 18, 1941, p. 4.

March 1
  Bulgaria signed protocol of adherence to Axis tripartite pact at Vienna; German troops occupied Bulgaria. *New York Times,* March 2, 1941, pp. 1, 38.

March 5
  Great Britain severed diplomatic relations with Bulgaria. *New York Times,* March 6, 1941, p. 2.
March 11
  Lend-Lease Act approved by U. S. President, Public Law 11, 77th Cong.
March 12
  Thai-Soviet exchange of notes establishing diplomatic relations. *New York Times,* March 13, 1941, p. 6.
March 24
  Turkish-Soviet *communiqué* promising neutrality if either should be attacked. *New York Times,* March 25, 1941, p. 5.
March 25
  Yugoslavia signed protocol of adherence to the Axis tripartite pact at Vienna. *New York Times,* March 26, 1941, p. 3.
  German war zone extended beyond Iceland. *New York Times,* March 26, 1941, p. 1.
March 27
  Anti-Axis *coup d'état* in Yugoslavia. *New York Times,* March 28, 1941, pp. 1, 6.
April 3
  Pro-Nazi *coup d'état* in Iraq. *New York Times,* April 5, 1941, p. 2.
April 5
  Yugoslav-Soviet treaty of friendship and non-aggression signed at Moscow. *New York Times,* April 6, 1941, pp. 1, 25.
April 6
  Germany attacked Yugoslavia and Greece; Hitler declared war on Yugoslavia. *New York Times,* April 6, 1941, pp. 1, 26.
April 7
  Great Britain severed diplomatic relations with Hungary. *New York Times,* April 8, 1941, p. 1.
April 9
  United States-Danish agreement relating to defense of Greenland by the United States. Department of State *Bulletin,* April 12, 1941, Vol. IV, pp. 443, 445.
April 10
  President Roosevelt's proclamation modifying the Red Sea combat zone.
April 13
  Japanese-Soviet five-year neutrality pact signed at Moscow, together with joint declaration regarding the frontiers of the Japanese protectorate at Manchukuo. *New York Times,* April 14, 1941, p. 8.

APPENDIX II 1107

April 15
Bulgaria severed diplomatic relations with Yugoslavia. *New York Times,* April 16, 1941, p. 3.

April 17
Yugoslav army surrendered. *New York Times,* April 18, 1941, p. 1.

April 23
Greece severed diplomatic relations with Bulgaria following invasion by the latter. *New York Times,* April 24, 1941, p. 3.

April 24
Bulgarian declaration of a state of war in its occupied areas of Greece and Yugoslavia. *New York Times,* April 25, 1941, p. 5.

April 27
German troops occupied Athens. *New York Times,* April 28, 1941, p. 1.

May 2
British-Iraqi fighting began in Iraq. *New York Times,* May 3, 1941, p. 1; May 4, p. 46.

May 6
Joseph Stalin became Soviet Premier. *New York Times,* May 7, 1941, p. 1.

May 9
French Indochinese-Thai peace treaty signed at Tokyo, with Japanese guaranty of new borders. *New York Times,* May 9, 1941, p. 8.

May 14
German proclamation of Red Sea danger zone. *New York Times,* May 14, 1941, p. 1.

May 15
Italian *communiqué* on the Croatian monarchy. *New York Times,* May 16, 1941, p. 6.
Marshal Pétain at Vichy announced replacement of Franco-German armistice agreement by a new collaboration scheme. *New York Times,* May 16, 1941, p. 1.

May 16
Iceland severed personal union with Denmark. *New York Times,* May 20, 1941, p. 11; May 21, p. 2.

May 16
Iraqi-Soviet exchange of notes at Ankara establishing diplomatic relations, etc. *New York Times,* May 18, 1941, p. 6.

May 21
United States announcement of German request that foreign diplomatic agents at Paris evacuate by June 10. *New York Times,* May 22, 1941, p. 1.
Sinking of the S.S. *Robin Moor* by German submarine in Atlantic

Ocean. Department of State *Bulletin,* June 21, 1941, Vol. IV, p. 741.
May 27
President Roosevelt's proclamation of unlimited national emergency. Department of State *Bulletin,* May 31, 1941, Vol. IV, p. 654.
May 31
British-Iraqi armistice signed at Baghdad. *New York Times,* June 1, 1941, p. 1.
June 2
United States statement of policy respecting French possessions in the Western Hemisphere. Department of State *Bulletin,* June 14, 1941, Vol. IV, p. 720.
June 6
Act authorizing acquisition of idle foreign merchant ships by the United States approved. Department of State *Bulletin,* June 7, 1941, Vol. IV, p. 701.
June 8
British and Free French troops entered French Syria and Lebanon. *New York Times,* June 8, 1941, p. 1; June 9, p. 4.
June 15
Croatia signed Axis protocol respecting its interests. *New York Times,* June 16, 1941, p. 3.
June 18
German-Turkish 10-year friendship pact signed at Ankara. *New York Times,* June 19, 1941, p. 4.
June 19
Germany and Italy requested United States consular staffs to evacuate territories under their control by July 15, following United States request of June 16 for German consular evacuation by July 10. *New York Times,* June 20, 1941, pp. 1, 6; Department of State *Bulletin,* June 21, 1941, Vol. IV, p. 743.
June 22
Germany invaded Soviet Union; the latter raided Finland; Hitler's speech and Ribbentrop's statement on declaration of war against Soviet Union. *New York Times,* June 23, 1941, pp. 1, 4.
Italy declared war on Soviet Union. *New York Times,* June 23, 1941, p. 5.
Rumanians entered Bessarabia to regain it. *New York Times,* June 23, 1941, p. 7.
Slovakia severed diplomatic relations with Soviet Union. *New York Times,* June 23, 1941, p. 5.
June 26
Finland announced state of war with Soviet Union. *New York Times,* June 27, 1941, p. 1.

APPENDIX II

June 27
Denmark severed diplomatic relations with Soviet Union. *New York Times,* June 28, 1941, p. 2.
Hungary declared war on Soviet Union following latter's air raids. *New York Times,* June 28, 1941, p. 2.

June 28
Albania announced state of war with Soviet Union. *New York Times,* June 29, 1941, p. 3.

June 30
France (Vichy) severed diplomatic relations with Soviet Union. *New York Times,* July 1, 1941, p. 6.

July 1
Icelandic-United States exchange of letters respecting defense of Iceland. Department of State *Bulletin,* July 12, 1941, Vol. V, pp. 16–18.

July 3
Denmark announced request for United States consular staffs to evacuate by July 15. *New York Times,* July 4, 1941, p. 4.

July 12
British-Soviet mutual-assistance agreement signed at Moscow. Department of State *Bulletin,* September 27, 1941, Vol. V, p. 240.

July 14
British-French Syria-Lebanon armistice signed at Acre, Palestine. *New York Times,* July 16, 1941, p. 4; July 17, p. 3.

July 26
British notice of denunciation of commercial agreements with Japan. *New York Times,* July 27, 1941, p. 13.

July 30
Polish-Soviet agreement of cooperation signed at London. *New York Times,* July 31, 1941, p. 4.
United States recognized Czechoslovak government-in-exile at London. Department of State *Bulletin,* August 2, 1941, Vol. V, p. 88.

August 2
United States-Soviet exchange of notes respecting economic assistance. Department of State *Bulletin,* August 9, 1941, pp. 109, 115.

August 12
British-Soviet declaration of aid to Turkey if attacked by European power. *New York Times,* August 13, 1941, pp. 1, 3.

August 14
Joint declaration by President Roosevelt and Prime Minister Churchill in Atlantic Charter. Department of State *Bulletin,* August 16, 1941, Vol. V, p. 125.

August 25
British-Soviet troops invaded Iran. *New York Times,* August 26, 1941, pp. 1, 4.
September 9
Iran accepted British-Soviet armistice terms. *New York Times,* September 10, 1941, p. 8.
September 11
President Roosevelt announced shoot-on-sight order to United States Navy in American defense waters, following U.S.S. *Greer* incident of September 4. Department of State *Bulletin,* September 13, 1941, Vol. V, p. 193.
September 14
Iran ordered departure of Axis diplomats. *New York Times,* September 15, 1941, p. 8.
October 16
Successful conclusion of Manchukuo–Outer Mongolia border talks at Harbin. *New York Times,* November 3, 1941, p. 5.
October 19
Afghanistan consented to British-Soviet request for ejection of Axis nationals. *New York Times,* October 20, 1941, p. 6.
November 17
Joint resolution to repeal sections 2, 3, and 6 of the Neutrality Act of 1939 approved.
November 24
United States announced occupation of Dutch Guiana (Surinam) in agreement with the Netherlands and Brazil. Department of State *Bulletin,* November 29, 1941, Vol. V, p. 425.
United States revocation of export licenses to French North Africa, Spain, and Tangier. *New York Times,* November 27, 1941, pp. 1, 7.
November 25
Renewal for five years of the Anti-Comintern Pact of November 25, 1936 at Berlin, by Germany, Japan, Italy, Hungary, Spain, Manchukuo, Bulgaria, Croatia, Denmark, Finland, Rumania, Slovakia, and the Nanking regime in China. *New York Times,* November 26, 1941, p. 12.
December 1
Reaffirmation by Marshals Pétain and Goering of Franco-German collaboration at St. Florentine. *New York Times,* December 2, 1941, p. 1.
December 6
President Roosevelt's message to the Japanese Emperor on the Pacific conversations. *New York Times,* December 8, 1941, p. 8.

APPENDIX II

British declaration of war against Finland, Hungary, and Rumania. *New York Times,* December 7, 1941, p. 19.

December 7 (Dec. 8, 6 a. m., Tokyo time)

Japan attacked the United States and Great Britain and occupied the International Settlement at Shanghai. *New York Times,* December 8, 1941, pp. 1, 4; December 9, p. 14.

December 7

Japanese reply rejecting United States note of November 26, delivered at Washington. *New York Times,* December 8, 1941, p. 6. Japan declared a state of war with United States and Great Britain. *New York Times,* December 9, 1941, p. 28.

Declarations of war by Netherlands East Indies and Canada against Japan. *New York Times,* December 8, 1941, p. 1; (late edition) p. 14.

December 8

British declared war against Japan. *New York Times,* December 9, 1941, p. 14.

United States declared by joint resolution a state of war with Japan. *New York Times,* December 9, 1941, p. 5.

Japan invaded Thailand, which capitulated. *New York Times,* December 9, 1941, p. 10.

Declarations of war against Japan by Nicaragua, Honduras, El Salvador, Guatemala, Haiti, the Dominican Republic, the Netherlands, the Free French, and Panama. *New York Times,* December 9, 1941, pp. 18, 22; December 10, p. 13.

Severance of diplomatic relations with Japan by Mexico, Colombia, Belgium, and Egypt. *New York Times,* December 9, 1941, pp. 18, 22.

December 9

Declarations of war against Japan announced by Australia, South Africa, and New Zealand; also against Japan, Germany, and Italy by China. *New York Times* (late edition), December 10, 1941, pp. 4, 8.

Costa Rica declared war against Japan. Department of State *Bulletin,* December 13, 1941, Vol. V, p. 490.

December 10

Cuba declared war against Japan. *New York Times* (late edition), December 11, 1941, p. 13.

December 11

Germany and Italy declared a state of war with the United States. *New York Times,* December 12, 1941, p. 1.

United States declared by joint resolutions a state of war with Ger-

many and Italy. *New York Times,* December 12, 1941, p. 1.
Costa Rica, Cuba, Guatemala, Nicaragua, and the Dominican Republic declared war against Germany and Italy. Department of State *Bulletin* of December 13, 1941, Vol. V, pp. 485–504 *passim; New York Times,* December 12, 1941, p. 9.
Poland declared a state of war with Japan. Department of State *Bulletin,* December 13, 1941, Vol. V, p. 507.
Mexico severed diplomatic relations with Germany and Italy. *New York Times,* December 12, 1941, p. 9.

December 12
Haiti, Panama, and Honduras declared war against Germany and Italy. Department of State *Bulletin,* December 13, 1941, Vol. V, pp. 485–504 *passim.*
Rumania declared a state of war with the United States. *Ibid.,* p. 483.

December 13
El Salvador declared war against Germany and Italy. *Ibid.,* p. 493.
Hungary declared a state of war with the United States. *Ibid.,* p. 482.
Bulgaria declared a state of war against the United States and the United Kingdom. *Ibid.,* p. 483.

INDEX

Albania, Hull's statement *re*, April 8, 1939, 138

Aloisi, Pompeo, Baron, *re* war with Ethiopia, Oct. 5, 1935, 820

American solidarity, 993 ff.; "Declaration of Lima," 993 f.; "Declaration of Panama," 994 f.; Joint declaration, 996 f.; declaration of reciprocal assistance, 997; declaration breaking diplomatic relations with the Axis, 998

Anglo-German Naval Agreement, June 18, 1935, 975 ff.; German memorandum to Great Britain *re*, April 27, 1939, 662

Anglo-Italian agreement, April 16, 1938, 1017

Anglo-Italian Declaration, April 14, 1935, 1001

Arita, Hachira, note to Grew, Nov. 18, 1938, 899; note from Craigie, Jan. 14, 1939, 433; address in the Imperial Diet, Feb. 1, 1940, 852

Atlantic Charter, 220, 1033

Australia, disarmament: Procès-verbal *re* submarine warfare, 985 f.; Treaty for the Limitation of Naval Armament, 978 ff.

Austria, acquisition of, 664 ff.; joint communiqué of France, Great Britain, and Italy *re* independence of, 1000

Avenol, Joseph, communication from Stimson, on relations with Japan, Feb. 25, 1933, 75; letter from Laval *re* German decisions on armaments, April 9, 1935, 483; Molotov's telegram *re* Finland, Dec. 5, 1939, 605

Axis agreements, 988 ff.

Baldwin, Stanley, address in the House of Commons, Nov. 28, 1934, 348

Barthou, Louis, memorandum to the British Embassy at Paris, April 17, 1934, 477

Bases, British, lease of, to U.S., 205

Belgium, invasion of, 759; reply of Japanese Government to invitation to Brussels Conference, Oct. 27, 1937, 890 ff.; German diplomatic office at Brussels, telegram from Weizsäcker, Nov. 15, 1940, 1070

"Black List," 216

Blum, Léon, statement in the French Senate, June 23, 1936, 455

Bonnet, Georges, communication from Poncet, Oct. 20, 1938, 500; instructions to the French ambassadors, Dec. 14, 1938, 507; communication from, and instruction to Coulondre, *re* Czechoslovakia, March 16, 17, 1939, 509 ff.; statement in the League Council, May 23, 1939, 470; communication to von Welczeck, July 1, 1939, 517; personal letter from Ribbentrop, July 13, 1939, 694; personal letter to Ribbentrop, July 21, 1939, 518; instruction to the French Ambassador to Poland, Aug. 24, 1939, 521; communication from Coulondre, Aug. 27, 1939, 526; telephone message from Coulondre, Sept. 3, 1939, 534

Boundary and Friendship Treaty between Germany and the U.S.S.R., 1029; confidential and secret protocols, Sept. 28, 1939, 1041

Briand, Aristide, address before the League of Nations Assembly, Sept. 11, 1931, 443

Brussels Conference, 1937, 890 ff.; 919 ff.; 954 ff.; report and declaration, Nov. 24, 1937, 1012 ff.

Bulgaria, Nyon Agreement, 1008 ff.

Canada, disarmament: Procès-verbal *re* submarine warfare, 985 f.; Treaty for the Limitation of Naval Armament, 978 ff.

Cecil, Viscount, address on British policy before the Assembly of the League of Nations, Sept. 10, 1931, 287

Chamberlain, Neville, *re* Czechoslovakia: letters to Hitler (1938), 362, 363, 364; message to Hull in reply to Roosevelt's appeal for peace, Sept. 26, 1938, 366; letter from Hitler, Sept. 23, 1938, 671; memorandum from Hitler, Sept. 23, 1938, 674; letter from Hitler, Sept. 27, 1938, 688; addresses in the House of Commons, Sept. 28, 1938, 367; Oct. 3, 1938, 381; joint communiqué issued at Munich, Sept. 30, 1938, 1023; address at Birmingham, March 17, 1939, 385; letter to Hitler, Aug. 22, 1939, 391; communication from Hitler, Aug. 23, 1939, 696; addresses in the House of Commons: Aug. 24, 1939, 392; Sept. 1, 1939, 405; Sept. 3, 1939, 408; radio address, Sept. 3, 1939, 409

Chicago, Roosevelt's address at the dedication of the Outerlink Bridge, 25

China, invasions of, 867 ff., 954 ff.

Churchill, Winston, radio address to the

Churchill, Winston (*Continued*)
Italian people, Dec. 23, 1940, 425; Atlantic Charter, Aug. 14, 1941, 1033; radio address *re* Japan, Aug. 24, 1941, 436; address in the House of Commons *re* Japan, Aug. 24, 1941, 436

Ciano, Galeazzo, German communiqué *re* visit of, Sept. 25, 1936, 723; visit to Germany, Oct. 25, 1936, 787; statement *re* Italy and German-Japanese Agreement, Nov. 25, 1936, 806; address before the Fascist Chamber, May 13, 1937, 793; conversation with Mussolini and Ribbentrop, May 13, 1941, 743

Cleveland, Ohio, Hull's address, Sept. 28, 1940, 98

Communist International, note from Krestinski to Bullitt *re,* Aug. 27, 1935, 600; German-Japanese agreement *re,* 988 ff.

Conference for the Limitation of Naval Armament at London, statement by Monsell, Jan. 15, 1936, 342; statement by Nagano, Jan. 15, 1936, 862 ff.; Grandi's statement, March 25, 1936, 818

Conference for the Reduction and Limitation of Armaments, minutes of the General Commission, Feb. 25, 1932, 582; May 29, 1934, 588; Five-Power Agreement, 971 f.; Neurath's communications to Henderson, Sept. 14, 1932, 637; Oct. 14, 1933, 638; communications from Henderson to Neurath, Sept. 18, 1932, 969; Oct. 16, 1933, 972; draft Disarmament Convention, March 16, 1933, 319; Hitler's proclamation of withdrawal from, Oct. 14, 1933, 639

Conference of Stresa, 1001

Coulondre, Robert, communication to Bonnet, March 16, 1939, *re* Czechoslovakia, 509; Bonnet's instruction, March 17, 1939, 516; communication to Bonnet, Aug. 27, 1939, 526; telephone message to Bonnet, Sept. 3, 1939, 534

Craigie, Sir Robert L., note to Hirota *re* bombing of British vessels, Dec. 16, 1937, 432; note to Arita, Jan. 14, 1939, 433

Curtius, Julius, address in the League Council, Jan. 20, 1931, 636; address before the League Assembly, Sept. 12, 1931, 609

Czechoslovakia, crisis, 362 ff.; proposals of France and Great Britain, Sept. 19, 1938, 1019; Litvinov's address before the League Assembly, Sept. 21, 1938, 601; letter from Chamberlain to Hitler, Sept. 23, 1938, 362; German acquisition of, 668 ff.; Coulondre's communication to Bonnet, March 16, 1939, 509; Bonnet's instruction to Coulondre, March 17, 1939, 516; note from Welles to Thomsen *re,* March 20, 1939, 137

Daladier, Edouard, address before the Radical-Socialist Congress, Oct. 8, 1933, 450; reply to Roosevelt's appeal for peace, Sept. 26, 1938, 491; address in the Chamber of Deputies, Oct. 4, 1938, 491; Hitler's message of Aug. 25, 1939, 524; personal letter from Hitler, Aug. 27, 1939, 701; address in the Chamber of Deputies, Sept. 2, 1939, 527; statement to the nation, Sept. 3, 1939, 535

Davis, Norman H., statement, at the General Disarmament Conference, Geneva, May 29, 1934, 51; statement on disarmament before the Senate Committee on Foreign Relations, May 13, 1936, 56

Dawes, Charles G., telegram from Stimson, on relations with Japan, Nov. 10, 1931, 67

Debuchi, Katsuji, memorandum from H. L. Stimson, Sept. 22, 1931, 65

"Declaration of Lima," Dec. 24, 1938, 993
"Declaration of Panama," Oct. 3, 1939, 994
Defense, American, 98, 166 ff., 993 ff.

Delbos, Yvon, address in the Chamber of Deputies, Nov. 19, 1937, 462

Denmark, agreement with the U.S. *re* Greenland, 210; invasion of, 758

Disarmament, policy *re:* France, 473 ff.; Germany, 636 ff.; Great Britain, 311 ff.; Italy, 812; Japan, 861 ff.; League of Nations and, 964 ff.; U.S.S.R., 582 ff.; U.S., 42 ff., 62, 971 ff., 978 ff., 985 f.; *see also* Conference for the Limitation of Naval Armament; Conference for the Reduction . . . of Armaments; Disarmament Conference

Disarmament Conference, First General, at Geneva, address by Hugh S. Gibson, Feb. 9, 1932, 42; message of F. D. Roosevelt, May 16, 1933, 49; statement by N. H. Davis, May 29, 1934, 51

Disarmament Convention, draft, submitted by MacDonald, 319

Drummond, Sir Eric, telegram from Uchida, March 27, 1933, 888

Eastern Pact, draft submitted by France to Great Britain, June 27, 1934, 480

Eden, Anthony, statements *re* Italy, July 1, 1935, 417; Oct. 12, 1935, 418; memorandum from Hoesch, March 7, 1936, 651; communication to Sir Eric Phipps, March 26, 1936, 350; memorandum from Rib-

INDEX

bentrop, April 1, 1936, 655; address in the House of Commons, Jan. 19, 1937, 360; address on disarmament and security, March 2, 1937, 346; address in the House of Commons, Nov. 1, 1937, 301; address before the League Assembly, Sept. 20, 1938, 298; address *re* Italy in the House of Commons, Nov. 2, 1938, 421

Egypt, Nyon Agreement, 1008 ff.

Ethiopian war, 819 ff., 938 ff.; Hull's statement *re*, Sept. 13, 1935, 133; Roosevelt's statement *re*, Oct. 30, 1935, 136

Finland, Molotov's radio address *re*, Nov. 29, 1939, 602; Molotov's telegram to Avenol, Dec. 5, 1939, 605

Five-Power Agreement, *re* disarmament, Dec. 11, 1932, 971

Flandin, Pierre-Etienne, statement *re* Germany, in the League Council, March 14, 1936, 487

Forbes, William Cameron, telegram from Stimson on relations with Japan, Jan. 7, 1932, 71; note from Yoshizawa, Jan. 16, 1932, 869

France, general statements of policy, 443 ff.; joint communiqué *re* Austria, Feb. 17, 1934, 1000; conference of Stresa, April 14, 1935, 1001; treaty of mutual assistance with the U.S.S.R., May 2, 1935, 1004; Blum's statement of June 23, 1936, 455; Nyon Agreement, Sept. 14, 1937, 1008 ff.; proposals to Czechoslovakia, Sept. 19, 1938, 1019; Munich agreements, Sept. 29, 1938, 1021; Daladier's address, Oct. 4, 1938, 491; and Germany, declaration, Dec. 6, 1938, 1024; U.S. aid to, in 1940, 201 f.; German diplomatic office in Paris, telegram from Weizsäcker, Nov. 15, 1940, 1070.

—— disarmament, 472 ff.; communication to Germany, Sept. 11, 1932, 473; Procès-verbal *re* submarine warfare, 985 f.; Treaty for the Limitation of Naval Armament, 978 ff.

—— relations with Germany, 483 ff., 693 ff.; outbreak of war, 527 ff.

Franco, Francisco, conversation with Hitler at Hendaye, Oct. 23, 1940, 727

Franco-German Declaration of Dec. 6, 1938, 1024; Ribbentrop's statement *re*, 693

Franco-Soviet Treaty, 1004; Hoesch's memorandum to Eden *re*, 651

German and Italian Aggressions, 129 ff.

German-Japanese Agreement, Nov. 25, 1936, 988

German News Agency, communiqué *re* the attack on the U.S.S. *Greer*, Sept. 6, 1941, 729

German-Polish Agreement of Jan. 28, 1934, 999

Germany, acquisition of Austria, 664 ff.; of Czechoslovakia, 668 ff.; assets frozen in the U.S., 212; Axis agreements, 988 ff.; consular offices and agencies in the U.S. closed, 213; disarmament, 636 ff., 971; and the disarmament conferences, 969 ff.; withdrawal, 972; economic and financial policy, 763 ff.; general statements of policy, 609 ff.; invasion of Belgium and the Netherlands, 759; of Denmark and Norway, 758 f.; of Yugoslavia, 760 ff.; the "New Plan," 765; relations with France, 483 ff., 693 ff., 701 ff.; with Great Britain, 348 ff., 696 ff., 705 ff.; with Italy, 723 f.; with Japan, 739 ff.; with Poland, 693 ff., 707 ff., 999 ff.; with the U.S.S.R., 747 ff., 1029, 1037 ff.; with the U.S., 725 ff.; declaration of state of war, 733 ff.; vs. the Treaty of Versailles, 937, 953; French statement *re* disarmament, Sept. 11, 1932, 473; Laval's letter to Avenol *re* armaments, April 9, 1935, 483; Ciano's visit, Oct., 1936, 787; Ciano *re* German-Japanese Agreement, Nov. 25, 1936, 806; Mussolini's visit, Sept., 1937, 804; Munich agreements and joint communiqué, Sept. 29, 30, 1938, 1021 ff.; and France, declaration, Dec. 6, 1938, 1024; notes from Gilbert to Ribbentrop, Dec. 14, 1938, 142; Jan. 11, 1939, 143; non-aggression treaty with the U.S.S.R., Aug. 23, 1939, 1025; Three-Power Pact, Sept. 27, 1940, 991; execution of hostages: Roosevelt's statement *re*, Oct. 25, 1941, 141

—— Foreign Office: memoranda, Sept. 16, 1938, 670; Sept. 20, 1938, 670; note to Gilbert, Dec. 30, 1938, 725; telegram from Ott, June 19, 1940, 740; telegram to Schulenburg, Nov. 26, 1940, 1071; telegrams from Schulenburg: Jan. 17, 1941, 1077; March 1, 1941, 1081 f.

—— Reichstag: Hitler's addresses, May 21, 1935, 647; Jan. 30, 1939, 694; Feb. 20, 1938, 628; Oct. 6, 1939, 747; Dec. 11, 1941, 734

Gibson, Hugh S., address, 1st General Disarmament Conference, Geneva, Feb. 9, 1932, 42

Gilbert, Prentiss B., telegram from Stimson, on relations with Japan, Oct. 9, 1931, 66; notes to Ribbentrop *re* U.S. citizens in Germany: Dec. 14, 1938, 142; Jan. 11,

Gilbert, Prentiss B. (*Continued*) 1939, 143; note from the German Foreign Office, Dec. 30, 1938, 725

Goebbels, Joseph, broadcast re Austria, July 11, 1936, 665

Goering, Hermann, conversation with Sztéjay, Sept. 16, 1938, 668

Grandi, Dino, address before the League of Nations, Sept. 8, 1931, 775; statement at Naval Armament Conference, London, March 25, 1936, 818

Great Britain, and Czechoslovakia, 362 ff., 1019; and Poland, 1025, 1027; general statements of policy, 287 ff.; relations with Germany, 348 ff., 696 ff.; with Italy, 417 ff.; with Japan, 430 ff., 436 ff.; joint communiqué re Austrian independence, Feb. 17, 1934, 1000; Embassy at Paris, Barthou's memorandum, April 17, 1934, 477; Conference of Stresa, April 14, 1935, 1001; declaration re the Mediterranean, Jan. 2, 1937, 1008; Nyon Agreement, Sept. 14, 1937, 1008 ff.; agreement with Italy, April 16, 1938, 1017; reply to Hitler's communications of Aug. 23, 25, 29, 1939, 399 ff.; Hitler's reply to the communication of Aug. 28, 1939, 705; proposals to Czechoslovakia, Sept. 19, 1938, 1019; Munich agreements and joint communiqué, Sept. 29, 30, 1938, 1021 ff.; bases leased to the U.S.: Roosevelt's message to Congress re, Sept. 3, 1940, 205

—— disarmament, 311 ff., 971, 985 f.; memorandum, March 16, 1933, 319; memorandum, Jan. 29, 1934, 640; Treaty for the Limitation of Naval Armament, 1936, 978 ff.

—— House of Commons: statement by Eden, re Italy, July 1, 1935, 417; address by Eden, Nov. 1, 1937, 420; address by Chamberlain, Aug. 24, 1939, 392; Churchill's address re Japan, Aug. 24, 1941, 436

Greece, Nyon Agreement, Sept. 14, 1937, 1008 ff.; communication from Grazzi re Italian occupation, Oct. 28, 1940, 830

Greenland, defense of, 210

Grazzi, Emmanuele, communication to the Greek government, Oct. 28, 1940, 830

Greer (U.S. ship), official German communiqué re the attack on, Sept. 6, 1941, 729

Grew, Joseph C., communication to Hull, Dec. 27, 1934, 76; telegram from Hull, Sept. 2, 1937, 81; note to Hirota, Dec. 14, 1937, 84; notes from Hirota, Dec. 14, 1937, 897; Feb. 12, 1938, 865; note from Arita, Nov. 18, 1938, 899; telegram to Hull, May 18, 1939, 91; pro-memoria from Nomura, Dec. 18, 1939, 905

Habicht, Theo, Manifesto re Austria, July 5, 1933, 664

Halifax, Lord, address in the House of Lords, Oct. 3, 1938, 383; address at Chatham House, June 29, 1939, 302

Havana, Meeting of Foreign Ministers, July 30, 1940, 997

Henderson, Arthur, communications from Neurath re disarmament, Sept. 14, 1932, and Oct. 14, 1933, 637, 638; communications to Neurath, Sept. 18, 1932, 969; Oct. 16, 1933; Five-Power Agreement, Dec. 11, 1932, 971

Henderson, Sir Nevile, verbal communication from Hitler, Aug. 25, 1939, 699; Hitler's reply to the British communication of Aug. 28, 1939, 705; communication received from Weizsäcker, Aug. 31, 1939, 707; communication from Ribbentrop, Sept. 3, 1939, 718; final report, on the termination of his mission, Sept. 20, 1939, 410

Hirohito, Emperor of Japan, Roosevelt's message, Dec. 6, 1941, 115

Hirota, Koki, addresses in the Imperial Diet: Jan. 23, 1934, 838; Jan. 21, 1936, 842; Jan. 22, 1938, 848; notes to Grew: Dec. 14, 1937, 897; note from Grew, Dec. 14, 1937, 84; note from Craigie re bombing of British vessels, 432

Hitler, Adolf, radio address, Oct. 14, 1933, 614; proclamation re withdrawal from the Disarmament Conference and the League, Oct. 14, 1933, 639; address before the Reichstag, May 21, 1935, 647; proclamation re Treaty of Versailles, March 16, 1935, 641, 937; Party Congress addresses, Nuremburg: Sept. 9, 1936, 659, 766; Sept. 13, 1937, 624; address during the visit of Mussolini, Sept. 28, 1937, 723; address before the Reichstag, Feb. 20, 1938, 628; address, March 12, 1938, following the entry into Austria, 666; joint communiqué issued at Munich, Sept. 30, 1938, 1023; address before the Reichstag, Jan. 30, 1939, 694, 767; letter from Chamberlain, Aug. 22, 1939, 391; communication to Chamberlain, Aug. 23, 1939, 696; communications to the British government, Aug. 23, 25, 29, 1939, 399 ff.; message to Daladier, Aug. 25, 1939, 522; verbal communication to Sir Nevile Henderson, Aug. 25, 1939, 699; personal letter to Daladier, Aug. 27, 1939, 701; reply to the

INDEX

British communication of Aug. 28, 1939, 705; address before the Reichstag, Sept. 1, 1939, 713; proclamation to the German army, Sept. 1, 1939, 712; address before the Reichstag, Oct. 6, 1939, 747; conversation with Franco, at Hendaye, Oct. 23, 1940, 727; communiqués *re* Roosevelt's address of Oct. 28, 1940, 730, 732; memoranda of conversations with Molotov: Nov. 12, 1940, 1043; Nov. 13, 1940, 1051; military directive for "Operation Barbarossa," Dec. 18, 1940, 1073; memoranda of conversations with Matsuoke: March 27, 1941, 1083; April 4, 1941, 1090; Order of the Day, April 6, 1941, 760; letter to Mussolini, June 21, 1941, 1093; proclamation, June 22, 1941, 749; address before the Reichstag, Dec. 11, 1941, 734

—— *re* Czechoslovakia: messages from Roosevelt in appeal for peace, 148, 150, 152, 157, 158; conversation with Imredy and de Kánya, Sept. 20, 1938, 670; letters from Chamberlain: Sept. 23, 1938, 362; Sept. 26, 1938, 364; letter to Chamberlain, Sept. 23, 1938, 671; memorandum to Chamberlain, Sept. 23, 1938, 674; radio address, Sept. 26, 1938, 676; reply to Roosevelt's appeal for peace, Sept. 26, 1938, 685; letter to Chamberlain, Sept. 27, 1938, 688

Hoare, Sir Samuel, note to Ribbentrop, and reply, June 18, 1935, 975 ff.

Hoesch, Leopold von, memorandum to Eden, March 7, 1936, 651

Hoover, Herbert, proposal *re* disarmament, 47; war-debts moratorium, 267; statements *re* war debts, 269-70

Horinouchi, Kensuke, note from Hull, July 26, 1939, 94; Hull's memorandum *re* conversation with, Aug. 26, 1939, 95; Hull's memorandum *re* conversation with, Oct. 8, 1940, 100

Hull, Cordell, address before the World Economic and Monetary Conference, July 27, 1933, 262; address, "The Foreign Policy of the United States," May 2, 1935, 276; radio address, "Our Foreign Policy with Respect to Neutrality," Nov. 6, 1935, 232; address, "Eight Pillars of Enduring Peace," Buenos Aires, Dec. 5, 1936, 14; statement on U.S. policy, July 16, 1937, 24; letter to Key Pittman, May 12, 1938, 235; telegrams from Phillips: May 27, 1940, 161; June 1, 1940, 164; telegram to Phillips, May 30, 1940, 163; statement, July 5, 1940, on European possessions in the Western Hemisphere, *re* the German reply to the U.S. note of June 18, 203; statement *re* national defense, Aug. 25, 1940, 172; address, "Our Foreign Policy," Oct. 26, 1940, 32; statement, Dec. 7, 1941, 251; statement, Jan. 2, 1942, 1036

—— *re* Germany and Italy: statement *re* Ethiopia, Sept. 13, 1935, 133; telegram, in appeal for peace to American diplomatic missions, Sept. 27, 1938, 149; statement *re* Albania, April 8, 1939, 138; note from Thomsen, March 17, 1939, 690; press conference statement, Aug. 4, 1941, 132; communication from Thomsen, Aug. 31, 1939, replying to Roosevelt's appeals for peace, 712; note from Thomsen *re* the sinking of the *Robin Moor*, Sept. 26, 1941, 730

—— *re* Japan: communication, from Grew, Dec. 27, 1934, 76; note *verbale* from Saito, Dec. 29, 1934, 861; telegram, Sept. 2, 1937, to Grew, 81; telegram from Grew, May 18, 1939, 91; note to Horinouchi, July 26, 1939, 94; memorandum *re* a conversation with Horinouchi, Aug. 26, 1939, 95; statement, March 30, 1940, 97; memorandum of conversation with Horinouchi, Oct. 8, 1940, 100; statement before the Foreign Affairs Committee of the House of Representatives, Jan. 15, 1941, 102; draft proposals from Nomura, Sept. 6, 1941, 908; Nov. 20, 1941, 909; communication to Nomura, Nov. 26, 1941, 107; memorandum *re* conversation with Nomura and Kurusu, Dec. 5, 1941, 112; memorandum from Nomura, Dec. 7, 1941, 910

Iceland, defense of, 215
Imredy, Béla, conversation with Hitler and de Kánya, Sept. 20, 1938, 670
India, disarmament: Procés-verbal *re* submarine warfare, 985 f.; Treaty for the Limitation of Naval Armament, 978 ff.
Indo-China, 742
International Road Congress, 7th, Berlin, address by Neurath, Oct. 12, 1934, 619
Invasions, Belgium and the Netherlands, 759; China, 867 ff.; Denmark and Norway, 758; Yugoslavia, 760
Irish Free State, Procès-verbal *re* submarine warfare, 985 f.
Italy, 775 ff.; Axis agreements, 988 ff.; closing of agencies in the U.S., 213 f.; disarmament and security, 775, 787, 789, 812 ff., 971, 985 f.; entry into the European War, 138, 825 ff.; freezing of assets in the U.S., 212; general statements of policy, 775 ff.; relations with Germany, 723 f.; with

Italy (*Continued*)
  Great Britain, 417 ff.; war with Ethiopia, 819 ff.; memorandum *re* disarmament and security, Rome, Jan. 31, 1934, 812; joint communiqué *re* Austrian independence, Feb. 17, 1934, 1000; Laval's statement on rapprochement with, Jan. 7, 1935, 481; Conference of Stresa, April 14, 1935, 1001; Agreement with Great Britain, April 16, 1938, 1017; Munich agreements, Sept. 29, 1938, 1021; Three-Power Pact, Sept. 27, 1940, 991

Japan, Axis agreements, 988 ff.; Brussels Conference, 890 ff.; disarmament, 835, 861 ff.; general statements of policy, 835 ff.; invasions of China, 867 ff., 919 ff., 954 ff.; relations with Germany, 739 ff.; with Great Britain, 430 ff.; with the U.S., 65 ff., 867 ff., 897 ff.; withdrawal from the League, 888 ff.; German-Japanese Agreement, Nov. 25, 1936, 988; Three-Power Pact, Sept. 27, 1940, 991; agreements with the U.S.S.R., April 13, 1941, 1031

Kánya, Kálmán de, conversation with Hitler and Imredy, Sept. 20, 1938, 670
Konoe, Prince, statements: Jan. 18, 1938, 898; Dec. 22, 1938, 903
Krestinski, N., note to Bullitt *re* Communist International, Aug. 27, 1935, 600
Kurusu, Saburo, statement from Roosevelt, Dec. 2, 1941, 111; Hull's memorandum *re* conversation with, Dec. 5, 1941, 112

Laval, Pierre, statement on rapprochement with Italy, Jan. 7, 1935, 481; letter to Avenol on German decisions *re* armaments, April 9, 1935, 483; address before the League Assembly, Sept. 13, 1935, 452
League of Nations, and the Ethiopian war, 820 ff., 938 ff.; expulsion of the U.S.S.R., 961 f.; German denunciation of the Treaty of Versailles, 937 f.; German denunciation of the Locarno treaty, 953 f.; Hitler's proclamation of withdrawal from, 639; *re* Japanese aggressions vs. China, 873 ff., 923, 954 ff.; Japanese withdrawal, from the League, 888; limitation of armaments, 964 ff.; *re* Manchuria, 919 ff.; *re* the Saar, 936; *re* Spain, 960 f.; statement of the Japanese Government *re* the Covenant, Feb. 25, 1933, 874
—— Assembly: address on policy by Viscount Cecil, 287; address by Anthony Eden, 298; Grandi's address, Sept. 8, 1931, 775; Briand's address, Sept. 11, 1931, 443; address by Curtius, Sept. 12, 1931, 609; statement by Matsuoka, Feb. 24, 1933, 873; Laval's address, Sept. 13, 1935, 452; Litvinov's address, Sept. 21, 1938, 560, 601
—— Council: Curtius's address, Jan. 20, 1931, 636; Flandin's statement *re* Germany, March 14, 1936, 487; Litvinov's statement *re* German denunciation of Locarno, March 17, 1936, 594; Bonnet's statement, May 23, 1939, 470
Lend-Lease Act, 206
"Lima, Declaration of," Dec. 24, 1938, 993
Limitation of Naval Armament, Treaty for, London, March 25, 1936, 978, 985
Litvinov, Maxim, address before the Central Executive Committee, Dec. 29, 1933, 540; letter to R. J. Sandler, *re* League membership, Sept. 15, 1934, 550; statement *re* German denunciation of Locarno, in the League Council, March 17, 1936, 594; address before the League Assembly, Sept. 21, 1938, 560, 601
Locarno, Treaty of, German denunciation, 594, 953; Hoesch's memorandum to Eden *re*, March 7, 1936, 651

MacDonald, J. Ramsay, address in the House of Commons, June 29, 1931, 311; draft Disarmament Convention, submitted at Geneva, March 16, 1933, 319; address at the Guildhall banquet, Nov. 9, 1934, 290; statement, March 1, 1935, 293
Manchuria, League of Nations *re*, 919 ff.
Matsuoka, Yosuke, statement at the League of Nations, Feb. 24, 1933, 873; memoranda of conversations with Hitler: March 27, 1941, 1083; April 4, 1941, 1090; memorandum of a conversation with Ribbentrop, March 29, 1941, 1086
Mediterranean Sea, declaration of England and Italy *re,* Jan. 2, 1937, 1008
Meeting of the Ministers for Foreign Affairs of the American Republics, 997 ff.
Molotov, Vyacheslav M., address before the Central Executive Committee, Jan. 11, 1936, 557; addresses before the Supreme Soviet, May 31, and Oct. 31, 1939, 564, 570; radio address *re* Finland, Nov. 29, 1939, 602; telegram to Avenol, Dec. 5, 1939, 605; memoranda of conversations with Hitler: Nov. 12, 1940, 1043; Nov. 13, 1940, 1051; memorandum of a conversation with Ribbentrop, Nov. 13, 1940, 1063

INDEX

Monsell, Viscount, statement at the Conference for the Limitation of Naval Armament at London, Jan. 15, 1936, 342

Morgenthau, Henry, Jr., statement on U.S. economic and financial policy, Sept. 25, 1936, 282

Morris, Leland B., note from Hitler, Dec. 11, 1941, 733

Moscicki, Ignace, message from Roosevelt in appeal for peace, Aug. 24, 1939, 156

Munich, agreements, Sept. 29, 1938, 1021; joint communiqué, Sept. 30, 1938, 1023

Mussolini, Benito, messages from Roosevelt in appeal for peace, 152, 159, 161; address to the General Staff of the army, Aug. 24, 1934, 779; address at Milan, Oct. 6, 1934, 781; address in the Chamber of Deputies, May 25, 1935, 782; radio address on war with Ethiopia, Oct. 2, 1935, 819; address at Milan, Nov. 1, 1936, 789; address at Avellino, Aug. 30, 1936, 785; Hitler's address in Berlin during visit of, Sept. 28, 1937, 723, 804; addresses at Rome: Dec. 11, 1937, 806; March 26, 1939, 808; Sept. 23, 1939, 825; communications to Roosevelt, May 2, 1940, 827; May 18, 1940, 827; radio address, June 10, 1940, 828; conversation with Ribbentrop and Ciano, May 13, 1941, 743; letter from Hitler, June 21, 1941, 1093; address, Dec. 11, 1941, 832

Nagano, Osami, at the London Naval Armament Conference, Jan. 15, 1936, 862 ff.

National Socialist Congress, Nuremberg, Sept. 13, 1937, Hitler's address, 624; Sept. 9, 1936, Hitler's address, 659

Navy Day, Roosevelt's address, Oct. 27, 1941, 228

Netherlands, The, invasion, 759

Neurath, Konstantin, Baron von, communication to Henderson *re* disarmament, Sept. 14, 1932, 637; communication from Henderson, Sept. 18, 1932, 969; at Berlin, Oct. 12, 1934, 619

Neutrality and Neutrality legislation, 232 ff.

New Zealand, procès-verbal *re* submarine warfare, 985 f.; Treaty for the Limitation of Naval Armament, 978 ff.

Nomura, Kichisaburo, statement, Oct. 27, 1939, 904; pro-memoria to Grew, Dec. 18, 1939, 905; draft proposals to Hull, Sept. 6, 1941, 909; Nov. 20, 1941, 909; communication from Hull, Nov. 26, 1941; statement from Roosevelt, Dec. 2, 1941, 111; Hull's memorandum *re* conversation with, Dec. 5, 1941, 112; memorandum to Hull, Dec. 7, 1941, 1910

Non-Aggression, treaty, between Germany and the U.S.S.R., Aug. 23, 1939, 1025; Secret additional protocol, Aug. 23, 1939, 1037

Norway, invasion of, 758

Nyon Agreement, Sept. 14, 1937, 1008; supplementary agreement, Sept. 17, 1937, 1011

"Operation Barbarossa," Hitler's military directive for, Dec. 18, 1940, 1073

Oshima, Hiroshi, conversation with Weizsäcker, Sept. 18, 1939, 739

Ott, Eugen, telegram to the German Foreign Office, June, 1940, 740

Outerlink Bridge, Chicago, Roosevelt's dedication address, 25

"Panama, Declaration of," Oct. 3, 1939, 994

Peace, appeals for, message from Roosevelt, Sept. 26, 1938, 148; telegram from Hull to American diplomatic missions, Sept. 27, 1938, 149; messages from Roosevelt to Hitler: Sept. 27, 1938, 150; April 14, 1939, 152; Aug. 24, 1939, 157; Aug. 25, 1939, 158; message from Roosevelt to King Victor Emmanuel, Aug. 23, 1939, 158; message from Roosevelt to Moscicki, Aug. 24, 1939; messages from Roosevelt to Mussolini: April 29, 1940, 159; May 14, 1940, 161; telegrams from Phillips to Hull: May 27, 1940, 161; June 1, 1940, 164; telegram from Hull to Phillips, May 30, 1940, 163

Phipps, Sir Eric, communication from Eden, March 26, 1936, 350

Poland, relations with Germany, 693 ff., 999; German-Polish Agreement of Jan. 28, 1934, 999 ff.; and Great Britain, communiqué, April 6, 1939, 1025; Bonnet's instruction to the French Ambassador, Aug. 24, 1939, 521; agreement of mutual assistance with Great Britain, Aug. 25, 1939, 1027

Poncet, André-François, communication to Bonnet, Oct. 20, 1938, 500

Radical-Socialist Party, Congress, Oct. 8, 1933, Daladier's address, 450

Reynaud, Paul, memorandum from Welles *re* U.S. economic and financial policy, March 9, 1940, 283; messages from Roosevelt *re* aid to France, 201, 202

Rhineland, demilitarized zone, Hoesch's memorandum to Eden *re*, March 7, 1936, 651

Ribbentrop, Joachim von, note from Hoare, and reply, June 18, 1935, 975 ff.; memorandum to Eden, April 1, 1936, 655; statement *re* Franco-German Declaration of Dec. 6, 1938, 693; notes from Gilbert *re* American citizens in Germany, Dec. 14, 1938, 142; Jan. 11, 1939, 143; personal letter to Bonnet, July 13, 1939, 694; personal letter from Bonnet, July 21, 1939, 518; communication handed to Sir Nevile Henderson, Sept. 3, 1939, 718; telegrams to Schulenburg: Sept. 15, 1939, 1038; Sept. 23, 1939, 1040; telegram from Schulenburg, Sept. 20, 1939, 1040; memorandum of a conversation with Molotov, Nov. 13, 1940, 1063; telegram to Weizsäcker, Jan. 21, 1941, 1078; telegram to Schulenburg, Feb. 27, 1941, 1080; memorandum of a conversation with Matsuoka, March 29, 1941, 1086; conversation with Mussolini and Ciano, May 13, 1941, 743; telegram to Ott, July 1, 1941, 744; note to Morris, Dec. 11, 1941, 733

Rio de Janeiro, Meeting of Foreign Ministers, Jan. 28, 1942, 998

Robin Moor, sinking of, message from Roosevelt to Congress, 144; note from Hull to Thomsen, 147; note from Thomsen to Hull, 730

Rome-Berlin-Tokyo Axis, 832; agreements, 988 ff., 991 f.

Roosevelt, Franklin D., inaugural address, March 4, 1933, 10; address at the dedication of the Outerlink Bridge, Chicago, 25; "Atlantic Charter," 220, 1033; messages to Reynaud on aid to France, 201, 202; message to the heads of nations participating in the Disarmament Conference and the World Monetary Economic Conference, May 16, 1933, 49; address at Washington, Dec. 28, 1933, on U.S. policy, 11; message to Congress, on economic policy, June 1, 1934, 267; radio address on U.S. policy, Oct. 26, 1938, 30; message to Congress *re* British naval and air bases, Sept. 3, 1940, 205; message to Congress *re* defense of Iceland, July 7, 1941, 215; addresses on the protection of American vessels: Sept. 11, 1941, 221; Oct. 27, 1941, 228

———— German and Italian aggressions: statement *re* Ethiopia, Oct. 30, 1935, 136; annual message to Congress, Jan. 3, 1936, 129; message to Benes, Hitler, and others, Sept. 26, 1938, 148; statement, Nov. 15, 1938, 132; address at the commencement exercises, Charlottesville, Va., June 10, 1940, 138; statement on German execution of hostages, Oct. 25, 1941, 141; Hitler's communiqués *re* the address of Oct. 28, 1941, 732

———— National defense: messages to Congress on defense and aid to the democracies: Jan. 28, 1938, 166; Jan. 12, 1939, 168; Jan. 6, 1941, 181; radio addresses: Dec. 29, 1940, 172; May 27, 1941, 189; proclamations, 199, 200

———— neutrality: radio address, Sept. 3, 1939, 236; messages to Congress: Sept. 21, 1939, 239; Oct. 9, 1941, 247

———— peace, appeals for: messages to Benes, Hitler, and others, Sept. 26, 1938, 148; messages to Hilter: Sept. 27, 1938, 150; April 14, 1939, 152; Aug. 24, 1939, 157; Aug. 25, 1939, 158; Daladier's reply, Sept. 26, 1938, 491; Hitler's reply, Sept. 26, 1938, 685; Chamberlain's reply, 366; Victor Emmanuel's reply, Aug. 23, 1939, 825; Thomsen's reply, Aug. 31, 1939, 712

———— relations with Japan: statement handed to Nomura and Kurusu, Dec. 2, 1941, 111; message to Emperor Hirohito, Dec. 6, 1941, 115; messages to Congress: Dec. 8, 1941, 252; Dec. 11, 1941, 260; radio address to the nation, Dec. 9, 1941, 254; message to Congress, Dec. 15, 1941, 117

Rumania, Nyon Agreement, 1008 ff.

Saar, 936
Saito, Hirosi, note *verbale* to Hull, Dec. 29, 1934, 861
Sandler, R. J., letter from Litvinov *re* League membership, Sept. 15, 1934, 550
Schacht, Hjalmar, address at Bad Eilsen, Aug. 30, 1934, 763; announcement of "New Plan," Sept., 1934, 765
Schulenburg, Count Friedrich Werner von der, telegrams from Ribbentrop: Sept. 15, 1939, 1038; Sept. 23, 1939, 1040; telegram to Ribbentrop, Sept. 20, 1939, 1040; telegram from the German Foreign Office, Nov. 26, 1940, 1071; telegram to the German Foreign Office, Jan. 17, 1941, 1077; telegram from Ribbentrop, Feb. 27, 1941, 1080; telegrams to the German Foreign Office, March 1, 1941, 1081 f.
Shipping, British, note from Craigie to Hirota *re* bombing of, 432 f.
Shipping, U.S., protection of, 221, 228; *Greer*, 729; *Robin Moor*, 230; *see also* Submarine warfare
South Africa, Union of, Procès-verbal *re* submarine warfare, 985 f.

INDEX

Spain, withdrawal of non-Spanish combatants, 960
Stimson, Henry L., memorandum on relations with Japan, Sept. 22, 1931, 65; telegram to Prentiss B. Gilbert, Oct. 9, 1931, 66; telegram to Dawes, Nov. 10, 1931, 67; telegram to Forbes, Jan. 7, 1932, 71; telegram to Wilson, Feb. 12, 1932, 71; address at Pittsburgh, Oct. 26, 1932, on U.S. policy, 3; communication to Avenol, Feb. 25, 1933, 75
Submarine warfare, Procès-verbal *re*, 985 f.; Nyon agreement, 1008 ff.
Sztéjay, Döme, conversation with Goering, Sept. 16, 1938, 668

Thomsen, Hans, note to Hull, March 17, 1939, 690; note from Welles, March 20, 1939, 137; reply, Aug. 31, 1939, to Roosevelt's appeals for peace, 712; note from Hull *re* the sinking of the *Robin Moor*, Sept. 19, 1941, 147; reply to Hull, Sept. 26, 1941, 730
Three-Power Pact (Axis), Sept. 27, 1940, 991
Togo, Shigenori, address in the Imperial Diet, Nov. 17, 1941, 857
Trade Agreements Act of 1934, 273
Turkey, Nyon Agreement, 1008 ff.

Uchida, Yasuya, Count, telegram to Drummond, March 27, 1933, 888
Union of Soviet Socialist Republics, *re* Czechoslovakia, 601 f.; disarmament and security, 582 ff.; expulsion from the League of Nations, 961; general statements of policy, 539 ff.; war with Finland, 602 ff.; responsibility for acts of the Communist International, 600 f.; Central Executive Committee, Litvinov's address, Dec. 29, 1933, 540; Molotov's address, Jan. 11, 1936, 557; treaty of mutual assistance with France, May 2, 1935, 1004; Nyon Agreement, Sept. 14, 1938, 1008 ff.; Supreme Soviet, Molotov's addresses, May 31 and Oct. 31, 1939, 564, 570; agreements with Japan, April 13, 1941, 1031
—— relations with Germany, 747 ff., 1037 ff.; boundary and friendship agreement, 570 ff., 1041; agreements, Sept. 29, 1939, 1029; non-aggression treaty, Aug. 23, 1939, 1025
United States, aid to France, 201 f.; appeals for peace, 1938–1940, 148 ff.; Atlantic Charter, 220, 1033; "Black List," 216 ff.; closing of German and Italian consular offices and other agencies, 213 ff.; declarations of a state of war, 253, 261, 733; defense of Greenland, 210 ff.; defense of Iceland, 215 f.; economic and financial policy, 262 ff.; entry into the war, 115 ff., 250 ff., 910 ff.; *re* European possessions in the Western Hemisphere, 203 ff.; freezing of German and Italian assets, 212 f.; general statements of policy, 3 ff.; *re* German and Italian aggressions, 129 ff., 133 ff., 142 ff.; lease of British bases, 205 f.; Lend-Lease Act, 206 ff.; National and continental defense, 98, 166 ff., 199 ff.; National emergency declarations, 199 ff.; neutrality and neutrality legislation, 232 ff.; protection of American vessels, 144-47, 221 ff.
—— Congress: war messages from Roosevelt, 252, 260; declaration of a state of war with Japan, 253; declarations of a state of war with Germany and Italy, 261; Roosevelt's message on economic policy, June 1, 1934, 267; the President's annual message, Jan. 3, 1936, 129; Senate Committee on Foreign Relations, statement of N. H. Davis on disarmament, May 13, 1936, 56; Roosevelt's message *re* British naval and air bases, Sept. 3, 1940, 205; House of Representatives Foreign Affairs Committee, Hull's statement on relations with Japan, Jan. 15, 1941, 102; message of Roosevelt *re* the sinking of the *Robin Moor*, June 20, 1941, 144; message of Roosevelt *re* defense of Iceland, July 7, 1941, 215; Roosevelt's message on the "Atlantic Charter," August, 1941, 220; Roosevelt's message on past policy in the Pacific, Dec. 15, 1941, 117
—— Department of State, statements on disarmament: Feb. 5, 1938, 60; June 30, 1938, 62; announcement on relations with Japan, April 22, 1938, 85; statement *re* European possessions in the Western Hemisphere, June 19, 1940, 203; announcement of agreement *re* Greenland, April 10, 1941, 210; statement on the "Black List," July 17, 1941, 216
—— disarmament, 42 ff., 62; Five-Power Agreement, 971 f.; Procès-verbal *re* submarine warfare, 985 f.; Treaty for Limitation of Naval Agreement, 978 ff.
—— relations with Germany, 725 ff.; German aggressions against, 142 ff.; declarations of a state of war, 261, 733 ff.
—— relations with Japan, 65 ff., 85, 102, 250 ff., 867 ff., 897 ff.; outbreak of war, 115 ff., 910 ff.; declaration of a state of war, 253
United Nations, joint declaration *re* cooperation vs. the Axis, Jan. 1, 1942, 1035

Versailles, Treaty of, German denunciation, 937; German violation of Article 43, 953; Hitler's proclamation *re,* March 16, 1935, 641

Victor Emmanuel, reply to Roosevelt's appeal for peace, Aug. 23, 1939, 825

Virginia, Univ. of, Roosevelt's commencement address, June 10, 1940, 138

Weizsäcker, Baron von, communication handed to Sir Nevile Henderson, Aug. 31, 1939, 707; conversation with Oshima, Sept. 18, 1939, 739; circular telegram to all German missions, Nov. 15, 1940, 1070; telegram from Ribbentrop, Jan. 21, 1941, 1078

Welczeck, Johannes, Count von, communication from Bonnet, July 1, 1939, 517

Welles, Sumner, note *re* Czechoslovakia to Thomsen, March 20, 1939, 137; memorandum to Reynaud, March 9, 1940, 283; address, "Our Foreign Policy and National Defense," Sept. 28, 1940, 98; note to Thomsen *re* closing of consular offices in the U.S., June 16, 1941, 213; note to Don Ascanio dei principi Colonna *re* closing of Consular offices in the U.S., June 20, 1941, 214; statement *re* Japan, July 24, 1941, 105

White House, statement on disarmament, June 22, 1932, 47; statement, Dec. 10, 1940, 102; statement, July 25, 1941, 106

Wilson, Hugh R., telegram from Stimson, Feb. 12, 1932, 71

Western Hemisphere, defense of, 166 ff.; European possessions in, 203 f.

World Monetary and Economic Conference, address of F. D. Roosevelt, May 16, 1933, 49; Hull's address, July 27, 1933, 262

Yoshizawa, Kenkichi, address to the League of Nations, Sept. 9, 1931, 835; note to Forbes, Jan. 16, 1932, 869

Yugoslavia, invasion, 760; Nyon Agreement, Sept. 14, 1937, 1008 ff.